A Howard Reader

EDITOR

Paul E. Logan

*Associate Professor of German and
    Associate Dean for the Humanities*
College of Arts and Sciences
Howard University

CONTRIBUTING EDITORS

Tritobia H. Benjamin

*Professor of Art and Director,
    The Howard University Gallery of Art*
College of Arts and Sciences
Howard University

Raymond G. Dobard

Professor of Art
College of Arts and Sciences
Howard University

Estelle Wormley Taylor

Professor emerita *of English*
Department of English
College of Arts and Sciences
Howard University

Barbara W. Williams

*Special Assistant to the Vice President for
    Enrollment Management and Director
    of Special Projects*
Office of Enrollment Management
Howard University

A Howard Reader

An Intellectual and Cultural Quilt of the African-American Experience

Edited, Compiled, and
with an Introduction by
Paul E. Logan

Foreword by
H. Patrick Swygert
President, Howard University

Houghton Mifflin
Custom Publishing

Manager, Custom Publishing: Rusty Johnson
Editor, Custom Publishing: Kelly Perkins
Administrator, Custom Publishing: Susanna Allshouse
Project Editor: Robin Hogan
Permissions Editor: Mary Dalton-Hoffman

Photo and text credits continue on page 519.

Chapter One   Toni Morrison   Excerpt from BELOVED by Toni Morrison. Reprinted by permission of International Creative Management, Inc. Copyright © 1987 by Alfred A. Knopf.
Chapter Two   Clinton Rossiter   "Introduction, pp. xii–xvi" by Clinton Rossiter, from THE FEDERALIST PAPERS by Alexander Hamilton et al., introduced by Clinton Rossiter. Copyright © 1961 by New American Library. Used by permission of Dutton Signet, a division of Penguin Books USA Inc.
Chapter Three   Toni Morrison   "Charter Day Address," delivered at Howard University, March 3, 1995. Reprinted by permission of International Creative Management, Inc. Copyright © 1987 by Toni Morrison.
Chapter Nine   Toni Morrison   Excerpt from SONG OF SOLOMON, pp. 336–337, Alfred A. Knopf, Inc. 1977. Reprinted by permission of International Creative Management, Inc. Copyright © 1977 by Toni Morrison.

Printed in the United States of America.

J I H G F E D C B A

ISBN: 0-395-88654-6
3-78729

Houghton Mifflin
Custom Publishing

222 Berkeley Street
Boston • MA • 02116 • (800) 813-5091

Address all correspondence and order information to the above address

Life is tragic simply because the earth
turns and the sun inexorably rises and
sets, and one day, for each of us, the sun
will go down for the last, last time.
Perhaps the whole root of our trouble, the
human trouble, is that we will sacrifice all
the beauty of our lives, will imprison
ourselves in totem, taboos, crosses, blood
sacrifices, steeples, mosques, races, armies,
flags, nations, in order to deny the fact of death,
which is the only fact we have. It
seems to me that one ought to rejoice in
the fact of death—ought to decide,
indeed, to earn one's death by
confronting with passion the conundrum
of life. One is responsible to life:
It is the small beacon in that terrifying
darkness from which we come and to which
we shall return.
One must negotiate this passage as nobly as possible,
for the sake of those who are coming after us.

James Baldwin, "The Fire Next Time"

Contents

CHAPTER THREE A Way of Looking at a University   129

[When we sang the Alma Mater] my soul stood on tiptoe and stretched up to take in all that it meant. So I was careful to do my class work and be worthy to stand there under the shadow of the hovering spirit of Howard. I felt the ladder under my feet.   Zora Neale Hurston

CHAPTER FOUR A Way of Responding   169

I now understood the pathway from slavery to freedom. . . . I set out . . . at whatever cost of trouble to learn how to read.   Frederick Douglass

CHAPTER FIVE The Emancipated Self   243

I am the hope and the dream of the slave . . .   Maya Angelou

CHAPTER SIX

The Observed Other 269

They failed to ask my name and called me negro.   Henry Dumas

CHAPTER SEVEN

A Disciplined Response 331

If you have run with men and they have wearied you, how can you compete with horses? Jeremiah 12:5

Foreword

The selections that comprise *A Howard Reader* affirm the seminal contributions made by African Americans to the historical and cultural legacy of our nation. The *Reader* gives all students access to exceptional writing, scholarship, and documentation about the intellectual and cultural heritage of African Americans. It compels one to recognize the indelible stamp that African Americans have placed on American history through their quest for freedom and equality, expressions of creative genius, and service to the country.

Woven into the documentary fabric of the *Reader* is the message that the goal of education is the improvement of our communities and the lives of our fellow men and women. *A Howard Reader* renders extraordinary texts that have served as responses to some of humankind's greatest challenges, triumphs, and tragedies. This text continues Howard University's legacy as a dynamic, academic environment that offers students unlimited opportunities to explore the full extent of their intellectual abilities. It supports Howard University's commitment to introduce students to the intellectual stimulation of found knowledge, the satisfaction of service, and the excitement and responsibility of leadership.

H. Patrick Swygert
President
Howard University

A Pieced Star[*]

" 'A Pieced Star'—that's what I call it" are the words of Mrs. Viola Canady whose vibrant quilt embraces the cover of *A Howard Reader: An Intellectual and Cultural Quilt of the African-American Experience*. Born near Goldsboro, North Carolina, on November 2, 1922, to African-American parents, Mrs. Canady is recognized as one of this nation's finest quilters. She is the founder of the Washington, D. C.-based quilting guild, the "Daughters of Dorcas," whose exhibits, workshops, classes for inner-city children, and charitable work are well known. With a memory as vivid as the colors of her quilt, Mrs. Canady stitches history into patterns—the fabric of heritage—which are signs and symbols of the African-American passage to freedom and self-definition.

The African-American quilt is all too often dismissed as something old, tattered, discolored, and "in pieces." One often fails to look deeper—fails to realize that which is old and torn is spiritually textured; that which is stained is marked by grace; and that which is fragmented comes together to create something new, whole, and beautiful. The quilt can be a visual metaphor for perseverance and continuity. The many scraps of fabric needed to make a quilt similar to "A Pieced Star" usually have special meaning because they are taken from garments of deceased relatives or given as tokens of friendship. The quilt then becomes a visible and tangible link to the past and a bridge to the future.

One may view Mrs. Canady's quilt as a family album in fabric or a textbook of community. Ideas, like fabric, require informed crafting by scholars who can make connecting stitches and create "a pieced star." *A Howard Reader* is such a "star."

Raymond G. Dobard, Ph.D.
Department of Art
College of Arts and Sciences
Howard University

---

[*]Save for the "Pieced Star" and "Log Cabin" quilts belonging to Mrs. Viola Canady, the quilts reproduced in *A Howard Reader* are from the collection of Raymond G. Dobard.

Acknowledgments

First and foremost, I am grateful to Barbara W. Williams, who suggested that I publish the essays and other creative documents that I had assembled and used in my Freshman Seminar course. Her advocacy of the project and support during the rather tumultuous initial stages will not be forgotten. My profound thanks also go to the other members of the team: Tritobia H. Benjamin and Raymond G. Dobard, whose artistic eyes and contributions have helped to give shape to the finished product, and Estelle W. Taylor, whose wise counsel has been my compass for more than twenty years and whose suggestions have made this anthology more seamless. I would also like to acknowledge Donna Brock of [Howard] University Communications for her singular vision and creative efforts at launching the text; Clifford Muse, Archivist of Howard University, and Donna Wells for researching and making available archival photographs from the Moorland-Spingarn Research Center as well as Thomas C. Battle, Director, Moorland-Spingarn Research Center, Howard University, for his support and generosity; Silvia Johnson, Editor, *Journal of Negro Education*, for her editorial suggestions; H. Patrick Swygert, President of Howard University, for his encouragement and contributions; and Clarence M. Lee, Dean, College of Arts and Sciences, for his patience and support. For their assistance throughout this project, I would like to thank Janet Sims-Wood (Moorland-Spingarn Research Center); Regina Drake (Office of the Provost, Howard University); Michele Bertrand (Office of the President, Howard University); Karen House (Office of the President, Howard University); Eleanor Murrell (University Communications); and Sally King McCoy (Administrative Assistant, Department of English, Howard University). Many thanks go to Michael Miller (Audio-Visual Center) and Charles Cooke & Sons for their assistance with photography. I would also like to thank warmly the staff of Houghton Mifflin Company, especially Garret White, Vice President and Director of Sales and Marketing (College Division); Rusty Johnson (Manager, Custom Publishing); Kelly Perkins (Editor, Custom Publishing); Jonelle Calon (Divisional Sales Manager); Jennifer Dinsmore (College Sales Representative); Mary Dalton-Hoffman (Permissions Editor); and Joan Cooke Newton.

For her hands and head steadied by years of editorial experience, for her enthusiasm, and support, I owe an enormous debt and gratitude to Robin Hogan, project editor, and, again, to Houghton Mifflin for having assigned her to this project.

Paul E. Logan
Editor

Introduction

In his essay "The Talented Tenth," which is included in the *Reader*, W. E. B. Du Bois maintains that we shall have educated African-American men [and women] only if we impart to them "*broad sympathy, knowledge of the world that was and is, and of [their] relation . . . to it.*" Aware that young African-American students come often to institutions of higher learning without a knowledge of the conditions under which their ancestors came to, lived in, and contributed to the New World—without an understanding of how their ancestors' emancipatory efforts challenged and helped define America's constitutional imperatives, the editors have quilted together essays, interviews, excerpts from legal documents, creative texts—some scattered in books long forgotten—in the hope that they will provide students a way of seeing the seamless pattern of the African-American cultural and intellectual cloth.

Through these essays and excerpts by and about African Americans, *A Howard Reader* bridges their past and present; recites their arduous journey from Africa over the Middle Passage to the Americas; confirms their contributions to the nation; and, most important, provides opportunities for students to sample and grapple with a number of great works of thought and literature. A springboard for class discussion, the *Reader* is designed to motivate students to familiarize themselves with the plethora of works written by, about, for, and against African Americans. *A Howard Reader*—a first attempt to explore that which many of Howard's colleges and schools define as their intellectual heritage—promotes the development of men and women who will become familiar with "the world that was and is," and who can discern what their relation to it is. It is this common thread—the development of men and women who can look at Western civilization, its principles of justice, freedom, government with the consent of the governed, and equality under the law through the critically focused lenses of the singular African-American experience—which is one of Howard's singular academic missions. While demanding that its students study the intellectual legacy of the West—the source of some of the most powerful and pervasive influences on America and all her people—Howard also affords its students opportunities to study critically their legacy as it is refracted through the lenses of America and to examine the legacy of the nation and the world as it is refracted through their people's cultural and intellectual identity and history.

More than four decades ago, Walter Lippman observed that "what enables men to know more than their ancestors is that they start with a knowledge of what their ancestors have already learned." "A society," he added, "can be progressive only if it conserves its tradition." The challenge for the editors of *A Howard Reader* was to select works that conserve and transmit that tradition and understanding, not merely to pay homage to the wisdom of the past, but to prepare wisely for the future. The common bond—inscribed partially in the *Reader*—seeks to assert who African Americans were and are, as well as where they have been and are going. The result of such an inquiry leads ultimately to African-American students' laying claim to a land that has been alien soil and to a culture that has given, through the enslaved's quest for freedom, new meaning to the concept of freedom.

The works included in the *Reader* resonate the African Americans' perceived "being" in and importance to America. In battling the nefarious forces that threatened and continue to threaten their rights to enjoy the fruits of this nation; in debating "conflicting views on solutions to highly complex, extremely volatile social problems" (Toni Morrison); and in remaining the constant, ever-present metaphor of the American "Declaration," African Americans and their institutions have fashioned—constructed—the national debate on the meaning of what America says it is—a nation of democracy, tolerance, liberty, justice, and equality. The nationally and internationally acclaimed historian John Hope Franklin maintained in his 1976 Jefferson Lecture for the National Endowment for the Humanities that the African American, as he observes waves of newcomers "enjoy [the] dignity of existence that only equality in a free society can provide," waits still his turn to "experience the inalienable right of equality." For him, Franklin states, it is still a "Dream Deferred."

In his seminal article, "What America Would Be Like Without Blacks," written for, published in *Time* (April 6, 1970), and included in the *Reader*, Ralph Ellison states that without the presence of African Americans, there would be no "need for that tragic knowledge which we try ceaselessly to evade: that the true subject of democracy is not simply material well-being, but the extension of the democratic process in the direction of perfecting itself." Furthermore, he states that "[t]he most obvious test and clue to that perfection is the inclusion, *not* assimilation, of the black man." Having been assigned the role of "outsider" by a state that denied and continues to deny their humanity, and in which, with notable exception of the abolitionists, countless American intellectuals of all political persuasions during the 18th and 19th centuries, learned to live with the paradox and moral contradictions of America's "peculiar institution" (slavery), African Americans deconstructed the world of slavery, intolerance, inequality, injustice and constructed one in which they could touch their humanity and thus achieve a sense of freedom and self-definition. This is the key to the spiritual and intellectual survival of African Americans—the ability to understand and to know the world, its perceptions, its ideas of good and evil; to effect the deconstruction of worlds in which they have been "undefined" and to the construction of worlds in which they find definition. America's "peculiar institution" was not, as some have maintained, an aberration that existed outside American political, legal, moral, economic, and religious development. The enslavement of the African American was the most crucial problem of antebellum America, the watershed of human history, and, according to Professor John T. Reilly (Department of English), that single event that "fostered the discourse of modernity."

This discourse of modernity—an exploration of ways in which man confronts and deconstructs reality in order to find a "self," in which he comes to terms with "self," his relationship to his world and its values—is evident in many of the works that are included here. To understand and appreciate their place in the world that their forefathers and foremothers helped create and define, African-American students must learn to appreciate the "deconstructive" and "constructive" measures that their ancestors undertook in order to survive spiritually and physically. It is through their coming to terms with the ways in which their ancestors responded to and debated the forces that enslaved them that African-American students will be able to achieve a unique and singular perception of the values and history of the land of their birth.

Forty years ago, in his essay "Stranger in the Village," James Baldwin confronted the challenge to the African American while reminiscing about his visit to the Cathedral at Chartres in the small medieval French town. According to the cultural historian Kenneth Clark, "Chartres is the epitome of the first great awakening in European civilisation. It is also the bridge between Romanesque and Gothic, between the world of Abelard and the world of St Thomas Aquinas, the world of restless curiosity and the world of system and order. Great things were to be done in the next centuries of high Gothic, great feats of construction, both

in architecture and in thought. But they rested on the foundations of the twelfth century. That was the age which gave European civilisation its impetus. Our intellectual energy, our contact with the great minds of Greece, our ability to move and change, our belief that God may be approached through beauty, our feeling of compassion, our sense of the unity of Christendom—all this, and much more, appeared in those hundred marvelous years between the consecration of Cluny and the rebuilding of Chartres" (*Civilisation*, 60). The Cathedral at Chartres, therefore, is to the cultural historian the cornerstone of modern European civilization. It centered European culture and defined the West's perception of beauty as well as its values.

For Baldwin, however, the Cathedral at Chartres "becomes not a paragon, but a speaking subject—a voice from the past" (Eleanor W. Traylor, "*The Humanities and Afro-American Literary Tradition*")—a voice, albeit a confirmation of the splendors of Western civilization, which reminds us that horrendous acts were done to human beings in the name of "civilization." It is this dichotomy of perception that Baldwin relates in "Stranger in the Village":

> The Cathedral at Chartres . . . says something to the people of this village which it cannot say to me; but it is important to understand that this Cathedral says something to me which it cannot say to them. . . . These [villagers], from the point of view of power, cannot be strangers anywhere in the world . . . even if they do not know it. The most illiterate among them is related, in a way that I am not, to Dante, Shakespeare, Michelangelo, Aeschylus, DaVinci, Rembrandt, and Racine; the Cathedral at Chartres says something to them which it cannot say to me. . . . Out of their hymns and dances come Beethoven and Bach. Go back a few centuries. . . . I am in Africa watching the conquerors arrive.

Baldwin concludes his essay and puts into clear focus the importance of the Cathedral at Chartres—this turning point in Western civilization—for the *villagers* and *himself*—and indeed for the African American. "*They* (emphasis added) are struck by the power of the spires and the glory of the stained glass windows. . . . *I* (emphasis added) am terrified by the slippery bottomless well to be found in the crypt down which heretics were hurled to death, and by the obscene inescapable gargoyles strutting out of the stone seeming to suggest that God and the devil can never be divorced. . . . Perhaps I have known God in a *different* (emphasis added) way."

Given the circumstances of their arrival in America and enslavement, which has no precedent in the history of the world in terms of length of time and the nature and specificity of its devastation, African Americans were compelled to see and perceive things differently. And it is their perception that has given unwittingly undeniable shape and form to America and her view of herself. No other minority in America has such a record of achievement in the face of what might have seemed to many as insurmountable odds. African Americans, collectively and singly, through the force of their will and intellect, be it in the halls of justice, in the churches, in the kitchens of white folks, within the walls of institutions of higher learning, or in the creative arts, have challenged and obliged the nation to live up to its promise of justice and equality under the law. The nation owes a great debt of gratitude to African Americans and, especially, to their institutions of higher learning. In her Charter Day Address at Howard University on March 3, 1995, Alumna and Nobel Laureate Toni Morrison reminds us that it was Howard University that "countered with a vengeance the prevailing 19th-century notion that education was not part of the future of African Americans—the prevailing 19th-century notion that, if by some odd chance higher education were to become available on a large scale, that it would be of no use to have it because the higher plateaus of achievement and influence were closed. Evidence to the contrary is overwhelming." The evidence presented in *A Howard Reader* confirms Morrison's assessment.

In discussing Duke Ellington's use of the idiomatic device "*break*"—a "temporary interruption of the established cadence . . . which usually requires a *fill*"—a fill which might consist of "an informal sequence of improvised choruses as the overall frame for a precisely controlled but still flexible instrumental composition," Albert Murray, in his essay "Storiella Americana as She is Swyung; or, The Blues as Representative Anecdote," sets the music for the African-American call-and-response. The "break" is, according to Murray, not "just another mechanical structural device. It is of its very nature, as dancers never forget, what the basic message comes down to: *grace under pressure, creativity in an emergency, continuity in the face of disjuncture.*" It is this "break" in the "pressured" and "disjunctured" lives of African Americans between the enslavement and emancipation, between emancipation and the continuing quest for equality, in which they moved and move still gracefully and creatively. *A Howard Reader* presents evidence of what the "dancers never forget"—evidence of how African Americans, in the words of Frederick Douglass, "agitated" and confronted creatively a nation that denied their humanity. But it offers, above all else, testimony and recitation of the African American's struggles, accomplishments, triumphs, and challenges—all negotiated for "those who are coming after us."

Paul E. Logan
Editor

CHAPTER ONE

A Way of Being

If you surrender to the air, you could *ride* it.

Toni Morrison, *Song of Solomon*

A Visit to the Slave Mother Who Killed Her Child

Last Sabbath, after preaching in the city prison, Cincinnati, through the kindness of the Deputy Sheriff, I was permitted to visit the apartment of that unfortunate woman, concerning whom there has been so much excitement during the last two weeks.

I found her with an infant in her arms only a few months old, and observed that it had a large *bunch* on its forehead. I inquired the cause of the injury. She then proceeded to give a detailed account of her attempt to kill her children.

She said, that when the officers and slave-hunters came to the house in which they were concealed, she caught a shovel and struck two of her children on the head, and then took a knife and cut the throat of the third, and tried to kill the other,—that if they had given her time, she would have killed them all—that with regard to herself, she cared but little; but she was unwilling to have her children suffer as she had done.

I inquired if she was not excited almost to madness when she committed the act. No, she replied, I was as cool as I now am; and would much rather kill them at once, and thus end their sufferings, than have them taken back to slavery, and be murdered by piecemeal. She then told the story of her wrongs. She spoke of her days of suffering, of her nights of unmitigated toll, while the bitter tears coursed their way down her cheeks, and fell in the face of the innocent child as it looked smiling up, little conscious of the danger and probable suffering that awaited it.

As I listened to the facts, and witnessed the agony depicted in her countenance, I could not but exclaim, Oh, how terrible is irresponsible power, when exercised over intelligent beings! She alludes to the child that she killed as being free from all trouble and sorrow, with a degree of satisfaction that almost chills the blood in one's veins; yet she evidently possesses all the passionate tenderness of a mother's love. She is about twenty-five years of age, and apparently possesses an average amount of kindness, with a vigorous intellect, and much energy of character.

The two men and the two other children were in another apartment, but her mother-in-law was in the same room. She says she is the mother of eight children, most of whom have been separated from her; that her husband was once separated from her twenty-five years, during which time she did not see him; that could she have prevented it, she would never have permitted him to return, as she did not wish him to witness her sufferings, or be exposed to the brutal treatment that he would receive.

She states that she has been a faithful servant, and in her old age she would not have attempted to obtain her liberty; but as she became feeble, and less capable of performing labor, her master became more and more exacting and brutal in his treatment, until she could stand it no longer; that the effort could result only in death, at most—she therefore made the attempt.

She witnessed the killing of the child, but said she neither encouraged nor discouraged her daughter-in-law,—for under similar circumstances she should probably have done the same. The old woman is from sixty to seventy years of age, has been a professor of religion about twenty years, and speaks with much feeling of the time when she shall be delivered from the power of the oppressor, and dwell with the Savior, 'where the wicked cease from troubling, and the weary are at rest.'

These slaves (as far as I am informed) have resided all their lives within sixteen miles of Cincinnati. We are frequently told that Kentucky slavery is very innocent. If these are its fruits, where it exists in a mild form, will some one tell us what we may expect from its more objectionable features? But comments are unnecessary.

FROM THE *American Baptist*, Fairmount Theological Seminary, Cincinnati, (Ohio,) Feb. 12, 1856.

TONI MORRISON

FROM *Beloved*

". . . Nephew walked over to the old nigger boy and took the ax from him. Then all four started toward the

Howard Players Edward Jenkins and Toni Wofford Morrison in King Richard III, *c. 1950.* (Courtesy of the Moorland-Spingarn Research Center)

shed. . . . Inside, two boys bled in the sawdust and dirt at the feet of a nigger woman holding a blood-soaked child to her chest with one hand and an infant by the heels in the other. She did not look at them; she simply swung the baby toward the wall planks, missed and tried to connect a second time, when out of nowhere—in the ticking time the men spent staring at what there was to stare at—the old nigger boy, still mewing, ran through the door behind them and snatched the baby from the arch of its mother's swing."

W. E. B. Du Bois

The Position of the Negro in the American Social Order: Where Do We Go from Here?

Reuter characterizes the period of Negro effort since Emancipation, as "blind fumbling for a new basis of racial accommodation," arising from the fact that "The Negroes are trying to achieve equal status in the common social order." The whites are trying to prevent democratic equality. "The Negro is a problem in the American social order because his aspiration and behavior are oriented toward a goal that a dominant majority does not want realized." This is a pill difficult for us to swallow. We have tried hard to believe that American race prejudice was the foible of a few; that the majority of white Americans were with us, if they realized our plight, or if they could be persuaded that the interests of their country were bound up with the interests of the Negro group.

Clearly it is not enough for us to prove that our rise, development and equality, will not hurt the whites; we are required to convince them that our survival and success are bound up with theirs. This at best requires a long, slow fight by intelligent, determined men, with infinite patience and unswerving ideals. Foreign observers, as Seiferth says, from Ratzel and Schurz and Hoetsch, see salvation only "by determination of the colored race itself"; while later observers see increased friction as the Negro grows more intelligent, and even a clash between the dogmas of human equality and racial exclusion.

Biology

This calls for a reexamination of the Negro in America, first as a biological entity, after the dogmas and prophecies of earlier days. Cobb makes a succinct and fair summation: the American Negro is a hybrid of African, Indian and European blood, interbreeding easily; he is fecund, strong and mentally able; with some special aptitudes, and with marked adaptability. The group, handicapped with a poverty death and disease rate, is shown by Dr. Cornely to have decreased its general death rate noticeably in the last decade, and between 1910 and 1934, to have reduced its mortality from tuberculosis from 447.7 per hundred thousand to 146.4; a rate indicating no inherent biological susceptibility to disease.

Of the Negro's mental ability, Jenkins says "Negroes of superior intelligence emerge under propitious environmental conditions. Negroes are found in the various highest levels of tested intelligence showing that differences in intelligence are individual rather than racial. Any program toward the development of the American Negro must be based on the assumption that the race is fully capable from the standpoint of mental ability, of assuming a position of equality in the social order." We can then conclude with Cobb "His future would appear to rest upon other factors than his biological quality."

Our Low Social Status

What are these other factors? They are two: the present inferior social status of the American Negro and the handicap of race prejudice. There is causal connection between these two, but not direct; low social status is not the sole cause of the color bar, and on the other hand present race discrimination is not the only cause of the Negro's low social status. Negro self-criticism recognizes that most Negroes in the United States today occupy a low cultural status; both low in itself and low as compared with the national average in the land. There are cultured individuals and groups among them. All Negroes do not fall culturally below all whites. But if one selects any one of the obviously low-cultured groups in the United States, the proportion of Negroes who belong to it will be larger than the Negro proportion in the total population. Nor is there anything singular about it; the real miracle would be if this were not so. Former slavery, present poverty and ignorance, with the inevitable resulting sickness and crime, are adequate social explanation.

This low social condition of the majority of Negroes is not merely a problem of the whites; a question of historic guilt in slavery and labor exploitation, and of present discrimination; it is not merely a matter of the social uplifting of an alien group within their midst; a problem of social contact and political power. Howsoever it may be thus rationalized and explained, it must be, at any current moment primarily an inner problem of the Negro group itself, a condition from which they themselves are prime sufferers, and a problem with which this group is itself forced to grapple. No matter what the true reasons are, or where the blame lies, the fact remains that among twelve million American Negroes there are today poverty, ignorance, disease and crime.

A determined fight has been made upon Negro ignorance, both within and without the group, and the results have been notable. Nevertheless, this is still an ignorant people. One in every six Negroes ten years of age and over, admitted in 1930 that he could not read and write. It is probable that one in every three would have been justified in confessing to practical illiteracy, to inexperience and lack of knowledge of the meaning of the modern world. In the South, not one-half the colored children from five to sixteen are regularly in school and the majority of these schools are not good schools. Any poor, ignorant people herded by themselves filled with more or less articulate resentment, are bound to be bad mannered, for manners are a matter of social environment; and the mass of American Negroes have retrograded in this respect.

There has been striking improvement in the Negro death rate. It was better than that of most South American countries, of Italy, Japan and Spain even before the war. But Cornely and Alexander conclude "that the health of the Negro in the United States as measured by mortality and morbidity statistics is not nearly so good as is that of the white population; that more needs to be done to meet his health needs particularly in the young adult group; that

progress has not been achieved through the media of private medical practice, hospital facilities, or public health facilities." Pneumonia, heart disease, syphilis and homicide are far too prevalent.

It is hard to know just what the criminal tendencies of the American Negroes are, for our crime statistics are woefully inadequate. We do know that in proportion to population three times as many Negroes are arrested as whites. The transgression of the poor and sick is always manifest among Negroes: disorder of all sorts, theft and burglary, fighting, breaking the gambling and liquor laws and especially fighting with and killing each other.

Above all the Negro is poor: poor by heritage from two hundred and forty-four years of chattel slavery, by emancipation without land or capital, and by seventy-five years of additional wage exploitation and crime peonage. Sudden industrial changes like the Civil War, the World War and the spree in speculation during the twenties have upset him. The Negro worker has been especially hard hit by the current depression. Of the nearly three million Negro families in the United States today probably the breadwinners of a million are unemployed and another million on the lower margin of decent subsistence. Analysis of 1930 census reports on occupations reveals for Negro workers says Wilkerson: "*first*, a disproportionate concentration in agricultural and domestic and personal service pursuits (six out of every ten Negro workers), both of which fields, especially agriculture, are experiencing the rapid inroads of technology; *second*, an even greater concentration in the social-economic group of unskilled workers (seven out of every ten gainfully employed Negroes), for which group the future seems to hold least promise; and *third*, a negligible degree of integration into the system of apprenticeship—1.4 per cent of the 77,452 apprentices in manufacturing and mechanical industries."

The Color Bar

The other consideration affecting Negro status is race prejudice. This prejudice is not entirely the result of the Negro's low social status. It is embalmed in the mores and institutions of the land and is manifest not only in the basic caste legislation of the South, but in the administration of law and the attitude of the courts in general. Thus social degradation of the Negro is intensified and emphasized by segregation, discrimination in employment and pay, difficulties of promotion and, more fundamentally, spiritual segregation from contact with those groups having the best manners and customs, and lack of incentives to effort despite handicaps. By outer pressure in most cases Negroes must live among themselves; neighbors to their own people in segregated parts of the city, in segregated country districts. The segregation is not complete and most of it is customary rather than legal. Nevertheless, most Negroes live with Negroes, in what are on the whole the least pleasant and healthful dwelling places.

This means that Negroes live in districts of low cultural level; that their contacts with their fellow men, involve contacts with people largely untrained and ignorant, and sometimes anti-social. These districts are not usually protected by the police—rather victimized and tyrannized over by them. Few realize what tyranny a low grade policeman can exercise in a colored neighborhood. In court his unsupported word cannot be disputed, and the only real defense against him is often mayhem and assassination by black criminals, with resultant hue and cry. City services of water, sewage, garbage-removal, street-cleaning, lighting, noise and traffic regulations, schools and hospitalization are usually neglected or withheld. Saloons, brothels and gambling seek these areas with open or tacit consent.

Ming emphasizes the fact that "The Negro suffers in the court not so much from the laws as from their administration. He suffers from the hostilities of jurors and judges." Nabrit says "The political impotence of the Negro in the South is due to the maladministration and malconstruction of the laws and not to the absence of laws."

In the basic matter of education, the discrimination is all too clear. Ransom shows that the equal protection clause of the Fourteenth Amendment is of little practical use, as the courts allow the authorities to give Negroes shorter terms, and lower salaries, and to divert funds from Negro to white schools. Wilkerson points out "that expenditures from Federal funds for vocational education in these eighteen (Southern) states aggregated $3,634,275 during 1934–35. Of this total, $3,279,341, or 90 per cent was spent for whites; and only $354,934, or ten per cent, for Negroes."

This race prejudice lies deeply entrenched in the minds of most Americans. Law and court decisions will not avail, until this fundamental attitude is changed. As Brown puts it, race prejudice "is not going to be appreciably weakened by preachments or mere assaults upon the stupid misconceptions current among whites about Negroes. Such approaches and programs attack the symptoms and manifestations of race prejudice, rather than its associated factors."

No matter in what degree or in what way the action of the white population may increase or decrease these social problems, they remain the present problems, which must be faced by colored people themselves and by colored people of widely different status.

What can be done, and done despite this prejudice which will last long and yield slowly?

Economic Emancipation

This symposium is arresting and unique in the emphasis put now for the first time on the underlying economic problem of the American Negro as pointing the next step in emancipation. It comes to the fore in nearly all the papers, but it has significant emphasis in a conspicuous few. Reuter says flatly "The Negro is a problem because he affords an easy means of exploiting prejudice for private profit." Johnson adds "In spite of many acute psychological aspects of race contact and relations, it is becoming increasingly evident to Southerners that the race problems are basically economic, and can only be soundly remedied by approaching them as such." Brown says "Any realistic program will take into account the economic foundations of race prejudice. It will recognize its relation to bread, security and prestige." Butler points out in the case of the main Negro occupational group, "No other occupational group of the American people is as disadvantaged as the Negro farmer. Not only does he suffer from the numerous diseases of a sick industry—which are popularly lumped together as the 'farm problem'—but he must operate under those additional handicaps imposed by the general poverty of the South and his racial proscription."

To what path does this point? Lewis says "The price of cotton is not a racial matter, nor the vicissitudes of the general economic cycle. . . . At every point the Negro's economic problem merges into a larger problem affecting men of either race. Yet this basic fact should not blind us to the comcomitant fact of racial discrimination." Lewis therefore advises "first, a successful attack upon the general economic problem of the country, second, an advance on the part of the working class as a whole, and finally, a degree of interracial cooperation on the economic level which will assure to the Negro a fair share in such advance."

The Labor Movement

Wesley and others believe that the Labor Movement is the most available present path for economic advance by Negroes. Wesley says "It can be well envisioned that racial lines may be broken at first in labor organizations, while inter-racial intellectuals are rationalizing differences, maintaining 'good' race relations and waving the 'red' flag above labor leaders who insist upon the importance of realizing, that fundamentally class lines are more determinative of labor's future than racial ones which are more dependent upon the accidents of birth. The future of white labor and of black labor will be tested by this realization as well as by its collective-bargaining power with American economic leadership." Brown adds "Any movement resulting in the economic, political or social collaboration of Negroes and whites, is far more important in the mitigation of prejudice than all the grand gestures *across* race lines."

This advice to the Negro worker, was already following before it was given. Butler points out that with the National Recovery Act and the National Labor Relations Board, there has been a large increase in Negro participation in labor unions. The Congress of Industrial Organization has given still further impetus. Johnson estimates 100,000 Negroes in the C.I.O. and a general increase of Negro union men among total union members in New York City from four to nine per cent in a decade. He points to increasing Negro membership in the Southern Tenant Farmers Union, and over a hundred interracial labor unions in the Northern Alabama industrial area, in the last five years.

Back of this strategic advice of the Negro intelligentsia, and defensive response of the Negro worker, lies the economic philosophy that, while the capitalists and other upper white groups are responding but slowly and reluctantly to the Negro demand for justice and equality, the white laborer, on the other hand, is forced by his necessities, to emphasize economic class interests rather than racial antagonisms. Lewis says "Casting up the evidence of the relative importance of these two factors, one is led inevitably to the conclusion that the economic rather than the racial factor is fundamental. . . . The history of American labor relations, in industry and agriculture, gives ample basis for the belief that the advance of labor in general is likely to suffer if there is a racial cleavage in its ranks."

But here it is necessary to ask what is the Labor Movement and whither is it headed? The symposium is significantly silent or vague here. In fact there is no one labor movement. The revolt of labor against present conditions exhibits three main directions: the American Federation of Labor is capitalistic, seeking a method of escape for fortunate individuals from the labor status to that of employer by monopoly, race discrimination and any available means. These means include the exploitation of less fortunate labor groups among the whites and of colored labor in general. This program is shared in by the Labor Party of England and by a considerable part of the labor movement of France. On the other hand, the Congress of Industrial Organization seeks greater income and better conditions of work for laborers as such, and does not envisage the rise of laborers into the ranks of capitalists or employers. To the end of raising the status of labor, it is willing to use all methods of bargaining, even to the

extent of forcible expropriation of property as exemplified by the sitdown strikes. Finally, the Communists seek a society without economic classes and would accomplish these by violent revolution, which they regard as the only method of overthrowing capitalism and enthroning the dictatorship of the proletariat.

Which now of these three paths shall we follow? There is in this symposium no clear answer to this, although most writers mention the Congress of Industrial Organization, and that not much because of agreement with objects, as because Negro labor force so large a proportion of the class which this organization is unionizing, that the recognition of black labor necessary to C.I.O.'s success. This inclusion of the Negro therefore, is not so much a matter of good will as of necessity; and above all, it is not due to any conviction on the part of white labor that the black labor movement is going to prove an asset and a help.

Our Economic Illiteracy

For this to be true, the Negro has got to study the world's economic plight. Bunche emphasizes this when he says "It is typical of Negro organizations that they concern themselves, not with the broad social and political implications of such policies as government relief, housing, socialized medicine, unemployment and old-age insurance, wages and hours laws, etc., but only with the purely racial aspects of such policies. They are content to let the white citizen determine the expediency of major policies, and the form and direction they will assume, while they set themselves up as watch dogs over relatively petty issues, as whether the Negro will get his proper share of the benefits and whether the laws, once made, will be fairly administered. They thus demark for the Negro a residual function in the society."

But why does not Mr. Bunche take a further and more searching step—and say, Regardless of what white folk are planning and doing, why do not Negroes boldly face the question, what do the best interests of our group demand in thought and action, and how far can a program to secure this be made to promote the best interests of all men? Mr. Bunche does not say this because he deplores and derides racial action as such. He lays down nevertheless a thirteen point program for racial organizations, thus clearly recognizing that Negroes must organize for certain ends; and while he insists that such organizations must not be "racial" they must necessarily be racial in effect, since they are carrying out the objects of the Negro-American group and for that reason must be predominantly Negro-American in membership and in ideology.

Such organization, he wishes to stress political and economic forces; raise the economic level of the Negro worker; encourage Negroes to join labor unions and carry on a program of propaganda among white and black workers to this end; support the organization of labor on an industrial basis; fight for the vote and court decisions, but subordinate this to the fight for economic justice; recognize that the best interests of the Negro are bound up with the best interests of the workers; encourage labor leaders to cooperate; relate the interests of the Negro to world events; recognize that the basic problem today is not that of the vote and the court, but of economic institutions; and that cultural uplift can and will overcome racial prejudice.

On the other hand Mr. Johnson's deductions from the same original thesis are more questionable. He says "With increasing social stratification in the Negro group and self-consciousness of labor generally, there will be closer class relationships between white and Negro professional and white and Negro workers. This is to say, the white and Negro workers will be closer in their interests than the Negro professional and the Negro worker. It is significant that no all-Negro racial movement exists in America, and there is no present indication that such will develop in the near future. The whole logic of present trends is toward the employment of the strategy of consolidating minority interests to enforce wider participation in the life of the community. There will be fewer and fewer objectives of the Negroes which are more racial than social and economic."

This seems to me a dangerous proposition. Instead of regimenting the members of the Negro group into a determined assault upon the racial barriers by economic methods, rather than simply by appeals to law and a sense of justice, Mr. Johnson would apparently have us throw overboard racial organizations just as quickly as possible, so that the Negro may land himself into the class structure of white social organizations and share their interests and hatreds. This assumes that the present economic class structure in the white world is satisfactory, and that class opposition between Negro capitalists, exploiters and professional men, as against Negro labor, is an ideal toward which Negroes should work.

This is dangerous advice and is partly shared in by other writers in this symposium; and by earlier writers who assume that the matter of acting as a racial group and organizing for objectives which the Negroes must attain if they survive, are matters of choice and blurred vision on the part of Negroes. Raphael Powell in 1937 published the last example of a long line of books and articles which try to say that the whole cause of the "Negro" problem, is that colored people allow themselves to be called Negroes and to think and act as Negroes. The obvious and inescapable answer is, that so long as the majority of white Americans believe in race and color discrimination, just so long we must act racially as Negroes. There is no alternative. Jews cannot avoid anti-Semitism by changing their names or refusing to cooperate with Jews for common objects. We have got to have racial organizations and recognize the group interests of American Negroes, so long as outer pressure compels this; that outer pressure does compel it is manifest in this symposium. Johnson and Bunche and I myself are working in Negro universities, not because the subject matter which we teach is purely "racial"; or because science should have a "racial" tinge; or because ability should be segregated by color; but for the obvious reason that no white university in the United States is going to give us a chance for teaching and research.

The Negro World

For this reason, we American Negroes have built, and in self defense have had to build, a singularly complete and separate Negro world in homes, schools, churches, hospitals, newspapers, literature and summer resorts. We lag in providing economic institutions, but present conditions are forcing us to at least examine the possibilities in this field.

What Mr. Bunche means to emphasize is the necessity of avoiding, in our unavoidable racial segregation, the adoption of narrowly racial objectives which hinder us from seeing the wider paths beckoning all humanity. This is not so clear in Mr. Johnson's thesis, since he apparently thinks that the avoidance of racial aims in our economic objectives is going to facilitate our escape into the economic classes of the whites; and that there we are going to be in a position to forget and ignore race. This procedure would lay our flanks bare to attack. Economic class division is not peace but war. Lewis and Wesley apparently recognize this, but believe that the planning of the Congress of Industrial Organization will result in such advance of labor as will create a new industrial world, although they do not indicate just what this world would be.

Into any new industrial objectives, however, the Negro must take thought lest the labor program consciously or unconsciously wreck itself upon the problem of race. To avoid this Bunche advises that Negroes take part in planning and that Negro labor leaders be invited into racial organizations in order to guide their thought and action. But here again comes difficulty: the program and ideology of white labor is continually being furnished them by an intelligentsia which sympathizes with their objects. This intelligentsia does not come down from above. It rises from the laboring mass itself. It is self uplift and not sympathy or philanthropy from above. But such intelligent leadership must come. Without this intelligent guidance, laborers will meet disaster in the future as in the past. And while they often repudiate their intelligentsia, in the long run it is cultural leadership that must guide the labor movement.

This must be true in the case of the Negro. The inferior culture status of the Negro American, means that his inclusion in any great forward movement, like that of labor, calls either for unselfish humanitarianism on the part of white labor, or such a strategic position on the part of Negroes that their exclusion would mean disaster to the whites. We cannot logically expect labor leaders to be more unselfish than the mass of the white world in which they have been trained and from which they have received their ideals. On the other hand it is not wise to assume that even in unskilled labor, the aims of white folk could not be accomplished with considerable success, even if they continued to

W. E. B. Du Bois (Courtesy of the Moorland-Spingarn Research Center)

discriminate against colored labor. We see that clearly in the attitude of white European labor toward colored colonial labor. It is more difficult to carry out such a policy in a country where the two groups are living side by side, and yet the post Civil War history of the South has been the rise of poor whites largely at the expense of black labor.

It is for this reason that I am apprehensive at a current tendency in the South which Johnson lauds. He says of a recent encouraging conference in Birmingham "The central feature . . . was the shift of attention from the Negro as a separate and embarrassing burden on the South, to an acceptance, in principle and practice, of the Negro as an organic part of its regional program of reconstruction." But does this make the burden less heavy or call for less attention and effort? I am worried because this current pattern enables the South to discuss its problems without separating the Negro problem and also to attack its problem without giving the Negro angle the attention it demands. It does not reduce Negro ignorance and poverty by calling the plight regional and proceeding to give the whites better schools and higher wages. It still remains true that the burden of the cultural uplift of the Negro and his advance in economic as well as intellectual and artistic lines must be assumed by his own cultural classes.

Negro Acculturation

It seems to me the most striking result of this symposium, that a young Negro scientist confirms from the most recent technique of anthropology and psychology, not only the fact that this must be true, but that it already is true in our own development. Allison Davis writes "There are major differences of behavior within Negro groups according to economic levels. In Negro groups today, parents are members of small social cliques which consist of intimate groups of two or more friends. These social cliques are the steps in the ladder of social rank and through them class sanctions are maintained and brought to bear upon the child's behavior. The upward or downward movement of an individual or family in the status system is a process of getting to know and associate freely with a small group of people just above or just below the position occupied by the individual. *The controls upon the relation between whites and Negroes are less important in the child's training than the class and clique control of the family in which he is trained.*" (My italics.)

Roucek and Brown emphasize this: "Every immigrant group is again subdivided into numerous socially stratified classes and castes disintegrated and frequently warring with each other. This applies also to the Negroes. Negroes are not just Negroes to each other. A multitude of status lines crisscross their social relationships." Davis continues "The colored group, therefore, takes the form of a steeple resting upon a tremendous base of lower class persons. The white group takes the form of a tower wider in the middle than at the bottom." Frazier emphasizes this differentiation in urban Negro family life. "The movement of the more stable elements in the Negro population toward the periphery of the Negro community is indicated by a gradual decline in the various forms of family disorganization."

This conclusion then seems to me inevitable: *The Negro in America occupies today a low cultural station. The acculturation of his masses must be mainly the task of his own intelligensia. If they refuse, the acculturation of this mass will continue at the hands of the whites, but slowly and hesitatingly, with possible regression and disaster, and with constant threat to the status of cultural Negroes the world over, so long as color and a low status can be coupled in the minds of men.*

What now are the norms of this Negro acculturation? First of all it must be primarily and fundamentally in economic lines. All else depends on this. If we can earn a decent living, we can fight race discrimination until it dies, if it takes a thousand years. In this fight for income, must it necessarily happen among us as among whites, that Class deserts Mass and exploits it? Acculturation follows even here, but slowly, haltingly; in slums, disease and crime. It is a long, discouraging tragedy. Must we follow this pattern? Is it inevitable and right because it is white? Most Negroes, especially the educated and well-to-do, thoroughly believe this. They do not for a moment question the right and duty of well-to-do Negroes to profit by the low wage and low status of the poor. Their conception of a fight against race prejudice is the right to conspicuous expenditure on the part of the colored well-to-do.

The mass of American Negroes especially in the upper classes, believe in the present economic régime so long as it does not discriminate against them. As Mr. Lewis says "It is difficult to see how the development of purely Negro business enterprise would bring benefit to the Negro population in general, whatever its effect on a favored few. Nor there is little reason, in theory or experience, to believe that labor relations under these circumstances would be much less 'business-like' than the relation between the Negro worker *or the white worker* and the present white employer." Mr. Bunche emphasizes the fact that "The Negro is sorely in need of organization and leadership, which is sufficiently independent and intelligent to give courageous orientation to the group and to guide it rationally through the bewildering maze of social forces which characterize the modern world." But he adds "Existing Negro organizations are philosophical and programatic paupers. They think and act entirely in a black groove. In a world in which events move rapidly and in which the very future of themselves and their group is at stake, they are unable to see the social forests for the racial saplings."

To which I would answer, the way to the social forest is through the racial saplings; or better, as it must appear to most of us today, the way to the saplings which are growing into the future social forest, is through the present stark and thick trunks of ancient trees with almost impassable undergrowth; through which the American Negro and other colored groups must force and cut a way. But seriously are we so ultra-racial, so proud of our color and convinced of our superiority, as to need warning? Bunche quotes Hitler "All that is not race is trash"; and apparently seeks to substitute "All save Race is our soul's salvation."

That the Negro must move in a racial groove today is clearly shown by our desperate educational plight. The majority of Negro children are not learning to read and write. Those in school are so poorly taught for such short terms that they cannot do first class college work. Instead of getting hysterical over the handicap of one graduate student, we must stir united group effort to teach a million unschooled children, to enlist better and more teachers, to found folk adult study circles—in fine to educate ourselves, instead of helplessly complaining that white folk do not train us in intelligence.

Thompson is concerned at the plight of Negro education, but apparently has a perfect phobia in regarding one cause of this as more important than the thing itself: cultural segregation from the whites undoubtedly slows up the process of Negro education; but the evil is in the lack of education itself, and not in the separate school; if despite the separate school, we can educate the Negro youth properly and completely, we have solved our problem. It seems to me less than sane to make more moan over "jim-crow" schools, than over Negro ignorance.

Of course the whites bar us from most of their schools. Most of them do not want us to be intelligent. On the other hand a majority of the whites are willing to let us teach ourselves. This we are doing. Most intelligent Negro-Americans today were taught by Negro teachers in Negro schools. Our job is not to neglect this major duty of teaching our own, by vain regrets at the fact that our schools are poorer and our teachers not so well-trained as the whites. Meet the problem of better Negro schools face-forward, and solve it.

This we are not doing. We are ashamed of Negro schools. We should be proud of them. They have given us this symposium. They can give us economic emancipation. But they are not doing this. They are failing in Vocational Guidance, as well as in other ways. Wilkerson says: "What is most disturbing about the guidance objectives reported is their platitudinous disregard for some of the most basic considerations which affect the vocational adjustment of Negro youth. . . . Only three of the eighty-two institutions reported 'a definite understanding of the occupational problems of Negroes' as an objective of their programs of vocational guidance."

In the same way Dr. Alexander insists that "Private medical practice among Negroes has progressed little if at all in this generation. The Negro physicians are not distributed according to the needs of the people. Negroes are excluded from taxed supported medical schools and have inadequate medical and hospital facilities. There is lack of insurance; waste and duplication of equipment; inability to practice preventive medicine; inability to keep up to date in knowledge of medicine; factions in professional ranks; exploitation of Negro patients and physicians by makers of patent medicines, drug companies, etc. Negro professional personnel are disadvantaged in industrial medicine, in the field of insurance examiners. Negro insurance companies are not responsive to health education needs of their clients."

A racial technique in art and propaganda is inevitable. The children of Charles Johnson have been taught about the deeds of great colored men; the children of Ralph Bunche are going to be carefully instructed in the vagaries of the color-line and trained not to be ashamed of their color. We all have to do this, much as we hate the necessity. But here too is opportunity: our Art can make black beautiful. It can be, not simply a "contribution to American culture," but a contribution to our own culture, which is and long will be a thing largely segregated and apart, despite all we think or do. Sterling Brown says: "American treatment of the Negro is now seen to be one of the greatest challenges to democracy. Negro writers, becoming more and more articulate and socially aware, are joining in the depiction of the problems faced by Negroes. Writing from the inside, they are often powerfully persuasive."

But Brown is here evidently thinking mainly of the white audience, as though Negro art must always have this as their goal; why not see Negro literature in terms of the Negro audience: as a means of expression of their feelings and aspiration; as a picture painted for their own enlightenment of the vast tragedy of their life, and the comedy of their very frustrations? This is possible; but only possible as a buying Negro clientele is deliberately and consciously built up to support such art. In the end such literature and only such will be authentic and true enough to join the Art Universal.

Economic Planning

The guiding of Negroes in their occupations by careful thought and planning is fundamental. Lewis points out that behind the walls of race segregation black institutions have developed, and among these black institutions are Negro business, Negro professional men and a considerable number of white collar workers. He points out that the more balanced and normal Negro institutions are those which have been forced by segregation and serve specific racial demands; but that even these have lacked vigor and opened no broad gate-way to respectability and self-sufficiency, because "basic industry, essential raw material, transportations and finance" are controlled by white capital.

This calls for on the part of Negroes a full-hearted attempt at new adjustment. Roucek and Brown reiterate what has so often been said: "The Negro being assigned a more definite place in the social ladder, has developed the art of adjustment to rules of social relations. Immigrant minorities have no such well developed patterns." Can then the Negro adjust and adapt himself to new economic institutions, so as to avoid being crushed by those which surround him, and establish such institutions as will lead out of his economic wilderness? The answer here again is that he must do this, and that he is already beginning to do it.

We cannot and must not follow the economic class structure of America. We have neither the economic nor political power, the ownership of machines and materials, the power to direct the processes of industry, the monopoly of capital and credit. On the other hand, even if we cannot follow this method of structure, nevertheless we are not helpless. With a magnificent new system of natural roads, transportation is no longer entirely the monopoly of Big Business; raw materials are only in part monopolized; cheap electric power can decentralize industry in some branches, and popular thrift is intimidated rather than impotent as a source of financial aid. We must do something. We cannot stand still; we cannot permit ourselves simply to be the victims of exploitation and social exclusion. It is from this paradox that arises the present frustration among American Negroes. We are afraid. We think it impossible to build economic institutions. Is this true or is it only true that we cannot and ought not to imitate the profit-making robbery and exploitation that has so long dominated American business ideals?

In the past the path seemed clearer. For a while it was education. When we had educated leaders all things else would be added unto us. This was not untrue; it was half-true. Then came faith in political power, but political power is limited by the power of wealth in the United States and even in its limited field we are partially disfranchised. Then came faith in agitation and the courts; but all this depends upon a responsive and sympathetic public opinion which is disposed to enforce rights and protest injustice done to Negroes. Such public opinion exists in some circles, but it is not yet a majority opinion. Its full development will demand several generations.

Meantime is there no way out? Yes, there is; because the American economic class structure—that system of domination of industry and the state, through income and monopoly, is breaking down; not simply in America but in the world. American Negroes realize this in widely differing degrees. Most of the well-to-do, with fair education, do not realize the imminence of profound economic change in the modern world. They are thinking in terms of work, thrift, investment and profit. They hope with the late Booker T. Washington to secure better economic conditions for Negroes by wider chances of employment and higher wages. They believe in savings and investment in Negro and in general business, and in the gradual evolution of a Negro capitalist class which will exploit both Negro and white labor. On the other hand some of the younger and better educated Negroes see the coming change in economic conditions, but envisage its ultimate accomplishment only through following the white labor movement. They, therefore, impress it upon Negroes that alliance with labor rather than with capital spells their salvation. They urge Negroes to join the labor unions and to advocate trade union methods of labor uplift.

The difficulty with this latter solution is that the same color line, the same racial repulsion persists in the labor movement as in the case of other cultural contacts. This is only natural. The white laborer has been trained to dislike and fear black labor; to regard the Negro as an unfair competitor able and willing to degrade the price of labor; and even if the Negro prove a good union man, his treatment as an equal would involve equal status, which the white laborer through his long cultural training bitterly resents as a degradation of his own status. Under these circumstances the American Negro faces in the current labor movement, especially in the A. F. of L. and also in the C.I.O., the current racial patterns of America.

The present economic order of the white world does not work. It has worked for considerable periods in the past and has accomplished miracles of efficiency, marvels of construction and dreams of power; it might continue to work today if not perfectly, at least to the satisfaction of most men, but for certain fatal weaknesses inherent to any system of irresponsible rule and uncurbed selfishness. The system continually and inevitably tempts individual owners and autocratic rulers of innumerable and semi-independent economic satrapies, kingdoms and empires, to accumulate profits at the expense of wages. And more fatal than this, combinations of these economic realms into national and international groups are made, from time to time, to work their will by world-wide war and murder, with use of all the resources of science, in order to enslave colonial labor and further monopolize goods.

The Consumer

The situation has become impossible; it cannot go on. It threatens the very foundations of civilization. Everyone recognizes this danger. Some government interference, some general control and regulation of private industry must take place or civilization collapses. First of all, it is clear that the interests of the intelligent consuming public and not the private profit of the owners of capital and directors of industry, must hereafter be the guiding and regulating force in industry. The production of goods and the rendering of services must be planned and directed for satisfying the wants of mankind and not primarily for enriching of the powerful few.

The consuming public, who should also be the real working producers of the world, must resume its logical and rightful place the final directing force in industry. This can be done without violence or revolution. Consumers today hold in their hands sufficient power first, to break down by their present ballot the legal institutions behind which monopoly of wealth is entrenched: land monopoly, mal-distribution of tax burdens, unjust allocation of the unearned increment of rents, unfair trade practices with adulteration of foods and misrepresentation of goods, tariff inequalities and bonuses, concealment of income and profits, unfair laws of contracts; cheating and gambling, unhampered judicial interference with law-making; patent monopoly; news suppression and distortion; and transfer of wealth and power by gift and inheritance, regardless of desert or the public good; above all, the laws and lack of laws which make group action by consumers in the interest of consumers, illegal or ineffective.

The second object of consumer groups should be themselves gradually to regain control of production, thus making the interests of producers and consumers identical. To do this, they must begin by creating a primary group of industrial democracy, corresponding to the New England townmeeting in political democracy. Indeed in mediaeval Africa, just this development was carried out in the village council, where every family was represented, and where economic action was controlled and guided as well as social and political. This was the basic communalism of the African tribe which the slave trade and colonial imperialism killed.

The new consumers' group will first essay to understand the real and essential needs of its members, and to supply these needs by goods and services at a reasonable price. Beginning merely as an intelligent distributing unit, it can buy at wholesale without retail profit, without risk of unsold stocks, useless advertising and rent. The inevitable attack upon this by modern business methods, by newspaper propaganda and even organized and purchased violence can be countered by uniting units for wholesale buying on a wider scale, and finally by cooperative production and wide planning of services in lines where monopoly permits.

It will be a hard fight, and its success depends, on the one hand, on how far intelligence, integrity, ability and high economic ideals, can be secured to serve these crusading groups; and a new industrial democracy established on a firm basis of individual knowledge and initiative built up to contest the occupation of the industrial field with the present individualists, monopolists, high-binders and free-booters. This will call for on the other hand, from the cooperating consumers and all friends of human culture, parallel, relentless fight against present secrecy, privilege and cheating; against the concentrated power of wealth in propaganda and for real freedom of the press. It does not seem impossible to establish gradually such little islands of industrial democracy and socialized wealth, clustered for defense and more complete economic autonomy, even though for a season, they continue to be surrounded by an ocean of monarchs and by the anarchists of present industry.

The Black Consumer

Right here the American Negro has his opportunity. As Bunche says, "No effective use has ever been made of the numerical strength of the Negro population, nor of its economic importance in labor and consuming power." The Negro is primarily a consumer in the sense that his place as a producer in the industrial process lacks power and income. He is disfranchised largely as a producer but not as a consumer. Moreover, he still has a remnant of his political power, and as Johnson shows, that is growing not only in the North but even in the South. He has in addition to that his

economic power as consumer, as one who can buy goods with some discretion as to what goods he buys. It may truly be said that his discretion is not large but it does exist, and it may be made the basis of a new instrument of democratic control over industry. During the days of economic equilibrium when under the capitalist system, wealth was fast accumulating and while far from being equitably distributed, yet was going in much larger proportion than ever before to the white laboring classes, the American Negro as a working class could depend upon increasing wage for himself; and the white philanthropic attitude made contribution toward his economic and social salvation. Today this is not true. Philanthropy for educational and social uplift is being increasingly curtailed; low wage and unemployment among white workers is widespread; the capitalistic system has been widely modified by government interference and control and in spite of powerful reaction, faces without doubt fundamental transformation.

The cultural differentiation among American Negroes has considerably outstripped the economic differences, which sets this group aside as unusual and at the same time opens possibilities for institutional development and changes of great importance. Fundamental in such change would be the building up of new economic institutions suited to minority groups without wide economic differences and with distinct cultural possibilities, as shown by the increasing number of college graduates among them, the varying but persistent development of a literature of expression and of a Negro-American art.

The fact that the number of Negro college graduates has increased from 215 between 1876 and 1880 to 10,000 between 1931 and 1935 shows that ability is there if it will act. In addition to mental ability there is demanded an extraordinary moral strength—the strength to endure discrimination and not become discouraged; to face almost universal disparagement and keep one's soul; and to sacrifice for an ideal which the present generation will hardly see fulfilled. This is an unusual demand and no one can say off-hand whether or not the present generation of American Negroes is equal to it. But there is reason to believe, that if the high emotional content of the Negro soul could once be guided into channels that promise success, the end might be accomplished.

Despite a low general level of income Negroes probably spend at least one hundred and fifty million dollars a month under ordinary circumstances and they live in an era when gradually economic revolution is substituting the consumer as the decisive voice in industry, rather than the all-powerful controller of production of the past. Already in the Negro group the consumer interest is dominant. His social institutions, therefore, are almost entirely the institutions of consumers and it is precisely along the development of these institutions that he can move in general accordance with the economic development of his time and of the larger white group and also in this way evolve unified organization for his own economic salvation.

The fact is, as the Census of 1930 shows, that there is almost no need that a modern group has, which Negro workers already trained and at work, are not able to satisfy. Already Negroes can raise their own food, build their own homes, fashion their own clothes, mend their own shoes, do much of their repair work, and raise some raw materials like tobacco and cotton. A simple transfer of Negro workers, with only such additional skills as can easily be learned in a few months, would enable them to weave their own cloth, make their own shoes, slaughter their own meat, prepare furniture for their homes, install electrical appliances, make their own cigars and cigarettes.

Appropriate direction and easy obtainable technique and capital, would enable Negroes further to take over the whole of their retail distribution, to raise, cut, mine and manufacture a considerable proportion of the basic raw material, to man their own manufacturing plants, to process foods, to import necessary raw materials, to invent and build machines. Processes and monopolized natural resources, they must continue to buy, but they could buy them on just as advantageous terms as their competitors if they bought in large quantities and paid cash, instead of enslaving themselves with white usury. Large numbers of other Negroes working as miners, laborers in industry and transportation could without difficulty be transferred to productive industries designed to cater to Negro consumers. The matter of skill in such industries is not as important as in the past with industrial operations massed and standardized.

Without doubt, there are difficulties in the way of this program. The Negro population is scattered. The mouths which the Negro farmers might feed might be hundreds of thousands of miles away, and carpenters and mechanics would have to be concentrated and guaranteed a sufficiency of steady employment. All this would call for careful planning and particularly, such an organization of consumers as would eliminate unemployment, risk and profit. Demand, organized and certain, must precede the production and transportation of goods. The waste of advertising must be eliminated. The difference between actual cost and selling price must disappear, doing away with exploitation of labor which is the source of profit.

All this would be a realization of democracy in industry, led by consumers organizations and extending to planned production. Is there any reason to doubt that such democracy among American Negroes could evolve the necessary leadership in technique, and the necessary social institutions which would so guide and organize the masses that a new economic foundation could be laid for a group which is today threatened with poverty and social subordination?

Segregation

To a degree, but not completely, this is a program of segregation. The consumer group is in important aspects a self-segregated group. We are now segregated largely without reason. Let us put reason and power beneath the segregation. Nothing is more utterly discouraging than to see the mass of intelligent American Negroes divide, hide, scuttle and run, at the very moment when united open mass effort would reveal to the world the power, ability, and genius of black folk. Englishmen do not die of shame if they are asked to work with Englishmen for the good of England. They even assume that the good of England is the good of all men, and that is often if not always true. Most men act in separate groups, nations, and races; and human unity will not leap at a bound from individual to humanity, but from neighborhood to nation, to internation to type and stock.

We are facing racial economic opportunity in the United States today. There are at present 31 Farm security projects in 13 Southern states open to 1700 Negro families. There are 14 Negro housing projects costing nearly 30 million dollars and housing 5,750 families already occupied. There are 15 other projects occupied by whites and Negroes, and housing 1200 Negro families at a proportional cost of forty million. Six more Negro projects are under construction, nine with contracts approved, while financial assistance has been promised to seventy-one others and earmarked for ninety-five others.

Here is an unrivalled opportunity for consumers' cooperation among perhaps 200,000 Negroes. Credit unions, home mortgages, farmers credit and even industrial capital are available for Negroes at the hands of the government. Rail if you will against the race segregation here involved and condoned, but take advantage of it by planting secure centers of Negro cooperative effort and particularly of economic power; to make us spiritually free for initiative and creation in other and wider fields, and for eventually breaking down all segregation based on color or curl of hair.

Have we the brains to do this?

Here in the past we have easily landed into a morass of criticism, without faith in the ability of

American Negroes to extricate themselves from their present plight. Our former panacea emphasized by Booker T. Washington was flight of class from mass in wealth with the idea of escaping the masses or ruling the masses through power placed in the hands of those with larger income. My own panacea of earlier days was flight of class from mass, through the development of a Talented Tenth; but the power of this aristocracy of talent was to lie in its knowledge and character, and not in its economic power. The problem which I did not then attack was that of leadership and authority within the group, which by implication left controls to wealth—a contingency of which I never dreamed. But now the whole economic trend of the world has changed. That mass and class must unite for the world's salvation is clear. We who have had least class differentiation in wealth, can follow in the new trend and indeed lead it.

Democracy

The discussion of leadership among American Negroes has not usually been associated with a parallel discussion of democracy. What Negroes have meant by democracy is the right to have their wishes and needs considered in the general social objects of the nation. They have sought to attain this with political power and followed this with a vision of economic power through control of capital. They are now forced to consider the building-up of democracy and democratic power among themselves. This calls for a new attempt to reorganize democracy.

Democratic control of the state or of a group without force, without power on the part of the cultured classes to compel the obedience of the masses has seldom succeeded and yet we all know that force defeats itself. Even a dictatorship of the proletariat, designed to hold the powers of the state in trust until the people have reached such a degree of intelligence, efficiency and social mindedness as to be able to conduct a government, may degenerate into the tyranny of a clique. This is what one fears today in Russia. We are used to seeing the force of a single tyrant or the force of an aristocracy degenerate into regarding the state as existing solely for them. We expect to see the same disaster overtake the totalitarian state. Can all this be avoided? Can ten million American Negroes led by cultured classes numbering less than a million, achieve efficient and voluntary democracy without force, without police power, without the domination of wealth and capital?

Most Negroes do not believe that this can be done. They not only share American public opinion in distrusting the inherent ability of the Negro group, but they see no way in which the present classes who have proven their intelligence and efficiency can gain leadership over their own people. On the contrary they fear desperately a vulgarization of emerging culture among them, by contact with the ignorant and anti-social mass. This fear has been accentuated by recent radical agitation; unwashed and unshaven demagogues have scared and brow-beaten the cultured Negroes; have convinced them that their leadership can only be secured through demagoguery. It is for this reason that we see in large Northern centers like Chicago and New York, intelligent, efficient Negroes conniving with crime, gambling and prostitution, in order to secure control of the Negro vote and gain place and income for black folk. Their procedure is not justified by the fact that excellent and well-trained Negro officials are thus often raised to power. The price paid is deliberate surrender of any attempt at acculturation of the mass, in exchange for increased income among the few.

Yet American Negroes must know that the advance of the Negro people since emancipation has been the extraordinary success in education, technique and character among a small number of Negroes and that the emergence of these exceptional men has been largely a matter of chance; that their triumph proves that down among the mass, ten times their number with equal ability could be discovered and developed, if sustained effort and sacrifice and intelligence were put to this task. That on the contrary today poverty, sickness and crime are choking the paths to Negro uplift, and that salvation of the Negro race is to come by planned and sustained efforts to open ways of development to those who now form the unrisen mass of the Negro group.

It is to be admitted that this will be a real battle. There are chances of failure, but there are also splendid chances of success. In the African communal group, ties of family and blood, of mother and child, of group relationship, made the group leadership strong, even if not always toward the highest culture. In the case of the more artificial group among American Negroes, there are sources of strength in common memories of suffering in the past; in present threats of degradation and extinction; in common ambitions and ideals, in emulation and the determination to prove ability and desert. Here in subtle but real ways the communalism of the African clan can be transferred to the Negro American group, implemented by higher ideals of human accomplishment through the education and culture which have arisen and may further arise through contact of black folk with the modern world. The emotional wealth of the American Negro, the nascent art in song, dance, and drama can all be applied, not to simply amuse the white audience, but to inspire and direct the acting Negro group itself. I can conceive no more magnificent nor promising crusade in modern times. We have a chance here to teach industrial and cultural democracy to a world that bitterly needs it.

When real and open democratic control is intelligent enough to select of its own accord on the whole the best, most courageous, most expert and scholarly leadership, then the problem of democracy within the Negro group is solved and by that same token the possibility of American Negroes entering into world democracy and taking their rightful place according to their knowledge and power is also sure. Here then is the economic ladder by which the American Negro, achieving new social institutions, can move pari passu with the modern world into a new heaven and a new earth.

CARTER G. WOODSON

Understand The Negro

"We do not offer here any course in Negro history, Negro literature, or race relations," recently said a professor of a Negro college. "We study the Negro along with other people."

"An excellent idea," the interviewer replied. "No one should expect you to do any more than this, but how do you do it when the Negro is not mentioned in your textbooks except to be condemned? Do you, a teacher in a Negro school, also condemn the race in the same fashion as the writers of your textbooks of history and literature?"

"No," said he, "we bring the Negro in here and there."

"How often does 'here and there' connote?"

"Well, you know," said he, "Negroes have not done much; and what they have accomplished may be briefly covered by referring to the achievements of a few men and women.

"Why do you emphasize the special study of the Negro?" said he further. "Why is it necessary to give the race special attention in the press, on the rostrum, or in the schoolroom? This idea of projecting the Negro into the foreground does the race much harm by singing continually of his woes and problems and thus alienating the public which desires to give its attention to other things."

It is true that many Negroes do not desire to hear anything about their race, and few whites of today will listen to the story of woe. With most of them the race question has been settled. The Negro has been assigned to the lowest drudgery as the sphere in which the masses must toil to make a living; and socially and po-

litically the race has been generally proscribed. Inasmuch as the traducers of the race have "settled" the matter in this fashion, they naturally oppose any effort to change this status.

Many Negro professional men who are making a living attending to the affairs of these laborers and servants in their mentally undeveloped state and many teachers who in conservative fashion are instructing their children to maintain the *status quo ante bellum*, also oppose any movement to upset this arrangement. They are getting paid for their efforts. Why should they try innovations? The gods have so decreed it. Human beings cannot change it. Why be foolish?

A Negro with sufficient thought to construct a program of his own is undesirable, and the educational systems of this country generally refuse to work through such Negroes in promoting their cause. The program for the uplift of the Negroes in this country must be handed over to an executive force like orders from the throne, and they must carry it out without question or get out of line and let the procession go on. Although the Negro is being daily forced more and more by segregation into a world peculiarly his own, his unusually perplexing status is given little or no thought, and he is not considered capable of thinking for himself.

The chief difficulty with the education of the Negro is that it has been largely imitation resulting in the enslavement of his mind. Somebody outside of the race has desired to try out on Negroes some experiment which interested him and his coworkers; and Negroes, being objects of charity, have received them cordially and have done what they required. In fact, the keynote in the education of the Negro has been to do what he is told to do. Any Negro who has learned to do this is well prepared to function in the American social order as others would have him.

Looking over the courses of study of the public schools, one finds little to show that the Negro figures in these curricula. In supplementary matter a good deed of some Negro is occasionally referred to, but oftener the race is mentioned only to be held up to ridicule. With the exception of a few places like Atlantic City, Atlanta, Tulsa, St. Louis, Birmingham, Knoxville, and the states of Louisiana and North Carolina no effort is made to study the Negro in the public schools as they do the Latin, the Teuton, or the Mongolian. Several mis-educated Negroes themselves contend that the study of the Negro by children would bring before them the race problem prematurely and, therefore, urge that the study of the race be deferred until they reach advanced work in the college or university. These misguided teachers ignore the fact that the race question is being brought before black and white children daily in their homes, in the streets, through the press and on the rostrum. How, then, can the school ignore the duty of teaching the truth while these other agencies are playing up falsehood?

The experience of college instructors shows that racial attitudes of the youth are not easily changed after they reach adolescence. Although students of this advanced stage are shown the fallacy of race superiority and the folly of social distinctions, they nevertheless continue to do the illogical thing of still looking upon these depised groups as less worthy than themselves and persist in treating them accordingly. Teachers of elementary and secondary schools giving attention to this interracial problem have succeeded in softening and changing the attitude of children whose judgment has not been so hopelessly warped by the general attitude of the communities in which they have been brought up.

In approaching this problem in this fashion to counteract the one-sided education of youth the thinking people of this country have no desire to upset the curricula of the schools or to force the Negro as such into public discussion; but, if the Negro is to be elevated he must be educated in the sense of being developed from what he is, and the public must be so enlightened as to think of the Negro as a man. Furthermore, no one can be thoroughly educated until he learns as much about the Negro as he knows about other people.

Upon examining the recent catalogues of the leading Negro colleges, one finds that invariably they give courses in ancient, mediæval, and modern Europe, but they do not give such courses in ancient, mediæval, and modern Africa. Yet Africa, according to recent discoveries, has contributed about as much to the progress of mankind as Europe has, and the early civilization of the Mediterranean world was decidedly influenced by Africa.

Negro colleges offer courses bearing on the European colonists prior to their coming to America, their settlement on these shores, and their development here toward independence. Why are they not equally generous with the Negroes in treating their status in Africa prior to enslavement, their first transplantation to the West Indies, the Latinization of certain Negroes in contradistinction to the development of others under the influence of the Teuton, and the effort of the race toward self-expression?

A further examination of their curricula shows, too, that invariably these Negro colleges offer courses in Greek philosophy and in that of modern European thought, but they direct no attention to the philosophy of the African. Negroes of Africa have and always have had their own ideas about the nature of the universe, time, and space, about appearance and reality, and about freedom and necessity. The effort of the Negro to interpret man's relation to the universe shows just as

much intelligence as we find in the philosophy of the Greeks. There were many Africans who were just as wise as Socrates.

Again, one observes in some of these catalogues numerous courses in art but no well defined course in Negro or African art which early influenced that of the Greeks. Thinkers are now saying that the early culture of the Mediterranean was chiefly African. Most of these colleges do not even direct special attention to Negro music in which the Negro has made his outstanding contribution in America. The unreasonable attitude is that because the whites do not have these things in their schools the Negroes must not have them in theirs. The Catholics and Jews, therefore, are wrong in establishing special schools to teach their principles of religion, and the Germans in America are unwise in having their children taught their mother tongue.

Such has been the education of Negroes. They have been taught facts of history, but have never learned to think. Their conception is that you go to school to find out what other people have done, and then you go out in life to imitate them. What they have done can be done by others, they contend; and they are right. They are wrong, however, in failing to realize that what others have done, we may not need to do. If we are to do identically the same thing from generation to generation, we would not make any progress. If we are to duplicate from century to century the same feats, the world will grow tired of such a monotonous performance.

In this particular respect "Negro education" is a failure, and disastrously so, because in its present predicament the race is especially in need of vision and invention to give humanity something new. The world does not want and will never have the heroes and heroines of the past. What this age needs is an enlightened youth not to undertake the tasks like theirs but to imbibe the spirit of these great men and answer the present call of duty with equal nobleness of soul.

Not only do the needs of generations vary, but the individuals themselves are not duplicates the one of the other; and being different in this respect, their only hope to function efficiently in society is to know themselves and the generation which they are to serve. The chief value in studying the records of others is to become better acquainted with oneself and with one's possibilities to live and to do in the present age. As long as Negroes continue to restrict themselves to doing what was necessary a hundred or a thousand years ago, they must naturally expect to be left out of the great scheme of things as they concern men of today.

The most inviting field for discovery and invention, then, is the Negro himself, but he does not realize it. Frederika Bremer, when reflecting upon her visit to America about 1850, gave this country a new thought in saying to Americans, "The romance of your history is the fate of the Negro." In this very thought lies unusual possibilities for the historian, the economist, the artist, and the philosopher. Why should the Negro writer seek a theme abroad when he has the greatest of all at home?

The bondage of the Negro brought captive from Africa is one of the greatest dramas in history, and the writer who merely sees in that ordeal something to approve or condemn fails to understand the evolution of the human race. Negroes now studying dramatics go into our schools to reproduce Shakespeare, but mentally developed members of this race would see the possibilities of a greater drama in the tragedy of the man of color. Negroes graduating from conservatories of music dislike the singing of our folk songs. For some reason such misguided persons think that they can improve on the productions of the foreign drama or render the music of other people better than they can themselves.

A knowledge of real history would lead one to think that slavery was one of the significant developments which, although evil in themselves, may redound sometimes to the advantage of the oppressed rather than to that of the oppressor. Some one has said that the music of Poland was inspired by incidents of a struggle against the despots invading and partitioning their prostrate land. The Greeks never had an art until the country was overrun by hostile Orientals. Some one then began to immortalize in song the sons who went forth to fight for the native land. Another carved in marble the thought evoked by the example of the Greek youth who blocked the mountain pass with his body or who bared his breast to the javelin to defend the liberty of his country. These things we call art.

In our own country the other elements of the population, being secure in their position, have never faced such a crisis; and the Europeans, after whose pattern American life is fashioned, have not recently had such experience. White Americans, then, have produced no art at all, and that of Europe has reached the point of stagnation. Negroes who are imitating whites, then, are engaged in a most unprofitable performance. Why not interpret themselves anew to the world?

If we had a few thinkers we could expect great achievements on tomorrow. Some Negro with unusual insight would write an epic of bondage and freedom which would take its place with those of Homer and Virgil. Some Negro with esthetic appreciation would construct from collected fragments of Negro music a grand opera that would move humanity to repentance. Some Negro of philosophic penetration would find a solace for the modern world in the soul of the Negro, and then men would be men because they are men.

The Negro in his present plight, however, does not see possibilities until it is too late. He exercises much "hindsight," and for that reason he loses ground in the hotly contested battles of life. The Negro as a rule waits until a thing happens before he tries to avert it. He is too much like a man whom the author once saw knocked down in a physical combat. Instead of dodging the blow when it was being dealt he arose from his prostration dodging it.

For example, the author has just received a letter from a lady in Pittsburgh complaining that the librarian in one of its schools insists upon reading to the children "a great deal of literature containing such words as 'nigger,' 'Blackie,' 'Little Black Sambo,' etc." This lady, therefore, would like to place in that school some books by Negro authors. This is a commendable effort, but it comes a little late; we hope not too late.

For centuries such literature has been circulated among the children of the modern world; and they have, therefore, come to regard the Negro as inferior. Now that some of our similarly mis-educated Negroes are seeing how they have been deceived they are awakening to address themselves to a long neglected work. They should have been thinking about this generations ago, for they have a tremendous task before them today in dispelling this error and counteracting the results of such bias in our literature.

There has just come, too, from a friend of humanity in Edinburgh, Scotland, a direful account of the increase in race prejudice in those parts. Sailors who had frequented the stronghold of race prejudice in South Africa undertook recently to prevent Negro men from socializing with Scotch women at a dance; and certain professors of the University of Edinburgh with the same attitude show so much of it in their teaching that this friend entreats us to send them informing books on the Negro. We are doing it.

Here again, however, the effort to uproot error and popularize the truth comes rather late. The Negro since freedom has gone along grinning, whooping, and "cutting capers" while the white man has applied himself to the task of defining the status of the Negro and compelling him to accept it as thus settled forever. While the Negro has been idle, propaganda has gone far ahead of history. Unfortunately, too, Negro "scholars" have assisted in the production of literature which gives this point of view.

The New Program

It seems only a reasonable proposition, then, that, if under the present system which produced our leadership in religion, politics, and business we have gone backward toward serfdom or have at least been kept from advancing to real freedom, it is high time to develop another sort of leadership with a different educational system. In the first place, we must bear in mind that the Negro has never been educated. He has merely been informed about other things which he has not been permitted to do. The Negroes have been shoved out of the regular schools through the rear door into the obscurity of the backyard and told to imitate others whom they see from afar, or they have been permitted in some places to come into the public schools to see how others educate themselves. The program for the uplift of the Negro in this country must be based upon a scientific study of the Negro from within to develop in him the power to do for himself what his oppressors will never do to elevate him to the level of others.

Being without actual education, we have very few persons prepared to help the Negroes whom they have set out to lead. These persons are not all dishonest men and women. Many of them are sincere, and believe that they are doing the race some great good in thus holding it backward. They must be awakened and shown the error of their ways.

We have very few teachers because most of those with whom we are afflicted know nothing about the children whom they teach or about their parents who influence the pupils more than the teachers themselves. When a boy comes to school without knowing his lesson he should be studied instead of being punished. The boy who does well in the beginning of the year and lags behind near the end of the term should not always be censured or ridiculed. As a rule, such children are not responsible for their failures. Their parents and their social status account mainly for these shortcomings. The Negro teacher, then, must treat the disease rather than its symptoms.

But can you expect teachers to revolutionize the social order for the good of the community? Indeed we must expect this very thing. The educational system of a country is worthless unless it accomplishes this task. Men of scholarship and consequently of prophetic insight must show us the right way and lead us into the light which shines brighter and brighter.

In the church where we have much freedom and independence we must get rid of preachers who are not prepared to help the people whom they exploit. The public must refuse to support men of this type. Ministers who are the creations of the old educational system must be awakened, and if this is impossible they must be dethroned. Those who keep the people in ignorance and play upon their emotions must be exiled. The people have never been taught what religion is, for most of the preachers find it easier to stimulate the superstition which develops in the unenlightened mind. Religion in such hands, then, becomes something with which you take advantage of weak people. Why try to enlighten the people in such matters when superstition serves just as well for exploitation?

The ministers with the confidence of the people must above all things understand the people themselves. They must find out the past of their parishioners, whether they were brought up in Georgia, Alabama or Texas, whether they are housed under desirable circumstances, what they do to make a living, what they do with their earnings, how they react to the world about them, how they spend their leisure, or how they function along with other elements of the social order.

In our schools, and especially in schools of religion, attention should be given to the study of the Negro as he developed during the ante-bellum period by showing to what extent that remote culture was determined by ideas which the Negro brought with him from Africa. To take it for granted that the ante-bellum Negro was an ignoramus or that the native brought from Africa had not a valuable culture merely because some prejudiced writers have said so does not show the attitude of scholarship, and Negro students who direct their courses accordingly will never be able to grapple with the social problems presented today by the Negro church.

The preachers of today must learn to do as well as those of old. Richard Allen so interpreted Christianity anew to his master that he was converted, and so did Henry Evans and George Bentley for other whites in North Carolina and Tennessee. Instead of accepting and trying to carry out the theories which the exploiters of humanity have brought them for a religious program the Negroes should forget their differences and in the strength of a united church bring out a new interpretation of Christ to this unwilling world. Following the religious teachings of their traducers, the Negroes do not show any more common sense than a people would in permitting criminals to enact the laws and establish the procedure of the courts by which they are to be tried.

Negro preachers, too, must be educated to their people rather than away from them. This, of course, requires a new type of religious school. To provide for such training the Negro church must get rid of its burdensome supervisory force. If the number of bishops of the various Negro Methodist churches were reduced to about twelve or fifteen, as they should be, the amount of a hundred thousand dollars or more now being paid to support the unnecessary number could be used to maintain properly at least one accredited college; and what is now being raised here and there to support various struggling but starving institutions kept alive by ambitious bishops and preachers could be saved to the peo-

Carter G. Woodson (Courtesy of the Moorland-Spingarn Research Center)

ple. With this money diverted to a more practical use the race would be able to establish some other things which would serve as assets rather than as liabilities.

We say liabilities, for practically all of our denominational schools which are bleeding the people for the inadequate support which they receive are still unable to do accredited work. There are so many of them that the one impoverishes the other. Outstanding men of the church, therefore, have to acquire their advanced education by attending other schools in the beginning or by taking additional training elsewhere after learning all our denominational schools can offer. This is a loss of ground which should be regained if the church is to go forward.

By proper unification and organization the Negro churches might support one or two much needed universities of their own. With the present arrangement of two or three in the same area and sometimes as many in one city there is no chance for emerging from the trying poverty-stricken state. And even if these institutions could do well what they undertake they do not

supply all educational needs. To qualify for certification in the professions Negroes must go to other schools, where, although they acquire the fundamentals, they learn much about their "inferiority" to discourage them in their struggle upward.

We should not close any accredited Negro colleges or universities, but we should reconstruct the whole system. We should not eliminate many of the courses now being offered, but we should secure men of vision to give them from the point of view of the people to be served. We should not spend less money for the higher education of the Negro, but should redefine higher education as preparation to think and work out a program to serve the lowly rather than to live as an aristocrat.

Such subjects of certitude as mathematics, of course, would continue and so would most of the work in practical languages and science. In theology, literature, social science, and education, however, radical reconstruction is necessary. The old worn-out theories as to man's relation to God and his fellowman, the system of thought which has permitted one man to exploit, oppress, and exterminate another and still be regarded as righteous must be discarded for the new thought of men as brethren and the idea of God as the lover of all mankind.

After Negro students have mastered the fundamentals of English, the principles of composition, and the leading facts in the development of its literature, they should not spend all of their time in advanced work on Shakespeare, Chaucer and Anglo-Saxon. They should direct their attention also to the folklore of the African, to the philosophy in his proverbs, to the development of the Negro in the use of modern language, and to the works of Negro writers.

The leading facts of the history of the world should be studied by all, but of what advantage is it to the Negro student of history to devote all of his time to courses bearing on such despots as Alexander the Great, Cæsar, and Napoleon, or to the record of those nations whose outstanding achievement has been rapine, plunder, and murder for world power? Why not study the African background from the point of view of anthropology and history, and then take up sociology as it concerns the Negro peasant or proletarian who is suffering from sufficient ills to supply laboratory work for the most advanced students of the social order? Why not take up economics as reflected by the Negroes of today and work out some remedy for their lack of capital, the absence of cooperative enterprise, and the short life of their establishments. Institutions like Harvard, Yale and Columbia are not going to do these things, and educators influenced by them to the extent that they become blind to the Negro will never serve the race efficiently.

To educate the Negro we must find out exactly what his background is, what he is today, what his possibilities are, and how to begin with him as he is and make him a better individual of the kind that he is. Instead of cramming the Negro's mind with what others have shown that they can do, we should develop his latent powers that he may perform in society a part of which others are not capable.

During his life the author has seen striking examples of how people should and should not be taught. Some of these are worth relating. Probably the most interesting was that of missionary work in China. In 1903 the author crossed the Pacific Ocean with twenty-six missionaries who were going to take the Orient by storm. One Todd, from North Carolina, was orating and preaching almost every day to stimulate his coworkers to go boldly to the task before them. Dr. De Forest, long a missionary to Japan, informed them that the work required more than enthusiasm; that they could not rush into the homes of the natives saying, "Peace be to this house," for it might turn out the other way and give somebody the opportunity to say, "Peace be to his ashes."

Dr. De Forest explained to them how he chose a decidedly different course, preferring first to study the history, the language, the manners and the customs of the people to approach them intelligently; and not until he had been in the country four years did he undertake to exhort, but after that time he had had great success and had been invited to preach before the Mikado himself. Now Todd did not take this advice, and he had not been in China five months before he and his wife had been poisoned by their native cook who had become incensed at the way they interfered with the institutions of his people.

Another striking illustration was the education of the Filipinos. Not long after the close of the Spanish-American War the United States Government started out to educate the Filipinos over night. Numbers of "highly trained" Americans were carried there to do the work. They entered upon their task by teaching the Filipinos just as they had taught American children who were otherwise circumstanced. The result was failure. Men trained at institutions like Harvard, Yale, Columbia, and Chicago could not reach these people and had to be dismissed from the service. Some of these "scholarly" Americans had to be maintained by the subscription of friends until they could be returned to this country on Government transportation.

In the meantime, however, there came along an insurance man, who went to the Philippines to engage in business. He had never taught at all, and he had never studied authorities like Bagley, Judd, and Thorndike; but he understood people. Seeing that others had

failed, he went into the work himself. He filled the schoolroom with thousands of objects from the pupil's environment. In the beginning he did not use books very much, because those supplied were not adapted to the needs of the children. He talked about the objects around them. Everything was presented objectively. When he took up the habits of the snake he brought the reptile to the school for demonstration. When he taught the crocodile he had one there. In teaching the Filipinos music he did not sing "Come shake the Apple-Tree." They had never seen such an object. He taught them to sing "Come shake the Lomboy Tree," something which they had actually done. In reading he did not concentrate on the story of how George Washington always told the truth. They had never heard of him and could not have appreciated that myth if some one had told them about it. This real educator taught them about their own hero, José Rizal, who gave his life as a martyr for the freedom of his country. By and by they got rid of most books based on the life of American people and worked out an entirely new series dealing with the life of Filipinos. The result, then, was that this man and others who saw the situation as he did succeeded, and the work of the public schools in the Philippines is today the outstanding achievement of the Americans in that country.

We do not mean to suggest here, however, that any people should ignore the record of the progress of other races. We would not advocate any such unwise course. We say, hold on to the real facts of history as they are, but complete such knowledge by studying also the history of races and nations which have been purposely ignored. We should not underrate the achievements of Mesopotamia, Greece, and Rome; but we should give equally as much attention to the internal African kingdoms, the Songhay empire, and Ethiopia, which through Egypt decidedly influenced the civilization of the Mediterranean world. We would not ignore the rise of Christianity and the development of the Church; but we would at the same time give honorable mention to the persons of African blood who figured in these achievements, and who today are endeavoring to carry out the principles of Jesus long since repudiated by most so-called Christians. We would not underestimate the achievements of the captains of industry who in the commercial expansion of the modern world have produced the wealth necessary to ease and comfort; but we would give credit to the Negro who so largely supplied the demand for labor by which these things have been accomplished.

In our own particular history we would not dim one bit the lustre of any star in our firmament. We would not learn less of George Washington, "First in War, First in Peace and First in the Hearts of his Countrymen"; but we would learn something also of the three thousand Negro soldiers of the American Revolution who helped to make this "Father of our Country" possible. We would not neglect to appreciate the unusual contribution of Thomas Jefferson to freedom and democracy; but we would invite attention also to two of his outstanding contemporaries, Phillis Wheatley, the writer of interesting verse, and Benjamin Banneker, the mathematician, astronomer, and advocate of a world peace plan set forth in 1793 with the vital principles of Woodrow Wilson's League of Nations. We would in no way detract from the fame of Perry on Lake Erie or Jackson at New Orleans in the second struggle with England; but we would remember the gallant black men who assisted in winning these memorable victories on land and sea. We would not cease to pay tribute to Abraham Lincoln as the "Savior of the Country"; but we would ascribe praise also to the one hundred and seventy-eight thousand Negroes who had to be mustered into the service of the Union before it could be preserved, and who by their heroism demonstrated that they were entitled to freedom and citizenship.

E. Franklin Frazier

Introduction

The presence of at least 19,000,000 persons of Negro ancestry among the people of the United States is the outcome of the expansion of Europe which began in the fifteenth century and became firmly established during the succeeding two centuries. As the result of this expansion Europeans met and conquered many primitive peoples, laid the basis for European settlements, and established commercial relations with the old civilizations of Asia and Africa. European expansion in the Americas became especially important for the economic development of Europe, since the production of tobacco, sugar, and cotton, which were exchanged for European manufactures, increased world trade and brought untold wealth to Europe. For the production of these raw materials and articles of commerce Negro slaves were transported to the New World and became the main support of the "triangular trade" involving the metropolis, Africa, and the colonies. Negro slaves thus became the creators of the wealth that made the flowering of capitalism possible in the nineteenth century.

E. Franklin Frazier, "Introduction" and "Behind the Masks." Reprinted with the permission of Simon & Schuster from BLACK BOURGEOISE by E. Franklin Frazier. Copyright © 1957, 1962 by Macmillan Publishing Company.

1. Negro Slavery and the Plantation

In the southern sections of what became the United States, the plantation system of agriculture developed on the basis of enslaved Negro labor. After the failure of the attempt to utilize the native Indian as a source of forced labor, white indentured servants were introduced into the colonies. But they were soon supplanted by Negro slaves, who proved a more efficient and a more economical source of labor. During the seventeenth and eighteenth centuries the importation of Negroes gradually increased to meet the growing need for laborers in the production of tobacco, rice, and indigo. But with the invention of the cotton gin, which enabled American producers to supply the increased demands of English manufacturers, the importation of Negro slaves was accelerated. As a result, the agitation against slavery, which had found expression along with the idealism respecting liberty during the American Revolution, died down when the declining productivity of slave labor on tobacco plantations was followed by a period of unprecedented profits in cotton production.

The condition of the Negro slaves on the southern plantations varied considerably. In the lower South, where the large cotton plantation tended to take on the character of a purely industrial organization, the treatment of the slaves was extremely brutal since they were regarded as mere work animals. They were treated even more inhumanely by the slave traders who supplied the needs of a commercial system of agriculture. As articles of commerce, the Negro slaves were treated in the same manner as the mules which were advertised for sale along with them. On the other hand, where the plantation became a social as well as an economic organization, under a semi-patriarchal regime, more consideration was shown for the personalities of the slaves. The lives of the masters and slaves became intertwined in a system of social relationships. The relations between whites and blacks thus came to be regulated by a complex system of social rituals and etiquette permitting a maximum degree of intimacy while maintaining the complete subordination of the blacks. The traditions governing race relations on the plantation became so firmly rooted in the South that they have persisted until the present day.

2. The Impact of Western Civilization

Where the plantation acquired the character of a social institution, it provided the means by which the Negro slaves could rapidly take over European culture. The basis for the rapid acculturation of the Negro slaves was created by the manner in which the slaves had been captured in Africa, sold on the slave markets, and integrated into the plantation system. The Negro slaves, who represented many different tribal backgrounds, had been captured in Africa during tribal wars and slave-hunting expeditions. They had been herded into the *baracoons* on the coast to await the arrival of slave ships. Then, during the Middle Passage they were transported in ships, in which they were packed spoon-fashion, to the West Indies where they were sold on the slave markets. In the West Indies they underwent a period of being "broken into" slavery before they were shipped to local plantations or to the plantations on the mainland. In the English colonies on the mainland, and later in the United States, they were widely scattered on plantations which had fewer slaves on the whole than did the plantations in the West Indies.

On the plantations in the southern states the Negro slave sloughed off almost completely his African cultural heritage. The African family system was destroyed and the slave was separated from his kinsmen and friends. Moreover, in the United States there was little chance that he could reknit the ties of kinship and old associations. If by chance he encountered fellow slaves with whom he could communicate in his native tongue, he was separated from them. From the very beginning he was forced to learn English in order to obey the commands of his white masters. Whatever memories he might have retained of his native land and native customs became meaningless in the New World. The very fact that the majority of the slaves were young males practically eliminated the possibility of recreating a social organization that could perpetuate and transmit the African cultural heritage.

While all of the slaves were always under the surveillance of the whites, the house servants lived constantly in close association with their masters. Very often these house servants had associated from childhood with their masters. Consequently, they early acquired the speech of their masters, a fact which set them off from the more isolated field hands, who spoke a dialect. Living in close association with whites, the house servants were subject to a type of discipline which caused them to identify themselves with their masters. This discipline included both moral and religious instruction. The slaves participated in the religious life of their white masters—including family prayers and attendance at the white churches, where a section was reserved for them.

Some recognition had to be given the individual qualities of the slaves, and it was most often among the house servants that these differences were recognized. For example, there was a division of labor on the plantation in which the intelligence and talents of the slaves found expression. Generally, the son of a house servant was apprenticed to some artisan to learn a skilled trade. These skilled mechanics, who constituted a large section of the artisans in the South, formed with the house servants a sort of privileged class in the slave community. The greater the integration of the slaves into the activities and family life of their white masters, the more nearly their behavior and ideals approximated those of the whites. On the other hand, the field hands, who had few intimate contacts with the whites and were subject to a more formal type of social control, could give expression to a more spontaneous type of behavior—especially in their religious life and in their musical creations. The field hands were especially attracted by the Methodist and Baptist missionaries who, in their revival meetings, preached a simple doctrine of salvation through conversion in which a highly emotional experience was of primary importance. Although the slaves were under the surveillance of the whites in order to prevent conspiracies and revolts, they were able to engage in a form of worship different from that of the whites and the more disciplined house servants. The Spirituals, or religious folksongs, grew out of these relatively independent religious meetings. The new slaves who were brought to the plantations from Africa had to adjust to a social world quite different from that from which they had come.

The close association of the races on the plantation, especially in the same household, resulted in considerable race mixture. The interbreeding of the races had begun in the seventeenth century soon after the introduction of Negroes into Virginia, and continued on a large scale as long as slavery existed. Many of the mulattoes were emancipated by their white fathers and formed the basis of the free Negro population that grew up in the South before the Civil War. In 1850, mulattoes or mixed-bloods constituted 37 per cent of the free Negro population but only 8 per cent of the slave population.

The free Negroes were not evenly distributed over the South, but were concentrated principally in cities and in those states where the plantation system of agriculture did not flourish. In Maryland and Virginia, where there were 83,942 and 58,042 free Negroes, respectively, in 1860, many of these free Negroes owed their freedom to the fact that they had been permitted to "hire their time" and work as semi-free laborers. With the money which they were able to accumulate after paying their masters for their "time" they bought their freedom. Although the majority of the free Negroes in the South did not live much above a subsistence level, many of them bought land and became independent farmers, or became successful mechanics and skilled artisans. In Charleston, South Carolina, and in New Orleans, the free Negroes or "free people of color" accumulated considerable wealth as skilled artisans, and as owners of plantations included slaves among their possessions.

The free Negroes constituted, in fact, the element in the Negro population that had made the greatest progress in acquiring European culture. The pattern of family life of the well-to-do free Negroes in the plantation South was the same as the patriarchal family pattern of the slaveholding whites. Moreover, their outlook on life and their values were the same as the white models. They occupied the position of an intermediate caste in some parts of the South, especially in New Orleans. As a group the free Negroes of the South were much better off economically than the free Negroes of the North, who had not been able to compete with the European immigrants. At one time the free Negroes in the South outnumbered the free Negroes in the North, but as the result of persecutions following the antislavery agitation in the North many of them migrated to the North. Nevertheless, half of the nearly 500,000 free Negroes in the United States at the outbreak of the Civil War were in the South.

3. A Nation within a Nation?

As the result of the Civil War and Emancipation, the future status of the Negro in American society became one of the most pressing problems facing the American government. This problem was tied up with the problem of re-integrating the southern states into the federal Union. Lincoln, although opposed to slavery, had never believed that Negroes and whites could be citizens of the same community. He had cautiously suggested that the educated free mulattoes in Louisiana who had fought on the Union side should be permitted to qualify as citizens in the reconstructed government of Louisiana. The assassination of Lincoln followed too soon for him to make known his general program for the future of the Negro. The successor of Lincoln, Andrew Johnson, who as a representative of the non-slaveholding "poor whites" had remained loyal to the Union, soon made it clear that he wanted to build a "democracy" in the South consisting only of white citizens, or white men of property. As the result of this policy, he was opposed by two factions of the Republican Party—the abolitionists among the Old Radicals, who were genuinely interested in creating a democracy in the South based upon the political participation of whites and Negroes; and the Republicans who, fearing that a white farming class would nullify the victory of the North, wanted to use Negro voters to support legislation that would give a legal basis to triumphant industrial capitalism.

The program of the Republican Congress for the reconstruction of the southern states gave promise of a democratic revolution in an area that had been ruled by a slaveholding oligarchy. Under the protection of the Union Army, the black freedmen along with the non-slaveholding whites were given the right to vote and hold office. Three amendments to the federal Constitution were necessary, however, to provide a legal basis for the citizenship of the Negro: the Thirteenth, abolishing slavery; the Fourteenth, making him a citizen; and the Fifteenth, forbidding restrictions upon his rights as a citizen on account of race or his previous status as a slave. Some of the more radical Republicans proposed that the plantations be divided in order to create a class of black and white small landowners. In fact, the black freedmen had been promised land by the federal government as a guarantee of their freedom. But since this program appeared too revolutionary for the majority of the Republican leaders, the vast majority of ex-slaves remained landless, except for a relatively small number of Negroes who had secured land during the Civil War.

The Negro has been blamed for the disorders and the graft on the part of politicians and speculators during the Reconstruction Period. But unprejudiced historians, who place the behavior of the Negro during this period in its proper perspective, agree that the Negro was the victim of the conflict of economic interests over which he had no control and that he exhibited considerable wisdom in attempting to help formulate social policies. The Negro gave his support to the establishment of a system of public education and sought to make land available to the great masses of black and white farmers. But the question of race was utilized to divide the whites and Negroes. The "redemption" of the South in 1876, which was hailed as the restoration of "white supremacy," really resulted in the political ascendancy of the "Bourbons," or the new middle classes and the planters. The state constitutions, which were supposed to be the legal instruments by which the "barbarous blacks" maintained their power but were, in fact, nothing more than the expression of middle-class interests, were retained for decades after the restoration of "white supremacy."

The restoration of "white supremacy" did not resolve the class conflict among whites in the South. In fact, the white planters sometimes used Negro voters to defeat the aspirations of the disinherited whites. When agrarian unrest among the "poor whites" of the South joined forces with the Populist movement, which represented the general unrest among American farmers, the question of race was used to defeat the cooperation of "poor whites" and Negroes. It was then that the demagogues assumed leadership of the "poor whites" and provided a solution to the class conflict among whites that offered no challenge to the political power and economic privileges of the industrialists and the planter class. The program, which made the Negro the scapegoat, obtained the following provisions: (1) the Negro was completely disfranchised by all sorts of legal subterfuges, with the threat of force in the background; (2) the funds which were appropriated on a per capita basis for Negro school children were diverted to white schools; and (3) a legal system of segregation in all phases of public life was instituted. In order to justify this program, the demagogues, who were supported by the white propertied classes, engaged for twenty-five years in a campaign to prove that the Negro was subhuman, morally degenerate, and intellectually incapable of being educated.

The North acquiesced in this program as a solution of the race problem. The rise to prominence of Booker T. Washington as the leader of the Negroes from 1895 onward was due to his apparent acceptance of racial segregation as a solution of the "Negro problem." Under his leadership, support of so-called "industrial education" for the Negro was provided by northern capitalists. During the quarter of a century from 1890 to 1915, when lynchings and mob violence were used to put the Negro "in his place" in the South, Negroes gave up their hope for freedom and equality in American life. Only a small group of northern Negro intellectuals, led by W. E. Burghardt DuBois and a few northern white "radicals" (on racial issues), attacked the so-called "solution" of the race problem. But more important than the attack of the radicals were changes in race relations which were set in motion by the northward migration of the Negro masses that began in 1915 as a result of the first World War.

But before analyzing the changes which occurred in race relations as the result of the northern migrations, let us consider the nature of the social world of the Negro which emerged as the result of the system of racial segregation. Until the first World War only about a tenth of the Negroes in the United States were in the North, and seven-eighths of those in the North lived in cities. The residents of the relatively small Negro communities in the northern cities gained their livelihood in domestic and personal service. Although they were restricted in their opportunities for employment in industry and white-collar occupations, they did not suffer much discrimination in utilizing public institutions. However, they had their own churches and their social life revolved chiefly about their own clubs and other organizations. In the South, on the other hand, the entire life of the Negro—except for his contacts with whites as a domestic or personal servant, or as a laborer—was restricted to the Negro community. Although this rigid system of racial segregation grew up in a region where, until 1920, more than three-fourths of the Negroes lived on farms and plantations, the "color line" in southern cities was as rigid as in rural areas. In the rural areas the majority of the Negroes worked as sharecroppers under a system closely resembling serfdom, while the majority of those in the cities gained a livelihood as domestic servants and as unskilled laborers. The church was the chief center of the Negro's social life in both the cities and in the rural areas. It provided the chief means for self-expression and leadership and erected a shelter against a hostile white world. In conjunction with the church there were the numerous mutual aid societies and fraternal organizations that offered not only an opportunity for social life, but provided aid in the time of sickness and death.

In this segregated world, especially in cities, a class structure slowly emerged which was based upon social distinctions such as education and conventional behavior, rather than upon occupation and income. At the top of the social pyramid there was a small upper class. The superior status of this class was due chiefly to its differentiation from the great mass of the Negro population because of a family heritage which resulted partly from its mixed ancestry. The family heritage consisted of traditions of civilized behavior and economic efficiency. The members' light skin-color was indicative not only of their white ancestry, but of their descent from the Negroes who were free before the Civil War, or those who had enjoyed the advantages of having served in the houses of their masters. This upper class constantly incorporated those Negroes who were able to acquire an education in the schools supported by northern philanthropy. The members of the upper class depended on a number of skilled occupations for a living, though there was a sprinkling of teachers, doctors, educated ministers, and small businessmen among them.

It was from this isolated social world that thousands of Negroes began migrating to northern industrial centers during the first World War. Although the migrants were attracted to northern cities because of opportunities for employment, the migrations were, in part, a flight from oppression to a Promised Land of freedom and equality. But many of the Negro migrants became disillusioned about the North when, without neighbors and friends, they faced the keen competition and racial discrimination of the cold, impersonal environment of northern cities. In their disillusionment many of them joined the Garvey Movement, the only serious Negro nationalist movement to arise in the United States. According to the leader of this movement, Marcus Garvey, who was a Negro of West Indian origin, the Negro would never achieve equality in America, a white man's country, and therefore the only salvation for the Negro was to return to Africa. Negro intellectuals and the middle-class Negroes generally were hostile to this movement, which gradually dissolved when the leader was sent to the federal penitentiary in Atlanta.

Despite the failure of the Negro to find a Promised Land in the North, the Negro enjoyed certain advantages in the North that changed his outlook on the world as well as his status in American society. In the North the Negro worker gained a foothold for the first time in American industry. Negro children had access for the first time on a large scale to a standard American education, generally in nonsegregated schools. Negroes enjoyed the right to vote and hold office, and as the result of their political power could resist racial discrimination. Through their experience with city life, Negroes acquired a certain sophistication towards the world and tended to redefine their problems in America. They did not seek a solution in a narrow program of racial exclusiveness such as the Garvey Movement. Especially during the Depression years some of them joined the Communist Party, which defined the Negro problem as a problem of "national liberation" from capitalist oppression. The vast majority of Negroes, however, gave up their sentimental allegiance to the Republican Party and supported the Democratic Party and the New Deal Program, which offered concrete economic advantages and a promise of satisfying their aspirations as citizens.

The greater economic and social freedom of the North accelerated the slow occupational differentiation of the Negro population. The rise of the industrial unions (C.I.O.) with their more liberal racial policy helped the integration of Negro workers into industry. But workers did not share immediately in the benefits of the economic revival that followed the decision of the United States to become the "arsenal of democracy." It was as the result of agitation, and the demand for manpower in a war against Nazism with its racial policy, that the Negro began to enjoy some of the fruits of an expanding American economy. Since the second World War, Negroes have continued to receive a larger share of the national income than they did before the War. Moreover, the racial barriers in the North, where nearly a third of the Negroes now live, have tended to be lowered in all phases of public life. Even in the South, the segregation of the Negro has been less rigid in public transportation, and Negro students have been admitted to some of the public universities. As the result of the changes in the economic status of the Negro, the Negro middle class, or the "black bourgeoisie," has grown in size and acquired a dominant position among Negroes.

4. Purpose of the Present Study

The primary purpose of this study is to make a sociological analysis of the behavior, the attitudes, and values of the "black bourgeoisie," a group which began to play an important role among American Negroes during the past two decades. Our analysis will deal with two aspects of the life of the "black bourgeoisie"—the first being the real or objectively existing economic condition and social status of the "black bourgeoisie" in the United States, and the second being the standards of behavior and values of the isolated social world of this segment of the Negro population, which has come into existence as a consequence of racial discrimination and racial segregation.

The first part of this study, which deals with the real status of the black bourgeoisie, will be concerned, first, with the process by which a black bourgeoisie has emerged in the United States as the result of a slow and difficult occupational differentiation of the Negro population. Against this background will be analyzed the present economic basis of this class, especially as regards the recent changes that have occurred in the economic position of the Negro in the American economy. The study of the economic position of the black bourgeoisie will include a realistic appraisal of the significance of "Negro business" in the American economy as well as in the economic life of the Negro. In this part of the study attention will also be given to the education of the Negro, since education has been the principal social factor responsible for the emergence of the black bourgeoisie. Special attention will be directed to the influence of the segregated schools and colleges on the aspirations and social outlook of the black bourgeoisie. Our analysis will be directed next to the political outlook of this class and the power which the black bourgeoisie exercises over Negroes—since the same economic and social forces in American life, which have been largely responsible for the existence of "Negro education" have shaped the political orientation of the black bourgeoisie.

The concluding chapter of the first part will deal with what, from a sociological standpoint, has been one of the most important consequences of the emergence of the black bourgeoisie, namely, the uprooting of this stratum of the Negro population from its "racial" traditions or, more specifically, from its folk background. As the result of the break with its cultural past, the black bourgeoisie is without cultural roots in either the Negro world with which it refuses to identify, or the white world which refuses to permit the black bourgeoisie to share its life. This chapter will provide a transition to the second part of the study, which will be devoted to the behavior of the black bourgeoisie in the social world that has grown up out of its isolation in American life.

Lacking a cultural tradition and rejecting identification with the Negro masses on the one hand, and suffering from the contempt of the white world on the other, the black bourgeoisie has developed a deep-seated inferiority complex. In order to compensate for this feeling of inferiority, the black bourgeoisie has created in its isolation what might be described as a world of make-believe in which it attempts to escape the disdain of whites and fulfill its wish for status in American life. One of the most striking indications of the unreality of the social world which the black bourgeoisie created is its faith in the importance of "Negro business," i.e., the business enterprises owned by Negroes and catering to Negro customers. Although these enterprises have little significance either from the standpoint of the American economy or the economic life of the Negro, a social myth has been created that they provide a solution to the Negro's economic problems. Faith in this social myth and others is perpetuated by the Negro newspapers, which represent the largest and most successful business enterprises established by Negroes. Moreover, the Negro newspapers help to create and maintain the world of make-believe in which Negroes can realize their desires for recognition and status in a white world that regards them with contempt and amusement. Much of the news featured in the Negro newspapers is concerned with the activities of the members of Negro "society," or it tends to make "socialites" out of most Negroes whose activities are considered newsworthy. "Society" is a phase of the world of make-believe which represents in an acute form the Negro's long preoccupation with "social life" as an escape from his subordinate status in America.

Since the world of make-believe can not insulate the black bourgeoisie completely from the world of reality, the members of this class exhibit considerable confusion and conflict in their personalities. Their emotional and mental conflicts arise partly from their constant striving for status within the Negro world, as well as in the estimation of whites. Moreover, they have accepted unconditionally the values of the white bourgeois world: its morals and its canons of respectability, its standards of beauty and consumption. In fact, they have tended to overemphasize their conformity to white ideals. Nevertheless, they are rejected by the white world, and this rejection has created considerable self-hatred, since it is attributed to their Negro characteristics. At the same time, because of their ambivalence towards Negroes, they are extremely sensitive to slights and discriminations which Negroes suffer. Since they do not truly identify themselves with Negroes, the hollowness of the black bourgeoisie's pretended "racial pride" is revealed in the value which it places upon a white or light complexion. Because of their social isolation and lack of a cultural tradition, the members of the black bourgeoisie in the United States seem to be in the process of becoming NOBODY. What significance, then, does the fate of the black bourgeoisie in the United States have for the bourgeoisie of other racial or cultural minorities that have come into existence as the result of the expansion of western civilization and European capitalism?

Behind the Masks

Self-Hatred and Guilt Feelings

One of the chief frustrations of the middle-class Negro is that he can not escape identification with the Negro race and consequently is subject to the contempt of whites.* Despite his "wealth" in which he has placed so much faith as a solvent of racial discrimination, he is still subject to daily insults and is excluded from participation in white American society. Middle-class Negroes do not express their resentment against discrimination and insults in violent outbreaks, as lower-class Negroes often do. They constantly repress their hostility toward whites and seek to soothe their hurt self-esteem in all kinds of rationalizations. They may boast of their wealth and culture as compared with the condition of the poor whites. Most often they will resort to any kind of subterfuge in order to avoid contact with whites. For example, in the South they often pay their bills by mail rather than risk unpleasant contacts with representatives of white firms. The daily repression of resentment and the constant resort to means of avoiding contacts with whites do not relieve them of their hostility toward whites. Even middle-class Negroes who gain a reputation for exhibiting "objectivity" and a "statesmanlike" attitude on racial discrimination harbor deep-seated hostilities toward whites.

---

*A Middle-class mulatto woman, a former school teacher, who was fearful of the impact of this book on European readers and southern detractors of "The Race," concluded her review of the original French edition with these words:

"Isn't it about time our sociologists and specialists on the 'race problem' in America, began to discuss and consider middle class Negroes as middle class Americans, or better, *all* U.S. Negroes as *Americans* with three hundred unbroken years of American tradition, way of life, cultural and spiritual contacts behind them—influences which have moulded them as they have moulded all others who are considered, even when not treated completely so, as members of the American community? Isn't it time to stop thinking of and talking about Negroes as a separate and distinct entity in the general scheme of things? And above all, isn't it time to realize that the melting pot has melted truly and fused together all the myriad (albeit conflicting) racial, cultural, educational, spiritual and social elements which have combined in such peculiar fashion to produce the American Negro of our time?" *Journal of Negro Education*, Vol. XXV, p. 141.

A Negro college president who has been considered such an inter-racial "statesman" once confessed to the writer that some day he was going to "break loose" and tell white people what he really thought. However, it is unlikely that a middle-class Negro of his standing will ever "break loose." Middle-class Negroes generally express their aggressions against whites by other means, such as deceiving whites and utilizing them for their own advantage.

Because middle-class Negroes are unable to indulge in aggressions against whites as such, they will sometimes make other minority groups the object of their hostilities. For example, they may show hostility against Italians, who are also subject to discrimination. But more often middle-class Negroes, especially those who are engaged in a mad scramble to accumulate money, will direct their hostilities against Jews. They are constantly expressing their anti-semitism within Negro circles, while pretending publicly to be free from prejudice. They blame the Jew for the poverty of Negroes and for their own failures and inefficiencies in their business undertakings. In expressing their hostility towards Jews, they are attempting at the same time to identify with the white American majority.

The repressed hostilities of middle-class Negroes to whites are not only directed towards other minority groups but inward toward themselves. This results in self-hatred, which may appear from their behavior to be directed towards the Negro masses but which in reality is directed against themselves. While pretending to be proud of being a Negro, they ridicule Negroid physical characteristics and seek to modify or efface them as much as possible. Within their own groups they constantly proclaim that "niggers" make them sick. The very use of the term "nigger," which they claim to resent, indicates that they want to disassociate themselves from the Negro masses. They talk condescendingly of Africans and of African culture, often even objecting to African sculpture in their homes. They are insulted if they are identified with Africans. They refuse to join organizations that are interested in Africa. If they are of mixed ancestry, they may boast of the fact that they have Indian ancestry. When making compliments concerning the beauty of Negroes of mixed ancestry, they generally say, for example, "She is beautiful; she looks like an Indian." On the other hand, if a black woman has European features, they will remark condescendingly, "Although she is black, you must admit that she is good looking." Some middle-class Negroes of mixed ancestry like to wear Hindu costumes—while they laugh at the idea of wearing an African costume. When middle-class Negroes travel, they studiously avoid association with other Negroes, especially if they themselves have received the slightest recognition by whites. Even when they can not "pass" for white they fear that they will lose this recognition if they are identified as Negroes. Therefore, nothing pleases them more than to be mistaken for a Puerto Rican, Philippino, Egyptian or Arab or any ethnic group other than Negro.

The self-hatred of middle-class Negroes is often revealed in the keen competition which exists among them for status and recognition. This keen competition is the result of the frustrations which they experience in attempting to obtain acceptance and recognition by whites. Middle-class Negroes are constantly criticizing and belittling Negroes who achieve some recognition or who acquire a status above them. They prefer to submit to the authority of whites than to be subordinate to other Negroes. For example, Negro scholars generally refuse to seek the advice and criticism of competent Negro scholars and prefer to turn to white scholars for such co-operation. In fact, it is difficult for middle-class Negroes to co-operate in any field of endeavor. This failure in social relations is, as indicated in an important study, because "in every Negro he encounters his own self-contempt." It is as if he said, "You are only a Negro like myself; so why should you be in a position above me?"

This self-hatred often results in guilt feelings on the part of the Negro who succeeds in elevating himself above his fellows. He feels unconsciously that in rising above other Negroes he is committing an act of aggression which will result in hatred and revenge on their part. The act of aggression may be imagined, but very often it is real. This is the case when middle-class Negroes oppose the economic and social welfare of Negroes because of their own interests. In some American cities, it has been the black bourgeoisie and not the whites who have opposed the building of low-cost public housing for Negro workers. In one city two wealthy Negro doctors, who have successfully opposed public housing projects for Negro workers, own some of the worst slums in the United States. While their wives, who wear mink coats, "drip with diamonds" and are written up in the "society" columns of Negro newspapers, ride in Cadillacs, their Negro tenants sleep on the dirt floors of hovels unfit for human habitation. The guilt feelings of the middle-class Negro are not always unconscious. For example, take the case of the Negro leader who proclaimed over the radio in a national broadcast that the Negro did not want social equity. He was conscious of his guilt feelings and his self-hatred in playing such a role, for he sent word privately to the writer that he never hated so much to do anything in his life, but that it was necessary because of his position as head of a state college which was under white supervision. The self-hatred of the middle-class Negro arises, then, not only from the fact that he does not want to be a Negro but also because of his sorry role in American society.

Escape into Delusions

The black bourgeoisie, as we have seen, has created a world of make-believe to shield itself from the harsh economic and social realities of American life. This world of make-believe is created out of the myth of Negro business, the reports of the Negro press on the achievements and wealth of Negroes, the recognition accorded them by whites, and the fabulous life of Negro "society." Some of the middle-class Negro intellectuals are not deceived by the world of make-believe. They will have nothing to do with Negro "society" and refuse to waste their time in frivolities. They take their work seriously and live in relative obscurity so far as the Negro world is concerned. Others seek an escape from their frustrations by developing, for example, a serious interest in Negro music—which the respectable black bourgeoisie often pretend to despise. In this way these intellectuals achieve some identification with the Negro masses and with the traditions of Negro life. But many more middle-class Negroes, who are satisfied to live in the world of make-believe but must find a solution to the real economic and social problems which they face, seek an escape in delusions.

They seek an escape in delusions involving wealth. This is facilitated by the fact that they have had little experience with the real meaning of wealth and that they lack a tradition of saving and accumulation. Wealth to them means spending money without any reference to its source. Hence, their behavior generally reflects the worst qualities of the gentleman and peasant from whom their only vital traditions spring. Therefore, their small accumulations of capital and the income which they receive from professional services within the Negro community make them appear wealthy in comparison with the low economic status of the majority of Negroes. The delusion of wealth is supported by the myth of Negro business. Moreover, the attraction of the delusion of wealth is enhanced by the belief that wealth will gain them acceptance in American life. In seeking an escape in the delusion of wealth, middle-class Negroes make a fetish of material things or physical possessions. They are constantly buying things—houses, automobiles, furniture and all sorts of gadgets, not to mention clothes. Many of the furnishings and gadgets which they acquire are never used; nevertheless they continue to accumulate things. The homes of many middle-class Negroes have the appearance of museums for the exhibition of American manufactures and spurious art objects. The objects which they are constantly buying are always on display. Negro school teachers who devote their lives to "society" like to display twenty to thirty pairs of shoes, the majority of which they never wear. Negro professional men proudly speak of the two automobiles which they have acquired when they need only one. The acquisition of objects which are not used or needed seems to be an attempt to fill some void in their lives.

The delusion of power also appears to provide an escape for middle-class Negroes from the world of reality which pierces through the world of make-believe of the black bourgeoisie. The positions of power which they occupy in the Negro world often enable them to act autocratically towards other Negroes, especially when they have the support of the white community. In such cases the delusion of power may provide an escape from their frustrations. It is generally, however, when middle-class Negroes hold positions enabling them to participate in the white community that they seek in the delusion of power an escape from their frustrations. Although their position may be only a "token" of the integration of the Negro into American life, they will speak and act as if they were a part of the power structure of American society. Negro advisers who are called into council by whites to give advice about Negroes are especially likely to find an escape from their feelings of inferiority in the delusion of power. Negro social workers, who are dependent upon white philanthropy, have often gained the reputation, with the support of the Negro press, of being powerful persons in American communities.

However, the majority of the black bourgeoisie who seek an escape from their frustrations in delusions seemingly have not been able to find it in the delusion of wealth or power. They have found it in magic or chance, and in sex and alcohol. Excessive drinking and sex seem to provide a means for narcotizing the middle-class Negro against a frustrating existence. A "social" function is hardly ever considered a success unless a goodly number of the participants "pass out." But gambling, especially poker, which has become an obsession among many middle-class Negroes, offers the chief escape into delusion. Among the black bourgeoisie it is not simply a device for winning money. It appears to be a magical device for enhancing their self-esteem through overcoming fate. Although it often involves a waste of money which many middle-class Negroes can not afford, it has an irresistible attraction which they often confess they can not overcome.

Despite the tinsel, glitter and gaiety of the world of make-believe in which middle-class Negroes take refuge, they are still beset by feelings of insecurity, frustration and guilt. As a consequence, the free and easy life which they appear to lead is a mask for their unhappy existence.

FRANTZ FANON

By Way of Conclusion

The social revolution . . . cannot draw its poetry from the past, but only from the future. It cannot begin with itself before it has stripped itself of all its superstitions concerning the past. Earlier revolutions relied on memories out of world history in order to drug themselves against their own content. In order to find their own content, the revolutions of the nineteenth century have to let the dead bury the dead. Before, the expression exceeded the content; now, the content exceeds the expression.

Karl Marx, *The Eighteenth Brumaire*

I can already see the faces of all those who will ask me to be precise on this or that point, to denounce this or that mode of conduct.

It is obvious—and I will never weary of repeating this—that the quest for disalienation by a doctor of medicine born in Guadeloupe can be understood only by recognizing motivations basically different from those of the Negro laborer building the port facilities in Abidjan. In the first case, the alienation is of an almost intellectual character. Insofar as he conceives of European culture as a means of stripping himself of his race, he becomes alienated. In the second case, it is a question of a victim of a system based on the exploitation of a given race by another, on the contempt in which a given branch of humanity is held by a form of civilization that pretends to superiority.

I do not carry innocence to the point of believing that appeals to reason or to respect for human dignity can alter reality. For the Negro who works on a sugar plantation in Le Robert, there is only one solution: to fight. He will embark on this struggle, and he will pursue it, not as the result of a Marxist or idealistic analysis but quite simply because he cannot conceive of life otherwise than in the form of a battle against exploitation, misery, and hunger.

It would never occur to me to ask these Negroes to change their conception of history. I am convinced, however, that without even knowing it they share my views, accustomed as they are to speaking and thinking in terms of the present. The few working-class people whom I had the chance to know in Paris never took it on themselves to pose the problem of the discovery of a Negro past. They knew they were black, but, they told me, that made no difference in anything. In which they were absolutely right.

In this connection, I should like to say something that I have found in many other writers: Intellectual alienation is a creation of middle-class society. What I call middle-class society is any society that becomes rigidified in predetermined forms, forbidding all evolution, all gains, all progress, all discovery. I call middle-class a closed society in which life has no taste, in which the air is tainted, in which ideas and men are corrupt. And I think that a man who takes a stand against this death is in a sense a revolutionary.

The discovery of the existence of a Negro civilization in the fifteenth century confers no patent of humanity on me. Like it or not, the past can in no way guide me in the present moment.

The situation that I have examined, it is clear by now, is not a classic one. Scientific objectivity was barred to me, for the alienated, the neurotic, was my brother, my sister, my father. I have ceaselessly striven to show the Negro that in a sense he makes himself abnormal; to show the white man that he is at once the perpetrator and the victim of a delusion.

There are times when the black man is locked into his body. Now, "for a being who has acquired consciousness of himself and of his body, who has attained to the dialectic of subject and object, the body is no longer a cause of the structure of consciousness, it has become an object of consciousness."[1]

The Negro, however sincere, is the slave of the past. None the less I am a man, and in this sense the Peloponnesian War is as much mine as the invention of the compass. Face to face with the white man, the Negro has a past to legitimate, a vengeance to exact; face to face with the Negro, the contemporary white man feels the need to recall the times of cannibalism. A few years ago, the Lyon branch of the Union of Students From Overseas France asked me to reply to an article that made jazz music literally an irruption of cannibalism into the modern world. Knowing exactly what I was doing, I rejected the premises on which the request was based, and I suggested to the defender of European purity that he cure himself of a spasm that had nothing cultural in it. Some men want to fill the world with their presence. A German philosopher described this mechanism as *the pathology of freedom*. In the circumstances, I did not have to take up a position on behalf of Negro music against white music, but rather to help my brother to rid himself of an attitude in which there was nothing healthful.

The problem considered here is one of time. Those Negroes and white men will be disalienated who refuse

---

[1]Maurice Merleau-Ponty, *La Phénoménologie de la perception* (Paris, Gallimard, 1945), p. 277.

to let themselves be sealed away in the materialized Tower of the Past. For many other Negroes, in other ways, disalienation will come into being through their refusal to accept the present as definitive.

I am a man, and what I have to recapture is the whole past of the world. I am not responsible solely for the revolt in Santo Domingo.

Every time a man has contributed to the victory of the dignity of the spirit, every time a man has said no to an attempt to subjugate his fellows, I have felt solidarity with his act.

In no way should I derive my basic purpose from the past of the peoples of color.

In no way should I dedicate myself to the revival of an unjustly unrecognized Negro civilization. I will not make myself the man of any past. I do not want to exalt the past at the expense of my present and of my future.

It is not because the Indo-Chinese has discovered a culture of his own that he is in revolt. It is because "quite simply" it was, in more than one way, becoming impossible for him to breathe. When one remembers the stories with which, in 1938, old regular sergeants described the land of piastres and rickshaws, of cut-rate boys and women, one understands only too well the rage with which the men of the Viet-Minh go into battle.

An acquaintance with whom I served during the Second World War recently returned from Indo-China. He has enlightened me on many things. For instance, the serenity with which young Vietnamese of sixteen or seventeen faced firing squads. "On one occasion," he told me, "we had to shoot from a kneeling position: The soldiers' hands were shaking in the presence of those young 'fanatics.' " Summing up, he added: "The war that you and I were in was only a game compared to what is going on out there."

Seen from Europe, these things are beyond understanding. There are those who talk of a so-called Asiatic attitude toward death. But these basement philosophers cannot convince anyone. This Asiatic serenity, not so long ago, was a quality to be seen in the "bandits" of Vercors and the "terrorists" of the Resistance.

The Vietnamese who die before the firing squads are not hoping that their sacrifice will bring about the reappearance of a past. It is for the sake of the present and of the future that they are willing to die.

If the question of practical solidarity with a given past ever arose for me, it did so only to the extent to which I was committed to myself and to my neighbor to fight for all my life and with all my strength so that never again would a people on the earth be subjugated. It was not the black world that laid down my course of conduct. My black skin is not the wrapping of specific values. It is a long time since the starry sky that took away Kant's breath revealed the last of its secrets to us. And the moral law is not certain of itself.

As a man, I undertake to face the possibility of annihilation in order that two or three truths may cast their eternal brilliance over the world.

Sartre has shown that, in the line of an unauthentic position, the past "takes" in quantity, and, when solidly constructed, *informs* the individual. He is the past in a changed value. But, too, I can recapture my past, validate it, or condemn it through my successive choices.

The black man wants to be like the white man. For the black man there is only one destiny. And it is white. Long ago the black man admitted the unarguable superiority of the white man, and all his efforts are aimed at achieving a white existence.

Have I no other purpose on earth, then, but to avenge the Negro of the seventeenth century?

In this world, which is already trying to disappear, do I have to pose the problem of black truth?

Do I have to be limited to the justification of a facial conformation?

I as a man of color do not have the right to seek to know in what respect my race is superior or inferior to another race.

I as a man of color do not have the right to hope that in the white man there will be a crystallization of guilt toward the past of my race.

I as a man of color do not have the right to seek ways of stamping down the pride of my former master.

I have neither the right nor the duty to claim reparation for the domestication of my ancestors.

There is no Negro mission; there is no white burden.

I find myself suddenly in a world in which things do evil; a world in which I am summoned into battle; a world in which it is always a question of annihilation or triumph.

I find myself—I, a man—in a world where words wrap themselves in silence; in a world where the other endlessly hardens himself.

No, I do not have the right to go and cry out my hatred at the white man. I do not have the duty to murmur my gratitude to the white man.

My life is caught in the lasso of existence. My freedom turns me back on myself. No, I do not have the right to be a Negro.

I do not have the duty to be this or that. . . .

If the white man challenges my humanity, I will impose my whole weight as a man on his life and show him that I am not that "sho' good eatin' " that he persists in imagining.

I find myself suddenly in the world and I recognize that I have one right alone: That of demanding human behavior from the other.

One duty alone: That of not renouncing my freedom through my choices.

I have no wish to be the victim of the *Fraud* of a black world.

My life should not be devoted to drawing up the balance sheet of Negro values.

There is no white world, there is no white ethic, any more than there is a white intelligence.

There are in every part of the world men who search.

I am not a prisoner of history. I should not seek there for the meaning of my destiny.

I should constantly remind myself that the real *leap* consists in introducing invention into existence.

In the world through which I travel, I am endlessly creating myself.

I am a part of Being to the degree that I go beyond it.

And, through a private problem, we see the outline of the problem of Action. Placed in this world, in a situation, "embarked," as Pascal would have it, am I going to gather weapons?

Am I going to ask the contemporary white man to answer for the slave-ships of the seventeenth century?

Am I going to try by every possible means to cause Guilt to be born in minds?

Moral anguish in the face of the massiveness of the Past? I am a Negro, and tons of chains, storms of blows, rivers of expectoration flow down my shoulders.

But I do not have the right to allow myself to bog down. I do not have the right to allow the slightest fragment to remain in my existence. I do not have the right to allow myself to be mired in what the past has determined.

I am not the slave of the Slavery that dehumanized my ancestors.

To many colored intellectuals European culture has a quality of exteriority. What is more, in human relationships, the Negro may feel himself a stranger to the Western world. Not wanting to live the part of a poor relative, of an adopted son, of a bastard child, shall he feverishly seek to discover a Negro civilization?

Let us be clearly understood. I am convinced that it would be of the greatest interest to be able to have contact with a Negro literature or architecture of the third century before Christ. I should be very happy to know that a correspondence had flourished between some Negro philosopher and Plato. But I can absolutely not see how this fact would change anything in the lives of the eight-year-old children who labor in the cane fields of Martinique or Guadeloupe.

No attempt must be made to encase man, for it is his destiny to be set free.

The body of history does not determine a single one of my actions.

I am my own foundation.

And it is by going beyond the historical, instrumental hypothesis that I will initiate the cycle of my freedom.

The disaster of the man of color lies in the fact that he was enslaved.

The disaster and the inhumanity of the white man lie in the fact that somewhere he has killed man.

And even today they subsist, to organize this dehumanization rationally. But I as a man of color, to the extent that it becomes possible for me to exist absolutely, do not have the right to lock myself into a world of retroactive reparations.

I, the man of color, want only this:

That the tool never possess the man. That the enslavement of man by man cease forever. That is, of one by another. That it be possible for me to discover and to love man, wherever he may be.

The Negro is not. Any more than the white man.

Both must turn their backs on the inhuman voices which were those of their respective ancestors in order that authentic communication be possible. Before it can adopt a positive voice, freedom requires an effort at disalienation. At the beginning of his life a man is always clotted, he is drowned in contingency. The tragedy of the man is that he was once a child.

It is through the effort to recapture the self and to scrutinize the self, it is through the lasting tension of their freedom that men will be able to create the ideal conditions of existence for a human world.

Superiority? Inferiority?

Why not the quite simple attempt to touch the other, to feel the other, to explain the other to myself?

MANNING MARABLE

Black America in Search of Itself

Conspiracy theories always tell you something, if not historical truth. They abound at present in the black community. Many believe that AIDS, which has struck disproportionately among people of color, is some kind of white-supremacist medical conspiracy. Many African-Americans remember the perverse medical experiment conducted by the federal government in Tuskegee, Alabama; for forty years beginning in the 1930s, 399 black men suffering from advanced stages of syphilis went untreated in this program.

In 1988, an aide to then-Mayor Eugene Sawyer of Chicago had to leave office after declaring that "Jewish doctors were infecting black babies with AIDS." In September 1990, *Essence,* a popular black women's magazine, featured an essay headed "AIDS: Is It Genocide?" When a *New York Times*/CBS News poll in August asked African-American and white residents of New York City whether AIDS "was deliberately created in a laboratory in order to infect black people," the differences in racial perceptions were striking. Only 1 per cent of all whites polled thought this statement was true, and another 4 per cent thought it could possibly be true. On the other hand, 10 per cent of all blacks accepted the statement as valid, with another 19 per cent agreeing it could be true.

When blacks were queried about the reasons for the accessibility of crack cocaine and other illegal drugs within the African-American community, the results were similar. One-fourth of all blacks questioned agreed that the federal government "deliberately makes sure that drugs are easily available in poor black neighborhoods." An additional 35 per cent thought that this assertion was "possibly true."

When millions of people are absolutely convinced that they are being systematically destroyed, whether by an onslaught of drugs, criminal violence, or medical mayhem, any nascent racial polemicist can gather a constituency around himself and acquire a degree of legitimacy. Blacks ask themselves: Why is it so much easier to obtain crack cocaine and heroin in our neighborhoods than it is to buy fresh milk, eggs, and bread? Why are so many white educators so hostile toward the introduction of African-American Studies and multicultural requirements within the core curricula of public schools and colleges?

Dr Leonard Jeffries, Jr., chair of the African-American Studies Department at New York's City College, started a firestorm in July at the Empire State Black Arts and Cultural Festival in Albany by delivering a public address that included several blatantly anti-Semitic remarks. Jeffries, whose speech was broadcast over an Albany cable-TV station, asserted that blacks were the victims of a "conspiracy planned and plotted out of Hollywood" by "people called Greenberg and Weisberg and Trigliani." He claimed that "Russian Jewry had a particular control" over the film industry and that "their financial partners, the Mafia, put together a financial system of destruction of black people." He criticized those who opposed the inclusion of African and African-American history and culture in the state's high-school curricula. He particularly condemned Diane Ravitch, assistant secretary of the De-partment of Education, a Bush appointee, as "a Texas Jew" and "a sophisticated debonair racist."

The response from the white political establishment, the media, and educational officials was swift. Many Democratic and Republican politicians, including New York governor Mario Cuomo, denounced Jeffries. Democratic senator Daniel Patrick Moynihan deplored the speech, noting that "conspiracy theories about 'rich Jews' are nothing new. What is new is for such things to be said by a professor at City College."

Moynihan insisted that Jeffries "ought to resign" and that if he was not removed the trustees of City College should resign. Harold Jacobs, a member of the City University board of trustees, declared that if Jeffries was "teaching bigotry in his classes, instead of African-American studies, that's consumer fraud being paid for by the state." The college's alumni association also demanded that Jeffries be fired as department head. Jewish leaders were particularly outraged. Michael Riff, local leader of the Anti-Defamation League of B'nai B'rith, said the controversial speech had "the tinge of classical anti-Semitism: to create a web of conspiracy by suggestion, innuendo and half-truths."

The Jeffries controversy generated more heat than light, because no dialogue exists between Jeffries' critics and defenders over the real issues that divide them. Neo-conservative writer Julius Lester, who is both black and Jewish, reviewed a videotape of the speech and found that the media "misrepresented some [of] Jeffries' statements." The speech certainly contained anti-Semitic assertions, but it had little to do with Jews or black–Jewish relations.

Many black scholars suspect that the condemnation of Jeffries is actually a smokescreen for a more general assault on multicultural perspectives in education. Jeffries served as principal consultant to a statewide curriculum-review committee for public schools in New York, which recently mandated a multicultural requirement. James De Jongh, chair of City College's faculty senate, admits that those who opposed the adoption of multiculturalism "are finding it easier to attack Jeffries on an obscure speech than to confront the curriculum."

Most black educators and leaders disagree with the expressions of anti-Semitism in Jeffries' public address, but they quietly question what the dispute is really about. It is difficult to take sympathetically the appeals of Moynihan, who a quarter of a century ago authored the notorious "black matriarchy" thesis, asserting that the black family is dysfunctional because it lacks patriarchal character. Blacks suspect that calls for the firing of the tenured professor, which in any case would be extremely difficult to accomplish legally, have little to do with anti-Semitism as such, and more with white hostility to affirmative action and the educational and political agenda of the black freedom struggle.

This perception hardened into certainty when another City College professor, Michael Levin, was vindicated by a federal court. Levin had made public statements declaring that African-Americans overall are "significantly less intelligent" than whites, and college administrators had established a committee in 1990 to investigate allegedly racist statements in his classroom lectures. The ruling said that the administrators were in error in ordering the investigation, and also erred in failing to discipline protestors who disrupted Levin's classes. Levin's statement following this decision targeted Jeffries as well as all other African-Americans who favor greater ethnic diversity within education. "This whole subject of Black Studies," Levin said, "is a made-up subject that shouldn't be at any college anywhere"; Jeffries and others teaching it only offer students "introductory resentment, intermediate resentment, and advanced resentment."

Many Jewish and white leaders were virtually silent about the Levin case and his legal victory, a fact not lost on black activists and scholars who reject both anti-Semitism and black chauvinism. The absence of media focus on Levin also seemed to reinforce the conspiracy thesis of Jeffries and other African-American nationalists. In this context, it is not difficult for some to ignore the objectionable and even odious elements of Jeffries' address and to insist that the attack against the black educator was racially and politically motivated.

Conversely, many Jewish leaders are upset about the apparent silence of blacks over the anti-Semitic smears of Jeffries. The Anti-Defamation League has recorded a 50 per cent increase in anti-Jewish harassment and violence on university campuses since the mid 1980s. Jewish stereotypes seem to be making a comeback in Hollywood: witness the Jewish-American princesses in *White Palace,* or the untrustworthy Jewish characters in *Bonfire of the Vanities, Class Action,* and *Regarding Henry.* "Kill-the-Jew" computer games are now being sold in Europe. From the perspective of many Jews, the Jeffries incident is the most threatening of a series of events—including Jesse Jackson's "Hymie" smear of 1984 and the rising popularity of Black Muslim Louis Farrakhan among young inner-city African-Americans. If mainstream black leaders fail to condemn vigorously a demagogue such as Jeffries, some reasoned, it must be because they quietly embrace anti-Semitism themselves.

Simmering racial grievances finally boiled over into violence this summer in Brooklyn's Crown Heights neighborhood, where Hasidic Jews and blacks dwell in uneasy coexistence. On an evening in August, Yosef Lifsh, a Hasidic Jew, lost control of his automobile and smashed into several black children on the sidewalk, killing one seven-year-old boy. Witnesses reported to police that Lifsh had run a red light and was speeding; others spread the rumor that he had been drinking, and that ambulance attendants assisted him before they saw to the black children. Outraged, hundreds of young black people took to the streets, hurling rocks and bottles at police and Jewish residents. Apparently in retaliation, a group of twenty or so young blacks surrounded and killed a visiting Hasidic scholar from Australia, reportedly chanting, "Kill the Jew!"

To most blacks, both deaths were criminal homicides. To New York's Jewish community and most whites, the deaths were entirely different—the first a regrettable accident, the second a deliberate murder provoked by vicious black anti-Semitism. Many black activists were troubled when attorney Barry Slotnick, who had represented subway murderer Bernhard Goetz, stepped forward as a spokesman for Lifsh. When Brooklyn district attorney Charles Hynes announced that no charges of criminally negligent homicide would be filed against Lifsh, the grief and resentment of thousands of blacks turned into deep outrage.

Instead of trying to understand the origins of black anger and violence in poverty and a sense of powerlessness, many whites leaped to the conclusion that anti-Semitism and violent sentiments have acquired a mass base of support among blacks. Few white commentators were more vehement on this baseless theme than the *New York Times* columnist (and former editor) A.M. Rosenthal. Blaming the recent upsurge of racial violence on "the black political marauders who goad mobs into the streets against Jews," Rosenthal asserted that their "strategy is to blow up all political and emotional bridges between blacks and nonblacks." Rosenthal linked the Crown Heights incident with the earlier Jeffries controversy, which he characterized as "weirdo speeches of a Jew-baiting professor on the public payroll and by bigotry's apologists, supporters, and conveyor belts in the black press and radio." Rosenthal offered his own self-fulfilling prophecy and warning to New York mayor David Dinkins and other black elected officials, wondering aloud whether "any black will be chosen mayor for a long time" because "so many nonblacks have been antagonized."

Nowhere in Rosenthal's diatribe did he recognize that many black politicians, and especially Dinkins, have taken a principled, public stance against anti-Semitism throughout their careers. To blame them for the actions of a small minority is, in effect, a concession to the worst form of racist bigotry. Nowhere in this none-too-subtle linkage of Dinkins with Jeffries did Rosenthal acknowledge that Jewish political behavior in recent years has grown more conservative ideologically—and has specifically opposed blacks' interests on such issues as affirmative action.

The sources of genuine tension between Jews and African-Americans cannot be so simplistically attributed to the actions of anti-Semites within the black community. From the vantage point of blacks, bridges with the liberal Jewish political establishment were torched by other, far more significant events—the gradual shift in political sympathies from Israel to the Palestinians among America's black leadership and activists, the geographical flight of many Jews from the problems of the inner city to the affluent suburbs, the general Jewish hostility toward the Rainbow Coalition and Jesse Jackson.

Rosenthal's feeble appeals to interracial dialogue were disingenuous precisely because he and others like him in the white media and political institutions refuse to face the legitimate differences which have separated African-Americans and Jewish interests in the old civil-rights coalition of a generation ago. This failure is particularly difficult for blacks such as myself, who still feel a special sympathy and political kinship with the historical struggles of Jewish people and a keen opposition to all forms of anti-Semitism. Why is this happening? Why are these disturbing and disruptive social trends emerging *now*? What is their long-term significance for black politics and culture?

Deeply embedded within the fabric of black American culture is the messianic myth of Moses and the ordeal of the ancient Hebrews. Gleaned from the Old Testament and reshaped to fit the contours of America's plantations and slave society, it became a beacon of hope and faith for successive generations of African-Americans yearning to be free. The sons and daughters of slaves saw themselves as the children of bondage, oppressed by a wicked and unjust power. But a gifted, charismatic figure would arise from their ranks, a figure who would embrace both the spiritual strivings and secular ambitions of his people. This black Messiah would lead his flock across the barren wilderness to the blessed banks of the River Jordan and into the golden horizon of the Promised Land.

A century ago, the Messiah's mantle rested on the shoulders of Frederick Douglass, the great abolitionist orator. A generation ago, the weight of moral leadership was borne by Martin Luther King, Jr. King recognized that his powerful presence in the lives of African-Americans was due not solely to his sonorous rhetoric, but rather to his kinship to the messianic cultural tradition of salvation and liberation. "The Bible tells the thrilling story of how Moses stood in Pharaoh's court centuries ago and cried, 'Let my people go,' " King once declared. In identical fashion, he thought, the

Southern desegregation movement demonstrated that "oppressed people cannot remain oppressed forever. The yearning for freedom eventually manifests itself." If the Hebrews found the courage to follow their convictions, African-Americans could do no less. But nearly a quarter of a century after the assassination of the civil-rights movement's Messiah, and after a decade of pain imposed by the Reagan–Bush conservative reaction, African-American political culture has taken a new and very disturbing direction.

The desegregation struggle had been informed by a political ideology of what I call "liberal integrationism." Its central tenets were the eradication of all legal barriers to blacks' gaining full access to civil society, economic exchange, and political institutions; an increase in the numbers of African-Americans representing their race in both real and symbolic positions of authority within the state; a strategic alliance with liberal whites, especially the national leaders of the Democratic Party, after the Great Depression. Several generations of African-American leaders were nurtured in this secular creed and unthinkingly accepted its implications. Blacks as a group could be guaranteed continued upward mobility within the system if the rules of the game were liberalized, as larger numbers of African-American elites were elevated into the federal judiciary, legislatures, and corporate board rooms.

Brown v. *Board of Education,* the 1954 Supreme Court decision outlawing segregated schools, had created the legal framework for a democratic, "color-blind" society within the structures of liberal capitalism. This liberal faith in the system was employed to justify all the sacrifices and hardships by the children of bondage. In destroying legal Jim Crow segregation, African-Americans had escaped the clutches of a dictatorial Pharaoh; their experiences since the 1960s seemed to represent a sojourn in the wilderness. But all along this bitter path, the image of a promised land of racial equality and economic democracy seemed to loom just ahead. Then the myth veered off course. The messianic figure of the former slaves was murdered several days into the difficult journey through the wilderness. None of his closest comrades and lieutenants seemed able to bear the dual burden of political emancipator and moral guide. The creed of liberal integrationism and color-blind institutions, once affirmed with Talmudic certainty, began to be perceived as strangely anachronistic and even counterproductive.

The new generation of the oppressed, born and raised not under the old Jim Crow order but in the sterility of a political wilderness, inevitably challenged the faith of their fathers and mothers. Speaking for this lost generation, Anthony Parker, writing recently in *Sojourners*, questions the future identity of African-

Americans as a people. "Unlike the generation of blacks who reached maturity before and during the early 1970s," Parker writes, "my generation has no memory of credible black leaders, such as Malcolm X or Martin Luther King, Jr. But the practice of integration created the illusion of equality with the wider culture, effectively wresting control of the black freedom movement by holding it hostage to Federal good will and weakening or destroying those institutions that influenced blacks' world view."

One major factor in the demise of black consciousness and identity was the materialism and greed inherent in the existing American political economy and secular society. By asking to be integrated into the existing structures of society, rather than demanding the basic transformation of the system, blacks became hostage to their own ideological demands. "Inoculated with secular values emphasizing the individual instead of the community," Parker observes, "young blacks rarely recognize each other as brothers and sisters, or as comrades in the struggle. We're now competitors, relating to each other out of fear and mistrust."

Other black intellectuals have also sensed that African-Americans have reached a secular epiphany, a moment of self-realization and uncertainty, when the old beliefs can no longer be sustained but the new insights into social reality cannot be fully comprehended. One of black America's most percpective critics, Professor Cornel West of Harvard University's Afro-American Studies Department, describes the contemporary spiritual crisis as a "profound sense of psychological depression, personal worthlessness, and social despair . . . widespread in black America." West recognizes that "black people have always been in America's wilderness in search of a promised land. Yet many black folk now reside in a jungle with a cutthroat mortality devoid of any faith in deliverance or hope for freedom."

On a national level, the mantle of leadership apparently passed to Jesse Jackson. Despite Jackson's incredible and largely unanticipated electoral success in the 1984 and 1988 Democratic presidential primaries, however, the promise of his Rainbow Coalition was never fulfilled. From its inception, the idea of the Rainbow brought together two contradictory currents: liberals who sought to make the Democrats a "social-democratic style" party, and leftists who wanted to launch a progressive third party from the bankrupt ruins of the New Deal and the Great Society.

In the wake of George Bush's election, Jackson tactically shifted to the right, siding with the liberals. He demanded and obtained the authority for his national board to veto all important political and legislative initiatives by local Rainbow chapters. In effect, the democratic grassroots leadership responsible for much of Jackson's electoral success was muzzled from above.

Efforts to build a more structured membership organization with a formal dues system and a regular newspaper were silenced. The results were inevitable. In 1989–90, the Rainbow Coalition's political action committee raised $549,973; in the first six months of 1991, the PAC raised only $33,657. Jackson's refusal to run for mayor of Washington DC reinforced perceptions that the "country preacher" has no stomach for the nitty-gritty work of actual governing.

Valuable state-wide leaders of the Rainbow defected in droves. In Louisiana, progressives bolted when Jackson ordered that all local initiatives be approved by his hand-picked lieutenant. Dissidents promptly created an independent group. In Vermont, New Jersey, and Pennsylvania, core Jackson activists are building their own local alliances. Elsewhere, there is a bitter sense of frustration and betrayal. As Kevin Gray, the 1988 campaign coordinator for Jackson in South Carolina, declared, "The movement is not supposed to be a continual photo opportunity for Jesse Jackson for President, but that's what it's been."

Unlike King, Jackson never succeeded in balancing his own personal ambitions with the broader goals of the democratic protest movement that thrust him into public prominence. But the real dilemma confronting Jackson and other African-American leaders is the limitations of their own political ideology, which is liberal integrationism. Jackson never believed that the American political system could be transformed from without, via the challenge of a third party or even a quasi-independent movement like the Rainbow Coalition. He retains a deep faith that the Democratic Party can be transformed from within into an effective vehicle for the aspirations of the poor, the working class, women, racial minorities, and others experiencing discrimination and social injustices. But what is strikingly clear after the crushing of Jimmy Carter, Walter Mondale, and Michael Dukakis in successive presidential elections, and the ideological capitulation of mainstream Democratic Party politics to many of the central tenets of Reaganism, is that American liberalism is bankrupt. The belief in an internal, progressive realignment of the Democrats is belief in a hopeless illusion never to be achieved or realized so long as the party has some utility to corporate capitalism. It is the activists themselves who become transformed.

The crisis within black political culture is also intensified by the fraying of the bonds among virtually all African-Americans. Once, segregation led to a sense of shared suffering and group identity. An artificial yet powerful wall of race had been built around our community, giving us simultaneously a sense of oppression and a collective will to resist. On Sunday mornings in the churches of my childhood, I can distinctly recall the people who came together for the ritual of spirit and unbowed faith—the school teacher and his family in the pew ahead, the automobile mechanics and sanitation workers beside me, the doctors and dentists in the pews behind. A wide range of vocations was represented, because segregation forced every class to cooperate with each other. A black lawyer looked to the black community for his or her clients. A black entrepreneur, anxiously opening a new business, had to depend on the faithful patronage of black consumers from her or his neighborhood, civic club, fraternity, and school.

Now, in the post-civil-rights era of the 1980s and 1990s, even the definition of the term "black community" is up for debate. The net result of affirmative action and civil-rights initiatives was to expand the potential base of the African-American middle class, which was located primarily outside the neighborhood confines of the old ghetto. By 1989, one out of seven African-American families had incomes exceeding $50,000 annually, compared to less than $22,000 for the average black household. Black college-educated married couples currently earn 93 per cent of the family income of comparable white couples.

But the general experience of the black working-class, low-income people, and families on welfare—the overwhelming majority of African-Americans—is one of steady deterioration. According to *African Americans in the 1990s,* a recent report by the Population Reference Bureau, the average annual income of African-Americans is only 56 per cent that of white income, significantly less than the 63 per cent ratio in 1975. Black female-headed households average less than $9,600 annually. Stark differences in patterns of home ownership, income, and education indicate that there are "two separate worlds inhabited by poor and middle-class black children," the report says. This strongly implies that "the African-American population will become more polarized as these children mature."

Many white liberals take such statistics to mean that the source of the material and social inequities which separate the races—institutional racism—no longer exists, or at least, in the words of influential black sociologist William Julius Wilson, has "declined in significance." A shift in liberal government policy from race-based remedies to economic, class-based programs is therefore required. From the vantage point of liberal Democrats, this would solve the perception problem among millions of white males that the party's social agenda is being held hostage to the interests of blacks. Class-based programs would eliminate the argument of "reverse discrimination" because all benefits would, theoretically, be distributed in a color-blind manner.

Stuart Eizenstat, domestic policy adviser in the Carter administration, defends this thesis. So does Richard Cohen, liberal columnist for the *Washington Post.* "If economic need, not race," Cohen writes, "became the basis for what we now call affirmative action, most Americans would not object. Whites, too, could be helped. . . . After all, poor is poor, although a disproportionate number of them are black." When minority community leaders read such statements, most cannot help but feel a sense of outrage and repudiation. The overwhelming majority of federal programs *were* based on income, not race. Poor whites shared substantial benefits from the initiatives of the Great Society. Currently, more than one-third of all students enrolled in the Upward Bound program, designed to prepare low-income students for college, are white. One-third of the children who attend the pre-school Head Start program are white. The majority of people living in public housing or who receive public assistance, are white.

The basis of affirmative action is the recognition that, within this society, there is systemic discrimination grounded in race and gender. Despite the passage of the Civil Rights Act of 1964, outlawing discrimination in public accommodations, race is a powerful factor in determining the actual conditions of life for any person of color, regardless of income and education. My children stand a much greater likelihood of being harassed or arrested by the police, for example, than the children of my white colleagues at the university, solely because they are black. Through practical experience, African-Americans of every social class recognize this reality. To argue that a shift in affirmative action policies from race to class will benefit them seems, at best, a gross distortion. At worst, it is taken as yet one more piece of evidence that liberal integrationism has failed as a political strategy. Black intellectuals and politicians are increasingly convinced that white liberals have turned their backs against us; both parties have repudiated our very presence at any serious debate on public policy.

Many millions of African-Americans believe that most whites live a racial double life, that whites follow a hypocritical racial etiquette in the presence of blacks which disappears whenever they are among themselves. This is the basic premise of the recent film *True Identity,* which features a black man who dons white make-up. He discovers that whites interact very differently with each other than they do with minorities. Abundant evidence supports this thesis. Earlier this year, a study of the American Bar Association published in *Harvard Law Review* indicated that car dealers charge African-Americans and women higher prices than white males. Male and female researchers, black and white, presented themselves as middle-class car shoppers at ninety car dealerships in the Chicago metropolitan area. They used identical negotiation styles and bartered for identical automobiles. The car dealers' offers to the consumers followed a pattern of gender and racial inequity. The final offer to white men averaged $11,352, and to white women, $11,504; to black men, $11,783, and to black women, $12,237.

Affirmative action is a particular sticking point in the 1990s. In the workplace, most white males behave publicly in a race-neutral manner. Virtually no one openly calls African-American employees or supervisors "niggers." But millions of whites harbor deep resentment against black and Latino co-workers, whom they believe have been unfairly advanced and receive excessively high wages because of affirmative action and equal-opportunity programs. In one recent survey of several thousand white male corporate employees, only 10 per cent expressed the opinion that "women were getting too much help" through affirmative action. But 50 per cent stated that blacks and Hispanics unfairly gained "too much" of an advantage by affirmative action. Conversely, 55 per cent of all Latino and black employees polled stated that "too little was being done for them" through corporate affirmative action efforts. Many whites perceive the presence of people of color in their workplace as a "zero-sum game"; the additional appointment of any single black person means that the potential job pool for whites has decreased. Instead of fighting to increase the size of the economic pie, many whites now want to take away the small slice served up to Latinos and blacks through affirmative action initiatives.

Such programs forced police departments to hire and promote thousands of minorities and women, partially in an attempt to respond to the changing urban demographics of race. But many whites have never reconciled themselves to these policy changes, which they perceive as an erosion of "standards" and "professionalism." This anger and alienation is projected onto black and Latino citizens, who are generally assumed to be guilty in any confrontation. For example, a public commission reviewing the Los Angeles Police Department reported several months ago that it found more than seven hundred racist, homophobic, and sexist remarks made by officers on the department's car-communications system over the previous eighteen months. Typical of the statements were: "Sounds like monkey-slapping time" and "I would love to drive down Slauson [a street in a black neighborhood] with a flame thrower. We would have a barbecue."

But the last evidence of the pervasiveness of white privilege is found in daily life. When inner-city blacks and Latinos return from work in the downtown district, they watch the striking changes in the allocation of commuter buses and trains, which shuttle upper-class whites in comfort to their suburban enclaves. They feel their worthlessness in white eyes as they wait for graffiti-scarred, filthy trains in stations pervaded with the stench of urine. They feel the anger held in check, seeing crack-cocaine merchants operate on their street corners as police cars casually drive by, doing nothing. Everything in daily life tells them that, to those with power and wealth within the system, African-American life, property, beliefs, and aspirations mean nothing.

In the ruins of ideology, bereft of messianic leadership, the African-American community reaches a moment of painful introspection. When hope of the New Jerusalem and the possibility of political liberation dies, part of the spirit dies as well. Locked in an urban abyss of poverty, drugs, and black-against-black violence, the working class and dispossessed increasingly retreat into themselves, psychologically and culturally. If the creed of liberal integrationism no longer makes sense, and if our leaders have failed to deliver us from the wilderness, then we must turn within our own group, reviving the images and symbols for survival. The temptation is to seek refuge in the narrow alleys of racial chauvinism and political parochialism.

Black America still sees itself as the litmus test of the viability and reality of American democracy. Indeed, the African-American striving for freedom and human rights embodies the country's best examples of sacrifice and struggle for the realization of democracy's highest ideals. A century ago, black scholar W.E.B. Du Bois suggested that the "concrete test of the underlying principles of the great republic is the Negro Problem." Yet this historic burden of race cannot be comprehended solely in legislative initiative or in the struggles for voting rights. This sojourn through the wilderness is a quest for full self-consciousness, a "spiritual striving of the freedmen's sons" which represents a "travail of souls whose burden is almost beyond the measure of their strength, but who bear it in the name of a historic race, in the name of this land of their fathers' fathers, and in the name of human opportunity."

It is precisely here, at the juncture of faith and political ambition, of spirit and struggle, that the black freedom movement must revive itself, casting aside the parochial chains of chauvinism and isolation. We can find value in our culture and heritage without fostering negative stereotypes and myths about other ethnic groups. We can express ourselves ethnically without resorting to the false discourse and rationales of race. In the process, we will discover that the proverbial promised land of full equality and economic equity can be achieved, but only in concert with other groups of the oppressed—especially Latinos, Native Americans, Arab Americans, Asian/Pacific Americans, and the unemployed and economically and socially disadvantaged of all ethnic backgrounds.

Ethnic pride and group awareness constitute a beginning stage, not an end in itself, for a richer understanding of the essential diversity and pluralism that constitute our America. That awareness of diversity must point toward the restructuring of the elaborate systems of ownership and power that perpetuate the unequal status of these ethnic groups and oppressed social classes. This leap of awareness depends on our willingness to define our political, educational, and social goals in a way that is truly majoritarian, that speaks for the commonwealth of the whole society, that realizes a new level of struggle for the black freedom movement.

WALT HARRINGTON

How Can Anyone Do Anything Else?

On the threshing-floor, in the center of the crying, singing saints, John lay astonished beneath the power of the Lord.

From *Go Tell It on the Mountain* by James Baldwin

I am not an expert on religion, far from it. But somewhere along the way, I learned that in ancient Jewish legend there is told the story of the *lamedvovniks,* the 36 Righteous Men who were sent by God to live and work among us, always poor, unnoticed and without glory, unaware of their own perfection. If a Righteous Man was ever discovered, various versions of the legend went, he would deny his identity, disappear and reappear, unknown and unknowing, in a distant place. I do not believe in *lamedvovniks.* I do not even believe in God. But over the years, I've sometimes puzzled at the *idea* of these Righteous Men living secretly among us, been reminded that what it means to be truly good was as mysterious to those who lived a thousand years ago as it is to us, with all our modern sophistication.

Lately, after meeting Bryan Stevenson, I've found myself puzzling over these questions once again. But then, that often happens to people after they meet Bryan Stevenson.

This morning, Bryan—31, a lawyer and a black man—is on the road out of Montgomery, Ala., where he lives, headed for Phenix City, a tiny Alabama town where Bryan's black client George Daniel has been locked in the Russell County jail awaiting his execution for murdering a white policeman. Just yesterday, a federal court overturned his conviction and ordered that he be given a new trial.

That is what Bryan Stevenson does. He files appeals. He is one of those much-maligned lawyers who

supposedly clog the courts with frivolous petitions meant only to postpone deserving men's dates with the electric chair, gas chamber or needle. He is one of the reasons Chief Justice William H. Rehnquist and countless politicians, including President Bush, have called for limits on the number of court reviews for those sentenced to death. He is one of the reasons that, with nearly 2,400 people on death row, only 143 have been executed since the Supreme Court declared the death penalty constitutional in 1976. Today, about 75 percent of Americans favor capital punishment, compared with 42 percent in 1966. For the first time, even a majority of blacks favor capital punishment. So far, this new public thirst for final vengeance has gone largely unquenched.

Bryan Stevenson is one of the reasons.

At the Russell County jail, Bryan is ushered into a small room where George Daniel is waiting. As Bryan tells him that he'll have a new trial—which might literally save George's life—the thin, 34-year-old man smiles blankly, squeezes his nose tightly, rocks his body gently and bounces his legs to some rapid, internal rhythm. He wears a white jail uniform that is filthy at the crotch. The last time Bryan visited George, his cell was dirty with his own urine. Court records show that at least once during his incarceration George Daniel ate his own feces and that he is mildly retarded. "I need cigarettes," he says finally. Bryan promises to get cigarettes, and George is led away. As Bryan leaves, a guard stops him at the jailhouse gate and says of George Daniel, "I think he's crazy. I really do. That's just my opinion. We have to make him take a shower and change clothes. I think he's crazy. Some people are playin'. I don't think he is."

Outside, past the electric door and the tall wire fence, Bryan says, "George is one of the men America believes is so evil he must be strapped into an electric chair and killed." He doesn't say this harshly or self-righteously. He says it gently, with eerie understatement. "You know, people always ask me how I can defend these 'animals.' I never understand how they can ask that. The criminal justice system is so corrupt, so racist. I wouldn't want George Daniel out fending for himself. He can't. He's ill. But a civilized society does not execute people like him. Rehnquist can restrict legal options for the convicted, because he can't imagine himself or anyone he loves ever being in George Daniel's situation. But how would Rehnquist feel if his son were in George's place?

"In the end, we are too frail to make these decisions."

I met Bryan Stevenson by chance while traveling through the South, which boasts more than half of

Bryan Stevenson, Director, Equal Justice Initiative of America (ABAJ/Paul Robertson, Jr.)

America's death-row inmates and about 85 percent of its executions since 1977. Right off, Bryan fascinated me. A graduate of Harvard's law school and John F. Kennedy School of Government, he's the director of the Alabama Capital Representation Resource Center, which is involved in some way with most of the 119 death-row inmates in Alabama. He was offered $50,000 to $60,000 a year to take the director's job, one of the center's board members told me, but Bryan said it was too much money. He settled on $18,000—now up to $24,000. In corporate law, he could make five to 10 times that.

Bryan worked seven days a week, still does, often from 8:30 in the morning to 11:30 at night. On Saturdays and Sundays, he knocks off early to do his laundry and maybe catch a movie. These days, he has little time to play his electric piano, compose music, play basketball or attend church, all of which he once did regularly. He hasn't had a vacation in years. Once a voracious reader, Bryan has read three books for pleasure in the last year. He sometimes worries that he doesn't laugh enough anymore.

Simply put, the man was hard to figure. A person didn't need to believe Bryan's cause was noble, or even correct, to be touched and fascinated by his passion.

All through the '80s, while most of his Harvard classmates got rich, he defended penniless murderers. His parents—working people from Milton, Del., near Rehoboth Beach—certainly didn't understand what their son was doing. "Take the money," Bryan's father said, more than once. With all his degrees, Bryan still drove a beat-up Honda Civic. His mother drove a jet-black BMW 325i. She couldn't figure her son either. What had made him so different—from his folks, his classmates, from America, really?

"I've asked him how he does this day in, day out," said William Newman, a Massachusetts lawyer in Alabama to work with Bryan on a death-row appeal. "It's Bryan. It's who Bryan is. I'm telling you, Bryan is a prince. I bet you won't find one person who *doesn't* say that. I'm telling you, he's a saint. You can't say that, I know, but he is. That's exactly what he is." Another Massachusetts lawyer, Stewart Eisenberg, also in Alabama working on an appeal, said, "I am extraordinarily impressed with Bryan, but I'm curious about why a black Harvard Law School graduate who could write his own ticket spends his time earning next to nothing in Klan country on the back roads of the South."

His curiosity was my curiosity. Bryan Stevenson had rejected America's reigning view of success and money, even justice. Perhaps understanding him—America's reverse image—would tell us something about ourselves. So, not yet having the legend of the *lamedvovniks* in mind, I set about trying to discover what had made Bryan Stevenson so unlike the rest of us.

The road is home to Bryan. He spends more time driving than he does in his apartment, which is furnished with a single folding director's chair, a stool, two end tables, two small ceramic lamps, a television and a mattress and boxspring on the floor. At the office, the phone rings incessantly. Bryan advises about 60 private lawyers who work on Alabama death-row cases pro bono. He handles an additional 24 death-row cases himself. He supervises a staff of five young lawyers who deal with about 30 cases. At the same time, he must raise about $200,000 a year in private or foundation grants to go with the $300,000 the federal government gives to the center. So it is only in his car, now a gray Toyota Corolla, on the back roads of the South, that Bryan has time to himself. He thinks, meditates, sometimes prays.

He is a thin, athletic man, just shy of six feet, a soccer star in high school and college. He wears short, natural hair and a short beard. He wears unstylish clothes and clunky sunglasses. He talks so softly that I must sometimes strain to hear him. He has no discernible accent, strictly Middle American. In phone conversations, prosecutors and defense attorneys who don't know him usually assume he's white. Once, when Bryan suggested that a defense lawyer try to plead his client down from a death sentence charge to life without parole, the lawyer said, "Didn't I tell you? He's a nigger. Can't get a life plea for a nigger in this county."

"I have always felt," Bryan says, as he drives toward Atlanta to visit another death-row client, "that I could just as easily have ended up as one of the men I am defending. I've had friends, cousins who fell into trouble. It could have been me." Bryan says this quietly and deliberately, with little emotion. When he talks about the death penalty, he talks mostly facts and fairness. He talks like a lawyer. Unless asked again and again, he rarely speaks about himself, not even in the little asides through which most people reveal so much. When I later read his words, I will see that he was, more or less, on a soapbox, plunging point by point through his list of horrors about the death penalty. But as I sit next to him, listening, a gentle intimacy in his manner masks his single-minded agenda.

"I could go through the South's prisons and put together five death rows of men not condemned whose crimes were far more vicious," Bryan says. "The people who end up on death row are always poor, often black. And almost always they had bad lawyers—real estate lawyers who never handled a capital case and who had to be dragged screaming into the courtroom. In one case, the judge actually sent the defense lawyer out to sleep off a drunk.

"Appointed lawyers, paid a maximum of $1,000 in Alabama and several other Southern states, often do almost no work on their cases. It takes 800 hours to do a capital case. The Supreme Court declared it unconstitutional, but prosecutors in the South still keep blacks off capital juries by giving bogus reasons to strike them. In one rural Alabama county we found potential jurors labeled by the prosecutor as 'strong,' 'medium,' 'weak' and 'black.'

"Maybe it would help the congressmen who are so hot for the death penalty if they thought of it this way: Imagine a senator is accused of stealing campaign funds and he is told that he gets a lawyer who's a drunk, who's being paid $1,000. Then the senator is told, if he's a Democrat, that only Republicans will sit on his jury—just as blacks are still tried by all-white juries. That's our system of justice today.

"Why do I do what I do? How can anyone do anything else?"

Bryan Stevenson was always different. In rural southern Delaware, he was the only black child in his first-grade class in 1965. His mother, who migrated from Philadelphia through marriage to Bryan's father, had volunteered to put Bryan and his older brother in the white school even before formal integration was in place. She had only to look at the ramshackle schoolhouse black children attended to know where her kids were going. Years later, when Bryan was put in a slow-learner class with the black children who had arrived with integration, it was Bryan's mother who went to the school and raised hell until he was bumped to the top class.

Alice Stevenson was a firebrand by the yardstick of southern Delaware. "Don't be a fool, don't be silly and grin," she'd tell her two sons and daughter. "You are here to make a mark. Otherwise you will be the mark." Appalled at the docility she perceived in southern Delaware's blacks, she admonished her children never to show false deference to whites. She insisted on perfect grammar, diction and pronunciation. And there was one absolute rule: "I never want to hear that you can't do something because you're black. You can do anything you want."

Bryan's father, Howard, a native of southern Delaware, gave less assertive advice. The child of a prominent black mechanic in nearby Georgetown, he had grown up playing with the children of the town's prominent whites. He recalls few incidents in which he was mistreated by whites. In fact, because he dressed nattily—refusing to wear the jeans and overalls then worn by most of the blacks he knew—it was more often blacks who insulted him with the charge that he was highfalutin. Howard's advice to his children—born of his own unusual experience—was that most white people will treat you well if you treat them well.

Between the two of them, Howard and Alice Stevenson sent a singular message: Whites were not to be feared.

Both had good jobs. She was an accounting clerk at the Air Force base in Dover, and he was a lab technician at the General Foods plant. They bought three acres on County Route 319 and built a little ranch house that was elegant by local black standards of the day. Up the road, their neighbors lived with dirt floors and no running water. In a sense, the Stevensons were local black gentry.

Alice worried about her children being in school all day with whites, worried they'd be picked on, worried they'd forget they were black. In high school, where Bryan was popular, she worried about the white girls who kept calling the house. "Please don't marry a white girl just to do it." Bryan's mother pleaded. Today, she says, "I didn't order him, but I did beg." On the other hand, Alice worried too about her children hanging around with too many black kids who said "mens" for "men" or who said "I be fixin' to go home now."

But most importantly, she worried about a more profound influence. Howard was a deeply religious man with a Pentecostal bent to his faith. Alice had realized this near the time of their wedding while they were attending a service at her white-gloved black Baptist church in Philadelphia. Out of the blue, Howard was struck by the power of the Holy Spirit. In the words of the Pentecostals, he "got happy"—and he stood and danced wildly in unconscious, joyful exultation. The ushers came to restrain him. The fiercely proud, urbane and proper Alice was mortified. And back in Delaware at Howard's Prospect AME Church, it was more of the same. To Alice, the congregation's emotionalism was ignorant and hickish. It did not fit with her plans for her children.

The Stevenson kids all did well, went to college and graduate school. But Bryan was always the family's darling. Howard Jr., the oldest, came to resent his father's strict discipline. Christy, the youngest, used to sneak off to listen to rock music. But Bryan—as far as anyone knows—did none of these things. Not to say he was perfect: He picked on his sister sometimes, fought with his brother, bent a few of his father's strict rules. But all in all he was about as good as kids come. A self-taught musician, he played organ and piano at the Prospect AME Church and learned to shift his tempo to the spontaneous outbursts of congregants as they, like his father, "got happy." He showed no interest in being a minister, but he could preach up a storm.

In his overwhelmingly white high school, Bryan was president of the student council. He was a star athlete. He was a straight-A student who would eventually graduate No. 1 in his class. He would be pursued by Ivy League schools but take a soccer scholarship to Eastern College, a small Baptist school in Pennsylvania, where he would lead the gospel choir and a Christian fellowship. In high school, he was a champion public speaker, and he played the lead in "A Raisin in the Sun." After 30 years of teaching drama, Harriet Jeglum still remembers it as the play of which she is the proudest. At Cape Henlopen High, Bryan held an odd status. He was one of only a handful of blacks in the advanced classes, and it was common for black kids in that situation to be teased, even harassed by other black kids—accused of "trying to be white." Bryan's sister, Christy, got some of that grief, but she and her brother and other old acquaintances of Bryan's say he never did.

"He was just so kind and decent," says Kevin Hopkins, a childhood neighbor of Bryan's. "Nobody would ever have thought of saying anything like that about Bryan, black or white."

Bryan's mother tells this story: When the kids were young, she always told them they could make requests for their favorite meals and she'd do what she could to fix them. Christy and Howard made requests, but Bryan never did. "He just ate whatever I cooked and said it was the best food he'd ever eaten," she says, still sounding a bit puzzled. "That's just the way he was about everything. If I was in a bad mood, he was always the first to notice it. He'd say, 'You all right, Mom?' "

Back on the road to Georgia's death row: "I had the happiest childhood," says Bryan, finally loosened up and talking about himself for a change. "I was at church two, three nights a week, all day on Sundays," he says. "At school, I knew everybody—the white kids from class, the black kids from sports. But we lived in the country, and I didn't hang with any clique. My parents cared about me and I wanted to do things to make them care about me more. Years later, at Harvard, so many kids I met felt that if they hadn't gone to Andover and Harvard, their lives would be over." He smiles. "But I always figured that people with even zillions of dollars couldn't be happier than me.

"I had fights with the white kids on the bus. They'd call me 'nigger.' In first grade, I remember holding my hand up and never being called on. In second grade, a teacher's aide made me get off the monkey bars while the white kids were on it. When they did integrate the schools, all the black kids were in 3-C. I was the only black kid in section A until junior high. Year after year, the counselors tried to get me to take vo-tech: 'Everybody needs to know how to make bricks,' they said." Finally, as Bryan talks, it becomes clear that the racism he has experienced, mild by the standards of the generation before him, is still tightly woven into his work against the death penalty.

"The reason I always say I've never met a client whose life isn't worth saving," he says, "is because they are like me—except they didn't get in 3-A. They were in 3-C. A few breaks the other way, and I could be on the other side of the table. You know, as a kid, I spent my summers at my aunt's in Philly. You couldn't get police to come to her neighborhood. You had to call and say a police officer had been shot. My grandfather was murdered, stabbed dozens of times, in his own home. The killers pleaded to a low charge. I had a black friend raped on campus, but the case was never pursued. She was leaving town, had no family there to pressure the prosecutor. That's our justice: We over-prosecute crimes against whites and under-prosecute crimes against blacks, because whites have political power and blacks don't. I saw it in my own life long before I studied the death penalty.

"But when I did, and discovered that a man who murders a white has a 4.3 times greater chance of getting the death penalty in Georgia, I saw it as a symbol of all the race and poverty bias in our society. We're not yet capable of valuing the life of a black mother of four in the projects the same way we value the life of, say, the ex-president of Chevron. We're just not capable.

"Do you know that in Montgomery, Alabama, there's a paper called the Bulletin Board that still runs ads seeking white renters? I spent weeks looking for an apartment. On the phone, a man said, 'You don't sound black, but I ask everyone.' I lost all humility. I told one woman I was a lawyer with a Harvard degree. She said the apartment was $250. I put on a suit, but when she saw me her whole body sagged. She said the rent was $450. It's very demoralizing and debilitating. None of my Harvard degrees, my suits, meant anything next to my little black face.

"All these things are of the same cloth."

At the Georgia Diagnostic and Classification Center, which houses that state's death row, Bryan's client, Roger Collins, is waiting in the visitors' room, a deep narrow place with a wall of screened bars and a long row of empty stools. After four years of handling his case, Bryan has come to think of Roger as a friend. Roger stands to greet him, takes away his sunglasses and puts them on, hams it up. He is a black man and Bryan's age exactly, 31, handsome, with short hair and a close-cut beard. He is on death row for brutally murdering a black woman 13 years ago. Roger was 18. His accomplice was 25. They had separate trials. Roger got death. His accomplice got life. Roger could get an execution date any day.

Bryan tells him about his appeal and about how Congress might pass a law that would help his case. (As it turned out, Congress did not.) "I understood right from wrong," Roger says. "I did, yeah. It just started out one thing and ended up another. I've done some hellful things in my past." When he was 13, Roger says, he and his father and brother would go to Florida from Georgia and rob places every weekend. In ninth grade, he still couldn't read. He thinks, but isn't sure, that his mother and brother are in prison. His father, who eventually went to prison for murder, is out now, and he visited a few weeks ago. "He said they went for the death sentence," Roger says, "and missed."

"It looks real good," Bryan says. "Don't get down."

Roger says, almost to himself, "Ain't set no date."

Outside, on the road again, Bryan says, "I meet people like Roger every day. Their lives are a mess. Half of my clients have had somebody in their families murdered. They are always getting their electric turned off, or their telephone. Or they mention that their daughter has been in jail for six months, and, by the way, what should they do about it? They live at the margins of society, with no sense of control over their lives. We've given up trying to help them. To mention it is to be ridiculed as naive and weak. You know, as a boy George Daniel was hung in a sheet from a tree when he wet the bed, and beaten with a bat." Bryan is quiet for a long time.

Then he says, "I'm afraid they're going to kill Roger."

Something happens to idealistic young people at Harvard Law School. On the first day, Bryan recalls, his entering class was asked how many planned to practice public interest law after graduation, and probably 70 percent of the hands went up. But very few entered the field. Last year, only about 3 percent of Harvard Law's graduates went directly into legal or public service organizations. In Bryan's class, the overwhelming majority of graduates took prestigious clerkships or cut to the chase and took $70,000-plus jobs with big law firms. "Everybody came into law school wanting to help the poor," Bryan says. "But when the big law firms offered $1,500 a week, they all went."

It was a seduction. On that first day, students were told to look around at their 500 classmates. "They tell you that you're sitting with future congressmen, leading partners of important law firms. You are pushed to compete, get to 'the top.' Only nobody ever stops to define 'the top.' There's no value orientation about finding meaning in what you do." Students are encouraged to feel special, he says, as if they are better than everyone else and therefore deserving of wealth, power and privilege. It can be a very appealing pitch, especially to youngsters from the bottom, who yearn to be accepted by the elite and who are willing to pay the price of distancing themselves from their roots. Bryan didn't bite. It sounds hokey, but Bryan seems instead to have cut a swath of goodness through his years at Harvard. In the remarks of his former classmates, there is an unmistakable tone of testimony.

"He is just this incredibly exceptional person," says Jeffrey Nussbaum, a lawyer in San Francisco and a former Harvard Law classmate. "Bryan radiated a sense of goodness and kindness, which sounds so mushy. But he definitely radiated it. He has some kind of inner peace." Nussbaum says Bryan was once harassed by a gang of whites in Cambridge. "He wasn't angry. That was the thing. How can I put it? He felt sorry for the people who had attacked him."

Another Harvard classmate, Jerry Salama, now an assistant to one of New York's deputy mayors, even remembers Bryan once talking about his opposition to the death penalty. "What about the guy who cuts people in 50 pieces?" Salama asked pointedly. First, Bryan mentioned that his grandfather had been savagely murdered. Then he said something Salama has never forgotten: "It's not right to kill them back." Says Salama, "He just couldn't fathom the idea of wanting to 'kill them back.' "

Again and again, old Harvard classmates mention that Bryan, who clearly didn't share the law school's dominant values, never criticized anyone for wanting to get rich and powerful by serving the already rich and powerful. "A lot of us were talkin', talkin' all the time about helping the poor, but very few of us did anything about it," says Kimberle Crenshaw, a former Harvard Law classmate and now a UCLA law professor. "Bryan never talked about it. He just did it. He didn't do it to win other people's approval. He did it for himself. He was one of the few people not tainted by Harvard. He's got something else that gives him energy. I don't know what it is. I don't know anybody like him. I think Bryan is religious. I don't know how religious."

Bryan's old classmates mention repeatedly that they "think" Bryan is religious, but they say he never talked about that either. They knew he went to church, but nobody knew where. In fact, Bryan went to church in a poor black Cambridge neighborhood, where as a volunteer he helped people fight their way through the city's housing and welfare bureaucracies and gave kids free piano lessons.

"Bryan is the kind of person who, even though I don't see much anymore, I will always consider a close friend," says Frederick Smith, a lawyer in New Jersey and a former Harvard Law classmate. "The word for Bryan is seminal. It's hard to be close to him and not be profoundly influenced and deeply changed. I very quickly fell under his wing. Bryan was from a little country town, and I had gone to prep school, Harvard College and spent two years at Oxford, but I had to run to keep up with Bryan, literally." He laughs. "It sounds like I'm talking about someone who is older, but I'm five years older than he is.

"I always assumed that what happened to me would happen to Bryan. 'Well, now's the time to grow up. We have bills to pay.' Everybody else in the class, like lemmings, hopped off the cliff and went to large law firms. But not Bryan. I have another friend from Harvard, and he and I still talk about the phenomenon of Bryan Stevenson. What makes him what he is? We talk about how much we hate what we're doing. Why did we fall so short and Bryan is out there as a beacon? I hate to admit to character flaws, but maybe Bryan is the clearest example of what true character is all about."

Bryan Stevenson doesn't like to hear this kind of talk about himself. It is, he believes, another kind of trap, not unlike the one Harvard lays for its "special" young students. "I know they are trying to be nice," he says, as he drives off to yet another rural Alabama town, this time Monroeville, to talk to the family of his death-row client Walter McMillian. "I hear it when I go to a reunion or I run into an old classmate who's doing something he hates. These people act like I'm a priest, making such sacrifices. I'm not. It's easy for me to do what I do. What people don't understand when they say I could be making all this money is that I *couldn't* be making all this money. I could *not* do it. I could not get up in the morning and go to work. If the death penalty were abolished tomorrow, I wouldn't be a corporate lawyer. I'd probably be a musician. When people say I'm great, what I'm doing is great, they aren't talking about me. They're talking about themselves, about what's missing in their lives."

Bryan has struggled with the idea that he is special, denied it, all his life. "Whites have always treated Bryan like he walked on water," says his brother, Howard Jr., a psychologist and visiting professor at the University of Pennsylvania. "But the label of specialness is impossible to swallow, because to be black and special to whites means you aren't really black, which puts a distance between you and your people, who are to whites very unspecial. To accept the label of special is to absolve people of their responsibility to be good. It's a different kind of control. It's the desire to take what you have and make it their own."

As Bryan cruises toward Monroeville, past cotton and cane and giant pecan trees, past Alabama's Holman Prison and its death row, I recall for the first time the legend of the *lamedvovniks*, the Righteous Men, who forever deny their own virtue. Bryan would understand why ancient legend required good men to deny their goodness: To believe you are good, special, better than the rest, is to be neither good nor special.

Finally, I ask, "How important is your faith?"

"It's very important," Bryan says. He explains that in the 1970s he was involved in the charismatic Christian movement. It was a modern version of the backwoods Pentecostalism—with its emotional and sublime encounters with the Holy Spirit—that Bryan's father had practiced all his life. In the 1960s, the faith burst forth and profoundly changed America's stodgy and ritualized mainline denominations. Yet, traditionally, Pentecostalism was a faith of the dispossessed—the poor and the uprooted, from white Appalachia to black Los Angeles. And Bryan knows this.

"Church is not so important to me today," he says, "but I still glory in the charisma and spontaneity of the black church, still love to play the piano for a person who stands and dances to the Spirit. It is restorative. A grandmother who stands up and says, 'I've lost my son and daughter in the fire, all my belongings, but I'm here with my grandson and we're gonna make it'—it is more restorative than praying with people who are thankful for their wealth. I must return to that well. If there is an afterlife, that's who it's for—those whose lives have been hellish and who've struggled to be better. That's who Christianity is for—the rejected, despised and broken. And those are my clients."

It's dark when Bryan arrives in Monroeville and meets Walter McMillian's sister, niece and nephew in the cold wind outside the IGA food market at Ollie's Corner. He tells them an appeals court has ordered the local court to consider whether the county prosecutor had secret deals with the two main witnesses against McMillian, a 49-year-old black man who was convicted of killing an 18-year-old white woman in cold blood during a robbery. One witness against McMillian was his alleged accomplice, who pleaded guilty to the murder and got a life sentence. In many of Bryan's cases, it's clear that his clients actually did murder someone. But the evidence against McMillian is strictly circumstantial. If Bryan can prove the secret deals, Walter McMillian gets a new trial.

"Is everything else going all right?" Bryan asks.

"Did my daughter call you?" McMillian's sister asks.

"From Mobile, yes. I haven't had a chance to call back."

"They got her son for capital murder."

"Is that right?" Bryan says, masking his shock with studied calmness. "Have her call me. Make sure she tells him not to say anything to the police. Does he have an attorney?"

"No."

"Make sure she calls tonight."

"How late?"

"Anytime, anytime."

Back on the road, Bryan says, "It's probably too late."

As always, Bryan worries first about the man accused, but right now I can't help thinking about the victim, for whom it is already too late. And I ask the question that is unavoidable, the one so many people believe challenges Bryan's entire work: "But what about the victims, the people your men kill? What about their husbands and wives, their kids? Don't these murderers deserve to die?"

Bryan is silent for a long moment. He has, of course, heard the question many times before. "I feel worse for the families than I do my clients. It's the hardest thing." He is silent again. "But I tell them, 'I don't care what you did, how awful it was. I'm here to get you off. I don't believe you should be killed.' "

"It's not right to kill them back?" I ask.

"It's not right to kill them back," he answers.

By now it's late, nearly 11, and on the drive back to Montgomery I close my eyes, very tired. But Bryan is wide awake, ready to go back to the office tonight to work on several briefs and to meet with Amnesty International representatives who are in town visiting his center. The schedule is grueling, and Bryan does sometimes yearn for regular hours, a wife, kids. But he finds working with his clients so absorbing that he doesn't think much about what he's missing. Besides, he figures he's still young, with plenty of time for a family later. After a while, when we are nearly back to Montgomery, I ask, "Your parents have never understood why you do this, have they? They think you could be earning gobs of money."

Bryan laughs. "They've come to understand me recently."

The next week, on a beautiful autumn day, I leave Washington and drive to Milton, Del., where Bryan grew up. I find his home, the little white ranch house on County Route 319, and his father, Howard Sr., a short, trim man with dark gray hair and black plastic glasses. He takes me to the Prospect AME Church on Railroad Avenue, past the road signs riddled with bullet holes, past Vern's Used Furniture.

It's a small, not so sturdy, white clapboard church about the size of some living rooms I've seen. The sanctuary is adorned with bright flowers, a cloth rendering of the Last Supper and a piano and an organ, much like the ones Bryan once played here on two, three nights a week and all day on Sundays. The church, with its vaguely musty aroma, is the very image of the tiny churches that dot rural America, particularly in the South, the very image of the backwoods church that embarrassed Bryan's mother when she first moved to Milton decades ago.

It's a long way form Prospect AME to Harvard Law School, but somehow Bryan made the distance look short and easy. I am marveling at this when I notice that Bryan's father is standing before the little altar, framed by the bright flowers and the cloth rendering of the Last Supper, lost in thought. He shakes his head, looks around at the empty sanctuary and says wistfully, "Bryan used to set me on fire when he prayed out loud." And once again I am reminded of how often Bryan's behavior—in childhood, in law school, still today—evokes inspiration in those around him, even his own father.

Back at the house, I see that Bryan's old room is filled with storage boxes now, but that the walls are still papered with dozens of his awards from childhood: the Golden Scroll for the Promise of Greatness, the Thespian Society Award, awards for music, sports, student council—you name it, the guy won it. His parents' pride is not disguised, and the dark-paneled walls of the house are covered with photographs of Bryan, Howard Jr. and Christy.

"Bryan said you only recently came to understand him," I say. "What did he mean by that?"

Without hesitation, Howard jumps up from the couch and dashes to the television. He roots around in a cabinet full of videotapes and pops one in the VCR. "This was last April," he says. "Bryan spoke to the national youth conference of the AME Church." In a few moments Bryan, all grainy, comes on the screen. And for half an hour, he speaks, starting slowly and then, moved by the power of his own emotions, quickly, like rapids. He says we execute the retarded, the young and the mentally ill. He says we execute men for killing whites far more often than we do for killing blacks. He talks of the defense lawyer who was drunk and of the blacks who are so often struck from murder juries. He talks of the judge who said of a convicted man's parents, "Since the niggers are here, maybe we can go ahead with the sentencing phase."

Then Bryan says, "It's not enough to see and deal with these things from a humanistic perspective. You've got to have a spiritual commitment. So many talk that talk, but they don't walk that walk. We've got to be prepared to pay the cost of what it means to save our souls." Then he quotes the Bible—Matthew 25:34-45: "Then the King will say to those at his right hand, 'Come, O blessed of my Father, inherit the kingdom prepared for you from the foundation of the world, for I was hungry and you gave me food; I was thirsty and you gave me drink; I was a stranger and you welcomed me; I was naked and you clothed me; I was sick and you visited me; I was in prison and you came to me . . . Truly, I say to you, as you did it to one of the least of these my bethren, you did it to me.' "

The place is bedlam. "I wouldn't exchange what I'm doing for anything," Bryan says, voice rising. "I feel the pleasure of God."

Bryan's father gets up quietly, rewinds the tape. Tears are in his eyes. "I didn't understand his faith until this talk," he says. "He never talked about himself, ever."

Sadly, Bryan's mother, Alice, is in the hospital being treated for a life-threatening illness, and his father and I go to visit. Her lean, elegant body and handsome face are the image of her son, as are her slow, deliberate mannerisms, perfect diction and clear, accentless voice. She sits in a robe in a chair next to her bed, illuminated by a single lamp. Seeming tired, she closes her eyes as she speaks. "I told him he was not going to live in the sticks all his life. Please do not be satisfied." She opens her eyes and laughs. "Sometimes I think he listened too well. He is so far away. I miss him so. Did Howard tell you we didn't understand him until April

of this year when we heard him speak? He never talked about himself. Me, I've been a money-grubber all my life. But now that I've been sick, I see that Bryan is right. Really, what are we here for? We're here to help one another. That's it." After a pause, she says, "You know, a college friend of Bryan's once asked me, quite seriously, 'Could Bryan be an angel?' "

Alice and Howard Stevenson talk into the evening, and just as I'm about to leave, Howard says, "The Lord touched him." And Alice tells this story: When Bryan was 13, in a hot little Pentecostal church in Camden, Del., where she's taken the Prospect youth choir to sing, "Bryan went off in the Spirit. He got happy. He danced." I ask what that means, and Alice and Howard chuckle at my naivete. "It is to be in a realm of complete and absolute joy," Alice says, although that day she did not feel joy. "I cried because I never wanted that to happen to Bryan. I didn't want him to be a backwoods cultist Christian. He broke out in a sweat, completely physically immersed, and Spirit took him over. I held him, hugged him and cried." Because for all the years Alice—proud, urbane Alice from her white-gloved Philadelphia Baptist church—had gone to Prospect AME, she'd never been a true Pentecostal believer.

"But this was my child, my darling, my flesh. I knew there was no falseness in him. So I knew this was a real gift from God. I stopped turning my nose up at it as something only ignorant people did." And looking out the window one morning soon afterward, watching the rising sun, Alice was suddenly overwhelmed with the presence of God. Simply put, Bryan had saved his mother.

"That feeling," she says, "can't be put into words."

Perhaps not, but I remember that James Baldwin seems to have come very close in the final pages of *Go Tell It on the Mountain.* And rereading his words at my home late that night, I try to imagine Bryan as Baldwin's character John, try to imagine how transforming must have been Bryan's experience—whether spiritual or psychological.

Baldwin wrote: "And something moved in John's body which was not John. He was invaded, set at naught, possessed. This power had struck John, in the head or in the heart . . . The center of the whole earth shifted, making of space a sheer void and a mockery of order, and balance, and time. Nothing remained: all was swallowed up in chaos . . . His Aunt Florence came and took him in her arms . . .

" 'You fight the good fight,' she said, 'you hear? Don't you get weary, and don't you get scared. Because I *know* the Lord's done laid His hands on you.'

" 'Yes,' he said, weeping, 'yes. I'm going to serve the Lord.' "

I put down the book, and I think again of the 36 Right-eous Men: The ancient legend, I now realize, isn't the answer to what it means to be truly good; it is only one more way of asking the question. With or without reli-gion, maybe that's all good people can ever really do: live their lives as a question posed to others. I think of a priest I once knew. He told me that Christians would have no need to evangelize if only they lived their lives as mirrors of goodness in which others could glimpse the goodness of Christ—and thus the goodness in themselves. And I think of Bryan: His deepest mission, I now see, is not to save the lives of convicted men, but to live in such a way that his own life is a question posed to others.

"I want to be a witness for hope and decency and commitment," Bryan had said, before I understood what he meant. "I want to show in myself the qualities I want to see in others." Bryan's own motive is to "feel the pleasures of God." Yet whether graced with the power of God, the power of a strong, decent family or the power of some buried psychological zeal, Bryan's life is like the priest's mirror: Looking into him, people see their failings and possibilities. Like the *lamedvov-niks*, Bryan must deny this power—not because he will disappear in a flash of God's will, but because if others can call him "special," they can excuse their failings and avoid struggling to find the goodness in them-selves.

Finally, I think of Frederick Smith, Bryan's friend from Harvard Law, the man who said he was for-ever changed by meeting Bryan: "If religion created Bryan Stevenson," he had said, "we all need a lot more religion."

Pray it were only that easy.

Is the Death Penalty Fair?

The death penalty in the United States today is, as the lawyers say, "settled law"—meaning the major consti-tutional challenges to its imposition have been recently considered and rejected by the U.S. Supreme Court. But the debate over whether the death penalty is im-posed fairly and impartially enough to suit not the le-gal but the moral conscience of America still rages.

That dispute centers on two main issues: First, does racial discrimination play a significant role in de-termining who is sentenced to die? And, second, is the quality of legal defense for indigent people facing the death penalty good enough to ensure that poor people are not unfairly treated?

The modern history of the death penalty begins in 1972, when a Supreme Court decision effectively de-clared all existing capital punishment laws unconstitu-tional for violating the Constitution's Eighth Amend-ment clause against "cruel and unusual punishment." The decision was based on the court's conclusion that death-sentencing procedures were arbitrary and poten-tially discriminatory. State legislatures—led by those in the South, where the death sentence was imposed most often—then wrote new statutes to meet the Supreme Court's objections.

In 1976, the Supreme Court ruled in favor of statutes that attempted to limit the death sentence to the most heinous murders. Today, 36 states (includ-ing Maryland and Virginia) have such death penalty statutes. The new laws also added to capital murder trials a "penalty" phase during which the prosecu-tion can present evidence supporting imposition of the death penalty and a guilty defendant's attorney can present evidence of mitigating factors, such as the de-fendant's poverty or possible mental illness or whether the defendant was abused as a child.

In more recent years, the Supreme Court has ruled that a capital murder defendant's legal defense is ade-quate if it is proven that defense counsel's decisions were reasonable at the time they were made and if the guilty verdict is supported by the weight of evidence presented at trial. The court also has ruled that statis-tical evidence of broad racial disparities in the impo-sition of the death penalty is not necessarily grounds for proving racial discrimination in any *given* case. To overturn a verdict on grounds of racial discrimination, the court ruled, defendants must prove discrimination in their particular cases.

Even the staunchest critics of the death penalty ac-knowledge that it is imposed far more equitably today than it was before 1972. But numerous statistical stud-ies by criminologists have established that capital defendants who kill whites are still far more likely to receive the death penalty than defendants who kill blacks. The critical distinction is the race of the victim, period," says University of Iowa law professor David C. Baldus, co-author of the recent book *Equal Justice and the Death Penalty.* "All of the white-victim crimes are treated more harshly than those with black vic-tims," adds Baldus, whose massive statistical studies of death sentencing are considered the most authoritative by criminologists. Baldus found that in Georgia, a cap-ital defendant—white or black—who killed a white person had on average a 4.3 times greater chance of re-ceiving the death penalty than a defendant who killed a black person under similar circumstances.

"The discrimination is against anybody who kills a white," says University of Michigan law professor

Samuel R. Gross, co-author of *Death & Discrimination*. His reviews of capital crime cases in Arkansas, Florida, Illinois, Mississippi, North Carolina, Oklahoma and Virginia have found race-of-victim sentencing disparities similar to those Baldus found in Georgia. "In every case the race of the victim makes a large difference in who gets sentenced to death and who doesn't."

The Bush administration Justice Department has disputed the findings of racial disparity in sentencing, pointing to a U.S. District Court review of Baldus's Georgia study that concludes that the study was seriously flawed and its conclusions invalid. (Numerous criminologists do not share the District Court's opinion. "The quality of the judge's report is laughable," says University of New Hampshire criminologist Michael Radelet. "He absolutely did not know what he was talking about. And that's not just my opinion, but the opinion of every criminologist I know.")

Justice officials also have argued that even if the studies that report a race-of-victim disparity are correct, the best way to redress such an imbalance isn't to end capital punishment but to more aggressively prosecute homicides committed against blacks.

In 1989 testimony before the Senate Judiciary Committee, Baldus argued that the race-of-victim disparities found in numerous academic studies flow mostly from the decisions of local prosecutors who decide in which cases they will seek the death penalty. Baldus called the disparities "the effect of political, personal and economic considerations" by prosecutors. In this view, the murder of whites more often results in public outrage, because whites can better identify with white victims, especially if they are middle-class victims. The political power of whites in most communities leads elected prosecutors—consciously or unconsciously—to respond. Murderers of blacks, as the Baldus and other studies suggest, are given less attention.

Anti-death-penalty activists such as Bryan Stevenson in Alabama and Stephen B. Bright at the Southern Prisoners' Defense Committee in Atlanta have compiled examples of alleged local judicial and prosecutorial bias in instances of black-on-white crime, many of which come from rural counties in the South. In one case in Swainsboro, Ga., the SPDC charged, the local prosecutor struck 10 of 10 blacks from the jury pool through use of his peremptory challenges, giving reasons such as "he appears to have the intelligence of a fence post" and "he looked a little slow." The SPDC also charged that the judge in the case was racially biased because he admitted having used racial epithets and because he belonged to an all-white country club.

Recent Supreme Court decisions limiting death penalty appeals on constitutional grounds have led to more aggressive legal strategies at the local level. The best capital murder defense is often the "scorched earth" defense, says Albert M. Pearson, a University of Georgia law professor and formerly the chief counsel to a committee headed by former Supreme Court justice Lewis Powell that studied the federal court review process for convicted death-penalty defendants. Stevenson and Bright use that approach, going into little towns and filing motion after motion, investigating the racial attitudes and behaviors of prosecutor and judge alike, charging violations of the Voting Rights Act if judges are elected in districtwide elections that dilute black voting strength. They mobilize black church leaders, hold rallies and fill the courtroom with black spectators. In Swainsboro Amnesty International representatives even came to town and held a press conference at which Swainsboro was compared to South Africa.

"We are trying to make a poor black man accused of murder be just like the mayor's nephew, somebody with clout," says Stevenson. But such scorched earth tactics aren't popular with local lawyers appointed by a court to defend indigent clients.

"One of the most difficult things for a lawyer in a rural locale to do is go in and defend the hell out of a case," says Pearson. "The community is against you, and you have to live there and go before that judge again. My experience is that they don't usually do a constitutionally improper job, but they don't use the motion process to impose costs on the prosecutor that would cause him to be cautious in asking for the death penalty. There is a consensus nationally that the quality of representation in capital cases has got to be improved. The question is to what level. Does everyone have the right to have a Bryan Stevenson defend them?"

Some believe the situation is urgent. In a devastating exposé of how indigent capital murder clients are actually defended in the South, the National Law Journal last year concluded: "The surprising cause of this failure in fairness lies not in the riveting legal and moral questions that usually animate the death penalty debate but in the way the death penalty really works in the small-town courthouse." The Journal's six-month investigation by a team of three reporters found that trial lawyers representing death-row inmates in the six states they studied had been disbarred, suspended or disciplined at rates ranging from 3 to 46 times the overall rates for those states. More than half of the dozens of capital defense lawyers interviewed said they were handling their first capital murder case when their client was convicted. Capital murder trials in those states often took one or two days—compared with two weeks to two months in states with sophisticated indigent defense systems. And the all-important penalty stage to set punishment took as little as 15 minutes to three hours, often with little or no defense lawyer effort to present mitigating evidence. Finally, the Journal found it was still common for blacks to be tried by all-white juries.

"There is a policy question of what's fair play," Pearson says of the present quality of defense counsel afforded indigent capital murder defendants. "There is no question that perfection is not now required."

ALBERT MURRAY

Storiella Americana as She is Swyung; or, The Blues as Representative Anecdote

It is a coincidence both appropriate and profoundly symbolic that the quintessential American composer was born, grew to young manhood, came to his vocation, and began his apprenticeship in the capital city of the nation. Such achievement as his is hardly predictable, to be sure. But in this instance it is easy enough to account for, because it is so consistent with uniquely local environmental factors that conditioned the outlook, direction, and scope of his ambition and development.

As little as has been made of it, there is in point of historical fact, much to suggest that circumstances in Washington during the first two decades of the century made it just the place to dispose a bright-eyed and ambitious young brownskin musician to become the composer who has indeed achieved the most comprehensive and sophisticated as well as the most widely infectious synthesis of the nation's richly diverse musical resources, both indigenous and imported.

Duke Ellington (*né* Edward Kennedy Ellington, a.k.a. Ellington and Duke), whose collected works represent far and away the most definitive musical stylization of life in the United States, was born in the house of his maternal grandparents on Twentieth Street on the twenty-ninth of April 1899, and shortly thereafter was taken by his parents, James Edward and Daisy

Albert Murray, "Storiella Americana as She is Swyung; or, The Blues as Representative Anecdote" from THE BLUE DEVILS OF NADA by Albert Murray. Copyright © 1996 by Albert Murray. Reprinted by permission of Pantheon Books, a division of Random House, Inc.

Kennedy Ellington, to their own residence in Wards Place off New Hampshire Avenue, about midway between Dupont Circle on Massachusetts Avenue and Washington Circle on Pennsylvania Avenue.

This was less than ten blocks from the White House of William McKinley, who was assassinated when Ellington was two years old. From then, until Ellington was ten it was the White House of Theodore Roosevelt, who was followed by four status quo ante years of William Howard Taft. From the time Ellington was fourteen until he was twenty-two, it was not only the White House but also very much the sharply segregated Washington of Woodrow Wilson.

The Washington of McKinley is said to have provided much more government employment for black citizens than any previous administration. But even so, post-Reconstruction disfranchisement continued apace, for McKinley's commitment was not to the implementation of the Thirteenth, Fourteenth, and Fifteenth Amendments, but to conciliation of the erstwhile Confederate states. Moreover, his capital city was also the seat of an American expansionism that was all too consistent with the underlying assumptions of the folklore of white supremacy and fakelore of black pathology.

Then there was the Washington of Theodore Roosevelt, whose admiration for the down-home Horatio Algerism of Booker T. Washington, the founder of Tuskegee and author of the best-selling autobiography *Up from Slavery*, was widely publicized, as was his defense of his appointment of William D. Crum as collector of the Port of Charleston. In point of fact Roosevelt's attitude toward black American aspirations was not only inconsistent and undependable, it was at times indistinguishable from that of those who were frankly opposed to anything except a subservient status for Negroes. The obvious immediate effect of his wrong-headed and high-handed overreaction in meting out dishonorable discharges to black soldiers allegedly involved in the so-called Brownsville Raid of 1906, was to embolden whites who advocated terrorism as a means of keeping black people from full citizenship, something against which Roosevelt spoke neither loudly nor softly and against which he seems to have carried no stick of any size.

During the administration of Taft, Washington was the city of a president who in his inaugural address announced that he would not appoint Negroes to any position where they were not wanted by white people. On one of his better days Roosevelt had once written that he would not close the door of hope to any American citizen. But to aspiring black Americans and white reactionaries alike Taft's statement seemed like official capitulation to the forces of white supremacy, not all of them in the South.

During Ellington's adolescence and young manhood his hometown was the Washington of the downright evil forces of Woodrow Wilson, whose campaign promises to black voters were forgotten as soon as he was inaugurated. Once in office, it was as if he had never expressed his "warmest wish to see justice done to the colored people in every matter, and not mere grudging justice, but justice executed with liberality and cordial good feeling. . . . I want to assure them that should I become president of the United States they may count on me for absolute fair dealing, for everything by which I could assist in advancing the interest of their race in the United States."

But whereas his predecessors had been, on balance, perhaps more indifferent to black aspirations than intolerant of gradual improvement, Wilson's two administrations turned out to be downright hostile. In less than three months he signed an executive order segregating dining and toilet facilities in federal service buildings whose black employees were already being rapidly reduced in number and significance. And this was only the beginning. During the next eight years every effort was made to turn the nation's capital into a typical peckerwood town with a climate of white supremacy. "I have recently spent several days in Washington," Booker Washington wrote to Oswald Garrison Villard in a letter (10 August 1913) that he knew was going to be passed on to Wilson, "and I have never seen the colored people so discouraged and bitter as they were at that time."

As inevitable as a direct effect of all this was on his daily life, Ellington did not grow up thinking of himself as downtrodden. On the contrary, as far back as he could remember he was treated as though he were a special child, and he never seems to have doubted his mother when she told him as she did time and again that he didn't have anything to worry about because he was blessed.

His father, who was a butler, then a caterer, and then a blueprint technician at the navy yard, was not only a good provider, but a man who saw to it that his family lived in good houses, in good neighborhoods (no slum dweller, he), and Ellington said that he "kept our house loaded with the best food obtainable and because he was a caterer we had the primest steaks and the finest terrapin." Ellington added, "He spent money and lived like a man who had money and he raised his family as though he were a millionaire. The best had to be carefully examined to make sure it was good enough for my mother."

No, James Ellington's outlook was neither negative nor provincial. Nor was young Edward's. Indeed, such were his horizons of aspiration even as a child that when at the age of about eight a slightly older playmate nicknamed him Duke, he accepted it as if it were his natural due, and so did his family and everybody else in Washington who knew him, and in time so did the world at large, including the royal family of England and the ever so proletarian bureaucrats and workers of the Soviet Union.

(Apropos of the personal vanity that this readiness to define himself in aristocratic terms may suggest to some pseudoegalitarians, let it be said that Ellington was always more charming than vain and not at all arrogant. The fact of the matter is that you would be hard put to find anybody who was ever more discerning and appreciative of other people's assets and as eager to develop and showcase them. His ability to utilize and feature specific nuances was one of the trademarks of his genius as a composer. And no other bandleader ever put up with so many exasperating personal faults in his sidemen just to have them on hand to supply shadings that perhaps most of his audiences would never have missed. What other bandleader always had so many *homegrown* superstars on hand at the same time?)

But to continue the chronology. What Ellington himself always emphasized when recounting the advantages of his coming of age in Washington was that he was born and raised among people to whom quality mattered and who required your personal best no less as a general principle than as a natural reaction to the folklore of white supremacy. In neither case would they accept excuses for failure. You either had what it took or you didn't, as somebody from less promising circumstances than yours would prove only too soon.

Not that Ellington would ever deny or ameliorate any of the atrocities perpetuated by the Wilson crowd between 1913 and 1921. He took them for granted much the same as the fairy tale princes and dukes of derring-do take the existence of the dragon (grand or not) for granted. Also like the fairy tale hero that he was by way of becoming, he seems to have been far too preoccupied with getting help to forge his magic sword (or magic means) to spend much time complaining about the injustice of the existence of the dragon. *Dispatching the dragon, after all, as devastating as dragons are, has always been only incidental to gaining the ultimate boon to which the dragon denies you access.*

According to Ellington himself, the hometown he grew up in was an exciting and challenging place of apprenticeship, in which there were many people of his kind to admire, learn from, and measure up to. As early on as the eighth grade there was Miss Boston. "She taught us that proper speech and good manners were our first obligations because as representatives of the Negro race we were to command respect for our people. This being an all-colored school, Negro

History was crammed into the curriculum so that we would know our people all the way back."

The mainstem hangout for the young man about town was Frank Holliday's poolroom next to the Howard Theatre on T Street between Sixth and Seventh. "Guys from all walks of life seemed to converge there: schoolkids over and under sixteen; college students and graduates, some starting out in law and medicine and science; and lots of Pullman porters and dining car waiters. These last had much to say about the places they'd been. The names of the cities would be very impressive. You would hear them say, 'I just left Chicago, or last night I was in Cleveland.'" You could do a lot of listening in the poolroom, where the talk "always sounded as if the prime authorities on every subject had been assembled there. Baseball, football, basketball, boxing, wrestling, racing, medicine, law, politics, everything was discussed with authority."

Then when he really began to focus his ambitions on the piano and music, there was a whole galaxy of virtuosi and theorists not only at Holliday's but all over town, and they were always willing to repeat and explain things. Among them were Lester Dishman with his great left hand, Clarence Bowser, a top ear man; Phil Wird from the Howard Theater; Louis Thomas, Sticky Mack, Blind Johnny, Gertie Wells, Carolynne Thornton, and the Man with a Thousand Fingers.

But most especially there was Louis Brown, who played chromatic thirds faster than most of the greats could play chromatic singles, and his left hand could reach an eleventh in any key. There was also Doc Perry, to whose house the young apprentice used to go as often as possible and "sit in a glow of enchantment until he'd pause and explain some passage. He never charged me a dime and he served food and drink during the whole thing."

There was also Henry Grant, a conservatory-trained teacher who directed the Dunbar High School Orchestra. He volunteered to give the promising young Ellington (a student at Armstrong High School, not Dunbar) private lessons in harmony, and was much impressed with his talent for melody and unusual harmonic nuances *and also with his indefatigable devotion to the mastery of fundamentals*. Hence the incomparable precision that was characteristic of all Ellington bands over the years!

As no true storyteller whether of fiction or the most precisely documented fact should ever forget—such as the indispensable function of the dynamics of antagonistic cooperation (or antithesis and synthesis, or competition or contention) in perhaps all achievement—there is neither irony nor mystery in the fact that Washington during the vicious years of Wilson and his

diehard Confederates was also the base of operations for Kelly Miller, dean of the College of Arts and Sciences at Howard (1907–19) and author of numerous essays on race relations, advocate of courses on the American Negro and on Africa, militant spokesman and pamphleteer, most notably of *As to the Leopard's Spots: An Open Letter to Thomas Dixon* (1905) and the widely distributed *The Disgrace of Democracy: An Open Letter to President Woodrow Wilson*.

It was likewise the Washington of Carter G. Woodson, with his B.A. and M.A. from Chicago and his Ph.D. from Harvard and his background of work and study in the Philippines, Asia, North Africa, and Europe, who taught French, Spanish, English, and history at the M Street School and at Dunbar and was later principal of Armstrong High School, and who was also cofounder of the Association for the Study of Negro Life and History from its beginning until his death in 1950.

And along with Miller and Woodson there was also Alain Locke from Philadelphia by way of Harvard and the Oxford of Rhodes scholars, who as a professor of arts and philosophy was especially concerned with making Howard a culture center for the development of black intellectuals and artists.

The national fallout of all of this (add to it *the work* of W. E. B. Du Bois) was such that by 1925 Locke could edit an anthology of poems, stories, plays, and essays by black contributors and call it *The New Negro* and introduce it by saying, "In the last decade something beyond the watch and guard of statistics has happened in the life of the American Negro, and the three *norms* that have traditionally presided over the Negro problem have a changeling in their laps. The sociologist, the philanthropist, the Race-leader are not unaware of the New Negro, but they are at a loss to account for him. . . ."

It was during this ten-year period, which included World War I, that Ellington came of age and left Washington for New York.

But a word about usage. The emphasis that Miller, Woodson, and Locke place on race consciousness and even race pride should not be confused with the shrill, chauvinistic, pseudoseparatism of the so-called Garvey Movement. As Arthur Schomburg, who knew very well how easy it was for such matters to degenerative into "puerile controversy and petty braggadocio," was to write in "The Negro Digs Up His Past" for Locke's anthology, race studies "legitimately compatible with scientific method and aim were being undertaken not only to correct certain omissions and not merely that we may not wrongfully be deprived on the spiritual nourishment of our cultural past, *but also that the full story of human collaboration and interdependence may be told and realized.*" And Locke himself wrote, "If after absorbing the new content of American life and experience, and after assimilating new patterns of art, the original (Afro-American) artistic endowment can be sufficiently augmented to express itself with equal power in more complex pattern and substance, then the Negro may well become what some have predicted, *the artist of American life.*" If not Ellington and Armstrong in music, who else?

Ellington's all-American outlook was a direct result not of Howard University but of the Howard Theatre and Frank Holliday's poolroom cosmopolitans, but the fallout from Professors Miller and Locke and from Woodson was there all the same. After all, his impact was not only citywide but also, like that of Du Bois, nationwide.

In all events, when the group of ambitious young musicians with whom Ellington went to New York in 1923 proudly advertised themselves as the Washingtonians they were not presenting themselves as a provincial novelty but rather as a band of sophisticated young men who were ready to get on with it, because they had grown up in the capital city checking out the best in the nation at the Howard Theatre, which, it should be remembered, was on the same T.O.B.A. circuit as the Lincoln and the Lafayette in Harlem. (There was no Savoy yet, no Cotton Club, no Apollo.) New York was a bigger league, to be sure, but the Washingtonians seem to have had no doubts that they were ready to make the most of the breaks. And they were right. In less than four years Ellington composed and recorded *East Saint Louis Toodle-oo, Birmingham Breakdown, Washington Wobble, Harlem River Quiver, New Orleans Low-Down, Chicago Stomp Down* (note the regional diversity), and also *Black and Tan Fantasie* and *Creole Love Call.*

Nor was he to encounter any musical authority in cosmopolitan New York that was more crucial to his development as a composer than that of Will Marion Cook, another Washingtonian. Cook, who was born in 1869, had been sent out to Oberlin to study violin at the age of thirteen and on to Berlin (with the encouragement and aid of the venerable Frederick Douglass) to be a pupil of Joseph Joachim, the greatest music master of the day, and had also studied composition in New York under Dvořák, who had been brought over from Bohemia in 1893 to head up an American conservatory and to encourage Americans to create a national music based on indigenous sources.

Cook, who had given up the violin to concentrate on composition and conducting, had become passionately committed to exploring and developing the possibilities of the Afro-American vernacular and had written the score for Paul Lawrence Dunbar's *Clorindy, or the Origin of the Cakewalk* in 1898, such musical comedies as *Bandanna Land, In Abyssinia,* and *In Dahomey* for the famous vaudeville team of Williams and Walker. He had also organized, directed, and toured with various jazz bands, most notably the Southern Syncopated Orchestra of some forty-one pieces, which he took to Europe in 1919. When he returned to New York, he became a pioneer arranger and conductor of radio music, leading a hundred-piece Clef Club Orchestra in some of the earliest live broadcasts.

Not only was Ellington, who had named his son Mercer after Cook's son Will Mercer, very much impressed and personally influenced by all of this, but he was especially taken by the fact that Cook, with all of his formal training and all his strictness about technical precision, also insisted, as James Weldon Johnson wrote, that the Negro in music and on the stage ought to be a Negro, a genuine Negro; he declared that the Negro should eschew "white" patterns, and not employ his efforts in doing what the white artist could always do as well, generally better. According to Ellington, Cook's advice was "first you find the logical way, and when you find it, avoid it, and let your inner self break through and guide you. Don't try to be anybody else but yourself."

Not the least of what Cook's advice may have done for young Ellington was to free him to compose in terms of what he liked about such stride or eastern ragtime masters as James P. Johnson, Willie "the Lion" Smith, and Lucky Roberts, such New Orleans pacesetters as Louis Armstrong, Sidney Bechet, King Oliver, and Jelly Roll Morton, and such special in-house talents as Charlie Irvis and Bubber Miley among others, including Johnny Hodges, Harry Carney, Jimmy Blanton, Ben Webster, and Ray Nance, who became stars even as they became Ellington "dimensions."

What Ellington went on beyond Will Marion Cook and everybody else to achieve was a steady flow of incomparable twentieth-century American music that is mostly the result of the extension, elaboration, and refinement of the traditional twelve-bar blues chorus and the standard thirty-two-bar pop song form. *And in doing so he has also fulfilled the ancestral aesthetic imperative to process folk melodies, and the music of popular entertainment as well as that of church ceremonies into a truly indigenous fine art of not only nationwide but universal significance, by using devices of stylization that are as vernacular as the idiomatic particulars of the subject matter itself.* It is not a matter of working folk and pop materials into established or classic European forms but of extending, elaborating, and refining (which is to say ragging, jazzing, and riffing and even jamming) the idiomatic into fine art. *Skyscrapers, not*

Gothic cathedrals. And as historians need not be reminded, barbarians eventually produce their own principles of stylization and standards of criticism.

Moreover, what Ellington's fully conjugated blues statement adds up to is a definitive American Storiella as she is *swyung*, which is to say, a musical equivalent to what Kenneth Burke calls the representative anecdote, the effect of which is to summarize a basic attitude toward experience; or a given outlook on life.

For many U.S. citizens, the representative anecdote would be any tale, tall or otherwise, or indeed any narrative tidbit or joke or even folk or popular saying or cliché that has to do with a self-made and free-spirited individual, or any variation on the Horatio Alger rags to riches, steerage to boardroom, log cabin to White House motif. Among the so-called Founding Fathers, Benjamin Franklin's career qualifies him as a veritable prototype of the picaresque Alger hero and two other classic examples are the *Narrative of the Life of Frederick Douglass, an American Slave, written by Himself*; and Booker T. Washington's *Up from Slavery*.

Everybody knows that even now there are people all over the world dreaming of the United States in the ever-so-materialistic image and patterns of Horatio Alger. Others, however, see definitive American characteristics in terms that are no less pragmatic but are more comprehensively existential. In their view, the anecdotes most fundamentally representative are those that symbolize (1) affirmation in the face of adversity, and (2) improvisation in situations of disruption and discontinuity.

To this end, nobody other than Ellington as yet has made more deliberate or effective use of basic devices of blues idiom statement, beginning with the very beat of the ongoing, upbeat locomotive onomatopoeia (the chugging and driving pistons, the sometimes signifying, sometimes shouting steam whistles, the always somewhat ambivalent arrival and departure bells) that may be as downright programmatic as in the old guitar and harmonica folk blues but that also function as the dead metaphoric basis of the denotative language of common everyday discourse. The obviously programmatic but always playfully syncopated pistons, bells, and whistles of "Daybreak Express," "Happy Go Lucky Local," and "The Old Circus Train Turn Around Blues" become as dead metaphors in "Harlem Airshaft" and "Mainstream." Incidentally, Ellington's use of locomotive onomatopoeia is resonant not only of metaphorical underground railroad but also the metaphysical gospel train.

As for the idiomatic devices that are basic to the structure of most Ellington compositions, there are the blues (mostly of twelve bars) and/or the popular song choruses (mostly of thirty-two bars), a series or sequence of which add up to a vernacular sonata form known as *the instrumental*, which is also made up of such special features as the *vamp* or improvised introduction or lead-in, the *riff* or repetition phrase, and the *break* or temporary interruption of the established cadence and which usually requires a *fill*.

An excellent instance of the break as both structural device and statement is "C-Jam Blues," which is also a perfect example of how Ellington used the jam session, which consists of an informal sequence of improvised choruses as the overall frame for a precisely controlled but still flexible instrumental composition. In an elementary sense it is as playful as a children's ring game or dance, and yet it is also a basic way of ordering a discourse, not unlike, say, that jam session of a social contract known as the Constitution with its neat piano vamp of a preamble followed by a sequence of articles and amendments. The point here, of course, is not one of direct derivation but of cultural consistency and perhaps a case could be made for occupational psychosis.

Nor is the break just another mechanical structural device. It is of its very nature, as dancers never forget, what the basic message comes down to: *grace under pressure, creativity in an emergency, continuity in the face of disjuncture.* It is on the break that you are required to improvise, to do your thing, to establish your identity, to write your signature on the epidermis of actuality which is to say entropy. The break is the musical equivalent to the storybook hero's moment of truth. It is jeopardy as challenge and opportunity, and what it requires is the elegant insouciance that Hemingway admired in bullfighters. Representative anecdote indeed. Talking about the American frontier Storiella as she is riffed!

As for any question of extended forms, so dear to the reactionary hearts of so many old-line academics, the number of choruses in a jazz composition is determined by the occasion, as is the number of floors in a given skyscraper, depends on the anticipated use and/or the budget! Once there was the three-minute phonograph record, then came the radio sound bite for voice-over, and suitelike sequence of bites that make a movie sound-track, and now there is the hour-plus L.P. Ellington took them all in stride.

The quintessential composer should be so called because he is the one who provides that fifth essence, beyond earth, air, water, and fire, that substance of the heavenly bodies that is latent in all things, that spirit, nay that soul which is the magic means that somehow makes life in a given time and place meaningful and thus purposeful.

Indeed, the fifth essence may well be nothing less than the ultimate boon that the storybook quest is usually, if not always, about. If so, then the golden fleece of the composer's quest is the musical equivalent to the representative or definitive anecdote. *The assumption here is that art is indispensable to human existence.*

Duke Ellington is the quintessential American composer because it is his body of work more than any other that adds up to the most specific, comprehensive, universally appealing musical complement to what Constance Rourke, author of *American Humor: A Study of the National Character,* had in mind when she referred to "emblems for a pioneer people who require resilience as a prime trait." Nor can it be said too often that at its best an Ellington performance sounds as if it knows the truth about all the other music in the world and is looking for something better. Not even the Constitution represents a more intrinsically American statement and achievement than that.

---

bell hooks

Revolutionary Black Women: Making Ourselves Subject

Sitting in a circle with several black women and one black man, children running in and out, on a hot Saturday evening at the office of the Council on Battered Women, after working all day, my spirits are renewed sharing with this group aspects of my development as a feminist thinker and writer. I listen intently as a sister comrade talks about her responses to my work. Initially she was disturbed by it. "I didn't want to hear it," she says. "I resented it." The talk in the group is about black women and violence, not just the violence inflicted by black men, but the violence black women do to children, and the violence we do to one another. Particularly challenged by the essay in *Talking Back,* "Violence in Intimate Relationships: A Feminist Perspective," because of its focus on a continuum of dominating violence that begins not with male violence against women but with the violence parents do to children, individual black women in the group felt they had to interrogate their parental practice.

There is little feminist work focusing on violence against children from a black perspective. Sharing our stories, we talked about the ways styles of parenting in diverse black communities support and perpetuate the

Reprinted from BLACK LOOKS by bell hooks with permission from the publisher, South End Press, 116 Saint Botolph Street, Boston, MA 02115.

use of violence as a means of domestic social control. We connected common acceptance of violence against children with community acceptance of male violence against women. Indeed, I suggested many of us were raised in families where we completely accepted the notion that violence was an appropriate response to crisis. In such settings it was not rare for black women to be verbally abusive and physically violent with one another. Our most vivid memories (in the group) of black women fighting one another took place in public settings where folks struggled over men or over gossip. There was no one in the group who had not witnessed an incident of black women doing violence to one another.

I shared with the group the declaration from Nikki Giovanni's "Woman Poem": "I ain't shit. You must be lower than that to care." This quote speaks directly to the rage and hostility oppressed/exploited people can turn inward on themselves and outward towards those who care about them. This has often been the case in black female encounters with one another. A vast majority of black women in this society receive sustained care only from other black women. That care does not always mediate or alter rage, or the desire to inflict pain; it may provoke it. Hostile responses to care echo the truth of Giovanni's words. When I first puzzled over them, I could hear voices in the background questioning, "How can you be worth anything if you care about me, who is worth nothing?" Among black women, such deeply internalized pain and self-rejection informs the aggression inflicted on the mirror image—other black women. It is this reality Audre Lorde courageously describes in her essay "Eye to Eye: Black Women, Hatred, and Anger." Critically interrogating, Lorde asks:

> . . . why does that anger unleash itself most tellingly against another Black woman at the least excuse? Why do I judge her in a more critical light than any other, becoming enraged when she does not measure up? And if behind the object of my attack should lie the face of my own self, unaccepted, then what could possibly quench a fire fueled by such reciprocating passions?

I was reminded of Lorde's essay while seated among black women, listening to them talk about the intensity of their initial "anger" at my work. Retrospectively, that anger was vividly evoked so that I would know that individual black women present had grappled with it, moved beyond it, and come to a place of political awareness that allowed us to openly acknowledge it as part of their process of coming to consciousness and go on to critically affirm one another. They wanted me to understand the process of transformation, the movement of their passions from rage to care and recognition. It is this empowering process that enables us to meet face to face, to greet one another with solidarity, sisterhood, and love. In this space we talk about our different experiences of black womanhood, informed by class, geographical location, religious backgrounds, etc. We do not assume that all black women are violent or have internalized rage and hostility.

In contrast, Lorde writes in "Eye to Eye":

> We do not love ourselves, therefore we cannot love each other. Because we see in each other's face our own face, the face we never stopped wanting. Because we survived and survival breeds desire for more self. A face we never stopped wanting at the same time as we try to obliterate it. Why don't we meet each other's eyes? Do we expect betrayal in each other's gaze, or recognition.

Lorde's essay chronicles an understanding of ways "wounded" black women, who are not in recovery, interact with one another, helping us to see the way in which sexism and racism as systems of domination can shape and determine how we regard one another. Deeply moved by her portrait of the way internalized racism and sexism informs the formation of black female social identity, the way it can and often does affect us, I was simultaneously disturbed by the presumption, expressed by her continual use of a collective "we," that she was speaking to an experience all black women share. The experience her essay suggests black women share is one of passively receiving and absorbing messages of self-hate, then directing rage and hostility most intensely at one another. While I wholeheartedly agree with Lorde that many black women feel and act as she describes, I am interested in the reality of those black women, however few, who even if they have been the targets of black female rage do not direct hostility or rage toward other black women.

Throughout "Eye to Eye," Lorde constructs a monolithic paradigm of black female experience that does not engage our differences. Even as her essay urges black women to openly examine the harshness and cruelty that may be present in black female interaction so that we can regard one another differently, an expression of that regard would be recognition, without hatred or envy, that not all black women share the experience she describes. To some extent Lorde's essay acts to shut down, close off, erase, and deny those black female experiences that do not fit the norm she constructs from the location of her experience. Never in Lorde's essay does she address the issue of whether or not black women from different cultural backgrounds (Caribbean, Latina, etc.) construct di-

verse identities. Do we all feel the same about black womanhood? What about regional differences? What about those black women who have had the good fortune to be raised in a politicized context where their identities were constructed by resistance and not passive acceptance? By evoking this negative experience of black womanhood as "commonly" shared, Lorde presents it in a way that suggests it represents "authentic" black female reality. To not share the critique she posits is to be made an "outsider" yet again. In Donna Haraway's essay "A Manifesto for Cyborgs," she warns feminist thinkers against assuming positions that "appear to be the telos of the whole," so that we do not "produce epistemologies to police deviation from official women's experience." Though Haraway is speaking about mainstream feminist practice, her warning is applicable to marginalized groups who are in the process of making and remaking critical texts that name our politics and experience.

Years ago I attended a small gathering of black women who were meeting to plan a national conference on black feminism. As we sat in a circle talking about our experiences, those individuals who were most listened to all told stories of how brutally they had been treated by "the" black community. Speaking against the construction of a monolithic experience, I talked about the way my experience of black community differed, sharing that I had been raised in a segregated rural black community that was very supportive. Our segregated church and schools were places where we were affirmed. I was continually told that I was "special" in those settings, that I would be "somebody" someday and do important work to "uplift" the race. I felt loved and cared about in the segregated black community of my growing up. It gave me the grounding in a positive experience of "blackness" that sustained me when I left that community to enter racially integrated settings, where racism informed most social interactions. Before I could finish speaking, I was interrupted by one of the "famous" black women present, who chastised me for trying to erase another black woman's pain by bringing up a different experience. Her voice was hostile and angry. She began by saying she was "sick of people like me." I felt both silenced and misunderstood. It seemed that the cathartic expression of collective pain wiped out any chance that my insistence on the diversity of black experience would be heard.

My story was reduced to a competing narrative, one that was seen as trying to divert attention from the "true" telling of black female experience. In this gathering, black female identity was made synonymous again and again with "victimization." The black female voice that was deemed "authentic" was the voice in pain; only the sound of hurting could be heard. No narrative of resistance was voiced and respected in this setting. I came away wondering why it was these black women could only feel bonded to each other if our narratives echoed, only if we were telling the same story of shared pain and victimization. Why was it impossible to speak an identity emerging from a different location?

A particular brand of black feminist "essentialism" had been constructed in that place. It would not allow for difference. Any individual present who was seen as having inappropriate thoughts or lingering traces of politically incorrect ideas was the target for unmediated hostility. Not surprisingly, those who had the most to say about victimization were also the ones who judged others harshly, who silenced others. Individual black women who were not a part of that inner circle learned that if they did not know the "right" thing to say, it was best to be silent. To speak against the grain was to risk punishment. One's speech might be interrupted or one might be subjected to humiliating verbal abuse.

At the close of this gathering, many black women gave testimony about how this had been a wonderful experience of sisterhood and black woman-bonding. There was no space for those individuals whose spirits had been assaulted and attacked to name their experience. Ironically, they were leaving this gathering with a sense of estrangement, carrying with them remembered pain. Some of them felt that this was the first time in their lives that they had been so cruelly treated by other black women. The oldest black woman present, an academic intellectual who had often been the target for verbal assault, who often wept in her room at night, vowed never again to attend such a gathering. The memory of her pain has lingered in my mind. I have not forgotten this collective black female "rage" in the face of difference, the anger directed at individual black women who dared to speak as though we were more than our pain, more than the collective pain black females have historically experienced.

Sitting at the offices of the Council on Battered Women was different. After many years of feminist movement, it seems to me that black women can now come together in ways that allow for difference. At the Council, women could speak openly and honestly about their experience, describe their negative and positive responses to my work without fear of rebuke. They could name their rage, annoyance, frustration, and simultaneously critique it. In a similar setting where black women had talked openly about the way my work "enraged" them, I had asked a sister if she would talk about the roots of her hostility. She responded by telling me that I was "daring to be different, to have a different response to the shit black

women were faced with everyday." She said, "It's like you were saying, this is what the real deal is and this is what we can do about it. When most of us have just been going along with the program and telling ourselves that's all we could do. You were saying that it don't have to be that way." The rage she articulated was in response to the demand that black women acknowledge the impact of sexism on our lives and engage in feminist movement. That was a demand for transformation. At the offices of the Council, I was among black comrades who were engaged in a process of transformation. Collectively, we were working to problematize our notions of black female subjectivity. None of us assumed a fixed essential identity. It was so evident that we did not all share a common understanding of being black and female, even though some of our experiences were similar. We did share the understanding that it is difficult for black women to construct radical subjectivity within white supremacist capitalist patriarchy, that our struggle to be "subject," though similar, also differs from that of black men, and that the politics of gender create that difference.

Much creative writing by contemporary black women authors highlights gender politics, specifically black male sexism, poverty, black female labor, and the struggle for creativity. Celebrating the "power" of black women's writing in her essay "Women Warriors: Black Women Writers Load the Canon" in the *Voice Literary Supplement*, dated May 1990, Michelle Cliff asserts:

> There is continuity in the written work of many African-American women, whether writer is their primary identity or not. You can draw a line from the slave narrative of Linda Brent to Elizabeth Keckley's life to *Their Eyes Were Watching God* to *Coming of Age in Mississippi* to *Sula* to *The Salteaters* to *Praisesong for the Widow*. All of these define a response to power. All structure that response as a quest, a journey to complete, to realize the self; all involve the attempt to break out of expectations imposed on black and female identity. All work against the odds to claim the *I*.

Passionate declarations like this one, though seductive, lump all black female writing together in a manner that suggests there is indeed a totalizing *telos* that determines black female subjectivity. This narrative constructs a homogenous black female subject whose subjectivity is most radically defined by those experiences she shares with other black women. In this declaration, as in the entire essay, Cliff glorifies black women writers even though she warns against the kind of glorification (particularly that accorded a writer that is expressed by sustained academic literary critique of their work) that has the potential to repress and contain.

Cliff's piece also contains. Defining black women's collective work as a critical project that problematizes the quest for "identity," she subsumes that quest solely by focusing on rites of passages wherein black women journey to find themselves. She does not talk about whether that journeying is fruitful. By focusing attention primarily on the journey, she offers paradigms for reading and understanding black women writers that invite readers (critics included) to stop there, to romanticize the journey without questioning the location of that journey's end. Sadly, in much of the fiction by contemporary black women writers, the struggle by black female characters for subjectivity, though forged in radical resistance to the *status quo* (opposition to racist oppression, less frequently to class and gender) usually takes the form of black women breaking free from boundaries imposed by others, only to practice their newfound "freedom" by setting limits and boundaries for themselves. Hence though black women may make themselves "subject" they do not become radical subjects. Often they simply conform to existing norms, even ones they once resisted.

Despite all the "radical" shifts in thought, location, class position, etc., that Celie undergoes in Alice Walker's novel *The Color Purple*, from her movement from object to subject to her success as a capitalist entrepreneur, Celie is reinscribed within the context of family and domestic relations by the novel's end. The primary change is that those relations are no longer abusive. Celie has not become a "feminist," a civil rights activist, or a political being in any way. Breaking free from the patriarchal prison that is her "home" when the novel begins, she creates her own household, yet radical politics of collective struggle against racism or sexism do not inform her struggle for self-actualization.

Earlier writing by black women, Linda Brent's slave narrative for example, records resistance struggles where black women confront and overcome incredible barriers in the quest to be self-defining. Often after those barriers have been passed, the heroines settle down into conventional gender roles. No tale of woman's struggle to be self-defining is as powerful as the Brent narrative. She is ever conscious of the way in which being female makes slavery "far more grievous." Her narrative creates powerful groundwork for the construction of radical black female subjectivity. She engages in a process of critical thinking that enables her to rebel against the notion that her body can be sold and insists on placing the sanctity of black ontological being outside modes of exchange. Yet this radical, visionary "take" on subjectivity does not inform who she becomes once she makes her way to freedom. After breaking the bonds of slavery, Harriet Jacobs takes on the pseudonym Linda Brent when she writes about the past and falls into the clutches of con-

ventional notions of womanhood. Does the radical invented self "Linda Brent" have no place in the life of Harriet Jacobs? Freed, descriptions of her life indicate no use of the incredible oppositional imagination that has been a major resource enabling her to transgress boundaries, to take risks, and dare to survive. Does Jacobs' suppression of the radical self chart the journey that black women will follow, both in real life and in their fictions?

More than any other novel by a contemporary black woman writer, Toni Morrison's *Sula* chronicles the attempt by a black female to constitute radical black female subjectivity. Sula challenges every restriction imposed upon her, transgressing all boundaries. Defying conventional notions of passive female sexuality, she asserts herself as desiring subject. Rebelling against enforced domesticity, she chooses to roam the world, to remain childless and unmarried. Refusing standard sexist notions of the exchange of female bodies, she engages in the exchange of male bodies as part of a defiant effort to displace their importance. Asserting the primacy of female friendship, she attempts to break with patriarchal male identification and loses the friendship of her "conservative" buddy Nel, who has indeed capitulated to convention.

Even though readers of *Sula* witness her self-assertion and celebration of autonomy, which Sula revels in even as she is dying, we also know that she is not self-actualized enough to stay alive. Her awareness of what it means to be a radical subject does not cross the boundaries of public and private; hers is a privatized self-discovery. Sula's death at an early age does not leave the reader with a sense of her "power," instead she seems powerless to assert agency in a world that has no interest in radical black female subjectivity, one that seeks to repress, contain, and annihilate it. Sula is annihilated. The reader never knows what force is killing her, eating her from the inside out. Since her journey has been about the struggle to invent herself, the narrative implies that it is the longing for "selfhood" that leads to destruction. Those black women who survive, who live to tell the tale, so to speak, and the "good girls," the ones who have been self-sacrificing, hardworking black women. Sula's fate suggests that charting the journey of radical black female subjectivity is too dangerous, too risky. And while Sula is glad to have broken the rules, she is not a triumphant figure. Sula, like so many other black female characters in contemporary fiction, has no conscious politics, never links her struggle to be self-defining with the collective plight of black women. Yet this novel was written at the peak of contemporary feminist movement. Given the "power" of Sula's black female author/creator, Toni Morrison, why does she appear on the page as an "artist without an art form"?

Is it too much like "treason"—like disloyalty to black womanhood—to question this portrait of (dare I say it) "victimization," to refuse to be seduced by Sula's exploits or ignore their outcome?

There are black female characters in contemporary fictions who are engaged in political work. Velma, the radical activist in Toni Cade Bambara's *The Salteaters,* has grounded her struggle for meaning within activist work for black liberation. Overwhelmed by responsibility, by the sense of having to bear too much, too great a weight, she attempts suicide. This novel begins with older radical black women problematizing the question of black female subjectivity. Confronting Velma's attempt at self-destruction and self-erasure, they want to know, "are you sure, sweetheart, that you want to be well?" Wellness here is synonymous with radical subjectivity. Indeed, the elders will go on to emphasize that Velma's plight, and that of other black women like her, reflects the loss of "maps" that will chart the journey for black females. They suggest that it is the younger generation's attempt to assimilate, to follow alien maps, that leads to the loss of perspective. Velma only came back to life (for though she fails to kill herself, she is spiritually dead) when she testifies to herself that she indeed will choose wellness, will claim herself and nurture that radical subjectivity. Like Paule Marshall's *Praisesong for the Widow* and Gloria Naylor's *Mama Day,* the "radical" black women elders with fresh memories of slavery holocaust, of the anguish of reconstruction, who sustain their courage in resistance, live fruitfully outside conventional gender roles. They either do not conform or they acknowledge the way conformity rarely enables black female self-actualization.

Representing a new generation of "modern" black women, Velma, even as she is in the process of recovery, critiques her desire to make a self against the grain, and questions "what good did wild do you, since there was always some low-life gruesome gang-bang raping lawless careless petty last straw nasty thing ready to pounce—put your shit under total arrest and crack your back?" Wild is the metaphoric expression of that inner will to rebel, to move against the grain, to be out of one's place. It is the expression of radical black female subjectivity. Law professor Regina Austin calls black women to cultivate this "wildness" as a survival strategy in her piece "Sapphire Bound." Significantly, she begins the essay by calling attention to the fact that folks seem to be more eager to read about wild black women in fictions than to make way for us in real life. Reclaiming that wildness, she declares:

> Well, I think the time has come for us to get truly hysterical, to take on the role of "professional Sapphires" in a forthright way, to declare that we are serious about ourselves, and to capture some of the intellectual power and resources that are necessary to combat the systematic denigration of minority women. It is time for Sapphire to testify on her own behalf, *in writing,* complete with footnotes.

If the writers of black women's fiction are not able to express the wilder, more radical dimensions of themselves, in sustained and fruitful ways, it is unlikely that they will create characters who "act up" and flourish. They may doubt that there is an audience for fictions where black women are not first portrayed as victims. Though fictions portray black women being wild in resistance, confronting barriers that impede self-actualization, rarely is the new "self" defined. Though Bambara includes passages that let the reader know Velma lives, there are no clues that indicate how her radical subjectivity will emerge in the context of "wildness."

Consistently, contemporary black women writers link the struggle to become subject with a concern with emotional and spiritual well-being. Most often the narcissistic-based individual pursuit of self and identity subsumes the possibility of sustained commitment to radical politics. This tension is played out again and again in Alice Walker's *The Third Life of Grange Copeland.* While the heroine, Ruth, is schooled by her grandfather to think critically, to develop radical political consciousness, in the end he fights against whites alone. It is not clear what path Ruth will take in the future. Will she be a militant warrior for the revolution or be kept in her place by "strong" black male lovers/patriarchs who, like her grandfather, will be convinced that they can best determine what conditions are conducive to producing black female well-being? Ironically, *Meridian* takes up where Ruth's story ends, yet the older black woman activist, like Ruth, remains confined and contained by a self-imposed domesticity. Is Meridian in hiding because there is no place where her radical black subjectivity can be expressed without punishment? Is the non-patriarchal home the only safe place?

Contemporary fiction by black women focusing on the construction of self and identity breaks new ground in that it clearly names the ways structures of domination, racism, sexism, and class exploitation, oppress and make it practically impossible for black women to survive if they do not engage in meaningful resistance on some level. Defiantly naming the condition of oppression and personal strategies of opposition, such writing enables the individual black woman reader who has not yet done so to question, and/or critically affirms the efforts of those readers who are already involved in resistance. Yet these writings often fail to depict any location for the construction of new identities. It is this textual gap that leads critic Sondra

O'Neale to ask in her essay "Inhibiting Midwives, Usurping Creators: The Struggling Emergence of Black Women in American Fiction":

> For instance, where are the Angela Davises, Ida B. Wellses, and Daisy Bateses of black feminist literature? Where are the portraits of those women who fostered their own action to liberate themselves, other black women, and black men as well? We see a sketch of such a character in *Meridian*, but she is never developed to a social and political success.

In an earlier essay, "The Politics of Radical Black Subjectivity," I emphasized that opposition and resistance cannot be made synonymous with self-actualization on an individual or collective level: "Opposition is not enough. In that vacant space after one has resisted there is still the necessity to become—to make oneself anew." While contemporary writing by black women has brought into sharp focus the idea that black females must "invent" selves, the question—what kind of self?—usually remains unanswered. The vision of selfhood that does emerge now and then is one that is in complete concordance with conventional western notions of a "unitary" self. Again it's worth restating Donna Haraway's challenge to feminist thinkers to resist making "one's own political tendencies to be the telos of the whole" so we can accept different accounts of female experience and also face ourselves as complex subjects who embody multiple locations. In "A Manifesto for Cyborgs," she urges us to remember that, "The issue is dispersion. The task is to survive in diaspora."

Certainly, collective black female experience has been about the struggle to survive in diaspora. It is the intensity of that struggle, the fear of failure (as we face daily the reality that many black people do not and are not surviving) that has led many black women thinkers, especially within feminist movement, to wrongly assume that strength in unity can only exist if difference is suppressed and shared experience is highlighted. Though feminist writing by black women is usually critical of the racism that has shaped and defined the parameters of much contemporary feminist movement, it usually reiterates, in an uncritical manner, major tenets of dominant feminist thought. Admonishing black women for wasting time critiquing white female racism, Sheila Radford-Hill, in "Considering Feminism as a Model for Social Change," urges black feminists:

> . . . to build an agenda that meets the needs of black women by helping black women to mobilize around issues that they perceive to have a direct impact on the overall quality of their lives. Such is the challenge that defined our struggle and constitutes our legacy . . . Thus, black women need to develop their own leadership and their own agenda based on the needs of their primary constituent base; that is, based around black women, their families, and their communities. This task cannot be furthered by dialoging with white women about their inherent racism.

While I strongly agree with Radford-Hill's insistence that black critical thinkers engaged in feminist movement develop strategies that directly address the concerns of our diverse black communities, she constructs an either/or proposition that obscures the diversity of our experiences and locations. For those black women who live and work in predominantly white settings (and of course the reality is that most black women work jobs where their supervisors are white women and men), it is an appropriate and necessary political project for them to work at critical interrogations and interventions that address white racism. Such efforts do not preclude simultaneous work in black communities. Evocations of an "essentialist" notion of black identity seek to deny the extent to which all black folk must engage with whites as well as exclude individuals from "blackness" whose perspectives, values, or lifestyles may differ from a totalizing notion of black experience that sees only those folk who live in segregated communities or have little contact with whites as "authentically" black.

Radford-Hill's essay is most insightful when she addresses "the crisis of black womanhood," stating that "the extent to which black feminists can articulate and solve the crisis of black womanhood is the extent to which black women will undergo a feminist transformation." The crisis Radford-Hill describes is a crisis of identity and subjectivity. When the major struggle black women addressed was opposition to racism and the goal of that struggle was equality in the existing social structures, when most black folks were poor and lived in racially segregated neighborhoods, gender roles for black women were more clearly defined. We had a place in the "struggle" as well as a place in the social institutions of our communities. It was easier for black women to chart the journey of selfhood. With few job options in the segregated labor force, most black women knew that they would be engaged in service work or become teachers. Today's black woman has more options even though most of the barriers that would keep her from exercising those options are still in place. Racial integration, economic changes in black class relations, the impact of consumer capitalism, as well as a male-centered contemporary black liberation struggle (which devalued the contributions of black females) and a feminist movement which called into question idealized notions of womanhood have radically altered black female reality. For many black women, especially the underclass, the dream of racial equality was intimately linked with the fantasy that once the struggle was over, black women would be able to assume conventional sexist gender roles. To some extent there is a crisis in black womanhood because most black women have not responded to these changes by radically reinventing themselves, by developing new maps to chart future journeys. And more crucially, most black women have not responded to this crisis by developing critical consciousness, by becoming engaged in radical movements for social change.

When we examine the lives of individual black women who did indeed respond to contemporary changes, we see just how difficult it is for black women to construct radical subjectivity. Two powerful autobiographies of radical black women were published in the early 1970s. In 1970, Shirley Chisholm published *Unbought and Unbossed,* chronicling the events that led to her becoming the first black congresswoman. In 1974, *Angela Davis: An Autobiography* was published. Both accounts demonstrate that the construction of radical black female subjectivity is rooted in a willingness to go against the grain. Though many folks may not see Chisholm as "radical," she was one of the first black female leaders to speak against sexism, stressing in the introduction to her book: "Of my two 'handicaps,' being female put many more obstacles in my path than being black." An outspoken advocate of reproductive and abortion rights for women, Chisholm responded to black males who were not opposed to compulsory pregnancy for black women by arguing: "Which is more like genocide, I have asked some of my black brothers—this, the way things are, or the conditions I am fighting for in which the full range of family planning service is fully available to women of all classes and colors; starting with effective contraception and extending to safe, legal termination of undesired pregnancies, at a price they can afford?"

Militant in her response to racism, Chisholm also stressed the need for education for critical consciousness to help eradicate internalized racism:

> It is necessary for our generation to repudiate Carver and all the lesser-known black leaders who cooperated with the white design to keep their people down. We need none of their kind today. Someday, when, God willing, the struggle is over and its bitterness has faded, those men and woman may be rediscovered and given their just due for working as best they could see to do in their time and place, for their brothers and sisters. But at present their influence is pernicious, and where they still control education in the North or the South, they must be

replaced with educators who are ready to demand full equality for the oppressed races and fight for it at any cost.

As a radical black female subject who would not allow herself to be the puppet of any group, Chisholm was often harassed, mocked, and ridiculed by colleagues. Psychological terrorism was often the weapon used to try and coerce her into silence, to convince her she knew nothing about politics, or worse yet that she was "crazy." Often her colleagues described her as mad if she took positions they could not understand or would not have taken. Radical black female subjects are constantly labeled crazy by those who hope to undermine our personal power and our ability to influence others. Fear of being seen as insane may be a major factor keeping black women from expressing their most radical selves. Just recently, when I spoke against the omnipresent racism and sexism at a conference, calling it terroristic, the organizers told folks I was "crazy." While this hurt and angered, it would have wounded me more had I not understood the ways this appellation is used by those in power to keep the powerless in their place. Remembering Chisholm's experience, I knew that I was not alone in confronting racist, sexist attacks that are meant to silence. Knowing that Chisholm claimed her right to subjectivity without apology inspires me to maintain courage.

Recently rereading the autobiography of Angela Davis, I was awed by her courage. I could appreciate the obstacles she confronted and her capacity to endure and persevere in a new way. Reading this work in my teens, her courage seemed like "no big deal." At the beginning of the work, Davis eschews any attempt to see herself as exceptional. Framing the narrative in this way, it is easy for readers to ignore the specificity of her experience. In fact, very few black females at the time had gone to radical high schools where they learned about socialism or traveled to Europe and studied at the Sorbonne. Yet Davis insists that her situation is like that of all black people. This gesture of solidarity, though important, at times obscures the reality that Davis' radical understanding of politics was learned as was her critical consciousness. Had she voiced her solidarity with underclass black people, while simultaneously stressing the importance of learning, of broadening one's perspective, she would have shared with black females tools that enable one to be a radical subject.

Like Chisholm, Davis confronted sexism when she fully committed herself to working for political change:

> I became acquainted very early with the widespread presence of an unfortunate syndrome among some Black male activists—namely to confuse their

political activity with an assertion of their maleness. They saw—and some continue to see—Black manhood as something separate from Black womanhood. These men view Black women as a threat to their attainment of manhood—especially those Black women who take initiative and work to become leaders in their own right.

Working the radical black liberation movement, Davis constantly confronted and challenged sexism even as she critiqued the pervasive racism in mainstream feminist movement. Reading her autobiography, it is clear that reading and studying played a tremendous role in shaping her radical political consciousness. Yet Davis understood that one needed to go beyond books and work collectively with comrades for social change. She critiqued self-focused work to emphasize the value of working in solidarity:

> Floating from activity to activity was no revolutionary anything. Individual activity—sporadic and disconnected—is not revolutionary work. Serious revolutionary work consists of persistent and methodical efforts through a collective of other revolutionaries to organize the masses for action. Since I had long considered myself a Marxist, the alternatives open to me were very limited.

Despite limited options, Davis' decision to advocate communism was an uncommon and radical choice.

When the Davis autobiography was written, she was thirty years old; her most militant expression of subjectivity erupted in her twenties. Made into a cultural icon, a gesture that was not in line with her insistence on the importance of collectivity and fellowship, she came to be represented in mass media as an "exceptional" black woman. Her experience was not seen as a model young black women could learn from. Many parents pointed to the prison sentence she served as reason enough for black women not to follow in her footsteps. Black males who wanted the movement to be male-centered were not trying to encourage other black women to be on the Left, to fully commit themselves to a revolutionary black liberation struggle. At public appearances, Angela Davis was not and is not flanked by other black women on the Left. Constantly projected as an "isolated" figure, her presence, her continued commitment to critical thinking and critical pedagogy, has not had the galvanizing impact on black females that it could have. Black women "worship" Davis from a distance, see her as exceptional. Though young black women adore Davis, they do not often read her work nor seek to follow her example. Yet learning about those black women who have dared to assert radical subjectivity, is a necessary part of black female self-actualization. Coming to power, to selfhood, to radical subjectivity cannot happen in isolation. Black women need to study the writings, both critical and autobiographical, of those women who have developed their potential and chosen to be radical subjects.

Critical pedagogy, the sharing of information and knowledge by black women with black women, is crucial for the development of radical black female subjectivity (not because black women can only learn from one another, but because the circumstances of racism, sexism, and class exploitation ensure that other groups will not necessarily seek to further our self-determination). This process requires of us a greater honesty about how we live. Black females (especially students) who are searching for answers about the social formation of identity want to know how radical black women think but they also want to know about our habits of being. Willingness to share openly one's personal experience ensures that one will not be made into a deified icon. When black females learn about my life, they also learn about the mistakes I make, the contradictions. They come to know my limitations as well as my strengths. They cannot dehumanize me by placing me on a pedestal. Sharing the contradictions of our lives, we help each other learn how to grapple with contradictions as part of the process of becoming a critical thinker, a radical subject.

The lives of Ella Baker, Fannie Lou Hamer, Septima Clark, Lucy Parson, Ruby Doris Smith Robinson, Angela Davis, Bernice Reagon, Alice Walker, Audre Lorde, and countless others bear witness to the difficulty of developing radical black female subjectivity even as they attest to the joy and triumph of living with a decolonized mind and participating in ongoing resistance struggle. The narratives of black women who have militantly engaged in radical struggles for change offer insights. They let us know the conditions that enable the construction of radical black female subjectivity as well as the obstacles that impede its development. In most cases, radical black female subjects have willingly challenged the *status quo* and gone against the grain. Despite the popularity of Angela Davis as a cultural icon, most black women are "punished" and "suffer" when they make choices that go against the prevailing social sense of what a black woman should be and do. Most radical black female subjects are not caught up in consumer capitalism. Living simply is often the price one pays for choosing to be different. It was no accident that Zora Neale Hurston died poor. Radical black female subjects have had to educate ourselves for critical consciousness, reading, studying, engaging in critical pedagogy, transgressing boundaries to acquire the knowledge we need. Those rare radical black women who have started organizations and groups are attempting to build a collective base that will support and enable their work. Many of these black women create sites of resistance that are far removed from conservatizing institutions in order to sustain their radical commitments. Those of us who remain in institutions that do not support our efforts to be radical subjects are daily assaulted. We persevere because we believe our presence is needed, is important.

Developing a feminist consciousness is a crucial part of the process by which one asserts radical black female subjectivity. Whether she has called herself a feminist or not, there is no radical black woman subject who has not been forced to confront and challenge sexism. If, however, that individual struggle is not connected to a larger feminist movement, then every black woman finds herself reinventing strategies to cope when we should be leaving a legacy of feminist resistance that can nourish, sustain, and guide other black women and men. Those black women who valiantly advocate feminism often bear the brunt of severe critique from other black folks. As radical subject, the young Michele Wallace wrote one of the first book length, polemical works on feminism that focused on black folks. She did not become a cultural icon; to a great extent she was made a pariah. Writing about her experience in "The Politics of Location: Cinema/Theory/Literature/Ethnicity/Sexuality/Me," she remembers the pain:

> I still ponder the book I wrote, *Black Macho and The Myth of the Superwoman*, and the disturbance it caused: how black women are not allowed to establish their own intellectual terrain, to make their own mistakes, to invent their own birthplace in writing. I still ponder my book's rightness and wrongness, and how its reception almost destroyed me so that I vowed never to write political and/or theoretical statements about feminism again.

Wallace suffered in isolation, with no group of radical black women rallying to her defense, or creating a context where critique would not lead to trashing.

Without a context of critical affirmation, radical black female subjectivity cannot sustain itself. Often black women turn away from the radicalism of their younger days as they age because the isolation, the sense of estrangement from community, becomes too difficult to bear. Critical affirmation is a concept that embraces both the need to affirm one another and to have a space for critique. Significantly, that critique is not rooted in negative desire to compete, to wound, to trash. Though I began this piece with critical statements about Audre Lorde's essay, I affirm the value of her work. The "Eye to Eye" essay remains one of the most insightful discussions of black female interaction. Throughout the essay, Lorde emphasizes the importance of affirmation, encouraging black women to be gentle and affectionate with one another. Tenderness should not simply be a form of care extended to those black women who think as we do. Many of us have been in situations where black females are sweet to the folks in their clique and completely hostile to anyone deemed an outsider.

In "Eye to Eye," Lorde names this problem. Offering strategies black women might use to promote greater regard and respect, she says that "black women must love ourselves." Loving ourselves begins with understanding the forces that have produced whatever hostility toward blackness and femaleness that is felt, but it also means learning new ways to think about ourselves. Often the black women who speak the most about love and sisterhood are deeply attached to essentialist notions of black female identity that promote a "policing" of anyone who does not conform. Ironically, of course, the only way black women can construct radical subjectivity is by resisting set norms and challenging the politics of domination based on race, class, and sex. Essentialist perspectives on black womanhood often perpetuate the false assumption that black females, simply by living in white supremacist/capitalist/patriarchy, are radicalized. They do not encourage black women to develop their critical thinking. Individual black women on the Left often find their desire to read or write "theory," to be engaged in critical dialogues with diverse groups, mocked and ridiculed. Often, I am criticized for studying feminist theory, especially writing by white women. And I am seen as especially "naive" when I suggest that even though a white woman theorist may be "racist," she may also have valuable information that I can learn from. Until black women fully recognize that we must collectively examine and study our experience from a feminist standpoint, there will always be lags and gaps in the structure of our epistemologies. Where are our feminist books on mothering, on sexuality, on feminist film criticism? Where are our autobiographies that do not falsely represent our reality in the interest of promoting monolithic notions of black female experience or celebrating how wonderfully we have managed to overcome oppression?

Though autobiography or any type of confessional narrative is often devalued in North American letters, this genre has always had a privileged place in African American literary history. As a literature of resistance, confessional narratives by black folks were didactic. More than any other genre of writing, the production of honest confessional narratives by black women who are struggling to be self-actualized and to become radical subjects are needed as guides, as texts that affirm our fellowship with one another. (I need not feel isolated if I know that there are other comrades with similar experiences. I learn from their strategies of resistance and from their recording of mistakes.) Even as the number of novels published by black women increases, this writing cannot be either a substitute for theory or for autobiographical narrative. Radical black women need to tell our stories; we cannot document our experience enough. Works like *Lemon Swamp, Balm in Gilead, Ready From Within,* and *Every Goodbye Ain't Gone,* though very different, and certainly not all narratives of radical black female subjectivity, enable readers to understand the complexity and diversity of black female experience.

There are few contemporary autobiographies by black women on the Left. We need to hear more from courageous black women who have gone against the grain to assert nonconformist politics and habits of being, folks like Toni Cade Bambara, Gloria Joseph, Faye Harrison, June Jordan, and so many others. These voices can give testimony and share the process of transformation black women undergo to emerge as radical subjects. Black females need to know who our revolutionary comrades are. Speaking about her commitment to revolution, Angela Davis notes:

> For me revolution was never an interim "thing-to-do" before settling down: it was no fashionable club with newly minted jargon, or a new kind of social life—made thrilling by risk and confrontation, made glamorous by costume. Revolution is a serious thing, the most serious thing about a revolutionary's life. When one commits oneself to the struggle, it must be for a lifetime.

The crisis of black womanhood can only be addressed by the development of resistance struggles that emphasize the importance of decolonizing our minds, developing critical consciousness. Feminist politics can be an integral part of a renewed black liberation struggle. Black women, particularly those of us who have chosen radical subjectivity, can move toward revolutionary social change that will address the diversity of our experiences and our needs. Collectively bringing our knowledge, resources, skills, and wisdom to one another, we make the site where radical black female subjectivity can be nurtured and sustained.

HOWELL RAINES

Grady's Gift

Grady showed up one day at our house at 1409 Fifth Avenue West in Birmingham, and by and by she changed the way I saw the world. I was 7 when she came to iron and clean and cook for $18 a week, and she stayed for seven years. During that time everyone in our family came to accept what my father called "those great long talks" that occupied Grady and me through many a sleepy Alabama afternoon. What happened between us can be expressed in many ways, but its essence was captured by Graham Greene when he wrote that in every childhood there is a moment when a door opens and lets the future in. So this is a story about one person who opened a door and another who walked through it.

It is difficult to describe—or even to keep alive in our memories—worlds that cease to exist. Usually we think of vanished worlds as having to do with far-off places or with ways of life, like that of the Western frontier, that are remote from us in time. But I grew up in a place that disappeared, and it was here in this country and not so long ago. I speak of Birmingham, where once there flourished the most complete form of racial segregation to exist on the American continent in this century.

Gradystein Williams Hutchinson (or Grady, as she was called in my family and hers) and I are two people who grew up in the 50's in that vanished world, two people who lived mundane, inconsequential lives while Martin Luther King Jr. and Police Commissioner T. Eugene (Bull) Connor prepared for their epic struggle. For years, Grady and I lived in my memory as child and adult. But now I realize that we were both children—one white and very young, one black and adolescent; one privileged, one poor. The connection between these two children and their city was this: Grady saw to it that although I was to live in Birmingham for the first 28 years of my life, Birmingham would not live in me.

Only by keeping in mind the place that Birmingham was can you understand the life we had, the people we became and the reunion that occurred one day not too long ago at my sister's big house in the verdant Birmingham suburb of Mountain Brook. Grady, now a 57-year-old hospital cook in Atlanta, had driven out with me in the car I had rented. As we pulled up, my parents, a retired couple living in Florida, arrived in their gray Cadillac. My father, a large, vigorous man of 84, parked his car and, without a word, walked straight to Grady and took her in his arms.

"I never thought I'd ever see y'all again," Grady said a little while later. "I just think this is the true will of God. It's His divine wish that we saw each other."

This was the first time in 34 years that we had all been together. As the years slipped by, it had become more and more important to me to find Grady, because I am a strong believer in thanking our teachers and mentors while they are still alive to hear our thanks. She had been "our maid," but she taught me the most valuable lesson a writer can learn, which is to try to see—honestly and down to its very center—the world in which we live. Grady was long gone before I realized what a brave and generous person she was, or how much I owed her.

Then last spring, my sister ran into a relative of Grady's and got her telephone number. I went to see Grady in Atlanta, and several months later we gathered in Birmingham to remember our shared past and to learn anew how love abides and how it can bloom not only in the fertile places, but in the stony ones as well.

I know that outsiders tend to think segregation existed in a uniform way throughout the Solid South. But it didn't. Segregation was rigid in some places, relaxed in others; leavened with humanity in some places, enforced with unremitting brutality in others. And segregation found its most violent and regimented expression in Birmingham—segregation maintained through the nighttime maraudings of white thugs, segregation sanctioned by absentee landlords from the United States Steel Corporation, segregation enforced by a pervasively corrupt police department.

Martin Luther King once said Birmingham was to the rest of the South what Johannesburg was to the rest of Africa. He believed that if segregation could be broken there, in a city that harbored an American version of apartheid, it could be broken everywhere. That is why the great civil rights demonstrations of 1963 took place in Birmingham. And that is why, just as King envisioned, once its jugular was cut in Kelly Ingram Park in Birmingham in 1963, the dragon of legalized segregation collapsed and died everywhere—died, it seems in retrospect, almost on the instant. It was the end of "Bad Birmingham," where the indigenous racism of rural Alabama had taken a new and more virulent form when transplanted into a raw industrial setting.

In the heyday of Birmingham, one vast belt of steel mills stretched for 10 miles, from the satellite town of Bessemer to the coal-mining suburb of Pratt City. Black and white men—men like Grady's father and mine—came from all over the South to do the work of these mills or to dig the coal and iron ore to feed them. By the time Grady Williams was born in 1933, the huge light of their labor washed the evening sky with an undying red glow. The division of tasks within these plants ran along simple lines: white men made the steel; black men washed the coal.

Henry Williams was a tiny man from Oklahoma—part African, part Cherokee, only 5 feet 3 inches, but handsome. He worked at the No. 2 Coal Washer at Pratt Mines, and he understood his world imperfectly. When the white foreman died, Henry thought he would move up. But the dead man's nephew was brought in, and in the natural order of things, Henry was required to teach his new boss all there was to know about washing coal.

"Oh, come on, Henry," his wife, Elizabeth, said when he complained about being passed over for a novice. But he would not be consoled.

One Saturday, Henry Williams sent Grady on an errand. "Go up the hill," he said, "and tell Mr. Humphrey Davis I said send me three bullets for my .38 pistol because I got to kill a dog."

In his bedroom later that same afternoon, he shot himself. Grady found the body. She was 7 years old.

Over the years, Elizabeth Williams held the family together. She worked as a practical nurse and would have become a registered nurse except for the fact that by the early 40's, the hospitals in Birmingham, which had run segregated nursing programs, closed those for blacks.

Grady attended Parker High, an all-black school where the children of teachers and postal workers made fun of girls like Grady, who at 14 was already working part-time in white homes. One day a boy started ragging Grady for being an "Aunt Jemima." One of the poorer boys approached him after class and said: "Hey, everybody's not lucky enough to have a father working. If I ever hear you say that again to her, I'm going to break your neck."

Grady finished high school in early 1950, four weeks after her 16th birthday. Her grades were high, even though she had held back on some tests in an effort to blend in with her older classmates. She planned to go to the nursing school at Dillard University, a black institution in New Orleans, but first she needed a full-time job to earn money for tuition. That was when my mother hired her. There was a state-financed nursing school in Birmingham, about 10 miles from her house, but it was the wrong one.

Between the Depression and World War II, my father and two of his brothers came into Birmingham from the Alabama hills. They were strong, sober country boys who knew how to swing a hammer. By the time Truman was elected in 1948, they had got a little bit rich selling lumber and building shelves for the A&P.

They drove Packards and Oldsmobiles. They bought cottages at the beach and hired housemaids for their wives and resolved that their children would go to college. Among them, they had eight children, and I was the last to be born, and my world was sunny.

Indeed, it seemed to be a matter of family pride that this tribe of hard-handed hill people had become prosperous enough to spoil its babies. I was doted upon, particularly, it occurs to me now, by women: my mother; my sister, Mary Jo, who was 12 years older and carried me around like a mascot; my leathery old grandmother, a widow who didn't like many people but liked me because I was named for her husband.

There was also my Aunt Ada, a red-haired spinster who made me rice pudding and hand-whipped biscuits and milkshakes with cracked ice, and when my parents were out of town, I slept on a pallat in her room.

Then there were the black women, first Daisy, then Ella. And finally Grady.

I wish you could have seen her in 1950. Most of the women in my family ran from slender to bony. Grady was buxom. She wore a blue uniform and walked around our house on stout brown calves. Her skin was smooth. She had a gap between her front teeth, and so did I. One of the first things I remember Grady telling me was that as soon as she had enough money she was going to get a diamond set in her gap and it would drive the men wild.

There is no trickier subject for a writer from the South than that of affection between a black person and a white one in the unequal world of segregation. For the dishonesty upon which such a society is founded makes every emotion suspect, makes it impossible to know whether what flowed between two people was honest feeling or pity or pragmatism. Indeed, for the black person, the feigning of an expected emotion could be the very coinage of survival.

So I can only tell you how it seemed to me at the time. I was 7 and Grady was 16 and I adored her and I believed she was crazy about me. She became the weather in which my childhood was lived.

I was 14 when she went away. It would be many years before I realized that somehow, whether by accident or by plan, in a way so subtle, so gentle, so loving that it was like the budding and falling of the leaves on the pecan trees in the yard of that happy house in that cruel city in that violent time, Grady had given me the most precious gift that could be received by a pampered white boy growing up in that time and place. It was the gift of a free and unhateful heart.

Grady, it soon became clear, was a talker, and I was already known in my family as an incessant asker of questions. My brother, Jerry, who is 10 years older than I, says one of his clearest memories is of my following Grady around the house, pursuing her with a constant buzz of chatter.

That is funny, because what I remember is Grady talking and me listening—Grady talking as she did her chores, marking me with her vision of the way things were. All of my life, I have carried this mental image of the two of us:

I am 9 or 10 by this time. We are in the room where Grady did her ironing. Strong light is streaming through the window. High summer lies heavily across all of Birmingham like a blanket. We are alone, Grady and I, in the midst of what the Alabama novelist Babs Deal called "the acres of afternoon," those legendary hours of buzzing heat and torpidity that either bind you to the South or make you crazy to leave it.

I am slouched on a chair, with nothing left to do now that baseball practice is over. Grady is moving a huge dreadnought of an iron, a G.E. with stainless steel base and fat black handle, back and forth across my father's white shirts. From time to time, she shakes water on the fabric from a bottle with a sprinkler cap.

Then she speaks of a hidden world about which no one has ever told me, a world as dangerous and foreign, to a white child in a segregated society, as Africa itself—the world of "nigger town." "You don't know what it's like to be poor and black," Grady says.

She speaks of the curbside justice administered with rubber hoses by Bull Connor's policemen, of the deputy sheriff famous in the black community for shooting a floor sweeper who had moved too slowly, of "Dog Day," the one time a year when blacks are allowed to attend the state fair. She speaks offhandedly of the N.A.A.C.P.

"Are you a member?" I ask.

"At my school," she says, "we take our dimes and nickels and join the N.A.A.C.P. every year just like you join the Red Cross in your school."

It seems silly now to describe the impact of this revelation, but that is because I cannot fully re-create the intellectual isolation of those days in Alabama. Remember that this was a time when television news, with its searing pictures of racial conflict, was not yet a force in our society. The editorial pages of the Birmingham papers were dominated by the goofy massive-resistance cant of columnists like James J. Kilpatrick. Local politicians liked to describe the N.A.A.C.P. as an organization of satanic purpose and potency that had been rejected by "our colored people," and would shortly be outlawed in Alabama as an agency of Communism.

But Grady said black students were joining in droves, people my age and hers. It was one of the most powerfully subversive pieces of information I had ever encountered, leaving me with an unwavering conviction about Bull Connor, George Wallace and the other segregationist blowhards who would dominate the politics of my home state for a generation.

From that day, I knew they were wrong when they said that "our Negroes" were happy with their lot and had no desire to change "our Southern way of life." And when a local minister named Fred L. Shuttlesworth joined with Dr. King in 1957 to start the civil rights movement in Birmingham, I knew in some deeply intuitive way that they would succeed, because I believed that the rage that was in Grady was a living reality in the entire black community, and I knew that this rage was so powerful that it would have its way.

I learned, too, from watching Grady fail at something that meant a great deal to her. In January 1951, with the savings from her work in our home, she enrolled at Dillard. She made good grades. She loved the school and the city of New Orleans. But the money lasted only one semester, and when summer rolled around Grady was cleaning our house again.

That would be the last of her dream of becoming a registered nurse. A few years later, Grady married Marvin Hutchinson, a dashing fellow, more worldly than she, who took her to all-black nightclubs to hear singers like Bobby (Blue) Bland. In 1957, she moved to New York City to work as a maid and passed from my life. But I never forgot how she had yearned for education.

Did this mean that between the ages of 7 and 14, I acquired a sophisticated understanding of the insanity of a system of government that sent this impoverished girl to Louisiana rather than letting her attend the tax-supported nursing school that was a 15-cent bus ride from her home?

I can't say that I did. But I do know that in 1963, I recognized instantly that George Wallace was lying when he said that his Stand in the School House Door at the University of Alabama was intended to preserve the Constitutional principle of states' rights. What he really wanted to preserve was the right of the state of Alabama to promiscuously damage lives like Grady's.

It is April 23, 1991. I approach the locked security gate of a rough-looking apartment courtyard in Atlanta. There behind it, waiting in the shadows, is a tiny woman with a halo of gray hair and that distinctive gap in the front teeth. Still no diamond. Grady opens the gate and says, "I've got to hug you."

Grady's apartment is modest. The most striking feature is the stacks of books on each side of her easy chair. The conversation that was interrupted so long ago is resumed without a beat.

Within minutes we are both laughing wildly over an incident we remembered in exactly the same way. Grady had known that I was insecure about my appearance as I approached adolescence, and she always looked for chances to reassure me, preferably in the most exuberant way possible. One day when I appeared in a starched shirt and with my hair slicked back for a birthday party, Grady shouted, "You look positively raping."

"Grady," my mother called from the next room, "do you know what you're saying?"

"I told her yeah. I was trying to say 'ravishing.' I used to read all those True Confession magazines."

Reading, it turned out, had become a passion of Grady's life, even though she never got any more formal education. For the first time in years, I recall that it was Grady who introduced me to Ernest Hemingway. In the fall of 1952, when I had the mumps and "The Old Man and the Sea" was being published in Life, Grady sat by my bed and read me the entire book. We both giggled at the sentence: "Once he stood up and urinated over the side of the skiff. . . ."

Partly for money and partly to escape a troubled marriage, Grady explains, she had left Birmingham to work in New York as a maid for $125 a month. Her husband had followed.

"So we got an apartment, and the man I worked for got him a job," Grady recalls. "And we got together and we stayed for 31 years, which is too long to stay dead."

Dead, I asked? What did that mean?

For Grady it meant a loveless marriage and a series of grinding jobs as a maid or cook. And yet she relished the life of New York, developing a reputation in her neighborhood as an ace gambler and numbers player. Through an employer who worked in show business, she also became a regular and knowledgeable attender of Broadway theater.

There were three children: Eric Lance, 37, works for the New York subway system; Marva, 33, is a graduate of Wilberforce University and works in the finance department at Coler Memorial Hospital in New York; Reed, 29, works for a bank in Atlanta, where Grady is a dietetic cook at Shepherd Spinal Center. It has not been a bad life and is certainly richer in experiences and perhaps in opportunities for her children than Grady would have had in Birmingham.

At one point Grady speaks of being chided by one of her New York-raised sons for "taking it" back in the old days in Birmingham.

"He said, 'I just can't believe y'all let that go on,'" she says. "I said: 'What do you mean *y'all?* What could you have done about it?' What were you going to do? If you stuck out, you got in trouble. I always got in trouble. I was headstrong. I couldn't stand the conditions and I hated it. I wanted more than I could have.

"I always wanted to be more than I was," she adds. "I thought if I was given the chance I could be more than I was ever allowed to be."

I felt a pang of sympathy for Grady that she should be accused of tolerating what she had opposed with every fiber of her being. But how can a young man who grew up in New York know that the benign city he saw on visits to his grandmother each summer was not the Birmingham that had shaped his mother's life?

Among black people in the South, Grady is part of a generation who saw their best chances burned away by the last fiery breaths of segregation. It is difficult for young people of either race today to understand the openness and simplicity of the injustice that was done to this dwindling generation. When you stripped away the Constitutional falderal from Wallace's message, it was this: He was telling Grady's mother, a working parent who paid property, sales and income taxes in Alabama for more than 40 years, that her child could not attend the institutions supported by those taxes.

Even to those of us who lived there, it seems surreal that such a systematic denial of opportunity could have existed for so long. I have encountered the same disbelief in the grown-up children of white sharecroppers when they looked at pictures of the plantations on which they and their families had lived in economic bondage.

Gradystein Williams Hutchinson (Ann States/SABA)

For people with such experiences, some things are beyond explanation or jest, something I learn when I jokingly ask Grady if she'd like her ashes brought back to Pratt City when she dies.

"No," she answers quite firmly, "I'd like them thrown in the East River in New York. I never liked Alabama. Isn't that terrible for you to say that? You know how I hate it."

Word that I had found Grady shot through my family. When the reunion luncheon was planned for my sister's house, my first impulse was to stage-manage the event. I had learned in conversations with Grady that she remembered my mother as someone who had nagged her about the housework. None of the rest of us recollected theirs as a tense relationship, but then again, none of us had been in Grady's shoes. In the end I decided to let it flow, and as it turned out, no one enjoyed the reunion more than Grady and my mother.

"You're so tiny," Grady exclaimed at one point. "I thought you were a great big woman. How'd you make so much noise?"

My mother was disarmed. In the midst of a round of stories about the bold things Grady had said and done, I heard her turn to a visitor and explain quietly, in an admiring voice, "You see, now, that Grady is a strong person."

Grady is also a very funny person, a born raconteur with a reputation in her own family for being outrageous. It is possible, therefore, to make her sound like some 50's version of Whoopi Goldberg and her life with my family like a sitcom spiced with her "sassy" asides about race and sex. But what I sensed at our gathering, among my brother, sister and parents, was something much deeper than fondness or nostalgia. It was a shared pride that in the Birmingham of the 50's this astonishing person had inhabited our home and had been allowed to be fully herself.

"She spoke out more than any person I knew of, no matter what their age," my sister observed. "She was the first person I'd ever heard do that, you see, and here I was 18 years old, and you were just a little fellow. This was the first person I'd ever heard say, 'Boy, it's terrible being black in Birmingham.' "

As Grady and my family got reacquainted, it became clear that my memory of her as "mine" was the narrow and selfish memory of a child. I had been blind to the bonds Grady also had with my brother and sister. Grady remembered my brother, in particular, as her confidant and protector. And although they never spoke of it at the time, she looked to him as her guardian against the neighborhood workmen of both races who were always eager to offer young black girls "a ride home from work."

"Even if Jerry was going in the opposite direction," Grady recalled, "he would always say: 'I'm going that way. I'll drop Grady off.' "

In my brother's view, Grady's outspokenness, whether about her chores or the shortcomings of Birmingham, was made possible through a kind of adolescent cabal. "The reason it worked was Grady was just another teen-ager in the house," he said. "There were already two teen-agers in the house, and she was just a teen-ager, too."

But it is also hard to imagine Grady falling into another family led by parents like mine. They were both from the Alabama hills, descended from Lincoln Republicans who did not buy into the Confederate mythology. There were no plantation paintings or portraits of Robert E. Lee on our walls. The mentality of the hill country is that of the underdog.

They were instinctive humanitarians. As Grady tells it, my father was well known among her relatives as "an open man" when it came to the treatment of his employees. I once saw him take the side of a black employee who had fought back against the bullying of a white worker on a loading dock—not a common occurrence in Birmingham in the 50's.

The most powerful rule of etiquette in my parents' home, I realize now, was that the word "nigger" was not to be used. There was no grand explanation attached to this, as I recall. We were simply people who did not say "nigger."

The prohibition of this one word may seem a small point, but I think it had a large meaning. Hill people, by nature, are talkers, and some, like my father, are great storytellers. They themselves have often been called hillbillies, which is to say that they understand the power of language and that the power to name is the power to maim.

Everyone in my family seems to have known that my great long afternoon talks with Grady were about race. Their only concern was not whether I should be hearing such talk, but whether I was old enough for the brutality of the facts.

"I would tell Howell about all the things that happened in the black neighborhoods, what police did to black people," Grady recalled to us. "I would come and tell him, and he would cry, and Mrs. Raines would say: 'Don't tell him that anymore. Don't tell him that. He's too young. Don't make him sad.' He would get sad about it."

Grady told me in private that she recalled something else about those afternoons, something precise and specific. I had wept, she said, on learning about the murder of Emmett Till, a young black boy lynched in Mississippi in 1955.

To me, this was the heart of the onion. For while some of the benefits of psychotherapy may be dubious, it does give us one shining truth. We are shaped by those moments when the sadness of life first wounds us. Yet often we are too young to remember that wounding experience, that decisive point after which all is changed for better or worse.

Every white Southerner must choose between two psychic roads—the road of racism or the road of brotherhood. Friends, families, even lovers have parted at that forking, sometimes forever, for it presents a choice that is clouded by confused emotions, inner conflicts and powerful social forces.

It is no simple matter to know all the factors that shape this individual decision. As a college student in Alabama, I shared the choking shame that many young people there felt about Wallace's antics and about the deaths of the four black children in the bombing of the Sixteenth Street Baptist Church in September 1963. A year later, as a cub reporter, I listened to the sermons and soaring hymns of the voting rights crusade. All this had its effect.

But the fact is that by the time the civil rights revolution rolled across the South, my heart had already chosen its road. I have always known that my talks with Grady helped me make that decision in an intellectual sense. But I had long felt there must have been some deeper force at work, some emotional nexus linked for me, it seemed now on hearing Grady's words, to the conjuring power of one name—Emmett Till—and to disconnected images that had lingered for decades in the eye of my memory.

Now I can almost recall the moment or imagine I can: Grady and I together, in the ironing room. We are islanded again, the two of us, in the acres of afternoon. We are looking at Life magazine or Look, at pictures of a boy barely older than myself, the remote and homely site of his death, several white men in a courtroom, the immemorial Mississippi scenes.

Thus did Grady, who had already given me so much, come back into my life with one last gift. She brought me a lost reel from the movie of my childhood, and on its dusty frames, I saw something few people are lucky enough to witness. It was a glimpse of the revelatory experience described by Graham Greene, the soul-shaking time after which all that is confusing detail falls away and all that is thematic shines forth with burning clarity.

Our reunion turned out to be a day of discovery, rich emotion and great humor. Near the end of a long lunch, my sister and my brother's wife began pouring coffee. In classic Southern overkill, there were multiple desserts. Grady spoke fondly of my late Aunt Ada's artistry with coconut cakes. Then she spoke of leaving Birmingham with "my dreams of chasing the rainbow."

"I used to say when I was young, 'One day I'm going to have a big house, and I'm going to have the white people bring me my coffee,' " Grady said, leaning back in her chair. "I ain't got the big house yet, but I got the coffee. I chased the rainbow and I caught it."

Of course, Grady did not catch the rainbow, and she never will. Among the victims of segregation, Grady was like a soldier shot on the last day of the war. Only a few years after she relinquished her dream of education, local colleges were opened to blacks, and educators from around the country came to Birmingham looking for the sort of poor black student who could race through high school two years ahead of schedule.

Grady's baby sister, Liz Spraggins, was spotted in a Pratt City high-school choir in 1964 and offered a music scholarship that started her on a successful career in Atlanta as a gospel and jazz singer. Grady's cousin Earl Hilliard, who is 10 years younger than she, wound up at Howard University Law School. Today he is a member of the Alabama Legislature. When Grady and I had lunch with the Hilliards, the family was debating whether Earl Jr. should join his sister, Lisa, at Emory or choose law-school acceptances at Stanford, Texas or Alabama.

If Grady had been a few years younger, she would have gone down the road taken by her sister and cousin. If she had been white, the public-education system of Alabama would have bailed her out despite her poverty. Even in 1950, fatherless white kids who zipped through high school were not allowed to fall through the cracks in Alabama. But Grady had bad timing and black skin, a deadly combination.

At some point during our reunion lunch, it occurred to everyone in the room that of all the people who knew Grady Williams as a girl, there was one group that could have sent her to college. That was my family. The next morning, my sister told me of a regretful conversation that took place later that same day.

"Mother said at dinner last night, 'If we had just known, if we had just known, we could have done something,' " Mary Jo said. "Well, how could we have not known?"

Yes, precisely, how could we not have known—and how can we not know of the carnage of lives and minds and souls that is going on among young black people in this country today?

In Washington, where I live, there is a facile answer to such questions. Fashionable philosophers in the think tanks that influence this Administration's policies will tell you that guilt, historical fairness and compassion are outdated concepts, that if the playing field is level today, we are free to forget that it was tilted for generations. Some of these philosophers will even tell you that Grady could have made it if she had really wanted to.

But I know where Grady came from and I know the deck was stacked against her and I know who stacked it. George Wallace is old, sick and pitiful now, and he'd like to be forgiven for what he, Bull Connor and the other segs did back then, and perhaps he should be. Those who know him say that above all else he regrets using the racial issue for political gain.

I often think of Governor Wallace when I hear about the dangers of "reverse discrimination" and "racial quotas" from President Bush or his counsel, C. Boyden Gray, the chief architect of the Administration's civil rights policies. Unlike some of the old Southern demagogues, these are not ignorant men. Indeed, they are the polite, well-educated sons of privilege. But when they argue that this country needs no remedies for past injustices, I believe I hear the grown-up voices of pampered white boys who never saw a wound.

And I think of Grady and the unrepayable gift she gave with such wit, such generosity, to such a boy, so many years ago.

Grady told me that she was moved when she went to a library and saw my book, an oral history of the civil rights movement entitled "My Soul Is Rested." It is widely used on college campuses as basic reading about the South, and of everything I have done in journalism, I am proudest of that book.

I was surprised that Grady had not instantly understood when the book came out in 1977 that she was its inspiration. That is my fault. I waited much too long to find her and tell her. It is her book really. She wrote it on my heart in the acres of afternoon.

CHAPTER TWO

A Way of Perception

We have the wolf by the ears; and we
can neither hold him, nor safely let
him go. Justice is in one scale, and
self-preservation in the other.

Thomas Jefferson, 1820

READING SELECTIONS

CLINTON ROSSITER

An Introduction to The Federalist Papers: Hamilton, Madison, and Jay

The Federalist is the most important work in political science that has ever been written, or is likely ever to be written, in the United States. It is, indeed, the one product of the American mind that is rightly counted among the classics of political theory.

This work has always commanded widespread respect as the first and still most authoritative commentary on the Constitution of the United States. It has been searched minutely by lawyers for its analysis of the powers of Congress, quoted confidently by historians for its revelations of the hopes and fears of the framers of the Constitution, and cited magisterially by the Supreme Court for its arguments in behalf of judicial review, executive independence, and national supremacy. It would not be stretching the truth more than a few inches to say that *The Federalist* stands third only to the Declaration of Independence and the Constitution itself among all the sacred writings of American political history. It has a quality of legitimacy, of authority and authenticity, that gives it the high status of a public document, one to which, as Thomas Jefferson put it, "appeal is habitually made by all, and rarely declined or denied by any" as to the "genuine meaning" of the Constitution.

In recent years respect for *The Federalist* has blossomed into admiration. It is now valued not merely as a clever defense of a particular charter, but as an exposition of certain timeless truths about constitutional government. It has caught the fancy of political scientists throughout the world, has been translated into a dozen languages, and—surely the most convincing evidence of its lofty status—has become one of the three or four staples of the American college curriculum in political science. General Washington, who was trying merely to be friendly, wrote some prophetic words to Alexander Hamilton in the summer of 1788: "When

the transient circumstances and fugitive performances which attended this crisis shall have disappeared, that work will merit the notice of posterity, because in it are candidly and ably discussed the principles of freedom and the topics of government—which will be always interesting to mankind so long as they shall be connected in civil society." The "notice of posterity" for the stern yet hopeful message of *The Federalist* has never been more attentive than in these drawn-out years of peril for constitutional democracy.

The immense prestige of this work seems especially remarkable when viewed in the light of its origins. *The Federalist* is essentially a collection of eighty-five letters to the public over the pseudonym of Publius that appeared at short intervals in the newspapers of New York City beginning on October 27, 1787. These letters were still appearing in late March, 1788, when the first thirty-six were issued in a collected edition. Continuous publication was halted with number 77 on April 4, then resumed June 14, and concluded August 16. In the meantime, a second volume containing numbers 37–85 was published May 28.

Conceived in the pressure of a great crisis in human events, written with a haste that often bordered on the frantic, printed and published as if it were the most perishable kind of daily news, *The Federalist* bore few marks of immortality at birth. It was, in fact, only one of several hundred salvos in the loud war of words that accompanied the protracted struggle over ratification of the Constitution. That new charter of government, it will be remembered, had been agreed upon and signed at Philadelphia, September 17, 1787, transmitted to the Congress then existing under the Articles of Confederation, and thereupon laid, with no great show of enthusiasm, before the people of the United States. The approval of ratifying conventions in nine of the thirteen states was to bring the Constitution into effect. Few of its authors and supporters imagined that it would be easy to win such a margin of approval in the chaotic political circumstances of the world's first experiment in popular government over an extended area; all recognized that a clear-cut vote against the Constitution in any one of four key states would be enough by itself to destroy their hopes for "a more perfect Union."

One of these states was New York, among whose claims to a vital role in the affairs of the new republic were a growing population, a lively commerce, a pivotal position on the Atlantic seaboard, and New York City, then the seat of the government of the United States. It was also the home of Governor George Clinton, a doughty politician whose principles and prejudices and skills made him the most formidable of opponents to the proposed Constitution. Plainly New York was a state that could easily be lost and yet had to be won; plainly it was a state in which arguments voiced in public debate or actions taken in the ratifying convention might influence the course of events in other states.

It was with such thoughts as these in mind that Alexander Hamilton, the recognized leader of the forces of ratification in New York, turned in the fall of 1787 to the task of winning his state to the cause of the new Constitution. The story of how Hamilton persuaded and plotted and bullied his way over the months to the narrowest of victories in the New York convention is an epic of American politics that deserves to be better known. What is important to us about this amazing effort is that Hamilton found it both practically expedient and psychologically comforting to supplement his political activities with a contribution to the literary war. Without his foresight, energy, and organizational skill there would have been no *Federalist* to stiffen the friends of the Constitution and to instruct the minds of posterity. He conceived the idea of a series of thoughtful communications that would explain and support the proposed Constitution; he scrambled for worthy contributors and finally found them in John Jay and James Madison; he wrote almost two thirds of the total of 175,000 words; he carried on the project to its scheduled end long after the other two men had been forced to leave the field. While the Publius we know and cherish today is a composite of three men, one of these men, Alexander Hamilton, must ever be regarded as the political magician who brought Publius to life.

The authors of *The Federalist* made up a first-class team of thinkers and doers. John Jay (1745–1829), the oldest and at that time most distinguished of the group, was a prosperous New York lawyer who had rendered three particularly eminent services to his state and country: authorship of the admirable New York Constitution of 1777, which was a prime source of ideas for the Convention at Philadelphia; negotiation, side-by-side with Benjamin Franklin and John Adams, of the Treaty of 1783 that gave America peace and final independence; and, as Secretary for Foreign Af-

fairs under the Articles of Confederation, direction of the diplomatic maneuverings of the almost friendless republic. James Madison (1751–1836), although he could hardly have known it at the time, had already won lasting fame as the most useful member of the Convention of 1787. The Constitution was the joint work of a half dozen or more superior men, yet even today, in part because of the notes he kept of the proceedings of the Convention, few historians begrudge Madison the title "Father of the Constitution." Alexander Hamilton (1755–1804) was another New York lawyer who had served his state and country well, notably as a youthful comrade-in-arms of General Washington and as a prime mover of the events that led to the Convention of 1787. He, like Madison, was a delegate to Philadelphia; unlike Madison, he was irregular in attendance and unpersuasive in argument. His principal services to the new Constitution came only after the Convention had adjourned.

All three authors of *The Federalist* went on after 1788 to even more splendid careers—Jay to the Chief Justiceship and to negotiation of the famous treaty that bears his name, Madison to a distinguished eight years as the leading figure in Congress and to somewhat less distinguished eight-year tenures as both Secretary of State and President of the United States, Hamilton to service under President Washington as the most influential of all Secretaries of the Treasury. For those who care about such things—and many readers of this introduction are sure to care—it should be recorded that both Hamilton and Jay were graduates of Columbia, Madison a son of Princeton.

Throughout the long months during which *The Federalist* was running in the New York newspapers, and indeed until several years after publication of the collected essays, the identity of Publius was a well-guarded secret. This mask of anonymity, put on by the authors for sound political purposes, made it possible for Hamilton, in a note written just before his death and discovered just after, to lay claim to a full sixty-three numbers of *The Federalist*, some of which very plainly belonged to Madison. Just why this man of honor and sound memory should have engaged in this extraordinary action is impossible to explain. In any case, he touched off a tortuous dispute that went on for generations between his political heirs and those of Madison over the authorship of the various papers, especially numbers 49–58, 62 and 63. Thanks chiefly to the scholarly labors of Professor Douglass Adair, we can say with some confidence that Hamilton wrote fifty-one numbers (1, 6–9, 11–13, 15–17, 21–36, 59–61, 65–85), Madison twenty-six (10, 14, 37–58, and probably 62, 63), and Jay five (2–5, 64), while three (18–20) were the product of a joint effort by Madison and Hamilton. The skimpiness of Jay's contribution is explained by an illness that overtook him in the fall of 1787, the impressive bulk of Hamilton's by the intensity of his commitment. Madison's contribution, which is far more important for the present reputation of Publius than its modest size would indicate, was made possible in the first place only because the Virginian was in New York in the fall of 1787 as a delegate to Congress. His participation ended abruptly upon his departure for home in March, 1788.

The Federalist worked only a small influence upon the course of events during the struggle over ratification. Promises, threats, bargains, and face-to-face debates, not eloquent words in even the most widely circulated newspapers, won hard-earned victories for the Constitution in the crucial states of Massachusetts, Virginia, and New York. Publius, by his own admission, spoke to a select audience of reasonable, responsible, and established men, and most such men had already been convinced of the necessity of a change in the system of government. The chief usefulness of *The Federalist* in the events of 1788 was as a kind of debater's handbook in Virginia and New York. Copies of the collected edition were rushed to Richmond at Hamilton's direction and used gratefully by advocates of the Constitution in the climactic debate over ratification.

The fame of *The Federalist* derives, therefore, not from the events of a single decisive year, but from the whole course of American history. It is a sign, as it were, of the prodigious success of the Constitution, which, as it has endured and evolved over the generations, has called attention ever more insistently to the men who, having helped to write it, first explained it. Viewed from this perspective, which is the one we are privileged to take, *The Federalist* appears as four books in one: an explanation of the blessings of federal government; an indictment of the Articles of Confederation for their failure to provide such government, or indeed to provide much in the way of government at all; an analysis and defense of the new Constitution as an instrument of federalism and constitutionalism; and, lighting up these more practical subjects with sudden bursts of brilliance, an exposition of certain enduring truths that provide an understanding of both the dangers and the delights of free government.

As an explanation of the federal form of government *The Federalist* comes closest to being an original piece of work. Other men, to be sure—most notably Althusius and "the celebrated Montesquieu"—had discoursed intelligently on some of the problems of unity and disunity among states with close emotional and commercial ties, but it remained for Publius to make the first real stab at expounding the merits of genuine federalism, which is, after all, a full and tricky step be-

yond mere federation in the direction of consolidation. *The Federalist* deserves lasting credit for the clarity with which it insists that both levels of government in a federal system must exercise direct authority over individuals, that the central government must enjoy unquestioned supremacy in its assigned fields, and that federalism is to be cherished not alone for its contributions to peace within the land and security without, but for the firm foundation it provides for the enjoyment of individual freedom over a wide expanse of territory. *The Federalist*, it could be said, converted federalism from an expedient into an article of faith, from an occasional accident of history into an enduring expression of the principles of constitutionalism.

Those pages of *The Federalist* which catalogue the weaknesses of the Articles of Confederation make much the least interesting reading today. In 1787–88, however, they made very interesting reading indeed, and many friends of the new Constitution valued *The Federalist* principally for its merciless indictment of the "palpable defects of the subsisting Confederation." Since the indictment was one that had to be made with force and in detail, one cannot begrudge Publius the joys he must have experienced in beating a horse that may look dead to us but was very much alive to him. And even in the muddiest parts of the hard going from numbers 15 to 22 there are solid observations on one of the major themes of *The Federalist*: the dreadful circumstance of a weak government in a disordered society.

Up to now, at least, *The Federalist* has worked its chief influence on the course of events as a uniquely authoritative commentary on the Constitution. Today, as all through the history of American constitutional development, a particular interpretation of some clause in that document can be given a special flavor of authenticity by a quotation from Publius. If he was understandably wrong in his interpretation of some details in the Constitution—for example, in assigning the Senate a share in the power of removal and in giving a purely military cast to the President's authority as commander-in-chief—he was remarkably right about many more. Publius the constitutional lawyer, in the bold person of Hamilton, reached the peak of intellectual power and of historical influence in the breathtaking assertion of judicial review in number 78.

Publius the political theorist, in the perceptive persons of both Hamilton and Madison, is the man who has brought fame and influence to *The Federalist* in recent years—this despite the fact that all the more or less speculative musings of *The Federalist* make up at best a fragment on government. What Hamilton and Madison were capable of producing as political theorists in the closet of leisurely detachment and what they managed to produce as political strategists in the arena of zestful engagement were, alas, two quite different matters. *The Federalist* is a contribution to political theory only by accident—by the happy accident, one might say, that neither of its chief authors could ever make a point in the most earth-bound debate without pausing, if only for a moment, to put the point in a larger and more abstract perspective. Yet this, after all, is the familiar way in which some of the greatest contributions to political theory were brought into being, and one should not spend too much time regretting the startling omissions and uneven quality of *The Federalist*, lest he be slow to pay the homage of painstaking study to such notable contributions as Madison's reflections on the plural society in numbers 10 and 51 and Hamilton's appraisal of executive power as an agency of free government in number 70.

If he does pay such homage, and if he also keeps an earnest eye out for the nuggets of speculation strewn all through these pages, the student of *The Federalist* will in time amass a respectable treasure of political wisdom about the problems and possibilities of freedom. While *The Federalist* has important things to say about all governments in general, it is popular government—in those days called "republican" government—with which Publius is principally concerned. His dislike of instability and downright fear of anarchy are writ large and often in these essays, but he offers us other and better ways than that recommended by Thomas Hobbes to bring peace and security to the community. To find "republican remedies" for the "diseases most incident to republican government" is the constant purpose of the authors of *The Federalist*.

In the course of their long search for these remedies, the chief of which turn out to be federalism, social pluralism, and constitutionalism (that is, divided, balanced, and limited government), Hamilton and Madison give their own answers to some of the oldest questions of political theory; and it is safe to say that no more eloquent, tough-minded, and instructive answers have ever been given by an American pen. Whether discoursing on the universal urge of mankind toward weakness and wickedness, demonstrating the existence of the saving graces of human reason and decency, accounting for the diverse interests that arise in a progressive society, finding a formula for liberty in the very fact of these clashing interests, setting both static and dynamic limits to the rule of the majority, or working out the balance of forces within a complex structure of government, *The Federalist* sends out messages of universal validity to all students of political man, and especially to those who wish him well. It is, in particular, the cold-eyed yet ultimately hopeful view of mankind that lifts *The Federalist* into the circle of classics in political theory. No one can read these pages without being reminded powerfully of both the light and dark sides of human nature—of man's capacity for reason and justice that makes free government possible, of his capacity for passion and injustice that makes it necessary.

It is, to be sure, a great pity that the authors of *The Federalist* had neither time nor inclination to sort out and restate in orderly, comprehensive fashion their many brilliant observations about the nature of political man, or indeed about liberty or society or the purposes and forms of government. It is a greater pity, a source of especially keen distress to students of political theory, that they apparently found it unnecessary to make more than a handful of explicit observations on private property as a right of man, a pillar of ordered society, and a force in politics. Nor is the occasional character of *The Federalist* as a tract in political theory its only fault. As a piece of very special pleading—some have called it a lawyer's brief—it says the same thing over and over in a half dozen ways, tiptoes delicately around many of the hard criticisms directed against the Constitution and slogs ponderously through some of the silliest, and makes at least a few arguments and appeals which its authors must have had trouble justifying to their own consciences. Hamilton, in particular, was hardly the enthusiast for the Constitution that he appears to be in these pages.

In recent years a good deal has been made of the fact that Publius was a "split personality," speaking through Madison as a federalist and an exponent of limited government, through Hamilton as a nationalist and an admirer of energetic government. Yet Publius was, on any large view, at least as whole a personality as any reasonable man can be when he has to deal with the everlasting tensions of free government. His own tensions, it might be argued, are only an honest reflection of those built into the Constitution. *The Federalist*, like the Constitution it expounds and the polity it celebrates, is a "bundle of compromises." The wonder must always be, not that Publius spoke some of the great truths of politics in an offhand manner and with a hoarse voice, but that, in the circumstances of the case, he spoke as pointedly and coherently as he did. He managed to do this principally because the thoughts of his creators, while hastily written down, had not been lightly conceived. They were, indeed, the product of years of learned study and hard experience.

Not every great political theorist has cared much for free and popular government. Of those who have cared, not every one has been candid enough to expose its diseases, or hopeful enough to counsel a broad scheme of prevention. *The Federalist* is a famous work in political science because it does just that, because it mixes candor and hope, realism and idealism, in a message to all friends of liberty wherever they ply their honorable trade. And the message of *The Federalist* reads: no happiness without liberty, no liberty without self-government, no self-government without constitutionalism, no constitutionalism without morality—and none of these great goods without stability and order.

TheFederalist Papers: Hamilton, Madison, and Jay: No. 54: Madison

The next view which I shall take of the House of Representatives relates to the apportionment of its members to the several States, which is to be determined by the same rule with that of direct taxes.

It is not contended that the number of people in each State ought not to be the standard for regulating the proportion of those who are to represent the people of each State. The establishment of the same rule for the apportionment of taxes will probably be as little contested; though the rule itself, in this case, is by no means founded on the same principle. In the former case, the rule is understood to refer to the personal rights of the people, with which it has a natural and universal connection. In the latter, it has reference to the proportion of wealth of which it is in no case a precise measure, and in ordinary cases a very unfit one. But notwithstanding the imperfection of the rule as applied to the relative wealth and contributions of the States, it is evidently the least exceptionable among the practicable rules, and had too recently obtained the general sanction of America not to have found a ready preference with the convention.

All this is admitted, it will perhaps be said; but does it follow, from an admission of numbers for the measure of representation, or of slaves combined with free citizens as a ratio of taxation, that slaves ought to be included in the numerical rule of representation? Slaves are considered as property, not as persons. They ought therefore to be comprehended in estimates of taxation which are founded on property, and to be excluded from representation which is regulated by a census of persons. This is the objection, as I understand it, stated in its full force. I shall be equally candid in stating the reasoning which may be offered on the opposite side.

"We subscribe to the doctrine," might one of our Southern brethren observe, "that representation relates more immediately to persons, and taxation more immediately to property, and we join in the application of this distinction to the case of our slaves. But we must deny the fact that slaves are considered merely as property, and in no respect whatever as persons. The true state of the case is that they partake of both these qualities: being considered by our laws, in some respects, as persons, and in other respects as property. In being compelled to labor, not for himself, but for a master; in being vendible by one master to another master; and in being subject at all times to be restrained in his liberty and chastised in his body, by the capricious will of another—the slave may appear to be degraded from the human rank, and classed with those irrational animals which fall under the legal denomination of property. In being protected, on the other hand, in his life and in his limbs, against the violence of all others, even the master of his labor and his liberty; and in being punishable himself for all violence committed against others—the slave is no less evidently regarded by the law as a member of the society, not as a part of the irrational creation; as a moral person, not as a mere article of property. The federal Constitution, therefore, decides with great propriety on the case of our slaves, when it views them in the mixed character of persons and of property. This is in fact their true character. It is the character bestowed on them by the laws under which they live; and it will not be denied that these are the proper criterion; because it is only under the pretext that the laws have transformed the Negroes into subjects of property that a place is disputed them in the computation of numbers; and it is admitted that if the laws were to restore the rights which have been taken away, the Negroes could no longer be refused an equal share of representation with the other inhabitants.

"This question may be placed in another light. It is agreed on all sides that numbers are the best scale of wealth and taxation, as they are the only proper scale of representation. Would the convention have been impartial or consistent, if they had rejected the slaves from the list of inhabitants when the shares of representation were to be calculated, and inserted them on the lists when the tariff of contributions was to be adjusted? Could it be reasonably expected that the Southern States would concur in a system which considered their slaves in some degree as men when burdens were to be imposed, but refused to consider them in the same light when advantages were to be conferred? Might not some surprise also be expressed that those who reproach the Southern States with the barbarous policy of considering as property a part of their human brethren should themselves contend that the government to which all the States are to be parties ought to consider this unfortunate race more completely in the unnatural light of property than the very laws of which they complain?

"It may be replied, perhaps, that slaves are not included in the estimate of representatives in any of the States possessing them. They neither vote themselves nor increase the votes of their masters. Upon what principle, then, ought they to be taken into the federal estimate of representation? In rejecting them altogether, the Constitution would, in this respect, have followed the very laws which have been appealed to as the proper guide.

"This objection is repelled by a single observation. It is a fundamental principle of the proposed Constitution that as the aggregate number of representatives allotted to the several States is to be determined by a federal rule founded on the aggregate number of inhabitants, so the right of choosing this allotted number in each State is to be exercised by such part of the inhabitants as the State itself may designate. The qualifications on which the right of suffrage depend are not, perhaps, the same in any two States. In some of the States the difference is very material. In every State, a certain proportion of inhabitants are deprived of this right by the constitution of the State, who will be included in the census by which the federal Constitution apportions the representatives. In this point of view the Southern States might retort the complaint by insisting that the principle laid down by the convention required that no regard should be had to the policy of particular States towards their own inhabitants; and consequently that the slaves, as inhabitants, should have been admitted into the census according to their full number, in like manner with other inhabitants, who, by the policy of other States, are not admitted to all the rights of citizens. A rigorous adherence, however, to this principle is waived by those who would be gainers by it. All that they ask is that equal moderation be shown on the other side. Let the case of the slaves be considered, as it is in truth a peculiar one. Let the compromising expedient of the Constitution be mutually adopted which regards them as inhabitants, but as debased by servitude below the equal level of free inhabitants; which regards the *slave* as divested of two fifths of the *man*.

"After all, may not another ground be taken on which this article of the Constitution will admit of a still more ready defense? We have hitherto proceeded on the idea that representation related to persons only, and not at all to property. But is it a just idea? Government is instituted no less for protection of the property than of the persons of individuals. The one as well as the other, therefore, may be considered as represented by those who are charged with the government. Upon this principle it is that in several of the States, and particularly in the State of New York, one branch of the government is intended more especially to be the guardian of property and is accordingly elected by that part of the society which is most interested in this object of government. In the federal Constitution, this policy does not prevail. The rights of property are committed into the same hands with the personal rights. Some attention ought, therefore, to be paid to property in the choice of those hands.

"For another reason, the votes allowed in the federal legislature to the people of each State ought to bear some proportion to the comparative wealth of the States. States have not, like individuals, an influence over each other, arising from superior advantages of fortune. If the law allows an opulent citizen but a single vote in the choice of his representative, the respect and consequence which he derives from his fortunate situation very frequently guide the votes of others to the objects of his choice; and through this imperceptible channel the rights of property are conveyed into the public representation. A State possesses no such influence over other States. It is not probable that the richest State in the Confederacy will ever influence the choice of a single representative in any other State. Nor will the representatives of the larger and richer States possess any other advantage in the federal legislature over the representatives of other States than what may result from their superior number alone. As far, therefore, as their superior wealth and weight may justly entitle them to any advantage, it ought to be secured to them by a superior share of representation. The new Constitution is, in this respect, materially different from the existing Confederation, as well as from that of the United Netherlands, and other similar confederacies. In each of the latter, the efficacy of the federal resolutions depends on the subsequent and voluntary resolutions of the States composing the union. Hence the States, though possessing an equal vote in the public councils, have an unequal influence, corresponding with the unequal importance of these subsequent and voluntary resolutions. Under the proposed Constitution, the federal acts will take effect without the necessary intervention of the individual States. They will depend merely on the majority of votes in the federal legislature, and consequently each vote, whether proceeding from a larger or a smaller State, or a State more or less wealthy or powerful, will have an equal weight and efficacy: in the same manner as the votes individually given in a State legislature, by the representatives of unequal counties or other districts, have each a precise equality of value and effect; or if there be any difference in the case, it proceeds from the difference in the personal character of the individual representative, rather than from any regard to the extent of the district from which he comes."

Such is the reasoning which an advocate for the Southern interests might employ on this subject; and although it may appear to be a little strained in some points, yet on the whole, I must confess that it fully reconciles me to the scale of representation which the convention have established.

In one respect, the establishment of a common measure for representation and taxation will have a very salutary effect. As the accuracy of the census to be obtained by the Congress will necessarily depend, in a considerable degree, on the disposition, if not on the co-operation of the States, it is of great importance that the States should feel as little bias as possible to swell or to reduce the amount of their numbers. Were their share of representation alone to be governed by this rule, they would have an interest in exaggerating their inhabitants. Were the rule to decide their share of taxation alone, a contrary temptation would prevail. By extending the rule to both objects, the States will have opposite interests which will control and balance each other and produce the requisite impartiality.

THOMAS JEFFERSON

Declaration of Independence

When in the course of human events it becomes necessary of one people to dissolve the political bands which have connected them with another, and to assume among the powers of the earth, the separate and equal station to which the Laws of Nature and of Nature's God entitles them, a decent respect to the opinions of mankind requires that they should declare the causes which impel them to the separation.

We hold these truths to be self-evident, that all men are created equal, that they are endowed by their Creator with certain unalienable rights, that among these are life, liberty and the pursuit of happiness. That to secure these rights, governments are instituted among men, deriving their just powers from the consent of the governed. That whenever any form of government becomes destructive of these ends, it is the right of the people to alter or to abolish it, and to institute new government, laying its foundation on such principles and organizing its powers in such form, as to them shall seem most likely to effect their safety and happiness. Prudence, indeed, will dictate that governments long established should not be changed for light and transient causes; and accordingly all experience hath shown, that mankind are more disposed to suffer, while evils are sufferable, than to right themselves by abolishing the forms to which they are accustomed. But when a long train of abuses and usurpations, pursuing invariably the same object, evinces a design to reduce them under absolute despotism, it is their right, it is their duty, to

throw off such government, and to provide new guards for their future security. Such has been the patient sufferance of these colonies; and such is now the necessity which constrains them to alter their former systems of government. The history of the present King of Great Britain is a history of repeated injuries and usurpations, all having in direct object the establishment of an absolute tyranny over these States. To prove this, let facts be submitted to a candid world:

He has refused to assent to laws, the most wholesome and necessary for the public good.

He has forbidden his governors to pass laws of immediate and pressing importance, unless suspended in their operation till his assent should be obtained; and when so suspended, he has utterly neglected to attend to them.

He has refused to pass other laws for the accommodation of large districts of people, unless those people would relinquish the right of representation in the legislature, a right inestimable to them and formidable to tyrants only.

He has called together legislative bodies at places unusual, uncomfortable, and distant from the depository of their public records, for the sole purpose of fatiguing them into compliance with his measures.

He has dissolved representative houses repeatedly, for opposing with manly firmness his invasions on the right of people.

He has refused for a long time, after such dissolutions, to cause others to be elected; whereby the legislative powers, in-capable of annihilation, have returned to the people at large for their exercise; the State remaining in the meantime exposed to all the dangers of invasion from without, and convulsions within.

He has endeavored to prevent the population of these States; for that purpose obstructing the laws for naturalization of foreigners; refusing to pass others to encourage their migrations hither, and raising the conditions of new appropriations of lands.

He has obstructed the administration of justice, by refusing his assent to laws for establishing judiciary powers.

He has made judges dependent on his will alone, for the tenure of their offices, and the amount and payment of their salaries.

He has enacted a multitude of new offices, and sent hither swarms of officers to harass our people, and eat out their substance.

He has kept among us, in times of peace, standing armies without the consent of our legislature.

He has affected to render the military independent of and superior to the civil power.

He has combined with others to subject us to a jurisdiction foreign to our constitution, and unacknowledged by our laws, giving his assent to their acts of pretended legislation:

For quartering large bodies of armed troops among us:

For protecting them, by a mock trial, from punishment for any murders which they should commit on the inhabitants of these States:

For cutting off our trade with all parts of the world:

For imposing taxes on us without our consent:

For depriving us in many cases of the benefits of trial by jury:

For transporting us beyond seas to be tried for pretended offenses:

For abolishing the free system of English laws in a neighboring province, establishing therein an arbitrary government, and enlarging its boundaries so as to render it at once an example and fit instrument for introducing the same absolute rule into these colonies:

For taking away our charters, abolishing our most valuable laws, and altering fundamentally the forms of our governments;

For suspending our own legislatures, and declaring themselves invested with power to legislate for us in all cases whatsoever.

He has abdicated government here, by declaring us out of his protection and waging war against us.

He has plundered our seas, ravaged our coasts, burnt our towns, and destroyed the lives of our people.

He is at this time transporting large armies of foreign mercenaries to complete the work of death, desolation and tyranny, already begun with circumstances of cruelty and perfidy scarcely paralleled in the most barbarous ages, and totally unworthy the head of a civilized nation.

He has constrained our fellow-citizens taken captive on the high seas to bear arms against their country, to become the executioners of their friends and brethren, or to fall themselves by their hands.

He has excited domestic insurrections amongst us, and has endeavored to bring on the inhabitants of our frontiers, the merciless Indian savages, whose known rule of warfare is an undistinguished destruction of all ages, sexes, and conditions.

In every stage of these oppressions we have petitioned for redress in the most humble terms: Our repeated petitions have been answered only by repeated injury. A prince, whose character is thus marked by every act which may define a tyrant, is unfit to be the ruler of a free people.

Nor have we been wanting in attentions to our British brethren. We have warned them from time to time of attempts by their legislature to extend an un-warrantable jurisdiction over us. We have reminded them of the circumstances of our emigration and settlement here. We have appealed to their native justice and magnanimity, and we have conjured them by the ties of our common kindred to disavow these usurpations, which would inevitably interrupt our connections and correspondence. They too have been deaf to the voice of justice and of consanguinity. We must, therefore, acquiesce in the necessity which denounces our separation, and hold them, as we hold the rest of mankind, enemies in war, in peace friends.

We, therefore, the Representatives of the United States of America, in General Congress, assembled, appealing to the Supreme Judge of the world for the rectitude of our intentions, do, in the name, and by the authority of the good people of these colonies, solemnly publish and declare, that these United Colonies are, and of right ought to be free and independent states; that they are absolved from all allegiance to the British Crown, and that all political connection between them and the state of Great Britain, is and ought to be totally dissolved; and that as free and independent states, they have full power to levy war, conclude peace, contract alliances, establish commerce, and do all other acts and things which independent states may of right do. And for support of this declaration, with a firm reliance on the protection of Divine Providence, we mutually pledge to each other our lives, our fortunes, and our sacred honor.

JOHN HOPE FRANKLIN

The Dream Deferred

On 28 August 1963, some 200,000 American citizens, black and white, converged on the nation's capital in the largest demonstration in the history of the United States. They gathered in the shadow of the Lincoln Memorial to present a "living petition" for jobs and freedom and equality. Among the several persons who presented the cause that they espoused, it was Martin Luther King who spoke most eloquently to the point of the traditional American dream of equality. He had a dream, he said, that one day the "sons of former slaves and the sons of former slaveholders will be able to sit down together at the table of brotherhood" and that "little black boys and black girls will be able to join hands with little white boys and white girls as sisters and brothers." This was merely the most recent expression of a sentiment that had been uttered, in one form or another, for more than three centuries.

Each generation of Americans, from the very first handful in the seventeenth century to the hundreds of millions in the twentieth century, has sought to create a social order in which equity and justice, as they understood it, would prevail. The Pilgrims in Massachusetts and the settlers in Virginia were matched in the vigor of their efforts by the ceaseless struggles of the Jeffersonians and Jacksonians and of the sectionalists and unionists of the nineteenth century. And this has surely been true of the numerous varieties of idealists and realists of our own time. Each individual and each group brought to this quest the varied backgrounds and experiences that defined their own objectives and fostered differences in methods as well as goals. On that August afternoon in 1963 Dr. King was defining the objectives of the group for which he spoke, and it goes without saying that there were others whose backgrounds and experiences prompted them to differ strongly with him in goals as well as methods.

Tensions and conflicts arising from these differences were inevitable, but in most cases—through the years—the participants demonstrated a remarkable capacity to resolve such difficulties. Religious conflicts gave way to a measure of toleration. Economic ques-

tions were mitigated by the numerous opportunities afforded by an expanding frontier as well as the diversity of economic pursuits. Political controversies moderated in the face of common enemies, the opportunity to explore alternatives on the local level, and common aspirations of self-determination. Perhaps neither perfect peace nor a perfect society would be achieved quickly, if ever; but the Americans moved toward a tolerable existence rather quickly, and this condition encouraged them to hope for and work for the higher goals.

One area which escaped the creative genius that had done so much to ease tensions in a dozen areas and chart the course for their ultimate solution was race. The problem was not with those troublesome native Americans, so strange and so different, who gave the colonists some moments of anxiety in the early years. Their strengths and weaknesses were soon accurately measured, and the formulas for their complete control or annihilation were worked out almost as soon. Nor was it with the several different groups of Europeans, whom Crèvecoeur, even in the Revolutionary years, would regard as belonging to different races. They were to be contrasted from the earlier settlers by their speech, their dress, their religion, or some other cultural attributes. But they had been known to each other and to the original colonists for centuries, and their membership in a common racial group was acknowledged by all but the most suspicious or the most uninformed. They could, moreover, accommodate themselves to each other by acts of mutual friendship and respect, including intermarriage.

But almost from the beginning such bonds of mutual friendship and respect were lacking in the relationship of Europeans and Africans in the New World. The decision to enslave Africans may well have been facilitated by an unfavorable assessment that Englishmen had already made before they settled in the New World. Surely the very act of enslavement served to generate still lower estimates of those held in bondage; and thus the twin acts of general debasement, as Winthrop Jordan in his *White over Black* calls slavery and prejudice, generated for blacks a status of degradation that remained operative for centuries. From the second decade of the seventeenth century to the eighth decade of the twentieth century this debasement would characterize race relations in this country. It could be seen in Virginia in 1642 when a magistrate sentenced a white indentured servant to an additional year of service for running away and a black indentured servant to labor for the remainder of his life for precisely the same offense. (In an interesting way certain absconding Negroes fared better by 1661, when a Virginia statute declared that when an "English servant shall run

John Hope Franklin (Courtesy of the Moorland-Spingarn Research Center)

away in company with any negroes who are incapable of making satisfaction by addition of time" he was required to serve for the Negroes' lost time as well as his own.) And the distinction could also be seen in 1963 when the governor of Alabama stood in the door of the state university in an attempt to block the enrollment of a Negro student. Even more revealing—and disturbing—was that this single act of "statesmanship" earned for the governor the most serious consideration by millions of Americans as a candidate in three presidential campaigns!

It was not merely the commitment to the perpetual enslavement of Africans that set the English colonists apart from their brethren at home, where the abhorrence of slavery was unequivocally expressed in 1773 by Lord Mansfield in the celebrated Somersett case. It was also the commitment to the principle of the inequality of blacks with whites, a condition that could not be significantly relieved even by emancipation, that seemed to confer on the colonists a special responsibility to promulgate and perpetuate the doctrine and practice of racial inequality. Free Negroes, whether or not they had ever been slaves, bore the burdens of inequality in a manner similar to that of slaves; and their inequality was likely to be clearly defined by law and custom that became all but universal. Differences in the punishment of whites and free blacks for the same offense, the prohibition against a free Negro's lifting his hand against a white person even in self defense, his exclusion from the militia, and his inclusion in the application of many parts of the slave code suggest that in the colonial years a black man who was *not* human chattel was nevertheless a human pariah.

The position of the colonists on African slavery was rendered extraordinarily difficult by the fact that human bondage was, as David B. Davis has observed, "an intrinsic part of American development from the first discoveries." Blacks had cleared the forests, felled the trees, drained the swamps, removed the boulders, and planted and harvested the crops. "To live in Virginia without slaves is morally impossible," an Anglican priest serving in the tidewater wrote his brother in London in 1757. Patrick Henry, who preferred death for himself if he could not have liberty, spoke almost casually of the "general inconvenience" of living in Virginia without slaves. By the end of the eighteenth century Negro slavery pervaded the atmosphere; and in many places where it did not flourish, as in Providence and Boston, the shippers and merchants grew wealthy on the profits from the slave trade. The longer this condition prevailed, the more difficult it would be to face up to the problem of slavery in a free society or to accommodate the institution of slavery to the ideology of the Revolution.

The decade before the beginning of hostilities between Britain and her colonies was one in which the colonists made the most eloquent statements of their rights. It was essential to their own freedom, they said, that "no taxes be imposed on them but with their own consent, given personally or by their representatives." The king's liege subjects in the colonies were entitled to "all the inherent rights and liberties of his natural born subjects within the kingdom of Great Britain," they cried. What is a man's own "is absolutely his own; and . . . no man hath a right to take it from him without his consent." The New York Sons of Liberty were subscribers "being influenced from a regard to liberty, and disposed to use all lawful endeavors in our power to defeat the pernicious project, and to transmit to our posterity, those blessings of freedom which our ancestors have handed down to us." If it was possible for men to believe that the "divine Author of our existence intended a part of the human race to hold an absolute property in, and an unbounded power over others . . . the inhabitants of these colonies might at least require from the Parliament . . . some evidence that this dreadful authority over them, has been granted to that body."

The situation was complicated by the fact that the colonists viewed themselves as slaves if they submitted to the policies England was imposing on them after 1763. Slavery was, in the words of Bernard Bailyn, "a crucial concept in eighteenth century political discourse. The ultimate political threat, the absolute political evil, it was embedded in the structure of political thought; it appears in every statement of political principle, in every discussion of constitutionalism or legal rights, in every exhortation to resistance." "Those who are taxed without their own consent are slaves," John Dickinson declared in his *Letters from a Farmer in Pennsylvania*. And yet, neither Dickinson nor any of his colleagues could accept such a lowly status or classify themselves in any sense with the Africans. The degraded status of the Africans was a dramatic and reprehensible reminder to the colonists of what the complete loss of freedom really meant. The mere thought was enough to embolden them not only to declare their independence but to fight for it.

When nothing could restrain the adversaries from armed conflict, there were several areas in which the colonists simply were not prepared for the consequences of the strong positions they had taken. They lacked an effective fighting force or even the military units that could be forged into one. They were without a real sense of mutual dependence or even a common purpose so necessary for nationhood. And the existence of slavery throughout the colonies, and especially among some of the most ardent patriots, compromised any arguments they dared to make regarding their own freedom from oppression. Circumstances required them to make the argument, but they could not possibly take it to the obvious conclusion, for that would be as damaging as it was logical.

There were some, nevertheless, who thought that it was not enough to fight in order to deliver themselves from the degradation of enslavement. For in the process they could not reconcile the institution of chattel slavery with a social order in which they were purchasing their own freedom, at least in part, with the labor of their bondsmen. "Does it follow," James Otis asked, "that 'tis right to enslave a man because he is black? Will short curled hair like wool instead of Christian hair . . . help the argument? Can any logical inference in favor of slavery be drawn from a flat nose, a long or short face?" Richard Wells of Philadelphia wondered in 1774 how the colonists could "reconcile the exercise of SLAVERY with our *professions of freedom.*" In the same year Abigail Adams wrote her husband, "It always appeared a most iniquitous scheme to me to fight ourselves for what we are daily robbing and plundering from those who have as good a right to freedom as we have."

It appeared for a time that the arguments of the opponents of slavery were not only unassailable but might indeed become overpowering. Slaves themselves began pressing their masters to grant them the freedom that the patriots were seeking from Britain. A group of Massachusetts blacks "detained in a State of slavery in the Bowels of a free and Christian country," in pleading for their freedom in 1774 told the legislature that "Every Principle from which America has Acted in the Cours of their unhappy dificultes with Great Briton Pleads Stronger than A Thousand arguments in favours of your petioners." Samuel Hopkins echoed their pleas with great eloquence when he said that the slavery of which the colonists complained "is lighter than a feather compared to their [the Africans'] heavy doom, and may be called liberty and happiness when contrasted with the most abject slavery and inutterable wretchedness to which they are subjected."

Surely some white colonists as well as some slaves and free Negroes believed that the dream of universal freedom and equality, described so movingly by Otis, Hopkins, and others, would become a reality in the crucible of the revolutionary struggle. But the caveats offered by the faint-hearted as well as the resistance put up by those unalterably opposed to any change in the status of blacks was a clear indication that any change would be postponed indefinitely, if not forever. Patrick Henry confessed an "abhorrence of slavery" and found it difficult to understand how it could flourish "in a country, above all others, fond of liberty." But

this was an opinion expressed privately to a Quaker friend; and the public was protected from his righteous wrath. Samuel Adams was careful to heap strictures on Great Britain for every transgression of which the Mother Country was conceivably guilty; but he was just as careful not to speak out against slavery, presumably for the reason that it might "jeopardize the unity of the colonies." The colonists needed all the unity they could get, for clearly they were fighting for a set of principles that did not transcend race, principles which only Englishmen or Europeans, committed by habit and choice, could understand and appreciate.

If the principles for which the colonists fought did not transcend race, the question of race, nevertheless, would not die, even as the colonists declared their independence. And if anyone, among all the colonists, could cope with the question it was Thomas Jefferson. As a large slaveholder, Jefferson knew well the interests of those who held men in bondage. As a man of the Enlightenment, he had a deep appreciation of the meaning of freedom as a state of existence that could scarcely be determined on the basis of class or race. As a very sensitive human being, he knew the warmth and depth of a personal relationship that could indeed transcend race, as his personal servant, Isaac, has told us. That he had serious reservations about slavery was attested by his early, futile efforts, in 1769, to change the Virginia law of manumission to facilitate the master's emancipation of a slave. How deeply he regretted his failure we do not know.

As the author of the Declaration of Independence Jefferson once more sought to strike at the institution of slavery. In the first draft of the historic document the young Virginian penned what John Adams called "a vehement philippic" against Negro slavery. Blaming the king for crimes in this as in numerous other areas, Jefferson said, "He has waged cruel war against human nature itself, violating its most sacred rights of life and liberty in the persons of a distant people who never offended him, captivating and carrying them into slavery in another hemisphere, or to incur miserable death in their transportation thither."

This was an auspicious beginning in the attempt to bring the antislavery cause into the movement for independence. And in placing on the king the onus of slavery and the slave trade, Jefferson obviously hoped to win wide support since he had implicated neither the southern slaveholders nor the northern slave traders. But he succeeded only in convincing both groups that an institution so close to the heart of American social and economic life should not be thrown away by placing it on the royal doorstep where it might die or disappear, especially if the patriots won their independence. Consequently, the Continental Congress voted to expunge the "vehement philippic" from the Declaration. The record does not indicate that Jefferson made any effort to save the section over which he had labored so diligently.

In his lively little book, *The Declaration of Independence,* Carl Becker expressed pleasure that Congress omitted the passage on slavery and the slave trade altogether. He argues that the discrepancy between fact and representation was too flagrant, for George III was not responsible for maintaining slavery and the slave trade in the colonies. But the other charges against the king could hardly receive high grades for their fidelity to the facts either. Becker further argues that it is in this part of the Declaration that Jefferson "conspicuously failed to achieve literary excellence," because he was attempting to achieve something he was temperamentally unfitted to achieve. It lacks warmth, Becker contends; and there was in it "a sense of labored effort, of deliberate striving for an effect that does not come." The passage seems to me to be at least as eloquent and as passionate as those sections that refer to the quartering of soldiers in the homes of the colonists or the cutting off of colonial trade with other parts of the world. But whether or not it lacked literary felicity, it clearly lacked appeal to the slaveholders and slave traders and, thus, was totally unacceptable to them.

As the most important document of the Revolution and easily one of the most important statements on the rights of man ever published, it seems unfortunate that the Declaration of Independence, in its final form, said nothing at all about the widespread practice of trading in human flesh and holding human beings in perpetual bondage. And it is insufficient to dismiss the omission as a happy resolution of a dilemma occasioned by stylistic infelicities or even by the resistance of slave traders and slaveholders. The unwillingness of the Revolutionary leaders to regard human freedom as having some palpable connection with their own fight for political freedom stems from what Donald L. Robinson has referred to as the "marginal consideration given to Negro slavery by a people who thought of little else, publicly, but the political slavery that threatened to engulf them." That all men were created equal was a phrase so hypothetical, so philosophical, so abstract as to have little bearing on the day-to-day status of those who, by failing to resist, conspired in their own enslavement. For all its emphasis on natural equality and human liberty, the ideology of the American Revolution was not really egalitarian.

Perhaps Jefferson could not have done very much about it had he wanted to, and there is considerable doubt that he really wanted to. For although Jefferson insisted he was strongly anti-slavery, his antipathy toward the institution never took him to the point of freeing his own slaves or of using his enormous prestige to oppose slavery unequivocally in word or deed. His status as a large slaveholder and his constant preoccupation with financial matters led him, on occasion, to sell his slaves to pay off his debts and blurred the distinction between him and his fellow slaveholders who generally regarded capital in slaves as more important than Revolutionary ideology. Indeed, William Cohen has observed that Jefferson's wealth, "his status, and his political position were tied to the system of slavery" and to "a societal environment which took for granted the enslavement of one race by another."

Jefferson's most profound indictment of slavery was his assertion that he trembled for his country when, as he said, "I reflect that God is just; that his justice cannot sleep forever." And yet, if he cheered the process of gradual emancipation in the North, he did so in silence. If the abolition of slavery in the Northwest Territory in 1787 pleased him, there is no record of it, although he had advocated the same in 1784. Perhaps the most charitable thing that can be said is that he suffered the torment of an inner conflict created by his owning slaves on the one hand and having a moral repugnance to the institution of slavery on the other.

It was doubtless the view of Jefferson and many of his contemporaries that blacks were inferior to whites, and this had much to do with their inability or their unwillingness to take any significant steps against slavery. Even if blacks as well as whites were endowed by their creator with certain inalienable rights, it did not follow that a social revolution should be effected in order to secure those rights to blacks. For Jefferson was no more certain than many of his spiritual descendants some two hundred years later, in 1976, that the social order should accommodate itself to the complete or even substantial equality of blacks and whites.

In the eighteenth century this sense of racial inequality was as pervasive as slavery itself and was often used to justify keeping blacks in bondage. The student at the Harvard commencement in 1773 who argued that slavery did not violate the law of nature insisted Negroes were inferior to whites and for the good of all they should be kept in subordination. And since the typical African was, in his view, part idiot, part madman, and part child, his consent was not required before exercising authority over him. "Why," he asked, "should anyone interfere with a stable and beneficent social order, just to pursue some mystical primeval equality?"

Perhaps Jefferson would never have been so gauche or so candid as the brash young commencement debater;

but his views on the inequality of the races were not very different. He set forth his views on the subject in his *Notes on Virginia*, written in 1781 for a limited private circulation and then reluctantly published by Jefferson when he realized that its contents were already becoming widely known. In defending a proposal in a draft of the revised Virginia code to deport slaves as they were emancipated, Jefferson saw no alternative. Should Negroes remain in the state, "deep-rooted prejudices" entertained by whites, "ten thousand recollections, by the blacks, of the injuries they have sustained; new provocations; the real distinctions which nature has made; and many other circumstances, will divide us into parties, and produce convulsions, which will probably never end but in the extermination of one or the other race." To these considerations he added others, including "physical and moral."

Jefferson found the skin color and other physical features of Africans unattractive and lacking in beauty. He asked, "Are not the fine mixtures of red and white, the expressions of every passion by greater or less suffusions of color in the one, preferable to that eternal monotony, which reigns in the countenance, that immovable veil of black which covers the emotions of the other race?" There followed a discussion in which Jefferson argued that the flowing hair and physical features of the whites were more attractive than those of blacks. He contended, moreover, that since blacks secrete less by the kidneys, and more by the glands of the skin, they have a "very strong and disagreeable odor." The nineteenth- and twentieth-century proponents of physiological differences between whites and blacks would not be able to put the case more succinctly or more crudely.

Jefferson thought he saw the mental and moral differences just as clearly and, if anything, attached more importance to them. Negroes, he said, required less sleep and thus, even after a hard day's work they could be induced by the slightest amusements to sit up until midnight. Yet, since their existence appeared to "participate more of sensation than reflection," they are disposed to sleep "when abstracted from their diversions, or unemployed in labor," like an animal whose body is at rest. "They are more ardent after their female," Jefferson was certain, "but love seems to them to be more an eager desire, than a tender delicate mixture of sentiment and sensation." In this connection one must recall that more than once Jefferson expressed a strong commitment only to those findings based on scientific observation. In memory, he said, "they are equal to whites; in reason much inferior, as I think one could scarcely be found capable of tracing and comprehending the investigations of Euclid."

Jefferson said he never found a black man who "had uttered a thought above the level of plain narra-

tion; never saw even an elementary trait of painting or sculpture." In purporting to use the language of natural history in discussing blacks, yet seeking to save himself from its rigorous axioms, Daniel J. Boorstin points out, Jefferson played "fast and loose with the concepts on which he had built his whole science." It would seem hardly likely that anyone with such pronounced views on the inferiority of blacks who, at the same time, believed blacks and whites could not live together as free persons could entertain a deeply serious belief that slaves should be emancipated.

For a new nation with extremely limited resources, the repatriation of three quarters of a million former slaves in their African homeland was beyond the wildest dreams of any eighteenth-century visionary. And since the deep-rooted prejudices of the whites and the "ten thousand recollections" by the blacks of the injuries they had sustained made it virtually impossible for manumitted slaves to remain within the country, exhortations against slavery were similar to a papal bull against the comet, to use Lincoln's apt phrase. If such views were held by Jefferson, whose natural sensibilities had been strengthened by the Enlightenment, it seems inconceivable that his less enlightened associates would have been more disposed to embrace antislavery views.

The view of the inferiority of blacks which was apparently held by most colonists did not relate merely to slaves but to all blacks, including those who were free. And the concept of racial inferiority was translated into law and custom which denied to free persons of color the minimum rights which other free persons enjoyed. Even before the Revolution any treatment of free blacks as equals was accidental or on a hit-or-miss basis. Limits were placed on Negro suffrage, and at best the colonial policy had a patchwork design, as Ira Berlin puts it in his *Slaves without Masters*. In the early eighteenth century, North and South Carolina barred free Negroes from the polls. By the time that Georgia joined in the proscription in 1761, North Carolina had reversed its position.

Blacks were officially excluded from the militia in all four New England colonies, but in practice they frequently served. Maryland excluded them, but Virginia allowed them to serve without arms. In some colonies they were barred from testifying against white persons, and in some they were taxed more heavily than whites or were prohibited from owning real estate. In dozens of other ways they suffered from legal distinctions and discriminations against them, not because they were not free but because they were not white.

Thus, at the time of the Revolution it was of doubtful significance to declare that blacks, free blacks, had been created equal when already the law that was written by the Patriots or their forebears had taken away those rights with which their Creator had endowed them. Free blacks, persuaded that their status conferred on them the right to bear arms against the enemy, were dismayed when the council of war, presided over by George Washington, in Cambridge in October 1775, excluded them from serving in the Continental Army. They had fought at Lexington and Concord and at Bunker Hill. Only their vigorous protest late in the year, together with the Patriots' fear that they would answer Lord Dunmore's call for them to join the British, brought forth a reversal of policy. There ensued, however, a long period in which states, acting on their own, excluded slaves or free blacks or both from service. Only the sagging fortunes of the Patriots' cause and the persistence of blacks in the assertion of their right to fight broke down the desire of the Americans to maintain an exclusively white man's army in the field.

Free Negroes also had to fight for their right, as taxpayers, to participate in the affairs of government. As property owners in Massachusetts, Paul and John Cuffe resented their exclusion from the suffrage and other citizenship rights. In a petition to the General Court in 1780 the Cuffe brothers, pointing out that they had "no vote or influence in the election with those that tax us," asked to be relieved from the duty of paying taxes. As a part of their running battle with the authorities, these two black brothers had refused to pay their taxes in 1778, 1779, and 1780. On his copy of the petition of 1780 John Cuffe wrote, "This is a copy of the petitions which we did deliver unto the honorable council and house for relief from taxation in the days of our distress. But we received none."

Accordingly, the authorities issued a warrant for the arrest of the Cuffe brothers. They were taken to the common jail in Taunton from which, after two hours, they were released on a writ of habeas corpus. After delays and postponements of their trial the young dissidents reluctantly agreed to pay their taxes and court costs in June 1781, and their case was dismissed. Four months before the British surrendered at Yorktown, Virginia, the free Negro brothers had surrendered at Taunton, Massachusetts. What they gave up had been a central issue in the war. The claim of no taxation without representation clearly did not extend to them.

It may be understandable, if regrettable, that the colonists could not bring themselves to incorporate the principles of human freedom into their struggle for political independence. After all, property was a central consideration in their immediate struggle; and to have taken a stand against slavery would be to take a stand against the very principle for which they perceived themselves to be fighting. As David Brion Davis has observed, a free society was by no means incom-

patible with dependent classes of workers. He could have added, of course, that a truly free society *is* incompatible with a slave society, one consisting not merely of dependent workers, but of chattel slaves, unless some free men in that society are so callous as to define freedom in a way that denies it to one-fourth of the population. In any case, the colonists had come to terms with a definition of their social order in which freedom was to be ensured to those who already had it; and the risk of undermining the entire social order, and especially property rights, was too great to extend it to human beings who happened to be property.

This explains not only the attitude toward slavery of the colonists and the Revolutionary leaders but the attitude of the framers of the Constitution as well. By 1787 the institution of slavery was more deeply entrenched than ever in the five slave states of the South. Meanwhile, some steps had been taken to arrange for the gradual abolition of slavery in some of the Northern states.

But even in the North the rhetoric of freedom was related to the dependence of Massachusetts, Connecticut, and Rhode Island manufacturers of rum and the elaborately organized program and practice of the merchants and shippers on slavery and the slave trade. Small wonder that they tolerated, even supported, provisions in the new Constitution to return fugitive slaves to their owners and to permit the slave trade for at least another twenty years. Of the slave trade provision, James Wilson, the learned delegate from Pennsylvania who had wanted to end the slave trade completely, acquiesced. He said, "If there was no other lovely feature in the Constitution but this one, it would diffuse a beauty over its whole countenance." Then, he confidently but naively predicted that since new states would be under the control of Congress, slavery would never be introduced among them.

It was one thing to reconcile the rhetoric of political freedom to the maintenance of Negro slavery, as incongruous as it may appear to the liberal, enlightened, or merely logical mind. It was quite another to withhold the elementary rights of political and economic freedom from persons—in this case, black persons—who were already free or who were becoming free. And yet this is precisely what the new national government and most of the state governments were doing. In 1790 Congress enacted a law limiting naturalization to white aliens, thus suggesting that blacks who were imprudent enough to enter the United States could not expect ever to become citizens. In 1792 Congress authorized the organization of a militia and restricted enrollment to ablebodied white citizens, thus declaring to the 5,000 Negroes who had fought in the War for Independence that their services were no longer required. In 1802

Congress, in a law signed by Jefferson, excluded blacks from carrying the United States mail, a gratuitous expression of distrust of free Negroes or an indication that mail carriers occupied a position of social respectability that should not be violated by the presence of blacks. And to confuse the issue completely, the House of Representatives in 1803 passed a resolution to inquire into the expediency "of granting protection to such American seamen citizens of the United States, as are free persons of color."

When Congress undertook the task of establishing a government for the new capital at Washington, it made certain that free blacks were not only excluded from participating in the affairs of that government but also that they would be reminded constantly of their degraded position. It specified that only free white males were eligible to be the mayor or to sit on the Board of Aldermen or the Board of the Common Council. The franchise, moreover, was restricted to free white males. The Board of Aldermen and other officials were to "restrain and prohibit the nightly and other disorderly meetings of slaves, free negroes, and mulattoes, and to punish such slaves by whipping . . . or by imprisonment not exceeding three months . . . and to punish free negroes and mulattoes, by penalties not exceeding twenty dollars for any one offence, and in case of the inability of such free negro or mulatto to pay such penalty and cost thereon, to cause him or her to be confined to labor for anytime not exceeding six calendar months." No state or local government, from whatever part of the country at whatever time in the nineteenth or twentieth century could have been more unequivocal than the First, Second, Eleventh, and Sixteenth Congresses of the United States in making certain that free persons who were also black were deprived of every semblance of equality within the legal and political system.

This is the new federal government that had pushed through the very first Congress the bill of rights that so many critics had demanded as they considered the ratification of the new Constitution. This was the new federal government dominated by Washington, Jefferson, Adams, Hamilton, Madison, Gallatin, Monroe, and other fighters for the rights of men. This was the new federal government to which the state and local governments were beginning to look for guidance on such matters as equal rights and even-handed justice. The example was there as far as racial equality was concerned, and most of them followed it, especially since it was consonant with practices they were already following.

In Massachusetts, where the question of Negro suffrage was unclear and where, as we have seen, two free persons of color had been jailed because they protested against being deprived of the ballot in 1781, there was general hostility to black aliens. And following the guidelines laid down in federal legislation, Boston authorities in 1800 ordered the immediate deportation of 240 Negroes from the state. In New Jersey they could be banished from the state if convicted of any crime more serious than petty larceny, and in any case they could not travel beyond their home county without a certificate proving their freedom. Even in the new state of Ohio, a law of 1807 barred free Negroes unless they presented a court certificate as evidence of their freedom and posted a $500 bond guaranteeing their good behavior. Even where slavery was dead or dying, racial equality did not exist; and there was no indication that the country was the least bit interested in moving toward it.

People who experience unequal treatment because of their race, religion, or national origin and are generally powerless to secure protection of the law, frequently look to some informal arrangement, some gesture of sympathetic understanding, or some custom that may grant them relief. And there are times when, as a result of the compassion, outrage, or whim of the more powerful, they are successful. The pages of history are filled with such acts of simple justice, without which life would hardly be tolerable for the despised and disinherited. But by the very nature of things, such hapless supplicants are just as often rejected in their quest for some expression of understanding on the part of persons or groups more advantageously placed. This happened so often to free persons of color that at times many must have been driven to the point of desperation.

By the time the Constitution was written in Philadelphia, the free blacks of that city, numbering about 2,500, were a solid and stable element in the community. They performed all kinds of domestic and common labor and much of the skilled labor. There were, moreover, some notable leaders, such as James Derham, whom Benjamin Rush called a "very learned" physician, Richard Allen, a talented spiritual leader of his people, and James Forten, a well-to-do sail maker, whom Anthony Benezet described as "a gentleman by nature, easy in manner and able in intercourse." They compared favorably with any other small, distinctive group in a city of almost a hundred thousand; and it was reasonable for them to expect civil treatment.

Richard Allen is credited with having increased Negro attendance at St. George's Methodist Episcopal Church in Philadelphia. When he began to use the facilities of the church for morning services at five o'clock, before the blacks reported for duty in the white homes, there was no objection. Indeed, his religious zeal was praised by the elders and trustees. As the number of Negroes attending regular services increased, however, the white members took steps to separate the blacks from the whites. First, blacks were seated in the rear and on the sides, but apparently this separation was not sufficient from the point of view of the whites.

In November 1787 it was announced that Negroes who attended St. George's would be seated in the gallery. When Allen and his group arrived they dutifully went to the gallery and proceeded to sit on the front rows. As they knelt to join in the prayer that was in progress, the white trustees began to tug at them, commanding them to move to the rear seats in the gallery. The blacks requested permission to complete their prayers, but the whites would not relent. When the prayers were over, as Allen reported, "all [of the blacks] went out of the church in a body and they were no more plagued with us in the church." Two months after the Constitution had been completed in Philadelphia, there was little evidence of Christian brotherhood in the City of Brotherly Love.

One can speculate on whether the denial of equality to a group is more painful to its members than it is to an individual who is singled out for such dubious distinction. If the group experiences the pain of humiliation, it can unite and take steps to protect its members from a repetition of the experience. That is what Allen and his group did in founding Bethel African Methodist Episcopal Church. Benjamin Banneker had no such recourse, and his bitterness over slights and condescension is abundantly clear in his writings. Banneker, a Maryland free Negro, had become quite proficient in mathematics and astronomy and in March 1791 had been engaged to assist in surveying the new District of Columbia. Although Jefferson, as Secretary of State, had some role in selecting persons to survey the District, Banneker could hardly have been unacquainted with the Secretary's views on the inferiority of Negroes. Perhaps he had not read the *Notes on Virginia,* already in print for almost a decade. But he would surely have been aware that the announcement of his own appointment in the Georgetown *Weekly Ledger* hailed it as proof that "Mr. Jefferson's concluding that that race of men were void of mental endowment was without foundation."

When Banneker published his first almanac in the fall of 1791, he sent Jefferson a copy. In an accompanying, polite letter he could not conceal his bitterness, some of which must have been occasioned by his knowledge of Jefferson's racial views. He appealed to Jefferson to "embrace every opportunity, to eradicate that train of absurd and false ideas and opinions that blacks were scarcely capable of mental endowments which so generally prevails with respect to us." To make certain Jefferson felt the full burden of his responsibilities as a white man and as a slaveholder, Banneker reminded him it was "the indispensable duty of those, who maintain for themselves the right of human nature, and who possess the obligations of Christianity, to extend their power and influence to the relief of every part of the human race, from whatever burden or

oppression they may unjustly labor under." Banneker did not presume to tell Jefferson by what methods the black people could be relieved of their degradation but he did recommend that "you and all others . . . wean yourselves from those narrow prejudices which you have imbibed."

Jefferson sent a courteous but ambiguous letter of thanks in which he assured Banneker that "No body wishes more than I do to see such proofs as you exhibit, that nature has given to our black brethren, talents equal to those of the other colors of men." In sending the almanac to his friend the Marquis de Condorcet, he noted that he would be delighted to *see* "these instances of moral eminence so multiplied as to prove to them that the want of talents observed in them is merely the effect of their degraded condition, and not proceeding from any difference in the structure of the parts on which intellect depends." Since Jefferson, of all people, held firmly to the view that the "moral sense" and the faculties of intellect were two quite separate entities, I am inclined to agree with Winthrop Jordan that what Jefferson said "simply made no sense."

Jefferson had his doubts not only about the mental capabilities of blacks but also about their intellectual honesty. He had told Condorcet about "very elegant solutions of Geometrical problems" by Banneker, but he told his friend Joel Barlow that Banneker's work was "not without suspicion of aid from Ellicot," Banneker's white friend and sponsor. He had cast a similar doubt regarding Phillis Wheatley, the Negro poetess, by discussing her poems as works "written under her name." In any case he declared that she was not a poet, but twenty years later he admitted that "of all men I am the last who should undertake to decide as to the merits of poetry." One would have thought that Jefferson could not have it both ways, but apparently he thought that he could.

There were later occasions when Jefferson's position on the problem of race made no sense. During his presidency he maintained a discreet silence on all matters pertaining to slavery, insisting that "Should an occasion ever occur in which I can interpose with decisive effect, I shall certainly know and do my duty with promptitude and zeal." The time never came. After he left the presidency, he declined to speak out, insisting that his views "had long since been in possession of the public," and in any case the younger generation seemed apathetic on the subject. Earlier, however, when he asserted that the cause of emancipation had the support of "nearly the whole of the young men as fast as they come into public life" he never even acknowledged the existence of the Virginia Abolition Society.

When Jefferson retired to Monticello and his exquisite surroundings and his vast retinue of slaves, he argued that the enterprise of opposing slavery was for the young. In 1785 he had expressed the hope that the way was preparing "under the auspices of heaven, for a total emancipation." By 1820 he could only despair that in the controversy over Missouri, Americans had a "wolf by the ears, and we can neither hold him, nor safely let him go. Justice is in one scale, and self-preservation in the other." It is clear that for Jefferson self-preservation was uppermost in his mind.

In some far-off day, perhaps, Americans would be courageous enough and strong enough to take the wolf by the ears and subdue him. Meanwhile, there was very little that could be done except to follow the counsel that Jefferson gave to Edward Coles, one of his young protégés, to remain in Virginia and take good care of his slaves. "I hope . . . you will reconcile yourself to your country and its unfortunate condition." If this was the best that the Revolution's quintessential egalitarian had to offer, one could hardly expect any better dream of equality from his fellows. New York's James Tallmadge had a better dream in 1819, when he sought to exclude slavery from the new state of Missouri. With the defect of slavery and inequality, Tallmadge told his colleagues in the House of Representatives, "your Government must crumble to pieces, and your people become the scoff of the world." Jefferson called the proposal a cheap Federalist party trick. "The leaders of federalism," he asserted, "defeated in their schemes of obtaining power by rallying partisans to the principle of monarchism . . . have changed their tack, and thrown out another barrel to the whale." One difficulty with Jefferson's analysis was that Tallmadge, who wanted to prohibit the spread of slavery, was not a Federalist but a member of Jefferson's own party! Whatever the motives of the Northerners—Democrats or Federalists—it was hardly becoming to one who for almost fifty years had been waiting for the opportunity to strike a blow for freedom to say, once again, that the time was not yet ripe.

The issue was as confusing fifty years after the Declaration of Independence as it had been in 1776. When men argued that blacks were innately inferior, they were not addressing the point at issue. It was, of course, unseemly for men of the Enlightenment, ardent in their adherence to the principles of science, to discuss texture of hair and alleged body odors as sound bases on which to make decisions regarding the fate of a people. When there were scarcely any opportunities for Negroes to learn to read and write and cipher, it would not seem to be a profound discovery that they could not trace and comprehend the investigations of Euclid. But the real point at issue was twofold: The first was whether slaves should be treated as property or men. If they were men, Gouverneur Morris had said to the Constitutional Convention, then make them citizens and let them vote. The view of Virginia's George Mason and his supporters prevailed, however, and the

Constitution did nothing to indicate that blacks were equal to others in the enjoyment of their rights.

The second point was whether blacks who were free should be treated as other free persons. In the first fifty years of the nation's history the dominant view was that they should not be. In the South free Negroes were nothing less than pariahs, while in the North they were an oppressed and underprivileged minority. Even if men did not violate the Constitution in maintaining slavery, they clearly violated it in denying full citizenship rights to free blacks.

The Revolutionary dream of equality of all peoples was deferred by the necessity, as the Founding Fathers saw it, of protecting the inviolability of property and maintaining a stable social order. It was also deferred because of the pervasive view that a man not only had to be free, but also white, in order to enjoy equality or even to aspire to it. Perhaps the men of the Revolution, in passing on to some later generation the task of solving the problem of race, did not know how difficult it would become in later years. It remained for those living two centuries later to discover that the intervening years would render the problem even more difficult to solve.

In this Bicentennial year, sixty-two windows were broken in the Chicago home of a young black nurse, who discovered that her property was not inviolable when it happened to be in a neighborhood whose ethnic purity was threatened by her presence. That same week our government warned Cuba against engaging in adventures in Africa, but no one warned the domestic hoodlums or even reminded them that the Revolution was fought to protect private property if not human freedom. In this Bicentennial year a black citizen of Boston was beaten up by white hoodlums near the city hall. When the mayor observed the bleeding man, whom he knew, he warned him that when it was *his* turn to be on top, he should deal more kindly with the Puerto Ricans than he had been dealt with. The mayor, who recounted the incident on public television, did not indicate whether or not his black friend responded. But the victim could have told the mayor that for two hundred years his black ancestors had been waiting their turn not to be on top or to engage in violence but merely to experience the inalienable right of equality. Each succeeding wave of newcomers had in time moved ahead of the blacks to the point where they could enjoy that dignity of existence that only equality in a free society can provide. For him and his ancestors the dream of equality was always deferred.

What happens to a dream deferred?

Does it dry up
like a raisin in the sun?

Or fester like a sore—
And then run?
Does it stink like rotten meat?
Or crust and sugar over—
like a syrupy sweet?

Maybe it just sags
like a heavy load.

Or does it explode?

FROM THE *CONSTITUTION OF THE UNITED STATES*

The Bill of Rights and Amendments

The Preamble

We, the people of the United States, in order to form a more perfect union, establish justice, insure domestic tranquility, provide for the common defense, promote the general welfare, and secure the blessings of liberty to ourselves and our posterity, do ordain and establish this Constitution for the United States of America.

Constitutional Amendments

Article I

Congress shall make no law respecting an establishment of religion, or prohibiting the free exercise thereof; or abridging the freedom of speech, or of the press; or the right of the people peaceably to assemble, and to petition the government for a redress of grievances.

Article II

A well-regulated militia being necessary to the security of a free state, the right of the people to keep and bear arms shall not be infringed.

Article III

No soldier shall, in time of peace, be quartered in any house, without the consent of the owner, nor in time of war, but in a manner to be prescribed by law.

Article IV

The right of the people to be secure in their persons, houses, papers, and effects against unreasonable searches and seizures shall not be violated, and no warrants shall issue, but upon probable cause, supported by oath or affirmation, and particularly describing the place to be searched, and the persons or things to be seized.

Article V

No person shall be held to answer for a capital or otherwise infamous crime, unless on a presentments or indictment of a grand jury, except in cases arising in the land or naval forces, or in the militia, when in actual service in time of war or public danger; nor shall any person be subject for the same offense to be twice put in jeopardy of life or limb; nor shall be compelled in any criminal case to be a witness against himself, nor be deprived of life, liberty, or property, without due process of law; nor shall private property be taken for public use, without just compensation.

Article VI

In all criminal prosecutions, the accused shall enjoy the right to a speedy and public trial, by an impartial jury of the state and district wherein the crime shall have been committed, which district shall have been previously ascertained by law, and to be informed of the nature and cause of the accusation; to be confronted by the witnesses against him; to have compulsory process for obtaining witnesses in his favor, and to have the assistance of counsel for his defense.

Article VII

In suits at common law, where the value in controversy shall exceed twenty dollars, the right in any court of the United States, than according to the rules of the common law.

Article VIII

Excessive bail shall not be required, nor excessive fines imposed, nor cruel and unusual punishments inflicted.

Article IX

The enumeration in the Constitution, a certain rights, shall not be construed to deny or disparage others retained by the people.

Article X

The powers not delegated to the United States by the Constitution, nor prohibited by it to the states, are reserved to the states respectively, or to the people.

Other Amendments

Article XIII   (Proposed in February and ratified by December 1865.)

Section 1.   Neither slavery nor involuntary servitude, except as a punishment for crime whereof the party shall have been duly convicted, shall exist within the United States, or any place subject to their jurisdiction.

Section 2.   Congress shall have power to enforce this article by appropriate legislation.

Article XIV (Proposed in 1866 and ratified in July 1868.)

Section 1.   All persons born or naturalized in the United States, and subject to the jurisdiction thereof, are citizens of the United States and of the state wherein they reside. No state shall make or enforce any law which shall abridged the privileges or immunities of citizens of the United States; nor shall any state deprive any person of life, liberty, or property, without due process of law; nor to deny to any person within its jurisdiction the equal protection of the laws.

Section 2.   Representatives shall be apportioned among the several states according to their respective numbers, counting the whole number of persons in each state, excluding Indians not taxed. But when the right to vote at any election for the choice of electors for President and Vice President of the United States, Representatives in Congress, the executive and judicial officers of the state, or the members of the legislature thereof, is denied to any of the male inhabitants of such state, being twenty-one years of age, and citizens of the United States, or in any way abridged, except for participation in rebellion, or other crime, the basis of representation therein shall be reduced in the proportion which the number of such male citizens shall bear to the whole number of male citizens twenty-one years of age in such state.

Section 3.   No person shall be a Senator or Representative in Congress, or elector of President and Vice-President, or hold any office, civil or military, under the United States, or under any state, who, having previously taken an oath, as a member of Congress, or as an officer of the United States, or as a member of any state legislature, or as an executive or judicial officer of any state, to support the Constitution of the United States, shall have engaged in insurrection or rebellion against the same, or given aid or comfort to the enemies thereof. But Congress may, by a vote of two-thirds of each House, remove such disability.

Section 4.   The validity of the public debt of the United States, authorized by law, including debts incurred for payment of pensions and bounties for services in suppressing insurrection or rebellion, shall not be questioned. But neither the United States nor any state shall assume or pay any debt or obligation incurred in aid of insurrection or rebellion against the United States, or any claim for the loss or emancipation of any slave; but all such debts, obligations, and claims shall be held illegal and void.

Section 5.   The Congress shall have power to enforce by appropriate legislation, the provisions of this article.

Article XV   (Proposed in 1869 and ratified in 1870.)

Section 1.   The right of citizens of the United States to vote shall not be denied or abridged by the United States or by any state on account of race, color, or previous condition of servitude.

Section 2.   The Congress shall have power to enforce this article by appropriate legislation.

Article XIX (Proposed in 1919 and ratified in 1920.)

Section 1.   The right of citizens of the United States to vote shall not be denied or abridged by the United States or by any state on account of sex.

Section 2.   The Congress shall have power to enforce this article by appropriate legislation.

Articles of the Constitution of the United States *Referring to Slavery and the Rights of Slaves*

Article 1, Section 2, Item 3

Representatives and direct taxes shall be apportioned among the several States which may be included within this Union according to their respective numbers, which shall be determined by adding to the whole number of free persons, including those bound to service for a term of years, and excluding Indians not taxed, three-fifths of all other persons. The actual enumeration shall be made within three years after the first meeting of the Congress of the United States, and within every subsequent term of ten years, in such manner as they shall by law direct. The number of representatives shall not exceed one for every thirty thousand, but each State shall have at least one Representative.

Article 1, Section 9, Item 1

The migration or importation of such persons as any of the states now existing shall think proper to admit shall not be prohibited by the Congress, prior to the year one thousand eight hundred and eight, but a tax or duty may be imposed on such importation, not exceeding ten dollars for each person.

Article 4, Section 2, Item 3

No person held in service or labor in one State under the laws thereof, escaping into another shall in consequence of any law or regulation therein, be discharged from such service or labor, but shall be delivered up on claim of the party to whom such service or labor may be due.

THE OPINION OF CHIEF JUSTICE ROGER BROOKE TANEY

The Dred Scott Decision of the United States Supreme Court, March 6, 1857

As a slave, Dred Scott (1795–1858) was inventoried under the name of "Sam" among the property of Peter Blow. When sold later to Dr. John Emerson, "Sam," an extremely short man, was named, as a whim, Dred Scott after the tall and imposing General Winfield Scott. Later, Dr. Emerson purchased for Scott a wife called Harriet and they had two children, Eliza and Lizzie, who were born in the Louisiana Territory and above the line where slavery, according to the Missouri Compromise, was permitted. Presenting evidence that they had been living in a "free state" as defined by the Missouri Compromise and claiming, therefore, that they were not subject to claims of ownership by another, the Scotts filed suit at the state level in 1853 which, having been reviewed by lower courts, finally was considered by the United States Supreme Court. Although the Supreme Court could have dismissed the suit by noting that Dred Scott, by virtue of his parentage, had no rights of citizenship, it heard the case in order to proffer its position on the national de-

bate relative to defining slaves as property and declared finally the Missouri Compromise unconstitutional.

It is maintained that the following Opinion of Chief Justice Roger Brooke Taney is in accordance with the Constitution:

"... The Territory being a part of the United States, the Government and the citizen both enter it under the authority of the Constitution, with their respective rights defined and marked out; and the Federal Government can exercise no power over his person or property beyond what that instrument confers, nor lawfully deny any right which it had reserved ...

"... the rights of private property are united with the rights of person, and placed on the same ground by the fifth amendment to the Constitution, which provides that no person shall be deprived of life, liberty, and property, without due process of law. And an act of Congress which deprives a citizen of the United States of his liberty or property, merely because he came himself or brought his property into a particular Territory of the United

Dred Scott (Courtesy of the Moorland-Spingarn Research Center)

States, and who had committed no offence against the laws, could hardly be dignified with the name due process of law . . .

". . . the powers of the Government, and the rights of the citizen under it, are positive and practical regulations plainly written down . . . And if the Constitution recognizes the right of property of the master in a slave, and makes no distinction between that description of property and other property owned by a citizen, no tribunal, acting under the authority of the United States, whether it be legislative, executive or judicial, has a right to draw such a distinction, of deny to it the benefit of the provisions and guarantees which have been provided for the protection of private property against the encroachments of the Government.

"Now . . . the right of property in a slave is distinctly and expressly affirmed in the Constitution. The right to traffic in it, like any ordinary article of merchandise and property, was guaranteed to the citizens of the United States, in every State that might desire it, for twenty years. And the Government in express terms is pledged to protect it in all future time, if the slave escape from his owner. This is done in plain words—too plain to be misunderstood . . .

". . . it is the opinion of the court that the act of Congress which prohibited a citizen from holding and owning property of this kind in the territory of the United States north of the line therein mentioned, is not warranted by the Constitution, and is therefore void; and that neither Dred Scott himself, nor any of his family, were made free by being carried into this territory; . . ."

ABRAHAM LINCOLN

Emancipation Proclamation by the President of the United States of America: A Proclamation

January 1, 1863

Whereas, on the twenty-second day of September, in the year of our Lord one thousand-eight hundred and sixty two, a proclamation was issued by the President of the United States, containing, among other things, the following, to wit:

"That on the first day of January, in the year of our Lord one thousand eight hundred and sixty-three, all persons held as slaves within any State or designated part of a State, the people whereof shall then be in rebellion against the United States, shall be then, thenceforward, and forever free; and the Executive

Government of the United States, including the military and naval authority thereof, will recognize and maintain the freedom of such persons, and will do no act or acts to repress such persons, or any of them in any efforts they may make for their actual freedom.

"That the Executive will, on the first day of January aforesaid, by proclamation, designate the States and parts of States, if any, in which the people thereof, respectively, shall then be in rebellion against the United States; and the fact that any State, or the people thereof, shall on that day be, in good faith, represented in the Congress of the United States by members chosen thereto at elections wherein a majority of the qualified voters of such State shall have participated, shall, in the absence of strong countervailing testimony, be deemed conclusive evidence that such State, and the people thereof, are not then in rebellion against the United States."

Now, therefore, I, Abraham Lincoln, President of the United States, by virtue of the power in me vested as Commander-in-Chief, of the Army and Navy of the United States in time of actual armed rebellion against authority and government of the United States, and as a fit and necessary war measure for suppressing said rebellion, do, on this first day of January, in the year of our Lord one thousand eight hundred and sixty three, and in accordance with my purpose so to do publicly proclaimed for the full period of one hundred days, from the day first above mentioned, order and designate as the States and parts of States where in the people thereof respectively, are this day in rebellion against the United States, the following towit:

Arkansas, Texas, Louisiana, (except the Parishes of St. Bernard, Plaquemines, Jefferson, St. Johns, St. Charles, St. James [,] Ascension, Assumption, Terrebonne, Lafourche, St. Mary, St. Martin, and Orleans, including the City of New Orleans) Mississippi, Alabama, Florida, Georgia, South-Carolina, North-Carolina, and Virginia, (except the fortyeight counties designated as West Virginia, and also the counties of Berkley, Accomac, Northampton, Elizabeth-City, York, Princess Ann, and Norwalk, including the cities of Norfolk & Portsmouth [)]; and which excepted parts are, for the present, left precisely as if this proclamation were not issued.

And by virtue of the power, and for the purpose aforesaid, I do order and declare that all persons held as slaves within said designated States, and parts of States, are, and henceforward, shall be free; and that the Executive government of the United States, including the military and naval authorities thereof, will recognize and maintain the freedom of said persons.

And I hereby enjoin upon the people so declared to be free to abstain from all violence, unless in necessary self-defence; and I recommend to them that, in all cases when allowed, they labor faithfully for reasonable wages.

And I further declare and make known, that such persons of suitable condition, will be received into the armed service of the United States to garrison forts, positions, stations, and other places, and to man vessels of all sorts in said service.

And upon this act, sincerely believed to be an act of justice, warranted by the Constitution, upon military necessity, I invoke the considerate judgment of mankind, and the gracious favor of Almighty God.

In witness whereof, I have hereunto set my hand and caused the seal of the United States to be affixed.

Done at the city of Washington, this first day of January, in the year of our Lord one thousand eight hundred and sixty three, and of the Independence of the United States of America the eighty-seventh.

JAMES M. MCPHERSON

Who Freed The Slaves?

If we were to go out on the streets of almost any town in America and ask the question posed by the title of this article, probably nine out of ten respondents would unhesitatingly answer, "Abraham Lincoln." Most of them would cite the Emancipation Proclamation as the key document. Some of the more reflective and better informed respondents would add the Thirteenth Amendment and point to Lincoln's important role in its adoption. And a few might qualify their answer by noting that without military victory the Emancipation Proclamation would never have been adopted, or at least would not have applied to the states where most of the slaves were held. But, of course, Lincoln was commander-in-chief of Union armies, so the credit for their victories would belong mainly to him. The answer would still be the same: Lincoln freed the slaves.

In recent years, though, this answer has been challenged as another example of elitist history, of focusing only on the actions of great white males and ignoring the actions of the overwhelming majority of the people, who also make history. If we were to ask our question of professional historians, we would receive a reply quite different from that described above. For one thing, it would not be simple or clear cut. Many of them would answer along the lines of "On the one hand . . . but on the other." They would speak of ambivalence, ambiguity, nuances, paradox, irony. They would point to Lincoln's gradualism, his slow and apparently reluctant decision for emancipation, his revocation of emancipation orders by Generals John C. Frémont and David Hunter, his exemption of border

states and parts of the Confederacy from the Emancipation Proclamation, his statements seemingly endorsing white supremacy. They would say that the whole issue is more complex than it appears—in other words, many historians, as is their wont, would not give a straight answer to the question.

But of those who did, a growing number would reply, as did an historian speaking to the Civil War Institute at Gettysburg two years ago: "THE SLAVES FREED THEMSELVES." They saw the Civil War as a potential war for abolition well before Lincoln did. By voting with their feet for freedom—by escaping from their masters to Union military camps in the South they forced the issue of emancipation on the Lincoln administration. By creating a situation in which northern officials would either have to return them to slavery or acknowledge their freedom, these "contrabands," as they came to be called, "acted resolutely to place their freedom—and that of their posterity—on the wartime agenda." Union officers, then Congress, and finally Lincoln decided to confiscate this human property belonging to the enemy and put it to work for the Union in the form of servants, teamsters, laborers, and eventually soldiers in northern armies. Weighed in the scale of the Civil War, these 190,000 black soldiers and sailors (and probably a larger number of black army laborers) tipped the balance in favor of Union victory. Even deep in the Confederate interior remote from the fighting fronts, with the departure of masters and overseers to the army, "leaving women and old men in charge, the balance of power gradually shifted in favor of slaves, undermining slavery on farms and plantations far from the line of battle."

The foremost exponent of the black self-emancipation theme is the historian and theologian Vincent Harding whose book *There is a River: The Black Struggle for Freedom in America*, published in 1981, has become almost a Bible for the argument. "While Lincoln continued to hesitate about the legal, constitutional, moral, and military aspects of the matter," Harding writes, "the relentless movement of the self-liberated fugitives into the Union lines" soon "approached and surpassed every level of force previously known. . . . Making themselves an unavoidable military and political issue . . . this overwhelming human movement . . . of self-freed men and women . . . took their freedom into their own hands." The Emancipation Proclamation, when it finally and belatedly came, merely "confirmed and gave ambiguous legal standing to the freedom which black people had already claimed through their own surging, living proclamations."

During the past decade this self-emancipation theme has become so pervasive among social historians that it has virtually achieved the status of the orthodox interpretation. The largest scholarly enterprise on the history of emancipation and the transition from a slave to a free society during the Civil War era, the Freedmen and Southern Society Project at the University of Maryland, has stamped its imprimatur on this interpretation. The slaves, write the editors of this project, were "the prime movers in securing their own liberty." The Columbia University historian Barbara J. Fields gave wide publicity to this thesis. On camera in the PBS television documentary "The Civil War" and in an essay in the lavishly illustrated volume accompanying the series, she insisted that "freedom did not come to the slaves from words on paper, either the words of Congress or those of the President, but from the initiative of the slaves" themselves. "It was they who taught the nation that it must place the abolition of slavery at the head of its agenda. . . . The slaves themselves had to make their freedom real."

Two important corollaries of the self-emancipation thesis are the arguments, first, that Lincoln hindered more than he helped the cause, and second, that the image of him as the great Emancipator is a myth created by whites to deprive blacks of credit for achieving their own freedom and making their own history. This "reluctant ally of black freedom," Harding remarks, "played an actively conservative role in a situation which . . . needed to be pushed toward its most profound revolutionary implications." Lincoln repeatedly "placed the preservation of the white Union above the death of black slavery"; even as late as August 1852, when he wrote his famous letter to Horace Greeley stating that "if I could save the Union without freeing any slave, I would do it," he was, Harding writes, "still trapped in his own obsession with saving the white Union at all costs, even the cost of continued black slavery." By exempting one-third of the South from the Emancipation Proclamation, Barbara Fields observes, "Lincoln was more determined to retain the goodwill of the slave owners than to secure the liberty of the slaves." Despite Lincoln, though, "no human being alive could have held back the tide that swept toward freedom" by 1863. Nevertheless, Harding laments, "while the concrete historical realities of the time testified to the costly, daring, courageous activities of hundreds of thousands of black people breaking loose from slavery and setting themselves free, the myth gave the credit for this freedom to a white republican president." By this myth, "the independent, radical action of the black movement toward freedom . . . was diminished, and the coerced, ambiguous role of a white deliverer . . . gained preeminence." University of Pennsylvania historian Robert Engs goes even farther; he thinks the "fiction" that " 'Massa Lincoln' freed the slaves" was a sort of tacit conspiracy among whites to convince blacks that "white America, personified by Abraham Lincoln, had *given* them their freedom [rather] than

allow them to realize the empowerment that their taking of it implied. The poor, uneducated freedman fell for that masterful propaganda stroke. But so have most of the rest of us, black and white, for over a century!"

How valid are these statements? First, we must recognize the considerable degree of truth in the main thesis. By coming into Union lines, by withdrawing their labor from Confederate owners, by working for the Union army and fighting as soldiers in it, slaves did play an active part in achieving their own freedom and, for that matter, in preserving the Union. Like workers, immigrants, women, and other so-called "non-elites," the slaves were neither passive victims nor pawns of powerful white males who loom so large in our traditional image of American history. They, too, played a part in determining their own destiny; they, too, made a history that historians have finally discovered. That is all to the good. But by challenging the "myth" that Lincoln freed the slaves, proponents of the self-emancipation thesis are in danger of creating another myth—that he had little to do with the destruction of slavery. It may turn out, upon close examination, that the traditional answer to the question "Who Freed the Slaves?" is closer to being the right answer than is the new and currently more fashionable answer.

First, one must ask what was the *siné qua non* of emancipation in the 1860s—the essential condition, the absolute prerequisite, the one thing without which it would not have happened. The clear answer is: the war. Without the Civil War there would have been no confiscation act, no Emancipation Proclamation, no Thirteenth Amendment (not to mention the Fourteenth and Fifteenth), certainly no self-emancipation, and almost certainly no end of slavery for several more decades at least. Slavery had existed in North America for more than two centuries before 1861, but except for a tiny fraction of slaves who fought in the Revolution, or escaped, or bought their freedom, there had been no self-emancipation during that time. Every slave insurrection or insurrection conspiracy failed in the end. On the eve of the Civil War, plantation agriculture was more profitable, slavery more entrenched, slave owners more prosperous, and the "slave power" more dominant within the South if not in the nation at large than it had ever been. Without the war, the door to freedom would have remained closed for an indeterminate length of time.

What brought war and opened that door? The answer, of course, is complex as well as controversial. A short and simple summary is that secession and the refusal of the United States government to recognize the legitimacy of secession brought on the war. In both of these matters Abraham Lincoln moves to center stage. Seven states seceded and formed the Confederacy because he won election to the presidency on an antislavery platform; four more seceded after shooting broke out when he refused to evacuate Fort Sumter; the shooting escalated to full-scale war because he called out troops to suppress rebellion. The common denominator in all the steps that opened the door to freedom was the decision making of Abraham Lincoln acting as antislavery political leader, president-elect, president, and commander-in-chief.

The statement quoted above, that Lincoln "placed the preservation of the white Union above the death of black slavery," while true in a narrow sense, is highly misleading when shorn of its context. From 1854, when he returned to politics, until nominated for president in 1860, the dominant, unifying theme of Lincoln's career was opposition to the expansion of slavery as the vital first step toward placing it on the course of ultimate extinction. A student of Lincoln's oratory has estimated that he gave 175 political speeches during those six years. The "central message" of these speeches showed Lincoln to be a "one-issue" man—the issue being slavery. Repeatedly, Lincoln denounced slavery as a "monstrous injustice," "an unqualified evil to the negro, to the white man, to the soil, and to the State." He attacked his main political rival, Stephen A. Douglas, for his "*declared* indifference" to the moral wrong of slavery. Douglas "*looks to no end of the institution of slavery*," said Lincoln. "That is the real issue. That is the issue that will continue in this country when these poor tongues of Judge Douglas and myself shall be silent. It is the eternal struggle between these two principles—right and wrong—throughout the world. . . . One is the common right of humanity and the other the divine right of kings. . . . No matter in what shape it comes, whether from the mouth of a king who seeks to bestride the people of his own nation and live by the fruit of their labor, or from one race of men as an apology for enslaving another race, it is the same tyrannical principle." The principles of the Declaration of Independence and the principle of slavery, said Lincoln, "cannot stand together. . . . Our republican robe is soiled" by slavery. "Let us repurify it. . . . Let us readopt the Declaration of Independence, and with it, the practices, and policy, which harmonize with it. . . . If we do this, we shall not only have saved the Union; but we shall have so saved it, as to make, and to keep it, forever worthy of the saving."

Southerners read Lincoln's speeches; they knew by heart his words about the house divided and the ultimate extinction of slavery. Lincoln's election in 1860 was a sign that they had lost control of the national government; if they remained in the Union, they feared that ultimate extinction of their way of life would be their destiny. That is why they seceded. It was not merely Lincoln's election, but his election as a *principled opponent of slavery on moral grounds* that precipitated secession. Militant abolitionists critical of

Lincoln for falling short of their own standard nevertheless recognized this truth.

No longer would the slave power rule the nation, said Frederick Douglass. "Lincoln's election has vitiated their authority, and broken their power." "We have passed the Rubicon," said Wendell Phillips. "For the first time in our history the *slave* has chosen a President of the United States." Without Lincoln's election, southern states would not have seceded in 1861, the war would not have come when and as it did, the door of emancipation would not have been opened as it was. Here, certainly, was an event that qualifies as a *siné qua non*, and it proceeded more from the ideas and agency of Abraham Lincoln than from any other single cause.

But, we must ask, would not the election of *any* Republican in 1860 have precipitated secession? Probably not, if the candidate had been Edward Bates, who might conceivably have won the election but had not even an outside chance of winning the nomination. Yes, almost certainly, if William H. Seward had been the nominee. Seward's earlier talk of a "higher law" and an "irrepressible conflict" had given him a more radical reputation than Lincoln. But Seward might not have won the election. More to the point, if he had won, seven states would undoubtedly have seceded. But Seward would have favored compromises and concessions to keep others from going out and perhaps to lure those seven back in. Most important of all, he would have evacuated Fort Sumter and thereby extinguished the spark that threatened to flame into war. As it was, Seward did his best to compel Lincoln into concessions and evacuation. But Lincoln stood firm. When Seward flirted with the notion of supporting the Crittenden Compromise, which would have repudiated the Republican platform by permitting the expansion of slavery, Lincoln stiffened the backbones of Seward and other key Republican leaders. "Entertain no proposition for a compromise in regard to the *extension* of slavery," he wrote to them. "The tug has to come, & better now, than any time hereafter." Crittenden's compromise "would lose everything we gained by the election." The proposal for concessions, Lincoln pointed out, "acknowledges that slavery has equal rights with liberty, and surrenders all we have contended for. . . . We have just carried an election on principles fairly stated to the people. Now we are told in advance, the government shall be broken up, unless we surrender to those we have beaten. . . . If we surrender, it is the end of us. They will repeat the experiment upon us *ad libitum*. A year will not pass, till we shall have to take Cuba as a condition upon which they will stay in the Union."

It is worth emphasizing here that the common denominator in these letters from Lincoln to Republican leaders was slavery. To be sure, on the matters of slavery where it already existed and enforcement of the fugitive slave provision of the Constitution, Lincoln was willing to reassure the South. But on the crucial issue of 1860, slavery in the territories, he refused to compromise, and this refusal kept his party in line. Seward, or any other man who might conceivably have been elected president in 1860, would have pursued a different course. This sheds a different light on the assertion that Lincoln "placed the preservation of the white Union above the death of black slavery." The Crittenden Compromise did indeed place preservation of the Union above the death of slavery. So did Seward; so did most white Americans during the secession crisis. But that assertion does *not* describe Lincoln. He refused to yield the core of his antislavery philosophy to stay the breakup of the Union. As Lincoln expressed it in a private letter to his old friend Alexander Stephens, "You think slavery is *right* and ought to be extended; while we think it is *wrong* and ought to be restricted. That I suppose is the rub." It was indeed the rub. Even more than in his election to the presidency, Lincoln's refusal to compromise on the expansion of slavery or on Fort Sumter proved decisive. If any other man had been in his position, the course of history—and of emancipation—would have been different. Here again we have without question a *siné qua non*.

It is quite true, of course, that once the war started, Lincoln moved more slowly and reluctantly toward making it a war for emancipation than black leaders, abolitionists, radical Republicans, and the slaves themselves wanted him to move. He did reassure southern whites that he had no intention and no constitutional power to interfere with slavery in the states. In September 1861 and May 1862, he revoked orders by Generals Frémont and Hunter freeing the slaves of Confederates in their military districts. In December 1861 he forced Secretary of War Cameron to delete a paragraph from his annual report recommending the freeing and arming of slaves. And though Lincoln signed the confiscation acts of August 1861 and July 1862 that provided for freeing some slaves owned by Confederates, this legislation did not come from his initiative. The initiative was taken out in the field by slaves who escaped to Union lines and officers like General Benjamin Butler who accepted them as "contraband of war."

All of this appears to support the thesis that slaves emancipated themselves and that Lincoln's image as emancipator is a myth. But let us take a closer look. It seems clear today, as it did to people in 1861, that no matter how many thousands of slaves came into Union lines, the ultimate fate of the millions who did not, as well as the fate of the institution of slavery itself, depended on the outcome of the war. If the North won, slavery would be weakened if not destroyed; if the Con-

federacy won, slavery would survive and perhaps grow stronger from the postwar territorial expansion of an independent and confident slave power. Thus Lincoln's emphasis on the priority of Union had positive implications for emancipation, while precipitate or premature actions against slavery might jeopardize the cause of Union and therefore boomerang in favor of slavery.

Lincoln's chief concern in 1861 was to maintain a united coalition of War Democrats and border-state Unionists as well as Republicans in support of the war effort. To do this he considered it essential to define the war as being waged solely for Union, which united this coalition, and not a war against slavery, which would fragment it. When General Frémont issued his emancipation edict in Missouri, on August 30, 1861, the political and military efforts to prevent Kentucky, Maryland, and Missouri from seceding and to cultivate Unionists in western Virginia and eastern Tennessee were at a crucial stage, balancing on a knife edge. If he had let Frémont's order stand, explained Lincoln to his old friend Senator Orville Browning of Illinois, it would have been "popular in some quarters, and would have been more so if it had been a general declaration of emancipation." But this would have lost the war by driving Kentucky into secession. "I think to lose Kentucky is nearly the same as to lose the whole game. Kentucky gone, we can not hold Missouri, nor, as I think, Maryland. These all against us, and the job on our hands is too large for us. We would as well consent to separation at once, including the surrender of this capitol."

There is no reason to doubt the sincerity and sagacity of this statement. Lincoln's greatest skills as a political leader were his sensitivity to public opinion and his sense of timing. He understood that while a majority of Republicans by the spring of 1862 favored a war against slavery, a decided majority of his Union coalition did not. During those spring months he alternately coaxed and prodded border-state Unionists toward recognition of the inevitable escalation of the conflict into a war against slavery and toward acceptance of his plan for compensated emancipation in their states. He warned southern Unionists and northern Democrats that he could not fight this war "with elder-stalk squirts, charged with rose water. . . . This government cannot much longer play a game in which it stakes all, and its enemies stake nothing. Those enemies must understand that they cannot experiment for ten years trying to destroy the government, and if they fail still come back into the Union unhurt."

Lincoln's meaning, though veiled, was clear; he was about to add the weapon of emancipation to his arsenal. When he penned these warnings, in July 1862, he had made up his mind to issue an emancipation proclamation. Whereas a year earlier, even three months earlier, Lincoln had believed that avoidance of the emancipation issue was necessary to maintain that knife-edge balance in the Union coalition, things had now changed. The war had escalated in scope and fury, mobilizing all the resources of both sides, including the slave labor force of the Confederacy. The imminent prospect of Union victory in the spring had been shredded by Robert E. Lee's successful counteroffensive in the Seven Days. The risks of alienating the border states and northern Democrats were now outweighed by the opportunity to energize the Republican majority and to mobilize part of the slave population for the cause of Union—and freedom. Lincoln was now convinced that emancipation was "a military necessity, absolutely essential to the preservation of the Union." "The slaves," he told his cabinet, were "undeniably an element of strength to those who had their service, and we must decide whether that element should be with us or against us." Lincoln had earlier hesitated to act against slavery in the states because the Constitution protected it there. But most slaves were the property of enemies waging war against the United States, and "the rebels," said Lincoln, "could not at the same time throw off the Constitution and invoke its aid. . . . Decisive and extensive measures must be adopted. . . . We [want] the army to strike more vigorous blows. The Administration must set an example, and strike at the heart of the rebellion"—slavery. Montgomery Blair, speaking for the forces of conservatism in the North and border states, warned of the consequences among these groups of an emancipation proclamation. But Lincoln was done conciliating these elements. He had tried to make the border states see reason; now "we must make the forward movement" without them. "They will acquiesce, if not immediately, soon." As for the northern Democrats, "their clubs would be used against us take what course we might."

In 1864, speaking to a visiting delegation of abolitionists, Lincoln explained why he had moved more slowly against slavery than they had urged. Having taken an oath to preserve and defend the Constitution, which protected slavery, "I did not consider that I had a *right* to touch the 'State' institution of 'Slavery' until all other measures for restoring the Union had failed. . . . The moment came when I felt that slavery must die that the nation might live! . . . Many of my strongest supporters urged *Emancipation* before I thought it indispensable, and, I may say, before I thought the country ready for it. It is my conviction that, had the proclamation been issued even six months earlier than it was, public sentiment would not have sustained it."

Lincoln actually could have made a case that the country had not been ready for the Emancipation Proclamation in September 1862, even in January 1863. Democratic gains in the northern congressional elections in the fall of 1869 resulted in part from a voter backlash against the preliminary Emancipation Proclamation. The crisis in morale in the Union armies and swelling Copperhead strength during the winter of 1863 grew in part from a resentful conviction that Lincoln had unconstitutionally transformed the purpose of the war from restoring the Union to freeing the slaves. Without question, this issue bitterly divided the North and threatened fatally to erode support for the war effort—the very consequence Lincoln had feared in 1861 and that Montgomery Blair feared in 1862. Not until after the twin military victories at Gettysburg and Vicksburg did this divisiveness diminish and emancipation gain a clear mandate in the off-year elections of 1863. In his annual message of December 1863, Lincoln acknowledged that his Emancipation Proclamation a year earlier had been "followed by dark and doubtful days." But now, he added, "the crisis which threatened to divide the friends of the Union is past."

Even that statement turned out to be premature and optimistic. In the summer of 1864, northern morale again plummeted and the emancipation issue once more threatened to undermine the war effort. By August, Grant's campaign in Virginia had bogged down in the trenches after enormous casualties, while Sherman seemed similarly stymied. War weariness and defeatism corroded the will of northerners as they contemplated the staggering cost of this conflict in the lives of their young men. Lincoln came under enormous pressure to open peace negotiations to end the slaughter. Even though Jefferson Davis insisted that Confederate independence was his essential condition for peace, northern democrats managed to convince a great many northern people that only Lincoln's insistence on emancipation blocked peace. A typical Democratic newspaper editorial declared that "tens of thousands of white men must yet bite the dust to allay the negro mania of the President."

Even Republicans like Horace Greeley, who had criticized Lincoln two years earlier for slowness to embrace emancipation, now criticized him for refusing to abandon it as a precondition for negotiations. The Democratic national convention adopted a platform for the 1864 presidential election calling for peace negotiations to restore the Union with slavery. Every political observer, including Lincoln himself, believed in August that the Republicans would lose this election. The *New York Times* editor and Republican national chairman Henry Raymond told Lincoln that "two special causes are assigned [for] this great reaction in public sentiment—the want of military success, and the impression . . . that we *can* have peace with Union if we would . . . [but that you are] fighting not for Union but for the abolition of slavery."

The pressure on Lincoln to back down on emancipation caused him to waver temporarily, but not to buckle. Instead, he told weak-kneed Republicans that "no human power can subdue this rebellion without using the Emancipation lever as I have done." Some 130,000 soldiers and sailors were fighting for the Union, Lincoln noted. They would not do so if they thought the North intended to "betray them. . . . If they stake their lives for us they must be prompted by the strongest motive . . . the promise of freedom. And the promise being made, must be kept. . . . There have been men who proposed to me to return to slavery the black warriors" who had fought for the Union. "I should be damned in time & in eternity for so doing. The world shall know that I will keep my faith to friends and enemies, come what will."

When Lincoln said this, he fully expected to lose the presidential election. In effect, he was saying that he would rather be right than president. In many ways this was his finest hour. As matters turned out, of course, he was both right and president. Sherman's capture of Atlanta, Sheridan's victories in the Shenandoah Valley, and military success elsewhere transformed the northern mood from deepest despair in August 1864 to determined confidence by November, and Lincoln was triumphantly reelected. He won without compromising one inch on the emancipation question.

It is instructive to consider two possible alternatives to this outcome. If the Democrats had won, at best the Union would have been restored without a Thirteenth Amendment; at worst the Confederacy would have achieved its independence. In either case the institution of slavery would have survived. That this did not happen was owing more to the steadfast purpose of Abraham Lincoln than to any other single factor.

The proponents of the self-emancipation thesis, however, would avow that all of this is irrelevant. If it is true, as Barbara Fields maintains, that by the time of the Emancipation Proclamation "no human being alive could have held back the tide that swept toward freedom," that tide must have been even more powerful by the fall of 1864. But I disagree. The tide of freedom could have been swept back. On numerous occasions during the war, when Union forces were compelled to retreat from areas of the Confederacy where their presence had attracted and liberated contrabands, the tide of slavery closed in behind them. Lee's army captured dozens of black people in Pennsylvania in June 1863 and sent them back South into slavery. Hundreds of black Union soldiers captured by Confederate forces were reenslaved. Lincoln himself took note of this phe-

nomenon when he warned that if "the pressure of the war should call off our forces from New Orleans to defend some other point, what is to prevent the masters from reducing the blacks to slavery again; for I am told that whenever the rebels take any black prisoners, free or slave, they immediately auction them off!" The editors of the Freedmen's and Southern Society Project, the most scholarly advocates of the self-emancipation thesis, concede that "Southern armies could recapture black people who had already reached Union lines. . . . Indeed, any Union retreat could reverse the process of liberation and throw men and women who tasted freedom back into bondage. . . . Their travail testified to the link between the military success of the Northern armies and the liberty of Southern slaves."

Precisely. That is the crucial point. Slaves did not emancipate themselves; they were liberated by Union armies. Liberation quite literally came from the barrel of a gun. And who was the commander-in-chief that called these armies into being, appointed their generals, and gave them direction and purpose? There, indubitably, is our *siné qua non*.

But let us acknowledge that once the war was carried into slave territory, no matter how it came out, the ensuing "friction and abrasion" (as Lincoln once put it) would enable thousands of slaves to escape to freedom. In that respect, a degree of self-emancipation *did* occur. But even on a large scale, such emancipation was very different from *the abolition of the institution of slavery*. That required Union victory; it required Lincoln's reelection in 1864; it required the Thirteenth Amendment. Lincoln played a vital role, indeed the central role, in all of these achievements. It was also his policies and his skillful political leadership that set in motion the processes by which the reconstructed or Unionist states of Louisiana, Arkansas, Tennessee, Maryland, and Missouri abolished the institution in those states during the war itself.

Regrettably, Lincoln did not live to see the final ratification of the Thirteenth Amendment. But if he had *never* lived, it seems safe to say that we would not have had a Thirteenth Amendment in 1865. In that sense, the traditional answer to the question "Who freed the slaves?" is the right answer. Lincoln did not accomplish this in the manner sometimes symbolically portrayed, breaking the chains of helpless and passive bondsmen with the stroke of a pen by signing the Emancipation Proclamation. But by pronouncing slavery a moral evil that must come to an end and then winning the Presidency in 1860, provoking the South to secede, refusing to compromise on the issue of slavery's expansion or on Fort Sumter, knitting together a Unionist coalition in the first year of war and committing it to emancipation in the second, refusing to compromise this policy once he had adopted it, and prosecuting the war to unconditional victory as commander-in-chief of an army of liberation, Abraham Lincoln freed the slaves.

PAUL FINKELMAN

The Union Army's Fighting 54th

They left Boston on May 28, 1863, with bayonets glistening, buttons shining brightly and glory in their eyes. This was the Massachusetts 54th Regiment, the first black regiment organized in the North during the Civil War. At the head of the regiment was Col. Robert Gould Shaw, the son of a prominent white abolitionist. The troops were black, the officers were white. That fact underscores the limited role for blacks in the Union Army even though blacks were armed. At the same time, it showed a measure of interracial cooperation. Blacks and whites could train together and fight together. Soon they would die together.

The troops marched down Beacon Street to be reviewed by the governor and cheered by crowds. It was a day for hope and pride. From the beginning of the war two years earlier, northern blacks had offered their services to the nation. Now, at last, the first regiment of northern blacks was on its way to the front—to South Carolina, the birthplace of the war and home of the most ardent secessionists and most passionate defenders of slavery. There free blacks from the North would first do battle.

Technically, the 54th was a Massachusetts unit. The soldiers' bounties were paid by the Bay State. The regiment was organized by Gov. John A. Andrew, an abolitionist committed to the idea that black freedom would only have meaning if won by black soldiers.

In reality, the 54th was a truly national regiment. Black men from all over the North volunteered for the regiment. Fugitive slaves returned from Canada for the chance to take up arms against their former oppressors. Some southern slaves and free blacks made their way to Boston to sign on. Most of the soldiers were common men, laborers, farmers, waiters, blacksmiths, carpenters. But some were from the elite of northern black society—among them Lewis and Charles Douglass, sons of the black abolitionist Frederick Douglass. This was not just another Massachusetts regiment: This was black America's regiment.

The Massachusetts 54th is the most famous black regiment in our military history. It is not famous for its great battlefield victories; rather, it is known for its

bravery in defeat and the circumstances surrounding that defeat. In the ill-fated attack on Fort Wagner in Charleston, S.C., Col. Shaw would die, along with about 150 of his troops. Another hundred would be captured. Before turning to the history of that charge, it is important to examine the events preceding the creation of the 54th and other black units in the Union Army.

When the war began, President Lincoln called for volunteers to save the nation. Blacks throughout the North stepped forward. Even before the firing of the first shot at Fort Sumter, Levin Tilmon, a black resident of New York City, wrote to Lincoln, offering to organize "colored volunteers." Shortly after the shooting started, Jacob Dodson, a black resident of Washington, D.C., informed Secretary of War Simeon Cameron that 300 blacks in the capital were ready to help defend the city.

Black men across the country were ready to serve. In May 1861, less than a month after the war began, Frederick Douglass wrote in his abolitionist newspaper that the way to win the war, and win it quickly, was to "LET THE SLAVES AND FREE COLORED PEOPLE BE CALLED INTO SERVICE, AND FORMED INTO A LIBERATING ARMY." Douglass predicted that 10,000 northern blacks could be recruited and in the field within a month. Private black militias were already training in preparation for the war.

Douglass' advice and the offers of numerous other blacks to serve, however, were rejected. In 1861 the war was not over slavery but over the Union. As such, it was to be a "white man's war." That, at least, was the official line. And so, officially, Lincoln and his secretary of war had no use for black troops.

Lincoln could not afford to make the war a crusade against slavery. To do so in 1861 would have sent the border slave states, such as Maryland, Kentucky, Missouri and Delaware, into the Confederacy.

Lincoln also knew that accepting black troops in 1861 would have undermined morale in the North. White prejudice against black soldiers centered on three sets of ideas and values. First, many whites believed blacks incapable of serving in the military. Accepting racist stereotypes of the era, they thought blacks could not learn military discipline, close-order drill or even how to care for their weapons. These whites predicted that black soldiers would break ranks under fire. Other whites were more concerned about the threat black soldiers posed to white supremacy. If you put a uniform on a man and gave him a gun, it would be hard then to deny him equal citizenship. Finally, there was simple prejudice.

Consequently, black offers to serve the Union cause were rejected. Officially the war remained a white man's war throughout 1861 and early 1862. Unofficially, some blacks served in individual units.

In Kansas, Brig. Gen. James H. Lane's units were integrated almost from the beginning of the war. Veterans of "Bleeding" Kansas would take any soldier who volunteered. They knew, from firsthand experience, that blacks could and would fight.

Lane said that fugitive slaves entered his camps "looking down" and fearful. But, "By-and-by they begin to straighten themselves, throw back their shoulders, stand erect, and soon look God straight in the face . . ." Soon, they were soldiers. "Give them a fair chance, put arms in their hands, and they will do the balance of the fighting in this war." Long before it was official policy, blacks in Kansas, including runaway slaves from Missouri and Arkansas, were fighting for not only the Union but for freedom.

In May 1862, Gen. David Hunter organized former slaves into the 1st South Carolina Volunteer Regi-

Detail of Augustus Saint Gaudens' bronze relief-tribute to the 54th Regiment entitled Robert Gould Shaw Memorial *(Michael Miller)*

ment, but this unit was quickly disbanded when the President refused to approve Hunter's actions.

The color line, however, was about to fall. In July 1862 Congress passed the Militia Act, which authorized the enlistment of black soldiers and, significantly, the emancipation of the families of any slaves leaving their Confederate masters and enlisting in the Army. Yet, even as the color line fell in one area, it rose in another. The act provided that black soldiers, no matter what their rank, be paid only $7 a month. White privates earned $13 a month, while corporals, sergeants and officers earned considerably more. The Massachusetts 54th refused all pay until August 1864, when Congress finally retroactively equalized their pay from the time of their enlistment.

By the time the Militia Act took effect, President Lincoln had written, but not yet announced, the Emancipation Proclamation. Freedom and the enlistment of black troops were on the horizon.

In September 1862 Gen. Benjamin Butler, acting under the Militia Act, began to organize three black regiments in New Orleans, which he and Adm. David Farragut had captured the previous April. Butler first turned to the large free black population in Louisiana, asking for volunteers for the Union army. He was driven more by events than ideology. Abolitionists in the North were demanding black troops to garrison south Louisiana. Significantly, his 1st Regiment of Louisiana Native Guards had black and mulatto officers. Shortly after Butler organized his units in Louisiana, Gen. Rufus Saxton organized the 1st South Carolina Colored Volunteers, a unit made up entirely of former slaves. Meanwhile, the 1st Kansas Colored was fighting in Missouri. In the South a revolution had begun.

On Jan. 1, 1863, Lincoln issued the Emancipation Proclamation and the war for the Union became the war for liberty. The War Department now officially endorsed proposals for the organization of black units in the North.

Massachusetts, with its abolitionist governor, was the first state to act. Gov. Andrew wanted a model for the world to see. He personally sought out Col. Robert Shaw and Lt. Col. Norwood P. Hallowell. These were battled-hardened veterans of other Massachusetts regiments. They would treat black troops with dignity and lead them with honor. Wealthy businessmen, prominent abolitionists and black leaders helped recruit soldiers not only in Massachusetts but throughout the North as well as in those parts of the South under Union control. Black activists, such as Martin Delany and Frederick Douglass (whose son, Lewis, was the first New Yorker to join the Massachusetts unit), recruited for the regiment, as did whites such as Wendell Phillips and William Lloyd Garrison. George Stearns, a wealthy abolitionist, used his personal fortune to send recruiters throughout the Union to raise a black regiment for the Bay State.

Arming former slaves in isolated areas in South Carolina or free blacks from Louisiana had little impact on the North. Abolitionists and supporters of equal rights wanted an effort on the home front that would breach the color line. The 54th led the way. By April its four companies were complete, but black recruits continued to arrive at the rate of 100 a week. Lt. Col. Hallowell was promoted to colonel of a second black regiment, the Massachusetts 55th.

By July the 54th was in South Carolina stationed on the Sea Islands near Charleston. Its first assignments were uneventful. They made a few raids against the mainland, including an attack on Darien, Ga.

From July 10 to 16, the 54th was part of an assault on James Island, in the Charleston harbor. On the night of July 16, the 54th was attacked by forces under the Confederate Gen. P.G.T. Beauregard. The attack was a surprise, intended to break the Union line. All that stood in the way of a Confederate victory was the untested 54th. Had the 54th given way, a regiment of Connecticut soldiers would have been caught in an indefensible position, unprepared for battle. But, the outnumbered 54th held, slowly giving ground, but neither panicking nor retreating. The Confederate attack failed. Fourteen men of the 54th died that night and another 13 were captured.

The commanding general, Alfred H. Terry, sent a message to Col. Shaw that he was "exceedingly pleased" with the 54th. A few days later a Connecticut newspaper story noted that "probably a thousand homes from Windham to Fairfield have in letters been told the story of how the dark-skinned heroes fought the good fight and covered with their own brave hearts the retreat of brothers, sons, and fathers of Connecticut." Doubts about the abilities of black soldiers no longer existed among the Union troops in South Carolina or the families and friends of the 10th Connecticut Volunteers.

After the battle, the 54th spent the next 48 hours being evacuated from James Island. With no food and little water, the men spent the entire day and night of July 17 waiting for transportation back to their main base. They arrived late afternoon on the 18th.

During the interim, the Union leadership decided to storm Fort Wagner, which guarded Charleston Harbor. The assault was an ill-conceived, poorly planned engagement. The commanding general asked Col. Shaw if he and his troops were able to lead the assault.

Shaw could have said no. Maybe he should have. His men had had no sleep and little food for the previous two days and nights. They were tired and hungry. Only two days earlier they had fought their first real battle. Now they were asked to be the vanguard of a charge against a fortified position. But, there was no hesitation among the officers or men. This was the chance for the soldiers to prove their worth in battle. The honor of black America was at stake. The men of the 54th sought glory, even if it meant death.

About 600 men from the 54th led a frontal assault on Fort Wagner. Behind them were white units from Connecticut, New York, New Hampshire, Maine and Pennsylvania. To reach the Fort, they had to cross about 200 yards of open beach, running through ocean that was knee deep, all the while under murderous fire from the fort. The Union command thought the fort was lightly manned with only 300 troops. In reality the Fort had about 1,700 defenders. Despite these circumstances the 54th breached the walls.

The second wave of troops—the white units—was late getting started, in part because of poor planning, in part because the 54th had reached the fort and breached the walls sooner than anyone expected they would.

For a few minutes the Stars and Stripes flew over this Confederate stronghold. But the handful of black soldiers were overwhelmed and outnumbered. Their officers were dead or wounded. Although black sergeants provided leadership, they could not provide the necessary firepower to sustain the charge. Before the other units attacked the fort, the first charge failed. Subsequent attackers did not even get close to the fort. It was a Union fiasco.

Before Fort Wagner whites had doubted the courage of black men. Would they run from battle? Would they cower in fear when facing their former masters? Could they obey orders? Could they fight? Could they die like men?

Northern whites—even those who hated blacks—could no longer doubt their courage. Abolitionists were thrilled. Northern blacks could hold their heads a little higher—their men had proven themselves a match for any soldier in bravery, honor and dignity.

During the battle Sgt. William H. Carney stood out even among the bravest. When a color bearer was shot down, Carney grabbed the flag and charged forward, waving it above the fray, rallying the troops and, for a short time, planting the star-spangled banner on the parapets of the rebel fort. When retreat became inevitable, Carney carried the flag back to the Union lines. He was wounded in the arms, the legs and the chest. But, he reported to his commanding officers, the flag had never touched the ground.

Carney was cited for bravery. He was the first black man to earn the Congressional Medal of Honor. During the war, 15 other black soldiers would earn this medal. Carney survived the battle and the entire war. Many of his comrades in the 54th were not so lucky.

When the battle at Fort Wagner was over, more than 250 of the 600 men of the 54th who had charged the fort were dead, captured or missing. Among the dead was Col. Robert Gould Shaw and three other officers.

The Confederates buried the Union dead of Fort Wagner. The bodies of those from other regiments were buried with dignity, as befitted soldiers. For the black men of the 54th, the Confederates dug a trench and dumped the bodies in. Col. Shaw was stripped of his uniform and thrown in with his men. The Confederate commander bragged: "He is buried with his niggers."

As news spread in the North of the 54th's gallantry and the death of Shaw, black enlistment increased tenfold. White respect for black troops increased even more dramatically.

When the war began it was a "white man's war" to save the Union. When the war ended, it had been transformed into a war of liberation. That freedom was partially won by those who had been slaves and those who were free only by the good fortune of their living in the North.

More than 180,000 black soldiers served the nation. About 130,000 of them came from the South and the border states, where they had been slaves before the war began. More than 37,000 black soldiers gave their lives for the Union cause. Sixteen blacks won the Congressional Medal of Honor for bravery. Many blacks won various other medals. An additional 200,000 or so blacks served in non-combatant roles as carpenters, blacksmiths, lumberjacks, teamsters, boat pilots, laborers, nurses, cooks and spies.

In the end, black soldiers made up about 10 percent of the Union Army. Their impact was somewhat greater because they came into the war in the last two years, when northern manpower sources were drying up. By helping to secure the Union victory blacks secured their own freedom. By fighting, and dying, side-by-side with whites, black soldiers disproved myths of racism and demonstrated that equality and integration were possible. Yet in the aftermath of the war many of these lessons were quickly forgotten or lost to history.

Plessy v. *Ferguson.*

Error to The Supreme Court of The State of Louisiana.

No. 210. Argued April 13, 1896.—Decided May 18, 1896.

The statute of Louisiana, acts of 1890, No. 111, requiring railway companies carrying passengers in their coaches in that State, to provide equal, but separate, accommodations for the white and colored races, by providing two or more passenger coaches for each passenger train, or by dividing the passenger coaches by a partition so as to secure separate accommodations; and providing that no person shall be permitted to occupy seats in coaches other than the ones assigned to them, on account of the race they belong to; and requiring the officers of the passenger trains to assign each passenger to the coach or compartment assigned for the race to which he or she belongs; and imposing fines or imprisonment upon passengers insisting on going into a coach or compartment other than the one set aside for the race to which he or she belongs; and conferring upon officers of the trains power to refuse to carry on the train passengers refusing to occupy the coach or compartment assigned to them, and exempting the railway company from liability for such refusal, are not in conflict with the provisions either of the Thirteenth Amendment or of the Fourteenth Amendment to the Constitution of the United States.

This was a petition for writs of prohibition and certiorari, originally filed in the Supreme Court of the State by Plessy, the plaintiff in error, against the Hon. John II. Ferguson, judge of the criminal District Court for the parish of Orleans, and setting forth in substance the following facts:

That petitioner was a citizen of the United States and a resident of the State of Louisiana, of mixed descent, in the proportion of seven eighths Caucasian and one eighth African blood; that the mixture of colored blood was not discernible in him, and that he was entitled to every recognition, right, privilege and immunity secured to the citizens of the United States of the white race by its Constitution and laws; that on June 7, 1892, he engaged and paid for a first class passage on the East Louisiana Railway from New Orleans to Covington, in the same State, and thereupon entered a passenger train, and took possession of a vacant seat in a coach where passengers of the white race were accommodated; that such railroad company was incorporated by the laws of Louisiana as a common carrier, and was not authorized to distinguish between citizens according to their race. But, notwithstanding this, petitioner was required by the conductor, under penalty of ejection from said train and imprisonment, to vacate said coach and occupy another seat in a coach assigned by said company for persons not of the white race, and for no other reason than that petitioner was of the colored race; that upon petitioner's refusal to comply with such order, he was, with the aid of a police officer, forcibly ejected from said coach and hurried off to and imprisoned in the parish jail of New Orleans, and there held to answer a charge made by such officer to the effect that he was guilty of having criminally violated an act of the General Assembly of the State, approved July 10, 1890, in such case made and provided.

That petitioner was subsequently brought before the recorder of the city for preliminary examination and committed for trial to the criminal District Court for the parish of Orleans, where an information was filed against him in the matter above set forth, for a violation of the above act, which act the petitioner affirmed to be null and void, because in conflict with the Constitution of the United States; that petitioner interposed a plea to such information, based upon the unconstitutionality of the act of the General Assembly, to which the district attorney, on behalf of the State, filed a demurrer; that, upon issue being joined upon such demurrer and plea, the court sustained the demurrer, overruled the plea, and ordered petitioner to plead over to the facts set forth in the information, and that, unless the judge of the said court be enjoined by a writ of prohibition from further proceeding in such case, the court will proceed to fine and sentence petitioner to imprisonment, and thus deprive him of his constitutional rights set forth in his said plea, notwithstanding the unconstitutionality of the act under which he was being prosecuted; that no appeal lay from such sentence, and petitioner was without relief or remedy except by writs of prohibition and certiorari. Copies of the information and other proceedings in the criminal District Court were annexed to the petition as an exhibit.

Upon the filing of this petition, an order was issued upon the respondent to show cause why a writ of prohibition should not issue and be made perpetual, and a further order that the record of the proceedings had in the criminal cause be certified and transmitted to the Supreme Court.

To this order the respondent made answer, transmitting a certified copy of the proceedings, asserting the constitutionality of the law, and averring that, instead of pleading or admitting that he belonged to the colored race, the said Plessy declined and refused, either by pleading or otherwise, to admit that he was in any sense or in any proportion a colored man.

The case coming on for a hearing before the Supreme Court, that court was of opinion that the law under which the prosecution was had was constitutional, and denied the relief prayed for by the petitioner. *Ex parte Plessy,* 45 La. Ann. 80. Whereupon petitioner prayed for a writ of error from this court which was allowed by the Chief Justice of the Supreme Court of Louisiana.

> *Mr. A. W. Tourgee* and *Mr. S. F. Phillips* for plaintiff in error. *Mr. F. D. McKenney* was on *Mr. Phillips's* brief.

> *Mr. James C. Walker* filed a brief for plaintiff in error.

> *Mr. Alexander Porter Morse* for defendant in error. *Mr. M. J. Cunningham,* Attorney General of the State of Louisiana, and *Mr. Lional Adams* were on his brief.

> Mr. Justice Brown, after stating the case, delivered the opinion of the court.

This case turns upon the constitutionality of an act of the General Assembly of the State of Louisiana, passed in 1890, providing for separate railway carriages for the white and colored races. Acts 1890, No. 111, p. 152.

The first section of the statute enacts "that all railway companies carrying passengers in their coaches in this State, shall provide equal but separate accommodations for the white, and colored races, by providing two or more passenger coaches for each passenger train, or by dividing the passenger coaches by a partition so as to secure separate accommodations: *Provided,* That this section shall not be construed to apply to street railroads. No person or persons, shall be admitted to occupy seats in coaches, other than, the ones, assigned, to them on account of the race they belong to."

By the second section it was enacted "that the officers of such passenger trains shall have power and are hereby required to assign each passenger to the coach or compartment used for the race to which such passenger belongs; any passenger insisting on going into a coach or compartment to which by race he does not belong, shall be liable to a fine of twenty-five dollars, or in lieu thereof to imprisonment for a period of not more than twenty days in the parish prison, and any officer of any railroad insisting on assigning a passenger to a coach or compartment other than the one set aside for the race to which said passenger belongs, shall be liable to a fine of twenty-five dollars, or in lieu thereof to imprisonment for a period of not more than twenty days in the parish prison; and should any passenger refuse to occupy the coach or compartment to which he or she is assigned by the officer of such railway, said officer shall have power to refuse to carry such passenger on his train, and for such refusal neither he nor the railway company which he represents shall be liable for damages in any of the courts of this State."

The third section provides penalties for the refusal or neglect of the officers, directors, conductors and employees of railway companies to comply with the act, with a proviso that "nothing in this act shall be construed as applying to nurses attending children of the other race." The fourth section is immaterial.

The information filed in the criminal District Court charged in substance that Plessy, being a passenger between two stations within the State of Louisiana, was assigned by officers of the company to the coach used for the race to which he belonged, but he insisted upon going into a coach used by the race to which he did not belong. Neither in the information nor plea was his particular race or color averred.

The petition for the writ of prohibition averred that petitioner was seven eighths Caucasian and one eighth African blood; that the mixture of colored blood was not discernible in him, and that he was entitled to every right, privilege and immunity secured to citizens of the United States of the white race; and that, upon such theory, he took possession of a vacant seat in a coach where passengers of the white race were accommodated, and was ordered by the conductor to vacate said coach and take a seat in another assigned to persons of the colored race, and having refused to comply with such demand he was forcibly ejected with the aid of a police officer, and imprisoned in the parish jail to answer a charge of having violated the above act.

The constitutionality of this act is attacked upon the ground that it conflicts both with the Thirteenth Amendment of the Constitution, abolishing slavery, and the Fourteenth Amendment, which prohibits certain restrictive legislation on the part of the States.

1. That it does not conflict with the Thirteenth Amendment, which abolished slavery and involuntary servitude, except as a punishment for crime, is too clear for argument. Slavery implies involuntary servitude—a state of bondage; the ownership of mankind as a chattel, or at least the control of the labor and services of one man for the benefit of another, and the absence of a legal right to the disposal of his own person, property and services. This amendment was said in the *Slaughter-house cases,* 16 Wall. 36, to have been intended primarily to abolish slavery, as it had been previously known in this country, and that it equally forbade Mexican peonage or the Chinese coolie trade, when they amounted to slavery or involuntary servitude, and that the use of the word "servitude" was intended to prohibit the use of all forms of involuntary slavery, of whatever class or name. It was intimated, however, in that case that this amendment was regarded by the statesmen of that day as insufficient to protect the colored race from certain laws which had been enacted in the Southern States, imposing upon the colored race onerous disabilities and burdens, and curtailing their rights in the pursuit of life, liberty and property to such an extent that their freedom was of little value; and that the Fourteenth Amendment was devised to meet this exigency.

So, too, in the *Civil Rights cases,* 109 U. S. 3, 24, it was said that the act of a mere individual, the owner of an inn, a public conveyance or place of amusement, refusing accommodations to colored people, cannot be justly regarded as imposing any badge of slavery or servitude upon the applicant, but only as involving an ordinary civil injury, properly cognizable by the laws of the State, and presumably subject to redress by those laws until the contrary appears. "It would be running the slavery argument into the ground," said Mr. Justice Bradley, "to make it apply to every act of discrimination which a person may see fit to make as to the guests he will entertain, or as to the people he will take into his coach or cab or car, or admit to his concert or theatre, or deal with in other matters of intercourse or business."

A statute which implies merely a legal distinction between the white and colored races—a distinction which is founded in the color of the two races, and which must always exist so long as white men are distinguished from the other race by color—has no tendency to destroy the legal equality of the two races, or reestablish a state of involuntary servitude. Indeed, we do not understand that the Thirteenth Amendment is strenuously relied upon by the plaintiff in error in this connection.

2. By the Fourteenth Amendment, all persons born or naturalized in the United States, and subject to the jurisdiction thereof, are made citizens of the United States and of the State wherein they reside; and the States are forbidden from making or enforcing any law which shall abridge the privileges or immunities of citizens of the United States, or shall deprive any person of life, liberty or property without due process of law, or deny to any person within their jurisdiction the equal protection of the laws.

The proper construction of this amendment was first called to the attention of this court in the *Slaughter-house cases,* 16 Wall. 36, which involved, however, not a question of race, but one of exclusive privileges. The case did not call for any expression of opinion as to the exact rights it was intended to secure to the colored race, but it was said generally that its main purpose was to establish the citizenship of the negro; to give definitions of citizenship of the United States and of the States, and to protect from the hostile legislation of the States the privileges and immunities of citizens of the United States, as distinguished from those of citizens of the States.

The object of the amendment was undoubtedly to enforce the absolute equality of the two races before the law, but in the nature of things it could not have been intended to abolish distinctions based upon color, or to enforce social, as distinguished from political equality, or a commingling of the two races upon terms unsatisfactory to either. Laws permitting, and even requiring, their separation in places where they are liable to be brought into contact do not necessarily imply the inferiority of either race to the other, and have been generally, if not universally, recognized as within the competency of the state legislatures in the exercise of their police power. The most common instance of this is connected with the establishment of separate schools for white and colored children, which has been held to be a valid exercise of the legislative power even by courts of States where the political rights of the colored race have been longest and most earnestly enforced.

One of the earliest of these cases is that of *Roberts v. City of Boston*, 5 Cush. 198, in which the Supreme Judicial Court of Massachusetts held that the general school committee of Boston had power to make provision for the instruction of colored children in separate schools established exclusively for them, and to prohibit their attendance upon the other schools. "The great principle," said Chief Justice Shaw, p. 206, "advanced by the learned and eloquent advocate for the plaintiff," (Mr. Charles Sumner,) "is, that by the constitution and laws of Massachusetts, all persons without distinction of age or sex, birth or color, origin or condition, are equal before the law. . . . But, when this great principle comes to be applied to the actual and various conditions of persons in society, it will not warrant the assertion, that men and women are legally clothed with the same civil and political powers, and that children and adults are legally to have the same functions and be subject to the same treatment; but only that the rights of all, as they are settled and regulated by law, are equally entitled to the paternal consideration and protection of the law for their maintenance and security." It was held that the powers of the committee extended to the establishment of separate schools for children of different ages, sexes and colors, and that they might also establish special schools for poor and neglected children, who have become too old to attend the primary school, and yet have not acquired the rudiments of learning, to enable them to enter the ordinary schools. Similar laws have been enacted by Congress under its general power of legislation over the District of Columbia, Rev. Stat. D. C. §§281, 282, 283, 310, 319, as well as by the legislatures of many of the States, and have been generally, if not uniformly, sustained by the courts. *State v. McCann*, 24 Ohio St. 198; *Lehew v. Brummell*, 15 S. W. Rep. 765; *Ward v. Flood*, 48 California, 36; *Bertonneau v. School Directors*, 3 Woods. 177; *People v. Gallagher*, 93 N. Y. 438; *Cory v. Carter*, 48 Indiana, 327; *Dawson v. Lee*, 83 Kentucky, 49.

Laws forbidding the intermarriage of the two races may be said in a technical sense to interfere with the freedom of contract, and yet have been universally recognized as within the police power of the State. *State v. Gibson*, 36 Indiana, 389.

The distinction between laws interfering with the political equality of the negro and those requiring the separation of the two races in schools, theatres and railway carriages has been frequently drawn by this court. Thus in *Strauder v. West Virginia*, 100 U. S. 303, it was held that a law of West Virginia limiting to white male persons, 21 years of age and citizens of the State, the right to sit upon juries, was a discrimination which implied a legal inferiority in civil society, which lessened the security of the right of the colored race, and was a step toward reducing them to a condition of servility. Indeed, the right of a colored man that, in the selection of jurors to pass upon his life, liberty and property, there shall be no exclusion of his race, and no discrimination against them because of color, has been asserted in a number of cases. *Virginia v. Rives*, 100 U. S. 313; *Neal v. Delaware*, 103 U. S. 370; *Bush v. Kentucky*, 107 U. S. 110; *Gibson v. Mississippi*, 162 U. S. 565. So, where the laws of a particular locality or the charter of a particular railway corporation has provided that no person shall be excluded from the cars on account of color, we have held that this meant that persons of color should travel in the same car as white ones, and that the enactment was not satisfied by the company's providing cars assigned exclusively to people of color, though they were as good as those which they assigned exclusively to white persons. *Railroad Company v. Brown*, 17 Wall. 445.

Upon the other hand, where a statute of Louisiana required those engaged in the transportation of passengers among the States to give to all persons travelling within that State, upon vessels employed in that business, equal rights and privileges in all parts of the vessel, without distinction on account of race or color, and subjected to an action for damages the owner of such a vessel, who excluded colored passengers on account of their color from the cabin set aside by him for the use of whites, it was held to be so far as it applied to interstate commerce, unconstitutional and void. *Hall v. De Cuir*, 95 U. S. 485. The court in this case, however, expressly disclaimed that it had anything whatever to do with the statute as a regulation of internal commerce, or affecting anything else than commerce among the States.

In the *Civil Rights case*, 109 U. S. 3, it was held that an act of Congress, entitling all persons within the jurisdiction of the United States to the full and equal enjoyment of the accommodations, advantages, facilities and privileges of inns, public conveyances, on land

or water, theatres and other places of public amusement, and made applicable to citizens of every race and
color, regardless of any previous condition of servitude, was unconstitutional and void, upon the ground
that the Fourteenth Amendment was prohibitory upon
the States only, and the legislation authorized to be
adopted by Congress for enforcing it was not direct
legislation on matters respecting which the States were
prohibited from making or enforcing certain laws, or
doing certain acts, but was corrective legislation, such
as might be necessary or proper for counteracting and
redressing the effect of such laws or acts. In delivering
the opinion of the court Mr. Justice Bradley observed
that the Fourteenth Amendment "does not invest Congress with power to legislate upon subjects that are
within the domain of state legislation; but to provide
modes of relief against state legislation, or state action,
of the kind referred to. It does not authorize Congress
to create a code of municipal law for the regulation of
private rights; but to provide modes of redress against
the operation of state laws, and the action of state officers, executive or judicial, when these are subversive of
the fundamental rights specified in the amendment.
Positive rights and privileges are undoubtedly secured
by the Fourteenth Amendment; but they are secured by
way of prohibition against state laws and state proceedings affecting those rights and privileges, and by
power given to Congress to legislate for the purpose
of carrying such prohibition into effect; and such legislation must necessarily be predicated upon such supposed state laws or state proceedings, and be directed
to the correction of their operation and effect."

Much nearer, and, indeed, almost directly in point,
is the case of the *Louisville, New Orleans &c. Railway*
v. *Mississippi*, 133 U. S. 587, wherein the railway company was indicted for a violation of a statute of Mississippi, enacting that all railroads carrying passengers
should provide equal, but separate, accommodations
for the white and colored races, by providing two or
more passenger cars for each passenger train, or by dividing the passenger cars by a partition, so as to secure
separate accommodations. The case was presented in
a different aspect from the one under consideration,
inasmuch as it was an indictment against the railway
company for failing to provide the separate accommodations, but the question considered was the constitutionality of the law. In that case, the Supreme Court
of Mississippi, 66 Mississippi, 662, had held that the
statute applied solely to commerce within the State,
and, that being the construction of the state statute by
its highest court, was accepted as conclusive. "If it be a
matter," said the court, p. 591, "respecting commerce
wholly within a State, and not interfering with commerce between the States, then, obviously, there is no

violation of the commerce clause of the Federal Constitution. . . . No question arises under this section, as to
the power of the State to separate in different compartments interstate passengers, or affect, in any manner,
the privileges and rights of such passengers. All that
we can consider is, whether the State has the power
to require that railroad trains within her limits shall
have separate accommodations for the two races; that
affecting only commerce within the State is no invasion of the power given to Congress by the commerce
clause."

A like course of reasoning applies to the case under
consideration, since the Supreme Court of Louisiana in
the case of the *State ex rel. Abbott* v. *Ilicks, Judge, et
al.*, 44 La. Ann. 770, held that the statute in question
did not apply to interstate passengers, but was confined
in its application to passengers travelling exclusively
within the borders of the State. The case was decided
largely upon the authority of *Railway Co.* v. *State*, 66
Mississippi, 662, and affirmed by this court in 133 U. S.
587. In the present case no question of interference with
interstate commerce can possibly arise, since the East
Louisiana Railway appears to have been purely a local
line, with both its termini within the State of Louisiana. Similar statutes for the separation of the two races
upon public conveyances were held to be constitutional
in *West Chester &c. Railroad* v. *Miles*, 55 Penn. St. 209;
Day v. *Owen*, 5 Michigan, 520; *Chicago &c. Railway*
v. *Williams*, 55 Illinois, 185; *Chesapeake &c. Railroad* v. *Wells*, 85 Tennessee, 613; *Memphis &c. Railroad* v. *Benson*, 85 Tennessee, 627; *The Sue*, 22 Fed.
Rep. 843; *Logwood* v. *Memphis &c. Railroad*, 23 Fed.
Rep. 318; *McGuinn* v. *Forbes*, 37 Fed. Rep. 639; *People*
v. *King*, 18 N. E. Rep. 245; *Houck* v. *South Pac. Railway*, 38 Fed. Rep. 226; *Heard* v. *Georgia Railroad Co.*,
3 Int. Com. Com'n, 111; S. C., 1 Ibid. 428.

While we think the enforced separation of the
races, as applied to the internal commerce of the State,
neither abridges the privileges or immunities of the
colored man, deprives him of his property without
due process of law, nor denies him the equal protection of the laws, within the meaning of the Fourteenth
Amendment, we are not prepared to say that the conductor, in assigning passengers to the coaches according to their race, does not act at his peril, or that the
provision of the second section of the act, that denies
to the passenger compensation in damages for a refusal
to receive him into the coach in which he properly belongs, is a valid exercise of the legislative power. Indeed, we understand it to be conceded by the State's
attorney, that such part of the act as exempts from liability the railway company and its officers is unconstitutional. The power to assign to a particular coach obviously implies the power to determine to which race

the passenger belongs, as well as the power to determine who, under the laws of the particular State, is to be deemed a white, and who a colored person. This question, though indicated in the brief of the plaintiff in error, does not properly arise upon the record in this case, since the only issue made is as to the unconstitutionality of the act, so far as it requires the railway to provide separate accommodations, and the conductor to assign passengers according to their race.

It is claimed by the plaintiff in error that, in any mixed community, the reputation of belonging to the dominant race, in this instance the white race, is *property,* in the same sense that a right of action, or of inheritance, is property. Conceding this to be so, for the purposes of this case, we are unable to see how this statute deprives him of, or in any way affects his right to, such property. If he be a white man and assigned to a colored coach, he may have his action for damages against the company, for being deprived of his so called property. Upon the other hand, if he be a colored man and be so assigned, he has been deprived of no property, since he is not lawfully entitled to the reputation of being a white man.

In this connection, it is also suggested by the learned counsel for the plaintiff in error that the same argument that will justify the state legislature in requiring railways to provide separate accommodations for the two races will also authorize them to require separate cars to be provided for people whose hair is of a certain color, or who are aliens, or who belong to certain nationalities, or to enact laws requiring colored people to walk upon one side of the street, and white people upon the other, or requiring white men's houses to be painted white, and colored men's black, or their vehicles or business signs to be of different colors, upon the theory that one side of the street is as good as the other, or that a house or vehicle of one color is as good as one of another color. The reply to all this is that every exercise of the police power must be reasonable, and extend only to such laws as are enacted in good faith for the promotion for the public good, and not for the annoyance or oppression of a particular class. Thus in *Yick Wo* v. *Hopkins,* 118 U. S. 356, it was held by this court that a municipal ordinance of the city of San Francisco, to regulate the carrying on of public laundries within the limits of the municipality, violated the provisions of the Constitution of the United States, if it conferred upon the municipal authorities arbitrary power, at their own will, and without regard to discretion, in the legal sense of the term, to give or withhold consent as to persons or places, without regard to the competency of the persons applying, or the propriety of the places selected for the carrying on of the business. It was held to be a covert attempt on the part of the municipality to make an arbitrary and unjust discrimination against the Chinese race. While this was the case of a municipal ordinance, a like principle has been held to apply to acts of a state legislature passed in the exercise of the police power. *Railroad Company* v. *Husen,* 95 U. S. 465; *Louisville & Nashville Railroad* v. *Kentucky,* 161 U. S. 677, and cases cited on p. 700; *Daggett* v. *Hudson,* 43 Ohio St. 548; *Capen* v. *Foster,* 12 Pick. 485; *State ex rel. Wood* v. *Baker,* 38 Wisconsin, 71; *Monroe* v. *Collins,* 17 Ohio St. 665; *Hulseman* v. *Rems,* 41 Penn. St. 396; *Orman* v. *Riley,* 15 California, 48.

So far, then, as a conflict with the Fourteenth Amendment is concerned, the case reduces itself to the question whether the statute of Louisiana is a reasonable regulation, and with respect to this there must necessarily be a large discretion on the part of the legislature. In determining the question of reasonableness it is at liberty to act with reference to the established usages, customs and traditions of the people, and with a view to the promotion of their comfort, and the preservation of the public peace and good order. Gauged by this standard, we cannot say that a law which authorizes or even requires the separation of the two races in public conveyances is unreasonable, or more obnoxious to the Fourteenth Amendment than the acts of Congress requiring separate schools for colored children in the District of Columbia, the constitutionality of which does not seem to have been questioned, or the corresponding acts of state legislatures.

We consider the underlying fallacy of the plaintiff's argument to consist in the assumption that the enforced separation of the two races stamps the colored race with a badge of inferiority. If this be so, it is not by reason of anything found in the act, but solely because the colored race chooses to put that construction upon it. The argument necessarily assumes that if, as has been more than once the case, and is not unlikely to be so again, the colored race should become the dominant power in the state legislature, and should enact a law in precisely similar terms, it would thereby relegate the white race to an inferior position. We imagine that the white race, at least, would not acquiesce in this assumption. The argument also assumes that social prejudices may be overcome by legislation, and that equal rights cannot be secured to the negro except by an enforced commingling of the two races. We cannot accept this proposition. If the two races are to meet upon terms of social equality, it must be the result of natural affinities, a mutual appreciation of each other's merits and a voluntary consent of individuals. As was said by the Court of Appeals of New York in *People* v. *Gallagher,* 93 N. Y. 438, 448, "this end can neither be accomplished nor promoted by laws which conflict with the general sentiment of the community upon whom they are designed to operate. When the government, therefore, has secured to each of its citizens equal rights before the law and equal opportunities for improvement and progress, it has accomplished the end for which it was organized and performed all of the functions respecting social advantages with which it is endowed." Legislation is powerless to eradicate racial instincts or to abolish distinctions based upon physical differences, and the attempt to do so can only result in accentuating the difficulties of the present situation. If the civil and political rights of both races be equal one cannot be inferior to the other civilly or politically. If one race be inferior to the other socially, the Constitution of the United States cannot put them upon the same plane.

It is true that the question of the proportion of colored blood necessary to constitute a colored person, as distinguished from a white person, is one upon which there is a difference of opinion in the different States, some holding that any visible admixture of black blood stamps the person as belonging to the colored race, (*State* v. *Chavers,* 5 Jones, [N. C.] 1, p. 11); others that it depends upon the preponderance of blood, (*Gray* v. *State,* 4 Ohio, 354; *Monroe* v. *Collins,* 17 Ohio St. 665); and still others that the predominance of white blood must only be in the proportion of three fourths. (*People* v. *Dean,* 14 Michigan, 406; *Jones* v. *Commonwealth,* 80 Virginia, 538.) But these are questions to be determined under the laws of each State and are not properly put in issue in this case. Under the allegations of his petition it may undoubtedly become a question of importance whether, under the laws of Louisiana, the petitioner belongs to the white or colored race.

The judgment of the court below is, therefore,

Affirmed.

Mr. Justice Harlan dissenting.

By the Louisiana statute, the validity of which is here involved, all railway companies (other than street railroad companies) carrying passengers in that State are required to have separate but equal accommodations for white and colored persons, "by providing two or more passenger coaches for each passenger train, *or* by dividing the passenger coaches by a *partition* so as to secure separate accommodations." Under this statute, no colored person is permitted to occupy a seat in a coach assigned to white persons; nor any white person, to occupy a seat in a coach assigned to colored persons. The managers of the railroad are not allowed to exercise any discretion in the premises, but are required to assign each passenger to some coach or compartment set apart for the exclusive use of his race. If a passenger insists upon going into a coach or compartment not set

apart for persons of his race, he is subject to be fined, or to be imprisoned in the parish jail. Penalties are prescribed for the refusal or neglect of the officers, directors, conductors and employees of railroad companies to comply with the provisions of the act.

Only "nurses attending children of the other race" are excepted from the operation of the statute. No exception is made of colored attendants travelling with adults. A white man is not permitted to have his colored servant with him in the same coach, even if his condition of health requires the constant, personal assistance of such servant. If a colored maid insists upon riding in the same coach with a white woman whom she has been employed to serve, and who may need her personal attention while travelling, she is subject to be fined or imprisoned for such an exhibition of zeal in the discharge of duty.

While there may be in Louisiana persons of different races who are not citizens of the United States, the words in the act, "white and colored races," necessarily include all citizens of the United States of both races residing in that State. So that we have before us a state enactment that compels, under penalties, the separation of the two races in railroad passenger coaches, and makes it a crime for a citizen of either race to enter a coach that has been assigned to citizens of the other race.

Thus the State regulates the use of a public highway by citizens of the United States solely upon the basis of race.

However apparent the injustice of such legislation may be, we have only to consider whether it is consistent with the Constitution of the United States.

That a railroad is a public highway, and that the corporation which owns or operates it is in the exercise of public functions, is not, at this day, to be disputed. Mr. Justice Nelson, speaking for this court in *New Jersey Steam Navigation Co.* v. *Merchants' Bank,* 6 How. 344, 382, said that a common carrier was in the exercise "of a sort of public office, and has public duties to perform, from which he should not be permitted to exonerate himself without the assent of the parties concerned." Mr. Justice Strong, delivering the judgment of this court in *Olcott* v. *The Supervisors,* 16 Wall. 678, 694, said: "That railroads, though constructed by private corporations and owned by them, are public highways, has been the doctrine of nearly all the courts ever since such conveniences for passage and transportation have had any existence. Very early the question arose whether a State's right of eminent domain could be exercised by a private corporation created for the purpose of constructing a railroad. Clearly it could not, unless taking land for such a purpose by such an agency is taking land for public use. The right of eminent domain nowhere justifies taking property for a private use. Yet it is a doctrine universally accepted that a state legislature may authorize a private corporation to take land for the construction of such a road, making compensation to the owner. What else does this doctrine mean if not that building a railroad, though it be built by a private corporation, is an act done for a public use?" So, in *Township of Pine Grove* v. *Talcott*, 19 Wall. 666, 676: "Though the corporation [a railroad company] was private, its work was public, as much so as if it were to be constructed by the State." So, in *Inhabitants of Worcester* v. *Western Railroad Corporation*, 4 Met. 564: "The establishment of that great thoroughfare is regarded as a public work, established by public authority, intended for the public use and benefit, the use of which is secured to the whole community, and constitutes, therefore, like a canal, turnpike or highway, a public easement." It is true that the real and personal property, necessary to the establishment and management of the railroad, is vested in the corporation; but it is in trust for the public."

In respect of civil rights, common to all citizens, the Constitution of the United States does not, I think, permit any public authority to know the race of those entitled to be protected in the enjoyment of such rights. Every true man has pride of race, and under appropriate circumstances when the rights of others, his equals before the law, are not to be affected, it is his privilege to express such pride and to take such action based upon it as to him seems proper. But I deny that any legislative body or judicial tribunal may have regard to the race of citizens when the civil rights of those citizens are involved. Indeed, such legislation, as that here in question, is inconsistent not only with that equality of rights which pertains to citizenship, National and State, but with the personal liberty enjoyed by every one within the United States.

The Thirteenth Amendment does not permit the withholding or the deprivation of any right necessarily inhering in freedom. It not only struck down the institution of slavery as previously existing in the United States, but it prevents the imposition of any burdens or disabilities that constitute badges of slavery or servitude. It decreed universal civil freedom in this country. This court has so adjudged. But that amendment having been found inadequate to the protection of the rights of those who had been in slavery, it was followed by the Fourteenth Amendment, which added greatly to the dignity and glory of American citizenship, and to the security of personal liberty, by declaring that "all persons born or naturalized in the United States, and subject to the jurisdiction thereof, are citizens of the United States and of the State wherein they reside," and that "no State shall make or enforce any law which shall abridge the privileges or immunities of citizens of the United States; nor shall any State deprive any person of life, liberty or property without due process of law, nor deny to any person within its jurisdiction the equal protection of the laws." These two amendments, if enforced according to their true intent and meaning, will protect all the civil rights that pertain to freedom and citizenship. Finally, and to the end that no citizen should be denied, on account of his race, the privilege of participating in the political control of his country, it was declared by the Fifteenth Amendment that "the right of citizens of the United States to vote shall not be denied or abridged by the United States or by any State on account of race, color or previous condition of servitude."

These notable additions to the fundamental law were welcomed by the friends of liberty throughout the world. They removed the race line from our governmental systems. They had, as this court has said, a common purpose, namely, to secure "to a race recently emancipated, a race that through many generations have been held in slavery, all the civil rights that the superior race enjoy." They declared, in legal effect, this court has further said, "that the law in the States shall be the same for the black as for the white; that all persons, whether colored or white, shall stand equal before the laws of the States, and, in regard to the colored race, for whose protection the amendment was primarily designed, that no discrimination shall be made against them by law because of their color." We also said: "The words of the amendment, it is true, are prohibitory, but they contain a necessary implication of a positive immunity, or right, most valuable to the colored race—the right to exemption from unfriendly legislation against them distinctively as colored—exemption from legal discriminations, implying inferiority in civil society, lessening the security of their enjoyment of the rights which others enjoy, and discriminations which are steps towards reducing them to the condition of a subject race." It was, consequently, adjudged that a state law that excluded citizens of the colored race from juries, because of their race and however well qualified in other respects to discharge the duties of jurymen, was repugnant to the Fourteenth Amendment. *Strauder* v. *West Virginia*, 100 U. S. 303, 306, 307; *Virginia* v. *Rives*, 100 U. S. 313; *Ex parte Virginia*, 100 U. S. 339; *Neal* v. *Delaware*, 103 U. S. 370, 386; *Bush* v. *Kentucky*, 107 U. S. 110, 116. At the present term, referring to the previous adjudications, this court declared that "underlying all of those decisions is the principle that the Constitution of the United States, in its present form, forbids, so far as civil and political rights are concerned, discrimination by the General Government or the States against any citizen because of his race. All citizens are equal before the law." *Gibson* v. *Mississippi*, 162 U. S. 565.

The decisions referred to show the scope of the recent amendments of the Constitution. They also show that it is not within the power of a State to prohibit colored citizens, because of their race, from participating as jurors in the administration of justice.

It was said in argument that the statute of Louisiana does not discriminate against either race, but prescribes a rule applicable alike to white and colored citizens. But this argument does not meet the difficulty. Every one knows that the statute in question had its origin in the purpose, not so much to exclude white persons from railroad cars occupied by blacks, as to exclude colored people from coaches occupied by or assigned to white persons. Railroad corporations of Louisiana did not make discrimination among whites in the matter of accommodation for travellers. The thing to accomplish was, under the guise of giving equal accommodation for whites and blacks, to compel the latter to keep to themselves while travelling in railroad passenger coaches. No one would be so wanting in candor as to assert the contrary. The fundamental objection, therefore, to the statute is that it interferes with the personal freedom of citizens. "Personal liberty," it has been well said, "consists in the power of locomotion, of changing situation, or removing one's person to whatsoever place one's own inclination may direct, without imprisonment or restraint, unless by due course of law," 1 Bl. Com. *134. If a white man and a black man choose to occupy the same public conveyance on a public highway, it is their right to do so, and no government, proceeding alone on grounds of race, can prevent it without infringing the personal liberty of each.

It is one thing for railroad carriers to furnish, or to be required by law to furnish, equal accommodations for all whom they are under a legal duty to carry. It is quite another thing for government to forbid citizens of the white and black races from travelling in the same public conveyance and to punish officers of railroad companies for permitting persons of the two races to occupy the same passenger coach. If a State can prescribe, as a rule of civil conduct, that whites and blacks shall not travel as passengers in the same railroad coach, why may it not so regulate the use of the streets of its cities and towns as to compel white citizens to keep on one side of a street and black citizens to keep on the other? Why may it not, upon like grounds, punish whites and blacks who ride together in street cars or in open vehicles on a public road or street? Why may it not require sheriffs to assign whites to one side of a court-room and blacks to the other? And why may it not also prohibit the commingling of the two races in the galleries of legislative halls or in public assemblages convened for the consideration of the political questions of the day? Further, if this statute of Louisiana is consistent with the personal liberty of citizens, why may not the State require the separation in railroad coaches of native and naturalized citizens of the United States, or of Protestants and Roman Catholics?

The answer given at the argument to these questions was that regulations of the kind they suggest would be unreasonable, and could not, therefore, stand before the law. Is it meant that the determination of questions of legislative power depends upon the inquiry whether the statute whose validity is questioned is, in the judgment of the courts, a reasonable one, taking all the circumstances into consideration? A statute may be unreasonable merely because a sound public policy forbade its enactment. But I do not understand that the courts have anything to do with the policy or expediency of legislation. A statute may be valid, and yet, upon grounds of public policy, may well be characterized as unreasonable. Mr. Sedgwick correctly states the rule when he says that the legislative intention being clearly ascertained, "the courts have no other duty to perform than to execute the legislative will, without any regard to their views as to the wisdom or justice of the particular enactment." Stat. & Const. Constr. 324. There is a dangerous tendency in these latter days to enlarge the functions of the courts, by means of judicial interference with the will of the people as expressed by the legislature. Our institutions have the distinguishing characteristic that the three departments of government are coordinate and separate. Each must keep within the limits defined by the Constitution. And the courts best discharge their duty by executing the will of the law-making power, constitutionally expressed, leaving the results of legislation to be dealt with by the people through their representatives. Statutes must always have a reasonable construction. Sometimes they are to be construed strictly; sometimes, liberally, in order to carry out the legislative will. But however construed, the intent of the legislature is to be respected, if the particular statute in question is valid, although the courts, looking at the public interests, may conceive the statute to be both unreasonable and impolitic. If the power exists to enact a statute, that ends the matter so far as the courts are concerned. The adjudged cases in which statutes have been held to be void, because unreasonable, are those in which the means employed by the legislature were not at all germane to the end to which the legislature was competent.

The white race deems itself to be the dominant race in this country. And so it is, in prestige, in achievements, in education, in wealth and in power. So, I doubt not, it will continue to be for all time, if it remains true to its great heritage and holds fast to the principles of constitutional liberty. But in view of the Constitution, in the eye of the law, there is in this country no superior, dominant, ruling class of citizens. There is no caste here. Our Constitution is color-blind, and neither knows nor tolerates classes among citizens. In respect of civil rights, all citizens are equal before the law. The humblest is the peer of the most powerful. The law regards man as man, and takes no account of his surroundings or of his color when his civil rights as guaranteed by the supreme law of the land are involved. It is, therefore, to be regretted that this high tribunal, the final expositor of the fundamental law of the land, has reached the conclusion that it is competent for a State to regulate the enjoyment by citizens of their civil rights solely upon the basis of race.

In my opinion, the judgment this day rendered will, in time, prove to be quite as pernicious as the decision made by this tribunal in the *Dred Scott case.* It was adjudged in that case that the descendants of Africans who were imported into this country and sold as slaves were not included nor intended to be included under the word "citizens" in the Constitution, and could not claim any of the rights and privileges which that instrument provided for and secured to citizens of the United States; that at the time of the adoption of the Constitution they were "considered as a subordinate and inferior class of beings, who had been subjugated by the dominant race, and, whether emancipated or not, yet remained subject to their authority, and had no rights or privileges but such as those who held the power and the government might choose to grant them." 19 How. 393, 404. The recent amendments of the Constitution, it was supposed, had eradicated these principles from our institutions. But it seems that we have yet, in some of the States, a dominant race—a superior class of citizens, which assumes to regulate the enjoyment of civil rights, common to all citizens, upon the basis of race. The present decision, it may well be apprehended, will not only stimulate aggressions, more or less brutal and irritating, upon the admitted rights of colored citizens, but will encourage the belief that it is possible, by means of state enactments, to defeat the beneficent purposes which the people of the United States had in view when they adopted the recent amendments of the Constitution, by one of which the blacks of this country were made citizens of the United States and of the States in which they respectively reside, and whose privileges and immunities, as citizens, the States are forbidden to abridge. Sixty millions of whites are in no danger from the presence here of eight millions of blacks. The destinies of the two races, in this country, are indissolubly linked together, and the interests of both require that the common government of all shall not permit the seeds of race hate to be planted under the sanction of law. What can more certainly arouse race hate, what more certainly create and perpetuate a feeling of distrust between these races, than state enactments, which, in fact, proceed on the ground that colored citizens are so inferior and degraded that they cannot be allowed to sit in public coaches occupied by white citizens? That, as all will admit, is the real meaning of such legislation as was enacted in Louisiana.

The sure guarantee of the peace and security of each race is the clear, distinct, unconditional recognition by our governments, National and State, of every right that inheres in civil freedom, and of the equality before the law of all citizens of the United States without regard to race. State enactments, regulating the enjoyment of civil rights, upon the basis of race, and cunningly devised to defeat legitimate results of the war, under the pretence of recognizing equality of rights, can have no other result than to render permanent peace impossible, and to keep alive a conflict of races, the continuance of which must do harm to all concerned. This question is not met by the suggestion that social equality cannot exist between the white and black races in this country. That argument, if it can be properly regarded as one, is scarcely worthy of consideration; for social equality no more exists between two races when travelling in a passenger coach or a public highway than when members of the same races sit by each other in a street car or in the jury box, or stand or sit with each other in a political assembly, or when they use in common the streets of a city or town, or when they are in the same room for the purpose of having their names placed on the registry of voters, or when they approach the ballot-box in order to exercise the high privilege of voting.

There is a race so different from our own that we do not permit those belonging to it to become citizens of the United States. Persons belonging to it are, with few exceptions, absolutely excluded from our country. I allude to the Chinese race. But by the statute in question, a Chinaman can ride in the same passenger coach with white citizens of the United States, while citizens of the black race in Louisiana, many of whom, perhaps, risked their lives for the preservation of the Union, who are entitled, by law, to participate in the political control of the State and nation, who are not excluded, by law or by reason of their race, from public stations of any kind, and who have all the legal rights that belong to white citizens, are yet declared to be criminals, liable to imprisonment, if they ride in a public coach occupied by citizens of the white race. It is scarcely just to say that a colored citizen should not object to occupying a public coach assigned to his own race. He does not object, nor, perhaps, would he object to separate coaches for his race, if his rights under the law were recognized. But he objects, and ought never to cease objecting to the proposition, that citizens of the white and black races can be adjudged criminals because they sit, or claim the right to sit, in the same public coach on a public highway.

The arbitrary separation of citizens, on the basis of race, while they are on a public highway, is a badge of servitude wholly inconsistent with the civil freedom and the equality before the law established by the Constitution. It cannot be justified upon any legal grounds.

If evils will result from the commingling of the two races upon public highways established for the benefit of all, they will be infinitely less than those that will surely come from state legislation regulating the enjoyment of civil rights upon the basis of race. We boast of the freedom enjoyed by our people above all other peoples. But it is difficult to reconcile that boast with a state of the law which, practically, puts the brand of servitude and degradation upon a large class of our fellow-citizens, our equals before the law. The thin disguise of "equal" accommodations for passengers in railroad coaches will not mislead any one, nor atone for the wrong this day done.

The result of the whole matter is, that while this court has frequently adjudged, and at the present term has recognized the doctrine, that a State cannot, consistently with the Constitution of the United States, prevent white and black citizens, having the required qualifications for jury service, from sitting in the same jury box, it is now solemnly held that a State may prohibit white and black citizens from sitting in the same passenger coach on a public highway, or may require that they be separated by a "partition," when in the same passenger coach. May it not now be reasonably expected that astute men of the dominant race, who affect to be disturbed at the possibility that the integrity of the white race may be corrupted, or that its supremacy will be imperilled, by contact on public highways with black people, will endeavor to procure statutes requiring white and black jurors to be separated in the jury box by a "partition," and that, upon retiring from the court room to consult as to their verdict, such partition, if it be a moveable one, shall be taken to their consultation room, and set up in such way as to prevent black jurors from coming too close to their brother jurors of the white race. If the "partition" used in the court room happens to be stationary, provision could be made for screens with openings through which jurors of the two races could confer as to their verdict without coming into personal contact with each other. I

cannot see but that, according to the principles this day announced, such state legislation, although conceived in hostility to, and enacted for the purpose of humiliating citizens of the United States of a particular race, would be held to be consistent with the Constitution.

I do not deem it necessary to review the decisions of state courts to which reference was made in argument. Some, and the most important, of them are wholly inapplicable, because rendered prior to the adoption of the last amendments of the Constitution, when colored people had very few rights which the dominant race felt obliged to respect. Others were made at a time when public opinion, in many localities, was dominated by the institution of slavery; when it would not have been safe to do justice to the black man; and when, so far as the rights of blacks were concerned, race prejudice was, practically, the supreme law of the land. Those decisions cannot be guides in the era introduced by the recent amendments of the supreme law, which established universal civil freedom, gave citizenship to all born or naturalized in the United States and residing here, obliterated the race line from our systems of governments, National and State, and placed our free institutions upon the broad and sure foundation of the equality of all men before the law.

I am of opinion that the statute of Louisiana is inconsistent with the personal liberty of citizens, white and black, in that State, and hostile to both the spirit and letter of the Constitution of the United States. If laws of like character should be enacted in the several States of the Union, the effect would be in the highest degree mischievous. Slavery, as an institution tolerated by law would, it is true, have disappeared from our country, but there would remain a power in the States, by sinister legislation, to interfere with the full enjoyment of the blessings of freedom; to regulate civil rights, common to all citizens, upon the basis of race; and to place in a condition of legal inferiority a large body of American citizens, now constituting a part of the political community called the People of the United States, for whom, and by whom through representatives, our government is administered. Such a system is inconsistent with the guarantee given by the Constitution to each State of a republican form of government, and may be stricken down by Congressional action, or by the courts in the discharge of their solemn duty to maintain the supreme law of the land, anything in the constitution or laws of any State to the contrary notwithstanding.

For the reasons stated, I am constrained to withhold my assent from the opinion and judgment of the majority.

Mr. Justice Brewer did not hear the argument or participate in the decision of this case.

RAYFORD W. LOGAN

The Supreme Court and the Negro

Practically all the relevant decisions of the United States Supreme Court during Reconstruction and to the end of the century nullified or curtailed those rights of Negroes which the Reconstruction "Radicals" thought they had written into laws and into the Constitution. Some of these decisions are still generally accepted—even though two of the most important were decided by a five to four vote. Another, Plessy *v.* Ferguson which laid down the doctrine of "separate but equal accommodations," is being challenged in the Supreme Court as this book goes to press. The rulings in the jury cases have been largely reversed. This fairly good record of the Supreme Court is, however, somewhat vitiated by expressions of social philosophy in some of the cases.*

The decisions of the Court were largely the handiwork of Northerners and Republicans. The first Southerner appointed to the Court since 1852 was William B. Woods, a Republican from Georgia, in 1880. John Marshall Harlan, appointed in 1881, came from the ex-slave state of Kentucky, but he had fought in the Union Army. The first Democrat after Stephen J. Field of California, appointed in 1862, was Lamar of Mississippi, appointed in 1888. There were thus only two Southerners, both of them Republicans, and one Democrat, from California, on the bench when it handed down the devastating Civil Rights decision in 1883. In 1896 when the Court wrote the more controversial decision, Plessy *v.* Ferguson, there was only one Southerner, Edward Douglass White of Louisiana (Woods and Lamar had died). There were only two Democrats, Field and White. An Ohio Republican, Morrison R. Waite, was Chief Justice from 1874 to 1888. Chief Justice Melville W. Fuller (1888–1910), was a graduate of Bowdoin College, Maine; he had attended Harvard Law School and practiced law in Illinois. Field, the California Democrat, and Joseph Bradley, the New Jersey Republican—who served from 1863 to 1897 and 1870 to 1892, respectively—were probably the most conservative. The most notable dissenter was the Ken-

tucky Republican Unionist, Harlan, 1877–1911. His dissenting opinions in the Civil Rights Cases and in Plessy *v.* Ferguson are still cited by lawyers and laymen who reject the validity of these decisions.*

In order to obtain a complete picture of the loopholes that the Supreme Court found in the efforts of the Reconstruction "Radicals" to protect the rights of Negroes, an examination of decisions from 1873 to 1877 is necessary. To some degree, the decisions against Negroes after 1877 followed the general pattern of the reaction against nationalism that had become evident, 1870–1873, under Chief Justice Salmon P. Chase. During the eighty-one years from 1789 to 1869 only four Acts of Congress had been declared invalid, but from 1870 to 1873 six such Acts were held unconstitutional. Since none of these six cases involved the rights of Negroes, it may be argued that subsequent decisions affecting Negro rights merely reflected the continued reaction of the Court against federal power. It can not be gainsaid, however, that some of these subsequent decisions also reflected the changing attitude in the nation at large with respect to the Negro.

It was during this early period of judicial reaction against nationalism that the Supreme Court first interpreted the Fourteenth Amendment. While the Slaughter-House Cases, 1873, did not directly involve the rights of Negroes, the Court frequently referred to these cases in later interpretations of those rights. The legislature of Louisiana had passed a statute which granted a monopoly of the slaughterhouse business within certain parishes of New Orleans in favor of one corporation, and thus deprived over one thousand persons of the right to engage in that business. Opponents of the monopoly contended that this state law created an involuntary servitude, abridged the privileges and immunities of citizens of the United States, denied them equal protection of the laws, and deprived them of their property without due process of law. By a majority of five to four the Court upheld the state law on all counts. The decision scoffed at the idea that the involuntary servitude forbidden by the Thirteenth Amendment could possibly refer to a servitude attached to property. But the real significance of the case involved the interpretation of the Fourteenth Amendment.

The five majority justices pointed out: "We do not deny that no one else but the negro can share in this protection." But, they declared, if the right to be freed from monopoly existed, it was not as a privilege or immunity

---

*Supreme Court decisions since 1941, the Civil Rights laws of 1957, 1960, 1964, and state laws now give evidence of attempts to apply these basic principles to almost 12 million American Negroes.

*The doctrine of "separate but equal" was reversed by the Supreme Court decision of May 17, 1954. This decision stated: "We conclude that in the field of public education the doctrine of 'separate but equal' has no place." Subsequent decisions expanded the thrust of this decision.

of a citizen of the United States. The majority opinion did not attempt to give a complete list of the privileges and immunities that inhered in state citizenship. The former, however, could all be comprehended under the following general heads: "protection by the government, with the right to acquire and possess property of every kind, and to pursue and obtain happiness and safety, subject, nevertheless, to such restraints as the government may prescribe for the general good of the whole." Having concluded that the privileges and immunities relied on in the argument belonged to citizens of states, as such, the Court held that it was excused from defining those privileges and immunities of citizens of the United States which no state can abridge, until some case involving those privileges and immunities made it necessary for the Court to define them. The Court, did, none the less, enumerate certain privileges and immunities that inhered in United States citizenship. Among these were the rights secured by the Thirteenth and Fifteenth Amendments and the clauses in the Fourteenth Amendment which the Court then considered.

The due process clause had been a part of the Constitution since the adoption of the Fifth Amendment which placed a restraint upon the federal government. But, under no construction of cases involving that Amendment could the Court find that the butchers in the Slaughter-House Cases had been deprived by Louisiana of their property without due process of law. The history of the Fourteenth Amendment showed clearly that the equal protection clause was clearly designed to forbid laws "which discriminated with gross injustice against them [the newly emancipated Negroes] as a class." The Court doubted whether any action of a state that did not fall within this category would ever be held to come within the purview of the equal protection provision. (In fact, however, between 1890 and 1910 only 19 of the 528 cases before the Court involving the Fourteenth Amendment applied to Negro rights; 288 of these cases referred to corporations which were considered "persons" within the language of the Fourteenth Amendment.) No such case was before the Court in this instance, the majority held.

The four dissenting judges, including Chief Justice Chase, pointed out that the majority opinion rendered the privileges and immunities clause a practical nullity. For, "with privileges and immunities pertaining only to citizens of the United States *as such*, no State ever could have interfered by its laws," and hence no new constitutional provision was necessary to prohibit such interference. The dissenting opinions added that, even before the Fourteenth Amendment, the supremacy of the Constitution and laws of the United States always controlled any legislation of that character. The clear purpose of the relevant clause was to prevent states from abridging the privileges and immunities which citizens enjoyed as citizens of states.

One of the most intriguing aspects of this case is the fact that the principal attorney for the plaintiffs argued frequently that the Fourteenth Amendment was intended to secure the rights of the recently emancipated slaves against their former masters. This attorney was John A. Campbell of Alabama, a former member of the United States Supreme Court who had concurred with the majority in the Dred Scott Case and who had resigned when Alabama seceded from the Union. Against a background of frequent references to the purpose of the amendment, he insisted that it "brought the federal government into immediate contact with every person and gave to every citizen a claim upon its protecting power." The Amendment, he continued, placed the privileges and immunities of national citizenship beyond the power of the state government. National citizenship and state citizenship were the same.

Campbell later declared that the decision was "probably best for the country." Had he deliberately portrayed the fulsome potentialities of the Fourteenth Amendment in protecting rights of Negroes in order to evoke a decision curtailing those potentialities? Whatever his purpose may have been, consideration of the privileges and immunities of national citizenship virtually disappeared from constitutional law until a tax case in 1935. A five to four decision nullified the aim of the Reconstruction "Radicals"—if Campbell was right—to protect, through the privileges and immunities clause, the freedmen against hostile state laws. One wonders how Campbell would have voted had he still been a member of the Court.

Three years later, in 1876, the Supreme Court found loopholes in the Civil Rights Enforcement Act of May 31, 1870. In United States *v.* Reese, the Court held that under the Fifteenth Amendment, congressional action was limited to that which prevented discrimination in the right to vote on account of race, color or previous condition of servitude. Since sections three and four of the Act were not confined to such a limited class of discrimination, those sections were unconstitutional. The sections of the Act of May 31, 1870, dealing with the right to vote were repealed by the Act of Congress of February 8, 1894.*

In the same year the Court held that section six of the Act of May 31, 1870, was constitutional, subject to a vital restriction of its scope. That section forbade two or more persons to "injure, oppress, threaten, or

---

*Title I of the Civil Rights Acts of 1957, 1960, and 1964 included provisions designed to protect the rights of Negroes to vote. The language can be construed as being based upon both the Fourteenth and Fifteenth Amendments.

intimidate any citizen with intent to prevent or hinder his free exercise and enjoyment of any right or privilege granted or secured to him by the Constitution or laws of the United States, or because of his having exercised the same." The penalty for violation of this section was a fine of not more than $5,000, imprisonment for not more than ten years, and ineligibility "to any office, or place of honor, or trust created by the Constitution and laws of the United States." The defendants were charged with conspiring to prevent two Negro citizens of the United States from the enjoyment of their rights peaceably to assemble with others, to petition for redress of grievances, to bear arms and to vote. They were further charged with conspiring falsely to imprison and murder the two Negroes and thus to deprive them of their lives and liberty without due process of law. The Court, in United States *v.* Cruikshank, with one dissenting opinion, rejected all the charges as not having been indictable under any act of Congress.*

In order for the case to be brought under the operation of the statute, the Court held that it would have to be demonstrated that the right in question was one granted or secured by the Constitution or laws of the United States. Since the rights peaceably to assemble and to bear arms had existed prior to the Constitution, they were therefore not derived from it. If the right to petition Congress had been involved, the case would have come within the statute, and within the scope of the sovereignty of the United States. The offense, as stated in the indictment, would have been established if it had been shown that the object of the conspiracy was to prevent a meeting for *any* lawful purpose. The United States had no more power to punish for a conspiracy falsely to imprison and to murder than to punish for false imprisonment or murder itself. This power was vested in the states. The Court also laid down the doctrine which is generally accepted, namely, that the due process clause in the Fourteenth Amendment did not add anything to the rights of one citizen against another. The due process clause merely furnished an additional procedural guarantee against any encroachment by the states upon the fundamental rights which belong to every citizen as a member of society. The counts in the indictment did not call for the exercise of any of the powers conferred by the due process clause of the Fourteenth Amendment.

The judgment of the Court with respect to equal protection of the laws is especially revealing. The Court pointed out that there was no allegation that the conspiracy under this count was because of the race or color of the persons conspired against. It then gave this interpretation of the meaning of the equal protection clause:

> The fourteenth amendment prohibits a State from denying to any person within its jurisdiction the equal protection of the laws; but this provision does not, any more than the one which precedes it, and which we have just considered, add any thing to the rights which one citizen has under the Constitution against another. The equality of the rights of citizens is a principle of republicanism. Every republican government is in duty bound to protect all its citizens in the enjoyment of this principle, if within its power. That duty was originally assumed by the States; and it still remains there. The only obligation resting upon the United States is to see that the States do not deny the right. This the amendment guarantees, but no more. The power of the national government is limited to the enforcement of this guaranty.

But this unequivocal statement of the responsibility resting upon the federal government did not define the equality of the rights of citizens. When the Court did rule on that question twenty years later, in Plessy *v.* Ferguson, it declared that equality of right did not prevent segregation.

The Court, meanwhile, invoked the equal protection clause to limit the exclusion of Negroes from jury service, the only cases during this period in which the Court interpreted the Fourteenth Amendment in favor of Negroes. The case of Strauder *v.* West Virginia established the precedent. West Virginia statutes of 1872–1873 excluded Negroes from grand and petit juries. The Court, in 1880, held that these laws flagrantly violated the equal protection clause and were therefore unconstitutional. In the same decision, the Court held valid that section of the Civil Rights Enforcement Act which authorized the removal of a case into the United States courts when the equal rights of a citizen were denied in a state court. During the same term, the Court ruled, in *Ex parte* Virginia, that acts by officers and agents of a state constituted state action under the Fourteenth Amendment. A county judge who had excluded Negroes from jury service had therefore violated that amendment.

In both these cases, Justice William Strong, a Pennsylvania Republican, made interesting observations that might be used today by organizations and individuals seeking congressional legislation in behalf of Negroes. In the first case, he expressed his conviction that the true spirit and meaning of the Reconstruction Amendments

---

*Section six of the Act of May 31, 1870 became, with immaterial changes, section 5508 of the revised statutes of 1874–1878. This section was repeated without change as section nineteen of the Criminal Code of 1909 (35 Stat. 1092). Section 241, United States Code, 1950 ed., repeated the terms of conspiracy, the fine and the imprisonment, but dropped the ineligibility clause.

could not be understood without keeping in view "the history of the times when they were adopted and the objects they plainly sought to accomplish." He repeated this conviction in the second case, and added that the amendments were intended to be and were "limitations of the power of the States and enlargements of the power of Congress." It made no difference that such legislation by Congress was restrictive of what a state might have done before the amendments were adopted. He affirmed:

> The prohibitions of the Fourteenth Amendment are directed to the States, and they are to a degree restrictions of State power. . . . No such enforcement is an invasion of State sovereignty. No law can be, which the people of the United States have, by the Constitution of the United States, empowered Congress to enact.

Justice Harlan was to take an even stronger tone in his dissenting opinion in the Civil Rights Cases, three years later.

The Supreme Court further strengthened the right of Negroes to serve on juries, in Neal *v.* Delaware, 1880. The Court held that the Fifteenth Amendment *ipso facto* rendered inoperative the constitution and laws of Delaware which, at the time the amendment was adopted, restricted jury service to white persons who were qualified to vote. Since, moreover, the state had not subsequently passed any law in violation of the Fifteenth Amendment, Delaware recognized its binding force. Consequently, there was no denial of equality on that score by the state. Since, however, the facts presented showed that no Negroes had been called to jury service, the discrimination constituted a "prima facie denial . . . of that equal protection which has been secured by the Constitution and laws of the United States."

Two years later, the Court declared void the indictment of a Negro who had been indicted and arraigned for trial under Kentucky laws which excluded Negroes from all jury service. But, in Virginia *v.* Rives, 1880, the Court had declared that the Fourteenth Amendment was not violated if, when the jury was all white, it could not be shown that Negroes were excluded solely on the ground of race or color.

To the traditional "man from Mars," it would be difficult to justify the ruling, in 1882, that an Alabama statute which provided a more severe punishment in cases of fornication and adultery between Negroes and whites than between members of the same race did not violate the equal protection clause. As will be seen later in this chapter, five other cases involving alleged exclusion of Negroes from juries resulted in decisions against federal intervention and only one in favor of it.

Meanwhile, the Supreme Court had handed down its first decision sanctioning segregation in interstate traffic. This decision, Hall *v.* De Cuir, 1878—the year after the withdrawal of federal troops from Louisiana and South Carolina—has not been accorded the importance that it deserves. The decision is all the more fascinating against the background of the complex struggle over the federal regulation of interstate commerce.

In the Granger Cases, 1877, the Court had upheld the right of states to regulate railroads. Since most of the traffic was interstate, such regulation was clearly a direct burden on interstate commerce. But, in Hall *v.* De Cuir, the Court held unconstitutional a Louisiana statute forbidding discrimination on account of race, because the law placed a direct burden on interstate commerce. In order to make clear that this was true, the Court pointed out: "A passenger in the cabin class set apart for the use of whites without the State must, when the boat comes within, share the accommodations of that cabin with such colored passengers as may come on board afterwards, if the law is enforced." The decision, written by Chief Justice Waite, observed that "it was to meet just such a case that the commercial clause in the Constitution was adopted." While this may be doubted, it is none the less true that, as the Court stated, it would be difficult to conduct business if, in one state white and colored passengers were separated by law, and in another were required by law to be put in cabins together. The racial aspects of this burden on interstate commerce were further pointed up when the Court observed:

> If this statute can be enforced against those engaged in interstate commerce, it may be as well against those engaged in foreign; and the master of a ship clearing from New Orleans to Liverpool, having passengers on board, would be compelled to carry all, white and colored, in the same cabin during his passage down the river, or be subject to an action for damages, "exemplary as well as actual," by any one who felt himself aggrieved because he had been excluded on account of his color.

If these two cases had stood alone, a logician would have been justified in concluding that state regulation of interstate commerce was less a violation of the Constitution if it dealt with commerce *per se* than if it involved the mingling of the races. But in 1886 the Court ruled, in the Wabash Case, that rates fixed by state law could not be applied to transportation beginning or ending outside the state. Even after this decision the Court found it difficult to fix the exact line of demarcation between a direct and an indirect burden on interstate commerce. One of the most interesting decisions was the Lake Shore Case in 1889, since it required consideration of the De Cuir Case. An Ohio law required some interstate passenger trains to stop at certain points in Ohio in order to let off and receive passengers. Rejecting the appositeness of the De Cuir decision, the Court declared that the Ohio law did not at all interfere with the "management" of trains outside the state and that it applied only to some trains. The Ohio law so manifestly subserved the public convenience, and was "in itself so just and reasonable, as wholly to preclude the idea that it was, as the Louisiana statute was declared to be, a direct burden upon interstate commerce, or a direct interference with its freedom."

It was easier for the Supreme Court to find that laws requiring segregation in intrastate commerce did not violate the interstate commerce clause. In 1890, the Court held that a Mississippi statute requiring separate but equal accommodations did not violate the interstate commerce clause, since the Mississippi Supreme Court had construed the law as applying only to intrastate commerce. At the turn of the century, the Court ruled that a separate coach law applicable only to passengers within the state of Kentucky was valid.

While the Supreme Court was seeking to define the precise line of demarcation between state laws that placed a direct, and those that placed an indirect, burden on interstate commerce, the Court had little trouble in fixing the limits between state action and individual action. The principle that the first section of the Fourteenth Amendment was prohibitory upon states only, and not upon individuals, was first upheld in United States *v.* Harris, 1882. Those sections of the so-called Ku-Klux Act of April 20, 1871, which had laid severe penalties upon anyone conspiring to impede the effects of the Fourteenth and Fifteenth Amendments, were therefore declared unconstitutional. In accordance with this same principle, the Court in 1883 held the Civil Rights Act of 1875 unconstitutional.

The preamble of this law stated that Congress deemed it essential to just government that "we recognize the equality of all men before the law, and hold it is the duty of government in all its dealings with the people to mete out equal and exact justice to all, of whatever nativity, race, color, or persuasion, religious or political," and that it is "the appropriate object of legislation to enact great fundamental principles into law." The Act provided that all persons within the jurisdiction of the United States should be entitled to "the full and equal enjoyment of the accommodations, facilities, and privileges of inns, public conveyances on land or water, theaters, and other places of public amusement; subject only to the conditions and limitations established by law, and applicable alike to citizens of every race and color, regardless of any previous condition of servitude." The person aggrieved by a violation could recover $500; the offender was guilty of a misdemeanor, and federal courts were given exclusive jurisdiction. This law was the culmination of the various federal laws that were passed to counteract the post-Civil War Black Codes in the Southern states. More than any of the other laws it rankled Southern views on the proper place of the free Negro.

The aversion of white men to personal contacts with Negroes after the Civil War stemmed largely from the new status of Negroes as free men. Masters and mistresses had had personal contacts with their house slaves. Indeed, the not infrequent practice of cohabitation had caused Mrs. Mary Boykin Chesnut, the wife of a rich planter, to pour out in poignant passages her bitterness against the slave system which permitted Southern gentlemen to live "like the patriarchs of old, . . . all in one house with their wives and concubines; and the mulattoes one sees in every family partly resemble the white children." After emancipation personal contacts became social relations. The etiquette of slavery permitted, for example, a slave girl to travel as maid for her mistress on a train. The etiquette of freedom found it intolerable that a colored woman paying her own fare should travel in the same coach with a white woman. The extramarital activities of white men with a free colored woman were considered even more reprehensible than similar infidelities with a slave woman. The myth of the faithful slave was replaced by the legend of the Negro as a rapist. Attempts to give the freedmen political and economic equality threatened the old way of life. Social equality—the mingling of the races in schools, inns, theaters and on public carriers—would encourage black men, it was asserted, to dream of cohabitation with white women. While these fears were most deeply rooted in recollections of the slave system in the South, they prevailed also to some degree in the North where free men had suffered economic, political and social inequality.

The case of the United States *v.* Stanley, and other cases, or the Civil Rights Cases as the decision is better known, involved seven different incidents. These included the denial of hotel accommodations to Negroes in Kansas and Missouri; the denial to a Negro of a seat in the dress circle of a theater in San Francisco; the denial to a person (presumably a Negro) of the full enjoyment of the accommodations of the Grand Opera in New York; the refusal by a conductor on a passenger train to allow a colored woman to travel in the ladies' car of the Memphis and Charleston Railroad Company. Only two of the five cases originated in the South. This fact should not lead to the conclusion that the aversion was greater in the North than in the South, but rather that Negroes in the North had more frequent personal contacts with whites in public places.

The decision was written by Justice Bradley, the "Fifth Judge" of the Electoral Commission which had decided every controversial issue of the Hayes-Tilden election in favor of Hayes. Woodward finds it appropriate that Bradley should have written the decision since it "constituted a sort of validation of the Compromise of 1877." The essential points in the decision are two: the first section of the Fourteenth Amendment is prohibitory upon states only; Congress is authorized by the amendment to adopt only corrective, not general legislation. In brief, the person wronged must look for vindication or redress to the laws of the state. Since the cases considered arose within states, the constitutionality of the act with respect to territories and to the District of Columbia was not presented. As in the Cruikshank Case, the Court held that if state laws were to make any unjust discrimination, Congress would have the power under the Fourteenth Amendment to afford remedy.

Harlan, the Kentucky Unionist, opened his classic dissent by stating that the majority opinion proceeded upon grounds

> entirely too narrow and artificial. I cannot resist the conclusion that the substance and spirit of the recent amendments of the Constitution have been sacrificed by a subtle and ingenious verbal criticism. Constitutional provisions, adopted in the interest of liberty, and for the purpose of securing, through national legislation, if need be, rights inhering in a state of freedom, and belonging to American citizenship, have been so construed as to defeat the ends the people desired to accomplish by changes in the fundamental law.

This far-reaching decision thus legalized race distinctions by individuals with respect to enjoyment of facilities in carriers and places of public accommodation and amusement. In addition, it virtually assured the subsequent development of Jim Crow laws, and other forms of race discrimination, and the passivity of the Federal government in the face of this discrimination. The sequel proved that Harlan was correct when he declared in his dissenting opinion: "We shall enter upon an era of constitutional law, when the rights of freedom and American citizenship cannot receive from the nation that efficient protection which heretofore was unhesitatingly accorded to slavery and the rights of the master."

But the nation, as a whole, rejoiced over the decision. It is still the law of the land. Charles Warren, whose book *The Supreme Court in United States History* is considered one of the most authoritative treatises on the subject, commented with respect to the Civil Rights Cases, the Harris Case and others of a similar character:

> Viewed in historical perspective now [1922], however, there can be no question that the decisions in

these cases were most fortunate. They largely eliminated from national politics the Negro question which had so long embittered Congressional debates; they relegated the burden and the duty of protecting the Negro to the states, to whom they properly belonged; and they served to restore confidence in the national court in the Southern states.

The decision, of course, had the reverse effect on many Negroes. Despite the admonition of the Court that Negroes were not justified in interpreting denials of equal accommodations as a badge of inferiority, they could hardly construe such discrimination otherwise. They found some solace in the fact that fifteen Northern states soon thereafter passed civil rights laws, and three others strengthened existing laws. But the lower courts frequently found loopholes which largely nullified these state laws. Moreover, the vast majority of Negroes still lived in the South where they were increasingly subjected to segregation and discrimination by law and custom.

While the Court upheld the right of individuals to discriminate in public places against Negroes on account of their race, in the following year, it construed the Civil Rights Act of 1870 as a valid exercise of the power granted under the Fifteenth Amendment. In the Cruikshank Case, the Court had dismissed the charge that Negroes had been denied the right to vote, because the allegations did not show that the denial had been based on race or color. But, in *Ex parte* Yarbrough, 1884, the Court ruled that the Fifteenth Amendment "does, *proprio vigore,* substantially confer on the negro the right to vote, and Congress has the power to enforce that right." The ineffectiveness of this 1870 law was so evident that Congress, in 1890, attempted to enact legislation that would give practical effect to the Fifteenth Amendment. That attempt not only failed but led to constitutional amendments by Southern states to "legalize" the disfranchisement of most Negroes.

No case involving the right of Negroes to engage in business came before the Supreme Court. But, in a case involving Chinese laundrymen in California, the Court construed the equal protection clause of the Fourteenth Amendment to the advantage of the Chinese. Chinese who conducted their business in wooden buildings were denied licenses while white persons conducting laundries under similar conditions were left unmolested. The Court vigorously ruled:

> Though the law itself be fair on its face and impartial in appearance, yet, if it is applied and administered by public authority with an evil eye and an unequal hand, so as practically to make unjust and illegal discriminations between persons in similar circumstances, material to their rights, the denial of

equal justice is still within the prohibition of the Constitution.

The Court pointed out that it had sanctioned this principle in a number of cases, including *Ex parte* Virginia, and Neal *v.* Delaware. In neither of these cases, however, did the Court use such strong language as it did in Yick Wo *v.* Hopkins. Moreover, the decision in this case was unanimous, whereas in the cases involving the right of Negroes to sit on juries, Justice Field of California had dissented in both, Justice Clifford in one and Chief Justice Waite in the other.

Thirteen years after the Supreme Court had sanctioned discrimination by individuals in public places and on public carriers, the Court approved separation of the races by state action. In Plessy *v.* Ferguson, 1896, the Court for the first time invoked the doctrine of police powers to deny in effect the equal protection which the framers of the Fourteenth Amendment thought they had established. It was this decision by which the Supreme Court accepted the doctrine of "separate but equal accommodations." Between 1882 and 1888, lower federal courts had upheld the principle in four cases. In three cases involving segregation on public carriers, the courts had held that separate cars were a proper exercise of the state's police powers. In the fourth case, dealing with an Ohio statute which authorized school boards to organize separate schools for colored children, the lower federal court ruled: "Equality of right does not mean identity of right and . . . so long as educational opportunities for Negroes were substantially equal to those for whites no denial of protection resulted." . . . 1888, and 1889 had approved this doctrine of separate but equal accommodations.

It was not until 1896, however, that the United States Supreme Court upheld this doctrine. A Louisiana law required separate but equal accommodations on public carriers and provided a penalty for passengers who sat in a car or compartment assigned to the other race. The petitioner, an octoroon in whom "Negro blood was not discernible," sat in a white car and was arrested. The Court held that the law was a reasonable exercise of the state police power and was therefore constitutional. Justice Henry B. Brown, a Republican from Michigan, speaking for the Court, made this revealing observation:

> The object of the [Fourteenth] Amendment was undoubtedly to enforce the absolute equality of the two races before the law, but in the nature of things it could not have been intended to abolish distinctions based on color, or to enforce social, as distinguished from political equality, or a commingling of the two races upon terms unsatisfactory to either.

The Court added, as it had done in the Civil Rights Case, that laws requiring segregation did not necessarily imply "the inferiority of either race to the other." Moreover, the Court pointed out that separate schools had been held valid in several Northern states by the state courts. Expanding even further the social philosophy which controlled the thinking of the judges, the Court continued:

> If the two races are to meet upon terms of social equality, it must be the result of natural affinities, a mutual appreciation of each other's merits and a voluntary consent of individuals. . . . If one race be inferior to the other socially, the Constitution of the United States cannot put them upon the same plane. The distinction between the two races, which was founded in the color of the two races, must always exist so long as white men are distinct from the other color.

Harlan, who had dissented in the Civil Rights Cases, again wrote a scorching dissent. Laws requiring segregation on public carriers, he declared, were unconstitutional, since they interfered with the personal freedom of citizens "under the guise of giving equal accommodations to whites and blacks." They fostered ideas of caste and inferiority and the majority decision would stimulate further aggressions upon the rights of Negroes. Giving his own social interpretation of the Constitution and laws, he insisted: "Our Constitution is blind, and neither knows nor tolerates classes among citizens. . . . The law regards man as man, and takes no regard of his surroundings or his color when his civil rights as guaranteed by the supreme law of the land are invoked."

It is easy enough, then, to understand why one student of the subject has written that "the invocation and application of the police power is nothing more than an appeal to the sociological method of interpreting our Constitution and laws." Justice Harlan prophesied that the decision—which is not mentioned in Warren's authoritative history of the Supreme Court—would prove as pernicious as the Dred Scott decision. The Washington *Post,* in 1949, editorially called Plessy *v.* Ferguson the "worst" decision in the history of the Supreme Court except the Dred Scott decision. But this decision is still the law of the land. In recent years the Supreme Court has sought to enforce "substantial equality" in the separate accommodations, but it has not yet ruled on the constitutionality of segregation itself under the equal protection clause.*

The principle of separate but equal accommodations was not again clearly presented to the Supreme Court during the period under study. The Court found

---

*Title II of the Civil Rights Act of 1964 was based upon both the equal protection clause of the Fourteenth Amendment and the interstate commerce clause.

an opportunity to avoid a direct ruling in a case originating in Richmond County, Georgia. Cummings, a Negro taxpayer, complained that the high school for Negroes in that county had been suspended "for economic reasons" while the high school for whites remained open. The constitutionality of all laws providing separate accommodations for whites and Negroes was attacked in the argument of the plaintiff's counsel, but the question was not presented in the record. Harlan, speaking for the Court, declared that the relief asked for was an injunction which would close the school for the whites without furnishing any additional opportunities for Negroes. The trial did not show any abuse of the discretion allowed by law to the County Board of Education. The Court further held that the education of people in schools maintained by state taxation was a matter belonging to the respective states, and interference could not be justified except in a case of "clear and unmistakable disregard of the rights secured by the supreme law of the land."

During the last six years of the century, Negroes found it increasingly difficult to establish that exclusion from juries violated the equal protection clause. In one case, the Court declared that the petitioner had used the wrong method of procedure, since the regular trial of a state court can not be reviewed by *habeas corpus* proceedings. The second case, Gibson *v.* Mississippi, 1895, is more significant, since it revealed a growing insistence by the Court that indisputable evidence be presented of the exclusion from juries because of race or color. The petitioner in this case sought removal of his case from a Mississippi state court on the ground that Negroes were excluded from the grand and petit juries in Mississippi. Counsel for the petitioner—this seems to have been the first case in which Negro lawyers appeared before the United States Supreme Court—contended that at the time of selecting jurors in Washington County there were 7,000 colored citizens competent to serve as jurors and only 1,500 whites. Nevertheless, no colored juror had been summoned for a number of years. The Court rejected the petition because no proof had been offered that Negroes were excluded solely because of race or color. In any event, as Justice Harlan pointed out: "It is clear in view of what has been said that these facts, even if they had been proved and accepted, do not show that the rights of the accused were denied by the Constitution and laws of the State." But the Court also declared that evidence of the failure to call Negroes to jury service would be for the consideration of the trial court upon motion by the accused to quash the indictment. The Court thus required the accused to establish proof in the court of a state which had rendered Negroes politically impotent. But in 1899, the Court reversed the decision of a Texas court and remanded the

case on the ground that the state court had erred in refusing to receive proof that Negroes were excluded from the grand jury solely because of their race or color. In two other cases, the Court based its rulings on failure to prove that the exclusion was due to discrimination.*

Perhaps the least defensible decision of the United States Supreme Court on the right of Negroes to serve on juries was handed down in the too little known case of Williams *v.* Mississippi. Cornelius J. Jones, one of the colored lawyers who had appeared in Gibson *v.* Mississippi was determined that he would this time give the Court no loopholes. The accused had been indicted for murder by a grand jury of white men. Jones had made a motion to quash the indictment, on the ground that the state constitution required the ability to read and write and understand any section of that constitution for service on a jury. The motion had been denied, and the defendant had then moved to remove the case to the United States Circuit Court on substantially the same ground. This motion had likewise been denied. The defendant had thereupon been tried by a jury of white men and convicted. When his motion for a new trial had been denied, he had appealed to the United States Supreme Court.

The ruling of the Court was based upon the doctrine that possibility of evil administration of a law was not necessarily proof of the fact that the law itself was evil. This case does not, therefore, offer an exact parallel with Yick Wo *v.* Hopkins, in which it was clearly demonstrated that Chinese laundrymen had been deprived of their right to conduct a business solely because of their race. But, the Court in this Mississippi case had to fall back upon a decision of the Mississippi Supreme Court for proof that Negroes were not excluded from the jury lists because of their color. The Court observed:

> We gather from the statements of the motion that certain officers are invested with discretion in making up lists of electors, and that this discretion has been exercised against the colored race and that from these lists the jurors are selected. The Supreme Court of Mississippi, however, decided in a case presenting the same question as that at bar that jurors are not selected from or with reference to any lists furnished by such election officers.

By the beginning of the twentieth century, the first section of the Fourteenth Amendment—except the definition of citizenship—had been virtually nullified by

---

*The Supreme Court ruled in Norris *v.* Alabama, 1935, that the systematic exclusion of Negroes from juries was *prima-facie* evidence of the denial of equal protection of the laws guaranteed by the Fourteenth Amendment.

decisions of the United States Supreme Court. The Court had ruled that most privileges and immunities of citizens inhered in state, rather than in United States, citizenship. The Fourteenth Amendment placed prohibitions upon states and not individuals. Under the doctrine of police powers the states could, however, do some of the very things which the framers of the Fourteenth Amendment thought they had prevented. Separation of the races, for example, was not a denial of equal protection of the laws, provided that the separate accommodations were substantially equal. Due process of law did not add to the rights of any citizens, but merely strengthened the procedure by which their rights were safeguarded. The only right of Negroes under the Fourteenth Amendment which the Court upheld was the right of Negroes to serve on juries when state laws and state officers clearly violated that right, and proof was presented at the trial that Negroes had been barred because of their race or color. The Supreme Court had further held that state law requiring separation of races was not a direct burden on interstate commerce and was, therefore, constitutional. The Interstate Commerce Commission had also upheld segregation in interstate travel, provided the accommodations were equal. The protection of the Negro was left to the states, which increasingly were relegating Negroes to what is today called second-class citizenship. The decision of the Supreme Court, that the Fifteenth Amendment did substantially confer on the Negro the right to vote, was being increasingly nullified by the revision of state constitutions that disfranchised most Negroes. No cases involving these new constitutions were presented to the Court during this period.

It is not clear whether Douglass meant abstract justice or the interpretation of the Constitution and laws when he listed "American justice" as the first principle which should apply alike to all Americans. Whichever he meant, the Supreme Court had been compelled to rule that, in substance, "Equal Justice under Law" did not guarantee to Negro Americans the same rights that other Americans enjoyed.

Southern Disturbances: Six Negroes Lynched at Trenton, Tenn.

Nashville, Tenn., Aug. 26—The negroes at Pickettsville, Gibson County, 6 miles from Humboldt, last Saturday and Sunday, threatened a riot on account of some supposed wrong done to them, and manifested a strong desire to kill two or three citizens, and fire and sack the town.

Yesterday sixteen of the ringleaders were arrested and taken to Trenton and placed in jail for safe-keeping.

About 1 o'clock this morning, between seventy-five and 100 masked men entered the town, rode up to the jail and compelled the Sheriff to deliver the keys to them. They then took the six negroes from the jail.

Four were killed and two mortally wounded at the edge of town. The masked men then rode off with the other ten, and are supposed to have killed them. Nothing has been heard from them since they left. Considerable excitement exists among the negroes there, and the whites are taking defensive steps in case of any outbreak.

A special to the *Union and American* from McKenzie, Tenn., reports as follows:

Trenton, Aug. 26—3 p.m.—Armed men are pouring in from the country to find all quiet. Scouts say they cannot find an armed negro. Two of the negroes found shot last night are still alive.

Humboldt, Aug. 26—5 p.m.—All quiet.

Pickettsville, Aug. 26—6 p.m.—The men are resting on their arms. All rumors of armed negro bands, and fighting in the country, are believed to be false.

Memphis, Aug. 26—The *Appeal's* special from Humboldt to-night says the excitement in Gibson County is subsiding. No further bloodshed is anticipated. Women and children have been coming in there during the day, and the wildest excitement existed throughout the county through rumors of negroes marching in strong force on Pickettsville, and rumors of their having murdered two women. On the other hand, the negroes were terribly alarmed, and many fled to the woods, fearing the fate of those taken from Trenton jail last night.

The origin of the troubles there occurred at a barbecue near Pickettsville five weeks since, in a difficulty between a white man named J. Hale and Josh Webb, colored, about the payment of half a dollar, since when the negroes had made numerous threats of violence. On Saturday night last, while two young men, named Morgan and James, were riding along the road, 3 miles from Pickettsville, they were fired upon by thirty or forty negroes hid in the woods. The young men abandoned their horses, took to the woods, and escaped to town, the citizens in which had become alarmed at the firing, in view of the reports that the negroes were organizing armed companies. Suspecting a negro named Ben Walker of complicity in the shooting, a constable, with a posse, proceeded to his house, where they captured a negro named Ben Ballard, who confessed that they had met on Saturday night and organized to protect Col. Webb, colored, from the Ku-Klux, and after that to kill Bassel Butler for divulging their plans to the whites, but after meeting and firing on Morgan and Warren, they separated. He also gave the names of a large number engaged in the plot for assassination and murder. When Ballard's confession was made public, the greatest excitement spread throughout the country, and the citizens gathered at Pickettsville, and a meeting was called, at which Squire Burnett presided. It was decided to summon a posse, and arrest the following negroes, who, according to Ballard, were the ringleaders: George Green, Steve Bryant, Dan Williams, Bob Love, Dick Shaw, Dug Jamison, Hays Peebles, Parret Burrows, Alfred Williams, and Nick Joey; which was done, and they were brought to Pickettsville. On Sunday night a band of masked men rode into town and demanded the prisoners, but Marshall Dungan refused to give them up, and the maskers left. On Monday they were arraigned before three Justice's of the Peace on a charge of shooting with intent to kill, and inciting a riot. One of them, Jarrett Burrows, turned State's evidence, and related the story of the cause, origin, purposes, and expectations of an extensive organization among the negroes of Gibson County, which was corroborated by Nelson McGhee, colored, who also said it was rumored for some time past that President Grant would back the negroes in whatever course they took against the whites, and, acting on this belief, the colored people had determined to extirpate the whites so as to obtain the lands, &c., but had not agreed upon the time for the outbreak. This measure for the murder of the whites was agreed to by all except Burrell Butler, of Pickettsville, and because of his opposition they intended to kill him on Saturday night, for fear he would tell the whites. Burrows also gave the names of several other persons who were to be killed on Saturday night, and told where the negroes met in the railroad cut and organized by electing Wesley Shields Captain, until they reached Col. Webb's house, who was then to take command. They expected to meet a company from Humboldt, under charge of John Regan, which failed to come. Their object in organizing thoroughly was to shoot the KuKlux, who they understood were raiding the country to persecute the negroes.

After the examination they were committed to jail at Trenton, and the result has been already announced. The lynching of the prisoners causes much indignation here.

Another Dispatch. Memphis, Aug. 26—A special from Trenton to the *Avalanche* gives the following additional particulars regarding the slaughter of the colored prisoners:

After the maskers, numbering about 100, had obtained possession of the prisoners, they tied them together and marched off on the Huntington road half a mile from town. Six of the number were cut loose and ordered to escape, and, as soon as that command was given, a full volley was fired upon them, killing four and wounding the other two,—one mortally. The remainder were carried up the river 2 miles and killed. Their remains were collected, and are being taken care of.

The Circuit Court was in session at this place. On the assembling of the Court this morning, several speeches were made by members of the Bar denouncing the conduct of the disguised men, who were from the country, and urging upon the Judge to give the Grand Jury an extra charge ordering them to send out for witnesses all along the road from here to Pickettsville in order to arrest and punish the criminals. While the charge was being delivered runners arrived in hot haste with a report that a large body of negroes, well armed, were marching to Trenton, which caused the adjournment of the Court. Scouts were sent out, and returned reporting all quiet.

There is no mistake but that the negroes are well organized in this county, and ready for action at a moment's warning. Two companies from Union City have arrived here. Other dispatches report everybody under arms.

Lynch Law in Mississippi.

Brookhaven, Miss., Aug. 23.—The three negroes, Dick Cooper, Anthony Grant, and Silas Johnson, who at 3 o'clock on Sunday morning last forcibly entered the residence of Mrs. Burnley, were taken from the jail at 4 o'clock on Saturday and hung by the citizens, about 1,000 of whom were present. Johnson was captured on Sunday. The other two were taken at Canton, brought here Saturday morning, and lodged in jail. They all confessed their guilt on the gallows. (*The Chicago Daily Tribune*, August 27, 1874.)

Marshall County. A letter from Marshall County of the 1st ult. gives a fearful account of the resurrected rebels in that district:

Marshall Co., July 1.—We have gathered some further particulars about the cruel inflictions of those infamous wretches, the Ku-Klux, or resurrected rebels as they call themselves. On the night of the 15th of July those infamous wretches went to the house of Mr. Lewis Strikally and abused him; as we learn their calculations were to serve in a like manner the person of Berryman Scales, Mr. Willis, and also R. Royster for the sole cause of boarding the teacher at his house. They expressed an intention to hang Mr. Jenkins for his habit of reading the Bible to those of his own race, thereby making them as wise as the white men, as they allege.

It is impossible at this time to give full reports of murders up to the 1st of July. The reports of the Sub-Assistant Commissioners of the Freedmen's Bureau for June have not all come in yet, and complete reports of outrages in that month will not be made until the first of August. But from the few reports received, and from other authentic sources, we have collected 96 additional homicides, so that the statistics of homicides committed in Texas during the three years since the conclusion of the rebellion stand thus:

Killed in 1865,	47	whites,	51	freedmen	96
Killed in 1866,	75	whites,	95	freedmen	170
Killed in 1867,	173	whites,	174	freedmen	347
Killed in 1868,	182	whites,	147	freedmen	319
Year unknown,	32	whites,	29	freedmen	61
Race unknown,	—		—		40
Total	509		486		1,035

We have thus a grand total of 1,035 homicides in three years, or 345 per year; and estimating our population since 1865, at 800,000, we have one person killed out of every 2,026 of the whole population per year. We doubt very much if such a record of blood can be exhibited in any Christian or civilized State in the world in a time of peace. It has been stated in the papers that the homicides in New York during the year 1867, numbered 47. If this be correct, there was one person killed out of every 80,000 of her population, and then in that year there were *forty times* as many homicides in Texas as in New York, according to the population of each. The eighth census of the United States for the year 1860, reports for that year 37 homicides and murders in New York, making one person killed out of every 104,000 of her whole population, so that Texas has averaged per year since the war, *forty-five times* more homicides than New York did in 1860. We note, also, that for 14 murders in New York there were three executions in 1860, while for the 1,000 in Texas since the war there has been but one execution.

It should be remembered that in New York and other States in the North, every murder is accurately reported, while the figures here presented come far short of representing the actual number of murders in Texas during the time specified. We have kept scrupulously within the number presented to us, of which fact any candid man can satisfy himself by patiently examining all the data. We assert, too, that the reports usually relied on do not present all the homicides committed in the section described by them. For example, from the ordinary sources of information we had reported only three homicides in Washington County since the 1st of December, 1867; but when a full report is obtained from that county it gives 16 in that time. Through the usual channels only two murders are reported in Tarrant County, whereas a more complete account gives 15, and so it is with other counties. Now, when it is remembered that we have full reports from about 30 of the 137 organized counties of the State, it becomes very evident that we have information only of a portion of the murders committed. It is proper to state further that the reports which we call full do not

profess to give full accounts of the murders in the counties represented by them. Many of them positively state that they do not report all, and witnesses tell us of men disappearing mysteriously, and of dead bodies being hid away in ravines, or floating down streams, of which cases no history is given. (*National Anti-Slavery Standard*, August 15, 1869)

Free Negroes in Arkansas. The Arkansas papers contain an address from a Committee appointed by the citizens of Little Rock, to the people of that State, upon the subject of the removal of free negroes from its limits. The address sets forth the undesirableness of that class of population in a slaveholding community, suggests that the necessary laws be passed by the Legislature to remove them from Arkansas, and forbid their return forever afterwards. The question was mooted two years ago, but failed. *(The Liberator*, September 3, 1858)

An Outrage.—We learn from a friend, who had his facts from a resident of Belbucle, on the Chattanooga Railroad, that Mrs. Long, the wife of Dr. Long of that place, a few days since, whipped a negro woman so severely that she died within an hour or two after the infliction. The coroner's verdict was in accordance with this statement. The woman and her husband, we learn, have fled from the country.—*Nashville Daily News.*

Slaves remanded to their masters. Cincinnati, Aug. 27.—Two fugitive slaves belonging to Robert W. Ingraham, who escaped in March from Kentucky, were arrested last night and taken before Commissioner Newhall, who remanded them to their master; whereupon they were taken to Covington. The arrest was made quietly.

Brown v. *Board of Education*

NO 1. Appeal From The United States District Court For The District of Kansas.*

Reargued on the question of relief April 11–14, 1955.— Opinion and judgments announced May 31, 1955.

---

*Together with No. 2, *Briggs et al.* v. *Elliott et al.*, on appeal from the United States District Court for the Eastern District of South Carolina; No. 3, *Davis et al.* v. *County School Board of Prince Edward County, Virginia, et al.*, on appeal from the United States District Court for the Eastern District of Virginia; No. 4, *Bolling et al.* v. *Sharpe et al.*, on certiorari to the United States Court of Appeals for the District of Columbia Circuit; and No. 5, *Gebhart et al.* v. *Belton et al.*, on certiorari to the Supreme Court of Delaware.

1. Racial discrimination in public education is unconstitutional, 347 U. S. 483, 497, and all provisions of federal, state or local law requiring or permitting such discrimination must yield to this principle. P. 298.

2. The judgments below (except that in the Delaware case) are reversed and the cases are remanded to the District Courts to take such proceedings and enter such orders and decrees consistent with this opinion as are necessary and proper to admit the parties to these cases to public schools on a racially nondiscriminatory basis with all deliberate speed. P. 301.

    (a) School authorities have the primary responsibility for elucidating, assessing and solving the varied local school problems which may require solution in fully implementing the governing constitutional principles. P. 299.

    (b) Courts will have to consider whether the action of school authorities constitutes good faith implementation of the governing constitutional principles. P. 299.

    (c) Because of their proximity to local conditions and the possible need for further hearings, the courts which originally heard these cases can best perform this judicial appraisal. P. 299.

    (d) In fashioning and effectuating the decrees, the courts will be guided by equitable principles—characterized by a practical flexibility in shaping remedies and a facility for adjusting and reconciling public and private needs. P. 300.

    (e) At stake is the personal interest of the plaintiffs in admission to public schools as soon as practicable on a nondiscriminatory basis. P. 300.

    (f) Courts of equity may properly take into account the public interest in the elimination in a systematic and effective manner of a variety of obstacles in making the transition to school systems operated in accordance with the constitutional principles enunciated in 347 U. S. 483, 497; but the vitality of these constitutional principles cannot be allowed to yield simply because of disagreement with them. P. 300.

    (g) While giving weight to these public and private considerations, the courts will require that the defendants make a prompt and reasonable start toward full compliance with the ruling of this Court. P. 300.

    (h) Once such a start has been made, the courts may find that additional time is necessary to carry out the ruling in an effective manner. P. 300.

    (i) The burden rests on the defendants to establish that additional time is necessary in the public interest and is consistent with good faith compliance at the earliest practicable date. P. 300.

    (j) The courts may consider problems related to administration, arising from the physical condition of the school plant, the school transportation system, personnel, revision of school districts and attendance areas into compact units to achieve a system of determining admission to the public schools on a nonracial basis, and revision of local laws and regulations which may be necessary in solving the foregoing problems. Pp. 300–301.

    (k) The courts will also consider the adequacy of any plans the defendants may propose to meet these problems and to effectuate a transition to a racially nondiscriminatory school system. P. 301.

    (l) During the period of transition, the courts will retain jurisdiction of these cases. P. 301.

3. The judgment in the Delaware case, ordering the immediate admission of the plaintiffs to schools previously attended only by white children, is affirmed on the basis of the principles stated by this Court in its opinion, 347 U. S. 483; but the case is remanded to the Supreme Court of Delaware for such further proceedings as that Court may deem necessary in the light of this opinion. P. 301.

98 F. Supp. 797, 103 F. Supp. 920, 103 F. Supp. 337 and judgment in No. 4, reversed and remanded.

91 A. 2d 137, affirmed and remanded.

Counsel for Parties.

Robert L. Carter argued the cause for appellants in No. 1 *Spottswood W. Robinson, III,* argued the causes for appellants in Nos. 2 and 3. *George E. C. Hayes* and *James M. Nabrit, Jr.* argued the cause for petitioners in No. 4. *Louis L. Redding* argued the cause for respondents in No. 5. *Thurgood Marshall* argued the causes for appellants in Nos. 1, 2 and 3, petitioners in No. 4 and respondents in No. 5.

On the briefs were *Harold Boulware, Robert L. Carter, Jack Greenberg, Oliver W. Hill, Thurgood Marshall, Louis L. Redding, Spottswood W. Robinson, III, Charles S. Scott, William T. Coleman, Jr., Charles T. Duncan, George E. C. Hayes, Loren Miller, William R. Ming, Jr., Constance Baker Motley, James M. Nabrit, Jr., Louis H. Pollak* and *Frank D. Reeves* for appellants in Nos. 1, 2 and 3, and respondents in No. 5; and *George E. C. Hayes, James M. Nabrit, Jr., George M. Johnson, Charles W. Quick, Herbert O. Reid, Thurgood Marshall* and *Robert L. Carter* for petitioners in No. 4.

Harold R. Fatzer, Attorney General of Kansas, argued the cause for appellees in No. 1. With him on the brief was *Paul E. Wilson,* Assistant Attorney General. *Peter F. Caldwell* filed a brief for the Board of Education of Topeka, Kansas, appellee.

S. E. Rogers and *Robert McC. Figg, Jr.* argued the cause and filed a brief for appellees in No. 2.

J. Lindsay Almond, Jr., Attorney General of Virginia, and *Archibald G. Robertson* argued the cause for appellees in No. 3. With them on the brief were *Henry T. Wickham,* Special Assistant to the Attorney General, *T. Justin Moore, John W. Riely* and *T. Justin Moore, Jr.*

Milton D. Korman argued the cause for respondents in No. 4. With him on the brief were *Vernon E. West, Chester H. Gray* and *Lyman J. Umstead.*

Joseph Donald Craven, Attorney General of Delaware, argued the cause for petitioners in No. 5. On the brief were *H. Albert Young,* then Attorney General, *Clarence W. Taylor,* Deputy Attorney General, and *Andrew D. Christie,* Special Deputy to the Attorney General.

In response to the Court's invitation, 347 U. S. 483, 495–496, *Solicitor General Sobeloff* participated in the oral argument for the United States. With him on the brief were *Attorney General Brownell, Assistant Attorney General Rankin, Philip Elman, Ralph S. Spritzer* and *Alan S. Rosenthal.*

By invitation of the Court, 347 U. S. 483, 496, the following State officials presented their views orally as *amici curiae: Thomas J. Gentry,* Attorney General of Arkansas, with whom on the brief were *James L. Sloan,* Assistant Attorney General, and *Richard B. McCulloch,* Special Assistant Attorney General. *Richard W. Ervin,* Attorney General of Florida, and *Ralph E. Odum,* Assistant Attorney General, both of whom were also on a brief. *C. Ferdinand Sybert,* Attorney General of Maryland, with whom on the brief were *Edward D. E. Rollins,* then Attorney General, *W. Giles Parker,* Assistant Attorney General, and *James H. Norris, Jr.,* Special Assistant Attorney General. *I. Beverly Lake,* Assistant Attorney General of North Carolina, with whom on the brief were *Harry McMullan,* Attorney General, and *T. Wade Bruton, Ralph Moody* and *Claude L. Love,* Assistant Attorneys General. *Mac Q. Williamson,* Attorney General of Oklahoma, who also filed a brief. *John Ben Shepperd,* Attorney General of Texas, and *Burnell Waldrep,* Assistant Attorney General, with whom on the brief were *Billy E. Lee, J. A. Amis, Jr., L. P. Lollar, J. Fred Jones, John Davenport, John Reeves* and *Will Davis.*

Phineas Indritz filed a brief for the American Veterans Committee, Inc., as *amicus curiae.*

Mr. Chief Justice Warren delivered the opinion of the Court.

These cases were decided on May 17, 1954. The opinions of that date,[1] declaring the fundamental principle that racial discrimination in public education is unconstitutional, are incorporated herein by reference. All provisions of federal, state, or local law requiring or permitting such discrimination must yield to this principle. There remains for consideration the manner in which relief is to be accorded.

Because these cases arose under different local conditions and their disposition will involve a variety of local problems, we requested further argument on the question of relief.[2] In view of the nationwide importance of the decision, we invited the Attorney General of the United States and the Attorneys General of all states requiring or permitting racial discrimination in public education to present their views on that question. The parties, the United States, and the States of Florida, North Carolina, Arkansas, Oklahoma, Maryland, and Texas filed briefs and participated in the oral argument.

These presentations were informative and helpful to the Court in its consideration of the complexities arising from the transition to a system of public education freed of racial discrimination. The presentations also demonstrated that substantial steps to eliminate racial discrimination in public schools have already been taken, not only in some of the communities in which these cases arose, but in some of the states appearing as *amici curiae,* and in other states as well. Substantial progress has been made in the District of

---

[1] 347 U. S. 483; 347 U. S. 497.

[2] Further argument was requested on the following questions, 347 U. S. 483, 495–496, n. 13, previously propounded by the Court:

"4. Assuming it is decided that segregation in public schools violates the Fourteenth Amendment

"*(a)* would a decree necessarily follow providing that, within the limits set by normal geographic school districting, Negro children should forthwith be admitted to schools of their choice, or

"*(b)* may this Court, in the exercise of its equity powers, permit an effective gradual adjustment to be brought about from existing segregated systems to a system not based on color distinctions?

"5. On the assumption on which questions 4 *(a)* and *(b)* are based, and assuming further that this Court will exercise its equity powers to the end described in question 4 *(b),*

"*(a)* should this Court formulate detailed decrees in these cases;

"*(b)* if so, what specific issues should the decrees reach;

"*(c)* should this Court appoint a special master to hear evidence with a view to recommending specific terms for such decrees;

"*(d)* should this Court remand to the courts of first instance with directions to frame decrees in these cases, and if so what general directions should the decrees of this Court include and what procedures should the courts of first instance follow in arriving at the specific terms of more detailed decrees?"

Columbia and in the communities in Kansas and Delaware involved in this litigation. The defendants in the cases coming to us from South Carolina and Virginia are awaiting the decision of this Court concerning relief.

Full implementation of these constitutional principles may require solution of varied local school problems. School authorities have the primary responsibility for elucidating, assessing, and solving these problems; courts will have to consider whether the action of school authorities constitutes good faith implementation of the governing constitutional principles. Because of their proximity to local conditions and the possible need for further hearings, the courts which originally heard these cases can best perform this judicial appraisal. Accordingly, we believe it appropriate to remand the cases to those courts.[3]

In fashioning and effectuating the decrees, the courts will be guided by equitable principles. Traditionally, equity has been characterized by a practical flexibility in shaping its remedies[4] and by a facility for adjusting and reconciling public and private needs.[5] These cases call for the exercise of these traditional attributes of equity power. At stake is the personal interest of the plaintiffs in admission to public schools as soon as practicable on a nondiscriminatory basis. To effectuate this interest may call for elimination of a variety of obstacles in making the transition to school systems operated in accordance with the constitutional principles set forth in our May 17, 1954, decision. Courts of equity may properly take into account the public interest in the elimination of such obstacles in a systematic and effective manner. But it should go without saying that the vitality of these constitutional principles cannot be allowed to yield simply because of disagreement with them.

While giving weight to these public and private considerations, the courts will require that the defendants make a prompt and reasonable start toward full compliance with our May 17, 1954, ruling. Once such a start has been made, the courts may find that additional time is necessary to carry out the ruling in an effective manner. The burden rests upon the defendants to establish that such time is necessary in the public interest and is consistent with good faith compliance at the earliest practicable date. To that end, the courts

may consider problems related to administration, arising from the physical condition of the school plant, the school transportation system, personnel, revision of school districts and attendance areas into compact units to achieve a system of determining admission to the public schools on a nonracial basis, and revision of local laws and regulations which may be necessary in solving the foregoing problems. They will also consider the adequacy of any plans the defendants may propose to meet these problems and to effectuate a transition to a racially nondiscriminatory school system. During this period of transition, the courts will retain jurisdiction of these cases.

The judgments below, except that in the Delaware case, are accordingly reversed and the cases are remanded to the District Courts to take such proceedings and enter such orders and decrees consistent with this opinion as are necessary and proper to admit to public schools on a racially nondiscriminatory basis with all deliberate speed the parties to these cases. The judgment in the Delaware case—ordering the immediate admission of the plaintiffs to schools previously attended only by white children—is affirmed on the basis of the principles stated in our May 17, 1954, opinion, but the case is remanded to the Supreme Court of Delaware for such further proceedings as that Court may deem necessary in light of this opinion.

It is so ordered.

KENNETH S. TOLLETT

The Strangling of Black Rights

The often referred to compromising, majority opinion of Justice Lewis Powell in the *Special-Minority-Admissions* case, *Regents of the University of California* v. *Bakke*, 438 U.S. 265 (1978), stated that the "one pervading purpose" or original intent of the Reconstruction Amendments was virtually strangled in its infancy by "judicial reactionism." The intent or one pervading purpose of the Civil War Reconstruction Amendments was to secure the liberty and freedom of Blacks and to protect them from their oppressors, Whites, who formerly exercised unlimited dominion and control over them. What I propose to do is to review briefly the judicial reactionism which strangled the rights of Blacks in the First Post-Reconstruction and comment upon the wavering protection and sometimes assaults on the rights of Blacks in the emerging Second Post-Reconstruction, particularly in the area of affirmative action and, sometimes, even Black colleges.

---

[3] The cases coming to us from Kansas, South Carolina, and Virginia were originally heard by three-judge District Courts convened under 28 U. S. C. §§2281 and 2284. These cases will accordingly be remanded to those three-judge courts. See *Briggs* v. *Elliott*, 342 U. S. 350.

[4] See *Alexander* v. *Hillman*, 296 U. S. 222, 239.

[5] See *Hecht Co.* v. *Bowles*, 321 U.S. 321, 329–330.

In the area of civil or Black rights, history may be more important than in any other area of social, political, and legal development. The often stated maxim, that those who ignore history are condemned to repeat it, is well worth repeating. I have put the matter this way: A people without a view of their past, have a dim view of their present, and are blind to their future. K.S. Tollett, Black Institutions of Higher Learning: Inadvertent Victims or Necessary Sacrifices?: With 1981 Prologue Update 4 (1981). This is especially noteworthy during the current controversy over the United States Constitution, the Supreme Court, and the Judges and Justices who interpret and apply laws, especially constitutional law and the issue of "original intent" versus a "living constitution."

In the First Reconstruction, through clever, subtle, ingenious, and disingenuous verbal analysis, the Court decided that whites murdering Blacks were not "affecting persons," *Blyew* v. *United States,* 80 U.S. (13 Wall) 581 (1871); recognized the Fourteenth Amendment and its Equal Protection Clause were "primarily designed" for the "protection" of Black rights (such as not excluding them from juries) without providing them effective remedies, *Strauder* v. *West Virginia,* 100 U.S. 303 (1880), *Virginia* v. *Rives,* 100 U.S. 313 (1880); sanctioned private violence and discrimination, *U.S.* v. *Cruikshank,* 92 U.S. 542 (1875); *United States* v. *Harris,* 106 U.S. 629 (1883); *Civil Rights Cases,* 109 U.S. 3 (1883); curtailed the power of Congress to protect Blacks from private violence directed at their employment, *Hodges* v. *United States,* 203 U.S. 1 (1906), overruled by *Jones* v. *Alfred H. Mayer Co.,* 392 U.S. 409 (1968); decreed the operation of an American-style *apartheid* in the fraudulent separate-but-equal doctrine, *Plessy* v. *Ferguson,* 163 U.S. 537 (1896) (public accommodations/transportation); *Cumming* v. *Richmond County School Board,* 175 U.S. 528 (1899) (education); and tolerated the disenfranchisement of Blacks, *U.S.* v. *Reese,* 92 U.S. 214 (1876).

More recently, in the name of a colorblind rhetoric which was first enunciated in Justice Harlan's dissent in the *Plessy* v. *Ferguson,* 163 U.S 537 (1896), separate-but-equal case, some courts have been playing ducks-and-drakes with affirmative action in employment and education. K. S. Tollett, Black Colleges As Instruments Of Affirmative Action (1982). Black higher education institutions, which are instruments of affirmative action, have been hassled with reverse discrimination suits. The threatened strangling of Black rights must be resisted, affirmative action and Black colleges must be maintained, and the human integrity and dignity of Blacks, male and female, young and old, must emphatically be reasserted. Lest we project insecurity and lack of self-esteem, we must stop being apologetic and defensive about affirmative action and Black colleges. K. S. Tollett, "Commentary: Disenchantment with the 'Egalitarian Revolution,'" 1979 *Washington University Law Quarterly* 421 (1979); K. S. Tollett, Jeanette J. Leonard, and Portia P. James, "A Color-Conscious Constitution: The One Pervading Purpose *Redux*," 52 *The Journal of Negro Education* 189 (1983). Insecurity and lack of self-esteem are twin outcomes of the internationalization of racism which undermine educational and economic achievement more than any other two evil products of racism.

We do not want to do others harm, we want our rights vindicated. We want a fair chance and opportunity to be a part of the mainstream of this country. Our twelve to sixteen percent unemployment rate will not do it. The forty to fifty percent unemployment rate of Blacks in the ghetto will not do it. We want a fair chance and if we are given a fair chance, we can more effectively, creatively, and positively contribute to the welfare and good of this country.

We only ask that we not be denied a fair chance by subtle, clever, and ingenious verbal rhetoric that turns affirmative action into reverse discrimination, education opportunity into test scores and hurdles, and a new beginning into a Second Post-Resconstruction.

CHAPTER THREE

A Way of Looking at a University

[When we sang the Alma Mater] my soul stood on tiptoe and stretched up to take in all that it meant. So I was careful to do my class work and be worthy to stand there under the shadow of the hovering spirit of Howard. I felt the ladder under my feet.

Zora Neale Hurston

Reading Selections

Ivan Earle Taylor

Gentle Mother

Heeding our urgent plea, you took us in;
Owing us nothing, still you promised all,
Willing to shelter, foster, and begin
Anew with us, your children communal,
Ranging in talent one to infinity,
Drawn from all states and climes from sea to sea.
Unstinting in your gracious amplitude,
Nothing withholding from the printed page,
Learned assemblage, scholars wise and good,
Valiant family, willing to engage,
Enduring scholars, strong in heart and mood,
Rise to your challenge, proud assemblage;
Stand fast, do battle when the turmoils rage.
In faith protect the weak against the crude;
Take courage from your sons and daughters proud.
Your name we honor, sing your praise aloud.

W. E. B. Du Bois

The Field and Function of the Negro College

At Fisk University a new president had come to power. The General Education Board had promised sorely needed money. A new regime and a new spirit were being built up. I myself was shortly to return to the academic world and take up again the teaching of sociology at the rebuilt Atlanta University. It seemed appropriate therefore, on the occasion of my forty-fifth anniversary of graduation, to utter a word of guidance. I think the authorities of Fisk would have preferred my silence. I had been in the past rather prodigal with advice, and the results had been almost disastrous. President [Thomas E.] Jones exhibited a little nervousness as he extended the invitation; but I explained to him frankly that I had no desire to prolong my hectic career of Fisk kingmaker. I was satisfied, in the main, with his administration, but I wanted to guide in general the

Negro college. I sensed a natural difficulty. When the Southern Negro college changed from a missionary school to a secular college, there was a tendency continually to say: this college is not a Negro college; it is a college; we are not teaching Negro science nor Negro art; we are teaching Art and Science. To this I wanted to oppose a word of warning. I wanted to say in all kindness and cooperation: you are and should and must remain a Negro college; but that involves no low ideals.

Once upon a time some four thousand miles east of this place, I saw the functioning of a perfect system of education. It was in West Africa, beside a broad river; and beneath the palms, bronze girls were dancing before the President of Liberia and the native chiefs, to celebrate the end of the Bush Retreat and their arrival at marriageable age.

There under the Yorubas and other Sudanese and Bantu tribes, the education of the child began almost before it could walk. It went about with mother and father in their daily tasks; it learned the art of sowing and reaping and hunting; it absorbed the wisdom and folklore of the tribe; it knew the lay of land and river. Then at the age of puberty it went into the bush and there for a season the boys were taught the secrets of sex and the girls in another school learned of motherhood and marriage. They came out of the bush with a ceremony of graduation, and immediately were given and taken in marriage.

Even after that, their education went on. They sat in council with their elders and learned the history and science and art of the tribe, and practiced all in their daily life. Thus education was completely integrated with life. There could be no uneducated people. There could be no education that was not at once for use in earning a living and for use in living a life. Out of this education and out of the life it typified came, as perfect expressions, song and dance and saga, ethics and religion.

Nothing more perfect has been invented than this system of training youth among primitive African tribes. And one sees it in the beautiful courtesy of black children; in the modesty and frankness of womanhood, and in the dignity and courage of manhood; and too, in African music and art with its world-wide influence.

If a group has a stable culture which moves, if we could so conceive it, on one general level, here would be the ideal of our school and university. But, of course, this can never be achieved by human beings on any wide stage.

First and most disconcerting, men progress, which means that they change their home, their work, their division of wealth, their philosophy. And how shall men teach children that which they themselves do not know, or transmit a philosophy or religion that is already partly disbelieved and partly untrue? This is a primal and baffling problem of education and we have never wholly solved it. Or in other words, education of youth in a changing world is a puzzling problem with every temptation for lying and propaganda. But this is but the beginning of trouble. Within the group and nation significant differentiations and dislocations appear, so that education of youth becomes a preparation not for one common national life but for the life of a particular class or group; and yet the tendency is to regard as real national education only the training for that group which assumes to represent the nation because of its power and privilege, and despite the fact it is usually a small numerical minority in the nation. Manifestly in such case if a member of one of the suppressed groups receives the national education in such a land, he must become a member of the privileged aristocracy or be educated for a life which he cannot follow and be compelled to live a life which he does not like or which he deeply despises.

This is the problem of education with which the world is most familiar, and it tends to two ends: it makes the mass of men dissatisfied with life and it makes the university a system of culture for the cultured.

With this kind of university, we are most familiar. It reached in our day perhaps its greatest development in England in the Victorian era. Eton and Harrow, Oxford and Cambridge, were for the education of gentlemen—those people who inherited wealth and who by contact and early training acquired a body of manners and a knowledge of life and even an accent of English which placed them among the well-bred; these were taken up and further trained for the particular sort of life which they were to live; a life which presupposed a large income, travel, cultivated society; and activity in politics, art, and imperial industry.

This type of university training has deeply impressed the world. It is foundation for a tenacious legend preserved in fiction, poetry, and essay. There are still many people who quite instinctively turn to this sort of thing when they speak of a university. And out of this ideal arose one even more exotic and apart. Instead of the university growing down and seeking to comprehend in its curriculum the life and experience, the thought and expression of lower classes, it almost invariably tended to grow up and narrow itself to a sublimated élite of mankind.

It conceived of culture, exquisite and fragile, as a thing in itself, disembodied from flesh and action; and this culture as existing for its own sake. It was a sort of earthly heaven into which the elect of wealth and privilege and courtly address, with a few chance neophytes from the common run of men, entered and lived in a region above and apart. One gets from this that ideal of cloistered ease for Science and Beauty, partaken of by those who sit far from the noise and fury, clamor and dust of the world, as the world's aristocrats, artists and scholars.

And yet, the argument against such an ideal of a university is more an argument of fact than logic. For just as soon as such a system of training is established or as men seek to establish it, it dies. It dies like a plant without root, withering into fantastic forms, that bring ridicule or hate. Or it becomes so completely disassociated from the main currents of real life that men forget it and the world passes on as though it was not, and had not been. Thus the university cut off from its natural roots and from the mass of men, becomes a university of the air and does not establish and does not hold the ideal of universal culture which it sought, in its earlier days, to make its great guiding end.

How is it now that failure to reach this often, if not always, kills the university? The reasons to me seem clear. Human culture in its broadest and finest sense can never be wholly the product of the few. There is no natural aristocracy of man, either within a nation or among the races of the world, which unless fed copiously from without can build up and maintain and diversify a broad human culture. A system, therefore, of national education which tries to confine its benefits to preparing the few for the life of the few, dies of starvation. And this every aristocracy which the world has ever seen can prove a thousand times. There are two ways in which this can be remedied: the aristocracy may be recruited from the masses, still leaving the aim of education as the preparation of men for the life of this privileged class. This has been the desperate effort of England and in this way English aristocracy has kept its privilege and its wealth more successfully than any modern or ancient land. But even here, the method fails because the life of the English aristocrat is after all not the broadest and fullest life.

It is only, therefore, as the university lives up to its name and reaches down to the mass of universal men and makes the life of normal men the object of its training—it is only in this way that the marvelous talent and diversity and emotion of all mankind wells up through this method of human training and establishes a national culture and a national art. Herein lies the eternal logic of democracy.

Thus in the progress of human culture you have not simply a development that produces different classes of men, because classes may harmonize more or less, and above the peasant, the artisan and the merchant, may exist a leisured aristocracy and on this leisured class a class culture may be built, which may flourish long and wide. But the difficulty goes further than the narrowness and ultimate sterility of this plan. Dislocations come within these classes. Their relation to each other may change and break and the foundations upon which the cultured class has been built, may crumble. In this case your system of human training becomes not only a system for the supposed benefit of the privileged few, but cannot, indeed, carry out its function even for them. Its system of learning does not fit the mass of men nor the relations of its constituents to that mass.

One can see examples of this the world over. In Kenya, which used to be German East Africa, there are millions of black natives, and a few thousand white Englishmen who have seized and monopolized the best land, leaving the natives scarcely enough poor land for subsistence. By physical slavery, economic compulsion, or legal sanction, the natives work the land of the whites.

What kind of education will suit Kenya? The minority of landed aristocracy will be taught by tutors in Africa and then go to the great English schools and universities. The middle class of immigrant Indian merchants will learn to read and write and count at home or in elementary schools. The great mass of the black millions will be taught something of the art of agriculture, something of the work of artisans, perhaps some ability to read and write, although whether this should be in English or merely in the native tongue is a question. But on this foundation there can grow in Kenya no national university of education, because there are no national ideals. No culture, either African or European, can be built on any such economic foundation.

Thus the university, if it is to be firm, must hark back to the original ideal of the bush school. It must train the children of a nation for life and for making a living. And if it does that, and insofar as it does it, it becomes the perfect expression of the life and the center of the intellectual and cultural expression of its age.

I have seen in my life three expressions of such an ideal; all of them imperfect, all of them partial, and yet each

tending toward a broad and singularly beautiful expression of universal education. My first sight of it was here at Fisk University in the fall of 1885 when I arrived as a boy of seventeen. The buildings were few, the cost of tuition, board, room and clothes was less than $200 a year; and the college numbered less than twenty-five. And yet the scheme of education as it existed in our minds, in the classroom, in the teaching of professors, in the attitude of students, was a thing of breadth and enthusiasm with an unusual unity of aim. We were a small group of young men and women who were going to transform the world by giving proof of our own ability, by teaching our less fortunate fellows so that they could follow the same path, by proclaiming to the world our belief in American democracy, and the place which Negroes would surely take in it. In none of these propositions did there exist in our minds any hesitation or doubt. There was no question as to employment and perfectly proper employment for graduates, for the ends which we had in view. There was no question of our remaining in school for no good or earnest student ever left.

Above all, to our unblinking gaze, the gates of the world would open—were opening. We never for a moment contemplated the possibility that seven millions of Americans who proved their physical and mental worth could be excluded from the national democracy of a common American culture. We came already bringing gifts. The song we sang was fresh from the lips that threw it round the world. We saw and heard the voices that charmed an emperor and a queen. We believed in the supreme power of the ballot in the hands of the masses to transform the world. Already the North was breaking the color line and for the South we were willing to wait.

I saw the same thing a few years later in Harvard University at the end of the nineteenth century. Harvard had broadened its earlier ideals. It was no longer simply a place where rich and learned New England gave the accolade to the social élite. It had broken its shell and stretched out to the West and to the South, to yellow students and to black. I had for the mere asking been granted a fellowship of $300—a sum so vast to my experience that I was surprised when it did not pay my first year's expenses. Men sought to make Harvard an expression of the United States, and to do this by means of leaders unshackled in thought and custom who were beating back bars of ignorance and particularism and prejudice. There were William James and Josiah Royce; Nathaniel Shaler and Charles Eliot Norton; George Santayana; Albert Bushnell Hart, and President Eliot himself. There were at least a dozen men—rebels against convention, unorthodox in religion, poor in money—who for a moment held in their hands the culture of the United States, typified it, expressed it, and pushed it a vast step forward. Harvard was not in 1888 a perfect expression of the American soul, or the place where the average American would have found adequate training for his life work. But perhaps it came nearer that high eminence than any other American institution had before or has since.

Again a few years later, I saw the University of Berlin. It represented in 1892 a definite and unified ideal. It did not comprehend at once the culture of all Germany, but I do not believe that ever in modern days and certainly not at Fisk or Harvard did a great university come so near expressing a national ideal. It was as though I had been stepping up from a little group college with a national vision to a provincial university with more than national outlook to a national institution which came near gathering to itself the thought and culture of forty million human beings. Every great professor of Germany, with few exceptions, had the life ambition to be called to a chair in the Friedrich Wilhelm's Universitaet zu Berlin. I sat beneath the voice of a man who perhaps more than any single individual embodied the German ideal and welded German youth into that great aggressive fist that literally put *Deutchland über Alles!* I remember well Heinrich von Treitschke. With swift flying words that hid a painfully stuttering tongue, he hammered into the young men who sat motionless and breathless beneath his voice, the doctrine of the inborn superiority of the German race. And out and around that university for a thousand miles, millions of people shared in its ideal teaching, and did this in spite of caste of birth and poverty, of jostling wealth, because they believed in an ultimate unity which Bismarckian state socialism promised. They sang their national songs and joined in national festivals with enthusiasm that brought tears to the onlooker. And it made you realize the ideal of a single united nation and what it could express in matchless poetry, daring science and undying music.

Yet in each of these cases, the ultimate ideal of a national, much less a universal university was a vision never wholly attained, and in the very nature of the case it could not be. Fisk had to be a Negro university because it was teaching Negroes and they were a caste with their own history and problems. Harvard was still a New England provincial institution and Berlin was sharply and determinedly German. Their common characteristic was that starting where they did and must, they aimed and moved toward universal culture.

Now with these things in mind, let us turn back to America and to the American Negro. It had been said many times that a Negro university is nothing more and nothing less than a university. Quite recently one of the great leaders of education in the United States,

Abraham Flexner, said something of that sort concerning Howard University. As President of the Board of Trustees, he said he was seeking to build not a Negro university but a university.[1] And by those words he brought again before our eyes the ideal of a great institution of learning which becomes a center of universal culture. With all good will toward them that speak such words, it is the object of this paper to insist that there can be no college for Negroes which is not a Negro college and that while an American Negro university, just like a German or a Swiss university, may rightly aspire to a universal culture unhampered by limitations of race and culture, yet it must start on the earth where we sit and not in the skies whither we aspire. May I develop this thought.

In the first place, we have got to remember that here in America, in the year 1933, we have a situation which cannot be ignored. There was a time when it seemed as though we might best attack the Negro problem by ignoring its most unpleasant features. It was not and is not yet in good taste to speak generally about certain facts which characterize our situation in America. We are politically hamstrung. We have the greatest difficulty in getting suitable and remunerative work. Our education is more and more not only being confined to our own schools but to a segregated public school system far below the average of the nation with one-third of our children continuously out of school. And above all, and this we like least to mention, we suffer a social ostracism which is so deadening and discouraging that we are compelled either to lie about it or to turn our faces toward the red flag of revolution. It consists of the kind of studied and repeated and emphasized public insult which during all the long history of the world has led men to kill or be killed. And in the full face of any effort which any black man may make to escape this ostracism for himself, stands this flaming sword of racial doctrine which will distract his effort and energy if it does not lead him to spiritual suicide.

We boast and have right to boast of our accomplishment between the days that I studied here and this forty-fifth anniversary of my graduation. It is a calm appraisal of fact to say that the history of modern civilization cannot surpass if it can parallel the advance of American Negroes in every essential line of culture in these years. And yet when we have said this we must have the common courage honestly to admit that every step we have made forward has been greeted by a step

---

[1] Abraham Flexner (1867–1959) was a founder of the Institute for Advanced Study, at Princeton and its director for nine years. Simon and Schuster published his autobiography, *I Remember*, in 1939. For the report of the committee on Howard University, which he headed, see *New York Times*, March 15, 1932, p. 23.

backward on the part of the American public in caste intolerance, mob law, and racial hatred.

I need but remind you that when I graduated from Fisk there was no "Jim Crow" car in Tennessee and I saw Hunter of '89 once sweep a brakeman aside at the Union Station and escort a crowd of Fisk students into the first-class seats for which they had paid. There was no legal disfranchisement and a black Fiskite sat in the legislature; and while the Chancellor of Vanderbilt University had annually to be reintroduced to the President of Fisk, yet no white Southern group presumed to dictate the internal social life of this institution.

Manifestly with all that can be said, pro and con, and in extenuation, and by way of excuse and hope, this is the situation and we know it. There is no human way by which these facts can be ignored. We cannot do our daily work, sing a song, or write a book or carry on a university and act as though these things were not.

If this is true, then no matter how much we may dislike the statement, the American Negro problem is and must be the center of the Negro university. It has got to be. You are teaching Negroes. There is no use pretending that you are teaching Chinese or that you are teaching white Americans or that you are teaching citizens of the world. You are teaching American Negroes in 1933, and they are the subjects of a caste system in the Republic of the United States of America and their life problem is primarily this problem of caste.

Upon these foundations, therefore, your university must start and build. Nor is the thing so entirely unusual or unheard of as it sounds. A university in Spain is not simply a university. It is a Spanish university. It is a university located in Spain. It uses the Spanish language. It starts with Spanish history and makes conditions in Spain the starting point of its teaching. Its education is for Spaniards, not for them as they may be or ought to be, but as they are with their present problems and disadvantages and opportunities.

In other words, the Spanish university is founded and ground in Spain, just as surely as a French university is French. There are some people who have difficulty in apprehending this very clear truth. They assume, for instance, that the French university is in a singular sense universal, and is based on a comprehension and inclusion of all mankind and of their problems. But it is not, and the assumption that it is arises simply because so much of French culture has been built into universal civilization. A French university is founded in France; it uses the French language and assumes a knowledge of French history. The present problems of the French people are its major problems and it becomes universal only so far as other peoples of the world comprehend and are at one with France in its mighty and beautiful history.

In the same way, a Negro university in the United States of America begins with Negroes. It uses that variety of the English idiom which they understand; and above all, it is founded, or it should be founded on a knowledge of the history of their people in Africa and in the United States, and their present condition. Without whitewashing or translating wish into facts, it begins with that; and then it asks how shall these young men and women be trained to earn a living and live a life under the circumstances in which they find themselves or with such changing of those circumstances as time and work and determination will permit.

Is this statement of the field of a Negro university a denial of aspiration or a change from older ideals? I do not think it is, although I admit in my own mind some change of thought and modification of method.

The system of learning which bases itself upon the actual condition of certain classes and groups of human beings is tempted to suppress a minor premise of fatal menace. It proposes that the knowledge given and the methods pursued in such institutions of learning shall be for the definite object of perpetuating present conditions or of leaving their amelioration in the hands of and at the initiative of other forces and other folk. This was the great criticism that those of us who fought for higher education of Negroes thirty years ago, brought against the industrial school.

The industrial school founded itself and rightly upon the actual situation of American Negroes and said: "What can be done to change this situation?" And its answer was: a training in technique and method such as would incorporate the disadvantaged group into the industrial organization of the country, and in that organization the leaders of the Negro had perfect faith. Since that day the industrial machine has cracked and groaned. Its technique has changed faster than any school could teach; the relations of capital and labor have increased in complication and it has become so clear that Negro poverty is not primarily caused by ignorance of technical knowledge that the industrial school has almost surrendered its program.

In opposition to that, the proponents of college training in those earlier years said: "What black men need is the broader and more universal training so that they can apply the general principles of knowledge to the particular circumstances of their condition."

Here again was indubitable truth but incomplete truth. The technical problem lay in the method of teaching this broader and more universal truth and here just as in the industrial program, we must start where we are and not where we wish to be.

As I said a few years ago at Howard University both these positions had thus something of truth and right. Because of the peculiar economic situation in our country the program of the industrial school came to grief first and has practically been given up. Starting even though we may with the actual condition of the Negro peasant and artisan, we cannot ameliorate his condition simply by learning a trade which is the transient technique of a passing era. More vision and knowledge is needed than that. But on the other hand, while the Negro college of a generation ago set down a defensible and true program of applying knowledge to facts, it unfortunately could not completely carry it out, and it did not carry it out because the one thing that the industrial philosophy gave to education, the Negro college did not take and that was *that the university education of black men in the United States must be grounded in the condition and work of those black men!*[2]

On the other hand, it would be of course idiotic to say, as the former industrial philosophy almost said, that so far as most black men are concerned, education must stop with this. No, starting with present conditions and using the facts and the knowledge of the present situation of American Negroes, the Negro university expands toward the possession and the conquest of all knowledge. It seeks from a beginning of the history of the Negro in America and in Africa to interpret all history; from a beginning of social development among Negro slaves and freedmen in America and Negro tribes and kingdoms in Africa, to interpret and understand the social development of all mankind in all ages. It seeks to reach modern science of matter and life from the surroundings and habits and aptitudes of American Negroes and thus lead up to understanding of life and matter in the universe.

And this is a different program than a similar function would be in a white university or in a Russian university or in an English university, because it starts from a different point. It is a matter of beginnings and integrations of one group which sweeps instinctive knowledge and inheritance and current reactions into a universal world of science, sociology, and art. In no other way can the American Negro college function. It cannot begin with history and lead to Negro history. It cannot start with sociology and end with[3] Negro sociology.

Why was it that the Renaissance of literature which began among Negroes ten years ago has never taken real and lasting root? It was because it was a transplanted and exotic thing. It was a literature written for the benefit of white people and at the behest of white readers, and starting out primarily from the white point of view. It never had a real Negro constituency and it did not grow out of the inmost heart and frank experience of Negroes; on such an artificial basis no real literature can grow.

On the other hand, if starting in a great Negro university you have knowledge, beginning with the particular, and going out to universal comprehension and unhampered expression, you are going to begin to realize for the American Negro the full life which is denied him now. And then after that comes a realization of the older object of our college—to bring this universal culture down and apply it to the individual life and individual conditions of living Negroes.

The university must become not simply a center of knowledge but a center of applied knowledge and guide of action. And this is all the more necessary now since we easily see that planned action especially in economic life is going to be the watchword of civilization.

If the college does not thus root itself in the group life and afterward apply its knowledge and culture to actual living, other social organs must replace the college in this function. A strong, intelligent family life may adjust the student to higher culture; and, too, a social clan may receive the graduate and induct him into life. This has happened and is happening among a minority of privileged people. But it costs society a fatal price. It tends to hinder progress and hamper change—it makes education propaganda for things as they are. It leaves the mass of those[4] without social standing—misfits and rebels who despite their education are uneducated in its meaning and application. The only college which stands for the progress of all—mass as well as aristocracy—functions in root and blossom as well as in the overshadowing and heaven-filling tree. No system of learning—no university—can be universal before it is German, French, Negro. Grounded in inexorable fact and condition, in Poland or Italy, it may seek the universal, and haply it may find it—and finding it bring it down to earth and to us.

We have imbibed from the surrounding white world a childish idea of progress. Progress means bigger and better results always and forever. But there is no such rule of life. In six thousand years of human culture, the losses and retrogressions have been enormous. We have no assurance that twentieth-century civilization will survive. We do not know that American Negroes will survive. There are sinister signs about us, antecedent to and unconnected with the great depression. The organized might of industry north and south is

---

[2] Italics added by Du Bois in manuscript.

[3] In the original this reads "lead to."

---

[4] In the original appear four words here omitted: "without family training and."

relegating the Negro to the edge of survival and using him as a labor reservoir on starvation wage. No secure professional class, no science, literature, nor art can live on such a subsoil. It is an insistent deep-throated cry for rescue, guidance, and organized advance that greets the black leader today and the college that trains him has got to let him know at least as much about the great black miners' strike in Alabama as about the Age of Pericles.[5] By singular accident—almost by compelling fate—I drove by, as I came here yesterday, the region where I taught a country school over forty years ago. There is no progress there. There is only space, disillusion, and death beside the same eternal hills. There where first I heard the "Sorrow Songs" are the graves of men and women and children who had the making of a fine intelligent upstanding yeomanry. There remains but the half-starved farmer, the casual laborer, the unpaid servant. Why, in a land rich with wealth, muscle, and colleges?

To the New Englander of wealth and family, Harvard and Yale are parts and only parts of a broad training which the New England home begins and a State Street or Wall Street business ends. How fine and yet how fatal! There lie root and reason for the World War and the Great Depression. To the American Negro, culture must adjust itself to a different family history and apply itself to a new system of social caste and in this adjustment comes new opportunity of making education and progress possible and not antagonistic.

We are on the threshold of a new era. Let us not deceive ourselves with outworn ideals of wealth and servants and luxuries, reared on a foundation of ignorance, starvation and want. Instinctively, we have absorbed these ideals from our twisted white American environment. This new economic planning is not for us unless we do it. Unless the American Negro today, led by trained university men of broad vision, sits down to work out by economics and mathematics, by physics and chemistry, by history and sociology, exactly how and where he is to earn a living and how he is to establish a reasonable life in the United States or elsewhere, unless this is done the university has missed its field and function and the American Negro is doomed to be a suppressed and inferior caste in the United States for incalculable time.

Here, then, is a job for the American Negro university. It cannot be successfully ignored or dodged without the growing menace of disaster. I lay the problem before you as one which you must not ignore.

_____

[5]As reprinted in the *Crisis*, August 1933, the conclusion of this paragraph and the entirety of the next is not included.

To carry out this plan, two things and only two things are necessary—teachers and students. Buildings and endowments may help, but they are not indispensable. It is necessary first to have teachers who comprehend this program and know how to make it live among their students. This is calling for a good deal, because it asks that teachers teach that which they have learned in no American school and which they never will learn until we have a Negro university of the sort that I am visioning. No teacher, black or white, who comes to a university like Fisk, filled simply with general ideas of human culture or general knowledge of disembodied science, is going to make a university of this school. Because a university is made of human beings, learning of the things they do not know from things they do know in their own lives.

And secondly, we must have students. They must be chosen for ability to learn. There is always the temptation to assume that the children of privileged classes, the rich, the noble, the white, are those who can best take education. One has but to express this to realize its utter futility. But perhaps the most dangerous thing among us is for us, without thought, to imitate the white world and assume that we can choose students at Fisk because of the amount of money which their parents have happened to get hold of. That basis of selection is going to give us an extraordinary aggregation. We want by the nicest methods possible, to seek out the talented and the gifted among our constituency, quite regardless of their wealth or position, and to fill this university and similar institutions with persons who have got brains enough to take fullest advantage of what the university offers. There is no other way. With teachers who know what they are teaching and whom they are teaching and the life that surrounds both the knowledge and the knower, and with students who have the capacity and the will to absorb this knowledge, we can build the sort of Negro university which will emancipate not simply the black folk of the United States, but those white folk who in their effort to suppress Negroes have killed their own culture—men who in their desperate effort to replace equality with caste and to build inordinate wealth on a foundation of abject poverty have succeeded in killing democracy, art, and religion.

Only a universal system of learning, rooted in the will and condition of masses and blossoming from that manure up toward the stars is worth the name. Once builded it can only grow as it brings down sunlight and star shine and impregnates the mud. The chief obstacle in this rich land endowed with every natural resource and with the abilities of a hundred different peoples— the chief and only obstacle to the coming of that kingdom of economic equality which is the only logical end of work, is the determination of the white world to keep the black world poor and make themselves rich. The disaster which this selfish and short-sighted policy has brought lies at the bottom of this present depression, and too, its cure lies beside it. Your clear vision of a world without wealth, of capital without profit, of income based on work alone, is the path out not only for you but for all men.

Is not this a program of segregation, emphasis of race and particularism as against national unity and universal humanity? It is, and it is not by choice but by force; you do not get humanity by wishing it nor do you become American citizens simply because you want to. A Negro university from its high ground of unfaltering facing of the Truth, from its unblinking stare at hard facts, does not advocate segregation by race, it simply accepts the bald fact that we are segregated, apart, hammered into a separate unity by spiritual intolerance and legal sanction backed by mob law, and that this separation is growing in strength and fixation; that it is worse today than a half century ago and that no character, address, culture, or desert is going to change it, in our day or for centuries to come.

Recognizing this brute fact, groups of cultured, trained, and devoted men gathering in great institutions of learning proceed to ask: What are we going to do about it? It is silly to ignore and gloss the truth; it is idiotic to proceed as though we were white or yellow, English or Russian. Here we stand. We are American Negroes. It is beside the point to ask whether we form a real race. Biologically we are mingled of all conceivable elements, but race is psychology, not biology; and psychologically we are a unified race with one history, one red memory, and one revolt. It is not ours to argue whether we will be segregated or whether we ought to be a caste. We are segregated; we are a caste. This is our given and at present unalterable fact. Our problem is: How far and in what way can we consciously and scientifically guide our future so as to insure our physical survival, our spiritual freedom and our social growth? Either we do this or we die. There is no alternative. If America proposes the murder of this group, its moral descent into imbecility and crime and its utter loss of manhood, self-assertion, and courage, the sooner we realize this the better. By that great line of McKay: "If we must die, let it not be like hogs."

But the alternative of not dying like hogs is not that of dying or killing like snarling dogs. It is rather conquering the world by thought and brain and plan; by expression and organized cultural ideals. Therefore, let us not beat futile wings in impotent frenzy, but carefully plan and guide our segregated life, organize in industry and politics to protect it and expand it, and above all to give it unhampered spiritual expression in art and literature. It is the council of fear and cowardice to say this cannot be done. What must be can and it is only a question of Science and Sacrifice to bring the great consummation.

What that will be, none knows. It may be a great physical segregation of the world along the color line; it may be an economic rebirth which insures spiritual and group integrity amid physical diversity. It may be utter annihilation of class and race and color barriers in one ultimate mankind, differentiated by talent, susceptibility and gift—but any of these ends are matters of long centuries and not years. We live in years, swift flying, transient years. We hold the possible future in our hands but not by wish and will, only by thought, plan, knowledge, and organization. If the college can pour into the coming age an American Negro who knows himself and his plight and how to protect himself and fight race prejudice, then the world of our dream will come and not otherwise.[6]

> The golden days are gone. Why do we wait
> So long upon the marble steps, blood
> Falling from our open wounds? and why
> Do our black faces search the empty sky?
> Is there something we have forgotten?
> Some precious thing we have lost,
> Wandering in strange lands?

What we have lost is the courage of independent self-assertion. We have had as our goal—American full citizenship, nationally recognized. This has failed—flatly and decisively failed. Very well. We're not dead yet. We are not going to die. If we use our brains and strength there is no way to stop our ultimate triumph as creators of modern culture—if we use our strength and brains.

And what pray stops us but our dumb caution—our fear—our very sanity. Let us then be insane with courage.

> Like a mad man's dream, there came
> One fair, swift flash to me
> Of distances, of streets aflame
> With joy and agony;
> And further yet, a moonlit sea
> Foaming across its bars
> And further yet, the infinity
> Of wheeling suns and stars.

---

[6]As published in the *Crisis*, August 1933, the essay ends at this point. The first stanza of poetry is from Arna Bontemps's "Nocturne at Bethesda" first published in the *Crisis*, December 1926. The last eight lines may have been Du Bois's own; they have not been otherwise identified.

ENVOY

There was no aftermath of this speech save perhaps a general satisfaction. But to me it was the beginning of a new line of thought. The argument of the Howard speech did not seem to me to be altogether final. Something was missing and from that day I began to read and study Karl Marx.[7] I began to understand my recent visit to Russia. I became interested in the New Deal and I wanted to supplement the liberalism of Charles Sumner with the new economic contribution of the twentieth century.

ZORA NEALE HURSTON

The Hue and Cry About Howard University

I went to Howard as a Prep in 1918–19. I had met Mae Miller and she liked me and urged me to transfer from Morgan to Howard. I still have her little letter of friendship and encouragement. I value it too. That was the beginning of a personal and literary friendship that has lasted.

The thrill Hannibal got when he finally crossed the Alps, the feeling of Napoleon when he finally placed upon his head the iron crown of Constantine, were nothing to the ecstasy I felt when I realized I was actually a Howardite.

We used to have "sings" in Chapel every Monday during services and nobody knows how I used to strive to eradicate all pettiness from my nature so that I might be fit to sing "Alma Mater." We always finished the service with that. I used to indulge in searching introspection to root out even those little meannesses that put us far below the class of the magnificent transgressor and leave us merely ridiculous.

It was during the next year (1919) while Howard was not recovered from the S. A. T. C., that Wienstein came to Howard under government pay to conduct the singing in the "camp." He had a magnificent tenor voice, and wore his khaki well. He had worked with Prof. Wesley, also a tenor, in the war camps of the country and together they had us singing lustily. We liked it. We sang lots of things: "Long, Long Trail a Winding," "K-K-Katy," "Roll Jordan Roll," and "Gointer Study War No Mo' " among other things but we always ended with "Alma Mater."

After Wienstein left, the singing was continued under Wesley. He used to come out before the faculty on the platform and lead the singing daily. The President would arise with beaming face and ask us to sing our songs for him. He said that Negro music began where "white" music left off. We used to respond cheerfully. Then we would select any song from the book we liked. Hymn 245, "God of Our Fathers" and 180, "Immortal Love Forever Full," were our favorites. This went on for weeks and weeks. Spring was approaching.

One day I wrote Dr. Durkee a note and left it on the pulpit as I came into chapel, asking him to read the 21st Psalm. He has a marvelous speaking voice and I would wish nothing better than hearing him read that beautiful piece of prose poetry. He did not read it. I felt snubbed and disappointed, but the next day he began that beautiful one, "The Heavens Declare the Glory of God." The sun shone in mellow tones through the stained windows, tendrils of the ivy vine crept in the open windows and the sparrows chirped incessantly in the midst of their nest building.

The President knew it perfectly and before he was fairly under way he had his audience on the edge of the seats so that the last tones left us still hanging there. And when we realized that he was really through we sank back tremendously moved.

Howard was unutterably beautiful to me that spring. I would give a great deal to call back my Howard illusion of those days:

Every day after that for a month the President read a psalm. It took a long time to reach the 91st, but I did not care. He never looked in the book—I am certain he knows them all by heart. E. H. Southern in "Hamlet" has nothing on Dr. Durkee reciting the psalms.

I dwell on these seemingly trifling details to give one a picture of Howard before the storm.

A few days later and the first storm broke. A great number of students but not the entire body of students by any means were holding indignation meetings alleging that they had been forced or commanded by the President to sing "Spirituals." He was denounced as a despot, a tyrant, who was dragging us back into slavery.

Though there were spokesmen among the students, various members of the faculty were credited as the real leaders. Among whom were Miss Childers, Mr. Tibbs and Miss Lewis. Some said Miss Childers didn't like the idea of Wesley leading the singing as she used to "raise" all the songs. The papers printed things down in the city and some members of the Senate denounced us as ingrates and accused us of being ashamed of ourselves and our traditions.

[7]Du Bois must mean here an intensive study of Marx—and by 1934 he taught a course on "Marx and the Negro Question" at Atlanta University. But he had read in Marx much earlier and by 1904 there are indications that he thought of himself as basically a socialist. His "visit to Russia" had occurred in 1926.

The President held a conference with the students one day after Chapel to find out how he had offended. There were speakers for and against the "Spirituals." John Miles, now of Yale Divinity School, was one of the "Pros," Mae Miller and another young lady whose name has slipped me, were "Antis."

The "Pro's" made the usual stand: (*a*) The beauty and workmanship of the songs. (*b*) Only American folk songs. (*c*) Only beauty that came out of slavery. The "Anti's" held: (*a*) They were low and degrading, being the product of slaves and slavery; (*b*) not good grammar; (*c*) they are not sung in white universities.

The thought that any Negro could or would be ashamed of Negro music, had never occurred to Dr. Durkee I am sure, for he seemed pained that he had unwittingly offended and never since has suggested them.

After a few days of bluster this affair died down but not before a perceptible rift had been made in the faculty and student group.

A little later that same year, Senator Smoot arose on the floor of the Senate with a book in hand which he informed the Senators was a highly culpable bolshevistic volume which he had received from the hands of a Howard student. He understood it came from the university library and insinuated that it was in the curriculum. He held forth that a government supported institution that was making bolshevists should be allowed to toddle along without government aid seeing that this was the U. S. and not Red Russia.

Rumors flew thick and fast among the students as to who had engineered the book into the Senator's hands. It is to be remembered that Smoot was head of the Appropriation Committee. Durkee hastened down to the Senate Committee room and explained that the book had been given by the Rand School and it was the policy of the university to accept all gifts. It was neither taught nor recommended. This satisfied the Senator evidently, for finally the appropriation came through. He was denounced by some on the Hill and some off for having cringed before the Senate. He should have informed that body that we could teach what we liked and if the money was withheld we could have the satisfaction of being untrammeled. I even saw a typewritten, unsigned card on the bulletin board on the second floor of the main building to the effect: "It is better to lose $250,000 than our manhood."

After the smoke had cleared away, a young man known to be socialistic, a close friend of mine, left Howard forever. I saw him recently in New York. He says he has been around the world twice since 1919 but never feels right to go back to any school.

More than one person was accused of having sent that book to Smoot by the student. Some say that a professor in the law school did it, others that a teacher in the department of history, to embarrass the administration. Perhaps it will not be known just who, but anyway, Senator Smoot never drew it from the library.

"The University Luncheonette," run by two law students, Dyett and McGhee, was a place where a great deal of discussion went on. Mr. Dyett being known as the anti-administration man.

About this time the "Contemptible puppy" rumors began to circulate. Students were beginning to see that there was something wrong somewhere. Some faculty members and the Administration were not so "clubby," so to speak, as they might be. There were stories flying about the campus that certain members were giving certain trusted students "tips" on faculty meeting doings.

Dr. Emmett J. Scott had been made secretary-treasurer of the university, succeeding both Cook and Parks in their respective jobs. This, some felt, was unjust and muttered that an attempt was being made to "Tuskegeeize" Howard. Dr. Scott being the first gun fired. There was no one to whom these rumors could be definitely traced, but the students passing along the complaints always claimed faculty sources. For instance a young lady friend of mine stopped me in the upper corridor of main building to tell me that Dr. Durkee should be thrown out. I was astonished and asked her why she thought this.

"Well," she said, "he called Kelly Miller a black dog to his face."

"How did you hear it?"

"A very high member of the faculty—an official told me, and I know he wouldn't lie."

This was the first time I had heard the story, but not the last by any means. I heard it variously repeated. In one story Mr. Miller had been called a "puppy dog;" in another "a black dog," in another a "contemptible puppy." From neither of the principals have I ever heard a syllable on this matter, but whether it is true in any part, it had a tremendous effect upon the students—a Negro professor being called out of his name by a white man—no matter what the provocation, if any.

More and more it came to be so that every official act of the faculty must be subject to student scrutiny. In some way or other Alexander Z. Looby, George Brown and Fred Jordan had a pretty thorough knowledge of what went on in the chamber. But Mr. Looby was President of the Student Council and perhaps had a chance to know things that way.

A great many of us took no stock in the hurly-burly, feeling that we could not as students act in the capacity of the Administration, but a great number were flattered at these rumored confidences. I discount most of it as being untrue—the figment of persons wishing to enhance their own importance in student eyes by appearing as the confident of the faculty. One instance I know to be true.

In political science Mr. Tunnell digressed one day from government in general to government in particular and told the class that Dr. Durkee was a joke; that some one (I forget who) had foisted that fisherman on us and that he was being paid a high salary to raise funds, but he was a failure. He then told us the President's salary was $7,000 per year and his house. He then told us that Emmett J. Scott had been brought on from Tuskegee and paid $5,000 ($4,500 salary, $500 incidentals) to divert the golden stream from that school to Howard but he was a white elephant.

Of course I was surprised at such confidences but so much was being said here and there on the campus that one could expect about anything. It was evident to me now that the faculty (I mean by that term the entire governing-teaching body) was a Spartan youth concealing a fox under its clothes.

Then there was the instance of the famous note on the desk of Senator Smoot written by Professor Kelly Miller. It had to do with the appropriation rules. The Administration was making a tremendous fight for the $500,000 for the Medical school. A number of Senators were doing battle for and against it, but a strong group had pledged themselves to see it through. President Coolidge in his message to Congress had urged that it be given Howard. Dr. Durkee is a Massachusetts man and his Senators had taken the field openly in his behalf. In the midst of this came Prof. Miller's note to Senator Smoot asking him not to ask for the half-million dollars for fear of losing the regular appropriation of $267,000, I think it was, and threw the Administration friends into confusion. The daily press of Washington accused the professor of attempting to embarrass the Administration since the President stated that Miller's action was unauthorized. I have never seen an authorized version of the affair from Prof. Miller's pen, and shall therefore suspend judgment until I do. There have been a number of stories pro and con, but so far as open statements are concerned, the affair remains where the press left it.

There are those who hold that Prof. Miller aspires to the presidency of the university. No one can deny the urge to ascend in humanity. If we do we preach stagnation. His ability to bring this about, if it is true, and if so rather to his credit than otherwise, what man is satisfied and his fitness for the job is being hotly debated all over the country at present. Some members of the alumnae claim that all that has happened at Howard in the way of disturbances is a part of the ladder up which Dean Miller prepares to ascend. The human mind unexpressed being unreadable, all these things pro and

Zora Neale Hurston (Courtesy of the Moorland-Spingarn Research Center)

con on the subject are still conjectures. Every one who reads or listens knows how often mole hills of trifling incidents are stretched to mountains and given special significance.

On the other hand there are those who contend that Dr. Durkee is an obstruction in the path of Howard's progress. This calls attention to the accomplishments of his administration. His bitterest enemy cannot but admit that more has been done for the advancement of the university under him than in all the other administrations put together. The following are excerpts from "Facts," a pamphlet issued by the university:

By vote of the Trustees, June 4, 1919, the offices of Secretary and Treasurer were combined, and Dr. Emmett J. Scott elected as Secretary-Treasurer. He began his services July 1, 1919.

The office of Registrar was created as a separate position, and a Howard alumnus, Dwight O. W. Holmes, was elected to that position, and succeeded by Mr. F. D. Wilkinson, upon the former's appointment as Dean of the School of Education.

Both the offices of Secretary-Treasurer and Registrar have been put by these officers on the most modern administrative basis with extensive rooms on the first floor of the Main Building.

The office of Dean of Men was created and to it elected Dr. Edward L. Parks, former Treasurer.

The office of Dean of Women was created and to it has been elected Miss Lucy D. Slowe, a Howard alumna, formerly principal of the M Street Junior High School of Washington. Miss Slowe is completing her first year most successfully.

For the academic deans has been created a group of offices on first floor of Main Building, with clerks. The Dean of Men and Dean of Women each have also been given fine offices with clerks.

There is also a University Council, composed of two members of each school of the University, including both undergraduate and graduate schools. The purpose of this Council is for a better understanding between the schools and for a more united purpose. This Council meets three or four times a year.

It has long been felt that an Alumni Secretary was necessary to our greatest success. In June, 1921, the Trustees voted as follows:

"Authority is granted to the President to secure an Alumni Secretary under conditions which will be of best advantage both to the University and to the alumni, paying such salary as shall be needed, money paid not to exceed $1,000 toward the salary of the person employed."

Mr. Norman L. McGhee, College '19, Law '22, a member of the Secretary-Treasurer's office force, is temporarily heading up this movement for closer affiliation with our alumni.

In February, 1920, the Board of Trustees voted as follows:

"One Trustee may be elected each year from a number recommended by the Alumni Association of the University, such Trustee to automatically retire at the expiration of his term of office."

Since the report of the Committee, no vacancies on the Board have occurred. It is interesting to note that eight Alumni of Howard University are now serving as members of the Board of Trustees.

Building and Grounds

New buildings erected: The Greenhouse, erected in 1919, at a cost of $8,000, and the Dining Hall Building with class rooms for the Department of Home Economics, erected in 1921, at a cost of $201,000. Plans are now under way for the new gymnasium and stadium. The General Statement, given below, will show numerous ren-

ovations made. Howard Hall, General O. O. Howard's old home, used for so many years as a detention house for incorrigible children, has been reclaimed, the old outbuildings torn away, and the home restored as a dormitory for girls. In the Main Building, a United States postoffice has been established, thus serving the postal needs of student body and faculty. In the Main Building, also, has been equipped a Rest Room for girls and also one for women teachers and workers. Both were greatly needed.

The items in the General Statement "Improvement of Grounds" includes the following: Reclaiming of the bank overlooking the Reservoir, formerly a dump for cans and a place for burning rubbish: trees on the campus have been treated twice; large flower beds of rare beauty have been placed; plaza and front of Thirkeld Hall made beautiful and splendid concrete walks and steps to Sixth Street provided; fence surrounding the lower half of main campus; unsightly plot of ground on Georgia Avenue changed into a beautiful little park with paths crossing and steps leading up to Sixth Street; surroundings of Howard Hall graded and granolithic walks and steps placed; grounds surrounding School of Music beautified; underground electric lighting system installed with posts and globes like those used in the District of Columbia—this latter one of the biggest improvements.

It also became necessary for the Trustees to appropriate certain amounts out of general funds so as to complete the improvements and repairs mentioned.

A summary of the amounts spent since July 1, 1919, up to the period ending December 30, 1922, follows:

Repairs to sundry buildings, including the Main Building, Science Hall, the Chapel, President's House, Spaulding Hall and various residence properties of the University	$55,487.34
Repairs to Clark and Miner Halls, dormitories for young men and young women	21,625.08
Improvement of grounds	15,896.98
Repairs to Law School Building	15,530.06
Improvements, Library Building	1,388.61
Repairs to Medical and Dental Schools Buildings	13,745.46
Installation New Electric Feeders, thereby making more efficient the heating and lighting facilities of the University	1,246.20

Repairs to Boarding Hall, while in basement of Miner Hall	478.30
Repairs to Manual Arts Building	732.56
	$126,130.59

Curriculum

At the close of school year 1918–19, all secondary schools were abolished, leaving a college registration of 1,057. Dire disaster was everywhere prophesied by the following year the college opened with 1,567 college students.

The whole plan of undergraduate work was changed. The four years' college course was divided into two periods of two years each—the first two years named the Junior College, and the second, the Senior Schools. A student entering the undergraduate department will take two years of general college subjects leading to his last two years of specialized work in whatever field he may choose, graduating at the end of four years with his degree from that particular school. The College of Liberal Arts cares for all those students who desire four full years of undergraduate non-professional work.

New courses of study authorized by the Trustees during the present administration:

Architecture

Art

Dramatics

Public Health and Hygiene

Reserve Officers' Training Corps

At the Trustee meeting of June, 1919, the old semester system was abolished. Under that system it took the college three weeks to register its students and get to work in its classes. We are now on the quarter system, and register two thousand students and more in two days at the opening of the year, and in one day for the winter and spring quarters, classes beginning recitations the following day.

The General Education Board required as a basis for its help that all finances of the School of Medicine be taken over by the general administration of the University and be handled in one office. When this was done, the Board pledged the University $250,000 as an endowment to the Medical School, providing the University would raise a like sum. This sum, in cash or pledges, must be raised by July 1, 1923, pledges to be redeemed by July 1, 1926. With such an endowment the Medical School may be kept in Class A. Without this endowment the Medical School will lose its Class A rating. Hence, the necessity for every friend of the

School to rally to its support now. To show the remarkable spirit among the student body, the President announces that the student body has pledged $24,843. The Trustees, administration, and faculty have pledged practically $15,000. The total gifts so far (May 21) amount to about $220,000.

During 1920–21 evening classes were established. The attendance for that year was 46. The registration for 1922–23 is 153. So far we have served 104 teachers from the public schools of Washington.

In 1919 the Trustees, on recommendation of the President, adopted a Faculty Salary Scale, toward which the administration should work. The scale is as follows:

Dean	$3,000 to $3,500
Professor	2,500 to 3,000
Associate Professor	2,000 to 2,500
Assistant Professor	1,500 to 2,000
Instructor	750 to 1,500

Over $63,000 have been added to the teachers' salaries alone during this administration. The minimum scale has now been practically reached, and the last two surpassed. Many salaries have been doubled in three years. Average increase of salaries 56 per cent; 26 new teachers have been added.

By recommendation of the President, the Trustees voted that teachers of professional rank may have the privilege of a sabbatical year of absence on half pay, providing they use that year's leave of absence for advance study in some standard institution of learning, the better to fit themselves for their particular field in teaching.

With the opening of the present administration, 1918–19, total financial income was $220,553.43, of which sum the Federal Government appropriation was $117,937.75.

Our auditors reported for the year 1921–22 a total budget figure of $589,033.87, of which sum the Government appropriation was $363,135.25; $116,000 of the $336,135.25 was appropriated for the New Dining Hall, which has been in use during the school year 1922–23.

We have a School of Public Health and Hygiene with a Director. Under that School comes the Department of Physical Education with a director in charge; also the Department of Military Education with six officers detailed from the United States Army to care for our Reserve Officers' Training Corps. But the Trustees voted to have student managers of the individual teams, such as football, baseball, track, etc., and also invited the alumni to elect three representatives from the alumni as an Advisory Committee who will meet with the staff of the Department of Physical Education concerning all matters of interest in that Department.

Congressional Appropriations for Five (5) Years as Contrasted With First Year of 1918–1919

Name of Appropriation	1918–19	1919–20	1920–21	1921–22	1922–23	1923–24	1924–25	1925–26
Maintenance, salaries, etc.	$72,437.75	$76,437.75	$90,000.00	$90,000.00	$100,000.00	$110,000.00	$125,000.00	$125,000.00
Buildings and grounds	10,000.00	10,000.00	32,500.00	32,500.00	42,500.00	20,000.00	20,000.00	30,000.00
Medical	7,000.00	7,000.00	7,000.00	8,000.00	8,000.00	9,000.00	9,000.00	9,000.00
Medical Addition, New Bldg	—	—	—	—	—	—	—	370,000.00
Laboratories	2,000.00	2,000.00	2,000.00	2,000.00	3,000.00	5,000.00	5,000.00	5,000.00
Libraries	1,500.00	1,500.00	1,500.00	1,500.00	1,500.00	3,500.00	3,500.00	3,000.00
Fuel and Light	5,000.00	5,000.00	5,000.00	10,000.00	15,000.00	15,000.00	15,000.00	15,000.00
Manual Arts	20,000.00	20,000.00	20,000.00	20,000.00	20,000.00	30,000.00	30,000.00	34,000.00
The New Dining Hall	—	—	85,000.00	116,000.00	—	—	157,500.00	—
*Athletic Field, Gymnasium, Armory and Administrative Headquarters for Department of Health and Hygiene	—	—	—	—	—	40,000.00	—	—
Totals	$117,937.75	$121,937.75	$243,000.00	$280,000.00	$190,000.00	$232,500.00	$365,000.00	$591,000.00

*Note: $157,500 to complete Gymnasium project also authorized, but not yet available.

With the opening of this administration there was but one department of the University approved by the rating associations of America. The School of Medicine was Class A.

In the autumn of 1921, the Association of Colleges and Preparatory Schools of the Middle States and Maryland, after most rigid personal investigation, placed our College of Liberal Arts on the Approved List. This means that now our graduates from such college have the same scholastic standing as graduates from any other first-class school in America.

In the spring of 1922, our Dental College was registered in the New York State Board of Regents, thus giving it the highest rating.

Our College of Pharmacy has just been given the highest rating with the Pharmacy Board of the State of Ohio.

Our School of Law is now applying for admission to the Association of American Law Schools, and we are confident of success.

A careful organization of the students has been approved, and under the title of "Student Council," the students have a very large measure of self-government.

The Board of Trustees in June, 1922, unanimously passed the following vote:

"INASMUCH as the past year has been marked by very substantial progress in the life of Howard University as indicated in the erection of a splendid new Dining Hall building at a cost of $200,000; in the registration of its Dental School in the A grade of dental schools by the Board of Regents of the State of New York; in the acceptance of Howard University on the Approved List of colleges and preparatory schools of the Middle States and Maryland; in the high quality of work done in the various departments and in other respects:

"BE IT RESOLVED, That the Board of Trustees of Howard University hereby expresses its hearty confidence in and its cordial approval of the energy, the sound judgment, and the administrative efficiency of the President and the other administrative officers in the conduct of the life of the institution;

"BE IT FURTHER RESOLVED, That the students, teachers and alumni of the University are cordially invited at any time to confer with the University authorities on matters pertaining to its welfare on the basis of mutual interest."

There is no doubt in the minds of fair people that the President has been maligned. The local alumni is responsible for this to a large extent. Whenever disturbances occur on the Hill, they never investigate but rush to press with bitter denunciations of the President, using that sure-fire gag to arouse the unthinking, "A group of intelligent, high-minded race persons being 'low-rated' and otherwise trampled under foot by a white tyrant." This never fails to stir, for we are yet too close to slavery, evidently to judge a case on its merits rather than on its relation to other groups.

The senseless criticism of the appointment of Dr. Scott has died down, for surely no one can deny that he has made good. No student has been forced to pick cotton as was predicted. The murmurs against Wilkinson as Registrar on the grounds that he was not a college man have proven untimely for he certainly has justified his appointment.

He has been misrepresented in connection with the Curry School at Boston. It is a very small private school founded over forty years ago by Dr. S. S. Curry of Tennessee. There have never been colored students at the school. He received a diploma from the school twenty-three years ago and knows of the great advantages of such training. When after the death of Dr. and

Mrs. Curry, Alumni asked him to head up the school for a little while. He did so with the statement in print (he wrote it to Mr. C. Murphy of the Afro-American) that he would slowly overcome the practice of forty years and have our colored students admitted. This he feels he could have done.

Notwithstanding the public statements, enemies distorted the whole question and made it seem to the public that he was playing double.

So after seven months as president of the school, Dr. Durkee resigned. Of course his name will appear for a few months, as in all similar cases of school catalogues, but when the board meets in the fall, his name will cease to be carried, as he is no longer connected with the school.

He has been criticized for preaching in the city pulpits of Washington. Some weeks ago he preached in one of the largest pulpits in the city. His services were freely given. At the close of the service a gentleman came up and gave Doctor a check for $500 for the School of Religion at Howard. Next week a check for $750.00 came from a good friend who had listened to him preach. He wanted him to place the money in the School of Religion drive. Another friend who listens to him preach in Washington gave him $400.00 per year for four years for the same drive. A Sunday School class of the city of Washington just sent him $105.00 for the same drive.

These are but a few touches—I could give you scores of such.

He is quoted as drawing a salary of $7,500 and certain perquisites from the school. That is false. His salary is but $7,000 and president's house.

You will note from "Facts" the scholastic standing. The struggle for such recognition may be imagined. Do not fancy that such a rating came to Howard by chance. He could tell you a long story of travel, conferences, writing, etc., with a great internal struggle to get the scholarship of the university up to the point where it could pass the test. Now our graduates go to the graduate schools of the leading universities of America on the strength of their work at Howard and the certification of their deans. There is no longer a question of "colored school." It is simply "Howard University," one of the sisterhood of the great universities. Note our teaching staff (President's Report, page 15).

Let me call your special attention to the close of the President's Report, pages 22–23. Also note Medical Report, page 18. You will see that he has secured $80,000.00 already of the $130,000.00 needed.

All these truths relating to great sums of money raised for

1. New buildings.
2. Endowment.
3. Repairs and improvement of grounds.
4. Teachers' salaries. (We have added to the salaries of teachers in six years, just about $70,000.00. Teachers who were receiving $800.00, $1,000.00, and $1,100.00 per year when he came seven years ago are to-day receiving $2,400.00, $2,600.00 and even $2,900.00. Two or three going over a total of $3,000.00.
5. Scholarship and scholastic standing.
6. General standing throughout America and the world. (A French scholar visiting Howard this past year, told Dr. Durkee that no group of scholars met for a conference on the European Continent, who did not discuss the growth and achievements of Howard University.)

Now all this vast achievement has been accomplished in the face of bitter opposition from certain persons on the faculty of the university and certain irresponsible persons outside the faculty. The active group on the outside are those who have contributed *scarcely one dollar to all this growth*. Dr. Durkee contributed $200.00 to the Medical Drive and has subscribed $500.00 to the School of Religion Drive. He yearly spends over $300.00 in aiding and helping students and societies of the university. The active opposition all together have not put as much money into the university as he has himself. (See article of Mr. Smith, Alumni and Field Secretary.)

Dr. Durkee often expresses his deepest debt and gratitude to Dr. Scott, without whom the work could not have succeeded; Dean Woodward, scholar, counsellor, loyal lover of Howard; Registrar Wilkinson than whom no university can have a finer, truer officer; Dr. Brady, Professor Coleman, and such like honest, upright, unswerving friends of the right and true. These have made possible what Dr. Leonard has said in his report regarding the wonderful work which the university has, and is, doing.

The following are excerpts from a recent statement of the Trustee Board:

Washington, D. C.—The Executive Committee of the Board of Trustees of Howard University, in joint session with the Budget Committee of the Board of Trustees of Howard University, Monday, June 15, 1925, authorized the release of the following statement:

The Statement

In response to requests which have reached the Trustees of Howard University from many loyal alumni and friends, making inquiry as to certain decisions of the Board of Trustees, at its annual meeting, held June 2,

1925, and subsequent meetings of the committees designated by the Board to carry its decision into effect, the following statement is made:

At a meeting of the Board of Trustees, held October 13, 1924, after a full discussion of the financial and academic condition of the university, it was decided that the general expansion of the university was running far ahead of the university's available resources. An intensive study on the part of officials of the university had led them to feel that there was much duplication of work and considerable expense in the way of overhead.

To relieve the situation of any suggestion of inside pre-judgment, or charge of prejudice, the Board of Trustees, upon recommendation to the Budget Committee, voted that a general survey of the various schools or departments should be made by an expert from the outside. The Board of Trustees considered itself most fortunate in being able to secure the services of Doctor Robert Josselyn Leonard, Director of the School of Education, Teachers' College, Columbia University, New York City, to make its first survey.

It was decided that a survey should be made first of the academic departments to be followed later by a survey of the departments of the School of Medicine. After a thorough-going study of the academic departments of the university, Doctor Leonard appeared in person and submitted a full and complete report, and made certain recommendations at the meeting of the Board of Trustees, held June 2, 1925. These recommendations were given very careful consideration by the members of the Board of Trustees. Some general idea as to Doctor Leonard's treatment of the situation is indicated by the following extracts from his report:

Retirement Plan for Teachers

Doctor Leonard, in his report, also recommended that the university look toward the adoption of a retirement plan. This whole matter, the retirement of teachers, has been before the Board of Trustees for a number of years. At the meeting of the Board, held February 3, 1925, the Budget Committee was requested to make a report at the June meeting of the Board of Trustees.

Professor Kelly Miller retains his professorship in the department of sociology. It was voted by the Executive Committee that his salary shall rank as $3,500 as dean.

Educational Organization

With reference to the present educational organization of the university, Doctor Leonard states that the present educational organization of the university is sound theoretically; *in fact, it represents the most advanced type*; but, in view of several practical difficulties, a number of important changes are proposed, looking toward consolidation for economy and efficiency, including the merger of the Junior College with the College of Liberal Arts.

"1. The university has neither the staff nor the financial resources to achieve fully the distinctive purpose of the Junior College; namely, to assist young men and women to determine upon the Senior College or professional school best adapted to their interests and abilities.

"2. Doctor Leonard also recommended that the work of the School of Commerce and Finance be merged under the College of Liberal Arts."

At the meeting of the Executive Committee, held June 15, 1925, carrying out the general program adopted by the Board of Trustees, making necessary contractions, eliminations and the discontinuance of some of the members of the faculty, it was decided to discontinue, as of June 30, 1925, the services of Alain L. Locke, Professor of Philosophy; Alonzo H. Brown, Professor of Mathematics; Metz. T. P. Lochard, Assistant Professor of French; Orlando C. Thornton, Instructor in Finance and Business Organization.

The Executive Committee devoted itself to a very full discussion of the whole matter in all of its phases and decided that the work of the university would not unduly suffer as the work of these professors would otherwise be carried. An expression of appreciation on behalf of the Board of Trustees was voted those discontinued for the services they have rendered the university since they have been in its employ.

Present Registration is 2,123 As Against 1,057 in 1919

A faculty member in criticising the Administration said, "everything that Dr. Durkee has done was needed and will be justified in the further growth of the university. His mistakes are he does the thing suddenly and without enough explanation; so that motives other than the real ones can and are attributed to him. He is rather boyish in his attitude; he will stake all on the word of some one in whom he believes, and a hard vindicative fighter for the things he thinks right. Full of primitive, youthful zeal and deadly serious in his efforts to build up Howard, he has faith in himself and a stomach for hard work. How else could he have done the things he has?"

What or who is behind the efforts to oust Dr. Durkee from the presidency at Howard? I do not know. But certainly this movement is on. In 1919–20 the "Spirituals" demonstration was pulled off. This singing was purely voluntary on the part of each student. Certainly not required of any one. But the president was blamed and denounced—for what?

In this same year (1919–20) the socialistic book found its way into the hands of Senator Smoot, head of the Appropriations Committee, who must decide on funds for Howard. Why? The president's efforts to placate the "watch dog of the treasury" were likewise denounced as "cringing."

A further rift in both teacher and student groups, and the year closed.

The following year when school opened, the third day of Chapel, the President appeared on the platform of the Chapel rather diffidently. Some one began handclapping. Instantly the crammed Chapel took it up and gave the President a most stirring reception full of yells, rah! rahs! with "Durkee" on the end.

Having the memory of those last bitter days of the preceeding term, he was tremendously moved. He advanced to the pulpit and stood with flushed face and those steel-blue eyes swimming.

"I see that the students realize what a tremendous strain the president has been laboring under for the past months. He—"

He could get no further and bowed his head, signifying dismissal. The students were themselves touched and went forth very pro-Durkee.

But in that same year came the Student Council fight headed by Looby, George Brown and Fred Jordan. More bitter Chapel sessions, more divisions on the campus, more denunciations from the city for the president.

Later also came the fight on compulsory Chapel attendance by students in the Engineering School led by Priestly, Hardwick and Goins.

This began a long struggle against Chapel attendance by compulsion. I believe few persons exist who do not object to forced spiritual life. The president's contention was that that was his only chance to meet the students. He wanted to keep in touch, to maintain a personal bond, feeling perhaps the need of this in his position. For in the services he always told of any new acquisitions, any new conquest, our athletes were called up and lauded—in general the life of the university was synchronized there. Then too, he had a chance to "tell his side of things."

In this same year or early in the next there was the dining room strike. The students paid $18.50 per month for board. Some said the food was poor, others more conservative said that the price was too high. The politicians of which there was no dearth accused the Administration and Mr. Scott in particular, of gouging.

The outcome of it all was that they were given permission to board in the city. But after a brief trial every one was again boarding on the hill.

The next year, 1921–22, the general protest against Chapel attendance won and no one but freshmen were required to go.

But other strikes have come and gone, more distracting of student attention from class room to problems of administration. Where will it end? We shrug.

No attempt has been made, nor will be made to show that the Administration is perfect or infallible. But their mistakes are made in an effort to arrive at something better than what they have to work with. Their efforts are *constructive*. That cannot be said of the harsh critics throughout the country who neither know what is being done nor wish to know in order that their unfavorable attitude may not change. Indeed, the facts in the case do not alter their opinion at all. Disentergration is the goal toward which they work for the university they profess to love. Never a dollar contributed, never a helpful word, never a constructive criticism from year to year. These are those who tear down in the name of love.

The question arises: Is it best to lend a helping hand to Howard—imperfect as it is, it is our only university—to raise it to our ideal of a university, or by destructive internal warfare, level it to the earth again? This is a world of compromises. Katabolism is easy, growth is hard.

MORDECAI WYATT JOHNSON

Inaugural Address

Mr. Chairman, Members of the Board of Trustees and Fellow-citizens:

I wish first of all to express my very great gratitude to the Secretary of the Interior, to the representative of the faculties of the University, and to the representative of the sister institutions who have greeted me with welcome today. Howard University is one among many agencies working for the development of the Negro people and for that enlargement of the life of our country which must inevitably follow every step of this development. I am proud to be a part of these agencies. I am deeply encouraged by the welcome that they are giving me. And I hope that during my administration Howard University may prove an increasingly worthy cooperator in our great common undertaking.

Howard University was conceived in the prayer meeting of a Congregational church, after the Civil War and the emancipation of the slaves. It was founded by a man who had been a soldier in that war, who rejoiced in the emancipation of the slaves and the preservation of the Union, but who wisely saw that these achievements were only the first and second steps toward a happy adjustment of the black people to the other elements of the American population. He believed that the next and most important step should be a strenuous undertaking to educate both the slaves themselves and the disadvantaged white people who under the slave regime had never had educational opportunity. So, with a broad heart, unembittered by strife, he spent the remainder of his life establishing educational institutions for the slaves and their children and for those disadvantaged whites.

This institution was originally planned to train preachers for the freed men, but the plan was soon expanded to include all the training given by a comprehensive university organization.

The beginnings of the university were very humble indeed. On May 1, 1867, the normal department was established in a little frame building with four students, one teacher and no money. Sixty years have passed since that day. What struggles there were during these years, what heroic sacrifices were made by presidents and faculties, and what joys there came as from time to time new sources of support appeared—these things are all well known to those who know and love the university's history. Today we are able to see that original normal department expanded into nine schools and colleges, embracing religion, medicine, dentistry, pharmacy, law, liberal arts, applied science, education and music. The four students have grown to two thousand two hundred sixty-eight students from thirty-seven states and ten foreign countries. The teaching force has grown from one to one hundred sixty. The rented frame building has grown to twenty-five buildings and grounds valued at three million dollars. The "no money" has grown to an annual income averaging five hundred thousand dollars. And now the university has seven thousand sixteen graduates living in every state of the Union where the Negro lives, and working in every rank of life. Two hundred forty-two graduates go out today to join that number.

But growth at Howard University has not been extensive expansion only. There has been intensive development as well. Little by little the curriculum has been concentrated and graded upward in quality. When Howard first opened her doors the curriculum was thinly stretched all the way from teaching an illiterate slave how to read a few verses in the Bible to the degrees of Doctor of Medicine and Bachelor of Divinity. As the years have passed the preparatory department has been taken away, and the high school division has been taken away, so that now no courses are given in the university under the freshman year, and every course given is of collegiate and university caliber. The standards of all the schools have been raised continuously, so that today at least six of the schools are rated in Class A by standard rating agencies; a seventh of them gives Class A work of its kind; and the two not yet recognized have come to the place where they can feel courageous to make application for Class A standing within the coming year.

There has been also a decided increase in the number of Negro scholars gathered on the several faculties, it being the purpose of the original white founders of the university not merely to train Negro men and women for practical life, but to train educational leaders who participate with them on a basis of uncondescending equality in the whole enterprise of Negro education. So that here during the years there has been gathered together the largest body of intelligent and capable Negro scholars to be found connected with any enterprise of its kind in the civilized world. These scholars have been able not only to teach their subjects, but some of them to venture into the field of creative scholarship and to make original contributions to the knowledge of the world. Negro scholars at Howard University have made original and creative contributions in the fields of botany, zoology, sociology and history. Just recently a Negro member of the faculty was invited to share with a number of other scholars in the field of the natural sciences, including several Nobel prize winners, in the preparation of a volume which they in common believe will be a notable contribution to the world's knowledge of living things.

Howard University is the first mature university organization to come to pass among Negroes in the modern civilized world. Its growth from the humblest beginnings is one of the great romances of American education. During all the early years, while the founder and his associates worked pseudo-scientific men were busily engaged in giving various reasons why serious education of the kind here undertaken should never be attempted among Negroes. History has answered these arguments. Howard University with its high caliber fruitfulness is a justifying monument to the faith of the founder and to all his hard working fellow-laborers. It is a monument also to the far-sighted wisdom of the Federal Government which, ever since the emancipation of the slaves, has not ceased to manifest an interest in their educational growth. Howard University has been made possible in its present efficiency very largely because for a period of nearly fifty years it has had the discriminating, judicious, far-sighted helpfulness of a sympathetic and understanding Government.

Howard University is also a monument to the capacity of the Negro himself. The coming of the Negroes from two hundred fifty years of slavery in which by far the most of them did not know even how to write their names, in a period of sixty years to constitute the majority of the members of the faculty of a full-fledged university and to have their names recorded as original and creative contributions to the knowledge of the world is certainly an indication that the human mind, whatever its color and under whatever serious embarrassments it may have worked, is essentially a dignified thing, and that all that Christianity and other great religions have dared to believe about it can possibly be true.

The development of Howard University has been, however, an unnatural thing, growing out of a desire to provide a monument. It has been a natural response to the claimant needs of a growing people. The Negro race today has needs that cannot be satisfied except by men trained in the way that Howard University attempts to train them. There are some needs of the people which may be met by servants trained in a brief period of time. There are other needs of the people which cannot be met except by slaves who spend one-third of their lives getting ready their powers to place them at the disposal of the people. When the humble woman in her crude cottage in Mississippi stands by the bedside of her child threatened with death, her heart reaches out with a great desire to conquer the disease about to take away her most precious possession. But the mind is not able to respond. It takes twenty-five years of training to be able to meet the needs of that simple woman's heart. Howard University exists in order that when the simple and the poor cry out for fundamental things that their hearts must have if they are to reach the goal of a normal and happy life, slaves shall be prepared with competent minds to see that the heart's desire of the people shall not fail. If it be the ambition of any institution to prepare servants for the American people, I say that Howard University seeks that preeminent greatness which comes to those who try to make ready themselves and their associates to be the slaves of the people.

The professional schools in Howard University have arisen to meet definite needs of the Negro people. Take the matter of health. When the Negro started out from slavery it was freely predicted that physically he would not be able to survive in the midst of civilized life. He has survived, and nobly, but his health standard is far below the general health of the American people. His death rate is higher and his losses from all causes are greater than among the other sections of the American population. Some three thousand medical men have gone out to serve the health needs of Negroes, and the progress which they have made in winning the confidence of their people, in the establishment of hospi-

tals, and in the public health service has been remarkable indeed. But their numbers are very inadequate. There is only one Negro physician to every three thousand three hundred Negroes in the United States, as compared with one white physician to every four hundred fifty members of the white race. As important as dentistry is today, there is only one Negro dentist for every twenty thousand needy Negro mouths. There is a great need for an increase in the number of efficient medical men, not only in curative medicine, but in preventive medicine, and for those public scientific measures by which we hope in the long run to prevent the rapid growth of disease among the people. Howard University is dedicated to supplying that need. This year her School of Medicine has been filled and she has had to turn away thirty-two qualified candidates for lack of space in her laboratories.

In recent years there has been a decided increase in the accumulation of Negro property and a vast growth in business. There has been manifested also an increasing desire on the part of enlightened communities to have Negroes themselves in the legislative halls, to represent the real interests of their people and to see to it that these real interests are taken account of in the legislative process. There is only one well qualified School of Law at work in the Negro race today. That is at Howard University. That the Negro shall have lawyers who are competent, living up to the highest standards of the legal profession, is the intention and one of the justifiably great measures of Howard University.

I turn now to the profession of teaching. Howard University has been able to come to the place where it stands today because of the rapid development in the field of fundamental education for Negroes. We have been able to do away with the high school department of Howard because there has been a widespread increase of primary and preparatory education for colored people. The time has come when the system of Negro education itself demands that there shall be a university organization specializing in the preparation of teachers. There is today in the United States a deeply recognized need for teachers of a certain caliber of mind and spirit, not only among the high schools, but among the growing colleges themselves. A few years ago, here at Howard University, a number of college presidents met, and, when they were asked to state in brief the one outstanding need in their institutions, every one of them, without previous conference, put his finger on this point: The greatest need is teachers who know their subjects, who understand the Negro mind and the difficulties under which our colleges labor, and who are willing to work with us, not counting hours or measuring units, but giving us all they have because they love the people. Howard University cannot presume to say at this moment that it is prepared to take care of that teacher need of the growing Negro colleges, but it is justifiable to hope that in this place in the coming years, with the proper class of graduate studies, there may be prepared a type of teacher for high schools and for the growing colleges whose competence and whose spiritual qualifications cannot be excelled anywhere in the United States.

I come now to the ministry of religion. There are forty-seven thousand Negro churches in the United States and there are in the whole country today less than sixty college graduates getting ready to fill these pulpits. The Negro church from every point of view is the most powerful and the most constructive organization now at work in the Negro race. There is no organization and no combination of organizations which can, at this stage in the history of the Negro race, begin to compare with the fundamental importance of the Negro church. And yet, we can see what is going to happen to that church if only sixty college men are preparing to enter the Negro pulpit. The simple, unsophisticated, mystical religion of the Negro cannot continue to endure, unless it is over and over reinterpreted to him by men who have a fundamental and far-reaching understanding of the significance of religion in its relation to the complexities of modern civilized life. Here at Howard University we have the ground-work laid for a great non-sectarian school of religion. It ought to be made a graduate school of religion, seeking the truth about the meaning of life, without bias, endeavoring to deliver the people from superstition and from uncharitable sectarianism, binding them into an understanding cooperation, clarifying their vision, and releasing their energies for constructive service to the common good.

This year there were one thousand seven hundred one students in the colleges of Howard University. That seems to be a large number, and to our hard-working deans and professors it sometimes appears to be too much. But there can be no danger in the next fifty years that there will be too many Negroes applying for college education. In all the days since the Civil War only ten thousand colored people have graduated from a college of any kind. There are today in the colleges of our country approximately eight hundred thousand youths studying for degrees. About ten thousand only of these are Negroes. This means that there are eighty times as many white young men and women studying in the colleges today as Negroes—a far too great disproportion that must be remedied as rapidly as it is possible for us to do so. There may be a danger in numbers for Howard University, but only the danger which comes from being overtaxed because of its limited plant, limited faculty, and limited income.

Mordecai Wyatt Johnson (Courtesy of the Moorland-Spingarn Research Center)

There can be no danger here of that thing now so greatly feared in many American institutions: that too many of our students will waste their time in a thin, incompetent, too liberal education. There is no leisure class among Negroes today, anxious to come to a university to produce a cultured aristocracy. Practically every Negro who comes to a college knows that he must earn his living by the sweat of his brow, and that whatever culture he gets must be in addition to fundamental specific preparation to do one thing by which he may earn his living. The great danger that confronts Howard University and all Negro institutions of learning is not that we shall have too much liberal education, but that we shall have too little of it—that we shall turn out competent physicians, competent lawyers, competent teachers in their several specialties, who are at the same time incompetent, shallow-sympathied men, ignorant of the fundamental human relations and not knowing how to take their part in the general development of a community. So that at Howard University, along with the training of the individual to render specific professional service, it is absolutely necessary that there shall go studies which fit a man sympathetically to understand the kind of country that he is living in, the progress which that country has made, the direction in which it is moving, the nature of the institutions with which he has to deal, and the relations and possibilities of his own people to his government and to the progress of his country. This is what is meant by a liberal education—not the preparation of a leisured aristocracy, simply spending its time in the discussion of things of cultural interest to incompetent men, but the broadening of the sympathies, and that deepening of the understanding which make the experienced physician able to cooperate with the experienced minister, the lawyer, and the teacher for the public good, together endeavoring to develop a country which shall have a deep sense of community and of brotherly cooperation.

Such preparation is all the more necessary by reason of the stage of development which the Negro himself has reached. A few years ago it was customary to assume that the Negro problem was a sectional problem and that the development of the Negro and the development of cooperative race relations were matters to be handed over almost entirely to the Southern States. But there are now two millions of Negroes living outside of the boundaries of the Southern States. It does not appear that there ever again will be a time when the Negro race will have a geographical unity and can be spoken of as involved in a mere sectional interpretation of the meaning of life. And yet these Negroes, distributed all over the country, from California to Maine and from New York to Texas, are more and more realizing that wherever they go they have certain common problems, and they are struggling today as never before to arrive at some unified understanding regarding what shall be their self-expression, what shall be their relation to the other members of the American population, and how they can maintain their creative self-respect in the midst of the communities where they live. These people must find some intelligent interpreter that shall not be sectional, some center of interpretation that shall look at the Negro question in its national aspect, and which is acquainted with the problem of the Negro wherever he goes. Howard University is the one great institution located and prepared by its history and organization to be that national center in which the Negro shall come to full self-consciousness about where he is, where he hopes to go, what difficulties are in the way, and how he can get there with the good will of his fellow-citizens. It is of the utmost importance to the Negro people that whatever studies may contribute to this end shall be developed here on the highest plane of efficiency and as rapidly as possible.

And this development is a matter of concern not alone to the Negro people themselves, but to the nation as a whole, for the Negro question is now a matter of national and of international significance. When Howard University was first established at Washington, this was a capital but recently subjected to attack, just recovering from the awful struggles of a Civil War, and looked upon with patronizing good will by many of the strong nations of the earth. But Washington today is the central throbbing heart of the most powerful and most hopeful republic that now exists on the face of the earth. The urgent question that now confronts the world regarding this republic is, What is going to be its relation to the weaker and disadvantaged peoples of the earth? The great nations of Europe for a century have been subordinating the undeveloped countries and the disadvantaged peoples of the world to the economic and political interests of the European powers. The urgent question today is whether there is going to arise in this place a country so deeply convinced of the possibilities of humanity that it is willing to keep its self-control, having no relations with even the weakest of peoples except such as it can justify in the light of its deepest conscience, committed to none by a purely open and above board practice of brotherliness to all men and to all countries of the earth.

It is not necessary for the world to wait to see what we are going to do in our foreign relations in order to find out what the trend is going to be, because the United States of America has a barometer within the nation. It has twelve millions of the disadvantaged peoples of the world in its own bosom. What is done as regards the Negro in this country is a signal and unfailing indication of the temper of the American spirit and of the character and intent of the American mind, and it will resound in the halls of all the world. It is in the interest, therefore, of our nation that it shall be assured from within not only that it is capable of getting along with a high degree of justice and good will in relation to Mexico, for example, but that right here in the experimental crucible where the great race problem of the world is crystallized it shall prove that it has the power publicly to assimilate twelve millions of Negroes, to give them every form of public justice, and to give it to them in ways persuasive of their own free consent and cooperation, making them an intimate part of the national life.

Years ago, when we were lead by our infantile imagination, we were accustomed to suppose that there were some one panacea by which we could achieve this result. We now know that there is no such single panacea. The Negro is now intermixed with all the complex activities of American life. Nothing but the application of intelligence persistent intelligence in a multitude of complex directions, with one solid good will, can possibly accomplish even in a great length of time the thing which we all desire and which we must have if the destiny of our country is to be fulfilled. Our country, therefore, needs an institution where those studies will be undertaken, in a large and comprehensive way, which will prepare not only the Negro but the nation to understand how the Negro is situated, where we want him to go, what the difficulties are in the way, and how, in spite of all the difficulties, by intelligence and persistent application of good will, he can get there.

I call attention to the special preparedness of Howard University to undertake those studies in Sociology, Economics, Social Philosophy, History, Biology and Anthropology that may give us the facts, inform the public mind, and set forth a light by which both the Negro and the nation may be advanced. Here we have a great university, situated in a southern city so far as practice is concerned. Atlanta, Georgia, Nashville, Tennessee, or Natchez, Mississippi, can make no claim to be more southern in spirit than Washington. And yet in the midst of this southern city you have something which you have nowhere else in the South. You have the continuously throbbing will of the whole American people, expressed in the Executive Government and in the Supreme Court, and a constant stream of noble characters who represent the best sentiment of the nation, interacting continually with the Southern mind, tending to assimilate and to transform it to the measure of the national will. Here we have a university with two thousand two hundred sixty-eight students, nearly one-fourth of all the Negroes in the United States engaged in college of professional education, taught by a bi-racial faculty, the white members of which constitute some of the most eminent minds in the life of America, and the Negro members of which constitute the largest and most competent body of trained Negro minds engaged in educational practice in the United States—Negro mind and white mind working together without condescension, a living example of what intelligent men can do with the race question when they have freedom to undertake it together. There is also a bi-racial Board of Trustees—white men among the most distinguished in America, and Negro products of higher educational institutions, working together with mutual respect, great capacity for cooperation, and a will to make this a creative, intellectual and spiritual center that shall have not only the patronage but the confidence of the Negro people. Here is an institution partly supported by the United States Congress so that every student who comes here can have daily and continuous evidence of the persistent good will of an enlightened government, and yet such a relationship to the Government as precludes

any form of political domination. It is an institution, therefore, in which the teaching can have no suspicion of political supervision by the Government, and which, therefore, can commend itself entirely to the free and spontaneous affection of the Negro people and to the continuous confidence of those men of good will of all races who want to see the Negro problem brought out well. In such an institution, so situated, so manned, so supported, and moreover, so richly blessed in having the resources of the Library of Congress and the other vast educational facilities of the national capital at its disposal, it is inevitable that far-reaching studies in race relations will be undertaken, and that these studies will be of benefit to Negroes in all parts of the country and to the nation as a whole.

I have high confidence also that these studies will add to the sum total of our knowledge of human life. If the Negro studies the human will, human motive, human organization, the philosophy of social life, in order to discover how he may become free, with the consent of the other elements of the American population, he is sure to discover something about the human will, something about human motives and human organization that may be to the advantage of mankind. The President of the United States has recently said that there is a residual unconquered territory in human nature which prevents us from carrying out in practice the ideals which we know to be the one to follow. The Negro situation is acute largely because the American population has not yet found the power to carry out its own ideals. If thinkers here can discover ways and means of eliciting that power and of bringing it to bear in race relations, they will make a contribution to the sum total of knowledge and to the ongoing of the human race.

As much, however, as the Negro may be interested in the professions and in those studies pointing to the solution of his problem he must not forget to cultivate those natural gifts which have come with him from the days of slavery. Though he does not have health as he should have it, he must continue to sing. Though the social problem may not be solved in his lifetime, he must develop his talent to tell a good story and act out a good part. Though he may not for years be fitted into the texture of American life, he must still keep alive that simple and beautiful faith whereby he has been able to get along and to bear the cross with a gentle and kindly heart. Howard University should be the place where the underdeveloped heritage of art in the soul of the Negro may be cultivated, a place where his music, his histrionic talents and his instinctive kindliness of disposition may be brought to its fullest self-consciousness and competency.

The support of an institution of this kind should be the common concern of all the American people. I do not hope that Howard University will become rich. I hope that it will always be poor enough to be responsive to the criticism and the stimulus of the current public will. But I do hope that it may be relieved from want. Howard University, with its great mission today, is in want. Over the heads of the people who work here hands an accumulated deficit of eighty-seven thousand dollars brought about by an annual current deficit over a period of six years. There has been an increase of one hundred per cent in the student body since 1919–20, yet the faculty has increased not more than twenty-eight per cent in numbers, and increase in equipment and in income has lagged far behind the needs. I should like to see that deficit removed. I should like to see an adequate income for maintenance. Every one of these buildings is in a low state of repair because we have now but a minimum of two per cent for repairs and maintenance of building and grounds. But above all I want that Howard University shall have salaries to give teachers a living wage. The work that it must do cannot be done by men who must be worried every night as to whether they can pay their board bill the first of the month. The highest salary for a professor at Howard University is $2,650—a salary below those paid in the public high school system in the city of Washington. There are teachers here teaching for $1,000 and $1,400 per year. How the work which we want to do can be done with these small salaries I am not yet able to say. But the gravest danger is not to the teachers themselves; it is to the product of the institution. Poorly paid teachers who must work in the night to supplement their salaries, preaching and selling—even coffins—as some of them have done and are doing, will find it impossible to turn out anything other than a mass product. A mass product in industry is a good thing, but a mass product in education is an abomination unto God and sure to be a disappointment to the public good. What we want to produce in Howard University is a self-conscious, self-directing, independent, responsible human being, who knows how to act, who knows where he is going, and has the courage to do what he believes to be right. Such a product cannot be trained in a machine university where the professors are financially strained and are obliged to spend their spare time in earning a living rather than in reflecting upon their studies and in personal conference with individual students.

Whence will come this support? For nearly fifty years the major portion of it has come from the fees of students and from the Government of the United States. I hope that during the next ten-year period the Government will not cease its support. Howard University cannot live without that support, and the product already established here is too precious to be allowed to go backward.

I hope also that an increased sum will come from student fees. Already we have increased them far beyond the limit of most of our students to endure. Eighty-five per cent of the male students are able to pay these fees only by working while they study. I hope an increased amount will come from the Negro people themselves. The way in which they have responded to the Government's challenge and to the challenge of the General Education Board is a thing which should be precious to the heart of every American. By far more than two-thirds of all the money now paid in the School of Medicine Endowment Campaign has been paid by the Negro people themselves. [Let me pause to say, to delight the hearts of those that are here, that the Endowment Campaign is now within fifteen thousand dollars of victory. Fifteen thousand dollars more than the first of July will bring us the first half million dollar endowment for the School of Medicine.]

I hope that discriminating philanthropy will supplement the gifts of the Government and of the Negro people themselves. I have seen encouraging signs that philanthropy intends to do this. Nowhere in America and nowhere else in the world can funds be spent with greater productiveness for the common good than they can now be spent at Howard University. We are so happy to be able to report that under the supervision of the Department of the Interior and by the determined will of the administration, Howard University has a financial system unequivocally honest and open to the inspection of any representative of any organization that desires to make that inspection on any day.

I am through now. Sixty-five years ago the Negro came from bondage. In a short a time he has come to this place. What is his destiny? I do not know. I hope, and I do not conceal my hope, that his destiny will be entire public equality and entire good-willed cooperative relations with every element of the American population, and that he will be especially understood by those men who have been his former masters and who have been accustomed to make him a slave. I hope that he will be delivered entirely from every form of public servitude and that he will be redelivered spontaneously by his own consent, into a willing slavery to the common good. I hope that this will be a moral accomplishment, not by amalgamation or by any expedient of any kind, even though that expedient should be brought to pass tomorrow morning. Amalgamation would be a beggarly solution of a problem which is essentially moral and which should be settled in a way that will result in the strengthening of the moral will of both of the peoples engaged in the enterprise. I want my country to conquer all of the inhibitions connected with blackness and all of the fears connected with blackness, but I want the original blackness there and I want that blackness to be unashamed and unafraid. That day is far off yet, but the existence of this institution tells something about the intent of the American mind. When I see that in sixty years it has been possible for such an institution as this to come to pass, I am encouraged for my country and my hopes are stimulated by a great inspiration.

Fellow-students of the graduating classes, you are among those who are prepared to take part in a great enterprise. You are going out to work among a people greatly undermanned. You are going to find it hard, most of you, to earn your living. You are going to be tempted to desert the public good and to seek merely your own self-aggrandizement. But I call upon you to keep in remembrance your university. Keep especially in remembrance those noble white men who founded it here. Existing in the form of Anglo-Saxon they thought it not a thing to be grasped after to be on equality with Anglo-Saxons and to enjoy the rights and privileges of Anglo-Saxons, but they humbled themselves, took upon themselves the form of servants, and made themselves obedient to the needs of slaves. They lived with us, ate with us, suffered ostracism and humiliation with us, in order that by their personal contact with us they might teach us the truth and the truth might set us free. They did these things because they loved a country which has never yet existed on land or sea, a country in which all men are free, all men are intelligent and all men are self-directing contributors to the common good.

That country has not yet been attained. It is still the goal of the American people. You are to participate in the bringing of that country to pass. You have here enjoyed the fruits of the labors of the founders. You cannot be self-respecting men and women unless you also participate in the spirit of the founders. Their country must be your country. You must salute it from afar, and, even while you fight with every ounce of energy for those public equalities by which you cannot live, you must also take upon yourself the cross—your proportionate share of the responsibility of bringing that country of intelligent good will to pass. You will have to keep in remembrance that many men of other races who seek to do you injury are men who have not had advantages that you have had. They do so because in their blindness regarding the meaning of life and the purposes of government they think that their welfare consists in the subordination of your own to theirs. But if they be blind in the mind, you cannot afford to strike a blind man. You must be patient to be just to them while they get wisdom and courage to be just to you. And you must remember that your disposition may be the decisive factor in the changing of their minds.

Keep in mind your university and in all of your labors cast no shame upon her. So live out in the real world that travellers from your city may come to this place because you have been trained here. Your institution is large, but still it is little known. She is like some humble mother that washes clothes in a country place while you go out to share the honor and the glory of the world. The world will never know much about your mother or respect her except what you make it do by the character of the life that you live. So live that when you are done men will eagerly ask where you were born, who were your teachers, where were you trained. And in your prayers, when you strip yourself of all dress parade of every kind, make mention of your university before the God and Father of us all, and make especial mention of your servant who now stands before you, the deans and members of the faculties, the Board of Trustees and all those men of good will in whose hands our destiny lies. And now may the beauty of the Lord our God be upon you. May He establish the work of your hands, yea, the work of your hands may He establish it.

A. LEON HIGGINBOTHAM, JR.

We Wish to Plead Our Cause. Too Long Have Others Spoken For Us

I look at a sea of happy and concerned faces. Many of you are happy because soon you will be graduates and will terminate your role as students. Parents, grandparents, relatives and friends are happy because you see an end in tuition bills and because you have shared the frustrations and joy leading up to this crowing event; others bask with pride under the halo of the personal triumphs of the graduates; the trustees and faculty know that their faith, sacrifices and dreams have once again been vindicated by the excellence of this year's graduating class. Yet, there are also concerned faces in the audience, faces of individuals who may be asking "Why should there ever be a commencement speech?", "How long will he take?", "Does he recognize that today's triumph is ours and not his?", "Does he know that this is no time to exploit a captive audience?" During calmer moments I would probably agree with all who question the relevance of a commencement speech. Perhaps someday your best Howard scientists will discern and diagnose a dreadful malady or disease which occurs most often in May or June—the commencement speaker's syndrome. It is a temporarily debilitating disease that causes delusions of grandeur and makes one believe that he has something significant to say, and even that the audience wants to hear him.

Because of the ambiance of this setting, I have become infected with that dreaded syndrome. Yet there is some realism left, for I know that I will not have as much to say, nor nearly as much wisdom to impart as did Dr. Mordecai Johnson for three decades. I cannot compete with the precise logic of Dr. Nabrit, the eloquence of Dr. Cheek or the stature of others such as President Lyndon Baines Johnson and Martin Luther King, Jr., who have stood here at this hour. But for a few moments I will share my malady with you.

In Search of a Theme

If I were to proffer a theme that would be as relevant a century from now as it was over a century and half ago, where would I find it? Though we meet here this morning on this 204th year of the Republic and on the 193rd year of our nation, in this setting of Howard University, it would seem somewhat inappropriate to rely on a theme from the Declaration of Independence—because when they spoke of "the self-evident truth, that all men are created equal," the framers did not mean to include either blacks or women. In fact, many of the signatories owned slaves, and others profited from the slavery system. Their daily conduct was a repudiation of the egalitarian concepts they proclaimed, and thus they cannot be perfect models for this occasion.

Similarly, it would not be appropriate to cite the preamble of the United States Constitution, because when it spoke of "we, the people, in order to form a more perfect union, establish justice, promote the general welfare, and secure the blessings of liberty to ourselves and our posterity," it did not recognize blacks either as people protected by that Constitution or as individuals entitled to justice or liberty.

In seeking a theme almost as old as the Republic, a theme from declarants who meant what they said and practiced what they declared, I would prefer the statements in the first editorial of *Freedom's Journal*, the first black newspaper to be published in this country. The editors, Samuel Cornish, a black Philadelphia abolitionist, and John Russwurm, the second black college graduate in this Nation, wrote:

> We wish to plead our own cause.
> Too long have others spoken for us.

In their editorial they noted the ambiguity of American democracy and emphasized "the neglect" and the repudiation of those "self-evident truths." They said that, "Though all men acknowledge the excellency of [Benjamin] Franklin's expressions of equality, yet compara-

tively few practice upon them." They recognized that "it avails little to mourn." But they were not willing to accept the past as a prologue for the future. They were determined to change the course of American history, and the key to that change would be pleading their own cause, and recognizing that "too long have others spoken for us."

Why Howard Is Unique

If one were to reflect on the history of Howard University, if one were to ask, why is Howard so unique, why has it been and why is it one of the great universities in the world, and why must it always remain so, the answer is that you have exemplified the dream of Russwurm and Cornish to "plead our own cause," and that you have recognized that "for too long others have spoken for us."

When I speak of Howard's profound contribution in "pleading our own cause," I do not speak of what Howard has meant only to blacks—yet if that were all that it had done, Howard would be entitled to one of the highest niches of esteem for American universities. Think of what our Nation would be today if there had not been a Howard University, or its equivalent; what would be the condition of America and of blacks if there had not been a Howard University which stayed on the cutting edge of excellence, providing better options for black Americans. Both blacks and the entire Nation would have suffered irrevocable losses.

You have been one of the major repositories for independent black scholars. Even though a few blacks received their graduate degrees from the most prestigious universities in the Nation, until the 1960s they were almost never invited back to teach at their graduate school *alma maters*. Hastie and Houston finished Harvard Law School with honors but taught at Howard Law School and a similar pattern followed for John Hope Franklin, Rayford Logan, Ralph Bunche, Carter Woodson, Alain Locke, Charles Wesley, James Nabrit, Mordecai Johnson, Charles Drew and hundreds of others.

Through your Law School you were the father and the mother, and the primary architect of the modern American Civil Rights Movement, developing the legal doctrines which led to *Brown* v. *Board of Education* and to earlier key civil rights decisions in employment, housing, fairness in the criminal justice system and voting. Until the 1960s you had trained almost 50% of the black doctors and lawyers.

It is frightening to envision how decadent America would be today if the Nation had not been the beneficiary of the contributions which Howard had made for more than a century. Think of it! What would have been the educational options for blacks today if we had been deprived of the thousands of teachers whom Howard was trained to nurture the minds and guide the aspirations of black school children. Similarly, it is appalling to contemplate what America would be today if there had not been a Howard to educate, to develop, to motivate and to train innumerable scholars, artists, scientists, architects, engineers, doctors, dentists, lawyers, activists, critics, and public officials who went on to plead the causes which others did not espouse.

Looking at the current national administration, we may have been deprived of illustrious Howard graduates such as Thurgood Marshall, Associate Justice of the United States Supreme Court; Patricia Roberts Harris, Secretary of Health, Education and Welfare; Andrew Young, former Ambassador to the United Nations; Mary Frances Berry, former Assistant Secretary of Education; and J. Clay Smith, Esq., Commissioner, Equal Employment Opportunity Commission. The Judiciary may have been deprived of William Bryant, Chief, Judge, United States District Court for the District of Columbia; Joseph Hatchett, United States Court of Appeals for the Fifth Circuit; Damon Keith, United States Court of Appeals for the Sixth Circuit; Robert Carter, United States District Court of the Southern District of New York, and several other distinguished judges on Federal and state courts. The Nation may have been deprived of great writers such as Toni Morrison, superb actors and actresses such as Deborah Allen and Ossie Davis; activists such as Vernon Jordan, James Farmer, Christopher Edley and, some might add, Stokely Carmichael; musicians and artists such as Roberta Flack and Elizabeth Catlett; physicians such as LaSalle Lefall. The list is almost endless.

But for Howard, thousands of black babies would have died unnecessarily; but for Howard, thousands of forums would not have had articulate minority spokespersons; but for Howard, thousands of black children would not have had the models of excellence which Howard has produced; and on the world scene, but for Howard, thousands of Africans would not have received the academic options which allowed them to return to their homelands to ultimately assume positions of world leadership. Just as Churchill on August 20, 1940, spoke of British airmen, similarly we can speak of Howard for "never . . . was so much owed by so many to so few."

Today some of those prestigious institutions which remained aloof from the fray when we needed them most are starting to pay recognition to the relatively few blacks who appeared on their campuses decades ago and who most often were lost in a well of anonymity. And while this belated recognition is far better than none at all, we must never forget how minuscule, if it existed at all, the black presence was at these educational institutions for the first two centuries of this Republic. Unlike those schools, whether we look at fifty years or a century ago, Howard did not have one or two blacks entering every other year or every other decade. Howard has graduated more than 39,000 men and women in the professions, the arts and sciences and the humanities. You have been a mass-producer of excellence.

Let us also not forget that, more so than most oth[er] [institutions, Howard has been a] model of inte-gra[tion ...] [so]lidly inte-gra[ted ...] [int]egrated stu-der[ts ...] [racia]l favoritism eve[n ...] [... duri]ng of the last dec[ades ...] [... at le]ast Howard an[d ...] [... a]ffirmative ac-tio[n ...] [... survive]d sur-vived dur-in[g ...] [... ver]y successful re-ve[...] [... a]ffirmative action pr[...] [...] or by undeviating p[...] [... di]scouraged blacks fr[...] [...] and almost every o[...] [... throu]gh it all, Howard w[...] [... opt]ions possible while c[...]

[...] have appeared on t[...] [...Johnny-Come]-Lately" who, like the institutions from which they were graduated, were never or seldom "around" when blacks needed them most, when racial barriers were the status quo and when integration was unpopular if not downright illegal. Yet today some of the alumni or those very institutions, which historically have done so little, seem anxious to punish or at least to denigrate the historic black colleges and universities—those colleges which were the victims of racism and which provided the only life raft, (regardless of how weak), when the seas of bigotry would otherwise have engulfed us.

Howard, A Benefactor for All America

During its century of caring, Howard was not merely aiding black Americans. In a very real and profound way, it was saving the soul of America. Howard Law School's victories in the courts in voting, housing, employment, and education, benefited all of America. Today, at the bargaining tables of the world, our Nation has greater credibility because of the victories which Howard pioneered in the courts of this land. Whether most Americans like it or not, they must face up to the stark reality that the destiny of the world will no longer be shaped exclusively or solely by persons with white skins. For our own national survival and ultimate success, the perception of this Nation's racial fairness by people in Tehran, Peking, Cairo and Lagos may be at least as significant as the views of citizens of Beverly Hills, California, or Peoria, Illinois. Think of how much more intense the opposition would be in the international forum if our courts still sanctioned state-imposed racial segregation. Think of how much greater the handicap would be in forming international alliances if blacks in this country could still be denied the right to vote in primary elections or denied the right to buy a Coke or a hot dog in a place of public accommodation. Think of how much less credible we would be before the high court of world opinion, if, under the sanction of law, governors were still espousing hatred from schoolhouse doors, and shouting "segregation forever." In eradicating some of the racial villainy of the past, Howard has helped our entire Nation.

Howard has been unique because it created a tradition which combined a dream of equality, a confidence in the future with an insistence for day-to-day excellence. That tradition must be maintained and, if possible, even improved. If the tradition of Howard's most noble hours and decades is maintained, you will always be a valuable national resource, as important as the technology for our anti-ballistic missiles, as important as the technology for our hospitals and medical care. This Nation and all of us have an obligation to keep Howard at the forefront of excellence as a great university where all Americans and particularly black Americans and other minorities can participate freely and totally in a truly comprehensive university experience.

Today you leave Howard superbly prepared. You will be able to compete with confidence anywhere in the world. Your individual success is assured. But as you leave here to make your mark on the future, never forget that Howard has done much to "plead our own cause" and that though in our Nation much has been accomplished, still far more must be done. There is still an urgent necessity for thousands of committed individuals of every color, religion and status to plead the causes of justice, dignity and fairness throughout our land. You must plead for these causes, since others will say, "Now is not the time." We must always be mindful that Cornish and Russwurm stressed that "too long others have spoken for us." They recognized that time is measured differently by those who have the power and those who do not. Regardless of how well-meaning those in power may be, there is always the danger of

which Cornish and Russwurm spoke. For there are always serious problems which can warrant delays. We will always be confronted with inflation or recession, depression or wars, global tensions or budget deficits. In the words of the late Dr. Martin Luther King, Jr.:

> We are faced with the fact that tomorrow is today. We are confronted with the fierce urgency of now. In this unfolding conundrum of life and history there is such a thing as being too late. Procrastination is still the thief of time. Life often leaves us standing bare, naked and dejected with a lost opportunity.

You must be a spokesman for broader opportunities for all the people, not merely for blacks. You must speak for the poor in Appalachia; the discouraged in our urban centers; the uneducated in our school systems; the handicapped; and the millions of Americans who still live in poverty and despair.

When I speak of pleading our own cause, of course, I am not urging polarization, divisiveness, hatred or antagonisms. I am speaking more of the cause of the weak, the poor, the disenfranchised and the powerless.

You have earned the crowning achievements of this hour because others have pled your cause. While forever mindful of the themes of Russwurm and Cornish, we must also plead the cause of all. For as Langston Hughes said so eloquently:*

There is a dream in the land.
With its back against the wall.
By muddled names and strange
Sometimes the dream is called.

There are those who claim
This dream for theirs alone—
A sin for which, we know,
They must atone.

Unless shared in common
Like sunlight and like air,
The dream will die for lack
Of substance anywhere.

The dream knows no frontier or tongue,
The dream no class or race.
The dream cannot be kept secure
In any one locked place.

This dream today embattled,
With its back against the wall—

---

*"Dream of Freedom" from COLLECTED POEMS by Langston Hughes. Copyright © 1994 by the Estate of Langston Hughes. Reprinted by permission of Alfred A. Knopf, Inc.

To save the dream for one
It must be saved for all.

I welcome you to the challenge to both plead our own cause and to save the dream for all.

JAMES E. CHEEK

If We Do Not, Then Who Will?: The Continuing Burden to Undo the Yoke of Bondage

I speak to you today in a period of grave peril to our nation's destiny. Despite the gravity of the international condition in which our nation is inevitably caught up, it is not the state of our foreign affairs that I now have in mind. It is rather the gravity of our domestic affairs, and those affairs as they specifically relate to the status and condition of black Americans and other dispossessed and oppressed minorities.

While this nation cannot escape playing a major role in the shaping of events on the international scene, its ability to contribute positively and honorably to resolving the differences among nations will be greatly determined by its ability and its willingness to resolve with honor, with morality and with nobility the disparities, the injustices and the differences among its own people on its own shores.

For it has long been my conviction that until America comes fully to grip with its most historic, endemic and pervasive characteristic at home, it will be incapable of coming to grip with the major problems abroad. And the historic, endemic, and pervasive characteristic to which I refer is "institutionalized racism."

It has been and remains the case that institutionalized racism, manifested in many forms, and exemplified in all areas of our national life—economic, social, cultural, political and educational—is the cancer which is destroying our ability to be a moral force in the affairs of mankind.

Near the beginning of this century, W. E. B. Du Bois was to write that the problem of the twentieth century is the problem of the "color line." That was 77 years ago. The issue of race that Du Bois perceived as a "problem," was perceived by Myrdal in the 1940's as a "dilemma," and by the Kerner Commission in the 1960's, as a "crisis." Many of us are now beginning to perceive this issue for our nation's present and its future as a catastrophe.

During the 1950's we achieved a victory in the courts in having laws sanctioning discrimination on the basis of race struck down. During the 1960's, through our acts of civil disobedience such as sitting-in, standing-in, praying-in, and because of the legislation of the Congress, we achieved further victories in public accommodations, in destroying disfranchisement in exercising our right to vote and in numerous other areas where there appeared to be a national moral commitment to eliminating the disparities and inequities between black and white, we embarked upon a program of eradicating poverty and to the building of a society in which there would exist no barriers to the development and preservation of an abundant life, to the making of true liberty and in making fundamental the pursuit of real happiness.

As the decade of the 1960's gave way to the dawning of the 1970's ominous signs begin to appear and as we lived through the 1970's, we discovered that much of our nation's transformation that we thought was fundamental was in reality, simply superficial. We discovered that voices and organizations and institutions which had supported our cause in the movement for civil rights became silent or adversaries in the emergence of our struggle for social justice.

"Benign neglect" which had become the theme setting the mood for the 1970's, had by the middle of that decade, evolved into a practice of malignant neglect.

I need not take the time to elaborate on all the factors and the characteristics of our national behavior that indicate a changing mood, an eroding commitment, more promise than fulfillment, a mania that has been described as being mean and ugly and as the Urban League notes the emergence of the new negativism.

I confine myself on this occasion to one aspect of our national life which for more than a century has been a foundation stone upon which the hopes and aspirations and the dreams of our people have been erected, and that foundation stone is the network of black colleges and universities.

Institutions serving primarily black Americans were created in response to American racism—a racism so thoroughly entrenched in our nation's mentality and so deeply engraved in our national social consciousness that it could be summed up in the words of Chief Justice Taney of the United States Supreme Court in the Dred Scott decision "that the Negro is so far inferior that he has no rights that a white man is bound to respect."

Although more than a hundred years have passed since those words were uttered from the highest court in the land, the concept that they embody has lingered on and continues to mold and to shape the contour and character of American economic, social, political, cultural and educational life for the almost thirty million black people who are citizens of this country.

During the institution of slavery and shortly after its abolition, the black colleges and universities were created to provide through education the development of leadership and equality to serve as instruments for

James E. Cheek (Courtesy of the Moorland-Spingarn Research Center)

the liberation of a people subjected, to a "bondage of the flesh" as well as to a "bondage of the spirit."

But our institutions were also founded to assist—indeed to force—this nation to act on its own declaration by living under God, by remaining indivisible and by preserving liberty and justice for all its people.

Never adequately funded, never enthusiastically supported, always cast to the outerfringes of the hinterlands of American higher education, these institutions have discharged their Herculean responsibilities and pursued their defying multiple mission with determination, with devotion, with compassion and with courage.

Like "trees planted in the rivers of waters" our black institutions, in the past, could not and would not be moved. And neither the lack of adequate finances, nor the absence of a broadscale public advocacy, nor the indifference of their alumni would deter them from their appointed tasks like the Rock of Gilbraltar, they have been and remain now impregnable defenders of our rights, the symbolic and realistic expressions of our culture and identity; and eloquent testimonies to

the lie that we are an inherently and genetically inferior people.

For it is from the campuses of these institutions that have emerged our clergymen, our physicians, our dentists, our lawyers, our engineers, our architects, our social workers, our teachers and our scholars.

It defies the imagination to even try and ponder where black people would be and where America would be today were it not for these colleges and universities.

Some educational experts and social commentators have characterized our black colleges and universities as the "wastelands" of American higher education.

In what they have done and in what they are and in what they represent, I consider them to be oases in America's deserts of oppression. They have not only educated the vast majority of our people, but they have enriched our black communities.

I had the good fortune to grow up in a southern city that had two predominantly black institutions, one privately supported, the other publicly supported. From the age of seven to the age of seventeen when I left home to attend college, I was privileged to hear and to meet the black giants of our country. From the pulpit of Peiffer Chapel at Bennett College and from the stage of Harrison Auditorium at A&T State, I and countless other thousands were exposed to Mary McLeod Bethune, to Walter White, Mordecai Johnson, Channing Tobias, Benjamin Mays, John W. Davis, Charles Wesley, Howard Thurmond, Charlotte Hawkins Brown, and numerous others. From the lips of these individuals and from their being issued forth words and a spirit that inspired, that motivated, that energized, that unified and illuminated. These two colleges, through the voices and the spirits of giant men and women, taught several generations of black people to be proud of our skin color, to guard and to protect our institutions, to allow no man to despise our race, that our worth as individuals was not to be determined by the color of our skin, the texture of our hair, the shape of our nose or the size of our lips. But rather our worth was to be measured by the nature of our character, the quality of our deeds and the nobility of our aspirations. And the experience made possible in Greensboro, North Carolina, because of two black colleges, was replicated throughout the southland and elsewhere wherever these kinds of institutions existed. They sent rays of hope like lightning bolts through our communities that banished fear and lifted despair; created courage and endowed hope. Black people, young and old, educated and uneducated, poor and not so poor, because of these institutions and what they gave, derived the ability—in the face of great adversity—to walk our streets and to live our lives enclosed in our bosom the radical audacity of faith.

And now we come face to face squarely with a serious and concerted effort to destroy these resources—the foundation stone of our past, our present and our future. To destroy them by starving them to death, though they have never been well nourished or by merging them with our predominantly white institutions, although they have always been submerged, by eliminating their racial identity despite the fact that in America today, nothing loses its racial identity; things in this country only change racial identity.

Those of us who advocate and defend the necessity for the preservation of our institutions have at various times been called "separatists," "racists in reverse," "black nationalists," and all kinds of other negative expressions. That kind of labeling and definition of our advocacy is intended to obfuscate, to divide us, and to divert our attention from the fundamental questions that are inherent in the ongoing debate about the presence of black people in a racist dominated society. As long ago as 1919, Du Bois addressed this question and wrote these words and I quote:

"Here then we face the curious paradox and we remember contradicting facts. Unless we fought segregation with determination, our whole race would have been pushed into an ill lighted, unpaved, unsewered ghetto. . . . Unless we had built great organizations and manned our own southern schools and colleges, we would be shepherdless sheep. . . ."

Our institutions were then, and continue to be the battering rams against the doors of discrimination, deprivation, disprivilege and injustice. Poor in resources, but rich in resolve, our colleges have been and continue to be the weapons of our peoples' liberation and the instruments of our nation's salvation and redemption.

We come now to the question and the issue of The Capstone, Howard University.

In the national atmosphere in which we must carry on our work, Howard University as has occurred so frequently in the past—will be looked upon to provide a haven and a sanctuary; to demonstrate both leadership and vision, to defend with courage and to protect with diligence, to chart and navigate a course that will cause our nation to unloose the yoke of bondage in order that the oppressed go free.

As always, from the time of our founding, in the endeavors in which we have engaged we have had few friends but many adversaries, weak supporters but strong opponents; little understanding, but much confusion, few advocates but numerous detractors.

During the years that I have been here, I have come strongly to believe that the mission and the purpose of this University are inextricably bound up with the future of the American nation as a free society. And it is abundantly clear to me that the future of black people will influence decisively the destiny of this Republic.

It was more than a symbolic act—as Dyson reports in his history of Howard—when the Board of Trustees voted unanimously on January 16, 1894, to adopt as the official colors of our University, the colors of the American Flag. In so doing they were in effect giving witness to the conviction that Howard University and the American nation would march hand in hand in forging a land where justice would have no tarnish, where opportunity would have no boundaries, where freedom would have no limitations, where equality would have no prescriptions and where fraternity would have no qualifications.

And whatever the founding fathers of our country may have intended in the hallowed language of the Declaration of Independence and in the Preamble to the Constitution, the founding fathers of Howard University were determined to make those words living realities in the lives and conditions of this nation's peoples no matter what the color of their skin or their ethnic background.

It was for this purpose that this institution was founded, and it is to this end that it continues.

To all of us to whom the preservation of this University has been entrusted, there is put the question to us that was put to the Prophet Jeremiah: *"If you have raced with men on foot and they have wearied you, how can you compete with horses? And if in a safe land you have fallen down, how will you do in the jungle of the Jordan?"*

Ours is neither the time nor is Howard University the place for those of faint heart, feeble courage, weak commitment, confused and purposeless ambition or selfish motives.

But this is the time and Howard University is the place for men and women who embody in their being, who demonstrate in their every action and who express in their every utterance that they are men and women who, in the words of our *alma mater*, are true and leal and strong and ever bold to battle wrong."

During the past eleven years we have devoted our energies and our efforts to strengthening the financial, the physical and the human resources of this institution toward the end that we shall have adequate resources to carry on the task we are obligated to perform.

Those efforts have been directed toward the private sector and the federal government. Our work in resource building remains incomplete and will be continued.

No one—who is enlightened—has questioned the appropriateness of Howard University seeking increased financial support from its alumni, from foundations or corporations.

But now, after a practice that has been in existence since the institution's founding and sanctioned by federal law since 1928, questions are being raised about the federal government providing direct financial support for Howard's academic programs and its physical facilities development. In ways both subtle and not so subtle; in a manner both covert and overt, this matter is being manifested in many forms and in several places—some you know—in forums where it would be least expected.

First, let me take note of the fact that the federal government for a long number of years has been supporting predominantly white institutions directly without anyone seriously raising the question or considering the matter an issue.

Secondly, Howard University has never received and does not now receive federal support commensurate with its needs or consistent with the intent and objectives of the Congress which authorized such support in 1928.

And thirdly, and most importantly, let us understand, if we understand nothing else in connection with this matter, that federal money is not one hundred percent white money.

Black people in the United States have a wealth in excess of 100 billion dollars. We pay income taxes into the federal treasury. And because our wealth is largely consumer wealth, for a large segment of American industry and commerce, our purchase of goods and products provide the margin of difference enabling those commercial enterprises to yield a profit on the basis of which they are taxed.

This nation achieved its economic supremacy largely on the backs of our black foreparents. Their sweat, their blood and their tears provided the fertilizer that was necessary to bring forth in this country an abundant economic harvest. And let everyone know that so long as I am here this University does not intend to cease aggressively to press its case for increased federal support. And this is the last time I am going to try to justify it to anybody.

But as we continue to press our cause and our case with the federal government, with foundations and corporations, we shall be no less aggressive in the pursuit of our alumni.

I have travelled around this country. I have been entertained in the homes of our alumni. I have ridden in their cars. I have gone riding on their horses. I have consumed their caviar and their wine. And I have yet to meet a graduate of this University who can lay a legitimate claim to being poor.

While we continue the effort to bring our resources to a level of parity with other comparable universities, let us be clear among ourselves that the campuses of Howard University are not playgrounds for the indolent who have come leisurely to go through the motions of an education. Our campuses are battlegrounds for the serious who seek out this place to confront ignorance with knowledge, where the truth grapples hand in hand with falsehood, where understanding comes face to face with confusion. And let us all understand that Howard University is no resting place, and there is no hiding place down here.

Other universities may/can afford the luxury of graduating students who cannot read or write, but not Howard University.

Some universities perhaps can be indifferent about whether their graduates are able to pass professional examinations required to practice their professions, but not Howard University.

Some universities may claim to be neutral, as Harvard does, on the great moral and social issues in our society, but not Howard University.

Some universities may/can afford to tolerate professors who do not teach though God sent them in the world to teach and students who refuse diligently to study and to learn as though God had sent them here to do so, but not Howard University.

Some universities perhaps may/can be at ease with discourteous staff, sloppy administrative procedures, people who are there to receive a paycheck, but not Howard University.

Our institution is in the business of not only educating but also of liberating; of not only discovering, but also of reconstructing. We are also in the business of undoing the yoke of bondage.

We make no apology for doing what our times and circumstances compel us to do. For the First Emancipation was the burden of the white man, and that is why it remained only a proclamation. But the Second Emancipation is the burden of the black man, and that is why it must be made a reality.

And I ask you, if we do not assume this burden, then who will?

TONI MORRISON

Charter Day Address

Thank you, thank you very much for that very warm and very sustained welcome. This is a very distinct pleasure for me to come to the place that has meant a great deal to me—to the place that was formative in ways that were social as well as intellectual. I made life-long friends here, and I felt always privileged in my encounters with faculty here who really knew how to develop a very fledging mind. Howard University, both as an institution and as a population, has had an extraordinary journey. It entered the world in an interventionist mode and has continued, throughout its history, to engage with and debate and respond to the most salient and the most passionately held and the most urgent issues of this nation. It countered with a vengeance the prevailing 19th-century notion that education was not part of the future of African Americans—the prevailing 19th-century notion that, if by some odd chance higher education were to become available on a large scale, that it would be of no use to have it because the higher plateaus of achievement and influence were closed. Evidence to the contrary is overwhelming. And the nation owes Howard University a great deal in terms of the countering of that 19th-century notion.

Howard struggled with distress, with shortages, with slashes and long periods, as well as intermittent periods, of national indifference. Yet among its alumni are men and women who raised the standards of morality, responsibility, and intellect all over the world. Howard negotiated and debated conflicting views on solutions to highly complex, extremely volatile social problems and regarded that debate as its duty. Howard has been much praised; it has also been much maligned. It has suffered a step back, even a setback, but it has never suffered defeat. And here it is—bigger and, in many ways, better than it was—at 128 years old, facing the 21st century with the vigor and vision we have come to take for granted. We have come to expect that vigor and that vision because, in addition to Howard's obvious triumphs, it has also, to its credit, tough scar tissue, nerves of steel, that walk-on-water determination that characterized its founders and our ancestors and was made testimony in the President [Ladner's] remarks this afternoon. Its bruises are testimonies accumulated through decades of battling nefarious forces—forces which we were led to believe despised our existence as a people. And Howard managed to keep a straight face and listen to segregationists' rhetoric because it knew that black people lived in those segregationists' houses, cooked their food, were all up in the intimate lives of their families and understood that our presence was not repellent but, in fact, sought after as long as they could control us. I don't know a leading racist who has not written about the perfect relationship he or she had with a loving black adult or child.

So members of the Howard community went right on disassembling these arguments and positions in order to become a leader in the early Civil Rights Movement. I am proud to have benefited from that tradition of argument—argument in the finest sense of the word: not to destroy an opponent but to discover truth; the tradition of managing dangerously limited resources, of cherishing excellence, of nurturing progeny, of reconfiguration, of invention, of creative problem-solving which are signs of modernity. These things—all—I learned here,

and they have informed that part of me of which I still approve.

I hope you will understand and forgive me for indexing here not the sweetness and the beauty, and the conviviality in my recollections of Howard. There are many, and, at least, one is seminal because it was here that I began, when I was an instructor on the faculty, to write the first book I ever published. So I have profoundly pleasant and exciting memories of this place. But I am listing the more sinewy of these impressions because they are the ones that represent aspects of knowledge and features of resilience very much in demand right now.

The vocabulary of our current dispossession has changed, but its desirability, in certain quarters, has not changed. And all of these strengths that I mentioned earlier, distributed among Howard alumni and among its students—all of these strengths have to be called upon now because they are urgently needed in 1995. Let me be clear in a little scenario that I want to paint that is not contrary to my mode: fiction.

Let us be reminded that before there is a final solution, there must be a first solution, a second one, even a third. The move toward a final solution is not a jump. It takes one step, then another, then another. Something, perhaps, like this:

1. Construct an internal enemy, as both focus and diversion.

2. Isolate and demonize that enemy by unleashing and protecting the utterance of overt and coded name-calling and verbal abuse. Employ *ad hominem* attacks as legitimate charges against that enemy.

3. Enlist and create sources and distributors of information who are willing to reinforce the demonizing process because it is profitable, because it grants power and because it works.

4. Palisade all art forms; monitor, discredit or expel those that challenge or destabilize processes of demonization and deification.

5. Subvert and malign all representatives of and sympathizers with this constructed enemy.

6. Solicit, from among the enemy, collaborators who agree with and can sanitize the dispossession process.

7. Pathologize the enemy in scholarly and popular mediums; recycle, for example, scientific racism and the myths of racial superiority in order to naturalize the pathology.

8. Criminalize the enemy. Then prepare, budget for and rationalize the building of holding arenas for the enemy—especially its males and absolutely its children.

Nobel Laureate Toni Morrison (Atoya Deans)

9. Reward mindlessness and apathy with monumentalized entertainments and with little pleasures, tiny seductions; a few minutes on television, a few lines in the press; a little pseudo-success; the illusion of power and influence; a little fun, a little style, a little consequence.

10. Maintain, at all costs, silence.

In 1995, racism may wear a new dress, buy a new pair of boots, but neither it nor its succubus twin fascism is new or can make anything new. It can only reproduce the environment that supports its own health: fear, denial and an atmosphere in which its victims have lost the will to fight.

The forces interested in these solutions to national problems are not to be found in one political party or another, or in one or another wing of a single political party. Democrats have no unsullied history of egalitarianism. Nor are liberals free of domination agendas. Republicans have housed abolitionists and white supremacists. Conservative, moderate, liberal; right, left, hard left, far right, religious, secular, socialist—we must not be blind-sided by these Pepsi-Cola, Coca-Cola labels because the genius of fascism is that any political structure can host the virus, and virtually any developed country can become a suitable home. Fascism talks ideology, but it really is just marketing—marketing for power.

It is recognizable by its need to purge, by the strategies it uses to purge and by its terror of truly democratic agendas. It is recognizable by its determination to convert all public services to private entrepreneurship; all nonprofit organizations to profit-making ones—so individuals become angry at even the notion of the public good. It changes neighbors into consumers—so the measure of our value as humans is not our humanity or our compassion or our generosity but what we own. It changes parenting into panicking—so that we vote against the interests of our own children; against *their* health care, *their* education, *their* safety from weapons. And in effecting these changes it produces the perfect capitalist, one who is willing to kill a human being for a product—a pair of sneakers, a jacket, a car—or kill generations for control of products—oil, drugs, fruit, gold.

When our fears have all been serialized, our creativity censured, our ideas "marketplaced," our rights sold, our intelligence sloganized, our strength downsized, our privacy auctioned; when the theatricality, the entertainment value, the marketing of life is complete, we find ourselves living not in a nation but in a consortium of industries, and wholly unintelligible to ourselves except for what we see as through a screen darkly.

The mission of Howard has withstood inclement political weather many, many, many times. And it will again have to be, perhaps, a forerunner. For universities all over the country will have ever greater difficulty—greater difficulty than they already have had of preserving freedoms that have already been won but are now threatened. Universities will have to convince themselves that it is still necessary to educate for critical intellects rather than for the receptacles of pre-digested knowledge. Howard may have to lead other universities into maintaining standards with garroted resources and the sort of national contempt for complicated, reflective thought. I am convinced that it will have to rely ever so strongly on its own historical wealth. Every discipline, every department, every program: the natural sciences—in an age when we are still, once again, defending or explaining the absence of a defense for racial and genetic inferiority; the humanities, while we witness the degradation of scholarship—our scholarship and our artists; law; the social sciences;—all have to be involved, as it has always been at this University, in that debate. This is life and death.

I have to tell you, nothing is more important than this generation. It is very difficult not to be enormously moved as I sat here listening to the 41st generation of Howard University Choirs. It is important to know that nothing, nothing, not even us, nothing is more important than our children. And if our children don't think they are important to us—if they don't think they are important to themselves—if they don't think they are important to the world it's because we have not told them. We haven't told them that they are our immortality. We have not told them that they are responsible for producing and leading generations after them. We have not told them the things that Howard University told me, for which I will always be grateful.

I congratulate you on your steadfastness, on the 128 years. And I resummon you to the heights—in fact, already cleared—in our past. Thank you.

H. PATRICK SWYGERT

Challenges, Change, and the Future of Howard University

Reverend Garrett, Dr. McKenzie, members of the Board of Trustees, members of my family, faculty, students, staff, alumni, emeriti, and friends of Howard University. I stand before you today with a deep sense of joy, pride, and humility. And with a deep sense of thanks to all of you for providing me with this opportunity to serve my *alma mater*.

Thirty-four years ago this month, I left 30th Street station in my hometown of Philadelphia to travel to Howard University to begin what became for me a defining and indelible journey that has shaped and formed my life.

When I arrived at Washington's Union Station, I was met by the Howard University Campus Pals. And I thought, "Gee, this is going to be really great. What a welcome. And just for me." Not knowing that the Campus Pals were there to greet all incoming students.

The welcome was great, but unfortunately my trunk did not arrive with me. For one week, some of the stalwart residents of Cook Hall took pity on this freshman from Philadelphia and provided me with the essentials and wherewithal to make my way through my first week at Howard. Eventually my trunk was found. And eventually I came to find and know Howard as well. For all of those in Cook Hall who gave so much of themselves, including their belongings, I thank you again.

I came to know of our institution as a dynamic, intellectual, and nurturing environment that allowed me the opportunity to explore the full extent of my intellectual abilities.

In my first few years here on campus, Dr. Mordecai Wyatt Johnson, whose 34-year tenure as president ended on June 30, 1960, still strolled about the campus wearing his customary Homburg. Dr. James M. Nabrit Jr. was his successor and my president through my seven years at Howard. Dr. Nabrit, as you all know, worked alongside of Justice Thurgood Marshall and many others in the valiant fight for civil rights. Dr. Nabrit was a delegate to the United Nations as well, and a national and world leader and a great president.

Today we find ourselves, 34 years later, at a critical juncture in the history of our great institution—a juncture of challenge, change, and opportunity—opportunity if we act decisively. And we will succeed in doing so. We will succeed if we have a vision that resonates with the constants that have kept and sustained us as Howard University.

These constants are our core values. And it is particularly important that all of us, in these times of challenge, pledge to renew our sense and knowledge of our core values.

The book of Proverbs tells us that where there is no vision, the people perish. *Where there is no vision, the people perish.* What then is our vision here at Howard University? In my vision, Howard University is a comprehensive research university, unique and irreplaceable, defined by its core values, the excellence of all its activities—its instruction, research and service, and by its enduring commitment to educating youth, African Americans and other people of color in particular, for leadership and service to our nation and the global community.

I believe this vision meets the test set out by one of our great leaders of the past, Dean Kelly Miller, dean and professor of mathematics and sociology, who served the University from 1890 to 1934. He wrote that, "Every institution of learning that has a distinctive sphere and function must have its ideals set forth in clearly defined terms." Dean Miller went on to define that essential element that propels and focuses Howard's vision and provides the very foundation of its core values. Dean Miller called that element the Howard spirit, which he described as an *esprit de corps*, or the elevated spirit of collected bodies exercising its influence over a coterie of kindred souls who are bound together by the subtle ties of common ideals.

Throughout our history, *we* have defined ourselves as an institution wedded to a common purpose. Our motto is *Veritas et Utilitas*, that is, truth and service. It is in the search for truth, and it is in the commitment to service, that we define our destiny—a destiny to lead and to serve. In the context of this destiny, as well, we must be aware of who we are, where we are, and where we are going.

Environmental, external forces, if you will, should not and cannot be permitted to define us. We must always define ourselves and contribute our energy and passion to making our definition of self real.

Now the mere articulation of our vision is not sufficient to attain it. We must have a plan that will make real the vision, integrate our core values, and our sense of self determination, while at the same time it must be a plan that positions us to be the leaders in the discussions, and indeed in the resolution, of the central issues of our day.

If we are to continue to be looked upon as the exemplars of leadership, "the Capstone," "the Mecca," then we must do what is necessary to meet this responsibility.

If I were asked to describe the fundamental challenge facing the University, I would say simply, that challenge is one of will and spirit. We can only talk about how to face that challenge of will and spirit again in the context of our core values.

Indeed, before I go any further, I would like to share with you what I believe are some of our core values. First, this University must continue to be dedicated to the unequivocal search for truth. The unequivocal, non-qualified search for truth. Second, this University must continue to be a place where African Americans and others can come to study, free of oppression of any type, stripe or kind. Third, this University must engender and nurture an environment that celebrates African-American culture in all its diversity. And fourth, this University must provide a caring, nurturing and respectful environment for all of the members of the Howard family: students, faculty, staff, trustees, and even the administration.

Indeed, perhaps the value most central to the mission may be the value that we most need to revisit and restate again and again and again—respect for this University, this institution and all that it stands for.

Everyone needs to understand that this is indeed a special place. And they need to understand as well the sacred environment that is Howard's—an environment that is steeped in a tradition of intellectual fervor, courageous leadership, and a "yes, we can," no-nonsense attitude to make our mission and our vision real.

Of course, there are challenges, but we know that challenge is not new to Howard University. The very idea of a Howard University was conceived by people in prayer who confronted great challenges. But those founders went on, after they prayed, to work to make their prayers a reality in this world. For surely, we need prayer as well. We also need to work just as hard to make our prayers real in this world. We can do so if we have the courage to stand up for our core values in the face of adversity.

Now, there are people who would argue that we should let our values languish, as the remnants of a bygone era, and move on to some notion that Howard can still be Howard and not be the best. Indeed there may be those who believe that this great school on this hill somehow should not aspire today to greatness. Well, we will continue to aspire to greatness because we should, we will, and we will succeed.

Let me be clear about what I mean by greatness. I refer to the Howard University that was founded to provide students with the very best in university education—for students of outstanding potential, regardless of their means, regardless of social class and status. At Howard, brains do count. Once we are clear about our history, and once we reaffirm our core values and come together to embrace a shared vision, we can then, but only then, turn our attention to the process, to the planning to make that vision real. But without a vision, the people shall perish.

Planning today, as it was in 1867, is not an easy task. Our issues, our challenges are difficult and complex. We should and we will avoid simple solutions to complex issues. Simple solutions most often are simply wrong. We must have a process that is informed by our unique history, by our aspirations, and by our values.

In 1867, when we received our charter from the federal government, we received that charter because in 1867 there was a perceived need for a national university. That need resonates and continues today. We should not, and we will not, permit anyone to go unchallenged who would suggest that the need for a national university, for Howard University, no longer exists, and, therefore, federal support for that institution is no longer required.

Our plan is a plan that will insist upon advocacy; it will insist upon our deep commitment to advocating on behalf of this great institution in the halls of Congress and elsewhere.

We know as practical people—and at Howard we have had to be practical people while at the same time dreamers—we know that we have to do more for ourselves. Well, we have always done for ourselves. That, too, is not a new phenomenon at Howard. In 1867 we had to do for ourselves. That has been our history. To the extent that we can, we will find more resources, and we will turn to every source available to us for those resources.

As you know, I am an alumnus of our great institution, and I am very familiar, very familiar, with the comment heard at so many gatherings of alumni and alumnae. Namely, "I would give, but I have never been asked." Or, "I would give, but to whom, to what program, to what activity on campus?" To those alumni who feel that we have not paid enough attention to them because we have not asked them to support *alma mater*, you may rest easy. You may take comfort in knowing that you soon will be asked, and asked often.

We will, as part of our plan, have a capital campaign, but we do not have to wait for that capital campaign to begin. There is so much that we can and should do today. When I came 34 years ago, Drew Hall was a new, magnificent facility. Yes, it was a long time ago. We do not have to wait to find the alumni who over the last three decades have called Drew Hall home. I simply say to them, the door is open. Yes, you may come home again. And yes, we expect you to bring something with you. So, when Drew Hall is air-conditioned and is a showcase on our campus, we will all know how that came about. It will have come about because alumni made it happen.

We do not have to wait for a campaign to make Howard Hall what it should be. We do not have to wait for any appropriations, for any external support to make Howard Hall real again on this campus. We can do that, and we will do that.

Our plan will also include ways and means of measuring the performance of all of us—to assess how we are doing. We have had more than a century of success. We have had that success largely because here in this sacred place we have continued to challenge one

H. Patrick Swygert—President, Howard University (Jim Wells)

another to do the best, to be the best. We will continue to do so. Everyone will be subject to assessment, from staff, most assuredly, to the president. We need to make sure that when we speak of our vision as giving our students the opportunity, the wherewithall to compete—not locally, not regionally, but globally—that indeed we are doing just that. And one of the ways of assuring that we are making the vision real is to examine our own performance.

We speak of the value of Howard as a caring and a nurturing place, a warm place, a safe harbor, if you will, for our students—whether those students be undergraduate, graduate students, or post doctoral students—a safe harbor, a place to live and breathe and grow. Well, that place is a place of people. People need to know, who have the opportunity to serve here at Howard, that that is a core value that they are responsible for making real—that every student should be treated with respect and courtesy. Every faculty member should know that his or her work is respected as the work of a member of an honored profession.

We have to put a plan together—all of us will participate in its formation—that provides our faculty, provides this University with the resources necessary to take our full place in the telecommunications world of today. The "superhighway" of information cannot bypass Howard University.

Our plan must speak as well to the organization of the University, its administration and all its programs, and all of its administrative and academic programs. All activities of the University will be reviewed in the context of a matrix comprising our core values, where we begin, our striving for excellence in all we do, our ability to sustain over time excellence, the extent to which our activities speak to the great issues of the day, and the extent to which those activities contribute to the education of our students so that they may succeed on a world stage.

Let me say a word about the great issues of today. In three retreats, one with our distinguished faculty, another with senior academic leaders and administrative leaders here at the University, and one with the loyal members of our staff, we talked about the great questions, and how great institutions respond to great questions.

The intellectual leaders of the ancient worlds of Africa and Greece had none of the resources that are so commonplace today—no computers, no library resources as they are known today, and hardly any budget. But the great intellectuals of the past had the ability to think, and to think critically. And in doing so, they were able to pose the great questions. They may not have had all of the answers, but the quest for the answers and the response to the questions themselves have fired our imaginations over a millennium.

Great institutions are about great questions. Howard University has been about great questions. Here again, like challenge, it is not new to our University. In 1867, there was a great question confronting this nation. That question was whether or not newly freed slaves could and should be the beneficiaries of a university-level education. In seeking the articles of incorporation and the charter in 1867, the debate was about whether there would be an academy, a college, or a university.

Our founders opted for a university. They were willing to raise the question, and for 128 years, because of their vision, we have answered that question.

In 1926, when a young Mordecai Johnson came to Howard University, there was another great question that Howard took on. That was whether or not this University, located in the nation's capital, largely dependent upon federal largesse, could serve as the platform for the completion of the freedom agenda. That was another great question. We did not shy away from the question of 1867; we did not shy away from the questions of 1926; and we cannot shy away today. We

cannot let our concerns for our resources so constrain and restrict us that we no longer have the capacity, or the willingness, or the courage, to take on the great questions.

I hope as well that the plan that we present to the trustees next spring also makes clear Howard's central place as the foremost repository of the African-American cultural experience.

Now some naysayers will say, "Well, we have the reality of resource limitations. That is real, Mr. President. Why do you now pose the question of Howard as a central and foremost repository of the African-American cultural experience?"

Let me remind you again of our history. The founders of what became Moorland-Spingarn did not have Moorland-Spingarn; they had an idea and a vision and a willingness. There was a Moorland-Spingarn before there was a Founders Library to house it. They had an idea, a vision, and a willingness to make it happen.

We must act on our ideas and our vision and have the courage to make it happen. We cannot wait until it is there. We have to make it happen. We will create, if we have the courage, the wit and the will, we will create our own reality. That speaks clearly of Howard University.

No plan, no matter how carefully crafted, no matter how articulate, no plan is self-actuating. All of us together have to make it real. All of us together have to support its purpose. To do so, all of us must be given the opportunity to participate and to participate fully in its formulation. I pledge to you that all the members of the University family will have that opportunity.

I began my address this morning by talking about values. I would like to conclude by returning to where I began. I spoke for just a moment about respect—respect for the history of this University, respect for the physical presence of all the University and our surroundings, but most important, respect for one another.

That means, among other things, that everyone on this campus, regardless of status, is to be respected as a member of a community of scholars. Scholarship, and the application of that scholarship to the great questions of the day, and our leadership in doing so, is really Howard University. So, respect for Howard is respect for the academy; it is the respect for that search for truth that will not only pose those great questions, but, hopefully, will lead us to the answers.

In the Psalms we find, "So teach us to number our days so that we may get a heart of wisdom." Throughout human experience we have sought to leave testimonies to our presence, to the time we spent on this earth—monuments built, institutions founded, facilities named—as if bricks and mortar will and can outlive eternity. We know as a family of scholars and those who support it that this is a sacred place. That Psalms refers not to bricks and mortar, but it refers to much of what occurs on this campus everyday, because everyday on this campus through our teaching, our service, our research, our scholarship, we do something that makes all of us just a bit immortal.

Through our students we touch the future. What we teach, what we share with them, what we introduce them to, the excitement of found knowledge, the excitement and the satisfaction of service, the excitement and responsibility of leadership takes place everyday on this campus. And everyday we touch the future.

Thank you.

CHAPTER FOUR

A Way of Responding

I now understood the pathway
from slavery to freedom. . . . I set
out . . . at whatever cost of trouble
to learn how to read.

—Frederick Douglass

Left to right: James M. Nabrit, Jr., Charles R. Drew, Sterling A. Brown, E. Franklin Frazier, Rayford W. Logan, Alain LeRoy Locke (Courtesy of the Moorland-Spingarn Research Center)

W. E. B. DU BOIS

The Talented Tenth (1903)

The Negro race, like all races, is going to be saved by its exceptional men. The problem of education, then, among Negroes must first of all deal with the Talented Tenth; it is the problem of developing the Best of this race that they may guide the Mass away from the contamination and death of the Worst, in their own and other races. Now the training of men is a difficult and intricate task. Its technique is a matter for educational experts, but its object is for the vision of seers. If we make money the object of man-training, we shall develop money-makers but not necessarily men; if we make technical skill the object of education, we may possess artisans but not, in nature, men. Men we shall have only as we make manhood the object of the work of the schools—intelligence, broad sympathy, knowledge of the world that was and is, and of the relation of men to it—this is the curriculum of that Higher Education which must underlie true life. On this foundation we may build bread winning, skill of hand and quickness of brain, with never a fear lest the child and man mistake the means of living for the object of life.

If this be true—and who can deny it—three tasks lay before me; first to show from the past that the Talented Tenth as they have risen among American Negroes have been worthy of leadership; secondly, to show how these men may be educated and developed; and thirdly, to show their relation to the Negro problem.

You misjudge us because you do not know us. From the very first it has been the educated and intelligent of the Negro and it has made the black man scorn the thought of enslavement, as does a white man, as far as its influence has extended. Strengthen that noble influence! Before its organization, the country only saw here and there in slavery some faithful Cudjoe or Dinah, whose strong natures blossomed even in bondage, like a fine plant beneath a heavy stone. Now, under the elevating and cherishing influence of the American Anti-slavery Society, the colored race, like the white, furnishes Corinthian capitals for the noblest temples.

Where were these black abolitionists trained? Some, like Frederick Douglass, were self-trained, but yet trained liberally; others like Alexander Crummell and McCune Smith, graduated from famous foreign universities. Most of them rose up through the colored schools of New York and Philadelphia and Boston, taught by college-bred men like Russworm, of Dartmouth, and college-bred white men like Neau and Benezet.

After emancipation came a new group of educated and gifted leaders: Langston, Bruce and Elliot,

Greener, Williams and Payne. Through political organization, historical and polemic writing and moral regeneration, these men strove to uplift their people. It is now the fashion of to-day to sneer at them and to say that with freedom Negro leadership should have begun at the plow and not in the Senate—a foolish and mischievous lie; two hundred and fifty years that black serf toiled at the plow and yet that toiling was in vain till the Senate passed the war amendments; and two hundred and fifty years more the half-free serf of to-day may toil at his plow, but unless he have political rights and righteously guarded civic status, he will still remain the poverty-stricken and ignorant plaything of rascals, that he now is. This all sane men know even if they dare not say it.

And so now we come to the present—a day of cowardice and vacillation, of strident wide voiced wrong and faint hearted compromise; of double-faced dallying with Truth and Right. Who are to-day guiding the work of the Negro people? The "exceptions" of course. And yet so sure as this Talented Tenth is pointed out, the blind worshippers of the Average cry out in alarm: "These are the exceptions, look here at death, disease and crime—these are the happy rule." Of course they are the rule, because a silly nation made them the rule: Because for three long centuries this people lynched Negroes who dared to be brave, raped black women who dared to be virtuous, crushed dark-hued youth who dared to be ambitious, and encouraged and made to flourish servility and lewdness and apathy. But not even this was able to crush all manhood and chastity and aspiration from black folk. A saving remnant continually survives and persists, continually aspires, continually shows itself in thrift and ability and character. Exceptional it is to be sure, but this is its chiefest promise; it shows the capability of Negro blood, the promise of black men. Do Americans ever stop to reflect that there are in this land a million men of Negro blood, well-educated, owners of homes, against the honor of whose womanhood no breath was ever raised, whose men occupy positions of trust and usefulness, and who, judged by any standard, have reached the full measure of the best type of modern European culture? Is it fair, is it decent, is it Christian to ignore these facts of the Negro problem, to belittle such aspiration, to nullify such leadership and seek to crush these people back into the mass out of which by toil and travail, they and their fathers have raised themselves?

Can the masses of the Negro people be in any possible way more quickly raised than by the effort and example of this aristocracy of talent and character? Was there ever a nation on God's fair earth civilized from the bottom upward? Never; it is, ever was and ever will be from the top downward that culture filters. The Talented Tenth rises and pulls all that are worth the saving up to their vantage ground. This is the history of human progress; and two historic mistakes which have hindered that progress were the thinking first that no more could ever rise save the few already risen; or second, that it would better the unrisen to pull the risen down.

How then shall the leaders of a struggling people be trained and the hands of the risen few be strengthened? There can be but one answer: The best and most capable of their youth must be schooled in the colleges and universities of the land. We will not quarrel as to just what the university of the Negro should teach or how it should teach it—I willingly admit that each soul and each race-soul needs its own peculiar curriculum. But this is true: A university is a human invention for the transmission of knowledge and culture from generation to generation, through the training of quick minds and pure hearts, and for this work no other human invention will suffice, not even trade and industrial schools.

All men cannot go to college but some men must; every isolated group or nation must have its yeast, must have for the talented few centers of training where men are not so mystified and befuddled by the hard necessary toil of earning a living, as to have no aims higher than their bellies, and no God greater than Gold. This is true training, and thus in the beginning were the favored sons of the freedmen trained. Out of the colleges of the North came, Cravath, Chase, Andrews, Bumstead and Spence to build the foundations of knowledge and civilization in the black South. Where ought they to have begun to build? At the bottom, of course, quibbles the mole with his eyes in the earth. Aye! truly at the bottom, at the very bottom; at the bottom of knowledge, down in the very depths of knowledge there where the roots of justice strike into the lowest soil of Truth. And so they did begin; they founded colleges, and up from the colleges shot normal schools, and out from the normal schools went teachers, and around the normal teachers clustered other teachers to teach the public schools; the colleges trained in Greek and Latin and mathematics, 2,000 men; and these men trained full 50,000 others in morals and manners and they in turn taught thrift and the alphabet to nine millions of men, who to-day hold $300,000,000 of property. It was a miracle—the most wonderful peace-battle of the nineteenth century, and yet to-day men smile at it, and in fine superiority tell us that it was all a strange mistake; that a proper way to found a system of education is first to gather the children and buy them spelling books and hoes; afterward men may look about for teachers, if haply they find them; or again they would teach men Work, but as for Life—why, what has Work to do with Life, they ask vacantly.

Was the work of these college founders successful; did it stand the test of time? Did the college graduates, with all their fine theories of life, really live? Are they useful men helping to civilize and elevate their less fortunate fellows? Let us see. Omitting all institutions which have not actually graduated students from college courses, there are to-day in the United States thirty-four institutions giving something above high school training to Negroes and designed especially for this race.

Three of these were established in the border States before the War; thirteen were planted by the Freedmen's Bureau in the years 1864–1869; nine were established between 1870 and 1880 by various church bodies; five were established after 1881 by Negro churches, and four are state institutions supported by United States' agricultural funds. In most cases the college departments are small adjuncts to high and common school work. As a matter of fact six institutions—Atlanta, Fisk, Howard, Shaw, Wilberforce and Leland, are the important Negro colleges so far as actual work and number of students are concerned. In all these institutions, seven hundred and fifty Negro college students are enrolled. In grade the best of these colleges are about a year behind the smaller New England colleges and a typical curriculum is that of Atlanta University. Here students from the grammar grades, after a three years' high school course, take a college course of 136 weeks. One-fourth of this time is given to Latin and Greek; one-fifth, to English and modern languages; one-sixth, to history and social science; one-seventh, to natural science; one-eighth to mathematics, and one-eighth to philosophy and pedagogy.

In addition to these students in the South, Negroes have attended Northern colleges for many years. As early as 1826 one was graduated from Bowdoin college, and from that time till to-day nearly every year has seen elsewhere, other such graduates. They have, of course, met much color prejudice. Fifty years ago very few colleges would admit them at all. Even to-day no Negro has ever been admitted to Princeton, and at some other leading institutions they are rather endured than encouraged. Oberlin was the great pioneer in the work of blotting out the color line in colleges, and has more Negro graduates by far than any other Northern college.

The total number of Negro college graduates up to 1899 (several of the graduates of that year not being reported), was as follows:

		Negro Colleges	White Colleges
Before	'76	137	75
	'75–80	143	22
	'80–85	250	31
	'85–90	413	43
	'90–95	465	66
	'95–99	475	88
Class Unknown		57	64
Total		1,940	389

Of these graduates 1,079 were men and 250 were women; 50 per cent of Northern-born college men come South to work among the masses of their people, at a sacrifice which few people realize; nearly 90 per cent of the Southern-born graduates instead of seeking that personal freedom and broader intellectual atmosphere which their training has led them, in some degree, to conceive, stay and labor and wait in the midst of their black neighbors and relatives.

The most interesting question, and in many respects the crucial question, to be asked concerning college-bred Negroes, is: Do they earn a living? It has been intimated more than once that the higher training of Negroes has resulted in sending into the world of work, men who could find nothing to do suitable to their talents. Now and then there comes a rumor of a colored college man working at menial service, etc. Fortunately, returns as to occupations of college-bred Negroes, gathered by the Atlanta conference, are quite full—nearly 60 per cent of the total number of graduates.

This enables us to reach fairly certain conclusions as to the occupations of all college-bred Negroes. Of 1,312 persons reported, there were:

	Per Cent	
Teachers,	53.4	XXXXXXXXXXXXXXXXX
Clergymen,	16.8	XXXXXX
Physicians, etc.	6.3	XXX
Students,	5.6	XX
Lawyers,	4.7	XX
In Govt. Service,	4.0	X
In Business,	3.6	X
Farmers and Artisans,	2.7	X
Editors, Secretaries and Clerks,	2.4	
Miscellaneous,	.5	

Over half are teachers, a sixth are preachers, another sixth are students and professional men; over 6 per cent are farmers, artisans and merchants, and 4 per cent are in government service. In detail the occupations are as follows:

OCCUPATIONS OF COLLEGE-BRED MEN

Teachers		
Presidents and Deans,	19	
Teachers of Music,	7	
Professors, Principals and Teachers,	675	Total 701
Clergymen		
Bishop,	1	
Chaplains, U.S. Army,	2	
Missionaries,	9	
Presiding Elders,	12	
Preachers,	197	Total 221
Physicians		
Doctors of Medicine,	76	
Druggists,	4	
Dentists,	3	Total 83
Students		74
Lawyers		62
Civil Service		
U.S. Minister Plenipotentiary,	1	
U.S. Consul,	1	
U.S. Deputy Collector,	1	
U.S. Gauger,	1	
U.S. Postmasters,	2	
U.S. Clerks,	44	
State Civil Service,	2	
City Civil Service,	1	Total 53
Business Men		
Merchants, etc.,	30	
Managers,	13	
Real Estate Dealers,	4	Total 47
Farmers		26
Clerks and Secretaries		
Secretary of National Societies,	7	
Clerks, etc.	15	Total 22
Artisans		9
Editors		9
Miscellaneous		5

These figures illustrate vividly the function of the college-bred Negro. He is, as he ought to be, the group leader, the man who sets the ideals of the community where he lives, directs its thoughts and heads its social movements. It need hardly be argued that the Negro people need social leadership more than most groups; that they have no traditions to fall back upon, no long established customs, no strong family ties, no well defined social classes. All these things must be slowly and painfully evolved. The preacher was, even before the war, the group leader of the Negroes, and the church their greatest social institution. Naturally this preacher was ignorant and often immoral, and the problem of replacing the older type by better educated men has been a difficult one. Both by direct work and by direct influence on other preachers, and on congregations, the college-bred preacher has an opportunity for refor-

matory work and moral inspiration, the value of which cannot be overestimated.

It has, however, been in the furnishing of teachers that the Negro college has found its peculiar function. Few persons realize how vast a work, how mighty a revolution has been thus accomplished. To furnish five millions and more of ignorant people with teachers of their own race and blood, in one generation, was not only a very difficult undertaking, but a very important one, in that, it placed before the eyes of almost every Negro child an attainable ideal. It brought the masses of the blacks in contact with modern civilization, made black men the leaders of their communities and trainers of the new generation. In this work college-bred Negroes were first teachers, and then teachers of teachers. And here it is that the broad culture of college work has been of peculiar value. Knowledge of life and its wider meaning, has been the point of the Negro's deepest ignorance, and the sending out of teachers whose training has not been simply for bread winning, but also for human culture, has been of inestimable value in the training of these men.

In the earlier years the two occupations of preacher and teacher were practically the only ones open to the black college graduate. Of later years a larger diversity of life among his people has opened new avenues of employment. Nor have these college men been paupers and spendthrifts; 557 college-bred Negroes owned in 1899, $1,342,862.50 worth of real estate (assessed value), or $2,411 per family. The real value of the total accumulations of the whole group is perhaps about $10,000,000, or $5,000 apiece. Pitiful, is it not, beside the fortunes of oil kings and steel trusts, but after all is the fortune of the millionaire the only stamp of true and successful living? Alas! it is, with many, and there's the rub.

The problem of training the Negro is to-day immensely complicated by the fact that the whole question of the efficiency and appropriateness of our present systems of education, for any kind of child, is a matter of active debate, in which final settlement seems still afar off. Consequently it often happens that persons arguing for or against certain systems of education for Negroes have these controversies in mind and miss the real question at issue. The main question, so far as the Southern Negro is concerned, is: What under the present circumstance, must a system of education do in order to raise the Negro as quickly as possible in the scale of civilization? The answer to this question seems to me clear: It must strengthen the Negro's character, increase his knowledge and teach him to earn a living. Now it goes without saying, that it is hard to do all these things simultaneously or suddenly, and that at the same time it will not do to give all the attention to one and neglect the others; we could give black boys trades, but that alone will not civilize a race of ex-slaves; we might simply increase their knowledge of the world, but this would not necessarily make them wish to use this knowledge honestly; we might seek to strengthen character and purpose, but to what end if this people have nothing to eat or to wear? A system of education is not one thing, nor does it have a single definite object, nor is it a mere matter of schools. Education is that whole system of human training within and without the school house walls, which molds and develops men. If then we start out to train an ignorant and unskilled people with a heritage of bad habits, our system of training must set before itself two great aims—the one dealing with knowledge and character, the other part seeking to give the child the technical knowledge necessary for him to earn a living under the present circumstances. These objects are accomplished in part by the opening of the common schools on the one, and of the industrial schools on the other. But only in part, for there must also be trained those who are to teach these schools—men and women of knowledge and culture and technical skill who understand modern civilization, and having the training and aptitude to impart it to the children under them. There must be teachers, and teachers of teachers, and to attempt to establish any sort of system of common and industrial school training, without *first* (and I say *first* advisedly) without *first* providing for the higher training of the very best teachers, is simply throwing your money to the winds. School houses do not teach themselves—piles of brick and mortar and machinery do not send out *men*. It is the trained, living human soul, cultivated and strengthened by long study and thought, that breathes the real breath of life into boys and girls and makes them human, whether they be black or white, Greek, Russian or American. Nothing, in these latter days, has so dampened the faith of thinking Negroes in recent educational movements, as the fact that such movements have been accompanied by ridicule and denouncement and decrying of those very institutions of higher training which made the Negro public school possible, and make the Negro industrial schools thinkable. It was Fisk, Atlanta, Howard and Straight, those colleges born of the faith and sacrifice of the abolitionists, that placed in the black schools of the South 30,000 teachers and more, which some, who depreciate the work of these higher schools, are using to teach their own new experiments. If Hampton, Tuskegee and the hundred other industrial schools prove in the future to be as successful as they deserve to be, then their success in training black artisans for the South will be due primarily to the white colleges of the North and the black colleges of

the South, which trained the teachers who to-day conduct these institutions. There was a time when the American people believed pretty devoutly that a log of wood with a boy at one end and Mark Hopkins at the other, represented the highest ideal of human training. But in these eager days it would seem that we have changed all that and think it necessary to add a couple of saw-mills and a hammer to this outfit, and, at a pinch, to dispense with the services of Mark Hopkins.

I would not deny, or for a moment seem to deny, the paramount necessity of teaching the Negro to work, and to work steadily and skillfully; or seem to depreciate in the slightest degree the important part industrial schools must play in the accomplishments of these ends, but I *do* say, and insist upon it, that it is industrialism drunk with its vision of success, to imagine that its own work can be accomplished without providing for the training of broadly cultured men and women to teach its own teachers, and to teach the teachers of the public schools.

But I have already said that human education is not simply a matter of schools; it is much more a matter of family and group life—the training of one's home, of one's daily companions, of one's social class. Now the black boy of the South moves in a black world—a world with its own leaders, its own thoughts, its own ideals. In this world he gets by far the larger part of his life training, and through the eyes of this dark world he peers into the veiled world beyond. Who guides and determines the education which he receives in his world? His teachers here are the group-leaders of the Negro people—the physicians and clergymen, the trained fathers and mothers, the influential and forceful men about him of all kinds; here it is, if at all, that the culture of the surrounding world trickles through and is handed on by the graduates of the higher schools. Can such culture training of group-leaders be neglected? Can we afford to ignore it? Do you think that if the leaders of thought among Negroes are not trained and educated thinkers, that they will have no leaders? On the contrary a hundred half-trained demagogues will still hold the places they so largely occupy now, and hundreds of vociferous busy-bodies will multiply. You have no choice; either you must help furnish this race from within its own ranks with thoughtful men of trained leadership, or you must suffer the evil consequences of a headless misguided rabble.

I am an earnest advocate of manual training and trade teaching for black boys, and for white boys, too. I believe that next to the founding of Negro colleges the most valuable addition to Negro education since the war, has been industrial training for black boys. Nevertheless, I insist that the object of all true education is not to make men carpenters, it is to make carpenters men; there are two means of making the carpenter a man, each equally important: the first is to give the group and community in which he works, liberally trained teachers and leaders to teach him and his family what life means; the second is to give him sufficient intelligence and technical skill to make him an efficient workman; the first object demands the Negro college and college-bred men—not a quantity of such colleges, but a few of excellent quality; not too many college-bred men, but enough to leaven the lump, to inspire the masses, to raise the Talented Tenth to leadership; the second object demands a good system of common schools, well-taught, conveniently located and properly equipped.

The Sixth Atlanta Conference truly said in 1901: "We call the attention of the Nation to the fact that less than one million of the three million Negro children of school age, are at present regularly attending school, and these attend a session which lasts only a few months.

"We are to-day deliberately rearing millions of our citizens in ignorance, and at the same time limiting the rights of citizenship by educational qualifications. This is unjust. Half the black youth of the land have no opportunities open to them for learning to read, write and cipher. In the discussion as to the proper training of Negro children after they leave the public schools, we have forgotten that they are not yet decently provided with public schools.

"Propositions are beginning to be made in the South to reduce the already meagre school facilities of Negroes. We congratulate the South on resisting, as much as it has, this pressure, and on the many millions it has spent on Negro education. But it is only fair to point out that Negro taxes and the Negroes' share of the income from indirect taxes and endowments have fully repaid this expenditure, so that the Negro public school system has not in all probability cost the white taxpayers a single cent since the war.

"This is not fair. Negro schools should be a public burden, since they are a public benefit. The Negro has a right to demand good common school training at the hands of the States and the Nation since by their fault he is not in position to pay for this himself."

What is the chief need for the building up of the Negro public school in the South? The Negro race in the South needs teachers to-day above all else. This is the current testimony of all who know the situation. For the supply of this great demand two things are needed—institutions of higher education and money for school houses and salaries. It is usually assumed that a hundred or more institutions for Negro training are to-day turning out so many teachers and college-bred men that the race is threatened with an oversupply. This is sheer nonsense. There are to-day less than 3,000 living Negro college graduates in the United States, and less than a 1,000 Negroes in college. Moreover, in the 164 schools for Negroes, 95 per cent of their students are doing elementary and secondary work, work which should be done in the public schools. Over half of the remaining 2,157 students are taking high school studies. The mass of so-called "normal" schools for the Negro are simply doing elementary common school work, or, at most, high school work, with a little instruction in methods. The Negro colleges and the postgraduate courses at other institutions are the only agencies for the broader and more careful training of teachers. The work of these institutions is hampered for lack of funds. It is getting increasingly difficult to get funds for training teachers in the best modern methods, and yet all over the South, from State Superintendents, county officials, city boards and school principals comes the wail, "We need *teachers*!" and teachers must be trained. As the fairest minded of all white Southerners, Atticus G. Haygood, once said: "The defects of colored teachers are so great as to create an urgent necessity for training better ones. Their excellencies and their successes are sufficient to justify the best hopes of success in the effort, and to vindicate the judgment of those who make large investments of money and service, to give to colored students opportunity for thoroughly preparing themselves for the work of teaching children of their people."

The truth of this has been strikingly shown in the marked improvement of white teachers in the South. Twenty years ago the rank and file of white public school teachers were not as good as the Negro teachers. But they, by scholarships and good salaries, have been encouraged to thorough normal collegiate preparation, while the Negro teachers have been discouraged by starvation wages and the idea that any training will do for a black teacher. If carpenters are needed it is well and good to train men as carpenters. But to train men as carpenters, and then set them to teaching is wasteful and criminal; and to train men as teachers and then refuse them a living wage, unless they become carpenters, is rank nonsense.

The United States Commissioner of Education says in his report for 1900: "For comparison between the white and colored enrollment in secondary and higher education, I have added together the enrollment in high schools and secondary schools with the attendance in colleges and universities, not being sure of the actual grade of work done in the colleges and universities. The work done in the secondary schools is reported in such detail in this office, that there can be no doubt of its grade."

He then makes the following comparisons of persons in every million enrolled in secondary and higher education:

	Whole Country	Negroes
1880	4,362	1,289
1900	10,743	2,061

And he concludes: "While the number in colored high schools and colleges had increased somewhat faster than the population, it had not kept pace with the average of the whole country, for it had fallen from 30 per cent to 24 per cent of the average quota. Of all colored pupils, one (1) in one hundred was engaged in secondary and higher work, and that ratio has continued substantially for the past twenty years. If the ratio of colored population in secondary and higher education is to be equal to the average for the whole country, it must be increased to five times its present average." And if this be true of the secondary and higher education, it is safe to say that the Negro has not one-tenth his quota in college studies. How baseless, therefore, is the charge of too much training! We need Negro teachers for the Negro common schools, and we need first-class normal schools and colleges to train them. This is the work of higher Negro education and it must be done.

Further than this, after being provided with group leaders of civilization, and a foundation of intelligence in the public schools, the carpenter, in order to be a man, needs technical skill. This calls for trade school. Now trade schools are not nearly such simple things as people once thought. The original idea was that the "Industrial" school was to furnish education, practically free, to those willing to work for it; it was to "do" things—i.e.: become a center of productive industry, it was to be partially, if not wholly, self-supporting, and it was to teach trades. Admirable as were some of the ideas underlying this scheme, the whole thing simply would not work in practice; it was found that if you were to use time and material to teach trades thoroughly, you could not at the same time keep the industries on a commercial basis and make them pay. Many schools started out to do this on a large scale and went into virtual bankruptcy. Moreover, it was found also that it was possible to teach a boy a trade mechanically, without giving him the full educative benefit of the process, and, vice versa, that there was a distinctive educative value in teaching a boy to use his hands and eyes in carrying out certain physical processes, even though he did not actually learn a trade. It has happened, there-

fore, in the last decade that a noticeable change has come over the industrial schools. In the first place the idea of commercially remunerative industry in a school is being pushed rapidly to the background. There are still schools with shops and farms that bring in an income, and schools that use student labor partially for the erection of their buildings and the furnishing of equipment. It is coming to be seen, however, in the education of the Negro, as clearly as it has been seen in the education of the youths the world over, that it is the *boy* and not the material product, that is the true object of eduction. Consequently the object of the industrial school came to be the thorough training of boys regardless of the cost of the training, so long as it was thoroughly well done.

Even at this point, however, the difficulties were not surmounted. In the first place modern industry has taken great strides since the war, and the teaching of trades is no longer a simple matter. Machinery and the long processes of work have greatly changed the work of the carpenter, the iron worker and the shoemaker. A really efficient workman must be to-day an intelligent man who has had good technical training in addition to thorough common school, and perhaps even higher training. To meet this situation the industrial schools began a further development; they established distinct Trade Schools for the thorough training of better class artisans, and at the same time they sought to preserve for the purpose of general education, such of the simpler processes of the elementary trade learning as were best suited therefor. In this differentiation of the Trade School and manual training, the best of the industrial schools simply followed the plain trend of the present educational epoch. A prominent educator tells us that, in Sweden, "In the beginning the economic conception was generally adopted, and everywhere manual training was looked upon as a means of preparing the children of the common people to earn their living. But gradually it came to be recognized that manual training has a more elevated purpose, and one, indeed, more useful in the deeper meaning of the term. It came to be considered as an educative process for the complete moral, physical and intellectual development of the child."

Thus, again, in the manning of trade schools and manual training schools we are thrown back upon the higher training as its source and chief support. There was a time when any aged and worn-out carpenter could teach in a trade school. But not so to-day. Indeed the demand for college-bred men by a school like Tuskegee ought to make Mr. Booker T. Washington the firmest friend of higher training. Here he has as helpers the son of a Negro senator, trained in Greek and the humanities, and graduated at Harvard; the son of a

Negro congressman and lawyer, trained in Latin and mathematics, and graduated at Oberlin; he has as his wife, a woman who read Virgil and Homer in the same class room with me; he has as college chaplain, a classical graduate of Atlanta University; as teacher of science, a graduate of Fisk; as teacher of history, a graduate of Smith—indeed some thirty of his chief teachers are college graduates, and instead of studying French grammars in the midst of weeds, or buying pianos for dirty cabins, they are at Mr. Washington's right hand helping him in a noble work. And yet one of the effects of Mr. Washington's propaganda has been to throw doubt upon the expediency of such training for Negroes, as these persons have had.

Men of America, the problem is plain before you. Here is a race transplanted through the criminal foolishness of your fathers. Whether you like it or not the millions are here, and here they will remain. If you do not lift them up, they will pull you down. Education and work are the levers to uplift a people. Work will not do it unless inspired by the right ideals and guided by intelligence. Education must not simply teach work—it must teach life. The Talented Tenth of the Negro race must be made leaders of thought and missionaries of culture among their people. No others can do this work and the Negro colleges must train men for it. The Negro race, like all other races, is going to be saved by its exceptional men.

CARTER G. WOODSON

The Migration of the Talented Tenth

What classes then have migrated? In the first place, the Negro politicians, who, after the restoration of Bourbon rule in the South, found themselves thrown out of office and often humiliated and impoverished, had to find some way out of the difficulty. Some few have been relieved by sympathetic leaders of the Republican party, who secured for them federal appointments in Washington. These appointments when sometimes paying lucrative salaries have been given as a reward to those Negroes who, although dethroned in the South, remain in touch with the remnant of the Republican party there and control the delegates to the national conventions nominating candidates for President. Many Negroes of this class have settled in Washington. In some cases, the observer witnesses the pitiable scene of a man once a prominent public functionary in the South now serving in Washington as a messenger or a clerk.

The well-established blacks, however, have not been so easily induced to go. The Negroes in business in the South have usually been loath to leave their people among whom they can acquire property, whereas, if they go to the North, they have merely political freedom with no assurance of an opportunity in the economic world. But now a few of these have given themselves up to unrelenting toil with a view to accumulating sufficient wealth to move North and live thereafter on the income from their investments. Many of this class now spend some of their time in the North to educate their children. But they do not like to have these children who have been under refining influences return to the South to suffer the humiliation which during the last generation has been growing more and more aggravating. Endeavoring to carry out their policy of keeping the Negro down, southerners too often carefully plan to humiliate the progressive and intelligent blacks and in some cases form mobs to drive them out, as they are bad examples for that class of Negroes whom they desire to keep as menials.

There are also the migrating educated Negroes. They have studied history, law and economics and well understand what it is to get the rights guaranteed them by the constitution. The more they know the more discontented they become. They cannot speak but for what they want. No one is likely to second such a protest, not even the Negroes themselves, so generally have they been intimidated. The more outspoken they become, moreover, the more necessary is it for them to leave, for they thereby destroy their chances to earn a livelihood. White men in control of the public schools of the South see to it that the subserviency of the Negro teachers employed be certified beforehand. They dare not complain too much about equipment and salaries even if the per capita appropriation for the education of the Negroes be one fourth of that for the whites.

In the higher institutions of learning, especially the State schools, it is exceptional to find a principal who has the confidence of the Negroes. The Negroes will openly assert that he is in the pay of the reactionary whites, whose purpose is to keep the Negro down; and the incumbent himself will tell his board of regents how much he is opposed by the Negroes because he labors for the interests of the white race. Out of such sycophancy it is easily explained why our State schools have been so ineffective as to necessitate the sending of the Negro youth to private institutions maintained by northern philanthropy. Yet if an outspoken Negro happens to be an instructor in a private school conducted by educators from the North, he has to be careful about contending for a square deal; for, if the head of his institution does not suggest to him to proceed conservatively, the mob will dispose of the complainant. Physicians, lawyers and preachers who are not so economically dependent as teachers can exercise no more freedom of speech in the midst of this triumphant rule of the lawless.

A large number of educated Negroes, therefore, have on account of these conditions been compelled to leave the South. Finding in the North, however, practically nothing in their line to do, because of the proscription by race prejudice and trades unions, many of them lead the life of menials, serving as waiters, porters, butlers and chauffeurs. While in Chicago, not long ago, the writer was in the office of a graduate of a colored southern college, who was showing his former teacher the picture of his class. In accounting for his classmates in the various walks of life, he reported that more than one third of them were settled to the occupation of Pullman porters.

The largest number of Negroes who have gone North during this period, however, belong to the intelligent laboring class. Some of them have become discontented for the very same reasons that the higher classes have tired of oppression in the South, but the larger number of them have gone North to improve their economic condition. Most of these have migrated to the large cities in the East and Northwest, such as Philadelphia, New York, Indianapolis, Pittsburgh, Cleveland, Columbus, Detroit and Chicago. To understand this problem in its urban aspects the accompanying diagram showing the increase in the Negro population of northern cities during the first decade of this century will be helpful.

Some of these Negroes have migrated after careful consideration; others have just happened to go north as wanderers; and a still larger number on the many excursions to the cities conducted by railroads during the summer months. Sometimes one excursion brings to Chicago two or three thousand Negroes, two thirds of whom never go back. They do not often follow the higher pursuits of labor in the North but they earn more money than they have been accustomed to earn in the South. They are attracted also by the liberal attitude of some whites, which, although not that of social equality, gives the Negroes a liberty in northern centers which leads them to think that they are citizens of the country.

This shifting in the population has had an unusually significant effect on the black belt. Frederick Douglass advised the Negroes in 1879 to remain in the South where they would be in sufficiently large numbers to have political power, but they have gradually scattered from the black belt so as to diminish greatly their chances ever to become the political force they formerly were in this country. The Negroes

once had this possibility in South Carolina, Georgia, Alabama, Mississippi and Louisiana and, had the process of Africanization prior to the Civil War had a few decades longer to do its work, there would not have been any doubt as to the ultimate preponderance of the Negroes in those commonwealths. The tendencies of the black population according to the censuses of the United States and especially that of 1910, however, show that the chances for the control of these State governments by Negroes no longer exist except in South Carolina and Mississippi. It has been predicted, therefore, that, if the same tendencies continue for the next fifty years, there will be even few counties in which the Negroes will be in a majority. All of the Southern States except Arkansas showed a proportionate increase in the white population over that of the black between 1900 and 1910, while West Virginia and Oklahoma with relatively small numbers of blacks showed, for reasons stated elsewhere, an increase in the Negro population. Thus we see coming to pass something like the proposed plan of Jefferson and other statesmen who one hundred years ago advocated the expansion of slavery to lessen the evil of the institution by distributing its burdens.

The migration of intelligent blacks, however, has been attended with several handicaps to the race. The large part of the black population is in the South and there it will stay for decades to come. The southern Negroes, therefore, have been robbed of their due part of the talented tenth. The educated blacks have had no constituency in the North and, consequently, have been unable to realize their sweetest dreams of the land of the free. In their new home the enlightened Negro must live with his light under a bushel. Those left behind in the South soon despair of seeing a brighter way and yield to the yoke. In the places of the leaders who were wont to speak for their people, the whites have raised up Negroes who accept favors offered them on the condition that their lips be sealed up forever on the rights of the Negro.

This emigration too has left the Negro subject to other evils. There are many first-class Negro business men in the South, but although there were once progressive men of color, who endeavored to protect the blacks from being plundered by white sharks and harpies there have arisen numerous unscrupulous Negroes who have for a part of the proceeds from such jobbery associated themselves with ill-designing white men to dupe illiterate Negroes. This trickery is brought into play in marketing their crops, selling them supplies, or purchasing their property. To carry out this iniquitous plan the persons concerned have the protection of the law, for while Negroes in general are imposed upon, those engaged in robbing them have no cause to fear.

ALAIN LOCKE

The New Negro

In the last decade something beyond the watch and guard of statistics has happened in the life of the American Negro and the three norns who have traditionally presided over the Negro problem have a changeling in their laps. The Sociologist, the Philanthropist, the Raceleader are not unaware of the New Negro, but they are at a loss to account for him. He simply cannot be swathed in their formulae. For the younger generation is vibrant with a new psychology; the new spirit is awake in the masses, and under the very eyes of the professional observers is transforming what has been a perennial problem into the progressive phases of contemporary Negro life.

Could such a metamorphosis have taken place as suddenly as it has appeared to? The answer is no; not because the New Negro is not here, but because the Old Negro had long become more of a myth than a man. The Old Negro, we must remember, was a creature of moral debate and historical controversy. His has been a stock figure perpetuated as an historical fiction partly in innocent sentimentalism, partly in deliberate reactionism. The Negro himself has contributed his share to this through a sort of protective social mimicry forced upon him by the adverse circumstances of dependence. So for generations in the mind of America, the Negro has been more of a formula than a human being—a something to be argued about, condemned or defended, to be "kept down," or "in his place," or "helped up," to be worried with or worried over, harrassed or patronized, a social bogey or a social burden. The thinking Negro even has been induced to share this same general attitude, to focus his attention on controversial issues, to see himself in the distorted perspective of a social problem. His shadow, so to speak, has been more real to him than his personality. Through having had to appeal from the unjust sterotypes of his oppressors and traducers to those of his liberators, friends and benefactors he has had to subscribe to the traditional positions from which his case has been viewed. Little true social or self-understanding has or could come from such a situation.

But while the minds of most of us, black and white, have thus burrowed in the trenches of the Civil War and Reconstruction, the actual march of development has simply flanked these positions, necessitating a sudden reorientation of view. We have not been watching in the right direction; set North and South on a sectional axis, we have not noticed the East till the sun has us blinking.

Recall how suddenly the Negro spirituals revealed themselves; suppressed for generations under the stereotypes of Wesleyan hymn harmony, secretive, half-ashamed, until the courage of being natural brought them out—and behold, there was folk-music. Similarly the mind of the Negro seems suddenly to have slipped from under the tyranny of social intimidation and to be shaking off the psychology of imitation and implied inferiority. By shedding the old chrysalis of the Negro problem we are achieving something like a spiritual emancipation. Until recently, lacking self-understanding, we have been almost as much of a problem to ourselves as we still are to others. But the decade that found us with a problem has left us with only a task. The multitude perhaps feels as yet only a strange relief and a new vague urge, but the thinking few know that in the reaction the vital inner grip of prejudice has been broken.

With this renewed self-respect and self-dependence, the life of the Negro community is bound to enter a new dynamic phase, the buoyancy from within compensating for whatever pressure there may be of conditions from without. The migrant masses, shifting from countryside to city, hurdle several generations of experience at a leap, but more important, the same thing happens spiritually in the life-attitudes and self-expression of the Young Negro, in his poetry, his art, his education and his new outlook, with the additional advantage, of course, of the poise and greater certainty of knowing what it is all about. From this comes the promise and warrant of a new leadership. As one of them has discerningly put it:

We have tomorrow
Bright before us
Like a flame.

Yesterday, a night-gone thing
A sun-down name.

And dawn today
Broad arch above the road we came.
We march!

This is what, even more than any "most creditable record of fifty years of freedom," requires that the Negro of today be seen through other than the dusty spectacles of past controversy. The day of "aunties," "uncles" and "mammies" is equally gone. Uncle Tom and Sambo have passed on, and even the "Colonel" and "George" play barnstorm rôles from which they escape with relief when the public spotlight is off. The popular melodrama has about played itself out, and it is time to scrap the fictions, garret the bogeys and settle down to a realistic facing of facts.

First we must observe some of the changes which since the traditional lines of opinion were drawn have rendered these quite obsolete. A main change has been, of course, that shifting of the Negro population which has made the Negro problem no longer exclusively or even predominantly Southern. Why should our minds remain sectionalized, when the problem itself no longer is? Then the trend of migration has not only been toward the North and the Central Midwest, but cityward and to the great centers of industry—the problems of adjustment are new, practical, local and not peculiarly racial. Rather they are an integral part of the large industrial and social problems of our present-day democracy. And finally, with the Negro rapidly in process of class differentiation, if it ever was warrantable to regard and treat the Negro *en masse* it is becoming with every day less possible, more unjust and more ridiculous.

In the very process of being transplanted, the Negro is becoming transformed.

The tide of Negro migration, northward and cityward, is not to be fully explained as a blind flood started by the demands of war industry coupled with the shutting off of foreign migration, or by the pressure of poor crops coupled with increased social terrorism in certain sections of the South and Southwest. Neither labor demand, the bollweevil nor the Ku Klux Klan is a basic factor, however contributory any or all of them may have been. The wash and rush of this human tide on the beach line of the northern city centers is to be explained primarily in terms of a new vision of opportunity, of social and economic freedom, of a spirit to seize, even in the face of an extortionate and heavy toll, a chance for the improvement of conditions. With each successive wave of it, the movement of the Negro becomes more and more a mass movement toward the larger and more democratic chance—in the Negro's case a deliberate flight not only from countryside to city, but from medieval America to modern.

Take Harlem as an instance of this. Here in Manhattan is not merely the largest Negro community in the world, but the first concentration in history of so many diverse elements of Negro life. It has attracted the African, the West Indian, the Negro American; has brought together the Negro of the North and the Negro of the South; the man from the city and the man from the town and village; the peasant, the student, the business man, the professional man, artist, poet, musician, adventurer and worker, preacher and criminal, exploiter and social outcast. Each group has come with its own separate motives and for its own special ends, but their greatest experience has been the finding of one another. Proscription and prejudice have thrown these dissimilar elements into a common area of contact and interaction. Within this area, race sympathy and unity have determined a further fusing of sentiment and experience. So what began in terms of segregation becomes more and more, as its elements mix and react, the laboratory of a great race-welding. Hitherto, it must be admitted that American Negroes have been a race more in name than in fact, or to be exact, more in sentiment than in experience. The chief bond between them has been that of a common condition rather than a common consciousness; a problem in common rather than a life in common. In Harlem, Negro life is seizing upon its first chances for group expression and self-determination. It is—or promises at least to be—a race capital. That is why our comparison is taken with those nascent centers of folk-expression and self-determination which are playing a creative part in the world today. Without pretense to their political significance, Harlem has the same rôle to play for the New Negro as Dublin has had for the New Ireland or Prague for the New Czechoslovakia.

Harlem, I grant you, isn't typical—but it is significant, it is prophetic. No sane observer, however sympathetic to the new trend, would contend that the great masses are articulate as yet, but they stir, they move, they are more than physically restless. The challenge of the new intellectuals among them is clear enough—the "race radicals" and realists who have broken with the old epoch of philanthropic guidance, sentimental appeal and protest. But are we after all only reading into the stirrings of a sleeping giant the dreams of an agitator? The answer is in the migrating peasant. It is the "man farthest down" who is most active in getting up. One of the most characteristic symptoms of this is the professional man himself migrating to recapture his constituency after a vain effort to maintain in some Southern corner what for years back seemed an established living and clientele. The clergyman following his errant flock, the physician or lawyer trailing his clients, supply the true clues. In a real sense it is the rank and file who are leading, and the leaders who are following. A transformed and transforming psychology permeates the masses.

When the racial leaders of twenty years ago spoke of developing race-pride and stimulating race-consciousness, and of the desirability of race solidarity, they could not in any accurate degree have anticipated the abrupt feeling that has surged up and now pervades the awakened centers. Some of the recognized Negro leaders and a powerful section of white opinion identified with "race work" of the older order have indeed attempted to discount this feeling as a "passing phase," an attack of "race nerves" so to speak, an "aftermath of the war," and the like. It has not abated, however, if we are to gauge by the present tone and temper of the Negro press, or by the shift in popular support from the officially recognized and orthodox spokesmen to those of the independent, popular, and often radical type who are unmistakable symptoms of a new order. It is a social disservice to blunt the fact that the Negro of the Northern centers has reached a stage where tutelage, even of the most interested and well-intentioned sort, must give place to new relationships, where positive self-direction must be reckoned with in ever increasing measure. The American mind must reckon with a fundamentally changed Negro.

The Negro, too, for his part, has idols of the tribe to smash. If on the one hand the white man has erred in making the Negro appear to be that which would excuse or extenuate his treatment of him, the Negro, in turn, has too often unnecessarily excused himself because of the way he has been treated. The intelligent Negro of today is resolved not to make discrimination an extenuation for his shortcomings in performance, individual or collective; he is trying to hold himself at par, neither inflated by sentimental allowances nor depreciated by current social discounts. For this he must know himself and be known for precisely what he is, and for that reason he welcomes the new scientific rather than the old sentimental interest. Sentimental interest in the Negro has ebbed. We used to lament this as the falling off of our friends; now we rejoice and pray to be delivered both from self-pity and condescension. The mind of each racial group has had a bitter weaning, apathy or hatred on one side matching disillusionment or resentment on the other; but they face each other today with the possibility at least of entirely new mutual attitudes.

It does not follow that if the Negro were better known, he would be better liked or better treated. But mutual understanding is basic for any subsequent co-operation and adjustment. The effort toward this will at least have the effect of remedying in large part what has been the most unsatisfactory feature of our present stage of race relationships in America, namely the fact that the more intelligent and representative elements of the two race groups have at so many points got quite out of vital touch with one another.

The fiction is that the life of the races is separate, and increasingly so. The fact is that they have touched too closely at the unfavorable and too lightly at the favorable levels.

While inter-racial councils have sprung up in the South, drawing on forward elements of both races, in the Northern cities manual laborers may brush elbows in their everyday work, but the community and business leaders have experienced no such interplay or far too little of it. These segments must achieve contact or the race situation in America becomes desperate. Fortunately this is happening. There is a growing realization that in social effort the co-operative basis must supplant long-distance philanthropy, and that the only safeguard for mass relations in the future must be provided in the carefully maintained contact of the enlightened minorities of both race groups. In the intellectual realm a renewed and keen curiosity is replacing the recent apathy; the Negro is being carefully studied, not just talked about and discussed. In art and letters, instead of being wholly caricatured, he is being seriously portrayed and painted.

To all of this the New Negro is keenly responsive as an augury of a new democracy in American culture. He is contributing his share to the new social understanding. But the desire to be understood would never in itself have been sufficient to have opened so completely the protectively closed portals of the thinking Negro's mind. There is still too much possibility of being snubbed or patronized for that. It was rather the necessity for fuller, truer self-expression, the realization of the unwisdom of allowing social discrimination to segregate him mentally, and a counter-attitude to cramp and fetter his own living—and so the "spite-wall" that the intellectuals built over the "color-line" has happily been taken down. Much of this reopening of intellectual contacts has centered in New York and has been richly fruitful not merely in the enlarging of personal experience, but in the definite enrichment of American art and letters and in the clarifying of our common vision of the social tasks ahead.

The particular significance in the re-establishment of contact between the more advanced and representative classes is that it promises to offset some of the unfavorable reactions of the past, or at least to re-surface race contacts somewhat for the future. Subtly the conditions that are molding a New Negro are molding a new American attitude.

However, this new phase of things is delicate; it will call for less charity but more justice; less help, but infinitely closer understanding. This is indeed a critical stage of race relationships because of the likelihood, if the new temper is not understood, of engendering sharp group antagonism and a second crop of more calculated prejudice. In some quarters, it has already done so. Having weaned the Negro, public opinion cannot continue to paternalize. The Negro to-day is inevitably moving forward under the control largely of his own objectives. What are these objectives? Those of his outer life are happily already well and finally formulated, for they are none other than the ideals of American institutions and democracy. Those of his inner life are yet in process of formation, for the new psychology at present is more of a consensus of feeling than of opinion, of attitude rather than of program. Still some points seem to have crystallized.

Up to the present one may adequately describe the Negro's "inner objectives" as an attempt to repair a damaged group psychology and reshape a warped social perspective. Their realization has required a new mentality for the American Negro. And as it matures we begin to see its effects; at first, negative, iconoclastic, and then positive and constructive. In this new group psychology we note the lapse of sentimental appeal, then the development of a more positive self-respect and self-reliance; the repudiation of social dependence, and then the gradual recovery from hypersensitiveness and "touchy" nerves, the repudiation of the double standard of judgment with its special philanthropic allowances and then the sturdier desire for objective and scientific appraisal; and finally the rise from social disillusionment to race pride, from the sense of social debt to the responsibilities of social contribution, and offsetting the necessary working and commonsense acceptance of restricted conditions, the belief in ultimate esteem and recognition. Therefore the Negro today wishes to be known for what he is, even in his faults and shortcomings, and scorns a craven and precarious survival at the price of seeming to be what he is not. He resents being spoken of as a social ward or minor, even by his own, and to being regarded a chronic patient for the sociological clinic, the sick man of American Democracy. For the same reasons, he himself is through with those social nostrums and panaceas, the so-called "solutions" of his "problem," with which he and the country have been so liberally dosed in the past. Religion, freedom, education, money—in turn, he has ardently hoped for and peculiarly trusted these things; he still believes in them, but not in blind trust that they alone will solve his life-problem.

Each generation, however, will have its creed, and that of the present is the belief in the efficacy of collective effort, in race co-operation. This deep feeling of race is at present the mainspring of Negro life. It seems to be the outcome of the reaction to proscription and prejudice; an attempt, fairly successful on the whole to convert a defensive into an offensive position, a handicap into an incentive. It is radical in tone, but not in purpose and only the most stupid forms of opposition, misunderstanding or persecution could make it otherwise. Of course, the thinking Negro has shifted a little toward the left with the world-trend, and there is an increasing group who affiliate with radical and liberal movements. But fundamentally for the present the Negro is radical on race matters, conservative on others, in other words, a "forced radical," a social protes-

tant rather than a genuine radical. Yet under further pressure and injustice iconoclastic thought and motives will inevitably increase. Harlem's quixotic radicalisms call for their ounce of democracy today lest tomorrow they be beyond cure.

The Negro mind reaches out as yet to nothing but American wants, American ideas. But this forced attempt to build his Americanism on race values is a unique social experiment, and its ultimate success is impossible except through the fullest sharing of American culture and institutions. There should be no delusion about this. American nerves in sections unstrung with race hysteria are often fed the opiate that the trend of Negro advance is wholly separatist, and that the effect of its operation will be to encyst the Negro as a benign foreign body in the body politic. This cannot be—even if it were desirable. The racialism of the Negro is no limitation or reservation with respect to American life; it is only a constructive effort to build the obstructions in the stream of his progress into an efficient dam of social energy and power. Democracy itself is obstructed and stagnated to the extent that any of its channels are closed. Indeed they cannot be selectively closed. So the choice is not between one way for the Negro and another way for the rest, but between American institutions frustrated on the one hand and American ideals progressively fulfilled and realized on the other.

There is, of course, a warrantably comfortable feeling in being on the right side of the country's professed ideals. We realize that we cannot be undone without America's undoing. It is within the gamut of this attitude that the thinking Negro faces America, but with variations of mood that are if anything more significant than the attitude itself. Sometimes we have it taken with the defiant ironic challenge of McKay:

Mine is the future grinding down today
Like a great landslip moving to the sea,
Bearing its freight of debris far away
Where the green hungry waters restlessly
Heave mammoth pyramids, and break and roar
Their eerie challenge to the crumbling shore.

Sometimes, perhaps more frequently as yet, it is taken in the fervent and almost filial appeal and counsel of Weldon Johnson's:

O Southland, dear Southland!
Then why do you still cling
To an idle age and a musty page,
To a dead and useless thing?

But between defiance and appeal, midway almost between cynicism and hope, the prevailing mind stands in the mood of the same author's *To America,* an attitude of sober query and stoical challenge:

How would you have us, as we are?
  Or sinking 'neath the load we bear,
Our eyes fixed forward on a star,
  Or gazing empty at despair?

Rising or falling? Men or things?
  With dragging pace or footsteps fleet?
Strong, willing sinews in your wings,
  Or tightening chains about your feet?

More and more, however, an intelligent realization of the great discrepancy between the American social creed and the American social practice forces upon the Negro the taking of the moral advantage that is his. Only the steadying and sobering effect of a truly characteristic gentleness of spirit prevents the rapid rise of a definite cynicism and counter-hate and a defiant superiority feeling. Human as this reaction would be, the majority still deprecate its advent, and would gladly see it forestalled by the speedy amelioration of its causes. We wish our race pride to be a healthier, more positive achievement than a feeling based upon a realization of the shortcomings of others. But all paths toward the attainment of a sound social attitude have been difficult; only a relative few enlightened minds have been able as the phrase puts it "to rise above" prejudice. The ordinary man has had until recently only a hard choice between the alternatives of supine and humiliating submission and stimulating but hurtful counter-prejudice. Fortunately from some inner, desperate resourcefulness has recently sprung up the simple expedient of fighting prejudice by mental passive resistance, in other words by trying to ignore it. For the few, this manna may perhaps be effective, but the masses cannot thrive upon it.

Fortunately there are constructive channels opening out into which the balked social feelings of the American Negro can flow freely.

Without them there would be much more pressure and danger than there is. These compensating interests are racial but in a new and enlarged way. One is the consciousness of acting as the advance guard of the African peoples in their contact with Twentieth Century civilization; the other, the sense of a mission of rehabilitating the race in world esteem from that loss of prestige for which the fate and conditions of slavery have so largely been responsible. Harlem, as we shall see, is the center of both these movements; she is the home of the Negro's "Zionism." The pulse of the Negro world has begun to beat in Harlem. A Negro newspaper carrying news material in English, French and Spanish, gathered from all quarters of America, the West Indies and Africa has maintained itself in Harlem for over five years. Two important magazines, both edited from New York, maintain their news and circulation consistently on a cosmopolitan scale. Under American auspices and backing, three pan-African congresses have been held abroad for the discussion of common interests, colonial questions and the future co-operative development of Africa. In terms of the race question as a world problem, the Negro mind has leapt, so to speak, upon the parapets of prejudice and extended its cramped horizons. In so doing it has linked up with the growing group consciousness of the dark-peoples and is gradually learning their common interests. As one of our writers has recently put it: "It is imperative that we understand the white world in its relations to the non-white world." As with the Jew, persecution is making the Negro international.

As a world phenomenon this wider race consciousness is a different thing from the much asserted rising tide of color. Its inevitable causes are not of our making. The consequences are not necessarily damaging to the best interests of civilization. Whether it actually brings into being new Armadas of conflict or argosies of cultural exchange and enlightenment can only be decided by the attitude of the dominant races in an era of critical change. With the American Negro, his new internationalism is primarily an effort to recapture contact with the scattered peoples of African derivation. Garveyism may be a transient, if spectacular, phenomenon, but the possible rôle of the American Negro in the future development of Africa is one of the most constructive and universally helpful missions that any modern people can lay claim to.

Constructive participation in such causes cannot help giving the Negro valuable group incentives, as well as increased prestige at home and abroad. Our greatest rehabilitation may possibly come through such channels, but for the present, more immediate hope rests in the revaluation by white and black alike of the Negro in terms of his artistic endowments and cultural contributions, past and prospective. It must be increasingly recognized that the Negro has already made very substantial contributions, not only in his folk-art, music especially, which has always found appreciation, but in larger, though humbler and less acknowledged ways. For generations the Negro has been the peasant matrix of that section of America which has most undervalued him, and here he has contributed not only materially in labor and in social patience, but spiritually as well. The South has unconsciously absorbed the gift of his folk-temperament. In less than half a generation it will be easier to recognize this, but the fact remains that a leaven of humor, sentiment, imagination and tropic nonchalance has gone into the making of the South from a humble, unacknowledged source. A second crop of the Negro's gifts promises still more largely. He now becomes a conscious contributor and lays aside the status of a beneficiary and ward for that of a collaborator and participant in American civilization. The great social gain in this is the releasing of our talented group from the arid fields of controversy and debate to the productive fields of creative expression. The especially cultural recognition they win should in turn prove the key to that revaluation of the Negro which must precede or accompany any considerable further betterment of race relationships. But whatever the general effect, the present generation will have added the motives of self-expression and spiritual development to the old and still unfinished task of making material headway and progress. No one who understandingly faces the situation with its substantial accomplishment or views the new scene with its still more abundant promise can be entirely without hope. And certainly, if in our lifetime the Negro should not be able to celebrate his full initiation into American democracy, he can at least, on the warrant of these things, celebrate the attainment of a significant and satisfying new phase of group development, and with it a spiritual Coming of Age.

ARTHUR A. SCHOMBURG

The Negro Digs Up His Past

The American Negro must remake his past in order to make his future. Though it is orthodox to think of America as the one country where it is unnecessary to have a past, what is a luxury for the nation as a whole becomes a prime social necessity for the Negro. For him, a group tradition must supply compensation for persecution, and pride of race the antidote for prejudice. History must restore what slavery took away, for it is the social damage of slavery that the present generations must repair and offset. So among the rising democratic millions we find the Negro thinking more collectively, more retrospectively than the rest, and apt out of the very pressure of the present to become the most enthusiastic antiquarian of them all.

Vindicating evidences of individual achievement have as a matter of fact been gathered and treasured for over a century: Abbé Gregoire's liberal-minded book on Negro notables in 1808 was the pioneer effort; it has been followed at intervals by less-known and often less discriminating compendiums of exceptional men and women of African stock, But this sort of thing was on the whole pathetically over-corrective, ridiculously over-laudatory; it was apologetics turned into biography. A true historical sense develops slowly and with difficulty under such circumstances. But today, even if

for the ultimate purpose of group justification, history has become less a matter of argument and more a matter of record. There is the definite desire and determination to have a history, well documented, widely known at least within race circles, and administered as a stimulating and inspiring tradition for the coming generations.

Gradually as the study of the Negro's past has come out of the vagaries of rhetoric and propaganda and become systematic and scientific, three outstanding conclusions have been established:

First, that the Negro has been throughout the centuries of controversy an active collaborator, and often a pioneer, in the struggle for his own freedom and advancement. This is true to a degree which makes it the more surprising that it has not been recognized earlier.

Second, that by virtue of their being regarded as something "exceptional," even by friends and well-wishers, Negroes of attainment and genius have been unfairly disassociated from the group, and group credit lost accordingly.

Third, that the remote racial origins of the Negro, far from being what the race and the world have been given to understand, offer a record of creditable group achievement when scientifically viewed, and more important still, that they are of vital general interest because of their bearing upon the beginnings and early development of culture.

With such crucial truths to document and establish, an ounce of fact is worth a pound of controversy. So the Negro historian today digs under the spot where his predecessor stood and argued. Not long ago, the Public Library of Harlem housed a special exhibition of books, pamphlets, prints and old engravings, that simply said, to sceptic and believer alike, to scholar and school-child, to proud black and astonished white, "Here is the evidence." Assembled from the rapidly growing collections of the leading Negro book-collectors and research societies, there were in these cases, materials not only for the first true writing of Negro history, but for the rewriting of many important paragraphs of our common American history. Slow though it be, historical truth is no exception to the proverb.

Here among the rarities of early Negro Americana was Jupiter Hammon's Address to the Negroes of the State of New York, edition of 1787, with the first American Negro poet's famous "If we should ever get to Heaven, we shall find nobody to reproach us for being black, or for being slaves." Here was Phillis Wheatley's Mss. poem of 1767 addressed to the students of Harvard, her spirited encomiums upon George Washington and the Revolutionary Cause, and John Marrant's St. John's Day eulogy to the 'Brothers of African Lodge No. 459' delivered at Boston in 1784.

Here too were Lemuel Haynes' Vermont commentaries on the American Revolution and his learned sermons to his white congregation in Rutland, Vermont, and the sermons of the year 1808 by the Rev. Absalom Jones of St. Thomas Church, Philadelphia, and Peter Williams of St. Philip's, New York, pioneer Episcopal rectors who spoke out in daring and influential ways on the Abolition of the Slave Trade. Such things and many others are more than mere items of curiosity: they educate any receptive mind.

Reinforcing these were still rarer items of Africana and foreign Negro interest, the volumes of Juan Latino, the best Latinist of Spain in the reign of Philip V, incumbent of the chair of Poetry at the University of Granada, and author of Poems printed Granatae 1573 and a book on the Escurial published 1576; the Latin and Dutch treatises of Jacobus Eliza Capitein, a native of West Coast Africa and graduate of the University of Leyden, Gustavus Vassa's celebrated autobiography that supplied so much of the evidence in 1796 for Granville Sharpe's attack on slavery in the British colonies, Julien Raymond's Paris exposé of the disabilities of the free people of color in the then (1791) French colony of Hayti, and Baron de Vastey's Cry of the Fatherland, the famous polemic by the secretary of Christophe that precipitated the Haytian struggle for independence. The cumulative effect of such evidences of scholarship and moral prowess is too weighty to be dismissed as exceptional.

But weightier surely than any evidence of individual talent and scholarship could ever be, is the evidence of important collaboration and significant pioneer initiative in social service and reform, in the efforts toward race emancipation, colonization and race betterment. From neglected and rust-spotted pages comes testimony to the black men and women who stood shoulder to shoulder in courage and zeal, and often on a parity of intelligence and public talent, with their notable white benefactors. There was the already cited work of Vassa that aided so materially the efforts of Granville Sharpe, the record of Paul Cuffee, the Negro colonization pioneer, associated so importantly with the establishment of Sierra Leone as a British colony for the occupancy of free people of color in West Africa; the dramatic and history-making exposé of John Baptist Phillips, African graduate of Edinburgh, who compelled through Lord Bathhurst in 1824 the enforcement of the articles of capitulation guaranteeing freedom to the blacks of Trinidad. There is the record of the pioneer colonization project of Rev. Daniel Coker in conducting a voyage of ninety expatriates to West Africa in 1820, of the missionary efforts of Samuel Crowther in Sierra Leone, first Anglican bishop of his diocese, and that of the work of John Russwurm, a leader in the work and foundation of the American Colonization Society.

When we consider the facts, certain chapters of American history will have to be reopened. Just as black men were influential factors in the campaign against the slave trade, so they were among the earliest instigators of the abolition movement. Indeed there was a dangerous calm between the agitation for the suppression of the slave trade and the beginning of the campaign for emancipation. During that interval colored men were very influential in arousing the attention of public men who in turn aroused the conscience of the country. Continuously between 1808 and 1845, men like Prince Saunders, Peter Williams, Absalom Jones, Nathaniel Paul, and Bishops Varick and Richard Allen, the founders of the two wings of African Methodism, spoke out with force and initiative, and men like Denmark Vesey (1822), David Walker (1828) and Nat Turner (1831) advocated and organized schemes for direct action. This culminated in the generally ignored but important conventions of Free People of Color in New York, Philadelphia and other centers, whose platforms and efforts are to the Negro of as great significance as the nationally cherished memories of Faneuil and Independence Halls. Then with Abolition comes the better documented and more recognized collaboration of Samuel R. Ward, William Wells Brown, Henry Highland Garnett, Martin Delaney, Harriet Tubman, Sojourner Truth, and Frederick Douglass with their great colleagues, Tappan, Phillips, Sumner, Mott, Stowe and Garrison.

But even this latter group who came within the limelight of national and international notice, and thus into open comparison with the best minds of their generation, the public too often regards as a group of inspired illiterates, eloquent echoes of their Abolitionist sponsors. For a true estimate of their ability and scholarship, however, one must go with the antiquarian to the files of the Anglo-African Magazine, where page by page comparisons may be made. Their writings show Douglass, McCune Smith, Wells Brown, Delaney, Wilmot Blyden and Alexander Crummell to have been as scholarly and versatile as any of the noted publicists with whom they were associated. All of them labored internationally in the cause of their fellows; to Scotland, England, France, Germany and Africa, they carried their brilliant offensive of debate and propaganda, and with this came instance upon instance of signal foreign recognition, from academic, scientific, public and official sources. Delaney's Principia of Ethnology won public reception from learned societies, Penington's discourses an honorary doctorate from Heidelberg, Wells Brown's three years mission the entree of the salons of London and Paris, and Douglass' tours receptions second only to Henry Ward Beecher's.

After this great era of public interest and discussion, it was Alexander Crummell, who, with the reaction already setting in, first organized Negro brains defensively through the founding of the American Negro Academy in 1874 at Washington. A New York boy whose zeal for education had suffered a rude shock when refused admission to the Episcopal Seminary by Bishop Onderdonk, he had been befriended by John Jay and sent to Cambridge University, England, for his education and ordination. On his return, he was beset with the idea of promoting race scholarship, and the Academy was the final result. It has continued ever since to be one of the bulwarks of our intellectual life, though unfortunately its members have had to spend too much of their energy and effort answering detractors and disproving popular fallacies. Only gradually have the men of this group been able to work toward pure scholarship. Taking a slightly different start, The Negro Society for Historical Research was later organized in New York, and has succeeded in stimulating the collection from all parts of the world of books and documents dealing with the Negro. It has also brought together for the first time cooperatively in a single society African, West Indian and Afro-American scholars. Direct offshoots of this same effort are the extensive private collections of Henry P. Slaughter of Washington, the Rev. Charles D. Martin of Harlem, of Arthur Schomburg of Brooklyn, and of the late John E. Bruce, who was the enthusiastic and far-seeing pioneer of this movement. Finally and more recently, the Association for the Study of Negro Life and History has extended these efforts into a scientific research project of great achievement and promise. Under the direction of Dr. Carter G. Woodson, it has continuously maintained for nine years the publication of the learned quarterly, The Journal of Negro History, and with the assistance and recognition of two large educational foundations has maintained research and published valuable monographs in Negro history. Almost keeping pace with the work of scholarship has been the effort to popularize the results, and to place before Negro youth in the schools the true story of race vicissitude, struggle and accomplishment. So that quite largely now the ambition of Negro youth can be nourished on its own milk.

Such work is a far cry from the puerile controversy and petty braggadocio with which the effort for race history first started. But a general as well as a racial lesson has been learned. We seem lately to have come at last to realize what the truly scientific attitude requires, and to see that the race issue has been a plague on both our historical houses, and that history cannot be properly written with either bias or counter-bias. The blatant Caucasian racialist with his theories and assumptions of race superiority and dominance has in turn bred his Ethiopian counterpart—the rash and rabid amateur who has glibly tried to prove half of the world's geniuses to have been Negroes and to trace the pedigree of nineteenth century Americans from the Queen of Sheba. But fortunately today there is on both sides of a really common cause less of the sand of controversy and more of the dust of digging.

Of course, a racial motive remains—legitimately compatible with scientific method and aim. The work our race students now regard as important, they undertake very naturally to overcome in part certain handicaps of disparagement and omission too well-known to particularize. But they do so not merely that we may not wrongfully be deprived of the spiritual nourishment of our culture past, but also that the full story of human collaboration and interdependence may be told and realized. Especially is this likely to be the effect of the latest and most fascinating of all of the attempts to open up the closed Negro past, namely the important study of African cultural origins and sources. The bigotry of civilization which is the taproot of intellectual prejudice begins far back and must be corrected at its source. Fundamentally it has come about from that depreciation of Africa which has sprung up from ignorance of her true role and position in human history and the early development of culture. The Negro has been a man without a history because he has been considered a man without a worthy culture. But a new notion of the cultural attainment and potentialities of the African stocks has recently come about, partly through the corrective influence of the more scientific study of African institutions and early cultural history, partly through growing appreciation of the skill and beauty and in many cases the historical priority of the African native crafts, and finally through the signal recognition which first in France and Germany, but now very generally the astonishing art of the African sculptures has received. Into these fascinating new vistas, with limited horizons lifting in all directions, the mind of the Negro has leapt forward faster than the slow clearings of scholarship will yet safely permit. But there is no doubt that here is a field full of the most intriguing and inspiring possibilities. Already the Negro sees himself against a reclaimed background, in a perspective that will give pride and self-respect ample scope, and make history yield for him the same values that the treasured past of any people affords.

ALAIN LOCKE

The Ethics of Culture

The "Ethics of Culture" is a published speech originally delivered to a freshman lecture course at Howard University. It explicates the importance of conversation and manner as cultural appointments, the development of which are necessary for a people to attain greatness. Locke is acutely aware of the way Afro-Americans are subject to being judged by whites. An individual black person's mode of being and the mode of being of black people as a group were commonly judged identically. Locke's elitism takes the form of admonishing students to be advance guards and models. This article also helps situate Locke's self-perception as an aesthete and an indication of the regard that he held for Du Bois' view of the Talented Tenth (that is, that the talented members of the black race should be the race's representatives to whites and models to be emulated by the rest of the race).

It should be remembered in reading this article that in the 1920s "ethics" entailed judgments of customs, manners, habits of speech, and dress codes and not simply, as is now commonly the case, general principles regulating institutional arrangements and the limits of personal expressions. The concepts of culture, duty, personality, and group responsibilities are thus considered ethical concepts.

I am to speak to you on the ethics of culture. Because I teach the one and try to practice the other, it may perhaps be pardonable for me to think of them together, but I hope at least not to leave you without the conviction that the two are in a very vital and immediate way connected. In my judgment, the highest intellectual duty is the duty to be cultured. Ethics and culture are usually thought out of connection with each other—as, in fact, at the very opposite poles. Particularly for our country, and the type of education which generally prevails, is this so. Quite unfortunately, it seems, duty toward the beautiful and the cultural is very generally ignored, and certainly, beauty as a motive has been taken out of morality, so that we confront beautiless duty and dutiless beauty. In an issue like this, it behooves education to try to restore the lapsing ideals of humanism, and to center more vitally in education the duty to be cultured.

It follows if there is any duty with respect to culture, that it is one of those that can only be self-imposed. No one can make you cultured, few will care whether you are or are not, for I admit that the world of today primarily demands efficiency—and further the only reward my experience can offer you for it is the heightened self-satisfaction which being or becoming cultured brings. There is, or ought to be, a story of a lad to whom some rather abstract duty was being interpreted who is said to have said, "If I only owe it to myself, why then I really don't owe it at all." Not only do I admit that culture is a duty of this sort, but I claim that this is its chief appeal and justification. The greatest challenge to the moral will is in the absence of external compulsion. This implies, young ladies and gentlemen, that I recognize your perfect right not to

be cultured, if you do not really want to be, as one of those inalienable natural-born privileges which so-called "practical minded," "ordinary" Americans delight to claim and exercise. As a touch-stone for the real desire and a sincere motive, the advocates of culture would not have it otherwise.

The way in which duty comes to be involved in culture is this: culture begins in education where compulsion leaves off, whether it is the practical spur of necessity or the artificial rod of the schoolmaster. I speak to a group that has already chosen to be educated. I congratulate you upon that choice. Though you have so chosen for many motives and with very diverse reasons and purposes, I fear that education for most of you means, in last practical analysis, the necessary hardship that is involved in preparing to earn a better living, perhaps an easier living. It is just such narrowing and truncating of the conception of education that the ideals and motives of culture are effective to remove or prevent. Education should not be so narrowly construed, for in the best sense, and indeed in the most practical sense, it means not only the fitting of the man to earn his living, but to live and to live well. It is just this latter and higher function of education, the art of living well, or, if I may so express it, of living up to the best, that the word *culture* connotes and represents. Let me offer you, if I may, a touchstone for this idea, a sure test of its presence. Whenever and wherever there is carried into education the purpose and motive of knowing better than the practical necessities of the situation demand, whenever the pursuit of knowledge is engaged in for its own sake and for the inner satisfaction it can give, culture and the motives of culture are present. I sense immediately that you may have quite other and perhaps more authoritative notions of culture in mind. Culture has been variously and beautifully defined. But I cannot accept for the purpose I have in view even that famous definition of Matthew Arnold's. "Culture is the best that has been thought and known in the world," since it emphasizes the external rather than the internal factors of culture. Rather is it the capacity for understanding the best and most representative forms of human expression, and of expressing oneself, if not in similar creativeness, at least in appreciative reactions and in progressively responsive refinement of tastes and interests. Culture proceeds from personality to personality. To paraphrase Bacon, it is that, and only that, which can be inwardly assimilated. It follows, then, that, like wisdom, it is that which cannot be taught, but can only be learned. But here is the appeal of it, it is the self-administered part of your education, that which represents your personal index of absorption and your personal coefficient of effort.

As faulty as is the tendency to externalize culture, there is still greater error in over-intellectualizing it. Defining this aspect of education, we focus it, I think, too much merely in the mind, and project it too far into the abstract and formal. We must constantly realize that without experience, and without a medium for the absorption and transfer of experience, the mind could not develop or be developed. Culture safeguards the educative process at these two points, and stands for the training of the sensibilities and the expressional activities. Mentioning the former as the neglected aspect of American education, former President Eliot contends that, since it is the business of the senses to serve the mind, it is reciprocally the duty of the mind to serve the senses. He means that properly to train the mind involves the proper training of the sensibilities, and that, without a refinement of the channels through which our experience reaches us, the mind cannot reach its highest development. We too often expect our senses to serve us and render nothing back to them in exchange. As a result they do not serve us half so well as they might: coarse channels make for sluggish response, hampered impetus, wastage of effort. The man of culture is the man of trained sensibilities, whose mind expresses itself in keenness of discrimination and, therefore, in cultivated interests and tastes. The level of mentality may be crowded higher for a special effort or a special pursuit, but in the long run it cannot rise much higher than the level of tastes. It is for this reason that we warrantably judge culture by manners, tastes, and the fineness of discrimination of a person's interests. The stamp of culture is, therefore, no conventional pattern, and has no stock value: it is the mold and die of a refined and completely developed personality. It is the art medallion, not the common coin.

On this very point, so necessary for the correct estimation of culture, most of the popular mistakes and misconceptions about culture enter in. Democracy and utilitarianism suspect tastes because they cannot be standardized. And if I should not find you over-interested in culture or over-sympathetic toward its ideals, it is because of these same prejudices of puritanism and materialism, which, though still typically American, are fortunately no longer representatively so. Yet it is necessary to examine and refute some of these prevalent misconceptions about culture. You have heard and will still hear culture derided as *artificial, superficial, useless, selfish, over-refined,* and *exclusive.* Let us make inquiry into the reasons for such attitudes. It is not the part of loyal advocacy to shirk the blow and attack of such criticism behind the bastions of dilettantism. Culture has its active adversaries in present-day life, indeed the normal tendencies of life today are not in the direction either of breadth or height of culture. The defense of culture is a modern chivalry, though of some hazard and proportional glory.

The criticism of culture as artificial first concerns us. In the mistaken name of naturalism, culture is charged with producing artificiality destructive of the fine original naturalness of human nature. One might as well indict civilization as a whole on this point; it, too, is artificial. But perhaps just a peculiar degree of artificiality is inveighed against—to which our response must be that it is just that very painful intermediate stage between lack of culture and wholesomeness of culture which it is the object of further culture to remove. All arts have their awkward stages: culture itself is its own cure for this. Closely associated, and touched by the same reasoning, is the argument that culture is superficial. Here we encounter the bad effect of a process undertaken in the wrong order. If the polished surface is, so to speak, the last coat of a consistently developed personality, it lends its final added charm to the total worth and effect. If, on the contrary, beginning with the superficial as well as ending with the superficial, it should be merely a veneer, then is it indeed both culturally false and artistically deceptive. No true advocacy of an ideal involves the defense or extenuation of its defective embodiments. Rather on the contrary, culture must constantly be self-critical and discriminating, and deplore its spurious counterfeits and shallow imitations.

More pardonable, especially for our age, is the charge of uselessness. Here we need not so much the corrective of values as that of perspective. For we only need to appreciate the perennial and imperishable qualities of the products of culture to see the fallacy in such depreciation. Fortified in ideas and ideals, culture centers about the great human constants, which, though not rigidly unchangeable, are nevertheless almost as durable as those great physical constants of which science makes so much. Indeed, if we count in the progressive changes of science through discovery, these are the more constant—the most constant then of all the things in human experience. Moreover, there is their superior representativeness by which posterity judges each and every phase of human development. Through their culture products are men most adequately represented; and by their culture-fruits are they known and rated. As we widen our view from the standpoint of momentary and partial judgment, this fact becomes only too obvious.

I take seriously, and would have you, also, the charge that culture is selfish. Being unnecessarily so is to be unduly so. Yet there is a necessary internal focusing of culture because true culture must begin with self-culture. Personality, and to a limited extent character also, are integral parts of the equation. In the earlier stages of the development of culture there is pardonable concentration upon self-cultivation. Spiritual capital must be accumulated; indeed, too early spending of the meager resources of culture at an early stage results in that shallow and specious variety which means sham and pretense at the start, bankruptcy and humiliation at the finish. Do not begin to spend your mental substance prematurely. You are justified in serious self-concern and earnest self-consideration at the stage of education. And, moreover, culture, even when it is rich and mature, gives only by sharing, and moves more by magnetic attraction than by transfer of material or energy. Like light, to which it is so often compared, it radiates, and operates effectively only through being self-sufficiently maintained at its central source. Culture polarizes in self-hood.

Finally we meet the criticism of exclusiveness, over-selectness, perhaps even the extreme of snobbery. Culture, I fear, will have to plead guilty to a certain degree of this: it cannot fulfill its function otherwise. Excellence and the best can never reside in the average. Culture must develop an elite that must maintain itself upon the basis of standards that can move forward but never backwards. In the pursuit of culture one must detach himself from the crowd. Your chief handicap in this matter as young people of today is the psychology and "pull" of the crowd. Culturally speaking, they and their point of view define vulgarity. As Professor Palmer says, "Is this not what we mean by the vulgar man? His manners are not an expression of himself, but of somebody else. Other men have obliterated him." There is no individuality in being ordinary: it is the boast of sub-mediocrity. Who in the end wishes to own that composite of everybody's average qualities, so likely to be below our own par? Culture's par is always the best: one cannot be somebody with everybody's traits. If to be cultured is a duty, it is here that that element is most prominent, for it takes courage to stand out from the crowd. One must, therefore, pay a moral as well as an intellectual price for culture. It consists in this: "Dare to be different—stand out!" I know how difficult this advice will be to carry out: America's chief social crime, in spite of her boasted freedoms, is the psychology of the herd, the tyranny of the average and mediocre; in other words, the limitations upon cultural personality. Strive to overcome this for your own sake and, as Cicero would say, "for the welfare of the Republic."

I am spending too much time, I fear, in pointing out what culture is when I would rather point out the way to its attainment. I must not trespass, however, upon the provinces of my colleagues who are to interpret culture more specifically to you in terms of the art of English speech, the fine arts, and music. I content myself with the defense of culture in general, and with the opportunity it gives of explaining its two most basic aspects—the great amateur arts of personal expression—conversation and manners. These personal arts are as important as the fine arts; in my judgment, they are their foundation. For culture without personal culture is sterile—it is that insincere and hypocritical profession of the love of the beautiful which so often discredits culture in the eyes of the many. But with the products of the fine arts translating themselves back into personal refinement and cultivated sensibilities, culture realizes itself in the fullest sense, performs its true educative function and becomes a part of the vital art of living. We too often estimate culture materialistically by what has been called "the vulgar test of production." On the contrary, culture depends primarily upon the power of refined consumption and effective assimilation; it consists essentially in being cultured. Whoever would achieve this must recognize that life itself is an art, perhaps the finest of the fine arts—because it is the composite blend of them all.

However, to say this is not to commit the man of culture to hopeless dilettantism, and make him a Jack of the arts. Especially for you, who for the most part work toward very practical professional objectives and who lack as Americans of our time even a modicum of leisure, would this be impossible. But it is not necessary to trouble much about this, for, even were it possible, it would not be desirable. There are, of course, subjects which are primarily "cultural" and subjects which are not, but I am not one of those who bewail altogether the departure from the old-fashioned classical program of education and the waning appeal of the traditional "humanities." Science, penetratingly studied, can yield as much and more culture than the humanities mechanically studied. It lies, I think, more in the point of view and the degree of intrinsic interest rather than in the special subject-matter or tradition of a subject. Nevertheless, to be sure of culture, the average student should elect some of the cultural studies; and, more important still, in his outside diversions, should cultivate a steady and active interest in one of the arts, aiming thereby to bring his mind under the quickening influence of cultural ideas and values. Not all of us can attain to creative productiveness and skill in the arts, though each of us has probably some latent artistic temperament, if it only expresses itself in love and day-dreaming. But each of us can, with a different degree of concentration according to his temperament, cultivate an intelligent appreciation of at least one of the great human arts, literature, painting, sculpture, music or what not. And if we achieve a high level of cultivated taste in one art it will affect our judgment and interest and response with respect to others.

May I at this point emphasize a peculiarly practical reason? In any community, in any nation, in any group, the level of cultural productiveness cannot rise much higher than the level of cultural consumption, cannot much outdistance the prevalent limits of taste. This is the reason why our country has not as yet come to the fore in the production of culture-goods. And as Americans we all share this handicap of the low average of cultural tastes. As educated Americans, we share also and particularly the responsibility for helping raise this average. A brilliant Englishman once characterized America as a place where everything had a price, but nothing a value, referring to the typical preference for practical and utilitarian points of view. There is a special need for a correction of this on your part. As a race group we are at the critical stage where we are releasing creative artistic talent in excess of our group ability to understand and support it. Those of us who have been concerned about our progress in the things of culture have now begun to fear as the greatest handicap the discouraging, stultifying effect upon our artistic talent of lack of appreciation from the group which it represents. The cultural par, we repeat, is always the best: and a group which expects to be judged by its best must live up to its best so that that may be truly representative. Here is our present dilemma. If the standard of cultural tastes is not rapidly raised in the generation which you represent, the natural affinities of appreciation and response will drain off, like cream, the richest products of the group, and leave the mass without the enriching quality of its finest ingredients. This is already happening: I need not cite the painful individual instances. The only remedy is the more rapid development and diffusion of culture among us.

It follows from this that it is not creditable nor your duty to allow yourselves to be toned down to the low level of average tastes. Some of you, many of you, I hope, will be making your life's work in sections of this country and among groups that are fittingly characterized as "Saharas of culture," that know culture neither by taste nor sight. You betray your education, however, and forego the influence which as educated persons you should always exert in any community if you succumb to these influences and subside to the mediocre level of the vulgar crowd. Moreover, you will find that, like knowledge or technical skill, culture to be maintained must be constantly practiced. Just as we saw that culture was not a question of one set of subjects, but an attitude which may be carried into all, so also we must realize that it is not a matter of certain moments and situations, but the characteristic and constant reaction of a developed personality. The ideal culture is representative of the entire personality even in the slightest detail.

I recall an incident of visiting with a friend a celebrated art connoisseur for his expert judgment upon a painting. He examined with a knife and a pocket magnifying glass a corner of the canvas. I perhaps thought for a moment he was searching for a signature, but it was not the signature corner. Without further scrutiny, however, he gave us his judgment: "Gentlemen, it is not a Holbein." The master painter puts himself into every inch of his canvas, and can be told by the characteristic details as reliably, more reliably even than by general outlines. Culture likewise is every inch representative of the whole personality when it is truly perfected. This summing up of the whole in every part is the practical test which I want you to hold before yourselves in matters of culture. Among cultivated people you will be judged more by your manner of speech and deportment than by any other credentials. They are meant to bear out your training and your heritage, and more reliably than your diplomas or your pedigree will they represent you or betray you. Manners are thus the key to personal relations, as expression is the key to intellectual intercourse. One meets that element in others which is most responsively tuned to a similar element in ourselves. The best fruits of culture, then, are the responses it elicits from our human environment. And should the environment be limited or unfavorable, then, instead of compromising with it, true culture opens the treasuries of art and literature, and lives on that inheritance.

Finally I must add a word about that aspect of culture which claims that it takes several generations to produce and make the truly cultured gentleman. Exclusive, culture may and must be, but seclusive culture is obsolete. Not all that are well-born are well-bred, and it is better to be well-bred. Indeed, one cannot rest satisfied at any stage of culture: it has to be earned and re-earned, though it returns with greater increment each time. As Goethe says, "What thou hast inherited from the fathers, labor for, in order to possess it." Thus culture is inbred—but we ourselves are its parents. With all of the possible and hoped for spread of democracy, we may say that excellence of this sort will always survive. Indeed, when all the other aristocracies have fallen, the aristocracy of talent and intellect will still stand. In fact, one suspects that eventually the most civilized way of being superior will be to excel in culture.

This much, then, of the ideals of humanism must survive; the goal of education is self-culture, and one must hold it essential even for knowledge's own sake that it be transmuted into character and personality. It must have been the essential meaning of Socrates' favorite dictum—"Know thyself"—that to know, one must be a developed personality. The capacity for deep understanding is proportional to the degree of self-knowledge, and by finding and expressing one's true self, one somehow discovers the common denominator of the universe. Education without culture, therefore, ignores an important half of the final standard, "a scholar and a gentleman," which, lest it seem obsolete, let me cite in those fine modern words which former President Eliot used in conferring the arts degree. "I hereby admit you to the honorable fellowship of educated men." Culture is thus education's passport to converse and association with the best.

Moreover, personal representativeness and group achievement are in this respect identical. Ultimately a people is judged by its capacity to contribute to culture. It is to be hoped that as we progressively acquire in this energetic democracy the common means of modern civilization, we shall justify ourselves more and more, individually and collectively, by the use of them to produce culture-goods and representative types of culture. And this, so peculiarly desirable under the present handicap of social disparagement and disesteem, must be for more than personal reasons the ambition and the achievement of our educated classes. If, as we all know, we must look to education largely to win our way, we must look largely to culture to win our just reward and recognition. It is, therefore, under these circumstances something more than your personal duty to be cultured—it is one of your most direct responsibilities to your fellows, one of your most effective opportunities for group service. In presenting this defense of the ideals and aims of culture, it is my ardent hope that the Howard degree may come increasingly to stand for such things—and especially the vintage of 1926.

MARTIN LUTHER KING, JR.

Letter From Birmingham Jail

AUTHOR'S NOTE: This response to a published statement by eight fellow clergymen from Alabama (Bishop C. C. J. Carpenter, Bishop Joseph A. Durick, Rabbi Hilton L. Grafman, Bishop Paul Hardin, Bishop Holan B. Harmon, the Reverend George M. Murray, the Reverend Edward V. Ramage and the Reverend Earl Stallings) was composed under somewhat constricting circumstances. Begun on the margins of the newspaper in which the statement appeared while I was in jail, the letter was continued on scraps of writing paper supplied by a friendly

Negro trusty, and concluded on a pad my attorneys were eventually permitted to leave me. Although the text remains in substance unaltered, I have indulged in the author's prerogative of polishing it for publication.

April 16, 1963

My Dear Fellow Clergymen:

While confined here in the Birmingham city jail, I came across your recent statement calling my present activities "unwise and untimely." Seldom do I pause to answer criticism of my work and ideas. If I sought to answer all the criticisms that cross my desk, my secretaries would have little time for anything other than such correspondence in the course of the day, and I would have no time for constructive work. But since I feel that you are men of genuine good will and that your criticisms are sincerely set forth, I want to try to answer your statement in what I hope will be patient and reasonable terms.

I think I should indicate why I am here in Birmingham, since you have been influenced by the view which argues against "outsiders coming in." I have the honor of serving as president of the Southern Christian Leadership Conference, an organization operating in every southern state, with headquarters in Atlanta, Georgia. We have some eighty-five affiliated organizations across the South, and one of them is the Alabama Christian Movement for Human Rights. Frequently we share staff, educational and financial resources with our affiliates. Several months ago the affiliate here in Birmingham asked us to be on call to engage in a nonviolent direct-action program if such were deemed necessary. We readily consented, and when the hour came we lived up to our promise. So I, along with several members of my staff, am here because I was invited here. I am here because I have organizational ties here.

But more basically, I am in Birmingham because injustice is here. Just as the prophets of the eighth century B.C. left their villages and carried their "thus saith the Lord" far beyond the boundaries of their home towns, and just as the Apostle Paul left his village of Tarsus and carried the gospel of Jesus Christ to the far corners of the Greco-Roman world, so am I compelled to carry the gospel of freedom beyond my own home town. Like Paul, I must constantly respond to the Macedonian call for aid.

Moreover, I am cognizant of the interrelatedness of all communities and states. I cannot sit idly by in Atlanta and not be concerned about what happens in Birmingham. Injustice anywhere is a threat to justice everywhere. We are caught in an inescapable network of mutuality, tied in a single garment of destiny. Whatever affects one directly, affects all indirectly. Never again can we afford to live with the narrow, provincial "outside agitator" idea. Anyone who lives inside the United States can never be considered an outsider anywhere within its bounds.

You deplore the demonstrations taking place in Birmingham. But your statement, I am sorry to say, fails to express a similar concern for the conditions that brought about the demonstrations. I am sure that none of you would want to rest content with the superficial kind of social analysis that deals merely with effects and does not grapple with underlying causes. It is unfortunate that demonstrations are taking place in Birmingham, but it is even more unfortunate that the city's white power structure left the Negro community with no alternative.

In any nonviolent campaign there are four basic steps: collection of the facts to determine whether injustices exist; negotiation; self-purification; and direct action. We have gone through all these steps in Birmingham. There can be no gainsaying the fact that racial injustice engulfs this community. Birmingham is probably the most thoroughly segregated city in the United States. Its ugly record of brutality is widely known. Negroes have experienced grossly unjust treatment in the courts. There have been more unsolved bombings of Negro homes and churches in Birmingham than in any other city in the nation. These are the hard, brutal facts of the case. On the basis of these conditions, Negro leaders sought to negotiate with the city fathers. But the latter consistently refused to engage in good-faith negotiation.

Then, last September, came the opportunity to talk with leaders of Birmingham's economic community. In the course of the negotiations, certain promises were made by the merchants—for example, to remove the stores' humiliating racial signs. On the basis of these promises, the Reverend Fred Shuttlesworth and the leaders of the Alabama Christian Movement for Human Rights agreed to a moratorium on all demonstrations. As the weeks and months went by, we realized that we were the victims of a broken promise. A few signs, briefly removed, returned; the others remained.

As in so many past experiences, our hopes had been blasted, and the shadow of deep disappointment settled upon us. We had no alternative except to prepare for direct action, whereby we would present our very bodies as a means of laying our case before the conscience of the local and the national community. Mindful of the difficulties involved, we decided to undertake a process of self-purification. We began a series of workshops on nonviolence, and we repeatedly asked ourselves: "Are you able to accept blows without retaliating?" "Are you able to endure the ordeal of jail?" We decided to schedule our direct-action pro-

gram for the Easter season, realizing that except for Christmas, this is the main shopping period of the year. Knowing that a strong economic-withdrawal program would be the by-product of direct action, we felt that this would be the best time to bring pressure to bear on the merchants for the needed change.

Then it occurred to us that Birmingham's mayoralty election was coming up in March, and we speedily decided to postpone action until after election day. When we discovered that the Commissioner of Public Safety, Eugene "Bull" Connor, had piled up enough votes to be in the run-off, we decided again to postpone action until the day after the run-off so that the demonstrations could not be used to cloud the issues. Like many others, we waited to see Mr. Connor defeated, and to this end we endured postponement after postponement. Having aided in this community need, we felt that our direct-action program could be delayed no longer.

You may well ask: "Why direct action? Why sit-ins, marches and so forth? Isn't negotiation a better path?" You are quite right in calling for negotiation. Indeed, this is the very purpose of direct action. Nonviolent direct action seeks to create such a crisis and foster such a tension that a community which has constantly refused to negotiate is forced to confront the issue. It seeks so to dramatize the issue that it can no longer be ignored. My citing the creation of tension as part of the work of the nonviolent-resister may sound rather shocking. But I must confess that I am not afraid of the word "tension." I have earnestly opposed violent tension, but there is a type of constructive, nonviolent tension which is necessary for growth. Just as Socrates felt that it was necessary to create a tension in the mind so that individuals could rise from the bondage of myths and half-truths to the unfettered realm of creative analysis and objective appraisal, so must we see the need for nonviolent gadflies to create the kind of tension in society that will help men rise from the dark depths of prejudice and racism to the majestic heights of understanding and brotherhood.

The purpose of our direct-action program is to create a situation so crisis-packed that it will inevitably open the door to negotiation. I therefore concur with you in your call for negotiation. Too long has our beloved Southland been bogged down in a tragic effort to live in monologue rather than dialogue.

One of the basic points in your statement is that the action that I and my associates have taken in Birmingham is untimely. Some have asked: "Why didn't you give the new city administration time to act?" The only answer that I can give to this query is that the new Birmingham administration must be prodded about as much as the outgoing one, before it will act. We are sadly mistaken if we feel that the election of Albert Boutwell as mayor will bring the millennium to Birmingham. While Mr. Boutwell is a much more gentle person than Mr. Connor, they are both segregationists, dedicated to maintenance of the status quo. I have hope that Mr. Boutwell will be reasonable enough to see the futility of massive resistance to desegregation. But he will not see this without pressure from devotees of civil rights. My friends, I must say to you that we have not made a single gain in civil rights without determined legal and nonviolent pressure. Lamentably, it is an historical fact that privileged groups seldom give up their privileges voluntarily. Individuals may see the moral light and voluntarily give up their unjust posture; but, as Reinhold Niebuhr has reminded us, groups tend to be more immoral than individuals.

We know through painful experience that freedom is never voluntarily given by the oppressor; it must be demanded by the oppressed. Frankly, I have yet to engage in a direct-action campaign that was "well timed" in the view of those who have not suffered unduly from the disease of segregation. For years now I have heard the word "Wait!" It rings in the ear of every Negro with piercing familiarity. This "Wait" has almost always meant "Never." We must come to see, with one of our distinguished jurists, that "justice too long delayed is justice denied."

We have waited for more than 340 years for our constitutional and God-given rights. The nations of Asia and Africa are moving with jetlike speed toward gaining political independence, but we still creep at horse-and-buggy pace toward gaining a cup of coffee at a lunch counter. Perhaps it is easy for those who have never felt the stinging darts of segregation to say, "Wait." But when you have seen vicious mobs lynch your mothers and fathers at will and drown your sisters and brothers at whim; when you have seen hate-filled policemen curse, kick and even kill your black brothers and sisters; when you see the vast majority of your twenty million Negro brothers smothering in an airtight cage of poverty in the midst of an affluent society; when you suddenly find your tongue twisted and your speech stammering as you seek to explain to your six-year-old daughter why she can't go to the public amusement park that has just been advertised on television, and see tears welling up in her eyes when she is told that Funtown is closed to colored children, and see ominous clouds of inferiority beginning to form in her little mental sky, and see her beginning to distort her personality by developing an unconscious bitterness toward white people; when you have to concoct an answer for a five-year-old son who is asking: "Daddy, why do white people treat colored people so mean?"; when you take a cross-country drive and find

it necessary to sleep night after night in the uncomfortable corners of your automobile because no motel will accept you; when you are humiliated day in and day out by nagging signs reading "white" and "colored"; when your first name becomes "nigger," your middle name becomes "boy" (however old you are) and your last name becomes "John," and your wife and mother are never given the respected title "Mrs."; when you are harried by day and haunted by night by the fact that you are a Negro, living constantly at tiptoe stance, never quite knowing what to expect next, and are plagued with inner fears and outer resentments; when you are forever fighting a degenerating sense of "nobodiness"—then you will understand why we find it difficult to wait. There comes a time when the cup of endurance runs over, and men are no longer willing to be plunged into the abyss of despair. I hope, sirs, you can understand our legitimate and unavoidable impatience.

You express a great deal of anxiety over our willingness to break laws. This is certainly a legitimate concern. Since we so diligently urge people to obey the Supreme Court's decision of 1954 outlawing segregation in the public schools, at first glance it may seem rather paradoxical for us consciously to break laws. One may well ask: "How can you advocate breaking some laws and obeying others?" The answer lies in the fact that there are two types of laws; just and unjust. I would be the first to advocate obeying just laws. One has not only a legal but a moral responsibility to obey just laws. Conversely, one has a moral responsibility to disobey unjust laws. I would agree with St. Augustine that "an unjust law is no law at all."

Now, what is the difference between the two? How does one determine whether a law is just or unjust? A just law is a man-made code that squares with the moral law or the law of God. An unjust law is a code that is out of harmony with the moral law. To put it in the terms of St. Thomas Aquinas: An unjust law is a human law that is not rooted in eternal law and natural law. Any law that uplifts human personality is just. Any law that degrades human personality is unjust. All segregation statutes are unjust because segregation distorts the soul and damages the personality. It gives the segregator a false sense of superiority and the segregated a false sense of inferiority. Segregation, to use the terminology of the Jewish philosopher Martin Buber, substitutes an "I-it" relationship for an "I-thou" relationship and ends up relegating persons to the status of things. Hence segregation is not only politically, economically and sociologically unsound, it is morally wrong and sinful. Paul Tillich has said that sin is separation. Is not segregation an existential expression of man's tragic separation, his awful estrangement, his terrible sinfulness? Thus it is that I can urge men to obey the 1954 decision of the Supreme Court, for it is morally right; and I can urge them to disobey segregation ordinances, for they are morally wrong.

Let us consider a more concrete example of just and unjust laws. An unjust law is a code that a numerical or power majority group compels a minority group to obey but does not make binding on itself. This is *difference* made legal. By the same token, a just law is a code that a majority compels a minority to follow and that it is willing to follow itself. This is *sameness* made legal.

Let me give another explanation. A law is unjust if it is inflicted on a minority that, as a result of being denied the right to vote, had no part in enacting or devising the law. Who can say that the legislature of Alabama which set up that state's segregation laws was democratically elected? Throughout Alabama all sorts of devious methods are used to prevent Negroes from becoming registered voters, and there are some counties in which, even though Negroes constitute a majority of the population, not a single Negro is registered. Can any law enacted under such circumstances be considered democratically structured?

Sometimes a law is just on its face and unjust in its application. For instance, I have been arrested on a charge of parading without a permit. Now, there is nothing wrong in having an ordinance which requires a permit for a parade. But such an ordinance becomes unjust when it is used to maintain segregation and to deny citizens the First-Amendment privilege of peaceful assembly and protest.

I hope you are able to see the distinction I am trying to point out. In no sense do I advocate evading or defying the law, as would the rabid segregationist. That would lead to anarchy. One who breaks an unjust law must do so openly, lovingly, and with a willingness to accept the penalty. I submit that an individual who breaks a law that conscience tells him is unjust, and who willingly accepts the penalty of imprisonment in order to arouse the conscience of the community over its injustice, is in reality expressing the highest respect for law.

Of course, there is nothing new about this kind of civil disobedience. It was evidenced sublimely in the refusal of Shadrach, Meshach and Abednego to obey the laws of Nebuchadnezzar, on the ground that a higher moral law was at stake. It was practiced superbly by the early Christians, who were willing to face hungry lions and the excruciating pain of chopping blocks rather than submit to certain unjust laws of the Roman Empire. To a degree, academic freedom is a reality today because Socrates practiced civil disobedience. In our own nation, the Boston Tea Party represented a massive act of civil disobedience.

We should never forget that everything Adolf Hitler did in Germany was "legal" and everything the Hungarian freedom fighters did in Hungary was "illegal." It was "illegal" to aid and comfort a Jew in Hitler's Germany. Even so, I am sure that, had I lived in Germany at the time, I would have aided and comforted my Jewish brothers. If today I lived in a Communist country where certain principles dear to the Christian faith are suppressed, I would openly advocate disobeying that country's antireligious laws.

I must make two honest confessions to you, my Christian and Jewish brothers. First, I must confess that over the past few years I have been gravely disappointed with the white moderate. I have almost reached the regrettable conclusion that the Negro's great stumbling block in his stride toward freedom is not the White Citizen's Counciler or the Ku Klux Klanner, but the white moderate, who is more devoted to "order" than to justice; who prefers a negative peace which is the absence of tension to a positive peace which is the presence of justice; who constantly says: "I agree with you in the goal you seek, but I cannot agree with your methods of direct action"; who paternalistically believes he can set the timetable for another man's freedom; who lives by a mythical concept of time and who constantly advises the Negro to wait for a "more convenient season." Shallow understanding from people of good will is more frustrating than absolute misunderstanding from people of ill will. Lukewarm acceptance is much more bewildering than outright rejection.

I had hoped that the white moderate would understand that law and order exist for the purpose of establishing justice and that when they fail in this purpose they become the dangerously structured dams that block the flow of social progress. I had hoped that the white moderate would understand that the present tension in the South is a necessary phase of the transition from an obnoxious negative peace, in which the Negro passively accepted his unjust plight, to a substantive and positive peace, in which all men will respect the dignity and worth of human personality. Actually, we who engage in nonviolent direct action are not the creators of tension. We merely bring to the surface the hidden tension that is already alive. We bring it out in the open, where it can be seen and dealt with. Like a boil that can never be cured so long as it is covered up but must be opened with all its ugliness to the natural medicines of air and light, injustice must be exposed, with all the tension its exposure creates, to the light of human conscience and the air of national opinion before it can be cured.

In your statement you assert that our actions, even though peaceful, must be condemned because they precipitate violence. But is this a logical assertion? Isn't

this like condemning a robbed man because his possession of money precipitated the evil act of robbery? Isn't
this like condemning Socrates because his unswerving
commitment to truth and his philosophical inquiries
precipitated the act by the misguided populace in which
they made him drink hemlock? Isn't this like condemning Jesus because his unique God-consciousness and
never-ceasing devotion to God's will precipitated the
evil act of crucifixion? We must come to see that, as the
federal courts have consistently affirmed, it is wrong to
urge an individual to cease his efforts to gain his basic
constitutional rights because the quest may precipitate
violence. Society must protect the robbed and punish
the robber.

I had also hoped that the white moderate would reject the myth concerning time in relation to the struggle
for freedom. I have just received a letter from a white
brother in Texas. He writes: "All Christians know that
the colored people will receive equal rights eventually,
but it is possible that you are in too great a religious
hurry. It has taken Christianity almost two thousand
years to accomplish what it has. The teachings of Christ
take time to come to earth." Such an attitude stems
from a tragic misconception of time, from the strangely
irrational notion that there is something in the very flow
of time that will inevitably cure all ills. Actually, time
itself is neutral; it can be used either destructively or
constructively. More and more I feel that the people of
ill will have used time much more effectively than have
the people of good will. We will have to repent in this
generation not merely for the hateful words and actions
of the bad people but for the appalling silence of the
good people. Human progress never rolls in on wheels
of inevitability; it comes through the tireless efforts of
men willing to be co-workers with God, and without
this hard work, time itself becomes an ally of the forces
of social stagnation. We must use time creatively, in the
knowledge that the time is always ripe to do right. Now
is the time to make real the promise of democracy and
transform our pending national elegy into a creative
psalm of brotherhood. Now is the time to lift our national policy from the quicksand of racial injustice to
the solid rock of human dignity.

You speak of our activity in Birmingham as extreme. At first I was rather disappointed that fellow
clergymen would see my nonviolent efforts as those of
an extremist. I began thinking about the fact that I
stand in the middle of two opposing forces in the Negro
community. One is a force of complacency, made up in
part of Negroes who, as a result of long years of oppression, are so drained of self-respect and a sense of
"somebodiness" that they have adjusted to segregation;
and in part of a few middle-class Negroes who, because
of a degree of academic and economic security and because in some ways they profit by segregation, have

become insensitive to the problems of the masses. The
other force is one of bitterness and hatred, and it comes
perilously close to advocating violence. It is expressed
in the various black nationalist groups that are spring-
ing up across the nation, the largest and best-known
being Elijah Muhammad's Muslim movement. Nourished by the Negro's frustration over the continued existence of racial discrimination, this movement is made
up of people who have lost faith in America, who have
absolutely repudiated Christianity, and who have concluded that the white man is an incorrigible "devil."

I have tried to stand between these two forces, saying that we need emulate neither the "do-nothingism"
of the complacent nor the hatred and despair of the
black nationalist. For there is the more excellent way of
love and nonviolent protest. I am grateful to God that,
through the influence of the Negro church, the way of
nonviolence became an integral part of our struggle.

If this philosophy had not emerged, by now many
streets of the South would, I am convinced, be flowing
with blood. And I am further convinced that if our
white brothers dismiss as "rabble-rousers" and "outside agitators" those of us who employ nonviolent direct action, and if they refuse to support our nonviolent
efforts, millions of Negroes will, out of frustration and
despair, seek solace and security in black-nationalist
ideologies—a development that would inevitably lead
to a frightening racial nightmare.

Oppressed people cannot remain oppressed forever.
The yearning for freedom eventually manifests itself,
and that is what has happened to the American Negro.
Something within has reminded him of his birthright
of freedom, and something without has reminded him
that it can be gained. Consciously or unconsciously, he
has been caught up by the *Zeitgeist*, and with his black
brothers of Africa and his brown and yellow brothers
of Asia, South America and the Caribbean, the United
States Negro is moving with a sense of great urgency
toward the promised land of racial justice. If one recognizes this vital urge that has engulfed the Negro community, one should readily understand why public demonstrations are taking place. The Negro has many pent-up
resentments and latent frustrations, and he must release
them. So let him march; let him make prayer pilgrim-
ages to the city hall; let him go on freedom rides—and
try to understand why he must do so. If his repressed
emotions are not released in nonviolent ways, they will
seek expression through violence; this is not a threat but
a fact of history. So I have not said to my people: "Get
rid of your discontent." Rather, I have tried to say that
this normal and healthy discontent can be channeled
into the creative outlet of nonviolent direct action. And
now this approach is being termed extremist.

But though I was initially disappointed at being cat-
egorized as an extremist, as I continued to think about

the matter I gradually gained a measure of satisfaction from the label. Was not Jesus an extremist for love: "Love your enemies, bless them that curse you, do good to them that hate you, and pray for them which despitefully use you, and persecute you." Was not Amos an extremist for justice: "Let justice roll down like waters and righteousness like an ever-flowing stream." Was not Paul an extremist for the Christian gospel: "I bear in my body the marks of the Lord Jesus." Was not Martin Luther an extremist: "Here I stand; I cannot do otherwise, so help me God." And John Bunyan: "I will stay in jail to the end of my days before I make a butchery of my conscience." And Abraham Lincoln: "This nation cannot survive half slave and half free." And Thomas Jefferson: "We hold these truths to be self-evident, that all men are created equal . . ." So the question is not whether we will be extremists, but what kind of extremists we will be. Will we be extremists for hate or for love? Will we be extremists for the preservation of injustice or for the extension of justice? In that dramatic scene on Calvary's hill three men were crucified. We must never forget that all three were crucified for the same crime—the crime of extremism. Two were extremists for immorality, and thus fell below their environment. The other, Jesus Christ, was an extremist for love, truth and goodness, and thereby rose above his environment. Perhaps the South, the nation and the world are in dire need of creative extremists.

I had hoped that the white moderate would see this need. Perhaps I was too optimistic; perhaps I expected too much. I suppose I should have realized that few members of the oppressor race can understand the deep groans and passionate yearnings of the oppressed race, and still fewer have the vision to see that injustice must be rooted out by strong, persistent and determined action. I am thankful, however, that some of our white brothers in the South have grasped the meaning of this social revolution and committed themselves to it. They are still all too few in quantity, but they are big in quality. Some—such as Ralph McGill, Lillian Smith, Harry Golden, James McBride Dabbs, Ann Braden and Sarah Patton Boyle—have written about our struggle in eloquent and prophetic terms. Others have marched with us down nameless streets of the South. They have languished in filthy, roach-infested jails, suffering the abuse and brutality of policemen who view them as "dirty nigger-lovers." Unlike so many of their moderate brothers and sisters, they have recognized the urgency of the moment and sensed the need for powerful "action" antidotes to combat the disease of segregation.

Let me take note of my other major disappointment. I have been so greatly disappointed with the white church and its leadership. Of course, there are some notable exceptions. I am not unmindful of the fact that each of you has taken some significant stands on this issue. I commend you, Reverend Stallings, for your Christian stand on this past Sunday, in welcoming Negroes to your worship service on a nonsegregated basis. I commend the Catholic leaders of this state for integrating Spring Hill College several years ago.

But despite these notable exceptions, I must honestly reiterate that I have been disappointed with the church. I do not say this as one of those negative critics who can always find something wrong with the church. I say this as a minister of the gospel, who loves the church; who was nurtured in its bosom; who has been sustained by its spiritual blessings and who will remain true to it as long as the cord of life shall lengthen.

When I was suddenly catapulted into the leadership of the bus protest in Montgomery, Alabama, a few years ago, I felt we would be supported by the white church. I felt that the white ministers, priests and rabbis of the South would be among our strongest allies. Instead, some have been outright opponents, refusing to understand the freedom movement and misrepresenting its leaders; all too many others have been more cautious than courageous and have remained silent behind the anesthetizing security of stained-glass windows.

In spite of my shattered dreams, I came to Birmingham with the hope that the white religious leadership of this community would see the justice of our cause and, with deep moral concern, would serve as the channel through which our just grievances could reach the power structure. I had hoped that each of you would understand. But again I have been disappointed.

I have heard numerous southern religious leaders admonish their worshipers to comply with a desegregation decision because it is the law, but I have longed to hear white ministers declare: "Follow this decree because integration is morally right and because the Negro is your brother." In the midst of blatant injustices inflicted upon the Negro, I have watched white churchmen stand on the sideline and mouth pious irrelevancies and sanctimonious trivialities. In the midst of a mighty struggle to rid our nation of racial and economic injustice, I have heard many ministers say: "Those are social issues, with which the gospel has no real concern." And I have watched many churches commit themselves to a completely other-worldly religion which makes a strange, un-Biblical distinction between body and soul, between the sacred and the secular.

I have traveled the length and breadth of Alabama, Mississippi and all the other southern states. On sweltering summer days and crisp autumn mornings I have looked at the South's beautiful churches with their lofty spires pointing heavenward. I have beheld the impressive outlines of her massive religious-education buildings. Over and over I have found myself asking: "What kind of people worship here? Who is their God? Where were their voices when the lips of Governor Barnett dripped with words of interposition and nullification? Where were they when Governor Wallace gave a clarion call for defiance and hatred? Where were their voices of support when bruised and weary Negro men and women decided to rise from the dark dungeons of complacency to the bright hills of creative protest?"

Yes, these questions are still in my mind. In deep disappointment I have wept over the laxity of the church. But be assured that my tears have been tears of love. There can be no deep disappointment where there is not deep love. Yes, I love the church. How could I do otherwise? I am in the rather unique position of being the son, the grandson and the great-grandson of preachers. Yes, I see the church as the body of Christ. But, oh! How we have blemished and scarred that body through social neglect and through fear of being nonconformists.

There was a time when the church was very powerful—in the time when the early Christians rejoiced at being deemed worthy to suffer for what they believed. In those days the church was not merely a thermometer that recorded the ideas and principles of popular opinion; it was a thermostat that transformed the mores of society. Whenever the early Christians entered a town, the people in power became disturbed and immediately sought to convict the Christians for being "disturbers of the peace" and "outside agitators." But the Christians pressed on, in the conviction that they were "a colony of heaven," called to obey God rather than man. Small in number, they were big in commitment. They were too God-intoxicated to be "astronomically intimidated." By their effort and example they brought an end to such ancient evils as infanticide and gladiatorial contests.

Things are different now. So often the contemporary church is a weak, ineffectual voice with an uncertain sound. So often it is an archdefender of the status quo. Far from being disturbed by the presence of the church, the power structure of the average community is consoled by the church's silent—and often even vocal—sanction of things as they are.

But the judgment of God is upon the church as never before. If today's church does not recapture the sacrificial spirit of the early church, it will lose its authenticity, forfeit the loyalty of millions, and be dismissed as an irrelevant social club with no meaning for the twentieth century. Every day I meet young people whose disappointment with the church has turned into outright disgust.

Perhaps I have once again been too optimistic. Is organized religion too inextricably bound to the status quo to save our nation and the world? Perhaps I must turn my faith to the inner spiritual church, the church within the church, as the true *ekklesia* and the hope of the world. But again I am thankful to God that some noble souls from the ranks of organized religion have broken loose from the paralyzing chains of conformity and joined us as active partners in the struggle for freedom. They have left their secure congregations and walked the streets of Albany, Georgia, with us. They have gone down the highways of the South on tortuous rides for freedom. Yes, they have gone to jail with us. Some have been dismissed from their churches, have lost the support of their bishops and fellow ministers. But they have acted in the faith that right defeated is stronger than evil triumphant. Their witness has been the spiritual salt that has preserved the true meaning of the gospel in these troubled times. They have carved a tunnel of hope through the dark mountain of disappointment.

I hope the church as a whole will meet the challenge of this decisive hour. But even if the church does not come to the aid of justice, I have no despair about the future. I have no fear about the outcome of our struggle in Birmingham, even if our motives are at present misunderstood. We will reach the goal of freedom in Birmingham and all over the nation, because the goal of America is freedom. Abused and scorned though we may be, our destiny is tied up with America's destiny. Before the pilgrims landed at Plymouth, we were here. Before the pen of Jefferson etched the majestic words of the Declaration of Independence across the pages of history, we were here. For more than two centuries our forebears labored in this country without wages; they made cotton king; they built the homes of their masters while suffering gross injustice and shameful humiliation—and yet out of a bottomless vitality they continued to thrive and develop. If the inexpressible cruelties of slavery could not stop us, the opposition we now face will surely fail. We will win our freedom because the sacred heritage of our nation and the eternal will of God are embodied in our echoing demands.

Before closing I feel impelled to mention one other point in your statement that has troubled me profoundly. You warmly commended the Birmingham police force for keeping "order" and "preventing violence." I doubt that you would have so warmly commended the police force if you had seen its dogs sinking their teeth into unarmed, nonviolent Negroes. I doubt that you would so quickly commend the policemen if you were to observe their ugly and inhumane treatment of Negroes here in the city jail; if you were to watch them push and curse old Negro women and young Negro girls; if you were to see them slap and kick old Negro men and young boys; if you were to observe them, as they did on two occasions, refuse to give us food because we wanted to sing our grace together. I cannot join you in your praise of the Birmingham police department.

It is true that the police have exercised a degree of discipline in handling the demonstrators. In this sense they have conducted themselves rather "nonviolently" in public. But for what purpose? To preserve the evil system of segregation. Over the past few years I have consistently preached that nonviolence demands that the means we use must be as pure as the ends we seek. I have tried to make clear that it is wrong to use immoral means to attain moral ends. But now I must affirm that it is just as wrong, or perhaps even more so to use moral means to preserve immoral ends. Perhaps Mr. Connor and his policemen have been rather nonviolent in public, as was Chief Pritchett in Albany, Georgia, but they have used the moral means of nonviolence to maintain the immoral end of racial injustice. As T. S. Eliot has said: "The last temptation is the greatest treason: To do the right deed for the wrong reason."

I wish you had commended the Negro sit-inners and demonstrators of Birmingham for their sublime courage, their willingness to suffer and their amazing discipline in the midst of great provocation. One day the South will recognize its real heroes. They will be the James Merediths, with the noble sense of purpose that enables them to face jeering and hostile mobs, and with the agonizing loneliness that characterizes the life of the pioneer. They will be old, oppressed, battered Negro women, symbolized in a seventy-two-year-old woman in Montgomery, Alabama, who rose up with a sense of dignity and with her people decided not to ride segregated buses, and who responded with ungrammatical profundity to one who inquired about her weariness: "My feets is tired, but my soul is at rest." They will be the young high school and college students, the young ministers of the gospel and a host of their elders, courageously and nonviolently sitting in at lunch counters and willingly going to jail for conscience' sake. One day the South will know that when these disinherited children of God sat down at lunch counters, they were in reality standing up for what is best in the American dream and for the most sacred values in our Judaeo-Christian heritage, thereby bringing our nation back to those great wells of democracy which were dug deep by the founding fathers in their formulation of the Constitution and the Declaration of Independence.

Never before have I written so long a letter. I'm afraid it is much too long to take your precious time. I can assure you that it would have been much shorter if I had been writing from a comfortable desk, but what else can one do when he is alone in a narrow jail cell, other than write long letters, think long thoughts and pray long prayers?

If I have said anything in this letter that overstates the truth and indicates an unreasonable impatience, I beg you to forgive me. If I have said anything that understates the truth and indicates my having a patience that allows me to settle for anything less than brotherhood, I beg God to forgive me.

I hope this letter finds you strong in the faith. I also hope that circumstances will soon make it possible for me to meet each of you, not as an integrationist or a civil-rights leader but as a fellow clergyman and a Christian brother. Let us all hope that the dark clouds of racial prejudice will soon pass away and the deep fog of misunderstanding will be lifted from our fear-drenched communities, and in some not too distant tomorrow the radiant stars of love and brotherhood will shine over our great nation with all their scintillating beauty.

Yours for the cause of Peace and Brotherhood,

MARTIN LUTHER KING, JR.

LYNDON BAINES JOHNSON
To Fulfill These Rights

Our earth is the home of revolution.

In every corner of every continent men charged with hope contend with ancient ways in the pursuit of justice. They reach for the newest of weapons to realize the oldest of dreams; that each may walk in freedom and pride, stretching his talents, enjoying the fruits of the earth.

Our enemies may occasionally seize the day of change. But it is the banner of our revolution they take. And our own future is linked to this process of swift and turbulent change in many lands in the world. But nothing in any country touches us more profoundly, nothing is more freighted with meaning for our own destiny, than the revolution of the Negro American.

In far too many ways American Negroes have been another nation: deprived of freedom, crippled by hatred, the doors of opportunity closed to hope.

In our time change has come to this Nation too. The American Negro, acting with impressive restraint, has peacefully protested and marched, entered the

Lyndon Baines Johnson, James M. Nabrit, and Howard Faculty (Courtesy of the Moorland-Spingarn Research Center)

courtrooms and the seats of government, demanding a justice that has long been denied. The voice of the Negro was the call to action. But it is a tribute to America that, once aroused, the courts and the Congress, the President and most of the people, have been the allies of progress.

Legal Protection For Human Rights

Thus we have seen the high court of the country declare that discrimination based on race was repugnant to the Constitution, and therefore void. We have seen in 1957, 1960, and again in 1964, the first civil rights legislation in this Nation in almost an entire century.

As majority leader of the United States Senate, I helped to guide two of these bills through the Senate. As your President, I was proud to sign the third. And now very soon we will have the fourth—a new law guaranteeing every American the right to vote.

No act of my entire administration will give me greater satisfaction than the day when my signature makes this bill too the law of this land.

The voting rights bill will be the latest, and among the most important, in a long series of victories. But this victory—as Winston Churchill said of another triumph for freedom—"is not the end. It is not even the beginning of the end. But it is, perhaps, the end of the beginning."

That beginning is freedom. And the barriers to that freedom are tumbling down. Freedom is the right to share fully and equally in American society—to vote, to hold a job, to enter a public place, to go to school. It is the right to be treated in every part of our national life as a person equal in dignity and promise to all others.

Freedom Is Not Enough

But freedom is not enough. You do not wipe away the scars of centuries by saying: Now you are free to go where you want, do as you desire, and choose the leaders you please.

You do not take a person who, for years, has been hobbled by chains and liberate him, bring him up to the starting line of a race and then say, "you are free to compete with all the others," and still justly believe that you have been completely fair.

Thus it is not enough just to open the gates of opportunity. All our citizens must have the ability to walk through those gates.

This is the next and more profound stage of the battle for civil rights. We seek not just freedom but opportunity—not just legal equity but human ability—not just equality as a right and a theory, but equality as a fact and as a result.

For the task is to give 20 million Negroes the same chance as every other American to learn and grow, to work and share in society, to develop their abilities—physical, mental and spiritual, and to pursue their individual happiness.

To this end equal opportunity is essential, but not enough. Men and women of all races are born with the same range of abilities. But ability is not just the product of birth. Ability is stretched or stunted by the family you live with, and the neighborhood you live in, by the school you go to and the poverty or the richness of your surroundings. It is the product of a hundred unseen forces playing upon the infant, the child, and the man.

Progress For Some

This graduating class at Howard University is witness to the indomitable determination of the Negro American to win his way in American life.

The number of Negroes in schools of higher learning has almost doubled in 15 years. The number of non-white professional workers has more than doubled in 10 years. The median income of Negro college women exceeds that of white college women. And there are also the enormous accomplishments of distinguished individual Negroes—many of them graduates of this institution, and one of them the first lady ambassador in the history of the United States.

These are proud and impressive achievements. But they tell only the story of a growing middle class minority, steadily narrowing the gap between them and their white counterparts.

A Widening Gulf

But for the great majority of Negro Americans—the poor, the unemployed, the uprooted and the dispossessed— there is a much grimmer story. They still are another nation. Despite the court orders and the laws, despite the legislative victories and the speeches, for them the walls are rising and the gulf is widening.

Here are some of the facts of this American failure.

Thirty-five years ago the rate of unemployment for Negroes and whites was about the same. Today the Negro rate is twice as high.

In 1948 the 8 percent unemployment rate for Negro teenage boys was actually less than that of whites. By last year that rate had grown to 23 percent, as against 13 percent for whites.

Between 1949 and 1959, the income of Negro men relative to white men declined in every section of this country. From 1952 to 1963 the median income of Negro families compared to white actually dropped from 57 percent to 53 percent.

In the years 1955 through 1957, 22 percent of experienced Negro workers were out of work at some time during the year. In 1961 through 1963 that proportion had soared to 29 percent.

Since 1947 the number of white families living in poverty has decreased 27 percent, while the number of poor nonwhite families decreased only 3 percent.

The infant mortality of nonwhites in 1940 was 70 percent greater than whites. Twenty-two years later it was 90 percent greater.

Moreover, the isolation of Negro from white communities is increasing, rather than decreasing, as Negroes crowd into the central cities and become a city within a city.

Of course Negro Americans as well as white Americans have shared in our rising national abundance. But the harsh fact of the matter is that in the battle for true equality too many are losing ground every day.

The Causes of Inequality

We are not completely sure why this is. The causes are complex and subtle. But we do know the two broad basic reasons. And we do know that we have to act.

First, Negroes are trapped—as many whites are trapped—in inherited, gateless poverty. They lack training and skills. They are shut in slums, without decent medical care. Private and public poverty combine to cripple their capacities.

We are trying to attack these evils through our poverty program, through our education program, through our medical care and our other health programs and a dozen more of the Great Society programs that are aimed at the root causes of this poverty.

We will increase, and accelerate, and broaden this attack in years to come until this most enduring of foes finally yields to our unyielding will. But there is a second cause—much more difficult to explain, more deeply grounded, more desperate in its force. It is the devastating heritage of long years of slavery; and a century of oppression, hatred and injustice.

Special Nature of Negro Poverty

For Negro poverty is not white poverty. Many of its causes and many of its cures are the same. But there are differences—deep, corrosive, obstinate differences— radiating painful roots into the community, the family, and the nature of the individual.

These differences are not racial differences. They are solely and simply the consequence of ancient brutality, past injustice, and present prejudice. They are anguishing to observe. For the Negro they are a constant reminder of oppression. For the white they are a constant reminder of guilt. But they must be faced and dealt with and overcome, if we are ever to reach the time when the only difference between Negroes and whites is the color of their skin.

Nor can we find a complete answer in the experience of other American minorities. They made a valiant and a largely successful effort to emerge from poverty and prejudice. The Negro, like these others, will have to rely mostly on his own efforts. But he just can not do it alone. For they did not have the heritage of centuries to overcome. They did not have a cultural tradition which had been twisted and battered by endless years of hatred and hopelessness. Nor were they excluded because of race or color—a feeling whose dark intensity is matched by no other prejudice in our society.

Nor can these differences be understood as isolated infirmities. They are a seamless web. They cause each other. They result from each other. They reinforce each other. Much of the Negro community is buried under a blanket of history and circumstance. It is not a lasting solution to lift just one corner of that blanket. We must stand on all sides and raise the entire cover if we are to liberate our fellow citizens.

The Roots of Injustice

One of the differences is the increased concentration of Negroes in our cities. More than 73 percent of all Negroes live in urban areas compared with less than 70 percent of the whites. Most of these Negroes live in slums. Most of them live together—a separated people. Men are shaped by their world. When it is a world of decay, ringed by an invisible wall—when escape is arduous and uncertain, and the saving pressures of a more hopeful society are unknown—it can cripple the youth and desolate the man.

There is also the burden that a dark skin can add to the search for a productive place in society. Unemployment strikes most swiftly and broadly at the Negro. This burden erodes hope. Blighted hope breeds despair. Despair brings indifference to the learning which offers a way out. And despair, coupled with indifference, is often the source of destructive rebellion against the fabric of society.

There is also the lacerating hurt of early collision with white hatred or prejudice, distaste, or condescension. Other groups have felt similar intolerance. But success and achievement could wipe it away. They do not change the color of a man's skin. I have seen this uncomprehending pain in the eyes of the little Mexican-American schoolchildren that I taught many years ago. It can be overcome. But, for many, the wounds are always open.

Family Breakdown

Perhaps most important—its influence radiating to every part of life—is the breakdown of the Negro family structure. For this, most of all, white America must accept responsibility. It flows from centuries of oppression and persecution of the Negro man. It flows from long years of degradation and discrimination, which have attacked his dignity and assaulted his ability to provide for his family.

This, too, is not pleasant to look upon. But it must be faced by those whose serious intent is to improve the life of all Americans.

Only a minority—less than half—of all Negro children reach the age of 18 having lived all their lives with both of their parents. At this moment little less than two-thirds are living with both of their parents. Probably a majority of all Negro children receive federally aided public assistance sometime during their childhood.

The family is the cornerstone of our society. More than any other force it shapes the attitude, the hopes, the ambitions, and the values of the child. When the family collapses it is the children that are usually damaged. When it happens on a massive scale the community itself is crippled.

So, unless we work to strengthen the family, to create conditions under which most parents will stay together—all the rest: schools and playgrounds, public assistance and private concern, will never be enough to cut completely the circle of despair and deprivation.

To Fulfill These Rights

There is no single easy answer to all of these problems.

Jobs are part of the answer. They bring the income which permits a man to provide for his family.

Decent homes in decent surroundings, and a chance to learn—an equal chance to learn—are part of the answer.

Welfare and social programs better designed to hold families together are part of the answer.

Care of the sick is part of the answer.

An understanding heart by all Americans is also a large part of the answer.

To all these fronts—and a dozen more—I will dedicate the expanding efforts of the Johnson Administration.

But there are other answers still to be found. Nor do we fully understand all of the problems. Therefore, I want to announce tonight that this fall I intend to call a White House conference of scholars, and experts, and outstanding Negro leaders—men of both races—and officials of government at every level.

This White House conference's theme and title will be "To Fulfill These Rights."

Its object will be to help the American Negro fulfill the rights which, after the long time of injustice, he is finally about to secure.

To move beyond opportunity to achievement.

To shatter forever not only the barriers of law and public practice, but the walls which bound the condition of man by the color of his skin.

To dissolve, as best we can, the antique enmities of the heart which diminish the holder, divide the great democracy, and do wrong—great wrong—to the children of God.

I pledge you tonight this will be a chief goal of my Administration, and of my program next year, and in years to come. And I hope, and I pray, and I believe, it will be a part of the program of all America.

What Is Justice

For what is justice?

It is to fulfill the fair expectations of man.

Thus, American justice is a very special thing. For, from the first, this has been a land of towering expectations. It was to be a nation where each man could be ruled by the common consent of all—enshrined in law, given life by institutions, guided by men themselves subject to its rule. And all—all of every station and origin—would be touched equally in obligation and in liberty.

Beyond the law lay the land. It was a rich land, glowing with more abundant promise than man had ever seen. Here, unlike any place yet known, all were to share the harvest.

And beyond this was the dignity of man. Each could become whatever his qualities of mind and spirit would permit—to strive, to seek, and, if he could, to find his happiness.

This is American justice. We have pursued it faithfully to the edge of our imperfections. And we have failed to find it for the American Negro.

It is the glorious opportunity of this generation to end the one huge wrong of the American Nation and, in so doing, to find America for ourselves, with the same immense thrill of discovery which gripped those who first began to realize that here, at last, was a home for freedom.

All it will take is for all of us to understand what this country is and what this country must become.

The Scripture promises: "I shall light a candle of understanding in thine heart, which shall not be put out."

Together, and with millions more, we can light that candle of understanding in the heart of all America.

And, once lit, it will never again go out.

James Baldwin

Stranger in the Village

From all available evidence no black man had ever set foot in this tiny Swiss village before I came. I was told before arriving that I would probably be a "sight" for the village; I took this to mean that people of my complexion were rarely seen in Switzerland, and also that city people are always something of a "sight" outside of the city. It did not occur to me—possibly because I am an American—that there could be people anywhere who had never seen a Negro.

It is a fact that cannot be explained on the basis of the inaccessibility of the village. The village is very high, but it is only four hours from Milan and three hours from Lausanne. It is true that it is virtually unknown. Few people making plans for a holiday would elect to come here. On the other hand, the villagers are able, presumably, to come and go as they please—which they do: to another town at the foot of the mountain, with a population of approximately five thousand, the nearest place to see a movie or go to the bank. In the village there is no movie house, no bank, no library, no theater; very few radios, one jeep, one station wagon; and, at the moment, one typewriter, mine, an invention which the woman next door to me here had never seen. There are about six hundred people living here, all Catholic—I conclude this from the fact that the Catholic church is open all year round, whereas the Protestant chapel, set off on a hill a little removed from the village, is open only in the summertime when the tourists arrive. There are four or five hotels, all closed now, and four or five *bistros*, of which, however, only two do any business during the winter. These two do not do any great deal, for life in the village seems to end around nine or ten o'clock. There are a few stores, butcher, baker, *épicerie*, a hardware store, and a money-changer—who cannot change travelers' checks, but must send them down to the bank, an operation which takes two or three days. There is something called the *Ballet Haus*, closed in the winter and used for God knows what, certainly not ballet, during the summer. There seems to be only one schoolhouse in the village, and this for the quite young children; I suppose this to mean that their older brothers and sisters at some point descend from these mountains in order to complete their education—possibly, again, to the town just below. The landscape is absolutely forbidding, mountains towering on all four sides, ice and snow as far as the eye can reach. In this white wilderness, men and women and children move all day, carrying washing, wood, buckets of milk or water, sometimes skiing on Sunday afternoons. All week long boys and young men are to be seen shoveling snow off the rooftops, or dragging wood down from the forest in sleds.

The village's only real attraction, which explains the tourist season, is the hot spring water. A disquietingly high proportion of these tourists are cripples, or semicripples, who come year after year—from other parts of Switzerland, usually—to take the waters. This lends the village, at the height of the season, a rather terrifying air of sanctity, as though it were a lesser Lourdes. There is often something beautiful, there is always something awful, in the spectacle of a person who has lost one of his faculties, a faculty he never questioned until it was gone, and who struggles to recover it. Yet people remain people, on crutches or indeed on deathbeds; and wherever I passed, the first summer I was here, among the native villagers or among the lame, a wind passed with me—of astonishment, curiosity, amusement, and outrage. That first summer I stayed two weeks and never intended to return. But I did return in the winter, to work; the village offers, obviously, no distractions whatever and has the further advantage of being extremely cheap. Now it is winter again, a year later, and I am here again. Everyone in the village knows my name, though they scarcely ever use it, knows that I come from America—though, this, apparently, they will never really believe: black men come from Africa—and everyone knows that I am the friend of the son of a woman who was born here, and that I am staying in their chalet. But I remain as much a stranger today as I was the first day I arrived, and the children shout *Neger! Neger!* as I walk along the streets.

It must be admitted that in the beginning I was far too shocked to have any real reaction. In so far as I reacted at all, I reacted by trying to be pleasant—it being a great part of the American Negro's education (long before he goes to school) that he must make people "like" him. This smile-and-the-world-smiles-with-you routine worked about as well in this situation as it had in the situation for which it was designed, which is to say that it did not work at all. No one, after all, can be liked whose human weight and complexity cannot be, or has not been, admitted. My smile was simply another unheard-of phenomenon which allowed them to see my teeth—they did not, really, see my smile and I began to think that, should I take to snarling, no one would notice any difference. All of the physical characteristics of the Negro which had caused me, in America, a very different and almost forgotten pain were nothing less than miraculous—or infernal—in the eyes of the village people. Some thought my hair was the color of tar, that it had the texture of wire, or the texture of cotton. It was jocularly suggested that I might let it all grow long and make myself a winter coat. If I sat in the sun for more than five minutes some daring creature was certain to come along and gingerly put his fingers on my hair, as though he were afraid of an electric shock, or put his hand on my hand, astonished that the color did not rub off. In all of this, in which it must be conceded there was the charm of genuine wonder and in which there was certainly no element of intentional unkindness, there was yet no suggestion that I was human: I was simply a living wonder.

I knew that they did not mean to be unkind, and I know it now; it is necessary, nevertheless, for me to repeat this to myself each time that I walk out of the chalet. The children who shout *Neger!* have no way of knowing the echoes this sound raises in me. They are brimming with good humor and the more daring swell with pride when I stop to speak with them. Just the same, there are days when I cannot pause and smile, when I have no heart to play with them; when, indeed, I mutter sourly to myself, exactly as I muttered on the streets of a city these children have never seen, when I was no bigger than these children are now: *Your*

mother *was a nigger*. Joyce is right about history being a nightmare—but it may be the nightmare from which no one *can* awaken. People are trapped in history and history is trapped in them.

There is a custom in the village—I am told it is repeated in many villages—of "buying" African natives for the purpose of converting them to Christianity. There stands in the church all year round a small box with a slot for money, decorated with a black figurine, and into this box the villagers drop their francs. During the *carnaval* which precedes Lent, two village children have their faces blackened—out of which bloodless darkness their blue eyes shine like ice—and fantastic horsehair wigs are placed on their blond heads; thus disguised, they solicit among the villagers for money for the missionaries in Africa. Between the box in the church and the blackened children, the village "bought" last year six or eight African natives. This was reported to me with pride by the wife of one of the *bistro* owners and I was careful to express astonishment and pleasure at the solicitude shown by the village for the souls of black folk. The *bistro* owner's wife beamed with a pleasure far more genuine than my own and seemed to feel that I might now breathe more easily concerning the souls of at least six of my kinsmen.

I tried not to think of these so lately baptized kinsmen, of the price paid for them, or the peculiar price they themselves would pay, and said nothing about my father, who having taken his own conversion too literally never, at bottom, forgave the white world (which he described as heathen) for having saddled him with a Christ in whom, to judge at least from their treatment of him, they themselves no longer believed. I thought of white men arriving for the first time in an African village, strangers there, as I am a stranger here, and tried to imagine the astounded populace touching their hair and marveling at the color of their skin. But there is a great difference between being the first white man to be seen by Africans and being the first black man to be seen by whites. The white man takes the astonishment as tribute, for he arrives to conquer and to convert the natives, whose inferiority in relation to himself is not even to be questioned; whereas I, without a thought of conquest, find myself among a people whose culture controls me, has even, in a sense, created me, people who have cost me more in anguish and rage than they will ever know, who yet do not even know of my existence. The astonishment with which I might have greeted them, should they have stumbled into my African village a few hundred years ago, might have rejoiced their hearts. But the astonishment with which they greet me today can only poison mine.

And this is so despite everything I may do to feel differently, despite my friendly conversations with the *bistro* owner's wife, despite their three-year-old son who has at last become my friend, despite the *saluts* and *bonsoirs* which I exchange with people as I walk, despite the fact that I know that no individual can be taken to task for what history is doing, or has done. I say that the culture of these people controls me—but they can scarcely be held responsible for European culture. America comes out of Europe, but these people have never seen America, nor have most of them seen more of Europe than the hamlet at the foot of their mountain. Yet they move with an authority which I shall never have; and they regard me, quite rightly, not only as a stranger in their village but as a suspect latecomer, bearing no credentials, to everything they have—however unconsciously—inherited.

For this village, even were it incomparably more remote and incredibly more primitive, is the West, the West onto which I have been so strangely grafted. These people cannot be, from the point of view of power, strangers anywhere in the world; they have made the modern world, in effect, even if they do not know it. The most illiterate among them is related, in a way that I am not, to Dante, Shakespeare, Michelangelo, Aeschylus, Da Vinci, Rembrandt, and Racine; the cathedral at Chartres says something to them which it cannot say to me, as indeed would New York's Empire State Building, should anyone here ever see it. Out of their hymns and dances come Beethoven and Bach. Go back a few centuries and they are in their full glory—but I am in Africa, watching the conquerors arrive.

The rage of the disesteemed is personally fruitless, but it is also absolutely inevitable; this rage, so generally discounted, so little understood even among the people whose daily bread it is, is one of the things that makes history. Rage can only with difficulty, and never entirely, be brought under the domination of the intelligence and is therefore not susceptible to any arguments whatever. This is a fact which ordinary representatives of the *Herrenvolk*, having never felt this rage and being unable to imagine it, quite fail to understand. Also, rage cannot be hidden, it can only be dissembled. This dissembling deludes the thoughtless, and strengthens rage and adds, to rage, contempt. There are, no doubt, as many ways of coping with the resulting complex of tensions as there are black men in the world, but no black man can hope ever to be entirely liberated from this internal warfare—rage, dissembling, and contempt having inevitably accompanied his first realization of the power of white men. What is crucial here is that, since white men represent in the black man's world so heavy a weight, white men have for black men a reality which is far from being reciprocal; and hence all black men have toward all white men an attitude which is designed, really, either to rob the white man of the jewel of his naïveté, or else to make it cost him dear.

The black man insists, by whatever means he finds at his disposal, that the white man cease to regard him as an exotic rarity and recognize him as a human being. This is a very charged and difficult moment, for there is a great deal of will power involved in the white man's naïveté. Most people are not naturally reflective any more than they are naturally malicious, and the white man prefers to keep the black man at a certain human remove because it is easier for him thus to preserve his simplicity and avoid being called to account for crimes committed by his forefathers, or his neighbors. He is inescapably aware, nevertheless, that he is in a better position in the world than black men are, nor can he quite put to death the suspicion that he is hated by black men therefore. He does not wish to be hated, neither does he wish to change places, and at this point in his uneasiness he can scarcely avoid having recourse to those legends which white men have created about black men, the most usual effect of which is that the white man finds himself enmeshed, so to speak, in his own language which describes hell, as well as the attributes which lead one to hell, as being as black as night.

Every legend, moreover, contains its residuum of truth, and the root function of language is to control the universe by describing it. It is of quite considerable significance that black men remain, in the imagination, and in overwhelming numbers in fact, beyond the disciplines of salvation; and this despite the fact that the West has been "buying" African natives for centuries. There is, I should hazard, an instantaneous necessity to be divorced from this so visibly unsaved stranger, in whose heart, moreover, one cannot guess what dreams of vengeance are being nourished; and, at the same time, there are few things on earth more attractive than the idea of the unspeakable liberty which is allowed the unredeemed. When, beneath the black mask, a human being begins to make himself felt one cannot escape a certain awful wonder as to what kind of human being it is. What one's imagination makes of other people is dictated, of course, by the laws of one's own personality and it is one of the ironies of black-white relations that, by means of what the white man imagines the black man to be, the black man is enabled to know who the white man is.

I have said, for example, that I am as much a stranger in this village today as I was the first summer I arrived, but this is not quite true. The villagers wonder less about the texture of my hair than they did then, and wonder rather more about me. And the fact that their wonder now exists on another level is reflected in their attitudes and in their eyes. There are the children who make those delightful, hilarious, sometimes astonishingly grave overtures of friendship in the unpredictable fashion of children; other children, having been taught that the devil is a black man, scream in genuine anguish as I approach. Some of the older women never pass without a friendly greeting, never pass, indeed, if it seems that they will be able to engage me in conversation; other women look down or look away or rather contemptuously smirk. Some of the men drink with me and suggest that I learn how to ski—partly, I gather, because they cannot imagine what I would look like on skis—and want to know if I am married, and ask questions about my *métier*. But some of the men have accused *le sale nègre*—behind my back—of stealing wood and there is already in the eyes of some of them that peculiar, intent, paranoiac malevolence which one sometimes surprises in the eyes of American white men when, out walking with their Sunday girl, they see a Negro male approach.

There is a dreadful abyss between the streets of this village and the streets of the city in which I was born, between the children who shout *Neger!* today and those who shouted *Nigger!* yesterday—the abyss is experience, the American experience. The syllable hurled behind me today expresses, above all, wonder: I am a stranger here. But I am not a stranger in America and the same syllable riding on the American air expresses the war my presence has occasioned in the American soul.

For this village brings home to me this fact: that there was a day, and not really a very distant day, when Americans were scarcely Americans at all but discontented Europeans, facing a great unconquered continent and strolling, say, into a marketplace and seeing black men for the first time. The shock this spectacle afforded is suggested, surely, by the promptness with which they decided that these black men were not really men but cattle. It is true that the necessity on the part of the settlers of the New World of reconciling their moral assumptions with the fact—and the necessity—of slavery enhanced immensely the charm of this idea, and it is also true that this idea expresses, with a truly American bluntness, the attitude which to varying extents all masters have had toward all slaves.

But between all former slaves and slave-owners and the drama which begins for Americans over three hundred years ago at Jamestown, there are at least two differences to be observed. The American Negro slave could not suppose, for one thing, as slaves in past epochs had supposed and often done that he would ever be able to wrest the power from his master's hands. This was a supposition which the modern era, which was to bring about such vast changes in the aims and dimensions of power, put to death; it only begins, in unprecedented fashion, and with dreadful implica-

tions, to be resurrected today. But even had this supposition persisted with undiminished force, the American Negro slave could not have used it to lend his condition dignity, for the reason that this supposition rests on another: that the slave in exile yet remains related to his past, has some means—if only in memory—of revering and sustaining the forms of his former life, is able, in short, to maintain his identity.

This was not the case with the American Negro slave. He is unique among the black men of the world in that his past was taken from him, almost literally, at one blow. One wonders what on earth the first slave found to say to the first dark child he bore. I am told that there are Haitians able to trace their ancestry back to African kings, but any American Negro wishing to go back so far will find his journey through time abruptly arrested by the signature on the bill of sale which served as the entrance paper for his ancestor. At the time—to say nothing of the circumstances—of the enslavement of the captive black man who was to become the American Negro, there was not the remotest possibility that he

James Baldwin (Courtesy of the Moorland-Spingarn Research Center)

would ever take power from his master's hands. There was no reason to suppose that his situation would ever change, nor was there, shortly, anything to indicate that his situation had ever been different. It was his necessity, in the words of E. Franklin Frazier, to find a "motive for living under American culture or die." The identity of the American Negro comes out of this extreme situation, and the evolution of this identity was a source of the most intolerable anxiety in the minds and the lives of his masters.

For the history of the American Negro is unique also in this: that the question of his humanity, and of his rights therefore as a human being, became a burning one for several generations of Americans, so burning a question that it ultimately became one of those used to divide the nation. It is out of this argument that the venom of the epithet *Nigger!* is derived. It is an argument which Europe has never had, and hence Europe quite sincerely fails to understand how or why the argument arose in the first place, why its effects are so frequently disastrous and always so unpredictable, why it refuses until today to be entirely settled. Europe's black possessions remained—and do remain—in Europe's colonies, at which remove they represented no threat whatever to European identity. If they posed any problem at all for the European conscience, it was a problem which remained comfortingly abstract: in effect, the black man, *as a man,* did not exist for Europe. But in America, even as a slave, he was an inescapable part of the general social fabric and no American could escape having an attitude toward him. Americans attempt until today to make an abstraction of the Negro, but the very nature of these abstractions reveals the tremendous effects the presence of the Negro has had on the American character.

When one considers the history of the Negro in America it is of the greatest importance to recognize that the moral beliefs of a person, or a people, are never really as tenuous as life—which is not moral—very often causes them to appear; these create for them a frame of reference and a necessary hope, the hope being that when life has done its worst they will be enabled to rise above themselves and to triumph over life. Life would scarcely be bearable if this hope did not exist. Again, even when the worst has been said, to betray a belief is not by any means to have put oneself beyond its power; the betrayal of a belief is not the same thing as ceasing to believe. If this were not so there would be no moral standards in the world at all. Yet one must also recognize that morality is based on ideas and that all ideas are dangerous—dangerous because ideas can only lead to action and where the action leads no man can say. And dangerous in this respect: that confronted with the impossibility of remaining faithful to one's beliefs, and the equal impossibility of becoming free of them, one can be driven to the most inhuman excesses. The ideas on which American beliefs are based are not, though Americans often seem to think so, ideas which originated in America. They came out of Europe. And the establishment of democracy on the American continent was scarcely as radical a break with the past as was the necessity, which Americans faced, of broadening this concept to include black men.

This was, literally, a hard necessity. It was impossible, for one thing, for Americans to abandon their beliefs, not only because these beliefs alone seemed able to justify the sacrifices they had endured and the blood that they had spilled, but also because these beliefs afforded them their only bulwark against a moral chaos as absolute as the physical chaos of the continent it was their destiny to conquer. But in the situation in which Americans found themselves, these beliefs threatened an idea which, whether or not one likes to think so, is the very warp and woof of the heritage of the West, the idea of white supremacy.

Americans have made themselves notorious by the shrillness and the brutality with which they have insisted on this idea, but they did not invent it; and it has escaped the world's notice that those very excesses of which Americans have been guilty imply a certain, unprecedented uneasiness over the idea's life and power, if not, indeed, the idea's validity. The idea of white supremacy rests simply on the fact that white men are the creators of civilization (the present civilization, which is the only one that matters; all previous civilizations are simply "contributions" to our own) and are therefore civilization's guardians and defenders. Thus it was impossible for Americans to accept the black man as one of themselves, for to do so was to jeopardize their status as white men. But not so to accept him was to deny his human reality, his human weight and complexity, and the strain of denying the overwhelmingly undeniable forced Americans into rationalizations so fantastic that they approached the pathological.

At the root of the American Negro problem is the necessity of the American white man to find a way of living with the Negro in order to be able to live with himself. And the history of this problem can be reduced to the means used by Americans—lynch law and law, segregation and legal acceptance, terrorization and concession—either to come to terms with this necessity, or to find a way around it, or (most usually) to find a way of doing both these things at once. The resulting spectacle, at once foolish and dreadful, led someone to make the quite accurate observation that "the Negro-in-America is a form of insanity which overtakes white men."

In this long battle, a battle by no means finished, the unforeseeable effects of which will be felt by many future generations, the white man's motive was the protection of his identity; the black man was motivated by the need to establish an identity. And despite the terrorization which the Negro in America endured and endures sporadically until today, despite the cruel and totally inescapable ambivalence of his status in his country, the battle for his identity has long ago been won. He is not a visitor to the West, but a citizen there, an American; as American as the Americans who despise him, the Americans who fear him, the Americans who love him—the Americans who became less than themselves, or rose to be greater than themselves by virtue of the fact that the challenge he represented was inescapable. He is perhaps the only black man in the world whose relationship to white men is more terrible, more subtle, and more meaningful than the relationship of bitter possessed to uncertain possessor. His survival depended, and his development depends, on his ability to turn his peculiar status in the Western world to his own advantage and, it may be, to the very great advantage of that world. It remains for him to fashion out of his experience that which will give him sustenance, and a voice.

The cathedral at Chartres, I have said, says something to the people of this village which it cannot say to me; but it is important to understand that this cathedral says something to me which it cannot say to them. Perhaps they are struck by the power of the spires, the glory of the windows; but they have known God, after all, longer than I have known him, and in a different way, and I am terrified by the slippery bottomless well to be found in the crypt, down which heretics were hurled to death, and by the obscene, inescapable gargoyles jutting out of the stone and seeming to say that God and the devil can never be divorced. I doubt that the villagers think of the devil when they face a cathedral because they have never been identified with the devil. But I must accept the status which myth, if nothing else, gives me in the West before I can hope to change the myth.

Yet, if the American Negro has arrived at his identity by virtue of the absoluteness of his estrangement from his past, American white men still nourish the illusion that there is some means of recovering the European innocence, of returning to a state in which black men do not exist. This is one of the greatest errors Americans can make. The identity they fought so hard to protect has, by virtue of that battle, undergone a change: Americans are as unlike any other white people in the world as it is possible to be. I do not think, for example, that it is too much to suggest that the American vision of the world—which allows so little

reality, generally speaking, for any of the darker forces in human life, which tends until today to paint moral issues in glaring black and white—owes a great deal to the battle waged by Americans to maintain between themselves and black men a human separation which could not be bridged. It is only now beginning to be borne in on us—very faintly, it must be admitted, very slowly, and very much against our will—that this vision of the world is dangerously inaccurate, and perfectly useless. For it protects our moral high-mindedness at the terrible expense of weakening our grasp of reality. People who shut their eyes to reality simply invite their own destruction, and anyone who insists on remaining in a state of innocence long after that innocence is dead turns himself into a monster.

The time has come to realize that the interracial drama acted out on the American continent has not only created a new black man, it has created a new white man, too. No road whatever will lead Americans back to the simplicity of this European village where white men still have the luxury of looking on me as a stranger. I am not, really, a stranger any longer for any American alive. One of the things that distinguishes Americans from other people is that no other people has ever been so deeply involved in the lives of black men, and vice versa. This fact faced, with all its implications, it can be seen that the history of the American Negro problem is not merely shameful, it is also something of an achievement. For even when the worst has been said, it must also be added that the perpetual challenge posed by this problem was always, somehow, perpetually met. It is precisely this black-white experience which may prove of indispensable value to us in the world we face today. This world is white no longer, and it will never be white again.

AMIRI BARAKA

The Negro as Non-American: Some Backgrounds

When black people got to this country, they were Africans, a foreign people. Their customs, attitudes, desires, were shaped to a different place, a radically different life. What a weird and unbelievably cruel destiny for those people who were first brought here. Not just the mere fact of being sold into slavery—that in itself was common practice among the tribes of West Africa, and the economic system in which these new slaves were to form so integral a part was not so strange either. In fact, Melville Herskovits points out, "Slavery [had] long existed in the entire region [of

West Africa], and in at least one of its kingdoms, Dahomey, a kind of plantation system was found under which an absentee ownership, with the ruler as principal, demanded the utmost return from the estates, and thus created conditions of labor resembling the regime the slaves were to encounter in the New World."[1] But to be brought to a country, a culture, a society, that was, and is, in terms of purely philosophical correlatives, the complete antithesis of one's own version of man's life on earth—that is the cruelest aspect of this particular enslavement.

An African who was enslaved by Africans, or for that matter, a Western white man who was, or is, enslaved by another Western white man can still function as a kind of human being. An economic cipher perhaps, even subject to unmentionable cruelties—but that man, even as the lowest and most despised member of the community, remains an essential part and member of whatever community he is enslaved in; the idea being, even if an African from the Guinea Coast is sold or beaten into slavery by an African from the Gold Coast, there continues to exist, at the very least, some understanding that what the victor has reduced into whatever cruel bondage is a man—another human being. There remains some condition of communication on strictly human terms between Babylonian and Israelite or Assyrian and Chaldean that allows finally for acceptance of the slave caste as merely an economically oppressed group. To the Romans, slaves were merely vulgar and conquered peoples who had not the rights of Roman citizenship. The Greeks thought of their slaves as unfortunate people who had failed to cultivate their minds and wills, and were thus reduced to that lowly but necessary state. But these slaves were still human beings. However, the African who was unfortunate enough to find himself on some fast clipper ship to the New World was not even accorded membership in the human race.

From the actress Frances Anne Kemble's *Journal of a Residence on a Georgia Plantation:* "The only exception that I have met with yet among our boat voices to the high tenor which they seem all to possess is in the person of an individual named Isaac, a basso profundo of the deepest dye, who nevertheless never attempts to produce with his different register any different effects in the chorus by venturing a second, but sings like the rest in unison, perfect unison, of both time and tune. By-the-by, this individual *does* speak, and therefore I presume he is not an ape, orangoutang, chimpanzee, or gorilla; but I could not, I confess, have conceived it possible that the presence of articulate sounds, and the ab-

sence of an articulate tail, should make, externally at least, so completely the only appreciable difference between a man and a monkey, as they appear to do in this individual 'black brother.' Such stupendous long thin hands, and long flat feet, I did never see off a large quadruped of the ape species. But, as I said before, Isaac speaks, and I am much comforted thereby."[2]

There was no communication between master and slave on any strictly human level, but only the relation one might have to a piece of property—if you twist the knob on your radio you expect it to play. It was this essential condition of nonhumanity that characterized the African slave's lot in this country of his captivity, a country which was later and ironically to become *his land* also.

Perhaps more weight will be added to the idea of the foreignness of the African in the New World if we consider that not only were the Africans completely different in appearance from their captors, but there was not even a semblance of similarity between the various dialects those Africans spoke and colonial English. In Greece, there were slaves who taught Greek children their grammar and conducted classes in botany, as well as performing more menial tasks. The Romans employed slaves in the theater, in gladiatorial combats, and utilized the highly-educated foreign slaves as instructors. Epictetus, Terence, and Phaedrus were slaves. But the black slave in America had no chance for such intelligent diversion based on his skills or prominence in his own country. The African's sole purpose in America was, for the most part, to provide the cheapest agricultural labor possible to procure. Any deviation from this purpose was either accidental or extremely rare. (Even such a normal phenomenon as the "house nigra" was nonexistent on the smaller farms; on the larger plantation there were only one or two. Sometimes the house slave was merely the oldest or most infirm member of the owner's retinue; even after the advent of the African slave, for some time house servants on the larger plantations were indentured white persons.)

It is certain that it was this foreignness and the reluctance of the white American to think of the African as another *man* that helped early to fix the African's, and later the Afro-American's, place in American society—just as the color of the African's skin set him apart from the rest of the society blatantly and permanently. A freed serf, if he was lucky, could hope at least to matriculate into the lower rungs of the general society and perhaps find some genuine niche in the mainstream of that society in which to function as a *citizen*, a man. But the African,

---

[1]*The Myth of the Negro Past* (Boston, Beacon Press, 1941), p. 62.

[2]*Journal of a Residence on a Georgia Plantation in 1838–1839* (New York, Alfred A. Knopf, 1961), p. 260.

and later even the freed black, was always apart. A freed Negro, and there were quite a few of them even before the so-called Emancipation, would always remain an *ex-slave*. Otherwise, what was he doing in this country?

I mentioned before that colonial America was the complete antithesis of the African's version of human existence. This idea seems to me one of the most important aspects of the enslavement of the African: the radically different, even opposing, *Weltanschauung's* which the colonial American and the African brought to each other. Each man, in whatever "type" of culture he inhabits, must have a way of looking at the world—whatever that means to him—which is peculiar to his particular culture. It is extremely important to understand that these diametrically opposed interpretations of life would be in conflict normally in the most minute human contacts. But when a man who sees the world one way becomes the slave of a man who interprets the world in an exactly opposite way, the result is, to my mind, the *worst* possible kind of slavery.

Colonial America was the country of the new *post-Renaissance* man, the largest single repository for *humanism* in the New World. It witnessed the complete emergence of secular man. The Church and religion had become only a part of a man's life. They were no longer, as in the pre-Renaissance Western World, the one reason for man's existence. The idea that came through in the Renaissance and took hold of the West was that life was no mere anteroom for something greater or divine. Life itself was of value—and could be made *perfect*. And if mysticism and the religious attitude were greatly weakened in Renaissance Europe, they were almost completely negated in the New World. If the England of Henry VIII was the beginning of the superiority of the "economic mind," as Brooks Adams says, the American colonies, and especially the English-speaking colonies, certainly demonstrated the ascendancy of this new species. The exaltation of secular man and man's life on earth, which we have called humanism, was responsible for the colonies and was the most salient characteristic of the *Weltanschauung* of the colonists. Only the Catholic countries conquered in the name of the Christian Church—which was largely a credo of convenience. The North American settlements were *strictly* economic enterprises, with the possible exception of the Pilgrims'.

Wars before the Renaissance were usually "holy" wars where one faith, sect, religion, would try to extend its beliefs in all directions throughout the known world. The Crusades, even admitting the hypocrisy and opportunism of the Christians, and the prostitution of Christianity in such debacles as the sack of Constantinople, etc., were still, in essence, "holy" wars.

The only other kind of war before the Renaissance was waged for the acquisition of more arable land, or any land that seemed more fertile to the conquerors, *viz.,* the Huns, or Genghis Khan. But the advent of Renaissance thought and the subsequent accumulation of monetary wealth in cities made war a strictly commercial enterprise. With the rise to prominence of the store-keeping class, war became one way to simplify bookkeeping, or at least to keep certain markets exclusive. The straw that broke the camel's back and sent the American colonists scrambling headlong for independence from Great Britain was *an excessive tax on dry goods*. Instead of "The Will of [our] God Must Be Done," the rallying cry for a war could be "No Taxation Without Representation."

I am stressing so emphatically the socio-economic psychological disposition of the colonial American only to set in full contrast the opposing *Weltanschauung* of the African. I believe that this drastic opposition of world-view contributed importantly not only to the attitude of the Americans to the African slaves but just as certainly to the *final* place of the Africans' descendants in the various societies of the New World.

So-called nonliterate peoples (called by Western man "primitive"), whose languages, and therefore whose cultural and traditional histories, are not written, are the antithesis of Western man and his highly industrialized civilization. But the idea of the "primordial man," or "undeveloped peoples," becomes absurd if we dismiss for a change the assumption that only the ideas and attitudes which the West finds useful or analogous to concepts forwarded within its own system are of any real value or profundity. For instance, a highly organized society predicated on the existence of mystical, omniscient superior beings who are in complete control of the lives and fates of all humans might seem a trifle "primitive" if viewed through the eyes of a society whose existence is predicated on exactly opposite hypotheses. That is, the *goals* or "canons of satisfaction," as T. E. Hulme called them, of a culture with complex concepts of predetermination and the subservience of the human being to a complex of gods cannot easily be understood by a culture which forwards the "ultimate happiness of mankind" as the sole purpose of the universe. And the cruelty of such ignorance when contained within the already terrifying circumstance of slavery should be readily apparent. The most profound concepts and beliefs of one culture become merely *absurd* fancies for the other. The cult of man must view the cult of the divine as absurd. Where the Renaissance cliché "Man is the measure" is the most salient attitude, the idea that "man is only a pawn of the gods" is ugly if looked at distantly, "childish" if one must deal with it intimately.

I am re-emphasizing what men like Hulme and Herskovits have pointed out in diverse ways a long time ago—that reference determines value. My only addition is that in a situation like slavery, and especially the enslavement of the West Africans by the American colonists, this concept is especially useful. Americans brought slaves to their country who were not only physical and environmental aliens but products of a completely alien philosophical system.

One of the main points of the Herskovits book is that most of the attitudes, customs, and cultural characteristics of the American Negro can be traced directly, or indirectly, back to Africa. And while I am inclined to accept this view, with whatever reservations my individual concepts propose, I would also have to insist that the African, because of the violent differences between what was native and what he was forced to in slavery, developed some of the most complex and complicated ideas about the world imaginable. Afro-Americans (by whom I mean the first few generations of American-born black people, who still retained a great many *pure* Africanisms), and later, American Negroes, inherited all these complexities with, of course, whatever individual nuances were dictated by their particular lives. But the ugly fact that the Africans were forced into an alien world where none of the references or cultural shapes of any familiar human attitudes were available is the determinant of the *kind* of existence they had to eke out here: not only slavery itself but the particular circumstances in which it existed. The African cultures, the retention of some parts of these cultures in America, and the *weight* of the stepculture produced the American Negro. A new race. I want to use music as my persistent reference just because the development and transmutation of African music to American Negro music (a *new* music) represents to me this whole process in microcosm.

Herskovits also points out that most of the "myths" about the Negro past were formed by the new masters' refusal to understand that the Africans were not governed by the same mores and culture references as Western man, that they had come from an alien land and culture. But one of the most persistent traits of the Western white man has always been his fanatical and almost instinctive assumption that his systems and ideas about the world are the most desirable, and further, that people who do not aspire to them, or at least think them admirable, are *savages* or *enemies*. The idea that Western thought might be *exotic* if viewed from another landscape never presents itself to most Westerners. As rulers of the world or as owners of these black people, they, Americans, were certainly in a position to declare that all thought outside their

known systems was at least "backward." But a Byzantine man *could not* understand the existence of a structure like the Empire State Building that was not erected to praise Jehovah. What made the American most certain that he was "superior" to the African (aside from the fact that the African *was* his slave)—as self-righteously certain as Cortez and his *conquistadores* when they had, in the name of Spain, the King, and their Spanish God, reduced to abject slavery the "heathen" race of Montezuma and brought to a horrifying end one of the longest-lived, most sophisticated and exalted traditions of human life on this planet—was the foreignness of African culture. This came to be the African's chief liability in the New World: in the context of slavery, the most undesirable attitudes the foreign slave and his many generations of American-born offspring could possess. In fact, twentieth-century American society finds many of these same offspring denying any connection with this culture, in what may seem to most Americans a perfectly natural attempt to dive headlong into and immerse themselves completely in the tepid safety of the mainstream of contemporary America.

But quite aside from any talk of what is known as complete "assimilation," which I think is *still* an imagined rather than a real concept, what seems most pertinent to the ideas I want to advance are Herskovits' thrusts at the question of "how, in the contact of Africans with Europeans and American Indians, cultural accommodation and cultural integration had been achieved."[3]

When a Yoruba tribesman from Dahomey, who thought that "the universe is ruled by fate and the destiny of each man worked out according to a predetermined scheme," but that "there were ways of escape through invoking the good will of the god," was enslaved and began to be reshaped by a philosophy that attributed all glory to the mind of man, what was the result? When the concept of "deification of Accident in a universe where predetermination is the rule" is thrown against the concept of a world where all things are explainable and the result of "rational processes," something emerges that must contain both ideas. Not immediately, but gradually. It is absurd to assume, as has been the tendency, among a great many Western anthropologists and sociologists, that all traces of Africa were erased from the Negro's mind because he learned English. The very nature of the English the Negro spoke and still speaks drops the lie on that idea. An idea like the attribution of an "innate and natural fear" (of everything) to Negroes must, as Herskovits

[3]*Op. cit.*, p. 62.

inferred, be given the same environment as its origin. The African's belief in the supernatural was carried over into the life of the American slave. The retort to the Western derision of the African's "fear" of the supernatural is simply that the white man conducts his life without thought to the gods. If the former idea seemed "childish" to the master, the latter idea seemed extremely dangerous to the slave. So one man becomes a child, and the other a fool.

"You are black . . . which means you lived too close to the sun. Black is evil." "You are white . . . which means you lived too far from the sun. You have no color . . . no soul." These are equally logical arguments. The twist is that if you are black and believe in the supernatural, and are issued from an ecological determinant that does not permit of such a psychological extreme as American Puritanism (which, said William Carlos Williams, is a "thing, strange, inhuman, powerful, like a relic of some died out tribe whose practices were revolting"), the circumstance of finding yourself in a culture of white humanist pseudo-Puritanical storekeepers must be revolting. And if you are the slave of such a culture, your sorrow must be indeterminable.

The Negro as Property

It is extremely important in a "study" of any aspect of the history of the American Negro to emphasize how strange and unnatural the initial contacts with Western slavery were for the African, in order to show how the black man was set apart throughout the New World from the start. This should enable one to begin to appreciate the amazing, albeit agonizing, transformation that produced the contemporary black American from such a people as were first bound and brought to this country.

Sociologists are always making fearsome analogies between minorities regarding their *acculturation* in this country (usually when confronted by, say, statistics on how many of the total crimes committed in any given year are attributable to Negroes). They claim that each one of the "newcomers" (a euphemism for "furriners") shows parallel development in the race toward ultimate Americanization. They say, flaunting their statistics, "See how, after such and such time, the sons and daughters of the once-despised Irish immigrants moved into genteel middle-class social respectability." So, with the Italians, they point out the decrease in crimes "directly attributable to persons of

Italian extraction" after enough time had passed to enable this minority also to enter into the mainstream of American life. And certainly, there are some analogies to be made between minority groups who have, since their initial removal to this country from their homelands, edged out from their first ghetto existences into the promise and respectability of this brave New World. But no such strict analogy will serve for Afro-Americans. There are too many aspects of these "newcomers' " existence in America that will not sit still under those kinds of statistics.

First of all, we know that of all the peoples who form the heterogeneous yet almost completely homogenous mass that makes up the United States population, Negroes are the only descendants of people who were not happy to come here. The African was brought to this country in bondage and remained in bondage more than two hundred and fifty years. But most of the black people who were freed from formal slavery in 1865 *were not* Africans. They were Americans. And whether or not we choose to characterize the post-Emancipation existence of Negroes in the United States as "freedom," we must still appreciate the idea that a group of people who became familiar with the mores, attitudes, language, and other culture references of this country while being enslaved by it cannot be seen as analogous to peoples who move toward complete assimilation of these same mores by *choice*, even though these peoples are also despised by the "natives" of the country as "furriners." The African as slave was one idea, *i.e.,* these people from another country were brought to this country against their wills. But the American-born slaves offer a less easily defined situation.

The first-born of these Africans in America knew about Africa only through the stories, tales, riddles, and songs of their older relatives. But usually the children born in this country were separated from their African parents. No mother could be sure she would see her child after it was weaned. The American-born African children were much prized, and the masters had to exercise extreme care that the women didn't do away with these children to save them from the ugliness of slavery. (Many African mothers smothered their first-born American children, and the owners thought this was the result of carelessness, or callousness, characteristic of "savages.") These children also had to learn about slavery, but there were no centuries of culture to unlearn, or old long-held habits to suppress. The only way of life these children knew was the accursed thing they had been born into.

If we think about the importation of Africans into the New World as a whole, rather than strictly into the United States, the most apparent difference that can be seen is that Africans throughout the rest of the Americas were much slower to become Westernized and "acculturated." All over the New World there are still examples of pure African traditions that have survived three hundred years of slavery and four hundred years of removal from their source. "Africanisms" are still part of the lives of Negroes throughout the New World, in varying degrees, in places like Haiti, Brazil, Cuba, Guiana. Of course, attitudes and customs of the noncontinental Negroes were lost or assumed other less apparent forms, but still the amount of pure Africanisms that have been retained is amazing. However, in the United States, Africanisms in American Negroes are not now readily discernible, although they certainly do exist. It was in the United States only that the slaves were, after a few generations, unable to retain any of the more obvious of African traditions. Any that were retained were usually submerged, however powerful their influence, in less recognizable manifestations. So after only a few generations in the United States an almost completely different individual could be born and be rightly called an American Negro.

Herskovits says about this phenomenon: "The contact between Negroes and whites in continental United States as compared to the West Indies and South America goes far to explain the relatively greater incidence of Africanisms in the Caribbean. In the earliest days, the number of slaves in proportion to their masters was extremely small, and though as time went on thousands and tens of thousands of slaves were brought to satisfy the demands of the southern plantations, nonetheless the Negroes lived in constant association with whites to a degree not found anywhere else in the New World. That the Sea Islands off the Carolina and Georgia coast offer the most striking retention of Africanisms to be encountered in the United States is to be regarded as but a reflection of the isolation of these Negroes when compared to those on the mainland."[1]

Some of this "constant association" between the white masters and the black slaves that took place in this country can be explained by comparing the circumstances of the slaves' "employment" in America with the circumstances of their employment in the rest of the New World. It was only in the United States that slaves were used on the smaller farms. Such a person as the "poor white" was a strictly American phenomenon. To turn again to Herskovits: "Matters were quite different in the Caribbean islands and in South America. Here racial numbers were far more disproportionate; estates where a single family ruled dozens, if not

hundreds, of slaves were commonplace and the 'poor white' was found so seldom that he receives only cursory mention . . . The white man with but a few slaves was likewise seldom encountered."[2]

But in the United States, the Utopia of the small businessman, the small farmer was the rule, rather than the exception, and these farmers could usually afford to own only a very small number of slaves.

On these small farms intimate contact between master and slave was unavoidable (I will just mention here the constant extra-curricular sexual activities that were forced on the slave women by their white masters). In 1863, Frederick Olmstead reported: "The more common sort of habitations of the white people are either of logs or loosely-boarded frame, a brick chimney running up outside, at one end; and black and white children, are commonly lying very promiscuously together, on the ground about the doors. I am struck with the close co-habitation and association of black and white—negro women are carrying black and white babies together in their arms; black and white children are playing together [not going to school together]; black and white faces constantly thrust together out of doors to see the train go by."[3] One result of this intimacy between the poorer master and his slaves was, of course, the invention of still another kind of Afro-American, the mulatto. But certainly the most significant result was the rapid acculturation of the African in this country. With no native or tribal references, except perhaps the stories of his elders and the performance of nonreligious dances and songs, the American-born slave had only the all-encompassing mores of his white master. Africa had become a foreign land, and none of the American-born slaves could ever hope to see it.

A graph could be set up to show just exactly what aspects of African culture suffered most and were most rapidly suppressed by this constant contact with Euro-American culture. It is certainly immediately apparent that all forms of political and economic thought, which were two of the most profound sophistications of African culture, were suppressed immediately. The extremely intricate political, social, and economic systems of the West Africans were, of course, done away with completely in their normal manifestations. The much praised "legal genius" that produced one of the strictest and most sophisticated legal systems known could not function, except very informally, in the cotton fields of America. The technology of the Africans, iron-working, wood-carving, weaving, etc., died out

---

[1] *Op. cit.*, p. 120.

[2] *Ibid.*, p. 121.

[3] *A Journey in the Seabord Slave States* (New York, 1863), p. 17.

quickly in the United States. Almost every material aspect of African culture took a new less obvious form or was wiped out altogether. (The famous wood sculpture of the Yoruba could not possibly have fallen into an area less responsive to its beauties than colonial America. The artifact was, like any other material manifestation of pure African culture, doomed. It is strange to realize that even in the realm of so-called high culture, Western highbrows have only in this century begun to think of African, Pre-Columbian, and Egyptian art, as well as the art of other pre-literate and/or "primitive" cultures, as art rather than archaeology. Of course, nowadays, it is a must in the home of any Westerner who pays homage to the arts to include in his collection of *objets d'art* at least a few African, Egyptian, and Pre-Columbian pieces.)

Only religion (and magic) and the arts were not completely submerged by Euro-American concepts. Music, dance, religion, do not have *artifacts* as their end products, so they were saved. These nonmaterial aspects of the African's culture were almost impossible to eradicate. And these are the most apparent legacies of the African past, even to the contemporary black American. But to merely point out that blues, jazz, and the Negro's adaptation of the Christian religion all rely heavily on African culture takes no great amount of original thinking. How these activities derive from that culture is what remains important.

African Slaves/American Slaves: Their Music

It is a comparatively short period of history that passes between the time, when Richard Francis Burton could say of African music that "it is monotonous to a degree, yet they delight in it," or when H. E. Krehbiel could ask (1914), "Why savages who have never developed a musical or other art should be supposed to have more refined aesthetic sensibilities than the peoples who have cultivated music for centuries, passes my poor powers of understanding . . ."[1] until the time (1920) when a great mass of white Americans are dancing a West African (Ashanti) ancestor dance they know as the "Charleston."

---

[1] H. E. Krehbiel, *Afro-American Folksongs* (New York, Schirmer, 1914), p. 73.

Jazz is commonly thought to have begun around the turn of the century, but the musics jazz derived from are much older. Blues is the parent of all legitimate jazz, and it is impossible to say exactly how old blues is—certainly no older than the presence of Negroes in the United States. It is a native American music, the product of the black man in this country: or to put it more exactly the way I have come to think about it, blues could not exist if the African captives had not become American captives.

The immediate predecessors of blues were the Afro-American/American Negro work songs, which had their music origins in West Africa. The religious music of the Negro also originates from the same African music. However, while the general historical developments of Negro secular and religious music can be said to be roughly parallel, *i.e.*, they follow the same general trends in their development, and in later forms are the result of the same kind of accultural processes, a Negro religious music contingent on Christianity developed later than the secular forms. An Afro-American work song could come about more quickly in slavery than any other type of song because even if the individual who sang it was no longer working for himself, most of the physical impetuses that suggested that particular type of singing were still present. However, Africans were not Christians, so their religious music and the music with which they celebrated the various cultic or ritualistic rites had to undergo a distinct and complete transfer of reference.

For the African in the United States there was little opportunity for religious syncretism (the identification of one set of religious dogma or ritual with analogous dogma or ritual in a completely alien religion). In the essentially Catholic New World cultures, the multitudes of saints were easily substituted for the many *loa* or deities in the various West African religions. But in Protestant America this was not possible.

So the music which formed the *link* between pure African music and the music which developed after the African slave in the United States had had a chance to become exposed to some degree of Euro-American culture was that which contained the greatest number of Africanisms and yet was foreign to Africa. And this was the music of the second generation of slaves, their work songs. The African slave had sung African chants and litanies in those American fields. His sons and daughters, and their children, began to use America as a reference.

As late as the nineteenth century, pure African songs could be heard and pure African dances seen in the Southern United States. Congo Square, in New Orleans, would nightly rock to the "master drums" of new African arrivals. In places like Haiti or Guiana, these drums still do remind the West that the black man came from Africa, not Howard University. But in the United States pure African sources grew scarce in a relatively short time after the great slave importations of the eighteenth century.

The work song took on its own peculiar qualities in America for a number of reasons. First, although singing to accompany one's labor was quite common in West Africa, it is obvious that working one's own field in one's own land is quite different from forced labor in a foreign land. And while the physical insistence necessary to suggest a work song was still present, the references accompanying the work changed radically. Most West Africans were farmers and, I am certain, these agricultural farm songs could have been used in the fields of the New World in the same manner as the Old. But the lyrics of a song that said, "After the planting, if the gods bring rain,/My family, my ancestors, be rich as they are beautiful," could not apply in the dreadful circumstance of slavery. Secondly, references to the gods or religions of Africa were suppressed by the white masters as soon as they realized what these were—not only because they naturally thought of any African religious customs as "barbarous" but because the whites soon learned that too constant evocation of the African gods could mean that those particular Africans were planning on leaving that plantation as soon as they could! The use of African drums was soon prevented too, as the white man learned that drums could be used to incite revolt as well as to accompany dancers.

So the work song, as it began to take shape in America, first had to be stripped of any purely African ritual and some cultural reference found for it in the New World. But this was difficult to do within the African-language songs themselves. The diverse labors of the African, which were the sources of this kind of song, had been funneled quite suddenly into one labor, the cultivation of the white man's fields. The fishing songs, the weaving songs, the hunting songs, all had lost their pertinence. But these changes were not immediate. They became the realized circumstances of a man's life after he had been exposed sufficiently to their source and catalyst—his enslavement.

And this is the basic difference between the first slaves and their offspring. The African slave continued to chant his native chants, sing his native songs, at work, even though the singing of them might be forbidden or completely out of context. But being forbidden, the songs were after a time changed into other forms that weren't forbidden in contexts that were contemporary. The African slave might have realized he was losing something, that his customs and the memory of his land were being each day drained from his life. Still

there was a certain amount of forbearance. No one can simply decree that a man change the way he thinks. But the first black Americans had no native cultural references other than the slave culture. A work song about fishing when one has never fished seems meaningless, especially when one works each day in a cotton field. The context of the Africans' life had changed, but the American-born slaves never knew what the change had been.

It is impossible to find out exactly how long the slaves were in America before the African work song actually did begin to have extra-African references. First, of course, there were mere additions of the foreign words—French, Spanish or English, for the most part, after the British colonists gained power in the United States. Krehbiel lists a Creole song transcribed by Lafcadio Hearn, which contains both French (or patois) and African words (the italicized words are African):

Ouendé, ouendé, macaya!
  Mo pas barrasse, *macaya!*
Ouendé, ouendé, macaya!
  Mo bois bon divin, *macaya!*
Ouendé, ouendé, macaya!
  Mo mange bon poulet, *macaya!*
Ouendé, ouendé, macaya!
  Mo pas barrasse, *macaya!*
Ouendé, ouendé, macaya!
        Macaya!

Hearn's translation was:

Go on! go on! eat enormously!
  I ain't one bit ashamed—*eat outrageously!*
Go on! go on! eat prodigiously!
  I drink good wine!—*eat ferociously!*
Go on! go on! eat unceasingly!
  I eat good chicken—*gorging myself!*
Go on! go on! etc.

It is interesting to note, and perhaps more than coincidence, that the portions of the song emphasizing excess are in African, which most of the white men could not understand, and the portions of the song elaborating some kind of genteel, if fanciful, existence are in the tongue of the masters. But there was to come a time when there was no black man who understood the African either, and those allusions to excess, or whatever the black man wished to keep to himself, were either in the master's tongue or meaningless, albeit rhythmical, sounds to the slave also.

Aside from the actual transfer or survival of African words in the songs and speech of the early slaves, there was also some kind of syntactical as well as rhythmical transfer since Africans and their descendants tended to speak their new languages in the same manner as they spoke their West African dialects. What is called now a "Southern accent" or "Negro speech" was once simply the accent of a foreigner trying to speak a new and unfamiliar language, although it was characteristic of the white masters to attribute the slave's "inability" to speak perfect English to the same kind of "childishness" that was used to explain the African's belief in the supernatural. The owners, when they bothered to listen, were impressed that even the songs of their native American slaves were "incomprehensible" or "unintelligible." However, as Herskovits says of early Afro-American speech:

"... since grammar and idiom are the last aspects of a new language to be learned, the Negroes who reached the New World acquired as much of the vocabulary of their masters as they initially needed or was later taught to them, pronounced these words as best they were able, but organized them into aboriginal speech patterns. Thus arose the various forms of Negro-English, Negro-French, Negro-Spanish and Negro-Portugese spoken in the New World, their "peculiarities" due to the fact that they comprise European words cast into an African grammatical mold. But this emphatically does not imply that those dialects are without grammar, or that they represent an inability to master the foreign tongue, as is so often claimed."[2]

A few of the "unintelligible" songs are not as unintelligible as their would-be interpreters would have it. For instance, Mr. Krehbiel lists as unintelligible two "corn songs"—songs sung while working the corn fields. Only a fragment of one song remains, the words "Shock along, John." It seems to me incredible that Krehbiel could not see that *shock* is the word *shuck*, meaning to strip the corn of its outer covering, which is what the slaves did.

Five can't ketch me and ten can't hold me—
  Ho, round the corn, Sally!
Here's your iggle-quarter and here's your count-aquils—
  Ho, round the corn, Sally!
  I can bank, 'ginny bank, 'ginny bank the weaver—
  Ho, round the corn, Sally!

All of the above seems obvious to me except the third and fifth lines. But *iggle* is, of course, *eagle*, and an eagle quarter was American money. It would also seem that *count* in the phrase "your count-aquils" is either a reference to that money or the count of merchandise being harvested—in this instance, the corn. *Aquil* could be either an appropriation of the Spanish

aquí, meaning *here*, or more likely an appropriation of the French word *kilo*, which is a term of measure.

Another less "obscure" song of probably an earlier period:

Arter you lub, you lub you know, boss. You can't
  broke lub. Man can't broke lub. Lub stan'—he ain't
  gwine broke—Man heb to be very smart for broke
  lub. Lub is a ting stan' just like tar, arter he stick, he
  stick, he ain't gwine move. He can't move less dan
  you burn him. Hab to kill all two arter he lub fo'
  you broke lub.[3]

Though the above should be considered an American song, it still retains so much of the African that it might be difficult for some people to understand. Yet I think the references quite American. But now, however, by *African*, I do not mean actual surviving African words, but rather the American accent and the syntactical construction of certain West African dialects. It is relatively easy to see the connection in the syntax of this song and the literal translation into English of African phrases. For example, the literal English rendering of an Ashanti (Twi dialect) phrase meaning "to calm a person" is "cool he heart give him." (And here, I think, even the word *cool* should bear further consideration.)

African speech, African customs, and African music all changed by the American experience into a native American form. But what was a pure African music? Were there similarities between African and European music before the importation of the slaves? What strictly musical changes occurred to transform African music into American? How did this come about?

The role of African music in the formulation of Afro-American music was misunderstood for a great many years. And the most obvious misunderstanding was one that perhaps only a Westerner would make, that African music "... although based on the same principles of European music, suffers from the African's lack of European technical skill in the fashioning of his crude instruments. Thus the strangeness and out-of-tune quality of a great many of the played notes." Musicologists of the eighteenth and nineteenth centuries, and even some from the twentieth, would speak of the "aberration" of the diatonic scale in African music. Or a man like Krehbiel could say: "There is a significance which I cannot fathom in the circumstance that the tones which seem *rebellious* [my italics] to the negro's sense of intervallic propriety are the fourth and

[2]*Op cit.*, p. 80.

[3]From Maud Cuney-Hare, *Negro Musicians and Their Music* (Washington, D.C., Associated Publishers, 1936), p. 27.

seventh of the diatonic major series and the fourth, sixth and seventh of the minor."[4] Why did it not occur to him that perhaps the Africans were using not a diatonic scale, but an African scale, a scale that would seem ludicrous when analyzed by the normal methods of Western musicology? Even Ernest Borneman says: "It seems likely now that the common source of European and West African music was a simple non-hemitonic pentatone system. Although indigenous variants of the diatonic scale have been developed and preserved in Africa, modern West Africans who are not familiar with European music will tend to become uncertain when asked to sing in a tempered scale. This becomes particularly obvious when the third and seventh steps of a diatonic scale are approached. The singer almost invariably tries to skid around these steps with slides, slurs or vibrato effects so broad as to approach scalar value."[5]

These sliding and slurring effects in Afro-American music, the basic "aberrant" quality of a blues scale, are, of course, called "blueing" the notes. But why not of "scalar value?" It is my idea that this is a different scale.

Sidney Finkelstein, in *Jazz: A People's Music:* ". . . these deviations from the pitch familiar to concert music are not, of course, the result of an inability to sing or play in tune. They mean that the blues are a non-diatonic music. . . . Many books on jazz . . . generally describe the blues as a sequence of chords, such as the tonic, subdominant and dominant seventh. Such a definition, however, is like putting the cart before the horse. There are definite patterns of chords which have been evolved to support the blues, but these do not define the blues, and the blues can exist as a melody perfectly recognizable as the blues without them. Neither are the blues simply a use of the major scale with the 'third' and 'seventh' slightly blued or flattened. The fact is that both this explanation, and the chord explanation, are attempts to explain one musical system in terms of another; to describe a non-diatonic music in diatonic terms."[6]

The most apparent survivals of African music in Afro-American music are its rhythms: not only the seeming emphasis in the African music on rhythmic, rather than melodic or harmonic, qualities, but also the use of polyphonic, or contrapuntal, rhythmic effects. Because of this seeming neglect of harmony and melody, Westerners thought music "primitive." It did

not occur to them that Africans might have looked askance at a music as vapid rhythmically as the West's.

The reason for the remarkable development of the rhythmic qualities of African music can certainly be traced to the fact that Africans also used drums for communication; and not, as was once thought, merely by using the drums in a kind of primitive Morse code, but by the phonetic reproduction of the words themselves—the result being that Africans developed an extremely fine and extremely complex rhythmic sense, as well as becoming unusually responsive to timbral subleties. Also, the elaborately developed harmonic system used in the playing of percussion instruments, *i.e.*, the use of drums or other percussion instruments of different timbres to produce harmonic contrasts, was not immediately recognizable to the Western ear; neither was the use of two and three separate rhythmic patterns to underscore the same melody, a concept easily recognizable to Westerners used to less subtle musical devices.

Melodic diversity in African music came not only in the actual arrangements of notes (in terms of Western transcription) but in the singer's vocal interpretation. The "tense, slightly hoarse-sounding vocal techniques" of the work songs and the blues stem directly from West African musical tradition. (This kind of singing voice is also common to a much other non-Western music.) In African languages the meaning of a word can be changed simply by altering the *pitch* of the word, or changing its stress—basically, the way one can change the word *yeh* from simple response to stern challenge simply by moving the tongue slightly. Philologists call this "significant tone," the "combination of pitch and timbre" used to produce changes of meaning in words. This was basic to the speech and music of West Africans, and was definitely passed on to the Negroes of the New World.

Another important aspect of African music found very readily in the American Negro's music is the antiphonal singing technique. A leader sings a theme and a chorus answers him. These answers are usually comments on the leader's theme or comments on the answers themselves in improvised verses. The amount of improvisation depends on how long the chorus wishes to continue. And improvisation, another major facet of African music, is certainly one of the strongest survivals in American Negro music. The very character of the first work songs suggests that they were largely improvised. And, of course, the very structure of jazz is the melodic statement with an arbitrary number of improvised answers or comments on the initial theme.

Just as some of the African customs survived in America in their totality, although usually given just a thin veneer of Euro-American camouflage, so pure African songs, dances, and instruments showed up on

---

[4]*Ibid.*, p. 73.

[5]"The Roots of Jazz," in Nat Hentoff and Albert J. McCarthy, eds., *Jazz* (New York, Rinehart, 1959), p. 13.

[6]*Jazz: A People's Music* (New York, Citadel, 1948), p. 68.

this side of the water. However, I consider this less significant because it seems to me much more important, if we speak of music, that features such as basic rhythmic, harmonic, and melodic devices were transplanted almost intact rather than isolated songs, dances, or instruments.

The very nature of slavery in America dictated the way in which African culture could be adapted. Thus, a Dahomey river god ceremony had no chance of survival in this country at all unless it was incorporated into an analogous rite that was present in the new culture—which is what happened. The Christians of the New World called it baptism. Just as the African songs of recrimination survive as a highly competitive game called "the dozens." (As any young Harlemite can tell you, if someone says to you, "Your father's a woman," you must say, as a minimal comeback, "Your mother likes it," or a similar putdown.) And in music: where the use of the African drum was strictly forbidden, other percussive devices had to be found, like the empty oil drums that led to the development of the Western Indian steel bands. Or the metal wash basin turned upside down and floated in another basin that sounds, when beaten, like an African hollow-log drum. The Negro's way in this part of the Western world was adaptation and reinterpretation. The banjo (an African word) is an African instrument, and the xylophone, used now in all Western concert orchestras, was also brought over by the Africans. But the survival of the *system* of African music is much more significant than the existence of a few isolated and finally superfluous features. The notable fact is that the only so-called popular music in this country of any real value is of African derivation.

Another important aspect of African music was the use of folk tales in song lyrics, riddles, proverbs, etc., which, even when not accompanied by music, were the African's chief method of education, the way the wisdom of the elders was passed down to the young. The use of these folk stories and legends in the songs of the American Negro was quite common, although it was not as common as the proportion of "Americanized" or American material grew. There are however, definite survivals not only in the animal tales which have become part of this country's tradition (the Uncle Remus/Br'er Rabbit tales, for example) but in the lyrics of work songs and even later blues forms.

And just as the lyrics of the African songs were usually as important or *more* important than the music, the lyrics of the work songs and the later blues were equally important to the Negro's concept of music. In fact the "shouts" and "field hollers" were little more than highly rhythmical lyrics. Even the purely instrumental music of the American Negro contains constant reference to vocal music. Blues-playing is the closest imitation of the human voice of any music I've heard; the vocal effects that jazz musicians have delighted in from Bunk Johnson to Ornette Coleman are evidence of this. (And it seems right to conclude that the African and blues scales proceed from this concept of vocal music, which produces note values that are almost impossible to reproduce on the fixed Western tempered scale, but can nevertheless be played on Western instruments.)

If we think of African music as regards its intent, we must see that it differed from Western music in that it was a purely *functional* music. Borneman lists some basic types of songs common to West African cultures: songs used by young men to influence young women (courtship, challenge, scorn); songs used by workers to make their tasks easier; songs used by older men to prepare the adolescent boys for manhood, and so on. "Serious" Western music, except for early religious music, has been strictly an "art" music. One would not think of any particular *use* for Haydn's symphonies, except perhaps the "cultivation of the soul." "Serious music" (a term that could only have extra-religious meaning in the West) has never been an integral part of the Westerner's life; no art has been since the Renaissance. Of course, before the Renaissance, art could find its way into the lives of almost all the people because all art issued from the Church, and the Church was at the very center of Western man's life. But the discarding of the religious attitude for the "enlightened" concepts of the Renaissance also created the schism between what was art and what was life. It was, and is, inconceivable in the African culture to make a separation between music, dancing, song, the artifact, and a man's life or his worship of his gods. *Expression* issued from life, and *was* beauty. But in the West, the "triumph of the economic mind over the imaginative," as Brooks Adams said, made possible this dreadful split between life and art. Hence, a music that is an "art" music as distinguished from something someone would whistle while tilling a field.

There are still relatively cultivated Westerners who believe that before Giotto no one *could* produce the human figure well, or that the Egyptians painted their figures in profile because they *could not* do it any other way. The idea of progress, as it has infected all other areas of Western thought, is thus carried over into the arts as well. And so a Western listener will criticize the tonal and timbral qualities of an African or American Negro singer whose singing has a completely alien *end* as the "standard of excellence." The "hoarse, shrill" quality of African singers or of their cultural progeny, the blues singers, is thus attributed to their lack of proper vocal training, instead of to a conscious desire dictated by their own cultures to produce a prescribed and certainly calculated effect. A blues singer and, say, a Wagnerian tenor cannot be compared to one another in any way. They issue from cultures that have almost nothing in common, and the musics they make are equally alien. The Western concept of "beauty" cannot be reconciled to African or Afro-American music (except perhaps now in the twentieth century, Afro-American music has enough of a Euro-American tradition to make it seem possible to judge it by purely Western standards. This is not quite true.) For a Westerner to say that the Wagnerian tenor's voice is "better" than the African singer's or the blues singer's is analogous to a non-Westerner disparaging Beethoven's Ninth Symphony because it wasn't improvised.

The Western concept of the cultivation of the voice is foreign to African or Afro-American music. In the West, only the artifact can be beautiful, mere expression cannot be thought to be. It is only in the twentieth century that Western art has moved away from this concept and toward the non-Western modes of art-making, but the principle of the beautiful thing as opposed to the natural thing still makes itself felt. The tendency of white jazz musicians to play "softer" or with "cleaner, rounder tones" than their Negro counterparts is, I think, an insistence on the same Western artifact. Thus an alto saxophonist like Paul Desmond, who is white, produces a sound on his instrument that can almost be called legitimate, or classical, and the finest Negro alto saxophonist, Charlie Parker, produced a sound on the same instrument that was called by some "raucous and uncultivated." But Parker's sound was *meant* to be both those adjectives. Again, reference determines value. Parker also would literally imitate the human voice with his cries, swoops, squawks, and slurs, while Desmond always insists he is playing an instrument, that it is an artifact separate from himself. Parker did not admit that there was any separation between himself and the agent he had chosen as his means of self-expression.

By way of further illustration of this, another quote from Mr. Borneman:

"While the whole European tradition strives for regularity—of pitch, of time, of timbre and of vibrato—the African tradition strives precisely for the negation of these elements. In language, the African tradition aims at circumlocution rather than at exact definition. The direct statement is considered crude and unimaginative; the veiling of all contents in ever-changing paraphrases is considered the criterion of intelligence and personality. In music, the same tendency towards obliquity and ellipsis is noticeable: no note is attacked straight; the voice or instrument always approaches it from above or below, plays around the implied pitch without ever remaining any length of time, and departs from it without ever having committed itself to a single meaning. The timbre is veiled and paraphrased by constantly changing vibrato, tremolo and overtone effects. The timing and accentuation, finally, are not *stated*, but *implied* or *suggested*. The denying or withholding of all signposts."[7]

JOHN OLIVER KILLENS

The Black Writer Vis-à-Vis His Country

I believe it was George Bernard Shaw who once said that America was the first country in history to move from barbarism to decadence without going through civilization. I construe the statement of this estimable British gentleman of letters to mean that our country has been in such a hurry becoming the wealthiest and the most powerful nation in the world, it has hardly had the time or stomach for the niceties of culture and civilization. Indeed, it has been in such unseemly haste, it has not even taken the time to bring into reality some of the most magnificent literature ever written about the rights of men. I refer, of course, to the Bill of Rights, the Declaration of Independence, and the Constitution of the United States.

So a cultural revolution is desperately needed, here and now, to un-brainwash the entire American people, black and white. For the people of this land have been the victims of a mighty brainwash that has continued unabated for the last four hundred years. Perhaps Negro artists must assume an uneven load in this cultural revolution because, as black folk, they know America better than she knows herself. The laws of survival dictate that the slave must know the many turns and twists and quirks of his master. Moreover, the Negro remembers better than anybody else the American dream, deferred and forgotten by most Americans. He remembers, because he lives constantly the dream's negation, yet lives for the day when the dream will become a reality. He could never take for granted the Declaration of Independence, the Bill of Rights, the Constitution of these United States. He could never become blasé about the dream. In a word, your humble servant, the black American, has borne the brunt of the millions of little white lies America has told the world about herself and about the Negro.

Since the so-called American Indian is practically extinct, it is highly probable that the only indigenous American culture is that of the American Negro. The

---

[7]*Loc. cit.*, pp. 23–24.

Negro was invented in America. Only in America. In the main, his has been a culture of revolt, of protest and revolution; a culture that is expressed very clearly in the Negro spirituals. More often than not, they are still interpreted as songs of a happy, childlike people, satisfied with their lot in this world and looking forward to the Hereafter, where the streets would be paved with gold and overflow with milk and honey. Why do Americans still hang on in desperation to the image of the happy and contented slave? "DIDN'T MY LORD DELIVER DANIEL? WHY NOT EVERY MAN?" is not exactly a happy and contented lyric!

From all sides pressure is put upon the Negro artist to deny his culture, his roots, his selfhood. How many black writers have you heard engage in this abject self-denial: "I am not a Negro writer. I am a writer who happens to be a Negro." But the truth of the matter is that we black Americans are all Negroes (African-Americans, if you prefer) who happen to have become writers, painters, lawyers, subway motormen, doctors, teachers, ditch-diggers, pickpockets, hustlers, or whatever. We see life from the vantage point of being Negro. A creative writer writes out of his particular frame of reference, which is the sum total of his life's experience, and he had better come to terms with it as hurriedly as possible.

Yet from Hollywood to Broadway to Madison Avenue, I hear variations of the same refrain: "John, why do you insist upon writing about Negroes? Why don't you write about people?" As often as I've heard that one, it never fails to jar me, laboring, as I always have, under the illusion that Negroes *are* people. Another goes like this: "The thing I liked about your story, John, it was universal. It could have been about anybody."

Well—I submit that a story that could have been about anybody is probably about precisely nobody at all. Negroes are the only people in this world who are set apart because of who they are, and at the same time told to forget who they are by the same people who set them apart in the first place.

Now, then, how could I, John Killens, write a valid story about a Chinese peasant in the hinterlands of China? No matter how *universal* my literary approach, I would never be able to get close to the Chinese peasant's specifics, the cultural and the idiomatic meanings of his life, the unique Chineseness of him, which are his and only his. Besides, I could never muster up that much racial arrogance.

I am convinced that when Western man speaks of universality, he is referring to an Anglo-Saxon universality, which includes a very meager sector of this young and aging universe. Every line of Sean O'Casey's works exudes a sense of Irishness. Dostoevski bared the Russian soul. No critic ever questioned their universality. But to write out of the frame of reference of an American Negro is *ipso facto* anti-universal.

Herbert Hill, newly blossoming literary expert on Negro affairs, in his introduction to *Soon, One Morning,* an anthology of "New Writing by American Negroes," acclaimed Ralph Ellison for all the wrong reasons, because Ellison's work, according to Hill, "transcends the traditional preoccupations of the Negro writer. . . . Today the Negro artist, as he enters into the mainstream of contemporary literature, feels a new strength and refuses to be limited to racial protest. . . . As the Negro writer moves beyond his anger, he develops a new concern for literary discipline and control . . ."

Well, Mr. Hill, the American mainstream contains some rather sickly fish; if Ellison did indeed enter the "mainstream," the mainstream got more than it gave. It is a pretty puny achievement to join the mainstream, and a puny achievement is precisely what Ellison's novel was not.

The mainstream is jammed with writers like Updike and Salinger, who write page after page of precious prose about absolutely nothing. With the whole Western world as their potential canvas, and swiftly going to pot and trying desperately to take the rest of civilization with it, such writers flee in panic because the New World is becoming too much for them. They escape into minutiae of tight little islands of personal insignificance and Oedipus complexes. The American mainstream has come up with a crop of literary nitpickers, most of them entirely without testicles. So now they want to castrate the Negro writer, too. Is this the stream Herb Hill would lead black writers into?

But the motley crew of little white fathers are saying nothing new. They merely repeat the old refrains pontifically, as if they're saying something startling and fresh. You say to yourself, I've heard that song before, for underneath there is always this veiled admonition to black writers: "You'll never win the prizes or the critics' adulation unless you cool your anger and lay that pistol down. Keep criticizing society and you'll continue to incur the wrath of us white reviewers, who are not bad fellows at all and would really like to bring you into the fold. Oh yes, in spite of the fact that you are a Negro, you too can join the club if you'll just play down your Negro-ness."

But a writer who writes to get into the mainstream and win National Book Awards and plaudits from the critics is in trouble with his muse. A creative writer is not a statesman. He must tell as much of the truth as he knows the painful truth to be, and let the flak fall where it may. Writing is a hazardous pursuit. The flak might very well fall back on the writer and put a large hole in his head. It has something to do with the law of gravity. What goes up must come down. Artists are forever at war with society, and if the artist is a black man in the Free World he is doubly at war and the war's consequences are especially dangerous for him. But he must fight in any event, for the consequences of his temporizing are fraught with even greater danger.

When Ernest Hemingway was interviewed by the *Paris Review* a few years before he died and asked what kind of advice he would give young writers, he answered that a writer needed two things—a sense of justice and a built-in, shock-proof shit detector. Obviously a writer also needs artistic talent, but granting his talent, he desperately needs these two attributes Mr. Hemingway so graphically described.

As a writer, I must believe with all my mind and heart and soul in the ancient adage "You shall know the truth and the truth shall set you free." In a far deeper sense even than men of the cloth, writers must be searchers for the truth; men and women whose life's mission is to explore the truth of man's relationship to man. And I, for one, believe the basic truth of what my grandmother used to say. "Aah Lord, honey, the half ain't never been told." There is nothing in the world that I believe more than the wisdom of that statement. If I believed, as some Western men continually assert, that everything has already been said and it's just a question now of how differently you say it, that all is semantics from now on, I would put the cover on my typewriter and never uncover it again. As a writer, I must believe that most of what has already been said is a pack of lies, or, in some instances, mistakes, to be more charitable to makers of the myths. It is up to the writer to create a new vision for mankind. He must be forever asking questions. He must ask the unaskable. Was "Plato's Republic" a Republic? Was Jefferson democrat or slaveholder? This world can't possibly be man's best effort, or we're all doomed to destruction or the madhouse. Life must make more sense than it has up to this point.

Did Shakespeare's "Macbeth" utter an everlasting truth? Have all our yesteryears lighted fools the way to dusty death? "Out, out, brief candle!" Macbeth shouts. "Life's but a walking shadow; a poor player, that struts and frets his hour upon the stage, and then is heard no more: it is a tale told by an idiot, full of sound and fury, signifying nothing." Or did Langston Hughes come closer to *our* truth when he asked: "What happens to a dream too long deferred?"

I am a writer, first of all, and precisely because the world stinks and I want to change it. Yes, I mean it, and any writer worth his salt is up to the same subversive business. This is the way things always were, the eternal confrontation between the artist and society. Every time I sit down to the typewriter, with every line I put on paper, I am out to change the world, to capture reality, to melt it down and forge it into something entirely different. The portrait of the artist as a human being is one of profound frustration, because although he knows that "change" is one of the inevitable laws of the universe in the context of time and space, change in human nature is imperceptible. That is why the French have a saying: "The more things change the more they remain the same." But the earth *does* move. And things *do* change.

Since everybody "knows" the artist is the maladjusted one, I plead guilty to the charge. To be perfectly adjusted in a crazy, impractical, unreasonable society hellbent for its own annihilation seems tantamount to remaining blissful in a raging booby hatch. This is what drove Van Gogh to suicide. He was naïve enough to want to make sense in a crazy world. His sin was that he took life seriously and he loved mankind. *Ergo*, he was an idiot before his peers. He wanted to make sense out of a senseless society, and therefore he was a damn fool. But what is the verdict a century after he departed? Whom does the world remember, Van Gogh or his contemporaries?

But despite the current Negro Revolt, which is not yet a revolution, rumors to the contrary, the American Negro remains a cultural nonentity as far as books, television, movies, and Broadway are concerned. It is as if twenty million Americans did not exist; as if twenty million people were committed to oblivion. A Negro child can read at home or go to school and look into his school books, come home and watch television or maybe go to an occasional movie, and follow this routine from day to day, month to month, year to year, and hardly, if ever, see a reflection of himself in the mass-communications media. This has a tremendously negative impact on a child, who must have a sense of belonging and not of being here by toleration. A child must have a sense of selfhood, a knowledge that he is not here by sufferance, that his forebears contributed to the country and to the world down through the years.

America knows that the blood, sweat, tears, and muscles of black folk helped to build this mighty country. You wouldn't be so high and mighty if it weren't for me. You built this country on the black backs of my forefathers. Slave labor, that's what it really was, slave labor at a time when slavery was already obsolete throughout much of the earth. That's how you constructed your great temples and stored them with riches. That's how you got so far ahead of the rest of man in treasures stored up here on earth. You cruelly exploited my forebears. And now you deny my children a cultural existence. You pretend they are invisible.

I know the impact. I was a black boy once in Georgia. I remember. And I know the impact now, because I am the father of two African-Americans in New York City. I remember when my son was nine or ten years old, my great friend Langston Hughes came to dinner and brought my son a book he had written called *Famous American Negroes*. In it Langston had written, for children, stories about the Negro heroes of American history. Of Harriet Tubman, Frederick Douglass, Crispus Attucks, and Benjamin Banneker. This book opened many doors for my son, Chuck. He was so thrilled he took it to school the next day and showed it to the teacher, then asked, demanded really, that she read it to the class.

We lived at the time in the now "infamous" Bedford-Stuyvesant area in Brooklyn and the school was about fifty-fifty in its composition (meaning Negro-white, not co-educational). This was just before the great white exodus from the community had developed into full-scale, panic-stricken, disorderly retreat. The teacher read passages of the book to my son's class and that night at the dinner table I asked him how it had gone.

"It was wonderful, Daddy! Everybody enjoyed the book." Then Chuck frowned and said, "But you know, Daddy, nobody at that school knows anything about Negro culture or Negro history."

"I suppose it's understandable that the white children don't know," I said.

"Oh no, Daddy, I mean the Negro children, too. Not even the teacher knows." And then he poked out his chest and said very proudly, "I'm the only one in that school that knows *anything* about Negro history or culture."

I looked at him and wanted to laugh and shout for the joy and pride he felt. At the same time I wanted to cry for all the black kids all over America caught up in what playwright Ted Ward has called the Big White Fog, never knowing that they have ever been anything and therefore never believing they'll ever amount to anything.

My daughter, Barbara, was then six years old. We lived in a brownstone on Lafayette Avenue, the parlor floor and basement. She would sit in the living room on the parlor floor and stare at the idiot box for hour upon hour. What program didn't matter, she even watched the commercials. We figured this was rather precocious for one of her tender age, for some of the commercials were better than the programs. Ultimately the fog lifted (for us, I mean), and we realized that our daughter was watching to see herself reflected on the television screen, a black man or woman presented with dignity, for she already knew the difference between dignity and *Amos 'n' Andy*. When once or twice during a long and arduous vigil she saw a black face on the white screen, she would run downstairs where we usually were, shouting, "Daddy! Mommy! Negro on

TV!" But by the time we got upstairs he or she would be gone.

When we first moved to the neighborhood where we now live, Barbara was the only Negro in her class. She came home from school one day in tears. The history teacher had told the class that the Civil War was fought too soon, that the slaves weren't ready for freedom, and were happy and contented on the old plantation. Barbara took on the entire class and the teacher. "I don't know if I said the right things, Daddy. But I knew that what that teacher was saying didn't sound like anything I'd heard at home."

She burst into tears again as if her heart would surely break. Barbara was a happy girl most of the time. She rarely cried. She ran headlong into life, smiling, laughing, tripping, falling, getting up and running smack dab into life again, with hardly ever a thought about the very high cost of living. How could a teacher be so vicious to such a tender-hearted child? Or was the lady just plain ignorant?

I know a young black artist whose art is a monument to black life in America. He renders a toast to life in every stroke of his talented brush. Yet when I saw Tom Feelings at a meeting a few months ago, he was disheartened and told me he was leaving America. He had been going to the public schools of Bedford-Stuyvesant and giving chalk talks to black children on Negro and African history. But he explained that he could no longer do so because he realized more and more that the Negro kids thought themselves ugly. Because they were black. He said it was just too much for him. He thought they were beautiful; they thought they were ugly. Obviously their parents agreed with them. How else can one interpret stocking caps and straightening combs and bleaching cream?

"John, I've got to get to Africa. I've got to go to a place where black children know who they are and what they are and know that they're beautiful and that they are somebody. I've got to go some damn place where black folk don't think of themselves as 'niggers.' "

He was almost in tears. I knew the desperate feeling. From generation to generation the "nigger" feeling is handed down from parent to child. The feeling that what is white is right, and what is black is wrong. White is the symbol of purity and virginity and everything else that is good and powerful and eternal. Oh, how many times in the days of my youth did I sit in the humble pews of black churches and hear the wonderful, soulful, beautiful, hard-working black sisters, young and old, shout supplications of utter futility: "Wash me, Heavenly Father, And I will be as white as snow!"

The Western world deliberately made black the symbol of all that was evil and ugly. Black Friday, black-list, Black Plague, black look, blackmail. Oh, the way the white Establishment made us hate ourselves. "A nigger ain't shit!" is a black password, a common utterance of black folks. You took a great people from a great continent and turned them into "niggers." That is the job you accomplished in the name of "civilizing the natives" and "Christianizing the pagans." That is the essence of what America is, from the black man's point of view. The land of the "niggermakers."

This distorted image of the Negro has its negative effect on your children too. It gives them a distorted picture of this earth and of human potential and ill-equips them to live in a world, three-quarters of which is colored and fast becoming free and independent.

That is why my friends from the African embassies run into difficulties "Down South" in Atlanta and New Orleans and even "Up South" in New York City. To the average American, they are simply "niggers." In a way, I cannot truthfully say that I am sorry. As long as indignities are commonplace for black Americans, it is all to the good for black brothers from across the seas to labor under no illusions as to the (universal) American attitude toward men and women of color. I am not sadistic. Neither am I masochistic. I just don't want America to hoodwink black folk throughout the world. Let us set things straight at home first.

Along with the fight to desegregate the schools, we must desegregate the entire cultural statement of America; we must desegregate the minds of the American people. If we merely succeed in desegregating the school buildings, we may very well find that we have won the battle and lost the war. Integration begins the day after the minds of the American people are desegregated. This is the great challenge to all American writers, but especially to the black writer. Who will tell the real story of America if the black writer doesn't? Certainly not the gentlemen of the "mainstream" who still believe in Gunga Din and Uncle Tom and Aunt Jemima, or the "avant-garde," the rebels who are really anti-revolutionary. Jean Genet and his genre, the "theater of the absurd," the "beatnik," the "new wave," would appear to be merely Johnny-come-lately Kiplings. Apologists for white supremacy die hard and recur in varying disguises.

Behind the "avant-garde's" beards and dark glasses, they rationalize, apologize, as they strut and posture. The underlying statements of *The Blacks* and *The Balcony* are the same, that all civilization stinks, *period.* "When the have-nots overthrow the *haves,* nothing will really change except the relative positions of the adversaries. It will be the same thing all over again. There is no revolution ever. It's the same merry-go-round, so stop the world, I want to get off." Well, pardon me, fellows, I don't want to get off. The world never looked so good to me before.

"Sure—don't worry how you treat the *blacks.* The blacks will do the same to you when they seize power." This is Genet's message, as far as I'm concerned. *The Blacks* was excellent therapy for many guilt-ridden white folk, which probably explains the long New York run it enjoyed, so much so that many whites went back to see it time and time again. Actually, the so-called "avant-garde" is really a rear-guard action in disguise. It is neither revolutionary, anti-bourgeois, as it sometimes makes pretentions of being, nor anti-white supremacy; it is not even anti-Establishment. It is essentially anti-people. "The West is humanity, humanity is the West, we're all sick to the guts, so let's, man, like all of us get into this here Western style pigsty, and have one final everlasting orgy."

There seems to be a growing tendency in the literature about black and white relationships to give the impression that everything could be solved on the analytical couch. I imagine this approach is a part of the so-called "sexual revolution." The whole "color" thing is merely a deeply rooted psychological sexual complexity and if we could only gather together 190 million black and white Americans into one gargantuan orgiastic group therapy, or perhaps one gigantic therapeutic orgy, all the problems would be solved. I submit that though we might have a ball, after the smoke and funk cleared away, the Great American Problem would still be with us; the Black Man's Burden would not have disappeared. Because the Problem and the Burden are historical, economic, cultural, and social, as well as psychological and sexual. The root of the problem is the Negro Invention.

So now comes the question: Who will uninvent the Negro? For nearly four hundred years the black man's personality has been under attack, his selfhood devastated. Ever since he was brought to this country in chains he has constantly been given the ultimatum: "Deny your humanity or perish!" Where are the artists and prophets who will undo this white destruction? Who will write the songs for us to sing of our black heroes? Who will tell our children of valiant Chalka? Who will re-create the ancient glory that was Timbuktu and Kush and Ghana and Songhay? It is important for us to know that our history on this earth did not begin with slavery's scars.

In order for a people to develop a highly political and revolutionary consciousness, they must hold a high regard for themselves. They must know that they came from *somewhere,* in order to believe themselves capable of going somewhere; they must have a past before they can create a future for themselves. A people needs legends, heroes, myths. Deny them these and you have won half the battle against them.

The French needed legendary figures like Joan of Arc in order to develop a national consciousness, without which any revolution is impossible. So we black folk need Saint Harriet of the Eastern Shore. We must build a literature of heroes, myths, and legends. The lives of Harriet Tubman, Frederick Douglass, Nat Turner, Sojourner Truth, are as formidable as George Washington's, and are based on a much more substantial reality. Our people, young and old, need such heroes desperately. Slavemasters Washington and Jefferson do not belong to *our* children. We need our own myths and legends to regain our lost self-esteem, our regard for each other as a people capable of working together to move the mountains that stand before us. We need such a heritage in order to really believe that we shall prevail.

I'm reminded of a story. A little boy had read numerous stories in his children's books about various life-and-death struggles between a man and lion. But no matter how ferociously the lion fought, each time the man emerged victorious. This puzzled the boy, so he asked his father, "Why is it, Daddy, that in all these stories the man always beats the lion, when everybody knows that the lion is the toughest cat in all the jungle?"

The father answered, "Son, those stories will always end like that until the lion learns how to write."

Few white American writers care enough about the country to criticize it fundamentally. Compared with the ambivalent lot who clutter up the mainstream, they make up a pitifully small pool of courageous talent. Mention James Jones, Norman Mailer, Warren Miller, Lillian Smith, Arthur Miller, Harvey Swados, Ginzburg, Buckmaster, Rosten, Williams, and you have very nearly run out of names. Regardless of how one feels about their views of this society, one must concede that they are writers who care about things deeply. One hopes that one day at least one of them will care deeply enough to dramatize or novelize the white folk who are completely taken in by the "righteous" cause of white supremacy, explain them to us and particularly to themselves in all their myriad contradictions. What is the metamorphosis of a racial bigot? Are they born retarded? Is it fed to them with their mother's milk? The public schools? The press? The church? The mass-communications media? How? Why? When? Where?

America needs to understand what goes into the making of a man who will go out on a Sunday morning in Birmingham, Alabama, and participate in the strange ritual of throwing bombs into a church and killing innocent little Negro children as they are being taught about Jesus, the same Jesus of Nazareth whom the killers profess to worship. And what about the sickness of men who will stand on the sidelines and watch such bloody rituals enacted, without daring to speak? What sort of unspeakable fear has locked their jaws? What is the true anatomy of racial prejudice? Here is a challenge for some writer who cares.

What happens to the dream too long deferred? What white writer will ask America Langston Hughes's question, and come up with some answers? For the dream has been deferred for all the country, black and white. But who will help convince white America that the dream is important to them also? Or have you, too, stopped dreaming? Come on, white brothers. Or don't you really give a damn?

Historically, white America put words in the black man's mouth and bade him sing improbable lyrics like:

*All the darkies am a weepin'
Massa's in de cold, cold ground.*

But my great-grandmother told me differently. "We wept all right, honey! Great God A'mighty! We cried for joy and shouted halleluyah!"

Even long after slavery, white America continued the black man singing such banalities as:

*I got plenty of nuthin'
And nuthin's plenty fo' me.*
                    or
Summertime and the livin' is easy.

Certainly the American Negro knows, more profoundly than anyone else, that the living is *never* easy.

Even a short while ago, you had us singing:

*It ain't no sin to dance and grin
That's why darkies were born.*

Yet a black poet once wrote:

*Carry me back to ol' Virginia—
That's the only way you'll get me there.*

And in our own songs we sang:

*Sometimes I feel like a motherless child,
A long ways from home.*

We sang:

Nobody knows the trouble I see.

Happy, contented people, we sang:

*Before I be a slave
I'll be buried in my grave
And go home to my Lord
And be free.*

How did all this begin, this billion-dollar misunderstanding? It started with your determination to have my labor without pay.

In order to justify slavery in a courageous New World spouting slogans of freedom and equality and brotherhood, the enslavers had to create the fiction that the enslaved were subhuman and undeserving of human rights and sympathies. The first job was to convince the outside world of the inherent inferiority of the enslaved. The second job was to convince the American people. And the third job, which was the cruelest hoax of all, was to convince the slaves themselves that they deserved to be the slaves. The propagandists for American slavery (the "creative writers" of that time) tackled their tasks with alacrity and a great measure of success, the effects of which still remain with us today, a hundred years after the Emancipation Proclamation, almost two hundred years after the Declaration of Independence. Thus was the Negro invented and the American Revolution thwarted. To this day, supposedly born in revolution, America is embarrassed by that word. Americans shy away from the word "revolution" like the plague, as if the American Revolution had never happened. Well, did it happen? Knock on any door in Harlem; in all the Harlems of the U.S.A. Ask any black man or woman in Alabama or Mississippi: Was 1776 for real? We black folk are the living proof of whether your revolution was a fake or not.

I attended a party some years ago near the Northwestern University campus, given by some university instructors to celebrate the publication of my first novel, *Youngblood*. One of them told me how much she had enjoyed *Youngblood*, but then asked, "Mr. Killens, do you think you could ever write about people, I mean, not just about Negroes? I mean about people." The nice lady was a trifle flustered.

"You mean, white people, don't you?"

She answered, "Well—yes. I suppose that is what I mean."

"Yes, I believe I could if I wanted to. In fact there are white folk in *Youngblood*. Actually, I believe that a black writer would find it easier writing about white folk than the white writer writing about black folk. The black man has had to know you in order to live in *your* world. I had to know what questions you were going to ask before you asked them, and I had to have the answers ready. But you've always taken me for granted. You come to me with all kinds of preconceptions about my innate inferiority. You never get past the myth to the real me."

My rejection slips reveal so much. I've gotten many a "Dear John" in my day, and I still get them.

Dear John:
Thank you for submitting your story to us. It is a powerful and beautiful job. Unfortunately the subject matter is not for us. Frankly, we are not a controversial house.

However, do keep us in mind when you write something else, especially if it has no racial overtones. Sincerely,

Meaning of course: "John, why do you insist on writing about Negroes? Why don't you write about people?" Why this pressure on the Negro writer to deny his roots? Because the Negro experience in this country is the most fundamental criticism of the American way of life. This reality America has refused to face. It always was and always will be, so long as black remains the symbol of human dispossession. As long as we black folk are D.P.'s in our native land, the controversy will continue to rage. It will always remain a stumbling block in our attempts to win friends and influence people among the African and Asian populations. Africans are concerned with the welfare of their American brothers, and the American brother is becoming more and more concerned with Mother Africa.

Don't write about the Negro, write about Americans. But surely the American Negro is the most uniquely American of all Americans, because he was created *here,* in this place, physically, psychologically, sociologically, culturally, economically. He is an American product. The Negro, in his black presence, is the barometer of this nation's Constitution, and all its democratic traditions yet unrealized. Still deferred. The black man's sojourn in this country is the universal story of man's inhumanity to man, capable of being understood in any language in any nation on the earth. Here is the place for the literary prophets! But maybe Western man is right. "Everything to be said has already been said by Western man." I mean, it may be true that Western man has said all he has to say. It may be that he has run out of meaningful dialogue. God knows, he has talked long enough.

But colored people throughout the world have been sentenced by Western man to centuries of silence. And now in the middle of the twentieth century, it is time for them to speak. Western man wrote his own history as if it were the history of the entire human race. I hope that colored men have watched Western men too long to commit the fatal folly of writing history with a "colored" pencil. For there is a great wisdom in the old Ghana proverb that says: "No one rules forever on the throne of time." Notwithstanding, in this cultural revolution, we must reconstruct the history of the last four hundred years and this time tell *How the West Was Really Won.*

There is much inhumanity, violence, and brutality in our country's history. We must face that. For neither a people nor a nation can free itself from its past by denying or distorting it. White Americans have been sheltered from their history. History is a people's memory, and people have a habit of remembering the very best about themselves. It is an all too human trait. But in the final analysis, a people must face its history squarely in order to transcend it.

RALPH ELLISON

What America Would Be Like Without Blacks

The fantasy of an America free of blacks is at least as old as the dream of creating a truly democratic society. While we are aware that there is something inescapably tragic about the cost of achieving our democratic ideals, we keep such tragic awareness segregated in the rear of our minds. We allow it to come to the fore only during moments of great national crisis.

On the other hand, there is something so embarrassingly absurd about the notion of purging the nation of blacks that it seems hardly a product of thought at all. It is more like a primitive reflex, a throwback to the dim past of tribal experience, which we rationalize and try to make respectable by dressing it up in the gaudy and highly questionable trappings of what we call the "concept of race." Yet despite its absurdity, the fantasy of a blackless America continues to turn up. It is a fantasy born not merely of racism but of petulance, exasperation and moral fatigue. It is like a boil bursting forth from impurities in the bloodstream of democracy.

In its benign manifestations, it can be outrageously comic, as in the picaresque adventures of Percival Brownlee, who appears in William Faulkner's story "The Bear." Exasperating to his white masters because his aspirations and talents are for preaching and conducting choirs rather than for farming, Brownlee is "freed" after much resistance and ends up as the prosperous proprietor of a New Orleans brothel. In Faulkner's hands the uncomprehending drive of Brownlee's owners to "get shut" of him is comically instructive. Indeed, the story resonates certain abiding, tragic themes of American history with which it is interwoven, and which are causing great turbulence in the social atmosphere today. I refer to the ex-

asperation and bemusement of the white American with the black, the black American's ceaseless (and swiftly accelerating) struggle to escape the misconceptions of whites, and the continual confusing of the black American's racial background with his individual culture. Most of all, I refer to the recurring fantasy of solving one basic problem of American democracy by "getting shut" of the blacks through various wishful schemes that would banish them from the nation's bloodstream, from its social structure, and from its conscience and historical consciousness.

This fantastic vision of a lily-white America appeared as early as 1713, with the suggestion of a white "native American," thought to be from New Jersey, that all the Negroes be given their freedom and returned to Africa. In 1777, Thomas Jefferson, while serving in the Virginia legislature, began drafting a plan for the gradual emancipation and exportation of the slaves. Nor were Negroes themselves immune to the fantasy. In 1815 Paul Cuffe, a wealthy merchant, shipbuilder and landowner from the New Bedford area, shipped and settled at his own expense thirty-eight of his fellow Negroes in Africa. It was perhaps his example that led in the following year to the creation of the American Colonization Society, which was to establish in 1821 the colony of Liberia. Great amounts of cash and a perplexing mixture of motives went into the venture. The slaveowners and many Border-state politicians wanted to use it as a scheme to rid the country not of slaves but of the militant free Negroes who were agitating against the "peculiar institution." The abolitionists, until they took a lead from free Negro leaders and began attacking the scheme, also participated as a means of righting a great historical injustice. Many blacks went along with it simply because they were sick of the black-and-white American mess and hoped to prosper in the quiet peace of the old ancestral home.

Such conflicting motives doomed the Colonization Society to failure, but what amazes one even more than the notion that anyone could have believed in its success is the fact that it was attempted during a period when blacks, slave and free, made up eighteen percent of the total population. When we consider how long blacks had been in the New World and had been transforming it and being Americanized by it, the scheme appears not only fantastic, but the product of a free-floating irrationality—indeed, a national pathology.

Nevertheless, some of the noblest of Americans were bemused. Not only Jefferson but later Abraham Lincoln was to give the scheme credence. According to historian John Hope Franklin, Negro colonization seemed as important to Lincoln as emancipation. In 1862, Franklin notes, Lincoln called a group of prominent free Negroes to the White House and urged them to support colonization, telling them, "Your race suffers greatly, many of them by living among us, while ours suffers from your presence. If this is admitted, it affords a reason why we should be separated."

In spite of his unquestioned greatness, Abraham Lincoln was a man of his times and limited by some of the less worthy thinking of his times. This is demonstrated both by his reliance upon the concept of race in his analysis of the American dilemma and by his involvement in a plan of purging the nation of blacks as a means of healing the badly shattered ideals of democratic federalism. Although benign, his motive was no less a product of fantasy. It envisaged an attempt to relieve an inevitable suffering that marked the growing pains of the youthful body politic by an operation which would have amounted to the severing of a healthy and indispensable member.

Yet like its twin, the illusion of secession, the fantasy of a benign amputation that would rid the country of black men to the benefit of a nation's health not only persists; today, in the form of neo-Garveyism, it fascinates black men no less than it once hypnotized whites. Both fantasies become operative whenever the nation grows weary of the struggle toward the ideal of American democratic equality. Both would use the black man as a scapegoat to achieve a national catharsis, and both would, by way of curing the patient, destroy him.

What is ultimately intriguing about the fantasy of "getting shut" of the Negro American is the fact that no one who entertains it seems ever to have considered what the nation would have become had Africans *not* been brought to the New World, and had their descendants not played such a complex and confounding role in the creation of American history and culture. Nor do they appear to have considered with any seriousness the effect upon the nation of having any of the schemes for exporting blacks succeed beyond settling some fifteen thousand or so in Liberia.

We are reminded that Daniel Patrick Moynihan, who has recently aggravated our social confusion over the racial issue while allegedly attempting to clarify it, is co-author of a work which insists that the American melting pot didn't melt because our white ethnic groups have resisted all assimilative forces that appear to threaten their identities. The problem here is that few Americans know who and what they really are. That is why few of these groups—or at least few of the children of these groups—have been able to resist

the movies, television, baseball, jazz, football, drum-majoretting, rock, comic strips, radio commercials, soap operas, book clubs, slang, or any of a thousand other expressions and carriers of our pluralistic and easily available popular culture. It is here precisely that ethnic resistance is least effective. On this level the melting pot did indeed melt, creating such deceptive metamorphoses and blending of identities, values and lifestyles that most American whites are culturally part Negro American without even realizing it.

If we can resist for a moment the temptation to view everything having to do with Negro Americans in terms of their racially imposed status, we become aware of the fact that for all the harsh reality of the social and economic injustices visited upon them, these injustices have failed to keep Negroes clear of the cultural mainstream; Negro Americans are, in fact, one of its major tributaries. If we can cease approaching American social reality in terms of such false concepts as white and nonwhite, black culture and white culture, and think of these apparently unthinkable matters in the realistic manner of Western pioneers confronting the unknown prairie, perhaps we can begin to imagine what the United States would have been, or not been, had there been no blacks to give it—if I may be so bold as to say—color.

For one thing, the American nation is in a sense the product of the American language, a colloquial speech that began emerging long before the British colonials and Africans were transformed into Americans. It is a language that evolved from the King's English but, basing itself upon the realities of the American land and colonial institutions—or lack of institutions—began quite early as a vernacular revolt against the signs, symbols, manners and authority of the mother country. It is a language that began by merging the sounds of many tongues, brought together in the struggle of diverse regions. And whether it is admitted or not, much of the sound of that language is derived from the timbre of the African voice and the listening habits of the African ear. So there is a *de'z* and *do'z* of slave speech sounding beneath our most polished Harvard accents, and if there is such a thing as a Yale accent, there is a Negro wail in it—doubtless introduced there by Old Yalie John C. Calhoun, who probably got it from his mammy.

Whitman viewed the spoken idiom of Negro Americans as a source for a native grand opera. Its flexibility, its musicality, its rhythms, freewheeling diction and metaphors, as projected in Negro American folklore, were absorbed by the creators of our great nineteenth-century literature even when the majority of blacks were still enslaved. Mark Twain celebrated it in the prose of *Huckleberry Finn;* without the presence of blacks, the book could not have been written. No Huck and Jim, no American novel as we know it. For not only is the black man a co-creator of the language that Mark Twain raised to the level of literary eloquence, but Jim's condition as American and Huck's commitment to freedom are at the moral center of the novel.

In other words, had there been no blacks, certain creative tensions arising from the cross-purposes of whites and blacks would also not have existed. Not only would there have been no Faulkner; there would have been no Stephen Crane, who found certain basic themes of his writing in the Civil War. Thus also there would have been no Hemingway, who took Crane as a source and guide. Without the presence of Negro American style, our jokes, tall tales, even our sports would be lacking in the sudden turns, shocks and swift changes of pace (all jazz-shaped) that serve to remind us that the world is ever unexplored, and that while a complete mastery of life is mere illusion, the real secret of the game is to make life swing. It is its ability to articulate this tragic-comic attitude toward life that explains much of the mysterious power and attractiveness of that quality of Negro American style known as "soul." An expression of American diversity within unity, of blackness with whiteness, soul announces the presence of a creative struggle against the realities of existence.

Without the presence of blacks, our political history would have been otherwise. No slave economy, no Civil War, no violent destruction of the Reconstruction, no K.K.K. and no Jim Crow system. And without the disenfranchisement of black Americans and the manipulation of racial fears and prejudices, the disproportionate impact of white Southern politicians upon our domestic and foreign policies would have been impossible. Indeed, it is almost impossible to conceive of what our political system would have become without the snarl of forces—cultural, racial, and religious—that make our nation what it is today.

Absent, too, would be the need for that tragic knowledge which we try ceaselessly to evade: that the true subject of democracy is not simply material well-being, but the extension of the democratic process in the direction of perfecting itself. The most obvious test and clue to that perfection is the inclusion, *not* assimilation, of the black man.

Since the beginning of the nation, white Americans have suffered from a deep inner uncertainty as to who they really are. One of the ways that has been used to simplify the answer has been to seize upon the presence of black Americans and use them as a marker, a symbol of limits, a metaphor for the "outsider." Many whites could look at the social position of blacks and feel that color formed an easy and reliable gauge for determining to what extent one was or was not American. Perhaps that is why one of the first epithets that many European immigrants learned when they got off the boat was the term "nigger"; it made them feel instantly American. But this is tricky magic. Despite his racial difference and social status, something indisputably American about Negroes not only raised doubts about the white man's value system, but aroused the troubling suspicion that whatever else the true American is, he is also somehow black.

Materially, psychologically and culturally, part of the nation's heritage is Negro American, and whatever it becomes will be shaped in part by the Negro's presence. Which is fortunate, for today it is the black American who puts pressure upon the nation to live up to its ideals. It is he who gives creative tension to our struggle for justice and for the elimination of those factors, social and psychological, which make for slums and shaky suburban communities. It is he who insists that we purify the American language by demanding that there be a closer correlation between the meaning of words and reality, between ideal and conduct, between our assertions and our actions. Without the black American, something irrepressibly hopeful and creative would go out of the American spirit, and the nation might well succumb to the moral slobbism that has always threatened its existence from within.

When we look objectively at how the dry bones of the nation were hung together, it seems obvious that some one of the many groups that compose the United States had to suffer the fate of being allowed no easy escape from experiencing the harsh realities of the human condition as they were to exist under even so fortunate a democracy as ours. It would seem that some one group had to be stripped of the possibility of escaping such tragic knowledge by taking sanctuary in moral equivocation, racial chauvinism or the advantage of superior social status. There is no point in complaining over the past or apologizing for one's fate. But for blacks there are no hiding places down here, not in suburbia or in penthouse, neither in country nor in city. They are an American people who are geared to what *is*, and who yet are driven by a sense of what it is possible for human life to be in this society. The nation could not survive being deprived of their presence because, by the irony implicit in the dynamics of American democracy, they symbolize both its most stringent testing and the possibility of its greatest human freedom.

TONI CADE BAMBARA

Deep Sight and Rescue Missions

It's one of those weird winter-weather days in Philly. I'm leaning against the wall of a bus kiosk in Center City brooding about this article that won't write itself. Shoppers unself-consciously divest themselves of outer garments, dumping woolly items into shopping bags. I'm scarfed to the eyes à la Jesse James, having just been paroled from the dentist. And I'm eager to get back to the 'Hood where I've been conducting an informal survey on assimilation. The term doesn't have the resonance it once had for me. I'm curious as to why that is.

At the moment, gums aching, I'm sure of only four things: ambivalence still hallmarks the integrationist-vs.-nationalist pull in Amero-African political life; social and art critics still disrespect, generally, actual differences in pluralistic United States and tend to collapse constructed ones instead into a difference-with-preference sameness, with White as major and People of Color (POCs) minor; media indoctrination and other strategies of coercive assimilation are endemic, ubiquitous, and relentless as ever; and the necessity of countering propaganda and deprogramming the indoctrinated as imperative as ever. I'm sure also that I am not as linguistically nimble as I used to be when interviewing various sectors/strata of the community, for I've just blown a gab fest on identity, belonging, and integration at the dentist's through an inability to bridge the gap between the receptionist, a working-class sister from the projects, who came of age in the sixties and speaks in nation-time argot, and the new dental assistant, a more privileged sister currently taking a break from Bryn Mawr, who speaks the lingo of postmodern theory.

Across from the bus stop is a new luxury high rise, a colossus of steel and glass with signs announcing business suites for lease. I wonder who's got bank these days to occupy such digs. Philly is facing economic collapse. Paychecks for municipal workers are often

weeks late. The hijacking of neighborhoods by developers, who in turn are being leaned on by the banks, which in turn are being scuttled by the robber barons, who in turn are being cornered by IRS investigators working for the Federal Reserve, whose covers have been pulled off by black and Latino task forces, who in turn are harassed by Hoover's heirs. And while many citizens are angry about the S & L bailout being placed on the backs of workers one paycheck away from poverty and obscurity, they are even more distressed by cuts in social services that have pushed homelessness beyond the crisis point. I roam my eyes over the building, wondering if the homeless union would deem it media-worthy for a takeover.

In the lobby of the high rise is a sister about my age, early fifties, salt-'n'-pepper 'fro, African brass jewelry, a woolly capelike coat of an Andean pattern. She's standing by a potted fern, watchful. She seems to be casing the joint. I get it in my head that she's a "checker," a member of a community group that keeps an eye on HUD and other properties suitable for housing the homeless. A brisk-walking young sister emerges from the bank of elevators. Briefcase tucked smartly under one elbow, coat draped over the left Joan Crawford shoulder pad, hair straight out of a Vidal Sassoon commercial, the sister strides past the visitors-must-sign-in information counter, and the older woman approaches her. I search for a word, rejecting "accosts," "buttonholes," "pounces," and "confronts," but can't find a suitable verb for the decisiveness and intensity of the older woman's maneuver. Obviously strangers, they, nonetheless, make short shrift of amenities and seem to hunker down to a heavy discussion forthwith, the older sister doing most of the talking. She's not panhandling. She's not dispensing literature of any kind. She doesn't reach over to pin a campaign button on the Armani lapel. But she's clearly on a mission. What kind of scam, then, could it be? And if not a scam, what?

I now get it in my head that the older sister is Avey Johnson, sprung from the pages of Paule Marshall's 1983 novel *Praisesong for the Widow.* Avey, having rejected her deracinated life of bleached-out respectability in White Plains, New York, fashions a new life's work, taking up a post in buildings such as the high rise to warn bloods of the danger of eccentricity and to urge them to (re)center themselves and work for the liberation of the people. I'm so certain it's Avey, I move away from the wall to go get in it. My daughter's voice chimes in my ear: "Mother, mind your own business." I head for the curb, muttering my habitual retort: "Black people are my business, sugar." A youngblood on a skateboard zooms by. His bulky down jacket, tied around his hips by the sleeves, brushes against my coat and stops me. The No. 23 bus is approaching. So is rush hour. And who knows how swiftly and mean the weather will turn any second. I board.

From my seat, I watch the briefcase sister spin out the revolving doors onto the sidewalk. She seems preoccupied, unsure, but not about whether to put on her coat. She walks to the corner. Her gait is no longer brisk. Her suit has lost its crispness. She swivels around, though, like a runway model and looks through the glass of the lobby. The older woman has a brother backed up against the newspaper rack. She's taken a wide-legged stance, coat swept back from her hips, fists planted on the rise of the bones, neck working, mouth going. He holds his attaché case in front of him with both hands as though to fend her off. The light changes and the bus moves on.

In *Praisesong*, it's the power of a handed-down tale that rescues Avey from an inauthentic life, from the bad bargain she made early on, surrendering up cultural authenticity in exchange for separate-peace acceptability. Through the tale's laying-on-of-hands potency, Avey undergoes a process of reading the signs and codes, a refamiliarization with blackness that releases the power of Nommo and grounds her, so that she can adopt a responsible life. The tale is still told today in the Georgia and Carolina Sea Islands. The self-same tale informs, too, Julie Dash's 1991 screen masterpiece *Daughters of the Dust*.

In the opening of the independent black feature film, a boat glides into view. The terrain looks tropical. Dragonflies hover over the green-thick water. At the prow of the boat stands a woman in a large, veiled, creamy-white hat. She wears a long, heavy, creamy-white dress. This image is straight out of a million colonialism-as-fun movies. But this woman is standing hipshot, one arm akimbo, cocked chin, all att-ti-tude. These ebonics signal the spectator that Sister Dash has appropriated the iconography from imperialist entertainment for an emancipatory purpose. The boat pulls into the shallows, where a carving of an African, a figure once attached to the prow of a slaver ship, bobs close to shore. The boat docks. A legend appears on screen: "Ibo Landing, 1902." Thereafter, the handed-down tale of the Ibos unfolds as part of the film's complex narrative.

When the boat brought the Ibos from the slaver ship, the story goes, the Africans stepped out onto the sand in their chains, took one look around, and with deep-sight vision saw what the Europeans further had in store for them, whereupon they turned right around and walked all the way home on the water to the motherland. In *Daughters*, various members of the Peazant family, gathered on a Carolina island for a final reunion picnic before migration splits them up, react to the tale in different ways. Several characters, urged by Nana, the family head, to remember, to resist amnesia, to take with them on their journey away from the ancestral place the faculty for deep-sight vision, draw strength from the story, as does Avey Johnson in the novel. "My body may be here," Avey's great-great-grandmother had said, passing along the tale, "but my mind's long gone with the Ibos." *Daughters*, like *Praisesong*, invites the viewer, the reader, to undergo a process to liberate the imperialized eye.

The No. 23 bus, heading for Chinatown, first cuts through a district that community workers call The Zone of Diminishing Options. In the three-block area around Race and Ninth streets are pawn shops that also sell used clothes, labor-pool agencies advertising dishwashing jobs in the Atlantic City casinos, a very busy blood bank, a drop-in shelter, the Greyhound terminal, an army recruiting office, and a hospice center. While draft counseling in the Zone, I'd often think of opening a gun shop, if only to disrupt the perverse visual gag. And while in the Zone, I caught a third of a provocative independent black film called *Drop Squad*. A community worker, cassette in hand, persuaded a pawn-shop owner to play it on a set in the window.

Written by David Taylor, produced by Butch Robinson, and directed by David Johnson, *Drop Squad* is a satire about hijacking the hijacked. A nationalist organization puts the snatch on an assimilated corporate blood, straps him down in a chair in a red-black-and-green-draped community center, and proceeds to try to deprogram him. "You need to reacquaint yourself with you, brother," they tell him, assigning him to read Toni Morrison's *The Bluest Eye*. They take turns chanting a roll-call reveille: Soul Train, Garvey, Eleanor Bumpers, Revolutionary Action Movement, Biko, Fannie Lou Hamer, W. E. B. Du Bois, Sharpeville, Billie Holiday, Frantz Fanon. They argue, threaten, cajole, insist, are determined to wake the brother up. He counters with equal passion for the individual right to be whatever and whomsoever he pleases. Frequently his arguments are sound, momentarily stumping his captors. But they are relentless in their campaign to call the brother home, to reclaim him for the collective mission of race recovery. Privileged as he has become through people's struggles, they argue that he has a debt both to himself and to his community blasted by drugs, violence, joblessness, homelessness, lack of access, and the politics of despair.

I reach Germantown. The Hawk, out now and bold, blows me toward the greengrocer on Chelten. Worker Khan Nguyen has been discussing assimilation for me with her customers, especially Vietnamese and African and East Indian Caribbeans new to the U.S. She reports that assimilation is synonymous with citizenship training. It's her take that while folks know that the intent of the training is to "domesticate" them, the emphasis on democracy and rights makes them "wildly expectant." Kahn winks. She has not been tamed by the process. "It may be naïve of me," she says, warming to the subject, but the fact that "new immigrants take democracy more seriously" than it is generally practiced in a society built on theft and bondage, riddled by a white-supremacist national ideology, motivated by profit and privilege, and informed by fascist relations between classes, races, sexes, and communities of various sexual orientations, cultural heritages, and political persuasions "means that, in time, they will become unruly." She leans on the phrase "in time," because I am frowning. I ask about citizenship as a bribe contract: We'll grant you citizenship, and in return you drop your cultural baggage and become "American," meaning defend the status quo despite your collective and individual self-interest. She repeats the phrase "in time," putting her whole body into it to drown me out. I stumble out of there, hugging a bottle of Jamaican vanilla extract (excellent wash for cleaning/deodorizing the refrigerator, by the by), hopeful.

I run into a young friend, Anthony (Buffalo Boy) Jackson, graffiti artist and comic-book maker. I ask for his help, easing into the topic by explaining "assimilation" as I first encountered it in Latin (the changing of letters to make them sound in accord with letters nearby, i.e., *absimilare* in Latin becomes *assimilar, eccentricus* in Medieval Latin or *ekkentros* in Greek becomes *eccentric* in English), and *bio* (the process by which the body converts food into absorbable substances for the maintenance of the system). Before I can get to the sociopolitical meaning, Anthony is off and running with "system," recounting a middle-school field trip to a marsh in the New Jersey Pine Barrens to study ecosystems. He loses me, but I chime in when I hear usable things like "symbiosis" and "parasites," and finally the ability of the amoeba to give alternate responses to its environment because of its shape-shifting ability.

"Hold it, Anthony, are you saying amoebas can transform the system? I mean, err rahh, are they capable of collective action or are they basically loners?"

My friend is dancing and laughing at me. "The amoeba shall overthrow, right?" Big joke.

I walk him toward Burger King 'cause now he has an idea—the amoeba as mantua, shape shifter, ninja—and the tables are big enough to spread out on. I bring him back to my needs, and he tells me the issue is rip-off, not assimilation.

"Everything we do," he says, meaning breaking, scratching, rapping, dressing, "gets snatched up and we get bumped off." Which is why, he explains, he admires Spike Lee, because of Lee's control over the films and especially over the spin-offs that come out of 40 Acres and a Mule—CDs, books, T-shirts, mugs, caps,

jackets. He ducks inside and shakes his head about me. I'm old enough to know what the deal is, and the deal is rip-off.

Down the block, toward Wayne Avenue, is a produce truck where people frequently gather to talk over the news of the day. Trucker Mr. Teddy, a blood from Minnesota, tells me that only Europeans were invited to become truly assimilated. "And assimilation went out when *Roots* came in and busted up the whole melting-pot con game." According to him, nobody's been melted—not Norwegians, not Germans, not Japanese, and definitely not Africans. He talks about the Swedes in the Midwest who, in reclaiming their heritage, particularly their seventeenth-century socialist tradition, have rejected assimilation. "Hmm," sez I and venture to ask if these unmelted Amero-Europeans he speaks of reject as well their race/skin privileges, the socio-eco-political and psychic profits derived from U.S. apartheid. "Now that would be un-Amurrican." He chuckles and slamdunks a cabbage into my bag.

Across the avenue in front of the newsstand where folks are lined up to buy lottery tickets, the daily floor show is in progress. It features an old white guy who shuffles along the strip panhandling from the newsstand, past the wall bordering the Super Fresh, past the Woolworth, to the area near the bank where vendors line the curbs all the way down to Germantown Avenue, where I got off the No. 23. Some black people derive great pleasure from helping a down-and-out white person. The same pleasure, I suspect, that film-buff friends of mine enjoy watching a wrecked Chet Baker fall totally apart on the screen in the docu *Let's Get Lost*. There are always folks about, fingering the videotapes on the tables—today "Highlights of the Clarence Thomas–Anita Hill Hearings" is selling for $8—who crack on the generous-minded who give money to panhandling whites. "Christian duty my ass! Let that ole cracker beg in his own neck of the woods." But the consensus notion is that Old Whiteguy is pretty much in his neck of the woods, that he lives, in fact, in posh quarters on Wissahickon Avenue. Should anyone voice that, they are charged with being proracist, at least stereotypic in thinking that all white people are well-off. "Well-off or not," someone is saying as I reach the performing arena, "he's getting fat off black people." That remark triggers a mention of jim crow, talking low, and slavery. So a few people make a point of jostling the old man. Should anyone object and call the behavior racist, as in reverse racism, that provokes still another discussion: that some in the race seem to live outside of history and don't appreciate the fact that a race war is going on and that it wasn't bloods who declared it; whereupon statistics are ticked off about infant mortality, life expectancy, illiteracy, unemployment, and other aspects of the war. Meanwhile, Old Whiteguy is steadily collecting loose change, wending his way toward a sister who vends around our way only occasionally.

I don't know her name yet, but I admire her titles: Sam Yette's *The Choice*, Chancellor Williams's *The Destruction of Black Civilization*, and everything that Angela Davis ever published. Should a youth bedecked in gold try to get past her, she'll beckon her/him over and give a mini workshop on black miners in South Africa, apartheid, and the international gold trade. Should a youngblood stroll by in a Malcolm T-shirt (*By Any Means Necessary*) she will get very generous with her wares. Old Whiteguy is another matter.

"You want a what—a quarter!?!" she says. "I'll give you a quarter." Images of Old Whiteguy tied to two horses being lashed in opposite directions flood my dentist-traumatized brain. She looks him up and down and says quite seriously, "Hey, you used to be a young peckerwood, so why ain't you president?" He grins his drooly grin, hand still stuck out. Book Sister turns to the incense seller in a crocheted cufi at the next table. "Come get this clown before I'm forced to hurt him."

Before dark, I reach home, a coop whose comfy lobby I'd thought would ensure me neighbors enough for a roundtable discussion on this article. But the lobby's empty. I drop in on my neighbor Vera Smith. She takes a hard line on both aggressive assimilationists and seemingly spaced denialists, folks quick to call behavior manifested by Book Sister and jostlers as racist, folks who swear that things are all right, or would be all right if Black people weren't so touchy, mean, and paranoid. I say something like "consciousness requires a backlog of certain experiences." Vera ain't going for it. From day one, she says, there's enough evidence around to peep the game and resist. "So it's a decision to be like that," she says. "And it takes a lot of energy to deny what's obvious." Denialists don't want to see, don't want to belong, don't want to struggle, says Vera, putting a pin in it.

We talk into the night about a lot of things. A first-generation U.S. Bajun, she shares with me her plan to have dual citizenship, from the U.S. which she automatically has, and from Barbados also. I'm profoundly pleased for her, and for us, for whenever a Brer Rabbit slip-the-yoke operation can be achieved, it puts another plank underfoot at home *base*.

I ride the elevator, thinking about people I've known growing up (not that all these years aren't my formative years) who worked tirelessly to maintain a deep connection with the briarpatch and its ways of being. No matter where they journeyed in the world or what kinds of bribes they were offered to become

amnesiacs, they knew their real vocation was to build home base, sanctuaries, where black people can stand upright, exhale, and figure out what to do about the latest attack. And so they kept faith with the church of their childhood, or the UNIA or Father Divine movement (both alive and well in Philly, by the by), or the family farm in Alabama, or the homestead in the Islands, sending money, cement, clothing, books, lumber, weapons, certain that home base is not where you may work or go to school, but where the folks are who named you daughter, daddy, mama, doctor, son, brother, sister, partner, dahlin', chile.

I rinse my ravaged mouth out with warm salt water and hit the keyboard. As my young friend said, the issue is rip-off. Invisibility is not a readily graspable concept for a generation that grew up on MTV, Cosby, Oprah, Spike Lee, Colin Powell, and black folks on soaps, quiz shows, and the nightly news. Not only are black folks ostensibly participating, so what the hell does invisibility mean?, but what is generally recognized at home and abroad as "American" is usually black. A hundred movies come to mind, but not their titles, sorry. For instance the one about two lost young Euro-Ams who find themselves in what they think is a time warp, the terrain woefully fiftyish, but discover that they've landed in a Soviet spy school, in an American village erected for the purpose of training infiltrators to pass as "American." The two are enlisted to update and authenticate the place and the curriculum. Everything they present as "American"—music, speech, gesture, style—is immediately identifiable, certainly to any black spectator, as black.

As for alienation, or as Dr. Du Bois limned it in numerous texts, double-consciousness and double vision, people coming of age in a period hallmarked by all-up-in-your-face hip-hop and an assertive pluralism/multiculturalism as well don't see barriers as a policy as old as Cortez, as deadly as COINTELPRO, as seductive as the Chris Columbus hype chugging down the pike, and more solid than the Berlin Wall, given the system's monstrous ability to absorb, coopt, deny, marginalize, deflect, defuse, or silence.

I don't know what goes on in classrooms these days, but in informal settings the advice of the Invisible Man's granddaddy, "Undermine 'em with grins," is inexplicable Tomism. The paradoxical paradigm of the Liberty Paint Factory episode in Ellison's novel, the necessity of mixing in black to concoct pure white, is just a literary joke thought up by some old-timey guy on an equally old-timey typewriter. The three aspects of alienation as traditionally experienced and understood by my elders, my age group, and the generation that came of age in the sixties—alienation from the African past (and present—Was there ever an American airline with direct flights to the motherland?), alienation from U.S. economic and political power, alienation from the self as wholly participating in history—don't register as immediately relevant.

I spend a fitful night fashioning questions to raise with myself in the morning. What characterizes this moment? There's a drive on to supplant "mainstream" with "multicultural" in the national consciousness, and that drive has been sparked by the emancipatory impulse, blackness, which has been the enduring model for other downpressed sectors in the U.S. and elsewhere. A repositioning of people of color (POCs) closer to the center of the national narrative results from, reflects, and effects a reframing of questions regarding identity, belonging, community. "Syncretism," "creolization," "hybridization" are crowding "assimilation," "alienation," "ambivalence" out of the forum of ideas. A revolution in thought is going on, I'm telling myself, drifting off. Modes of inquiry are being redevised, conceptual systems overturned, new knowledges emerging, while I thrash about in tangled sheets, too groggy to turn off the TV.

It drones on about Maxwell, the publishing baron who allegedly went over the side of his private yacht at two in the morning. All commentary reduced to the binary, as is typical of thought in the "West": suicide or homicide? I smirk in my sleep, sure that Maxwell used a proxy corpse and is alive and chortling in, say, Belo Horizonte, Brazil. Jim Jones, no doubt, is operating, courtesy of the CIA's answer to the Witness Relocation Program.

Still half-asleep, I rummage around in dualisms which keep the country locked into delusional thinking. The Two-Worlds obsession, for example: Euro-Ams not the only book reviewers that run the caught-between-two-worlds number into the ground when discussing works by Maxine Hong Kingston, Leslie Marmon Silko, Rudolfo Anaya, and other POCs, or rather, when reducing complex narrative dramas by POCs to a formula that keeps White World as a prominent/given/eternal factor in the discussion. Two-Worlds functions in the cultural arena the way Two-Races or the Black-and-White routine functions in the sociopolitical arena. It's a bribe contract in which Amero-Africans assist in the invisibilization of Native Americans and Chicanos in return for the slot as *the* "indigenous," the former slaves who were there at the beginning of the great enterprise called America.

The limits of binary opposition were in evidence in a manuscript I'd been reading on the way to the dentist's office. Articles that called black cinema "oppositional cinema" to Hollywood totally ignored practitioners operating in the independent circuit, and focused instead on Spike Lee, Matty Rich, John Singleton, Joe Vasquez, and Mario Van Peebles—filmmakers who take, rather than oppose, Hollywood as their model of filmmaking. The articles reminded me of the way the establishment press during the so-called Spanish-American War labeled the gung-ho, shoot-em-up, Manifest Destiny-without-limits proponents as imperialists, and the let's-move-in-in-the-name-of-hemispheric-hegemony proponents as anti-imperialists. Meanwhile, only the black press was calling for a genuine help-liberate-then-cooperate-not-dominate anti-imperialism. All that is to say, there are at least three schools of black filmmaking in the U.S.: that which produces within the existing protocol of the entertainment industry and may or may not include a critique (Fred Williamson, for example); that which uses enshrined genres and practices but disrupts them in order to release a suppressed voice (Spike Lee, for example, who freed up the B-Boy voice in his presentations, not to be confused with interrogations, offering a critique of U.S. society but not rising above its retrograde mindset *re* women and homosexuals in order to produce a vision); and that which does not use H'wood as its point of departure, but is deliberate and self-conscious in its commitment to building a socially responsible cinema, fashioning cinematic equivalents for our socio-political/cultural specificity and offering transformation dramas (Julie Dash, Hailie Gerima, Larry Clarke, and other insurgents of "La Rébellion," who, in the late sixties, drafted a declaration of independence in the overturning of the UCLA film school curriculum).

The limits of binary thinking are spooky enough, I'm thinking, as the birds begin, but what are the prospects for sound sense in the immediate future now that conglomerates have escalated their purchase on the national mind? Since the 1989 publication of the Chomsky-Herman tome *orechestraing* and the fall 1991 issues of *Media Fair,* which drew a scary enough picture of media control by white men of wealth, the noose has tightened. And today seventeen corporations own more than 50 percent of U.S. media—textbook companies, newspapers, magazines, TV stations, radio stations, publishing houses, film-production companies. And computerization makes it all the easier to expunge from available reference material those figures, movements, and lessons of the past that remind us that radicalism is also a part of the U.S. tradition. Without models, how does any citizen break out of the basic dualism that permeates social, educational, political, economic, cultural, and intimate life in this country? I refer to the demonic model abridged below:

We are ordained	You are damned
We make history	You make dinner

We speak	You listen
We are rational	You are superstitious, childlike (as in minor)
We are autonomous and evolved	You are shiftless, unhinged, underdeveloped, primitive, savage, dependent, criminal, a menace to public safety, are needy wards and clients but are not necessarily deserving
We live center stage, the true heroes (and sometimes heroines)	You belong in the wings or behind the scrim providing the background music
We are pure, noble, upright	You are backward, fallen, tainted, shady, crafty, wily, dark, enigmatic, sly, treacherous, polluted, deviant, dangerous, and pathological
We are truly human	You are grotesques, beasts, pets, raisins, Venus flytraps, dolls, vixens, gorillas, chicks, kittens, utensils
We were born to rule	You were born to serve
We own everything	Even you are merely on loan to yourself through our largess
We are the dicks	You are the pussies
We are entitled	You are obliged

I slap the alarm clock quiet and roll over, pondering my own journey out of the lockup. Pens crack under me, paper rustles. When in doubt, hew close to the autobiographical bone, I instruct myself. But my own breakout(s) from the lockup where black/woman/cultural worker in the binary scheme is a shapeless drama with casts of thousands that won't adhere to any outline I devise. I opt instead for a *faux* family portrait to narrate what I can't essay.

Split Vision and America the Beautiful

José Feliciano is on the radio singing "Ohhh beautiful for spacious skies." Everyone holds still, alert to meaning in each stressed note, breath, and strum. Elbows on the table, Aunt Clara studies the pattern of kernels in her corn-on-the-cob as Feliciano builds, reining in his passion then unleashing it. Cousin Claude, the barbecue fork his baton, stands on tiptoe to hit the high notes. "America, America" comes out in preposterous falsetto, but nobody laughs or complains. Fragments of the tune, raspy and offkey, snag in the throat of Granddaddy Daniels. He leaves off singing to say that nobody lets loose on "America" like Aretha or Ray Charles. It takes a blood to render the complex of longing, irony, and insistence that characterizes our angular relationship to this country.

The song over, Cousin Claude forgets he came indoors to take orders; he drifts around the living room while the burgers burn out back. Aunt Clara makes pulp of her corn on the cob; the attack has less to do with food, more with what a hunger the song has stirred up. Granddaddy Daniels clears his throat, spits phlegm into a hanky, then makes a big production out of folding the paper and backing it to the crossword puzzle. The youngsters on the floor doing homework lean in the old man's direction. Clearing the throat is usually a prelude to storytelling, but his pencil point keeps piercing the newsprint, a signal that he's not in a storying mood about, say, why he never rises when "The Star-Spangled Banner" is sung at the stadium, but will shush everybody and strain forward when a "cullid person" is doing the hell out of "America, the Beautiful." Eventually he bobs his head up and down and says that the Latino brother kicked much butt.

Cousin Claude waltzes into the kitchen and dances one of the Moten sisters away from the chopping board. He's humming the last few lines of the song, his lips tucked in and "brotherhood" growling in the throat then richocheting off the roof of his mouth, the final notes thin and trailing out to sea as, the dance over, he bows and heads through the door. The Moten twins, "healthy" women who cook in their black slips and stockinged feet, resume arguing about whether or not hard-boiled eggs are going into the potato salad this day, goddamnit.

Cousin Claude goes down the back steps one at a time like a child. He ponders aloud the mystery and history of Africans in the U.S. The elders, squinched together on the back-porch glider, call out, "Shut up," "Preach," or "Your food's on fire, sugah," depending on how worked up they wish to get on the subject. When the call-and-response reaches a pitch, drowning out the DJ on the radio overhead in the kitchen window, Cousin Claude tries, without success, to lure the elders into a discussion of his childhood days when the household wars between the Danielses and the Motens threatened to split the family up and drive all the children crazy.

War One: Assimilation vs. Transformation

It was Great Aunt Zala, a Daniels, who would shake us awake when Mr. Paul came calling. We'd scramble up and brace ourselves against each other in order to reach our assigned-by-age positions on the horsehair couch that my daddy, a Moten, went and bought anyway during the 1930s Don't-Buy-Where-You-Can't-Work campaign in Harlem. Legs stuck out, heels hooked in the welting that edged the cushions, we'd manage not to yawn, suck our thumbs, or otherwise disgrace ourselves in front of a race man or race woman, who always seemed to come in the night to do their talking.

Some of the grownups didn't think children should be privy to conversations about the state of the race—our struggles, our prospects, our allies, our enemies. They kept us away from Speakers Corner, union halls, poetry readings, outdoor rallies, tenant meetings, and even our own basement, where longshoremen—"Negroes," West Indians, Puerto Ricans, and Cubans—would meet to strategize against the bosses, landlords, merchants, union sellouts, cops, the FBI, the draft board, Immigration, Murder Incorporated, and other white forces in easy collusion when it came to keeping colored folks down.

The less the children know, the easier it'll be for them to fit in and make their way, seemed to be the thinking of half the household. They lobbied for lobotomy, in other words, convinced that ignorance was the prime prerequisite for assimilation, and assimilation the preferred path to progress. But Great Aunt Zala went right on opening the door to Robeson, Du Bois, Claudia Jones, Rose Garner, J. A. Rogers, the Sleeping Car Porters and Maids, the dockworkers, and members of the Ida B. Wells clubs. The woman would just not let us sleep.

War Two: Repatriation vs. Self-Determination

Cousin Claude entered high school the year of the World's Fair in New York. Grown, to hear him tell it, he had the right to join the Garveyites collecting signatures on a petition demanding reparations from the government and rematriation to the motherland. On April 24, 1939, the petition, signed by two-point-five million African souls, was introduced into Congress. Claude's mother, Aunt Billy, let it be known that she wasn't going no damn where on account of (a) she was part Narragansett on her father's side, (b) she was grandchild of many an enslaved African whose labor had further purchased her place in this land, (c) what was the point in going over there when the thing to do was to fight the good fight over here and change the government's policies that made life here and there and everywhere unbearable for colored people.

By freeing up this country from the robber barons and their brethren in sheets, the argument went, we'd free up half the world. So the first thing was to work hard and develop a firm base here from which to challenge the state. Forget this place, was Uncle Charlie's position; in Africa, we could build bigger armies with which to defeat colonialists and imperialists. Yeah, tell it to freedmen in Liberia slaving on Firestone's plantations, Aunt Billy would say right back. The children were drawn into the debates. Posters made from board-of-education oaktag filled the halls of the brownstone: BACK TO AFRICA *vs.* SELF-DETERMINATION IN THE BLACK BELT AND THE REST OF THE PLANET. Arguments waxed hot. Kinship loyalties frayed. Even after Congress tabled the bill and turned its attention to the war raging in Europe, there was no sleeping in that house.

War Three: Swing-Vote Politics vs. Independent Formations

After what the black press called "Fighting the Two Hitlerisms" at home and abroad, the Cold War chill set in, which we, in Harlem, experienced as heat—HUAC ushering in a new Inquisition. Patriotism against Hitler made the blacks-as-inferior line too blatant, as Gerald Horne points out in his work on Du Bois, *Black and Red*. Blacks-as-subversives became the new line. We experienced a crackdown on thinkers, speakers, writers, organizers, and coalition builders. Independent thought was a threat to national security, the state mouthpieces said at the Smith Act trials.

The household split into ever-shifting factions over the 1948 presidential election. Play ward politics for local spoils and concessions and never mind the "big picture" *vs.* hitch our collective wagon to the NAACP and bloc vote *vs.* Up the Party! and Down with HUAC! *vs.* build the American Labor Party and campaign for Henry Wallace *vs.* establish an independent black national party and to hell with all this switch hitting that only keeps us locked into other people's tournaments.

An insomniac at twenty-two, Cousin Claude began reading everything he could get his hands on, haunting the Michaux Memorial Bookstore on 125th street and Seventh Avenue and haunting us too, day and night. He took to quizzing his less-than-peers at the kitchen table: Did we know about Palmares, the sovereign nation self-emancipated Africans in Brazil created? Did we know about the maroon communities in the Sea Islands off the Georgia and Carolina coasts? Did we know that Oklahoma was going to come into the union as either an "Indian" state or a "Negro" state? Did we have any idea how stupid we were? If we weren't going to improve our minds, would we kindly change our names?

Cousin Claude was reading Du Bois as well, who in 1948 had just been bounced for the second time in fifteen years from the NAACP. Cousin Claude took to waking us up at night for our opinion of Dr.'s divided-self proposition: should we invest our time, energy, money, and African genius struggling to become first-class citizens in an insanely barbarous country whose majority despises both us and our efforts to humanize the place; or should we gather our genius together and create a society of our own, in this country or someplace else? Not an elder yet, Cousin Claude could be told to get lost and let us rest. But being a Daniels, he never did.

White Sight and the Bee in the Hexagon

When I first ran across Dr. Du Bois's passage as a girl, I had a problem straightaway. It conflicted with what I'd learned early on through Eldersay, namely, that the seventh son (or seventh son of the seventh son) who was born with a "veil" (some said "caul," which I heard as "call" as in having a calling) was enhanced by it, was gifted, not afflicted (unless the parents or godparents failed to perform particular rites with the caul, in which case the cauled might see ghosts; but that seemed to me no big deal, for a people who've come through the Middle Passage are surely predisposed to see ghosts, right?).

Second sight enabled the person to see things others couldn't see. Persons born with the veil were, if not clairvoyants, at least clearseeing. They could see through guise and guile. They were considered wise, weird, blessed, tetched, or ancient, depending on the bent of the describer. But they were consulted in the neighborhoods, occasionally revered. It was a vice-versa thing too—that is, people in the community known for unusually imaginative good sense were said to have been born with second sight, both with a veil, even if the sayer had not been present at the birth or could otherwise verify the existence of a gauzy membrane surrounding the eyes of the newborn.

When I came to the bit about looking at your own self all the time through the eyes of people who either pity you or hate you, that did not sound like the second sight I'd heard of. That sounded like white sight, the way your eyeballs roll around in a sea of white when you've totally lost track of yourself because of drinking or some other foolishness. My classmate Kyoto had a name for the condition where a lot of white is visible between the bottom round of the pupil and the eyelid, *sanpaku*. The person is disoriented, out of touch with self, surroundings, the universe. In this disconnected state, the person lacks vitality, lacks precision in thought and movement, has

poor instinctual self-preservation reactions, and is very prone to accidents. *Sanpaku* is considered a state of serious physical and spiritual imbalance. You need a doctor, preferably a Japanese doctor, preferably one who can start you on a macrobiotic diet.

Kyoto's family were in the U.S. concentration camps during the forties. He used to say that many of the inmates suffered from white sight. Several, to prove their loyalty to America, enlisted and helped kill Japanese and other members of the Axis powers. I can't say for sure whether he said those volunteers manifested the gravest forms of white sight or not, because we mostly liked to talk about the Japanese American battalions and African American units that liberated the German concentration camps and how the State Department was determined to keep the participation of colored people secret. So in the newsreels we only saw white heroism. It was propaganda designed to promote white sight, we instructed each other.

Frenchy, a neighborhood friend whose bio homework I used to do in exchange for safe passage through the neighborhood, especially through Morningside Park, was a member of the Chapmans and used to refer to a moment in gang rumbling as white sight. Say you've been cold-cocked from behind. Your eyeballs commence to roll up in your head like they're seeking asylum in the mass of neuromelanin surrounding the pineal gland. You definitely need to get to Sydenham or Harlem Hospital. You could have brain damage. You could die.

According to Dear Diary, I'd been at camp shortly before reading the passage in *Souls of Black Folk*, and bees were very much on my mind. So while I was reading about the affliction of viewing the self from an outside and unloving vantage point, Dr.'s "veil" began to take on the look of one of those wood-frame screens beekeepers slide down into the apiary so as to collect the honey from the caged-up bees. Dr.'s seventh son sounded like he needed to see a healer, a seer, someone whose calling was to pierce that screen that somebody, who clearly does not wish the seventh son well, shoved down split the self, because they wanted his sweetness. And his eyes.

By the time I read the passage again, I had experienced enough to know that I needed my eyes, my sweetness, and my stingers. I did not know, though, that I'd already become addicted to the version of the world and my community as promoted by Hollywood movies. I merely noticed that race movies, like race records, were no longer on the scene. But I did not fully appreciate that my celluloid jones made me as up for grabs as a sleeping bee. I interpreted "twoness" as the split-version struggle I thought I was valiantly waging to stay centered in the community's core-culture perspective and at the same time excel in the schools' and various chump-change workplaces'. I got poleaxed. I got sandbagged and *sanpakued*. I got stuck in the mask. I lost my eyes. I became unmoored.

But blessed, as many of us are, I never left the gaze of the community; that is, folks did not avert their eyes from me. And so I did not stay caged up long in secondary consciousness (Dr. says second sight) or false consciousness (as opposed to primary consciousness, or what Dr. calls true self-consciousness); at least not chronic not-consciousnesshood. For in the community, then as now, were at least four discernible responses to the way in which we are positioned in the U.S.: accommodation, opportunism, denial/flight, and resistance. Long before I learned to speak of these responses as "tendencies," I encountered the living examples, neighbors.

Accommodationists recommended that I read (not to be confused with analyze) white we-are-great books and Negro we-too-are-clean-so-please-white-folks-include-us-in works, and that I speak good English and stay off the streets. Opportunists taught me how to move through the streets and capitalize on the miserable and gullible, 'cause what the hell, the point was to beat Whitey at his own game, which was, don't you know?, taking off black folks. The I-have-never-experienced-prejudice-in-the-all-white-school-and-church-I-attend types urged me not to regard as belligerent every racial encounter, for there were good white people if I looked hard enough and overlooked some of their ideas. All of which was helpful for "breaking the ice" at camps, integrating ballet schools, "proving" we were not what Dem said we were. Of course, many of us did not understand then how dangerous a proposition proving could be. James Baldwin put his mighty mouth on it a bit later, though talking to Dem: "If I'm not who you say I am, then you're not who you say you are. And the battle is on!"

While others saw in me an icebreaker, a law-breaker, or a potential credit to the race, neighborhood combatants saw something else and spent a great deal of time, energy, and imagination encouraging and equipping me to practice freedom in preparation for collective self-governance (the very thing Hoover and the Red Squads called a danger to the national security—black folks thinking they had the capacity to rule themselves). I became acquainted with black books that challenged, rather than mimicked, white or Negro versions of reality. I became acquainted with folks who demonstrated that their real work was creating value in the neighborhoods—bookstores, communal gardens, think tanks, arts and crafts programs, community-organizer training, photography workshops. Many of them had what I call second sight—the ability to make reasoned calls to the community to cre-

ate protective spaces wherein people could theorize and practice toward future sovereignty, while at the same time watching out for the sharks, the next wave of repression, or the next smear campaign, and preparing for it.

Insubordinates, dissidents, iconoclasts, oppositionists, change agents, radicals, and revolutionaries appealed to my temperament and my earliest training at home. They studied, they argued, they investigated. They had fire, they had analyses, they had standards. They had respect for children, the elders, and traditions of struggle. They imparted language for rendering the confusing intelligible, for naming the things that warped us, and for clarifying the complex and often contradictory nature of resistance.

Through involvement in tenants' actions, consumer groups, and other community-based activism, I began to learn how and why an enterprise prompted by an emancipatory impulse might proceed in the early stages as a transform-as-we-move intervention, but soon take on an assimilationist character. The original goal might be to oust the slum landlord and turn the building into a coop. But soon rank-and-file men are complaining about the authority exercised by the women officers. Founding members are opting for historical privilege, arguing that their votes and opinions are weightier than newcomers'. More solvent members begin objecting to the equal-shares policy of the association and start calling the less than solvent chiselers and freeloaders. Finally, everybody's got it in for the elected chairperson. And nobody trusts the treasurer. Then there's a purge, a splintering, or the hardening of factions. And each falls back on the surrogate lingo: "Same o, same o, niggers just can't get it together."

The situation, in some respects, is worse in these days of *Dallas* and *Lifestyles of the Rich and Famous*. Bigger-is-better and grassroots-ain't-shit drive many a budding organization to grab any ole funding in order to enlarge. Say a community organization comes together in response to a crisis government agencies ignore. For a while folks operate in the style of the neighborhood culture. But soon they begin to duplicate the very inequities and pathologies that gave rise to the original crisis: Setting up hierarchal structures that cut less aggressive members out of the decision-making process. Underdeveloping the staff in favor of the stars. Deferring to "experts" whether they live on the turf, share the hardships, and understand the conditions or not. Devaluing the opinion of the experienced because they are less articulate than others. Smoothing over difference and silencing dissent in the name of unity.

Sometimes the virus in the machine is the funding, or a clique with a hidden agenda, or the presence of agents provocateurs, or media seduction. Most often the replication is the result of the failure to build a critical mechanism within the organization, the failure to recognize that close, critical monitoring of process is necessary in order to overcome the powerful pull domination and demonizing exert in this society. That is to say, we often underestimate the degree to which exploitative behavior has been normalized and the degree to which we've internalized these norms. It takes, then, a commitment to an acutely self-conscious practice to be able to think and behave better than we've been taught by the commercial media, which we, addicted, look to for the way we dress, speak, dance, shop, cook, eat, celebrate, couple, rear, think, solve problems, and bury each other.

Fortunately, a noncommercial media exists. Independent-minded students, teachers, parents, fundraisers, spectators, readers, theoreticians, programmers, curators, and practitioners are increasingly drawn to the independent media movement—the films and video, in particular, produced outside of the industry structure. The Independent Black Cinema Movement and now the Independent Multicultural Media Movement are generally made up of progressive-minded POCs who wage a battle against white sight, disconnectedness, indoctrination, assimilation.

POCs, for example, who have challenged white privilege over language have been producing in the last fifteen years books, films, videos, radio formats, poetry, performance art, sculpture, paintings, audio programs, criticism, theory, dramas, at a rate not previously recorded. It is more than a "heritage of insult," as Dr. often phrased it, that draws POCs together to organize neighborhoods, devise curricula, convene conferences, compare notes, collaborate on projects, or form coalitions. Frequently the moves are motivated by acknowledgment of multiple cultural heritage or biraciality. Sometimes they are compelled by a hunch that the answers to questions of identity lie in another's culture. Sometimes alliances are sparked by a determination to understand what is going on in this country that doesn't reach the nightly news or the campuses. As David Mura, Amero-Japanese writer in Minnesota, has frequently said, POCs find in the cultural work of other POCs what they can't find in the Saul Bellows and Updikes, or in Descartes and Plato.

Unfortunately, it is not always easy to locate independent film programs mentioned in the quarterly *Black Film Review*, the Asian *Cinevision* newsletter, *Independent Film & Video* journal, or the publications put out by the Latino Film Collaborative and the Native American Broadcasting Consortium, or the National Black Programming Consortium's *Take One*. It's no simple task to locate the periodicals themselves, *In-dependent* the only one that is found with any regularity in well-stocked book and magazine stores.

What's particular about this new crop of films and videos? For one, they don't flatten our cultural specificity in favor of "crossover." What is observable about them of late is the awareness that POCs are part of the authenticating audience. What might that mean in the future should artists of, say, the Chicano/Chicana community direct their work with Native Americans readers or spectators in mind? For one, it would probably mean the end of victim portraiture, the kind of characterization the downpressed frequently engage in when addressing "the wider audience," as is said, based on the shaky premise that if only Dem knew the situation they would lighten up. Victim portraits are an insult to those struggles. Victim portraits send a dispiriting message to one's own constituency. What might happen if, say, Amero-Africans pitched our work toward Pacific Islander readers and spectators? We'd have to drop the Two-Race delusion, for one. What is and can be the effect of this swapmeet, now that one out of every four persons in the U.S. is a POC? A reconceptualization of "America" and shift in the power configuration of the U.S.A.

CORNEL WEST

Learning to Talk of Race

What happened in Los Angeles this past April was neither a race riot nor a class rebellion. Rather, this monumental upheaval was a multiracial, trans-class, and largely male display of justified social rage. For all its ugly, xenophobic resentment, its air of adolescent carnival, and its downright barbaric behavior, it signified the sense of powerlessness in American society. Glib attempts to reduce its meaning to the pathologies of the black underclass, the criminal actions of hoodlums, or the political revolt of the oppressed urban masses miss the mark. Of those arrested, only 36 percent were black, more than a third had full-time jobs and most claimed to shun political affiliation. What we witnessed in Los Angeles was the consequence of a lethal linkage of economic decline, cultural decay, and political lethargy in American life. Race was the visible catalyst, not the underlying cause.

The meaning of the earthshaking events in Los Angeles is difficult to grasp because most of us remain trapped in the narrow framework of the dominant liberal and conservative views of race in America, which with its worn-out vocabulary leaves us intellectually debilitated, morally disempowered, and personally depressed. The astonishing disappearance of the event from public dialogue is testimony to just how painful and distressing a serious engagement with race is. Our truncated public discussions of race suppress the best of who and what we are as a people because they fail to confront the complexity of the issue in a candid and critical manner. The predictable pitting of liberals against conservatives, Great Society Democrats against self-help Republicans, reinforces intellectual parochialism and political paralysis.

The liberal notion that more government programs can solve the problems is simplistic—precisely because it focuses *solely* on the economic dimension. And the conservative idea that what is needed is a change in the moral behavior of poor black urban dwellers (especially poor black men, who, they say, should stay married, support their children, and stop committing so many crimes) highlights immoral actions while ignoring public responsibility for the immoral circumstances that haunt our fellow citizens.

The common denominator of these views of race is that each still sees black people as a "problem people," in the words of Dorothy I. Height, president of the National Council of Negro Women, rather than as fellow American citizens with problems. Her words echo the poignant "unasked question" of W. E. B. Du Bois, who wrote:

> They approach me in a half-hesitant sort of way, eye me curiously or compassionately, and then instead of saying directly, How does it feel to be a problem? they say, I know an excellent colored man in my town. . . . Do not these Southern outrages make your blood boil? At these I smile, or am interested, or reduce the boiling to a simmer, as the occasion may require. To the real question, How does it feel to be a proble5m? I answer seldom a word.

Nearly a century later, we confine discussions about race in America to the "problems" black people pose for whites rather than considering what this way of viewing black people reveals about us as a nation.

This paralyzing framework encourages liberals to relieve their guilty consciences by supporting public funds directed at "the problems"; but at the same time, reluctant to exercise principled criticism of black people, they deny them the freedom to err. Similarly, conservatives blame the "problems" on black people themselves—and thereby render black social misery invisible or unworthy of public attention.

Hence, for liberals, black people are to be "included" and "integrated" into "our" society and culture, while for the conservatives they are to be "well behaved" and "worthy of acceptance" by "our" way

of life. Both fail to see that the presence and predicaments of black people are neither additions to nor defections from American life, but rather *constitutive elements of that life.*

To engage in a serious discussion of race in America, we must begin not with the problems of black people but with the flaws of American society—flaws rooted in historic inequalities and longstanding cultural stereotypes. How we set up the terms for discussing racial issues shapes our perception and response to these issues. As long as black people are viewed as a "them," the burden falls on blacks to do all the "cultural" and "moral" work necessary for healthy race relations. The implication is that only certain Americans can define what it means to be American—and the rest must simply "fit in."

The emergence of strong black-nationalist sentiments among blacks, especially young people, is a revolt against this sense of having to "fit in." The variety of black-nationalist ideologies, from the moderate views of Supreme Court Justice Clarence Thomas in his youth to those of Louis Farrakhan today, rest upon a fundamental truth: white America has been historically weak-willed in ensuring racial justice and has continued to resist accepting fully the humanity of blacks. As long as double standards and differential treatment abound—as long as the rap performer Ice-T is harshly condemned while former Los Angeles Police Chief Daryl F. Gates's antiblack comments are received in polite silence, as long as Dr. Leonard Jeffries's anti-Semitic statements are met with vitriolic outrage while presidential candidate Patrick J. Buchanan's are received with a genteel response—black nationalisms will thrive.

Afrocentrism, a contemporary species of black nationalism, is a gallant yet misguided attempt to define an African identity in a white society perceived to be hostile. It is gallant because it puts black doings and sufferings, not white anxieties and fears, at the center of discussion. It is misguided because—out of fear of cultural hybridization, silence on the issue of class, retrograde views on black women, homosexuals, and lesbians, and a reluctance to link race to the common good—it reinforces the narrow discussions about race.

To establish a new framework, we need to begin with a frank acknowledgment of the basic humanness and Americanness of each of us. And we must acknowledge that as a people—*E Pluribus Unum*—we are on a slippery slope toward economic strife, social turmoil, and cultural chaos. If we go down, we go down together. The Los Angeles upheaval forced us to see not only that we are not connected in ways we would like to be but also, in a more profound sense, that this failure to connect binds us even more tightly together. The paradox of race in America is that our common destiny is more pronounced and imperiled precisely when our divisions are deeper. The Civil War and its legacy speak loudly here. Eighty-six percent of white suburban Americans live in neighborhoods that are less than one percent black, meaning that the prospects for the country depend largely on how its cities fare in the hands of a suburban electorate. There is no escape from our interracial interdependence, yet enforced racial hierarchy dooms us as a nation to collective paranoia and hysteria—the unmaking of any democratic order.

The verdict that sparked the incidents in Los Angeles was perceived to be wrong by the vast majority of Americans. But whites have often failed to acknowledge the widespread mistreatment of black people, especially black men, by law-enforcement agencies, which helped ignite the spark. The Rodney King verdict was merely the occasion for deep-seated rage to come to the surface. This rage is fed by the "silent" depression ravaging the country—in which real weekly wages of all American workers since 1973 have declined nearly twenty percent, while at the same time wealth has been upwardly distributed.

The exodus of stable industrial jobs from urban centers to cheaper labor markets here and abroad, housing policies that have crated "chocolate cities and vanilla suburbs" (to use the popular musical artist George Clinton's memorable phrase), white fear of black crime, and the urban influx of poor Spanish-speaking and Asian immigrants—all have helped erode the tax base of American cities just as the federal government has cut its supports and programs. The result is unemployment, hunger, homelessness, and sickness for millions.

Driving that rage is a culture of hedonistic self-indulgence and narcissistic self-regard. This culture of consumption yields coldhearted and meanspirited attitudes and actions that turn poor urban neighborhoods into military combat zones and existential wastelands.

And the pervasive spiritual impoverishment grows. The collapse of meaning in life—the eclipse of hope and absence of love of self and others, the breakdown of family and neighborhood bonds—leads to the social deracination and cultural denudement of urban dwellers, especially children. We have created rootless, dangling people with little link to the supportive networks—family, friends, school—that sustain some sense of purpose in life. We have witnessed the collapse of the spiritual communities that help us face despair, disease, and death and that transmit through the generations dignity and decency, excellence, and elegance.

The result is lives of what we might call "random nows," of fortuitous and fleeting moments preoccupied with "getting over"—with acquiring pleasure, property, and power by any means necessary. (This is not what Malcolm X meant by this famous phrase.) Postmodern culture is more and more a market culture dominated by gangster mentalities and self-destructive wantonness. This culture engulfs all of us—yet its impact on the disadvantaged is devastating, resulting in extreme violence in everyday life. Sexual violence against women and homicidal assaults by young black men on one another are only the most obvious signs of this empty quest for pleasure, property, and power.

Lastly, this rage is fueled by a political atmosphere in which images, not ideas, dominate, where politicians spend more time raising money than issues. The functions of parties have been displaced by public polls, and politicians behave less as thermostats that determine the climate of opinion than as thermometers registering the public mood. American politics has been rocked by an unleashing of greed among opportunistic public officials—following the lead of their counterparts in the private sphere, where, as of 1989, one percent of the population owned thirty-seven percent of the wealth—leading to a profound cynicism and pessimism among the citizenry.

And given the way in which the Republican party since 1968 has appealed to popular xenophobic images—playing the black, female, and homophobic cards and realigning the electorate along race, sex, and sexual-orientation lines—it is no surprise that the notion that we are all part of one garment of destiny is discredited. Appeals to special interests rather than public interests reinforce this polarization. The Los Angeles upheaval was an expression of utter fragmentation by a powerless citizenry that includes not just the poor but all of us.

What is to be done? How do we capture a new spirit and vision to meet the challenges of the postindustrial city, post modern culture, and postparty politics?

First, we must admit that the most valuable sources for help, hope, and power consist of ourselves and our common history. As in the ages of Lincoln, Roosevelt, and King, we must look to new frameworks and languages to understand our multilayered crisis and overcome our deep malaise.

Second, we must focus our attention on the public square—the common good that undergirds our national and global destinies. The vitality of any public square ultimately depends on how much we *care* about the quality of our lives together. The neglect of our public infrastructure, for example—our water and sewage systems, bridges, tunnels, highways, subways, and streets—reflects not only our myopic economic policies, which impede productivity, but also the low priority we place on our common life.

The tragic plight of our children clearly reveals our deep disregard for public well-being. With about one out of five children living in poverty in this country and one out of two black children and two out of five Hispanic children doing so—and with most of our children ill-equipped to live lives of spiritual and cultural quality, neglected by overburdened parents, and bombarded by the market values of profit-hungry corporations—how do we expect ever to constitute a vibrant society?

One essential step is some form of large-scale public intervention to ensure access to basic social goods—housing, food, health care, eduction, child care, and jobs. We must invigorate the common good with a mixture of government, business, and labor that does not follow any existing blueprint. After a period in which the private sphere has been sacralized and the public square gutted, the temptation is to make a fetish of the public square. We need to resist such dogmatic swings.

Last, the major challenge is the need to generate new leadership. The paucity of courageous leaders—so apparent in the response to the events in Los Angeles—requires that we look beyond the same elites and voices that recycle the older frameworks. We need leaders—neither saints nor sparkling television personalities—who can situate themselves within a larger historical narrative of this country and world, who can grasp the complex dynamics of our peoplehood and imagine a future grounded in the best of our past, yet attuned to the frightening obstacles that now perplex us. Our ideals of freedom, democracy, and equality must be invoked to invigorate all of us, especially the landless, propertyless, and luckless. Only a visionary leadership that can motivate "the better angels of our nature," as Lincoln said, and activate possibilities for a freer, more efficient, and stable America—only that leadership deserves cultivation and support.

This new leadership must be grounded in grassroots organizing that highlights democratic accountability. Regardless of whether Bill Clinton's cautious neoliberal programs or George Bush's callous conservative policies prevail in November, the challenge to America will be determining whether a genuine multiracial democracy can be created and sustained in an era of global economies and a moment of xenophobic frenzy.

Let us hope and pray that the vast intelligence, imagination, humor, and courage in this country will not fail us. Either we learn a new language of empathy and compassion, or the fire this time will consume us all.

TONI MORRISON

On the Backs of Blacks

Fresh from Ellis Island, Stavros gets a job shining shoes at Grand Central Terminal. It is the last scene of Elia Kazan's film *America, America*, the story of a young Greek's fierce determination to immigrate to America. Quickly, but as casually as an afterthought, a young black man, also a shoe shiner, enters and tries to solicit a customer. He is run off the screen—"Get out of here! We're doing business here!"—and silently disappears.

This interloper into Stavros' workplace is crucial in the mix of signs that make up the movie's happy-ending immigrant story: a job, a straw hat, an infectious smile—and a scorned black. It is the act of racial contempt that transforms this charming Greek into an entitled white. Without it, Stavros' future as an American is not at all assured.

This is race talk, the explicit insertion into everyday life of racial signs and symbols that have no meaning other than pressing African Americans to the lowest level of the racial hierarchy. Popular culture, shaped by film, theater, advertising, the press, television and literature, is heavily engaged in race talk. It participates freely in this most enduring and efficient rite of passage into American culture: negative appraisals of the native-born black population. Only when the lesson of racial estrangement is learned is assimilation complete. Whatever the lived experience of immigrants with African Americans—pleasant, beneficial or bruising—the rhetorical experience renders blacks as noncitizens, already discredited outlaws.

All immigrants fight for jobs and space, and who is there to fight but those who have both? As in the fishing ground struggle between Texas and Vietnamese shrimpers, they displace what and whom they can. Although U.S. history is awash in labor battles, political fights and property wars among all religious and ethnic groups, their struggles are persistently framed as struggles between recent arrivals and blacks. In race talk the move into mainstream America always means buying into the notion of American blacks as the real aliens. Whatever the ethnicity or nationality of the immigrant, his nemesis is understood to be African American.

Current attention to immigration has reached levels of panic not seen since the turn of the century. To whip up this panic, modern race talk must be revised downward into obscurity and nonsense if antiblack hostility is to remain the drug of choice, giving headlines their kick. PATTERNS OF IMMIGRATION FOLLOWED BY WHITE FLIGHT, screams the *Star-Ledger* in Newark. The message we are meant to get is that disorderly newcomers are dangerous to stable (white) residents. Stability is white. Disorder is black. Nowhere do we learn what stable middle-class blacks think or do to cope with the "breaking waves of immigration." The overwhelming majority of African Americans, hard-working and stable, are out of the loop, disappeared except in their less than covert function of defining whites as the "true" Americans.

So addictive is this ploy that the fact of blackness has been abandoned for the theory of blackness. It doesn't matter anymore what shade the newcomer's skin is. A hostile posture toward resident blacks must be struck at the Americanizing door before it will open. The public is asked to accept American blacks as the *common* denominator in each conflict between an immigrant and a job or between a wannabe and status. It hardly matters what complexities, contexts and misinformation accompany these conflicts. They can all be subsumed as the equation of brand X vs. blacks.

But more than a job is at stake in this surrender to whiteness, more even than what the black intellectual W.E.B. Du Bois called the "psychological wage"—the bonus of whiteness. Racist strategies unify. Savvy politicians always include in the opening salvos of their campaigns a quick clarification of their position on race. It is a mistake to think that Bush's Willie Horton or Clinton's Sister Souljah was anything but a candidate's obligatory response to the demands of a contentious electorate unable to understand itself in any terms other than race. Warring interests, nationalities and classes can be merged with the greatest economy under that racial banner.

Race talk as bonding mechanism is powerfully on display in American literature. When Nick in F. Scott Fitzgerald's *The Great Gatsby* leaves West Egg to dine in fashionable East Egg, his host conducts a kind of class audition into WASP-dom by soliciting Nick's support for the "science" of racism. "If we don't look out the white race will be . . . utterly submerged," he says. "It's all scientific stuff; it's been proved." It makes Nick uneasy, but he does not question or refute his host's convictions.

The best clue to what the country might be like without race as the nail upon which American identity is hung comes from Pap, in Mark Twain's *Huckleberry Finn*, who upon learning a Negro could vote in Ohio, "drawed out. I says I'll never vote ag'in." Without his glowing white mask he is not American; he is Faulkner's character Wash, in *Absalom, Absalom!*, who, stripped of the mask and treated like a "nigger," drives a scythe into the heart of the rich white man he has loved and served so completely.

For Pap, for Wash, the possibility that race talk might signify nothing was frightening. Which may be why the harder it is to speak race talk convincingly, the more people seem to need it. As American blacks occupy more and more groups no longer formed along racial lines, the pressure accelerates to figure out what white interests really are. The enlisted military is almost one-quarter black; police forces are blackening in large urban areas. But welfare is nearly two-thirds white; affirmative-action beneficiaries are overwhelmingly white women; dysfunctional white families jam the talk shows and court TV.

The old stereotypes fail to connote, and race talk is forced to invent new, increasingly mindless ones. There is virtually no movement up—for blacks or whites, established classes or arrivistes—that is not accompanied by race talk. Refusing, negotiating or fulfilling this demand is the real stuff, the organizing principle of becoming an American. Star spangled. Race strangled.

CHAPTER FIVE

The Emancipated Self

I am the hope and the dream of the slave . . .

—Maya Angelou

READING SELECTIONS

Further Particulars Concerning the Schooner Amistad

The following letter from the New London Gazette office, gives further particulars concerning the Spanish schooner, and as every thing relating to this subject is read with interest, we lay it before our readers.

New London Gazette Office.
August 30th, 1839.

We regret to see in some of your papers complaints that they were not duly supplied with the particulars concerning the capture of the Amistad. As one of the conductors of the press in your city, from whom we have received repeated marks of editorial courtesy, expresses some surprise that we had not furnished him with the earliest intelligence on this subject, we deem it due to ourselves to state, that when we were called on by Captain Gedney at 12 o'clock on the night of the 26th, the first thing we did, after despatching an express for the Marshal, was to write a minute account to one of your daily papers, with a request that yourself and others should be supplied immediately with a copy of the same. As we had seen no publication of this, it, probably owing to the tardiness and irregularity of the mail, was not received till after the publication of the Gazette. In addition to this, the first papers that we printed at this office on the evening of the 28th, were sent by private conveyance to Stonington to the agents of the New York boats, who delivered them promptly the next morning. This much to exonerate ourselves from any imputation of a want of professional courtesy.

It is a source of regret that several of your papers, with no other authority than mere rumor, have published accounts, which, if credited, must deprive those to whom it is due, of their just share of credit in this capture. It has been stated that Captain Gedney was not on board the Washington at the time the schooner was seized. The truth is, that he was on board, and was, at the time the schooner was discovered, engaged in running a line of soundings. The Amistad was first observed by Lieut. R. W. Meade, who at that time had charge of the deck. Capt. Gedney scrutinized her with his glass, and observing wagons and people on the shore, concluded that she was a smuggler, and accordingly despatched a boat, with six men, and arms, in charge of Lieut. Meade and Passed Midshipman D. D. Porter, for the purpose of seizing her. On approaching the schooner, the two Spanish gentlemen made their appearance on deck, and exclaimed, "Bless the Holy Virgin, you are our preservers." The boat laid aboard the prize, and Lieut. Meade and Mr. Porter, followed by two of the men, jumped on deck, and drove the Africans below. Lieut. Meade then demanded in Spanish who was their captain, and where were their colors; when a torn Spanish ensign was produced, and by his orders it was set in the main rigging as a signal of distress to Capt. Gedney to send another boat alongside. The joy of the two passengers was unbounded. One of them, Senor Montez, the elder, who had been threatened every day during his captivity with death, threw his arms around Mr. Meade, who, under the circumstances, and from the by no means gentle nature of the embrace, being led to think that his intention was any thing but amicable, presented a pistol at his face, with a threat that unless he relaxed his hold he would shoot him. He was, however, soon convinced of the sincerity of his intentions by the tears of delight and thankfulness of the poor old man. Mr. Meade and two men remained in charge of the prize, while Mr. Porter, with four others, went ashore to arrest the leader and his accomplices, who were on the beach. On their approach, the blacks leapt into their boat, and pulled towards the schooner, when Mr. Porter discharged a pistol and they hove to. They were taken on board the brig, when Cinques, watching a convenient opportunity, leapt overboard, diving and swimming like a fish, till he was caught with a boat-hook. Meantime, Capt. Gedney came up with the Washington, and took the prize in tow for New London.

It has been stated that the schooner was taken by boys; this is also incorrect; she was taken by able-bodied men, who were prepared for the worst, and who would have been hard customers to deal with in case of a brush. On board the Washington there are several naval apprentices, and it is not out of place here to bear testimony to their neat and healthy appearance as well as their orderly deportment. We have cause to hope that from the adoption of this system, our navy, whilst it protects our commerce throughout the world, will at the same time be educating a class of mariners, in seamanship and character equal to those of any other nation, at the same time providing for a large class of indigent boys, who otherwise would become the inmates of our prisons.

The advantage of the surveying squadron to our revenue in preventing smuggling is also proved. In fact, we have long been of the opinion that it would be well for the service and for our commerce, if the revenue cutters were placed in charge of the junior officers of the navy, who would be thus qualifying themselves for more important duties. We have no doubt that they would prove equally as efficient as those who now make a sinecure of what was originally intended as a safeguard against frauds on the revenue.

You have doubtless received ere this a report of the investigation in presence of Judge Judson.—Segnor Montez is writing a history of his sufferings, which a friend has kindly offered to translate for us, and should it develop any additional facts of importance, they shall be transmitted to you at once. The negroes have been taken to New Haven, where they will await in jail their trial, which is to take place at Hartford on the 17th day of September next. The schooner is discharging at New London, where probably both vessel and cargo will be sold at auction.

If the Washington had not fallen in with the Amistad at the time and under the circumstances she did, the lives of the two passengers must inevitably have been sacrificed, and the cargo and vessel destroyed. They had supplied themselves with water, and were going to sea that night. Cinques had always declared that in case they were likely to be taken, he should kill the passengers, and that he would die sooner than be taken, and he enjoined upon his comrades to take his knife and avenge his death—that they had better die in self-defence, than be hung as they would be if taken.

The old gentleman says he never shall recover from the effects of his trouble, and that if he had been chained for ten years in a dungeon, it would not thus have broken him down. For some time previous to their deliverance, their only drink was the water of the sea. For more minute particulars, I would refer you to the Sun, of your city.

The schooner is of faultless model, and foul as her bottom is at present, she would have been able to work to windward of almost any of our cutters.

Names of the slaves as furnished by Lieutenant Meade:

> Cinques, the chief.
>
> Quash, his brother.
>
> Faquorna, assisted in killing the captain.
>
> Quimboo, also one of the murderers.
>
> Maum, helped to kill the captain and cook.
>
> Faa, concerned also in murder.
>
> Gabzo, one of the ringleaders, fat and short.
>
> Funny, cook, apparently amiable.
>
> Pana, alias Juan, speaks little English.
>
> Llamani, very severe with passengers and cabin boy.
>
> Guana, Sissi, Con, Sua, (sick) Zabray.
>
> Paulo Dama, great friend of cabin boy—saved his life.
>
> Conorno, cannibal with six large tusks projecting at right angles from his mouth.
>
> Jaoni, Pie, Naquai, Cnba, Baa, Berry, Prumuco, Faha, Huebo, Fuerre 1st, Fuerre 2d, Saa, Faguana, Chockamaw, Fasoma, Panguna, Kinna, Carri, Cuperi.
>
> Antonio Gonzalez, cabin boy.
>
> Cane, boy, 9 years old.
>
> *Females*—Ferue, Kene, Margra, about 13 years of age.

NEW LONDON, Aug. 29, 1839.

A Card.—The subscribers, Don Jose Ruiz and Don Pedro Montez, in gratitude for their most unhoped for and providential rescue from the hands of a ruthless gang of African buccaneers, and an awful death, would take this means of expressing, in some slight degree, their thankfulness and obligation to Lieut. T. R. Gedney, and the officers and crew of the U. S. surveying brig Washington, for their decision in seizing the Amistad, and their unremitting kindness and hospitality in providing for their comfort on board their vessel, as well as the means they have taken for the protection of their property.

We also must express our indebtedness to that nation whose flag they so worthily bear, with an assurance that this act will be duly appreciated by our most gracious sovereign Her Majesty the Queen of Spain.

DON JOSE RUIZ.
DON PEDRO MONTEZ.

Notice issued by the slavers aboard the *Amistad*

The African Prisoners

NEW HAVEN, Sept. 9, 1839.
To the committee on behalf of the African Prisoners:

I arrived here last Friday evening, with three men who are natives of Africa, and who were joined the next day by two others, to act as interpreters in conversing with Joseph Cinquez and his comrades. On going to the jail, the next morning, we found, to our great disappointment, that only one of the men, J.F., was able to converse with the prisoners. He is about 30 years of age, a native of Geshee or Gishe, which is about 100 or 150 miles from the mouth of the river Gallinus, in the interior, which is about a day's journey south of Sierra Leone. He was kidnapped when about 12 years of age, and was liberated in Columbia, by Bolivar. He is able to converse a little in the Mandingo dialect, but understands better that of Gallinao, which some of the prisoners can speak. Most of the prisoners can understand him, although none of them can speak his Geshee dialect. You may imagine the joy manifested by these poor Africans, when they heard one of their own color address them in a friendly manner, and in a language they could comprehend!

The prisoners are in comfortable rooms.—They are well clothed in dark striped cotton trowsers, called by some of the manufacturers "hard times," and in striped cotton shirts. The girls are in calico frocks, and have made the little shawls that were given them into turbans. The prisoners eyed the clothes some time, and laughed a good deal among themselves before they put them on. Their food is brought to them in separate tin pans, and they eat it in an orderly manner. In general, they are in good health. One of their number, however, died on Tuesday last, and two or three more are on the sick list and considered dangerous. They probably suffer for want of exercise in the open air. The four children are apparently from 10 to 12 years of age. The boy and two of the girls (who appeared to be sisters) are Mandingos, and the other girl is from Congo. They are robust, and full of hilarity, especially the Mandingos. The sheriff of the county took them to ride in a wagon on Friday. At first their eyes were filled with tears, and they seemed to be afraid, but soon they enjoyed themselves very well, and appeared to be greatly delighted. The children speak only their native dialects. Neither Cinquez nor any of his comrades have been manacled since they have been here. Their demeanor is altogether quiet, kind and orderly.

Most of the prisoners told the interpreter that they are from Mandingo. The district of Mandingo, in the Senegambia country, is bounded by the Atlantic Ocean, and is directly north of Liberia. Two or three of the men, besides one of the little girls, are natives of Congo, which is on the coast just south of the equator. The man with some of his teeth like tusks, is from Gahula in Congo. The teeth are said to be sharpened and made thus prominent by artificial means. One of the men from Mandingo, named Dama, talks Mandingo, and is a good looking and intelligent man. Cinquez is about five feet eight inches high, of fine proportions, with a noble air. Indeed, the whole company, although thin in flesh, and generally of slight forms and limbs, especially, are as good looking and intelligent a body of men as we usually meet with. All are young, and several are quite striplings. The Mandingos are described in books as being a very gentle race, cheerful in their dispositions, inquisitive, credulous, simple hearted, and much given to trading propensities. The Mandingo dialects are spoken extensively, and it is said to be the commercial language of nearly the whole coast of West Africa. We found that the following words are nearly the same in the Gallinas of the interpreter, in the Mandingo of the prisoners, in the Mandingo of Mungo Park, and in Jallowka of the German author, Adeburg, viz:—Sun, moon, woman, child, father, head, hand and foot. The numerals do not agree so well. If any person, who reads this statement, can furnish the Committee information concerning the Mandingo language, and its different dialects, particularly for vocabularies, they may render important service in the future examination of these unfortunate Africans. Professor Gibbs, of Yale College, has Adeburg's Mithridates, Park's Travels, and Mollien's Travels in Africa, and Professor Silliman has Prichard's Physical History of Mankind, which are at the service of the Committee.

Previous to this the Captain was very cruel and beat them senselessly. They would not take it, to use their own expression, and therefore turned to and fought for it. After this they did not know which way to go. But at length they told the Spaniards to take them to Sierra Leone. "They made fools of us," said Shinquau, "and did not go to Sierra Leone." In the day time they said they could tell very well which way to go by the sun, but at night the Spaniards deceived them, and put the vessel the other way. After this, said they, we got here, and did not know where we were.

Cinque by Nathaniel Jocelyn (Courtesy of New Haven Colony Historical Society)

Captain Green, of Sag Harbor, who was one of the first men the prisoners met ashore before their capture by Lieut. Gedney, of the U.S. brig Washington, and who has given me a circumstantial account, differing in many respects from what has been published, of all that took place, says that the Africans asked him of one of their number who speaks a little broken English, "What country is this?" He replied, this is America. They immediately asked, "Is it a slave country?" Captain Green answered, it is free here, and safe, and there are no Spanish law here. Shinquau then gave a sort of whistle, when they all sprang upon their feet and shouted. Captain Green and his associates sprang to their wagon for their guns, supposing the Africans were about to attack them. But Shinquau came up, delivered up his cutlass and gun, and even offered his hat &c., and the rest did the same, indicating that they would give all up, that Capt. G. might take charge of the schooner and everything on board. They however begged of him to take them to Sierra Leone. Shinquau positively assured Capt. G. at the time, and he re-

peats it now, that they threw nothing overboard. The stories about his loosening his girdle, and letting three or four hundred doubloons drop into the sea, and of diving and keeping under water forty minutes, are considered fabulous. The Africans assert that there was a quantity of doubloons in the trunks that were carried on shore on Long Island, and Capt. Green says he heard the money rattle as the trunks were returned to the schooner by order of Lieut. Gedney. On examining the contents of the trunks afterwards no gold was found! Some person, or persons, are supposed to have the money, *but who, is a secret.* While on shore, at Long Island, Shinquau and his companions, although hungry, and with arms in their hands, would not kill a single animal, or take an article even to satisfy their hunger, without paying generously for it. They appeared, it is true, to know very little about the value of money, and gave a doubloon for a dog, and a small gold piece for some victuals.

The African prisoners are orderly and peaceable among themselves. Some of them sing well, and appear to be in good spirits and grateful for the kindness shewn them. Col. Stanton Pendleton, at whose house I stop, is the jailor, and is kind and attentive to the prisoners. He provides them wholesome food in sufficient quantities, and gives every reasonable indulgence to the numerous visitors, from the neighboring towns and elsewhere, who throng the prison continually to see these interesting strangers from a distant land. Col. P. has allowed me to take copies of the warrants of commitment. The little girls, and the negro boy, Antonio, are committed as witnesses, "for neglecting to become recognized to the United States with surety," and Shinquau and his comrades are bound over "for murder on the high seas."

I have read an ingenious and well written article in the Evening Post signed Veto, in which the learned writer presents a pretty full examination of the case of the schooner Amistad. He says that it seems but too probable that the slaveholders, Messrs. Ruez and Montez, conscious of the invalidity of their claim in the Civil Courts, have drawn this criminal prosecution (the charge of murder) to give time to their government to make a demand: and he rather singularly says "this raises a far more difficult question." If Veto will turn to Niles' Register for 1823, he will find an elegantly written and very able opinion of Chief Justice Tilghman, of Pa., on this subject, in which that eminent jurist, in giving his own judgment against the claim of a foreign government in the case of a fugitive charged with treason or for said District, against Simon, Lucis, Joseph, Peter, Mortine, Manuel and fifty two others (whose names are enumerated) for the murder of Ramon Ferrer on the 20th day of June, 1839, on the high seas within the admiralty and maritime jurisdiction of the United States, it was ordered and adjudged by the undersigned that they against whom said information and complaint was made, stand committed to appear before the Circuit Court of the United States for the District of Connecticut, to be holden at Hartford, in said District, on the 17th day of September, 1839, to answer to the crime of murder, as set forth in said information and complaint.

You are therefore commanded to take the said persons, named as above, and charged with said crime, and them safely keep in the jail in New Haven, in said District, and them have before the Circuit Court of the United States to be holden at Hartford, in said District, on the 17th day of September A. D. 1839. Here of fail not, &c. Dated at New London, Aug. 29, 1839.

(Signed)   ANDREW T. JUDSON,
Judge of the United States for the District of Connecticut.

The Interesting Narrative of the Life of Olaudah Equiano, or Gustavus Vassa, the African; by Himself

The author is carried to Virginia—His distress—Surprise at seeing a picture and a watch—Is bought by Captain Pascal, and sets out for England—His terror during the voyage—Arrives in England—His wonder at a fall of snow—Is sent to Guernsey, and in some time goes on board a ship of war with his master—Some account of the expedition against Louisburg under the command of Admiral Boscawen, in 1758.

I now totally lost the small remains of comfort I had enjoyed in conversing with my countrymen; the women too, who used to wash and take care of me were all gone different ways, and I never saw one of them afterwards.

I stayed in this island for a few days, I believe it could not be above a fortnight, when I, and some few more slaves, that were not saleable amongst the rest, from very much fretting, were shipped off in a sloop for North America. On the passage we were better treated than when we were coming from Africa, and we had plenty of rice and fat pork. We were landed up a river a good way from the sea, about Virginia county, where we saw few or none of our native Africans, and not one soul who could talk to me. I was a few weeks

weeding grass and gathering stones in a plantation; and at last all my companions were distributed different ways, and only myself was left. I was now exceedingly miserable, and thought myself worse off than any of the rest of my companions, for they could talk to each other, but I had no person to speak to that I could understand. In this state, I was constantly grieving and pining, and wishing for death rather than anything else. While I was in this plantation, the gentleman, to whom I suppose the estate belonged, being unwell, I was one day sent for to his dwelling-house to fan him; when I came into the room where he was I was very much affrighted at some things I saw, and the more so as I had seen a black woman slave as I came through the house, who was cooking the dinner, and the poor creature was cruelly loaded with various kinds of iron machines; she had one particularly on her head, which locked her mouth so fast that she could scarcely speak; and could not eat nor drink. I was much astonished and shocked at this contrivance, which I afterwards learned was called the iron muzzle. Soon after I had a fan put in my hand, to fan the gentleman while he slept; and so I did indeed with great fear. While he was fast asleep I indulged myself a great deal in looking about the room, which to me appeared very fine and curious. The first object that engaged my attention was a watch which hung on the chimney, and was going. I was quite surprised at the noise it made, and was afraid it would tell the gentleman anything I might do amiss; and when I immediately after observed a picture hanging in the room, which appeared constantly to look at me, I was still more affrighted, having never seen such things as these before. At one time I thought it was something relative to magic; and not seeing it move, I thought it might be some way the whites had to keep their great men when they died, and offer them libations as we used to do our friendly spirits. In this state of anxiety I remained till my master awoke, when I was dismissed out of the room, to my no small satisfaction and relief; for I thought that these people were all made up of wonders. In this place I was called Jacob; but on board the *African Snow,* I was called Michael. I had been some time in this miserable, forlorn, and much dejected state, without having anyone to talk to, which made my life a burden, when the kind and unknown hand of the Creator (who in very deed leads the blind in a way they know not) now began to appear, to my comfort; for one day the captain of a merchant ship, called the *Industrious Bee,* came on some business to my master's house. This gentleman, whose name was Michael Henry Pascal, was a lieutenant in the royal navy, but now commanded this trading ship, which was somewhere in the confines of the county many miles off. While he was at my master's house, it happened that he saw me, and liked me so well that he made a purchase of me. I think I have often heard him say he gave thirty or forty pounds sterling for me; but I do not remember which. However, he meant me for a present to some of his friends in England: and as I was sent accordingly from the house of my then master (one Mr. Campbell) to the place where the ship lay; I was conducted on horseback by an elderly black man (a mode of travelling which appeared very odd to me). When I arrived I was carried on board a fine large ship, loaded with tobacco, &c., and just ready to sail for England. I now thought my condition much mended; I had sails to lie on, and plenty of good victuals to eat; and everybody on board used me very kindly, quite contrary to what I had seen of any white people before; I therefore began to think that they were not all of the same disposition. A few days after I was on board we sailed for England. I was still at a loss to conjecture my destiny. By this time, however, I could smatter a little imperfect English; and I wanted to know as well as I could where we were going. Some of the people of the ship used to tell me they were going to carry me back to my own country, and this made me very happy. I was quite rejoiced at the idea of going back, and thought if I could get home what wonders I should have to tell. But I was reserved for another fate, and was soon undeceived when we came within sight of the English coast. While I was on board this ship, my captain and master named me *Gustavus Vassa,* I at that time began to understand him a little, and refused to be called so, and told him as well as I could that I would be called Jacob; but he said I should not, and still called me Gustavus: and when I refused to answer to my new name, which I at first did, it gained me many a cuff; so at length I submitted, and by which I have been known ever since. The ship had a very long passage; and on that account we had very short allowance of provisions. Towards the last, we had only one pound and a half of bread per week, and about the same quantity of meat, and one quart of water a day. We spoke with only one vessel the whole time we were at sea, and but once we caught a few fishes. In our extremities the captain and people told me in jest they would kill and eat me; but I thought them in earnest, and was depressed beyond measure, expecting every moment to be my last. While I was in this situation, one evening they caught, with a good deal of trouble, a large shark, and got it on board. This gladdened by poor heart exceedingly, as I thought it would serve the people to eat instead of their eating me; but very soon, to my astonishment, they cut off a small part of the tail, and tossed the rest over the side. This renewed my consternation; and I did not know what to think of these white people, though I very

much feared they would kill and eat me. There was on board the ship a young lad who had never been at sea before, about four or five years older than myself: his name was Richard Baker. He was a native of America, had received an excellent education, and was of a most amiable temper. Soon after I went on board, he showed me a great deal of partiality and attention, and in return I grew extremely fond of him. We at length became inseparable; and, for the space of two years, he was of very great use to me, and was my constant companion and instructor. Although this dear youth had many slaves of his own, yet he and I have gone through many sufferings together on shipboard; and we have many nights lain in each other's bosoms when we were in great distress. Thus such a friendship was cemented between us as we cherished till his death, which, to my very great sorrow, happened in the year 1759, when he was up the Archipelago, on board his Majesty's ship the *Preston:* an event which I have never ceased to regret, as I lost at once a kind interpreter, an agreeable companion, and a faithful friend; who, at the age of fifteen, discovered a mind superior to prejudice; and who was not ashamed to notice, to associate with, and to be the friend and instructor of one who was ignorant, a stranger, of a different complexion, and a slave! My master had lodged in his mother's house in America; he respected him very much, and made him always eat with him in the cabin. He used often to tell him jocularly that he would kill and eat me. Sometimes he would say to me—the black people were not good to eat, and would ask me if we did not eat people in my country. I said, No; then he said he would kill Dick (as he always called him) first, and afterwards me. Though this hearing relieved my mind a little as to myself, I was alarmed for Dick, and whenever he was called I used to be very much afraid he was to be killed; and I would peep and watch to see if they were going to kill him; nor was I free from this consternation till we made the land. One night we lost a man overboard; and the cries and noise were so great and confused, in stopping the ship, that I, who did not know what was the matter, began, as usual, to be very much afraid, and to think they were going to make an offering with me, and perform some magic; which I still believed they dealt in. As the waves were very high, I thought the Ruler of the seas was angry, and I expected to be offered up to appease him. This filled my mind with agony, and I could not any more, that night, close my eyes again to rest. However, when daylight appeared, I was a little eased in my mind; but still, every time I was called, I used to think it was to be killed. Some time after this, we saw some very large fish, which I afterwards found were called grampusses. They looked to me exceedingly terrible, and made their appearance just at dusk, and were so near as to blow the water on the ship's deck. I believed them to be the rulers of the sea; and as the white people did not make any offerings at any time, I thought they were angry with them; and, at last, what confirmed my belief was, the wind just then died away, and a calm ensued, and in consequence of it the ship stopped going. I supposed that the fish had performed this, and I hid myself in the fore part of the ship, through fear of being offered up to appease them, every minute peeping and quaking; but my good friend Dick came shortly towards me, and I took an opportunity to ask him, as well as I could, what these fish were. Not being able to talk much English, I could but just make him understand my question; and not at all, when I asked him if any offerings were to be made to them; however, he told me these fish would swallow anybody which sufficiently alarmed me. Here he was called away by the captain, who was leaning over the quarter-deck railing, and looking at the fish; and most of the people were busied in getting a barrel of pitch to light for them to play with. The captain now called me to him, having learned some of my apprehensions from Dick; and having diverted himself and others for some time with my fears, which appeared ludicrous enough in my crying and trembling, he dismissed me. The barrel of pitch was now lighted and put over the side into the water. By this time it was just dark, and the fish went after it; and, to my great joy, I saw them no more.

However, all my alarms began to subside when we got sight of land; and at last the ship arrived at Falmouth, after a passage of thirteen weeks. Every heart on board seemed gladdened on our reaching the shore, and none more than mine. The captain immediately went on shore, and sent on board some fresh provisions, which we wanted very much. We made good use of them, and our famine was soon turned into feasting, almost without ending. It was about the beginning of the spring 1757, when I arrived in England, and I was near twelve years of age at that time. I was very much struck with the buildings and the pavement of the streets in Falmouth; and, indeed, every object I saw, filled me with new surprise. One morning, when I got upon deck, I saw it covered all over with the snow that fell over night. As I had never seen anything of the kind before, I thought it was salt: so I immediately ran down to the mate, and desired him, as well as I could, to come and see how somebody in the night had thrown salt all over the deck. He, knowing what it was, desired me to bring some of it down to him. Accordingly I took up a handful of it, which I found very cold indeed; and when I brought it to him he desired me to taste it. I did so, and I was surprised beyond measure. I then asked him what it was; he told me it was snow, but I could not in anywise understand him. He asked me, if we had no

such thing in my country; I told him, No. I then asked him the use of it, and who made it; he told me a great man in the heavens, called God. But here again I was to all intents and purposes at a loss to understand him; and the more so, when a little after I saw the air filled with it, in a heavy shower, which fell down on the same day. After this I went to church; and having never been at such a place before, I was again amazed at seeing and hearing the service. I asked all I could about it, and they gave me to understand it was worshipping God, who made us and all things. I was still at a great loss, and soon got into an endless field of inquiries, as well as I was able to speak and ask about things. However, my little friend Dick used to be my best interpreter; for I could make free with him, and he always instructed me with pleasure. And from what I could understand by him of this God, and in seeing these white people did not sell one another as we did, I was much pleased; and in this I thought they were much happier than we Africans. I was astonished at the wisdom of the white people in all things I saw; but was amazed at their not sacrificing, or making any offerings, and eating with unwashed hands, and touching the dead. I likewise could not help remarking the particular slenderness of their women, which I did not at first like; and I thought they were not so modest and shame-faced as the African women.

I had often seen my master and Dick employed in reading; and I had a great curiosity to talk to the books as I thought they did, and so to learn how all things had a beginning. For that purpose I have often taken up a book, and have talked to it, and then put my ears to it, when alone, in hopes it would answer me; and I have been very much concerned when I found it remained silent.

My master lodged at the house of a gentleman in Falmouth, who had a fine little daughter about six or seven years of age, and she grew prodigiously fond of me, insomuch that we used to eat together, and had servants to wait on us. I was so much caressed by this family that it often reminded me of the treatment I had received from my little noble African master. After I had been here a few days, I was sent on board of the ship; but the child cried so much after me that nothing could pacify her till I was sent for again. It is ludicrous enough, that I began to fear I should be betrothed to this young lady; and when my master asked me if I would stay there with her behind him, as he was going away with the ship, which had taken in the tobacco again, I cried immediately, and said I would not leave him. At last, by stealth, one night I was sent on board the ship again; and in a little time we sailed for Guernsey, where she was in part owned by a merchant, one Nicholas Doberry. As I was now amongst a people who had not their faces scarred, like some of the African nation where I had been, I was very glad I did not let them ornament me in that manner when I was with them. When we arrived at Guernsey, my master placed me to board and lodge with one of his mates, who had a wife and family there; and some months afterwards he went to England, and left me in care of this mate, together with my friend Dick. This mate had a little daughter, aged about five or six years, with whom I used to be much delighted. I had often observed that when her mother washed her face it looked very rosy, but when she washed mine it did not look so. I therefore tried oftentimes myself if I could not by washing make my face of the same color as my little play-mate, Mary, but it was all in vain; and I now began to be mortified at the difference in our complexions. This woman behaved to me with great kindness and attention, and taught me everything in the same manner as she did her own child, and, indeed, in every respect, treated me as such. I remained here till the summer of the year 1757, when my master, being appointed first lieutenant of his Majesty's ship the *Roebuck*, sent for Dick and me, and his old mate. On this we all left Guernsey, and set out for England in a sloop, bound for London. As we were coming up towards the Nore, where the *Roebuck* lay, a man-of-war's boat came along side to press our people, on which each man run to hide himself. I was very much frightened at this, though I did not know what it meant, or what to think or do. However I went and hid myself also under a hencoop. Immediately afterwards, the press-gang came on board with their swords drawn, and searched all about, pulled the people out by force, and put them into the boat. At last I was found out also; the man that found me held me up by the heels while they all made their sport of me, I roaring and crying out all the time most lustily; but at last the mate, who was my conductor, seeing this, came to my assistance, and did all he could to pacify me; but all to very little purpose, till I had seen the boat go off. Soon afterwards we came to the Nore, where the *Roebuck* lay; and, to our great joy, my master came on board to us, and brought us to the ship. When I went on board this large ship, I was amazed indeed to see the quantity of men and the guns. However, my surprise began to diminish as my knowledge increased; and I ceased to feel those apprehensions and alarms which had taken such strong possession of me when I first came among the Europeans, and for some time after. I began now to pass to an opposite extreme; I was so far from being afraid of anything new which I saw, that after I had been some time in this ship, I even began to long for an engagement. My griefs, too, which in young minds are not perpetual, were now wearing away; and I soon enjoyed myself pretty well, and felt tolerably easy in my present situation. There was a number of boys on board, which still made it more agreeable; for we were always together, and a great part of our time was spent in play. I remained in this ship a considerable time, during which we made several cruises, and visited a variety of places; among others we were twice in Holland, and brought over several persons of distinction from it, whose names I do not now remember. On the passage, one day, for the diversion of those gentlemen, all the boys were called on the quarter-deck, and were paired proportionable, and then made to fight; after which the gentlemen gave the combatants from five to nine shillings each. This was the first time I ever fought with a white boy; and I never knew what it was to have a bloody nose before. This made me fight most desperately, I suppose considerably more than an hour; and at last, both of us being weary, we were parted. I had a great deal of this kind of sport afterwards, in which the captain and the ship's company used very much to encourage me. Sometime afterwards, the ship went to Leith in Scotland, and from thence to the Orkneys, where I was surprised in seeing scarcely any night; and from thence we sailed with a great fleet, full of soldiers, for England. All this time we had never come to an engagement, though we were frequently cruising off the coast of France; during which we chased many vessels, and took in all seventeen prizes. I had been learning many of the manœuvres of the ship during our cruise; and I was several times made to fire the guns. One evening, off Havre de Grace, just as it was growing dark, we were standing off shore, and met with a fine large French built frigate. We got all things immediately ready for fighting; and I now expected I should be gratified in seeing an engagement, which I had so long wished for in vain. But the very moment the word of command was given to fire, we heard those on board the other ship cry, "Haul down the jib"; and in that instant she hoisted English colors. There was instantly with us an amazing cry of—"Avast!" or stop firing; and I think one or two guns had been let off, but happily they did no mischief. We had hailed them several times, but they not hearing, we received no answer, which was the cause of our firing. The boat was then sent on board of her, and she proved to be the *Ambuscade*, man-of-war, to my no small disappointment. We returned to Portsmouth, without having been in any action, just at the trial of Admiral Byng (whom I was several times during it); and my master having left the ship, and gone to London for promotion, Dick and I were put on board the *Savage*, sloop-of-war, and we went in her to assist in bringing off the *St. George*, man-of-war, that had run ashore somewhere on the coast. After staying a few weeks on board the *Savage,* Dick and I were sent on shore at Deal, where we remained some short time, till my master sent for us to London, the place I had long desired exceedingly to see. We therefore both with great pleasure got into a wagon, and came to London, where we were received by a Mr. Guerin, a relation of my master. This gentleman had two sisters, very amiable ladies, who took much notice and great care of me. Though I had desired so much to see London, when I arrived in it I was unfortunately unable to gratify my curiosity; for I had at this time the chilblains to such a degree that I could not stand for several months, and I was obliged to be sent to St. George's hospital. There I grew so ill that the doctors wanted to cut my left leg off, at different times, apprehending a mortification; but I always said I would rather die than suffer it, and happily (I thank God) I recovered without the operation. After being there several weeks, and just as I had recovered, the smallpox broke out on me, so that I was again confined; and I thought myself now particularly unfortunate. However, I soon recovered again; and by this time, my master having been promoted to be first lieutenant of the *Preston,* man-of-war, of fifty guns, then new at Deptford, Dick and I were sent on board her, and soon after, we went to Holland to bring over the late Duke of —— to England. While I was in the ship an incident happened, which, though trifling, I beg leave to relate, as I could not help taking particular notice of it, and considered it then as a judgment of God. One morning a young man was looking up to the foretop, and in a wicked tone, common on shipboard, d——d his eyes about something. Just at the moment some small particles of dirt fell into his left eye, and by the evening it was very much inflamed. The next day it grew worse, and within six or seven days he lost it. From this ship my master was appointed a lieutenant on board the *Royal George.* When he was going he wished me to stay on board the *Preston,* to learn the French horn; but the ship being ordered for Turkey, I could not think of leaving my master, to whom I was very warmly attached; and I told him if he left me behind, it would break my heart. This prevailed on him to take me with him; but he left Dick on board the *Preston,* whom I embraced at parting for the last time. The *Royal George* was the largest ship I had ever seen, so that when I came on board of her I was surprised at the number of people, men, women, and children, of every denomination; and the largeness of the guns, many of them also of brass, which I had never seen before. Here were also shops or stalls of every kind of goods, and people crying their different commodities about the ship as in a town. To me it appeared a little world, into which I was again cast without a friend,

for I had no longer my dear companion Dick. We did not stay long here. My master was not many weeks on board before he got an appointment to the sixth lieutenant of the *Namur,* which was then at Spithead, fitting up for Vice-admiral Boscawen, who was going with a large fleet on an expedition against Louisburg. The crew of the *Royal George* were turned over to her, and the flag of that gallant admiral was hoisted on board, the blue at the maintop gallant mast head. There was a very great fleet of men-of-war of every description assembled together for this expedition, and I was in hopes soon to have an opportunity of being gratified with a sea-fight. All things being now in readiness, this mighty fleet (for there was also Admiral Cornish's fleet in company, destined for the East Indies) at last weighed anchor, and sailed. The two fleets continued in company for several days, and then parted; Admiral Cornish, in the *Lenox,* having first saluted our Admiral in the *Namur,* which he returned. We then steered for America; but, by contrary winds, we were driven to Tenerife, where I was struck with its noted peak. Its prodigious height, and its form, resembling a sugar loaf, filled me with wonder. We remained in sight of this island some days, and then proceeded for America, which we soon made, and got into a very commodious harbor called St. George, in Halifax, where we had fish in great plenty, and all other fresh provisions. We were here joined by different men-of-war and transport ships with soldiers; after which, our fleet being increased to a prodigious number of ships of all kinds, we sailed for Cape Breton in Nova Scotia. We had the good and gallant General Wolfe on board our ship, whose affability made him highly esteemed and beloved by all the men. He often honored me, as well as other boys, with marks of his notice, and saved me once a flogging for fighting with a young gentleman. We arrived at Cape Breton in the summer of 1758; and here the soldiers were to be landed, in order to make an attack upon Louisburg. My master had some part in superintending the landing; and here I was in a small measure gratified in seeing an encounter between our men and the enemy. The French were posted on the shore to receive us, and disputed our landing for a long time; but at last they were driven from their trenches, and a complete landing was effected. Our troops pursued them as far as the town of Louisburg. In this action many were killed on both sides. One thing remarkable I saw this day. A lieutenant of the *Princess Amelia,* who, as well as my master, superintended the landing, was giving the word of command, and while his mouth was open, a musket ball went through it, and passed out at his cheek. I had that day, in my hand, the scalp of an Indian king, who was killed in the engagement; the scalp had been taken off by an Highlander. I saw the king's ornaments too, which were very curious, and made of feathers.

Our land forces laid siege to the town of Louisburg, while the French men-of-war were blocked up in the harbor by the fleet, the batteries at the same time playing upon them from the land. This they did with such effect, that one day I saw some of the ships set on fire by the shells from the batteries, and I believe two or three of them were quite burnt. At another time, about fifty boats belonging to the English men-of-war, commanded by Captain George Belfour, of the *Etna*, fire ship, and Mr. Laforey, another junior Captain, attacked and boarded the only two remaining French men-of-war in the harbor. They also set fire to a seventy-gun ship, but a sixty-four, called the *Bienfaisant*, they brought off. During my stay here, I had often an opportunity of being near Captain Belfour, who was pleased to notice me, and liked me so much that he often asked my master to let him have me, but he would not part with me; and no consideration could have induced me to leave him. At last, Louisburg was taken, and the English men-of-war came into the harbor before it, to my very great joy; for I had now more liberty of indulging myself, and I went often on shore. When the ships were in the harbor, we had the most beautiful procession on the water I ever saw. All the Admirals and Captains of the men-of-war, full dressed, and in their barges, well ornamented with pendants, came alongside of the *Namur*. The Vice-admiral then went on shore in his barge, followed by the other officers in order of seniority, to take possession, as I suppose, of the town and fort. Some time after this, the French governor and his lady, and other persons of note, came on board our ship to dine. On this occasion our ships were dressed with colors of all kinds, from the top-gallant mast head to the deck; and this, with the firing of guns, formed a most grand and magnificent spectacle.

As soon as everything here was settled, Admiral Boscawen sailed with part of the fleet for England, leaving some ships behind with Rear-admirals Sir Charles Hardy and Durell. It was now winter; and one evening, during our passage home, about dusk, when we were in the channel, or near soundings, and were beginning to look for land, we descried seven sail of large men-of-war, which stood off shore. Several people on board of our ship said, as the two fleets were (in forty minutes from the first sight) within hail of each other, that they were English men-of-war; and some of our people even began to name some of the ships. By this time both fleets began to mingle, and our Admiral ordered his flag to be hoisted. At that instant, the other fleet,

which were French, hoisted their ensigns, and gave us a broadside as they passed by. Nothing could create greater surprise and confusion among us than this. The wind was high, the sea rough, and we had our lower and middle deck guns housed in, so that not a single gun on board was ready to be fired at any of the French ships. However, the *Royal William* and the *Somerset*, being our sternmost ships, became a little prepared, and each gave the French ships a broadside as they passed by. I afterwards heard this was a French squadron, commanded by Monsieur Constans; and certainly, had the Frenchmen known our condition, and had a mind to fight us, they might have done us great mischief. But we were not long before we were prepared for an engagement. Immediately many things were tossed overboard, the ships were made ready for fighting as soon as possible, and about ten at night we had bent a new main-sail, the old one being split. Being now in readiness for fighting, we wore ship, and stood after the French fleet, who were one or two ships in number more than we. However we gave them chase, and continued pursuing them all night; and at day-light we saw six of them, all large ships of the line, and an English East Indiaman, a prize they had taken. We chased them all day till between three and four o'clock in the evening, when we came up with, and passed within a musket shot of one seventy-four–gun ship, and the Indiaman also, who now hoisted her colors, but immediately hauled them down again. On this we made a signal for the other ships to take possession of her; and, supposing the man-of-war would likewise strike, we cheered, but she did not; though if we had fired into her, from being so near we must have taken her. To my utter surprise, the *Somerset*, who was the next ship astern of the *Namur*, made way likewise; and, thinking they were sure of this French ship, they cheered in the same manner, but still continued to follow us. The French Commodore was about a gun-shot ahead of all, running from us with all speed; and about four o'clock he carried his foretopmast overboard. This caused another loud cheer with us; and a little after the topmast came close by us; but, to our great surprise, instead of coming up with her, we found she went as fast as ever, if not faster. The sea grew now much smoother; and the wind lulling, the seventy-four–gun ship we had passed, came again by us in the very same direction, and so near that we heard her people talk as she went by, yet not a shot was fired on either side; and about five or six o'clock, just as it grew dark, she joined her Commodore. We chased all night; but the next day we were out of sight, so that we saw no more of them; and we only had the old Indiaman (called *Carnarvon*, I think) for our trouble. After this we stood in for the channel, and soon made the land; and, about the close of the year 1758–9, we got safe to St. Helen's. Here the *Namur* ran aground, and also another large ship astern of us; but, by starting our water, and tossing many things overboard to lighten her, we got the ships off without any damage. We stayed for a short time at Spithead, and then went into Portsmouth harbor to refit. From whence the Admiral went to London; and my master and I soon followed, with a press-gang, as we wanted some hands to complete our complement.

FREDERICK DOUGLASS

Life and Times of Frederick Douglass Written by Himself

Established in my new home in Baltimore, I was not very long in perceiving that in picturing to myself what was to be my life there, my imagination had painted only the bright side, and that the reality had its dark shades as well as its light ones. The open country which had been so much to me was all shut out. Walled in on every side by towering brick buildings, the heat of the summer was intolerable to me, and the hard brick pavements almost blistered my feet. If I ventured out on to the streets, new and strange objects glared upon me at every step, and startling sounds greeted my ears from all directions. My country eyes and ears were confused and bewildered. Troops of hostile boys pounced upon me at every corner. They chased me, and called me "eastern-shore man," till really I almost wished myself back on the Eastern Shore. My new mistress happily proved to be all she had seemed, and in her presence I easily forgot all outside annoyances. Mrs. Sophia was naturally of an excellent disposition—kind, gentle, and cheerful. The supercilious contempt for the rights and feelings of others, and the petulance and bad humor which generally characterized slaveholding ladies, were all quite absent from her manner and bearing toward me.

She had never been a slaveholder—a thing then quite unusual at the South—but had depended almost entirely upon her own industry for a living. To this fact the dear lady no doubt owed the excellent preservation of her natural goodness of heart, for slavery could change a saint into a sinner, and an angel into a demon. I hardly knew how to behave towards "Miss Sopha," as I used to call Mrs. Hugh Auld. I could not approach her even as I had formerly approached Mrs. Thomas Auld. Why should I hang down my head, and speak with bated breath, when there was no pride to scorn me, no coldness to repel me, and no hatred to inspire me with fear? I therefore soon came to regard her as something more akin to a mother than a slaveholding mistress. So far from deeming it impudent in a slave to look her straight in the face, she seemed ever to say, "Look up, child; don't be afraid." The sailors belonging to the sloop esteemed it a great privilege to be the bearers of parcels or messages for her, for whenever they came, they were sure of a most kind and pleasant reception. If little Thomas was her son, and her most dearly loved child, she made me something like his half-brother in her affections. If dear Tommy was exalted to a place on his mother's knee, "Freddy" was honored by a place at the mother's side. Nor did the slave-boy lack the caressing strokes of her gentle hand, soothing him into the consciousness that, though motherless, he was not friendless. Mrs. Auld was not only kind-hearted, but remarkable pious, frequent in her attendance at public worship and much given to reading the Bible and to chanting hymns of praise when alone.

Mr. Hugh was altogether a different character. He cared very little about religion, knew more of the world and was more a part of the world, than his wife. He doubtless set out to be, as the world goes, a respectable man and to get on by becoming a successful ship-builder, in that city of shipbuilding. This was his ambition, and it fully occupied him. I was of course of very little consequence to him, and when he smiled upon me, as he sometimes did, the smile was borrowed from his lovely wife, and like borrowed light, was transient, and vanished with the source whence it was derived. Though I must in truth characterize Master Hugh as a sour man of forbidding appearance, it is due to him to acknowledge that he was never cruel to me, according to the notion of cruelty in Maryland. During the first year or two, he left me almost exclusively to the management of his wife. She was my lawgiver. In hands so tender as hers, and in the absence of the cruelties of the plantation, I became both physically and mentally much more sensitive, and a frown from my mistress caused me far more suffering than had Aunt Katy's hardest cuffs. Instead of the cold, damp floor of my old master's kitchen, I was on carpets; for the corn bag in winter, I had a good straw bed, well furnished with covers; for the coarse corn meal in the morning, I had good bread and mush occasionally; for my old tow-linen shirt, I had good clean clothes. I was really well off. My employment was to run of errands, and to take care of Tommy, to prevent his getting in the way of carriages, and to keep him out of harm's way generally.

So for a time everything went well. I say for a time, because the fatal poison of irresponsible power, and the natural influence of slave customs, were not very long in making their impression on the gentle and loving disposition of my excellent mistress. She at first regarded me as a child, like any other. This was the natural and spontaneous thought; afterwards, when she came to consider me as property, our relations to each other were changed, but a nature so noble as hers could not instantly become perverted, and it took several years before the sweetness of her temper was wholly lost.

The frequent hearing of my mistress reading the Bible aloud, for she often read aloud when her husband was absent, awakened my curiosity in respect to this *mystery* of reading, and roused in me the desire to learn. Up to this time I had known nothing whatever of this wonderful art, and my ignorance and inexperience of what it could do for me, as well as my confidence in my mistress, emboldened me to ask her to teach me to read. With an unconscious and inexperience equal to my own, she readily consented, and in an incredibly short time, by her kind assistance, I had mastered the alphabet and could spell words of three or four letters. My mistress seemed almost as proud of my progress as if I had been her own child, and supposing that her husband would be as well pleased, she made no secret of what she was doing for me. Indeed, she exultingly told him of the aptness of her pupil and of her intention to persevere, as she felt it her duty to do, in teaching me, at least, to read the Bible. And here arose the first dark cloud over my Baltimore prospects, the precursor of chilling blasts and drenching storms. Master Hugh was astounded beyond measure and, probably for the first time, proceeded to unfold to his wife the true philosophy of the slave system, and the peculiar rules necessary in the nature of the case to be observed in the management of human chattels. Of course he forbade her to give me any further instruction, telling her in the first place that to do so was unlawful, as it was also unsafe, "for," said he, "if you give a nigger an inch he will take an ell. Learning will spoil the best nigger in the world. If he learns to read the Bible it will forever unfit him to be a slave. He should know nothing but the will of his master, and learn to obey it. As to himself, learning will do him no good, but a great deal of harm, making him disconsolate and unhappy. If you teach him how to read, he'll want to know how to write, and this accomplished, he'll be running away with himself." Such was the tenor of Master Hugh's oracular exposition, and it must be confessed that he very clearly comprehended the nature and the requirements of the relation of master and slave. His discourse was the first decidedly anti-slavery lecture to which it had been my lot to listen. Mrs. Auld evidently felt the force of what he said, and, like an obedient wife, began to shape her course in the direction indicated by him. The effect of his words *on me* was neither slight nor transitory. His iron sentences, cold and harsh, sunk like heavy weights deep into my heart, and stirred up within me a rebellion not soon to be allayed.

This was a new and special revelation, dispelling a painful mystery against which my youthful understanding had struggled, and struggled in vain, to wit, the white man's power to perpetuate the enslavement of the black man. "Very well," thought I. "Knowledge unfits a child to be a slave." I instinctively assented to the proposition, and from that moment I understood the direct pathway from slavery to freedom. It was just what I needed, and it came to me at a time and from a source whence I least expected it. Of course I was greatly saddened at the thought of losing the assistance of my kind mistress, but the information so instantly derived, to some extent compensated me for the loss I had sustained in this direction. Wise as Mr. Auld was, he underrated my comprehension, and had little idea of the use to which I was capable of putting the impressive lesson he was giving to his wife. He wanted me to be a slave; I had already voted against that on the home plantation of Col. Lloyd. That which he most loved I most hated, and the very determination which he expressed to keep me in ignorance only rendered me the more resolute to seek intelligence. In learning to read, therefore, I am not sure that I do not owe quite as much to the opposition of my master as to the kindly assistance of my amiable mistress. I acknowledge the benefit rendered me by the one, and by the other, believing that but for my mistress I might have grown up in ignorance.

I lived in the family of Mr. Auld, at Baltimore, seven years, during which time, as the almanac makers say of the weather, my condition was variable. The most interesting feature of my history here was my learning, under somewhat marked disadvantages, to read and write. In attaining this knowledge I was compelled to resort to indirections by no means congenial to my nature, and which were really humiliating to my sense of candor and uprightness. My mistress, checked in her benevolent designs toward me, not only ceased instructing me herself, but set her face as a flint against my learning to read by any means. It is due to her to say, however, that she did not adopt this course in all its stringency at first. She either thought it unnecessary, or she lacked the depravity needed to make herself forget at once my human nature. She was, as I have said, naturally a kind and tender-hearted woman, and in the humanity of her heart and the simplicity of her mind, she set out, when I first went to live with her, to treat me as she supposed one human being ought to treat another.

Nature never intended that men and women should be either slaves or slaveholders, and nothing but rigid training long persisted in, can perfect the character of the one or the other.

Mrs. Auld was singularly deficient in the qualities of a slaveholder. It was no easy matter for her to think or to feel that the curly-headed boy, who stood by her side, and even leaned on her lap, who was loved by little Tommy, and who loved Tommy in turn, sustained to her only the relation of a chattel. I was more than that; she felt me to be more than that. I could talk and sing; I could laugh and weep; I could reason and remember; I could love and hate. I was human, and she, dear lady, knew and felt me to be so. How could she then treat me as a brute, without a mighty struggle with all the noblest powers of her soul? That struggle came, and the will and power of the husband were victorious. Her noble soul was overcome, and he who wrought the wrong was injured in the fall no less than the rest of the household. When I went into that household, it was the abode of happiness and contentment. The wife and mistress there was a model of affection and tenderness. Her fervent piety and watchful uprightness made it impossible to see her without thinking and feeling that "that woman is a Christian." There was no sorrow nor suffering for which she had not a tear, and there was no innocent joy for which she had not a smile. She had bread for the hungry, clothes for the naked, and comfort for every mourner who came within her reach.

But slavery soon proved its ability to divest her of these excellent qualities, and her home of its early happiness. Conscience cannot stand much violence. Once thoroughly injured, who is he who can repair the damage? If it be broken toward the slave on Sunday, it will be toward the master on Monday. It cannot long endure such shocks. It must stand unharmed, or it does not stand at all. As my condition in the family waxed bad, that of the family waxed no better. The first step in the wrong direction was the violence done to nature and to conscience in arresting the benevolence that would have enlightened my young mind. In ceasing to instruct me, my mistress had to seek to justify herself *to* herself, and once consenting to take sides in such a debate, she was compelled to hold her position. One needs little knowledge of moral philosophy to see where she inevitably landed. She finally became even more violent in her opposition to my learning to read than was Mr. Auld himself. Nothing now appeared to make her more angry than seeing me, seated in some nook or corner, quietly reading a book or newspaper. She would rush at me with the utmost fury, and snatch the book or paper from my hand, with something of the wrath and consternation which a traitor might be supposed to feel on being discovered in a plot by some dangerous spy. The conviction once thoroughly established in her mind, that education and slavery were incompatible with each other, I was most narrowly watched in all my movements. If I remained in a separate room from the family for any considerable length of time, I was sure to be suspected of having a book, and was at once called to give an account of myself. But this was too late—the first and never-to-be-retraced step had been taken. Teaching me the alphabet had been the "inch" given, I was now waiting only for the opportunity to "take the ell."

Filled with the determination to learn to read at any cost, I hit upon many expedients to accomplish that much desired end. The plan which I mainly adopted, and the one which was the most successful, was that of using as teachers my young white playmates, with whom I met on the streets. I used almost constantly to carry a copy of *Webster's Spelling-Book* in my pocket, and when sent on errands, or when playtime was allowed me, I would step aside with my young friends and take a lesson in spelling. I am greatly indebted to these boys—Gustavus Dorgan, Joseph Bailey, Charles Farity, and William Cosdry.

Although slavery was a delicate subject and, in Maryland, very cautiously talked about among grown-up people, I frequently talked with the white boys about it, and that very freely. I would sometimes say to them, while seated on a curbstone or a cellar door, "I wish I could be free, as you will be when you get to be men." "You will be free, you know, as soon as you are twenty-one, and can go where you like, but I am a slave for life. Have I not as good a right to be free as you have?" Words like these, I observed, always troubled them, and I had no small satisfaction in drawing out from them, as I occasionally did, that fresh and bitter condemnation of slavery which ever springs from natures unseared and unperverted. Of all consciences, let me have those to deal with, which have not been seared and bewildered with the cares and perplexities of life. I do not remember ever while I was in slavery, to have met with a *boy* who defended the system, but I do remember many times, when I was consoled by them, and by them encouraged to hope that something would yet occur by which I would be made free. Over and over again, they have told me that "they believed I had as good a right to be free as *they* had," and that "they did not believe God ever made any one to be a slave." It is easily seen that such little conversations with my playfellows had no tendency to weaken my love of liberty, nor to render me contented as a slave.

When I was about thirteen years old, and had succeeded in learning to read, every increase of knowledge, especially anything respecting the free states, was an additional weight to the almost intolerable burden of my thought—*"I am a slave for life."* To my bondage I could see no end. It was a terrible reality, and I shall never be able to tell how sadly that thought chafed my young spirit. Fortunately or unfortunately, I had, by blacking boots for some gentlemen, earned a little money with which I purchase of Mr. Knight, on Thames street, what was then a very popular school book, viz., *The Columbian Orator*, for which I paid fifty cents. I was led to buy this book by hearing some little boys say that they were going to learn some pieces out of it for the exhibition. This volume was indeed a rich treasure, and, for a time, every opportunity afforded me was spent in diligently perusing it. Among much other interesting matter, that which I read again and again with unflagging satisfaction was a short dialogue between a master and his slave. The slave is represented as having been recaptured in a second attempt to run away, and the master opens the dialogue with an upbraiding speech, charging the slave with ingratitude, and demanding to know what he has to say in his own defense. Thus upbraided and thus called upon to reply, the salve rejoins that he knows how little anything that he can say will avail, seeing that he is completely in the hands of his owner, and with noble resolution, calmly says, "I submit to my fate." Touched by the slave's answer, the master insists upon his further speaking, and recapitulates the many acts of kindness which he has performed toward the slave, and tells him he is permitted to speak for himself. Thus invited, the quondam slave made a spirited defense of himself, and thereafter the whole argument for and against slavery is brought out. The master was vanquished at every turn in the argument, and, appreciating the fact, he generously and meekly emancipates the slave, with his best wishes for his prosperity.

It is unnecessary to say that a dialogue with such an origin and such an end, read by me when every nerve of my being was in revolt at my own condition as a slave, affected me most powerfully. I could not help feeling that the day might yet come when the well-directed answers made by the slave to the master, in this instance, would find a counterpart in my own experience. This, however, was not all the fanaticism which I found in *The Columbian Orator*. I met there one of Sheridan's mighty speeches on the subject of Catholic Emancipation, Lord Chatham's speech on the American War, and speeches by the great William Pitt, and by Fox. These were all choice documents to me, and I read them over and over again, with an interest ever increasing, because it was ever gaining in intelligence, for the more I read them the better I understood them. The reading of these speeches added much to my limited stock of language, and enabled me to give tongue to many interesting thoughts which had often flashed through my mind and died away for want of words in which to give them utterance. The mighty power and heart-searching directness of truth, penetrating the heart of a slaveholder and compelling him to yield up his earthly interests to the claims of eternal justice, were finely illustrated in the dialogue, and from the speeches of Sheridan I got a bold and powerful denunciation of oppression and a most brilliant vindication of the rights of man.

Here was indeed a noble acquisition. If I had ever wavered under the consideration that the Almighty, in some way, had ordained slavery and willed my enslavement for His own glory, I wavered no longer. I had now penetrated to the secret of all slavery and of all oppression, and had ascertained their true foundation to be in the pride, the power, and the avarice of man. With a book in my hand so redolent of the principles of liberty, and with a perception of my own human nature and of the facts of my past and present experience, I was equal to a contest with the religious advocates of slavery, whether white or black, for blindness in this matter was not confined to the white people. I have met, at the South, many good, religious colored people who were under the delusion that God required them to submit to slavery and to wear their chains with meekness and humility. I could entertain no such nonsense as this, and I quite lost my patience when I found a colored man weak enough to believe such stuff. Nevertheless, eager as I was to partake of the tree of knowledge, its fruits were bitter as well as sweet. "Slaveholders," thought I, "are only a band of successful robbers, who, leaving their own homes, went into Africa for the purpose of stealing and reducing my people to slavery." I loathed them as the meanest and the most wicked of men. And as I read, behold! the very discontent so graphically predicted by Master Hugh had already come upon me. I was no longer the light-hearted, gleesome boy, full of mirth and play, that I was when I landed in Baltimore. Light had penetrated the moral dungeon where I had lain, and I saw the bloody whip for my back and the iron chain for my feet, and my *good, kind* master was the author of my situation. The revelation haunted me, stung me, and made me gloomy and miserable. As I writhed under the sting and torment of this knowledge I almost envied my fellow slaves their stupid indifference. It opened my eyes to the horrible pit, and revealed the teeth of the frightful dragon that was ready to pounce upon me, but alas, it opened no way for my escape. I wished myself a beast, a bird, anything rather than a slave. I was wretched and gloomy beyond my ability to describe. This everlasting thinking distressed and tormented me, and yet there was no getting rid of this subject of my thoughts. Liberty, as the inestimable birthright of every man, converted every object into an asserter of this right. I heard it in every sound, and saw it in every object. It was ever present to torment me with a sense of my wretchedness. The more beautiful and charming were the smiles of nature, the more horrible and desolate was my condition. I saw nothing without seeing it, and I heard nothing without hearing it. I do not exaggerate when I say that it looked at me in every star, smiled in every calm, breathed in every wind and moved in every storm.

I have no doubt that my state of mind had something to do with the change in treatment which my mistress adopted towards me. I can easily believe that my leaden, downcast, and disconsolate look was very offensive to her. Poor lady! She did not understand my trouble, and I could not tell her. Could I have made her acquainted with the real state of my mind and given her the reasons therefor, it might have been well for both of us. As it was, her abuse fell upon me like the blows of the false prophet upon his ass; she did not know that an angel stood in the way. Nature made us friends, but slavery had made us enemies. My interests were in a direction opposite to hers, and we both had our private thoughts and plans. She aimed to keep me ignorant, and I resolved to *know,* although knowledge only increased my misery. My feelings were not the result of any marked cruelty in the treatment I received; they sprung from the consideration of my being a slave at all. It was *slavery,* not its mere *incidents* that I hated. I had been cheated. I saw through the attempt to keep me in ignorance. I saw that slaveholders would have gladly made me believe that, in making a slave of me and in making slaves of others, they were merely acting under the authority of God, and I felt to them as to robbers and deceivers. The feeding and clothing me well could not atone for taking my liberty from me. The smiles of my mistress could not remove the deep sorrow that dwelt in my young bosom. Indeed, these came, in time, but to deepen the sorrow. She had changed, and the reader will see that I too, had changed. We were both victims to the same overshadowing evil, she as mistress, I as slave. I will not censure her harshly.

BOOKER T. WASHINGTON

The Struggle for an Education

One day, while at work in the coal-mine, I happened to overhear two miners talking about a great school for coloured people somewhere in Virginia. This was the first time that I had ever heard anything about any kind of school or college that was more pretentious than the little coloured school in our town.

In the darkness of the mine I noiselessly crept as close as I could to the two men who were talking. I heard one tell the other that not only was the school established for the members of my race, but that opportunities were provided by which poor but worthy students could work out all or part of the cost of board, and at the same time be taught some trade or industry.

As they went on describing the school, it seemed to me that it must be the greatest place on earth, and not even Heaven presented more attractions for me at that time than did the Hampton Normal and Agricultural Institute in Virginia, about which these men were talking. I resolved at once to go to that school, although I had no idea where it was, or how many miles away, or how I was going to reach it; I remembered only that I was on fire constantly with one ambition, and that was to go to Hampton. This thought was with me day and night.

After hearing of the Hampton Institute, I continued to work for a few months longer in the coal-mine. While at work there, I heard of a vacant position in the household of General Lewis Ruffner, the owner of the salt-furnace and coal-mine. Mrs. Viola Ruffner, the wife of General Ruffner, was a "Yankee" woman from Vermont. Mrs. Ruffner had a reputation all through the vicinity for being very strict with her servants, and especially with the boys who tried to serve her. Few of them had remained with her more than two or three weeks. They all left with the same excuse: she was too strict. I decided, however, that I would rather try Mrs. Ruffner's house than remain in the coal-mine, and so my mother applied to her for the vacant position. I was hired at a salary of $5 per month.

I had heard so much about Mrs. Ruffner's severity that I was almost afraid to see her, and trembled when I went into her presence. I had not lived with her many weeks, however, before I began to understand her. I soon began to learn that, first of all, she wanted everything kept clean about her, that she wanted things done promptly and systematically, and that at the bottom of everything she wanted absolute honesty and frankness. Nothing must be sloven or slipshod; every door, every fence, must be kept in repair.

I cannot now recall how long I lived with Mrs. Ruffner before going to Hampton, but I think it must have been a year and a half. At any rate, I here repeat what I have said more than once before, that the lessons that I learned in the home of Mrs. Ruffner were as valuable to me as any education I have ever gotten anywhere since. Even to this day I never see bits of paper scattered around a house or in the street that I do not want to pick them up at once. I never see a filthy yard that I do not want to clean it, a paling off of a fence that I do not want to put it on, an unpainted or unwhitewashed house that I do not want to paint or whitewash it, or a button off one's clothes, or a grease-spot on them or on a floor, that I do not want to call attention to it.

From fearing Mrs. Ruffner I soon learned to look upon her as one of my best friends. When she found that she could trust me she did so implicitly. During the one or two winters that I was with her she gave me an opportunity to go to school for an hour in the day during a portion of the winter months, but most of my studying was done at night, sometimes alone, sometimes under some one whom I could hire to teach me. Mrs. Ruffner always encouraged and sympathized with me in all my efforts to get an education. It was while living with her that I began to get together my first library. I secured a dry-goods box, knocked out one side of it, put some shelves in it, and began putting into it every kind of book that I could get my hands upon, and called it my "library."

Notwithstanding my success at Mrs. Ruffner's I did not give up the idea of going to the Hampton Institute. In the fall of 1872 I determined to make an effort to get there, although, as I have stated, I had no idea of the direction in which Hampton was, or what it would cost to go there. I do not think that any one thoroughly sympathized with me in my ambition to go to Hampton unless it was my mother, and she was troubled with a grave fear that I was starting out on a "wild-goose chase." At any rate, I got only a half-hearted consent from her that I might start. The small amount of money that I had earned had been consumed by my stepfather and the remainder of the family, with the exception of a very few dollars, and so I had very little with which to buy clothes and pay travelling expenses. My brother John helped me all that he could, but of course that was not a great deal, for his work was in the coal-mine, where he did not earn much, and most of what he did earn went in the direction of paying the household expenses.

Perhaps the thing that touched and pleased me most in connection with my starting for Hampton was the interest that many of the older coloured people took in the matter. They had spent the best days of their lives in slavery, and hardly expected to live to see the time when they would see a member of their race leave home to attend a boarding-school. Some of these older people would give me a nickel, others a quarter, or a handkerchief.

Finally the great day came, and I started for Hampton. I had only a small, cheap satchel that contained what few articles of clothing I could get. My mother at the time was rather weak and broken in health. I hardly expected to see her again, and thus our parting was all the more sad. She, however, was very brave through it all. At that time there were no through trains connecting that part of West Virginia with eastern Virginia. Trains ran only a portion of the way, and the remainder of the distance was travelled by stage-coaches.

The distance from Malden to Hampton is about five hundred miles. I had not been away from home many hours before it began to grow painfully evident that I did not have enough money to pay my fare to Hampton. One experience I shall long remember. I had been travelling over the mountains most of the afternoon in an old-fashioned stage-coach, when, late in the evening, the coach stopped for the night at a common unpainted house called a hotel. All the other passengers except myself were whites. In my ignorance I supposed that the little hotel existed for the purpose of accommodating the passengers who travelled on the stage-coach. The difference that the colour of one's skin would make I had not thought anything about. After all the other passengers had been shown rooms and were getting ready for supper, I shyly presented myself before the man at the desk. It is true I had practically no money in my pocket with which to pay for bed or food, but I had hoped in some way to beg my way into the good graces of the landlord, for at that season in the mountains of Virginia the weather was cold, and I wanted to get indoors for the night. Without asking as to whether I had any money, the man at the desk firmly refused to even consider the matter of providing me with food or lodging. This was my first experience in finding out what the colour of my skin meant. In some way I managed to keep warm by walking about, and so got through the night. My whole soul was so bent upon reaching Hampton that I did not have time to cherish any bitterness toward the hotel-keeper.

By walking, begging rides both in wagons and in the cars, in some way, after a number of days, I reached the city of Richmond, Virginia, about eighty-two miles from Hampton. When I reached there, tired, hungry, and dirty, it was late in the night. I had never been in a large city, and this rather added to my misery. When I reached Richmond, I was completely out of money. I had not a single acquaintance in the place, and, being unused to city ways, I did not know where to go. I applied at several places for lodging, but they all wanted money, and that was what I did not have. Knowing nothing else better to do, I walked the streets. In doing this I passed by many foodstands where fried chicken and half-moon apple pies were piled high and made to present a most tempting appearance. At that time it seemed to me that I would have promised all that I expected to possess in the future to have gotten hold of one of those chicken legs or one of those pies. But I could not get either of these, nor anything else to eat.

I must have walked the streets till after midnight. At last I became so exhausted that I could walk no longer. I was tired, I was hungry, I was everything but discouraged. Just about the time when I reached extreme physical exhaustion, I came upon a portion of a street where the board sidewalk was considerably elevated. I waited for a few minutes, till I was sure that no passersby could see me, and then crept under the sidewalk and lay for the night upon the ground, with my satchel of clothing for a pillow. Nearly all night I could hear the tramp of feet over my head. The next morning I found myself refreshed, but I was extremely hungry, because it had been a long time since I had had sufficient food. As soon as it became light enough for me to see my surroundings I noticed that I was near a large ship, and that this ship seemed to be unloading a cargo of pig iron. I went at once to the vessel and asked the captain to permit me to help unload the vessel in order to get money for food. The captain, a white man, who seemed to be kind-hearted, consented. I worked long enough to earn money for my breakfast, and it seems to me, as I remember it now, to have been about the best breakfast that I have ever eaten.

My work pleased the captain so well that he told me if I desired I could continue working for a small amount per day. This I was very glad to do. I continued working on this vessel for a number of days. After buying food with the small wages I received there was not much left to add to the amount I must get to pay my way to Hampton. In order to economize in every way possible, so as to be sure to reach Hampton in a reasonable time, I continued to sleep under the same sidewalk that gave me shelter the first night I was in Richmond. Many years after that the coloured citizens of Richmond very kindly tendered me a reception at which there must have been two thousand people present. This reception was held not far from the spot where I slept the first night I spent in that city, and I must confess that my mind was more upon the sidewalk that first gave me shelter than upon the reception, agreeable and cordial as it was.

When I had saved what I considered enough money with which to reach Hampton, I thanked the captain of the vessel for his kindness, and started again. Without any unusual occurrence I reached Hampton, with a surplus of exactly fifty cents with which to begin my education. To me it had been a long, eventful journey; but the first sight of the large, three-story, brick school building seemed to have rewarded me for all that I had undergone in order to reach the place. If the people who gave the money to provide that building could appreciate the influence the sight of it had upon me, as well as upon thousands of other youths, they would feel all the more encouraged to make such gifts. It seemed to me to be the largest and most beautiful building I had ever seen. The

sight of it seemed to give me new life. I felt that a new kind of existence had now begun—that life would now have a new meaning. I felt that I had reached the promised land, and I resolved to let no obstacle prevent me from putting forth the highest effort to fit myself to accomplish the most good in the world.

As soon as possible after reaching the grounds of the Hampton Institute, I presented myself before the head teacher for assignment to a class. Having been so long without proper food, a bath and change of clothing, I did not, of course, make a very favourable impression upon her, and I could see at once that there were doubts in her mind about the wisdom of admitting me as a student. I felt that I could hardly blame her if she got the idea that I was a worthless loafer or tramp. For some time she did not refuse to admit me, neither did she decide in my favour, and I continued to linger about her, and to impress her in all the ways I could with my worthiness. In the meantime I saw her admitting other students, and that added greatly to my discomfort, for I felt, deep down in my heart, that I could do as well as they, if I could only get a chance to show what was in me.

After some hours had passed, the head teacher said to me: "The adjoining recitation-room needs sweeping. Take the broom and sweep it."

It occurred to me at once that here was my chance. Never did I receive an order with more delight. I knew that I could sweep, for Mrs. Ruffner had thoroughly taught me how to do that when I lived with her.

I swept the recitation-room three times. Then I got a dusting-cloth and I dusted it four times. All the woodwork around the walls, every bench, table, and desk, I went over four times with my dusting-cloth. Besides, every piece of furniture had been moved and every closet and corner in the room had been thoroughly cleaned. I had the feeling that in a large measure my future depended upon the impression I made upon the teacher in the cleaning of that room. When I was through, I reported to the head teacher. She was a "Yankee" woman who knew just where to look for dirt. She went into the room and inspected the floor and closets; then she took her handkerchief and rubbed it on the woodwork about the walls, and over the table and benches. When she was unable to find one bit of dirt on the floor, or a particle of dust on any of the furniture, she quietly remarked, "I guess you will do to enter this institution."

I was one of the happiest souls on earth. The sweeping of that room was my college examination, and never did any youth pass an examination for entrance into Harvard or Yale that gave him more genuine satisfaction. I have passed several examinations since then, but I have always felt that this was the best one I ever passed.

I have spoken of my own experience in entering the Hampton Institute. Perhaps few, if any, had anything like the same experience that I had, but about that same period there were hundreds who found their way to Hampton and other institutions after experiencing something of the same difficulties that I went through. The young men and women were determined to secure an education at any cost.

The sweeping of the recitation-room in the manner that I did it seems to have paved the way for me to get through Hampton. Miss Mary F. Mackie, the head teacher, offered me a position as janitor. This, of course, I gladly accepted, because it was a place where I could work out nearly all the cost of my board. The work was hard and taxing, but I stuck to it. I had a large number of rooms to care for, and had to work late into the night, while at the same time I had to rise by four o'clock in the morning, in order to build the

Booker T. Washington (Courtesy of the Moorland-Spingarn Research Center)

fires and have a little time in which to prepare my lessons. In all my career at Hampton, and ever since I have been out in the world, Miss Mary F. Mackie, the head teacher to whom I have referred, proved one of my strongest and most helpful friends. Her advice and encouragement were always helpful and strengthening to me in the darkest hour.

I have spoken of the impression that was made upon me by the buildings and general appearance of the Hampton Institute, but I have not spoken of that which made the greatest and most lasting impression upon me, and that was a great man—the noblest, rarest human being that it has ever been my privilege to meet. I refer to the late General Samuel C. Armstrong.

It has been my fortune to meet personally many of what are called great characters, both in Europe and America, but I do not hesitate to say that I never met any man who, in my estimation, was the equal of General Armstrong. Fresh from the degrading influences of the slave plantation and the coal-mines, it was a rare privilege for me to be permitted to come into direct contact with such a character as General Armstrong. I shall always remember that the first time I went into his presence he made the impression upon me of being a perfect man: I was made to feel that there was something about him that was superhuman. It was my privilege to know the General personally from the time I entered Hampton till he died, and the more I saw of him the greater he grew in my estimation. One might have removed from Hampton all the buildings, classrooms, teachers, and industries, and given the men and women there the opportunity of coming into daily contact with General Armstrong, and that alone would have been a liberal education. The older I grow, the more I am convinced that there is no education which one can get from books and costly apparatus that is equal to that which can be gotten from contact with great men and women. Instead of studying books so constantly, how I wish that our schools and colleges might learn to study men and things!

General Armstrong spent two of the last six months of his life in my home at Tuskegee. At that time he was paralyzed to the extent that he had lost control of his body and voice in a very large degree. Notwithstanding his affliction, he worked almost constantly night and day for the cause to which he had given his life. I never saw a man who so completely lost sight of himself. I do not believe he ever had a selfish thought. He was just as happy in trying to assist some other institution in the South as he was when working for Hampton. Although he fought the Southern white man in the Civil War, I never heard him utter a bitter word against him afterward. On the other hand, he was constantly seeking to find ways by which he could be of service to the Southern whites.

It would be difficult to describe the hold that he had upon the students at Hampton, or the faith they had in him. In fact, he was worshipped by his students. It never occurred to me that General Armstrong could fail in anything that he undertook. There is almost no request that he could have made that would not have been complied with. When he was a guest at my home in Alabama, and was so badly paralyzed that he had to be wheeled about in an invalid's chair, I recall that one of the General's former students had occasion to push his chair up a long, steep hill that taxed his strength to the utmost. When the top of the hill was reached, the former pupil, with a glow of happiness on his face, exclaimed, "I am so glad that I have been permitted to do something that was real hard for the General before he dies!" While I was a student at Hampton, the dormitories became so crowded that it was impossible to find room for all who wanted to be admitted. In order to help remedy the difficulty the General conceived the plan of putting up tents to be used as rooms. As soon as it became known that General Armstrong would be pleased if some of the older students would live in the tents during the winter, nearly every student in school volunteered to go.

I was one of the volunteers. The winter that we spent in those tents was an intensely cold one, and we suffered severely—how much I am sure General Armstrong never knew, because we made no complaints. It was enough for us to know that we were pleasing General Armstrong, and that we were making it possible for an additional number of students to secure an education. More than once, during a cold night, when a stiff gale would be blowing, our tent was lifted bodily, and we would find ourselves in the open air. The General would usually pay a visit to the tents early in the morning, and his earnest, cheerful, encouraging voice would dispel any feeling of despondency.

I have spoken of my admiration for General Armstrong, and yet he was but a type of that Christlike body of men and women who went into the Negro schools at the close of the war by the hundreds to assist in lifting up my race. The history of the world fails to show a higher, purer, and more unselfish class of men and women than those who found their way into those Negro schools.

Life at Hampton was a constant revelation to me; was constantly taking me into a new world. The matter of having meals at regular hours, of eating on a tablecloth, using a napkin, the use of the bathtub and of the toothbrush, as well as the use of sheets upon the bed, were all new to me.

I sometimes feel that almost the most valuable lesson I got at the Hampton Institute was in the use and value of the bath. I learned there for the first time some of its value, not only in keeping the body healthy, but in inspiring self-respect and promoting virtue. In all my travels in the South and elsewhere since leaving Hampton I have always in some way sought my daily bath. To get it sometimes when I have been the guest of my own people in a single-roomed cabin has not always been easy to do, except by slipping away to some stream in the woods. I have always tried to teach my people that some provision for bathing should be a part of every house.

For some time, while a student at Hampton, I possessed but a single pair of socks, but when I had worn these till they became soiled, I would wash them at night and hang them by the fire to dry, so that I might wear them again the next morning.

The charge for my board at Hampton was ten dollars per month. I was expected to pay a part of this in cash and to work out the remainder. To meet this cash payment, as I have stated, I had just fifty cents when I reached the institution. Aside from a very few dollars that my brother John was able to send me once in a while, I had no money with which to pay my board. I was determined from the first to make my work as janitor so valuable that my services would be indispensable. This I succeeded in doing to such an extent that I was soon informed that I would be allowed the full cost of my board in return for my work. The cost of tuition was seventy dollars a year. This, of course, was wholly beyond my ability to provide. If I had been compelled to pay the seventy dollars for tuition, in addition to providing for my board, I would have been compelled to leave the Hampton school. General Armstrong, however, very kindly got Mr. S. Griffitts Morgan, of New Bedford, Mass., to defray the cost of my tuition during the whole time that I was at Hampton. After I finished the course at Hampton and had entered upon my lifework at Tuskegee, I had the pleasure of visiting Mr. Morgan several times.

After having been for a while at Hampton, I found myself in difficulty because I did not have books and clothing. Usually, however, I got around the trouble about books by borrowing from those who were more fortunate than myself. As to clothes, when I reached Hampton I had practically nothing. Everything that I possessed was in a small hand satchel. My anxiety about clothing was increased because of the fact that General Armstrong made a personal inspection of the young men in ranks, to see that their clothes were clean. Shoes had to be polished, there must be no buttons off the clothing, and no grease-spots. To wear one suit of clothes continually, while at work and in the schoolroom, and at the same time keep it clean, was rather a hard problem for me to solve. In some way I managed to get on till the teachers learned that I was in earnest and meant to succeed, and then some of them were kind enough to see that I was partly supplied with second-hand clothing that had been sent in barrels from the North. These barrels proved a blessing to hundreds of poor but deserving students. Without them I question whether I should ever have gotten through Hampton.

When I first went to Hampton I do not recall that I had ever slept in a bed that had two sheets on it. In those days there were not many buildings there, and room was very precious. There were seven other boys in the same room with me; most of them, however, students who had been there for some time. The sheets were quite a puzzle to me. The first night I slept under both of them, and the second night I slept on top of both of them; but by watching the other boys I learned my lesson in this, and have been trying to follow it ever since and to teach it to others.

I was among the youngest of the students who were in Hampton at that time. Most of the students were men and women—some as old as forty years of age. As I now recall the scene of my first year, I do not believe that one often has the opportunity of coming into contact with three or four hundred men and women who were so tremendously in earnest as these men and women were. Every hour was occupied in study or work. Nearly all had had enough actual contact with the world to teach them the need for education. Many of the older ones were, of course, too old to master the text-books very thoroughly, and it was often sad to watch their struggles; but they made up in earnestness much of what they lacked in books. Many of them were as poor as I was, and, besides having to wrestle with their books, they had to struggle with a poverty which prevented their having the necessities of life. Many of them had aged parents who were dependent upon them, and some of them were men who had wives whose support in some way they had to provide for.

The great and prevailing idea that seemed to take possession of every one was to prepare himself to lift up the people at his home. No one seemed to think of himself. And the officers and teachers, what a rare set of human beings they were! They worked for the students night and day, in season and out of season. They seemed happy only when they were helping the students in some manner. Whenever it is written—and I hope it will be—the part that the Yankee teachers played in the education of the Negroes immediately after the war will make one of the most thrilling parts of the history of this country. The time is not far distant when the whole South will appreciate this service in a way that it has not yet been able to do.

To the Union Convention of Tennessee Assembled in the Capitol at Nashville, January 9th, 1865

We the undersigned petitioners, American citizens of African descent, natives and residents of Tennessee, and devoted friends of the great National cause, do most respectfully ask a patient hearing of your honorable body in regard to matters deeply affecting the future condition of our unfortunate and long suffering race.

First of all, however, we would say that words are too weak to tell how profoundly grateful we are to the Federal Government for the good work of freedom which it is gradually carrying forward; and for the Emancipation Proclamation which has set free all the slaves in some of the rebellious States, as well as many of the slaves in Tennessee.

After two hundred years of bondage and suffering a returning sense of justice has awakened the great body of the American people to make amends for the unprovoked wrongs committed against us for over two hundred years.

Your petitioners would ask you to complete the work begun by the nation at large, and abolish the last vestige of slavery by the express words of your organic law.

Many masters in Tennessee whose slaves have left them, will certainly make every effort to bring them back to bondage after the reorganization of the State government, unless slavery be expressly abolished by the Constitution.

We hold that freedom is the natural right of all men, which they themselves have no more right to give or barter away, than they have to sell their honor, their wives, or their children.

We claim to be men belonging to the great human family, descended from one great God, who is the common Father of all, and who bestowed on all races and tribes the priceless right of freedom. Of this right, for no offence of ours, we have long been cruelly deprived, and the common voice of the wise and good of all countries, has remonstrated against our enslavement, as one of the greatest crimes in all history.

We claim freedom, as our natural right, and ask that in harmony and co-operation with the nation at large, you should cut up by the roots the system of slavery, which is not only a wrong to us, but the source of all the evil which at present afflicts the State. For slavery, corrupt itself, corrupted nearly all, also, around it, so that it has influenced nearly all the slave States to rebel against the Federal Government, in order to set up a government of pirates under which slavery might be perpetrated.

In the contest between the nation and slavery, our unfortunate people have sided, by instinct, with the former. We have little fortune to devote to the national cause, for a hard fate has hitherto forced us to live in poverty, but we do devote to its success, our hopes, our toils, our whole heart, our sacred honor, and our lives. We will work, pray, live, and, if need be, die for the Union, as cheerfully as ever a white patriot died for his country. The color of our skin does not lessen in the least degree, our love either for God or for the land of our birth.

We are proud to point your honorable body to the fact, that so far as our knowledge extends, not a negro traitor has made his appearance since the beginning of this wicked rebellion.

Whether freeman or slaves the colored race in this country have always looked upon the United States as the Promised Land of Universal freedom, and no earthly temptation has been strong enough to induce us to rebel against it. We love the Union by an instinct which is stronger than any argument or appeal which can be used against it. It is the attachment of a child to its parent.

Devoted as we are to the principles of justice, of love to all men, and of equal rights on which our Government is based, and which make it the hope of the world. We know the burdens of citizenship, and are ready to bear them. We know the duties of the good citizen, and are ready to perform them cheerfully, and would ask to be put in a position in which we can discharge them more effectually. We do not ask for the privilege of citizenship, wishing to shun the obligations imposed by it.

Near 200,000 of our brethren are to-day performing military duty in the ranks of the Union army. Thousands of them have already died in battle, or perished by a cruel martyrdom for the sake of the Union, and we are ready and willing to sacrifice more. But what higher order of citizen is there than the soldier? or who has a greater trust confided to his hands? If we are called on to do military duty against the rebel armies in the field, why should we be denied the privilege of voting against rebel citizens at the ballot-box? The latter is as necessary to save the Government as the former.

The colored man will vote by instinct with the Union party, just as uniformly as he fights with the Union army.

This is not a new question in Tennessee. From 1796 to 1835, a period of thirty-nine years, free colored men voted at all her elections without question. Her leading politicians and statesmen asked for and obtained the suffrages of colored voters, and were not ashamed of it. Such men as *Andrew Jackson,* President of the United States, Hon. *Felix Grundy,* John Bell, Hon. *Hugh L. White, Cave Johnson,* and *Ephraim H. Foster,* members of the United States Senate and of the Cabinet, *Gen. William Carroll, Samuel Houston,* Aaron V. Brown, and, in fact, all the politicians and candidates of all parties in Tennessee solicited colored free men for their votes at every election.

Nor was Tennessee alone in this respect, for the same privileges was granted to colored free men in North Carolina, to-day the most loyal of all the rebellious States, without ever producing any evil consequences.

If colored men have been faithful and true to the Government of the United States in spite of the Fugitive Slave Law, and the cruel policy often pursued toward them, will they not be more devoted to it now than ever, since it has granted them that liberty which they desired above all things? Surely, if colored men voted without harm to the State, while their brethren were in bondage, they will be much more devoted and watchful over her interests when elevated to the rank of freemen and voters. If they are good law-abiding citizens, praying for its prosperity, rejoicing in its progress, paying its taxes, fighting its battles, making its farms, mines, work-shops and commerce more productive, why deny them the right to have a voice in the election of its rulers?

This is a democracy—a government of the people. It should aim to make every man, without regard to the color of his skin, the amount of his wealth, or the character of his religious faith, feel personally interested in its welfare. Every man who lives under the Government should feel that it is his property, his treasure, the bulwark and defence of himself and his family, his pearl of great price, which he must preserve, protect, and defend faithfully at all times, on all occasions, in every possible manner.

This is not a Democratic Government if a numerous, law-abiding, industrious, and useful class of citizens, born and bred on the soil, are to be treated as aliens and enemies, as an inferior degraded class, who must have no voice in the Government which they support, protect and defend, with all their heart, soul, mind, and body, both in peace and war.

This Government is based on the teachings of the Bible, which prescribes the same rules of action for all members of the human family, whether their complexion be white, yellow, red or black. God no where in his revealed word, makes an invidious and degrading distinction against his children, because of their color. And happy is that nation which makes the Bible its rule of action, and obeys principle, not prejudice.

Let no man oppose this doctrine because it is opposed to his old prejudices. The nation is fighting for its life, and cannot afford to be controlled by prejudice. Had prejudice prevailed instead of principle, not a single colored soldier would have been in the Union army to-day. But principle and justice triumphed, and now near 200,000 colored patriots stand under the folds of the national flag, and brave their breasts to the bullets of the rebels. As we are in the battlefield, so we swear before heaven, by all that is dear to men, to be at the ballot-box faithful and true to the Union.

The possibility that the negro suffrage proposition may shock popular prejudice at first sight, is not a conclusive argument against its wisdom and policy. No proposition ever met with more furious or general opposition than the one to enlist colored soldiers in the United States army. The opponents of the measure exclaimed on all hands that the negro was a coward; that he would not fight; that one white man, with a whip in his hand could put to flight a regiment of them; that the experiment would end in the utter rout and ruin of the Federal army. Yet the colored man has fought so well, on almost every occasion, that the rebel government is prevented, only by its fears and distrust of being able to force him to fight for slavery as well as he fights against it, from putting half a million of negroes into its ranks.

The Government has asked the colored man to fight for its preservation and gladly has he done it. It can afford to trust him with a vote as safely as it trusted him with a bayonet.

How boundless would be the love of the colored citizen, how intense and passionate his zeal and devotion to the government, how enthusiastic and how lasting would be his gratitude, if his white brethren were to take him by the hand and say, "You have been ever loyal to our government; henceforward be voters." Again, the granting of this privilege would stimulate the colored man to greater exertion to make himself an intelligent, respected, useful citizen. His pride of character would be appealed to this way most successfully; he would send his children to school, that they might become educated and intelligent members of society. It used to be thought that ignorant negroes were the most valuable, but this belief probably originated from the fact that it is almost impossible to retain an educated, intelligent man in bondage. Certainly, if the free colored man be educated, and his morals enlightened and improved, he will be a far better member of society, and less liable to transgress its laws. It is the brutal, degraded, ignorant man who is usually the criminal.

One other matter we would urge on your honorable body. At present we can have only partial protection from the courts. The testimony of twenty of the most intelligent, honorable, colored loyalists cannot convict a white traitor of a treasonable action. A white rebel might sell powder and lead to a rebel soldier in the presence of twenty colored soldiers, and yet their evidence would be worthless so far as the courts are concerned, and the rebel would escape. A colored man may have served for years faithfully in the army, and yet his testimony in court would be rejected, while that of a white man who had served in the rebel army would be received.

If this order of things continue, our people are destined to a malignant persecution at the hands of rebels and their former rebellious masters, whose hatred they may have incurred, without precedent even in the South. Every rebel soldier or citizen whose arrest in the perpetration of crime they may have effected, every white traitor whom they may have brought to justice, will torment and persecute them and set justice at defiance, because the courts will not receive negro testimony, which will generally be the only possible testimony in such cases. A rebel may murder his former slave and defy justice, because he committed the deed in the presence of half a dozen respectable colored citizens. He may have the dwelling of his former slave burned over his head, and turn his wife and children out of doors, and defy the law, for no colored man can appear against him. Is this the fruit of freedom, and the reward of our services in the field? Was it for this that colored soldiers fell by hundreds before Nashville, fighting under the flag of the Union? Is it for this that we have guided Union officers and soldiers, when escaping from the cruel and deadly prisons of the South through forests and swamps, at the risk of our own lives, for we knew that to us detection would be death? Is it for this that we have concealed multitudes of Union refugees in caves and cane-brakes, when flying from the conscription officers and tracked by bloodhounds, and divided with them our last morsal of food? Will you declare in your revised constitution that a pardoned traitor may appear in court and his testimony be heard, but that no colored loyalist shall be believed even upon oath? If this should be so, then will our last state be worse than our first, and we can look for no relief on this side of the grave. Has not the colored man fought, bled and died for the Union, under a thousand great disadvantages and discouragements? Has his fidelity ever had a shadow of suspicion cast upon it, in any matter of responsibility confided to his hands?

There have been white traitors in multitudes in Tennessee, but where, we ask, is the black traitor? Can you forget how the colored man has fought at Fort Morgan, at Milliken's Bend, at Fort Pillow, before Petersburg, and your own city of Nashville?

When has the colored citizen, in this rebellion been tried and found wanting?

In conclusion, we would point to the fact that the States where the largest measure of justice and civil rights has been granted to the colored man, both as to suffrage and his oath in court, are among the most rich, intelligent, enlightened and prosperous. Massachusetts, illustrious for her statesmen and her commercial and manufacturing enterprises and thrift, whose noble liberality has relieved so many loyal refugees and other sufferers of Tennessee, allows her colored citizens to vote, and is ever jealous of their rights. She has never had reason to repent the day when she gave them the right of voting.

Had the southern states followed her example the present rebellion never would have desolated their borders.

Several other Northern States permit negro suffrage, nor have bad effects ever resulted from it. It may be safely affirmed that Tennessee was quite as safe and prosperous during the 39 years while she allowed negro suffrage, as she has been since she abolished it.

In this great and fearful struggle of the nation with a wicked rebellion, we are anxious to perform the full measure of our duty both as citizens and soldiers to the Union cause we consecrate ourselves, and our families, with all that we have on earth. Our souls burn with love for the great government of freedom and equal rights. Our white brethren have no cause for distrust as regards our fidelity, for neither death nor life, nor angels, nor principalities, nor powers, nor things present, nor things to come, nor height, nor depth, nor any other creature, shall be able to separate us from the love of the Union.

Praying that the great God, who is the common Father of us all, by whose help the land must be delivered from present evil, and before whom we must all stand at last to be judged by the rule of eternal justice, and not by passion and prejudice, may enlighten your minds and enable you to act with wisdom, justice, and magnanimity, we remain your faithful friends in all the perils and dangers which threaten our beloved country.

[*59 signatures*]
And many other colored citizens of Nashville

The convention adopted an amendment to the state constitution abolishing slavery, which was ratified on February 22, 1865. The delegates took no action to extend the rights of suffrage or testimony to black Tennesseans.

Letters Dated September 3, 1864, and January 9, 1865, from Spotswood Rice

Drawing strength from both the Union's commitment to emancipation and its march toward victory, a black soldier from Missouri assured first his daughters and then the woman who owned one of them that the federal army would do the Lord's work, and that he would be there when it did. The moment of liberation was at hand.

[Benton Barracks Hospital, St. Louis, Mo., September 3, 1864]

My Children I take my pen in hand to rite you A few lines to let you know that I have not forgot you and that I want to see you as bad as ever now my Dear Children I want you to be contented with whatever may be your lots be assured that I will have you if it cost me my life on the 28th of the mounth. 8 hundred White and 8 hundred blacke solders expects to start up the rivore to Glasgow and above there thats to be jeneraled by a jeneral that will give me both of you when they Come I expect to be with, them and expect to get you both in return. Dont be uneasy my children I expect to have you. If Diggs dont give you up this Government will and I feel confident that I will get you Your Miss Kaitty said that I tried to steal you But I'll let her know that god never intended for man to steal his own flesh and blood. If I had no confidence in God I could have confidence in her But as it is If I ever had any Confidence in her I have none now and never expect to have And I want her to remember if she meets me with ten thousand soldiers she [will?] meet her enemy I once [*thought*] that I had some respect for them but now my respects is worn out and have no sympathy for Slaveholders. And as for her cristianantty I expect the Devil has Such in hell You tell her from me that She is the frist Christian that I ever hard say that aman could Steal his own child especially out of human bondage

You can tell her that She can hold to you as long as she can I never would expect to ask her again to let you come to me because I know that the devil has got her hot set against that that is write now my Dear children I am a going to close my letter to you Give my love to all enquiring friends tell them all that we are well and want to see them very much and Corra and Mary receive the greater part of it you sefves and dont think hard of us not sending you any thing I you father have a plenty for you when I see you Spott & Noah sends their love to both of you Oh! My Dear children how I do want to see you
HL

[Benton Barracks Hospital, St. Louis, Mo., September 3, 1864]

I received a leteter from Cariline telling me that you say I tried to steal to plunder my child away from you now I want you to understand that mary is my Child and she is a God given rite of my own and you may hold on to hear as long as you can but I want you to remembor this one thing that the longor you keep my Child from me the longor you will have to burn in hell and the qwicer youll get their for we are now makeing up a bout one thoughsand blacke troops to Come up tharough and wont to come through Glasgow and when we come wo be to Copperhood rabbels and to the Slaveholding rebbels for we dont expect to leave them there root neor branch but we thinke how ever that we that have Children in the hands of you devels we will trie your [vertues?] the day that we enter Glasgow I want you to understand kittey diggs that where ever you and I meets we are enmays to each orther I offered once to pay you forty dollers for my own Child but I am glad now that you did not accept it Just hold on now as long as you can and the worse it will be for you you never in you life befor I came down hear did you give Children any thing not eny thing whatever not even a dollers worth of expencs now you call my children your pro[per]ty not so with me my Children is my own and I expect to get them and when I get ready to come after mary I will have bout a powrer and autherity to bring hear away and to exacute vengencens on them that holds my Child you will then know how to talke to me I will assure that and you will know how to talk rite too I want you now to just hold on to hear if you want to iff your conchosence tells thats the road go that road and what it will brig you to kittey diggs I have no fears about geting mary out of your hands this whole Government gives chear to me and you cannot help your self

Like Private Rice, many slaves-turned-soldiers took "chear" from their new status. As slaves, they had been subject to the personal power of their owners, with no means to appeal arbitrary or violent acts. As soldiers, they belonged to a bureaucracy ruled by impersonal laws to which officers and enlisted men were equally accountable. Although orders proceeded from superior to subordinate, men with grievances had access to formal channels of redress. Moreover, soldiers accused of violating army regulations or particular orders were subject to a regular process of court-martial. In principle, court-martial procedures provided a framework in which every case—whether it involved a private or a general, a black soldier or a white one—could be tried impartially. In practice, military justice was not always impartial, and even when it was, it often imposed severe penalties for minor infractions. Many a black soldier discovered that the law of the army, though fundamentally different in character from the law of slavery, could be every bit as harsh. A sergeant from Louisiana asked President Lincoln to reverse his conviction for disobedience of orders, breach of arrest, and mutinous conduct.

CHAPTER SIX

The Observed Other

They failed to ask my name and called
me negro.

—Henry Dumas

READING SELECTIONS

HARRIET JACKSON SCARUPA

W. Montague Cobb: His Long, Storied, Battle-Scarred Life

The old fighter looks fragile now, his walk reduced to a tentative, slow motion shuffle, his voice sometimes winding down in fatigue or interrupted by coughs, his eyes squinting as he tries to read print that seems to him so very small. But his mind is still keen, overflowing with its treasure chest of memories, quotations, opinions, facts. And his will is still strong. Oh so strong.

Nobody—but nobody—has ever accused W. Montague Cobb of being passive.

"I'm a seasoned fighter and the battle never bothered me," says the 83-year-old teacher, anatomist, physical anthropologist, editor, writer, historian, medical, civic and civil rights leader. As for all those roles and then some:

As a full-time faculty member at the Howard University College of Medicine for 41 years (1932–73) and a visiting professor at 12 other medical schools, he has taught anatomy to some 6,000 medical students (by his count).

As an anatomist and physical anthropologist, his research has covered topics as diverse as the development of teeth in the walrus, aging changes in the human skeleton, the cranio-facial union in man, the role of anatomical records in city history and the physical anthropology of the Black American.

As an editor of the *Journal of the National Medical Association (JNMA)* for 28 years (1949–77), he is credited with transforming what was once a modest house organ into a lively, informative and influential medical journal.

On the pages of the *JNMA* and elsewhere, his documentation of the achievements, activities and concerns of the nation's Black physicians has earned him a reputation as the foremost living authority on Black medical history.

As a writer, he has been almost embarrassingly prolific. His 52-page list of publications runs to 1,113 titles, encompassing a book on the nation's first Black medical society, scientific monographs and abstracts, book reviews, tributes, editorials, book chapters and articles on just about every subject under the sun for scholarly, professional and popular magazines.

His leadership skills have found expression through a wide variety of outlets, including those as president of the American Association of Physical Anthropologists, the Anthropological Society of Washington, the National Medical Association, the Medico–Chirurgical Society of the District of Columbia, the Washington Society for the History of Medicine, the Venice Beach (Maryland) Citizens Association—and the NAACP.

Alongside the many serious roles he has played are those in a more carefree vein: the violinist who "treated" his students to the strains of a Handel sonata as they dissected cadavers in the anatomy laboratory; the self-acknowledged "ham" who entertained freshmen medical students with dramatized recitals of "Casey at the Bat" or "The Cremation of Sam McGee" and his friends with a legendary imitation of the late Howard University President Mordecai Wyatt Johnson; the bon vivant and raconteur who, with Arthur P. Davis, Sterling Brown and other members of the much storied Gourmet Club, turned fellowship, good eating, good drinking and questionable singing into a high art; the "captain" who strutted around his summer home in Venice Beach sporting the requisite cap, in keeping with his stature as owner of that mighty seagoing vessel, the Tuscarora, i.e. a rowboat; the author of a variety of light pieces in the *JNMA*, among them, a mock-treatise on an affliction suffered by many a middle-aged man of his acquaintance: "stomachus convivous or banquet belly."

Whatever role W. Montague Cobb has played at any given moment or any given decade, he has played it with verve. Whatever role W. Montague Cobb has played at any given moment or any given decade, he has seldom strayed from battle. Observes surgeon LaSalle D. Leffall Jr., his friend and former student: "He has been willing to enter the fray. That's one thing

I can say about Dr. Cobb: *he has been willing to enter the fray.*"

Not surprisingly, then, controversy has touched Cobb's life more than once.

The Battles

Some 50 years before Jimmy "The Greek" Snyder caused an outcry by attributing the prowess of Black athletes to "big thighs that run up their backs," among other alleged "reasons," Cobb was demolishing the myth that Blacks are more anatomically equipped to excel in athletics than whites. The corollary of this myth—sometimes stated, sometimes not—was that Blacks were less anatomically equipped for strictly cerebral endeavors.

In a January 1936 article, "Race and Runners," published in *The Journal of Health and Physical Education,* he took aim at the then popularly held view that the success of Black sprinters and broad jumpers was due to such supposedly racially determined characteristics as "a longer heel bone," "a long Achilles tendon" and a "short-bellied calf." His weapon: simple scientific investigation. He compared X-rays of 1936 Olympic champion Jesse Owens' heel with that of a randomly selected white man of the same age and found, lo and behold, that Owens' heel bone was shorter, supposedly a "white" characteristic.

Cobb also compared Owens' legs to that of Frank Wykoff, the white co-holder of the world's record for the 100-yard dash at that time, and discovered, lo and behold, that the white runner had the allegedly "Black" calves and vice versa. He concluded: "The physiques of champion Negro and white sprinters in general and Jesse Owens in particular reveal nothing to indicate Negroid physical characters are anatomically concerned with the present dominance of Negro athletes in national competition in the short dashes and the broad jump." Settling the whole silly matter once and for all (he thought), he wrote in a May 1947 article in *Negro Digest:* "Science has not revealed a single trait peculiar to the Negro alone, to which his athletic achievements could be attributed."

Around the same time, Cobb was addressing such other pseudoscientific bits of racism as the notions that Blacks were constitutionally more sexually promiscuous than whites (the term of the day was "oversexed") and that they were lower on the evolutionary chart, i.e. closer to apes, than whites.

The first issue he laid to rest in a May 1947 article in *Our World* entitled "Are Negroes Oversexed?" "No known scientific fact can support the lie that Negroes as a race are oversexed," he wrote. "Absurd claims like these were seriously used by self-styled scientists as propaganda to keep the Negro enslaved and to maintain him in a degraded status after liberation."

The second issue he tackled in an article "Education in Human Biology: An Essential for the Present and Future" in the April 1943 issue of *The Journal of Negro History.* His method was simple. He drew a new hierarchical chart to illustrate human ascent. By turning the tree-like branches traditionally used to depict evolution sideways, he was able to show the races of mankind at levels of equality—as, in fact, they are—instead of the white man in the higher or superior position as had been the style of such charts in the past. (See "What Is Man? An Anatomist's View," *New Directions,* April 1976.)

He advocated that his chart or one like it be introduced to schoolchildren as part of a required instructional program in physical anthropology. Through such a program, they could be exposed to "the full and honest exposition of the nature and import of racial differences," he wrote. Thus they would come to see that "Race as a biological is no index of physical, mental or cultural capacity." It was a theme that also permeated his own teaching at Howard.

Attacking segregation and discrimination in medical education, professional training and hospital customs constituted another grand Cobb crusade. Some particulars:

In 1947 in the Bulletin of *The Medico-Chirurgical Society of the District of Columbia* (of which he was founding editor), he lambasted the practice of turning outmoded hospitals to Blacks in an allegorically titled article, "Old Clothes to Sam: The Negro's Hospital Dilemma." Indeed, the phrase "old clothes to Sam" made its way into the general lexicon as a shorthand to describe Black Americans' second-class treatment.

As president of the Medico-Chirurgical Society in the '40s and '50s, he led the fight for the admission of Black physicians to the city's predominantly white hospitals and headed the organization's negotiating team which in 1952 successfully forced the Medical Society of the District of Columbia to admit Blacks.

Looking beyond his native city, in 1957 he conceived and organized a national conference on hospital integration under the sponsorship of the National Medical Association, the NAACP and the National Urban League. Through the First Imhotep National Conference on Hospital Integration and its six successors, hospital administrators across the nation were pressured to open their doors to Black residents, interns, patients and physicians. At the same time, the pressure he and others put on the nation's medical schools helped open those doors as well.

Related to all this was Cobb's crusade to begin to redress the deplorable health conditions so endemic in so much of Black America. "Even though health conditions in this country as a whole are far from satisfactory, the plight of the Negro is worse than that of the white," he told members of a Senate committee as part of his testimony on behalf of the NAACP in support of a 1946 bill to establish national health insurance. He did so in defiance of the stance taken by the powerful American Medical Association, which equated the intent of the bill with that old bugaboo, "socialized medicine." As a result, according to Cobb, "Some people came to Mordecai [Wyatt Johnson] and said, 'Why don't you throw that fellow off the faculty?' . . . But Mordecai never bothered me."

Cobb and his NAACP brethren saw the controversial bill as "a means whereby the economic barrier to the extension of medical care to the millions of American citizens who so sorely need, but cannot afford, such care, may be overcome," as he testified. The bill didn't pass, but Cobb remained loyal to the principles enshrined in it. As he wrote in an article in *The Crisis* a year later, "Health care . . . has to be readily available to *all* in a successful democracy, without regard to status or pocketbook."

In another arena of his life, he was waging still another battle against the status quo.

In the '50s, Cobb boycotted meetings of the American Association for the Advancement of Science and the American Association of Anatomists to protest the organizations' decisions to hold their annual meetings in cities where segregation was practiced in hotels, restaurants and public transportation. These well-publicized boycotts ["Dr. Cobb Sets an Example," ran a headline above an article in the January 14, 1956 *Afro-American*] helped the organizations' members face the contradiction between being scientists in pursuit of truth and tacitly supporting racially exclusionary practices for which there could be no scientific justification whatsoever. The result: both organizations formally resolved to refuse to hold any future meetings in cities where segregation was the norm.

Later, in 1965, he put far more than his intellect and influence on the line when he journeyed to Selma as president of the National Medical Association to give moral and other support to Black Alabama physicians who had volunteered to treat besieged participants of the historic Selma to Montgomery march.

The '80s, a quieter time for many, have not necessarily been a quieter time for Cobb. In 1982, the Metropolitan Washington YMCA announced its intent to close its 12th Street (Anthony Bowen) branch which was located in the neighborhood of Cobb's birth, an area now sullied with drug trafficking and desperately in need of constructive recreational outlets for youth.

The Y made the announcement at a time it was promoting a posh new downtown facility whose high entrance fees put it out of reach of most D.C. residents.

Cobb was among those outraged. In a letter to the City Council, he charged that the action was "arrogant and presumptuous in the extreme, and may mildly be termed bigoted and irresponsible," a charge highlighted in a front page Metro section article in *The Washington Post* on March 7. A picture of an angry Cobb ran with the article.

Cobb found the action not only galling in light of the neighborhood's needs, but also because it seemed to desecrate history. The Anthony Bowen branch was the first Black YMCA in the nation, one that had enriched the lives of many a Black boy like himself when so many doors in the nation's capital had been closed to them because of race. In light of the protests, the YMCA backed down, agreeing to retain the Anthony Bowen branch in the neighborhood but to house it in a building that was in better structural condition than the original.

As he moves through the eighth decade of his life, Cobb has tended to dwell less on the concerns of any one particular constituency, whether Black physicians or poor D.C. youth, but on an issue of crucial import to *all*: survival. In his writing and speeches, he has again and again phrased the issue as a conflict between "*Homo sanguinis*, or Man the Bloody" and "*Homo sapiens*, or Man the Wise." Speaking, for instance, at a meeting of the American Anthropological Association last November, he elaborated:

"Man has been a bloody predatory primate always given to the overkill for over a million years, but only during the last 3,000 years or so, has he developed anything like ethical systems.

"At the present time it would seem that *Homo sanguinis* has the upper hand. Can *Homo sapiens* win? . . .

"Let us hope that *Homo sapiens* will prevail . . . and that we may use reason more in the solution of our problems. Otherwise we may eliminate our species, along with many others, and ruin our planet in the process."

And so the old gadfly/crusader/fighter carries on. He even, briefly, adopts a pugilistic stance as he confronts a writer who has come to his house near Howard's main campus to try to find out why one man has been so drawn to battle, what compelled him to take on many diverse roles and what thread ties them all together.

As he sits in his formal Victorian-styled living room in his impeccably tailored grey suit, puffing on his ever-present pipe filled with his favorite Captain Black tobacco, he looks very much the dignified elder statesman he is. Then he pounces. In no uncertain terms he lets the writer know that if she wants to know what his life is all about, she's going to have to go about it *his* way. "You come to me with a list of things you want to know and you want to ask them the way you want to ask them," he scolds. "But, after all, you have to take the subject into consideration. He or she has some points of view too."

His point of view right now, he scolds anew, is that in order to understand the things he's done and the thoughts he has "you have to know what lies behind them." You have to look at a life—his life—from the beginning and see how one thing has led to another. And if in the process it means pausing for a good story or two or three or four or a burst of song, a bit of pantomime, a recitation of verse or a tour of the house, well, then, so be it.

The Cobb House

If ever a dwelling reflects the character of the occupant, this sturdy three-story brick rowhouse (circa 1890) does. Indeed, it is a veritable museum to the life and times of W. Montague Cobb.

Almost every available inch of wall space is covered with: his own watercolors; paintings done by his mother and friends; family photographs (of his earliest known ancestors, his grandmother, parents, wife, two daughters, four grandchildren); photographs of teachers, friends, students and public figures he has known; an old print of Vesalius (the father of anatomy) dissecting in secret; a reproduction of Rembrandt's "The Lesson in Anatomy;" his 1930 license to practice medicine and surgery in the District of Columbia; a large drawing showing Amherst College during his student days there in the '20s; honorary degrees from 10 institutions; honorary plaques from some two dozen organizations; photographs galore of Cobb, of course—sitting in a deck chair on the Battleship USS Missouri when he was an honored guest of the Secretary of the Navy; surrounded by skeletons in his Howard anatomy lab; playing the violin with a string quartet; witnessing President Lyndon B. Johnson signing the Medicare Bill in 1965; being presented with a "Living Legacy" award by President Jimmy Carter 14 years later. . . .

Then too: small family photographs crowd tables throughout the house; bookshelves hold weathered volumes on a wide array of subjects, carefully labeled photo albums, notebooks filled with scientific notations; a bed serves as an improvised file cabinet supporting piles of reprints of articles, correspondence, magazines. . . .

"I live in a kind of organized chaos," Cobb admits. "And somehow due to my archeological system of knowing in what layer a thing is, I make out."

Childhood Years

The house where Cobb has lived for more than half a century is eight blocks away from his boyhood home. In that modest rowhouse near 13th and T Streets, N.W., the only child of William Elmer and Alexzine Montague Cobb was delivered on October 12, 1904 by a Howard trained physician, Dr. Austin Maurice Curtis. "So Howard has touched my life from the beginning," Cobb says.

His father was a printer, who had come to Washington from Selma, Ala., in 1889 to work in the U.S. Government Printing Office and later opened his own small printing shop not far from the family home. "My father never had any money, but he was never afraid of anybody," Cobb reflects.

Through his father, he says, he learned the importance of standing up for one's principles. Through both parents, he learned "not to hate." Imhotep, the name he was later to choose for those '50s conferences on hospital integration, reflects that teaching. The name of the Egyptian demigod of medicine, Imhotep means "He who cometh in peace," Cobb explains.

The Washington of his childhood was, of course, rigidly segregated. As he ironically observes, "The first time somebody tried to explain apartheid to me, I said, 'You don't need to' because all of my early life had been lived under apartheid in the capital city of the great nation declaimed as the 'Land of the Free and the Home of the Brave.' "

He attended Patterson Elementary School and then went on to Dunbar High School, the alma mater of generations of high achievers. He started kindergarten at four and it was there, he says, that he got his first interest in "what education is." "The teachers, Miss Montgomery and Miss Williams [yes, he remembers their names] made the classroom so happy," he recalls. "So I learned then unconsciously that good teaching involves making the pupils enjoy learning."

At Dunbar, Cobb received what he considers the finest of educations. "I used to later tell my good white friends, 'It's a pity that all the white kids in town could not be exposed to somebody like Clyde McDuffie' [a Dunbar Latin teacher]. He would come in and put the daily paper on the board showing the movement of the Germans and the Allies [during World War I] and talk about it and then he'd say, 'Now, let's see how Caesar

Augustus fought it out on those same lines.' And you'd learn."

From Dunbar, he headed for Amherst College, his interest in attending the Massachusetts liberal arts college having been sparked by the visits of some Amherst students to Dunbar. In his Amherst class, ('25), he was part of a quartet of young Black men who were to make distinctive marks on history. The other members: Mercer Cook, the diplomat and scholar; William Hastie, the first Black federal judge; and Ben Davis, the U.S. Communist Party leader who was once a popular city councilman from Harlem. Charles Drew, Cobb's boyhood friend, who later carved out his own niche of fame as surgeon and blood plasma storage developer, was in the class behind him.

Except for his interaction with Amherst's few Black students, his college years were spent in an essentially all-white world. That provided some lessons in itself. As he puts it, "As I got a chance to observe the white man, I recognized he didn't have an exceptional amount of brains. Some Black boys were brighter than I was—not too many, but some. [No one ever has accused Cobb of inordinate modesty.] And I saw a lot of dumb white boys. So I thought, 'What is all this race stuff about?' "

At Amherst, Cobb proved to be a top student—and a star athlete. He excelled at track and boxing, so for a while he was literally—not just symbolically—a fighter. By his senior year, he had racked up the best record in his class in zoology, which earned him a scholarship the following summer to study and conduct research at the prestigious Marine Biological Laboratory in Woods Hole, Mass. Traditionally, winners of the scholarship went on to academic careers in biology. But Cobb was already committed to a career in medicine, having been accepted to the Howard University College of Medicine.

Cobb the Student

Why medicine? "I knew Dr. Curtis had delivered me in the home and over the years I got to know other doctors who would treat people in the neighborhood. I just felt a doctor was respected and made sick people well." Teasing now, he adds, "And at the time all hospitals used iodophor (a disinfectant) and it smelled good. [He takes an exaggerated sniff.] I thought, 'That's what I'd like to be: a doctor.' "

Returning to the subject of that summer at Woods Hole, Cobb takes out his perfectly preserved notebook filled with the notations and drawings he made for the course he took there in embryology. Before long he embarks on what the visiting writer considers a long diversionary discourse on such topics as how to catch specimens for laboratory studies and the mating habits of seaworms. The latter subject even inspires a quotation from "Romeo and Juliet" which he delivers in full theatrical style: "Violent delights have violent ends and in their triumph die." [No wonder his good friend Arthur P. Davis calls him an "aborted great actor" as well as "a first class ham, no make that 'a 24-carat ham.' "]

When the writer tries to get the conversation back to what she considers the right track, he refuses. "*No,*" he practically shouts, and proceeds to share new details of what he learned in that embryology course more than 60 years ago.

Finally, he says, "On the basis of the training I had in the course, when I was a senior in medical school, I was asked to be an instructor in embryology. You get it? And on the basis of *that* Numa P.G. Adams, who was the first Black dean of the medical school, asked me if I was interested in pursuing a full-time academic career. So the Woods Hole experience is what led to my whole teaching career."

Continuing the narrative, Cobb says, "I told Adams, 'Yes, I would be interested in an academic career . . . if I could pick my field.' He said, 'What field do you want?' I said, 'Anatomy.' " Why Anatomy?, he is later asked. "Anatomy is the kindergarten [i.e., the foundation] of medicine," he recites as if he's said it many times before, as he has.

Once Adams gave his assent to Cobb's choice, Cobb says, "We had to hunt around for a suitable place for me to go for further study." That suitable place turned out to be Western Reserve University [now Case Western] in Cleveland where he enrolled in the graduate program in physical anthropology and anatomy—two fields that have a natural affinity.

But before he embarked on those studies, he had a few things to get out of the way—earning his M.D. from Howard, completing an internship at Freedmen's Hospital, (now Howard University Hospital), obtaining his license to practice medicine and surgery in the District of Columbia and marrying a young schoolteacher named Hilda B. Smith. It was a marriage that was to last for 47 years before her death from cancer in 1976 and today Cobb's conversation is sprinkled with abundant references to "the voice of authority," as he teasingly used to call his wife.

Cobb the Investigator

He obtained his Ph.D. in anatomy and physical anthropology from Western Reserve in 1932 and then embarked directly on a full-time teaching career at Howard.

It was at Western Reserve, which boasted an excellent anatomy laboratory and museum, that he first investigated the physical differences between Blacks and whites. He took a comprehensive series of measurements on Black and white cadavers in order to come up with some hard data on the subject and reviewed the data of other researchers in the field as well.

Among the conclusions he drew from this investigation, as he reported in a 1934 article in *The Journal of Negro Education*, "The Physical Constitution of the American Negro:" "The evidence now available shows clearly that racial characters are largely variations of form which have no distinct functional survival value in modern civilization."

Today, the very notion of actually measuring a bunch of dead people to make such a point seems not only ghoulish and bizarre, but totally unnecessary. "Sure there's no need to do that now," Cobb agrees. No one, for instance, rushed out to measure Black athletes' thighs after Jimmy "The Greek's" comments as Cobb had so measured Jesse Owens' heel bone after similar comments were made 50 years ago. But the kind of harmful racial stereotyping reflected in such comments is still around, Cobb believes. "That substrate has been there all the time. And it must be fought."

So his narrative comes back to the issue of fighting racism. "As I began to hear this race stuff I decided the whole set-up was wrong," reflects a man whose own hue is so light he easily could "pass," as they used to say in the old days. "So I just made up my mind that I would try to do something about it. I didn't know what, but something."

Gradually, alongside his Howard teaching career, he began defining what those "somethings" would be.

Because he was a teacher of future Black physicians and had no interest in sending them out into a circumscribed world, segregated hospitals and medical societies became a natural target for his concern and activism. And his activism in behalf of Black physicians led him naturally to the kind of activism in behalf of his race as a whole that found its expression in his work for the NAACP.

Because he was at Howard, historically the premier training ground for the nation's Black physicians, it became likewise natural for him to develop an interest in the history of Blacks in medicine and want to pursue that interest in a concrete way.

Because he was "Will Cobb, the printer's boy," and a long term lover of all things literary, there was perhaps both ink in his blood and a bit of the muse in his soul. So it was natural that he embrace the roles of editor and writer.

"One thing just sort of led to another," says Cobb. And what links them all, he believes, is "a constructive outlook." To illustrate what he means, he proffers a verse he learned as a child: "If you're not getting better, you're bound to be worse, for nothing stands still in the universe." Looking very proud of himself, he adds, "So I decided many years ago that when I went out in the world, I would be trying to move forward."

Many are those who are grateful for that decision.

"Dr. Cobb has really dedicated his whole life to service," says orthopedic surgeon Charles H. Epps, a Cobb protégé and friend, who for eight years was an assistant editor of the *JNMA*. "I'm sure he has a treasury of people who feel, as I do, indebted by all he's done."

Consider that indebtedness as it relates to just one issue: opening the doors of the nation's hospitals to Black residents, interns and physicians. "Dr. Cobb didn't even practice clinical medicine, but was concerned about having Black physicians get hospital privileges in predominantly white hospitals," says LaSalle Leffall, who was once also an assistant editor of the *JNMA*. "To me that's the mark of a big man. He had nothing personal to gain from it [gaining hospital privileges]. It was just a part of his concern with striving for social justice.

"Young Black physicians coming up today take these privileges for granted. I talk to students about where they're going to do a residency and one says, 'Oh, I'm going to Johns Hopkins' or 'I'm going to Georgetown' or 'I'm going to The Washington Hospital Center,' wherever. They don't even think about it. They don't know what it was like then. But people like me and others who followed know the great efforts Dr. Cobb has made in our behalf and we are grateful."

Consider, also, his service to just two of the organizations that bear his imprint: the National Medical Association and the NAACP.

Observes John Joyner, the current president of the NMA, the 93-year-old organization that represents the nation's 16,000 Black physicians: "Dr. Cobb is certainly one of the most distinguished past presidents of the NMA and we are certainly appreciative of all the contributions he has made to the NMA and that he continues to make to it." When asked if he ever studied under Cobb, the Indianapolis neurosurgeon replies, "Not formally. But to know Dr. Cobb is to study and to learn."

Observes the Rev. Edward Hailes, president of the Washington branch of the NAACP and vice chairman of its national board of directors who served on the board for many years with Cobb: "In addition to the tangible contributions Dr. Cobb has made to the NAACP—such as the giving of his talents—he has been a constant motivator of people, always getting the members of the board to keep their minds focused on the issues. People get emotional when it comes to civil rights, but Dr. Cobb was able to rise above emotionalism. When he became president of the NAACP [1976–82] he made what had been a ceremonial office into an operative office and he spoke courageously from that office to the issues of the day."

So the plaudits roll in, as do multiple honors. Cobb has had a medical education building named for him (at the Charles R. Drew Postgraduate Medical School in Los Angeles), a medical society (the NMA's Columbia, Md., affiliate), a medical library (within the NMA office in Washington), a high school science club (at Armstrong High School in Richmond, Va.) and has been the recipient of a slew of other honors—honorary degrees, citations, certificates, medals, scrolls, plaques, keys to the city. When asked how he feels about all this, he replies, "I think I've been blessed because I'm alive to see it."

Cobb the Teacher

Notwithstanding all the honors and plaudits, there has been one role Cobb has played in his long, full life that seems to have earned him mixed reviews. That is his role as teacher.

From his days as a four-year-old in Miss Montgomery's and Miss Williams' classroom, Cobb had been convinced that the role of the teacher was "to make the educational process a pleasure." In keeping with this spirit, he often referred to the course he taught freshmen medical students at Howard as "our one-year frolic in anatomy, the kindergarten of medicine" and did more than his share of frolicking himself.

One day he might come into class jumping rope, another imitating the movements of an embryo in the womb, all in the interest of explaining some point about anatomy, of course. Sometimes he would bring his trusty violin into the anatomy laboratory, and take it out and play some soothing music, all in the interest of getting students to relax about this whole messy, unnerving business of dissecting a cadaver, of course. "This is to help you relax, doctor, just relax," his voice would caress as the strains of the slow movement from a Handel sonata would fill the air.

Some of his students were delighted by such antics. Others thought he was a nut.

Then there was the matter of the way he interjected into lectures quotations from the Bible or Shakespeare or the classics or whatever; his own reflections on history or philosophy or sociology or current events, or whatever; and his miscellaneous comments on subjects ranging from the structure of Jesse Owens' heel bone (again) to sexual practices through the ages.

About all this, too, the student verdict was mixed. While most found Cobb's lectures interesting, many couldn't see what some of the information presented in them had to do with what they needed to know as physicians.

"Oh, some students would get very annoyed with Dr. Cobb, sure," recalls Epps. "And the thing about Dr. Cobb, which I think is true for most professors who are very bright and have a wide range of interests, is that you often don't appreciate them as a student, you only appreciate them afterwards."

Many of Cobb's students did later come to see that the parts of his lectures they once had judged irrelevant or tangential had behind them a sound educational purpose. "One of the things Dr. Cobb tried to make students realize," says Epps, "is that knowledge is ever so expansive and that we need to know a lot about not only anatomy, but everything. In general, doctors tend to be one-sided; we know a lot about the sciences, but don't get enough exposure to other branches of knowledge. Well, Dr. Cobb was a man who mastered the sciences and excelled in the humanities and he delighted in trying to spur us to do the same, not always with much success, I might add."

Similarly, Leffall applauds Cobb's ambition to turn out "the broad physician," an idea that has come back into currency with recent reform movements in medical education: "Dr. Cobb used to tell us the more well-rounded you are, the more tolerant, the more compassionate, the more human."

Still, through the years some rumblings of discontent with the content and style of Cobb's teaching persisted. This was true, though to a lesser degree, with the graphic method of learning anatomy he pioneered and promoted. Through this method, students were required to demonstrate their knowledge of the structure of the human body by making detailed, carefully labeled drawings, using as models a dissected cadaver, a skeleton and a live person. A typical exam question might be, "Draw on a blank sheet of paper an outline of the ventral aspect of the male figure with the skeleton in correct proportions," as he described it in a 1946 *JNMA* article.

Critics of this method contended that it tended to favor and reward those with good drawing skills but that such skills may or may not have anything to do with the kind of understanding of the body's structure needed by physicians. Cobb dismissed this objection, citing "the tremendous mental disciplinary value of the graphic method in compelling thorough analytical and accurate observation, a habit invaluable to a physician."

Today, the graphic method as Cobb promoted it has been pretty much abandoned, though not entirely. Explains Raymond L. Hayes Jr., the current chairman of Howard's anatomy department, "We don't require students to develop line drawing reproductions of the anatomy [of the body]. In many respects, though, the students do it on their own. It becomes obvious to any student taking anatomy that you have to boil things down to a basic skeleton in order to carry the information around with you. But we don't ask students to do any kind of drawing [on an exam] because we don't want their artistic abilities to be the criterion for evaluation.

"What we try to emphasize in our teaching is the *application* of the material the students have learned. In other words, it is not enough to be able to create a line drawing showing the structure of a particular part of the body. You have to be able to use that information in some kind of practical context, be able to figure out what happens when that particular part isn't working right, for instance. For the last five to seven years most anatomy courses around the country have become problem oriented."

Ever combative, Cobb predicts that the graphic method will make a comeback. "Here's what we're getting now," he says. "The computer industry has gotten into it [medicine] and computers are doing this scanning now. But the physicians who interpret the scans don't have the background of actually visualizing what is there. And so, I am perfectly content to wait, because one of my themes is 'Man is a slow learner.' "

'69 Protest

As the '60s were coming to a close and strident demands for Student Power and Black Power were convulsing campuses throughout the nation, a vocal group of Howard medical students thought more than Cobb's graphic method might be out of date. These students thought *he* was. "Medical Students Boycott Class to Protest Anachronistic Professor" ran the headline above a front page *Hilltop* article on February 7, 1969. The outcome of the boycott was the ouster of Cobb as anatomy department chairman, a post he had held since 1947.

The leader of the boycott was the president of the College of Medicine's freshman class, Ewart Brown, who as president of the Howard University Student Association had helped lead a successful takeover of Howard's administration building the previous spring. Today, Brown is a successful Los Angeles physician and a strong booster of Howard, currently a candidate for West Coast representative of the national alumni association. When asked about the Cobb protest, he urges that it be placed within the context of the times. In his view:

"What you had was an entering class that was fresh from the most tumultuous year in college life in America and which contained a core of students steeped in principles of radical activity. So the atmosphere was ripe for students to reject anything that smacked of paternalism and inadequacy. At the time the Howard medical school had a reputation of producing people who did not do well on the National Board exams. We determined early in the game that one of the reasons for that, particularly in anatomy, was that students weren't given the material that would ultimately appear on the Boards. When Dr. Cobb refused to come to a meeting we called to discuss our concerns, we successfully were able to convert that refusal into the initiation of a boycott."

Brown contends the boycott was never meant as a personal attack on Cobb. "Dr. Cobb is an amazing individual," he says. "Dr. Cobb is a brilliant man. I don't want to give any impression other than that I have a deep and lasting respect for his abilities. He had a unique and powerful way of presenting basic concepts in anatomy, talking about the heart and likening it to a pump, that sort of thing. But at the point where we met up with him he was more interested in entertaining than in the hard academics. So you'll find that most of my classmates will remember Dr. Cobb in terms of the theatrics—playing the violin while we dissected cadavers, offering $10 to anybody who could remember the source of a quote. . . .

"It was the way he ran the department, though, that most concerned us. He was the responsible leader of the anatomy department, charged with providing students with an adequate curriculum. And we found out he hadn't had a faculty meeting in years . . . We thought that Howard deserved better, that we deserved better and we took the necessary steps."

Others viewed the protest and its outcome in far less lofty terms. For Epps, for instance, what happened to Cobb in 1969 was "a travesty." "I was a young faculty person then," he recalls, "and I was distressed by what I perceived to be a program of persecution. The students who put the medical school under siege had been the same ones who had caused a lot of disruption on the campus when they were undergraduates; so when they came to the medical school they were determined to do the same thing. And they decided, 'Let's knock off the biggest one here. Well, that's got to be Montague Cobb. So, let's get rid of Cobb.' They didn't like his style and they went after him.

"They would be out there in front of the television cameras every day calling for his dismissal, his resignation, saying anything they wanted with complete indemnity. But Dr. Cobb, as a man of restraint and propriety and decorum, wasn't interested in doing the same thing. It was not his style to fight the battle in the media."

In April 1969, Epps and 57 other faculty members of the College of Medicine submitted a petition to Howard University President James N. Nabrit Jr., and Howard's Board of Trustees protesting the "abrupt removal" of Cobb from the anatomy chairmanship, concluding: "We deplore the use of intimidation, boycott or strike as instruments of change in the College of Medicine and further deplore what may be considered recent submission to these instruments by the Administration."

Cobb's case was taken up by the medical school's grievance committee, which recommended he be reinstated as chairman. He never was. The executive committee of the Board of Trustees took up the matter the following September and in what Cobb views as vindication and some others saw as a face-saving gesture, the committee moved to appoint Cobb distinguished professor of anatomy, the first distinguished professor in the university's history. The announcement of the appointment was made by Howard's then new president, James E. Cheek.

The Testimonial

On November 10, 1973, 500 people attended a testimonial dinner for Cobb organized by Epps and Leffall, two of the three men Cobb considers "sons" [the other is his internist son-in-law Robert S. Wilkinson Jr.]. The two prominent surgeons conceived of the affair as a formal way to express support and appreciation for one they believed had been so beleaguered but who had given so much to so many. Among those in attendance were some of the participants in the '69 boycott.

"When many in that class became seniors they realized how unfair they had been to Dr. Cobb," says Epps. "By then they had a chance to become familiar with and reflect on what the man had accomplished under very difficult circumstances and at great financial sacrifice. He worked at a time when medical school salaries were just deplorable. So it was gratifying to see that some in that class realized it had mistreated him and made efforts to make amends."

Ask Cobb what that "mess in '69" was all about and how he feels about it and you get a variety of responses. A bit of conspiracy theory: "During that time, you know, there were squads of hell raisers who would move from campus to campus." A Biblical reference: "A fellow came to me and said, 'Dr. Cobb, why are you taking this so calmly?' I said, 'Because it's not in our hands. The Lord giveth and the Lord taketh away.'" Another Biblical reference, this one referring to the pro-

testing students: "None so blind as those who will not see." And finally a boxing analogy: "I beat them. I was taught that when you've got a man helpless [as he claims he had the students] you shake a glove in his face and if he can't respond, well, then the referee steps in. I just shook a glove in the face of those people and they hurt permanently." Perhaps.

Cobb spent the balance of his years on the Howard faculty in relative tranquility and found himself more than welcome on a number of other campuses as a visiting professor, as well. Says Epps, "No matter what people ever felt about him at Howard, he was always highly respected away from it. He had a little saying to that effect, something about a man being a king everywhere but in his own country, something like that. When I have traveled I have never met a person in the anatomy department of any university who did not know W. Montague Cobb."

Cobb is no fan of mandatory retirement, but when he became 70 he settled not uncomfortably into his emeritus faculty status. During his post-retirement years, three ambitious projects have vied for his attention: a textbook designed to compress the rudiments of anatomy into 100 pages; a comprehensive history of the Black American in medicine; an autobiography. Of the latter, he notes dryly, "I don't think it will be dull."

During these years, other new challenges have beckoned. He was 77 when he made his debut as a serious actor (after years as an accomplished "ham") at the Kennedy Center for the Performing Arts no less. He did so in a June 17, 1982 performance of "Without A Doubt," a collage of poetry, speeches and songs exemplifying the history of Afro-Americans which had been compiled and directed by his daughter, Amelia Cobb Gray, a University of the District of Columbia theater professor. Cobb portrayed the scholar-activist W.E.B. Du Bois, a man he had known and admired.

The role Cobb more typically has been asked to play in recent years is that of wise elder statesman. As one who has helped push open the doors of opportunity for Black Americans, he frequently is asked to evaluate how Blacks are faring today. "The doors are technically open," he is wont to answer, "but you've still got to fight your way in. The analogy I use is that the generation to which I belong is like the offensive linemen on a football team. Their job is to hit and make holes. But you've got to have fast backs there ready to rush right through or those holes will close up.

"Our situation today is that we've got the holes, but we're short on the fast backs to run through. One of the problems is that our people aren't oriented to studying. We've got to get our youngsters oriented to education so they will have the rigor to compete and forge ahead."

Ask him to predict how it will all come out and he demurs. "I don't go in for prophecy," he answers. "Prophecy has been given to those with Divine Light. I don't have that. I can just say as [journalist] Heywood Broun would write, 'It seems to me.' "

Ask him to share his formula for a satisfying old age, he keeps it simple as befitting "lowly Mr. Will Cobb, the printer's boy," as he often describes himself. "Keep moving forward," he says. "Just keep moving forward."

Then the fragile-looking old fighter adds a post-script: "I'd rather be moving forward ever more slowly than to be sliding back. And so when I go down, I hope I'll go down still pushing for something in the forward direction."

KENNETH R. MANNING

Ernest Everett Just: The Beginning of a Professional Career, 1907–1916

Early in the summer of 1912, Just returned to Washington from Woods Hole to consummate a long-standing courtship. On 26 June he married Ethel Highwarden. The ceremony took place at the Highwarden home, and was attended only by close relatives.

On her wedding day, Ethel displayed a youthful charm and vigor that did not in any way betray her twenty-seven years. She was pretty, delicate, and petite, with a serious and subdued countenance. Her long straight hair, jet black, revealed traces of white ancestry. Unmistakably dark-skinned, she was blended of the lightest hues of brown with the darkest hues of charcoal gray. She carried herself in a gracious manner, which could often seem arrogant and haughty. Alongside her sophistication and refinement stood her determination and sternness of character—qualities befitting the daughter of a riverboat captain.

Ethel had grown up in Ripley, Ohio, a small town on the banks of the Ohio River. Her father, William H. Highwarden, was a man of means. He ran freight up and down the Ohio. Through him Ethel traced her ancestry back to William Whipple, a signer of the Declaration of Independence. Her mother, Belle Johnson, a woman of dignity, was one of the first black female graduates of Oberlin College. She worked as a teacher and businesswoman throughout Ohio. She was admired, in particular, for her management skills: the way she operated her store convinced people that women could "carry on business as successfully as men." Her

family had been among the early black settlers in Ohio, where they had enjoyed freedom and education even during the days of slavery. Though somewhat prosperous, the Johnsons had not been as well off as the older, more established black families in the northern part of the state. Black settlements along the river had generally been poor, comprised of recent runaway slaves and older free blacks without the means to remove themselves from the perils of slave hunters along the banks of the Ohio. The sharp and dangerous boundary of the Ohio River was vividly portrayed by Harriet Beecher Stowe in *Uncle Tom's Cabin*. One of the novel's most memorable scenes is Eliza's flight with an infant across the water from Kentucky to Ohio, from slavery to freedom, on sheets of melting ice. Legend has it that a similar crossing actually took place at Ripley.

By the 1880s and '90s Ripley was emerging as a vibrant community of blacks and whites, the latter mostly German immigrants. Ethel grew up in a bilingual community, speaking German and English interchangeably in the town and in the local grammar school. As a teenager she left Ripley to matriculate at Ohio State University in Columbus. There she pursued a broad course of study and developed a special interest in German literature. After graduation in June 1906 she took up an appointment at Howard, a year before Just arrived.

She began as an instructor in the College of Arts and Sciences and the Academy, a preparatory school run by the university. She and Miss Cook made up the Department of Modern Languages, offering German and French respectively at the college and preparatory levels. Ethel put special stress on literature in her classes. A demanding teacher, she introduced her students early to the works of German writers such as Goethe, Lessing, Vilmar, and Sturm. German culture interested her, but it did not captivate her imagination as it would her future husband's over two decades later.

The two met in the fall of 1908 during a faculty tea at the home of President Thirkield. Just was attracted by Ethel's stately, even noble appearance, her knowledge of German language and culture, her relative aloofness from what he regarded as the philistine mentality of the black middle class. Ethel admired the cultivated demeanor of this Dartmouth man, his keen intellect, and, above all, his professional ambition. He courted her persistently thereafter, making calls at 1903 Third Street, where she lived under the watchful eye of her mother. Only after receiving his promotion to full professor, in the spring of 1912, did he propose and she accept.

Soon after their engagement, Ethel began to plan a honeymoon abroad. They both were anxious to visit Europe, especially Germany. She longed to see the art and architecture of the Continent's cities and towns, and he hoped to take a look at the universities and research institutes. Their plans were rare but not unique, for the black bourgeoisie had begun to take European tours in earnest by the early 1910s. Though Just and Ethel had more reason than most to visit Europe, it must have appeared a little pretentious to other young faculty to propose such an elaborate trip.

The honeymoon never took place. As summer approached, Just was forced to face facts: he needed to consolidate his work on *Nereis* and Lillie needed him at Woods Hole. He was in too formative a stage of his career to take the prime months of summer off from his research. A week's leave was about all he could afford. The marriage took place on a Wednesday. Just arrived from Woods Hole a day or two early and then spent the rest of the week in Washington with his bride before returning to his laboratory. Ethel no doubt was disappointed by the decision, but she gave up a honeymoon so that her husband could get on with his career.

Just did not focus on his work to the exclusion of starting a family, however. A child, Margaret, was born to Ethel on 28 April 1913, within a year of the marriage. At the time the family did not have a permanent residence; they were living with Just's sister Inez at 1853 Third Street. In the summer and autumn of 1914 they tried to find their own place. They moved twice before finally settling, around Christmas, at 412 T Street in the fashionable Le Droit Park section. The community was plush, made up mainly of black professionals and academics who had secure positions and incomes. The Justs began making payments on their new home, a stately three-story dwelling with a carriage house in back. A typically Victorian structure, rambling and spacious, it was large enough to accommodate two other children, Highwarden and Maribel, born in 1917 and 1922. The family lived in comfort, even elegance, while Just pursued his career in science.

The summer of 1912 marked the beginning of many things for Just. It was then that he met Jacques Loeb, the eminent biologist of the Rockefeller Institute for Medical Research. This early encounter enhanced Just's reputation as a prominent black scientist. Just knew that Loeb was deeply concerned with social issues and the plight of the oppressed, but he could hardly have hoped that Loeb's interest would focus as intensely as in fact it did on him and the situation at Howard.

Born in Germany in 1859, Loeb moved to the United States in 1891. He held a position at Bryn Mawr before moving to the University of Chicago in 1899 and the Rockefeller Institute in 1910. Even early in life he had been concerned with politics, especially the condition of oppressed peoples. As a Jew, he had endured the racial antagonism and anti-Semitism of the Germans under Bismarck, and had left Germany for that reason. He understood the problems of the Filipinos and Japanese in the United States, and he fought the evils of the "yellow peril" mentality in American society. Socialism, he believed, was the one political philosophy that would remove oppression from the world. Nothing pleased him more than to meet Just in 1912. Here was a chance for him to direct his political energies; here was a living specimen, downtrodden and oppressed, whom he could get to know and help firsthand.

If Loeb's concern was to help Just and black people generally, Just's was to make that help possible. Throughout 1913 and 1914 Loeb received many invitations from Just—as well as from the dean and the secretary of the Howard Medical School—to visit the campus, inspire the student body, and lend prestige to the effort to strengthen the financial status of the school. Because of his failing health and chronic "throat trouble," he never made the visit, although he accepted several invitations to go. He continued, however, to express "great interest" in the Howard cause. In October 1914 he contacted Simon Flexner of the Rockefeller Institute and Simon's brother Abraham, of the Rockefeller Foundation, about what could be done to improve things at Howard. He also told Jerome D. Greene, a high-ranking official at the foundation, that there was no question but that Rockefeller funds should be channeled into support for Howard's medical program. "A rather large amount of good," he assured Greene, could be done with "comparatively little" financial outlay. Moreover, he linked Howard's success as an institution with Just's brilliance as a scientist. Just, he felt, was "certainly a superior man."

Loeb's concern for the improvement of medical education went hand in hand with his interest in the practice of medicine in the black community. Well-trained physicians, according to his assessment of the social problem, were "the best missionaries for uplift that could be sent to the Negro." Black doctors were effective because in the South white physicians did not "care to practice among Negroes," and Negroes, in many cases, did not "care to be treated by their white oppressor." It was Just, or men like Just, who would train black doctors; it was Howard, or schools like Howard, where they would be trained. Loeb wanted to visit the Howard Medical School to see Just and gather information for the Rockefeller Foundation, which he hoped was "above the racial prejudice which would deny help to the colored people."

Loeb's interest in black medical education was part of his larger concern for the improvement of the general education of the Negro. Through Just, his awareness of the predicament of Negroes increased, and he came to the firm conclusion that help for blacks lay "purely in educational directions." One efficient and humanitarian method of eliminating prejudice in America, he insisted, was "to uplift the Negro" and thus remove the myth that "his low status" was due to "racial inferiority." The black man's status was the result not of any inherent limitations but of "poor educational facilities" and the poverty that existed in his home.

Though Loeb championed the black cause, Just was one of the few blacks he knew personally. The two enjoyed long, intimate conversations at Woods Hole during the summer of 1913 and 1914. They shared thoughts on what could be done to improve the lot of black people. And more important, perhaps, Just gained through Loeb the inspiration to try and become a first-rate scientist.

One evening as he was leaving the laboratory Just met Loeb on the steps of the MBL. They once again began talking about the problems of blacks in America, one of Loeb's favorite topics. This night, however, Just was tired and frustrated, and concerned about his work, not his race. He tried to explain his anxiety over the results of some experiments. Loeb said nothing about the experiments, but held forth instead on the importance of Just's work for the uplift of black people. He had a vision of Just serving as a model in the black community and as an excellent teacher for future black doctors. In conclusion he assured Just of the general importance of his work for the advancement of science, and encouraged him to further heights in the world of biology. Impressed by Loeb's patience and sympathy, Just made the rather odd remark that "colored men" were like "dumb animals" in their gratitude for "kindness and interest" from others. Through Loeb, he was beginning to view his work from a global perspective and to relate it to the larger cause of black people.

Loeb had successfully touched Just, one individual black, but he wanted to work on many levels at the same time. He would continue to lend his support to Just and medical education at Howard; there was much work to be done in that direction. He also wanted, however, to reach out directly to the black population. He was aware that the National Association for the Advancement of Colored People (NAACP) was the one organization concerned with social and political reform for blacks throughout the country and the world. In 1913 he began to support the causes of that organization.

Loeb was introduced to the NAACP at a reception for Miss Lillian D. Wald, a member of the association's board of directors, in the spring of 1913. There he met the wealthy donors and the various board members, mostly Jewish, who had guided the organization from its birth in 1909. His attention was less on them, however, than on the famous black radical W.E.B. Du Bois, also a board member and the editor of the organization's official journal, *The Crisis*. Du Bois's radicalism impressed Loeb deeply. The two men talked about politics and the evils of racism in America. They parted that night close comrades, united in a cause. Loeb was to be involved with two major NAACP campaigns over the next two years.

The NAACP had always held its national conferences in Northern cities such as New York, Boston, Chicago, and Philadelphia, but in 1913 it planned to convene in Baltimore, a stone's throw from the Southern states of Virginia and North Carolina. Important figures like Jane Addams, Franz Boas, William Hayes Ward, and John Dewey had been guest speakers in the past, and this year Oswald Garrison Villard and Belle Case (Mrs. Robert M.) La Follette were scheduled. While previous conferences had focused on questions of education, voting, and employment for the Negro, this one was to stress the "scientific side" of the race question. Not surprisingly, Loeb was invited to play a major role.

Du Bois asked Loeb to deliver a lecture on "The Theory of Race Inferiority as Modified by Recent Biological Knowledge." Loeb agreed to speak at the main session of the conference on Tuesday, 5 May, in McCoy Hall at Johns Hopkins University. He was to be part of a program to "impress the public by the weight of its scientific authority." But when the time came he could not attend the forum owing to "a very unpleasant attack of lumbago." Instead, he wrote out a short paper which Du Bois read to the association on the last night of the conference and subsequently published in *The Crisis*.

That year Loeb wrote several articles on the question of racial inferiority, but never once did he appear on the NAACP podium. Perhaps he felt uncomfortable. He knew so few black people personally. He had developed a friendship with Just, met Du Bois, and heard of C. H. Turner, another black scientist engaged in biological research, but that was the extent of his acquaintance with blacks. Still, he was devoted to their cause. His commitment to the uplift of blacks was part of his larger goal, dearly held, of eradicating racism internationally. He would continue to take an interest in the NAACP as long as men like Just were confronted with racism in American society.

In 1914 one of the NAACP's big concerns was D. W. Griffith's film *The Birth of a Nation*. The film glorified the brutality of the Ku Klux Klan in particular and white supremacy in general. Loeb was involved from the beginning. Stunned and bewildered by the film, he emerged from a theater in New York one cold evening in mid-March 1915 feeling as if "the most ghastly nightmare" had "taken possession" of him. His mind was spinning, so much so that he did not remember being introduced in the lobby to Joel Spingarn, a pioneering leader of the NAACP. Loeb felt tired and nauseated, anxious only to get home. The film and the audience had made him sick. The film exhibited "a display of homicidal paranoia with the special grievance against the Negro," and, even more horrifying, the "homicidal paranoia" seemed to take possession of the audience. To call "this diabolical appeal to race hatred" *The Birth of a Nation* was, Loeb thought, "the worst insult" that had "ever been heaped upon this country." But he would not support the NAACP in its efforts to censor or suppress the film. He felt that this would only be an advertisement for it. A better course, he suggested, was to appeal to "the common sense and the decency" of actors, directors, and producers "to unite against performances of this kind in the future and to quietly drop 'The Birth of a Nation.' " No doubt Loeb thought that these people were different from the authors of *Birth of a Nation*'s script.

Spingarn, chairman of the board of directors of the NAACP, shared Loeb's feelings about censorship, but in this case he found himself confronted by "a condition and not a theory." The tangible results of the film, in terms of social bitterness, unrest, even violence, might be devastating. He intended to push forward against "this hideous libel" disguised as historical truth. He only wanted permission to quote Loeb's characterization of the film "in its pathological aspects." After consulting legal authorities, Loeb agreed to allow the NAACP to make use of his remarks.

Loeb's contact with the NAACP, by anchoring his theoretical politics to real situations, allowed him to see more clearly the pernicious effects of racism on the everyday lives of black Americans. He also became more aware of the feelings that a black like Just experienced when confronted by racist theories in science. He was inspired to fight racism within the scientific professions as well as in society at large. One of his goals was to rid the scientific literature of racist tendencies. Science was rational; racism was emotional. For Loeb, the two had nothing to do with each other.

In 1916 a relatively unknown scientist, J. E. Wodsedalek, published an article entitled "Causes of Sterility in the Mule." The article appeared in the *Biological Bulletin*, the official journal of the MBL. One paragraph compared the Negro with the ass:

> The cause of the difference of opinion is probably due to the fact that Guyer used Negro material in his investigation, while Von Winiwarter studied tissue obtained from a white man. In view of the difference between these two human races it is not at all improbable that a difference in the number of chromosomes also exists. The Negro is fully as far removed from the white man as is the ass from the horse, where a great difference in the number of chromosomes apparently exists. This vast difference in number appears to be, at least in part, responsible for the sterility of the mule. The difference between the white man and the Negro in regard to the number of chromosomes according to Guyer and Von Winiwarter is equally as great, but unfortunately the mulatto is fertile.

Loeb was outraged. He felt that the editorial board of the *Bulletin* should disavow any association with the statement, especially since Just and C. H. Turner were regular contributors.

Just's sponsor Frank Lillie, who was the managing editor of the *Bulletin*, felt otherwise. Though he admitted that the choice of words in the article was "extremely unfortunate," he did not believe that there was any "derogatory" intention on Wodsedalek's part. Still, he apologized for not having read and edited the article more carefully. T. H. Morgan, to whom Loeb also appealed for help, agreed with Lillie. He doubted that Wodsedalek intended "to compare the Negro with the ass." In his opinion, the phrasing was "merely a piece of stupidity" on Wodsedalek's part. It was best, in any case, to give Wodsedalek "the benefit of the doubt," since the statement could be interpreted in several ways.

Both Lillie and Morgan felt that Loeb's interpretation might have been erroneous and, further, that any notice given to Wodsedalek's remarks would only serve to publicize them too much. Lillie agreed, however, to contact Wodsedalek personally. His position was clear: he would submit the entire matter to the editorial board should Wodsedalek admit racial animosity. Wodsedalek admitted none, stating that he had not intended to insult the Negro in his article. Loeb found Wodsedalek's disavowal "a sufficient safeguard" against further "persecution of the Negro." He dropped the issue; a rebuttal he had written was never published, and Wodsedalek's comparison received no further attention.

Just, who would certainly have felt "the sting" of Wodsedalek's remarks, never mentioned the article. He read it, just as he read every article published in the *Biological Bulletin*. But the matter was best left alone. Just was still feeling his way at Woods Hole, trying to learn the routes necessary for smooth traveling along his career path. Loeb could afford to criticize: he was in a different position, accomplished, recognized, entrenched.

As Just struggled to advance professionally, Loeb and the NAACP played a major role in helping him along. In 1913 the association developed plans to present an award the following year. Sponsored by Spingarn, the award would go to the man or woman of "African descent" who had performed "the foremost service to his race." A selection committee was formed, comprising Bishop John Hurst (chairman), William Howard Taft, John Hope, James H. Dillard, and Oswald Garrison Villard. At first it seemed it might be difficult to find anyone worthy of the honor; but when the nominations began to pour in, members of the committee were astonished at the number of people who had made significant contributions. The nominees—thirty in all—included Meta Warwick Fuller, the sculptress; William Monroe Trotter, publisher of the *Guardian* and militant agitator; Heman Perry, founder and president of the first major black life insurance company, in Atlanta; Major John R. Lynch, the Reconstruction statesman and author; Major R. R. Moton, principal of Hampton Institute; Isaac Fisher, the essayist of Tuskegee Institute; Howard Drew, world recordholder for the hundred-yard dash; and Cornelia Bowen, principal of Mt. Meigs School in Alabama. The nominations reflected a predominant interest in art, politics, social work, business, literature, education, and athletics—the fields in which black achievement had traditionally been concentrated.

Apparently the association decided that science should also be represented: a black scientist had to be found. Publicity for his or her achievements would demonstrate the intellectual depth of people of "African descent"; furthermore, it would help place black people and the NAACP in particular in the mainstream of Western tradition. Science, unlike music, literature, and art, was held to be objective in its approach and method, culture-free and universal. Scientific truth could be denied by no one, white or black. If this was the first time the whole world was to know of the achievements of blacks, then those achievements should be as universal as possible. What better way to command the respect of all than to consider a scientist for the Spingarn Medal? No longer would the white scientific world find it easy to perpetuate the idea that blacks had never done creditable scientific work. Ironically, a close friend of Loeb's, J. McKeen Cattell, made a remark to that effect in a speech entitled "Science, Education and Democracy" at the annual conference of the American Association for the Advancement of Science in Atlanta, Georgia, in December 1913. Du Bois was quick to take issue with him in *The Crisis*, calling attention to the work of Just and C. H. Turner.

Loeb was asked to recommend possible candidates for the medal. He explained that his acquaintance with "colored people" was so limited that a recommendation might do an "injustice." He did suggest, however, that the medal be awarded to "one of the few colored people who, in the face of great difficulties," had done important scientific research. The person he had in mind was E. E. Just, professor of physiology at the Howard Medical School. He knew Just "personally very well," and considered him to be "a very able researcher." Just had "sacrificed a good deal for the advancement of the medical schools for colored people," and would do "a good deal more if . . . given a chance." Loeb knew of another black "by the name of Turner" engaged in scientific research, but he was unfamiliar with Turner's work. It was Just whom Loeb had come to know intimately, though personally more than professionally. When asked by Villard for a letter recounting Just's scientific achievements, he said that he did not feel competent to provide detailed information. Instead of submitting an inadequate statement, he referred Villard to Lillie as the person most knowledgeable in the matter. His recommendation simply asserted a general impression that Just's "attitude of scientific subjects, his knowledge of biology, and his critical ability" were of an "unusually high and lofty order." Most importantly, Just seemed to be "guided by very high motives" in his work within the black community. He would not give up his position at Howard in order to increase his income. This Loeb particularly admired.

Just had championed the cause of the Howard Medical School and sought funds for its survival because he believed in its integrity and high quality. His motives were not, however, entirely altruistic. The medical school provided a substantial part of his income and even paid his room rent at Woods Hole during the summers. The exact amount of his salary depended, among other things, on the level of the medical school's enrollment. While most of its faculty members derived their major income from medical practice, he was dependent upon teaching alone and so had to "bear the hazards of a fluctuating salary." Yet in any case, he was willing "to sink the personal for the larger cause." This attitude impressed Loeb. Who was more deserving of the Spingarn Medal than Just?

The American public did not know Just as well as they knew some of the other nominees, especially Trotter. Newspapers at the time were filled with stories of Trotter's dramatic exploits: his involvement with the Niagara Movement; his opposition to Booker T. Washington; his confrontation with Woodrow Wilson on the issue of jim crow in Washington's federal office buildings. When Just won the medal, everyone was surprised. The exchange of telegrams between the editor of the Chisholm News Service in Denison, Texas, and the secretary of the NAACP captures this:

EDITOR: Is Trotter winner Spingarn Medal?
SECRETARY: Ernest Everett Just winner of medal.

EDITOR: Who is Ernest Everett what?
SECRETARY: Ernest Everett Just is head Howard University Medical School.

Perhaps Just was selected precisely because of his relative obscurity, because the NAACP wanted the public to recognize a black man of science, his great promise and lasting achievement. Notification of the award reached Just at the beginning of February 1915. It was not the first time he had been honored by the association; three years earlier he had been chosen their "man of the month," and his photograph had appeared in *The Crisis* along with an article detailing his accomplishments. But the Spingarn Medal was a far more prestigious honor, involving a great deal of publicity and an elaborate ceremony. Just informed the committee that he would be embarrassed to face a large audience, and he attacked publicity as incompatible with scientific endeavors. Still, in the cold of winter he journeyed to New York to accept the award.

On the evening of 12 February 1915, Governor Charles Whitman presented Just the first Spingarn Medal. The ceremony took place in Ethical Culture Hall. There were crowds and crowds of spectators and several important speakers, including Charlotte Perkins Gilman and Oswald Garrison Villard. The hall was buzzing with talk of the new "flood of anti-negro legislation" in Washington and of how timely the Spingarn award was as a reminder to the country of "the spirit of brotherhood, fellowship, and Americanism." Just watched and listened attentively. His speech was brief and to the point: "I thank the Association for the award not so much for myself as for the students whom I represent."

The NAACP managed to secure good press coverage for this ceremony in honor of black achievement. It did not matter that Just was relatively unknown. That a black, any black, had done brilliant work in marine biology was startling news in itself. Presses throughout the country, even Southern newspapers, commented extensively on the fact that a medal had been awarded a Negro for scientific achievement. The *Courier-Journal* of Louisville, Kentucky, a white Southern paper, astounded the black community by referring favorably to Just's "scholarly research, original, not imitative work, in the field of biology."

The award and the accompanying publicity made Just known to the American public. But the question in his mind was: How would the award appear to the scientific world? At first he feared that it represented a popular and perhaps vulgar watering down of his scholarly pursuits: it was an award given specifically to a black, unlike any he had ever received before, so different from the notion of general merit on which he believed science was based. After the ceremony, Lillie explained to him the value of the award and informed him that Loeb had been instrumental in calling the committee's attention to his work. Only then did Just feel comfortable, and start to look at the award as an object of pride, as a possible factor in building his career and scientific reputation. That Loeb was interested in the medal eased his "deep-seated fear . . . that real biologists would rather deride the whole business and especially the paltry recipient." Lillie's words of congratulation "removed a deep burden" from his mind. He had thought that Lillie would consider the award "a travesty." Quite the contrary—Lillie was pleased that the award had gone to someone in pure science rather than a more practical field. He felt that the award was good for Just, the country, and the Negro race. Loeb, more narrow in his perspectives, considered it a harbinger of ambassadorial possibilities for Just in the black medical world.

Just perhaps never thought of the award in its larger context. To him it was mainly a stepping-stone to a successful career. He rarely mentioned it later, but he did feel its effects at the time. The award, he confessed, signified "a new day" in his life; it allowed him suddenly to become "a real human being alive and anxious to work." He would continue to make sacrifices, at Howard and elsewhere, now that there was appreciation for his "striving."

The Spingarn Medal may have called attention to Just's scientific accomplishments and helped build his scientific stature, but a Ph.D. from a major university was nevertheless essential to expand opportunities, to maintain and further a reputation. This was especially true for Just, one of the first blacks to join the professional ranks of science. If he was to have a serious career in science, Just had to have a Ph.D. Lillie understood this and began to encourage him more strongly than before to obtain the "official stamp of approval."

In June 1915 Lillie decided that Just had completed the research requirements for the Ph.D., and he agreed to accept previously published articles as a doctoral thesis. Only minor subject and residence requirements remained, all of which could be completed in three quarters at the University of Chicago. Eager to finish up, Just requested a leave of absence, with pay, from the Howard Medical School. Lillie lent support to this request, urging the leave as necessary for Just to establish a "scientific reputation" that would in turn be of "greatest advantage" to Howard. He persuaded the administration that the reputation of faculty members was an important consideration for any medical school and that a leave of absence for Just would be an "investment" for the further development of medical education at Howard. The Howard administration recognized its indebtedness to Just for past loyal service and understood the wisdom of Lillie's argument of cost-benefit. The dean, W. C. McNeill, vowed that his office would "do its part" to find sufficient funds for the leave of absence. Sacrifices would be made to help Just obtain the Ph.D.

Just began to make plans for his year of study in Chicago. His wife Ethel and their two-year-old daughter, Margaret, would remain in Washington so that he could focus full attention on his studies and avoid the distractions of domestic life. He would board with his kinsfolk, the Bentleys, who lived on East Forty-first Street within walking distance of the university. He would return to Washington from time to time, certainly at Christmas, but he could not promise how often. His priority was to take full advantage of resources at the university, of opportunities to meet people and to get to know the city. Sabbaticals were almost unheard of at Howard, and he could hardly hope to have another chance like this any time in the near future.

Just went to Chicago for the 1915–16 academic year and was awakened to the life of a big city. Washington was still an oversized town of sorts, whereas Chicago had already taken its place as America's second-largest and most flourishing metropolis. There he found "much-needed rest and mental refreshment." The high-powered intellectual atmosphere of the University of Chicago was a welcome change from the dull routine of Howard Medical School. Opportunities abounded. Just gained perspective on his life and work by establishing contact with many high-ranking professionals in and out of his field in the black and white communities.

What inspired him most was the prosperity of blacks in Chicago. Cloistered in his Washington and Woods Hole laboratories, he had not realized that "anywhere in the United States colored could get even half a chance." The large number of "highly respected, competent . . . Negro surgeons, dentists, and lawyers" in Chicago was a revelation to him. Also, he was surprised to observe that a young black Ph.D. had been working for some time under H. G. Wells at the Sprague Research Institute—probably a reference to Julian H. Lewis, the pathologist who later became the first black member of the faculty at the University of Chicago. Of course, black professionals at this educational level were the exception rather than the rule. Law, medicine, and research may have attracted a privileged few, but business was the occupation of most middle-class blacks. It did not demand long, expensive years of study at a university, just a little capital and a lot of hard work. No doubt Just was astonished by the number of black Chicagoans in proprietary and managerial positions. His daily activities must have brought him into contact with many who ran their own factories, restaurants, hotels, funeral parlors, printing plants, and real estate offices.

Just's kinsfolk the Bentleys were in the vanguard of black social and professional life in Chicago, part of a circle that included E. M. A. Chandler, chief chemist with the Dicks, David, and Heller Company; William E. Quinn, a well-known physician who maintained a plush residence on Indiana Avenue; Jesse Binga, president of the Binga State Bank; Edward H. Wright, the lawyer who reputedly grossed over thirty thousand dollars in fees each year; Willard Landry, the surgeon who standardized the method of childbirth by caesarean section; Robert S. Abbott, founder and editor of the weekly *Defender*; Charles S. James, the first black to be appointed dentist to the city's public schools; Sheadrick B. Turner, member of the Illinois legislature; Anthony Overton, head of the Overton Hygienic Manufacturing Company; Charles S. Duke, bridge-designing engineer for the city; and Daniel H. Williams, the first cardiologist to perform a successful operation on the human heart. The list could go on. Chicago was one city where blacks had established a reputation for "their work, their education, their prosperity, and their political power." Anyone who claimed that there was "not a single Negro" in Chicago, other than those who "black shoes, transport . . . luggage, or serve . . . in . . . restaurants," was sorely out of touch with reality.

Just's hosts exemplified the best in cultured black life. C. E. Bentley had grown up in Cincinnati, where he studied voice and began a career in concert singing. In his early twenties he moved to Chicago and enrolled in the College of Dental Surgery. A diligent and independent worker, he opened private offices in the city shortly after graduation. Before long he numbered among his patients "some of the most distinguished and discrimination citizens of Chicago." His social and professional activities came to cover a broad spectrum: he could be found delivering an address at the Appomattox Club in remembrance of the birth of Samuel Coleridge-Taylor, the black composer; lecturing at Howard University on systemic infections due to pyorrhea and inadequate root therapy; attending a dinner given in his honor by administrators of Provident Hospital; organizing a dental congress in St. Louis for three thousand members of the profession; and developing a program of dental hygiene in the Chicago public schools. Nor was he the only distinguished member of the family. His wife, Florence Lewis Bentley, was an experienced literary editor and "a strong social force in the city," while his daughter, Vilma E. Bentley, was a highly respected music teacher in the public school system.

Yet if some blacks were able to achieve social status in Chicago, others were plagued by insuperable social difficulties. Just did not comment on the seamy side of Chicago life, but he could not have been unaware of the problems faced by destitute blacks there. Decent housing and worthwhile employment were difficulty to come by. Forced into ghettos on the southern and western sides of the city, blacks had to pay extortionate rents for tiny apartments in run-down buildings. Job opportunities were by and large restricted to domestic work or manual labor; the average black put in an eight- to nine-hour day for a one- to two-dollar wage. Weekly earnings often fell short of covering the cost of rent and food, and at times a choice had to be made between the comforts of a warm room and a full stomach. The situation, dismal indeed, was aggravated by racial hostility. Lurid stories of white violence against blacks appeared daily in the newspapers. Over the course of a month, the *Chicago Tribune* reported six beatings (one fatal) of blacks by police, one illegal execution, two lynchings, three attempted lynchings, and assorted minor street confrontations. Meanwhile the trial of "Chicken Joe" Campbell, a black accused of murdering his white employer, made headlines throughout October and November. After his conviction, unrest increased. The problem was getting out of hand. Civic organizations decided to make a move. The Progressive Negroes' League and the Chicago chapter of the NAACP arranged lectures and conferences. Du Bois spoke at a meeting in February 1916, sponsored in part by Julius Rosenwald, the Chicago philanthropist. But nothing could be done to prevent trouble. The situation simmered for the next three years and finally bubbled over into near race war in 1919.

How much Just was aware of all this is unclear, but he could not easily have ignored such a potentially explosive setup. His evenings at the Bentleys' usually were spent playing cards, but there can be little doubt that the conversation often turned from whist bids and poker bets to the urgent social and political issues facing blacks. Bentley was one of the original members of the Niagara Movement, "that first bitter protest against the program of surrender and segregation," and one of the founder-directors of the NAACP. His passion for reform ran deep: "no cause that involved emancipation of the Negro failed of his enthusiastic support, so long as it did not involve any surrender of human rights." As chairman of the Chicago chapter of the NAACP, he spearheaded the investigation of certain racial incidents in the city: two of the most publicized cases involved the fatal beating of a black drayman in 1911 and the burning of the home of a black chauffeur in 1914. More important, perhaps, was Bentley's firm stand against discrimination in general. He spoke his mind on the brazen efforts of state legislators to introduce anti-intermarriage and jim crow car bills, as well as on the more subtle attempts of city administrators to institute segregation in schools and hospitals. Concerned by the unemployment and poor housing plaguing blacks, he was a leader in the effort to solve the problem of indigent and displaced families. Another concern of black Chicagoans in 1915 and 1916 was whether or not the city would grant a license for the showing of *The Birth of a Nation*. Bentley led the NAACP's Committee on Grievances straight to the mayor's office each time a nickelodeon manager put in an application.

Just did not talk about Bentley's activism, just as he did not mention any of the depressing aspects of black life in Chicago. He preferred calling the attention of people like Loeb to the status and accomplishments of black Chicagoans, perhaps as a way of suggesting possibilities for his own professional advancement. The bright side appealed to him; unlike Du Bois, he did not find the "murk and shadows" intolerable.

Trouble in Chicago in 1915–16 was not exclusively racial; there were also well-publicized political struggles along class lines. On 8 December Just wrote Loeb about the "strike situation," noting in particular that Mrs. Frank Lillie had been taking "a great part in the movement to give the workers fair play." He knew this would fascinate Loeb, who could never have imagined that a woman of Frances Crane Lillie's piety, wealth, and social standing would throw herself headlong into the most radical kind of political activism. She was a daughter of the multimillionaire Richard T. Crane and the wife of a conservative academician; it was indeed out of the ordinary that she should commit herself as she did—not only to the special cause of the strikers but also to a socialist philosophy, including public control of essential services. Just's interest in the strike perhaps was prompted more by Mrs. Lillie's participation than by any special concern about what was happening. The daily reports in the *Chicago Tribune* seem, however, to have aroused his political consciousness to some extent. He was beginning to wonder whether "freedom and justice" would ever be prevalent anywhere and whether "brute force" might not be the only viable political tool for the oppressed. This was a far cry from the anti-union sentiments expressed in his first article, "Government Ownership of Monopolies," published thirteen years earlier in the Kimball Union Academy school newspaper.

The garment workers' strike began in late September. It was caused by the clothing manufacturers' refusal to negotiate a wage agreement and accept collective bargaining. From the beginning the workers received support from several groups, including the Socialist Party, the Hull House organization under Jane Addams, and "a number of wealthy Chicago women." Mrs. Lillie first showed interest in mid-October, when she signed a resolution drawn up by Addams condemning the "suffering and waste" caused by the strike and demanding immediate settlement by arbitration. Upset by the manufacturers' continued rejection of pleas for peaceful mediation, she joined the front ranks of the picket lines, alongside Ellen Gates Starr of Hull House. Their signs read, "*We Are Picketing for the Pickets Driven from the Line,*" a reference to the brutality with which the police had been implementing a court order prohibiting public protest. No matter what the time or weather, Mrs. Lillie could be seen marching to and fro with her placard outside Kuppenheimer's factory on Western Avenue and Twenty-second Street. In mid-November she loudly ridiculed a policeman who had arrested Starr, accusing him of being afraid to arrest someone rich. Her activism became more and more vocal. In early December she took out a full-page advertisement in the *Daily Maroon,* inviting all interested parties to a strike meeting in Kent Hall at the University of Chicago. She also sent out several hundred postcards to members of women's clubs, civic organizations, and church societies assailing the police as "obscene."

Soon Mrs. Lillie found herself in direct conflict with the police. On 6 December (two days before Just wrote Loeb) she created a scene by accusing a policeman of allowing "sluggers," hired by manufacturers, to attack strikers. The officer arrested her for interfering in the performance of his duty. Far from daunted, she protested all the way to the police station and the courtroom. Her language was radical and impassioned: "I protest against the mayor of Chicago using the police to crush the desire of liberty in the working people's breast through terrorism; . . . I protest against the power that seeks to perpetuate industrial slavery in America." The incident only served to reaffirm her commitment to the struggle for workers' rights. She returned to picket duty the next day.

As expected, her husband's attitude towards all this was diplomatically neutral. Lillie neither condoned nor condemned; he simply went about his business at the university. Everyone know that Lillie did not involve himself in politics. The contrast between him and his wife may have been amusing to some and upsetting to others, but it was a fact that had to be accepted. Just accepted it, and was probably amused. Unlike Loeb, he was not enough of a political activist to be either upset by Lillie's apathy or ecstatic over Mrs. Lillie's commitment. He was, after all, in Chicago to get on with completing the requirements for the doctorate. He had neither the time nor the inclination to think as deeply about political issues as he had done in his youth.

The academic atmosphere at the university was as much of an awakening to him as the social and political life of the city. The two were not, however, unre-

lated; the university's growth was undoubtedly connected with the flourishing aspects of the city. Having established itself as one of America's top universities, on a par with Columbia and Harvard, the University of Chicago had come a long way since it opened in the fall of 1892. John D. Rockefeller, who gave the original gift of $600,000 to found the university, had given well over $35 million to its various parts by 1916. William Rainey Harper, the university's first president and its organizer, at once brought together a distinguished faculty—one that engaged itself in both first-class teaching and research—and managed to attract superb students from the start. Included on the faculty were nine former presidents of other universities who brought with them not only scholarly credentials but also administrative acumen. The benefactors and trustees were, for the most part, Chicago's leading businessmen, who gave the university the entrepreneurial force needed to take it to the forefront of education, men who took an active part in the affairs of the institution. In this respect the University of Chicago was different from older Eastern universities, whose donors and trustees were usually old-line families who observed school affairs from afar.

In general science research and teaching were riding high when Just entered for the academic year 1915–1916, the closing year in the first quarter-century in the history of the university. The university laboratory system, comprising laboratories from the various disciplines, had mushroomed under the direction of Julius Stieglitz, a renowned chemist. Most of the science departments had come to be among the best in any American university. The physics department in particular boasted A. A. Michelson, who had received the Nobel Prize in 1907, and R. A. Millikan, who was to receive the prize in 1923. The zoology department had distinguished itself, first under the direction of C. O. Whitman and from 1910 under Lillie, and had been associated in the 1890s with Jacques Loeb and T. H. Morgan. It was still a growing department, and in the winter quarter of 1915 it had just gained a laboratory of its own; previously the laboratories for the departments of pathology and bacteriology were housed in the zoology laboratory. When Just arrived on campus, he not only was inspired by the vibrant scientific community within the university, but he also felt a strong sense of identity with the upwardly moving zoology department.

The department required its graduate students to complete a rigorous program of course work for the doctorate. A major and a minor field had to be selected. Fortunately, Just was permitted to use his previous course work at the MBL to satisfy a substantial part of the zoology requirement. He had passed the invertebrate zoology and embryology courses with highest praise. In Lillie's view, each of these courses, involving five hours of lecture, four hours of field work, and thirty hours of laboratory work per week, was the equivalent of two major graduate credits. Just also received credit equivalent to five courses for the independent research he had done under Lillie's supervision at Woods Hole between 1911 and 1915. There was still much to be done, however, to complete the course requirements in his major field, not to mention the problem of selecting a minor. Physiology, a subject combining important aspects of biological research and medical teaching, seemed to be the right choice as a minor. Just was becoming as fascinated by the living organism's internal processes as he had been by its external habits; further, he was growing more and more convinced of the significance of his work at the Howard Medical School. With these factors in mind, he registered for one zoology course and three physiology courses in the fall of 1915.

Zoology 45 was perhaps the most stimulating of the courses he took at Chicago. Entitled "Physiology of Development," it considered a broad spectrum of data and views as material for a theory of development and heredity. Lillie was in charge, exuding his usual air of calm authority. Each week he delivered a two-hour lecture and presided over a one-hour conference session. A good thing about the course was its small enrollment. Only seven students registered, several of whom, including Elinor Behre and Tadachika Minoura, had been at Woods Hole.

The course began with a consideration of the basic structure and function of the egg. In October the topic was fused eggs in the marine hermaphroditic animal *Ctenophora* and the sea worm *Ascaris,* and in November, germinal localization and nuclear determination in the eggs of the worm-like chordate *Amphioxus,* the slipper limpet *Crepidula,* and the frog *Rana.* Questions that would later figure prominently in Just's own research came up for detailed analysis: the rapidity of the cleavage process, the possibility of nuclear differentiation, the interdependence of nucleus and cytoplasm. Lillie was careful not to allow his students to become enmeshed in theoretical questions at the expense of practical problems. He took up next the topic of tissue culture, a subject requiring a sophisticated treatment of both the idea of cell specificity and the fact of physical development. These were the most inspiring classes. Just and his fellow students argued over the various interpretations by Hammar, Rhumbler, Harrison, Burrows, and the Lewises. Just argued for the position taken by Hammar, a German biologist who in 1847 had insisted on the significance of "ectoplasm." Later, in the 1930s, Just's own work would center on this theme.

From tissue culture Lillie went on to consider the law of genetic restriction, as prelude to an analysis of the development of the nervous system. He linked Hertwig's ideas on biogenesis to experiments with the optic vesicle of various animals, using Hans Spemann's *The Development of the Vertebrate Eye* (1912) as the starting point for further discussion and research. In early December the students completed individual research projects applying genetic theory to the problem of physiological development. Just followed up some of T. H. Morgan's work in 1902 on muscular regeneration in the earthworm.

The course concluded with a summary of the various approaches to *Entwicklungsmechanik,* developmental mechanics—Wilhelm Roux's theory of nuclear analysis, Hertwig's principle of correlation, vitalism, and so on. Lillie insisted on the importance of keeping an open mind, especially in so complex a field of research. He referred several times to Roux's opinion that the attempt to understand *Entwicklungsmechanik* is "very difficult, the most difficult task that the human intellect can undertake." Finally, he stressed that genetics and embryology had not yet been closely enough applied to each other. Scientists still seemed more interested in tissue processes than in the activity of the egg. Zoology 45 was supposed to correct that imbalance, to impress on rising young biologists the need to approach embryology with greater sophistication and respect.

Zoology 45 stood out in Just's mind as the most rewarding of all seventeen courses he took or audited at Chicago. He vowed to do at least one important "piece of work" which would show how he had "caught part" of Lillie's teaching. It was a demanding course and assumed that the students were knowledgeable, independent, and motivated. It increased Just's interest in the physiological approach to embryology and sharpened his awareness of the international dimensions of science. Much of the source material came from German journals, especially Wilhelm Roux's *Archiv für Entwicklungsmechanik der Organismen.* Lillie brought up the theories and interpretations of no less than forty-seven scientists–twenty-three Germans, thirteen Americans, five Englishmen, three Frenchmen, one Chinese, one Italian, and one Pole.

Just felt he had a duty to prepare himself for medical teaching as well as for biological research. He looked for relevant courses, but was not impressed by the offerings. Though pathology and pharmacology seemed interesting in the catalog description, they turned out to be a complete waste of time. Just attended pharmacology once, "more than enough," and pathology twice, "three times too much." Besides, he had decided on physiology as the perfect compromise between zoology and medicine. In the end he restricted

Ernest Everett Just (Courtesy of the Moorland-Spingarn Research Center)

his course selections to the physiology department. He registered for three physiology courses in the fall quarter, two in the winter, and three in the spring.

Most of the physiology offerings were undergraduate survey courses designed primarily for premedical students, but registration by graduate students with physiology as a minor field was also encouraged. There was no chance for theoretical discussion and independent research. Students simply read the assigned texts, took lecture notes, and performed required experiments. Though he was beyond this kind of regimen, Just took it in stride, keeping his duties at the Howard Medical School always at the back of his mind. He was one of a few graduate students surrounded by a crowd of eager undergraduates. For the most part, the graduate students received poor grades. Unlike the undergraduates, they had neither the time nor the desire to compete for top honors, especially in a field outside their major area of interest. Just always received the highest grade of any graduate student, but, like the others, he was less involved than in the conference courses in his major field.

In addition to the basic physiology courses Just registered for A. P. Mathews's advanced course, which involved a detailed analysis of the chemistry of cell constituents such as carbohydrates, lipids, proteins, and nucleic acids. The prerequisites for admission were general chemistry, qualitative and quantitative analysis, and organic chemistry. Though the chemistry prerequisite caused him some anxiety at first, he was assured by Mathews, a Woods Hole regular, that this would be no problem considering his experience and maturity. Mathews did, however, advise him to audit a few chemistry courses so as to fill in any gaps of knowledge. So Just attended courses in qualitative analysis and organic chemistry regularly and took detailed notes, a practice he was to continue in the winter and spring quarters. Of twelve students registered, ten were graduates; many were regular investigators at Woods Hole. Classes met in conference style for three hours each week, and each student was expected to put in a minimum of six hours per week of independent research in the laboratory and close reading of articles in foreign journals. Just enjoyed this type of course and its emphasis on the creative exchange of ideas.

Mathews's course, stressing the physiological properties of the cell, laid the foundation for Just's future work on the protoplasmic systems of marine invertebrates. Mathews later recalled that Just seemed to understand cell chemistry "wonderfully well," certainly "better than any other student in the class." He was impressed by Just's insight and ability; he knew that Just would go on to advance "original ideas" and accomplish "great things," to become "one of the most original and creative men in zoology in the United States."

Just's choice of courses for the winter quarter followed the pattern of the fall, with minor variations. In January he enrolled for two zoology and two physiology courses: William L. Tower's graduate course on organic evolution and C. M. Child's graduate seminar on reproduction; an elementary course on the nervous system and the senses and Mathews's seminar on digestion. He also decided to audit A. J. Carlson's course on the physiology of the digestive tract.

The spring quarter, from April to June, was the last opportunity he would have for full-time study, satisfying requirements for the Ph.D. and acquiring knowledge for future research. He planned to go to Woods Hole in the summer, and he was obligated to return to Washington for the start of the fall term at Howard in September. The spring quarter in Chicago therefore had to be a time of relentless effort and concentration on his part. Besides taking three basic physiology courses, Just audited Carlson's advanced course on the physiology of blood circulation and respiration, Lillie's course on vertebrate embryology for medical students, and Kyes's anatomy course on immunity. Kyes and his course had special significance for Just.

Preston Kyes was professor of preventive medicine at Chicago, and there was a strictly medical side to his course involving consideration of the physiological mechanisms of disease production and prevention. Just noted Kyes's ideas on the relative susceptibility of blacks and Semites to diseases such as tuberculosis and diabetes. But he did not sit in on the course primarily for medical information; rather, he wanted to gain familiarity with the language of immunity, with the terminology Lillie had used to put forward the fertilizin theory which was to be so important to Just's work later. J. G. Adami's textbook on pathology provided the basic definitions for terms such as "agglutination" and "specificity." Just paid close attention to Kyes's analyses of Ehrlich's work, in order to grasp the full meaning of the terminology and how Lillie had used it in formulating his theory of fertilization.

But it was in Lillie's own seminar on the historical development and current status of problems of fertilization that Just gained a new perspective on his past work and his plans for the future. The seminar dealt with the questions on which he and Lillie had worked together for years at Woods Hole. Lillie led lively discussions on the mechanism of fertilization. Just listened carefully and read and reread Lillie's articles, seeking new answers to old problems. To do research in this area would place him close to Lillie; it would make his reputation as a scientist; and ultimately it would produce work he could call his own.

The spring quarter ended in early June. The department had already agreed to accept two of Just's articles as the main text for a doctoral thesis entitled "Studies of Fertilization in *Platynereis megalops*." All he had left to do was receive his diploma.

One of a handful of blacks in the country seeking a doctorate in science, let alone receiving one, Just could hardly be calm about his accomplishment; he was jubilant and afraid at the same time. He would certainly take part in the ceremony and mark the occasion. The convocation services were, however, to be a multifaceted celebration. The university had set aside from 2 to 6 June to commemorate its quarter-centennial. Just's self-pride was heightened and magnified by the numerous celebrations hailing the university for being the pioneering educational institution it was. Ceremonies took place in every department, and scholars from all over the country converged on the campus—renowned scholars such as William Henry Welch, the medical professor from Johns Hopkins, whom Just listened to with all attention as he dreamed of the future for the Howard Medical School.

On Tuesday, 6 June, Just attended the school's ninety-ninth convocation (the university graduated students after each quarter). The commencement addresses were made by representatives of various groups at the

university, from the trustees to the alumni to the students, even one by the founder himself. John D. Rockefeller spoke briefly to the crowd, and Just, in cap and gown, was dazzled by the power and legend of the man. He hardly knew what to think, moving among the wealthy. He knew, however, that it was people like Rockefeller who had helped to make the university move, who embodied the American dream. What these people would mean for him he could not predict; he hoped no doubt that he himself would keep moving.

Badly worn out and in desperate need of a vacation, proud but tired, he passed up the opportunity to go to Woods Hole. He boarded the train on Sixty-third Street and headed home for a well-deserved two-month rest from the pressures and pleasures of academia. He left Chicago overjoyed that he had finally completed a rigorous program under eminent biologists at a leading university, had finally equipped himself with the technical training necessary for success in science. As he approached Washington, his doctoral diploma was uppermost in his mind. How would he use his "union card," as Loeb would have labeled it, his "official stamp of approval," as Lillie had called it earlier? He knew now he could be a more valuable asset to Howard, establish himself within the university system, and begin his career in the white world of science.

Milton Viorst

E. D. Nixon: The New Expectations

"The third person I called was Martin Luther King. He said, 'Brother Nixon, let me think about it a while and call me back.' And when I called him back he was number nineteen. He said, 'Brother Nixon, you know I been thinking about that and I believe you got something there and I'll go along with it.' I said, 'I'm glad to hear you say that, Reverend, because I've told everybody to meet at your church this evening.' "

The spring bloomed hopefully for American blacks in 1954. Jim Crow, the devil that had brutalized black people for so long, appeared doomed to die. After twenty years of lawsuits by the NAACP, the Supreme Court in *Brown* v. *Board of Education* had at last ruled that segregation in the nation's public schools was unconstitutional. It seemed reasonable that the courts would forthwith abolish the remaining racial barriers in American society, and that blacks would be included at last within the promise of equality before the law.

"All of us thought our problems was over with," E. D. Nixon told me. The man I spoke to was a tall, leather-skinned black whose deep voice communicated authority, a touch of humor, deep pride and perhaps even some grandeur. We talked in the living room of his little house in Montgomery, Alabama, its surfaces covered with mementos of the civil rights struggle. Nixon shook his head as we spoke, as if reproaching himself for his brief lapse into innocence. "We really thought we had it made," he remembered ruefully.

In 1954, E. D. Nixon was the acknowledged leader of the black community in Montgomery. He was head of the local organizations of both the National Association for the Advancement of Colored People and the Brotherhood of Sleeping Car Porters. Apart from the black church, these were the two strongest and most influential black institutions in the country. Already toughened by the fight against discrimination, Nixon was preparing for a new round of struggle against the racial practices of the white South.

E. D. Nixon, as much as any man, planted the seed of the 1960s. It was he who led the cause for civil rights from the courtroom to the streets. He conceived of the Montgomery bus boycott, the first battle that used the strategy of direct action to challenge the established practices of the society. Subsequently overshadowed by the greatness of his early subordinate, Martin Luther King, Jr., he has been largely bypassed by history. But it was Nixon who applied the spark to the tinder which blazed forth as the era of the 1960s. In the fall of 1954, he took the first tentative steps when he led a handful of black children to enroll at William Harrison, a white school a few blocks from the black neighborhood where he lived.

"We is two or three members of the NAACP," Nixon said in his rolling Southern tongue. "We met with the parents and talked about it, and everybody was ready for it. We told the parents to stay out of it, let us have the children, and all the children just followed us right on over. We thought it was wonderful but the superintendent thought it was the worst thing in the world, and the police was there and they pushed us out.

"That's when our feets hits the ground. We found out that if we really wanted to have integration, we was going to have to fight for it."

The weakness of the *Brown* decision, scarcely noticed in the euphoria of the moment, was that it contained no enforcement provisions. Nixon recalled that, shortly after the incident at the Harrison school, he received a directive from the NAACP's national office in New York. It said that the NAACP would take the desegregation issue back to the courts, and that no more challenges were to be made at the schoolhouse door.

Because he was not happy with the directive, Nixon turned his mind to finding another way, less tortuous than the lawsuit, to break down the barriers of segregation. He proposed the boycott, and fifty thousand blacks in Montgomery rallied to him. Not since the Civil War had blacks reached out so massively, or so courageously, for their own freedom.

The boycott drew not just upon Nixon's roots in the Brotherhood and the NAACP but, much more importantly, it mobilized the force of the black church in the South. It inspired blacks everywhere, and particularly the young, to a militant assertion of their rights, and it won sympathizers throughout the world. It became a popular movement—in a few years, it would be known as *the* movement—and it changed American society permanently.

Son of a sharecropper, Edgar Daniel Nixon was born in rural Alabama just before the turn of the century. He managed to finish a few years of school before leaving the countryside at the age of fourteen to go off on his own to Montgomery. After holding a series of jobs, he was hired in the baggage room at the Montgomery railroad station. In 1923, he was taken on as a Pullman porter, one of the most prestigious jobs then available to blacks.

"Until I started working for the Pullman Company," Nixon told me, "I'd felt that the whole world was like Montgomery. I figured if there was segregation here, there was segregation everywhere. I just didn't think about it.

"I first went to St. Louis, and then to Jacksonville, Florida. I went to Atlanta and then I went to Chicago, to Detroit, to Canada, to Los Angeles, to Texas, to New York, to Washington.

"When I first went into St. Louis, I remember I couldn't hardly believe it. St. Louis was a Jim Crow town, yet in the station black and white peoples sat down together. You couldn't go to one of the hotels outside, but you could eat at the same counter in the railroad station. Then I went out the station and I saw a black policeman. I was talking to a friend of mine and he said they had fifty-two parks in St. Louis, and black people could go into any of them. And we in Montgomery didn't have any black policemans and couldn't go into any parks. I came back here and started thinking about things."

In the late 1920s, Nixon remembered, he first met A. Philip Randolph. From the perspective of the 1970s, it is difficult to imagine the daring required of a young man like Randolph in the era between the wars to assert the equality of blacks in America. In much of America blacks were still lynched with impunity, and in the North no less than the South, the Ku Klux Klan swaggered through the streets. But the principle Randolph believed in he did not espouse softly. From every rostrum he could find, he preached that a black was any man's equal. Nixon said A. Philip Randolph was to be forever his inspiration and ideal.

"When I heard Randolph talk the first time, I had never heard a black man talk like that before. Let me tell you, that guy could talk! Today peoples don't realize that there was no way Martin Luther King could take Randolph. Reverend King could talk, all right, don't let nobody fool you, but I don't know if any boy could talk any better than S. Philip Randolph. From the first time on, whenever I had an opportunity just to listen to him, I made every effort to go hear him.

"And let me tell you, Randolph made me see myself as a different type of man. He pointed out things that men ought to be manly enough to stand up for. He said that if you had a conviction that what you were doing was right, then you oughtn't to let nobody stop you. And when I heard how he handled Pullman officials, who were all white at that time, it changed my view about life. Randolph said that if life isn't worth dying for, then it isn't worth living for. Nobody in all my years influenced me or made me feel like A. Philip Randolph did."

Born in 1889, Phil Randolph was tall and slim, with cordovan skin and fine features, and a voice which conveyed an elegance that belied his impoverished Southern origins. In 1911, Randolph arrived in Harlem, a tempest of men and ideas, and in the ensuing decade of war and postwar reaction, he became increasingly known, and a trifle notorious, as an outspoken partisan of pacifism, Socialism and Negro power.

In those days, racial equality was a farfetched idea. Debate between blacks tended to be between the partisans of Booker T. Washington, who argued that his people should resign themselves to serving as a permanent underclass of artisans, and of W. E. B. Du Bois, who responded that the "talented tenth" of the race should be fully admitted to the nation's intellectual and professional life. Later, Marcus Garvey captured the black imagination, arguing not for equality but a doctrine of withdrawal from American life, in favor of a massive return to Africa.

Randolph rejected Garvey's separatism, as he did the submissiveness of Washington and the elitism of Du Bois. He maintained that the black masses had to organize themselves to acquire economic and political strength, and be prepared to struggle as a people until they established their rights to full equality in American society.

In 1925, Randolph set out on his lifework, to organize the Brotherhood of Sleeping Car Porters, which he saw as an opportunity "to carry the gospel of union-

ism in the colored world." It was the chance he had dreamed of to forge black strength through unity, through the instrument of the strike, through black economic might. The union, as Randolph envisaged it, would create a new black man, vigorous, self-respecting, tough.

But the effort, begun in antiunion times and carried on during depression, was discouraging and painful. A breakthrough came in 1929, when the Brotherhood was admitted into the American Federation of Labor. The affiliation assured the Brotherhood's stability, and established its respectability. Organizing and bargaining would never be easy and, compared to other unions, it would never be very powerful. But the Brotherhood raised the banner of black economic power and, as its spokesman, Randolph became the preeminent spokesman of the black working classes. He also came to be recognized as the country's strongest black leader.

E. D. Nixon said he first encountered Randolph on a run to St. Louis, and went to hear him speak there at a Negro Y. Porters, Nixon said, were then earning $72 a month, and Randolph promised them that if they signed up with him they would soon be earning $150. Nixon said he was skeptical, but gave Randolph a dollar for dues anyhow.

Nixon remembered that when he walked up to the podium that night to shake Randolph's hand, Randolph asked him to organize a Brotherhood unit in Montgomery. Nixon said he promised to try, but as soon as he got back home his superintendent was waiting menacingly for him on the platform. With a touch of laughter, he recalled the encounter like this:

" 'They tell me you went to one of the meetings of the Brotherhood out there in St. Louis the other day,' the superintendent said, and I answered, 'Yes, I did.' And he said, 'Well, I'm going to tell you right now, we're not going to have any of our porters joining the Brotherhood.' And I said, 'Well, I was just about to tell you, after I heard Mr. Randolph talk I thought it was a good thing, and I agreed to join up with him. I also figured you was going to come out here and tell me I couldn't, so the next thing I decided is that anybody mess with my job I'm going to haul them into court, 'cause I've got the right to join any type of organization that I want and you or nobody else can't stop me.'

"Now that was nothing but a bluff. I doubt whether I knew a lawyer's name at that time. But I bluffed him out of it, and I organized a local union here and I served as president for twenty-five years."

Persuaded by Randolph's arguments that blacks had to organize on a massive scale, Nixon set out at about the same time to found a Montgomery chapter of the NAACP. Inspired by W. E. B. Du Bois, the National Association for the Advancement of Colored People had been established in 1909 in reaction to Booker T. Washington's advocacy of lower-caste ranking for blacks. Its ideology was integrationist, and its leadership throughout its early decades was largely, sometimes preponderantly, white. Its strategy was chiefly judicial, and from its early years it regularly won important decisions in the Supreme Court. For decades it reflected Du Bois's early elitism, and attracted the "better class" of blacks.

By the 1930s, Du Bois had moved significantly to the left in his politics, and he regarded the NAACP as hopelessly middle class. Randolph agreed with him. But it was the closest thing that blacks had to a nationwide, mass-based organization of their own, and it was a major step to have its presence established in the Southern city of Montgomery.

Nixon said he and a postman named William G. Porter embarked on a campaign to sign up members, and in the first years it was hard to persuade enough people out into the open to attend meetings. As president he finally got some preachers to join, Nixon said, then some women, and then some socially prominent business people. Finally the momentum picked up, he said, and by the late 1930s the chapter had more than two thousand members, many from the black working class, all paying dues of $1 a year.

In 1941, Nixon recalled, he led a march of 750 people to the county courthouse to register to vote. Before the authorities closed the doors, 42 of them actually got on the rolls. That was the year, Nixon said, that he established his own right to vote, after a lawsuit and a decade of persistence. But white resistance to the black vote remained implacable, he said, and even though a few brave souls regularly went down to the courthouse, the registration campaign died.

Instead, the NAACP chapter turned its attention to abusive police practices, Nixon said, which were much more central to the daily life of Montgomery's Negroes. He acquired considerable court experience, Nixon said, trying to assure a fair trial for blacks who faced charges that were often patently trumped up. Sometimes, crosses were burned on the lawn of black houses, and with some frequency he himself received phone calls in the night threatening him with beatings and death. Whites commonly exacted economic retribution against unsubmissive blacks, Nixon said, but he noted that the Brotherhood protected his own job. Nixon acknowledged that it was the strength of the Brotherhood that permitted him to take certain stands which others could not.

Nixon offered no claim that the NAACP made much of an improvement in the life of Montgomery's blacks in those days. But it kept contact with the masses of blacks, for whom the simple act of paying $1 in dues

was commitment to a cause. Whatever its failures, however, Nixon remained faithful to Randolph's ideal that blacks had to stand together against a hostile world. Nixon said the NAACP, if only by its persistent presence, helped build a sense of solidarity within the black community, which burst forth at the time of the boycott in 1955.

The day-to-day concerns of the NAACP's Montgomery chapter were far removed from the work of the NAACP's national office in New York, which was waging an antisegregation campaign through the medium of the courts. After a series of promising rulings, the NAACP resolved in 1934 to fritter away its resources no longer on efforts to attain a dubious equality for blacks under the "separate but equal" doctrine that American courts had accepted as constitutional since the 1890s. The NAACP adopted a strategy of striking at segregation directly, by persuading the Supreme Court to banish Jim Crow altogether.

Concentrating first on graduate education, NAACP lawyers won one lawsuit after another, on the grounds that equal facilities could not be assured in a segregated graduate school. By 1950, more than a thousand blacks were attending the graduate and professional schools of white Southern universities. But the ultimate test still loomed, when the NAACP would be required to persuade the Supreme Court that all segregated education was unequal, at any level, and therefore unconstitutional.

In December of 1953 Thurgood Marshall, the NAACP's legal director, appeared before the Supreme Court to deliver his final argument in the *Brown* case. In his seventeen years as a lawyer for the NAACP, Marshall had pleaded before a thousand magistrates in the shabby courtrooms of the rural South. He had slept in hundreds of segregated fleabag hotels, and many times had had his life threatened by racist whites. Now he was at the pinnacle of the judicial structure, arguing before the nine judges who embodied federal justice. Marshall's long years of services, and his earlier successes before the Supreme Court, had made him "Mr. Civil Rights." Analysts considered him likely to win the *Brown* case, which would become his crowning triumph.

On an ideological level, Chief Justice Earl Warren's decision in the *Brown* case was indeed a victory for Marshall. Warren wrote that "in the field of public education the doctrine of 'separate but equal' has no place." But on a practical level the Court was less decisive.

Rather than provide for immediate relief, the justices called for further arguments on enforcement. Thurgood Marshall, of course, pleaded for immediate integration. Lawyers for the Southern states proposed a gradual transition, implemented according to local circumstances within each school district. President Dwight Eisenhower said nothing in support of *Brown*, and his attorney general quietly endorsed the South's position.

A full year after *Brown*, the Supreme Court decreed no date for the enforcement of its decision but said desegregation should be accomplished district by district "with all deliberate speed." It was the first time the Court had vindicated a constitutional right, then deferred its exercise to a more convenient time.

By the fall of 1955, Southern whites had taken courage from the faintheartedness of the federal authorities, and begun to entertain the notion that they could hold off any change indefinitely. This was still the era of witch-hunting, of McCarthyism, and of the conservative Eisenhower, when any effort, from whatever quarter, to change society was looked upon with suspicion. Most Americans probably rejected the Southern claim that the civil rights campaign was a Communist conspiracy but they were apprehensive, nonetheless, of its potential to invoke disorder. Within a few months of the Supreme Court's order to proceed, the South had made up its mind not to comply.

Senator Harry Byrd of Virginia, one of the esteemed members of the South's Old Guard, issued a call for "massive resistance" to the Court's decision. Nineteen senators and twenty-seven representatives from eleven Southern states endorsed a "Southern Manifesto" containing the same message. Alabama declared *Brown* "null, void and of no effect" and defied a court order to admit a black woman to the state university. In response to Alabama's action the federal government did nothing.

Emboldened by the message of federal indifference, working-class whites in the South swelled the ranks of a resurgent Ku Klux Klan. White violence against blacks, ranging from psychological humiliation to beatings and lynchings, had deep roots in the South, and in the mid-1950s it took on a renewed vigor. Middle-class whites founded a network they called "citizens councils," a white-collar version of the Klan. White supremacy hardly seemed in jeopardy as NAACP lawyers in places like E. D. Nixon's Montgomery filed desegregation suits, which Southern lawyers handily tied up in local courts.

Such was the treacherous atmosphere when E. D. Nixon in 1955 contemplated the available options. The *Brown* decision had made Southern whites more fearful, angrier, more resourceful, more violent than before. But it had made blacks hungrier than ever for equality. Within the country there was no discernible wave of support for civil rights, but a concern for the integrity of the Constitution was emerging. A quiet consensus was building, which held that, whatever the South's hostility to *Brown*, there could be no turning back.

What E. D. Nixon understood better than the others, however, was that the system could not be left to proceed at its own leisurely pace. Thurgood Marshall's very victory had rendered him an anachronism. Civil rights lawyers, and their liberal allies, might one day redeem the promise of *Brown*, but the legal process could have taken a half-century, or more, and blacks did not want to wait. E. D. Nixon concluded that it was time for his people to act on their own to obtain their rights, not in the courtroom but in the streets.

"We'd talked about the bus boycott all year," Nixon recounted to me with ardor. "I kept saying the only way we're going to do any good is to hit these people right where it hurts, and that's in the pocketbook. I kept telling people every time we had police brutality on the bus and everything—and they would come to me about it—there ain't but one way we're going to break it up and that's we goin' to have to boycott these buses. I started telling about if we stayed off the bus, at least we could make them know we mean business."

The bus system in Montgomery, as in many Southern cities, was a particular torment to the black community. Blacks were its principal patrons, yet it had no black drivers, and the white drivers took it as their personal prerogative to abuse and degrade their black customers. Montgomery's particular version of segregation required that blacks pay their fare in the front, then get out and reenter the bus through the rear. It was an uncomfortable system in winter and in the rain, and in rush hour bus drivers sometimes pulled away before blacks, having paid their money, reached the rear door. More obnoxious were the seating practices inside. Blacks were required to seat themselves from back to front, whites from front to back, and when the bus filled, the driver was empowered to order blacks to vacate their places to whites. "Niggers, move back!" was the driver's conventional command. The humiliation of having to relinquish a seat already occupied was a special irritant to black pride, and it assured a recurrence of acrimonious incidents.

Throughout the painful months of 1955, when civil rights seemed to be everywhere in retreat, Nixon bided his time, confident that the right incident for starting the boycott would come along. "You think anybody that got arrested would be good," he said, ". . . but my training with the NAACP and the Brotherhood of Sleeping Car Porters taught me different. I've handled so many cases that I know when a man would stand up and when he wouldn't." Nixon rejected a minister's daughter because he sensed she was too weak, a schoolgirl because she had a promiscuous reputation, a woman who lived with a father who was a notorious drunk. Then, on December 1, Rosa L. Parks was arrested on a charge of violating the Alabama segregation law, and Nixon knew he had his case.

Rosa Parks has been depicted in many accounts as a chance player in the Montgomery drama, a seamstress who took it into her head to defy a white driver because she was tired from a hard day at work. Indeed, Mrs. Parks's decision that afternoon was spontaneous, but the role was one for which she had spent many years preparing. Nixon remembered Mrs. Parks as one of the first women with the courage to join the Montgomery chapter of the NAACP. Later she became the chapter secretary, and for some years she managed the office in downtown Montgomery which served as Nixon's headquarters when he was, simultaneously, state president of the NAACP and regional director of the Brotherhood. Mrs. Parks was widely known in Montgomery as a woman with a steely belief in racial equality.

On several earlier occasions Rosa Parks, without being arrested, had been evicted from Montgomery buses for refusing to obey the drivers. But now the line between the races was more tautly drawn than before. Mrs. Parks was taken off the bus by two policemen and driven to the jail, where she was charged, photographed and fingerprinted. Nixon arrived a few hours later to sign the bond for her release.

"The next morning, I called Reverend Ralph D. Abernathy," Nixon recalled, "and told him what had happened and that I expected him to support me in the boycott, and he said, 'I'll go along with you.' I called the late Reverend H. H. Hubbard and he said, 'Brother Nick'—you see, everybody called me Brother Nick in those days—'you know I'll to along with you.' Abernathy was secretary of the Baptist Ministers Alliance and the Reverend Hubbard was president.

"The third person I called was Martin Luther King. He said, 'Brother Nixon, let me think about it awhile and call me back.' And when I called him back he was number nineteen. He said, 'Brother Nixon, you know I been thinking about that and I believe you got something there and I'll go along with it.' I said, 'I'm glad to hear you say that, Reverend, because I've told everybody to meet at your church this evening.'* The reason I set it up at his church was I wanted it right

_____
* King's account of the start of the bus boycott, published in his *Strive Toward Freedom*, differs substantially from Nixon's. It tends to emphasize his own role, though not necessarily in a self-serving way. King simply seemed to be unaware of what Nixon was doing during these days and he never bothered to find out.

downtown. Reverend King didn't even know Mrs. Parks at that time."

The Montgomery bus boycott would not have happened without the hope engendered among blacks by the Supreme Court's *Brown* decision the year before, and the despair which accompanied the recognition that desegregation would not be enforced. The boycott would surely not have happened without Nixon, who introduced to the community the ideological militancy of A. Philip Randolph and the organizational mission of the NAACP. But, having begun, it could not have endured until victory without Martin Luther King's genius for imparting to it a moral quality, which in turn mobilized the churches to sustain it. Conditions were no worse in Montgomery than they were elsewhere in the South, and they were better than in many cities. Only a unique convergence of men and ideas distinguished Montgomery from so many other places in the South and transformed it into the first major battleground in the new uprising for equality.

Martin Luther King, Jr., had arrived from Atlanta only the year before. Bearer of a reputation for erudition, he was the son of an esteemed family. His maternal grandfather had been pastor of the Ebenezer Baptist Church in Atlanta, and a charter member of the NAACP. His father, a self-taught sharecropper's son, had taken over at Ebenezer after marrying the pastor's daughter.

Raised in the secure comfort of Atlanta's black middle class, Martin Luther King, Jr., attended Morehouse, one of the well-regarded black colleges in the South, the Crozer Theological Seminary in Chester, Pennsylvania, and Boston University, where he received a doctorate in theology. At the age of twenty-five, he was invited to become the pastor of the Dexter Avenue Baptist Church in the center of Montgomery, one of the black South's most prestigious churches.

Some forty leaders of the black community, more than half of them ministers, attended the meeting that night in King's church. E. D. Nixon, off on his regular run on the railroad, was absent, but his will dominated the proceedings. There was a mood of defiance among the men, but they argued lustily until they reached a consensus that the black community was prepared to support them. Then they voted unanimously to begin the boycott on Monday, two days hence.

King and the staff of the church got out leaflets announcing the boycott the next morning. The *Montgomery Advertiser* acquired a copy and reproduced it in the Sunday editions. The publicity was indispensable to the boycott. Proof to whites of a heinous conspiracy, the leaflet was to blacks a call to act.

It was a cold winter Monday, December 5, when Montgomery's buses first rode empty, while blacks by the thousands traveled in improvised car pools, or trudged back and forth, many of them for miles, to their jobs. At police court that morning, Rosa Parks was found guilty of violating the city's Jim Crow ordinance and fined $14. Fred Gray, a young black lawyer who had worked with Nixon on NAACP cases, announced his intention to appeal. In the afternoon, the black leadership met to form an organization to keep the boycott going.

Some of the men at the meeting, out of a reflexive fear of provoking the white community, wanted to operate the organization in secret. E. D. Nixon, who was back in town now, would not hear of it. "We are acting like little boys," King's book quotes Nixon as saying. ". . . If we are afraid, we might as well fold up right now . . . The white folks are eventually going to find it out anyway. We'd better decide now if we are going to be fearless men or scared boys."

Nixon had a more pungent recollection of the episode. "Well, I was sittin' there boiling over," he told me, "so mad I didn't know what to do, so I jumped up, and I forgot about we was up in the balcony of the church. I said, 'What the hell you people talkin' 'bout?' Just like that, see, and I cussed. I said, 'How you gonna have a mass meeting, gonna boycott a city bus line without the white folks knowing it? You guys have went around here and lived off these poor washerwomen all your lives and ain't never done nothing for 'em. And now you got a chance to do something for 'em, you talkin' about you don't want the white folks to know it. Unless'n this program is accepted and brought into the church like a decent, respectable organization, . . . I'll take the microphone and tell 'em the reason we don't have a program is 'cause you all are too scared to stand on your feet and be counted.' "*

Whichever account may be more accurate, neither left any doubt that Nixon settled the dispute, but he was not the only brave man in the church that evening. In the atmosphere of December 1955, the act of chartering an organization to confront the power of the white majority in Montgomery, Alabama, required huge courage. It also required the daring to cast off old habits of mind, which were the accomplice of white supremacy. These black men, only a generation or two away from slavery, broke new ground in the South that day by standing up for what they believed were their rights. They called the organization they founded the Montgomery Improvement Association.

E. D. Nixon agreed to serve as treasurer of the MIA. He told me he ruled out being a candidate for the

presidency because he knew that the boycott would be long and the crises recurring, and that too much of the time he would be away riding the trains. He also told me he felt the MIA needed "a man who is intelligent enough to meet with any class of people," which he said disqualified him. It was a touching, self-effacing admission from a man who had spent a lifetime defying persecution, and in whose mind the boycott had taken shape, but who doubted whether he, a Pullman porter, was equal to the more wide-ranging public responsibilities that he foresaw for the MIA.

Without debate, Martin Luther King, Jr., was elected the MIA's president. The mythology holds that King was selected because special qualities were recognized in him. It is more likely true that the choice was made, unanimously, because King, being new in town, had not been compromised by his dealing with the whites, or weakened in factional disputes during his dealing with the blacks.

"The action had caught me unawares," King wrote in *Stride Toward Freedom.* "It happened so quickly that I did not even have time to think it through. It is probable that if I had, I would have declined the nomination."

The statement is credible, and corresponds with what we know of King's character. King was not conventionally ambitious. He drew self-assurance from his social rank in the black community, from a sense of *noblesse oblige.* It is likely he would have been content to spend his life at the center of an observant and dutiful Christian congregation, a pastor recognized for his scholarship and good works, not for political leadership.

During his first year in Montgomery, King had given no evidence of great secular concern. He lingered over the final touches of his doctoral dissertation, and proceeded circumspectly to shape new pastoral programs. With civil rights a growing public preoccupation, he delivered excellent sermons on racial issues, but he made no effort to draw his congregation, the most influential in the black community of Montgomery, into social activism. A month before the boycott began, he had declined nomination to the presidency of the city's chapter of the NAACP.

Throughout his life, in fact, there was a side of King, discernible even in his finest moments, of ambiguity and self-doubt. This was not a man endowed with a feeling of God-given righteousness. He did not claim to be an oracle. Unable to summon the certainty of a fanatic, he agonized at every juncture over the morality and the prudence of the choices he faced. Instead of dogmatism, there burned in him an unquenchable faith in God, which transcended his fears and vacillation and, transmitted to his followers, gave them strength.

---

* This, and several other quotes from Nixon, are drawn from Howell Raines, *My Soul Is Rested.*

King would probably have been satisfied to play a lesser role in the boycott, as he would have been happy, in the years that followed, to relinquish responsibility and withdraw to lesser prominence in the civil rights struggle. King was not comfortable with leadership. He accepted it only reluctantly. And yet, without King's leadership, the civil rights movement is unlikely ever to have become the dynamic force which moved the nation.

King sat at the center of the platform in the Holt Street Baptist Church, awaiting his turn to speak, the night the boycott started. It was a mass meeting of the Montgomery Improvement Association, the kind that would be repeated twice a week throughout the yearlong campaign. The hall was filled to its remotest corners. The outside world sensed that something important was happening, and television cameras whirred. Rosa Parks was introduced and received a standing ovation. A series of ministers delivered prayers and invocations.

E. D. Nixon, who also spoke, provided the following recollection:

"I told the people there, this is going to be a long-drawn-out affair. What I'm going to tell you right now is before this thing is over with, somebody is gonna die. It might be me, for all I know, but the only thing I ask is if it be me, don't let me die in vain. And nobody got up and got their hat and left that night.

"And then I said, for twenty-some-odd years I been fightin' and sayin' to myself that I didn't want the children to come along and have to suffer all the insults that I've suffered. Well, hell, I changed my mind tonight. Just like that, I decided that I wanted to enjoy some of this freedom myself. And everybody hollered when I said that.

"And the paper will tell you that forty-five hundred hymn-singing niggers were at the Holt Street Baptist Church and organized the Montgomery Improvement Association. But I'm telling you that if it weren't seventy-five hundred people down there, there weren't a single soul."

For Martin Luther King that night, the speech he was called upon to make represented a major effort at self-examination. He had never before thought seriously about the social implications of his religious beliefs. In his theological studies, he had been attracted to the activist interpretation of the church contained in the social gospel. He had been drawn by his personal religious credo to the concept of society shaped by Christian pacifism. He had acquired some familiarity with Gandhi's ideas of nonviolent direct action and Thoreau's of civil disobedience. But he had never tried to put them together in a practical program, and he was troubled by the apparent contradiction in inspir-

ing his listeners to show courage in behalf of a just cause without engendering in them un-Christian feelings of resentment and hate.

"How could I make a speech," he later wrote, "that would be militant enough to keep my people aroused to positive action and yet moderate enough to keep this fervor within controllable Christian bounds?"

What King articulated was a dilemma he would never permanently resolve, nor were his successive formulations to resolve it ever completely accepted by those who followed him. Still, in Montgomery, King forged the ideas of nonviolent direct action into a powerful weapon. With this weapon, he was able to mobilize Christian morality and apply its force to the cause of racial equality. It was a weapon he would work to refine, but from which he never turned, throughout the remainder of his life. It was his transcendent achievement that he was able to harness the latent dynamism of the black church, as a religious and social force, and put it to the service of civil rights.

In a large sense, this dynamism had always lain concealed beneath the surface of the black man's Christianity, waiting to be tapped. For many years, the black church had been a passive force in Southern society, even an accomplice of Jim Crow. King himself attributed this complicity to the Fundamentalist doctrine imbedded in the black church which held that "ministers are not supposed to get mixed up in such earthy, temporal matters as social and economic improvement; they are to 'preach the gospel.'" He did not find it easy himself making the leap in his professional preoccupation from personal salvation to public weal.* In later years, he would acknowledge a resentment toward "preachers riding around in big cars, living in fine homes, but not willing to take part in the fight." Yet, over the years, there had been an ambiguity in the black church that made it far more than a passive partner in the status quo.

The black church, from the beginning, took from Christianity a dual, and contradictory, message: submission to slavery and the equality before God of the human soul. The whites, in offering blacks their faith, emphasized the virtues of the former. The blacks, in accepting it, dwelled upon the implications of the latter.

---

*King's ideas had matured enough by 1963 for him, in his celebrated "Letter from a Birmingham Jail," to write: "I have watched white churchmen stand on the sidelines and mouth pious irrelevancies and sanctimonious trivialities. In the midst of a mighty struggle to rid our nation of racial and economic injustice, I have heard many ministers say: 'Those are social issues, with which the gospel has no real concern.' And I have watched many churches commit themselves to a completely otherworldly religion which makes a strange un-Biblical distinction between body and soul, between the sacred and the secular."

During the decades of slavery the black church, shunned by whites, acquired increasing autonomy, and drew further and further from the influence of the masters. The Negro church in American history served as the incubator and transmitter of an indigenous black culture, and the mainstay of the concept of black dignity. By the nineteenth century, black Christianity possessed a clear political character, which whites hardly noticed. The Negro spiritual was a signpost on the road that black culture traveled. Whites countenanced it as a lament, and a statement of resignation. Blacks upheld it as a hymn of faith in the ultimate triumph of justice for all men. To many blacks, the mission of the church lay not so much in the gospel as in pursuing that triumph.

But whatever its role, the church created leaders. "The Preacher," wrote W. E. B. Du Bois in *The Souls of Black Folk*, "is the most unique personality developed by the Negro on American soil. A leader, a politician, an orator, a 'boss,' an intriguer, an idealist—all these he is, and ever, too, the centre of a group of men, now twenty, now a thousand in number." The church was the only training ground that blacks had.

Of the slave revolts in American history, most were led by preachers, but more often preachers kept the flame of freedom alive more discreetly, within the church's walls. After the Civil War, preachers became the political chiefs of the emancipated slaves but, like black political power generally, they went into eclipse near the end of the century. Martin Luther King, Jr., and the many black preachers who followed along with him, represented not a new phenomenon in leading black resistance to white oppression, but the reemergence of an old one.

King followed long-standing church practice, too, in eliciting, and controlling, the emotions of his congregation from the pulpit. His practice had deep roots in the black ministry, perhaps in Africa itself. One Sunday morning, in the Ebenezer Baptist Church in Atlanta, I saw that side of King, and I understood that the political inspiration he gave his followers came, first, from his powers as a preacher of the gospel. King excelled in the pulpit, and enjoyed it, both its high theatrics and warm spontaneity.

Dressed in his black robe, King performed like an orchestra conductor, rolling out pronouncements in his deep baritone voice, to which the crowded pews responded on cue. Almost mystically, the congregation answered with handclaps and shouts of approval, periodic laughter, with the rhythmic counterpoint of "yessir, yessir," by an occasional shriek of pain or a rapturous moan of deep involvement. Du Bois called it the "frenzy," and considered it a means of achieving a collective spiritual union. King's contribution was that he put this worship openly to political ends, in direct challenge to the system of segregation.

It was only through the medium of the church, in fact, that King could imagine a movement to assert the rights of blacks. When the question was asked, "Why Montgomery, in December of 1955?" King had little doubt about the answer. He addressed it in *Stride Toward Freedom*, and concluded that "every rational explanation breaks down at some point . . . it cannot be explained without a divine dimension." A divine dimension may indeed have been present in Montgomery, but it was Martin Luther King who moved it out of the churches and into the streets to create real political power.

In the first few months of the boycott, King deepened his grasp of the concept of nonviolence, gradually transforming it from a personal commitment to a strategy for provoking political change. He was helped by at least two others, whose experience with nonviolence dated back to the Fellowship of Reconciliation, a pacifist organization which in the 1940s set out to apply to the United States the new ideas that Mohandas Gandhi was practicing in India within an altogether different context. Though never more than a tiny organization, the FOR had a profound influence on the development of the civil rights movement.

One of King's teachers was Glenn E. Smiley, a white Methodist minister from Texas, who was then field secretary for the Fellowship of Reconciliation. The other was Bayard Rustin, a black pacifist, former FOR activist, a protégé of A. Philip Randolph and an organizer of great renown. Rustin fed King on the thinking of Gandhi, worked to organize support services for the boycott outside Montgomery and finally signed on as King's secretary and factotum.

Yet what distinguished Montgomery from the experiences of these two men in FOR was that, for the first time in America, nonviolence had acquired a mass following. The work of Smiley and Rustin had always been with small groups, selflessly practicing nonviolence to desegregate a restaurant here or a theater there; but in Montgomery blacks were marching by the thousands. These two men, and others familiar with Gandhian principles who passed through Montgomery, shared their understanding, both theoretical and practical, with King. But it was King himself who had to make the leap, to apply nonviolent direct action on a massive scale, on the inhospitable terrain of the American South.

In *Stride Toward Freedom*, King wrote that, until he read Gandhi as a divinity student, he was convinced that the ethics of Jesus had application only to individual relationships. He said he accepted the view that "turn the other cheek," while a valid personal philosophy, was irrelevant to the conflict between races. Gandhi, he wrote, was "probably the first person in history to lift the love ethic of Jesus above mere interaction between individuals to be a power and effective social force on a large scale." Gandhi convinced him, he said, that nonviolent resistance, lovingly conducted, was a strategy in the freedom struggle that was not only moral but practical.

But only after the bus boycott began, King wrote, did he come to understand the real power of nonviolence. "Many of the things that I had not cleared up intellectually," he noted, "were now solved in the sphere of practical action."

In Montgomery, the campaign was limited to a boycott, a quiescent, even stoic, form of nonviolent direct action. In future years, King's nonviolent strategy would become more aggressive, evolving into mass marches and other forms of physical confrontation with authority. Near the end of his life, he was seeking tactics which would be still more dynamic, and he spoke of massive "dislocation" of transportation systems, of local bureaucracies, perhaps of the government itself. But Montgomery was the start.

King acknowledged that, even for him, it was not easy to reach an appreciation of how love could serve as an instrument of social change. Nonetheless, he made a commitment in Montgomery to pursue no other political course. His example persuaded thousands of others, black and white, that this was the right road to the achievement of racial equality.

King made a basic distinction: nonviolent direct action was not to be confused with passive nonresistance to evil. It was an active nonviolent *attack* upon evil. Its aim was not to defeat or humiliate an opponent but to win his friendship, and persuade him of his error. Its target was not the evildoer but the evil, and its practitioner had to be willing to turn the other cheek to violence, and even to accept jail when necessary. King believed that the suffering of a nonviolent activist would educate his opponent, and transform him.

Nonviolence, furthermore, contained a pledge to shun "internal violence of the spirit," King believed, no less than physical violence. The nonviolent activist had to refuse to hate. He was to seek to create a community of *agape*, a Greek work which King defined as an overflowing love, or a redeeming goodwill for all men, even toward those who do one evil. King also said that the nonviolent activist had to understand that suffering without retaliation was an act of faith in the future, and had to believe that the universe was ultimately on the side of justice.

These were the principles that King worked to impart to the blacks of Montgomery, chiefly during the biweekly mass meetings that became an intrinsic part of the MIA movement. The meetings rotated from church to church and in many ways, were indistinguishable from religious services. They regularly drew thousands of people, cutting sharply across class lines in the black community. The agenda of the meetings was unvarying in its sequence of songs, prayer, Scripture reading, remarks by the leader, donations, reports from various MIA committees and an inspirational talk.

King presided over a large proportion of the meetings, but whether it was he or another minister who spoke, their purpose was, more often than not, indoctrination in the theories and practices of nonviolence. The meetings made Gandhi a household word, King noted, and "people who had never heard of the little brown saint were now saying his name with an air of familiarity."

By insisting upon the principles of nonviolence, King asked a great deal of those who gave him their allegiance. The doctrine was foreign to the experience, the history and the vision of life of most blacks. Only a few in Montgomery ever really grasped it, and most accepted it only out of confidence in King, and in his assurance that it represented "Christianity in action." But the doctrine's prospects for survival as a commanding force depended on the results it yielded.

E. D. Nixon, for one, had no use for it. He had been raised in the atmosphere of savagery that was intrinsic to race relations in the South. His life had many times been threatened, sometimes because he was a black leader, sometimes simply because he was black. He envisaged the boycott not as King did, as a witness against evil, but as a means for applying pressure, inflicting pain, demonstrating a power of revenge over the whites who had brutalized him. Nixon's experiences told him that brute force was the method to which whites would turn to maintain the structure of their supremacy. And it told him that force was the only way for blacks to deal with them in return. To E. D. Nixon, nonviolence was an incomprehensible folly.

"I had all kinds of guns here in the house," he told me, "and a whole lot of times I carried one in my pocket. I told Reverend King that I didn't go along with non-violence, and I told him I wouldn't. 'Cause I knew if anybody hit me in the face, I was goin' to hit them back.

"Now Reverend King wouldn't do that. But I told him point blank that I couldn't agree with him. And he said don't go around and preach it, and I said I won't. But I told him I'll stay out of your parades where I might get hit, 'cause I know I'm going to fight back."

The personal test of King's commitment, and the black community's, came when the boycott was two months old. Though blacks complained of long walks, sore feet and lost time, the sight of the empty buses buoyed their satisfaction and sense of solidarity. Hundreds of volunteers had been enlisted for the car pools. Despite the wintry weather, seventeen thousand people got to work each day, while whites looked on in angry impotence. Then, on January 30, when King was at the pulpit leading a mass meeting, his house was bombed, and only by chance did his wife and ten-week-old baby escape unharmed. Later that night, a thousand angry black men and women assembled on his lawn, many of them carrying guns, knives, clubs or broken bottles. They were ready to spill blood, even their own, and waited only for a command from King when he appeared on his devastated front porch. It was a climactic moment for the movement, and for nonviolent protest, and King did not hesitate.

"If you have weapons, take them home," he told the wrathful crowd. "If you do not have them, please do not seek to get them. We cannot solve this problem through retaliatory violence . . . We must love our white brothers, no matter what they do to us. We must make them know that we love them. Jesus still cries out in words that echo across the centuries: 'Love your enemies; bless them that curse you; pray for them that despitefully use you.' This is what we must live by. We must meet hate with love."

The crowd responded grudgingly with cries of "Amen," and fitfully drifted away.

The demands formulated by the Montgomery Improvement Association at the start of the boycott were extremely modest. That the MIA did not call for an immediate end to segregation was an index of what appeared realistic, even proper, in the American South at that time. It is true that when Rosa Parks was found guilty of violating the Jim Crow ordinance and fined $14, the MIA looked to the Supreme Court to vindicate its efforts by sweeping bus segregation away. But that was for the federal government, in its majesty, to do. The program submitted by the MIA to the city fell far short of such a demand.

The MIA's three conditions for ending the boycott were (1) courteous treatment of blacks by bus drivers, (2) seating on a first-come-first-served basis, blacks back to front, whites front to back, (3) employment of black operators on routes through predominantly black neighborhoods. This proposed modification of Montgomery's Jim Crow system was hardly audacious. It was, in fact, the procedure followed in Atlanta, Mobile and other Southern cities. But a committee composed of Montgomery's mayor, several city commissioners and representatives of the bus company insisted the demands would violate the local segregation laws, and turned them down cold.

Within a few days after the start of the boycott, all negotiations collapsed, and were never resumed. The feeling among whites toward the MIA was not quite unanimous. A businessman's group called Men of Montgomery promoted compromise as preferable to economic disruption and bad publicity for the city. A few white ministers, and a handful of private citizens, spoke out courageously for a new attitude toward blacks. But an overwhelming majority opposed any concessions, and seemed to sense—as did Montgomery's blacks—that a victory for the MIA would be the beginning of the end of the structure of white supremacy. So, after the initial flurry of meetings, the city's white leadership turned its attention to destroying the blacks' organization.

On January 22, 1956, the *Montgomery Advertiser* ran an article containing an announcement by the city commission that it had reached a "settlement" with three prominent black ministers. King was tipped off to the story the night before and found the three ministers, none of them prominent, who admitted having been cajoled into a meeting by white leaders, but denied making any agreement with them at all. That night, King and other MIA members made the rounds of the black community to denounce the hoax and the next morning, Sunday, all of the city's black ministers reaffirmed from their pulpits that the boycott was still on. The city commission was confounded, and the buses continued to ride empty.

The police then embarked on a series of harassments to disrupt the MIA's car pools. Drivers were stopped for questioning about their licenses and insurance, ticketed on dubious charges and sometimes jailed. People waiting for rides were threatened with arrest for hitchhiking or vagrancy. King himself was arrested on a traffic charge, intimidated during a long ride in a police car and locked in a cell for several hours. The tactic brought the city some success, frightening away a number of volunteer drivers, but the car pools survived and the boycott went on.

Then came a profusion of threatening letters and phone calls, followed by the bombings. King's home was the first target, E. D. Nixon's the second. "I was coming down from Chicago and I got to Birmingham that morning," Nixon recalled. "A redcap came out when he saw me and gave me a paper and said, 'Hey, Nick, they blowed up your house.' They tried to throw the bomb in the upstairs window but it hit the side of the building and slid off the porch and hit the driveway."

King wrote in *Stride Toward Freedom* that, after this savagery, he felt intimations of impending death, and urged his followers to face up to carrying on without him. It was a feeling that was to stay with him for the rest of his life. King understood by now that the violence in Montgomery was not random. If the bombings were not actually ordered by the white hierarchy, the lackadaisical investigation by the Montgomery police was persuasive evidence that violence had its sanction. Some reports indicated, in fact, that the dynamite had passed through the hands of the police.

Then late in February, 1956, a Montgomery County grand jury indicted King and more than a hundred other activists in the MIA, at least a fourth of them preachers, on an obscure state antiboycott law. King was out-of-town that day and, according to a diarist,* Nixon was the first to appear at the police station to surrender. "You are looking for me? Here I am," he declared.

Soon hundreds of blacks assembled outside the police station to applaud as, one by one, the other indicted leaders appeared. "A once fear-ridden people had been transformed," King wrote. "Those who had previously trembled before the law were now proud to be arrested for the cause of freedom." Many who were not arrested on the indictment were disappointed, King reported, and checked at the police station in the hope that they had been inadvertently overlooked.

King was tried in a test of the law on March 19. His team of NAACP attorneys brought twenty-eight defense witnesses to the stand to show, as the statute required, that the boycott had just cause, and they testified at length on the indignities they had suffered on the buses. After four days of trial, the two sides rested and the judge immediately found King guilty. The sentence was a fine of $500 or 386 days at hard labor. The indictments against the other defendants, now reduced to eighty-nine, were stayed pending King's appeal.

Meanwhile, the city's white leadership continued the campaign against the car pools, reasoning now that they were the MIA's weakest link. The city succeeded in having the MIA's liability insurers cancel the policies on its station wagons, several of which it had acquired through donations. King, in bewilderment, turned to a black insurance broker in Atlanta, who then went to Lloyd's of London, which solved the problem by issuing new policies.

Then the mayor instructed the city's legal department to file a suit to stop the operation of the car pools outright. It alleged that the car pools were an illegal private enterprise, operating without license or franchise, depriving the city of legitimate tax revenues. An

MIA petition in Federal court to have the suit dismissed was rejected. As summer turned to fall, and blacks looked forward to a second winter without buses, it appeared quite possible that the city's suit would succeed, thereby bringing MIA and the entire boycott effort to collapse.

But the city was up against more than a local association of blacks, for, within a few months after it was founded, the MIA had become a cause that captured imaginations, and contributions, everywhere. The heaviest response came from black church groups throughout the country and local chapters of the NAACP. Whites were also enthusiastic, however, and important gifts were made by labor and civic organizations. Individual contributions came from as far away as Europe and Asia. Every mail brought in checks, King reported, a few as large as $5000. More often, the letters contained one or two dollar bills.

E. D. Nixon, who was treasurer of the MIA, recalled that he was always out trying to raise money. "I'd come in here at nine o'clock in the morning on my run, take a bath and catch a flight out of here, and at nine o'clock at night I'd be in Detroit, Chicago, New York and so forth," Nixon said. "I raised ninety-seven thousand dollars and brought back five automobiles. The United Automobile Workers one night gave me thirty-five thousand dollars."

For Nixon, the most exhilarating event of the year was a fundraiser for the MIA in New York's Madison Square Garden at the end of May, 1956. Eleanor Roosevelt and A. Philip Randolph were there. So were Roy Wilkins, executive secretary of the NAACP, and Congressman Adam Clayton Powell of Harlem. Tallulah Bankhead, Sammy Davis, Jr., and Pearl Bailey were the entertainers, and eighteen thousand enthusiastic supporters were in the audience. Nixon and Rosa Parks were guests of honor.

"When it got to me to talk it was five minutes of twelve," Nixon reminisced, "and I'd been sitting there so long I could hardly stand up. I got up and thanked the people, and I said that, according to this program, I'm supposed to speak thirty minutes, but if that's true it means I'll start talking today and end tomorrow. They didn't catch that at first, and then someone started laughing in the corner and they all started applauding.

"I don't think I talked for over ten or fifteen minutes. I started out by saying, 'I'm E. D. Nixon from Montgomery, Alabama, a city that is known as the Cradle of the Confederacy and the city that has stood still for more than ninety-three years until Rosa Parks was arrested and thrown in jail like a common criminal, and

*Bayard Rustin kept a diary on some of his Montgomery experiences. It was published in the April 1956 issue of *Liberation*, and reprinted in Rustin's book, *Down the Line*.

fifty thousand Negroes—"We weren't using the word 'black' then," he whispered to me—rose up and caught hold to the cradle and began to rock it till the Jim Crow rocker began to reel and the segregated slats began to fall. I'm from that city.' The people screamed. I never shall forget it."

As MIA treasurer, Nixon had more unusual financial responsibilities, too. One of the MIA's fears was that the city would somehow manage to seize its bank accounts, or at least freeze its balances, leaving it financially impotent. So the executive board decided to deposit MIA's money outside Alabama. "You know what," Nixon told me, "I left here once with eighty-five thousand dollars in a briefcase. I went to Atlanta, Raleigh, Richmond, Washington, Philadelphia and New York, and I scattered that money out and put it in the bank."

King has written that the MIA collected $250,000 during the boycott. But Nixon, who was often unhappy about the organization's loose bookkeeping procedures, said the figure was too low. "I cut checks myself for four hundred and fifteen thousand," he said, and there may have been more.

More than money came to Montgomery. The boycott was the object of incessant attention from the press and television, which kept it constantly before the eyes of the nation and the world. Without television to maintain a level of popular concern, the boycott would not have been able to endure. Without television, in fact, it is probable there would not have been a civil rights movement. Television and the press kept up heavy coverage because the country was interested in Montgomery, but it is also true that the country remained interested in Montgomery because television and the press kept up heavy coverage.

King proved to be a luminous media personality, receptive to questioning, invariably articulate, always composed. He quickly became nationally, then internationally, known, and he was deluged with invitations to appear before audiences to tell the Montgomery story. He made regular visits to black colleges, where he carried the doctrine of nonviolence to a generation of black students. He preached in the nation's most celebrated churches, where he helped turn the religious impulses of whites toward civil rights.

In August of 1956, King appeared before the Democratic National Convention in Chicago. He urged the Democrats to commit themselves to strong federal action in behalf of civil rights, but they were scarcely more supportive of the Supreme Court's *Brown* decision in 1956 than Eisenhower was. Adlai Stevenson, the Democratic nominee, failed to sense that civil rights was a rapidly maturing political issue. He pre-

ferred being vague, in the hope of retaining the electoral votes of what had once been the Solid South. In spite of Montgomery, civil rights was hardly discussed in the 1956 campaign. But four years later, and for the rest of the decade, civil rights would be central to American politics.

From the start of the boycott, an underlying assumption of Martin Luther King and the MIA was that, ultimately, the Supreme Court would come along to declare bus segregation unconstitutional. The boycott gave urgency to the cause. It tested the political strength of blacks. It gave a moral component to the court deliberations. But, by itself, it would not end Jim Crow. The MIA's strategy was an acknowledgment that, even with the weapon of nonviolent direct action, Southern blacks were still dependent on the federal government to change the law.

The city of Montgomery had made a serious mistake in charging Rosa Parks with violating the local desegregation ordinance. Had it brought her to court on a conventional disorderly conduct charge, the MIA's lawyers would have had no real case to appeal. But by convicting her on the basis of a law whose constitutionality could be challenged, Montgomery defined the MIA's case. MIA's lawyers felt confident that they had only to hold out while the appeals ascended, slowly but surely, through the judicial system. They underestimated, however, the canny ability of Southern officials to rectify their blunders by manipulating justice.

"One day it came to me, I just thought about it off the top of my head," E. D. Nixon told me, "about this woman named Viola White, and her case had never been heard after ten years. It was a bus case just like Mrs. Parks'. The only thing was she didn't get up and the bus driver attacked her, and she beat him almost to death on the bus. They arrested her and put her in jail, and I hired a lawyer to represent her. They found her guilty, and we appealed her case to the Circuit Court of Alabama. The case never got docketed on appeal and she died. That was ten years before."

Nixon said he shared his fears with J. Clifford Durr, a white lawyer in Montgomery. One of the few whites to support civil rights, Durr confirmed that the state was likely never to put the Parks case on the appeals court calendar. It was Durr's opinion that the MIA was wasting its time trying to get the Parks case to the Supreme Court via the Alabama court system. He said it would be better to get four or five plaintiffs to swear they had been mistreated on the bus, and then file a civil suit directly in federal court.

"I came in from my run on the second Sunday in January 1956," Nixon recalled, "and I called Reverend King and Reverend Abernathy, and I told them, I got news for you boys. I said I can call you 'boys' because I got a son that's older than either of you. I said, you all think we goin' to the Supreme Court in Mrs. Parks's case. The city fathers knows we feels that the only outlet we got is that case, and they goin' to freeze us out. I told them what we would have to do."

The MIA found some women who were willing to join a complaint in federal court, and Fred Gray, the NAACP lawyer who represented Mrs. Parks, put the case together. Four women filed at first. Later one dropped out, and the city used the pretext to seek disbarment of Gray, on grounds that he had sought to represent her without permission. The woman, who worked for the city, subsequently told Bayard Rustin, "I had to do what I did or I wouldn't be alive today," and the disbarment was averted only after Nixon, who had been forewarned of the trap, produced a tape recording of the MIA's negotiations with the women. Later, the MIA paid off Mrs. Parks's sentence with a check to the Alabama courts, and a hearing on the women's civil suit was set in Federal Court on May 11, 1956.

"No one can understand the feeling that comes to a Southern Negro on entering a Federal court," King wrote, "unless he sees with his own eyes and feels with his own soul the tragic sabotage of justice in the city and state courts of the South. The Negro goes into these courts knowing that the cards are stacked against him . . . But the Southern Negro goes into the Federal court with the feeling that he has an honest chance of justice before the law."

The case was argued before a panel of three federal judges. Robert Carter of the NAACP's national office, representing the MIA, contended that the judges should apply the *Brown* precedent to overthrow the separate-but-equal doctrine which guided Montgomery's bus operations. The city's attorneys responded that, if segregation were abolished, Montgomery would become a bloody battleground.

King wrote that he knew the MIA would win when one of the judges asked, "Is it fair to command one man to surrender his constitutional rights, if they are his constitutional rights, in order to prevent another man from committing a crime?" The judges deliberated for about three weeks, and on June 4 ruled in the MIA's favor by a two-to-one margin, declaring the municipal bus segregation ordinance unconstitutional.

King and his followers then waited with anxiety while the Supreme Court considered the city's appeal. Throughout the summer and into the fall, meanwhile, city officials raced the court by applying their heaviest pressure against the car pools in a last-ditch effort to break the MIA.

The Supreme Court did not speak until November 13, 1956. That very day, King was sitting in municipal court with E. D. Nixon and Ralph Abernathy, listening to the city present its case for the injunction to break the MIA transportation system. As King had foreseen, the Supreme Court vindicated the MIA position, and affirmed the lower court judgment without argument. It was irrelevant that the municipal court judge later granted the city's bid for the injunction. Segregation on the city buses was declared illegal, and the fight in Montgomery was over.

Yet the city did not concede gracefully. The city commission refused to make any move until it received official notification from the Court, which was to be more than a month away. In the interval, King's people put great stress at the continuing mass meetings on the need for nonviolence in the integration of the buses, and they made special visits to black schools to impress on students their responsibility for averting conflict. Neither the city nor private white organizations, however, would take the initiative in preparing the white community for the change.

On December 18, 1956, the city commission promised that it "will not yield one inch, but will do all in its power to oppose the integration of the Negro race with the white race." The White Citizens Council, to which several members of the city commission publicly belonged, threatened that enforcement of the decision would lead to riot and bloodshed. The Ku Klux Klan had already initiated a campaign of terror, and rumors of new bombings circulated throughout the city. But having stood fast through a year of struggle, Montgomery's blacks were not tempted to surrender at the moment of triumph. The MIA would not let Montgomery ignore the law.

On December 20, 1956, the Court's order finally reached Montgomery. At the MIA's mass meeting that night, King said, "As we go back to the buses, let us be loving enough to turn an enemy into a friend. We must now move from protest to reconciliation." Later King asked the ministers from the MIA to ride the buses during rush hour for a few days, to give blacks the courage to integrate and to handle provocations nonviolently.

Before television cameras and newsmen, King and E. D. Nixon boarded an early bus together the next morning. They were joined by Abernathy and Glenn Smiley, the white minister from the Fellowship of Reconciliation. The boycott officially over, the bus driver greeted them politely. The relative quiet of the next few days provided hope that Montgomery would accept the blacks' offer of reconciliation cordially.

Montgomery, however, did not. King noted that the public officials who had predicted violence needed violence to save face. Within a week, bus riders were being subjected to a reign of terror. Shots were fired at buses as they rode through poorly lighted neighborhoods, and at least one black was struck by a bullet. A teenage girl was beaten by a band of white thugs as she left a bus. The city commission, rather than protect the buses, chose to suspend runs after 5:00 P.M., leaving black workers once again without transportation. The white leadership's prophecy that integrated transportation would not work was now self-fulfilled.

By the start of the new year, tension had grown even worse. King was in Atlanta with Abernathy when, early in the morning of January 10, 1957, he received a phone call that bombs had again exploded throughout Montgomery. Abernathy's home was struck. So, for the second time, was that of Reverend Robert Graetz, a white Lutheran minister of a black church. Three black Baptist churches had also been hit. Though a few responsible white voices were finally raised in protest, King said he had never felt so depressed, not even during the grimmest days of the boycott.

Then, on January 28, twelve sticks of smoldering dynamite were found unexploded on the front porch of King's home. Blacks at two other sites were less fortunate; a home and service station were leveled by bombs. King wrote that, in touring the wreckage, he witnessed the arrest of two blacks who had done nothing more than berate policemen aloud for acquiescing in the bombings. Montgomery's blacks had never been angrier than they were that day, but there was no riot, and nonviolence prevailed.

Whatever King had hoped, the Christian nonviolence practiced by the blacks had not transformed the hearts of white Southerners. If the brutal character of Southern resistance had not been apparent before, it became unmistakable during and after the Montgomery confrontation. Since the beginning of King's campaign, relations between the races in the South had become more fragile than ever. It seemed possible that any kind of incident could snap the self-restraint of blacks, and provoke a catastrophe.

In fact, King wondered after it was over what, apart from the desegregation of the buses in Montgomery, the boycott had accomplished. By the peculiarities of the American judicial system, the decision the courts rendered for Montgomery applied nowhere else. The Supreme Court had set a precedent in the Montgomery case to which civil rights lawyers could refer, but blacks in every city in the South needed to file lawsuits to get all the buses desegregated. Meanwhile, bus segregation remained, along with job dis-

crimination, a devious judicial system, disenfranchisement, brutal police forces and segregated restaurants, theaters, sports, housing and—the *Brown* decision notwithstanding—schools. Even in victory King could not underestimate the magnitude of the task of desegregation that lay ahead.

Nonetheless, King had proven something fundamental in Montgomery. It was that nonviolence was not a strategy of weakness, passivity and cowardice, as many had once believed. Nonviolence was not valuable merely in demonstrating the moral superiority of the oppressed over the oppressors. The experience had shown that it was a positive strategy, to which blacks could adapt, which the South could not ignore, and which the world would applaud. The challenge would now be to apply it to other situations, for more grandiose ends.

King was not at all sure after his victory in Montgomery how to proceed. Three weeks after the integration of the buses, he called a meeting in Atlanta of some sixty black activists, most of them ministers who had been part of a network of MIA supporters in the South. They founded an organization which, shortly afterward, they named the Southern Christian Leadership Conference. King was elected its president. None of its members knew how next to apply the strategy of nonviolence, either, but ideas were fermenting among them, and their banding together in itself represented a commitment to continue the struggle.

What was clear was that the white South intended to defy the school desegregation order, and every other desegregation order the courts issued, as long as it could. When blacks realized they faced this defiance, as E. D. Nixon put it, "That's when our feets hits the ground." Recognizing they would have to fight, they knew they could not win alone. They needed the Supreme Court. They needed the moral sanction of a white majority to pressure the government. They needed money. But, until Montgomery, the white South never thought it had an adversary. At Montgomery, blacks showed not only that they could come together for the struggle, but knew how to win.

The Montgomery bus boycott did not instantly ignite the blacks of the South. Few Southern black communities had a man like Martin Luther King, Jr., to inspire and lead them. Fewer still had such a man in combination with a strong force like E. D. Nixon to transform an angry sense of grievance into active resistance. Many Americans in the late 1950s dismissed Montgomery as an isolated episode, praiseworthy perhaps but without important consequences. King himself was unsure of the influence it would have on others. But within the mass of Southern blacks the lesson of Montgomery was incubating, and a new decade had barely begun before it blossomed forth spectacularly.

TRITOBIA H. BENJAMIN

A Rich Legacy: Lois Mailou Jones and the Howard Years

Two institutions have played an influential role in shaping African American cultural production: the black church and Historically Black Colleges and Universities (HBCUs). The story of the black church has been widely told. The story of HBCUs is less well known, particularly the roles that individuals at these institutions have played in formulating concepts of African American cultural identity through visual means.

Floyd W. Coleman[1]

HBCUs have served as incubators for the currency of ideas and a place for growth in every discipline; the arts were no exception. As departments of art were formulated in the opening decades of the twentieth century, many individuals who had active careers as practicing and competing artists were also the backbones of these newly emerging programs. Artists/educators such as James V. Herring at Howard University; Hale Woodruff at Atlanta University; Aaron Douglas at Fisk University; James D. Parks at Lincoln University, Jefferson City, Missouri; Viktor Lowenfield at Hampton Institute (now University); Lawrence Jones at Fort Valley State College (now University) and Jackson State University; John Howard at A. M. & N College, Pine Bluff, Arkansas (now University of Arkansas at Pine Bluff); Hayward Oubre at Florida A & M University and Alabama State College (now University); John Biggers and Carroll Simms at Texas Southern University; and William Fletcher at Southern University, Baton Rouge, Louisiana, to cite a few, nurtured the artistic genius of our artists today.

As professor of design and watercolor painting from 1930–1977 at Howard University, Lois Mailou Jones also played an important role in formulating the theoretical underpinnings of ideas, the application of design principles, the physics of color and color theory, and related technical knowledge of artistic pursuits to more than 2500 students—young and old, amateur and professional, of many racial and ethnic backgrounds. Over a course of five decades, her importance to their artistic development is evident through the distinguished careers they have created as designers, graphic artists, educators, painters, sculptors, scholars and administrators. The range of her influence was amazingly

Lois Mailou Jones (Photo by Marvin T. Jones. ©1989, Marvin T. Jones)

broad, having an important effect on the succeeding generations of African American artists.

Because Jones considered teaching a noble profession, she transmitted more than just the fundamentals of theories and practical applications; she became a beloved mentor and guide, and an inspiration to those who admired her artistry. As a professional artist who exhibited regularly, Jones was a model for those aspiring young artists who wanted to engage in a career as successful as hers. The many and varied tributes made by her dedicated students remain as a testimony to her contribution in the field of pedagogy. Described variously as a master of technique, one who could easily convey her love of art and her knowledge of painting in an effective way, she has also been characterized as dynamic, inspiring, and, able to challenge her charges. This exhibition underscores that Lois Mailou Jones's unfailing inspiration and devotion to her students has shaped an artistic tradition in American art history. Their art embraces every "ism" practiced today, and many of them are in the forefront of their professions. As products of the Howard tradition, and as progeny of Lois Mailou Jones, the artist/educator, they too pass on the mantle to successive generations.

When Lois Jones arrived in August, 1930 on the campus of Howard University, it was entering the fourth phase of its drawing history.[2] Under the stewardship of

James Vernon Herring, from 1921 to 1953, Howard moved to the forefront of higher education, especially among HBCUs. As Walter Dyson observed in *Howard University, The Capstone of Negro Education*:

> For the first time at the University illustrated lectures in the history of architecture, sculpture and painting were given by Herring. And new courses, such as water-color, painting and drawing from life, were added to the curriculum. By the autumn of 1921 Herring had organized these subjects into the first official Department of Art at the University.[3]

The department was permitted to grant two degrees: B.S. in education for teachers in art, and a B.S. for professional work in design and painting. As chairman of the new department, Herring expanded the curriculum with free-hand drawing, composition, watercolor painting, and life sketch.

A stellar teaching staff guided the young students who flocked to the new Department of Art: May Howard Jackson, (1877–1931) sculptor, was hired in 1922; Gwendolyn Bennett (1902–19 ?) taught design in 1924, and from 1926–1927; James A. Porter (1905–1970), scholar, historian, author of *Modern Negro Art*, and a 1927 graduate of the department, was hired that same year to teach drawing and painting; James Lesesne Wells (1902–1993) was appointed as an instructor in graphic arts in 1929; Alice E. Bailie, taught the history of fine arts from 1931–1933; and Sidney Kellner replaced her from 1934–1935.

While visiting the campus of Palmer Memorial Institute in 1930 in Sedalia, North Carolina, where Lois Mailou Jones's teaching career began in 1928, Herring aggressively recruited the young artist to teach design at Howard University. Excited by his offer, (she had applied in 1927 but James A. Porter had just been hired), she accepted, and began a career that lasted forty seven years. Jones joined Porter, Wells and Herring and together they forged a fine arts curriculum unique among HBCUs.

Because drawing was viewed as the foundation of training in the arts, Jones, a product of the Boston Museum School of Fine Arts (1919–1927), had been trained under a system of rigorous aesthetic canons where an insistence on drawing was indeed the basis for all artistic enterprises. This conventional regimen was at the core of her teaching at Howard. Yet, there was room for the development of original and innovative forms of expression in her classroom, not inhibiting students, but allowing their inner resources free play. Jones's methodology was an important component in the development of the fledgling department of art.

Her initial appointment included two courses in design, with an additional course added in the winter of 1931. By the spring, Jones taught a full schedule of six courses with one design class offered in the evening. A total of sixty seven students received instructions during her first year. And, for the next six years, Jones's course load varied between two to seven courses per quarter.[4]

By 1936 the department was under the auspices of the College of Liberal Arts and offered only an A.B. in both art education and in the studio professions of design, painting, and graphics. The reputation of the department grew as an institution of the highest caliber. It attracted some of the best and most talented students in those early decades: Gwendolyn Knight Lawrence, Albert J. Carter, Alice Elizabeth Catlett, Malkia Roberts, Henry Hudson, Delilah Pierce, Humbert Howard, Percy Ricks, Peter Robinson, Wendell P. Taylor, Georgia Mills Jessup, Samuel Green, Kenn Simpson, David Driskell, and many other illustrious artists.[5]

In the early years, the department was located on the southeast and southwest wings of the third floor of Thirkeld Hall, a science building in "the valley". Art history courses were held in the first floor lecture room while seminar classes met in the basement of Founders Library. Beginning in 1954 temporary quarters were established in Quonset huts on the site of the proposed fine arts complex.[6] The new structure, which included Cramton Auditorium, Ira Aldridge Theatre, and the Lulu Vere Childers Hall (College of Fine Arts) was opened in 1961. This location was a dramatic improvement. Located on the second floor, the large rooms with a flood of natural light from oversized windows, provided a more perfect setting for the teaching of art than the previous studios in Thirkeld Hall; it remains the site of the department today.

In the 1960s and 70s, Jones taught a new generation of artists such as: Sylvia Snowden, Lou Stovall, Mary Lovelace O'Neal, Stephanie Pogue, Cecilia Washington, Bernard Brooks, Richard Fitzhugh, Starmanda Bullock, Lloyd McNeil, Leo Robinson, William Lanier, Franklin White, Rose Powhattan, Michael Auld, William H. Harris, Irma Francis, James A. Davis, Harvey Boyd, Yvonne Pickering Carter, Akili Ron Anderson, Houston Conwill, and Martha Jackson Jarvis, to cite only a few.

Jones took a personal interest in the development and success of each of her students. She would provide loans for tuition when needed by deserving students, and purchase their art as a form of encouragement. She also saw that her pupils' works were included in important exhibitions throughout the city.

On a regular basis, Jones gave critiques of her student's work, benefitting the individual and the class as a whole. Generally, these critiques were of an encouraging and constructive nature. Her method of instruction, as one student recalled, was "relaxed, not tense or rigidly formal, casual, non-judgmental and highly encouraging. She didn't try to make you paint as she painted—she was able to show you what was good about what you were doing."[7] When warranted, the critique could be harsh and unrelenting, especially if the student was languid towards his or her art. "She did not spare your feelings in her comments," surmised another student, "if your work did not measure up to her expectations."[8] Another student recalled that "critiques were dreaded by less talented students who viewed them as a time of reckoning. 'Shall we give this a number one or a number two?' she would ask us melodiously. Earning the distinction of a number one indicated superior execution."[9]

Although concise, colorful, and sometimes devastating, Jones's critiques were meant to benefit the students, and to help them grow. "Those in-classroom critiques were extremely beneficial to me. Not only did I learn some important practices and skills in the medium of watercolor, I learned interpretive skills, the language of art," recalled a student who currently works as a museum educator. "Some of the first opportunities for me to learn these skills," she continued, "began in Lois Jones's classes."[10] A professor of graphic design and painting at the University of the District of Columbia also stated that he "uses the same critique procedures today that Jones used thirty years ago in her class."[11]

Jones considered the painting process a labor of love, and she demanded that her students put forth their best efforts, advising them that, "Talent is the basis of your career, but hard work determines your success. You must love your art as though you are married to it."[12] This creed, so to speak, was the pithy reminder issued to her charges annually.

Jones admonished her students to study other works of art, and she encouraged them to attend exhibitions. Washington, D.C. offered great advantages by having original art available at the many museums in the city. She required her students to attend exhibitions, and to study the works on view. She conducted gallery tours and on-site discussions to many classes. Trips to the Corcoran Gallery of Art, the National Gallery of Art, the Franz Bader Gallery, the Washington Watercolor Club, the Phillips Collection, and the Howard University Gallery of Art were scheduled. Students were required to critique and report on each gallery visit. These exercises reinforced their ability to articulate many of the principles and theories taught in class, and it allowed Jones to determine their level of comprehension. One student recalled enthusiastically:

> I remember an exhibition at the National Gallery of Art which focused on the roots of abstract art in

Lois Mailou Jones, "Jennie," 1943. Oil on canvas, 35¼" × 28¼". (The Howard University Gallery of Art)

America. The exhibit was comprehensive and Professor Jones considered it important enough to cancel class and required us to attend the pre-arranged tour given by a staff lecturer. At the conclusion of the tour, Professor Jones discussed further the geometric elements in the works of Dove, O'Keeffe, and Hartley. Having just seen these works, I made associations between these objects and the exercises we were doing in class. I saw the practical aspect of learning by doing; I was then beginning to understand modernist theories. We experienced art and we were not isolated from the mainstream of the art gallery and the museum.[13]

Exhibitions at the Howard University Gallery of Art were of the highest caliber. Founded in 1928, it officially opened with an exhibition in April, 1930, the year of Jones's arrival. The gallery was in the forefront of showing most of the major artists in Washington.[14] As chairman of the department and director of the gallery, Herring's "instincts led toward diversity because he worked with the knowledge that much more national contemporary art needed to seen in Washington, for the good of the students at Howard and the city as a whole."[15] During those years, the gallery exhibited international works by Matisse, Klee, Kandinsky, Picasso, and those of the German Expressionists, as well as American artists such as Max Weber, Thomas Hart Benton and Charles White.[16] And as Floyd Coleman has so astutely observed: "The permanent collections at Hampton, Howard, Fisk, Texas Southern and Morgan State Universities were, and still are, most important to the development of an African American fine arts tradition."[17]

Studio majors in advertising design courses were encouraged to build a strong portfolio which would aid them in securing employment after graduation. In this connection, businesses that requested designs for productions, both on and off campus, were assigned to those majors which encouraged and facilitated building student portfolios. Many of Jones's students worked as layout and design artists for *The Hilltop*, the Howard University newspaper. Other projects resulted in honors for the art department as students took top awards in city-wide competitions.[18]

Hands-on activity outside the classroom augmented museum and gallery visits. These exercises would include workshops and clinics offered by reputable art-oriented companies, such as the George F. Muth Company, where students were introduced to airbrush techniques, photo stenciling, design demonstrations, state of the art technical equipment such as the Camera Lucikon for graphic arts, use of Reifler Graphic pens, and new procedures for quick drying oil techniques.[19] Visits were also made to Colortone Press, where students were introduced to the offset process by on-site personnel. In other words, Jones made certain that these young artists were not denied access to or knowledge of new equipment when the department lacked the resources. Jones was zealous in her efforts to gain experience for her students and she was determined that they would be on the cutting edge of the discipline. "Young black professionals have to be overqualified in order to compete," said Jones, "or even to be considered as viable applicants."

Practicing professionals were invited to the class/studio to give lectures and demonstrations. Jones felt that it was mandatory for students majoring in design to have current information concerning the trends, materials, and techniques used in advertising design studios of the day. Towards achieving this goal, noted artists of local and national reputation were invited to give demonstrations or lectures in their respective fields. Among the visiting lecturers were Elliot O'Hara, Lucner Lazard, T. Tany, Meta Warrick Fuller, Sam Gilliam, and Frank Bonitto.[20]

Convinced that travel would broaden their knowledge of the world, Jones began to plan tours for students to Europe and Africa in 1962. The first trip, approved by the central administration and supported by James A. Porter, then chairman of the department, and Warner Lawson, dean of the College of Fine Arts, was a tour of France. Specifically prepared for students of the art department, Art 016 was conceived as a course covering the "use of all contemporary media with emphasis on aqueous media."[21] Students received three hours credit for the session (July 16–August 3) at the Academie de la Grande Chaumiere. Twenty seven students attended and were required to submit ten finished works upon completion. After the session, Jones and the students traveled to Montmarte, Lyon, Aix-en-Provence, Menton, Cannes, Cabris, Grenoble, and Dijon, sketching the countryside and rounding out their first trip abroad.

The tour was a success! Many of the participants still fondly remember the summer of 1962, and their experiences at the Academie.

> The tour . . . was the most important influence in my artistic and social development. That trip taught me more about life, people(s), art and attitude than any other experience. It was especially beneficial at that young age. . . . The experience also earned me a certificate of attendance from L'Academie de la Grand Chaumiere. Sessions of figure drawing and painting influenced by the local as well as fellow artists had an enormous effect on current techniques and my point of view.[22]

Other former student artists voiced similar responses. Upon their return, the paintings of these students were assembled and exhibited as *Paintings by Americans in Paris, with Lois Mailou Jones, 1962*. On view at the DuPont Theatre Gallery of Art, April 30–June 1, 1963, in Washington, D.C., it received good reviews.

The second tour in 1965 included six countries: Austria, Yugoslavia, Greece, Italy, Switzerland, and France in five weeks (June 23–July 28). Students, faculty, alumni, and friends of the University participated in this cultural program touring museums, opera houses, churches and monuments. The following summer Jones conducted a five-week "Around the World Tour" for Howard University alumni. She suspended the tours, however, in 1966, and began to focus on individual research projects with grants received from the University.

Between 1968–1976, Jones was awarded five grants under the title "The Black Visual Arts", to conduct research in Haiti, America and eleven countries in Africa. Her classes were strengthened by her travels and research. Not only did her own works shift stylistically to reflect the cultural explorations in Haiti and

Africa, but the students were also stimulated with new challenges offered by the multicultural studies presented in classes. She lectured at the University, in Washington, D.C. and throughout the country on her research. A slide set of the artist's work and a report were submitted to the University, and were available for review by the students. Having access to this resource supplemented the in-class room discussions given by this artist/educator/scholar.

As one of her students during the 1960s, I, too, was grounded in the fundamentals of color theory and the elements of basic design. And although the studio arts would not retain my interest as a professional goal, my respect for Lois Jones as a teacher, as an artist, and as a professional woman grew exponentially throughout the decades. For thirty years, I have been able to call Lois Jones teacher, mentor, friend, sister, colleague, and confidant. She taught me and countless others how to pursue lofty and ambitious goals, regardless of the obstacles—real or imagined. To the young woman art aspirant, Jones was a beacon to follow—for while sexism and racism prevailed within the profession and within society, Lois Mailou Jones overcame these obstacles and made significant and measurable achievements despite the adversities facing her. As her students, we particularly noted how she triumphed with a personal resolve and a determination that propelled her into the profession of her choice; her continued productivity is a source of inspiration. In addition to the technical knowledge obtained in her classroom, other important issues were learned that have sustained us beyond those hallowed walls. And for that, we thank you Ms. Jones!

Notes

[1] Floyd Coleman, "Black Colleges and the Development of an African American Visual Arts Tradition," in *The International Review of African American Art* 11:3 (Summer, 1994): 31.

[2] Walter Dyson chronicled the early history of drawing at the University in *Howard University, The Capstone of Negro Education, A History: 1867–1940* (Washington, D.C.: The Graduate School, 1941). He states the following: "The history of drawing at Howard University may be divided into five periods - the first from 1871–1891, the second from 1891 to 1917, the third from 1917 to 1921, the fourth from 1921 to 1936 and the fifth from 1936 to [1940]." see Dyson pp, 139–145, for an extensive discussion of the evolution of drawing from its placement in the Industrial Department as "mechanical drawing" between 1871–1891, and its transfer to the Normal Department designated as "drawing" in 1891 which suggested that the emphasis was beginning to be placed upon the educative value of drawing.

[3] Ibid., p. 141.

[4] Information regarding the number of students and the courses taught were drawn from the 1930–1931 class lists/grade sheets located in the archives of the Office of the University Registrar, Howard University.

[5] Ibid. Names obtained from class lists/grade sheets between 1931 and 1955.

[6] Conversation with David C. Driskell, September 5, 1995.

[7] Questionnaire response from R.F., Watercolor Painting II, spring, 1964. A structured questionnaire was sent to former students of Lois Jones throughout the decades. These comments were drawn from their responses. Some students requested anonymity, and only initials are being used. Survey conducted 1989–1990.

[8] Questionnaire response from S.B. enrolled in Design I and II, fall 1968 and spring 1969.

[9] Questionnaire response from T.B. enrolled in Watercolor Painting I, fall 1968.

[10] Ibid.

[11] Questionnaire response from R.D.W. enrolled in Advertising Design and Watercolor Painting, 1959–1963.

[12] Interviews with Lois Mailou Jones, September, October, November, 1986. All quotes are from those sessions.

[13] Questionnaire response from T.H., Watercolor Painting I, 1965–66.

[14] The Howard University Gallery of Art was formally opened on April 7, 1930, with a distinguished assembly of art patrons. During the year, 16 exhibitions were shown at the Gallery. Many of these exhibitions were circulated by organizations and institutions such as the College Art Association, the American Federation of Arts and the Roerich Museum. See Dyson, p. 142.

The New York Times, October 26, 1930, reported ". . . never until now have Howard students or students in other Negro schools and colleges, had an opportunity to study within the walls of their institutions products of artists of the highest rank at home and abroad." And the *Crisis* magazine, November, 1932, determined that "Art at Howard University has passed the stage of experimentation and is designed to make the university one of the distinguished centers of the country."

Of the other galleries in the area, the Phillips Collection had the most important influence in modernism in Washington during that time. It opened in 1921. The American University's Art Department opened in 1942, and the National Gallery of Art opened in 1941. See Keith Morrison, *Art in Washington and Its Afro-American Presence: 1940–1970*, (Washington, D.C.: Washington Project for the Arts, 1985), p. 18.

[15] Ibid., p. 14.

[16] Ibid.

[17] Coleman, p. 32.

[18] Beginning with the 1949 *Annual Report*, and subsequent years as well, Jones highlighted some of the student's achievements. A few are as follows:

    1949: Juletta Randolph—$500 scholarship (source not designated)

    1953: David Driskell—The Charles Allen Award for Outstanding Work in Watercolor Painting

1955: James Stone won the 3rd Prize award in the 1955 International Human Poster Contest

1957: Ray Manley won the 1st Prize award, $50 for the Washington Post Christmas Painting Contest

1966: Albert M. Auld—1st Prize award in Design from the Muth Co. in Student Exhibition (also noted for 1st Prize in Design, 1964)

1966: Rose Jessup (Rose Powhattan)—1st Prize award in Watercolor Painting, Annual Student Exhibition

[19]*Annual Reports* of 1957–58; 1958–59; 1960–61.

[20]See *Annual Reports*, 1948–1977.

[21]Communication to Dean Warner Lawson from Lois Jones, Recommendation and Justification Re: Tour of France, dated March 3, 1962, personal files of the artist.

[22]Questionnaire response from R.D.W. enrolled in Advertising Design and Water Color Painting, 1959–63.

CALVIN H. SINNETTE

Rudolph Fisher: Harlem Renaissance Physician-Writer

Within the last two decades there has been a revival of interest in a period during which there was a proliferation of creative activities by blacks in the United States. Centered in New York City, it is referred to as either the Harlem Renaissance or the Negro Renaissance. The period lasted roughly from 1920 to 1930 and coincided with a time when the rest of the nation was living through the Roaring Twenties. Not surprisingly it occurred at a time when Harlem was a "cultural mecca" for blacks from every section of the United States as well as from the Caribbean and Africa.[1] Among the notable black literary figures to emerge during the Harlem Renaissance were Langston Hughes, Zora Neale Hurston, Claude McKay, and Countee Cullen. Somewhat less known but mentioned prominently by virtually all scholars of the period is Rudolph Fisher, M.D.

Biographical Details

Born in Washington, D.C. on May 9, 1897, Rudolph John Chauncey Fisher was the last of six children born to the Reverend John Wesley and Glendora Williamson Fisher. Originally from Memphis, Tennessee, the Fishers lived at various times in Little Rock, Arkansas, New York City, and Fall River, Massachusetts. In 1905, the

family settled in Providence, Rhode Island, where Reverend Fisher was attached initially to the Macedonia Baptist Church and later to the Olney Baptist Church. Three children died before the family reached Providence, and it is not known if any of them was alive when Rudolph was born. Young Rudolph attended elementary school and high school in Providence, and upon graduating in 1915 with honors from Classical High School, he enrolled at Brown University in the same city.

An outstanding student at Brown, where he majored in English and biology, Fisher was elected to Phi Beta Kappa, Sigma Xi, and Delta Sigma Rho, the national honorary debating fraternity. During his four years at Brown, he received two of the university's prestigious scholarships while winning prizes in German and public speaking. He received the Bachelor of Arts degree in 1919 with the distinction of being chosen by his peers to be one of the Class Day orators and by the faculty to be the Commencement Day speaker. The following year, he received the Master of Arts degree in biology, also from Brown University. While an undergraduate at Brown, Fisher also furthered his formal education in music. As he was already an accomplished pianist, the courses he took in theory, harmony, and composition strengthened his musical abilities to the extent that he was able to persuade his friend Paul Robeson to join him on a concert tour. In 1918, with Fisher as arranger/accompanist and Robeson providing the vocal renditions, the pair gave a series of small recitals in the black communities of New York, Philadelphia, Baltimore, and Washington, D.C. Although the tour was a financial failure, the two handsome and gifted young men attracted considerable attention in the social circles of the communities in which they appeared. In later years, Robeson would achieve world renown as an actor and concert singer.

In 1920, Fisher entered Howard University Medical School in Washington, D.C. With the death of his father the year before, Fisher soon ran into financial difficulties. Ever resourceful, however, he succeeded in obtaining an appointment to the medical faculty in his sophomore year as a lecturer in embryology. He also was required to give lectures in pharmacology and scientific English to dental students. Unable to continue his teaching obligations because of clerkship responsibilities, in his junior and senior years Fisher persuaded university authorities to provide him with a room at the medical school in exchange for his services as the night watchman. Despite his studies and employment obligations, Fisher, now known to his friends as "Bud," began to turn his attention to creative writing. Moving in Washington's literary circles, Fisher soon met Alain Locke, the brilliant Rhodes scholar and savant, who was a member of the Howard University faculty and who later played a significant role as architect and spokesman for the Harlem Renaissance. Inspired and encouraged by Locke and others, Fisher secured a private cubicle at the Library of Congress to pursue his literary activities. While a senior in medical school, he published his first short story, "The City of Refuge." The work, which appeared in *Atlantic Monthly,* was reprinted five times and singled out in a 1925 review as one of the best short stories of the year.[2]

On June 6, 1924, "Bud" Fisher graduated from Howard University Medical School, again with high honors, and in September of the same year married Jane Ryder of Washington, D.C. He then completed a year's internship at Freedmen's Hospital, the former teaching hospital of Howard University. During this period, under the tutelage of a favorite clinical mentor, he developed an interest in radiology. In 1925, Fisher received a National Research Council fellowship. He was one of a small group of young Howard University Medical School graduates to garner this coveted award.[3, 4] It was renewed the following year, thereby enabling Fisher to complete two years of postgraduate study in the Department of Bacteriology at Columbia University College of Physicians and Surgeons. Nineteen twenty-six was also the year that Hugh Fisher, "Bud" and Jane's only child, was born.

After completing his fellowship, Fisher decided to enter private practice, specializing in roentgenology. He opened an office in one of Harlem's more affluent neighborhoods but never developed a large patient clientele. Although he had a wide circle of friends, Fisher did not participate actively in medical affairs of the community. Consequently, he did not establish a significant base of patient referrals. Nor could he withstand the competition of Clilian B. Powell, Harlem's other x-ray specialist, who was well known in both medical and lay circles. At the same time, Fisher also ran up against the formidable racial barriers faced by black physicians when they sought to obtain staff privileges in white hospitals. Even though he was befriended by Walter Gray Crump, an influential white member of the hospital medical staff, Fisher's application for a staff appointment at Broad Street Hospital on Manhattan's lower east side was opposed on racial grounds by other members of the staff and ultimately rejected.*

Shortly after the stock market crash of 1929, Fisher was offered a high level administrative position at Howard University Medical School. He declined the

offer because he did not want to forsake the stimulating artistic environment of New York City for the intrigue and bicker of academe. Since he was unable to realize financial security from private practice, Fisher sought a salaried position. He applied to the New York City Health Department for employment as a staff roentgenologist, but his application was rejected. Caught in the throes of the Depression with a young family to support, Fisher took the only job that the city agency was prepared to offer him—as an x-ray technician. He remained on this job until illness forced him to retire. Although not a person to brood over disappointment, having to endure the humiliation of being employed in a position beneath his intellectual and professional stature rankled Fisher for the rest of his life.

It is difficult to pinpoint the onset of his illness, but it seems probable that his symptoms began in late 1932, before he moved with his family from upper Manhattan to Jamaica, Queens. Gradually his condition worsened, so that in his last year of life he underwent three major abdominal operations.* He seemed to improve briefly following the last procedure only to succumb somewhat unexpectedly on the day after Christmas, 1934.

Even if life had been kinder, it is problematic that Dr. Rudolph Fisher would have prospered as a medical practitioner. While he recognized an obligation to provide for his family's well-being, financial rewards were a relatively minor concern. Diagnostic challenges piqued his curiosity, but true intellectual satisfaction came from experimental and theoretical science rather than from their clinical applications. Conversations with his widow reveal that he longed to have a research laboratory and the opportunity to work with and teach young graduate students.† The bedside was not the setting for Rudolph Fisher to show his compassion for humanity. He needed a different terrain to display that facet of his personality.

Literary and social figure

After leaving Brown University and the sheltered home environment of Providence, Fisher began to develop an interest in the black communities where he lived. The summers spent in New York, both before and after entering medical school, revealed to him fascinating vistas on black life in the metropolis. To a lesser extent, he was able to explore the comings and goings of Washington's black inhabitants but his studies re-

---

*Jane Fisher 1987: personal communication

*All attempts to ascertain the exact nature of Fisher's illness and the surgical procedures he underwent have been unsuccessful.
†Jane Fisher 1988, 1989: personal communication.

stricted such activities. After moving permanently to New York in 1925, "Bud" Fisher thoroughly immersed himself in the everyday life of Harlem. Particularly attracted to the "common people," Fisher enjoyed listening to and participating in the banter of audiences in neighborhood movie houses. He went to local speakeasies, card parties, and ballroom casinos. Gamblers and nightclub entertainers became well known to him and he to them. While some of his professional colleagues frowned on his association with the lower stratum, Fisher found the more plebian locales to be a fertile source for the characters he sought to portray. He derived great satisfaction from capturing the style, anguish, and aspirations of the ghetto dwellers, and in a 1933 radio interview he stated that he would be pleased to be identified and recognized as "Harlem's Interpreter."[5] Indeed, Harlem was the setting for Fisher's works, and it provided the background for the major themes that characterize those works. The conflict between rural and urban values appears frequently in his fiction and is evident in such short stories as "Ringtail," and "Miss Cynthie," and "The City of Refuge." Of particular note in these works is Fisher's keen ear for the language, dialects, and accents of Harlem residents. Another recurrent theme in Fisher's works is the strain and stress in the lives of Harlemites produced by differences, both imagined and real, in social class and status. *The Walls of Jericho,* "High Yaller," and "Fire by Night" are examples of works in which these communal tensions play a large part. Finally, mention should be made of Fisher's second novel, *The Conjure Man Dies,* which is one of the earliest detective stories written by a black American. Fifteen months after his death, an adaptation of the novel was staged by the Federal Theatre Project and played to enthusiastic audiences at Harlem's Lafayette Theater.[6]

Though disparaged by some for his unconventional attitudes, "Bud" Fisher was a popular figure in the social and literary circles of the Harlem Renaissance. His carefree manner, sardonic wit, musical talents, and cleverness with words were widely known. In fact, it was the latter that led his friend, the widely acclaimed writer Langston Hughes, to comment,

> The wittiest of these New Negroes of Harlem, whose tongue was flavored with the sharpest and saltiest humor, was Rudolph Fisher. . . . His novel, [sic] *Walls of Jericho,* captures but slightly the raciness of his own conversation. He was a young medical doctor and X-ray specialist, who always frightened me a little, because he could think of the most incisively clever things to say—and I could never think of anything to answer. He and Alain Locke together were great for intellectual wise-cracking. The two would fling big and witty words about with such swift and punning innuendo that an ordinary mortal just sat and looked wary for fear of being caught in a net of witticisms beyond his cultural ken. I used to wish I could talk like Rudolph Fisher.[7]

With his poise, quick-wittedness, and personal magnetism, "Bud" Fisher was equally at ease and a center of attraction at an uptown house-rent party or at a downtown Bohemian cocktail affair.

Comparison with A. J. Cronin

The contributions of physicians to the arts and letters have received the attention of many observers. The article on the life of A. J. Cronin that appeared in the Fall 1988 issue of *The Pharos* is a recent example. Not only did it provide illuminating insights on the life of the Scottish physician-writer, but it led me to compare the life of Rudolph Fisher with that of Cronin. Both were born near the turn of nineteenth century into strongly religious households, and from early life each distinguished himself as a scholar. Neither family was well-to-do, and both men encountered financial difficulties in obtaining medical education. The mothers of both were eager for their sons to become medical doctors, and Fisher and Cronin lost their fathers while they were relatively young. Not surprisingly, the medical profession played a significant role in their fictional works, perhaps to a somewhat greater degree with Cronin than with Fisher. Neither of the two confined himself to a particular literary genre, with each writing short stories, novels, and plays. Intestinal ailments plagued both men, leading Cronin to relinquish his medical practice briefly, while causing Fisher an untimely demise.

Other than the obvious dissimilarities of race and national origin, there were, to be sure, significant differences in the two lives. Cronin achieved such financial success from his writing that he could retire from medical practice in the 1930s. Fisher, on the other hand, was in financial straits throughout his lifetime. Fisher had considerable musical talents, possessing a fine baritone voice in addition to being a capable amateur pianist. There is no information to suggest that Cronin was musically inclined. One of the most important differences between the two men was their comparative life spans. Cronin wrote until his seventies. "Bud" Fisher died at age thirty-seven, and his full flowering never materialized. Commenting on "Miss Cynthie," which many believe to be Fisher's finest short story, Columbia University professor and noted critic of African-

American literature Robert Bone sums up by stating, "Published in the shadow of impending death, it testifies to Fisher's inner growth and aggravates our loss of his maturing powers."[8]

Postscript

It is clear that Rudolph Fisher's life was split between two separate orbits. His intellectual fulfillment came from confronting the rigors of "pure" science. Medicine was a vehicle that partially satisfied his scientific appetite while providing a relatively stable financial base. On the other hand, Fisher's creative and spiritual needs were answered by his literary and musical pursuits. Recognizing the precarious existence of the creative person in the Depression period, especially if he or she were black, Fisher had no intentions of sacrificing his well-being or that of his family to the uncertainties of a creative career. While it cannot be said that he made outstanding contributions to science, medicine, literature, or music, Fisher was remarkably successful in accommodating the demands of the several disciplines and in juggling two rather separate careers.

Blessed with a superior intellect and an artistic yet unromantic vision of his people's struggle, Dr. Rudolph "Bud" Fisher and his creative works deserve to be better known to his medical colleagues. Hours of reading pleasure await those who choose to acquaint themselves with his literary legacy.

References

1. Excellent studies of the Harlem Renaissance are to be found in *(a)* Huggins, NI: Harlem Renaissance. New York, Oxford University Press, 1971; *(b)* Bontemps, A, ed: The Harlem Renaissance Remembered. New York, Dodd, Mead & Co., 1972; and *(c)* Lewis, DL: When Harlem Was in Vogue. New York, Alfred A. Knopf, 1981.

2. Fisher, R: The city of refuge. *In:* O'Brien, EJ, ed: The Best American Short Stories of 1925, pp. 105–21. Boston, Small, Maynard & Co., 1926.

3. The first black recipient of a National Research Council fellowship was Ernest Everett Just, professor of biology at Howard University, who received his award in 1920. Manning, KR: Black Apollo of Science: The Life of Ernest Everett Just. New York, Oxford University Press, 1983, p. 125.

4. Cobb, WM: The first hundred years of the Howard University College of Medicine. J Natl Med Assoc 59: 408–20, 1967.

5. Clarke, JL: Mystery novel writer is interviewed over the radio. Pittsburgh Courier, January 21, 1933.

6. Over the years, a number of scholarly reviews of Fisher's works have appeared. Among them are: *(a)* Bone, R:

Down Home: Origins of the Afro-American Short Story. New York, Columbia University Press, 1988; *(b)* Davis, AP: From the Dark Tower: Afro-American Writers 1900 to 1960. Washington, D.C., Howard University Press, 1981; *(c)* Perry, M, ed: The Short Fiction of Rudolph Fisher. Westport, Connecticut, Greenwood Press, 1987; and *(d)* McCluskey, Jr, J, ed: The City of Refuge: The Collected Stories of Rudolph Fisher. Columbia, Missouri, University of Missouri Press, 1987.

7. Hughes, L: The Big Sea: An Autobiography. New York, Hill & Wang, 1940, pp. 240–41.

8. Fisher, PM: Compilation prepared for the Schomburg Collection of Negro Literature, New York, May 9, 1951.

JENNIFER JORDAN

James Baldwin: A Voice in the Wilderness

It is written that a prophet has no honor in his own country. In America this maxim applies only to living prophets. Dead ones are much admired. So when James Baldwin succumbed to stomach cancer on December 1, 1987, the litanies of praise resounded over the land. While he was alive, his voice was heard primarily on National Public Radio; his face seen mainly at odd hours on PBS. But in death Jimmy Baldwin made the national evening news on ABC, NBC and CBS. At his memorial service he was mourned by the superstars of the Black literary community—writers like Toni Morrison and Amiri Baraka.

It is fitting that Establishment America should honor James Baldwin in death. For he spent his life trying to awaken European Americans to the reality of Black existence and confronting them with their failure to deal with that reality candidly and ethically. And although Baldwin felt Black Americans were more willing to look at life without blinking, he often had to make them admit their denials and to shore them up when they lacked the courage to do what they knew had to be done.

James Baldwin was a valuable guide to us all because he was one of those rare realists in Afro-American literature who saw life very clearly and called it as he saw it. Unfortunately, Americans have never been very fond of realism. They prefer the bang and crash of romanticism—weird whale captains, flying Africans, wild rebels giving the high sign to life and winning against all odds. Occasionally, the American literary scene will give the nod to a so-called naturalist like Theodore Dreiser and Richard Wright. But often that naturalist is merely a romanticist turned inside out and is fond of the super-crazed, the down and out struggling mightily yet losing to an insuperable universe, the psychotic Negro shoving white girls into furnaces.

Realism avoids hyperbole and instead examines the typical with an intimate particularity. Characters exist in a specific social framework, a particular time and place that can both destroy and nurture. They are surrounded by other people whose relationships with them are clear. Sometimes these characters perform heroically, but generally they are not larger than life. The object of realism is to make them the same size as life, a job which demands above all balance and a realization that, although people can be as wretched as Bigger Thomas in Wright's *Native Son* and as magical as Pilate in Toni Morrison's *Song of Solomon,* they usually fall somewhere in between.

Baldwin gave us a look at the ordinary and the human. His best fiction, *Go Tell It On The Mountain* (1953) and *If Beale Street Could Talk* (1974), focuses on the people he knew the best—Black people living in what we like to call the ghetto. But it is obvious that Baldwin approaches that place with the same kind of emotions that Lucille Clifton expresses in her 1969 book of poems, *Good Times:* "We hang on to our place/happy to be alive/and in the inner city/or/like we call it/home." And when one is at home, one can be brutally but mercifully frank about the flaws of the homefolk. One also knows what one can be honestly proud of.

Baldwin never shrank from the depravity in Black life. He acknowledged that the terror around him as a child in Harlem forced him to seek sanctuary in the church, "for the wages of sin were visible everywhere, in every wine-stained and urine-splashed hallway, in every clanging ambulance bell, in every scar on the faces of the pimps and their whores, . . . in every knife and pistol fight on the Avenue, and in every disastrous bulletin." (*The Fire Next Time,* 1963.) It is the hell around the saints of *Go Tell It on the Mountain* that makes them so hysterical in their struggle for exclusivity and isolation. Those who find no protection soon find themselves victims of the environment around them. Heroin destroys Red in *Just Above My Head* (1979) and captures Sonny in "Sonny's Blues." Julia, the child evangelist in *Just Above My Head,* is forced into an incestuous relationship with her father, who beats her until she miscarries the child that may be his own.

But for Baldwin those Blacks who succumb to the traps that life sets for everyone, but especially for dark people in America, do so not because of the inherent insufficiencies of their blackness or the omnipotence of racist America. They merely share in a human frailty that is Baldwin's secular notion of a kind of original sin. Every living soul has within himself or herself this imperfection. Sometimes it is a flaw so grievous that it leads to self-destruction and rains down misery on the heads of others.

Baldwin, however, was no Calvinist ready to condemn the fallen to hell fire. There is a tolerance for the most flawed of men. Gabriel in *Go Tell It on the Mountain* is miserly of heart, unable to love his stepchild, John. His hypocrisy allows him to pretend to sainthood as he hides a past life of failed responsibility. He is capable of brutalizing his family while praying fervently for its salvation. Yet we never forget Gabriel's humanity and understand him as a man driven by a desire to deny his own inadequacy and to protect his family from a hostile world that terrifies him.

Baldwin created men like Gabriel because he was guided by the conviction that "most people are not, in action, worth very much; and yet, every human being is an unprecedented miracle." (*No Name in the Street,* 1972.) He, thus, presented Black life with all its sins but refused to succumb to the assumptions that he believed marred Richard Wright's *Native Son:* the beliefs that "black is the color of damnation" and that "Negro life is . . . as debased and impoverished as our theology claims." (*Notes of a Native Son,* 1955.)

According to Baldwin, the greatest limitation of a protest novel like *Native Son* is that it leads "us to believe that in Negro life there exists no tradition, no field of manners, no possibility of ritual or intercourse." (*Notes.*) The strength of that tradition was obvious to him; it was those talents, institutions, and powers that made it possible for us to survive despite the brutalization, deprivation and rejection. So without avoiding the debilitating legacies of our past, Baldwin also set for himself the task of looking at what is wondrous in Black life. The entire corpus of his work celebrates the power that is Black culture, especially the music; the bridge over troubled water that is the Black family; and the salvation that is love.

Baldwin made the mistake in the early 1950s of admitting that he had once "despised" Black people "because they failed to produce Rembrandt." (*Notes.*)

Despite the fact that Black people as a group were a bit confused in the '50s about the notion of self-hatred and the question of cultural identity, Addison Gayle, in *We Walk the Way of the New World* (1975)—on the basis of this remark and a myopic reading of Baldwin's *Another Country* (1962)—cast the first stone and condemned Baldwin as a lap dog of the whites, a sycophant who treasured all things white and hated all that was Black. Such a conclusion makes one suspect

Gayle of a cursory reading of Baldwin before 1962 and a refusal to read him afterwards.

Baldwin, like Langston Hughes before him, had his hand on the pulse of Black culture. Despite his condemnation of the Black church as a "racket" feeding off the "Blindness, Loneliness, and Terror" of its people, Baldwin recognized in *The Fire Next Time* its excitement, "power and glory": "There is no music like that music, no drama like the drama of the saints rejoicing, the sinners moaning, the tambourines racing, and all those voices coming together and crying holy unto the Lord."

Just Above My Head, despite its other flaws, is a moving tribute to the spiritual and to gospel music. "Sonny's Blues," in *Going to Meet the Man* (1965), includes one of the most effective descriptions of the jazz musician at work and commemorates the blues as "the tale of how we suffer, and how we are delighted, and how we may triumph."

Despite Baldwin's obvious love of Afro-American culture, critics like Addison Gayle are greatly offended by his refusal to recognize the significance of Africa in the diaspora (Gayle). And indeed, Baldwin revealed a serious ignorance of African traditions and their resilient survival in Afro-American life. He assumed that the African past was irrecoverable and that Black Americans were tabulae rasae writ upon by only their 350 years in America. His prose revealed a continual grappling question of Blacks' relationship with Africa, but even as he learned more about African culture and politics (see "Princes and Power" in *Nobody Knows My Name*—1960), he insisted that Black Americans were aliens who had no choice but America. That choice was a cross to bear, according to Baldwin, who coveted Africans' firmly rooted identities and their enviably clear destiny—the wresting of their lands from European hands. But Baldwin was convinced that the African past could not change the Afro-American present. He saw Black Americans as condemned to a torturous but indestructible link to America and implied that we must save white Americans—and thus ourselves—by aiding them to become like us. (*The Fire Next Time*.)

The culture with the survival techniques which ensured America's salvation resided for Baldwin in the traditional Black family. Although his portrayal of this family may have conflicted greatly with the sociological projections of the last 20 years, Baldwin wrote of the Black family as he knew it: a source of a great deal of pain but ultimately the lifeline which anchors those who are to survive. Without the family there is no future for John in *Go Tell It on the Mountain*, no life for Tish and her baby in *If Beale Street Could Talk*, no witness for Rufus in *Another Country*, and no prop for Arthur Montana in *Just Above My Head*. There is a description in "Sonny's Blues" of a Black family quietly enjoying a Sunday in the slums of New York that conveyed perfectly what the family meant to James Baldwin:

> *Maybe somebody's got a kid in his lap and is absent-mindedly stroking the kid's head. . . . The silence, the darkness coming, and the darkness in the faces frightens [sic] the child obscurely. He hopes that the hand which strokes his forehead will never stop—will never die. He hopes that there will never come a time when the old folks won't be sitting around the living room, talking about where they've come from, and what they've seen. . . ."*

Of course, in "Sonny's Blues" the old folks have to die eventually, but not before they leave behind maps for those who follow. In the '80s we hear that there is no longer a connection between the elders and the young, that the Black family has disintegrated under the force of unemployment, drugs, and crime. If this is so, we must appreciate Baldwin for having recorded the poor, Black, urban family at its best and wait for another chronicler to come along to document the present desolation.

For Baldwin, it was love that held the family together, and love that made life possible. On first glance it seems to be the one thing about which he was an incurable romantic. In *Just Above My Head*, he spoke of an ideal love which provides support when it is needed and which allows others to be themselves by repudiating judgment and possessiveness. It is the kind of love that Hall Montana feels for his brother Arthur and for Julia, his former lover. It is a kind of spiritual bond that exists between Arthur and his male lovers, Crunch and Jimmy.

It is, however, no panacea. Happiness, especially happiness which is the result of romantic love, is transient. Baldwin compared it to the joy of being given someone else's lost "wallet containing a fortune." You know you don't deserve it, but you claim it anyway. Unfortunately, "the wallet will, one day, be empty, and money spent. God knows where happiness goes." (*Just Above My Head*.)

Love also is helpless against the internal demons that plague every living soul. Hall Montana's love, despite its intensity and unselfishness, can not save Arthur from his self-doubt and excesses.

Of course, Baldwin's notion of love grows far more complicated when sex is added, and his novels add a great deal of graphic sex, at least when compared to other Black fiction. Baldwin presented sex as something both powerful and mundane. It is also obvious that he thought it important to make homosexual love something real for the heterosexual, who usually peers at it with a mixture of revulsion and prurient fascination.

Baldwin spent a great deal of energy trying to evoke empathy from a sometimes hostile reader by focusing on the human emotions of homosexual love and sex. Arthur Hall is an especially sensitive lover who is concerned that he never use another and who, in his lack of cynicism about both sex and love, seems the eternal naif. Arthur, in effect, is the very opposite of the indiscriminate, phallic-centered stereotype of the homosexual.

Despite the emphasis that Baldwin placed on sexuality—whether heterosexual, homosexual or bisexual—his portrayal of sex was not without ambivalence. At times he wrote about sexual encounters with the kind of breathless purple prose one might expect from a long reluctant virgin discovering the miracle of orgasm or from a writer spewing out another one of those bad drugstore romances. At other moments sex was viewed with a tremendous casualness, which allowed for a free-wheeling exchange of partners and disregarded the little differences of sex and race.

At one point in *Just Above My Head,* Arthur's lover, Crunch, explains why he has slept with Julia: "Sometimes a person just needs somebody's arms around them, then anything can happen. . . . That's life." But ultimately sex is merely an exchange of bodily fluids if there is no love.

Hall Montana reaches manhood when he arrives at the understanding that he must be able "to accept my nakedness as sacred, and to hold sacred the nakedness of another. . . . There must be a soul within the body you are holding, a soul which you are striving to meet, a soul which is striving to meet you."

Love is also the corrective which Baldwin offered to an America drowning in a sea of racial conflict. Before the death of Dr. Martin Luther King he honestly felt that Black people must relinquish their justifiable fury and forgive white Americans, whom he perceived as highly destructive toddlers unable to grasp the magnitude of the devastation they wreak on the rest of the world. He writes his nephew in *The Fire Next Time:* "You must accept them with love. For these innocent people have no other hope. They are, in effect, still trapped in a history which they do not understand; and until they understand it, they cannot be released from it."

Even when Baldwin grew tired of trying to pierce the impenetrable and purposeful ignorance of white Americans, he still maintained a reluctant sympathy. The long trail of bodies left by the civil rights struggle and the multitude of imprisoned and murdered radicals of the '60s' rebellion led Baldwin to a sad recognition of "the fraudulent and expedient nature of the American innocence which has always been able to persuade itself that it does not know what it knows too well." (*No Name in the Street.*)

But even when he began to feel he had been duped, perhaps by his own generosity, he insisted that to be a Black American is to condemn America "out of the most passionate love, hoping to make the kingdom new . . . honorable and worthy of life." (*No Name.*)

Despite all the talk of love, Baldwin was a man who knew, with a great deal of intimacy and intensity, the reality of rage. In 1955, in his first book of essays *Notes of a Native Son,* he wrote: "There is . . . no Negro living in America who has not felt . . . simple, naked and unanswerable hatred, who has not wanted to smash any white face he may encounter in a day, . . . to break the bodies of all white people and bring them low, as low as that dust into which he himself has been and is being trampled."

Baldwin never spoke of this rage as anything other than a natural and vindicable response to American racism. But he rejected it and the violence it demands, not only because he insisted on trying to save America from itself, but also because he felt that such anger acted out would destroy Black people psychologically and morally. In *The Fire Next Time,* he wrote: "I am very much concerned that American Negroes achieve their freedom. . . . But I am also concerned for their dignity, for the health of their souls, and must oppose any attempt that Negroes may make to do to others what has been done to them."

Despite his refusal to embrace violence, Baldwin at the end seemed to think it inevitable. America would not listen; America would not change. The result, according to Baldwin, would be a violent struggle on the part of the world's non-white people to effect a new order: "There will be bloody holding actions all over the world, for years to come: but the Western party is over, and the white man's sun has set. Period." (*No Name.*)

Despite, or maybe because of, this frightening message, it is fitting that white America commemorate the passing of this man of large spirit and vision.

On one level white Americans send him away with loud hosannas because they are glad to have him gone. No longer do they have to hear that unrelenting voice, crying out of the wilderness, warning them to repent and enter into fellowship with the rest of mankind.

On a deeper, subconscious level, however, they understand they have lost an invaluable ally, for James Baldwin belonged to an almost extinct breed: a Black articulate voice who still had credibility with other Blacks and who still felt for white America a kind of love that survived the palpable pity and contempt he struggled vainly to contain. He was among those Blacks who achieved adulthood in the '50s and felt they had formed sincere relationships with a tiny but significant group of whites, who in their youth, rushed madly away from their own whiteness. The Blacks of that generation became quite ironic and sometimes quite bitter trying to balance the love and the hatred that white America elicited from them.

White America must be grateful for Baldwin and the others like him, for the next generation—the one of the '60s—had no patience for the balancing act and reached out for the rage. Of course, the ones from the '60s are quite calm these days and struggle like the rest of America to feed the children and pay the mortgage. But white America remembers and fears they can not be trusted. The children of the late '70s and '80s elicit even greater discomfort. How can white Americans turn their backs on a group that shows signs of becoming too much like them and thus capable of terrible things in the struggle for money and power?

Black Americans are still uncertain about what Baldwin had to offer them. They too came to praise him in death. But many Blacks, fearful and hypocritical, despise him for talking about the rage; and a significant group, insisting on the need for retribution, reject the message of love. And an alarming number, especially males, can not see past the homosexuality.

Whatever one's position, one must admit that Baldwin was a man of tremendous talent, honesty and intellect, who created enduring works of art and brought his genius to a lifelong consideration of problems that will carry us well into the next century. We do well to heed him.

E. ETHELBERT MILLER

Stephen E. Henderson: A Conversation with a Literary Critic

The following was edited from a taped conversation with Stephen E. Henderson, co-author of "The Militant Black Writer" and editor of the anthology "Understanding the New Black Poetry." Before his death in 1996, Professor Henderson taught for many years in the Department of Afro-American Studies and directed the Institute for the Arts and the Humanities at Howard University. The contributions of Stephen Henderson, according to E. Ethelbert Miller, Director, Afro-American Resource Center at Howard, "have enhanced our insight into and appreciation of Afro-American literature."

MILLER: Dr. Henderson, let us begin with your growing up in Key West, Florida. I remember you talking about that experience as something that shaped your character and personality and probably grounded you in certain positions that you took in terms of analyzing Afro-American literature and Afro-American culture. Can you tell us something about growing up in Key West and what makes that part of the country so unique in terms of Afro-American culture?

HENDERSON: Well, Key West is very well known now. But when I was in college and after I began my graduate work, if you said Key West most people looked at you twice. Growing up in Key West is growing up in a semi-tropical or even sub-tropical environment. And you even remember specific colors like the special kind of ultramarine blue, then the red-orange of poincianas. That combination just stays in my mind. I used to paint watercolors when I was younger and that was one of the things I couldn't get away from. But in addition to the sheer beauty of the place, Key West was isolated physically from the mainland of Florida and, until World War II, Key West people used to refer to other people as "mainland people." And most of the Black population is derived from either Afro-Cuban or Bahamian descent. My folks on my mother's side were derived from Bahamian ancestry. Coming to Howard in 1970 I used to hear the West Indian students talk. I always would be surprised when I turned around and noticed their ages because they sounded like the older people at home. And I felt, I still feel, a certain kind of gravitational pull toward that part of the world. Key West is 90 miles from Cuba.

MILLER: What about the music?

HENDERSON: Well, the music is calypso. We used to call it the Nassau dance which covers a multitude of sounds, but as I said Cuba is only 90 miles away so Afro-Cuban music was heard all day long. There was indigenous music which later became known as Junkanoo music—a sort of a modern rediscovery of the Nassau flavor. My high school in Key West had a tremendous influence on me, particularly some of the teachers. And as far as literature was concerned, we memorized Paul Laurence Dunbar, we memorized Shakespeare, we memorized quite a few things.

MILLER: So you were pretty equipped before you went to Morehouse in Atlanta in the 1940s. There was a certain tradition that had been presented to you. Did that have a lot to do with your decision to go to a Black college?

Stephen Henderson (Bill Rose/Ltd.)

HENDERSON: Well, going to a Black college was just the way you thought if you came from a poor family such as mine. In fact, I wasn't really considering college in a serious way until I was discharged from the army and my staff sergeant asked me what I was going to do. I said I was going to get married. He said "why don't you go to college?" That was good advice. That is how it happened . . . Everybody knew about Tuskegee and Hampton, but I learned about Morehouse through a fellow hospital inmate from Atlanta.

MILLER: Who were some of the people who were at Morehouse because I think you were in school with a number of people who are very prominent today.

HENDERSON: Well, Lerone Bennett and I were classmates. I was there when Lerone was editor of the campus newspaper, *The Maroon Tiger*, which was on par with [Howard's] *The Hilltop*. He did the yearbook. Lerone was also a musician, which most people didn't know. He was philosophical but also a very talented musician and poet. He played tenor saxophone and had his own orchestra. Martin Luther King had been there as an early admission student. I never knew him then, just heard talk about

him. They called him M.L., Jr. in contrast to his father M.L., Sr. And Dr. Benjamin Mays, of course, was the guiding light to all of us. That was one of the most significant experiences in my life, particularly the chapel. You grumbled and kicked about going to chapel but in the chapel I saw Alain Locke. Mordecai Johnson gave our commencement address. That's all I remember. But Morehouse gave you a sense of identity and identification because of the whole emphasis on building men—Morehouse men. We were obnoxious in some people's way of handling things but I think both for little lost sheep and people who had made up their minds it was a good experience.

MILLER: You left Morehouse and later went to teach in Richmond. If I'm not mistaken, you roomed with Wyatt T. Walker.

HENDERSON: Yeah, well my first job was at Virginia Union University in Richmond and I was pretty young. I had gone right out of Morehouse to the University of Wisconsin with a scholarship, and I had to finish very quickly because I didn't have any money. So I got the master's degree in nine months or two semesters [and later a Ph.D. in English and art history]. And then I had to get a job so I went by Morehouse to check out my English teacher and he said, "you write everybody but check this one." So I wrote to Virginia Union and they had an opening. Wyatt T. Walker was a chemistry major when we were roommates, but he was called to the Baptist ministry. He came from a brilliant family. We were friends and I learned a lot from him. There were other people, too. I had a good friend who was an artist then and I had, and still have, a strong interest in art. I sort of hung around his gallery and workshop and picked up a few things. Virginia Union was a very good experience because, as I look back, and this is the first time I've had the occasion to look back, some of the programs that I participated in there later became incorporated into other kinds of things. They had an annual fine arts festival, for example, which is one of the experiences. I met Lois Jones Pierre-Noel there. I said I used to fool around with watercolor and . . .

MILLER: You didn't just fool around. You also had some exhibits if I'm not mistaken.

HENDERSON: I exhibited twice—in '61 and '62. But one of the interesting things was that I put these on for a local show and Lois was there and she saw certain things she liked and she offered me a job at

Howard teaching watercolor. That was fabulous. I drop that on people when I try to impress them.

MILLER: You think that offer still stands?

HENDERSON: No.

MILLER: After Richmond, you went back to Atlanta, I think around 1962. Could you talk a little about not only returning to Atlanta, but also about the mood of the country at that time? Also, could you talk about what was happening on the campus of Atlanta University?

HENDERSON: Before Atlanta you have to think in terms of the civil rights movement and the sit-ins in 1960. Some Virginia Union students were involved in the sit-ins. One of the leaders, Charles Sherrod, a student in my class, was among those picketing downtown department stores. He came to me for advice. I lived, at that time, in a dormitory with divinity students and Sherrod was one of the undergraduates who was planning to enter the ministry so I think that gave him some feeling of ease with being around me. That was the connection. I went to Atlanta because you heard all these good things, all these exciting things coming out of the South. And people were being attacked not only physically but intellectually. The Virginia Union students were being attacked, for example, in the newspapers. And when the students sat in at the counters, a columnist named Ross Valentine poked fun at them because they sat there with books. And it was unfortunate for him that he mentioned two of the books that were being used in one of the classes that I was teaching—Goethe's *Faust*—and he talked about that. So I used the words "pandering to white supremacy" in my response to him, and I know I got to him because he wrote several articles after that and he kept using the word "pander." Dr. Mays came frequently to Virginia Union. Martin Luther King spoke at Virginia Union around 1960. He asked to see me because I had sent a contribution to the Montgomery Project and it was sort of a strange kind of feeling to have somebody that you know being transformed as if something special had happened to him. He had reached a sort of plateau in his life. It was Dr. Mays who recruited me . . . I hated to leave Virginia Union but I went and Atlanta was just a fantastic place then. There was a great deal of excitement among the students, among the faculty.

MILLER: You took an active role in terms of new ideas for curriculum, especially in terms of some of the things you felt could be improved, particularly the treatment of the Black experience.

HENDERSON: Well, maybe what you're referring to is the students' idea of "the Black curriculum." I didn't know how localized that was. I suspect that it was something that occurred in other places. But they talked about a Black curriculum. And they talked about making courses "relevant." Of course that was the catch word and the bass note of the '60s. So those of us who were young, who were liberal, and who were crazy, felt that we ought to side with the students. I learned a lot from the students. One of the majors questioned why there wasn't any course on LeRoi Jones or why LeRoi Jones wasn't included in American literature courses. Eventually the Council of Presidents of the Atlanta University Center—it was the summer of '67, I think—organized a group of faculty and students, including some visiting students from Wesleyan, to study the whole business of a Black curriculum. What we did was to look at all of the catalog offerings of all of the schools and check out the courses that seemed fit and pertinent to the Black experience . . . And we did that and made recommendations and some of those recommendations were followed. But one of the immediate things that happened was that in the summer of '67 Spelman College inaugurated a cultural series and a program—an institute—to train teachers in the significant aspects of the Black experience, areas that border on the arts and particularly the humanities and social sciences.

MILLER: Did some of these ideas eventually help in the development of the Institute of the Black World?

HENDERSON: Well, the thing about it is that some of us who were in that group, in that committee, became part of the Institute of the Black World. In this particular case, Vincent Harding and myself. But the Institute of the Black World is another kind of story because we were not exactly welcomed with open arms.

MILLER: Let's just talk a little about that because I think that when we look at the Institute of the Black World and the people who were involved in it we see it had a tremendous impact in terms of Black thought in this country. You served from, I think, 1969–1971, as a senior research fellow but even before that your conversations with Vincent Harding pretty much shaped the development of that institute. Could you elaborate on what your aims were at that particular time, what you were trying to outline or accomplish?

HENDERSON: Well, the idea of an institute probably was floating around the country in a sort of embryonic form. The night that Dr. King was killed Vincent Harding came to my house to hammer out some ideas. We had talked earlier about literary and historical kinds of things. He said this is a golden opportunity to make our point to the nation and we ought to get the presidential candidates here to speak out on issues which affect Blacks and minority people. There was always in Vincent's mind the realization that we were a part of something larger than just the United States, than just Black people. But what we wanted was to have a series of open forums . . . And I remember staying up until about four o'clock in the morning waiting at Ralph Abernathy's house for him to come so that we could make contact with him. That didn't work. But after the raw edges of the loss had been set into the healing process, Mrs. King called Vincent Harding to help her set up some kind of memorial to her husband. And what we had in mind, based on previous kinds of conversations coming out of the curriculum movement, was that Dr. King's life—the memory of his life—could be served in a living way by having his ideas and thoughts incorporated into the history of the protest, the history of the civil rights struggle, the history and culture of Black people. And we had a very elaborate scheme and conception in nine parts. I don't remember all of the parts now but the Institute of the Black World was going to be one, the tomb/mausoleum was going to be two, the library documentation project, which actually got started, which was to be a repository of the papers of SNCC, and SCLC and other civil rights organizations were going to be included. The civil rights museum was going to be another. There were several other portions. But we split up as a result of ideological differences.

MILLER: One thing which I find amazing is some of the individuals—such as Robert Hill, William Strickland, yourself, Vincent Harding, Howard Dodson—were all involved with the institute back then. Today, they are still doing tremendous work and it seems as if the institute gave them a sense of purpose and direction.

HENDERSON: That was really the objective of the institute, to shape and give direction; help give direction to the Black studies movement. That's the initial thing, but beyond that was the idea of acting as a catalyst, a kind of obstetrician to a new way of thinking which wasn't really all that new on reflection. A new way of thinking about the integration of art, humanities and political struggle.

MILLER: Well, talking about that, I want to make a link here and if I'm incorrect you can let me know. There was a conference held, I think, in Idlewild, Michigan, about 1970–71, in which you gave a paper on Black culture. Also at that conference, I believe, was Andrew Billingsley who eventually came to Howard as vice president for academic affairs. It seems as if you were putting forth certain ideas in terms of culture and people like Billingsley were looking at how they could affect or change Black institutions in terms of incorporating these ideas and disseminating them to students and teachers and preserving Black culture. It seems as if the two of you came together at that conference and one of the results was the Institute for the Arts and the Humanities at Howard a few years later.

HENDERSON: That's essentially correct, except that was earlier in 1969, to trace the institute's story a little more precisely. In 1969, in November, all of the Black studies directors that we could corral—about 40 or 50 of them—came to Atlanta to a conference. You had people who were art majors or history majors or whatever and suddenly they were thrust into the position of administrators for a highly volatile subject matter. From that meeting in which those directors told us, "You lead and we'll follow," we realized that we had to get our sense of direction and our sense of organization straight. That called for the Idlewild conference on the Black agenda on March 24. I think it was 1970. Dr. Billingsley was there because he was also connected with the Black studies movement in California at Berkeley.

MILLER: He's also responsible for bringing you from Atlanta to Howard.

HENDERSON: That was part of what he wanted. What he really wanted and what he really offered us, and we debated this, because we were working on slim budgets and all of us had families, was to move the Institute of the Black World here. As I said, Atlanta didn't appreciate us too much and some of us were encouraged to leave at one time or another anyhow.

MILLER: Let me focus on that because when you look at Black colleges across the country there are similarities. One is that they have a tendency to be conservative. Even looking back today and looking at the things that Andrew Billingsley was writing even about the Black family, they were radical in terms of how to view Black culture and consciousness. Did you think that the ideas could be successful at an institution like Howard University?

HENDERSON: Yeah, I thought they would work in a number of schools, in fact. Those ideas that Billingsley had were meshing into what was the beginning of a national debate on the idea of a Black university and you all recall in . . . it was around 1969–'70 that there was a conference here at Howard and I saw the original proposal to the Mellon Foundation for funds for the Institute for the Advanced Study of the Arts and the Humanities and it quoted from the position paper I had presented at Idlewild.

MILLER: You left a position where you were chairman of the English department at Morehouse to come to Howard University and then you took on another administrative job as director of the Institute for the Arts and the Humanities. Did you have any reluctance about going back into administration?

HENDERSON: I was very reluctant about being the director of the Institute for the Arts and the Humanities because I had heard all kinds of stories . . . I didn't want to be a part of because I had my domestic life to look after. And I was very ambitious in an academic sense and I wanted to write. But I was part of the planning group that formed the Institute for the Arts and the Humanities for which Dr. Billingsley deserves a lot of credit. I think people have a tendency to forget who is responsible for what but what he did at Howard during his tenure was to set up a series of alternate force fields around these departments and a lot of people at Howard didn't like that. But if there is anything that approaches positive radicalism that was it. And I eventually acceded to the request to take the position. But it was offered to other people. The person that we really wanted was Hoyt Fuller. The others included James Turner and a Chicago artist . . . Murray DePillars. And, of course, another person who would have been ideal because of his energy and his scholarship was Houston Baker. But Houston at that time was sort of split between the offer from Howard and going to the University of Virginia. So they tapped me and the price was right, too. That helped. I'm not going to be reluctant to say that was one of the deciding factors. But I had had some experience with a small group. I felt that as long as the staff was small I could be effective. I don't have any particular administrative skills that would be useful in a large situation. So as long as it was small I felt I would try it.

MILLER: Well, you tried it and immediately a number of things occurred which affected two individuals. One is that you were able to bring Sterling Brown out of retirement, and you also brought Frank Marshall Davis whom you had been corresponding with from Hawaii to Howard. And these two writers are very important in terms of looking back at literature in the 1920s and 1930s. Could you comment about their work and also about what these men meant to you personally?

HENDERSON: Well, I'm always delighted to talk about Sterling and about Frank Marshall Davis. I was in touch with Frank Marshall Davis through my request for permission to quote from his work in "The Militant Black Writer" and he continued to write. He sent me Christmas cards and all that. You know, a lot of people didn't even know that he still existed and he's a very lively guy. And when I got a small grant from the administration I used that to bring Frank Marshall Davis here . . . He was a tremendous man . . . when he was young he looked like Joe Louis. He told all kinds of stories, very raunchy. That's why I like him. I remember the day I took Frank over to meet Sterling. Sterling was in Michael Winston's office—the old office in Moorland-Spingarn. So they sat down and started talking. Sterling Brown was setting up one of his anecdotes to tell and the anecdote was how long it took him to do such and such. Of course Sterling Brown is a brilliant man. So he said, "Steve was taping my life, Frank, and we've been here now for about four or five sittings and I'm just through the fourth grade and it's just taking a long time." So Frank said, "You must be a slow learner." So if you can imagine anybody calling Sterling Brown a slow learner. Understand? And Sterling had immense control. So he put this, what I'd call "Slim Greer" grin, on his face but he was boiling. But they got along well and respected one another. I learned a lot from Sterling. Sterling has been a model for me of what an academic can be, among a few others. In a very personal way some teachers have been to me sort of surrogate fathers. My father died when I was 15; my mother when I turned 18. I got certain aspects of my model from Sterling. I read Langston Hughes for the first time when I was about 19. And it was the first time I had seen blues as poetry on the page in "Shakespeare in Harlem." And then with Sterling the introduction was "The Blues As Folk Poetry" which he published in 1930. That's the first time I had seen anybody take the time to treat, intellectually, this folk material. And this folk material is very important to me . . . I suppose the basic thing that motivated me as far as language study was concerned was that when I was about 14 or 15 people coming from the "mainland," you understand, would be making fun of the way we talked. And when I went into the service people would call me geechee. My father was from Savannah, Ga. They would call me geechee. That was a pejorative term. And then I heard some real geechees talk and I said, what the hell, they sound like us so what's the problem!

MILLER: Along with Sterling Brown and Frank Marshall Davis are a number of other writers who came to Howard because of your work with the institute and the National Afro-American Writers Conferences. Let me preface a question about the conferences with a quote by Harold Cruse, in "The Crisis of the Negro Intellectual," where he writes about writers conferences: "During the first half of the 1960s there were no events that mirror the utter impoverishment of Negro creative intellectuals so much as those publicized glamorous meetings that go under the imposing title of Negro Writers Conferences. These literary conventions in black and tan are without a doubt the nearest thing imaginable to those congressional talk fetes in Washington, D.C. where every elected representative knows it's his bounden duty to be present for the record.

"But only for the record because no one has any intention of passing one bit of positive pending legislation. This is another way of saying that Negro Writers Conferences settle nothing, solve nothing, pose nothing, analyze nothing, plan nothing, create nothing, not even a decent new literary review which is the least any bunch of serious, self-respecting writers with a gripe ought to do." Cruse goes on to talk about a conference that John Killens organized. We know that Killens was also with the Institute for the Arts and the Humanities and he, along with yourself and Haki Madhubuti, were key people in the development of writers conferences at Howard. Looking at the ones which were held over the years—I think we had them in '74, '76, '77, '78 and '83—do you think they accomplished anything?

HENDERSON: I think they accomplished a great deal. Cruse—you know—looking back, I wish I had time to reread "The Crisis of the Negro Intellectual" but part of that, which I try to stay out of, is the fact that some writers during the '60s and '70s—particularly with a certain mandate coming out of the Black aesthetic—misunderstood what it is that they could do. Haki Madhubuti (Don Lee) said it very, very eloquently: "I ain't seen no metaphors stop a tank/I ain't seen no words kill." You understand? And that's a difference because people would come to a John Killens at a conference that deals with ideas and expect him to give a blueprint for the new Jerusalem. Well, of course, the problem becomes com-

pounded when you believe that you can do that. I think writers conferences, not only writers conferences but also scientific conferences where you're talking about nuclear physics, serve a purpose in addition to the solution of problems or the posing of questions. I think that what they do is allow people to interact . . . You're rejuvenated; you get an exposure to people's works in progress and things of that sort. With regard to these particular conferences, I'm distressed at the fact that they haven't been continued, although lip service had been given to them. But just think that of the mileage that we have with regard to the tapes—anybody can do a dozen Ph.Ds on these conference tapes. You even have a chance to get even with your enemies or people who insult you. You just put them on a conference panel between two of their opponents. But, you know, seriously, you get people together in all kinds of combinations. And you allow the students to see real-in-the-flesh Black writers. And they do discuss technique and things of that sort.

MILLER: When you look at some of the themes which were selected for the conferences do you think they were themes which enhanced one's appreciation of the literature at that particular time?

HENDERSON: I would think so because out of the writers conferences came other kinds of conferences. I am sorry that Ginny (Virginia Blandford) is not here because the institute was a small unit but everybody participated democratically. People say "secretary" with a slur on the word but our secretaries participated in the planning of the conferences and sometimes had good ideas. But in the particular case of Ginny, the idea of conferences flowered into a conference that dealt with Black women in liberation movements. That's one aspect of it. Another aspect of it is that we not only had these writers conferences but we had two conferences on folklore.

MILLER: Talking about folklore, I think one of the key things accomplished was the fact that it removed the isolation many individuals suffered. That means that many times people got into folklore because they had a particular interest, not realizing that there might be someone across the country with the same interest. Could you talk about some of the people who were involved in those folklore conferences?

HENDERSON: Well, the folklore conferences were in '75 and '76 and Gerald Davis is the person who first comes to mind who was working, I think part-time, at the Smithsonian. He has recently published his Ph.D. thesis as a book and it's on the structural analysis of the preaching style of selected ministers from the Bay area. And he deals with this material as literature. So James Early was here with the institute and he was interested in folklore. Early was one of the young radicals from the Atlanta community, also connected with the Institute of the Black World first and then the Institute for the Arts and the Humanities. But Early was connected with the Smithsonian and he told me that Jerry was interested in setting up some kind of organization. But he was there, and then there was a very elderly man . . . as I think of him now . . .

MILLER: Folklorist?

HENDERSON: Folklorist? Oh, yeah, William Faulkner. William Faulkner was there and a tremendous man. We have him on videotape. Worth Long was there. Long eventually got a Ph.D. He was one of the poets from the '60s and '70s and a field secretary for SNCC. He brought a railroad man—Anderson—a gandy dancer to one conference. We had authentic stuff. Leon Damas was there for the '76 conference, I think it was. Damas gave a paper on the decolonization of folklore. And Damas, of course to say the name Damas is to speak history. Just the name. He was here with us. And that's the marvelous part of having the opportunity to try these things. Even if they did not continue, the record is here. I just hope the record becomes more easily accessible to those who want to see it.

MILLER: The institute closed in June 1985 and I was wondering how much of that is because Andrew Billingsley is no longer here. Do you think that makes a difference or did the institute outgrow its usefulness?

HENDERSON: Well, it's hard to say because usefulness depends on budget. And you can have all the ideas in the world and if you don't have the budget you can't do anything with them. And for five or six years the institute was starved for lack of funds . . . I know that with Billingsley you had another kind of ideological framework. So maybe the cutting back and the retrenchment is part of the mood and the spirit coming out of the White House . . . into the Black House.

MILLER: There has been a lot of discussion about that period in terms of literature and art. But I would like you to comment on something which I find one en-

counters for instance when one examines the Harlem Renaissance. When does the Black arts movement begin and when does it end in terms of history? People have a tendency to use the term and just throw it out. But are there any events or things that one could point to and say this is the beginning of the Black arts movement, this is its demise? I know in an essay you cited the ending of *Black World* as a symbolic demise of the Black arts movement. I was wondering if you could elaborate on that.

HENDERSON: Well, it's problematical to me because the Black arts movement is a kind of New York term and almost a kind of New York concept. But I have always had problems with that. I know that probably the prestige, the visibility and the genius of LeRoi Jones (Amiri Baraka) did a lot to put this thing on the map nationally. But I know personally that there are people from the Umbra group, for example, who resent having the Black arts movement date from 1964 and Umbra's first publishing was 1962. And then you had a group here at Howard who called themselves the Howard Poets—Percy Johnston and others—and they were my original contact with this new spirit. I was a professor down at Richmond then. Then, of course, people resent the fact that they don't get exclusive entitlement to it. I've heard Baraka called a Johnny-come-lately. I've heard Haki Madhubuti called the same; the whole Chicago thing I've seen set up against the New York thing. I think what has influenced me has been Larry Neal's essay in *The Drama Review* and he dates the Black arts movement from 1964, the Black arts repertory theatre. I think, whatever your ideological persuasion, you have to give credit to the fact that one thing we had that we don't have today was that network of communication established by *Black World*. There would not have been any kind of vehicle for dissemination of these ideas if it hadn't been for such organizations.

MILLER: Within the Black arts movement there was one discussion which quite a number of people wrote about and debated and that was the whole idea of the Black aesthetic. Addison Gayle edited a volume of various essays on this. Looking back one sees a certain grappling in many of those essays in terms of trying to determine exactly what the Black aesthetic was. Was there some failure in terms of actually developing a critical framework by which we could assess and evaluate our arts?

HENDERSON: Well, I wouldn't really call it a failure. I think that the questions are still there. And I think you would find similar kinds of confusion and similar kinds of attempts when people examine the Harlem Renaissance or the Negritude movement. You have people who belong to various points on the political spectrum. I think I saw a typewritten program of the Newark Black Power Conference in 1967 and the Black aesthetic was on the agenda then. The whole business of the Black aesthetic is associated very intimately with Hoyt Fuller's attempt. In the January 1968 issue of *Negro Digest,* he corrals, condenses and synthesizes responses that 20-odd writers gave to a series of questions, including the purpose of Black art and such a thing as a Black aesthetic. And I think that it largely has been associated with him. But on that I used to say that the most intelligent thing that was said was said by Larry Neal. He said that there's no need to create a Black aesthetic. One already exists, and you start from here. And when he made that statement Larry Neal linked himself almost organically with people like Langston Hughes, Sterling Brown and James Weldon Johnson in his good days.

MILLER: In some of your recent essays I notice a change. You started to use the blues aesthetic. Is this shift from Black aesthetic to blues a clarification or is it something completely different?

HENDERSON: It's really the same thing and this is one of the things I love Larry for. Larry would jump on people who said that. Well, like Sonia Sanchez said it, and Haki said it—We ain't blue, we're Black—and Larry said in effect "Well, what is blacker than blues?" You see? So Baraka and Larry in particular, with his tremendous elegance and eloquence, made it possible to do all kinds of things. It's become very popular now to talk about blues. But a lot of people who talk about blues haven't really listened to many blues and they even correct the speech and the grammar of the people who sing the blues.

MILLER: In some of your essays you criticize a number of younger writers in terms of not building on certain traditions which were there and have been established by Langston Hughes and Sterling Brown . . . You mention them not having an appreciation for the blues.

HENDERSON: Well, it's not only blues. I think a lot of things have been said, enough has been said to reveal to any sensitive writer who is really ambitious that the Black experience is capable of supporting a multitude of epical expressions, and we have these epical expressions, some in the music . . . In Duke Ellington's music for example. And if you deal with

Langston Hughes in *Ask Your Mama* all kinds of possibilities are there. And if you put all of Sterling Brown's work together it's there. I think maybe Jay Wright would do some of that. Michael Harper has some of that. June Jordan has some of it.

MILLER: We've been receiving a number of new texts put out by Houston Baker and Henry Louis Gates, Jr. Do you see these books raising our understanding of literature?

HENDERSON: Well, I think what they're doing is a very vital service now that some of the misunderstanding has dissipated because they have to deal with some of the things that were dealt with in the '60s. And I think that what they are doing is translating into another language. They're translating the Black experience into another kind of language or they're applying a different critical vocabulary to the Black experience. And whether that's the best or most effective way to deal with it, I don't know, but it's still legitimate. And the struggle has to be maintained in all directions and all situations. So I don't have any problem with it. I have problems when people don't acknowledge their sources, when they don't acknowledge their indebtedness. They have a tendency to acknowledge the new French and Swiss and German critics but they don't acknowledge Sterling Brown and other people.

MILLER: How do you think Black literature should be taught in the classroom?

HENDERSON: I should defer to some of my distinguished colleagues who have had more recent and extended experience. Some of the things about myself that I needed to realize are these: When you read for yourself it's one thing and when you read to teach it's something else. And when you do research on specialized problems that's one thing. When you try to give in a semester or a year a kind of capsule summary and to get people to think about the way literature works, that's another thing. So I have had a lot of problems this semester, but I think I have worked out some of them and the key is the human voice, the Black voice, and if I were to teach a course on Black poetry again I would begin with Fannie Lou Hamer's "Songs That My Mother Taught Me." I mean that's the struggle. In the Black arts movement we talk about struggle and political dimension of struggle. Lerone Bennett in an article in a recent issue of *Ebony* says it well. One of the things we have to get rid of, he suggests, is this business of old Negroes and new Black folks. It's one struggle, and the people who are struggling now are standing on the shoulders of the Negroes of the past, in so many words. And that's what I think the crucial role of a teacher of any subject ought to be.

MILLER: One of the things many teachers today are faced with is the shortage of textbooks. You've spoken openly of doing another anthology similar to "Understanding the New Black Poetry." If you did compile another anthology what would you do differently?

HENDERSON: Well, I think I would have some of the same problems that I had with the first anthology except for the fact that the ideas and notions that I had in the first anthology are fairly well known so I wouldn't have to do that again. I think I'd take a page from Arnold Adoff. I'd get as many different poems as I could get but one of the problems that I think would plague me or anybody else would be just to find out who the new writers are. Because we don't have any national publication to provide a forum for the younger and the newer writers. So it would be a tremendous job.

MILLER: Talking about new writers and the future, my question is tied into something that the Institute of the Black World used to do and that was develop the idea of a Black agenda for a particular decade. As a former member of the Institute of the Black World and a person who is respected for his opinions on Black culture and education, what do you see as being on the Black agenda for the 1990s?

HENDERSON: That scares me. I think that, for myself, some of the same things that were always on the agenda, or should have been on the agenda, would still be on the agenda. In the Idlewild paper I talked about certain kinds of problems and I see those problems still taking form . . . the problem of discontinuous knowledge, the problem of neglected knowledge, the problem of inferiority feelings about Black culture and things of that sort. I still see those as issues that have to be addressed. My students today were talking about the persistence of stereotypes in the media. Well, that's the same thing that's been going on and on and on. I don't think it's going to be solved until you get certain kinds of political power . . . At the Institute of the Black World's meeting at Idlewild, they talked about everything because they realized the interconnectedness of things. And what strikes me is how optimistic, how energetic and how confident and believing everybody was. I think that is still there, that it is still a part of

what makes us tick—what makes any people who survive tick. But I would be foolhardy, I think, to venture anything else except to say that many of the same problems still exist, but in addition to that there are all kinds of new possibilities in terms of developing artistic formats. And they're all around us. I think you know more about them than I do. But if you just take the music video as an art form, a potential art form, they're all of those things that could be done. But I would like to see some of the problems that Lerone Bennett has been talking about, Leo Hansberry has been talking about, Sterling Brown has been talking about, James Weldon Johnson has been talking about, Leon Damas and others, I would like to see them just continued, to be addressed. The chief problem I see is that there's such a tremendous discontinuity between the '70s and the '80s and a student honestly doesn't know who Malcolm X was, who hasn't heard "We Shall Overcome," except indirectly. And that's a kind of gut level problem that has to be dealt with and I don't know how.

MICHAEL R. WINSTON

James Madison Nabrit, Jr.

One standard of greatness in a law school is its impact on law and society. By that measure the Howard law school holds special distinction in its leading role in the destruction of statutory segregation in the United States, arguably the most significant social reform of the twentieth century. Of the constellation of brilliant lawyers who participated in that remarkable effort, one of the brightest stars was James M. Nabrit, Jr., who was appointed to the law faculty in 1936 and served as Dean from 1958 until 1960, when he became President of Howard University.

James M. Nabrit Jr. was born in Atlanta, Georgia on September 24, 1900, the eldest of eight children of the Reverend James M. Nabrit and Gertrude West Nabrit.[1] The turn of the century was the high tide of the white supremacy movement in the South, when the legal status of Black Americans was at its lowest point since the Emancipation. When James Nabrit, Jr. was about ten years old he saw a black man beaten and burned to death by a white mob in Americus, Georgia because he had cheered too heartily when Jack Johnson, the famous prizefighter, defeated a white opponent, Jim Jeffries, at that time called "The Great White Hope". Not surprisingly, this made a deep impression on him.[2] When his father had a pastorate in Augusta, the young James Nabrit saw that whites had three public high schools, and blacks had none (which the Supreme Court of the United States had held did *not* "violate any of the privileges belonging to [Negroes] as citizens of the United States" in its decision in *Cumming v. Richmond County Board of Education*, 1899).

He entered the Academy of Morehouse College in 1915 to pursue his high school education. While there he was inspired by the school's impressive President, John Hope, its legendary Dean, Samuel H. "Big Boy" Archer, and by some of the outstanding teachers, including John W. Davis, Mordecai W. Johnson, and Benjamin Brawley. Continuing his education at Morehouse, he entered the College in 1919. An end on the football team and short stop on the baseball team, Nabrit was undefeated as a debater. Coached in debate by Benjamin Mays, he was also greatly influenced by E. Franklin Frazier, whose uninhibited thinking and sharp attacks on segregation were unusual, particularly in the South. While he was a Morehouse student Nabrit was arrested in downtown Atlanta for getting off a streetcar at the white exit rather than the colored exit. More and more, he saw that "something was wrong with the law."

During the summers he worked in a number of the northern and midwestern industrial plants opened for the first time to black employees by the manpower shortage of World War I, including the Jones and Laughlin Steel Mills in Pittsburgh and the Riggs Body Company in Detroit. In Washington and Chicago he also had the opportunity to meet a number of young black attorneys—George E. C. Hayes and Charles H. Houston in Washington, and J. Alston Atkins and Carter Wesley in Chicago. As a result of these associations, and his own ideas about his experiences in the South, he decided to pursue a career in law as a way to change things. "As soon as I found out what the law was, then I knew that was what I wanted. That was all I could think of, that's all I ever thought of studying."

After graduating from Morehouse with honors in 1923, James Nabrit entered the Northwestern University School of Law. There he was free of Atlanta's style of racial domination, but not from the common idea that the profession of law was for whites. When he first arrived at Northwestern, the white students drummed their feet to drown out his voice whenever he started to recite in class. In response, characteristically, he moved to the front row, and as he recalled later, "I would hold my hand up. The professor would be right there and he wouldn't pay any attention, but I kept on and after several days he stopped and said 'Yes?' I asked my question. And he said, 'As I was saying' and went on." Not long thereafter, the Dean, John H. Wigmore, gave all of the first year students an examination of 200 questions based on required reading. For the first time a student had 200 correct answers—James

M. Nabrit. After that result was posted, the heckling of Nabrit ceased. This result is all the more remarkable in light of the fact that he had no financial assistance and was working his way through law school. He went to law classes until three in the afternoon, then from 4 to 10 P.M Nabrit worked as a red cap at the railroad station, then studied much of the night for the next day's classes.[3] After two years of law school he went to teach English for a year at Leland College in Baker, Louisiana (1925–1926), then returned to Northwestern. Elected to the Order of the Coif because of his outstanding academic record, he graduated with honors, but unlike his white classmates, he received no offers for employment in the law. He returned to Leland to teach, 1927–1928, then was appointed Professor of English and Dean at Arkansas A.M. & N. College, Pine Bluff, Arkansas, 1928–1930.

Finally, in 1930 he was able to pursue his dream of a legal career by moving to Houston, Texas, where he joined J. Alston Atkins, a Yale Law graduate and Carter W. Wesley, a Northwestern Law graduate, to form the firm of Nabrit, Atkins and Wesley. Atkins and Wesley had practiced earlier in Oklahoma, successfully representing Indians and Negroes who had oil interests, and as a result had the means to start in Houston a newspaper, an insurance company and a real estate business. Atkins and Wesley handled the business and political side of the firm, and Nabrit was the principal litigator and manager of the firm's legal portfolio. Handling all sorts of cases, including many criminal cases, Nabrit developed a very broad and thriving practice, including representation of clients defending their rights to oil properties. As he later said, practicing in Houston at that time was in a "wild west" atmosphere, with large sums of money at stake, ruthlessness the norm, and whites as well as blacks heavily armed. Despite the business and legal success of the firm, Nabrit was dissatisfied. From his first days in Texas he was seeking ways to attack the various forms of segregation imposed on Negroes. He believed the key to removing many of the civic disabilities of the black population was access to the power of the ballot. In Texas, the "white primary" system was in force, in which no blacks could vote in the primary, but only in the general election, which was meaningless since the Democratic candidates selected in the primary would win overwhelmingly in the general election. While in Houston Nabrit began his relentless assault on the disfranchisement of blacks in Texas, starting with the case *Nixon v. Condon*, (1932).[4]

Meanwhile, Dean Charles H. Houston of the Howard Law School, William H. Hastie of the Howard faculty and the NAACP, and President Mordecai W. Johnson had written to him and talked with him for several years about leaving his Houston practice to join the Howard law faculty. Despite the success of his law practice, Nabrit was dissatisfied with the prospects for making headway on his most cherished projects in the civil rights field if he stayed in Texas. He had no access to the library of the Texas Bar Association, restricted to its white members, and no access to any other law libraries in the state. There was also the practical reality that his Houston law firm could only take on civil rights cases as a sideline. At Howard there was developing a unique mobilization of legal talent focused on attacking legally required and enforced racial domination in all of the former slave states.

Nabrit joined the Howard Law faculty in 1936, but his razor-sharp mind and administrative ability caused the University's President to appoint him Administrative Assistant to the President (1938–1939) in addition to his law school duties, and a year later, Secretary of Howard University, one of the top three administrative positions in the University at that time. What for others might have been a fatal distraction from professional objectives was simply a parallel responsibility for Nabrit. For the entire period 1938 to 1960, when he became President, he carried multiple responsibilities, teaching in the law school, serving as Director of Public Relations (1940–1950), Dean of the Law School (1958–1960) and full-time Secretary of the Board of Trustees and the University (1939–1960).

Upon his arrival at the Howard Law School, Professor Nabrit proposed to the faculty the adoption of a course in Civil Rights. Approved and offered for the fist time in 1937, it was the first such formal course in any law school in the United States. The purpose of the course was to "discover what the law was in respect to minorities in this area of civil rights; second, to develop techniques for raising constitutional questions in respect to disabilities affecting minorities . . . and third, to separate those disabilities for which legislative action would be required for their elimination."[5]

While many brilliant civil rights lawyers taught for a time at the Howard Law School, one of the striking things about Nabrit's career was that he remained at the core of the faculty for a quarter of a century, with a single-minded focus on destroying the legal foundations of segregation in the United States. As he later described the Howard Law School in the 1930's and 1940's, it was the intellectual anchor for an emerging system that he has called the "Howard Law School—NAACP Nexus." At that time the NAACP was understaffed, with Thurgood Marshall working with little direct legal assistance, and a network of cooperating attorneys in various jurisdictions. The Law School provided a reservoir of talent for legal research. Outstanding students, such as Spottswood Robinson, III, Oliver

Hill, Joseph Waddy and Robert L. Carter, were fully involved during their student years in cutting-edge legal research on constitutional issues. This connection with the NAACP's effort also gave the law faculty the opportunity to test new ideas in litigation. The Howard Law School was transformed by this new emphasis. "Our students," Nabrit later said, "who had formerly been just reciting and listening to the professor lecture, were now made to start drafting documents, drafting pleadings and procedure." The law school, he added "was focusing on the mechanism of pleading, trying cases and appealing cases."[6] As is now well known, a crucial part of this new system was the massive preparation for Supreme Court cases, in which the highlight was the Howard Law School Moot Court, on the Saturday before oral argument, in which Howard faculty, students, and alumni, along with invited members of the Washington Bar, would critique the arguments and propound questions that might be asked by the Justices of the Supreme Court.

The whole process created a new environment in the Howard Law School, embodying Charles Hamilton Houston's concept of the school as "The West Point of the Civil Rights Movement." According to Nabrit, an unsung hero of this whole development was President Mordecai W. Johnson, who not only "took in the significance of the law for us as a people," but put the resources of the University behind the effort. Considering the politically volatile potential of such cases as Nabrit's *Lane* v. *Wilson* (Oklahoma, 1939) and *Terry* v. *Adams,* (Texas, 1953), voting rights cases affecting the jurisdictions of Members of Congress involved in Howard's annual federal appropriation, the courage required to support the battalion of Howard civil rights lawyers, year after year, was formidable. The stimulus of working on civil rights cases, and the intense pressures of high level appellate litigation "was the centralizing factor in the development of the Howard Law School."[7] In those years Professor Nabrit not only participated in the major voting rights and education cases, but developed a set of theories in constitutional law that were more aggressive than the consensus views of the National Legal Committee of the NAACP and the NAACP Legal Defense Fund. He was, for example, an early advocate of the class-action suit as a strategy to leapfrog over Houston's earlier, protracted case-by-case approach. Most importantly, he was the boldest advocate of an attack on the constitutionality of segregation *per se.* Nabrit argued that in the so-called "equalization cases" attacking public school segregation, judicial relief tended to be temporary, since within a relatively short time southern jurisdictions created new inequalities, forcing the civil rights forces to be on an endless treadmill of litigation about unequal teachers' salaries, facilities, per-pupil expenditures, and so forth. Moreover, the Houston-Marshall equalization strategy left *Plessy* v. *Ferguson* intact as constitutional doctrine.

In what is perhaps his greatest case, *Bolling v. Sharpe*, (the District of Columbia school desegregation case decided along with *Brown* v. *Board of Education*, 1954) argued with his Howard colleague and friend, George E. C. Hayes. Nabrit did not maintain that segregated public schools in the District of Columbia were unconstitutional because they were unequal, but that racial segregation itself was unconstitutional. The system of segregated schools constituted, he said, a bill of attainder, since it deprived, as a class, black citizens of rights without due process of law. The prevailing view among civil rights lawyers at the time was that an attack on segregation *per se* was too risky because the Supreme Court might re-affirm *Plessy*, destroying in the eyes of many lawyers the gains made in the twenty years of litigation attacking inequality on the premises of the *Plessy* doctrine. Nabrit thought that any temporizing was playing into the hands of the segregationists.

To those who said it was foolish to put the white South's back to the wall, which might provoke widespread violence, Nabrit replied with his characteristic toughness: "Suppose it does? Shall the Negro child be required to wait for his constitutional rights until the white South is educated, industrialized, and ready to confer these rights on his children's children?" No concessions were to be made to "southern custom" and the Supreme Court's habit of deferring issues that might be politically and socially explosive: "Wherever the Negro is laboring under constitutional disabilities in the South, there is the best place to attack. The attack should be waged with the most devastating forces at hand. . . . The Supreme Court will have to worry over community attitudes. Let us worry over the problem of pressing for our civil rights. . . . Let the Supreme Court take the blame if it dares say to the entire world, 'Yes, democracy [in the United States] rests on a legalized caste system. Segregation of races is legal.' Make the Court choose. . . ."[8] In 1952 Nabrit closed his oral argument in *Bolling* v. *Sharpe*, with an eloquent statement of his position. The attorney for the defendants, Nabrit said, had "dwelt in the past upon the white man's burden, and he has seemed to feel that for some reason that exists today."

"It would appear to me," Nabrit continued, "that in 1952 the Negro should not be viewed as anybody's burden." Furthermore:

He is a citizen. He is performing his duties in peace and in war, and today, on the bloody hills of Korea, he is serving in an unsegregated war.

All we ask of this Court is that it say under the Constitution he is entitled to live and send his children to school in the District of Columbia unsegregated, with the children of his war comrades. That is simple. The Constitution gives him that right.

The basic argument here is one of liberty, and under liberty, under the due process clause, you cannot deal with it as you deal with equal protection of laws, because there you deal with it as a quantum of treatment, substantially equal.

You either have liberty or you do not. When liberty is interfered with by the state, it has to be justified, and you cannot justify it by saying that we only took a little liberty. You justify it by the reasonableness of the taking.

We submit that in this case, in the heart of the nation's capital, in the capital of democracy, in the capital of the free world, there is no place for a segregated school system. This country cannot afford it, and the Constitution does not permit it and the statutes of Congress do not authorize it.[9]

Although he was best known in the legal profession for his brilliant work as a civil rights lawyer in such landmark cases as *Lane* v. *Wilson*, *Sweatt* v. *Painter*, and *Bolling* v. *Sharpe*, for many Howard Law students Professor Nabrit was simply the best teacher they had ever encountered. Genial, easy to talk to, he was also demanding, skeptical, and breath-takingly analytical. He could cut through a case, an issue, or student filibuster with awesome speed and precision. "With Nabrit," one law student said, "you don't simply learn law, you argue it."[10] Students were also impressed by Nabrit's great versatility. He was a member of the President's Committee on Government Contracts during the Eisenhower administration, a participant in the International Labor Conferences in Geneva, Switzerland, and Legal Adviser to the Governor of the Virgin Islands on the Reorganization of the Executive Branch.

By the time Dr. Nabrit became Dean of the Law School in 1958, many thought of him as embodying the best in the legal profession. He had also shown how intellect, harnessed to firm purpose and disciplined inquiry could reshape the law, and through it the operation of society itself. In 1960, at the end of his deanship, the graduating seniors of the law school dedicated their section of the yearbook to James M. Nabrit, Jr. The students wrote that just as he was an "indispensable leader of society," his qualities of "humility, good humour, sincerity, competence, and friendliness" had made him "just as indispensable" to his students.

Dean Nabrit's elevation to the Presidency of Howard University opened a new era at Howard. He was President during one of the most turbulent periods of United States history. Swept into the multiplying tensions generated by white backlash against the civil rights, black identity and black power movements, colleges and universities had to cope also with the growing anti-war and women's rights movements. Always a place where controversies could thrive because of its many national and international constituencies, Howard also became during Dr. Nabrit's Presidency a national center of protest thought and student upheaval. With his usual aplomb and frankness, he met the roughest days of his career. Students and faculty alike saw once again his courage under fire. During the time he served as U.S. Permanent Deputy Representative to the United Nations, he gave the commencement address at Howard, June 3, 1966. Despite the enormous pressures generated by the sudden popularity of anti-integration leaders such as Malcolm X, President Nabrit insisted on holding to his lifelong faith in the United States Constitution and the ideals of democracy. To the rising voices of the black nationalists and those who would abandon the goal of achieving an integrated society based on the Constitution, he said:

Frustrated and bitter, disillusioned and skeptical men do foolish and violent things. But having fought all my life for the rights and privileges of an American citizen, which I am, and for the rights to which all are entitled under the Constitution of the United States, which they are, I would not give up hope for their achievement at the very time when the first clear hopeful view of their attainment comes into sight—I would not at the very moment when integration begins to appear on the horizon, turn my back on this revolutionary struggle and steep myself in racial hatred and loneliness and misery in a chauvinistic embrace of black nationalism. . . . Let us not apologize either for uniformed or ill-advised Negroes who do feel hatred, or frustration or pursue black nationalistic myths—for if the white man who is richer, better educated, with more political power—who enjoys to the limits all of his constitutional rights can produce Ku Klux Klansmen, John Birchites, and Rockwell Nazis, why cannot we be permitted to have our share of the lunatic fringe and of aberrant groups too? As for me, I not only will not apologize for them, but I do not even intend to engage in any more criticism of them than I do with respect to any group with which I personally do not agree.

When he retired as President of the University on June 30, 1969, James Madison Nabrit, Jr., ended a brilliant career of service to his country. Lawyer, dean, diplomat, and university president, he has been one of the shapers of a new American society in the twentieth century. He continues to this day, at the age of 94, to watch with enthusiasm the work of Howard University, and especially his beloved Law School, where he was able to pursue his dream of Equal Justice Under Law for all Americans.

Notes

[1] Basic biographical data for this article was drawn from the James M. Nabrit, Jr. biographical file, Moorland-Spingarn Research Center, Howard University. For assistance in the University Archives, I am indebted to Dr. Clifford L. Muse, Jr., University Archivist, and for assistance in the Library Division of the Research Center, Mrs. Avril Madison, Reference Librarian.

[2] Richard Kluger, *Simple Justice: The History of Brown v. Board of Education and Black America's Struggle for Equality* (New York: Alfred A. Knopf, 1976), p. 518.

[3] James M. Nabrit, Jr., Interview with Michael R. Winston, Washington, D.C., September 25, 1979.

[4] For the significant role of the Nabrit, Atkins and Wesley firm in the Texas disfranchisement cases, see August Meier and Elliott Rudwick, "Attorneys in Black and White: A Case Study of Race Relations with the NAACP" in Meier and Rudwick, *Along the Color Line: Explorations in the Black Experience* (Urbana: University of Illinois Press, 1976), pp. 147–154.

[5] James M. Nabrit, Jr., *Cases and Materials on Civil Rights*, quoted in J. Clay Smith, Jr., *Emancipation: The Making of the Black Lawyer, 1844–1944* (Philadelphia: University of Pennsylvania Press, 1993), p. 51.

[6] James M. Nabrit, Jr., Interview with Michael R. Winston, October 11, 1979.

[7] *Ibid.*

[8] James M. Nabrit, Jr., quoted in Kluger, *op. cit.*, pp. 536–537.

[9] James M. Nabrit, Jr., Oral Argument, *Spottswood Thomas Bolling, et al., vs. C. Melvin Sharpe et al.* before the Supreme Court of the United States, December 10, 1952, in *Argument: The Oral Argument Before the Supreme Court in Brown v. Board of Education of Topeka, 1952–55*, edited by Leon Friedman (New York: Chelsea House Publishers, 1969), p. 142.

[10] "James M. Nabrit, Jr." in "Six Howard Professors" [Nabrit, Charles Drew, Sterling Brown, E. Franklin Frazier, Rayford W. Logan and Alain Locke] in *Our World* (January, 1950), p. 29.

CHAPTER SEVEN

A Disciplined Response

If you have run with men and they
have wearied you, how can you
compete with horses?

Jeremiah 12:5

READING SELECTIONS

STEPHEN JAY GOULD

Curveball

The Bell Curve, by Richard J. Herrnstein and Charles Murray (Free Press; $30), subtitled *Intelligence and Class Structure in American Life,* provides a superb and unusual opportunity to gain insight into the meaning of experiment as a method in science. The primary desideratum in all experiments is reduction of confusing variables: we bring all the buzzing and blooming confusion of the external world into our laboratories and, holding all else constant in our artificial simplicity, try to vary just one potential factor at a time. But many subjects defy the use of such an experimental method—particularly most social phenomena—because importation into the laboratory destroys the subject of the investigation, and then we must yearn for simplifying guides in nature. If the external world occasionally obliges by holding some crucial factors constant for us, we can only offer thanks for this natural boost to understanding.

So, when a book garners as much attention as *The Bell Curve,* we wish to know the causes. One might suspect the content itself—a startlingly new idea, or an old suspicion newly verified by persuasive data—but the reason might also be social acceptability, or even just plain hype. *The Bell Curve,* with its claims and supposed documentation that race and class differences are largely caused by genetic factors and are therefore essentially immutable, contains no new arguments and presents no compelling data to support its anachronistic social Darwinism, so I can only conclude that its success in winning attention must reflect the depressing temper of our time—a historical moment of unprecedented ungenerosity, when a mood for slashing social programs can be powerfully abetted by an argument that beneficiaries cannot be helped, owing to inborn cognitive limits expressed as low IQ scores.

Stephen Jay Gould, "Curveball," first published in THE NEW YORKER, November 28, 1994. Reprinted by permission of the author.

The Bell Curve rests on two distinctly different but sequential arguments, which together encompass the classic corpus of biological determinism as a social philosophy. The first argument rehashes the tenets of social Darwinism as it was originally constituted. "Social Darwinism" has often been used as a general term for any evolutionary argument about the biological basis of human differences, but the initial nineteenth-century meaning referred to a specific theory of class stratification within industrial societies, and particularly to the idea that there was a permanently poor underclass consisting of genetically inferior people who had precipitated down into their inevitable fate. The theory arose from a paradox of egalitarianism: as long as people remain on top of the social heap by accident of a noble name or parental wealth, and as long as members of despised castes cannot rise no matter what their talents, social stratification will not reflect intellectual merit, and brilliance will be distributed across all classes; but when true equality of opportunity is attained smart people rise and the lower classes become rigid, retaining only the intellectually incompetent.

This argument has attracted a variety of twentieth-century champions, including the Stanford psychologist Lewis M. Terman, who imported Alfred Binet's original test from France, developed the Stanford-Binet IQ test, and gave a hereditarian interpretation to the results (one that Binet had vigorously rejected in developing this style of test); Prime Minister Lee Kuan Yew of Singapore, who tried to institute a eugenics program of rewarding well-educated women for higher birth rates; and Richard Herrnstein, a co-author of *The Bell Curve* and also the author of a 1971 *Atlantic Monthly* article that presented the same argument without the documentation. The general claim is neither uninteresting nor illogical, but it does require the validity of four shaky premises, all asserted (but hardly discussed or defended) by Herrnstein and Murray. Intelligence, in their formulation, must be depictable as a single number, capable of ranking people in linear order, genetically based, and effectively immutable. If any of these premises are false, their entire argument collapses. For example, if all are true except immutability, then programs for early intervention in education might work to boost IQ permanently, just as a pair of eyeglasses may correct a genetic defect in vision. The central argument of *The Bell Curve* fails because most of the premises are false.

Herrnstein and Murray's second claim, the lightning rod for most commentary, extends the argument for innate cognitive stratification to a claim that racial differences in IQ are mostly determined by genetic causes—small difference for Asian superiority over Caucasian, but large for Caucasians over people of African descent. This argument is as old as the study of race, and is most surely fallacious. The last generation's discussion centered on Arthur Jensen's 1980 book *Bias in Mental Testing* (far more elaborate and varied than anything presented in *The Bell Curve*, and therefore still a better source for grasping the argument and its problems), and on the cranky advocacy of William Shockley, a Nobel Prize-winning physicist. The central fallacy in using the substantial heritability of within-group IQ (among whites, for example) as an explanation of average differences between groups (whites versus blacks, for example) is now well known and acknowledged by all, including Herrnstein and Murray, but deserves a restatement by example. Take a trait that is far more heritable than anyone has ever claimed IQ to be but is politically uncontroversial—body height. Suppose that I measured the heights of adult males in a poor Indian village beset with nutritional deprivation, and suppose the average height of adult males is five feet six inches. Heritability within the village is high, which is to say that tall fathers (they may average five feet eight inches) tend to have tall sons, while short fathers (five feet four inches on average) tend to have short sons. But this high heritability within the village does not mean that better nutrition might not raise average height to five feet ten inches in a few generations. Similarly, the well-documented fifteen-point average difference in IQ between blacks and whites in America, with substantial heritability of IQ in family lines within each group, permits no automatic conclusion that truly equal opportunity might not raise the black average enough to equal or surpass the white mean.

Disturbing as I find the anachronism of *The Bell Curve*, I am even more distressed by its pervasive disingenuousness. The authors omit facts, misuse statistical methods, and seem unwilling to admit the consequences of their own words.

The ocean of publicity that has engulfed *The Bell Curve* has a basis in what Murray and Herrnstein, in an article in *The New Republic* last month [Oct. 31, 1994], call "the flashpoint of intelligence as a public topic: the question of genetic differences between the races." And yet, since the day of the book's publication, Murray (Herrnstein died a month before the book appeared) has been temporizing, and denying that race is an important subject in the book at all; he blames the press for unfairly fanning these particular flames. In *The New Republic* he and Herrnstein wrote, "Here is what we hope will be our contribution to the discussion. We put it in italics; if we could, we would put it in neon lights: *The answer doesn't much matter.*"

Fair enough, in the narrow sense that any individual may be a rarely brilliant member of an averagely dumb group (and therefore not subject to judgment by the group mean), but Murray cannot deny that *The Bell Curve* treats race as one of two major topics, with each given about equal space; nor can he pretend that strongly stated claims about group differences have no political impact in a society obsessed with the meanings and consequences of ethnicity. The very first sentence of *The Bell Curve*'s preface acknowledges that the book treats the two subjects equally: "This book is about differences in intellectual capacity among people and groups and what those differences mean for America's future." And Murray and Herrnstein's *New Republic* article begins by identifying racial differences as the key subject of interest: "The private dialogue about race in America is far different from the public one."

Furthermore, Herrnstein and Murray know and acknowledge the critique of extending the substantial heritability of within-group IQ to explain differences between groups, so they must construct an admittedly circumstantial case for attributing most of the black-white mean difference to irrevocable genetics—while properly stressing that the average difference doesn't help in judging any particular person, because so many individual blacks score above the white mean in IQ. Quite apart from the rhetorical dubiety of this old ploy in a shopworn genre—"Some of my best friends are Group X"—Herrnstein and Murray violate fairness by converting a complex case that can yield only agnosticism into a biased brief for permanent and heritable difference. They impose this spin by turning every straw on their side into an oak, while mentioning but downplaying the strong circumstantial case for substantial malleability and little average genetic difference. This case includes such evidence as impressive IQ scores for poor black children adopted into affluent and intellectual homes; average IQ increases in some nations since the Second World War equal to the entire fifteen-point difference now separating blacks and whites in America; and failure to find any cognitive differences between two cohorts of children born out of wedlock to German women, reared in Germany as Germans, but fathered by black and white American soldiers.

The Bell Curve is even more disingenuous in its argument than in its obfuscation about race. The book is a rhetorical masterpiece of scientism, and it benefits from the particular kind of fear that numbers impose on non-professional commentators. It runs to 845 pages, including more than a hundred pages of appendixes filled with figures. So their text looks complicated, and reviewers shy away with a knee-jerk claim that, while they suspect fallacies of argument, they really cannot judge. In the same issue of *The New Republic* as Murray and Herrnstein's article, Mickey Kaus writes, "As a lay reader of 'The Bell Curve,' I am unable to judge fairly," and Leon Wieseltier adds, "Murray, too, is hiding the hardness of his politics behind the hardness of his science. And his science, for all I know, is soft. . . . Or so I imagine. I am not a scientist. I know nothing about psychometrics." And Peter Passell, in the *Times*: "But this reviewer is not a biologist, and will leave the argument to experts."

The book is in fact extraordinarily one-dimensional. It makes no attempt to survey the range of available data, and pays astonishingly little attention to the rich and informative history of its contentious subject. (One can only recall Santayana's dictum, now a cliché of intellectual life: "Those who cannot remember the past are condemned to repeat it.") Virtually all the analysis rests on a single technique applied to a single set of data—probably done in one computer run. (I do agree that the authors have used more appropriate technique and the best source of information. Still, claims as broad as those advanced in *The Bell Curve* simply cannot be properly defended—that is, either supported or denied—by such a restricted approach.) The blatant errors and inadequacies of *The Bell Curve* could be picked up by lay reviewers if only they would not let themselves be frightened by numbers—for Herrnstein and Murray do write clearly, and their mistakes are both patent and accessible.

While disclaiming his own ability to judge, Mickey Kaus, in *The New Republic*, does correctly identify the authors' first two claims that are absolutely essential "to make the pessimistic 'ethnic difference' argument work": "1) that there is a single, general measure of mental ability; 2) that the IQ tests that purport to measure this ability . . . aren't culturally biased."

Nothing in *The Bell Curve* angered me more than the authors' failure to supply any justification for their central claim, the sine qua non of their entire argument: that the number known as *g*, the celebrated "general factor" of intelligence, first identified by the British psychologist Charles Spearman, in 1904, captures a real property in the head. Murray and Herrnstein simply declare that the issue has been decided, as in this passage from their *New Republic* article: "Among the experts, it is by now beyond much technical dispute that there is such a thing as a general factor of cognitive ability on which human beings differ and that this general factor is measured reasonably well by a variety of standardized tests, best of all by IQ tests designed for that purpose." Such a statement represents extraordinary obfuscation, achievable only if one takes "expert" to mean "that group of psychometricians working in the tradition of *g* and its avatar IQ." The authors even admit that there are three major schools of psychometric interpretation and that only one supports their view of *g* and IQ.

But this issue cannot be decided, or even understood, without discussing the key and only rationale that has maintained *g* since Spearman invented it: factor analysis. The fact that Herrnstein and Murray barely mention the factor-analytic argument forms a central indictment of *The Bell Curve* and is an illustration of its vacuousness. How can the authors base an 800-page book on a claim for the reality of IQ as measuring a genuine, and largely genetic, general cognitive ability—and then hardly discuss, either pro or con, the theoretical basis for their certainty?

Admittedly, factor analysis is a difficult mathematical subject, but it can be explained to lay readers with a geometrical formulation developed by L. L. Thurstone, an American psychologist, in the 1930s and used by me in a full chapter on factor analysis in my 1981 book *The Mismeasure of Man*. A few paragraphs cannot suffice for adequate explanation, so, although I offer some sketchy hints below, readers should not question their own IQs if the topic still seems arcane.

In brief, a person's performance on various mental tests tends to be positively correlated—that is, if you do well on one kind of test, you tend to do well on the other kinds. This is scarcely surprising, and is subject to interpretation that is either purely genetic (that an innate thing in the head boosts all performances) or purely environmental (that good books and good childhood nutrition boost all performances); the positive correlations in themselves say nothing about causes. The results of these tests can be plotted on a multidimensional graph with an axis for each test. Spearman used factor analysis to find a single dimension—which he called *g*—that best identifies the common factor behind positive correlations among the tests. But Thurstone later showed that *g* could be made to disappear by simply rotating the dimensions to different positions. In one rotation Thurstone placed the dimensions near the most widely separated attributes among the tests, thus giving rise to the theory of multiple intelligences (verbal, mathematical, spatial, etc., with no overarching g). This theory (which I support) has been advocated by many prominent psychometricians, including J. P. Guilford, in the 1950s, and Howard Gardner today. In this perspective g cannot have inherent reality, for it emerges in one form of mathematical representation for correlations among tests and disappears (or greatly attenuates) in other forms, which are entirely equivalent in amount of information explained. In any case, you can't grasp the issue at all without a clear exposition of factor analysis—and *The Bell Curve* cops out on this central concept.

As for Kaus's second issue, cultural bias, the presentation of it in *The Bell Curve* matches Arthur Jensen's and that of other hereditarians, in confusing a technical (and proper) meaning of "bias" (I call it "S-bias," for "statistical") with the entirely different vernacular concept (I call it "V-bias") that provokes popular debate. All these authors swear up and down (and I agree with them completely) that the tests are not biased—in the statistician's definition. Lack of S-bias means that the same score, when it is achieved by members of different groups, predicts the same thing; that is, a black person and a white person with identical scores will have the same probabilities for doing anything that IQ is supposed to predict.

But V-bias, the source of public concern, embodies an entirely different issue, which, unfortunately, uses the same word. The public wants to know whether blacks average 85 and whites 100 because society treats blacks unfairly—that is, whether lower black scores record biases in this social sense. And this crucial question (to which we do not know the answer) cannot be addressed by a demonstration that S-bias doesn't exist, which is the only issue analyzed, however correctly, in *The Bell Curve*.

The book is also suspect in its use of statistics. As I mentioned, virtually all its data derive from one analysis—a plotting, by a technique called multiple regression, of social behaviors that agitate us, such as crime, unemployment, and births out of wedlock (known as dependent variables), against both IQ and parental sociometric status (known as independent variables). The authors first hold IQ constant and consider the relationship of social behaviors to parental socioeconomic status. They then hold socioeconomic status constant and consider the relationship of the same social behaviors to IQ. In general, they find a higher correlation with IQ than with socioeconomic status; for example, people with low IQ are more likely to drop out of high

school than people whose parents have low socioeconomic status.

But such analyses must engage two issues—the form and the strength of the relationship—and Herrnstein and Murray discuss only the issue that seems to support their viewpoint, while virtually ignoring (and in one key passage almost willful hiding) the other.

Their numerous graphs present only the form of the relationships; that is, they draw the regression curves of their variables against IQ and parental socioeconomic status. But, in violation of all statistical norms that I've ever learned, they plot only the regression curve and do not show the scatter of variation around the curve, so their graphs do not show anything about the strength of the relationships—that is, the amount of variation in social factors explained by IQ and socioeconomic status. Indeed, almost all their relationships are weak: very little of the variation in social factors is explained by either independent variable (though the form of this small amount of explanation does lie in their favored direction). In short, their own data indicate that IQ is not a major factor in determining variation in nearly all the social behaviors they study—and so their conclusions collapse, or at least become so greatly attenuated that their pessimism and conservative social agenda gain no significant support.

Herrnstein and Murray actually admit as much in one crucial passage, but then they hide the pattern. They write, "It [cognitive ability] almost always explains less than 20 percent of the variance, to use the statistician's term, usually less than 10 percent and often less than 5 percent. What this means in English is that you cannot predict what a given person will do from his IQ score. . . . On the other hand, despite the low association at the individual level, large differences in social behavior separate groups of people when the groups differ intellectually on the average." Despite this disclaimer, their remarkable next sentence makes a strong causal claim. "We will argue that intelligence itself, not just its correlation with socioeconomic status, is responsible for these group differences." But a few percent of statistical determination is not causal explanation. And the case is even worse for their key genetic argument, since they claim a heritability of about 60 percent for IQ, so to isolate the strength of genetic determination by Herrnstein and Murray's own criteria you must nearly halve even the few percent they claim to explain.

My charge of disingenuousness receives its strongest affirmation in a sentence tucked away on the first page of Appendix 4, page 593: the authors state, "In the text, we do not refer to the usual measure of goodness of fit for multiple regressions, R^2, but they are presented here for the cross-sectional analyses." Now, why would they exclude from the text, and relegate to an appendix that very few people will read, or even consult, a number that, by their own admission, is "the usual measure of goodness of fit"? I can only conclude that they did not choose to admit in the main text the extreme weakness of their vaunted relationships.

Herrnstein and Murray's correlation coefficients are generally low enough by themselves to inspire lack of confidence. (Correlation coefficients measure the strength of linear relationships between variables; the positive values run from 0.0 for no relationship to 1.0 for perfect linear relationship.) Although low figures are not atypical for large social-science surveys involving many variables, most of Herrnstein and Murray's correlations are very weak—often in the 0.2 to 0.4 range. Now, 0.4 may sound respectably strong, but—and this is the key point—R^2 is the square of the correlation coefficient, and the square of a number between zero and one is less than the number itself, so a 0.4 correlation yields an R-squared of only .16. In Appendix 4, then, one discovers that the vast majority of the conventional measures of R^2, excluded from the main body of the text, are less than 0.1.

These very low values of R^2 expose the true weakness, in any meaningful vernacular sense, of nearly all the relationships that form the meat of *The Bell Curve*.

Like so many conservative ideologues who rail against the largely bogus ogre of suffocating political correctness, Herrnstein and Murray claim that they only want a hearing for unpopular views so that truth will out. And here, for once, I agree entirely. As a card-carrying First Amendment (near) absolutist, I applaud the publication of unpopular views that some people consider dangerous. I am delighted that *The Bell Curve* was written—so that its errors could be exposed, for Herrnstein and Murray are right to point out the difference between public and private agendas on race, and we must struggle to make an impact on the private agendas as well. But *The Bell Curve* is scarcely an academic treatise in social theory and population genetics. It is a manifesto of conservative ideology; the book's inadequate and biased treatment of data displays its primary purpose—advocacy. The text evokes the dreary and scary drumbeat of claims associated with conservative think tanks: reduction or elimination of welfare, ending or sharply curtailing affirmative action in schools and workplaces, cutting back Head Start and other forms of preschool education, trimming programs for the slowest learners and applying those funds to the gifted. (I would love to see

more attention paid to talented students, but not at this cruel price.)

The penultimate chapter presents an apocalyptic vision of a society with a growing underclass permanently mired in the inevitable sloth of their low IQs. They will take over our city centers, keep having illegitimate babies (for many are too stupid to practice birth control), and ultimately require a kind of custodial state, more to keep them in check—and out of high IQ neighborhoods—than to realize any hope of amelioration, which low IQ makes impossible in any case. Herrnstein and Murray actually write, "In short, by *custodial state*, we have in mind a high-tech and more lavish version of the Indian reservation for some substantial minority of the nation's population, while the rest of America tries to go about its business."

The final chapter tries to suggest an alternative, but I have never read anything more grotesquely inadequate. Herrnstein and Murray yearn romantically for the good old days of towns and neighborhoods where all people could be given tasks of value, and self-esteem could be found for people on all steps of the IQ hierarchy (so Forrest Gump might collect clothing for the church raffle, while Mr. Murray and the other bright ones do the planning and keep the accounts—they have forgotten about the town Jew and the dwellers on the other side of the tracks in many of these idyllic villages). I do believe in this concept of neighborhood, and I will fight for its return. I grew up in such a place in Queens. But can anyone seriously find solutions for (rather than important palliatives of) our social ills therein?

However, if Herrnstein and Murray are wrong, and IQ represents not an immutable thing in the head, grading human beings on a single scale of general capacity with large numbers of custodial incompetents at the bottom, then the model that generates their gloomy vision collapses, and the wonderful variousness of human abilities, properly nurtured, reemerges. We must fight the doctrine of *The Bell Curve* both because it is wrong and because it will, if activated, cut off all possibility of proper nurturance for everyone's intelligence. Of course, we cannot all be rocket scientists or brain surgeons, but those who can't might be rock musicians or professional athletes (and gain far more social prestige and salary thereby), while others will indeed serve by standing and waiting.

I closed my chapter in *The Mismeasure of Man* on the unreality of *g* and the fallacy of regarding intelligence as a single-scaled, innate thing in the head with a marvelous quotation from John Stuart Mill, well worth repeating:

The tendency has always been strong to believe that whatever received a name must be an entity or being, having an independent existence of its own, and if no real entity answering to the name could be found, men did not for that reason suppose that none existed, but imagined that it was something particularly abstruse and mysterious.

How strange that we would let a single and false number divide us, when evolution has united all people in the recency of our common ancestry—thus undergirding with a shared humanity that infinite variety which custom can never stale. *E pluribus unum.*

LEE BROWN

IQ, Nurture, and the Realization of Excellence

The Bell Curve: Intelligence and Class Structure in American Life, by Richard J. Herrnstein and Charles Murray is a recent addition to decades of efforts to employ the honorific status of science to demonstrate the purported inherent superiority of people of European descent over people of African descent. Concerning the categories, people of European descent have an ancestry that is tied to Europe and are characterized as caucasian or white. People of African descent have an ancestry that is tied to Africa and are characterized as negroid or black.

During the latter half of the 19th Century, noted hereditarins used cranial studies to support racialism and to confirm the racist ideology that caucasians are by nature superior to negroids. Negroids were viewed as the least evolved of all humans, and they were viewed as mentally and morally inferior to caucasians. Since being moral was tied to being adept at abstract reasoning, and since caucasians were viewed as intellectually superior to negroids, caucasians were characterized as morally superior to negroids. Given such a characterization, caucasians were viewed as having the moral authority to oppress and abuse non-caucasians. The cranial studies were offered as proof that caucasians were by nature—via evolution—intellectually superior to all others. Brains of caucasians were claimed to be larger than those of others, and larger brains were associated with higher intelligence. In brief, those with the largest heads were characterized as the most evolved. The results of such studies were used also to justify sexism.

The combination of racism and sexism gave Negroid women a horrendously dehumanizing status. Cranial studies were later dismissed as unscientific and disreputable: the studies were rigged, and the interpretations of the data were dishonest.

Like previous efforts, *The Bell Curve* employs science to support race-based intellectual and moral elitism. Unlike previous efforts, *The Bell Curve* uses state of the art statistical research to ground its message. *The Bell Curve* is a particularly dangerous work, because it supports both racialism and racism, and because its claims are grounded upon well documented statistics. The work suggests that in the arena where humans are thought to be most evolved—the capacity to reason abstractly—blacks are biologically inferior to whites, and the nature of the inferiority is alleged to be such that nurture is not capable of accounting for or ameliorating the claimed deficiencies.

Stephen J. Gould's "Curveball"[1] shows significant short-comings in the findings of Richard J. Herrnstein and Charles Murray. Gould argues that *The Bell Curve*'s conclusions are not warranted by the data upon which they are claimed to have been derived. Gould also aptly points out that IQ tests, as a measure of native intelligence, is not a reliable predictor of the attainment of intellectual excellence. With rare exception, successes and failures in life do not turn on IQ. Except in cases of obvious dysfunctionality, one's ability to achieve academic or professional excellence is not determined by the features that are measured by IQ tests. He argues that nurture is significantly more important than native capacities. Gould's point is that we should focus upon the positive contributions that nurture makes upon the abilities of people to excel in arenas that nature may leave wanting—not all great basketball players are over 6'4" tall. Just as we have corrective lenses and hearing aids, we have educational institutions and mentors. In keeping with this observation, one's successes and failures are influenced more by the quality of one's nurture and by fate than by any other factors in one's life. Little can be done about fate, but one typically has significant control over what one learns and how one uses what one learns.

Concerning nurture, a college education is arguably the most significant investment one can make in oneself. The knowledge and tools that one acquires in college will determine the quality of one's future life experiences. The broader and deeper one's education, the richer will be one's quality of life. Society requires

Lee Brown, "IQ, Nurture, and the Realization of Excellence." Reprinted by permission of the author.

[1]Gould's essay first appeared in *The New Yorker,* November 28, 1994.

a multitude of skills and talents in order to flourish. An individual's ability to contribute in any given arena depends upon a range of characteristics: determination and courage, educational preparation, personality and character, physical aptitude, psychological disposition and fit, and a willingness and capacity to adapt. IQ is not a factor for any of the aforementioned characteristics. Nurture is a factor in all of them. Moreover, if one were to look at the lives of those purported to be geniuses, one will see tremendous dedications to learning. Most of genius is sweat, and those who think otherwise have little sensitivity to what is required for achieving excellence. Alexander Pushkin, Albert Einstein, Marian Anderson, Paul Robeson, Shaka Zulu, Wolfgang A. Mozart, Matthew Henson, Louis Leakey, George Washington Carver, Leonardo da Vinci, Jacob Lawrence, Sitting Bull, Osceola, Red Beard, Barbara Jordan, Alain Locke, Frederick Douglass, Mohandas Ghandi, Thurgood Marshall, W. E. B. Du Bois, Richard Hunt, Charles Drew, and Andrew Hill are noted for having burned the midnight oil. Both Kathleen Battle and Wynton Marsalis have mentors.

For broader perspectives on these issues see: Steven Fraser, 1995: *The Bell Curve Wars: Race, Intelligence and the Future of America,* (New York: Basic Books, 1995); Richard J. Herrnstein and Charles Murray, *The Bell Curve: Intelligence and Class Structure in American Life,* (New York: Free Press, 1994).

STEPHEN JAY GOULD

American Polygeny and Craniometry before Darwin: Blacks and Indians as Separate, Inferior Species

Order is Heaven's first law; and, this confessed,
Some are, and must be, greater than the rest.
ALEXANDER POPE, *Essay on Man (1733)*

Appeals to reason or to the nature of the universe have been used throughout history to enshrine existing hierarchies as proper and inevitable. The hierarchies rarely endure for more than a few generations, but the arguments, refurbished for the next round of social institutions, cycle endlessly.

The catalogue of justifications based on nature traverses a range of possibilities: elaborate analogies between rulers and a hierarchy of subordinate classes with the central earth of Ptolemaic astronomy and a ranked order of heavenly bodies circling around it; or appeals to the universal order of a "great chain of being," ranging in a single series from amoebae to God, and including near its apex a graded series of human races and classes. To quote Alexander Pope again:

> Without this just gradation, could they be
> Subjected, these to those, or all to thee?
>
> From Nature's chain whatever link you strike,
> Tenth, or ten thousandth, breaks the chain alike.

The humblest, as well as the greatest, play their part in preserving the continuity of universal order; all occupy their appointed roles.

This book treats an argument that, to many people's surprise, seems to be a latecomer: biological determinism, the notion that people at the bottom are constructed of intrinsically inferior material (poor brains, bad genes, or whatever). Plato, as we have seen, cautiously floated this proposal in the *Republic*, but finally branded it as a lie.

Racial prejudice may be as old as recorded human history, but its biological justification imposed the additional burden of intrinsic inferiority upon despised groups, and precluded redemption by conversion or assimilation. The "scientific" argument has formed a primary line of attack for more than a century. In discussing the first biological theory supported by extensive quantitative data—early nineteenth-century craniometry—I must begin by posing a question of causality: did the introduction of inductive science add legitimate data to change or strengthen a nascent argument for racial ranking? Or did a priori commitment to ranking fashion the "scientific" questions asked and even the data gathered to support a foreordained conclusion?

A Shared Context of Culture

In assessing the impact of science upon eighteenth- and nineteenth-century views of race, we must first recognize the cultural milieu of a society whose leaders and intellectuals did not doubt the propriety of racial ranking—with Indians below whites, and blacks below everybody else. Under this universal umbrella, arguments did not contrast equality with inequality. One group—we might call them "hard-liners"—held that blacks were inferior and that their biological status justified enslavement and colonization. Another group—the "soft-liners," if you will—agreed that blacks were inferior, but held that a people's right to freedom did not depend upon their level of intelligence. "Whatever be their degree of talents," wrote Thomas Jefferson, "it is no measure of their rights."

Soft-liners held various attitudes about the nature of black disadvantage. Some argued that proper education and standard of life could "raise" blacks to a white level; others advocated permanent black ineptitude. They also disagreed about the biological or cultural roots of black inferiority. Yet, throughout the egalitarian tradition of the European Enlightenment and the American revolution, I cannot identify any popular position remotely like the "cultural relativism" that prevails (at least by lip-service) in liberal circles today. The nearest approach is a common argument that black inferiority is purely cultural and that it can be completely eradicated by education to a Caucasian standard.

All American culture heroes embraced racial attitudes that would embarrass public-school mythmakers. Benjamin Franklin, while viewing the inferiority of blacks as purely cultural and completely remediable, nonetheless expressed his hope that America would become a domain of whites, undiluted by less pleasing colors.

> I could wish their numbers were increased. And while we are, as I may call it, scouring our planet, by clearing America of woods, and so making this side of our globe reflect a brighter light to the eyes of inhabitants in Mars or Venus, why should we . . . darken its people? Why increase the Sons of Africa, by planting them in America, where we have so fair an opportunity, by excluding all blacks and tawneys, of increasing the lovely white and red?* (*Observations Concerning the Increase of Mankind*, 1751).

Others among our heroes argued for biological inferiority. Thomas Jefferson wrote, albeit tentatively: "I advance it, therefore, as a suspicion only, that the blacks, whether originally a distinct race, or made distinct by time and circumstance, are inferior to the whites in the endowment both of body and of mind" (in Gossett, 1965, p. 44). Lincoln's pleasure at the performance of black soldiers in the Union army greatly increased his respect for freedmen and former slaves.

But freedom does not imply biological equality, and Lincoln never abandoned a basic attitude, so strongly expressed in the Douglas debates (1858):

> There is a physical difference between the white and black races which I believe will forever forbid the two races living together on terms of social and political equality. And inasmuch as they cannot so live, while they do remain together there must be the position of superior and inferior, and I as much as any other man am in favor of having the superior position assigned to the white race.

Lest we choose to regard this statement as mere campaign rhetoric, I cite this private jotting, scribbled on a fragment of paper in 1859:

> Negro equality! Fudge! How long, in the Government of a God great enough to make and rule the universe, shall there continue knaves to vend, and fools to quip, so low a piece of demagogism at this (in Sinkler, 1972, p. 47).

I do not cite these statements in order to release skeletons from ancient closets. Rather, I quote the men who have justly earned our highest respect in order to show that white leaders of Western nations did not question the propriety of racial ranking during the eighteenth and nineteenth centuries. In this context, the pervasive assent given by scientists to conventional rankings arose from shared social belief, not from objective data gathered to test an open question. Yet, in a curious case of reversed causality, these pronouncements were read as independent support for the political context.

All leading scientists followed social conventions. In the first formal definition of human races in modern taxonomic terms, Linnaeus mixed character with anatomy (*Systema naturae*, 1758). *Homo sapiens afer* (the African black), he proclaimed, is "ruled by caprice"; *Homo sapiens europaeus* is "ruled by customs." Of African women, he wrote: *Feminis sine pudoris; mammae lactantes prolixae*—Women without shame, breasts lactate profusely. The men, he added, are indolent and annoint themselves with grease.

The three greatest naturalists of the nineteenth century did not hold blacks in high esteem. Georges Cuvier, widely hailed in France as the Aristotle of his age, and a founder of geology, paleontology, and modern comparative anatomy, referred to native Africans as "the most degraded of human races, whose form approaches that of the beast and whose intelligence is nowhere great enough to arrive at regular government" (Cuvier, 1812, p. 105). Charles Lyell, the conventional founder of modern geology, wrote:

> The brain of the Bushman . . . leads towards the brain of the Simiadae [monkeys]. This implies a

---

*I have been struck by the frequency of such aesthetic claims as a basis of racial preferences. Although J. F. Blumenbach, the founder of anthropology, had stated that toads must view other toads as paragons of beauty, many astute intellectuals never doubted the equation of whiteness with perfection. Franklin at least had the decency to include the original inhabitants in his future America; but, a century later, Oliver Wendell Holmes rejoiced in the elimination of Indians on aesthetic grounds: ". . . and so the red-crayon sketch is rubbed out, and the canvas is ready for a picture of manhood a little more like God's own image" (in Gossett, 1965, p. 243).

connexion between want of intelligence and structural assimilation. Each race of Man has its place, like the inferior animals (in Wilson, 1970, p. 347).

Charles Darwin, the kindly liberal and passionate abolitionist,* wrote about a future time when the gap between human and ape will increase by the anticipated extinction of such intermediates as chimpanzees and Hottentots.

> The break will then be rendered wider, for it will intervene between man in a more civilized state, as we may hope, than the Caucasian, and some ape as low as a baboon, instead of as at present between the negro or Australian and the gorilla (*Descent of Man*, 1871, p. 201).

Even more instructive are the beliefs of those few scientists often cited in retrospect as cultural relativists and defenders of equality. J. F. Blumenbach attributed racial differences to the influences of climate. He protested rankings based on beauty or presumed mental ability and assembled a collection of books written by blacks. Nonetheless, he did not doubt that white people set a standard, from which all other races must be viewed as departures:

> The Caucasian must, on every physiological principle, be considered as the primary or intermediate of these five principal Races. The two extremes into which it has deviated, are on the one hand the Mongolian, on the other the Ethiopian [African blacks] (1825, p. 37).

Alexander von Humboldt, world traveler, statesman, and greatest popularizer of nineteenth-century science, would be the hero of all modern egalitarians who seek antecedents in history. He, more than any other scientist of his time, argued forcefully and at length against ranking on mental or aesthetic grounds. He also drew political implications from his convictions, and campaigned against all forms of slavery and subjugation as impediments to the natural striving of all people to attain mental excellence.

He wrote in the most famous passage of his five-volume *Cosmos*:

> Whilst we maintain the unity of the human species, we at the same time repel the depressing assumption of superior and inferior races of men. There are nations more susceptible of cultivation than others—but none in themselves nobler than others. All are in like degree designed for freedom (1849, p. 368).

Yet even Humboldt invoked innate mental difference to resolve some dilemmas of human history. Why, he asks in the second volume of *Cosmos*, did the Arabs explode in culture and science soon after the rise of Islam, while Scythian tribes of southeastern Europe stuck to their ancient ways; for both peoples were nomadic and shared a common climate and environment? Humboldt did find some cultural differences—greater contact of Arabs with surrounding urbanized cultures, for example. But, in the end, he labeled Arabs as a "more highly gifted race" with greater "natural adaptability for mental cultivation" (1849, p. 578).

Alfred Russel Wallace, codiscoverer of natural selection with Darwin, is justly hailed as an antiracist. Indeed, he did affirm near equality in the innate mental capacity of all peoples. Yet, curiously, this very belief led him to abandon natural selection and return to divine creation as an explanation for the human mind—much to Darwin's disgust. Natural selection, Wallace argued, can only build structures immediately useful to animals possessing them. The brain of savages is, potentially, as good as ours. But they do not use it fully, as the rudeness and inferiority of their culture indicates. Since modern savages are much like human ancestors, our brain must have developed its higher capacities long before we put them to any use.

Preevolutionary Styles of Scientific Racism: Monogenism and Polygenism

Preevolutionary justifications for racial ranking proceeded in two modes. The "softer" argument—again using some inappropriate definitions from modern perspectives—upheld the scriptural unity of all peoples in the single creation of Adam and Eve. This view was called *monogenism*—or origin from a single source. Human races are a product of degeneration from Eden's perfection. Races have declined to different degrees, whites least and blacks most. Climate proved most popular as a primary cause for racial distinction. Degenerationists differed on the remediability of modern deficits. Some held that the differences, though developed gradually under the influence of climate, were now fixed and could never be reversed. Others argued that the fact of gradual development implied reversibility in appro-

---

*Darwin wrote, for example, in the *Voyage of the Beagle:* "Near Rio de Janeiro I lived opposite to an old lady, who kept screws to crush the fingers of her female slaves. I have stayed in a house where a young household mulatto, daily and hourly, was reviled, beaten, and persecuted enough to break the spirit of the lowest animal. I have seen a little boy, six or seven years old, struck thrice with a horse-whip (before I could interfere) on his naked head, for having handed me a glass of water not quite clean. . . . And these deeds are done and palliated by men, who profess to love their neighbors as themselves, who believe in God, and pray that his Will be done on earth! It makes one's blood boil, yet heart tremble, to think that we Englishmen and our American descendants, with their boastful cry of liberty, have been and are so guilty."

priate environments. Samuel Stanhope Smith, president of the College of New Jersey (later Princeton), hoped that American blacks, in a climate more suited to Caucasian temperaments, would soon turn white. But other degenerationists felt that improvement in benevolent climes could not proceed rapidly enough to have any impact upon human history.

The "harder" argument abandoned scripture as allegorical and held that human races were separate biological species, the descendants of different Adams. As another form of life, blacks need not participate in the "equality of man." Proponents of this argument were called "polygenists."

Degenerationism was probably the more popular argument, if only because scripture was not to be discarded lightly. Moreover, the interfertility of all human races seemed to guarantee their union as a single species under Buffon's criterion that members of a species be able to breed with each other, but not with representatives of any other group. Buffon himself, the greatest naturalist of eighteenth-century France, was a strong abolitionist and exponent of improvement for inferior races in appropriate environments. But he never doubted the inherent validity of a white standard:

> The most temperate climate lies between the 40th and 50th degree of latitude, and it produces the most handsome and beautiful men. It is from this climate that the ideas of genuine color of mankind, and of the various degrees of beauty ought to be derived.

Some degenerationists cited their commitments in the name of human brotherhood. Etienne Serres, a famous French medical anatomist, wrote in 1860 that the perfectability of lower races distinguished humans as the only species subject to improvement by its own efforts. He lambasted polygeny as a "savage theory" that "seems to lend scientific support to the enslavement of races less advanced in civilization than the Caucasian":

> Their conclusion is that the Negro is no more a white man than a donkey is a horse or a zebra— a theory put into practice in the United States of America, to the shame of civilization (1860, pp. 407–408).

Nonetheless, Serres worked to document the signs of inferiority among lower races. As an anatomist, he sought evidence within his speciality and confessed to some difficulty in establishing both criteria and data. He settled on the theory of recapitulation—the idea that higher creatures repeat the adult stages of lower animals during their own growth (Chapter 4). Adult blacks, he argued, should be like white children, adult Mongolians like white adolescents. He searched dili-

gently but devised nothing much better than the distance between navel and penis—"that ineffaceable sign of embryonic life in man." This distance in small relative to body height in babies of all races. The navel migrates upward during growth, but attains greater heights in whites than in yellows, and never gets very far at all in blacks. Blacks remain perpetually like white children and announce their inferiority thereby.

Polygeny, though less popular, had its illustrious supporters as well. David Hume did not spend his life absorbed in pure thought. He held a number of political posts, including the stewardship of the English colonial office in 1766. Hume advocated both the separate creation and innate inferiority of nonwhite races:

> I am apt to suspect the negroes and in general all the other species of men (for there are four or five different kinds) to be naturally inferior to the whites. There never was a civilized nation of any other complexion than white, nor even any individual eminent either in action or speculation.* No ingenious manufacturers amongst them, no arts, no sciences. . . . Such a uniform and constant difference could not happen in so many countries and ages, if nature had not made an original distinction betwixt these breeds of men. Not to mention our colonies, there are negroe slaves dispersed all over Europe, of which none ever discovered any symptoms of ingenuity, tho' low people without education will start up amongst us, and distinguish themselves in every profession. In Jamaica indeed they talk of one negroe as a man of parts and learning: but 'tis likely he is admired for very slender accomplishments like a parrot who speaks a few words plainly (in Popkin, 1974, p. 143; see Popkin's excellent article for a long analysis of Hume as a polygenist).

Charles White, an English surgeon, wrote the strongest defense of polygeny in 1799—*Account of the Regular Gradation in Man*. White abandoned Buffon's criterion of interfertility in defining species, pointing to successful hybrids between such conventionally separate groups as foxes, wolves, and jackals.† He railed

---

*This "inductive" argument from human cultures is far from dead as a defense of racism. In his *Study of History* (1934 edition), Arnold Toynbee wrote: "When we classify mankind by color, the only one of the primary races, given by this classification, which has not made a creative contribution to any of our twenty-one civilizations is the Black Race" (in Newby, 1969, p. 217).

†Modern evolutionary theory does invoke a barrier to interfertility as the primary criterion for status as a species. In the standard definition: "Species are actually or potentially interbreeding populations sharing a common gene pool, and reproductively isolated from all other groups." Reproductive isolation, however, does not mean that individual hybrids never arise, but only that the two species maintain their integrity in natural contact. Hybrids may be sterile (mules). Fertile hybrids may even arise quite frequently, but

against the idea that climate might produce racial differences, arguing that such ideas might lead, by extension, to the "degrading notion" of evolution between species. He disclaimed any political motivation and announced an untainted purpose: "to investigate a proposition in natural history." He explicitly rejected any extension of polygeny to "countenance the pernicious practice of enslaving mankind." White's criteria of ranking tended toward the aesthetic, and his argument included the following gem, often quoted. Where else but among Caucasians, he argued, can we find

> . . . that nobly arched head, containing such a quantity of brain. . . . Where that variety of features, and fulness of expression; those long, flowing, graceful ring-lets; that majestic beard, those rosy cheeks and coral lips? Where that . . . noble gait? In what other quarter of the globe shall we find the blush that overspreads the soft features of the beautiful women of Europe, that emblem of modesty, of delicate feelings . . . where, except on the bosom of the European woman, two such plump and snowy white hemispheres, tipt with vermillion (in Stanton, 1960, p. 17).

Louis Agassiz—America's Theorist of Polygeny

Ralph Waldo Emerson argued that intellectual emancipation should follow political independence. American scholars should abandon their subservience to European styles and theories. We have, Emerson wrote, "listened too long to the courtly muses of Europe." "We will walk on our own feet; we will work with our own hands; we will speak our own minds" (in Stanton, 1960, p. 84).

In the early to mid-nineteenth century, the budding profession of American science organized itself to follow Emerson's advice. A collection of eclectic amateurs, bowing before the prestige of European theorists, became a group of professionals with indigenous ideas and an internal dynamic that did not require constant fueling from Europe. The doctrine of polygeny acted as an important agent in this transformation; for it was one of the first theories of largely American origin that won the attention and respect of European scientists—so much so that Europeans referred to polygeny as the "American school" of anthropology. Polygeny had European antecedents, as we have seen, but Americans developed the data cited in its support and based a large body of research on its tenets. I shall concentrate on the two most famous advocates of polygeny—Agassiz the theorist and Morton the data analyst; and I shall try to uncover both the hidden motives and the finagling of data so central to their support.* For starters, it is obviously not accidental that a nation still practicing slavery and expelling its aboriginal inhabitants from their homelands should have provided a base for theories that blacks and Indians are separate species, inferior to whites.

Louis Agassiz (1807–1873), the great Swiss naturalist, won his reputation in Europe, primarily as Cuvier's disciple and a student of fossil fishes. His immigration to America in the 1840s immediately elevated the status of American natural history. For the first time, a major European theorist had found enough of value in the United States to come and stay. Agassiz became a professor at Harvard, where he founded and directed the Museum of Comparative Zoology until his death in 1873 (I occupy an office in the original wing of his building). Agassiz was a charmer; he was lionized in social and intellectual circles from Boston to Charlestown. He spoke for science with boundless enthusiasm and raised money with equal zeal to support his buildings, collections, and publications. No man did more to establish and enhance the prestige of American biology during the nineteenth century.

Agassiz also became the leading spokesman for polygeny in America. He did not bring this theory with him from Europe. He converted to the doctrine of human races as separate species after his first experiences with American blacks.

Agassiz did not embrace polygeny as a conscious political doctrine. He never doubted the propriety of racial ranking, but he did count himself among the opponents of slavery. His adherence to polygeny flowed easily from procedures of biological research that he had developed in other and earlier contexts. He was, first of all, a devout creationist who lived long enough to become the only major scientific opponent of evolution. But nearly all scientists were creationists before 1859, and most did not become polygenists (racial differentiation within a single species posed no threat to the doctrine of special creation—just consider breeds

---

if natural selection acts preferentially against them (as a result of inferiority in structural design, rejection as mates by full members of either species, etc.) they will not increase in frequency and the two species will not amalgamate. Often fertile hybrids can be produced in the laboratory by imposing situations not encountered in nature (forced breeding between species that normally mature at different times of the year, for example). Such examples do not refute a status as separate species because the two groups do not amalgamate in the wild (maturation at different times of the year may be an efficient means of reproductive isolation).

---

*An excellent history of the entire "American school" can be found in W. Stanton's *The Leopard's Spots.*

of dogs and cattle). Agassiz's predisposition to polygeny arose primarily from two aspects of his personal theories and methods:

1. In studying the geographic distribution of animals and plants, Agassiz developed a theory about "centers of creation." He believed that species were created in their proper places and did not generally migrate far from these centers. Other biogeographers invoked creation in a single spot with extensive migration thereafter. Thus, when Agassiz studied what we would now regard as a single widespread species, divided into fairly distinct geographical races, he tended to name several separate species, each created at its center of origin. *Homo sapiens* is a primary example of a cosmopolitan, variable species.

2. Agassiz was an extreme splitter in his taxonomic practice. Taxonomists tend to fall into two camps—"lumpers," who concentrate on similarities and amalgamate groups with small differences into single species, and "splitters," who focus on minute distinctions and establish species on the smallest peculiarities of design. Agassiz was a splitter among splitters. He once named three genera of fossil fishes from isolated teeth that a later paleontologist found in the variable dentition of a single individual. He named invalid species of freshwater fishes by the hundreds, basing them upon peculiar individuals within single, variable species. An extreme splitter who viewed organisms as created over their entire range might well be tempted to regard human races as separate creations. Nonetheless, before coming to America, Agassiz advocated the doctrine of human unity—even though he viewed our variation as exceptional. He wrote in 1845:

> Here is revealed anew the superiority of the human genre and its greater independence in nature. Whereas the animals are distinct species in the different zoological provinces to which they appertain, man, despite the diversity of his races, constitutes one and the same species over all the surface of the globe (in Stanton, 1960, p. 101).

Agassiz may have been predisposed to polygeny by biological belief, but I doubt that this pious man would have abandoned the Biblical orthodoxy of a single Adam if he had not been confronted both by the sight of American blacks and the urgings of his polygenist colleagues. Agassiz never generated any data for polygeny. His conversion followed an immediate visceral judgment and some persistent persuasion by friends. His later support rested on nothing deeper in the realm of biological knowledge.

Agassiz had never seen a black person in Europe. When he first met blacks as servants at his Philadelphia hotel in 1846, he experienced a pronounced visceral re-

vulsion. This jarring experience, coupled with his sexual fears about miscegenation, apparently established his conviction that blacks are a separate species. In a remarkably candid passage, he wrote to his mother from America:

> It was in Philadelphia that I first found myself in prolonged contact with negroes; all the domestics in my hotel were men of color. I can scarcely express to you the painful impression that I received, especially since the feeling that they inspired in me is contrary to all our ideas about the confraternity of the human type [*genre*] and the unique origin of our species. But truth before all. Nevertheless, I experienced pity at the sight of this degraded and degenerate race, and their lot inspired compassion in me in thinking that they are really men. Nonetheless, it is impossible for me to repress the feeling that they are not of the same blood as us. In seeing their black faces with their thick lips and grimacing teeth, the wool on their head, their bent knees, their elongated hands, their large curved nails, and especially the livid color of the palm of their hands, I could not take my eyes off their face in order to tell them to stay far away. And when they advanced that hideous hand towards my plate in order to serve me, I wished I were able to depart in order to eat a piece of bread elsewhere, rather than dine with such service. What unhappiness for the white race—to have tied their existence so closely with that of negroes in certain countries! God preserve us from such a contact! (Agassiz to his mother, December 1846.) (The standard *Life and Letters*, compiled by Agassiz's wife, omits these lines in presenting an expurgated version of this famous letter. Other historians have paraphrased them or passed them by. I recovered this passage from the original manuscript in Harvard's Houghton Library and have translated it, verbatim, for the first time so far as I know.)

Agassiz published his major statement on human races in the *Christian Examiner* for 1850. He begins by dismissing as demagogues both the divines who would outlaw him as an infidel (for preaching the doctrine of multiple Adams) and the abolitionists who would brand him as a defender of slavery:

> It has been charged upon the views here advanced that they tend to the support of slavery. . . . Is that a fair objection to a philosophical investigation? Here we have to do only with the question of the origin of men; let the politicians, let those who feel themselves called upon to regulate human society, see what they can do with the results. . . . We disclaim, however, all connection with any question involving political matters. It is simply with reference to the possibility of appreciating the differences existing between different men, and of eventually determining whether they have originated all over the world,

and under what circumstances, that we have here tried to trace some facts respecting the human races (1850, p. 113).

Agassiz then presents his argument: The theory of polygeny does not constitute an attack upon the scriptural doctrine of human unity. Men are bound by a common structure and sympathy, even though races were created as separate species. The Bible does not speak about parts of the world unknown to the ancients; the tale of Adam refers only to the origin of Caucasians. Negroes and Caucasians are as distinct in the mummified remains of Egypt as they are today. If human races were the product of climatic influence, then the passage of three thousand years would have engendered substantial changes (Agassiz had no inkling of human antiquity; he believed that three thousand years included a major chunk of our entire history). Modern races occupy definite, nonoverlapping, geographic areas—even though some ranges have been blurred or obliterated by migration. As physically distinct, temporally invariant groups with discrete geographical ranges, human races met all Agassiz's biological criteria for separate species.

> These races must have originated . . . in the same numerical proportions, and over the same area, in which they now occur. . . . They cannot have originated in single individuals, but must have been created in that numeric harmony which is characteristic of each species; men must have originated in nations, as the bees have originated in swarms (pp. 128–129).

Then, approaching the end of his article, Agassiz abruptly shifts his ground and announces a moral imperative—even though he had explicitly justified his inquiry by casting it as an objective investigation of natural history.

> There are upon earth different races of men, inhabiting different parts of its surface, which have different physical characters; and this fact . . . presses upon us the obligation to settle the relative rank among these races, the relative value of the characters peculiar to each, in a scientific point of view. . . . As philosophers it is our duty to look in the face (p. 142).

As direct evidence for differential, innate value Agassiz ventures no further than the standard set of Caucasian cultural stereotypes:

> The indomitable, courageous, proud Indian—in how very different a light he stands by the side of the submissive, obsequious, imitative negro, or by the side of the tricky, cunning, and cowardly Mongolian! Are not these facts indications that the dif-

ferent races do not rank upon one level in nature (p. 144).

Blacks, Agassiz declares, must occupy the bottom rung of any objective ladder:

> It seems to us to be mock-philanthropy and mock-philosophy to assume that all races have the same abilities, enjoy the same powers, and show the same natural dispositions, and that in consequence of this equality they are entitled to the same position in human society. History speaks here for itself. . . . This compact continent of Africa exhibits a population which has been in constant intercourse with the white race, which has enjoyed the benefit of the example of the Egyptian civilization, of the Phoenician civilization, of the Roman civilization, of the Arab civilization . . . and nevertheless there has never been a regulated society of black men developed on that continent. Does not this indicate in this race a peculiar apathy, a peculiar indifference to the advantages afforded by civilized society? (pp. 143–144).

If Agassiz had not made his political message clear, he ends by advocating specific social policy. Education, he argues, must be tailored to innate ability; train blacks in hand work, whites in mind work:

> What would be the best education to be imparted to the different races in consequence of their primitive difference, . . . We entertain not the slightest doubt that human affairs with reference to the colored races would be far more judiciously conducted if, in our intercourse with them, we were guided by a full consciousness of the real difference existing between us and them, and a desire to foster those dispositions that are eminently marked in them, rather than by treating them on terms of equality (p. 145).

Since those "eminently marked" dispositions are submissiveness, obsequiousness, and imitation, we can well imagine what Agassiz had in mind. I have treated this paper in detail because it is so typical of its genre—advocacy of social policy couched as a dispassionate inquiry into scientific fact. The strategy is by no means moribund today.

In a later correspondence, pursued in the midst of the Civil War, Agassiz expressed his political views more forcefully and at greater length. (These letters are also expurgated without indication in the standard version published by Agassiz's wife. Again, I have restored passages from the original letters in Harvard's Houghton Library.) S. G. Howe, a member of Lincoln's Inquiry Commission, asked Agassiz's opinion about the role of blacks in a reunited nation. (Howe, known best for his work in prison reform and education of the blind, was the husband of Julia Ward Howe, author of the "Battle

Hymn of the Republic".) In four long and impassioned letters, Agassiz pleaded his case. The persistence of a large and permanent black population in America must be acknowledged as a grim reality. Indians, driven by their commendable pride, may perish in battle, but "the negro exhibits by nature a pliability, a readiness to accommodate himself to circumstances, a proneness to imitate those among whom he lives" (9 August 1863).

Although legal equality must be granted to all, blacks should be denied social equality, lest the white race be compromised and diluted: "Social equality I deem at all time impracticable. It is a natural impossibility flowing from the very character of the negro race" (10 August 1863); for blacks are "indolent, playful, sensuous, imitative, subservient, good natured, versatile, unsteady in their purpose, devoted, affectionate, in everything unlike other races, they may but be compared to children, grown in the stature of adults while retaining a childlike mind. . . . Therefore I hold that they are incapable of living on a footing of social equality with the whites, in one and the same community, without being an element of social disorder" (10 August 1863). Blacks must be regulated and limited, lest an injudicious award of social privilege sow later discord:

> No man has a right to what he is unfit to use. . . . Let us beware of granting too much to the negro race in the beginning, lest it become necessary to recall violently some of the privileges which they may use to our detriment and their own injury (10 August 1863).

For Agassiz, nothing inspired more fear than the prospect of amalgamation by intermarriage. White strength depends upon separation: "The production of halfbreeds is as much a sin against nature, as incest in a civilized community is a sin against purity of character. . . . Far from presenting to me a natural solution of our difficulties, the idea of amalgamation is most repugnant to my feelings, I hold it to be a perversion of every natural sentiment. . . . No efforts should be spared to check that which is abhorrent to our better nature, and to the progress of a higher civilization and a purer morality" (9 August 1863).

Agassiz now realizes that he has argued himself into a corner. If interbreeding among races (separate species to Agassiz) is unnatural and repugnant, why are "halfbreeds" so common in America? Agassiz attributes this lamentable fact to the sexual receptiveness of housemaids and the naïveté of young Southern gentlemen. The servants, it seems, are halfbreeds already (we are not told how their parents overcame a natural repugnance for one another); young men respond aesthetically to the white half, while a degree of black heritage loosens the natural inhibitions of a higher race. Once acclimated, the poor young men are hooked, and they acquire a taste for pure blacks:

> As soon as the sexual desires are awakening in the young men of the South, they find it easy to gratify themselves by the readiness with which they are met by colored [halfbreed] house servants. . . . This blunts his better instincts in that direction and leads him gradually to seek more spicy partners, as I have heard the full blacks called by fast young men (9 August 1863).

Finally, Agassiz combines vivid image and metaphor to warn against the ultimate danger of a mixed and enfeebled people:

> Conceive for a moment the difference it would make in future ages, for the prospect of republican institutions and our civilization generally, if instead of the manly population descended from cognate nations the United States should hereafter be inhabited by the effeminate progeny of mixed races, half indian, half negro, sprinkled with white blood. . . . I shudder from the consequences. We have already to struggle, in our progress, against the influence of universal equality, in consequence of the difficulty of preserving the acquisitions of individual eminence, the wealth of refinement and culture growing out of select associations. What would be our condition if to these difficulties were added the far more tenacious influences of physical disability. . . . How shall we eradicate the stigma of a lower race when its blood has once been allowed to flow freely into that of our children (10 August 1863).*

Agassiz concludes that legal freedom awarded to slaves in manumission must spur the enforcement of rigid social separation among races. Fortunately, nature shall be the accomplice of moral virtue; for people, free to choose, gravitate naturally toward the climates of their original homeland. The black species, created for hot and humid conditions, will prevail in the Southern lowlands, though whites will maintain dominion over the seashore and elevated ground. The new South will contain some Negro states. We should bow before this necessity and admit them into the

---

*E. D. Cope, America's leading paleontologist and evolutionary biologist, reiterated the same theme even more forcefully in 1890 (p. 2054): "The highest race of man cannot afford to lose or even to compromise the advantages it has acquired by hundreds of centuries of toil and hardship, by mingling its blood with the lowest. . . . We cannot cloud or extinguish the fine nervous susceptibility, and the mental force, which cultivation develops in the constitution of the Indo-European, by the fleshy instincts, and dark mind of the African. Not only is the mind stagnated, and the life of mere living introduced in its stead, but the possibility of resurrection is rendered doubtful or impossible."

Union; we have, after all, already recognized both "Haity and Liberia."[†] But the bracing North is not a congenial home for carefree and lackadaisical people, created for warmer regions. Pure blacks will migrate South, leaving a stubborn residue to dwindle and die out in the North: "I hope it may gradually die out in the north where it has only an artificial foothold" (11 August 1863). As for the mulattoes, "their sickly physique and their impaired fecundity" should assure their demise once the shackles of slavery no longer provide an opportunity for unnatural interbreeding.

Agassiz's world collapsed during the last decade of his life. His students rebelled; his supporters defected. He remained a hero to the public, but scientists began to regard him as a rigid and aging dogmatist, standing firm in his antiquated beliefs before the Darwinian tide. But his social preferences for racial segregation prevailed—all the more because his fanciful hope for voluntary geographic separation did not.

Samuel George Morton—Empiricist of Polygeny

Agassiz did not spend all his time in Philadelphia reviling black waiters. In the same letter to his mother, he wrote in glowing terms of his visit to the anatomical collection of Philadelphia's distinguished scientist and physician Samuel George Morton: "Imagine a series of 600 skulls, most of Indians from all tribes who inhabit or once inhabited all of America. Nothing like it exists anywhere else. This collection, by itself, is worth a trip to America" (Agassiz to his mother, December 1846, translated from the original letter in Houghton Library, Harvard University).

Agassiz speculated freely and at length, but he amassed no data to support his polygenic theory. Morton, a Philadelphia patrician with two medical degrees—one from fashionable Edinburgh—provided the "facts" that won worldwide respect for the "American school" of polygeny. Morton began his collection of human skulls in the 1820s; he had more than one thousand when he died in 1851. Friends (and enemies) referred to his great charnel house as "the American Golgotha."

Morton won his reputation as the great data-gatherer and objectivist of American science, the man who would raise an immature enterprise from the mires of fanciful speculation. Oliver Wendell Holmes praised Morton for "the severe and cautious character" of his works, which "from their very nature are permanent data for all future students of ethnology" (in Stanton, 1960, p. 96). The same Humboldt who had asserted the inherent equality of all races wrote:

> The craniological treasures which you have been so fortunate as to unite in your collection, have in you found a worthy interpreter. Your work is equally remarkable for the profundity of its anatomical views, the numerical detail of the relations of organic conformation, and the absence of those poetical reveries which are the myths of modern physiology (in Meigs, 1851, p. 48).

When Morton died in 1851, the *New York Tribune* wrote that "probably no scientific man in America enjoyed a higher reputation among scholars throughout the world, than Dr. Morton" (in Stanton, 1960, p. 144).

Yet Morton gathered skulls neither for the dilettante's motive of abstract interest nor the taxonomist's zeal for complete representation. He had a hypothesis to test: that a ranking of races could be established objectively by physical characteristics of the brain, particularly by its size. Morton took a special interest in native Americans. As George Combe, his fervent friend and supporter, wrote:

> One of the most singular features in the history of this continent, is, that the aboriginal races, with few exceptions, have perished or constantly receded, before the Anglo-Saxon race, and have in no instance either mingled with them as equals, or adopted their manners and civilization. These phenomena must have a cause; and can any inquiry be at once more interesting and philosophical than that which endeavors to ascertain whether that cause be connected with a difference in the brain between the native American race, and their conquering invaders (Combe and Coates, in review of Morton's *Crania Americana*, 1840, p. 352).

Moreover, Combe argued that Morton's collection would acquire true scientific value *only if* mental and moral worth could be read from brains: "If this doctrine be unfounded, these skulls are mere facts in Natural History, presenting no particular information as to the mental qualities of the people" (from Combe's appendix to Morton's *Crania Americana*, 1839, p. 275).

Although he vacillated early in his career, Morton soon became a leader among the American polygenists. He wrote several articles to defend the status of human races as separate, created species. He took on the strongest claim of opponents—the interfertility of all human races—by arguing from both sides. He re-

---

[†]Not all detractors of blacks were so generous. E. D. Cope, who feared that miscegenation would block the path to heaven (see preceding footnote), advocated the return of all blacks to Africa (1890, p. 2053): "Have we not burdens enough to carry in the European peasantry which we are called on every year to receive and assimilate? Is our own race on a plane sufficiently high, to render it safe for us to carry eight millions of dead material in the very center of our vital organism?"

lied on travelers' reports to claim that some human races—Australian aborigines and Caucasians in particular—very rarely produce fertile offspring (Morton, 1851). He attributed this failure to "a disparity of primordial organization." But, he continued, Buffon's criterion of interfertility must be abandoned in any case, for hybridization is common in nature, even between species belonging to different genera (Morton, 1847, 1850). Species must be redefined as "a primordial organic form" (1850, p. 82). "Bravo, my dear Sir," wrote Agassiz in a letter, "you have at last furnished science with a true philosophical definition of species" (in Stanton, 1960, p. 141). But how to recognize a primordial form? Morton replied: "If certain existing organic types can be traced back into the 'night of time,' as dissimilar as we see them now, is it not more reasonable to regard them as aboriginal, than to suppose them the mere and accidental derivations of an isolated patriarchal stem of which we know nothing?" (1850, p. 82). Thus, Morton regarded several breeds of dogs as separate species because their skeletons resided in the Egyptian catacombs, as recognizable and distinct from other breeds as they are now. The tombs also contained blacks and Caucasians. Morton dated the beaching of Noah's Ark on Ararat at 4,179 years before his time, and the Egyptian tombs at just 1,000 years after that—clearly not enough time for the sons of Noah to differentiate into races. (How, he asks, can we believe that races changed so rapidly for 1,000 years, and not at all for 3,000 years since then?) Human races must have been separate from the start (Morton, 1839, p. 88).

But separate, as the Supreme Court once said, need not mean unequal. Morton therefore set out to establish relative rank on "objective" grounds. He surveyed the drawings of ancient Egypt and found that blacks are invariably depicted as menials—a sure sign that they have always played their appropriate biological role: "Negroes were numerous in Egypt, but their social position in ancient times was the same that it is now, that of servants and slaves" (Morton, 1844, p. 158). (A curious argument, to be sure, for these blacks had been captured in warfare; sub-Saharan societies depicted blacks as rulers.)

But Morton's fame as a scientist rested upon his collection of skulls and their role in racial ranking. Since the cranial cavity of a human skull provides a faithful measure of the brain it once contained, Morton set out to rank races by the average sizes of their brains. He filled the cranial cavity with sifted white mustard seed, poured the seed back into a graduated cylinder and read the skull's volume in cubic inches. Later on, he became dissatisfied with mustard seed because he could not obtain consistent results. The seeds

did not pack well, for they were too light and still varied too much in size, despite sieving. Remeasurements of single skulls might differ by more than 5 percent, or 4 cubic inches in skulls with an average capacity near 80 cubic inches. Consequently, he switched to one-eighth-inch-diameter lead shot "of the size called BB" and achieved consistent results that never varied by more than a single cubic inch for the same skull.

Morton published three major works on the sizes of human skulls—his lavish, beautifully illustrated volume on American Indians, the *Crania Americana* of 1839; his studies on skulls from the Egyptian tombs, the *Crania Aegyptiaca* of 1844; and the epitome of his entire collection in 1849. Each contained a table, summarizing his results on average skull volumes arranged by race. I have reproduced all three tables here (Tables 2.1 to 2.3). They represent the major contribution of American polygeny to debates about racial ranking. They outlived the theory of separate creations and were reprinted repeatedly during the nineteenth century as irrefutable, "hard" data on the mental worth of human races (see p. 84). Needless to say, they matched every good Yankee's prejudice—whites on top, Indians in the middle, and blacks on the bottom; and, among whites, Teutons and Anglo-Saxons on top, Jews in the middle, and Hindus on the bottom. Moreover, the pattern had been stable throughout recorded history, for whites had the same advantage over blacks in ancient Egypt. Status and access to power in Morton's America faithfully reflected biological merit. How could sentimentalists and egalitarians stand against the dictates of

TABLE 2-1   MORTON'S SUMMARY TABLE OF CRANIAL CAPACITY BY RACE

| Race | N | Internal Capacity (IN³) | | |
		Mean	Largest	Smallest
Caucasian	52	87	109	75
Mongolian	10	83	93	69
Malay	18	81	89	64
American	144	82	100	60
Ethiopian	29	78	94	65

TABLE 2-2   CRANIAL CAPACITIES FOR SKULLS FROM EGYPTIAN TOMBS

People	Mean Capacity (IN³)	N
Caucasian		
Pelasgic	88	21
Semitic	82	5
Egyptian	80	39
Negroid	79	6
Negro	73	1

TABLE 2-3   MORTON'S FINAL SUMMARY OF CRANIAL CAPACITY BY RACE

| Races And Families | N | Cranial Capacity (IN³) | | | |
		Largest	Smallest	Mean	Mean
MODERN CAUCASIAN GROUP					
Teutonic Family					
Germans	18	114	70	90	
English	5	105	91	96	92
Anglo-Americans	7	97	82	90	
Pelasgic Family	10	94	75	84	
Celtic Family	6	97	78	87	
Indostanic Family	32	91	67	80	
Semitic Family	3	98	84	89	
Nilotic Family	17	96	66	80	
ANCIENT CAUCASIAN GROUP					
Pelasgic Family	18	97	74	88	
Nilotic Family	55	96	68	80	
MONGOLIAN GROUP					
Chinese Family	6	91	70	82	
MALAY GROUP					
Malayan Family	20	97	68	86	85
Polynesian Family	3	84	82	83	
AMERICAN GROUP					
Toltecan Family					
Peruvians	155	101	58	75	79
Mexicans	22	92	67	79	
Barbarous Tribes	161	104	70	84	
NEGRO GROUP					
Native African Family	62	99	65	83	83
American-born Negroes	12	89	73	82	
Hottentot Family	3	83	68	75	
Australians	8	83	63	75	

nature? Morton had provided clean, objective data based on the largest collection of skulls in the world.

During the summer of 1977 I spent several weeks reanalyzing Morton's data. (Morton, the self-styled objectivist, published all his raw information. We can infer with little doubt how he moved from raw measurements to summary tables.) In short, and to put it bluntly, Morton's summaries are a patchwork of fudging and finagling in the clear interest of controlling a priori convictions. Yet—and this is the most intriguing aspect of the case—I find no evidence of conscious fraud; indeed, had Morton been a conscious fudger, he would not have published his data so openly.

Conscious fraud is probably rare in science. It is also not very interesting, for it tells us little about the nature of scientific activity. Liars, if discovered, are excommunicated; scientists declare that their profession has properly policed itself, and they return to

work, mythology unimpaired, and objectively vindicated. The prevalence of *unconscious* finagling, on the other hand, suggests a general conclusion about the social context of science. For if scientists can be honestly self-deluded to Morton's extent, then prior prejudice may be found anywhere, even in the basics of measuring bones and toting sums.

The Case of Indian Inferiority: Crania Americana*

Morton began his first and largest work, the *Crania Americana* of 1839, with a discourse on the essential

---

*This account omits many statistical details of my analysis. The complete tale appears in Gould, 1978. Some passages in pp. 56–69 are taken from this article.

character of human races. His statements immediately expose his prejudices. Of the "Greenland esquimaux," he wrote: "They are crafty, sensual, ungrateful, obstinate and unfeeling, and much of their affection for their children may be traced to purely selfish motives. They devour the most disgusting aliments uncooked and uncleaned, and seem to have no ideas beyond providing for the present moment. . . . Their mental faculties, from infancy to old age, present a continued childhood. . . . In gluttony, selfishness and ingratitude, they are perhaps unequalled by any other nation of people" (1839, p. 54). Morton thought little better of other Mongolians, for he wrote of the Chinese (p. 50): "So versatile are their feelings and actions, that they have been compared to the monkey race, whose attention is perpetually changing from one object to another." The Hottentots, he claimed (p. 90), are "the nearest approximation to the lower animals. . . . Their complexion is a yellowish brown, compared by travellers to the peculiar hue of Europeans in the last stages of jaundice. . . . The women are represented as even more repulsive in appearance than the men." Yet, when Morton had to describe one Caucasian tribe as a "mere horde of rapacious banditti" (p. 9), he quickly added that "their moral perceptions, under the influence of an equitable government, would no doubt assume a much more favorable aspect."

Morton's summary chart (Table 2.1) presents the "hard" argument of the *Crania Americana*. He had measured the capacity of 144 Indian skulls and calculated a mean of 82 cubic inches, a full 5 cubic inches below the Caucasian norm. In addition, Morton appended a table of phrenological measurements indicating a deficiency of "higher" mental powers among Indians. "The benevolent mind," Morton concluded (p. 82), "may regret the inaptitude of the Indian for civilization," but sentimentality must yield to fact. "The structure of his mind appears to be different from that of the white man, nor can the two harmonize in the social relations except on the most limited scale." Indians "are not only averse to the restraints of education, but for the most part are incapable of a continued process of reasoning on abstract subjects" (p. 81).

Since *Crania Americana* is primarily a treatise on the inferior quality of Indian intellect, I note first of all that Morton's cited average of 82 cubic inches for Indian skulls is incorrect. He separated Indians into two groups, "Toltecans" from Mexico and South America, and "Barbarous Tribes" from North America. Eighty-two is the average for Barbarous skulls; the total sample of 144 yields a mean of 80.2 cubic inches, or a gap of almost 7 cubic inches between Indian and Caucasian averages. (I do not know how Morton made this elementary error. It did permit him, in any case, to

retain the conventional chain of being with whites on top, Indians in the middle, and blacks on the bottom.)

But the "correct" value of 80.2 is far too low, for it is the result of an improper procedure. Morton's 144 skulls belong to many different groups of Indians; these groups differ significantly among themselves in cranial capacity. Each group should be weighted equally, lest the final average be biased by unequal size of subsamples. Suppose, for example, that we tried to estimate average human height from a sample of two jockeys, the author of this book (strictly middling stature), and all the players in the National Basketball Association. The hundreds of Jabbars would swamp the remaining three and give an average in excess of six and a half feet. If, however, we averaged the averages of the three groups (jockeys, me, and the basketball players), then our figure would lie closer to the true value. Morton's sample is strongly biased by a major overrepresentation of an extreme group—the small-brained Inca Peruvians. (They have a mean cranial capacity of 74.36 cubic inches and provide 25 percent of the entire sample). Large-brained Iroquois, on the other hand, contribute only 3 skulls to the total sample (2 percent). If, by the accidents of collecting, Morton's sample had included 25 percent Iroquois and just a few Incas, his average would have risen substantially. Consequently, I corrected this bias as best I could by averaging the mean values for all tribes represented by 4 or more skulls. The Indian average now rises to 83.79 cubic inches.

This revised value is still more than 3 cubic inches from the Caucasian average. Yet, when we examine Morton's procedure for computing the Caucasian mean, we uncover an astounding inconsistency. Since statistical reasoning is largely a product of the last one hundred years, I might have excused Morton's error for the Indian mean by arguing that he did not recognize the biases produced by unequal sizes among subsamples. But now we discover that he understood this bias perfectly well—for Morton calculated his high Caucasian mean by consciously eliminating small-brained Hindus from his sample. He writes (p. 261): "It is proper, however, to mention that but 3 Hindoos are admitted in the whole number, because the skulls of these people are probably smaller than those of any other existing nation. For example, 17 Hindoo heads give a mean of but 75 cubic inches; and the three received into the table are taken at that average." Thus, Morton included a large subsample of small-brained people (Inca Peruvians) to pull down the Indian average, but excluded just as many small Caucasian skulls to raise the mean of his own group. Since he tells us what he did so badly, we must assume that Morton did not deem his procedure improper. But by what rationale did he keep Incas and exclude Hindus, unless it were the a priori assumption of a truly higher Caucasian mean? For one might then throw out the Hindu sample as truly anomalous, but retain the Inca sample (with the same mean as the Hindus, by the way) as the lower end of normality for its disadvantaged larger group.

I restored the Hindu skulls to Morton's sample, using the same procedure of equal weighting for all groups. Morton's Caucasian sample, by his reckoning, contains skulls from four subgroups, so Hindus should contribute one-fourth of all skulls to the sample. If we restore all seventeen of Morton's Hindu skulls, they form 26 percent of the total sample of sixty-six. The Caucasian mean now drops to 84.45 cubic inches, for no difference worth mentioning between Indians and Caucasians. (Eskimos, despite Morton's low opinion of them, yield a mean of 86.8, hidden by amalgamation with other subgroups in the Mongol grand mean of 83). So much for Indian inferiority.

The Case of the Egyptian Catacombs: Crania Aegyptiaca

Morton's friend and fellow polygenist George Gliddon was United States consul for the city of Cairo. He dispatched to Philadelphia more than one hundred skulls from tombs of ancient Egypt, and Morton responded with his second major treatise, the *Crania Aegyptiaca* of 1844. Morton had shown, or so he thought, that whites surpassed Indians in mental endowment. Now he would crown his story by demonstrating that the discrepancy between whites and blacks was even greater, and that this difference had been stable for more than three thousand years.

Morton felt that he could identify both races and subgroups among races from features of the skull (most anthropologists today would deny that such assignments can be made unambiguously). He divided his Caucasian skulls into Pelasgics (Hellenes, or ancient Greek forebears), Jews, and Egyptians—in that order, again confirming Anglo-Saxon preferences (Table 2.2). Non-Caucasian skulls he identified either as "negroid" (hybrids of Negro and Caucasian with more black than white) or as pure Negro.

Morton's subjective division of Caucasian skulls is clearly unwarranted, for he simply assigned the most bulbous crania to his favored Pelasgic group and the most flattened to Egyptians; he mentions no other criteria of subdivision. If we ignore his threefold separation and amalgamate all sixty-five Caucasian skulls into a single sample, we obtain an average capacity of 82.15 cubic inches. (If we give Morton the benefit of all doubt and rank his dubious subsamples equally—as we did in computing Indian and Caucasian means for

the *Crania Americana*—we obtain an average of 83.3 cubic inches.)

Either of these values still exceeds the negroid and Negro averages substantially. Morton assumed that he had measured an innate difference in intelligence. He never considered any other proposal for the disparity in average cranial capacity—though another simple and obvious explanation lay before him.

Sizes of brains are related to the sizes of bodies that carry them: big people tend to have larger brains than small people. This fact does not imply that big people are smarter—any more than elephants should be judged more intelligent than humans because their brains are larger. Appropriate corrections must be made for differences in body size. Men tend to be larger than women; consequently, their brains are bigger. When corrections for body size are applied, men and women have brains of approximately equal size. Morton not only failed to correct for differences in sex or body size; he did not even recognize the relationship, though his data proclaimed it loud and clear. (I can only conjecture that Morton never separated his skulls by sex or stature—though his tables record these data—because he wanted so much to read differences in brain size directly as differences in intelligence.)

Many of the Egyptian skulls came with mummified remains of their possessors, and Morton could record their sex unambiguously. If we use Morton's own designations and compute separate averages for males and females (as Morton never did), we obtain the following remarkable result. Mean capacity for twenty-four male Caucasian skulls is 86.5 cubic inches; twenty-two female skulls average 77.2 (the remaining nineteen skulls could not be identified by sex). Of the six negroid skulls, Morton identified two as female (at 71 and 77 cubic inches) and could not allocate the other four (at 77, 77, 87, and 88).* If we make the reasonable conjecture that the two smaller skulls (77 and 77) are female, and the two larger male (87 and 88), we obtain a male negroid average of 87.5, slightly above the Caucasian male mean of 86.5, and a female negroid average of 75.5, slightly below the Caucasian value of 77.2. The apparent difference of 4 cubic inches between Morton's Caucasian and negroid samples may only record the fact that about half his Caucasian sample is male, while only one-third the negroid sample may be male. (The apparent difference is magnified by Morton's incorrect rounding of the negroid

---

*In his final catalogue of 1849, Morton guessed at sex (and age within five years!) for all crania. In this later work, he specifies 77, 87, and 88 as male, and the remaining 77 as female. This allocation was pure guesswork; my alternate version is equally plausible. In the *Crania Aegyptiaca* itself, Morton was more cautious and only identified sex for specimens with mummified remains.

TABLE 2-4   CRANIAL CAPACITY OF INDIAN GROUPS ORDERED BY MORTON'S ASSESSMENT OF BODY STATURE

Stature And Group	Cranial Capacity (IN³)	N
LARGE		
Seminole-Muskogee	88.3	8
Chippeway and		
related groups	88.8	4
Dacota and Osage	84.4	7
MIDDLE		
Mexicans	80.2	13
Menominee	80.5	8
Mounds	81.7	9
SMALL		
Columbia River		
Flatheads	78.8	10
Peruvians	74.4	33

average down to 79 rather than up to 80. As we shall see again, all of Morton's minor numerical errors favor his prejudices.) Differences in average brain size between Caucasians and negroids in the Egyptian tombs only record differences in stature due to sex, not variation in "intelligence." You will not be surprised to learn that the single pure Negro skull (73 cubic inches) is a female.

The correlation of brain and body also resolves a question left hanging in our previous discussion of the *Crania Americana*: What is the basis for differences in average brain size among Indian peoples? (These differences bothered Morton considerably, for he could not understand how small-brained Incas had built such an elaborate civilization, though he consoled himself with the fact of their rapid conquest by the conquistadores). Again, the answer lay before him, but Morton never saw it. Morton presents subjective data on bodily statures in his descriptions of the various tribes, and I present these assessments along with average brain sizes in Table 2.4. The correlation of brain and body size is affirmed without exception. The low Hindu mean among Caucasians also records a difference in stature, not another case of dumb Indians.

The Case of the Shifting Black Mean

In the *Crania Americana*, Morton cited 78 cubic inches as the average cranial capacity for blacks. Five years later, in the *Crania Aegyptiaca*, he appended the following footnote to his table of measurements: "I have in my possession 79 crania of Negroes born in Africa. . . . Of the whole number, 58 are adult . . . and give 85 cubic inches for the average size of the brain" (1844, p. 113).

Since Morton had changed his method of measurement from mustard seed to lead shot between 1839 and 1844, I suspected this alteration as a cause for the rising black mean. Fortunately, Morton remeasured most of his skulls personally, and his various catalogues present tabulations of the same skulls by both seed and shot (see Gould, 1978, for details).

I assumed that measures by seed would be lower. Seeds are light and variable in size, even after sieving. Hence, they do not pack well. By vigorous shaking or pressing of the thumb at the foramen magnum (the hole at the base of a skull), seeds can be made to settle, providing room for more. Measures by seed were very variable; Morton reported differences of several cubic inches for recalibrations of the same skull. He eventually became discouraged, fired his assistants, and redid all his measurements personally, with lead shot. Recalibrations never varied by more than a cubic inch, and we may accept Morton's judgment that measures by shot were objective, accurate, and repeatable—while earlier measures by seed were highly subjective and erratic.

I then calculated the discrepancies between seed and shot by race. Shot, as I suspected, always yielded higher values than seed. For 111 Indian skulls, measured by both criteria, shot exceeds seed by an average of 2.2 cubic inches. Data are not as reliable for blacks and Caucasians because Morton did not specify individual skulls for these races in the *Crania Americana* (measured by seed). For Caucasians, 19 identifiable skulls yield an average discrepancy of only 1.8 cubic inches for shot over seed. Yet 18 African skulls, remeasured from the sample reported in *Crania Americana*, produce a mean by shot of 83.44 cubic inches, a rise of 5.4 cubic inches from the 1839 average by seed. In other words, the more "inferior" a race by Morton's a priori judgment, the greater the discrepancy between a subjective measurement, easily and unconsciously fudged, and an objective measure unaffected by prior prejudice. The discrepancy for blacks, Indians, and Caucasians is 5.4, 2.2, and 1.8 cubic inches, respectively.

Plausible scenarios are easy to construct. Morton, measuring by seed, picks up a threateningly large black skull, fills it lightly and gives it a few desultory shakes. Next, he takes a distressingly small Caucasian skull, shakes hard, and pushes mightily at the foramen magnum with his thumb. It is easily done, without conscious motivation; expectation is a powerful guide to action.

The Final Tabulation of 1849

Morton's burgeoning collection included 623 skulls when he presented his final tabulation in 1849—an overwhelming affirmation of the ranking that every Anglo-Saxon expected.

The Caucasian subsamples suffer from errors and distortions. The German mean, reported at 90 in the summary, is 88.4 from individual skulls listed in the catalogue; the correct Anglo-American average is 89 (89.14), not 90. The high English mean of 96 is correct, but the small sample is entirely male.* If we follow our procedure of computing averages among subsamples, the six modern Caucasian "families" yield a mean of 87 cubic inches.† The ancient Caucasian average for two subsamples is 84 cubic inches (Table 2.5).

Six Chinese skulls provide Morton with a Mongolian mean of 82, but this low value records two cases of selective amnesia: First, Morton excluded the latest Chinese specimen (skull number 1336 at 98 cubic inches), though it must have been in his collection when he published his summary because he includes many Peruvian skulls with higher numbers. Secondly, although Morton deplored the absence of Eskimos from his collection (1849, p. iv), he did not mention the three Eskimo skulls that he had measured for *Crania Americana*. (These belonged to his friend George Combe and do not appear in Morton's final catalogue.)

Morton never remeasured these skulls with shot, but if we apply the Indian correction of 2.2 cubic inches to their seed average of 86.8 we obtain a mean of 89. These two samples (Chinese with number 1336 added, and Eskimo conservatively corrected) yield a Mongolian average of 87 cubic inches.

By 1849 Morton's Indian mean had plummeted to 79. But this figure is invalid for the same reason as before, though now intensified—inequality of numbers

---

*To demonstrate again how large differences based on stature can be, I report these additional data, recovered from Morton's tabulations, but never calculated or recognized by him: 1) For Inca Peruvians, fifty-three male skulls average 77.5; sixty-one female skulls, 72.1. 2) For Germans, nine male skulls average 92.2; eight females, 84.3.

†My original report (Gould, 1978) incorrectly listed the modern Caucasian mean as 85.3. The reason for this error is embarrassing, but instructive, for it illustrates, at my expense, the cardinal principle of this book: the social embeddedness of science and the frequent grafting of expectation upon supposed objectivity. Line 7 in Table 2.3 lists the range of Semitic skulls as 84 to 98 cubic inches for Morton's sample of 3. However, my original paper cited a mean of 80—an obvious impossibility if the smallest skull measures 84. I was working from a Xerox of Morton's original chart, and his correct value of 89 is smudged to look like an 80 on my copy. Nonetheless, the range of 84 to 98 is clearly indicated right alongside, and I never saw the inconsistency—presumably because a low value of 80 fit my hopes for a depressed Caucasian mean. The 80 therefore "felt" right and I never checked it. I am grateful to Dr. Irving Klotz of Northwestern University for pointing out this error to me.

TABLE 2-5   CORRECTED VALUES FOR MORTON'S FINAL TABULATION

People	Cranial Capacity (IN³)
Mongolians	87
Modern Caucasians	87
Native Americans	86
Malays	85
Ancient Caucasians	84
Africans	83

among subsamples. Small-headed (and small-statured) Peruvians provided 23 percent of the 1839 sample, but their frequency had risen to nearly half (155 of 338 skulls) by 1849. If we use our previous criterion and compute the average of all subsamples weighted equally, the Indian average is 86 cubic inches.

For the Negro average, we should drop Morton's australoids because he wanted to assess the status of African blacks and we no longer accept a close relationship between the two groups—dark skin evolved more than once among human groups. I also drop the Hottentot sample of 3. All skulls are female, and Hottentots are very small in stature. Native and American-born blacks, amalgamated to a single sample, yield an average value between 82 and 83, but closer to 83.

In short, my correction of Morton's conventional ranking reveals *no* significant differences among races for Morton's own data (Table 2.5). All groups rank between 83 and 87 cubic inches, and Caucasians share the pinnacle. If western Europeans choose to seek their superiority in high averages for their subsamples (Germanics and Anglo-Saxons in the Caucasian tabulations), I point out that several Indian subsamples are equally high (though Morton amalgamated all North American Indians and never reported averages by subgroup), and that all Teutonic and Anglo-Saxon averages are either miscalculated or biased in Morton's table.

Conclusions

Morton's finagling may be ordered into four general categories:

1. Favorable inconsistencies and shifting criteria: Morton often chose to include or delete large subsamples in order to match group averages with prior expectations. He included Inca Peruvians to decrease the Indian average, but deleted Hindus to raise the Caucasian mean. He also chose to present or not to calculate the averages of subsamples in striking accord with desired results. He made calculations for Caucasians to demonstrate the superiority of Teutons and Anglo-

Saxons, but never presented data for Indian subsamples with equally high averages.

2. Subjectivity directed toward prior prejudice: Morton's measures with seed were sufficiently imprecise to permit a wide range of influence by subjective bias; later measures with shot, on the other hand, were repeatable, and presumably objective. In skulls measured by both methods, values for shot always exceed values for the light, poorly packing seed. But degrees of discrepancy match a priori assumptions: an average of 5.4, 2.2, and 1.8 cubic inches for blacks, Indians, and whites, respectively. In other words, blacks fared poorest and whites best when the results could be biased toward an expected result.

3. Procedural omissions that seem obvious to us: Morton was convinced that variation in skull size recorded differential, innate mental ability. He never considered alternate hypotheses, though his own data almost cried out for a different interpretation. Morton never computed means by sex or stature, even when he recorded these data in his tabulations—as for Egyptian mummies. Had he computed the effect of stature, he would presumably have recognized that it explained all important differences in brain size among his groups. Negroids yielded a lower average than Caucasians among his Egyptian skulls because the negroid sample probably contained a higher percentage of smaller-statured females, not because blacks are innately stupider. The Incas that he included in the Indian sample and the Hindus that he excluded from the Caucasian sample both possessed small brains as a consequence of small body size. Morton used an all-female sample of three Hottentots to support the stupidity of blacks, and an all-male sample of Englishmen to assert the superiority of whites.

4. Miscalculations and convenient omissions: All miscalculations and omissions that I have detected are in Morton's favor. He rounded the negroid Egyptian average down to 79, rather than up to 80. He cited averages of 90 for Germans and Anglo-Saxons, but the correct values are 88 and 89. He excluded a large Chinese skull and an Eskimo subsample from his final tabulation for mongoloids, thus depressing their average below the Caucasian value.

Yet through all this juggling, I detect no sign of fraud or conscious manipulation. Morton made no attempt to cover his tracks and I must presume that he was unaware he had left them. He explained all his procedures and published all his raw data. All I can discern is an a priori conviction about racial ranking so powerful that it directed his tabulations along preestablished lines. Yet Morton was widely hailed as the objectivist of his age, the man who would rescue American science from the mire of unsupported speculation.

The American School and Slavery

The leading American polygenists differed in their attitude toward slavery. Most were Northerners, and most favored some version of Squier's quip: "[I have a] precious poor opinion of niggers . . . a still poorer one of slavery" (in Stanton, 1960, p. 193).

But the identification of blacks as a separate and unequal species had obvious appeal as an argument for slavery. Josiah Nott, a leading polygenist, encountered particularly receptive audiences in the South for his "lectures on niggerology" (as he called them). Morton's *Crania Aegyptiaca* received a warm welcome in the South (in Stanton, 1960, pp. 52–53). One supporter of slavery wrote that the South need no longer be "so much frightened" by "voices of Europe or of Northern America" in defending its "peculiar institutions." When Morton died, the South's leading medical journal proclaimed (R. W. Gibbs, *Charleston Medical Journal*, 1851, quoted in Stanton, 1960, p. 144): "We of the South should consider him as our benefactor, for aiding most materially in giving to the negro his true position as an inferior race."

Nonetheless, the polygenist argument did not occupy a primary place in the ideology of slavery in mid-nineteenth-century America—and for a good reason. For most Southerners, this excellent argument entailed too high a price. The polygenists had railed against ideologues as barriers to their pure search for truth, but their targets were parsons more often than abolitionists. Their theory, in asserting a plurality of human creations, contradicted the doctrine of a single Adam and contravened the literal truth of scripture. Although the leading polygenists held a diversity of religious attitudes, none were atheists. Morton and Agassiz were conventionally devout, but they did believe that both science and religion would be aided if untrained parsons kept their noses out of scientific issues and stopped proffering the Bible as a document to settle debates in natural history. Josiah Nott stated his goal in a forceful way (Agassiz and Morton would not have put it so baldly): ". . . to cut loose the natural history of mankind from the Bible, and to place each upon its own foundation, where it may remain without collision or molestation" (in Stanton, 1960, p. 119).

The polygenists forced defenders of slavery into a quandary: Should they accept a strong argument from science at the cost of limiting religion's sphere? In resolving this dilemma, the Bible usually won. After all, scriptural arguments for supporting slavery were not wanting. Degeneration of blacks under the curse of Ham was an old and eminently functional standby. Moreover, polygeny was not the only quasi-scientific defense available.

John Bachman, for example, was a South Carolina parson and prominent naturalist. As a committed monogenist, he spent a good part of his scientific career attempting to refute polygeny. He also used monogenist principles to defend slavery:

> In intellectual power the African is an inferior variety of our species. His whole history affords evidence that he is incapable of self-government. Our child that we lead by the hand, and who looks to us for protection and support is still of our own blood notwithstanding his weakness and ignorance (in Stanton, 1960, p. 63).

Among nonpolygenist, "scientific" defenses of slavery, no arguments ever matched in absurdity the doctrines of S. A. Cartwright, a prominent Southern physician. (I do not cite these as typical and I doubt that many intelligent Southerners paid them much attention; I merely wish to illustrate an extreme within the range of "scientific" argument.) Cartwright traced the problems of black people to inadequate decarbonization of blood in the lungs (insufficient removal of carbon dioxide): "It is the defective . . . atmospherization of the blood, conjoined with a deficiency of cerebral matter in the cranium . . . that is the true cause of that debasement of mind, which has rendered the people of Africa unable to take care of themselves" (from Chorover, 1979; all quotes from Cartwright are taken from papers he presented to the 1851 meeting of the Louisiana Medical Association.).

Cartwright even had a name for it—*dysesthesia*, a disease of inadequate breathing. He described its symptoms in slaves: "When driven to labor . . . he performs the task assigned to him in a headlong and careless manner, treading down with his feet or cutting with his hoe the plants he is put to cultivate—breaking the tools he works with, and spoiling everything he touches." Ignorant Northerners attributed this behavior to "the debasing influence of slavery," but Cartwright recognized it as the expression of a true disease. He identified insensibility to pain as another symptom: "When the unfortunate individual is subjected to punishment, he neither feels pain of any consequence . . . [nor] any unusual resentment more than stupid sulkiness. In some cases . . . there appears to be an almost total loss of feeling." Cartwright proposed the following cure:

> The liver, skin and kidneys should be stimulated to activity . . . to assist in decarbonizing the blood. The best means to stimulate the skin is, first, to have the patient well washed with warm water and soap; then to anoint it all over with oil, and to slap the oil in with a broad leather strap; then to put the patient to some hard kind of work in the open air and sunshine that will compel him to expand his lungs, as chopping wood, splitting rals, or sawing with the crosscut or whip saw.

Cartwright did not end his catalogue of diseases with dysesthesia. He wondered why slaves often tried to flee, and identified the cause as a mental disease called *drapetomania*, or the insane desire to run away. "Like children, they are constrained by unalterable physiological laws, to love those in authority over them. Hence, from a law of his nature, the negro can no more help loving a kind master, than the child can help loving her that gives it suck." For slaves afflicted with drapetomania, Cartwright proposed a behavioral cure: owners should avoid both extreme permissiveness and cruelty: "They have only to be kept in that state, and treated like children, to prevent and cure them from running away."

The defenders of slavery did not need polygeny. Religion still stood above science as a primary source for the rationalization of social order. But the American debate on polygeny may represent the last time that arguments in the scientific mode did not form a first line of defense for the status quo and the unalterable quality of human differences. The Civil War lay just around the corner, but so did 1859 and Darwin's *Origin of Species*. Subsequent arguments for slavery, colonialism, racial differences, class structures, and sex roles would go forth primarily under the banner of science.

Claude M. Steele

Black Students Live Down to Expectations

The debate over affirmative action on college campuses has become dangerously distanced from facts. The issue has taken on such an ideological fervor that votes, Presidential and otherwise, are hanging in the balance. In the fray, the image of African-American college students has taken a beating.

Opponents of affirmative action claim that it pushes African-American students into schools where they can't compete and where, with the stigma they bear as "special admits," they get lower grades and drop out more than other students.

It is true that these students have their troubles, suffering a college dropout rate hovering near 70 percent (against 40 percent for other students), with lower grades to match. Given such statistics, even supporters of affirmative action have faltered, too unsure themselves about the students' abilities to rise quickly or publicly to their defense.

In fact, most black college students are in school on the same terms as anyone else, not as a result of any racial preference. Still, as their fate goes, so goes our faith in affirmative action and in the ability of public policy to address racial and social problems. So a few facts and some new evidence can help in addressing some central questions.

- *Do the academic troubles of black students stem from their being underprepared for the competition?*

This is a common complaint that has turned into conventional wisdom. But in fact there isn't much evidence of it. Very few minority students are admitted to any college beneath that school's cut-off for other students.

It is true that blacks have lower S.A.T. scores than other entering students. But the deficit in test scores—which are certainly flawed as predictors anyway—doesn't begin to explain why black students are more likely to drop out and get bad grades once they begin college. Besides, this "underperformance" is just as common among black students entering with very high test scores and grades as it is among those with weaker credentials.

One thing is clear: If affirmative action is failing by not producing more successful black college students, it is not because they have been placed where they can't compete.

- *If it isn't a lack of preparation, then what is depressing their performance?*

Recent research by my colleagues and me points to a disruptive pressure tied to racial stereotypes that affects these students. The pressure begins simply enough, with a student's knowledge that negative stereotypes about his group could apply to him—that he could be judged by this perception, treated in terms of it, even that he could fulfill it.

Black students know that the stereotypes about them raise questions about their intellectual ability. Quite beside any actual discriminatory treatment, they can feel that their intelligence is constantly and everywhere on trial—and all this at a tender age and on difficult proving ground.

They may not believe the stereotype. But it becomes a threatening hypothesis that they can grow weary of fending off—much as a white student, for example, can grow weary of fending off the stereotype that his group is racist.

Everyone is subject to some form of what I call "stereotype vulnerability." The form that black students suffer from can hurt them where it matters, in academic performance. My research with Joshua Aronson shows that "stereotype vulnerability" can cost these students many points on exams like the S.A.T.

Over time, the pressure can push the students to stop identifying with achievement in school. They may even band together in doing this, making "disidentification" the pattern. For my money, the syndrome is at the root of black students' troubles in college.

If affirmative action contributes to this problem, it is less from the policy itself than from its implementation, often through a phalanx of "minority support" programs that, however well intended, reinforce negative stereotypes. Almost certainly, there would be persistent, troubling underperformance by minority students even if affirmative action programs were dismantled, just as there was before they existed.

- *Is there any reason to believe that affirmative action programs can alleviate this problem?*

In the diagnosis may lie the seeds of a cure: Schools need to reduce the burden of suspicion these students are under. Challenging students works better than dumbing down their education. Framing intelligence as expandable rather than as a set, limiting trait makes frustration a signal to try harder, not to give up. Finally, it is crucial that the college convey, especially through relationships with authoritative adults, that it values them for their intellectual promise and not just because of its own openness to minorities.

My colleagues (Steven Spencer, Mary Hummel, David Schoem, Kent Harber and Richard Nisbett) and I incorporated these and other principles into a program at the University of Michigan for the last four years. The students, both white and minority, were selected randomly for the project and as freshmen were housed in the same dorm.

Through workshops and group study, all placing emphasis on the students' intellectual potential, the program eliminated the differential between black and white students' grades in freshman year for the top two-thirds of the black students.

It helped others as well; 92 percent of all the students in the group, white and black, were still in school after four years.

The success of comparable programs—Urie Treisman's math workshops at the University of Texas, Georgia State's pre-engineering program, John Johnides's faculty mentoring project, also at Michigan—show that this approach can work.

- *But what about reverse discrimination? How much does this policy of inclusion cost in exclusion of others?*

To know if affirmative action is displacing whites in admissions, you have to know if, among comparably qualified applicants, more minorities get in than whites.

Thomas Kane of Harvard University's Kennedy School of Government found that this seems to happen only in elite colleges, where the average S.A.T. score is above 1,100. These schools make up only 15 percent of our four-year colleges. There was no evidence of preference in admissions among the rest.

Moreover, in the elite schools, blacks don't often use the preference they get, choosing schools closer to home, perhaps, for various reasons. They rarely exceed 7 percent of the student body at the top schools. Overall, affirmative action causes little displacement of other students—less by far than other forms of preferences, like the one for children of alumni.

In our society, individual initiative is an indisputable source of mobility. But a stream of resources including money, education and contacts is also important. After all this time, even the black middle class has only tentative access to this stream. Affirmative action in college represents a commitment to fixing this, allowing those with initiative a wider aperture of opportunity.

If its opponents prevail and affirmative action is dumped, will the same people, so ostensibly outraged by the racial injustice of it, then step forward to address the more profound racial injustices?

I wouldn't bet on it and, in the meantime, let's talk about this policy frankly and pragmatically: how to improve it, when it should be more inclusive, and how it should be made fairer.

To dump it now would be to hold some people, just beginning to experience a broader fairness in society, to a tougher standard than the rest of us have had to meet.

SHELBY STEELE

Affirmative Action: The Price of Preference

In a few short years, when my two children will be applying to college, the affirmative action policies by which most universities offer black students some form of preferential treatment will present me with a dilemma. I am a middle-class black, a college professor, far from wealthy, but also well-removed from the kind of deprivation that would qualify my children for the label "disadvantaged." Both of them have endured racial insensitivity from whites. They have been called names, have suffered slights, and have experienced firsthand the peculiar malevolence that racism brings out in people. Yet, they have never experienced racial discrimination, have never been stopped by their race on any path they have chosen to follow. Still, their society now tells them that if they will only designate themselves as black on their college applications, they will likely do better in the college lottery than if they conceal this fact. I think there is something of a Faustian bargain in this.

Of course, many blacks and a considerable number of whites would say that I was sanctimoniously making affirmative action into a test of character. They would say that this small preference is the meagerest recompense for centuries of unrelieved oppression. And to these arguments other very obvious facts must be added. In America, many marginally competent or flatly incompetent whites are hired everyday—some because their white skin suits the conscious or unconscious racial preference of their employer. The white children of alumni are often grandfathered into elite universities in what can only be seen as a residual benefit of historic white privilege. Worse, white incompetence is always an individual matter, while for blacks it is often confirmation of ugly stereotypes. The Peter Principle was not conceived with only blacks in mind. Given that unfairness cuts both ways, doesn't it only balance the scales of history that my children now receive a slight preference over whites? Doesn't this repay, in a small way, the systematic denial under which their grandfather lived out his days?

So, in theory, affirmative action certainly has all the moral symmetry that fairness requires—the injustice of historical and even contemporary white advantage is offset with black advantage; preference replaces prejudice, inclusion answers exclusion. It is reformist and corrective, even repentent and redemptive. And I would never sneer at these good intentions. Born in the late forties in Chicago, I started my education (a charitable term in this case) in a segregated school and suffered all the indignities that come to blacks in a segregated society. My father, born in the South, only made it to the third grade before the white man's fields took permanent priority over his formal education. And though he educated himself into an advanced reader with an almost professorial authority, he could only drive a truck for a living and never earned more than ninety dollars a week in his entire life. So yes, it is crucial to my sense of citizenship, to my ability to identify with the spirit and the interests of America, to know that this country, however imperfectly, recognizes its past sins and wishes to correct them.

Yet good intentions, because of the opportunity for innocence they offer us, are very seductive and can blind us to the effects they generate when implemented. In our society, affirmative action is, among other things, a testament to white goodwill and to black power, and in the midst of these heavy investments, its effect can be hard to see. But after twenty years of implementation, I think affirmative action has shown itself to be more bad than good and that blacks—whom I will focus on in this essay—now stand to lose more from it than they gain.

In talking with affirmative action administrators and with blacks and whites in general, it is clear that supporters of affirmative action focus on its good intentions while detractors emphasize its negative effects. Proponents talk about "diversity" and "pluralism"; opponents speak of "reverse discrimination," the unfairness of quotas and set-asides. It was virtually impossible to find people outside either camp. The closest I came was a white male manager at a large computer company who said, "I think it amounts to reverse discrimination, but I'll put up with a little of that for a little more diversity." I'll live with a little of the effect to gain a little of the intention, he seemed to be saying. But this only makes him a halfhearted supporter of affirmative action. I think many people who don't really like affirmative action support it to one degree or another anyway.

I believe they do this because of what happened to white and black Americans in the crucible of the sixties when whites were confronted with their racial guilt and blacks tasted their first real power. In this stormy time white absolution and black power coalesced into virtual mandates for society. Affirmative action became a meeting ground for these mandates in the law, and in the late sixties and early seventies it underwent

a remarkable escalation of its mission from simple anti-discrimination enforcement to social engineering by means of quotas, goals, timetables, set-asides and other forms of preferential treatment.

Legally, this was achieved through a series of executive orders and EEOC guidelines that allowed racial imbalances in the workplace to stand as proof of racial discrimination. Once it could be assumed that discrimination explained racial imbalances, it became easy to justify group remedies to presumed discrimination, rather than the normal case-by-case redress for proven discrimination. Preferential treatment through quotas, goals, and so on is designed to correct imbalances based on the assumption that they always indicate discrimination. This expansion of what constitutes discrimination allowed affirmative action to escalate into the business of social engineering in the name of anti-discrimination, to push society toward statistically proportionate racial representation, without any obligation of proving actual discrimination.

What accounted for this shift, I believe, was the white mandate to achieve a new racial innocence and the black mandate to gain power. Even though blacks had made great advances during the sixties without quotas, these mandates, which came to a head in the very late sixties, could no longer be satisfied by anything less than racial preferences. I don't think these mandates in themselves were wrong, since whites clearly needed to do better by blacks and blacks needed more real power in society. But, as they came together in affirmative action, their effect was to distort our understanding of racial discrimination in a way that allowed us to offer the remediation of preference on the basis of mere color rather than actual injury. By making black the color of preference, these mandates have reburdened society with the very marriage of color and preference (in reverse) that we set out to eradicate. The old sin is reaffirmed in a new guise.

But the essential problem with this form of affirmative action is the way it leaps over the hard business of developing a formerly oppressed people to the point where they can achieve proportionate representation on their own (given equal opportunity) and goes straight for the proportionate representation. This may satisfy some whites of their innocence and some blacks of their power, but it does very little to truly uplift blacks.

A white female affirmative action officer at an Ivy League university told me what many supporters of affirmative action now say: "We're after diversity. We ideally want a student body where racial and ethnic groups are represented according to their proportion in society." When affirmative action escalated into social engineering, diversity became a golden word. It grants whites an egalitarian fairness (innocence) and blacks an entitlement to proportionate representation (power). *Diversity* is a term that applies democratic principles to races and cultures rather than to citizens, despite the fact that there is nothing to indicate that real diversity is the same thing as proportionate representation. Too often the result of this on campuses (for example) has been a democracy of colors rather than of people, an artificial diversity that gives the appearance of an educational parity between black and white students that has not yet been achieved in reality. Here again, racial preferences allow society to leapfrog over the difficult problem of developing blacks to parity with whites and into a cosmetic diversity that covers the blemish of disparity—a full six years after admission, only about 26 percent of black students graduate from college.

Racial representation is not the same thing as racial development, yet affirmative action fosters a confusion of these very different needs. Representation can be manufactured; development is always hard-earned. However, it is the music of innocence and power that we hear in affirmative action that causes us to cling to it and to its distracting emphasis on representation. The fact is that after twenty years of racial preferences, the gap between white and black median income is greater than it was in the seventies. None of this is to say that blacks don't need policies that ensure our right to equal opportunity, but what we need more is the development that will let us take advantage of society's efforts to include us.

I think that one of the most troubling effects of racial preferences for blacks is a kind of demoralization, or put another way, an enlargement of self-doubt. Under affirmative action the quality that earns us preferential treatment is an implied inferiority. However this inferiority is explained—and it is easily enough explained by the myriad deprivations that grew out of our oppression—it is still inferiority. There are explanations, and then there is the fact. And the fact must be borne by the individual as a condition apart from the explanation, apart even from the fact that others like himself also bear this condition. In integrated situations where blacks must compete with whites who may be better prepared, these explanations may quickly wear thin and expose the individual to racial as well as personal self-doubt.

All of this is compounded by the cultural myth of black inferiority that blacks have always lived with. What this means in practical terms is that when blacks deliver themselves into integrated situations, they encounter a nasty little reflex in whites, a mindless, atavistic reflex that responds to the color black with alarm. Attributions may follow this alarm if the white cares to

indulge them, and if they do, they will most likely be negative—one such attribution is intellectual ineptness. I think this reflex and the attributions that may follow it embarrass most whites today, therefore, it is usually quickly repressed. Nevertheless, on an equally atavistic level, the black will be aware of the reflex his color triggers and will feel a stab of horror at seeing himself reflected in this way. He, too, will do a quick repression, but a lifetime of such stabbings is what constitutes his inner realm of racial doubt.

The effects of this may be a subject for another essay. The point here is that the implication of inferiority that racial preferences engender in both the white and black mind expands rather than contracts this doubt. Even when the black sees no implication of inferiority in racial preferences, he knows that whites do, so that—consciously or unconsciously—the result is virtually the same. The effect of preferential treatment—the lowering of normal standards to increase black representation—puts blacks at war with an expanded realm of debilitating doubt, so that the doubt itself becomes an unrecognized preoccupation that undermines their ability to perform, especially in integrated situations. On largely white campuses, blacks are five times more likely to drop out than whites. Preferential treatment, no matter how it is justified in the light of day, subjects blacks to a midnight of self-doubt, and so often transforms their advantage into a revolving door.

Another liability of affirmative action comes from the fact that it indirectly encourages blacks to exploit their own past victimization as a source of power and privilege. Victimization, like implied inferiority, is what justifies preference, so that to receive the benefits of preferential treatment one must, to some extent, become invested in the view of one's self as a victim. In this way, affirmative action nurtures a victim-focused identity in blacks. The obvious irony here is that we become inadvertently invested in the very condition we are trying to overcome. Racial preferences send us the message that there is more power in our past suffering than our present achievements—none of which could bring us a *preference* over others.

When power itself grows out of suffering, then blacks are encouraged to expand the boundaries of what qualifies as racial oppression, a situation that can lead us to paint our victimization in vivid colors, even as we receive the benefits of preferences. The same corporations and institutions that give us preference are also seen as our oppressors. At Stanford University minority students—some of whom enjoy as much as $15,000 a year in financial aid—recently took over the president's office demanding, among other things, more financial aid. The power to be found in victimization, like any power, is intoxicating and can lend itself to the creation of a new class of super-victims who can feel the pea of victimization under twenty mattresses. Preferential treatment rewards us for being underdogs rather than for moving beyond that status—a misplacement of incentives that, along with its deepening of our doubt, is more a yoke than a spur.

But, I think, one of the worst prices that blacks pay for preference has to do with an illusion. I saw this illusion at work recently in the mother of a middle-class black student who was going off to his first semester of college. "They owe us this, so don't think for a minute that you don't belong there." This is the logic by which many blacks, and some whites, justify affirmative action—it is something "owed," a form of reparation. But this logic overlooks a much harder and less digestible reality, that it is impossible to repay blacks living today for the historic suffering of the race. If all blacks were given a million dollars tomorrow morning it would not amount to a dime on the dollar of three centuries of oppression, nor would it obviate the residues of that oppression that we still carry today. The concept of historic reparation grows out of man's need to impose a degree of justice on the world that simply does not exist. Suffering can be endured and overcome, it cannot be repaid. Blacks cannot be repaid for the injustice done to the race, but we can be corrupted by society's guilty gestures of repayment.

Affirmative action is such a gesture. It tells us that racial preferences can do for us what we cannot do for ourselves. The corruption here is in the hidden incentive *not* to do what we believe preferences will do. This is an incentive to be reliant on others just as we are struggling for self-reliance. And it keeps alive the illusion that we can find some deliverance in repayment. The hardest thing for any sufferer to accept is that his suffering excuses him from very little and never has enough currency to restore him. To think otherwise is to prolong the suffering.

Several blacks I spoke with said they were still in favor of affirmative action because of the "subtle" discrimination blacks were subject to once on the job. One photojournalist said, "They have ways of ignoring you." A black female television producer said, "You can't file a lawsuit when your boss doesn't invite you to the insider meetings without ruining your career. So we still need affirmative action." Others mentioned the infamous "glass ceiling" through which blacks can see the top positions of authority but never reach them. But I don't think racial preferences are a protection against this subtle discrimination; I think they contribute to it.

In any workplace, racial preferences will always create two-tiered populations composed of preferreds and unpreferreds. This division makes automatic a perception of enhanced competence for the unpreferreds and of questionable competence for the preferreds—the former earned his way, even though others were given preference, while the latter made it by color as much as by competence. Racial preferences implicitly mark whites with an exaggerated superiority just as they mark blacks with an exaggerated inferiority. They not only reinforce America's oldest racial myth but, for blacks, they have the effect of stigmatizing the already stigmatized.

I think that much of the "subtle" discrimination that blacks talk about is often (not always) discrimination against the stigma of questionable competence that affirmative action delivers to blacks. In this sense, preferences scapegoat the very people they seek to help. And it may be that at a certain level employers impose a glass ceiling, but this may not be against the race so much as against the race's reputation for having advanced by color as much as by competence. Affirmative action makes a glass ceiling virtually necessary as a protection against the corruptions of preferential treatment. This ceiling is the point at which corporations shift the emphasis from color to competency and stop playing the affirmative action game. Here preference backfires for blacks and becomes a taint that holds them back. Of course, one could argue that this taint, which is, after all, in the minds of whites, becomes nothing more than an excuse to discriminate against blacks. And certainly the result is the same in either case—blacks don't get past the glass ceiling. But this argument does not get around the fact that racial preferences now taint this color with a new theme of suspicion that makes it even more vulnerable to the impulse in others to discriminate. In this crucial yet gray area of perceived competence, preferences make whites look better than they are and blacks worse, while doing nothing whatever to stop the very real discrimination that blacks may encounter. I don't wish to justify the glass ceiling here, but only to suggest the very subtle ways that affirmative action revives rather than extinguishes the old rationalizations for racial discrimination.

In education, a revolving door; in employment, a glass ceiling.

I believe affirmative action is problematic in our society because it tries to function like a social program. Rather than ask it to ensure equal opportunity we have demanded that it create parity between the races. But preferential treatment does not teach skills, or educate, or instill motivation. It only passes out entitlement by color, a situation that in my profession has created an unrealistically high demand for black professors. The social engineer's assumption is that this high demand will inspire more blacks to earn Ph.D.'s and join the profession. In fact, the number of blacks earning Ph.D.'s has declined in recent years. A Ph.D. must be developed from preschool on. He requires family and community support. He must acquire an entire system of values that enables him to work hard while delaying gratification. There are social programs, I believe, that can (and should) help blacks *develop* in all these areas, but entitlement by color is not a social program; it is a dubious reward for being black.

It now seems clear that the Supreme Court, in a series of recent decisions, is moving away from racial preferences. It has disallowed preferences except in instances of "identified discrimination," eroded the precedent that statistical racial imbalances are *prima facie* evidence of discrimination, and in effect granted white males the right to challenge consent degrees that use preference to achieve racial balances in the workplace. One civil rights leader said, "Night has fallen on civil rights." But I am not so sure. The effect of these decisions is to protect the constitutional rights of everyone rather than take rights away from blacks. What they do take away from blacks is the special entitlement to more rights than others that preferences always grant. Night has fallen on racial preferences, not on the fundamental rights of black Americans. The reason for this shift, I believe, is that the white mandate for absolution from past racial sins has weakened considerably during the eighties. Whites are now less willing to endure unfairness to themselves in order to grant special entitlements to blacks, even when these entitlements are justified in the name of past suffering. Yet the black mandate for more power in society has remained unchanged. And I think part of the anxiety that many blacks feel over these decisions has to do with the loss of black power they may signal. We had won a certain specialness and now we are losing it.

But the power we've lost by these decisions is really only the power that grows out of our victimization—the power to claim special entitlements under the law because of past oppression. This is not a very substantial or reliable power, and it is important that we know this so we can focus more exclusively on the kind of development that will bring enduring power. There is talk now that Congress will pass new legislation to compensate for these new limits on affirmative action. If this happens, I hope that their focus will be on development and anti-discrimination rather than entitlement, on achieving racial parity rather than jerry-building racial diversity.

I would also like to see affirmative action go back to its original purpose of enforcing equal opportunity—a purpose that in itself disallows racial preferences. We cannot be sure that the discriminatory impulse in

America has yet been shamed into extinction, and I believe affirmative action can make its greatest contribution by providing a rigorous vigilance in this area. It can guard constitutional rather than racial rights, and help institutions evolve standards of merit and selection that are appropriate to the institution's needs yet as free of racial bias as possible (again, with the understanding that racial imbalances are not always an indication of racial bias). One of the most important things affirmative action can do is to define exactly what racial discrimination is and how it might manifest itself within a specific institution. The impulse to discriminate *is* subtle and cannot be ferreted out unless its many guises are made clear to people. Along with this there should be monitoring of institutions and heavy sanctions brought to bear when actual discrimination is found. This is the sort of affirmative action that America owes to blacks and to itself. It goes after the evil of discrimination itself, while preferences only sidestep the evil and grant entitlement to its *presumed* victims.

But if not preferences, then what? I think we need social policies that are committed to two goals: the educational and economic development of disadvantaged people, regardless of race, and the eradication from our society—through close monitoring and severe sanctions—of racial, ethnic, or gender discrimination. Preferences will not deliver us to either of these goals, since they tend to benefit those who are not disadvantaged—middle-class white women and middle-class blacks—and attack one form of discrimination with another. Preferences are inexpensive and carry the glamour of good intentions—change the numbers and the good deed is done. To be against them is to be unkind. But I think the unkindest cut is to bestow on children like my own an undeserved advantage while neglecting the development of those disadvantaged children on the East Side of my city who will likely never be in a position to benefit from a preference. Give my children fairness; give disadvantaged children a better shot at development—better elementary and secondary schools, job training, safer neighborhoods, better financial assistance for college, and so on. Fewer blacks go to college today than ten years ago; more black males of college age are in prison or under the control of the criminal justice system than in college. This despite racial preferences.

The mandates of black power and white absolution out of which preferences emerged were not wrong in themselves. What was wrong was that both races focused more on the goals of these mandates than on the means to the goals. Blacks can have no real power without taking responsibility for their own educational and economic development. Whites can have no racial innocence without earning it by eradicating discrimination and helping the disadvantaged to develop. Because we ignored the means, the goals have not been reached, and the real work remains to be done.

ETHAN WATTERS

Claude Steele Has Scores to Settle

Gathered here at the Harris School of Public Policy at the University of Chicago on this warm morning is an unusually interdisciplinary group of two dozen academic heavyweights. Hailing from the nation's most elite departments of education, economics, public policy, social psychology and sociology, these scholars have come together to discuss the hot topic of the year. Inspired by last year's controversial book "The Bell Curve," the question today is: Why do African-Americans score significantly worse on standardized tests than whites? As people take their seats around the long wood table, one professor silently reads down the list of presenters, leans to a colleague and asks, "Who's this Claude Steele from Stanford?"

"I don't know," the other says. Looking around the room, they locate Steele by name tag. Across the table, Steele, wearing a dark tweed jacket, striped dress shirt and tie, shuffles some papers in preparation for his talk.

"Oh, maybe he's that black essayist," the first professor suggests. "Why would he be presenting here? Some literary angle perhaps?"

Although Steele can't hear the exchange, it would not surprise him that he was mistaken for his estranged brother, the well-known conservative author Shelby Steele. The two are identical twins, right down to their closely trimmed peppered mustaches.

A professor of social psychology, Steele, 49, has a different take than the other scholars presenting today. While they have tried to find an answer to the black-white testing gap by analyzing factors like economic status, family structure and educational opportunities, Steele has looked into the test-taking situation itself and has found new evidence of "a beast" stalking black test takers.

"Our idea," Steele says to the group, "was that whenever black students concentrate on an explicitly scholastic task, they risk confirming their group's negative stereotype. This extra burden, in situations with certain characteristics, can be enough to drag down

their performance. We call this burden stereotype vulnerability."

In the first experiment Steele describes, he and Joshua Aronson from the University of Texas gave two groups of black and white Stanford undergraduates a test composed of the most difficult verbal-skills questions from the Graduate Record Exam. Before the test, one group was told that the purpose of the exercise was only to research "psychological factors involved in solving verbal problems," while the other group was told that the exam was "a genuine test of your verbal abilities and limitations."

"This is what we found," Steele says, placing a transparency onto the overhead projector. As the information in the bar charts sinks in, people sit up in their chairs. There are several audible "hmmms," a muffled "wow!" Then a professor at the back of the room asks: "Did you give the groups the same test?"

Steele smiles and says, "Yes." The question speaks to the startling nature of the results. As the graphs indicate, the blacks who thought they were simply solving problems performed as well as the whites (who performed equally in both situations). However, the group of black students who labored under the belief that the test could measure their intellectual potential performed significantly worse than all the other students.

Steele's idea of stereotype vulnerability is not that the student consciously or unconsciously accepts the stereotype (as other social scientists have speculated), but rather, as Steele says, that they have to *contend* with this whisper of inferiority at the moment when their mental abilities are most taxed. In trying not to give credence to the stereotype, Steele theorizes, the students may redouble their efforts only to work too quickly or inefficiently. The cues that can spark the vulnerability can be subtle—like suggesting the test can measure ability or making students mark down their races before the test begins. While there might be no perceptible bias in a given test or in the test-taking situation, an exam might still be weighted against blacks because the possibility of performing badly has a more devastating meaning.

As Steele goes on to describe his experiments—more than a dozen over the last four years—the audience remains riveted. With his colleague Steve Spencer at Hope College, he has run eight additional experiments showing that stereotype vulnerability can negatively affect women who believe a given math test shows "gender differences." The negative impact of stereotype vulnerability has even appeared in white men who took a difficult math test after being told that Asians tended to outperform whites on that particular exam.

"Have you told anyone about this work?" one professor asks Steele after the conference. "The

Ethan Watters, "Claude Steele Has Scores to Settle," THE NEW YORK TIMES MAGAZINE, September 17, 1995. Copyright © 1995 by The New York Times Co. Reprinted by permission.

ramifications are enormous." Janellen Huttenlocher, a professor of psychology at the University of Chicago, says, "I've never heard of him but his work is fascinating." Glenn Loury, an African-American Boston University economist, adds, "He hit a home run." The professor who didn't know who Steele was an hour ago is now whispering to a colleague, "So how did we miss him in our hiring searches?"

A few weeks after the Chicago conference in June, Steele takes the afternoon to further explain his work during a walk in the grassy hills behind his Stanford home. Steele has the patient demeanor of a teacher taking time with a student after class. Handsome and engaging, he is a favorite among the graduate students at the Stanford psychology department.

He began his research on the psychological aspects of race in 1987 while studying the dropout rates of black students at the University of Michigan, where he had just taken a position. This was the year before his brother entered the bitter national debate over race with two essays, one in Harper's and the other in Commentary. Over the next several years, his brother became a prominent commentator and collected his essays into the best-selling book "The Content of Our Character: A New Vision of Race in America," in which he argued that blacks must stop trying to gain power by claiming victim status.

At Michigan, Steele found a puzzle in the statistics on the performance of black students that drew his interest. According to university data, no matter how well qualified a black student was at a given level, he or she was more likely than an equally qualified white student to fall behind at the next level of achievement. Steele figured that the more well known factors like discrimination, bad schools, broken homes and the poverty and crime that disproportionately damage black communities couldn't fully account for the plight of highly motivated, middle-class African-Americans. "Black students with 1,300 S.A.T. scores were going home from college with 2.4 G.P.A.'s," Steele says. "When I realized that the smartest black students were having these terrible troubles, I figured something else was going on."

After talking with students, Steele decided that the answer was not a lack of a desire to succeed. Nor could he find significant overt or covert racism on the part of the school. He began formulating theories on how the ebbs and flows of anxiety and confidence that all students experience might be exaggerated in black students by the deeper currents in a racially focused society.

As Steele describes it, stereotype vulnerability is a "patient predator" that affects black students not just in testing situations, but in every area of their academic lives. "At each new proving ground the problem can re-emerge," Steele says. "The student who has risen above the stereotype in high school—proving to everyone that he is smart—goes off to college, where a new level of performance is expected."

Eventually, even minor failures—a lapse in grammar while talking to a professor—can discourage. At some point, students may begin to "disidentify" or pull away from the challenge of school.

But Steele doesn't just want to explain away the overall poor showing of black students. "One of the thrills of doing this research," Steele says, "is that I can provide an optimistic take without being political—it's in the results." The results he's referring to are not the ones that demonstrate that stereotype vulnerability exists, but those that show that it disappears with the subtlest of changes. Take away the situational clues that make the setting racially charged (like having to identify race before the exam), and the vulnerability can vanish from the student's performance. If this vulnerability can be consistently kept at bay, Steele says, the downward spiral may never start.

Detractors are hard to find, partly because the research hasn't yet had wide circulation. Steele presented his findings last month in New York at the American Psychological Association's annual meeting. A paper, co-written by Aronson, is being published this fall by the association's Journal of Personality and Social Psychology. A few fellow academics strike a pose of reserved interest. "As with most experimental work, it is hard to judge the magnitude of the effect in real-life testing situations," says Sandra Scarr, the Commonwealth Professor of Psychology at the University of Virginia. "Still, it's novel work." Even Charles Murray, co-author of "The Bell Curve," which argued that blacks were intellectually inferior to other races, is inclined to give it some credence. "I think he probably has hold of something that might be one source of poor academic performance among blacks," Murray says. "The question I have is whether you can extend this theory to tests that exclusively measure cognitive functioning. I doubt he can. I wish him well though. I think it's fascinating stuff."

While Steele's experiments thus far have focused on tests that measure both learning and intelligence—verbal G.R.E. tests for African-Americans and math tests for women—he intends to try his theory on the various I.Q. and cognitive ability tests to which Murray refers.

From the top of the path behind Steele's house, he can survey the red-tile roofs of the Stanford Campus and the bell tower that marks home of the conservative Hoover Institution, where his brother began a fellowship this summer. From this perspective, the bell tower is only a compass point or two away from the psychology building where Steele has his office. He won't talk specifically about his brother's work or their relationship except to say that it has been alternatively close and estranged for much of their lives. They are currently not talking.

When the conversation with Steele accidentally lands on the topic of Shelby or his work, Steele sighs and chooses his words carefully. "He blew a hole open in the debate about the black student's experience on campus, which has allowed a lot of people, including myself, to walk into the discussion. I think of it as almost an unfortunate detail that we wound up following similar terrain and coming down on an issue like affirmative action on different sides. It suggests a bigger difference than there really is."

Despite efforts on both their parts to chart separate life courses, fate seems intent on drawing them back together. Like their father, both have married white women. Not only did they both end up at the University of Utah at the same time in the 1970's (where Claude took his first teaching job and Shelby was getting his English Ph.D.), Claude's appointment at Stanford in 1991 has landed him within an hour's drive of Shelby, who has a professorship at San Jose State. Although Shelby will not be taking an office at the Hoover Institution during his fellowship, his frequent presence on the Stanford campus will only make quarters tighter.

Claude and Shelby grew up in the thick of the civil rights movement. Their parents met while active in the Congress of Racial Equality. "Our household was like a graduate school in race relations," Claude recalls. "My mother was a social worker and my father was a truck driver, but they were both very intellectual people."

Although Shelby and Claude were not talking during the years when they both started exploring the psychology of race, they have followed remarkably similar lines of thinking. Co-opting a term from his field of literary study, for instance, Shelby has written of "objective correlatives," that is, objective events—as simple as seeing a Band-Aid tinted to match pink skin—that evoke a sense of what he calls "racial vulnerability." Objective correlatives "evoke the painful thicket of emotions—vulnerability, self-doubt, helplessness, terror and rage." Shelby's idea of *racial* vulnerability and Claude's *stereotype* vulnerability vary little. Put in Shelby's terms, Claude might be said to have found how different cues function as "objective correlatives"—the pink Band-Aids—of the test-taking situation.

Where the brothers' ideas diverge is over the questions of who is responsible for the predicament and what is to be done about it. Like a number of conserva-

tive writers and social critics, Shelby argues that the onus remains on the individual who must, through superior will, achieve despite these insecurities. Shelby has angered many by charging that black students "voluntarily perceive themselves as inferior."

While Claude Steele won't attack his brother's work in particular, he's openly critical of what he calls "that other school of thought" to which many black conservatives, including Thomas Sowell and Clarence Thomas, belong. Steele says that those who have seized on the apparent willful pulling away of the black student have unfairly focused on the very end of a long descent that can begin with a vulnerability so subtle that not even the student can identify its origin.

"These kids want to make it," Steele says. "These kids are in their dorm rooms confronting the beast of their deepest fears. Instead of telling them that it is their responsibility to overcome the psychology that they are feeling in their gut, let's get rid of the beast."

Although one might think that it would be Claude who would worry about being in the shadow of his famous sibling, it's Shelby who can throw a tantrum when the subject of his brother comes up. Asked to comment on his brother's research for this story, Shelby first gave an angry telephone interview during which be dismissed the entire discipline of social psychology as all but worthless, only to call the next day to demand that he be left completely out of this story.

In arguing that he should not be compared with his brother, Shelby became enraged. "I could kill you for this," he said at one point and then, falling into language he criticizes liberal blacks for, yelled, "You're victimizing me!" Shortly after these conversations, the brothers broke a six-month silence—which began after an argument over the November elections—only to agree that they would not comment publicly on each other's work or about their relationship. "To be compared all your life to your twin," Shelby says, "is a form of existential Hell."

While Shelby is most adamant, the brothers share the worry that their twinship will overshadow their ideas. "We have the same abhorrence of playing the brother-act sideshow," Claude admits. The fear is not unfounded. Ed Bradley recently called the two with the idea that they might debate racial preferences on "60 Minutes." The barker's call was not hard to hear: "Step right up and see the handsome black twins who disagree on affirmative action!"

No doubt it would have been a lively debate, for it is over the issue of affirmative action that the brothers are most at odds. While Shelby says that affirmative action has done more to trigger blacks' vulnerability "than any other social policy this side of segregation,"

Claude favors carefully designed programs. He says that any increase in vulnerability a black student feels for receiving admissions preference can be overcome when the student shows up on campus.

In this respect, Steele has taken his ideas outside the laboratory. During his time at Michigan, he lobbied for and helped create a 250-student integrated dorm program. The 21st Century Program, inaugurated the year Steele left Michigan, tries to maintain an integrated environment by requiring that all the students take a certain number of classes with other dorm members. The hope is that students with a challenging workload will intertwine their academic and social lives instead of self-segregating. The results have been striking: for three out of four years, the program has significantly reduced the grade gap between white and black students.

Because the 21st Century Program avoids emphasizing race, it was assailed by some at Michigan as "assimilationist." "Claude got incredible static from the party line among black faculty and their self-appointed liberal allies," says one university source who asked not to be identified. "It was very difficult for him. Of course, he had a big strike against him being Shelby Steele's brother."

Steele admits that he got verbally roughed. "It looked like I was blaming the victim," he remembers. "Some took it as if I were saying: 'All black students have to do to succeed is stop disidentifying.' I learned a lot from being hammered on. It forced me to try to trace the reason for this phenomenon and the idea of stereotype vulnerability came out of that process. I owe them a lot."

How Steele and his theories will fare in this national dialogue he's entering remains to be seen. So far, Steele reports that most people he has explained the idea of stereotype vulnerability to have had something of an "aha!" reaction, which is often followed by what he calls the "I-knew-it-all-along phenomenon." Stereotype vulnerability is a seductive idea with breathtakingly broad implications.

"I think much of what is mistaken for racial animosity in America today is really stereotype vulnerability," he says. "Imagine a black and a white man meeting for the first time. Because the black person knows the stereotypes of his group, he attempts to deflect those negative traits, finding ways of trying to communicate, in effect, 'Don't think of me as incompetent.' The white, for his part, is busy deflecting the stereotypes of his group: 'Don't think of me as a racist.' Every action becomes loaded with the potential of confirming the stereotype, and you end up with two people struggling with these phantoms they're only

half aware of. The discomfort and tension is often mistaken for racial animosity."

The parallel is instructive. The white person who has felt how much energy it takes to communicate the message "I am not the racist person you might think I am" can perhaps also understand how distracting such an effort might be during a standardized test. Following the idea of white vulnerability, he says he can even explain something of the current frustration with racial issues.

"Many whites are just like the black kid in the school situation," Steele says. "When racial issues become frustrating—when there are setbacks—the suspicions about their sincerity re-emerges. If they feel that, in continuing to try, they will only give more evidence to the conclusion that they are really racist they'll eventually want to withdraw. That is what is happening: the whole thing has become too loaded, and we're seeing whites walking away."

Michael Bérubé

Public Academy: A New Generation of Black Thinkers is Becoming the Most Dynamic Force in the American Intellectual Arena Since the Fifties

Ten years ago, writing in the inaugural issue of the academic journal *Cultural Critique*, Cornel West surveyed the scene of black intellectual activity in the United States and found it barren. "The quantity and quality of black intellectual exchange is at its worst since the Civil War," he wrote. "There is no major black academic journal; no major black intellectual magazine; no major black periodical of highbrow journalism; not even a major black newspaper of national scope. In short, the black infrastructure for intellectual discourse and dialogue is nearly nonexistent." West fingered two primary causes of this intellectual impoverishment: integration, "which has yielded mere marginal black groups within the professional disciplines of a fragmented academic community"; and "the wide-

Michael Bérubé, "Public Academy: A New Generation of Black Thinkers is Becoming the Most Dynamic Force in the American Intellectual Arena Since the Fifties," THE NEW YORKER, January 9, 1995. Reprinted courtesy of the author; originally published in THE NEW YORKER.

spread refusal of black intellectuals to remain, in some visible way, organically linked with African-American cultural life." In West's view, one of the unintended effects of the civil-rights movement was that élite, formerly all-white universities wound up institutionalizing the African-American intelligentsia, thereby insuring that its work would never again roam free in—or keep its "organic" links to—the world outside the academy.

It is strange to relate, then, that a few weeks ago, in a shopping mall somewhere on the American prairie, I wandered into the local McBooks store to find fully half its "Current Affairs" section occupied by the work of black intellectuals, chief among them Cornel West himself, peering back at me from the cover of "Race Matters." In the picture he looks calm and composed, an Emersonian sage sitting on a rooftop in East Harlem; but, as he tells his readers in the book's preface, he showed up late for the photo shoot that day, because not a single midtown taxi would stop for him. It is symptomatic of America in the nineteen-nineties that—as he also writes in his preface—the internationally renowned director of a black-studies program at an Ivy League university would be stopped by police three times in ten days for driving too slowly in his own neighborhood. And yet it is also symptomatic that above his photograph on the jacket of "Race Matters" are the words "National Bestseller."

West's book is flanked by two new books, "Outlaw Culture" (Routledge; $49.95 cloth, $15.95 paper) and "Teaching to Transgress" (Routledge; $49.95 cloth, $15.95 paper), both by Bell Hooks. Three shelves above them is the latest book from Michael Eric Dyson, "Making Malcolm: The Myth and Meaning of Malcolm X" (Oxford; $19.95). I look over the blurbs on the back cover. Weighing in are Cornel West, Angela Davis, the Reverend Jesse Jackson, and Senator Carol Moseley-Braun. That's an impressive range already, but it's the last blurb that really raises my eyebrows. It's from Chuck D, of the rap group Public Enemy, who says of Dyson, "He's a bad brother. Check out his new book 'Making Malcolm' by all means." Well, I think, it's a rare book from Oxford that gets plugs from a philosopher, a couple of politicians, *and* a rapper.

Such a thing may not be rare much longer. Something new is happening in American cultural history, and it can be gauged neither by tales of racist traffic cops nor by flattering endorsements from hip-hop superstars. A decade after Cornel West issued his baleful diagnosis, a new African-American intelligentsia has become part of this country's cultural landscape. It's a development as noticeable as the ascendancy of the New York intellectuals after the Second World War. Like the New York intellectuals, the new black intel-

lectuals are, to varying degrees, public figures, and, like the New York intellectuals, they seek to redefine what it means to be an intellectual in the United States. Whether lecturing in churches or testifying on Capitol Hill, they have the burden and the blessing of a constituency, a public—which is something that most so-called public intellectuals can only invoke.

They didn't all attend City College, they don't all live in the same city, and they have no journal as powerful as *Partisan Review* was in its heyday. But they are identifiable—and not only for being young, gifted, and black, as the saying goes. They *are* young in academic terms (that is, under forty-five); they tend to be concentrated along the Eastern Seaboard; and they can usually be found in humanities departments and law schools. But they are coming of age at an extraordinary cultural moment, amid a myriad of explosions in black popular culture, from Hollywood to hip-hop, and a series of staggering implosions in American race relations, from Howard Beach to the Clarence Thomas–Anita Hill debacle and the 1992 riots in Los Angeles. Where Lionel Trilling's "The Liberal Imagination" set the measure for cultural criticism in its time, Cornel West's "Race Matters" may set the measure for ours. It's a disquieting prospect, of course, to be "measured" by a book on racial injustice. Even so, when one recalls that Trilling's epochal collection of essays sold an astonishing hundred thousand copies (thereby helping to establish the genre of the "serious" paperback), it may seem all the more significant that Cornel West's collection has already sold well over twice that many. And though Bell Hooks (née Gloria Watkins) looks and sounds nothing like the late Irving Howe, she now has the same title at City College that he once held at CUNY; namely, distinguished professor.

Michael Eric Dyson appeared on the scene only in the past few years, but Hooks and West have been working away since the early eighties, publishing books every few years with small houses like South End Press or the University of Wisconsin Press, and earning themselves a devoted, but still limited, following. West's star really began rising with the nineties, and in the fall of 1994 Hooks, too, hit her stride, with Routledge, the large trade and scholarly publisher, releasing two hefty books by her simultaneously—in apparent accord with the Bruce Springsteen approach to product placement. Though no one has yet proposed a boxed set of Bell Hooks' greatest hits, the impact of her books on students and teachers has been palpable. In the movies, underemployed college graduates may sit around in coffee shops reading Heidegger's "Being and Time" (as does a character in Ben Stiller's twenty-something flick "Reality Bites"), but real campus coffee shops these days are much more likely to be filled with waiters reading "Making Malcolm" and riot girls perusing "Outlaw Culture."

Perhaps it's one of history's ironies that, in the past half century, the New York intellectual has become a popular American icon: the learned cosmopolitan whose erudition once marked the difference between "culture" and "mass culture" is now a standard reference point in mass culture. And yet when wistful scholars of the twenty-first century look back on the golden age of the American public intellectual, they may think not only of the audiences served by Trilling and Irving Howe but of those belonging to the black intellectuals of the nineteen-nineties.

Of course, there have been black intellectuals on these shores from 1619 or so, and Frederick Douglass, Anna Julia Cooper, and Ida B. Wells were about as effective in their day as any nineteenth-century public intellectual could hope to be. What was lacking, until very recently, was a black public sphere of commensurate size. Even in the nineteen-twenties, when writers of the Harlem Renaissance set out to theorize about the relation between lumpen black folk and what Zora Neale Hurston wryly called the "niggerati," black intellectuals were playing to a small crowd indeed. As Langston Hughes put it, "The ordinary Negroes hadn't heard of the Negro Renaissance. And if they had, it hadn't raised their wages any."

Until the nineteen-sixties, America's nationally known black intellectuals tended also to be its nationally known black novelists—the triumvirate of Richard Wright, Ralph Ellison, and James Baldwin, two of whom eventually chose exile over life in their native land. Meanwhile, within the tiny public arena bounded by segregation, African-American intellectuals like Oliver Cromwell Cox, W. E. B. Du Bois, James Weldon Johnson, Alain Locke, J. Saunders Redding, and Carter G. Woodson were creating African-American history, sociology, and literary criticism in black colleges, black journals like *Phylon* and *The Crisis*, and black newspapers like the Pittsburgh *Courier* and the *Afro-American* (published in five Eastern cities). But as long as segregation prevailed in higher education and in the publishing world it was quite easy for white Americans to believe that—Wright, Ellison, and Baldwin aside—the most important books on race in this country were written by white Americans.

That much, anyway, has changed about the American mind. Thirty years after Du Bois gave up on America and renounced his citizenship, African-Americans have emphatically taken the lead in the national conversation about "the Negro problem." Indeed, what's distinctive about this generation of African-American intellectuals is that their work has become a fixture of mall bookstores, talk shows, élite universities, and black popular culture. Plainly, they have consolidated the gains of the civil-rights and Black Power movements in at least this regard: they have the ability and the resources to represent themselves in public on their own terms.

That's not to say that their attitude toward desegregation is simply celebratory. In "Teaching to Transgress" Bell Hooks warmly recalls "the messianic zeal to transform our minds and beings that had characterized teachers and their pedagogical practices in our all-black schools" (as opposed to desegregated white schools, where, she writes, "too much eagerness to learn could easily be seen as a threat to white authority"); Cornel West and Michael Eric Dyson speak of the pathologies that come from constantly seeking white peer approval; and "Confronting Authority: Reflections of an Ardent Protester" (Beacon; $20), by their elder colleague Derrick Bell, relates how, in the late nineteen-fifties, he joined the newly formed Civil Rights Division of the Department of Justice only to be told that his membership in the N.A.A.C.P. constituted a "conflict of interest." So they've had good reason to be circumspect about integration. And yet it's one of the two developments that have made possible the emergence of black academics as public intellectuals. The other, of course, is the expansion of academe itself—and its gradual incorporation of the American intelligentsia.

To be sure, there are still plenty of black intellectuals who aren't college professors, among them activists like Marian Wright Edelman; cultural critics like Stanley Crouch, Lisa Jones, and Darryl Pinckney; and poets like Essex Hemphill. But even Gerald Early, Michele Wallace, and Shelby Steele, whose reputations rest almost entirely on their general-audience publications, hold full-time academic appointments; and when you add to that list figures like Patricia Williams, Stephen L. Carter, Lani Guinier, Henry Louis Gates, Jr., and Randall Kennedy you find that the black intellectuals of the eighties and nineties have decisively rebutted the claim that academe has been the death of the public intellectual. Though their positions of privilege have occasioned a certain amount of soul-searching (Hooks' "Teaching to Transgress" opens with a description of her violently mixed emotions about being granted tenure—having job security yet feeling walled in), there's a sense in which this dilemma reprises that of many New York intellectuals in the fifties, when they found themselves both threatened and energized by their academic embourgeoisement. Where Daniel Bell was criticized for buying nice furniture in his forties, Bell Hooks now draws stares for driving a BMW.

What Marxism was to Lionel Trilling, Clement Green-berg, Philip Rahv, and company, black nationalism is to West, Gates, Hooks, et al.: the inspiration, the spring-board, the template, but also the antagonist and the goad. Just as the postwar Jewish intelligentsia largely abandoned radical politics but remained committed to rethinking America's progressivist traditions (often by delivering scathing critiques of radical politics), the black intelligentsia of our fin de siècle has largely abandoned cultural nationalism while remaining committed to rethinking forms of African-American collectivity (often by delivering scathing critiques of cultural nationalism). But the new intellectuals have a markedly different relation to the vernacular of their time. A major part of what the New York intellectuals represented, in cultural politics, was a collocation of the politics of anti-Communism with the literature of high modernism—something that required its inventors to erect a cordon sanitaire protecting "real" culture from contamination by the kitsch, dreck, schlock, pop, and camp that surrounded it. One cannot imagine, given the past decade's controversies over black popular culture, the new black intelligentsia adopting the same cultural politics. Nor should it. As West writes in "Race Matters," "One irony of our present moment is that just as young black men are murdered, maimed, and imprisoned in record numbers, their styles have become disproportionately influential in shaping popular culture"—and black intellectuals have become singularly influential as interpreters of this moment and its ironies.

Nowhere are the terms of the new dispensation clearer than in the debates over the legacy of Malcolm X. By any standard, that legacy is vast: Malcolm's life and career resound through the recent history of black nationalism, of black music, art, and religion. And as Martin Luther King, Jr., has been at once deified and depoliticized, his contentious career boiled down to a few words he uttered about a dream he had in 1963, Malcolm's stature has grown to the point where he now serves as an icon of the black urban underclass—and, more narrowly, black urban masculinity—in crisis. But, unlike their Afrocentric colleagues, West, Dyson, and company take Malcolm not merely as an exemplar of black nationalism's political potency but as a test case of its political limitations. "Like most black nationalists, Malcolm X feared the culturally hybrid character of black life," West writes in "Race Matters" Dyson's view of black nationalism is still more severe. "Those most aided by its successes have rarely stuck around to witness the misery of those most hurt by its failures," he maintains. "The greatest irony of contemporary black nationalism may be its use by members of the

black middle class—for instance, black intellectuals and artists thoroughly insulated in niches of protection within the academy—to consolidate their class interests *at the expense* of working-class and poor blacks."

Yet both contemporary hardcore rap and contemporary black cinema have been shaped by Malcolm's influence, and that means that any intellectual recasting of his legacy must take account of nineties neo-nationalism in a profusion of popular-cultural forms—forms that few traditional intellectuals are at home with. Dyson's book is clearly the most ambitious effort to come to terms with this profusion. It not only analyzes nearly every important biography and scholarly study of Malcolm to date but takes on hip-hop culture and a cluster of recent films centered on the crisis of black masculinity (films like "Boyz N the Hood," "New Jack City," and "Menace II Society"). Charting Malcolm's "ideological blindnesses, his strategic weakness, his organizational limitations, and his sometimes bristling moral contradictions" alongside his deeply principled denunciations of white racism and black accommodationism, Dyson gives us Malcolm as "public moralist"—and a study that is as substantive and comprehensive as "public" cultural criticism of such a figure can hope to be.

A full chapter of the book is devoted to Spike Lee's "Malcolm X"—our era's preëminent black nationalist in the hands of our preëminent black neo-nationalist director. Few films have sparked so wide-ranging a debate in the African-American community, and Dyson's treatment of the film is lucid and balanced—weighing Lee's "commercialization of Malcolm's memory" against his "richly textured and subtly nuanced evocation" of Malcolm's life. Dyson is *so* lucid and balanced, in fact, that I almost began to prefer Bell Hooks' decidedly gnarled and skewed treatment of the film in "Outlaw Culture." According to Hooks, Lee is really a Hollywood insider pretending to be an outsider; she maintains that "Lee's work cannot be revolutionary and generate wealth at the same time." It follows that Lee has simply sold out, by "reproducing conservative and even stereotypical images of blackness so as not to alienate that crossover audience," and leaving filmgoers with a Malcolm who "has more in common with Steven Spielberg's representation of Mister in the film version of 'The Color Purple' than with real-life portraits of Malcolm X."

This is an outrageously unfair reading of Lee's film, but, as is often the case with Bell Hooks' work, the essay's impact as critical provocation is in part a function of its audacity. Hooks' forays into popular culture often undertake the kind of sweeping, indiscriminate critique that one finds oneself arguing with on every page. There's hardly a book, record, or film in circulation that she can't denounce as reactionary, whether she's berating "What's Love Got to Do with It" for giving us "Ike's story" on Tina Turner, or Madonna for exploiting gay culture. Where Hooks is reckless, however, she is also fearless: Michael Eric Dyson stops at merely remarking on Malcolm X's sustained inattention to gender politics, but Hooks starts by noting that "critical scholarship on Malcolm X contains no *substantial* work from a feminist standpoint," and proceeds to criticize no less sainted a figure than Malcolm's widow. Indeed, Hooks is at her best in debates over the meaning and the future of feminism—particularly when she's taking on the post-feminists who seem to have captured the hearts of C-SPAN, *Playboy*, the *Times Literary Supplement*, and *Esquire*. Here, for example, as a setup from that renowned motormouth Camille Paglia: "I'm very loud. I've had a hell of a time in academe. This is why I usually get along with African Americans. I mean, when we're together, 'Whooo!' It's like I feel totally *myself*—we just let everything go!" And here's how Hooks, in "Outlaw Culture," handles this slow, fat pitch over the middle of the plate: "Naturally, all black Americans were more than pleased to have Miss Camille give us this vote of confidence, since we live to make it possible for white girls like herself to have a place where they can be 'totally' themselves."

The occasional Manichaeanism of Hooks' rhetoric—the sense that the merit of a work can be determined by its contribution to the cause—is a common feature of political criticism, whether practiced by Granville Hicks or by Hilton Kramer. For black intellectuals, however, the problem has another dimension, which affects their assessment not only of popular culture but of their social roles as well. Because non-black audiences are still the ones that have the power to put black artists at the top of the charts, African-American intellectuals' uneasiness about black commercial and professional success stems in part from the long-standing fear that "crossing over" must entail selling out. It's what leads to Hooks' attack on Lee—the unstated suspicion that any critical or commercial success with white audiences is, de facto, political failure.

So if black public intellectuals are legitimated by their sense of a constituency, they're hamstrung by it, too: they can be charged with betraying that constituency as easily as they can be credited with representing it. On the one hand, they have an unprecedented opportunity to speak from, to, and for a public, since their professional bona fides depend not on their repudiation of vernacular African-American culture but on their engagement with it. On the other hand,

they inhabit an intellectual tradition of extreme sensitivity toward the issue of who represents what to whom—a tradition in which the weightiest term of disapprobation is that familiar bludgeon "Uncle Tom."

For Cornel West, the uneasiness about representing "the public" also stems from his pointed critique of American consumer culture: the world of brand names and product placement, of corporate campaigns designed, he writes, to "entice and titillate consumers," constructing "the public" not as a citizenry but as a market for Air Jordans and St. Ides malt liquor. In West's distinctive blend of socialist politics and preacherly appeals to black spiritual renewal, this culture of consumption is cast as one of the prime causes of black "nihilism" and social disarray. The public, West insists, is coextensive with the commodity: Visa is everywhere we want to be. West is far from sanguine about what this means for the African-American public; his latest collection is entitled "Keeping Faith," but it sounds a sombre basso continuo of near-despair.

"The proper starting point for the crucial debate about the prospects for black America is an examination of the nihilism that increasingly pervades black communities," he writes in "Race Matters." This is a risky position for any progressive social critic, and particularly for any black social critic who appeals for the remediation of black poverty but does not wish to present poor blacks as, yet again, passive "targets" for social reform or as participant-victims of a dysfunctional culture. West wants to generate concern about the black poor without pathologizing them (or construing the black middle class as greedy wannabes); at the same time, he wants to defend "traditional morality" and traditional institutions, like churches and schools, from that dread culture of consumption without simply reciting the neoconservative mantras—religion, family values, private associations—of our day. It's a tricky double play, and he doesn't always pull it off. The fact is that it's often difficult to distinguish between conservative and progressive critiques of the social corrosiveness of consumer capital. For one thing, both points of view tend to rely on the idea of some once unalienated human community that has been violated by modernity: leftists can look back at precapitalist gemeinschaft and conservatives can long for the agrarian pastoral with more or less the same ardor. It's remarkable but altogether fitting that West's work turns out to make some common cause with that of the cultural conservative Daniel Bell—who "in stark contrast to black conservatives," West writes, "highlights the larger social and cultural forces, for example, consumerism and hedonism, which undermine the Protestant ethic and its concomitant values." Maybe it's safer to run the risk of exaggerating the hopelessness of the black underclass than to run the risk of soft-pedalling its plight. But though West's reading of black nihilism is compelling, it's not the only story worth telling—particularly to white folks who hear nothing else. For every posse of nihilists on the streets, there may well be a housing activist at work, or a graffiti artist on his way to the Whitney.

And what of the black conservative intellectuals? They may not be coffee-shop mainstays, but they've been busy nonetheless. In fact, Thomas Sowell has just published his most important book since "Race and Economics" (1975), the book that made him the right's point man in the fight against affirmative action. But, though it will certainly get its hearing at the Heritage Foundation, Sowell's "Race and Culture: A World View" (Basic; $25) is in danger of being lost in the crush of his younger and more agile competitors, who can leap from Kierkegaard to KRS-One in a single bound. One might well take Sowell's resolute unhipness as a sign of his intellectual strength. But at times his analysis looks frankly dated, as when he faults contemporary social science for not attending to the details of "culture"—apparently oblivious of the culturalist turn of the past two decades. "Race and Culture" may aspire to a role in national policy debates, but it's not clear what role it can plausibly play. For instance, in a crucial section of the book Sowell argues against the presumption that intelligence tests are "biased" against underprivileged groups, noting that such groups do worst on abstract test questions with no "cultural" content, and that performance is independent of variation in income within the group. "This does not prove that cultural bias is not present," he admits, "but it does indicate that any such bias must take a very different form from what is usually assumed or portrayed." Fair enough, but then the critical issue is whether that more nebulous bias can be redressed. Sowell notes that the United States' first foray into comprehensive intelligence testing, during the First World War, showed a kind of reverse Lake Wobegon effect: most Irish, Russian, Italian, and Polish immigrants had below normal intelligence. Sixty-seven per cent of Anglo-American test-takers, by contrast, were above normal. The question for policymakers, therefore, is this: Did America's European-immigrant populations get smarter in three generations thanks to their own pluck and initiative, or do I.Q. scores reflect groups' histories of access to high-quality education? Sowell refuses to say. "For many practical purposes," he concludes, "it makes no real difference whether poor performances in abstract thinking are due to neglect or to lack of capacity." But this is no conclusion at all, since if groups' differences *are* attributable to

"neglect"—or, worse, to active discrimination—then Sowell has inadvertently demonstrated the necessity for precisely the kind of ambitious social programs that his career has been dedicated to attacking.

Still, criticizing Sowell is not so simple as this. For, despite its weaknesses, his oeuvre stands—or should stand—as a powerful reminder to his progressive counterparts that public intellectual work does not consist exclusively of deconstructing Spike Lee, historicizing Malcolm X, deliberating over gangsta rap on "Donahue," or debating the future of feminism in *Ms.* The current crop of left public intellectuals may take on matters of public concern, but, a few law professors aside, they don't always take on matters of public policy—and, needless to say, they don't always have the impact on public debate that Sowell (or such conservative co-religionists as Alan Keyes and Glenn Loury) has thus far enjoyed.

One reason for that, surely, is the sometimes unconvincing mixture of rarefied theoretical discourse and heartfelt populist rhetoric you find among many academics on the left. It's hard to know what any professional legislator would make of Bell Hooks' critique of Madonna: "Within the sphere of Madonna's pornographic gaze, gayness is reinscribed as a trope within the cultural narrative of patriarchal pornographic sexual hedonism." Yet there's a broader reason for the poor fit between left public intellectuals and public policy, and it has to do with contemporary cultural criticism's uncertain sense of the "political." Of course, any self-respecting progressive intellectual will tell you (repeatedly) that intellectual work is "political" work. But not every kind of "political" work has political effects, and at times it seems that you can redraw the map of cultural politics without touching the practical-political map of precincts, districts, policymakers, and appropriations committees. Where the left tends to address itself to culture, the right—even when it takes up the topic of "culture"—tends to address itself to policy. It's all too clear who does, and who doesn't, benefit from this curious division of labor. West, Dyson, and Hooks define themselves as "radical democrats"—committed, they would say, to the principle that every citizen should participate as fully as possible in the debates that shape his or her society and culture. And yet democracy is but a form; it does not specify outcomes, nor does it dictate political affiliations of the radicals working at its roots. In a sense, therefore, Ralph Reed, the thirty-three-year-old executive director of the Christian Coalition, has been a better—that is, a more effective—radical democrat than most of those who aspire to that label.

Nor is fluency in popular culture a guarantor of popular influence. In the preface to "Making Malcolm," Michael Eric Dyson recounts that when he quoted Snoop Doggy Dogg during a United States Senate subcommittee hearing on gangsta rap he was told by a young black admirer that "for a guy your age, you really can flow." He's right to be pleased at the compliment. An intellectual generation that responds broadly and sympathetically to popular culture has numerous advantages over an intellectual generation that defines itself against popular culture. But for cultural critics the danger of popular acclaim is that it can tempt them to pay more attention to the responses of young admirers than to the deliberations of Senate subcommittees. And it can tempt them to pull their punches, as when Bell Hooks, in an interview with the rap artist Ice Cube that appears in "Outlaw Culture," sounds uncharacteristically tentative about Cube's misogynistic lyrics and declines even to ask about his role as a pitchman for St. Ides. Intellectuals need not be so arrogant as to claim to occupy the cultural vanguard, but in renouncing that role they need not settle for the role of fan, disk jockey, or press agent.

Nothing about the new black intellectuals' work so far suggests that they will settle for such a role; the political stakes are too high, the crisis of the African-American underclass is too urgent. And the crisis of African-American intellectual life is not without its own urgency: traditional intellectuals ridicule the members of the rising generation as being more concerned with hip-hop than with health care, more worried about getting tenure than about stopping torture; nationalist intellectuals excoriate them for appearing in "white-controlled" media, from C-SPAN to publishing houses owned by Time Warner. For every critic who laments that progressive black intellectuals are not sufficiently incorporated into the machinery of social policy, there's an equal and opposite critic lamenting that progressive black intellectuals are too thoroughly incorporated—that they've crossed over, sold out.

Whether or not they can possibly sell out in a way that makes a difference to national politics is another question. Indeed, watching the American left redefine the terrain of cultural politics while practical political positions to the left of Bill Clinton disappear from the map, one begins to wonder if there isn't a sense, even in the work of the most prolific and capable black public intellectuals, that cultural politics is a kind of compensation for practical politics—more satisfying, more supple, more susceptible to sheer intellectual virtuosity, because it involves neither revenues nor statutes. Not that the celebrated New York intellectuals of yesteryear held any clear advantage in the realm of practical politics: Lionel Trilling had no hand in Truman's Far East policies, nor did Philip Rahv help enforce Brown *v.* Board of Education. My guess is that the new black intellectuals will have a significant influence on

the American political agenda when, and only when, a national party runs on the slogan "It's the social justice, stupid." I'm not counting on seeing this anytime soon.

The overwhelming irony here is that black public intellectuals are doing their work—at colleges, in churches, and on cable TV—at a time when the very idea of "the public" has become nearly unthinkable in national politics. Such has been the signal achievement of the New Right, whose religious wing has built its organizations on the bedrock of home, school, and family while attacking the realm of the public in the name of the people. Public housing, public education, public health, public ownership, public welfare—to much of the American electorate these terms signify that which is not in the public interest. Black public intellectuals like West and Hooks may have a large following, but the paradoxical conditions under which they operate dictate that they will have to revivify the nation's faith in "the public" if their work is going to have broad political consequences. The measure of their success will be the degree to which they help generate a sense of the public as elastic and capacious as their sense of the intellectual.

ELEANOR TRAYLOR

The Humanities and Afro-American Literary Tradition

A system of education that fails to nurture memory of the past denies its students the satisfaction of mature thought, an attachment to abiding concerns, a perspective on human existence.

> *American Memory: A Report on the Humanities in the Nation's Public Schools* by Lynne V. Cheney, Chairman, National Endowment for the Humanities

. . . they ask me to remember but they want me to remember their memories and I keep remembering mine.

> Lucille Clifton (Afro-American Poet)

There was nothing remarkable about the Saturday afternoon's excursion. We were a small group of friends happy to be gathered at Arundel on the Bay. The heat of the August day had scorched the city, but here, facing the water from a shady porch, we were happy to be cool, to eat our lunches, and to talk about the world which had disappeared beyond the water. "But," said the friend who was a

Eleanor W. Traylor, "The Humanities and Afro-American Literary Tradition." Reprinted by permission of the author.

lawyer, in reply to an observation that all had not heard, "Why must it always be fantasy? After all, what are we to make of a ghost—a woman fully clothed who walks from the sea into the lives of people and seems to ruin them?" The world, for a moment, had become a book. We had plunged into the world of Toni Morrison's Beloved (1987). The friend from Trinidad answered her. "Memory," he said, "is sometimes the ghost of a forgotten or unadmitted past, like the stories of the Duennes and La Diablesse." The friend who was a lawyer was annoyed. "There we go again!" she said. But another voice interrupted, "Who are they—the Duennes and La Diablesse?" "Well," said the friend from Trinidad, "according to the lore of the island, Duennes are spirits of children who died without the sacrament of burial and are fated to roam the forests practicing their repertoire of pranks. Their feet are turned backward, for they belong on the other side. They wish to be there, but they must be properly buried before they can go. On the other hand, La Diablesse is really an old crone whose petticoats rustle like the sound of chains. Sometimes, she appears as a tall beautiful woman who catches the eye of a man. The man proceeds to follow her but, never able to catch her, finds himself bewildered, far from home, and maybe quite mad." "But this is what I mean," cried the objector. "Why dwell on painful old stories? We live now, and in a world which requires of us as much reality. . . ." The friend who had asked to hear the stories interrupted the objector. "It is what we avoid—what we do not admit—what we impose in its place that challenges what is real," said the friend. The company of friends agreed.

I

The insistence upon a recall of memory, a review of the past, characteristic of Afro-American intellectual and artistic productions, emphasizes the constant humanistic observation that we find living value in remembering our ancestry: "the sweep of human experience" (Cheney, *American Memory,* 6) which has preceded us. Or as James Baldwin has put it: "how we may suffer, how we are defeated, how we may triumph" ("Sonny's Blues," 121) are the great lessons of the past. Yet when Baldwin, the storefront preacher from Harlem, the Black writer from America, visits the medieval French town at Chartres and stands before the great Cathedral there, his response to what he views as a living text from the past is decidedly different than that of his countryman, Henry Adams, historian, scholar, man of letters, who had also read the text of the Cathedral. "We come to Chartres," said Adams, "for our ideals" (*Chartres,* 9). To the contrary, for Baldwin, the Cathe-

dral becomes not a paragon, but a speaking subject—a voice from the past. He tells us:

> The Cathedral at Chartres . . . *says* something to the people of this village which it cannot *say* to me; but it is important to understand that this Cathedral says something to me which it cannot say to them ("Stranger in the Village," 88, emphasis added).

The past, for the writer, inspires a conversation between memory and the moment. It is a call which empowers a creative and recreative responsive present. He muses:

> These [villagers], from the point of view of power, cannot be strangers anywhere in the world . . . even if they do not know it. The most illiterate among them is related, in a way that I am not, to Dante, Shakespeare, Michelangelo, Æschylus, Da Vinci, Rembrandt, and Racine; the Cathedral at Chartres says something to them which it cannot say to me . . . Out of their hymns and dances came Beethoven and Bach. Go back a few centuries . . . I am in Africa watching the conquerors arrive ("Stranger," 83).

The dialogue between past and present conjures from the writer a canonical recitation and a review of two histories: in one of these, the Cathedral, the text being read, is representative; the other history is the one by which the reader, speaker, writer views the text. Yet the viewer is participant in both histories and, for that reason, is released to a plenitude unavailable, by exclusion, in one history alone. The viewer, thus enabled, renders a responsible mediation. For in his investigation of the many-layered meanings abiding in the Cathedral, as text of the past, he has also confronted himself in relation to it. The outcome has included us in a drama wherein the Self examines itself in relation to an other. The examination results in "overcoming the other's strangeness without assimilating it wholly to oneself" (Bakhtin, 24). Such an examination is the *être de rigueur,* the traditional behavior, of the Afro-American legacy in literature.

In this case, Baldwin concludes his study of the Cathedral by assessing its probable impact upon the villagers and its actual effect upon himself:

> Perhaps, they are struck by the power of the spires and the glory of the stained glass windows. . . . I am terrified by the slippery bottomless well to be found in the crypt down which heretics were hurled to death, and by the obscene inescapable gargoyles strutting out of the stone seeming to suggest that God and the devil can never be divorced . . . Perhaps I have known God in a different way ("Stranger," 89).

II

In a different way. The difference has been the substance and fine tuning of the products shaped by the Afro-American mind. Perhaps the difference becomes apparent in Miz Eva's tale about visit another village and witness another text. Now, "we have this [little] church in the village," (Lovelace, *Wine*, 32) begins Miz Eva. Miz Eva is a Trinidadian villager who is wife of the Reverend Bee Raymond, pastor of the Spiritualist Baptist Church, in Earl Lovelace's novel *The Wine of Astonishment* published in 1982. Miz Eva is the central vision and narrator of the novel, through her eyes, we see the situation surrounding the little church in the village. Indeed, through her sensibility do we apprehend the meaning of "we church" for its members:

> We have this church. The walls make out of mud. The roof covered with carrot leaves; a simple hut with no steeple or cross or acolytes or priests or latin ceremonies. But is our own. Black people own it. Government ain't spent one cent helping us build it or put bench in it or anything; the bell that we ring when we call to the Spirit is our money that pay for it. So we have this church.

> We have this church where we gather to sing hymns and ring the bell and shout hallelujah and speak in tongues when the Spirit come; and we carry the Word to the downtrodden and the forgotten and the lame and the beaten, and we touch black people soul.

> We have this church where in this tribulation country far away from Africa, the home that we don't know, we can come together and be ourselves (*Wine*, 32–33).

By 1903, Dr. W.E.B. Du Bois had inscribed the far reaching implication of "we church" in the development of Black new world literature and art. In his landmark study, *The Souls of Black Folk* he had written:

> They that walked in darkness sang songs in the olden days. Sorrow songs—for they were weary of heart. And so before each thought that I have written in this book I have set a phrase, a haunting echo of these weird old songs in which the soul of the Black slave spoke to men. Ever since I was a child these songs have stirred me strongly. They come out of the South unknown to me, one by one, and yet at once I knew them [to be] of me and mine (181).

But even before that, in his now classic *Narrative* of 1845 written before the first gun of the Civil War had pronounced the waning of the age of slavery in the United States and, therefore, before the ban prohibiting the literacy of the enslaved had been lifted, Frederick Douglass had written of those songs which we may call the first living monument of "we church." He said:

> . . . they were tones, loud, long and deep . . . revealing at once the highest joy and the deepest sadness . . . they breathed the prayer and complaint of souls boiling over with the bitterest anguish. Every tone was a testimony against slavery and a prayer to God for deliverance . . . to those songs, I trace my first glimmering conception [of humanity] (30–31).

From then to now, interview a range of artists speaking across the wide diversity of humanistic and aesthetic endeavor. Ask them the inevitable question: Wherein and how from and to what do you attribute your extraordinary and brilliant and powerful and unique expression? From

Marian Anderson to Leontyne Price

Paul Robeson to William Warfield

Ma Rainey to Aretha Franklin

Ella Fitzgerald to Betty Carter

Edward Ellington to John Coltrane

Mahalia Jackson to James Cleveland

Huddie Leadbetter to Bobby McFerrin

Hale Wodruff to Romare Bearden and Jacob Lawrence

Augusta Savage to Valerie Maynard

Laura Wheeler Waring to Mildred Thompson

Katherine Dunham to Alvin Ailey

Rose McClendon to Ruby Dee

Phyliss Wheatley to Gwendolyn Brooks

Langston Hughes to Sterling Brown

Claude McKay to Amiri Baraka

Anna J. Cooper to Maya Angelou

Zora Neale Hurston to Toni Morrison

W.E.B. Du Bois to C.L.R. James

(to say nothing of the myriad unnamed of whom those names are representative and to say nothing of the now and emergent present). Ask the question. The answer? Always, "there was this little church."

"We church," say Miz Eva, is a place where "you could hear your own voice . . . feel your own spirit, and catch your own power" (*Wine*, 33). The church, then, is not a land, not an army, not a flag. No, "we church" is the sign of a very different matter. It is a tabernacle of human witness where every voice hears itself speaking; every tear, each acknowledged, fertilizes every shout of joy. It is the place of authentic human feeling—the residence of language which admits the existence of the human heart: that sentient drum beating one insistent message:

> this is your urgency: Live!
> and have your blooming . . .
>
> (Brooks, "The Second Sermon," 453)

Here at the altar of the little church is the daily round of life whose expression we may call the Humanities. No walls or boundary lines restrict "we church." It is a community of memory and shared experience where all the old stories begin, are recalled, are transformed anew. Here where "the old decapitations and dispossessions" (Brooks, "The Wall," 445) are remembered, where the small and large victories of being are rehearsed, "something profound and unanswerable [stirs] in the consciousness of all . . ." (Baldwin, *The Evidence*, 122). Here, the litany admits no categorical distinction between the Aesthetic and the ethical: "the apostle of Beauty thus becomes the apostle of Truth and Right not by choice but by inner and outer compulsion. Free he is but his freedom is ever bounded by Truth and Justice . . ." (Du Bois, *Criteria*, 258). And here, a common faith abounds: "the world is full of [beauty]. . . its variety is infinite, its possibility endless. In normal life all may have it . . ." (253). Yet, the congregation shares a tacit understanding: "the mass of humanity is locked away from [beauty] and their lives distorted and made ugly . . ." (253). Thus, "we church" intones the common weal: "who shall right this well-nigh universal failing? Who shall let this world be beautiful?" (253). It is here where "our endless connections with and responsibilities for each other" (*The Evidence*, 122) are, somehow clarified by the memory of our particular passage through the world: who in the slave ship's pit was the first to lift his head? Who on the southern fields east of Eden was to lift her voice in defiant cry? Who was the first to ratify the daring proclamation: this child shall not be eaten!

> *Jésus, Estrella, Esperanza, Mercy. . .*
>
> (Hayden, *Ballad*, 48–50)

> *The Nation's hoop was broken, and there was no center any longer . . . and the sacred tree is dead . . . a people's dream died there. It was a beautiful dream . . .*
>
> (Black Elk, 182–230).

> *Runs falls rises stumbles on from darkness into darkness and the darkness thicketed with shapes of terror and the hunters pursuing and the hounds pursuing and the night cold and the night long and the river to cross and the jack-muh-lanterns beckoning beckoning and blackness ahead and where*

> *shall I reach that somewhere morning and keep on going and never turn back . . .*

> *And this was the way of it, brethren brethren. Way we journeyed from can't to can. Moon so bright and no place to hide, the cry up and the patterollers riding, bounty dogs belling in the bladed air. And fear starts a-murbling. Never make it, We'll never make it. Hush that now, and she's turned upon us, levelled pistol glinting in the moon light: [Hush that now] you keep on going keep on going now, she says*
>
> (Hayden, *Ballad*, 59–61).

"We church," say Miz Eva, "*ain't do the white man or his brown tools any wrong . . . We preach the Word and who have ears to hear, hear. And the lost souls scattered in every religion in Babylon was coming home to a Church that is their own, whereafter the service finish the brethren could discuss together how the corn growing, how the children doing, for what price cocoa selling, and the men could know which brother they should lend a hand to the coming week, and the sisters could find out who sick from the congregation so we could go and sit with her a little and help her out with the cooking for her children or the washing or the ironing. And it was nice at last to have a place to be together, where you could hear your own voice shouting hallelujah and feel the spirit spreading over the Church as the brethren sing and dance and catch the power*" (*Wine*, 33).

Yet in the world of the novel from which Miz Eva speaks, the little church is banned. For the novel recreates "the history of a spiritualist Community on the island from the passing of the [British] Prohibition Ordinance of 1917 until the lifting of the ban in 1951" (Thorpe, viii). But the beauty of *The Wine of Astonishment* is its orchestration of the island's many voices; its choreography of images painting the epic faces of life; its lyrical evocation of the enduring spirit of a people whose urgency is the humanistic moment:

> Then we was singing a hymn, soft and low, sweet with our rhythm:

> *The Lion of Judah shall break every chain And bring us to victory over Satan again.*

> Then it cool down, die away with sweet, soft humming and low moaning, and a cleanness and a lightness come over the church, and the rain stop falling, and we was fresh and wash like new grass in the morning (*Wine*, 62).

III

A rigorous examination of the texts of the past in the present; the inclusion of two histories in dialectical conversation: one's own history and that of an other; a practical application of the fruit of the inquiry toward the amelioration of both the individual and society; the creation of a community of memory where we hear our own voices, in multiplicity, articulate what we need and what we feel to be the best in human life—these have been the traditions of the Afro-American legacy in literature. From the texts arising from "we church," we receive a vocabulary naming major and broad-reaching conditions of modern humanity: *the veil* (Du Bois), the distorting, warping, dwarfing myopia preventing a clear vision of reality; *the river* (Hughes), the stream of consciousness mapping the journey back, the journey forward; *the native son* (Wright), the dispossessed and dispossessing pariah denied the rites of passage essential to self-knowledge and, therefore, self-fulfillment; *the conjurer,* (Chesnutt-Bambara), the healing power of insight and imagination; *invisibility* (Ellison), the denial of authentic being; the slave (Baraka), a delusion; *the bluest eye* (Morrison), the dementia of delusion; *Sula* (Morrison), the conundrum of modern woman; *ark of bones* (Dumas), the ship of memory, resisting deluge, conveying "the whole house of thy brothers" (*Ark*, 6).

Nor do the texts which speak from the present of "we church" lack the resonance of the whole humanistic past: the rage of Achilleus, the plight of Andromache, the bold assertion of Antigone, the vengeance of Medea, the mission of Moses, the dreams of Joseph, the insistence of Job, the courage of Judith, the quest of Dante, the outrage of Caliban, the arrogance of Prospero, the triumph of Sundiata, the quaking soul of the G. All these memories are alive in "we church." But memory "involves not just an act of retrieval by the mind of the poet, but simultaneously the perception of what lies before him and he the present as deficient, as a vice, a lack that memory will fill' (Vance, 382).

Nevertheless, the Prohibition Ordinance is no respecter of virtue beyond its own prescription. The ban of exclusion is, at least as old as the hemlock and the cross, and, today, it projects its monolithic voice in current policy pronouncements regarding the state of the Humanities and the Nation. Since 1984, when former Chairman of the National Endowment for the Humanities William Bennett, issued his report, *To Reclaim a Legacy* through the present Chairman, Lynne V. Cheney's 1987 report, *American Memory: A Report on the Humanities in the Nation's Public Schools to her 1988 Report to the President, the Congress and American People: Humanities in America*, the recommendation of the National Endowment have voiced a consensus: to re-enter the great (and phallic) Cathedral of Culture (the great books of the elect of Western tradition) whose seminal flow, by these accounts, is the sure engenderer of "what it means to be human . . . [of] truths that, transcending *accidents* of class, race,

and gender, speak to us all" (*Humanities*, 14, *emphasis* added). Something seems avoided here—something unadmitted. And, once again, the "we churches" in the villages, speaking through the silences of the great cathedral, are the heretics hurled down the slippery bottomless well to be found in the crypt.

At Arundel on the Bay, the evening shadows had deepened, the tide was coming in, and the sound of the water crashing against the rock reminded the company of friends of the world beyond the water. But there was yet a question lurking. The quiet friend who had not spoken all afternoon asked the question: "But, really, who is Beloved?" asked the friend. "Oh!" answered the student, the youngest of the friends, who had charmed the company by speaking of the theory of signs as easily as she had nibbled her papaya. "By its signifying system, the text can't tell us that," said the student. "It exists to ask us that," said the student. "It works like a praise song," she explained. "The praise song is very old. It is the old griot's song whose job it was to hold in memory the history of the noble houses. It is called by another name in the literary history that we study, but it's the same." The student said, "The song must be regularly sung to the young and old, high and low, rich and poor." It tells of the heroic and evil deeds of the past and of the struggles that the tribe has suffered through. The quiet friend raised a finger to ask another question: "Is that why they gather around the troubled house to sing?"

"Well, yes," said the student, "they sing a song . . ." the quiet friend finished her query. "That's the anthem isn't it?" Sing a song

Full of the hope that the dark past has taught us.

"Yes," whispered the student. The company of friends agree.

References

Adams, Henry. *Mont Saint-Michel and Chartres* (1905), Princeton, NJ: Princeton UP, 1981.

Bakhtin, Mikhail. *The Dialogical Principle.* ed. Tzvetan Todorov, *Theory and History of Literature,* 13. Minneapolis: U of Minnesota P, 1984.

Baldwin, James. "Sonny's Blues," *Going to Meet the Man.* New York: Dell, 1966.

———. "Stranger in the Village," *Notes of a Native Son* (1955). rpt. *The Price of the Ticket: Collected Non Fiction.* New York: St. Martin's Marek, 1985. Toni Morrison contrasts Adams' and Baldwin's perspectives on Chartres in "City Limits Village Values: Concepts of Urbanism in Black Fiction."

HENRY LOUIS GATES, JR.

Race and the Humanities: The Transforming of the American Mind

When I am asked to talk about the opening of the American mind, or the decentering of the humanities, or the new multiculturalism—or any number of such putative "developments"—I have to say my reaction is pretty much Mahatma Gandhi's when asked what he thought about Western Civilization. He said he thought it would be a very good idea. My sentiments exactly.

This decade has, to be sure, witnessed an interesting coupling of trends. On the one hand, we have seen calls from on high to reclaim a legacy, to fend off the barbarians at the gates, and return to some prelapsarian state of grace. On the other hand (or is it the same hand?), we have seen a disturbing resurgence of campus racism sweeping the nation. Many of you will have seen the lead article about this in the recent *Chronicle of Higher Education*, but the topic has been in the news for quite some time.[1] For people who agitated in the civil rights era, and saw real gains in the college curriculum in the 1970's, the new conservatism seems to have succeeded their own efforts rather as the Redemption politicians followed the Reconstruction, threatening to undo what progress had been made.

One thing is clear. Education in a democratic society (or one that aspires to that ideal) has particular burdens placed upon it: few theorists of American education, in this century or the preceding one, separated pedagogy from the needs of citizenship. The usual term here is often given a sinister intonation: *social reproduction*. Yet this country has always had an evolutionary view of what reproduction entails; we have never been content with mere replication, we have sought improvement. We want our children to be better than we are.

So it is discouraging, even painful, to look about our colleges, bastions of liberal education, and find that people are now beginning to talk—and with justice, it seems—about the "new racism." I do not want to offer a simple diagnosis, but perhaps the phenomenon is not completely unconnected to larger political trends. It has been pointed out that today's freshmen were ten years old when the Reagan era began. Presumably the public discourse of the '80s may have

had something to do with the forming of political sensibilities. But whatever the causes, the climate on campus has been worsening. According to one monitoring group, racial incidents have been reported at over one hundred and seventy-five colleges since the 1986–87 school year. And that is just counting the cases that made the papers.[2]

At the same time, there has been a marked decline in overall black enrollment in colleges since 1977. The evidence suggests the decline is connected to a slipping economic situation, and cuts in available federal aid. In the decade since 1977, federal grants and scholarships have fallen 62 percent, and that, of course, disproportionately affects minority students. Almost half of all black children (46.7 percent) lives under the poverty line, according to the Congressional Research Service. Indeed, if you look at students at traditionally black colleges, you find that 42 percent of them come from families with income below the poverty line; a third of these students comes from families with a total family income less than $6,000 a year.[3] So when it comes to larger economic trends, blacks are like the canaries in the coal mine: the first to go when things are going wrong.

But there is an even bigger problem than getting these students, and that is keeping them. The attrition rate is depressing. At Berkeley, one in four black students will graduate. The fact is, according to the National Center of Education Statistics, of freshmen blacks in 1980, only 31% had graduated by 1986.[4] And while financial pressures explain some of it, they do not explain all of it. Down the educational pike, things get worse. Just 2.3% of our full-time college professors are black, and the number is said to be decreasing. In 1986, only 820 of the 32,000 PhDs awarded went to blacks; less than half of that 820 plan a college career[5] (that's 0.015 percent of our new PhDs).

In short, it is a bad situation. But it is not a conspiracy. Nobody wants it to be the way it is. In general, our colleges really are devoted to diversity. People are genuinely upset when they fail to incorporate diversity among their students and faculty. I said before that the peculiar charge of our education system is the shaping of a democratic polity. It is a reflection of the public consensus on this matter that one of the few bipartisan issues in the last presidential campaign had to do with equitable access to higher education. Pollsters on both sides found that this was an issue that made the American heart skip a beat. Equal opportunity in education is an idea with very broad appeal in this country. And that has something to do with what education means to us. So one thing I want to bring out is that the schools are a site where real contradictions and ambivalences are played out.

Henry Louis Gates, Jr., "Race and the Humanities: The Transforming of the American Mind." Reprinted by permission of the author.

I would like to talk today about institutions for higher learning in terms of the larger objectives of what we call a liberal education. As unfashionable as it is among many of my fellow theorists, I do believe in the humanities, very broadly conceived. But it is that breadth of conception I want to address. We hear the complaints. Allan Bloom, for example, laments that "just at the moment when everyone else has become 'a person,' blacks have become blacks . . ." (Needless to say, "everyone else" can become a person precisely when the category "person" comes to be defined in contradistinction to "black.") Many thoughtful educators are dismayed, even bewildered, when minority students—at Berkeley or Stanford or Texas or Oberlin, (the sentiment's widespread)—say that they feel like visitors, like guests, like foreign or colonized citizens in relation to a traditional canon that fails to represent their cultural identities. I am not interested in simply endorsing that sentiment. It is not a reasoned argument, this reaction. It is a playing out, a logical extension, of an ideology resident in the traditional rhetoric about Western Civilization. And I want to consider it in that light.

Once upon a time, there was a race of men (the rhetoric stipulated that they were men) who could claim all of knowledge as their purview. Someone like Francis Bacon really did try to organize all of knowledge into a single capacious but coherent structure. And even into the nineteenth century, the creed of universal knowledge—*mathesis universalis*—still reigned. There is a wonderful piece of 19th-century student doggerel about Jowett, the Victorian classicist and master of Balliol College, Oxford, which rather sums up the philosophy:

Here stand I, my name is Jowett,
    If there's knowledge, then I know it;
I am the master of this college,
    What I know not, is not knowledge.[6]

The question this raises for us, of course, is: how does something get to count as knowledge? Intellectuals, Gramsci famously observes, can be defined as experts in legitimation, and the academy today is an institution of legitimation—establishing what counts as knowledge, what counts as culture. In the most spirited attacks on the movement toward multiculturalism in the academy today, there is a whiff of "we are the masters of this college, what we know not, is not knowledge." So that in the wake of Bacon's epistemic megalomania, there has been a contrary movement, a constriction of what counted as even worth knowing. We have got our culture, what more do we need? Besides, there was Heidigger on stage right, assuring us that "philosophy

speaks Greek." And beyond the cartography of Western culture? A cryptic warning: Here Be Monsters.

I got mine: the rhetoric of liberal education remains suffused with the imagery of possession, patrimony, legacy, lineage, inheritance . . . Call it cultural geneticism (in the broadest sense of that term). At the same moment, the rhetoric of possession and lineage subsists upon, and perpetuates, a division between us and them: we the heirs of *our* tradition, and you, the Others, whose difference defines our identity. (In the French colonies, in Africa and the Caribbean, a classroom of African students would dutifully read from their textbook, "Our ancestors, the Gauls . . ." Well, you could see that was not going to last.)

What happens, though, if you buy into that rhetoric—if you accept its terms and presuppositions about cultural geneticism? Then you will say, "Yes, I am Other," and if the aim of education is to reinforce an individual's rightful cultural legacy, then I do not belong here—I am a guest at someone else's banquet. Foucault called this kind of contestation that of "reverse discourse." It remains entrapped within the presuppositions of the discourse it means to oppose, enacts a conflict internal to that "master discourse," but when the terms of argument have already been defined, it may look like the only form of contestation possible. One of the most eloquent reflections on this sense of entrapment is James Baldwin's, where the rhetoric of dispossession turns to that of cultural reappropriation:

> I know, in any case, that the most crucial time in my own development came when I was forced to recognize that I was a kind of bastard of the West; when I followed the line of my past I did not find myself in Europe but in Africa. And this meant that in some subtle way, in a really profound way, I brought to Shakespeare, Bach, Rembrandt, to the stones of Paris, to the cathedral at Chartres, and to the Empire State Building, *a special attitude*. These were not really my reactions, they did not contain my history; I might search in them in vain forever for any reflection of myself. I was an interloper; this was not my heritage. At the same time, I had no other heritage which I could possibly hope to use—I had certainly been unfitted for the jungle or the tribe. I would have to appropriate these white centuries, I would have to make them mine—I would have to accept my special attitude, my special place in this scheme—otherwise I would have no place in any scheme.

(This terror of having no place in any scheme contrasts oddly with the more familiar modernist anxiety of the Western writer, the anxiety that one fits into a scheme all too easily, all too well.)

If Richard Wright's comments are characteristically blunter, they are no less anxious: "I'm black. I'm a man of the West. . . . I see and understand the non- or anti-Western point of view. . . ." But, Wright confesses, "when I look out upon the vast stretches of this earth inhabited by brown, black and yellow men . . . my reactions and attitudes are those of the West" (*White Man Listen*). Wright never had clearer insight into himself, but his ambivalent relation to both the Western and non-Western cultures was satisfactorily resolved. So long as we retain a vocabulary of heritage and inheritance in defining our putative national cultures, it cannot be resolved.

This suggests (if I may invoke the relevant stereotypes) that the old fogey and the young turk have a lot more in common then they realize; that they may, in fact, be two sides of the same debased coin, and that those of us who really care about humane learning should convert to another currency.

The argument has been made that cultural nationalism has been a constitutive aspect of Western education. As humanists, our challenge today is, simply, to learn to live without it. Indeed, it saddens me that there should be any perceived conflict between the ideal of humanistic learning, and what I think of as the truly human, and humane, version of the humanities: one that sees the West not as some mythical, integrative whole, but as a part of a still larger whole. In the resonant words of W.E.B. Du Bois: "I sit with Shakespeare, and he winces not . . ."

Which is then to say, I believe we can change the terms of argument. I believe we can rethink the role of a liberal education without the conceptual residue of cultural nationalism or geneticism. I believe it, because I do think many scholars have already begun to do so.

Some people have begun to realize that broadening our educational vistas is not only sweet, but useful. As most of you will know, a panel of United States governors recently concluded that America's economic and cultural dominance has been endangered by our vast ignorance of the languages and cultures of other nations. In a report made public on February 25, 1989, the National Governors Association argued for broad changes in the way we teach foreign languages and basic geography. Among the report's more startling findings are the following:

- A recent Gallop poll revealed that young American adults know less about geography than their peers in six developed countries.
- One in seven American adults cannot locate the United States on a world map.

- Twenty-five percent of a sample of high school seniors in Dallas did not know that Mexico was the country bordering the U.S. to the south.
- Only twenty percent of American high school graduates receive more than two years instruction in a foreign language.

In response to this report, Ernest L. Boyer, the President of the Carnegie Foundation for the Advancement of Teaching, remarked that "a curriculum with international perspective [is] critically important to the future of our nation."

Americans know so little about world history and culture in part because high school and college core curricula in this country center upon European and American societies, with America represented as the logical conclusion or summary of civilization since the Greeks, in the same way that Christians believe that Christ is the culmination of the Old Testament prophesies. Our ignorance of physical geography is a symptom of a much broader ignorance of the world's cultural geography. Since the trivium and quadrivium of the Latin Middle Ages, "the humanities" has *not* meant the best that has been thought by all human beings; rather, "the humanities" has meant the best that has been thought by white males in the Graeco-Roman, Judeo-Christian traditions. A tyrannical pun exists between the words "humanity," on the one hand, and the "humanities," on the other.

We need to reform our entire notion of the core curricula to account for the comparable eloquence of the African, the Asian, the Latin American, and the Middle Eastern traditions, to prepare our students for their roles in the twenty-first century as citizens of a world culture, educated through a truly human notion of the humanities.

I talked earlier about the long-dead ideal of universal knowledge. Today, you look back to C.P. Snow's complaint about the gulf between the "two cultures" and you think, *two?* Keep counting, C.P. The familiar buzzwords here are the "fragmentation of humanistic knowledge." And there are people who think that the decentering of the humanities that I advocate just makes a bad situation worse—bring on the ivory towers of Babel. So I want to say a few words about this.

Certainly there are different kinds of fragmentation. One is knowledge explosion; specialized fields produce specialized knowledge, and there is too much to keep up with. But there is another kind of fragmentation which does deserve scrutiny: the ways in which knowledge produced in one discipline is inaccessible to scholars in another discipline, even when it would be useful for them in solving their problems. And here, what I call the de-centering of the humanities can help us rethink some of the ways traditional subjects are constituted, and allow us a critical purview helpful in cultural studies quite generally. Indeed, far from being inimical to traditional Western scholarship, humanistic scholarship in Asian and African cultures can be enriching mutually and to the humanities in general. And that is as you would expect. The study of the humanities is the study of the possibilities of human life in culture. It thrives on diversity. And when you get down to cases, it is hard to deny that what you could call the new scholarship has invigorated the traditional disciplines.

Historians of black America have pioneered work in oral history that has had a significant effect on the way nineteenth century social history is done. Or for a much older example think of the upheavals in Homeric scholarship from Milman Parry's work on those Yugoslavian bards; or the advances in understanding the epic from Jack Goody's studies of northern Ghanaian orature. In art history, many Africanists have helped introduce ways of approaching artwork that takes a rich and sophisticated account of cultural context. Often it is when unfamiliar cultural formations are explored that the inadequacies of traditional disciplinary boundaries in the Western academy are most clearly revealed. The gap between the social sciences and the humanities is often bemoaned by those studying the complexities of African history and cultural forms. As Kwame Appiah observes, "methods normally used in anthropology and in art history, for example, can provide profound and mutually reinforcing illumination of the cultural significance of a masquerade or the architecture of a shrine, but students and scholars who are taught to see these methods as radically incommensurable are bound to fail to achieve these insights."

Those scholars who have faced up to these challenges have had to develop theoretical and methodological tools and data resources that promise help in thinking creatively about the ways in which society and culture relate to each other quite generally. For example, the challenges posed by African materials and the new approaches and techniques developed to deal with the varieties of African experience, offer an opportunity to enrich and expand the perspectives of all humanities disciplines and to aid in casting off disciplinary blinders.

In literary theory, our understanding of expressive acts and the symbolic have been influenced by, for instance, Victor Turner's work on the Ndembu; and if you are reading a new historicist essay on drama in Renaissance England, do not be surprised to encounter references to Clifford Geertz's work on the Balinese. I do not want to exaggerate the gains. The opening up of traditional disciplines to the scholarly insights of the new has only just begun, and has not progressed as far as it might have.

But I do want to emphasize that a true decentering of the humanities can not be just a matter of new content in old forms. We have to get away from the paradigm of disciplinary essentialism—imagining the boundaries of disciplines as hermetic, imagining our architectures of knowledge as natural or organic. Granted, sometimes conversation is neither possible nor productive. But we do not need a lazy sort of Platonism that can pretend to "cut nature at the joints"—sustaining the illusion only as long as we do not inquire too closely about the peculiar institutional history of our own particular discipline.

I have suggested that moving toward this human notion of the humanities moves us away from the divisive us/them implications of traditional defenses of the humanities, and removes a source of cultural alienation that is clearly breeding disenchantment and disillusionment among those for whom the experience of higher education may matter the most. But I also think—and here my Whiggish triumphalism is revealed—that it is the natural conclusion of scholarly enlightenment, in which ethnocentric presuppositions have fallen under scholarly critique, auto-critique—and been found wanting.

We need, for instance, to rethink the whole notion of comparative literature. The most influential, and innovative programs in comparative literature have usually embraced just three languages, Latin, French, German, and one other. I look forward to truly comparative programs of comparative literature that embrace the languages and literatures of Yoruba, Urdu, or Arabic as well as the traditional European literatures. I think we should design a required humanities course that is truly humanistic—with the Western segment comprising a quarter or a third—in addition to the traditional Western Civilization course, so that students can begin to understand the histories of civilization itself, in a truly comparative manner.

Such an embracive posture honors the best, the noblest traditions and ambitions of the academy, and while I have decried cultural nationalism, I hope you will permit me to bow to it in citing something Ishmael Reed has said on the subject of multiculturalism. He said it is possible here "because the United States is unique in the world: *the world is here.*"

Or listen to a great canonical author, Herman Melville, writing a century earlier in his novel *Redburn:* "There is something in the contemplation of the mode in which America has been settled, that, in a noble breast, should forever extinguish the prejudices of national dislikes. Settled by the people of all nations, all nations may claim her for their own. You cannot spill a drop of American blood without spilling the blood of the whole world . . . We are not a nation so much as a world."

In a more practical vein, it turns out that the affirmative action programs for recruiting minority faculty have only been successful at institutions where strong ethnic studies programs exist. Many ambitious "minority" scholars of my generation, feeling secure in their academic credentials and their ethnic identities, have tried to fill a lacuna they perceived in their own education by producing scholarship about, well—"their own people." A lot of the social commitment that emerged during the 1960s has been redirected toward the scholarly arena: continents of ignorance have been explored and charted. At the same time, so called "minority studies" are not *for* minorities, any more than "majority studies" (let's say) are for majorities. And it is wrong simply to conflate affirmative action objectives in employment with the teaching of such subjects.

I respect what Robert Nisbet calls the Academic Dogma—knowledge for its own sake (I suspect it does not quite exist; but that is another matter). At the same time, I believe that truly humane learning can not help but expand the constricted boundaries of human sympathy, of social tolerance. Maybe the truest thing to be said about racism is that it represents a profound failure of imagination. I have talked a good deal about multiculturalism as a good in itself, as the natural shape of scholarship untrammeled by narrow ethnocentrism; and also as a response to the persistence of racism on campuses. And the best ethnic studies departments have made a real contribution to this ideal of scholarly diversity. As I said, I respect the ideal of the disinterested pursuit of knowledge, however unattainable, and I do not think classes should be converted into "consciousness raising" sessions. Lord knows, at the same time anyone who is not a positivist realizes that "moral education" is a pleonasm—in the humanities, facts and values do not exist in neatly disjunct regimes of knowledge. (Allan Bloom is right to ask about the effect of higher education on our kids' moral development, even if that is the only thing he is right about.)

Amy Gutmann said something important in her recent book *Democratic Education:* "In a democracy, political disagreement is not something that we should generally seek to avoid. Political controversies over our educational problems are a particularly important source of social progress because they have the potential for educating so many citizens." I think

that is true. I think a lot of us feel that any clamor or conflict over the curriculum is just a bad thing in itself, that it somehow undermines the legitimacy of the institutions of knowledge. And this sort of no-news-is-good-news attitude on the subject of education is all too widespread. In fact, I think one of the most renewing activities we can do is to rethink the institutions where we teach people to think: we invest in myths of continuity, but universities have constantly been molting and creating themselves anew for the last millennium, and there is no reason to think that will change in the next.

Gerald Graff has been saying that where there is no consensus—and there is no consensus—teach the conflicts. In fact, I think at the better colleges, we do. We do not seem to be able not to. And that is nothing to be embarrassed about. College is not kindergarten, our job is not to present a seemly, dignified, unified front to the students. College students are too old to form, we should not delude ourselves; but they are not too old to challenge. I am reminded of something that the college president and educator Robert Maynard Hutchins wrote in a book he published during the height of the McCarthy era. He recounted a conversation he'd had with a distinguished doctor about the attempt of the Board of Regents of the University of California to extort, as Hutchins put it, "an illegal and unconstitutional oath of loyalty from the faculty of that great institution." "Yes, but" the doctor said, "if we are going to hire these people to look after our children we are entitled to know what their opinions are." And Hutchins grandly remarks: "I think it is clear that the collapse of liberal education in the United States is related as cause or effect or both to the notion that professors are people who are hired to look after children."[7] Wise words, those.

In all events, the sort of pluralism I have been recommending has one evolutionary advantage over its opponents. If you ask, how do we form a consensus around such a "de-centering" proposal, the answer is that it does not exactly require a consensus. Which is why, in the words of John Dewey, "pluralism is the greatest philosophical idea of our times." Not that this puts us home free. As Dewey also said,

> What philosophers have got to do is to work out a fresh analysis of the relations between the one and the many. Our shrinking world presents that issue today in a thousand different forms . . . How are we going to make the most of the new values we set on variety, difference, and individuality—how are we going to realize their possibilities in every field, and at the same time not sacrifice that plurality to the

cooperation we need so much? How can we bring things together as we must without losing sight of plurality?

Learning without center is not learning without focus. We have all seen undigested eclecticism posing as a bold new synthesis; but to read and write culture anew means additional demands for rigor and coherence, not emancipation from these things. I take Dewey's question seriously, but there is nothing vaporous about the form the answer takes: it is made of brick and mortar, and sometimes a little ivy about the architrave. For us scholars and teachers it is the university whose constant refashioning is our charge, burden, and privilege.

Endnotes

1. "Blacks and Whites on the Campuses: Behind Ugly Racist Incidents, Student Isolation and Insensitivity," *The Chronicle of Higher Education*, April 26, 1989. See also general articles on racial incidents on campuses in: *New York Times*, December 15, 1986, A18; *Los Angeles Times*, May 8, 1981, 1; *Christian Science Monitor*, March 26, 1987, 3; and John Wiener's "Racial Hatred on Campus," *The Nation*, February 27, 1989, 260-264.

   Other news reports on particular incidents can be found in the *New York Times*, February 13, 1988, 7; April 8, 1987, 24; November 15, 1986, 6; March 9, 1987, A12; January 31, 1988, 20.

2. Cited in the *Chronicle of Higher Education*, above.

3. Robert M. Press, "College Enrollment Rate for Black Students is Falling," *Christian Science Monitor*, May 24, 1985, 4 and "Students at Black Colleges Hit Hard by Grant Cuts," *New York Times*, April 1, 1987, A19.

4. Robert Marquand, "Racism on Campus, Part II," *Christian Science Monitor*, June 15, 1988.

5. Marquand, above.

6. Thomas McFarland, *Shapes of Culture* (Iowa City: University of Iowa Press, 1987), 6.

7. Robert M. Hutchins, *The Conflict in Education in Democratic Society* (New York: Harper and Brothers, 1953), 93-94.

Further Reading

Stanley Aronowitz and Henry Giroux, *Education Under Seige: The Conservative, Liberal, and Radical Debate Over Schooling* (South Hadley, MA: Bergin and Garvey, 1985).

Pierre Bourdieu and Jean-Claude Passeron, *Reproduction in Education, Society, and Culture*, translated by Richard Nice (Beverly Hills, London: Sage Publications, 1977).

Gerald Graff, *Professing Literature: An Institutional History* (Chicago: University of Chicago, 1987).

Amy Guttman, *Democratic Education* (Princeton: Princeton University Press, 1987).

Robert Maynard Hutchins, *The Conflict in Education in Democratic Society* (New York: Harper & Brothers, 1953).

James Lynch, *Multicultural Education in a Global Society* (London: The Falmer Press, 1989).

JOHN LOVELL, JR.

Afro-American Spiritual: Radical Change in the Existing Order of Things

Sense of Change: Evolutionary and Revolutionary

The fundamental theme, though perhaps not the greatest, that pervades the spiritual is the need for a change in the existing order. No one can deny that this theme is equally fundamental in Biblical Christianity. A close reader of the spiritual is compelled to conclude that this fact provides the prime reason for the slave poet's selecting the Bible for his main source when a harvest of sources (his work, his fellow slaves, the people he worked for, the phenomena of nature, his legends handed down from African ancestors, and many others) were available.

If this declaration of key theme seems to deny the religious motivation of the songs, let us quickly explain. No doubt, as we have demonstrated, the spiritual is often a religious song; it is just not a simple religious song and nothing else. What we are examining here is why it is a religious song. As shown above, in Chapter 15, religion was adopted by the greatest leaders of the slave revolts, undoubtedly because it was the most radical method by which their personal feelings, their criticism of slavery, and their need for a frame of secrecy could be expressed. So the slave folk poet and all his band chose religion as the chief field of their expression. This choice did not mean that they thought any less of their religion or, on the other hand, that they were necessarily predominantly religious. Religion does not automatically inspire literature in its practitioners. But if a slave, even a religious slave, seeks an outlet for expression, he wants and needs a system capable of direct language and undercurrent symbolism at the same time.

Nothing fits this need better than the Christian religion. It has a firm base in traditionalism. But it strikes out in two other directions, a much better and radically different life on earth and a supremely better and revolutionary life in a world beyond the grave. Since poets are helpless without symbolism and since slave poets find symbolism indispensable (as self-protection and as prevention of the destruction of their creative product, if for no other reasons), the Christian religion was made to order for the slave poet we are studying. He seized upon it and put it to as good use as poets anywhere have done.

In his expression of radical change he relies first upon the evolutionary process. Things will happen, he declares, in a certain way as to make things different. Not for a moment does it occur to him that anyone will doubt that things need changing, from top to bottom; a world with the bitter, degrading injustice of slavery in it obviously could not be a good or a tolerable world. This poet is sure that the folk band who will join in his choruses fully agree in the need for radical change. His song naturally assumes that this view is the consensus everywhere.

His own troubles are the symptoms of the most immediate level of change.

> All my troubles will soon be over with,
> Soon be over with, soon be over with,
> All my troubles will soon be over with,
> All over this world.

In only two ways can this prophecy come true. He will die and go to a better world for him, or the current world will be transformed to eliminate his troubles. Since he says nothing about dying in this particular song, suppose we assume the latter way. To change his troubles means a very big change either in the slave system or in his removal from it. This sense of change recurs hundreds of times in these songs.

If the die-hard believer in death has his own solution upheld, that fact does not change in the slightest the slave poet's concept that a fundamental overhaul of things is desirable and required.

In a similar song, the poet takes himself, as individual, out of the picture. He talks about trouble in general. Obviously, he means to suggest a system of troubles that need eradicating. And he predicts with great joy—note the "Hallelujah"—that the eradication is sure to come.

> I'm so glad Trouble don't last always; . . .
> Hallelujah, I'm so glad trouble don't last always.

Naturally, the poet uses death as a symbol of change. This does not necessarily mean physical death as an infinite number of poets before and since these have shown. Whether or not it means physical death (and new life beyond the grave), the point about need for evolutionary change is sharp and deeply embedded.

> Death's gwineter lay its cold icy hands on me.
> I'm ready fo' to cross ol' Jordan's stream.

He would certainly not be ready to accept this deepest of changes if his current situation were profitable.

Evolutionary change is often credited as God's work:

> Oh, yes, bow yo' knees upon de groun' . . .
> An' ask yo' Lord to turn your roun',

or

> Oh, can't you rise an' tell what de Lord has done
> for you?
> Yes he's taken my feet out of de miry clay
> An' he's a placed 'em on de right side of my Father.

And note that all this took place before the robber death intervened.

Occasionally the radical change is perpetrated by the individual himself, and once in a while he will specifically ask that others keep hands off.

> Do don't touch-a my garment . . .
> Good Lord,* I'm gwine home
> (Also do don't touch-a my slippers)
> Touch me not little Mary,
> Good Lord,* I'm gwine home.

The most striking declarations of change, however, are revolutionary, not evolutionary. The slave poet saw too many things wrong with the existing order to hope that a few alterations here and there would satisfy. He was too impatient, generally speaking, to accept the slow process of gradual development and improvement by enlightened forces. Directly or indirectly, therefore, there had to be revolution. Once more using the Bible, he projected both bloodless and bloody revolution. In hundreds of songs, it should be noted, his root thinking is more important than his surface words. Considering that the songs came from individual creators all over the South, representing folk opinion everywhere, the consistency and persistency of these views is inescapable.

---

*The injunction not to touch is not directed against the Lord; "Good Lord" here is merely a holy byword.

Let us begin with songs in which revolution is implied rather than planned and developed. These songs stress situations that cannot take place unless the old (current) order is abolished and a new order is established. Since we are dealing with the poet's mind and his intentions, whether the new order is in heaven (the next life) or on earth (this life, South or North) is irrelevant. From a study of the social history, however, there is little doubt that the slave singers were talking about this world, not some other (see Chapters 13 and 15).

Since John the Apostle wrote the Book of Revelation, projecting and predicting a complete new order, he is a favorite point of departure,

> Tell all the world, John, Tell all the world, John.
> Tell all the world, John, I know the other world is
> not like this.

As in all folk literature, repetition here is not only for mnemonic convenience but for deep and varied emphasis.

Switching from John to Mary (who ran to the supposedly occupied tomb of Jesus on Easter morning and found it empty), the poet reaches very nearly the same position,

> Run, Mary, run, (repeated twice)
> I know de udder worl' is not like dis.
> [Changes probably due to local transcription]
> Fire in de Eas', an' fire in de Wes',
> I know de udder worl' is not like dis.
> Boun' to burn de wilderness,
> I know de udder worl' is not like dis.

In the New Testament of the Bible are several references to great healing operations conducted when a deformed or paralytic individual waded in a stream after the water had been "troubled" by an angel of the Lord. This sort of belief is age-old and worldwide, being very much alive in India (and other places) today. The theory of the spiritual poet is that, if one person can be transformed by such a process, why cannot the same thing work for a whole crowd or nation of people. This theory is very little different, in the poetic sense, from a doctrine of implied revolution; only the method needs working out. If God is going to supply the method, you do not have to worry about that part anyway; thus,

> Wade in de water, children (repeated twice)
> God's a-gwineter trouble de water.

So far, the revolutionary principle has inhered in God or other outside forces. The spiritual poet often initiates the revolution in himself. The *I* of the spiritual, however, is not a single person. It is every person who

sings, everyone who has been oppressed and, therefore, every slave anywhere.

The slave poet sometimes finds himself utterly disgusted. His patience gives out. In his heart he can no longer bring himself to work and pray and wait. The patchwork here and there suggests nothing so much as futility. And so he sings,

> If I had my way,
> O Lordy, Lordy,
> If I had my way;
> If I had my way,
> I would tear this building down.

In other songs the poet says,

> I'm a-goin' to lay down this world,
> Goin' to shoulder up my cross,

or

> Yes, one o' dese mornin's 'bout twelve o'clock,
> Dis ol' worl' am gwineter reel and rock.

Either way, the revolutionary spirit is satisfied especially if you read the first one (as from the evidence you have every right to do) to mean that he is going to accept all the hazards and run away to freedom.

In the civil rights legislative discussion of the 1960s there was much talk of the revolutionary effect which would derive from digging up and throwing away the deep-seated tradition of separate eating facilities for white and black races. Orators and pseudo-sociologists equated the tradition with deep ramifications of an orderly society; they likewise equated the destruction of the tradition with social disorder, mongrelization, white genocide, and other dire outcomes.

Although the slave was probably not interested in intermarriage as such, he was certainly an integrationist, largely on the grounds that anything less was degrading and insulting. To be denied the ordinary treatment of a human being was unbearable to him. He was not in position to say so flatly, but he did not hesitate to say so poetically,

> I'm goin' to eat at the welcome table,
> O yes I'm goin' to eat at the welcome table some of
> these days hallelujah!

Not only was he going to have the right to eat at a table where good food was served (note the impossible food of the slave). He was also going to live in a world where he would be welcomed to a good table. Later in the song he was going to be equally welcome to "drink at the crystal fountain." From the viewpoint of the late 1700s and early 1800s, the probable time of the creation of most of these songs, such practices would involve the mightiest of revolutions.

Nothing could be more revolutionary than the slave running away to freedom, inducing others to run away, or advocating running away. First, the slave was a chattel and his departure was a violation of the laws of property. Second, the slave system was considered by the South an economic and political necessity; any loss of slaves undermined the system, any advocacy of running away was economic and political revolution. Third, the religious leaders of the South, relying upon the Biblical passages which they said supported slavery, demonstrated that inducing a slave to leave his bondage was morally wrong and religiously sinful.

Even so, the slave advocated running away in his songs. Set aside for now the "Go Down, Moses" series. It is beyond question that the chief desire of the slave (see Chapter 15) was for physical freedom here and now. He had many friends in the North and the example of many runaway slaves to encourage him in his desire.

One of the creative singers wishes to remind the crowd that freedom is not an impossible way out of their troubles. He comes by a suitable rhythm and stretches it into song,

> Steal away,
> Steal away,
> Steal away.

And then the danger of his position confronts him. He cannot openly advocate escape and insurrection; it would do no good. He knows that his yearning is already shared by the crowd around him and that they all understand what he is trying to say. He searches for a medium with appeal and force. Knowing the religious bent of his companions, he settles on "To Jesus!"

Now, he is in the clear. From now on, he can say whatever he pleases. The oppressor, always close by, is satisfied that this is a purely religious enterprise; his suspicion, aroused by the first "Steal away" is fully allayed. But the slave poet goes on,

> Steal away, steal away home,
> I ain't got long to stay here!

The trusting oppressor never knew (or believed) until too late that the slave had probably already made contact with a representative of the Underground Railroad or some other slave stealing organization. But the surrounding slaves knew well the implications of the first verse,

> My Lord calls me, He calls me by the thunder;
> The trumpet sounds within-a my soul,
> I ain't got long to stay here.

To support this interpretation is the testimony of one of many hundreds of testifying slaves, Frederick Douglass, who ran away successfully and became a great man in a free society. Of the spirituals he writes,

> They were tones, loud, long and deep, breathing the prayer and complaint of souls boiling over with the bitterest anguish. Every tone was a testimony against slavery, and a prayer to God for deliverance from chains (*My Bondage and My Freedom*, p. 99).

The revolutionary song at its best is a powerful production. As nearly always, the slave chooses a revolutionary chapter from the Bible. Note that nearly all of the Biblical personages the slave poet deals with were involved in upheaval and revolution (Moses, Daniel, David, the Hebrew children, Samson, Elijah, Gideon, Jesus, Paul). This fact alone should warn the reader what the songs import if the reader were genuinely interested in reading the literature, rather than in singing or in being lulled to quasi-religious sleep.

One of these big productions is called "Joshua Fit de Battle ob Jericho." Historically, Joshua, Moses' successor, is in the final stages of a major conquest by a group of recently freed slaves over a well-equipped and superior army of Philistines. The walls of Jericho are symbolic of a long-standing tradition which kept the ex-slaves out of Canaan, their promised land. If the above characteristics and their revolutionary implications had not been inherent in the subject matter, the slave poet would certainly have passed over Joshua and his prize battle as a dramatic theme.

The basic ingredients established, the poet gives Joshua's pedigree,

> You may talk about yo' king ob Gideon,
> You may talk about yo' man ob Saul,
> Dere's none like good ole Joshua,
> At de battle ob Jericho.

Step by step the poet follows Joshua. (1) "Up to de walls of Jericho, He marched with spear in han'," (2) " 'Go blow dem ram horns,' Joshua cried, 'Kase de battle am in my hand.' " (3) After the horns and trumpets blow, "Joshua commanded de chillen to shout, An' de walls come tumblin' down."

Only the most naïve reader misses the point that what Joshua did can be done again and again, wherever wrong and evil are to be overthrown, wherever promised good and right are to be established. Once the walls are down, the ex-slaves walk into the capital of Canaan, free men in a free land. Getting into the singing heart and mind of the slave poet (especially when the song is sung with the proper vigor and gusto), you can appreciate the thrill of a group of singing slaves, with a certain expectation in their hearts, following their leader through:

Dat mornin', Joshua fit de battle ob Jericho,
An' de walls come tumblin' down.

Deliverance Through Power and Association with Power

It perhaps needs to be repeated that religion was an essential quality and ingredient of the spiritual. The chief injunction remains the avoidance of overemphasis upon conventional religion or upon religion as something relaxing and taken for granted. The slave relied upon religion, not primarily because he felt himself "converted," but because he recognized the power inherent in religious things.

What he needed most was power and a feeling of closeness with power. It is probably strange that one must say that he cared little for subtle power or mystical power (usually religion's greatest selling point). The slave had to have physical, realistic, and even material power. Those who say he was singing quietly religious songs associate his creative mind with ultimate, distant power; they seem to think he conceded immediate power because he was a helpless slave.

This view is unsupported by the songs. Of course he believed in ultimate power; but he believed in immediate power too, lots of it, close at hand. His relationship with the Deity presupposed anthropomorphic as well as omnipresent beings, capable of miraculous performance and always on call. His reading of the Bible had conditioned him to miracles and mighty feats of power. In his predicament, only this kind of deity was worth trusting. He trusted, but he demanded every resource of his contract.

The slave's association with power naturally meant a radical change in the existing order, heralded by his songs. This change was reflected in his everyday life, in the prospect of doom for his enemies (just as it was with "the chosen people" of the Bible), and in the assurance of the best possible life beyond the grave. Since he was in bondage, the key concept of the change he sang about was deliverance.

Hardly a song is without some evidence of this sense of powerful deliverance and of the slave's reliance upon it. In refrain or verses the recurrence of the symbols of power, Jesus, the Lord, God, the angels, and various inanimate things, is so great that a comprehensive list of examples would be little less than a dozen volumes of poems and poetic phrases. Some effort is made here, however, to give examples that are representative of this widespread display.

One example purports to be representative of one other phase of the subject, the rank of the symbols.

For instance, if one makes a close examination of 260 spirituals, carefully selected for their representativeness, one will find about fifty developmental references (not simple mentions) of Jesus, the Lord, and God. Of these fifty, a little over half talk of Jesus, a little more than one-third of the Lord, and less than one-tenth of God. Rarely does the spiritual poet mix up the three except in bywords like "O my good Lord" or "Yes, my Lord" mingled with a reference to Jesus or God.

On the basis of this examination one might, very cautiously, say that the spiritual poet thought of God as the ultimate and final source of power, more or less removed like an unbelievably massive and inexhaustible dynamo; of the Lord as a more available series of power stations; and of Jesus as readily available, always at hand. Angels are the messengers of any one of the three.

The functions of Jesus as a deliverer are far-reaching. He is, first of all, an indomitable ruling king who does not hesitate a second in favoring his subjects, "Ride on King Jesus! No man can hinder him," or "Ride on King Jesus, I want to go to heav'n in the mornin'." He rides "on a milk-white horse" and performs all manner of useful and difficult services,

When I was blind and could not see,
King Jesus brought that light to me.

Since he favors his people on earth, he will certainly extend his benevolence to the extracurricular world:

When every star refuses to shine, . . .
I know King Jesus will be mine.

Occasionally, the poet bursts into a paean of praise for his gracious King. Although he works with and for men, he is clearly above them and capable of cutting down wrongs and building up rights.

He is King of Kings, He is Lord of Lords,
Jesus Christ the first and last, no man works
like him.

He built his throne up in the air, . . .
And called his saints from everywhere, . . .

He pitched his tents on Canaan's ground
And broke the Roman kingdom down.

But Jesus, in the poet's eyes, can also be powerful as a Lamb (often a dying Lamb), who rescued man from sin by pulling the destructive sting from death. "I'm purchased by the dyin' Lamb" constantly recurs. He is a tender, sympathetic Lamb as the song "Sittin' Down beside O' the Lamb" proves. But these inherent qualities detract nothing from his delivering power.

In the river of Jordan John* baptized,
How I long to be baptized,
In the river of Jordan John baptized unto the dying
Lamb. . . .

We baptize all that come by faith unto the dying
Lamb. . . .

Here's another one come to be baptized unto the
dying Lamb.

It is always touching when the poet, after recognizing the power and the deliverance conferred on
him by his closest friend (Jesus), unabashedly gives
his heart,

O Lamb, beautiful Lamb; I'm going to serve God
til I die. . . .
Never felt such love before, I'm going to serve God
til I die. . . .
Looked at my hands, and they looked new, . . .
Looked at my feet, and they did too.
I'm going to serve God til I die.

In "Jesus Will Come Bye-an'-bye" the slave poet
learns a great fact about power. If you are deserving
and if you move persistently in the right direction,
power will meet you halfway,

Keep a-inchin' along,
Keep a-inchin' along,
Jesus will come bye-an'-bye.

One reason the poet leans so heavily on the power
of Jesus is that he has conquered even a meaner world
than the slave confronts, the world of death. Many songs
speak of the crucifixion; many more of the resurrection,

Go and tell ev'rybody
Yes, Jesus is risen from the dead.

If a power can overcome death, the poet reasons, he
can certainly handle slavery, all personal troubles, and
all sinful weaknesses of all the people. But Jesus did not
stop with mere overcoming. He maintains a dynamic
victorious attitude afterwards, one that is more appealing to an imaginative slave.

Jesus rides in the middle of de air, . . .
He's callin' sinners from ev'rywhere.

"Jesus rides" is not a rare, but a favorite phrase. It carries the implication that if you are pinned down (as the
slave was at the time), you can still hope for deliverance from a benevolent king who moves about.

The delivering Jesus of the afterlife is impressive,
but he is the more conventional symbol. "I'm goin'

up to see my Jesus, O some sweet day after 'while" is
pretty much what you would expect from a slave song-
writer. The following lines, however, are somewhat off
the beaten track,

You needn't min' my dyin' (repeated twice)
Jesus goin' to make up my dyin' bed. . . .

I'll be sleepin' in Jesus, . . .

I'll be restin' easy.

And a very generous thought,

When I get to heav'n I want you to be there too,
When I cry "holy" I want you to say so too.

He obviously infers that Jesus will make up more than
one dying bed and will try to keep friends together. Another mildly unconventional touch delineating deliverance in the afterlife is in a military vein,

We'll shout o'er all our sorrows, An' sing forever
more,
With Christ an' all his army, On dat celestial shore.

Without a doubt, however, the really powerful
Jesus of the spiritual works on earth, in this life, in the
here and now, today and tomorrow. At his very best
the spiritual poet sings,

Nobody knows de trouble I see,
Nobody knows like [or but] Jesus
Nobody knows de trouble I see,
Glory, Hallelujah!

A sad song is turned into exultation by sudden appreciation of Jesus' delivering power.

Again and again, in wonderful strokes of his
brush, the amazing poet echoes poignant variations
on this idea,

I'm troubled, I'm troubled, I'm troubled in mind,
If Jesus don't help me I sho'ly will die. . . .

When you see me on my knees—
Come here, Jesus, if you please. . . .

When you hear me calling, Jesus,
Hear me, Jesus, if you please.

The pathos of the last two songs is matched only by
their gentle courtesy.

Sometimes, Jesus is not expected to do a major act
of salvation. Sometimes, a bit of psychoanalytic listening or talking will do.

O a little talk with Jesus makes it right, all
right, . . .
Troubles of ev'ry kind, Thank God I'll always find
That a little talk with Jesus makes it right.

---

*John the Baptist, differentiated from John the Apostle.

It is therefore not surprising that the poet declares, "You may have all this world, Give me Jesus." Or that he is grateful for that happy day "when Jesus wash'd my sins away." Or that he appreciates more deeply a King who preached to the poor,

> Did you ever see such love before, . . .
> King Jesus preaching to the poor,
> I do love the Lord.

If the reader is beginning to wonder how these private services relate to radical change, let us remind him that the slave felt that he had to be sustained from day to day before he could accomplish his transformation. American slavery with its isolation, its backbreaking toil under hot sun or in inclement weather, its lack of family life, its poor food and housing, its persistent threat of being sold "down the river," and its other disabilities was very hard to take. Even the first acts of the slave stealers were related to upholding the prospective escapee until he could be delivered. These concepts of Jesus were, in this regard, effective and necessary.

But Jesus contributed a greater concept than any of these to the slave mind through the spiritual—the feeling that he was already free at heart and already a denizen of democracy.

> When Jesus shook the manna tree, . . .
> He shook it for you and He shook it for me, . . .
>
> Hallelujah to the lamb! . . . Jesus died for ev'ry man.

And the more expressive lines, because of their Biblical implications,

> Jesus Christ, He died for me, Way down in Egypt land:
> Jesus Christ, He set me free, Way down in Egypt land.

The fact that Jesus was not around when Moses and the Hebrew children were freed from Egyptian bondage is irrelevant. The poet is not a theologian or historian, as so many people have apparently given him credit for being. He is concerned with his private desires, and the greatest of these is freedom. The quickest route to freedom is through the transforming power of Jesus.

The Lord in the spiritual is somewhat more comprehensive than Jesus and definitely farther away. But he is power beyond all the needs of the slave. The Lord readily cuts through laws, conventions, power structures, and all other sociopolitical forms to make things right for those he favors, for those who return his trust. Thus, the slave creator appeals directly to the Lord when the need is great. The implied answers to his appeals often connote radical departures from natural as well as social law. Note these two,

> My Lord's done just what He said,
> Healed the sick and raised the dead. . . .
>
> Didn't my Lord deliver Daniel, deliver Daniel, deliver Daniel,
> Didn't my Lord deliver Daniel, An' why not every man.

The song containing the second quotation also refers to Jonah's delivery from the belly of the whale and the saving of "de Hebrew chillun" from the fiery furnace. The rescues of Daniel, Jonah, and the trio Shadrach, Meshach, and Abednego were not ordinary acts of deliverance. They involved suspension or repeal of the laws of nature, the nature of hungry lions to eat available flesh, the nature of whales to retain their food, the nature of fire to burn human flesh. In the slave's mind, his situation within the rigid and crushing system of slavery, which seemed to all others immovable and unchangeable, was in the category of hopelessness with Daniel, Jonah, and the three fire-eaters. But the Lord had proved He was equal to the occasion; and the slave had proved he was deserving. Thus the miraculous deliverance was inevitable.

To the slave, Pharaoh was earthly power to the highest degree. He was in the class with the slave master. The Israelites were in a hopeless position against such power. So is the slave in a hopeless position. Both hopeless, except for one thing—the existence of the Lord and His determination to side with the helpless good against the powerful bad. Not just his determination; also, his command of power, supreme power, unlimited power. He had such power that he could pronounce,

> Your enemies you see today,
> You never shall see more.

All the helpless good had to do was to call upon him. For Pharaoh read the combined power of the slave owners of America, their errand-running, subservient politicians, their military might,

> When the children were in bondage,
> They cried unto the Lord,
> To turn back Pharaoh's army,
> He turned back Pharaoh's army.
>
> When Pharaoh crossed the water,
> The waters came together,
> And drowned ole Pharaoh's army,
> Hallelu!

Using the same logic and magnificent poetic faith, the spiritual poet told of other great deliverances which he intended to be relative to his own. Through the creative strength of his idea and his simple, but overwhelming, directness, he carved out marvelously touching lines:

O, de blin' man stood on de road an' cried.
O, de blin' man stood on de road an' cried.
Cryin' O, my Lord, save-a me,
De blin' man stood on de road an' cried.

The poet's blind man, like the poet, and like the reader if he is sensitive, is fully aware of the bigness of the job he is asking the Lord to do. The job involves preeminent social and psychological, as well as medical, skills. But the poet is never doubtful of the Lord's ability to perform it.

The poet often projects himself into this complex field of sociopsychological welfare. Listen to this,

Lord help the po' and the needy,
In this lan' . . .
In this great getting up morning we shall face another sun,
Lord help the po' and the needy,
In this lan', In this lan'. . . .

Lord help the widows and the orphans, In this lan' . . .

Lord help the motherless children, In this lan' . . .

Lord help the hypocrite members, In this lan' . . .

Lord help the long-tongue liars, In this lan' . . .

Note several things: The poet does not join the poor and the needy; he separates them. He does not request help for just the worthy; he includes the unworthy and the obnoxious. And most radical of all, he indicates that this kind of help points toward a time when all the conditions that cry for help will be removed.

Although the slave poet's personal appeals to the Lord imply more limited changes, they are radical enough. First, they are far more numerous than all other appeals combined; when their total weight is added up, they cover a broad range of changes and of implicit modifications in the social structures. For example, "O Lord I'm hungry, I want to be fed" and "O Lord I'm naked, I want to be clothed" would assault the economic structure by adding greatly to the slave owner's food and clothing bills. Second, if the prayers are answered, the slave himself would be so basically transformed that he might be much less useful, and more uneconomic, as a slave. Third, the slave would acquire elements of character and personality that would make slavery even less palatable than it was, if that were possible, and would increase the slave's desire to escape. Study the implications in the following,

Do Lord, do Lord, Do remember me, . . .
When I'm in trouble, Do remember me, . . .

It seems that the Lord with his gigantic whip would be standing above the overseer who overshadowed the slave.

Oh, Lord, Oh, my Lord! Oh my good Lord!
Keep me f'om sinkin' down,

obviously meaning, don't let me give in to threats, overwork, and oppression; stiffen my resistance.

It's me, it's me, O Lord,
Standing in the need of pray'r
[Not my brother, my sister, my mother, my elder].

In spite of the deep sense of community in the spiritual as a whole (see Chapter 19) songs like this reinforce the sense of individual identity. Again and again the spiritual poet stresses the need for strength of individual character (see also Chapter 19, "Development Through Character and Right Living") as opposed to group unity. Such individual spiritual strength, derived from the Lord, would not be conducive to good slave psychology and was a commodity the slave owner, dealer, and overseer greatly deplored and feared, even fought against. Not Emerson himself ever preached a sharper sermon on self-reliance.

We have several times referred to peaks in spiritual poetry, and shall again. One of these peaks is the poet's immersing himself within the boundless power of the Lord and emerging into everyday life clothed in and invigorated by that power, like some Achilles dipped completely (not held by a heel) into the Styx.

At first, he gradually launches in, almost like a toe trying the water, "Lord, I want to be a Christian/ In my heart, in-a my heart." Being a Christian means being more loving, more holy, less like Judas, more like Jesus, all in his heart.

Next, he loses any modesty and dives in, partly because, like the Biblical people, he has found the Lord wholly reliable,

O, ain't I glad I've got out the wilderness, . . .
Leaning on the Lord.

At length, he reaches complete understanding. Adapting one of his inscrutably glorious figures of speech from the world of work, he declares,

In de Lord, in de Lord,
My soul's been anchored in de Lord. . . .

Befo' I'd stay in hell one day,
My soul's been anchored in de Lord.
I'd sing an' pray myself away,
My soul's been anchored in de Lord.

I'm gwineter pray an' never stop, . . .
Until I reach de mountaintop,

My soul's been anchored in de Lord,
O Lord, my soul's been anchored in de Lord.

See my father in the gospel
Come wagging* up the hill so slow,
He's crying new as he cried before
My soul's been anchored in the Lord.

To go from the Lord to God is to go from the top to the topmost top. The slave's god is the God of Moses and Daniel and other such Old Testament heroes; His prime function is in His role as the Deliverer. In being the Deliverer, He is at times not gentle,

My God is mighty man of war, man of war,
(repeated twice)
Sinner, please don't let this harvest pass,
And die and lose your soul at last.

The emphasis is strong that all of God's might and martial strength cannot deliver a man who refuses the opportunity to believe and the action necessary to meet deliverance partway. As we have seen, He can trouble the water and turn it into a gigantic hospital and great society. Although standing in proper "fear" and respect, who would not love such a God and strive to be in his presence.

O mother, don't you weep when I'm gone.
For I'm going to Heav'n above,
Going to the God I love.

Like Christians from everywhere, the spiritual poet and his band, from "dat great gittin' up mornin' " on, will "live wid God forever."

That God is his friend and protector no one can ever doubt. In these phrases he must have included overseers and other brutalizers in his warning,

I'm gonna tell God how you treat me (repeated
twice) . . . some of these days.

In spite of the poet's gratitude for all other manifestations and associations with God, nothing surpasses his pride over the fact that this friend of his is the greatest power in reality or imagination.

God is a God! God don't never change!
God is a God! An' He always will be God!
He made the sun to shine by day, He made the
sun to show the way,
He made the stars to show their light, He made
the moon to shine by night, sayin'
God is a God, God don't never change! . . .

The earth his footstool an' heav'n his throne,
The whole creation all his own,
His love an' power will prevail, His promise

will never fail, sayin'
God is a God! An' always will be God!

With such a friend and deliverer, the slave poet has every right to warn enemies, detractors, and oppressors that their day of control and dominance will be short. God would certainly carry out his just requirements. "My God ain't no lyin' man," the poet sang.

The angels are important only because they carry out the edicts of Jesus, the Lord, and God. From time to time, however, they can be quite colorful. At one place the poet demands that you "Listen to the angels shoutin'." One thing they shout gives them parallelism with the slaves: "I hear them shoutin' 'I've been redeemed.' " And much is said of the angel chorus "that hailed our Savior's birth."

But mostly the angels (and archangels) are engaged, under orders, in the work of deliverance, with notable efficiency. One of them is celebrated in spirituals because he rolled the stone away at some time between Good Friday evening and Easter sunrise. (Rarely, though, does the angel of the spiritual work alone.) Others are busy with difficult chores,

Way over yonder in the harvest fields,
The angels shoving at the chariot wheels.

The slave poet does not hesitate to ask for the services of the angels as if they were a regular transportation company,

O bretheren, my way, my way's cloudy, my way,
Go sen'-a dem angels down.

Or from a very famous song,

I look'd over Jordan, an' what did I see
Comin' for to carry me home,
A band of angels comin' after me,
Comin' for to carry me home.

An extremely interesting responsibility for angels is to make certain that all the good folk get their rewards. There is little doubt that in the following song the poet is projecting one or both sides of a double meaning—reward in the afterlife and assurance that he will be in the next batch from his plantation to be carried up to freedom on the Underground Railroad.

O, write my name, (repeated twice)
De Angels in de heav'n gwineter write my
name. . . .

Write my name in de Book of life,
Yes, write my name in de drippin' blood,
De Angels in de heav'n gwineter write my name.

Death and Judgment Day are likewise methods of defeating the system of slavery. It cannot be repeated

---

*Means "toiling, moving slowly," a truly wonderful usage.

too often, however, that very likely death means merely deliverance into a system of freedom, that is, a free land, and Judgment Day merely that great day (like V.E. or V.J. Day) when the liberation is accomplished.

Considering the background and psychology of the slave and the nature of folk expression, as clarified in Chapter 15 above, only a weak or perverse imagination could overlook the implications in such a song as the following, and there are hundreds like it. "The heavy load" is certainly slavery, not life; the "robe" is the opportunity to live freely; the "gate of hell" is the tribulations of the slave that defeat his true expression; Jesus, as usual, is the deliverer. Why go all the way to heaven when you can begin your deliverance on earth?

> O Bye and bye, bye and bye,
> I'm goin' to lay down my heavy load. . . .
>
> I know my robe's goin' to fit me well, . . .
> I tried it on at the gate of hell. . . .
>
> O Christians, can't you rise and tell
> That Jesus hath done all things well,
> I'm goin' to lay down my heavy load.

The same pattern of interpretation will fit "Somebody's Buried in the Graveyard," "O My Little Soul," "Deep River," "Mos' Don Toilin' Here," "My Ship Is on de Ocean," "O Wasn't Dat a Wide River," "Po' Mourner's Got a Home at Las'," "Roll, Jordan, Roll," "Walk in Jerusalem Jus' Like John," and hundreds of other so-called death spirituals. Likewise, "You May Bury Me in de Eas'," "When the Roll Is Called up Yonder," "See the Signs of Judgment," the fabulous "In Dat Great Gittin' Up Mornin'," and perhaps a hundred other judgment day spirituals.

Deliverance is often expressed in the spiritual in impersonal ways and things. Note the following, each of which is a mere sample of a very large group,

Balm:	"There is a Balm in Gilead, To make the wounded whole, There is a Balm in Gilead, To heal the sin-sick soul."
Chariot:	"Roll de Ol' Chariot Along" ("Ef de devil's in the way Jus' roll right over")
City:	"You'd Better Run, Run, Run-a-run . . . to the City of Refuge" "I'm Seeking for a City, Hallelujah"
Rock:	"Got a Home in That Rock" "O Hide Me over in the Rock of Ages" ("O Rock of Ages cleft for me")
Ship:	"I'm Gwine Cling to de Ship o' Zion" ("Try my bes' for to serve my Lord")

Train:	"Same Train" "De gospel train's a-comin', I hear it jus' at han', I hear de car wheels movin' An' rumblin' thru de lan' . . . Git on board, little chillen, Dere's room for many a mo'."

There is thus little doubt that the spiritual poet thought always of his deliverance or that he could approach the subject from a thousand directions. He realized that only the greatest power could deliver him; he discovered and sang of the power and of its multifarious manifestations. In spite of his confidence in ultimate victory, he devoted many songs and parts of songs to the terrible hazards of the course. But when he rose to the heights in "Nobody Knows de Trouble I See," "My Soul's Been Anchored in the Lord," or "God Is a God, God Don't Never Change," he was at his very best. This best was as good as a folk song ever gets to be.

RALPH J. BUNCHE

The Programs of Organizations Devoted to the Improvement of the Status of the American Negro

Minority groups, such as the American Negro, inevitably tend to become introverted in their social thinking. Attention of the group is so firmly riveted on the struggle to attain release from suppression, that its social perspective becomes warped. The group discovers early that the barriers between it and the status of the dominant majority are sturdy and formidable. Progress is insufferably slow, and the necessity for constant battering against the solid walls of majority prejudice and domination—a social heritage of each succeeding minority generation—gives rise to a psychological fixation in the minority population.

The problems of the group come to be analyzed in progressively narrow terms. Thinking, feeling, life itself, revolve about the narrow axis of "minority

Ralph J. Bunche, "The Programs of Organizations Devoted to the Improvement of the Status of the American Negro," THE JOURNAL OF NEGRO EDUCATION, 8(3), (1939), 673–680. Copyright 1939 by Howard University. All rights reserved.

Ralph J. Bunche (Courtesy of the Associated Publishers, Inc.)

It is precisely the minority group organizations and their leadership which portray minority chauvinism in boldest relief. Organizations and leaders seek only escape for their group. They flounder about, desperately and often blindly, in their ghettoes of thought, seeking a break in the dams of oppression through which they may lead their flock to a more dignified and secure existence. The tiniest crevice in the barriers is magnified into a brilliant ray of hope. So great is the desperation that daily disillusionments are angrily shaken off; they pound away at impregnable walls, dash triumphantly down blind alleys, yet dare not stop to calculate lest it is learned that ultimate escape is generations, even centuries removed.

American Negro organizations and leaders run true to minority type. Color is their phobia; race their creed. The Negro has problems and they are all racial ones; ergo, their solution must be in terms of race. In general, whites must be regarded with suspicion, if not as enemies. White allies are recruited, it is true, but only from those who think of Negro problems as Negroes think of them. There is impatience with any but race problems. There is little appetite for social theories and limited ability to digest social forces. There is but one social force for the Negro, and that is color. As long as the Negro is black and the white man harbors prejudice, what has the Negro to do with class or caste, with capitalism, imperialism, fascism, communism or any other "ism"? Race is the black man's burden.

Generally speaking, it may be stated that the weakness of organizations devoted to the salvation of the Negro is implicit in their structure and philosophy. In the course of the Negro's post-Emancipation history, numerous organizations, black, white, and mixed, have directed their efforts toward lifting him out of the muck of subjection. These organizations, in varying degree and with minor exceptions, have had the following fundamental characteristics:

(1) adherence to policies of escape, based upon racialism and nationalism;

(2) lack of mass support among Negroes, and mass appeal;

(3) dependence upon white benefactors for finance;

(4) reluctance to encourage the development of working-class psychology among Negroes and avoidance of class interpretations;

(5) tendency, directly or indirectly, to take their main ideological cues from white sympathizers;

(6) lack of a coherent, constructive program;

(7) lack of broad social perspective and the ability to relate the problems of the Negro to the main so-

status." All agitation and protest, all programs and tactics, operate within this circumscribed framework.

If the assumed basis of minority group status is race rather than culture, as in the case of the American Negro, race ineluctably tends to become the overwhelmingly dominant factor in the social equation devised by the group to interpret its problem. Thus, with the Negro, racial interpretations are generally considered the only "realistic" ones. Events that cannot be explained on the color chart are relegated to categories of inconsequence to the Negro. The Negro is an American citizen, but his thinking is often more Negro than American. The white American may look with subjective interest upon Munich, but the American Negro regards the latest lynching as infinitely more important to him. The white American may recoil with horror at the German barbarisms against the Jew. But the American Negro cries, "Hitler be damned, and the Jew too; what about the Jim Crow here?" The Negro may evidence some momentary excitation about Italy's rape of Ethiopia, but the dismemberment of Czecho-Slovakia is the white man's business.

cial currents and forces of the American society; and

(8) pursuit of policies of immediate relief and petty opportunism.

The two principal historical schools of Negro thought had as their ideological leaders Booker T. Washington and W. E. B. Du Bois. Washington, who founded Tuskegee Institute in 1881, was the great exponent of what has come to be known as the policy of conciliation.[1] In this policy of appeasement Negroes were advised to cast down their buckets where they were; to avoid conflict with the white man; to accept racial separation and its implication of inferiority as inescapable; to rely upon the good-will of the white upper classes; to work hard, develop thrifty habits and strive for economic independence. Washington discouraged the Negro worker from the identification of his interests and organized efforts with the white working class, whose objectives he mistrusted. That he should advocate the dignity of labor but not the importance of its organized unity in an industrial society, did not appear inconsistent to him. In short, his was a policy of cautious expediency, designed to win the approbation of Southern whites and Northern philanthropists. This was a very racial sort of "realism," and its immediate objectives were realized. It has left an indelible impression on the South, and landmarks in the form of industrial schools for Negroes. But the great problems of Negro-white relationships remain unaffected.

Du Bois early began a vigorous assault on the teachings of Booker T. Washington.[2] He instituted an insistent campaign for full social and political equality for the Negro. Where Washington advised the Negro to eschew politics, Du Bois made the attainment of the franchise a cardinal objective in his program of Negro betterment. Du Bois went back beyond Washington to Frederick Douglass in thus exalting the indispensable virtue of the ballot.

Though Washington and Du Bois differed sharply on the issues of political and social equality for the Negro, and industrial versus cultural education, they were never very far apart in their basic philosophies. Both confined their thinking within the periphery of race. Though Du Bois emphasized the helplessness of a disfranchised working class, the direction of his effort was toward Negro enfranchisement rather than toward working class unity. In recent years he has expressed strongly the view that union between white and black workers is a futile hope, and has advocated the full exploitation of Negro segregation as a means of increasing group strength, especially in economic matters. Both Washington and Du Bois strove for: (1) improved living conditions for Negro city-dwellers; (2) greatly increased educational facilities; (3) equality of economic opportunity; (4) equal justice in the courts; (5) emphasis on racial consciousness and dignity.

Two of the more important Negro betterment organizations sprung up under the aegis of these two influential Negro leaders: the National Negro Business League, established by Washington in 1900, and the National Association for the Advancement of Colored People, which Du Bois helped to form in 1910. Du Bois had organized the Niagara Movement in 1905, which protested against racial discrimination in all of its forms.

In the decade prior to Emancipation Martin Delaney and McCune Smith had advocated the principles of thrift, industry, and exploitation of economic separatism as a means of economic escape for free black men. Some fifty years later Washington made these principles the foundation stones for his National Negro Business League. In terms of its influence on economic betterment of the Negro the National Business League has been inconsequential. As a factor in shaping the psychology and thinking of Negroes, however, it has been vastly important, especially in the period following the migrations under the leadership of Dr. Washington's successor, Major Robert R. Moton. It has fed the Negro on the traditional American illusion that even the man or group on the very lowest rung of the economic ladder can, by industry, thrift, efficiency, and perseverance, attain the top rung. It has pursued the narrowest type of racial chauvinism, for it has organized not business, but "Negro" business, and has employed the racial situation as its main stock in trade in bidding for the support of Negro patronage. The League is the ideological parent to the traditionally reactionary philosophy of Negro business advocates. This is cogently stated in the resolution formulated by the Business section of the first meeting of the National Negro Congress in Chicago, in February, 1936:

> The development of sound and thriving Negro business is most indispensable to the general elevation of the Negro's social and economic security . . . all Negroes consider it their inescapable duty to support Negro business by their patronage.[3]

---

[1]Booker T. Washington, *Up From Slavery; Future of the American Negro, passim.*

[2]W. E. B. Du Bois, *The Souls of Black Folk, passim.*

---

[3]Cf. "Triumph! Or Fiasco!", by R. J. Bunche, *Race*, 1: (No. 2) Summer, 1936.

This hope for the salvation of the Negro masses by the erection of black business within the walls of white capitalism is clearly futile. It is obvious that the advocates of Negro business attempt to labor a policy of "expediency" through exploitation of the segregation incident to the racial dualism of America. Negro business suckles at the breast of the poverty-stricken Negro ghettoes and is inevitably undernourished. And must remain so. It exists only on the sufferance of that dominant white business world which controls credit, basic industry, and the state. The appeal which Negro business makes for the support of Negroes is a racial one, viz.: that the race can advance only through economic unity. Yet the small, individually-owned Negro businesses cannot meet the price competition of the larger-capitalized, more efficient white businesses. The very poverty of the Negro consumer dictates that he must buy where he can find cheapest prices. Negroes in the United States spend approximately $4,150,000,000 per year for the three essential items of food, clothing and shoes,[4] but only some $83,000,000 of this sum is spent with Negro retailers.

In 1929 the National Negro Business League organized the Colored Merchants' Association (C.M.A.) stores. These were individually-owned stores which attempted to reduce overhead by cooperative buying and group advertising, and by consequent lower prices to attract Negro trade. The membership fees were modest, but only a few Negro businesses were attracted to the scheme. The Negro consuming public did not take to the untested brands sold by the C.M.A. stores, preferring the nationally advertised standard brands offered by the white chain stores. In 1934, in the midst of the depression, the C.M.A. experiment met a quiet demise.

At best, Negro business becomes a parasitical growth on the Negro society. It must eke out a meager existence from the segregated Negro community, as a middleman between large white business and the Negro market, through exploitation of the "race problem." Negro business, recognizing its inability to compete with white business on equal terms, demands for itself special privilege and marches under the chauvinistic banner of "race loyalty," thus further exploiting an already sorely harassed group. It represents the interests only of the pitifully small Negro middle-class group, though receiving support for its ideology from the race conscious masses.

The development of Negro capitalism in America, even granting its possibility, would offer no hope for the betterment of the Negro masses. There is no evidence that the 12,561 employees of the Negro retail stores[5] reported in 1937, worked under better conditions for their Negro employers than did Negroes working for white employers. There is no reason to believe that the Negro employer is any less profit-minded than the white, or that he is any less reluctant to exploit his fellow blacks as employees than any other employer. The Negro population is a working-class population. Negro business may offer an uncertain escape from economic oppression for a handful of the more able or more fortunate members of the group. But the overwhelming majority of Negroes in America will continue to till the soil and toil in the industries of the white employer.[6]

A logical corollary of the Negro business philosophy has recently come to the fore in the guise of the "don't buy where you can't work" or "buy where you can work" credo. This movement began about 1931 in Chicago, and rapidly spread to the East. It has been sponsored by organizations such as the "League for Fair Play," the "Afro-American Federation of Labor" and the "New Negro Alliance." These organizations occasionally have employed the labor weapons of boycott and picketing against white stores in Negro districts which refuse to employ Negro white-collar workers. This has been of educational value to the Negro less in that it has given him some inkling of his latent economic power and an acquaintance with the recognized weapons of labor. The most violent manifestation of this movement was in the Harlem riot of 1935, when thousands of Harlem Negroes vented their fury, born of poverty, against the small white shop-owners on Lennox and Seventh Avenues.

The philosophy of this movement is narrowly racial. If successful, it could only result in a vicious cycle of job displacement, since it creates no new jobs but only struggles to displace white workers, and since Negro communities do not offer sufficient economic activity to absorb even a small number of the Negroes now employed in white industries. Its appeal has been primarily in the interest of the Negro white-collar worker, and its support has come chiefly from Negro middle-class professional and intellectual groups. It appears unable to realize that there is an economic system as well as a race problem in America and that when a Negro is unemployed, it is not just because he is a Negro, but more seriously, because of the defective operation of the economy under which we live—an economy that finds it impossible to provide an adequate number of jobs and economic security for the population. More seriously still, this movement tends

---

[4]*Negro Year Book,* 1931–2, p. 132.

[5]*Negro Year Book,* 1937–8, p. 92.

[6]Abram L. Harris, *The Negro as Capitalist, passim.*

to widen the menacing gap between white and black workers, by insisting that jobs be distributed on a racial basis. It is a philosophy which, like that of Negro business, offers only racialism, with no significant hope for the mass Negro population.

In 1910 the National League on Urban Conditions Among Negroes was founded, as a social-service agency devoted to the task of aiding rural Negroes in their adjustment to urban life, and securing positions for them in industry. The work of this organization, subsequently named the National Urban League, assumed increasing importance with the great migration of Negroes to Northern cities after 1916. The chief financial support of the Urban League is from white philanthropy. Its headquarters are in New York and it has some forty local offices in the large industrial centers. Negroes hold all responsible executive offices, but the local directing boards are interracial. Its slogan is "not alms but opportunity", i.e., economic opportunity.

This organization advocates a policy of racial expediency and conciliation, which is characterized by extreme opportunism. It tries to make the most out of the condition of racial separatism and appeals to the conscience and good-will of the white community, especially the employing class. It maintains an industrial department, which attempts to place city Negroes in white industry. It runs "Negro-in-industry-weeks"; it sends its secretaries to white employers in an effort to sell them the idea of employing more Negroes; some of the local offices run employment bureaus, and send welfare agents into the plants to aid in the adjustment of Negro employees. Feeble attempts have been made toward lifting trade-union bars against Negro workers, but there has been no real effort to advance the doctrine of solidarity between white and black workers. In fact there have been instances in which Urban League locals have encouraged scabbing and strikebreaking by Negro workers.[7]

That the Urban League has rendered valuable services for urban Negro populations throughout the country, can scarcely be disputed. But it is equally true that its policy operates within the genteel frame-work of conciliation and interracial good-will. Moreover its efforts have been directed at winning the sympathies of white employers, professional and intellectual groups, and the top ranks of the hierarchy of organized labor.

There is no single element of economic realism in this policy. It barters away the economic future of the Negro worker for an immediate but transitory "gain" in the form of a temporary job. It is severely race-conscious, but socially blind. It encourages the develop-

ment of a racial caste within the American working class and it lacks the independence and courage necessary to give honest direction to the Negro working population.

The programs of organizations like the Y.M.C.A., the Y.W.C.A., the interracial groups, such as the Atlanta Interracial Commission and the Department of Race Relations of the Federal Council of the Churches of Christ in America, are similarly committed to the rather dubious task of developing interracial fellow feeling. Their appeal is to the enlightened groups in the dominant population. They divorce race and economics. They operate on the assumption that when the two races know and understand each other better, the principal incidents of the race problem will disappear. They almost invariably shy away from the harsher aspects of the problem, such as the Negro's relation to organized labor, and therefore, even when sincere, tend to confuse and obscure the vital issues. They are exclusively middle-class, and have but slight contact with the working masses of either race. For these they offer no effective program.

The most extreme example of black chauvinism is found in Marcus Garvey's U.N.I.A.[8] Garvey came to the United States from Jamaica in 1916, and began to preach the gospel of a return to Africa, and international pan-Africanism. His movement developed into a sort of black Zionism. But in its immediate objectives and its influence on the thought of American Negroes, it conformed to the typical pattern of Negro betterment organizations. It was intensely nationalistic; it sought to arouse race consciousness and pride among Negroes. It boasted a realism of sorts, in that it adopted a fatalistic attitude toward the Negro dream of attaining equality in a white man's country. Garveyism was opposed to the policy of unity of black and white labor, regarding all white labor unions with suspicion, and counseling the Negro worker to ally himself with the white employer until such time as the Negro could become economically independent and his own employer.

The movement received amazing support from Negro masses of both North and South. No other organization has ever been able to reach and stir the masses of Negroes to the same degree, or to receive from them such generous financial support.

Garveyism collapsed when its leader was convicted of fraud. It had made but feeble gestures toward Africa but it did afford a psychological escape for the black masses. It provided an emotional release, through its highly charged "race" meetings, its fiery, race-conscious

---

[7]Spero and Harris, *The Black Worker*, p. 140.

[8]Universal Negro Improvement Association.

orators, its emphasis on pride in things black, its elaborate parades, ceremonials, brilliant uniforms, and the pomp and circumstance of its meetings. When the curtain dropped on the Garvey theatricals, the black man of America was exactly where Garvey had found him, though a little bit sadder, if not wiser.

Dr. Du Bois had organized the Niagara Movement in 1905, as a broadside of protest against racial discrimination of every kind. This beginning sounded the tocsin of Negro civil libertarianism and it was designed as a militant departure from the Booker T. Washington philosophy. Out of the Niagara Movement there emerged, in 1910, in New York City, the National Association for the Advancement of Colored People, with a bold program of complete political and cultural assimilation.

The N.A.A.C.P. accepted struggle on the political front as the most promising means of attaining equality for Negroes. Through the use of the ballot and the courts strenuous efforts were exerted to gain social justice for the group. Full faith was placed in the ability of these instruments of democratic government to free the minority from social proscription and civic inequality. Under this banner the N.A.A.C.P. has fought for full equality for the Negro, involving the eradication of all social, legal, and political disabilities tending to draw a line of distinction between the black citizen and the white. The Negro, like the white American, is to quaff the full draught of eighteenth-century democratic liberalism. The Negro citizen must have the franchise, freedom of economic opportunity (consisting of the right to employment without discrimination), the right to accommodations in public places and on common carriers, the right to voluntary choice of place of residence, the right to jury service, equal expenditures of public funds for education and other public services, and protection against lynch violence.

In the pursuit of this great struggle, the Negro has been seriously handicapped, in that he has never yet been able to win any large measure of suffrage. Thus, his political pressure power is limited to those relatively few sectors in which the Negro votes and holds or threatens to hold the political balance of power. Perhaps 90 per cent of the potential black voting strength of the South is eliminated by the devices of disfranchisement employed by the states of the solid South.

The N.A.A.C.P. has carried on its struggle valiantly and has won many notable local victories, in both the political and judicial arenas. Its collaboration with labor in the Senate's rejection of Judge Parker's nomination to the Supreme Court; its recent fight on the educational front, culminating in the celebrated Gaines case triumph; and its unceasing demand for an anti-lynching law, deserve prominent mention. Yet it has never succeeded in developing a program which has that bread-and-butter appeal necessary to command the support of the mass section of the Negro population. Its court successes have often proved to be pyrrhic victories, even as the Gaines case promises to be, in that they merely reassert rights that the Constitution clearly promises to all citizens, but which the white population stubbornly refuses to recognize as exercisable by Negroes. Nor has the N.A.A.C.P. broadened its interests to include a constructive, clearly-defined and practical program for the economic betterment of the race.

The inherent fallacy in this type of political militancy is found in the failure to recognize that the instrumentalities of the state, constitution, government and laws, can do no more than reflect the political, social and economic ideology of the dominant population, and that the political arm of the state cannot be divorced from the prevailing economic structure.

Thus the N.A.A.C.P. policy of civil libertarianism is circumscribed by the dominant mores of the society. In the final analysis, whatever success it may have, must depend upon its ability to elicit a sympathetic response to its appeals from among influential elements in the advantaged population. In the long run, therefore, its militancy must be toned down and the inevitable result is that the programs of organizations such as the N.A.A.C.P. tend gradually to conform to the general pattern of the genteel programs of interracial conciliation, which strive to cultivate the good-will of the white "better classes." They are forced to cajole, bargain, compromise, and even capitulate in order to win petty gains or hollow victories. The N.A.A.C.P. has elected to fight for civil liberties rather than for labor unity; it has never reached the masses of Negroes, and remains strictly Negro middle-class, Negro-*intelligentsia*, in its leadership and appeal. It has received increasing financial support from Negroes, but has often had to lean heavily upon its white benefactors for monetary aid and advice; and it has cautiously maintained its respectability.

The first meeting of the National Negro Congress was held in Chicago in February 1936. This organization, taking its cue from India, was an attempt to develop a Negro united front, and to work out a minimum program of action which could win wide acceptance among Negro as well as sympathetic white organizations. The Congress has held two national meetings, and has many regional and local branches. These undertake to unify the local protest movements against injustices on the united front principle. That is to say the Congress has proceeded on the assumption that the common denominator of race is enough to weld together in thought and action, such divergent segments of the Negro society as preachers and labor organizers, lodge officials and black workers, Negro business men, Negro radicals, professional politicians, professional men, domestic servants, black butchers, bakers and candle stick makers. The Congress mountain has twice labored and has brought forth many contradictions,[9] but no program of action in advance of that already formulated by previously-established Negro organizations.

A Negro Congress with a strong labor bias and with its representation less diffuse and more homogeneous in its thinking could conceivably work out a clearer, more consistent and realistic program than has yet come from the National Negro Congress.

The Negro churches and schools reach more deeply into the Negro masses than do any of the deliberate and formal Negro protest organizations. But it cannot be said that either church or school is a tower of strength in its influence on the social thinking of Negroes and in its contribution toward the improvement of the status of the group. Negro schools, even more than white schools, are controlled by the dominant group, and have never been characterized by their courage in leading any frontal attack upon the problems of the group.[10] The schools are responsive to the interests of those who provide the money for their support, and they are not free. The churches have more independence, but they are controlled by reactionary and often ambitious, self-seeking gentlemen of the frock, and they too lack courage, as well as intelligent leadership.

It is a sad but true commentary that despite the universal grievances endured by the harshly buffeted Negro, there is no single organization, save the church, the school, and in lesser degree, the fraternal order, which can boast any intimate contact with and support from the common man who represents the mass Negro population. The Negro church has consecrated itself to the spiritual salvation of its charges, and has leaned heavily on the side of social reaction and racialism whenever it has concerned itself with the black man's worldly life. The Negro lodges and fraternal orders have contributed little of a constructive nature to the social thought of their Negro membership, though they indulge abundantly in ritual and social activity. The Negro schools are socially vacuous and have shown no disposition to meet the challenge offered by the problems of the group whose interests they are designed to serve. The Negro school, its principal or president and its teachers, are content to seek refuge in the tranquil atmosphere of the academic cloister and to look down upon the problems of the group and its neglected masses, in "scholarly" detachment. The students are infected by this false isolation and are not equipped to understand nor to attack the social problems with which they are confronted in their post-school life.

It is not surprising that the narrowly racial conceptions of the Negro have caused him to be seduced by antisemitism. He thinks only in terms of jobs for Negroes, business for Negroes, Negro landlords, bankers and employers, and vents his emotional spleen on the Jewish shop-keeper in the Negro neighborhood, who exploits the black trade quite as enthusiastically as would the black shopkeeper. The Negro anti-Semite does not reason, nor does it matter, that all Jews are neither shopkeepers nor prejudiced. It is sufficient that the Jew makes profit from a store in a Negro section that Negroes ought to own and work in, or that a Jewish professor holds a position at a Negro university that a Negro, if even a less competent one, should occupy. Such bigoted attitudes are deliberately nurtured by the self-seeking, sensitive Negro middle-class—the business and professional groups, who seek an economic base for their middle-class aspirations.

In view of the obvious social implications for the Negro of this sort of blind, suicidal emotionalism, and the certain truth that racial generalizations and prejudices are luxuries which the Negro can ill afford, it is a bitter indictment of Negro organizations that none has been rational or bold enough to wage a vigorous campaign against Negro anti-Semitism.

Again, in a world in which the major issues affecting the future of humanity are increasingly defined in terms of fascism, with its fundamental racial and totalitarian dogmas, versus democracy, imperfect as it has been for minority groups, no Negro organization makes any serious attempt to define these issues in terms of Negro interest, or to align the full power of Negroes with those forces which are struggling heroically to preserve the last vestiges of human liberty in a world gravely threatened with enslavement. Negro organizations herald the Gaines Case and the anti-lynching bill while the eyes of the rest of the world are turned on Munich, Prague and Memel, Albania, Spain and China.

It is typical of Negro organizations that they concern themselves not with the broad social and political implications of such policies as government relief, housing, socialized medicine, unemployment and old-age insurance, wages and hours laws, etc., but only with the purely racial aspects of such policies. They are content to let the white citizen determine the expediency of major policies, and the form and direction they will assume, while they set themselves up as watch dogs over relatively petty issues, as whether the Negro will get his proper share of the benefits and whether

---

[9]Cf. "Triumph! Or Fiasco!", *op. cit.*

[10]Cf. "Black and White in Education," by R. J. Bunche, JOURNAL OF NEGRO EDUCATION, 5: J1, 1936.

the laws, once made, will be fairly administered. They thus demark for the Negro a residual function in the society.

There is no coordination of thought or serious collaboration in action among these several important Negro organizations and their numerous satellites. Each has marked off its little sphere of action and guards it with professional jealousy. No effective use has ever been made of the numerical strength of the Negro population, nor of its economic importance in labor and consuming power. Race pride does not permit most Negro organizations to make intelligent and practical overtures to the white working population, since a rebuff would result in loss of dignity.

The Negro is sorely in need of organization and leadership which is sufficiently independent and intelligent to give courageous orientation to the group and to guide it rationally through the bewildering maze of social forces which characterize the modern world. This organization and leadership would presumably adhere to some such policies as the following: (1) it would place less emphasis on race and more on economics and broad political and economic forces; (2) it would understand that the major problems of Negroes are not entirely attributable to race but are intimately linked up with the operation of the economy; (3) it would attempt to gain a mass basis among Negroes by a simple program designed to raise the economic level of the Negro worker; (4) it would devote its full energy toward the incorporation of Negro workers in labor unions, and would carry on incessant educational propaganda among both black and white workers toward this end; (5) it would attempt to throw the full support of Negro workers behind the movement to organize labor on an industrial basis, since the vast majority of Negroes are unskilled workers; (6) it would not cease to fight on the political and judicial fronts but would subordinate this to the fight on the economic and union fronts; (7) it would recognize that the future interests of Negroes are closely related to every general effort to improve the lot and increase the security of the working man of whatever color, and it would back every such measure to the limit; (8) it would include Negro labor leaders in its leadership and among its most influential advisers, and avoid dependence on professional Negro leaders and professional white interracialists; (9) it would interpret for Negroes, and relate their interests to, every world event and every foreign policy of importance; (10) its interpretations would be less in terms of race and more in terms of group economic interest; (11) it would recognize that the problems of the Negro cannot be solved in the courts, nor yet by the ballot, even under American democracy; (12) it would take its cue from the share-croppers' and tenant-farmers' unions formed in the South in recent years, and realize that above all, these successful efforts have broken down once and for all the stubborn legend that prejudice between white and black in the South is invested with a mystical quality and is insurmountable; (13) it would recognize that under oppressive conditions identity of economic interests can overcome racial prejudices, and that black and white unity is possible.

Existing Negro organizations are philosophical and programatic paupers. They think and act entirely in a black groove. In a world in which events move rapidly and in which the very future of themselves and their group is at stake, they are unable to see the social forests for the racial saplings. They, like Hitler, even though for different reasons, think that "all that is not race in this world is trash."[11]

Because of the extreme provincialism of its organizations and leadership, the Negro population of America suffers from stagnation in its social thought. The traditional stereotypes and clichés of Negro thought have become outmoded and a new set of values, tooled to fit the political and economic conditions of the modern world, are indicated. Negro organizations should take close inventory of their policies and discard shop-worn doctrines; and should realize that freedom in the modern world is not to be bought at bargain-basement prices. Unless the Negro can develop, and quickly, organization and leadership endowed with broad social perspective and fore-sighted, analytical intelligence, the black citizen of America may soon face the dismal prospect of reflecting upon the tactical errors of the past from the gutters of the black ghettoes and concentration camps of the future.

ROBERT D. BULLARD

Anatomy of Environmental Racism and the Environmental Justice Movement

Communities are not all created equal. In the United States, for example, some communities are routinely poisoned while the government looks the other way. Environmental regulations have not uniformly bene-

[11]Adolf Hitler, *Mein Kampf* (Reynal and Hitchcock unexpurgated edition, 1939), p. 406.

Reprinted from CONFRONTING ENVIRONMENTAL RACISM: VOICES FROM THE GRASSROOTS edited by Robert D. Bullard with permission from the publisher, South End Press, 116 Saint Botolph Street, Boston, MA 02115.

fited all segments of society. People of color (African Americans, Latinos, Asians, Pacific Islanders, and Native Americans) are disproportionately harmed by industrial toxins on their jobs and in their neighborhoods. These groups must contend with dirty air and drinking water—the byproducts of municipal landfills, incinerators, polluting industries, and hazardous waste treatment, storage, and disposal facilities.

Why do some communities get "dumped on" while others escape? Why are environmental regulations vigorously enforced in some communities and not in others? Why are some workers protected from environmental threats to their health while others (such as migrant farmworkers) are still being poisoned? How can environmental justice be incorporated into the campaign for environmental protection? What institutional changes would enable the United States to become a just and sustainable society? What community organizing strategies are effective against environmental racism? These are some of the many questions addressed in this book.

This chapter sketches out the basic environmental problems communities of color face, discusses how the mainstream environmental movement does not provide an adequate organizational base, analysis, vision, or strategy to address these problems, and, finally, provides a glimpse of several representative struggles within the grassroots environmental justice movement. For these purposes, the pervasive reality of racism is placed at the very center of the analysis.

Internal Colonialism and White Racism

The history of the United States has long been grounded in white racism. The nation was founded on the principles of "free land" (stolen from Native Americans and Mexicans), "free labor" (cruelly extracted from African slaves), and "free men" (white men with property). From the outset, institutional racism shaped the economic, political, and ecological landscape, and buttressed the exploitation of both land and people. Indeed, it has allowed communities of color to exist as internal colonies characterized by dependent (and unequal) relationships with the dominant white society or "Mother Country." In their 1967 book, *Black Power*, Carmichael and Hamilton were among the first to explore the "internal" colonial model as a way to explain the racial inequality, political exploitation, and social isolation of African Americans. As Carmichael and Hamilton write:

> The economic relationship of America's black communities [to white society] . . . reflects their colonial status. The political power exercised over those

communities goes hand in glove with the economic deprivation experienced by the black citizens.

> Historically, colonies have existed for the sole purpose of enriching, in one form or another, the "colonizer"; the consequence is to maintain the economic dependency of the "colonized" (pp. 16–17).

Generally, people of color in the United States—like their counterparts in formerly colonized lands of Africa, Asia, and Latin America—have not had the same opportunities as whites. The social forces that have organized oppressed colonies internationally still operate in the "heart of the colonizer's mother country" (Blauner 1972, p. 26). For Blauner, people of color are subjected to five principal colonizing processes: they enter the "host" society and economy involuntarily; their native culture is destroyed; white-dominated bureaucracies impose restrictions from which whites are exempt; the dominant group uses institutionalized racism to justify its actions; and a dual or "split labor market" emerges based on ethnicity and race. Such domination is also buttressed by state institutions. Social scientists Omi and Winant (1986, pp. 76–78) go so far as to insist that "every state institution is a racial institution." Clearly, whites receive benefits from racism, while people of color bear most of the cost.

Environmental Racism

Racism plays a key factor in environmental planning and decisionmaking. Indeed, environmental racism is reinforced by government, legal, economic, political, and military institutions. It is a fact of life in the United States that the mainstream environmental movement is only beginning to wake up to. Yet, without a doubt, racism influences the likelihood of exposure to environmental and health risks and the accessibility to health care. Racism provides whites of all class levels with an "edge" in gaining access to a healthy physical environment. This has been documented again and again.

Whether by conscious design or institutional neglect, communities of color in urban ghettos, in rural "poverty pockets," or on economically impoverished Native-American reservations face some of the worst environmental devastation in the nation. Clearly, racial discrimination was not legislated out of existence in the 1960s. While some significant progress was made during this decade, people of color continue to struggle for equal treatment in many areas, including environmental justice. Agencies at all levels of government, including the federal EPA, have done a poor job protecting people of color from the ravages of pollution and industrial encroachment. It has thus been an up-hill battle convincing white judges, juries, government officials, and policymakers that racism exists in environmental protection, enforcement, and policy formulation.

The most polluted urban communities are those with crumbling infrastructure, ongoing economic disinvestment, deteriorating housing, inadequate schools, chronic unemployment, a high poverty rate, and an overloaded health-care system. Riot-torn South Central Los Angeles typifies this urban neglect. It is not surprising that the "dirtiest" zip code in California belongs to the mostly African-American and Latino neighborhood in that part of the city (Kay 1991a). In the Los Angeles basin, over 71 percent of the African Americans and 50 percent of the Latinos live in areas with the most polluted air, while only 34 percent of the white population does (Ong and Blumenberg 1990; Mann 1991). This pattern exists nationally as well. As researchers Wernette and Nieves note:

> In 1990, 437 of the 3,109 counties and independent cities failed to meet at least one of the EPA ambient air quality standards . . . 57 percent of whites, 65 percent of African Americans, and 80 percent of Hispanics live in 437 counties with substandard air quality. Out of the whole population, a total of 33 percent of whites, 50 percent of African Americans, and 60 percent of Hispanics live in the 136 counties in which two or more air pollutants exceed standards. The percentage living in the 29 counties designated as nonattainment areas for three or more pollutants are 12 percent of whites, 20 percent of African Americans, and 31 percent of Hispanics (pp. 16–17).

Income alone does not account for these above-average percentages. Housing segregation and development patterns play a key role in determining where people live. Moreover, urban development and the "spatial configuration" of communities flow from the forces and relationships of industrial production which, in turn, are influenced and subsidized by government policy (Feagin 1988; Gottdiener 1988). There is widespread agreement that vestiges of race-based decisionmaking still influence housing, education, employment, and criminal justice. The same is true for municipal services such as garbage pickup and disposal, neighborhood sanitation, fire and police protection, and library services. Institutional racism influences decisions on local land use, enforcement of environmental regulations, industrial facility siting, management of economic vulnerability, and the paths of freeways and highways.

People skeptical of the assertion that poor people and people of color are targeted for waste-disposal sites should consider the report the Cerrell Associates provided the California Waste Management Board. In their 1984 report, *Political Difficulties Facing Waste-to-Energy Conversion Plant Siting*, they offered a detailed profile of those neighborhoods most likely to organize effective resistance against incinerators. The policy conclusion based on this analysis is clear. As the report states:

> All socioeconomic groupings tend to resent the nearby siting of major facilities, but middle and upper socioeconomic strata possess better resources to effectuate their opposition. Middle and higher socioeconomic strata neighborhoods should not fall within the one-mile and five-mile radius of the proposed site (p. 43).

Where then will incinerators or other polluting facilities be sited? For Cerrell Associates, the answer is low-income, disempowered neighborhoods with a high concentration of nonvoters. The ideal site, according their report, has nothing to do with environmental soundness but everything to do with lack of social power. Communities of color in California are far more likely to fit this profile than are their white counterparts.

Those still skeptical of the existence of environmental racism should also consider the fact that zoning boards and planning commissions are typically stacked with white developers. Generally, the decisions of these bodies reflect the special interests of the individuals who sit on these boards. People of color have been systematically excluded from these decisionmaking boards, commissions, and governmental agencies (or allowed only token representation). Grassroots leaders are now demanding a shared role in all the decisions that shape their communities. They are challenging the intended or unintended racist assumptions underlying environmental and industrial policies.

Toxic Colonialism Abroad

To understand the global ecological crisis, it is important to understand that the poisoning of African Americans in South Central Los Angeles and of Mexicans in border *maquiladoras* have their roots in the same system of economic exploitation, racial oppression, and devaluation of human life. The quest for solutions to environmental problems and for ways to acheive sustainable development in the United States has considerable implications for the global environmental movement.

Today, more than 1,900 *maquiladoras*, assembly plants operated by American, Japanese, and other foreign countries, are located along the 2,000-mile U.S.-Mexico border (Center for Investigative Reporting 1990; Sanchez 1990; Zuniga 1992, p. 22A). These plants use cheap Mexican labor to assemble products from imported components and raw materials, and then ship them back to the United States (Witt 1991). Nearly half a million Mexicans work in the *maquiladoras*. They earn an average of $3.75 a day. While these plants bring jobs, albeit low-paying ones, they exacerbate local pollution by overcrowding the border towns, straining sewage and water systems, and reducing air quality. All this compromises the health of workers and nearby community residents. The Mexican environmental regulatory agency is understaffed and ill-equipped to adequately enforce the country's laws (Working Group on Canada-Mexico Free Trade 1991).

The practice of targeting poor communities of color in the Third World for waste disposal and the introduction of risky technologies from industrialized countries are forms of "toxic colonialism," what some activists have dubbed the "subjugation of people to an ecologically-destructive economic order by entities over which the people have no control" (Greenpeace 1992, p. 3). The industrialized world's controversial Third World dumping policy was made public by the release of an internal, December 12, 1991, memorandum authored by Lawrence Summers, chief economist of the World Bank. It shocked the world and touched off a global scandal. Here are the highlights: "Dirty" Industries: Just between you and me, shouldn't the World Bank be encouraging MORE migration of the dirty industries to the LDCs [Less Developed Countries]? I can think of three reasons:

1) The measurement of the costs of health impairing pollution depends on the foregone earnings from increased morbidity and mortality. From this point of view a given amount of health impairing pollution should be done in the country with the lowest cost, which will be the country with the lowest wages. I think the economic logic behind dumping a load of toxic waste in the lowest wage country is impeccable and we should face up to that.

2) The costs of pollution are likely to be nonlinear as the initial increments of pollution probably have very low cost. I've always thought that underpolluted areas in Africa are vastly UNDER-polluted; their air quality is probably vastly inefficiently low compared to Los Angeles or Mexico City. Only the lamentable facts that so much pollution is generated by non-tradable industries (transport, electrical generation) and that the unit transport costs of solid waste are so high prevent world welfare-enhancing trade in air pollution and waste.

3) The demand for a clean environment for aesthetic and health reasons is likely to have very high income elasticity. The concern over an agent that causes a one in a million change in the odds of prostate cancer is obviously going to be much higher in a country where people survive to get prostate cancer than in a country where under 5 [year-old] mortality is 200 per thousand. Also, much of the concern over industrial atmosphere discharge is about visibility impairing particulates. These discharges may have very little direct health impact. Clearly trade in goods that embody aesthetic pollution concerns could be welfare enhancing. While production is mobile the consumption of pretty air is a non-tradable.

The problem with the arguments against all of these proposals for more pollution in LDCs (intrinsic rights to certain goods, moral reasons, social concerns, lack of adequate markets, etc.) could be turned around and used more or less effectively against every Bank proposal . . .

Beyond the Race vs. Class Trap

Whether at home or abroad, the question of who *pays* and who *benefits* from current industrial and development policies is central to any analysis of environmental racism. In the United States, race interacts with class to create special environmental and health vulnerabilities. People of color, however, face elevated toxic exposure levels even when social class variables (income, education, and occupational status) are held constant (Bryant and Mohai 1992). Race has been found to be an independent factor, not reducible to class, in predicting the distribution of 1) air pollution in our society (Freeman 1972; Gianessi, Peskin, and Wolff 1979; Gelobter 1988; Wernette and Nieves 1992); 2) contaminated fish consumption (West, Fly, and Marans 1990); 3) the location of municipal landfills and incinerators (Bullard 1983, 1987, 1990, 1991a); 4) the location of abandoned toxic waste dumps (United Church of Christ Commission for Racial Justice 1987); and 5) lead poisoning in children (Agency for Toxic Substances and Disease Registry 1988).

Lead poisoning is a classic case in which race, not just class, determines exposure. It affects between three and four million children in the United States—most of whom are African Americans and Latinos living in urban areas. Among children five years old and younger, the percentage of African Americans who have excessive levels of lead in their blood far exceeds the percentage of whites at all income levels (Agency for Toxic Substances and Disease Registry 1988, p. I-12).

The federal Agency for Toxic Substances and Disease Registry found that for families earning less than $6,000 annually an estimated 68 percent of African-American children had lead poisoning, compared with 36 percent for white children. For families with incomes exceeding $15,000, more than 38 percent of African-American children have been poisoned, compared with

12 percent of white children. African-American children are two to three times more likely than their white counterparts to suffer from lead poisoning independent of class factors.

One reason for this is that African Americans and whites do not have the same opportunities to "vote with their feet" by leaving unhealthy physical environments. The ability of an individual to escape a health-threatening environment is usually correlated with income. However, racial barriers make it even harder for millions of African Americans, Latinos, Asians, Pacific Islanders, and Native Americans to relocate. Housing discrimination, redlining, and other market forces make it difficult for millions of households to buy their way out of polluted environments. For example, an affluent African-American family (with an income of $50,000 or more) is as segregated as an African-American family with an annual income of $5,000 (Denton and Massey 1988; Jaynes and Williams 1989). Thus, lead poisoning of African-American children is not just a "poverty thing."

White racism helped create our current separate and unequal communities. It defines the boundaries of the urban ghetto, *barrio*, and reservation, and influences the provision of environmental protection and other public services. Apartheid-type housing and development policies reduce neighborhood options, limit mobility, diminish job opportunities, and decrease environmental choices for millions of Americans. It is unlikely that this nation will ever achieve lasting solutions to its environmental problems unless it also addresses the system of racial injustice that helps sustain the existance of powerless communities forced to bear disproportionate environmental costs.

The Limits of Mainstream Environmentalism

Historically, the mainstream environmental movement in the United States has developed agendas that focus on such goals as wilderness and wildlife preservation, wise resource management, pollution abatement, and population control. It has been primarily supported by middle- and upper-middle-class whites. Although concern for the environment cuts across class and racial lines, ecology activists have traditionally been individuals with above-average education, greater access to economic resources, and a greater sense of personal power (Buttel and Flinn 1978; Morrison 1980, 1986; Dunlap 1987; Bullard, 1990; Bullard and Wright 1987; Bachrach and Zautra 1985; Mohai, 1985, 1990).

Not surprisingly, mainstream groups were slow in broadening their base to include poor and working-class whites, let alone African Americans and other people of color. Moreover, they were ill-equipped to deal with the environmental, economic, and social concerns of these communities. During the 1960s and 1970s, while the "Big Ten" environmental groups focused on wilderness preservation and conservation through litigation, political lobbying, and technical evaluation, activists of color were engaged in mass direct action mobilizations for basic civil rights in the areas of employment, housing, education, and health care. Thus, two parallel and sometimes conflicting movements emerged, and it has taken nearly two decades for any significant convergence to occur between these two efforts. In fact, conflicts still remain over how the two groups should balance economic development, social justice, and environmental protection.

In their desperate attempt to improve the economic conditions of their constituents, many African-American civil rights and political leaders have directed their energies toward bringing jobs to their communities. In many instances, this has been achieved at great risk to the health of workers and the surrounding communities. The promise of jobs (even low-paying and hazardous ones) and of a broadened tax base has enticed several economically impoverished, politically powerless communities of color both in the United States and around the world (Center for Investigative Reporting and Bill Moyers 1990; Bullard 1990; Bryant and Mohai 1992). Environmental job blackmail is a fact of life. You can get a job, but only if you are willing to do work that will harm you, your families, and your neighbors.

Workers of color are especially vulnerable to job blackmail because of the greater threat of unemployment they face compared to whites and because of their concentration in low-paying, unskilled, nonunionized occupations. For example, they make up a large share of the nonunion contract workers in the oil, chemical, and nuclear industries. Similarly, over 95 percent of migrant farmworkers in the United States are Latino, African-American, Afro-Caribbean, or Asian, and African Americans are overrepresented in high-risk, blue-collar, and service occupations for which a large pool of replacement labor exists. Thus, they are twice as likely to be unemployed as their white counterparts. Fear of unemployment acts as a potent incentive for many African-American workers to accept and keep jobs they know are health threatening. Workers will tell you that "unemployment and poverty are also hazardous to one's health." An inherent conflict exists between the interests of capital and that of labor. Employers have the power to move jobs (and industrial hazards) from the Northeast and Midwest to the South and Sunbelt, or they may move the jobs offshore to Third World countries where labor is even cheaper and where there are even fewer health and safety regulations. Yet, unless an environmental movement emerges that is capable of addressing these economic concerns, people of color and poor white workers are likely to end up siding with corporate managers in key conflicts concerning the environment.

Indeed, many labor unions already moderate their demands for improved work-safety and pollution control whenever the economy is depressed. They are afraid of layoffs, plant closings, and the relocation of industries. These fears and anxieties of labor are usually built on the false but understandable assumption that environmental regulations inevitably lead to job loss (Brown 1980, 1987).

The crux of the problem is that the mainstream environmental movement has not sufficiently addressed the fact that social inequality and imbalances of social power are at the heart of environmental degradation, resource depletion, pollution, and even overpopulation. The environmental crisis can simply not be solved effectively without social justice. As one academic human ecologist notes, "Whenever [an] in-group directly and exclusively benefits from its own overuse of a shared resource but the costs of that overuse are 'shared' by out-groups, then in-group motivation toward a policy of resource conservation (or sustained yields of harvesting) is undermined" (Catton 1982).

The Movement for Environmental Justice

As this book testifies, activists of color have begun to challenge both the industrial polluters and the often indifferent mainstream environmental movement by actively fighting environmental threats in their communities and raising the call for environmental justice. This groundswell of environmental activism in African-American, Latino, Asian, Pacific Islander, and Native-American communities is emerging all across the country. While rarely listed in the standard environmental and conservation directories, grassroots environmental justice groups have sprung up from Maine to Louisiana and Alaska (see map below).

These grassroots groups have organized themselves around waste-facility siting, lead contamination, pesticides, water and air pollution, Native self-government, nuclear testing, and workplace safety (Alston 1990; Bullard 1990, 1992; Bryant and Mohai 1992). People of color have invented and, in other cases, adapted existing organizations to meet the disproportionate environmental challenges they face. A growing number of grassroots groups and their leaders have adopted confrontational direct action strategies similar to those used in earlier civil rights conflicts. Moreover, the in-

creasing documentation of environmental racism has strengthened the demand for a safe and healthy environment as a basic right of all individuals and communities (Commission for Racial Justice 1991; Bullard and Wright 1987, 1990; Bryant and Mohai forthcoming).

Drawing together the insights of *both* the civil rights and the environmental movements, these grassroots groups are fighting hard to improve the quality of life for their residents. As a result of their efforts, the environmental justice movement is increasingly influencing and winning support from more conventional environmental and civil rights organizations. For example, the National Urban League's *1992 State of Black America* included—for the first time in the seventeen years the report has been published—a chapter on the environmental threats to the African-American community (Bullard 1992b). In addition, the NAACP, ACLU, and NRDC led the fight to have poor children tested for lead poisoning under Medicaid provisions in California. The class-action lawsuit *Matthews v. Coye*, settled in 1991, called for the state of California to screen an estimated 500,000 poor children for lead poisoning at a cost of $15 to $20 million (Lee 1992). The screening represents a big step forward in efforts to identify children suffering from what federal authorities admit is the number one environmental health problem of children in the United States. For their part, mainstream environmental organizations are also beginning to understand the need for environmental justice and are increasingly supporting grassroots groups in the form of technical advice, expert testimony, direct financial assistance, fundraising, research, and legal assistance. Even the Los Angeles chapter of the wilderness-focused Earth First! movement worked with community groups to help block the incinerator project in South Central Los Angeles.

Case Studies from the Grassroots

For all of their current and potential significance, however, little research has yet been done on these African-American, Latino, Asian, Pacific Islander, and Native American organizations which make up the grassroots environmental justice movement. The research discussed here focuses on environmentally threatened communities of color in Houston (TX), Dallas (TX), Los Angeles (CA), Richmond (CA), Kettleman City (CA), Alsen (LA), and Rosebud (SD). Each of these communities is embroiled in a wide range of environmental disputes against both government and private industry.

We had three major objectives in looking at these nine communities: 1) to examine the organizations and the dispute mechanisms people of color use in resolving environmental conflicts, 2) to explore the conditions and circumstances under which communities of color mobilize against an environmental threat, and 3) to assess the level of external support that grassroots groups of color receive from environmental, social justice, and other groups. To gather this information, in-depth interviews were conducted with opinion leaders, who were identified through a "reputational" approach. We started out with a small number of local informants. The informants were asked to "identify the *most* influential person or persons who had played a role in resolving the local dispute." These influential leaders were later asked the same question, and this second group of leaders was also interviewed.

The interviews focused on a number of key issue areas, including the nature of the dispute, leadership and external support, opposition tactics, and dispute outcomes. The questions included: Were the environmental problems caused by the government and/or corporations? Did the dispute involve a proposed or existing facility? Was the community group started as an environmental group? Do its leaders and members see themselves as environmentalists? Were equity and social justice concerns dominant organizing themes? Who led the local citizen opposition in the disputes? What kind of support did the local groups receive from environmental and other organizations? What tactics did the groups use? Which were most effective? How was the dispute resolved?

A summary of the various communities, grassroots groups, and types of environmental disputes included in this study are presented in Table 1. Here is a more detailed overview of each community's situation.

Houston: In the 1970s, Houston was dubbed the "golden buckle" of the Sunbelt (Bullard 1987, 1990). In 1982, it became the nation's fourth largest city with 1.7 million inhabitants. Its black community of some 450,000 is the largest in the South. For decades, Houston boasted that it was the only major city without zoning. During the "boom" years of the 1970s, this no-zoning policy contributed to haphazard and irrational land-use planning and infrastructure chaos (Bullard 1983). A mostly African-American suburban neighborhood was selected as the site for a municipal landfill. The Northeast Community Action Group (NECAG) formed to block the construction of the landfill.

Dallas: Dallas is the seventh largest city in the nation with a population of just under one million. The 265,594 African Americans who live in Dallas represent 29.4 percent of the city's population. West Dallas is one of many segregated black enclaves in the city. It has a population of 13,161, of which 85 percent is black. The neighborhood has lived with a polluting lead smelter for five decades (Nauss 1983; Bullard 1990). Early on, West Dallas residents formed the Neighborhood Coalition on Lead Pollution to get the smelter closed and the area cleaned up. Another group, West Dallas Coalition for Environmental Justice, continued the fight after the Neighborhood Coalition for Lead Pollution was disbanded.

Alsen (LA): Alsen is an unincorporated community on the Mississippi River several miles north of Baton Rouge, Louisiana's state capital. It had a population of 1,104 individuals in 1980, of which 98.9 percent were African Americans. Alsen lies at the beginning of "Cancer Alley," the 85-mile stretch of land from Baton Rouge to New Orleans, an area that accounts for one-fourth of the nation's petro-chemical production (See Maraniss and Weisskopf 1987; Anderson, Dunn, and Alabarado 1985; Bullard 1990; Bullard and Wright 1990). Much of Louisiana's hazardous waste is disposed of in the Rollins Environmental Services incinerators located near Alsen. The residents formed Coalition for Community Action to challenge the Rollins hazardous waste incinerator operation.

Los Angeles: Los Angeles is the nation's second largest city with a population of 3.5 million. It is one of

TABLE 1   SUMMARY OF COMMUNITY DISPUTES

Group (Year Founded), Location	Type of Dispute	Facility
Northeast Community Action Group (1979), Houston, TX	Solid waste landfill	Existing
Neighborhood Committee on Lead Pollution (1981), Dallas, TX	Lead smelter	Existing
West Dallas Coalition for Environmental and Economic Justice (1989), Dallas, TX	Lead smelter	Existing
Coalition for Community Action (1979), Alsen, LA	Hazardous waste incinerator	Existing
Concerned Citizens of South Central Los Angeles (1985), Los Angeles, CA	Solid waste incinerator	Proposed
Mothers of East Los Angeles (1985), Los Angeles, CA	Hazardous waste incinerator	Proposed
People for Clean Air and Water (1990), Kettleman City, CA	Hazardous waste incinerator	Proposed
West County Toxics Coalition (1989), Richmond, CA	Petrochemical refinery	Existing
Good Road Coalition (1991), Rosebud, SD	Solid waste landfill	Proposed

the nation's most culturally and ethnically diverse big cities. People of color (Latinos, Asians, Pacific Islanders, African Americans, and Native Americans) now constitute 63 percent of the city's population. Residents of South Central Los Angeles, a neighborhood that is over 52 percent African-American and about 44 percent Latino, was slated to host the city's first state-of-the-art municipal solid waste incinerator. Local residents organized Concerned Citizens of South Central Los Angeles to fight the incinerator (Sanchez 1988; Russell 1989; Blumberg and Gottlieb 1989; Hamilton 1990).

Just as Los Angeles's largest African-American community was selected as a site for a city-sponsored municipal incinerator, East Los Angeles, the city's largest Latino community, was chosen as a site for a hazardous waste incinerator (Russell 1989). Officially, the incinerator was planned for Vernon, an industrial suburb that has only 96 people. But, several East Los Angeles neighborhoods (made up of mostly Latino residents) are located only a mile away and downwind from the proposed site. The group Mothers of East Los Angeles (MELA) took the lead in fighting the proposed hazardous waste site (Pardo 1991).

Richmond (CA): Richmond has a population of 80,000. Over half are African Americans and about 10 percent are Latinos. Most of the African-American population live next to the city's petrochemical corridor—a cluster of 350 facilities that handle hazardous waste (Citizens for a Better Environment 1989). The five largest industrial polluters in the city are the Chevron oil refinery, Chevron Ortho pesticide plant, Witco Chemical, Airco Industrial Gases, and an ICI pesticide plant (formerly Stauffer Chemical). Chevron Ortho generates over 40 percent of the hazardous waste in Richmond. The bulk of it is incinerated on the plant's grounds. Local citizens founded the West County Toxics Coalition to address the problem of toxic emissions.

Kettleman City (CA): Kettleman City is a small farmworker community of approximately 1,200. Over 95 percent of the residents are Latino. It is home to a hazardous waste landfill operated by the world's largest waste-disposal company, Chemical Waste Management (see Corwin 1991; Siler 1991). The company proposed that a new incinerator be built in Kettleman City. Residents organized an opposition group called El Pueblo para el Aire y Agua Limpio (People for Clean Air and Water).

Rosebud Reservation (SD): As state environmental regulations have become more stringent in recent years, Native-American reservations have become prime targets of waste disposal firms (Beasley 1990b; Tomsho 1990; Kay 1991b). Many waste-disposal companies have attempted to skirt state regulations (which are often tougher than the federal regulations) by

targeting Native lands (Angel 1992). Because of their quasi-independent status, Native-American reservations are not covered by state environmental regulations. The threat to Native lands exists for the Mohawk Indians in New York to the Mission Indians (i.e., Campo, La Posta, Los Coyotes, Morongo, Pala, and Soboda) in southern California to the Gwichin people in Alaska (Kay 1991b). The problem is typified in the case of the Rosebud Reservation in South Dakota. RSW, a Connecticut-based company, proposed in 1991 to build a 6,000-acre municipal landfill on Sioux lands (Daschle 1991). Local residents founded the Good Road Coalition to block the landfill.

What We Learned

Eight of the nine community opposition groups were started as environmental groups. Mothers of East Los Angeles was the only exception. It grew out of a six-year dispute involving a proposed 1,450-bed state prison in East Los Angeles (Pardo 1991). MELA also fought a proposed underground pipeline through their neighborhood. Its fight against the incinerator is an extension of this earlier battle.

All of the groups have multi-issue agendas and incorporate social justice and equity as their major organizing themes. The leaders see their communities as "victims" and are quick to make the connection between other forms of discrimination, the quality of their physical environment, and the current dispute. Some of the leaders have worked in other organizations that fought discrimination in housing, employment, and education.

It is clear that the local grassroots activists in the impacted communities provided the essential leadership in dealing with the disputes. The typical grassroots leader was a woman. For example, women led the fight in seven of the nine cases examined. Only the West Dallas Coalition for Environmental Justice and Richmond's West County Toxics Coalition were headed by men.

Women activists were quick to express their concern about the threat to their family, home, and community. The typical organizer found leadership thrust upon her by immediate circumstances with little warning or prior training for the job. Lack of experience, however, did not prove an insurmountable barrier to successful organizing.

The manner in which the local issue was framed appears to have influenced the type of leadership that emerged. Local activists immediately turned their energies to what they defined as environmental discrimination, for discrimination is a fact of life in all of these communities. Most people of color face it daily.

The quest for environmental justice thus extends the quest for basic civil rights. Actions taken by grassroots activists to reduce environmental inequities are consistent with the struggle to end the other forms of social injustice found throughout our society—in housing, education, employment, health care, criminal justice, and politics.

The mainstream environmental groups do not have a long history of working with African-American, Latino, Asian, Pacific Islander, and Native-American groups. For the most part, they have failed to adequately address environmental problems that disproportionately impact people of color. Despite some exceptions, the national groups have failed to sufficiently make the connection between key environmental and social justice issues.

The experience of the organizations discussed here suggests that the situation is beginning to change for the better. While still too little, the mainstream environmental movement's support of environmental justice struggles has visibly increased between the first Earth Day in 1970 and Earth Day 1990. Certainly, the early environmental struggles by communities of color were less likely than more recent ones to attract significant support from the mainstream groups.

Because of the redefinition of "environmentalism" spurred on by grassroots challenges to the elitism and environmental racism of the mainstream groups, more mainstream groups now acknowledge and try to address the widespread inequities throughout our society. Many of these groups are beginning to understand and embrace the cause of social justice activists mobilizing to protect their neighborhoods from garbage dumps or lead smelters. These first steps have been a long time in coming, however. For many conservationists, the struggle for social justice is still seen as separate from environmental activism. Because of this, environmental activists of color have usually had better luck winning support for their cause by appealing to more justice-oriented groups. For example, Houston's Northeast Community Action Group (NECAG) was able to enlist support from a number of local social justice activists in their dispute with Browning-Ferris Industries. The anti-discrimination theme was a major tool in enlisting the Houston Black United Front (an African-American self-help group), the Harris County Council of Organizations (an African-American voter education and political group), and a Houston chapter of ACORN (Association of Community Organizations for Reform Now).

The situation in Dallas somewhat resembled that found in Houston. Leaders of West Dallas's Neighborhood Committee on Lead Pollution received no assistance from any outside environmental group in resolving their dispute. Instead, they relied exclusively on a grassroots self-help group, the Common Ground Community Economic Development Corporation, to get their grievances publicly aired. Common Ground not surprisingly has a long history of working on equity issues in the city's African-American community.

The Neighborhood Committee on Lead Pollution disbanded after the lead-smelter dispute was resolved. In 1989, the West Dallas Coalition for Environmental Justice, a multiracial group, formed to fill the leadership vacuum. It pressed for cleanup of the RSR site in West Dallas, closure of the Dixie Metals lead smelter in Dallas's East Oak Cliff neighborhood, and pollution prevention measures for the remaining industries in the neighborhood. The multiracial coalition has about 700 members and 20 volunteers. It has worked closely with Common Ground and Texas United, a grassroots environmental group affiliated with the Boston-based National Toxics Campaign. The local Sierra Club also wrote several letters endorsing the actions taken by the West Dallas group to get their neighborhood cleaned up.

Leaders in Alsen, on the other hand, did receive support (although late in their struggle) from several environmental groups. Rollins' proposal to burn PCBs in the Alsen incinerator had gotten the attention of several national environmental groups, including Greenpeace, Citizens' Clearinghouse for Hazardous Waste, and the National Toxics Campaign.

Alsen residents also enlisted the support of the Louisiana Environmental Action Network (a mostly white group) and Gulf Coast Tenants Organization (a mostly African-American group). Gulf Coast has, for example, led Earth Day "toxics marches" from New Orleans to Baton Rouge.

The four California community groups examined in this study all had great success in getting support from and forming alliances with both grassroots and national environmental groups. Again, the level of outside support was greatest for the groups fighting new facilities proposals.

The African-American leaders of Concerned Citizens of South Central Los Angeles found allies and built strong working relationships with a diverse set of international, national, and grassroots environmental groups. Greenpeace was the first national group to join Concerned Citizens in their fight to kill LANCER 1 (Russell 1989; Blumberg and Gottlieb 1989). Others joined later, including Citizens for a Better Environment (CBE), National Health Law Program, and the Center for Law in the Public Interest. Concerned Citizens also forged alliances with two white Westside "slow-growth" groups: Not Yet New York (a coalition of environmental and homeowner groups) and the anti-incineration group California Alliance in Defense of Residential Environments (CADRE).

Mothers of East Los Angeles lined up the support of groups such as Greenpeace, the Natural Resources Defense Council, the Environmental Policy Institute, the Citizens' Clearinghouse on Hazardous Waste, the National Toxics Campaign, and the Western Center on Law and Poverty. These allies provided valuable technical advice, expert testimony, lobbying, research, and legal assistance.

The Kettleman City dispute attracted widespread attention and became a topic on prime-time newscasts. The local group, El Pueblo para el Aire y Agua Limpio (People for Clean Air and Water), got a lot of support from both national and grassroots environmental and social justice groups. The dispute brought together environmental leaders of color from inside and outside California. The decision to site a hazardous waste incinerator in Kettleman City also acted as a rallying point for many environmental justice groups ranging from Greenpeace to the Albuquerque-based Southwest Network for Environmental and Economic Justice (a coalition of environmental activists of color from eight states in the Southwest).

The Richmond-based West County Toxics Coalition was founded with assistance from the National Toxics Campaign. It then got the Sierra Club (headquartered just across the Bay in San Francisco) involved in their struggle. The San Francisco-based Citizens for a Better Environment (CBE) furnished the group with technical assistance and documentation of the local environmental problem (see the 1989 report *Richmond at Risk*). The report offers graphic evidence of the threat posed by polluting industries in the city's African-American and Latino communities.

Disputes involving Native lands present special problems to conventional environmental movements. Given the long history of exploitation and genocide directed at Native Americans by whites, environmental disputes take on larger historical and cultural meanings. However, the Good Road Coalition was able to enlist the support of Greenpeace activists and two Native-American groups (the Indigenous Environmental Network and the Natural Resource Coalition).

Organizing Tactics

The grassroots environmental groups and their allies have used a wide range of tactics to fend off what they see as a threat to family, home, and community. The leaders have borrowed many of their tactics from the earlier civil rights movement. All of the groups have used public protest, demonstrations, petitions, lobby-

ing, reports and fact-finding, and hearings to educate the community and intensify public debate on the dispute. In addition, leaders organized community workshops and neighborhood forums to keep local residents informed on the disputes and new developments.

All of the grassroots groups targeted local, state, and federal governments for their direct or indirect influence in siting and enforcement decisions. For example, the leaders of Houston's Northeast Community Action Group directed their actions toward both the local and state government bodies responsible for permitting the facility.

A number of tangible results emerged from the Houston dispute. First, the Houston City Council, acting under intense political pressure from local residents, passed a resolution in 1980 that prohibited city-owned garbage trucks from dumping at the controversial landfill in the Northwood Manor subdivision. Second, the council also passed an ordinance restricting the construction of solid-waste sites near public facilities such as school and parks. (This action was nothing less than a form of protective zoning.) And, third, the Texas Department of Health updated its requirements for landfill permit applicants. Applications now must include detailed land-use, economic impact, and sociodemographic data on areas where proposed municipal solid waste landfills are to be sited.

The Neighborhood Committee on Lead Pollution challenged the Dallas Health Department for its lax enforcement of the city's lead ordinance and the repeated violations by the nearby smelter. Grassroots leaders in West Dallas extended their influence beyond the neighborhood by pressuring the Dallas mayor to appoint a government-sanctioned city-wide task force (the Dallas Alliance Environmental Task Force) to address lead contamination. The impetus for the task force came from the local West Dallas group.

The two Los Angeles neighborhood groups also sought to have the city intervene in their dispute. The LANCER dispute was injected into local city politics and became a contributing factor in both the defeat of the pro-LANCER City Council President Pat Russell and the election of environmental advocate Ruth Galanter. Concerned Citizens of South Central Los Angeles and its allies proved that local citizens can fight city hall and win. Opponents of the city-initiated incinerator project applied pressure on key elected officials, including Mayor Tom Bradley. Bradley reversed his position and asked the city council to kill the project, which had been in the planning stage since 1969 and included a commitment to contribute $12 million (Russell 1989).

Mothers of East Los Angeles, in its struggle, targeted the South Coast Air Quality Management District

(AQMD), the California Department of Health Services (DHS), and the U.S. Environmental Protection Agency (EPA)—the agencies responsible for awarding a permit for the Vernon hazardous waste incinerator project. The facility was to be California's first "state-of-the-art" toxic-waste incinerator.

To block the project, Mothers of East Los Angeles and its allies arranged for more than 500 residents to attend a 1987 DHS hearing on it. They pressed their demands in other public forums as well. The alliance questioned DHS's 1988 decision that allowed California Thermal Treatment Services (CTTS) to move the project forward without preparing an environmental impact report (EIR). The City of Los Angeles, MELA, and others joined in a lawsuit to review the decision. The federal EPA, however, approved the permit without an EIR.

This prompted California Assemblywoman Lucille Roybal-Allard to lead a successful fight to change the California law and require EIRs for all toxic waste incinerators. In December 1988, as CTTS was about to start construction, the AQMD decided that the company should do the environmental studies and redesign its original standards to meet the new, more stringent clean air regulations. CTTS legally challenged the AQMD's decision all the way up to the State Supreme Court and lost.

The Coalition for Community Action (Alsen, LA) focused its attack on the Louisiana Department of Environmental Quality and its less-than-enthusiastic enforcement of air quality standards in North Baton Rouge and the African-American communities affected by emissions from the nearby polluting industries. The group also worked on getting the federal EPA more actively involved in pollution prevention efforts in "Cancer Alley."

Richmond's West County Toxics Coalition worked to get both state and federal government agencies involved in reducing emissions from the nearby polluting industries. On the other hand, Kettleman City's People for Clean Air and Water focused its attention on the Kings County Board of Supervisors, the California Department of Health Services, and the federal EPA.

The Native Americans who founded the Good Road Coalition appealed to their Tribal Council (the government of the sovereign Sioux Nation on the Rosebud Reservation) to rescind the contract signed with RSW to build the 6,000-acre landfill on the reservation. Tribal Chairman Ralph Moran had supported the construction. It is interesting that six of the nine grassroots groups used litigation as a tactic. The three groups that did not were the West Dallas Coalition for Environmental Justice (its predecessor

had already filed a lawsuit), Richmond's West County Toxics Coalition, and Rosebud's Good Road Coalition. All of the groups that filed lawsuits used their own lawyers. Three of them (Concerned Citizens of South Central Los Angeles, Mothers of East Los Angeles, and People for Clean Air and Water) applied to public interest law centers to file their lawsuits.

The West Dallas and East Los Angeles groups were joined in their lawsuits by the local government: both the city of Dallas and the Texas Attorney General joined the West Dallas plaintiffs, while the city of Los Angeles joined MELA.

Three of the neighborhood groups (the two in West Dallas and the one in Richmond) used negotiations as a dispute resolution tactic. The West Dallas groups were able to negotiate two different cleanup plans—the first in 1984, the second in 1992.

Richmond's West County Toxics Campaign brought in the Reverend Jesse Jackson of the National Rainbow Coalition to negotiate with Chevron, the major polluter in the community. Richmond's Mayor George Livingston helped arrange the May 7, 1990 meeting with Chevron that included representatives from the West County Toxics Coalition, the National Rainbow Coalition, and the Sierra Club. Jackson described the negotiations as a "test case, a test example, both with dangers and possibilities." He and the West County Toxics Coalition presented Chevron with a six-point plan (Reed 1990, p. A1):

- Annually set aside 1 percent of the cost of Chevron's proposed $1 billion modernization for a cleanup fund. The fund should employ Richmond's unemployed to help clean up the environment, and should also be used to finance health care and new pollution-reduction technology;
- Establish a 24-hour, fully funded clinic to provide medical attention to those harmed by the dozens of polluting industries in Richmond;
- Reduce the tons of toxic waste destroyed in Chevron's Ortho Chemical plant incinerator. (Chevron, which currently burns about 75,000 tons annually in the furnace, is seeking state permits to double the incinerator's capacity);
- Bring together representatives of other polluting industries and pressure them to reduce their companies' toxic emissions;
- Divest from South Africa; and
- Negotiate a timetable for accomplishing the above goals.

Nobody knows what these negotiations will yield or how long it will take to get tangible results. Nevertheless, both sides appear willing to talk. Of course, talking about emission reduction is different from actual emission reduction. But the Coalition and its allies did get Chevron to agree not to bring in outside waste to burn at the Richmond site.

The other concrete result of the negotiations was an agreement to meet again to negotiate specifics. Nevertheless, the meeting itself represented a major community victory in that the West County Toxics Coalition finally won the right to bargain with Chevron, something local leaders had unsuccessfully attempted to do since 1987.

Resolutions and Outcomes

These case studies demonstrate that African Americans, Latino Americans, and Native Americans are actively pursuing strategies to improve the overall quality of life in their neighborhoods. The grassroots leaders have not waited for "outsiders" or "elites" to rush to their rescue; they have taken the initiative themselves.

As expected, the groups had more success in blocking proposed facilities than closing those already operating. The West Dallas residents were successful in shutting down the lead smelter and in winning an out-of-court settlement worth over $45 million—one of the largest awards ever in a lead pollution case in the country. It was made on behalf of 370 children—almost all of whom were poor, black residents of the West Dallas public housing project—and 40 property owners.

The lawsuit was finally settled in June 1983 when RSR agreed to a soil cleanup program in West Dallas, a blood-testing program for the children and pregnant women, and the installation of new antipollution equipment. The equipment, however, was never installed. In May 1984 the Dallas Board of Adjustments, a city agency responsible for monitoring land-use violations, requested that the city attorney order the smelter permanently closed for violating the zoning code. It had operated in the neighborhood for some 50 years without the necessary use permits.

The 1984 lead cleanup proved inadequate. A more comprehensive cleanup of West Dallas was begun in December 1991—20 years after the first government study of lead smelters. Some 30,000 to 40,000 cubic yards (roughly 1,800 truckloads) of lead-tainted soil are to be removed from several West Dallas sites, including schoolyards and about 140 private homes (Loftis 1992). The project will cost between $3 to $4 million. The contaminated soil was originally planned to be shipped to a landfill in Monroe, Louisiana—a city that is 60 percent African-American.

The municipal landfill in Houston, the hazardous waste incinerator in Alsen, and the petrochemical plant (and on-site hazardous waste incinerator) in Richmond are still operating. Although the three groups and their allies fell short of completely eliminating the threat by bringing about actual plant closures, they were able to extract concessions from the polluting industries in the form of capacity reduction and emission controls. In Alsen, after more than six years, a 1987 out-of-court settlement was reached between Rollins and the residents. It was reported to be worth an average of $3,000 per resident. The company was also required to reduce emissions from its facilities.

Construction of four proposed facilities were prevented: the two waste facilities in Los Angeles (South Central and East Los Angeles), the one on Rosebud Reservation in South Dakota, and the one in Kettleman City. The two lawsuits filed on behalf of South Central and East Los Angeles residents never reached the trial or settlement stage, for the two construction proposals were withdrawn. The city-sponsored LANCER project was killed by the mayor and city council. In May 1991, CTTS decided to "throw in the towel" because the lawsuits threatened to drive up costs beyond the $4 million the company had already spent on the project (Dolan 1991). The Vernon hazardous waste incinerator became a dead issue.

On the other hand, the Good Road Coalition blocked plans to build the 6,000-acre landfill on the Rosebud Reservation through the electoral process. A majority of the residents voted the proposal down. In 1991, former tribal chairman Ralph Moran, who had favored the landfill proposal, was defeated in the tribal primary election and residents convinced the tribal council to cancel the agreement to build the facility. The proposal was resurrected in 1992 in yet another offer to the tribal council by RSW. Again, the plan was rejected by the council.

Although part of the lawsuit involving the Kettleman City incinerator dispute is still pending, People for Clean Air and Water won a major victory in delaying construction. A superior court judge in January 1992 overturned the Kings County Board of Supervisors' approval of the Kettleman City incinerator, citing its detrimental impact on air quality in the agriculture-rich Central Valley of California.

The judge ruled that Kings County's environmental impact report was inadequate and that county leaders had failed to involve the local residents in the decision by not providing Spanish translations of material about the project. This court ruling represents a victory since the waste-disposal company must now begin the permit process all over again if it is still interested in siting the facility.

Conclusion

The mainstream environmental movement has proven that it can help enhance the quality of life in this country. The national membership organizations that make up the mainstream movement have clearly played an important role in shaping the nation's environmental policy. Yet, few of these groups have actively involved themselves in environmental conflicts involving communities of color. Because of this, it's unlikely that we will see a mass influx of people of color into the national environmental groups any time soon. A continuing growth in their own grassroots organizations is more likely. Indeed, the fastest growing segment of the environmental movement is made up by the grassroots groups in communities of color which are increasingly linking up with one another and with other community-based groups. As long as U.S. society remains divided into separate and unequal communities, such groups will continue to serve a positive function.

It is not surprising that indigenous leaders are organizing the most effective resistance within communities of color. They have the advantage of being close to the population immediately affected by the disputes they are attempting to resolve. They are also completely wedded to social and economic justice agendas and familiar with the tactics of the civil rights movement. This makes effective community organizing possible. People of color have a long track record in challenging government and corporations that discriminate. Groups that emphasize civil rights and social justice can be found in almost every major city in the country.

Cooperation between the two major wings of the environmental movement is both possible and beneficial, however. Many environmental activists of color are now getting support from mainstream organizations in the form of technical advice, expert testimony, direct financial assistance, fundraising, research, and legal assistance. In return, increasing numbers of people of color are assisting mainstream organizations to redefine their limited environmental agendas and expand their outreach by serving on boards, staffs, and advisory councils. Grassroots activists have thus been the most influential activists in placing equity and social justice issues onto the larger environmental agenda and democratizing and diversifying the movement as a whole. Such changes are necessary if the environmental movement is to successfully help spearhead a truly global movement for a just, sustainable, and healthy society and effectively resolve pressing environmental disputes. Environmentalists and civil rights activists of all stripes should welcome the growing movement of African Americans, Latinos, Asians, Pacific Islanders, and Native Americans who are taking up the struggle for environmental justice.

RONALD WALTERS

Black Politics and Democratic Theory: "Two Unreconciled Strivings"

Introduction

In conceptualizing the phenomenon of Black Politics—or the way in which African descendant people have used power within American society—it is necessary to understand the sociological situation they face, living in a racially stratified, white dominant system, with blacks and other non-white minorities as subordinate cultural groups. And although this model of American society has changed somewhat over the years, its manifestations have remained remarkably constant. Black Politics, therefore, takes place both within the black community and the white community in a way that will be described below as a two-level process. After describing this basic frame of reference, the author will enter into a longer narrative which defines the manner in which the dynamics of this two-level process have worked to achieve the political objectives of the black community in specific eras.

The Black Community

The orientation of black people toward politics, in the context of their relationship with America began at the very moment that Africans slaves organized to obtain their freedom, by whatever means available. To the extent that organization was necessary which implied the construction of leadership, a process of decision-making and goal setting, politics was at the heart of the enterprise. "Politics" in this sense, was the development of power through organization and its use in the formulation of strategies designed to achieve objectives.

Ronald Walters, "Black Politics and Democratic Theory: 'Two Unreconciled Strivings.'" Reprinted by permission of the author.

Therefore, the first level was the internal politics of the black community. The substance of that politics was not only the question of organization, but grappling with the issues of community survival and development. The first task of such politics was to regulate the cultural coherence and communing of black people. The issues involved in this more often dealt with subjects such as work, education, non-discriminatory treatment and others, but since these activities were often regulated by the dominant community, the nature of Black Politics was to fashion the demands for these resources. Thus, much of the internal character of Black Politics involved the "sorting process" with respect to these demands and the way in which the community might be structured and mobilized to achieve them.

National Political Institutions

The second level of black politics has been characterized by the participation of blacks in the wider society. The problem here, however, was that most blacks were prohibited from normal participation in society because of their initial status as slaves, while those who not enslaved enjoyed severely restricted access to such participation, such as voting and taking part in political parties and other methods of authoritative decision-making at both the local and national levels.

Historically, the white majority has not easily accommodated the entry of black Americans into political participation and in many eras of history has violently sought to prevent such participation. So, the character of Black Politics has been defined by not only an offensive nature, but an oppositional character as well, opposing those attempts to subjugate the black community through repressive laws or social practices and attempting to affect social change. It has often found blacks responding to the shifting currents which, at one time in history, have denied black participation as part of the process of racial subordination and oppression, and in another time, forward movement has been made by the initiative of blacks having been accommodated by the dominant institutions.

So, the major objective of those involved in Black Politics was first to obtain the right to participate. This often called for such tactics as individual or collective protest and legal representation in the courts. The second objective was that once such a right to participate was obtained, to utilize it for the benefit of the black community and the wider society. This concept might be regarded as a theory of Black Politics, and the general nature of the elements of the Black Political system might be represented below as follows:

FIG. 1   THE BLACK POLITICAL SYSTEM

Expectations and Demands →	Wider Political system →	Goals
Organization; mobilization of tactics and strategies	authoritative decision making in major political institutions	laws/resources development social acceptance

This model is often used to describe the general working of the main political system. (8) The major problem with the general model of the political system is that its functioning depends upon how well the authoritative structures of the main political institutions (government) succeeds in addressing the needs and goals of citizens. When it does not, that is to say, when it does not provide the proper equilibrium between citizen demands and the satisfaction of those demands, citizens have a right to seek redress through other non-institutional lawful means through the right of assembly and free speech such as the basis of political protest.

Thus, the black community addressed the wider society through the political system as a group, since its original status as slaves was maintained on a group basis, and since after slavery, laws governing racial segregation and other forms of subordination were meted out on a group basis. The theory of black politics, then, was that if the right of the group could be established in law and practice and the access to social mobility and resources secured, then the exercise of those rights by the individual might be expanded. In this sense, as the most oppressed segment of society, for blacks to test the system of political participation, test the very character of American democracy itself.

The emphasis on group action was also necessary for blacks because, as a minority, it was the most effective way to leverage power, the only power black possessed which was "people power." The necessity to use group power was also critical because of the power arrayed against blacks and because of their need to change an often desperate socio-economic status. Indeed Political Scientist Robert Dahl, a theorist of the democratic process, suggests that the effective functioning of the political system for individuals depended upon the amount of change required:

> . . . your chances of gaining a favorable action from the government depends on still another factor: how much change you require in the behavior of other people in order for government to do what you want it to do. The greater the amount of

change required, the less your chances of success—other things being equal of course.[1]

The logic of his observation, then is that in order for individuals to make substantial amounts of change, they must enter into arrangements that yield them more power in order for them to participate successfully. This has also defined the context in which blacks would utilize institutional procedures of change such as the courts and extra-institutional methods such as direction-action.

The Framework of Politics Within the Black Community

Organizational Forms

The forms of organization in the black community oriented toward "politics" evolved with the nature of the community itself. Originally, in the plantation society, authoritative decision-making was performed by the white master and to some extent, his overseers, who in some cases were black. However, this was the dominant system within the slaves worked and lived. Slowly, as it became fashionable to "christianize" slaves as a method of legitimizing slavery, black ministers became figures of moral authority; and as the Christian religion was used also as a tool of the socialization of slaves into English culture, black churches were permitted and the role of the black minister expanded.[2]

Thus, the church emerged as the first social organization of blacks in America and it also was the strongest because it performed a multiplicity of purposes in the practical life of the African. It came to participate in rituals of spiritual celebration that encompassed such practical aspects of life as, birth, marriage, moral living, financial support, and death. And although there were no political clubs, even in the so-called "freed" black communities, the church provided a source of internal organization for the black community and, as such, a vehicle for the representation of black interests to the larger white community.

Education was also a route to leadership, as the slave understood very quickly the power of English culture and its relationship to his emancipation. The English settlers understood this also, thus, they prohibited the slave from learning to read and write the English language. Lerone Bennett cites a poignant expression of the thirst for education from Rev. Thomas Calahan, a missionary of the United Presbyterian Church:

> Go out in any direction and you meet negroes on horses, negroes on mules, negroes with oxen, negroes by the wagon, cart and buggy load, negroes on foot, men, women, and children; negroes in uniform, negroes in rags, negroes in frame houses, negroes living in tents, negroes living in rail pens covered with brush, and negroes living under brush piles without any rails, negroes living on the bare ground with the sky for their covering; all hopeful, almost all cheerful, everyone pleasing to be taught, willing to do anything for learning. They are never out of our rooms, and their cry is for 'Books! Books!' and 'when will school begin?'[3]

Notwithstanding the formidable impediments to their education, free blacks and slaves alike became educated and as they did so, their community organizational structure elaborated itself to accommodate new roles. There were elite black organizations which mirrored those in the white community, comprised of social clubs, professional, educational clubs, secret societies, civic clubs and the like. Most of these did not adopt political roles overtly, but because in the typical black community, they were all members of the same churches, the church came to express a collective sentiment of many other such organizations.

The Men's clubs which sprang up in cities in the early 1800s, became the first such political clubs with a civic function. They formed the basis of a national movement, the Negro Convention movement that began to meet in 1831 until 1854. This movement was important in building a platform of free blacks against slavery and for participation in political parties and elections. They, therefore, considered many issues attendant to these choices such as whether to leave America or stay and fight for citizenship; whether in deciding to stay, to fight for the vote as the badge of full citizenship rights; whether to vote for the Republican, Free Soil, Liberty, Democrat, Greenback or other such parties of the 19th Century.

Leadership

Small wonder, then, that many of the leaders of the black community have been ministers. In the 19th Century, they abounded, as Nat Turner, who led one of the major slave rebellions in the 1830s, was said to have been a minister whose visions led him to take up arms against the white masters; Rev. Henry Highland Garnet, fiery

---

[1]Robert Dahl, *Democracy in the United States*, Second ed., Chicago: Rand McNally, 1972, p. 389.

[2]V. P. Franklin, *Black self-determination: A Cultural History of the Faith of the Fathers*, Westport: Lawrence Hill, 1984, pp. 27–68.

[3]Lerone Bennett, Jr., *The Shaping of Black America*, Chicago: Johnson Publishing Co., 1974, p. 199.

abolitionist and diplomat; Bishop Henry McNiel Turner, Pan Africanists, and many others. However, the black class structure also began to diversify in the 19th century, as the first black lawyer was admitted to the bar in 1845, and other professionals began to develop. In fact, some of the most famous leaders of the 19th century were non-ministers, such as Frederick Douglass, (civil rights leader), Booker T. Washington (educator), George T. Downing (business), W. E. B. Du Bois (educator), William Monroe Trotter (newspaper publisher), and etc.[4]

There were also those who dedicated themselves to politics when the opportunity arose after the Civil War and at the close, 21 blacks had served in the Congress of the United States, hundreds more at the local levels, especially in the South. However, by 1901, they had nearly all been eliminated.[5]

The most important fact was that this pattern of diversification continued into the 20th Century, as government bureaucrats, labor leaders, college presidents, magazine publishers, scientists, all came to fruition. However, the opportunities for dedicated political leadership were severely restricted in the first quarter of the 20th Century as blacks in the South were still largely prohibited from electoral participation and blacks in the North, who were relatively fewer in number, had just begun to make their presence felt.

In any case, many of the problems of the black community were addressed increasingly using a variety of tactics and strategies as the leadership cadre grew in many arenas of life.

Political Structure and Issue Mobilization

Here, it will be necessary to operationalize the theory discussed above utilizing more concrete examples in the categories such as the black community, the majority community exhibiting patterns of conflict and cooperation in the achievement of the political objectives of the black community's status rights, socio-economic rights and resources.

Leadership Structure:

The natural political leadership of the black community has been a combination of the major civil rights leaders and elected officials. This combination illustrates both community/political institution relationship. However, as the civil rights protests and legal battles opened up

opportunities for blacks to vote and hold office in the major political institutions, the national leaders status of ministers and civil rights leaders declined. Thus, Professor Robert Smith illustrates, using the database of the "100 Most Influential Negroes," an annual listing composed by *Ebony Magazine*, that between 1963 and 1980, the most significant changes were in the category of Civil Rights leaders (18%–7%) and glamorous personalities (10%–2%), as the number of ministers remained low and steady, and the number of appointed government officials, grew strongly (9%–13%), and elected officials (9%–25%), increased strongest of all.[6] Smith says that seven factors may be responsible for the changes in the leadership categories: population changes, changes in the Negro class structure, the civil rights revolution, the community action program, the ghetto revolts, the Black Power movement, and changes in white attitudes toward black people.[7]

The changes among the various categories have continued into the '90s, as the growth of the black middle class, and the expansion of the opportunities to serve in both appointed and elected office have increased. I will revisit the nature of this expansion below. However, having observed that the *categories* of leadership have expanded, it should be said, they have a concomitant affect upon the *structure* of national leadership.

It should be posited, first of all, that there is a black leadership structure at both local and national levels. At the local level, the leadership structure manifests itself by the presence of a black political class. In cities, for example, where there is no affective black class, or a small class, of elected and appointed officials, the leadership class tends to be comprised of black community leaders.[8] In that case, it will typically include the ministers of the largest churches, the head of the civil rights organization, the head of business organizations and the press, and perhaps an educator or two. However, in localities where blacks dominate the political structure, the members of the City Council, Mayor, school board members, members of Congress and other figures often form the top of the leadership structure pyramid.

Nationally, an organizational group structure dominates the black leadership structure. At the top are the heads of recognized national black organizations such as the Congressional Black Caucus, the NAACP, the

---

[4]Vincent Harding, *There is a River: The Black Struggle for Freedom in America*, New York: Harcourt Brace and Jovanovitch, 1981.

[5]William Clay, *Just Permanent Interests: Black Americans in Congress, 1870–1991*, Amistad Publishers, 1992.

[6]Robert Smith, "Black Leadership: A Survey of Theory and Research," Institute of Urban Affairs and Research, Howard University, p. 47.

[7]Ibid., p. 35.

[8]Matthew Holden, Jr., *The Politics of the Black Nation*, New York: Chandler Publishing Co., pp. 26–33.

National Urban League, the Southern Christian Leadership Conference, the National Council of Negro Women, the National Rainbow Coalition/PUSH and others. The heads of these organizations and several others have formed a National Black Leadership Forum that is comprised of 13 top organizations, including the Joint Center for Political and Economic Studies, heads of black fraternities and sororities, and the National Conference of Black Mayors.

There are also a plethora of organizations of black elected officials, headed by the CBC, there is the National Conference of Black Mayors, the National Black Caucus of Local Elected Officials (of the National League of Cities), the International Conference of Black Mayors, the Association of Black County officials, School board officials, National Political Caucus of Black Women, and etc. The status relationship among these organizations, of course, complies with their level of government.[9]

There is also a considerable degree of overlap among these organizations in their individual membership, as a member of one is likely to be a member of another. This means that the effective leadership class of the black community has a high degree of coherence and integrated membership.

Issues Mobilization

The mobilization of black leadership traditionally has been directed toward the attainment of concrete objectives as represented by the original threat of the March on Washington by black labor leader A. Philip Randolph in 1941. The mere fact that so much of the black leadership was willing to mobilize their organizations to follow Randolph achieved the objective of opening up many of the Defense industries to black employment during World War II.

The decade of the 1960s, however, was different in that protest demonstrations became the major tool of the Civil Rights movement. Emboldened by the success of the 1954 Supreme Court decision of *Brown* v *Board of Education* of Topeka, Kansas mandating integrated education, and the Montgomery, Alabama Bus Boycott, blacks in both the North and South launched a series of physical challenges to all forms of racial segregation that have not, as yet, ended. Fueled by the student movement of the late 1950s and early 1960s, testing segregated eating facilities, the adults began to protest segregation in employment, public accommodations and the right to vote and participate in the

Southern society at large. One major high point of the Civil Rights movement was the 1963 March on Washington, organized by A. Philip Randolph. This massive protest demonstration provided an opportunity for all Americans to witness the broad cross-racial consensus that the Civil Rights movement enjoyed at that moment in history.[10]

Black protests, however, grew violent in the 1960s, as the temper of the Northern movement became expressed in an urgency that was incomparable to the more defensive tactics utilized by Martin Luther King, Jr. in the South. By 1967, a "Black Power movement" was born with Stokeley Carmichael as its leader, and by 1969, 500 cities were burning in an exorcism of violence. The impact of the more militant politics spawned a renewed appreciation of African culture and the push for Black studies became a political objective of black student and faculty members on white college campuses all over the country. Thus, many major colleges and universities were politicized as the struggle for black studies was joined by the struggle for Women's rights and protests against the Viet Nam War.[11]

Other protest demonstrations have occurred since the 1970s by black organizations with the objectives of seeking to commemorate the goals of the 1963 March on Washington, or to signal the public objection of blacks and others to the emerging anti-Civil Rights Supreme Court decisions of the 1980s. However, the largest demonstration in American history was the Million Man March, held in October 1995, which was organized by Minister Louis Farrakhan, head of the Nation of Islam. This March, which brought nearly 2 million black men to Washington, D. C. on October 12, 1995, was not a traditional protest demonstration, but carried the theme of "atonement and reconciliation," as a way of seeking the recommitment of African American males to their basic responsibilities to their families and their communities.[12]

As important an issue as the size of the March was to become, far more important was the fact that it unleashed a new phase of grassroots activity in local black communities all across the country. In cities such as Baltimore, Maryland, Denver, Colorado, Buffalo, New York, Newark, New Jersey and many others, thousands of black men began to meet and take action to improve aspects of the local quality of life, confronting the drug trade, adopting orphaned black children, registering to

[9]Ronald Walters, "Serving the People: African American Leadership and the Challenge of Empowerment," in *The State of Black America, 1994*, National Urban League, January 1994, pp. 153–170.

[10]James Forman, *The Making of Black Revolutionaries*, New York: Macmillan, 1972, pp. 331–337.

[11]August Meier, ed., *Black Experience: The Transformation of Activism*, Transaction/Aldine Publishing Co., 1970.

[12]Haki Madthubuti and Maulana Karenga, eds., *The Million Man March: A Documentary*, Chicago: Third World Press, 1996.

vote, demanding peaceful communities and urging increased economic development.

Thus, community mobilization has historically contributed to raising issues for attention and evolving strategies with which to confront them, as a regular strategy of attempting to achieve progress.

Electoral Politics

Voting

Since the beginning of the Constitution, blacks have voted in both some local and national elections as persons born free. Thus, the issue of the juxtaposition of the dominant political system to achieve black objectives through the vote was an issue. Immediately after the Civil War, there was the issue of whether or not blacks would seek their right to vote as free men (women could not vote at this time). Frederick Douglass, who, in the 1850s, had broken with the white abolitionists over this issue to pursue it as an affirmative agenda item of the black abolitionists, felt as strongly in 1865. He said: "Our work will not be done, until the colored man is admitted as a full member in good standing in the American body politic."[13] In this, he confirmed the view of the Virginia Freedmen's Convention which resolved that: "the only salvation for us besides the power of the Government is the 'possession of the ballot.' "[14]

Four million blacks were released from slavery in 1865, and six hundred thousand participated in the election in 1868 and for several years, they assured the Republicans of political dominance in national elections. In fact, the transition in the black vote did not come until 1932, when the New Deal program of President Franklin Roosevelt made it attractive for blacks to do as T. Thomas Fortune said: for blacks to go home and turn their pictures of Lincoln to the wall. From that point, blacks gave a majority of their vote to Democrats, except for the equally attractive post-war candidacies of General Dwight D. Eisenhower in 1952 and 1956, coming back to the Democratic party to ensure that John F. Kennedy was elected president in 1960.

Despite the passage of the Fifteenth Amendment to the Constitution ensuring the right to vote, blacks have in practice, been prohibited from voting, especially in the South, by force and terror. It became an important aspect of the Civil Rights movement, then, to enforce that amendment in the words of Martin Luther King, Jr., in a speech on May 17, 1957 at a mass rally at the Lincoln Memorial to commemorate the third anniversary of the Brown decision of 1954:

> Give us the ballot and we will no longer plead to the federal government for passage of an anti-lynching law; we will by the power of our vote write the law on the statute books of the southern states and bring an end to the dastardly acts of the hooded perpetrators of violence.
> Give us the ballot and we will transform the salient misdeeds of bloodthirsty mobs into the calculated good deeds of orderly citizens.
> Give us the ballot and we will fill our legislative halls with men of good will, and send to the sacred halls of Congress men who will not sign a Southern Manifesto, because of their devotion to the manifesto of justice.
> Give us the ballot and we will place judges on the benches of the South who will "do justly and love mercy," and we will place at the head of the southern states governors who have felt not only the tang of the human, but the glow of the divine.
> Give us the ballot and we will quietly and nonviolently, without rancor or bitterness, implement the Supreme Court decisions of May 17, 1954.[15]

It is worth citing the long passage from Dr. King's speech above because it transmits to the reader the expansive expectations alive in the civil rights movement overall for the actions that were being taken to sacrifice lives for justice, and the nature of their ultimate realization of the laws. The Voting Rights was won on the battlefield of "bloody Sunday" in Selma, Alabama, on March 6, 1965, when televisions in the living rooms of America, showed peaceful civil rights marchers being beaten unmercifully by Bull Connor's mounted policemen. The public outcry jolted President Lyndon Johnson and the Congress into actions and the Bill was signed on August 6, 1965.

In fact, considerable progress has been made since that time. In the 1992 election, Census data indicates that the black vote constituted 10 percent (11,371,000) of the electorate 113,866,000.[16] And as figures below will show, the gap between black and white voters has been narrowing.

Thus, while the gap in black-white political participation narrowed in 1988, it increased moderately in the presidential election of 1992. A major observation from these data may be that there is no linear correlation in the expected convergence in the black-white

---

[13]Bess Beatty, *A Revolution Gone Backward*, New York: Greenwood, 1987, p. 1.

[14]Ibid., p. 2.

[15]James Washington, ed., *A Testament of Hope: The Essential Writings of Martin Luther King, Jr.*, San Francisco: Harper and Row, 1986, p. 198.

[16]Jerry Jennings, "Vote and Registration in the United States in the Election of 1992," P20–466, Bureau of the Census, U.S. Department of Commerce, pp. 4–5.

TABLE 1 PERCENT BLACK-WHITE ELECTORAL PARTICIPATION GAP IN NATIONAL PRESIDENTIAL ELECTIONS, 1968, 1988, 1992.

	1968	1988	1992
Registration Gap	9.2	3.4	6.0
Turnout Gap	11.5	7.6	9.0

(Voting and Registration in the Election of November 1968, 1988, 1992, Bureau of the Census, U. S. Department of Commerce.)

vote, that different factors influence black and white turnout and thus, the gap will fluctuate in any given election. It also means, that, for example, convergence may occur when it is least expected.

The Political Parties

Blacks have given most of their votes to the Democratic party, as indicated above. For example, in the 1988 Presidential election, approximately 86% of the vote went to the Democratic candidate, and in 1992, 76% went to the Democratic candidate.

Nevertheless, there is some slight indication that black allegiance to the Democratic party has waned. Black turnout in 1988 for example, constituted a drop from 1984 levels and from the data above, black support for the president in 1992 dropped 10 percentage points. In addition, the black vote for Ross Perot in 1992 amounted to 7 percent, or 6 percent more than the combined vote of two black candidates running that year, Dr. Lenora Fulani (.08%) and Ron Daniels (.02%).

TABLE 2 PARTY ID AMONG BLACK VOTERS BY PERCENT

Party	1980	1984	1988
Strong Democrat	45	55	50
Weak Democrat	27	21	22
Independent Democrat	9	12	10
Independent	7	5	3
Independent Republican	3	3	3
Weak Republican	2	3	4
Strong Republican	3	*	3

Source: Paul Abramson and David Rhode, *Change and Continuity in the 1984 Elections*, Washington, D. C.: Congressional Quarterly Press, 1986. Gallup Poll Survey, Joint Center for Political Studies, Washington, DC.

These changes in party identification of blacks has been relatively modest over time, with whatever significant changes there have been accruing to strong Democrats and Independent Democrats both in 1984, with both dropping in 1988. Again these changes in party

ID apparently do not forecast long-term linear trends in any one direction, but may fluctuate with the circumstances of the election. However, the basic pattern of Democratic voting has held.

Elected Officials

One significant long-term trend has been the growth of black elected officials. Before the Voting Act was passed in 1965, there were an estimated 300 Black elected officials at all levels of government. As is indicated below, the growth since that time has been dramatic.

By 1994, there were 8,406 black elected officials total in office, and although the *number* of officials continues to grow, the *rate* at which they are growing has slowed dramatically from the early 1970s, when the annual increases were sometimes quite striking. The slower rate of growth at 2% and 3% per year in the 1990s is an indication of the fact that many of the available places where blacks could be elected easily (black majority political jurisdiction, for example) have been filled by black representatives. Thus, for the continued growth of black elected officials, blacks will have to run for office in non-majority black political jurisdictions. This will likely change the nature of the agenda of black candidates, because they will not be able to pursue black politics.

TABLE 3 GROWTH IN BLACK ELECTED OFFICIALS

Year	Total	Federal	State	Municipal
1970	1,469	10	169	623
1975	3,503	18	281	1,573
1980	4,912	17	323	2,356
1985	6,056	20	396	2,898
1991*	7,490	26	458	3,696

*January 1991

Source: Joint Center for Political and Economic Studies, Washington, D. C. *Black Elected Officials: A National Roster* (Given year).

The Strategic Role of the Black Vote

The Jackson Campaigns: Besides voting and running for office, there is a strategic role for black politics. That is to say, running for office is not always intended to produce an electoral victory. Nevertheless, one must use this strategy of attempting to win, if the strategic objective is to be realized. For example, the 1984 and 1988 presidential campaigns of the Rev. Jesse Jackson were significant examples of the way in which it is possible to influence national politics without winning office.

In 1984, Jackson ran for President devoting his campaign to advocate for those in the most severe conditions of life from all races and ethnic groups. He lost the primary election for the Nominee of the Democratic party to Walter Mondale, but collected 3.2 million votes, suggesting that a base of voters was indeed possible to be expanded.[17] In 1984, he had an impact upon the Platform of the Democratic party, placing issues such as opposing South African Apartheid, and support for financing economic development in urban areas on its agenda. In 1988, he again mounted a campaign for the Democratic nomination for President, and although he won several primaries and caucuses, ran second to Michael Dukakis, the eventual winner. Nevertheless, his campaign attracted 7 million votes (2.4 million white votes), and again influenced the party platform, placing issues such as "rebuilding America" through financing infrastructure development, financing urban investment with public pension funds, and other issues.[18] In particular, his foreign policy issues of building majority rule in South Africa, peace in the Middle East through mutual dialogue and negotiation, approaching the Sandinistas in Nicaragua with peace and participation for fair elections and other issues have been enacted into law.

The mobilization caused by the Jackson campaigns had a significant effect upon coalition building in several states and the electoral coalitions he constructed which won the primary in Virginia and carried New York City in 1992 led to such subsequent victories as electing David Dinkins to be Mayor of New York City, and Doug Wilder to be Governor of the State of Virginia.

The Margin of Difference: Although the impact of the Jackson campaign was felt in the primary elections, the importance of the black vote in the General election is that it may often be the margin of difference for the Democratic victor. This was the case in both 1976 and 1992.

In the 1976 election, Jimmy Carter won by what was then called the "new arithmetic of power"—a combination of white and black votes in the Southern states comprising the electoral majority. This was the case in states such as Georgia, Louisiana and Mississippi where the black vote constituted 20–30 percent of the total electorate because of the large black population in those states.

Then again in 1992, Bill Clinton won a narrow victory by 43 percent of the vote and in some southern states, the black vote constituted his margin of victory. For example, Clinton won the state of Louisiana, where the black share of Clinton's vote was 50.6%, an historic first that the black vote should comprise most of the vote of a winning candidate in a state or nationally.[19] However, the black vote was also critical to Clinton's vote in other states such as South Carolina and Mississippi because Ross Perot split the Republican vote with George Bush in the South, a region that was becoming more Republican.

The Ideology of Black Politics

Two Strivings

The enterprise of Black Politics does not take place without purpose and intention and as such, is informed by the identify and experiences of the people who are considered black or who consider themselves to be part of the African descendant community in the United States and around the world. These people, "African Americans" like other ethnic groups have to reconcile what W. E. B. Du Bois defined as "two strivings" to be both part of their ethnic cultural diaspora—or homeland group—and to be full citizens of the United States at the same time.[20] Therefore, the first determination that influences the strength of one's ideology is the degree to which one considers himself or herself to be identified on the spectrum of African-Americaness. If one considers himself or herself to be more on the African side in terms of the strength of identity, extent of non-racist treatment from the wider society, perception of the openness of the opportunity structure, etc., that person is more likely to adopt a Black nationalist or system-opposing ideology.

On the other hand, if one considers himself or herself closer to the American ideal in terms previously specified, one is more likely to adopt an ideology toward the American side of the spectrum. These two poles of ideology might be represented by the Marcus Garvey / Malcolm X / Stokeley Carmichael tradition of Black nationalism. This belief is characterized by a

[17]William Crotty, "Jesse Jackson's Campaign: Constituency Attitudes and Political Outcomes," in Lucius J. Barker and Ronald W. Walters, eds., *Jesse Jackson's 1984 Presidential Campaign: Challenge and Change in American Politics*, Chicago: University of Illinois Press, 1989, pp. 59–95.

[18]Frank Clemente and Frank Watkins, eds., *Keep Hope Alive: Jesse Jackson's 1988 Presidential Campaign*, Boston: South End Press/Keep Hope Alive PAC, 1989.

[19]David Bositis, Joint Center for Political and Economic Studies, Washington, D. C., 1992.

[20]Du Bois said: "One ever feels his twoness,—an American, a Negro; two souls, two thoughts, two unreconciled strivings; two warring ideals in one dark body, whose dogged strength alone keeps it from being torn asunder." (W. E. Burghardt Du Bois, *The Souls of Black Folk*, first edition, 1903, New York: Fawcett Publications, 1961, p. 17)

strong belief in a connection with Africa as the cultural origin of black peoples, that there is integrity and worth in the values of the black community and its culture, and that there is a social value to behaving as a member of the black community and protecting its legacy.[21]

The Civil Rights integrationist position might be represented by Frederick Douglass / Martin Luther King, Jr. / Roy Wilkins. And here, there is a tendency to take the cultural integrity of the black community for granted or to believe that it should be rehabilitated with integration into the social and institutional reality of the dominant culture. That only with such integration will the rights of blacks to enjoy the perquisites of an open society be acquired and protected.[22]

So, whether or not one adhered to the Black nationalist tradition or to the Civil Rights integrationist tradition was a product of where one evaluated the fortunes of the group to which he/she belonged and also himself/herself as an individual part of that group. The result of the evaluation often depends upon the satisfaction of a person with the perceived efficiency and accuracy with which a given ideology is able to answer questions such as, why racial inequality persists.[23]

Within that spectrum, an important factor that influences how one is socialized to one side of the spectrum or another is concrete experiences. To be "black" in America is not merely a question of color, it is also a question of shared experience. It is a question of shared history and consciousness of that history and its meaning; it is a question of one's daily lived experiences in relation to that history and the people who have experienced it. However, to be an American is also to avail oneself of a highly individualistic social experience and to experience the richness of different and culturally diverse group experiences. Indeed, the openness of the society itself has the capacity to influence concrete experiences and therefore, one's evaluation of the possibilities of interracial life and thus, one's identity.[24] Thus, ideology must reconcile these "two strivings" in the pursuit of both cultural outlook and political outlook.

The ideologies of those who are members of the black community are not static, but change according to historical events and personal experiences. For ex-

ample, the country has changed from a period in the 1960s and 1970s where whites engaged in the relative acceptance of racial integration in many aspects of life as a response both to changes in the law and demonstrated racial unfairness. To many, the pendulum has now swung to a more conservative mood, where public and private acts of racial intolerance and changes in the law toward eliminating prohibitions against racial discrimination have occurred.

The dominant ideology of the Black community is a curious blend of conservatism and liberal/progressivism. The value system originated—and persists—to conserve life and cultural values of the group and the maintenance of institutions. Thus, there is dominant support in the black community for such issues as prayer in the schools, restriction on illegal immigration, restrictions on gay rights such as same sex marriages, toughness on crime, opposed to the legalization of marijuana, and etc.[25]

On the other hand, black opinion manifest a civil libertarian attitude toward the acquisition and distribution of rights, and fairness toward all groups. The perceived lack of fairness, for example, can foster levels of alienation that can increase forms of political participation such as lobbying, community activism, electoral activism and voting.[26]

Therefore, it is possible to predict that as the Democratic party, the traditional party of blacks, increasingly adapts to the conservative tenor of this era, that conflict will grow among blacks with respect to whether or not to continue high levels of support. There is historical precedent for this position, in that when the 1877 Hays bargain occurred that withdrew Federal troops from the South and facilitated the restoration of white power, a debate occurred within the black community as to continued support for the Republican party. This debate simmered for several decades until blacks openly began to break with the party in opposition to its growing racially exclusive practices. Thus, when Roosevelt appeared on the scene, blacks were ready for a political transition.

Perhaps another political transition is in the near future for blacks. Already, survey data indicates growing support for a Black Political party, nearing 50 percent of blacks nationally in 1992.[27] The factors that may cause this sentiment to grow will have much

---

[21]Kinfe Abraham, *The Politics of Black Nationalism*, Trenton: Africa World Press, 1991, pp. 10–138.

[22]Celeste Michelle Condit and John Louis Lucaites, *Crafting Equality: America's Anglo-African World*, Chicago: The University of Chicago Press, 1993, pp. 11–13.

[23]John T. McCartney, *Black Power Ideologies: An Essay in African-American Political Thought*, Philadelphia: Temple University Press, 1992, pp. 5–13.

[24]Thomas F. Pettigrew, *Racially Separate or Together?*, New York: McGraw-Hill, 1971, pp. 295–328.

[25]Robert Smith and Richard Seltzer, *Race, Class and Culture: A Study of Afro-American Mass Opinion*, Albany: State University of New York Press, 1992, pp. 39–40.

[26]Ibid, p. 134.

[27]Michael Dawson, "Black Discontent: The Preliminary Report on the 1993–1994 National Black Politics Study," NBPS Report No. 1, University of Chicago, April 1994.

to do with the political affect of ideology upon both the dominant white majority and blacks in the future.

Conclusion

Of course, Black Politics cannot "reconcile the strivings" of which Du Bois spoke, because the task is much larger than the capabilities within the black community, and must involve the society as a whole. However, properly understood, the task of black politics to regulate aspects of black culture and community affairs and to mobilize the interest of black community and its participation in the major political institutions of the nations, will contribute substantially to this reconciliation.

CHAPTER EIGHT

A Way of Looking at Africa and Afrocentricity

I am a lioness
and will never allow my body
to be anyone's resting place.
But if I did,
I would not yield to a dog—
and O! the lions I have turned away!

Aisha bint Ahmadalz-Qurtubiyya

READING SELECTIONS

ROBERT J. CUMMINGS

Africa Between the Ages

Africa is the second largest continent in the world. Partitioned into what is now fifty-one or more territorial units at the Berlin Conference of 1884–85, the continent presently has the largest number of states represented at the United Nations. This numerical strength has advantages and disadvantages for Africans. It is advantageous because it gives Africa greater visibility in the international voting process. It is disadvantageous because it turns this vast continent into a highly fragmented sector of the international community. Yet Africa's size and fragmentation have great significance for Africanists because together these factors make the continent a major laboratory for research on human society. Africa's numerous political and socio-economic units provide many examples of political and social engineering for students of underdeveloped world societies.

My presidential address tonight deals with Africa and its role and position in world history between two ages. The two ages addressed are the ancient/medieval and the modern/contemporary. As a historian, I see ancient African history as going back to the appearance of Homo Sapiens whose origins are now conclusively identified with East Africa. In tracing the historical past of Africa, I do not wish to travel so far back as to link up with those early Homo Sapiens, rather I wish to go only as far back on the world continuum as ancient Egypt to show in time how this magnificent civilization served as the birthplace of many cultural ideas that later travelled in all directions from the Nile Valley.

By entitling this presentation "Africa Between the Ages," I intend to argue that the African peoples of today face a major challenge, in that they are being asked—dare I say demanded—by history to define themselves, and to establish economic and political systems capable of meeting the basic needs of their respective populations. This has been the recurrent theme in African history beginning with ancient Egypt where biblical accounts claim that one Joseph admonished

Pharoah of the impending "seven lean years and the subsequent seven fat years." Coming down to our own age, the Africans of the Sahel and elsewhere are dying of starvation because human institutions have failed to stem the tide of desiccation which historians have traced back some five thousand years.

What the last five thousand years of African history reveals to us is that the continent was the historical (not biblical) Garden of Eden which prepared the diverse races of humankind to embark upon global human civilization. It also has been a place where foreign influences and foreign invaders have assumed historically a great deal of power and influence. As a result of these experiences, it is not surprising to see that throughout African history, the dominant themes generally have been self-identification and the quest for self-development within one's own ecosystem. The proliferation of ethnic languages and groupings on the African continent is unparalleled in human history. No area of the earth has a greater concentration of ethnic groups than Africa. Perhaps one can assert, if only in jest, that this ethnic diversity is a living testimony to the fact that Africa is not only the birthplace of humankind, as Leakey (1971) would affirm,[1] but it is the very site where the biblical Tower of Babel was located. Even if Africa is not the honored locus of such a major biblical event, it remains a fact that Africa is the land out of which ancient Egypt flourished as a primary location for human civilization and habitation.

With this understanding, one can assert that recent scholarly research into ancient Egyptian history has made it abundantly clear that the old notion of separating Egypt and North Africa from the rest of the African continent is both fallacious and untenable.[2] We know that ancient Egypt influenced Kush and Meroe and that many ideas and cultural patterns were borrowed from Egypt and spread to other African locations west, east and south of the Nile. Although we do not know for certain how the influences entered the west and central Sudan, for example, we do understand how specific ideas about divine kingship and social organization became diffused throughout the African continent.[3]

Because of this new scholarship, the former experts on ancient Egypt and their students must now come to terms with Africanists. In effect, they must treat Egypt as the African territory it is and work to link and integrate Egypt's history with that of the rest of the continent. For those of us writing on African affairs, the studies of Fage (1978), Oliver (and Fagan, 1975), Drake (1977), Diop (1955, 1974, 1978), Obenga (1973), Curtin (1964), Ranger (1968), Ogot (1974), and Kimambo (1971), among many others, have made significant contributions to our knowledge of the African past.[4] The scholarship of Africanists has made it glaringly clear that African history cannot be fragmented and treated as independent pieces of cloth with nothing in common. Rather, the evidence indicates that the African past is a thread of unity which links, for example, the Nilotic peoples whose lives were tied to the waterways of the Nile. This linkage provides us now with a significant bridge over which we can commence valuable historical discussions regarding African affairs between the ancient and the contemporary ages.

I

When I say that the two most dominant themes in African history were the attempts toward self-definition and self-development within one's ecosystem, I mean that African peoples generally were affected by alien influences and by questions of subsistence. For many centuries the ancient Egyptians saw themselves as beneficiaries of the Nile and this ecological relationship defined their attitudes toward the cosmos, life, and human society. As a result of the act of self-definition, the Egyptian saw himself as master of a world differentiated from others and inhabited by groups with strange languages, strange cultures, and strange racial origins. This sense of cultural self-sufficiency was later challenged and overthrown by invasions from Asia and Africa. The conquests of Egypt by the Assyrians, the Hyksos, and the Kushites, former colonial subjects of the Egyptian Empire itself, threatened and, in effect, diluted ancient Egyptian identity.[5] This fact of foreign invasion and domination is a recurrent theme in Egyptian history. Indeed, the decline of Egypt as a major power and center of world and African civilization, recognized as supporting the primary needs of its inhabitants, gave rise also to the series of invasions by such external forces as the Phoenicians.

The Phoenician settlement along the north African coast, near present day Tunisia and Libya, was significant on two grounds. First, it gave rise to the colonization of Africa by an alien people whose closer ties to Mediterranean people would affect historians' per-

ceptions of African history. Secondly, the supremacy of these Mediterranean peoples reduced the level of human traffic between Africa north and south of the Sahara. This was very much the case after the desiccation process began more than 5000 years ago.

With the Sahara serving as a wedge between the Berber descendants of Cro-Magnon people and the Sub-Saharan successors of the San-Goan culture, two African histories began to develop. The northern history became an extension of Mediterranean regional history and, since foreign colonists were the major actors in the drama, no attempts were made to bring the two together. Whereas in ancient Egypt, Egyptian history occasionally recorded events involving Egyptian interests in areas south of the empire. In the Phoenician-occupied portion of the continent, history was almost totally the acts of foreigners living on the African side of the Mediterranean (Harden, 1963).

Here, too, we see the question of self-definition emerging as a major theme. It is true that African Berbers resisted the Phoenicians just as fiercely as they later resisted the Arab invaders in the medieval period, but the fact remains that those who lived within the orbit of Phoenician culture were assimilated. Hannibal, the African who tried to use his elephants to bring down Roman hegemony in the African Mediterranean, is a good example of this. For, in his case, we have an assimilated African who identified so strongly with Phoenician culture that he decided to do battle against another imperial power that also was interested in establishing an African empire. Of course, we all know what happened to Hannibal: in the end, Rome conquered and destroyed his home base of Carthage (Bennett, 1975).

Yet, in the story of Carthage, we learn a great deal of the self-definition theme in African history. It should be pointed out that "Africa" itself is a word of Punic origin, meaning corn. Although other interpretations of the word are available,[6] I lean toward the Punic origin. If my assumption is correct, then I can continue to argue that the Phoenicians in their conquest of North Africa and in their use of the term "Africa" set a precedence which was destined to affect the course of African history. The destruction of Carthage by Rome and the retention of the term "Africa" for the conquered territory on the Carthaginian side of the Mediterranean Sea together made North Africa a part of Roman history (Bennett, 1984).

To return to the question of self-definition as a major theme in African history, I would argue further that the Roman occupation of North Africa was destined historically to be significant in the sense that it led to the introduction in 525 B.C. of the Dromedary camel, the Arabian one humped camel,[7] whose ability to travel long distances without food or water made it the ideal beast of burden for carrying people across the Sahara. The camel was an important force, moreover, in "communications between the Nile and the Red Sea" (Obenga, 1981:77). In our quest for historical threads linking African history, Euro-American history, and Middle Eastern history, the camel provides a symbolic thread. The camel made it possible for the Arab or Arabized Muslims to venture much deeper into the Sahara and Sub-Saharan regions than the Romans before them. Thus, in retrospect, we can maintain that the introduction of the camel to the Saharan region helped create two conditions which were destined to affect the course of world history. First, it gave Muslims greater access to the African gold fields and thus granted monopoly of the trade to the Muslim powers in the Mediterranean areas. Secondly, the trade in gold heightened the curiosity and jealousy of European traders who were effectively cut off from the trade across the Sahara and the rich spices of the Orient. Indeed, it was this sense of deprivation and denial of access which led Prince Henry (later called the Navigator) to establish a Maritime Academy dedicated to the study and exploration of the seas (Sanceau, 1969; Boorstein, 1983). As a result of his efforts, Africa, the continent, became known to Europe; and "Africa," the limited northern geographic region known to the Phoenicians, Romans and Arabs, lost its significance among cartographers and scholars.

The Age of Exploration,[8] as students of Portuguese expansion call it, was significant for European and African history on three grounds. It led first to the gradual realization by humankind that the biblical unity of people was now reinforced by the unity of feelings regarding being residents of the same world space. Hence the slogan, "one humanity and one world," which later reverberated in the firmaments of Enlightenment debates and entered the vocabulary of the secular humanists of Europe. At the same time that the Age of Discovery and Exploration ushered in this spirit of human brotherhood, it led also to the greatest tragedy of human history. This was the trade in human cargo and the death of thousands, nay millions, of Africans during the infamous Atlantic Slave Trade.

It is certainly true that slavery existed in Africa long before the Portuguese slavers ferried their cargo in the 1440s. It is also true that Arab slavers preceded Europeans in this diabolical trade in human bodies, but this does not necessarily reduce the magnitude of the crime or the level of human sufferings. Certainly, the slave trade was the historical event that altered both African and American history. When Africans read about the slave trade they wonder in astonishment about what happened to their clansmen whose descendants were dissolved in the vast ocean of human faces and names now called America. When Euro-Americans study the slave trade, they remember the excesses of their ancestors and the divisive nature of slavery in their own society. To their counterparts, the Afro-Americans, the peculiar institution which evolved from the slave trade and its destructive legacies, among others, of "strange fruits hanging on the poplar tree,"[9] raises again the old historical issues of self-definition and self-sufficiency. Once more the effects of foreign intrusions in Africa manifest themselves.

For this and related reasons, therefore, the Afro-American Africanists see in African studies both an intellectual as well as a historic emotional bridge which provides a self-defining link between Africa and the United States. Obviously, this must have been the consideration in the minds of such personalities as H. Sylvester Williams (Mathurin, 1976) and W.E.B. Du Bois (1947) when they embarked upon the idea of Pan Africanism (Esedebe, 1982; Thompson, 1969).

The third significance of the Age of Exploration was that it provided Europe with more room for expansion. The founding of colonies in the Americas and the Caribbean brought millions of Europeans to these respective shores. The comingling and coexistence resulted in the establishment of a new center of civilization. African studies is the result of this experience in America, especially the United States of America. Today, many Africanists are of European ancestry and their contributions add much to a greater understanding of Africa and African peoples. As descendants of immigrants themselves, one expects they can provide the sensitivity to relate to and understand the emotional and intellectual yearnings of peoples struggling to define and assert their identities. In studying Africa, many of these Africanists see much of themselves in their subjects of study for the quest for self-definition and self-sufficiency is a universal phenomenon.

II

After identifying several of the main features of African history in the previous section of this paper, let us now proceed to the elaboration of four issues in African history that form the basis of my discussion of "Africa Between the Ages."

The first issue is the African encounter with Islam; the second is Africa's relationship with Europe; the third issue is Africa's American connection; and the fourth is Africa's contemporary involvement in world affairs.

Africa's encounter with Islam goes back to the beginning of the Islamic Movement under the Prophet

Mohammed. It is now known that many Ethiopians lived in the Arabian Peninsula long before Islam. The history of the Horn of Africa provides enough data to show the cultural, linguistic, and racial ties between the South Arabians and the ancestries of present inhabitants of the Horn. The history of Axum shows the South Arabians coming to the African side of the Red Sea and comingling with the indigenous ethnic groups. Indeed it was these Habasha peoples who established the political system which later provided sanctuary to the Muslim Meccans fleeing from Arabia because of persecution.

Another historical evidence which has implications for the development of Afro-Semitic relations was the presence of Africans (in this case, Ethiopians) in the Arabian Peninsula. Although the history of the Africans and the Semites, particularly the Arabs, has been tumultuous on several occasions in the past, the evidence clearly notes that there were moments when Ethiopia had a significant impact on Arabian society and vice versa. There is reference to the hospitality of the Ethiopian Negus (the Sea King) to the Muslim refugees from Mecca. What needs to be added here is that apart from the living legacies of the Afro-Semitic connections, now symbolized by the variety of languages in the Horn of Africa, and by the large number of Falashas (Ethiopian Jews) who traced their geneological roots back to biblical times, there are historical and linguistic residues of the African past which remind us of the bonds between the peoples of the African continent and the inhabitants of the Semitic world.[10]

The Arabic word *fil* (elephant), experts tell us, is derived from the name of the Ethiopian general who first introduced elephants into the Arabian Peninsula. This campaign against Arabia by an African was repeated later by another Ethiopian called Abraha. Allusion to Abraha's expedition against Mecca is contained in the Quranic chapter entitled "The Companion of the Elephants."[11]

Indeed, from the wider perspective of world history, one could argue that Hannibal and Abraha represent, from a contemporary African point of view, the efforts of Africans to affect the course of European and Mediterranean history on the one hand and Arabian history on the other. Although both Hannibal and Abraha failed in their respective missions, their campaigns dramatize once again Africa's attempt to define itself vis-a-vis alien forces. Their efforts also make it clear to all of us that the African peoples' challenge of self-definition and self-development grew out of the historical legacies of Rome and Arabia. To put it another way, Africa's quest even today is to define itself while maintaining its *lebensraum* (distance or leaving space) between "Rome" and "Arabia."

Of course, not all Africans see their continent in this light. Some are either disillusioned with the work and legacy of the Christianity of Rome and the Islam of Arabia, or are convinced that these two spiritual traditions are irrelevant to the new struggle for existence in contemporary Africa. Those who embrace this position generally are identified as socialists or Marxists, perhaps to reduce or ignore the value of their observations and/or analyses.

Returning to the Islamic theme in African history and its significance in African studies, I should like to note that the Ethiopian connection in the Islamic Movement was one Bilal Ibn Rabah (Rauf, 1974), the Ethiopian slave who was elevated by prophet Muhammad to the position of Muezzin (caller to prayer). But the African presence in Arabia was not limited to Bilal.

Amr Ibn al-As, the conqueror of Egypt, was believed to be of Ethiopian ancestry. If this is true, then with the benefit of hindsight, we can maintain that Africa's encounter with an alien culture produced in Arabia another assimilated descendant of Africa who, like Hannibal, joined the imperial caravan of a rising non-African empire. Indeed, in the case of men like Bilal and Amr Ibn al-As, we find examples of the African who returned to Africa generations after his ancestors to propagate the culture of his new identity (Nyang, 1984:48). This indeed was the universal strength or weakness, some would argue, of the African peoples. Starting with the East and ending in the West (America), African peoples, together with the Jews and Chinese, proved to be men and women willing to allow themselves to be absorbed into alien civilizations. The difference among these three is that while the Chinese and the Jews tended to be cautious in their entanglements, the Africans proved to be assimilationists. This differential approach to alien cultures could be attributed to the nature of the slave trade to the New World and to the manner in which ancient Semites—both Arabic and Hebrew speaking—handled the racial question.

If the common experience of the African in the Semitic World and the African in the New World is that of assimilation, we can argue that this dispersal of the African peoples led to the overlapping of African and Middle Eastern studies. The whole concept of Afro-Arab Studies or, more broadly, Afro-Semitic Studies, illustrates the kind of intellectual challenges students of the African experience face in our times. Indeed, we cannot understand the history and substance of the Pan-African Movement without drawing heavily upon sources now classified as Afro-American and American Studies on the one hand, and Caribbean and African Studies on the other. The triangular relationship between Africa, Europe, and America has spawned more recently new areas of scholarly research which presently are lumped together under Atlantic Studies, Mediterranean Studies, and Lusophone Studies, among what must be others.

The second issue that deserves attention is the African encounter with Europe. References have already been made to the exploration of Prince Henry the Navigator. The Age of Vasco da Gama, as the period after da Gama's successful circumnavigation of the Cape of Good Hope is known, affected African history in several ways as well. First of all, this Age of Discovery launched Europe on a global mission of conquest which brought her peoples much closer to the gold mines of Boure, Bambuk, and other points in Wangara country. Secondly, it led to the gradual termination of the trans-Saharan trade which accounted for the West Sudanic civilizations of Ghana, Mali, and Songhai. Although historians still argue whether or not early European colonization of the West African coast put an end to Arabo-Berber monopoly of the gold trade, the evidence is quite clear that a century after having staked its claims in West Africa, Portugal had only 30% of the gold trade (Duffy, 1963; Rodney, 1965:307–22). This was to change later after other European rivals joined Portugal in the feverish search for African gold.

The third consequence of the Age of Discovery for Africa was the induction of Africa into the international capitalistic system. Between the fifteenth and late eighteenth centuries, African gold became the most precious item on the European list of African export commodities. The passing away of the mercantilistic period ushered in a new development, one which its originators initially were not sufficiently knowledgable to see. The slave trade which had been the most tragic result of Africa's encounter with external cultures and societies came about, in many ways, as a result of certain contradictions in the economic and value systems of Europe.

After displacing their Mediterranean and North African rivals in the contest for access to African gold-mines, the European countries soon found themselves engaged in trade in human cargo. Although historians and others have debated continuously the exact number of African slaves brought to the New World (Rodney, 1974:95),[12] the consensus is that the slave trade wrought havoc in those African communities where large numbers of able-bodied men and women were captured and sold into slavery. There is also a unanimity of view that millions of Africans were lost to this holocaust whose magnitude was taken less than seriously until recent times. Regardless of one's interpretation of this great human tragedy, the evidence is unequivocal in its demonstration that the economic system of trading in slaves served both to destabilize

African societies and to transplant Africa's children in unimaginable numbers to the Americas.

The fourth consequence of the Age of Discovery was the sowing of the seeds of Euro-Western culture in African society. This process of westernization went through two stages, and affected the material, institutional, and value foundations of African cultures. First it took root in the various colonial outposts created by Europeans along Africa's coastline. In these European settlements, the planting of European culture took place and within the span of several centuries a small but growing population of Africans became perfectly, or imperfectly, acculturated to western culture. Many of these Africans were repatriates from the New World, but a significant number were from the African hinterlands. Between those peoples from the hinterland who were attracted by European culture and those who came back from the New World a new culture took shape.

This Euro-African phenomenon was most evident in the chain of settlements which dotted the African coastline. Starting from Senegambia, where the French established Goree and St. Louis, and the British founded Fort James and Bathurst (Banjul), one finds these European settlements, among others, in Sierra Leone, Liberia, Ghana, and Nigeria. Sierra Leone and Liberia are particularly significant because their respective capitals are direct results of European involvement in both the slave trade and in the colonization of African territories.[13] Liberia's Monrovia was the principal settlement chosen by the leader of the American Colonization Society for the repatriation of American based and recruited blacks.[14]

These developments had significant implications for African identity and for the identity of peoples of African descent. Indeed, these historical events once again raised the recurring theme in African history—the quest for self-identity and self-development. To the students of American and African history, this period was critical in the sense that the identity question featured prominently in the debates of Afro-American intellectuals, among others. Long before the end of slavery in America, many blacks had raised the issue: who are we? Are we Americans or Africans? Frederick Douglass, the prominent abolitionist, sought to resolve the issue once and for all. In a now famous statement, Douglass told Americans, black and white, that Afro-Americans are Americans, although descendants of Africa (cf. 1962:513). While Douglass raised the standard for Americanism, other contemporaries of his such as Martin R. Delany (1852, 1969) and Bishop Henry McNeal Turner (M. Cummings, 1972) championed their own back-to-Africa movements. With the benefit of hindsight, we now can assert that Douglass won the debate and the Civil Rights Movement led by Martin Luther King, Jr. in the 1960s reaffirmed his position.

This question of identity featured also in the early debates in West Africa where in both Sierra Leone and Liberia returnees and recaptives from the New World faced the question of readjustment to African societies (Shick, 1980; West, 1970). From the limited numbers of studies on the Creoles of West Africa and on the Americo-Liberians, we now know the forces and factors that affected the social dynamics of their identity building. In retrospect, we can say that the encounter between Africa and the New World not only resulted in the transplantation of millions of Africans to the Americas and the Caribbeans, but it also led to the assimilation of a sizable number of Africans whose traditional African culture was altered by their decisions to settle in the colonial enclaves along the West African coast.

If the encounter with the West gave rise to a breed of Africans who were perfectly, or imperfectly, acculturated to western culture, the encounter with the Semitic World, namely the Arab World, gave rise to different experiences. In East Africa, where foreigners began to deal with Africans much earlier, the cumulative effect was felt most clearly in the string of city states along the coast. Kilwa, Mombasa, Malindi, Dar es Salaam, and Pemba are living testimonies of the results of Africa's encounter with Arabia. Indeed, this encounter created Afro-Arabs by blood and to a limited degree by culture and language. Afro-Arab culture also penetrated deeply into the East African hinterland through the medium of Swahili. Speaking comparatively, one can argue that although Creole (or Pidgin English) is spoken widely by many West Africans, it is not on a par with Swahili, a language that is guaranteed a place among African languages by its rich literary heritage and by its numerous speakers in East and Central Africa specifically, and beyond.

To return to the European encounter with Africa, let me state that Africa was negatively affected by Europe, although in fairness to Europe, one must acknowledge the contributions of European civilization to African life and society. It is true that Europe brought slavery and colonialism to Africa along with other accoutrements. Of these the alphabet, medicine, and modern technology were the most significant. The alphabet revolutionized the world including Africa, and especially those parts of the continent where the Arabic script had not reached during the pre-colonial era. One cannot talk about the introduction of the alphabet without saying something about its peddlers. The role of the missionary in African society is well documented[15] and is noted briefly below.

What we can emphasize is that, in spite of the excesses attributed to it, Europe made some contributions to the development, for example, of literacy in many parts of Africa. Evidence for this claim can be gleaned from official statistics on African students studying in schools and colleges around the continent. Most significantly, Europe affected Africa both through the alphabet and through the various European languages adopted by the African leaders at the time of political independence.

As a result of the African decision to keep European languages, Africans are now tied to the language communities of Europe. Indeed, Africa is the only geographical area whose people have decided to conduct official national and international business in adopted languages. Of course, there have been numerous debates over the relevance and appropriateness of adopting a foreign language. Regardless of one's position on the matter, the current state of research seems to arrive at several conclusions.

First, many studies have pointed out (a) that language choice in present-day Africa was determined by colonialism; (b) that African elites have a vested interest in maintaining the status quo in this area; (c) that African languages would need to be officially and intellectually stimulated to make them viable and effective media of communication; and (d) that Africa's ethnic diversity mitigates against the imposition of a single language in a heterogeneous society.[16] Most significantly, we learn that except for Ethiopia, Somalia, Kenya, and Tanzania, none of the African states outside the Arabic-speaking areas ventured toward the adoption of an African language. This problem of language, which is part of the baggage unloaded in Africa from the European train of colonialism, is bound to affect Africa for a long time to come. African intellectuals are badly divided on this issue.

Former President Leopold S. Senghor of Senegal resisted throughout his presidency the calls from Senegalese nationalists that Wolof be adopted as the official language of this West African state. Instead of pursuing an Africanization policy, President Senghor decided to embrace and popularize the French language. His Negritude notwithstanding, President Senghor felt that the French language was an important and useful tool which the African Personality could employ in the service of African civilization. Committed to realizing the universal civilization, and seriously convinced that the African has a mission to make a significant international contribution, President Senghor identified and idealized the French language as an anvil upon which to forge African contributions to the world community.

It is well known that Senghor's position was opposed by other Senegalese such as Cheikh Anta Diop, whose researches into early African history led him to conclude that Africans should take pride in the achievements of ancient Egypt in the same way that westerners take pride in the achievements of Greece and Rome (both of which, of course, are linked historically to Africa's Egypt). Diop's argument for the adoption of Wolof as the official language of Senegal follows logically from his cultural nationalist conclusions. To strengthen his claim, this Senegalese scholar translated Einstein's theory of relativity and several portions of western literary texts into Wolof.[17]

If Diop is the cultural nationalist who sees the need for Wolof to serve as a national language, Ousmane Sembene is the Senegalese intellectual and writer who has tried to advance the course of indigenous national language through the use of the cinema or film. His outstanding films certainly raised the relevance of local languages in the modernization of Africa. Sembene and his fellow Senegalese cultural nationalists tried to raise the language question in their now defunct publication, CADU. Written in Wolof, this publication was designed to disseminate information on national affairs and to sensitize the Senegalese to the need for cultural autonomy.

Although the language question has not been resolved in favor of Wolof in Senegal, the debates in that country have certainly made it clear to many Senegalese that while French is an important medium of communication in the international community, the Senegalese identity would be greatly affected if the authorities do not respond to the need for indigenization at some levels. The Senghor administration addressed this issue through the creation of an Institute for the Study of Local Languages.

In reviewing the positive and negative sides of the Senghorian era in Senegal, it is not unfair to note that Senghor's personal and emotional involvement with the French language affected his decision, for example, to adopt and push forward vigorously the Wolof language. Although his international political strategy drove him to bridge the Muslim-Christian divide across the Sahara through the construction of the edifice of Francophonie, there is some evidence that the former President did not neglect totally the idea of developing the local languages. Today, as a result of Senghor's policy, Wolof and several Senegalese vernacular languages are alphabetized. Wolof, moreover, is taught to the national community via television.

Huge and multilingual in the typical African sense, Nigeria is the English-speaking African counterpart to Senegal. The evidence from Nigeria seems to support the conclusion that a national language other than English was never seriously considered or supported by major political parties. The linguistic conclusions identified earlier in this address alluded to the political difficulties which have mitigated against the adoption of an African language in Africa, south of the Sahara.

In Nigeria, the most widely publicized suggestion for a national language was made by Soyinka, who asked his fellow countrymen to consider the adoption of Swahili as the national Nigerian language. Soyinka's idea was not favorably received, to put it mildly, and some members of the Nigerian press dismissed the suggestion off-handedly as part of the outpourings of a non-conformist Nigerian. While Soyinka suggested Swahili as a possibility, Chinua Achebe finds European languages necessary evils for communication with the wider world. Achebe feels that the African choice is limited and Africans might as well content themselves with literature written in English or other European languages.

On this question of language, there is once again the recurring theme of self-definition. Leopold Senghor and Chinua Achebe conclude that while the politics of Africa can be decolonized, the language question cannot be sufficiently decolonized because of certain practical realities peculiar to the African scene. This debate will continue. Yet, one of the areas of agreement, that is to say silent agreement, between the radical and more conservative elements in Africa is the elevation of the language question to the status of a sacred cow.

The American connection is the third issue that deserves attention. Earlier I spoke about the triangular relationship between Africa, Europe, and America. Now, let us see how Africa's American connection manifested itself in history. The slave trade came to North America in the early 17th century but its beginnings date back to South America in the 16th century. Africanists studying the Lusophone World are very much aware of the Brazilian connection in the African slave trade. In fact, in Brazil we witness the uneasy co-existence of the legacies of Ancient Africa, Arabia, and Europe. From the old Africa were the various traditional religions whose presence is felt in a significant portion of Brazilian life and culture today. This is particularly true in Bahia where persons of African descent are more numerous (Herskovits, 1958).[18]

That the slave trade affected the course of African history is undoubted. What is not widely noted is that the African, even in these times of terrible dehumanization and humiliation, affected the emerging colonial society in the New World. Brazil, unlike the United States, was more affected by Africans, but if Brazil was affected (both biologically and culturally), North America was destined instead to evolve differently from the rest of the

West primarily because of the presence of the large number of Afro-Americans.

Traditional Africa, which was the source of most of the slaves that entered the New World, passed on to the future residents of these emerging societies many contributions. Some of these cultural retentions are more evident than others, and some areas of the New World are more affected by them than the others. This issue was hotly disputed between the advocates of African retentions and the opponents of such retentions. Melville Herskovits and E. Franklin Frazier are recognized as the major contenders in this debate—the former supported and the latter opposed the claims for African retentions in North America (Herskovits, 1941; Frazier, 1957). Regardless of which side one takes in the Herskovits/Frazier Debate,[19] the fact remains that in the New World Africans had a tremendous impact upon the physical population and the cultural systems developed in the region. Today, the African presence is evident from certain parts of Argentina to Newfoundland in Canada. Between these two points lies a vast mosaic of peoples reflecting the diversity that has resulted from the triangular relationship between the Africans, the Europeans, and the old (Indian populations) and new Americans during the past four hundred or more years.

If traditional Africa was the source of slaves, there is also evidence that many of those who came to the New World were identified with Islam and Muslim culture. In fact, one intellectual bridge connecting some Middle Eastern historians and Africanists interested in certain aspects of New World history, was the Islamic connection of some of these slaves. Brazilian scholars such as Roger Bastide (1967, 1978) and Nina Rodrigues (1932) have studied the Muslims in Brazilian civilization. Their findings seem to lend more support to our theme of the African quest for self-definition and self-development over the historic past.

These Lusophone scholars teach us that the triangular relationship between Africa, Europe, and America led to the importation of a minority of Muslim slaves whose limited numbers did not deter them from leading conspiracies and rebellious revolts in Brazil. As a matter of fact, one can argue that the eruption of what Brazilian historians described as the Male (ma-lay) rebellion was an American reverberation of the confrontations and conflicts between Europe and Islam in Africa. It should be borne in mind also that at the very moment that the Muslims (Male) were up in arms against the Portuguese colonists in Brazil, their co-religionists elsewhere in Africa and beyond were fighting to stem the tide of European hegemony. As history would have it, the Male were defeated and today, thanks to the efforts of Brazilian scholars like Gilberto Freyre[20] and French scholars

like Vincent Montel, we know much more about this obscure segment of African slaves who landed in the New World. If Brazilian slaves were able to hold onto their African religions, borrowed or home-grown, the historical evidence for North America provides striking contrast to the Brazilian experience.

In the original thirteen colonies, the slave masters denied slaves the opportunity to develop structures necessary for cultural continuity. As a result, Africans in the United States had little choice but to adopt the culture, language, and religion of the slave master. This was the legacy of the slave system in North America and today this society has within its borders a large number of persons of African descent, whose identity is defined by the biological legacy of Africa, and by the intellectual and political legacies of the founding fathers of this North American Republic.

As a result, I am arguing that the presence of the Afro-American in the United States was, until recently, the single most important factor that differentiated American civilization from European civilization. Although Europe and even Australia and Canada are now becoming Americanized in the sense of becoming more racially pluralistic, the truth is that the experience in the United States is still unique in terms of the history of Africans on this continent and the role they have played in this particular society. Indeed, Africanists from the U.S. will always labor under the shadow of the African past found within their own national boundaries. Realizing this, our researches would better enrich our understanding of Africans and their continent and eliminate some of the assumptions and myths we have unconsciously acquired in the formative years of our respective intellectual training.

Another aspect of the African encounter with America is the heritage of Afro-Americans. Reading through the writings of some American and African musicologists, one comes across strong arguments for African influences in certain aspects of American music (cf. Nketia, 1973:7–15). These arguments are made particularly for Jazz and Blues, although some musicologists may go even farther. Even if one does not share the extreme position among the historians of Afro-American and American music, there is no denying the fact that one of Africa's links with America, and in the special case of Afro-America, is music, among others. As Africanists writing in this period of African-American historical encounters, we have the responsibility to conduct serious studies on the continuities and discontinuities of African culture in the New World. In this regard, Africanists may have to collaborate more closely with American culture historians and other specialists in the same fields from Latin America.

III

After having sought to examine the Islamic, European, and American connections with Africa, let us discuss Africa's contemporary involvement in World Affairs.

If we take the Berlin Conference as the historical point of departure, we can identify three major phases in the recent history of Africa. The first phase was the conclusion of the chapter which began with the Portuguese explorations of the African continent and gradual expansion of the European sphere of influence. The second phase begins with the formal colonization of all Africa by Europe and the effective induction of all African peripheral areas into the expanding global capitalistic system. The third phase was the Second World War and the weakening of Europe by the Nazi bid for power in this region of the world.

The first phase was significant for African and world history because it ushered into Africa five processes which were destined to affect the identity and place of Africa in our age. These processes, namely, are the:

1. balkanization of Africa;
2. westernization of Africa's elites;
3. planting of Christianity;
4. monetization of African economies; and the
5. incorporation of all African peoples in world history.

This last process, which is now very advanced within African intellectual circles, has led to the transplantation of foreign ideologies and the attendant conflicts.

The balkanization process (deBenoist, 1979; Lucas, 1970), which African historians usually describe as the partitioning process, gave rise to a British African Empire, a French African Empire, a German African Empire, a Portuguese African Empire, an Italian African Empire, and a Spanish African Empire. Although these European Powers were of different strengths and exercised jurisdiction over unequal territories, the Africa of 1985 is very much a result of this particular process.

From the history of colonial Africa, we learned a great deal about Africans and Europeans. We learned about the resistance to colonial rule, and about the efforts of European colonial governments to affect social and political changes with very limited resources and personnel. But the data from colonial history that address our main argument are those which relate to the identity questions for Africans. As a direct result of the African encounters with Europe and, indeed, as a result of the African's reluctance to accept colonial administration, Africa is today divided into more than fifty states. These territories were colonial fiefs and so served colonial interests from the time they were created until the end of the colonial era. The legacy of the individual colonial empires has been addressed by a number of scholarly studies written by individuals within our own African Studies Association.

Although the partition of Africa has affected Africa's identity and role in the international system, the system of administration and the kinds of policies that emerged out of that history drastically changed the power relationship between African groups in the post-colonial period. The might of power, we can argue retrospectively, was the anvil that forged the personalities of the variegated states we identify with modern Africa. This was evident in the different forms of administration set up by the different European powers. The indirect rule policy of Britain, which is now called Lugardian, certainly conserved the old traditions of Africa while laying the foundations for the gradual if not rapid colonization and Anglicization of the land and peoples. This willingness to allow the uneasy co-existence between the old pre-colonial African traditions on the one hand, and the Islamic or western Christian elements on the other, paved the way for the development of what Kwame Nkrumah (1964) identified as the three strands of African thought, viz., the traditional African, the Arabo-Islamic, and the Euro-western Christian. If British indirect rule helped create the necessary conditions for the emergence of Nkrumah's three strands of African thought, French and Portuguese colonialism drove the African intellectuals to another position. Because these two colonial powers were bent on promoting their civilization in an open, direct, and enthusiastic way, Africans were told that being French or Portuguese was more "civilized" and rewarding than being totally immersed in the traditional African culture. This attitude toward things African in both French and Portuguese Africa led to the emergence of two African intellectual forums of resistance: Negritude and armed socialism.

In the case of the former, its advocates were highly assimilated blacks, Africans, and West Indians, who saw in total assimilation the negation of their being. Leopold Senghor (1946, 1964), Leon Damas (1934, 1956, 1972; Racine, 1982:94–105), and Aime Cesaire (1955, 1959; Frutkin, 1973) championed this intellectual position and their efforts affected the content and the direction of the discourse between blacks and whites in the French civilization.[21]

If the creations of European empires unified ethnic groups and territories that were separate and distinct in the pre-colonial period, their successful consolidation during the colonial era helped create new, and sometimes alien, identities among Africans. In addition to the pre-colonial ethnic identities, colonialism also has created an embryonic territorial nationalism and a continental fellowship among speakers of a borrowed European tongue.

(The Africanists from America should recognize these new realities and study them not only with sympathy and understanding, but with objectivity. While doing that, however, we must remember that what distinguishes American political history from African political history is that, whereas America and Africa were field objects of European expansionism in the Age of Discovery, it was in America that Europe reproduced itself through colonization. This significant distinction has affected America's images of Africa and Africa's images of America. Although the two geographical regions have different historical experiences, there are areas where Africanists with American backgrounds can use their own history to understand African society and history to the benefit of both. There is a history of success in many areas in this regard. The history of the Pan-African Movement, as I pointed out above, can be better understood itself through an effective synthesis of American and African history.)

The second process which orginated from the first phase in the European encounter with Africa is the westernization of Africa's elites. The establishment of colonial settlements along the African coast was the beginning of westernization. Through such settlements the Europeans and later others were able to penetrate African culture and society. The first group of persons to be inducted into this gradually expanding Western cultural universe were often times the "socially inferior"—Africans who had virtually no standing in their society. These persons were attracted to the European settlements for a variety of reasons. Some were runaway slaves; some were sold as slaves themselves to European masters; still others were adventurers who had committed some crime or offense against their old society and wanted to start a new life under European protection.

Regardless of the social origins of these people, it is quite clear that they were the first fruits of western education. Many became cultural brokers between their societies and the foreigners living in their midst. In this new role, they linked the foreign culture to the local; they actually became the purveyors and peddlers of western goods, ideas, and tastes among their African contemporaries. As a result, Africa gradually became a continent receptive to European culture through these persons, themselves once societal outcasts who clearly benefitted from their associations with the new arrivals.

It is against this background that one can discuss the role of the missionary in the propagation of western ideas and values in Africa. Although it is true that one cannot make sweeping generalizations about Africa,

the fact remains that the westernization of Africa's elites began with the importation and purchase of luxury items by traditional African chiefs and became more diversified and popularized through the missionary schools. Whereas in the Sahelian zone, the trans-Saharan trade affected primarily the material base of traditional culture, in the centuries after the Age of Discovery the process of westernization altered, as noted earlier, the institutional, value, and material bases of African society.

The coming of the missionaries did not affect the material base of African societies. Rather it was the mental or psychological world of the African that the missionary gradually affected through the use of the Roman alphabet to promote their gospels. By teaching the alphabet and the contents of the gospels, the missionary exposed the African to a new world-view. The African's acceptance of this world-view was the beginning of his westernization. Soon his mental estate became the gallery for the display and celebration of western images. Moreover, his conscience became the theater wherein traditional African values complemented or competed against western religious values.

Among the first generation of westernized Africans were so-called "mission boys and girls" who were weaned away from African cultures by the successful religious teachings of western Christians. Included in this first generation were also Africans who returned to Africa during and after the Slave Trade. As a result of the successes of these men and women, the number of westernized Africans began to increase. Two developments were responsible for the speed and direction of westernization.

The first was the expansion of full scale trade and commerce into the interior of Africa; and the second was the colonial policy of recruiting Africans into the embryonic civil service. The first development led to the employment of many partially westernized Africans to serve as middle-men in the trade between the European merchants on the African coast and the Africans in the interior. This relationship varied from place to place. In some areas it was a transaction which embraced an ethnically diverse group. In others it was the monopoly of a particular group.

The second development, which is inextricably linked to the geo-strategic and geo-political calculations of European empire builders, resulted in the pursuit of different educational policies by the different colonial powers. In French-speaking Africa, the republican spirit helped to limit the greater participation of French religious groups in the field of education. As a result, many Africans were educated under French patronage without too much exposure to Christian teachings. The pattern was somewhat different in British Africa where the indirect rule system and the toleration of missionary activities in unrestricted areas opened the door for the Christianization of African education. Even if one concedes this difference between French policy and British policy, up to the beginning of the Second World War, missionaries organized and operated most of the African schools.

This new trend in the westernization of African education later gave rise to the present generation of African leaders. This group had two advantages over those preceeding them. First, they went to schools that were better structured and organized. Second, they went beyond the steady diet of missionary instruction, which in the early days of colonialism was heavily laden with Biblical knowledge. While we acknowledge the presence of the Christian missionary factor in the education of these peoples, let us not forget that it was this colonial educational system which opened the flood gates of African nationalism. Yet, the African nationalist and the western missionary grew out of a similar historical experience in Africa. The main difference between the two is their respective attitudes toward the colonial period. Indeed, the missionary, who was the emerging symbol of Christian fellowship, was the one who brought into being the African nationalist.

Here we see the fruits of transnational encounters. Through their schools, missionaries successfully captured the fancy and imagination of Africans, and as a result of this development, the basis for African nationalism was laid.

Thus, in recounting the evolution of colonial rule in Africa and its effects on the westernization of African peoples, one must point to the manner in which the balkanization of Africa tied rather directly into the processes of westernization, Christianization, and monetization. All of these processes, as noted by the dependency scholars,[22] for example, set the stage for the incorporation of all Africa into world history. This is to say that whereas in pre-colonial Africa only certain geographic areas and peoples of Africa participated in world affairs ("world history" being what it was/is at that time), in the modern period the entire continent and all of its peoples are somehow participating in this new experience called world history.

Indeed, Africa is now in the heart of this world history. Africa may not be a superpower in world affairs, but it is attractive enough in the political power struggle to be a major bone of contention between world powers and world ideologies. In noting these realities of the African condition, we must hasten to stress the great need for Americans and others to respect Africa's right to define itself and its socio-economic and political priorities. Yet in our desires to respect, we must not abdicate our responsibility to

help Africa and its peoples in their search for self-development in the political, economic, cultural, and social domains of societal life.

IV

It is against this history that we look at the last but not the least important factor in this discussion. This factor is economic development and priority identification for and by Africans.

"The complaint of the poor nations against the present [international economic] system is not only that we are poor both in absolute terms and in comparison with the rich nations," noted President Julius Nyerere of Tanzania. "It is also that within the existing structure of economic interaction we must remain poor, and get relatively poorer, whatever we do" (1977:9). This fact of poverty for Tanzania and other African nations does not evolve exclusively from their actions or lack thereof.

The present international economic and legal structure developed gradually out of the interaction between the different nations of Europe, and then the United States and the British Dominions. Their cultures were basically similar, and their knowledge and access to it were primarily similar. Even so, President Nyerere observed, "there were great economic conflicts, and even wars, before the evolution of those conventions, institutions, and practices which are now regarded as the normal, and even natural, rules and mechanisms of international exchange." The underdeveloped world, however, was not a party to either the early efforts or the later ones at Bretton Woods in 1945 to establish rules of international trade. They were either colonies of one or the other major powers, or were so weak or so far away from the mainstream of economic intercourse that they could be (and were) totally ignored.

The free market philosophy or theory of trade inherited at independence continues to bear little relation to fact. Equality between nations of the twentieth century is only a legal equality. It is not an economic reality. Even though the Bretton Woods/General Agreement for Trade and Tariffs rules of international trade, to my mind, are simply obsolete in today's world, there is not much hope for change in the near future. Africa has found no truth in the economic theory that prices are determined by the operations of a free market, that is, by discussion and compromise between sellers and buyers. Rather, they have found that prices of primary products are fixed by the purchasers. Their so-called comparative advantages have been of little consequence since their need to import manufactured goods is so great. They are de facto price-takers, not price-makers, both as seller and buyer. They sell cheap and buy dear, regardless.

> The international financial system is regulated by the I.M.F. and the World Bank, helped or hindered by unilateral actions of major powers like the U.S.A., E.E.C., Japan and a few other developed nations. Given that voting power in the Governing Bodies of the I.M.F. and the World Bank is determined by the proportion of the capital contributed by different nations, the results are perhaps inevitable. The richer you are, and the more you trade in the world, the greater the support you can get in times of crisis, and the greater will be your allocation of international credit when Special Drawing Rights are created (Nyerere, 1977:8).

It is the low international purchasing power of the underdeveloped nations which is a major factor in keeping poor nations locked in their poverty. It is a fact that success breeds success and riches breed riches. Poverty also breeds poverty. Nyerere (1977:16) concluded:

> The present economic order governing international production, development, and exchange does not in practice ensure progress towards meeting those basic needs for all people, all over the world. The plea of the poor is a New International Economic Order 'which embraces for its objective the happiness of mankind.'

It was out of this concern that Africans finally raised these questions for themselves: Is there a correct path for Africa's economic development? What kind of development does Africa need? What kind of African should Africa begin to mold for the future? These questions reached a new peak during the early 1980s when they became crystallized around two documents, the *Lagos Plan of Action for the Economic Development of Africa, 1980–2000* (O.A.U., 1981) and *Accelerated Development in Sub-Saharan Africa: an Agenda for Action* (World Bank, 1981). Each purported to identify a proper path for Africa's development future.[23] *Lagos Plan of Action* (LPA) is a genuinely historic document because it represents the first continental-wide attempt by Africans themselves to create a comprehensive unified approach to the economic development of their continent.

While there are a number of problems with the document as a planning device, it does outline, however ambiguously, a set of priorities, with self-sufficiency in food as the first. It stresses the need for Africa to strive actively to reduce its dependency on external nations and replace this dependence with a self-sustaining development strategy based on the maximum internal employment of the continent's natural and related resources. This is known now as a "self-reliant" strategy of development and it is becoming the over-arching theme for Africa for the balance of this century—and well it should.

The LPA calls for an Africa which relies primarily on its own technical skills and not on those of foreigners, and an Africa which develops an industrial base and consumption patterns suitable to African needs and customs rather than to adopt blindly models from abroad. This Plan rails against the historic export-led development model of the World Bank, arguing for regional and sub-regional commercial-trade groupings which will gradually expand into continental efforts and eventually evolve into an African Common Market and later an Economic Community of Africa. In short, this multi-sectoral plan of action calls for a restructuring of the continent's economic base and the transformation of social and economic systems, many of them inherited from the colonial past, as a means of promoting integrated and self-reliant development. This planning approach advances a different vision of economic development strategy and priorities for Africa from that of the "Berg Report."[24]

Over the short term, it will be necessary to maintain close associations with the World Bank and other international donors and therefore to continue to follow the export-oriented economic model. This is done, however, with a sense of the need to acquire the financial support necessary to develop sufficient infrastructure and skilled manpower for the long term.

> Sub-regional groupings to help facilitate intra-African trade are now evolving, but their potentials cannot reach full fruition until national policies, production capacities and trade structures are adapted accordingly (Economic Commission for Africa, 1985:20).

The Food and Agricultural Organization (FAO) developed a set of indices for monitoring trends in the achievement of targets and objectives for African countries via the LPA. The indices cover population, gross domestic product, land use, domestic agricultural production, domestic food production, agriculture imports/exports, food imports/exports, fish catches and landings and forestry production and exploitation. In addition to these, methodologies have been formulated by the FAO to measure post-harvest food losses, food security levels and improved agricultural practices, forestry management, research extension service levels, and agricultural services resources. Some governments in the region are said to be developing these systems, but this is an area where technical and financial assistance may be required to enhance the effectiveness of such monitoring and to wed it with other information needs (Economic Commission for Africa, 1985:21).

Famine, drought, and desertification emergencies in much of Africa have forced many national governments to direct their attention to activities and programs which bear quick results/relief. However, the severity of the food and agricultural problems facing the region demands that the continent place more direct emphasis on long-term strategies which address not only Africa's current food needs, for example, but also prepare for sustained increases in production of food and raw materials. Research, development, and the introduction of technologies and institutions adapted to African conditions must be considered as high-priority measures which merit considerable human and financial investments.

Africanists must join together to assist in providing the human capital necessary to assure the success of the larger development plan. Our help is a necessity, although solutions to Africa's development problems must be found internally and articulated by Africans themselves.

At this time, the LPA targets for most of Africa have remained largely elusive. The production levels for crops, livestock, fishery, and forestry as set out in the LPA are far from being achieved. No significant progress has been made toward reduction of food losses. Food insecurity has worsened and the establishment of foundations for food self-sufficiency is yet to be achieved. Current economic policies continue to owe their origins to the past and, therefore, have not changed much, if at all. As a consequence, institutions, infrastructure, and investment patterns continue to follow past historic and colonial legacies. In addition to the non-realization of the LPA targets, several internal and external factors, primarily structural in nature, have played havoc with the implementation efforts (Economic Commission for Africa, 1985:25).

Internally, development strategies of the 1960s and 1970s gave the agricultural sector a lower-priority ranking in African economies than industry and services. Those strategies have created structural problems, including infrastructure which is not attuned to domestic food needs. Transport, communication, storage, marketing and input-supply systems are inadequate to serve the majority of farmers in Africa, especially small farmers in distant locations. Trained manpower to provide important agricultural services is in short supply.

A second internal factor is that of African leadership and its acquisition of the political will necessary to break with past developmental strategies to give agriculture the highest ranking among the respective sectors in a sustained manner. Drought and population growth rates ranks as further internal factors.

Several external factors in this connection include sharp declines in terms of trade, extraordinary shortages in foreign exchanges or revenues, severe import restrictions which have affected the importation of capital goods, and the tendency for Africa's exports, which are predominantly agricultural commodities, to face a low annual rate of growth in the international market. Yet, imports to African economies have been characterized, at the same time, by rapid annual rates of growth. High debt-servicing costs together with these developments have resulted in large negative balances. This structural problem in turn causes adverse terms of trade between dependent and underdeveloped African nations and the overdeveloped countries with which they trade. In short, as Julius Nyerere (1977:7) wrote, "The poor nations of the world remain poor because they are poor, and because they [are forced to] operate as if they were equals in a world dominated by the rich."

While I have tended to mention only Africanists in this context, the Middle Eastern scholars and researchers are not to be left out. Indeed, if the Sudan, among others, can be made to produce food, for example, sufficient to become the bread basket of the region, as many believe it can, then the Middle East too will benefit. There is, in short, a task, a responsibility, for us all. Let us get on with it before it is too late.

Notes

1. Thanks to the potassium-argon isotope chronological dating method, "the birth of East African man [sic] (the oldest of all according to the present state of our knowledge) is actually the birth of [humankind] as a whole . . ." (Obenga, 1981:73).

2. The United States Department of State made this initial geographical division/distinction primarily for administrative reasons. This now, however, has become general practice by foreign policy makers around the globe.

3. For this aspect of the relationship between Egypt and other parts of Africa, see Murphy (1972) and Mokhtar (1981).

4. See also Fage and Oliver (1970), Shinnie (1971), Harris (1982), and Williams (1974).

5. For a concise discussion of ancient Egypt and its neighbors, see Hayes (1965).

6. Some scholars have identified the term *Africa* with the Berber group called "Ifriqi."

7. Indeed, the dromedary was no latecomer to Africa according to the Chad Sahara rock painting which dates from the Third Century B.C. (Obenga, 1981:77).

8. See, for example, such works as Oliver (1965), Fagan (1984), Tholfsen (1984), Cobban (1960), Previte-Orton (1951), Waugh (1980), Folz (1980), Niane (1982), Mauro (1967), Clapham (1941), and Wolf (1982).

9. As performed by Nina Simone (Phillips Records, 1965):

> Southern trees bearing strange fruits,
>   Blood on the leaves and blood at the roots.
> Black bodies swinging in the southern breeze—
>   Strange fruits hanging from the poplar trees.
>
> Pastoral scenes of the gallant south—
>   them big bulging eyes and the twisted mouth.
> Scent of magnolia, clean and fresh;
>   then the sudden smell of burning flesh.
>
> Here is a fruit for the crows to pluck,
>   for the rain to gather, for the wind to suck,
> for the sun to rot, for the leaves to drop.
>   Here is a strange, and bitter, crop.

10. Cheik Anta Diop (1974:123–24) argues forcefully that the earliest inhabitants of Arabia were racially "Negro" and that they were invaded later by a coarse Jectanide people who gradually became assimilated into Black life and culture:

> These facts, on which even Arab authors agree, prove . . . that the Arab race cannot be conceived as anything but a mixture of Blacks and Whites, a process continuing even today. These same facts also prove that traits common to Black culture and Semitic [Muslim and Jewish] culture have been borrowed from the Blacks.

The relationship between the peoples of East Africa and the Arabs/Muslims of the East are described in Chittick (1965:275–94), de Graft-Johnson (1957), Casely-Hayford (1969), and Mazrui (1978:19–36).

11. Abraha's name, in fact, is not mentioned in the Holy Qur'an although Islamic commentators make direct references to this Ethiopian general as if it were.

12. For a review of the debate, cf. especially Du Bois (1970), Curtin (1969), and Inikori (1982:13–60; 1976:17/2:197–223 and 17/4:595–627).

13. Research data available on this development include Shick (1980), Fyfe (1979), Kup (1961), West (1970), Azikiwe (1970), Alexander (1969), and Blyden (1978).

14. Note the attitudes generated by American Colonization Society's activities among Afro-American and other leaders in Delany (1852, 1969), Rollin (1883:313–27), Douglass (1962), Billington (1953:12–19), M. Cummings (1972), Redkey (1969), Fisher (1922), and Mehlinger (1916). The conflicting debate notwithstanding, some outstanding personalities who supported colonization included Alexander Crummell, Daniel A. Payne, Lott Cary, and Colin Teague. However, Cary, for example, refused to have anything to do with the ACS, seeking instead to work with the African settlers and expecting to extend Christianity into Africa.

15. See, among others, Oliver (1952), Jacobs (1982), Christy (1854), Livingstone (1971), Berman (1975), Ayandele (1967), and Ajayi (1971).

16. See Senghor (1959, 1964); and Sembene (1962) and his films: Tauw (1970), Emitai (1971), Xala (1974), and Ceddo (1978); Mafeje (1967:193), Ngugi (1981), Amin (1973, 1977), Burness (1977), Williams (1976), and Chezan (1978:15–38).

17. For comparable East African examples, see Julius Nyerere's translation of Shakespeare and the Kikuyu language play of Ngugi wa Thiong'o. See also the "Appendix" in Ngugi (1972) for an East African initiative on the issue of language: The fundamental debate questioned the assumption that the English tradition and the emergence of the modern west was/is somehow the central root of African consciousness and cultural heritage. In their response, "On the Abolition of the English Department" at the University of Nairobi, Kenyan professors rejected the primacy of English literature, language, and culture.

18. Additional references are Bastide (1974:111–23), Ramos (1934), Kent (1965:169–75), J. Rodriques (1962, 1968), van den Berghe (1967), and Pierson (1942).

19. Cf. Ofuatey-Kodjoe (1977), Turner (1949), Skinner (1972), and Wright (1954).

20. Gilberto Freyre (1946) is known also to have assisted the popularization of the historical interpretation (similar to that of U.B. Phillips) that the black historical experience is "defined by certain pervasive European cultural impulses and institutional mechanisms" and, therefore, is nothing more than "a function of some white-oriented external character." See Uya (1982:75).

21. On the question of black self-negation via assimilation, see Fanon (1967).

22. The "dependency" reference here is used only as a form of shorthand to identify a group of prolific theoreticians, such as Samir Amin (1977), Walter Rodney (1972), Paul Baran (1957), Argihiri Emmanuel (1972), Immanuel Wallerstein (1979), and Andre Gunder Frank (1978).

23. The World Bank (1984) sought to distance itself somewhat from the original Berg Report (which seems to have ignored completely the LPA). The World Bank document is more moderate and flexible in its approach to African development and recognizes the need for a long-term strategy and Africans' right to speak for themselves.

24. See Browne and Cummings (1985) for an accurate summary and comparative analysis of these two documents.

References

Alexander, Archibald. 1969. *A History of Colonization on the Western Coast of Africa*. Connecticut: Negro Universities Press.

Ajayi, J. Ade. 1971. *Christian Missions in Nigeria, 1845–1891*. New York: International Publications.

Amin, Samir. 1973. *Neocolonialism in West Africa*. New York: Penguin.

———. 1977. *Imperialism and Unequal Development*. London: Monthly Review Press.

Ayandele, E. A. 1960. *The Missionary Impact on Modern Nigeria, 1842–1914*. London: Longman.

Azikiwe, Nnamdi. 1970. *Liberia in World Politics*. Connecticut: Negro Universities Press.

Baran, Paul. 1957. *The Political Economy of Growth*. New York: Marzani and Munsel Publishers.

Bastide, Roger. 1967. *Les Ameriques Noire, Les Civilizations Africaines Dans Le Nouveau Monde*. Paris: Payot.

———. 1978. *The African Religions of Brazil: Toward a Sociology of the Interpenetration of Civilizations*. Baltimore: Johns Hopkins University Press.

Bennett, Norman. 1975. *Africa and Europe From Roman Times to the Present*. New York: Africana Press.

———. 1984. *Africa and Europe From Roman Times to National Independence*. 2nd ed. New York: Africana.

Berman, Edward H. 1975. *African Reactions to Missionary Education*. New York: Columbia University Press.

Billington, James A. (ed.). 1953. *The Journal of Charlotte L. Forten*. New York: Collier Books.

Blyden, E. W. 1978. *Selected Letters of Edward Wilmot Blyden*. Reprint. New York: KTO Press.

Boorstein, Daniel J. 1983. *The Discoveries: A History of Man's Search to Know His World and Himself*. New York: Vintage Books.

Browne, R. S. and R.J. Cummings. 1985. *The Lagos Plan of Action vs. The Berg Report: Contemporary Issues In African Economic Development*. Lawrenceville, VA.: Brunswick Publishing Company.

Burness, Donald. 1977. *Fire: Six Writers From Angola, Mozambique, and Cape Verde*. Washington: Three Continents Press.

Casely-Hayford, J. C. 1969. *Ethiopia Unbound*. Reprint. London: Frank Cass.

Cesaire, Aime. 1955. *Discours Sur Le Colonialisme*. 3rd ed. Paris: Presence Africaine.

———. 1959. "L'Homme de Culture et Ses Responsabilities." *Presence Africaine, Deuxieme Congres Des Escrivains Et Artistes Noirs*. No. Special, March 26–April 1. Tome 1.

Chazan, Naomi. 1978. "The Africanization of Political Change: Some Aspects of the Dynamics of Political Culture in Ghana and Nigeria." *African Studies Review* XXI, 3:15–38.

Chittick, H. N. 1965. "The Shirazi Colonization of East Africa." *Journal of African History*, 6:275–94.

Christy, David. 1854. *African Colonization By the Free Colored People of the United States: An Indispensible Auxillary to African Mission*. Cincinnati: J.A. James.

Clapham, (Sir) John H. 1941. *The Cambridge Economic History of Europe from the Decline of the Roman Empire*. Edinburgh: Cambridge University Press.

Cobban, Alfred. 1960. *In Search of Humanity: The Role of The Enlightenment in Modern History*. New York: Brazilier.

Cummings, Melbourne S. 1972. "The Rhetoric of Bishop Henry McNeil Turner: Leading Advocate in the African Emigration Movement, 1866–1907." Los Angeles: UCLA Ph.D. Diss.

Cummings, Robert J. 1986. "Internal Factors Which Generate Famine: A Critique," Chapter 8 in M. Glantz (ed.) *Drought and Hunger in Africa: Denying Famine a Future in Africa*. Cambridge: University Press.

Curtin, Philip D. 1964. *The Image of Africa*. Madison: University of Wisconsin Press.

———. 1969. *The Atlantic Slave Trade: A Census*. Madison: University of Wisconsin Press.

Damas, Leon-Gontran. 1934. *L'Etudiant Noir*. Paris: Gallimard.

———. 1956. *Black Label*. Paris: Gallimard.

———. 1972. *Pigments*. Reprint. Paris: Presence Africaine.

deBenoist, Joseph-Roger. 1979. *La Balkanization De L'Afrique Occidentale Francaise*. Abidjan, Dakar, Lome: Les Nouvelle Editions Africaines.

De Graft-Johnson, J. C. 1957. *African Empires of the Past*. Paris: Presence Africaine.

Delany, Martin R. 1969. *The Condition, Elevation, Emigration, and Destiny of the Colored People of the United States*. Reprint. New York: Arno Press.

——— (with R. Campbell). 1969. *Search for a Place: Black Separation and Africa, 1860*. Ann Arbor: University of Michigan Press.

Diop, Cheik Anta. 1955. *Nations Negre et Culture*. Paris: Presence Africaine.

———. 1974. *African Origins of Civilization: Myth or Reality*. Mercer Cook, ed. & trans. New York: Lawrence Hill.

———. 1978. *The Cultural Unity of Black Africa*. Chicago: Third World Press.

Douglass, Frederick. 1962. *Life and Times of Frederick Douglass*. London: Collier-Macmillan Ltd.

Drake, St. Clair. 1977. *The Redemption of Africa and Black Religion*. Chicago: Third World Press.

Du Bois, W. E. B. 1947. *The World and Africa*. New York: Viking Press.

———. 1970. *The Suppression of the African Slave Trade to the United States of America, 1638–1870*. New York: Dover.

Duffy, James. 1963. *Portugal in Africa*. Baltimore: Penguin.

Economic Commission for Africa. 1985. *Evaluation of the Implementation of the Regional Food Plan for Africa (1978–1984): A Preliminary Assessment of the Food and Agricultural Aspects of the Lagos Plan of Action*. New York: United Nations.

Emmanuel, Argihiri. 1972. *Unequal Exchange*. New York: Monthly Review Press.

Esedebe, P. O. 1982. *Pan-Africanism: The Idea and Movement, 1776–1963*. Washington: Howard University Press.

Fagan, Brian M. 1984. *Clash of Cultures*. New York: W. H. Freeman.

Fage, J. D. 1978. *Cambridge History of Africa, vol. 2, c. 500 B.C.–A.D. 1050*. Cambridge: University Press.

Fage, J. D. and R. Oliver (eds.). 1970. *Papers in African Prehistory*. Cambridge: University Press.

Fanon, Frantz. 1967. *Black Skin, Whited Masks*. New York: Grove Press.

Fisher, M. M. 1922. "Lott Cary, the Colonizing Missionary." *Journal of Negro History*. 7 (October): 17–32.

Folz, Robert. 1980. *The Concept of Empire in Western Europe from the Fifth to the Fourteenth Century*. Connecticut: Greenwood.

Frank, A. G. 1978. *Dependent Accumulation and Underdevelopment*. London: Monthly Review Press.

Frazier, E. Franklin. 1957. *Race and Cultural Contacts in the Modern World*. New York: Knopf.

Freyre, Gilberto. 1946. *The Masters and the Slaves: A Study in the Development of Brazilian Civilization*. New York: Knopf.

Frutkin, Susan. 1973. *Aime Cesaire, Black Between Worlds*. Coral Gables: University of Miami Press.

Fyfe, Christopher. 1979. *A Short History of Sierra Leone*. London: Longman.

Harden, Donald. 1963. *The Phoenicians*. Rev. ed. London: Longman.

Harris, Joseph E. 1982. *Global Dimensions of the African Diaspora*. Washington: Howard University Press.

Hayes, William C. 1965. *Most Ancient Egypt*. Chicago: University Press.

Herskovits, M. J. 1941. *The Myth of The Negro Past*. New York: Harper.

———. 1943. *Pesquisa Ethnologicas Na Bahia*. Bahia: Publicacoe de Museu da Bahia.

———. 1962. *The Human Factor in Changing Africa*. New York: Knopf.

Inikori, Joseph E. (ed.). 1982. *Forced Migrations: The Impact of the Export Slave Trade on African Societies*. New York: Africana Publishing Company.

———. 1976. "Measuring the Atlantic Slave Trade: An Assessment of Curtin and Anstey." *Journal of African History* XVII, 2:197–223; and XVII, 4:595–627.

Jacobs, Sylvia M. 1982. *Black Americans and The Missionary Movement in Africa*. Connecticut: Greenwood Press.

Kent, R. R. 1965. "Palmares: An African State in Brazil." *Journal of African History* 6:169–75.

Kimambo, I. N. 1971. *A Political History of The Pare of Tanzania*. Nairobi: East African Publishing House.

———. 1972. (with T. O. Ranger). *Historical Study of African Religion*. Berkeley: University of California Press.

Ki-Zerbo, J. (ed.). 1981. *General History of Africa I: Methodology and African Prehistory*. Paris: UNESCO.

Kup, A. P. 1961. *A History of Sierra Leone, 1400–1787*. Cambridge: University Press.

Leakey, Mary D. 1971. *Olduvai Gorge: Excavations in Beds I & II, 1960–1963*. Cambridge: University Press.

Livingstone, David. 1971. *Missionary Travels and Researches in South Africa*. Reprint. New York: Johnson Publishing.

Lucas, J. O. 1970. *Religions in West Africa and Ancient Egypt*. Lagos: CMS Bookshop.

Mafeje, Archie. 1967. "The Role of the Bard in a Contemporary African Community." *Journal of African Languages* VI:193–223.

Mathew, G. 1963. "The East African Coast Until the Coming of the Portuguese." *History of East Africa*. R. Oliver, G. Mathew (eds.). Vol. 1. Oxford: University Press.

Mathurin, Owen C. 1976. *Henry Sylvester Williams and The Origins of the Pan-African Movement, 1869–1911*. Connecticut: Greenwood Press.

Mauro, F. 1967. *L'Expansion Europene (1600–1870)*. 2nd ed. Paris: Presses Universitaires de France.

Mazrui, Ali. 1978. "Negritude, the Talmudic Tradition and Intellectual Performance of Blacks and Jews." *Ethnic and Racial Studies* 1 (January):19–36.

Mehlinger, Louis R. 1916. "The Attitudes of the Free Negro Toward Colonization." *Journal of Negro History* 1 (July):10–19.

Moktar, Go. (ed.). 1981. *General History of Africa, II: Ancient Civilizations of Africa*. Berkeley: University of California Press.

Murphy, E. Jefferson. 1972. *History of African Civilization*. New York: Crowell.

Niane, D. T. (ed.). 1982. *UNESCO General History of Africa, IV: Africa From the Twelfth to the Sixteenth Century*. Berkeley: University of California.

Nketia, J. H. K. 1963. "The Study of African and Afro-American Music." *The Black Perspective In Music* 1, 1:7–15.

Nkrumah, Kwame. 1964. *Consciencism*. London: Heinemann.

Nyang, Sulayman S. 1984. *Islam, Christianity, and African Identity*. Brattleboro: Amana Books.

Nyerere, Julius. 1977. "The Plea of the Poor." (August) *Presidential Address* (unpublished). Washington: Howard University.

Obenga, Theophile. 1973. *Afrique Dan l'e Antique*. Paris: Editions du Seuil.

———. 1981. "Sources and Specific Techniques Used in African History: General Outline," in J. KiZerbo (ed.), *General History of Africa, 1: Methodology and African Prehistory*. Paris: UNESCO.

Ofuatey-Kodjoe, W. 1977. "The Ideological Triangle: Reciprocal Ideological Influences among Afro-West Indians, Afro-Americans and Africans." *Studia Africana* 1 (Spring).

Ogot, B. A. 1974. *Zamani: A Survey of East African History*. Nairobi: East African Publishing House.

Oliver, Roland. 1952. *The Missionary Factor in East Africa*. London: Longman.

———. 1965. *Africa in the Days of Exploration*. New Jersey: Prentice Hall.

——— and Brian Fagan. 1975. *Africa in the Iron Age, c. 500 B.C. to A. D. 1400*. Cambridge: University Press.

Organization of African Unity. 1981. *Lagos Plan of Action for the Economic Development of Africa, 1980–2000.* Geneva: International Institute for Labor Studies.

Pierson, Donald. 1942. *Negroes in Brazil.* Chicago: University Press.

Previte-Orton, C. W. 1951. *A History of Europe From 1198 to 1378.* London: Methuen.

Racine, Daniel. 1982. "Concepts of Diaspora and Alienation as Privileged Themes in Negritude Literature," J. Harris (ed.). *Global Dimensions of the African Diaspora.* Washington: Howard University Press.

Ramos, Artur. 1934. *Negroes in Brazil.* Trans. from *O Negro Brasileiro.* Rio de Janeiro: Civilizacao Brasileira.

Ranger, T. O. 1968. *Emerging Themes of African History.* Evanston: Northwestern.

Rauf, Abdur. 1974. *Bilal Ibn Rabah.* Washington: Islamic Center.

Redkey, Edwin S. 1969. *Black Exodus: Black Nationalism and Back-to-Africa Movements, 1890–1910.* New Haven: Yale.

Rodney, Walter. 1965. "Portuguese Attempts at Monopoly on the Upper Guinea Coast, 1580–1650." *Journal of African History* 6, 3:307–22.

———. 1974. *How Europe Underdeveloped Africa.* Washington: Howard University Press.

Rodriques, Jose Honorio. 1962. "The Influence of Africa on Brazil and of Brazil on Africa." *Journal of African History.* 3:45–72.

———. 1968. *Brazil and Africa.* Berkeley: University of California Press.

Rodriques, Nina. 1932. *Los Africanos no Brasil.* Sao Paulo: Cia. Editora Nacional.

Rollin, Frank A. 1883. *Life and Public Services of Martin R. Delany.* Boston: Lee and Shepard.

Sanceau, Elaine. 1969. *Henry the Navigator.* Connecticut: Archon Books.

Shick, Tom W. 1980. *Behold the Promised Land: A History of Afro-American Settler Society in Nineteenth Century Liberia.* Baltimore: Johns Hopkins.

Shinnie, P. L. 1971. *The African Iron Age.* Oxford: University Press.

Skinner, Elliott P. 1972. *Drums and Shadows: Survival Studies Among the Georgia Coastal Negroes.* New York: Doubleday.

Sembene, Ousmane. 1962. *Les Bouts De Bois De Dieu.* Paris: Le Livre Contemporain.

Senghor, Leopold Sedar. 1959. *African Socialism.* New York: American Society of Culture.

———. 1964. *Liberte 1: Negritude et Humanisme.* Paris: Le Seuil.

Tholfsen, T. R. 1984. *Ideology and Revolution in Modern Europe: An Essay on the Role of Ideas in History.* New York: Columbia University Press.

Thompson, V. P. 1969. *Africa and Unity: The Evolution of Pan-Africanism.* London: Harlow, Longman.

Turner, Lorenzo D. 1949. *Africanisms in the Gullah Dialect.* Chicago: University Press.

Uya, Ukon Edet. 1982. "Conceptualizing Afro-American/ African Relations: Implications for African Diaspora Studies." *Global Dimensions of the African Diaspora.* Washington: Howard University Press.

Van den Berghe, Pierre. 1967. *Race and Racism.* New York: Wiley.

Wallerstein, Immanuel. 1979. *The Capitalist World Economy.* New York: Cambridge University Press.

wa Thiong'o, Ngugi. 1972. *Homecomings: Essays on African and Caribbean Literature, Culture and Politics.* London: Heinemann.

Waugh, W. T. 1980. *A History of Europe from 1378 to 1494.* Connecticut: Greenwood.

———. 1981. *Writers in Politics.* London: Heinemann.

West, Richard. 1970. *Back to Africa: A History of Sierra Leone and Liberia.* New York: Holt, Rinehart & Winston.

Ann Macy Roth

Egypt, African Americans, and Afrocentrism: An Egyptologist's View

Palm trees and pyramids, camels and Cleopatra, mummies and Moses: these are the images that spring to the minds of most Americans when Egypt is mentioned. For many African-Americans, however, Egypt has other associations, too: the land of an African people who, long before the rise of Greece and Rome, built a great and sophisticated civilization that created beautiful works of literature and art and imposing architectural monuments. While other African civilizations are equally worthy of admiration and study, only ancient Egypt is both familiar and impressive to all Americans. Only for ancient Egypt does the traditional American history curriculum depart from its well-beaten westward path in the progress of civilization—Mesopotamia to Israel to Greece to Italy to England to America—and sojourn briefly on the continent that, for lack of more specific histories, many African-Americans view in its entirety as their ancestral home.

The society and culture of ancient Egypt has been the object of my own study, research, and teaching for several decades now, and for the last three years I have taught Egyptology courses to African-American students at Howard University. I have been delighted at the interest and enthusiasm that many of my students feel about the subject of ancient Egypt. Students who specialize in many different disciplines take my courses, not (or not only) because they fill a requirement, but because they can provide information about a corner of Africa. They are often inspired by learning about an African people who created a civilization that was admired by the early European civilizations of

Greece and Rome. Occasionally, my students go on to further study of Egypt, Nubia, or other African cultures, and perhaps even to a career in African history, archaeology, Egyptology, or anthropology; but most of them will concentrate on other areas of academic or professional endeavor, taking from their brief exposure to Egyptology an understanding of other cultures, an increased interest in African history, and perhaps a greater confidence in their own abilities.

Some of my most enthusiastic students, however, are troubled by their contact with traditional Egyptology. They are reluctant to believe the evidence for phenomena such as homosexuality, human sacrifice, and sexism in ancient Egypt. "Ancient Egypt was not like that," they tell me, "The translations can't be accurate," or "These burials can't really mean that." They seem to approach Egyptian culture assuming that all ancient Egyptians were superhumanly moral and perfect, *by modern ethical standards*. The interpretation of evidence can always be debated; but it is unrealistic and unscholarly to discard an interpretation simply because it contradicts the assumption that no ancient Egyptian ever committed an act that some of us might find distasteful. If the study of Egyptian culture is to be viewed as a scholarly enterprise, and not merely an exercise in confirming what we want to believe, it must be based on the evidence; and the interpretation of that evidence must, as far as possible, be approached without preconceived ideas.

Many of the students who find this kind of evidence troubling have read deeply in popular Afrocentric literature, in books that have perhaps been recommended by their teachers as a welcome antidote to the Eurocentric approach of most traditional teaching materials. The authors of such works have usually not had specialized training in Egyptian language, art, and archaeology, and they must thus depend upon general sources that synthesize this evidence for them. Such sources are, in turn, often themselves one or two steps removed from the scholarly work they cite, or are long out of date (for example, the ubiquitous popular writings of E. A. Wallis Budge, which were written at the turn of the 20th century, although the reprint editions often give more recent dates). Afrocentric authors also have a different aim from traditional Egyptologists: reacting against a Western tradition which often downplays Africa and its cultures, their intent is to emphasize and celebrate Egypt's positive achievements. These achievements are, of course, impressive; but many writers, anxious to make their case, misinterpret or exaggerate their sources, often out of an inability to test the speculative or wishful writings of others against the primary evidence. For such writers, it is not enough that the Egyptians made important contributions to religion, medi-

cine, art, architecture, and literature. They must also be credited with the invention of light bulbs, airplanes, and philosophical argument.

Such contentions are not generally accepted by traditional Egyptologists. We are not skeptical because we wish to disparage the achievements of the Egyptians—quite the contrary: had the Egyptians in fact achieved such things, our field of study would undoubtedly be immensely more respected and we would be far better paid than we are now. We would have no interest at all in suppressing evidence for such achievements if that evidence existed. But it does not; and indeed there is considerable evidence against such propositions. The argument that the ancient Egyptians harnessed electricity and invented some sort of light bulb is contradicted by the archaeological and textual evidence that buildings were lit by torches, oil lamps, and candles. The argument that the Egyptians flew using gliders (argued on the basis of a single wooden model of a bird) is very doubtful, if only in view of the many Greek visitors who wrote accounts of the marvels of Egypt and could hardly have failed to note such a spectacular achievement. And the claim that the Egyptians invented philosophical argument is made unlikely by the Egyptian texts that speculate about the nature of the world, which invariably present their reconstructions and explanations as facts, never as arguments from established premises. It is true that such philosophical texts may have existed—it is notoriously difficult to prove a negative—but if they did, they did not survive, and it is hard to believe that they would not have had some effect on the writers of the very sophisticated cosmological and ethical texts that have come down to us.

One of the most painful—and most necessary—scholarly tasks is to relinquish the ideas we like when the evidence turns out to contradict them. Because we want to believe that history was the way we would like it to have been, we have to make very certain that all the available evidence supports our reconstructions. It is comparatively easy to build convincing structures of argument to support patterns that we want to see: we need only select from all of the available evidence the pieces that seem to support our ideas, and then present those pieces in detail and at great length. Such arguments can often be very convincing to people who are not very familiar with the subject (which in the case of Egyptology means most people), and who therefore do not know about all the evidence that we have either overlooked or decided not to present. Honest researchers, in contrast, not only must present the evidence against their conclusions, but they must seek it out. Sometimes this means having a skeptical colleague look at the conclusion and try to find arguments against it; but after some practice, most scholars become adept at criticizing their own work. They search through older scholarship on the subject, looking for evidence that would show that they were wrong. If earlier writers make statements that contradict their ideas, they track down the evidence for those statements. (This is why scholars hate books with no footnotes—it is impossible to look up the evidence—if any—for the author's claims and argue against it.) The evidence may have been misinterpreted; or it may be proof that the theory is wrong, in which case the theory must be abandoned.

Sometimes we can find no absolute evidence against our claims, but on consideration of the whole question, we find that the balance of the evidence is against us. I had a recent example of this in my own research: I was writing an article on the four Egyptian bricks of birth and their use to ensure rebirth after death, as part of a larger project to show how important birth metaphors were in Egyptian mortuary religion. Because I wanted to believe that there were many examples of these bricks, I was very pleased to notice four rectangles painted on the footboard of a queen's coffin. Earlier scholars had called these rectangles basins of purification, but since birth bricks were used to support a woman while she gave birth, a footboard, particularly on a woman's coffin, would be an appropriate place to find them depicted. Even more convincingly, two of the bricks were marked with the emblem of Hekat, the goddess of birth, and the other two with the name of Khepri, a creator god. The fact that they were divided into two pairs (as birth bricks were under a woman's feet) also supported my idea. The text accompanying them was short and unclear; while it said nothing about birth, it did not contradict my interpretation, either. In researching the text, however, I found that it occurred with similar rectangles on the footboards of two other coffins, one belonging to a man. On these examples, the corners of each rectangle were joined by short diagonal lines to the corners of a smaller inner rectangle. These examples looked, in other words, like rectangular basins seen from above. I might have argued that these side panels were just a rendering in Egyptian perspective of the sides of bricks, but other pictures of bricks do not have sides, and pictures of basins often do. Since it would have been dishonest to present only the evidence from the first coffin, I decided that the balance of the evidence was against me, and I was probably wrong. Regretfully (since I still think the birth goddess might be significant), I took the whole argument out of my article.

This is not to say that all scholars, or even all Egyptologists, are perfect at this business of balancing pro against con, that we can unerringly winnow away

the chaff of incorrect ideas and collect the golden kernels of truth that survive. Far from it. Not only are we humans and prone to human error, but we are limited by the history of our field. When Egyptology began, less than two hundred years ago, almost all of its early practitioners viewed the Egyptians through the eyes of better known cultures: the classical civilizations of Greece and Rome, and the peoples of the Bible. Naturally, the questions these scholars asked, and the answers they found, were framed in the context of their desire to illuminate Egyptian connections to the Biblical and Classical worlds. Moreover, as in the Classical and Biblical traditions, most early Egyptologists were concerned with language and texts, and this too tended to focus their attention on ancient Egypt's ties with Europe and Western Asia, where other early languages and texts could be found. Even today, our discoveries are given more attention when there is some tie-in with these better known civilizations, as witness the recent journalistic furor over Tomb 5 in the Valley of the Kings. The tomb seems to belong to the sons of Ramesses II, who ruled around the time that some people think the Exodus occurred. Much was said in the press about the possibility that his eldest son might be buried there, and might provide evidence for or against the question whether Ramesses II was the pharaoh of the Exodus. Today's Egyptologists are less Eurocentric, but as inheritors of the tradition, we are sometimes affected by the prejudices of our predecessors.

Only with the advent of anthropological research into modern African cultures did a few Egyptologists begin to look at ancient Egypt's ties and similarities to other African cultures, but this early work was generally limited to borrowing recent African models to illuminate obscure aspects of Egyptian religion. To trace the connections suggested by these similarities, with 5000 years of history and little archaeological or written evidence between them, was practically impossible. More intensive scientific examination of these connections began with the salvage excavations that took place in Nubia under pressure of the construction of the Aswan High Dam in the late 1960s, which have been slowly published in the decades following. These excavations and the analysis of them have changed our view of Nubian culture, which used to be seen as a poor, derivative cousin to the Egyptian culture. Recent research has allowed us to see the Nubians as a separate and equally creative culture, which selectively borrowed some Egyptian ideas, but adapted those borrowings to their own needs while developing other forms of cultural expression that were quite different from those of the Egyptians. At the same time, this research shows underlying connections between these two Nilotic cultures, perhaps going back to shared cultures during their prehistories.

So how do the Afrocentric movement and African-Americans' interest in their African heritage relate to traditional Egyptology? Some Afrocentrists (and even some Egyptologists) would say, not at all. Nonetheless, the two groups share an interest in ancient Egypt and in learning more about what it was really like, and there are encouraging signs that both Afrocentrists and Egyptologists are coming to appreciate what the other group has to offer. Already, I think, as a result of popular American interest in the connections between Egypt and the rest of Africa, Egyptologists have begun to investigate these connections more seriously, and there has been increased interest in the cultures of Nubia and Libya. At the same time, African-Americans interested in Egypt have begun to study in traditional programs and attend Egyptological lectures, seminars, and professional meetings. Ultimately, one hopes, the result will be a reduction of Eurocentrism in Egyptology and an increase in the scholarly solidity of popular Afrocentrism. Such improvements can only benefit us all.

RUSSELL ADAMS

Epistemology, Afrocentricity, and Ideology

Epistemology is defined by *Webster's Unabridged Dictionary* as "the theory or science of the *methods and grounds* of knowledge, esp. with reference to its limits and validity" (emphasis added). Epistemology involves the understanding of how groups of people come to hold the ideas and viewpoints characteristic of them and their cultural heritage. Afro-American Studies specialists claim that, since the traditional disciplines were shaped without awareness of the nature of the subjective, internal communities of persons of African descent, their vaunted "objectivity" is compromised by their practitioners' a) social distance from blacks, b) basically tourist/anthropologist methods of research on blacks, c) lack of intimate familiarity with the real effects of the actions of the larger societies on black social formations and psyche, and d) deliberate distortion of the African-American and African social record, past and present. The rising black research groups reject the intrinsic elitism and cultural ethnocentrism of establishment academics as flawed at best and degradingly unfair at worst.

This rejection of establishment academic perceptions has deep roots in the black intellectual experience. Carter G. Woodson, the best-known exponent of this view (and founder of the Black History Week, now Month, in 1926), saw his work as a corrective endeavor. Over the three-quarters of a century since the establishment of the Association for the Study of Afro-American Life and History by Woodson (a Harvard Ph.D.), in 1915, critical black thought has moved from accepting the "myths of the Negro past" through a rejection of epistemological viewpoints of blacks as deviations from the stock of humankind and from the standards of "host" societies to an assertiveness which recently has sprung forth as Afrocentrism. For the first time, the concern of professional Afro-Americanists have spilled over into the popular media and public discussion. For this reason, attention here will be given to this new concern.

The purest form of Afrocentrism places Africa at its center as the source of the world's peoples and its most fundamental ideas and inventions. As a term, however, it also refers to African and African-American culture, education, ideologies, and social interests. Perhaps it is not surprising that the foremost exponents of a proactive epistemological stance toward the assumptions of Afro-American Studies have emerged most fully in historically white institutions and in conjunction with the search of predominantly black urban school systems for answers to problems of student self-concept, motivation and performance. Nor is it surprising that the leading exponent of Afrocentrism, Molefe Asante, is developer and star of Temple University's African-American Studies Department, the most advanced in the nation. Through his many writings, Asante, with the assistance of black professors at other historically white institutions, has made "Afrocentrism" a buzz word. The collection of supporting scholars around Professor Asante often are identified as *"Nile Valley" Afrocentrists*.

Adherents to this school of thought assert the primacy of Egyptian Africa as the creative locus of the major ideas and practices which undergird the foundations of humanity. They declare that not only did humankind split off from the simian or ape world in East Africa, but assert that this African segment of humankind generated a still-living stock of ideas produced by its long history alongside the Nile. In one of his recent works, Asante said of the Nile that "it played a vital role in the creation of Kemetic (black) philosophy, agriculture, technology, and religion." Consequently, black people in particular, and the rest of the world, in general, should acknowledge their debt to black Egypt (Kemet) and revive those ideas which contributed to black achievement in many areas of life during antiquity. This school asserts that recovery of ancient Egyptian knowledge would fill the spiritual void and raise the self-esteem of those peoples with clearly African legacies and that curricula based on Nile Valley philosophy and values are most appropriate for Egypt's African-American descendants and are of great use to others.

Continental Afrocentrists assert that the entire African continent is the true cultural source of black trans-Atlantic communities. Adherents of this school celebrate their version of authentic black cultural values and practices in the diaspora and declare that they are prerequisites for the revitalization of African-American communities. They also hold that a common Afrocentric world view can be synthesized out of the complex of traditional African life and history through careful study of existing artifacts and print materials. *It is a conviction of this group that African social values are more humanistic than those derived from Europe.*

Afrocentric Infusionists assert, instead, the positive value of infusion or blending Africa-based ideas, concepts, values, and historical data into the curricula. This school holds that all Americans can profitably share positive African viewpoints, experiences and practices. While such blending would have the effect of reducing stereotypes and enhancing conceptions of others about blacks, sharing would enable people to discern the common humanity of European and African societies. *This group seeks close collaboration with public school curriculum specialists.* Afrocentric infusionists see black people as Americans of African descent with a rich and valuable heritage, which has been ignored and under-used. Professor Asa Hilliard of Georgia State University is perhaps the leading advocate of infusionism, even though he also is partial to the Nile Valley school.

Social Afrocentrists, on the other hand, place greater stress on the *use of knowledge and resources in protecting and promoting the best interests of black people as interacting members of the societies where they live.* They do not use the African background as much as the other Afrocentrists. They agree that the heritage of America's black population is insufficiently appreciated, but hold that it is not possible nor desirable to try to reproduce ancient Africa in a world headed toward the twenty-first century. Adherents of this school take an interest group approach to the topic of Afrocentrism and hold that intellectual fads come and go but group interests are permanent. Thus, *social Afrocentrists do not see the black experience as so specialized that only blacks may be involved in exploring it.* This version of Afrocentrism is "less hard line" about who can participate in the work of using education to promote the concerns of African-Americans. It recognizes the complexity of human experience and the difficulties in identifying the "culturally African" from the non-African elements which societies absorb over time. Africa per se is more of a target of interest than of inspiration. *In a sense, this conception of Afrocentrism is but a continuation of the position taken by the first wave of individual black scholars in the era of forced segregation.*

The types of Afrocentrism cited above represent the *thinking* about how to avoid the negative aspects and consequences of traditional curricula and attitudes toward people of color. The very concept of Afrocentrism has stimulated a great deal of debate about the role of different perspectives in guiding instruction and research in the field of Afro-American Studies. At the level of practice, Afro-American Studies departments are 1) endeavoring to create an independent world view free of the defects of misleading claims of Eurocentric "universality" and "objectivity," 2) still trying to develop and present once-omitted factual material to their students, 3) hoping to evolve from multi-disciplinary to inter-disciplinary instruction, 4) responding more effectively to issues of curriculum balance in the area of academic skills, and 5) enhancing their institutional foundations. Although only a quarter-century old, the institutional field of Afro-American Studies has already made a major contribution to education by raising anew questions about the nature, content, and direction of American education in this era of ethnic and cultural diversity. The debate over Afrocentricity is generally an epistemological and a pedagogical one. The differences in ideology within the black studies programs and among black intellectuals, however, have generated a more heated debate, sometimes used by the establishment as well as by students to indict the programs as venues of "indoctrination" rather than of intellectual exposure to facts, theories, and opinions which might assist young men and women, both black and white, in determining, for themselves, the best course of action in their lives and relationships with their fellow citizens. The controversy heightens tensions because these ideologies are action-oriented thought systems or philosophies, advanced as solutions to the problems of the African-American community in a predominantly white, Anglo-Saxon, and male-dominated society, which, throughout the centuries, has shown little concern for the plight of minorities, blacks in particular.

Following is a brief summary of the most popular ideologies of which students of Africa and African-America ought to be aware. One of the most concise discussions of the issue appears in the volume edited by James Turner, *The Next Decade: Theoretical and Research Issues in African Studies* (1984), in an article authored by Tilden LeMelle of Hunter College titled "The Status of Black Studies in the Second Decade: The Ideological Imperative."

LeMelle classifies black ideologies into two broad categories: the assimilationist and the self-determinationist (the latter also known as the nationalist ideology). While the first category comprises the accomodationist, the reconciliationist, the liberal idealist, and the Marxist-Leninist, the second category encompasses the psychological and the separatist nationalist ideologies.

The accommodationist, exemplified by the philosophy of Booker T. Washington, who advocated economic self-help taken to a higher level through vocational training, is conciliatory and appeasing toward the white majority, does not dare to challenge the status quo, and is geared toward accommodating and accepting the white set parameters within which blacks can advance. The followers of this course of action are often dubbed as "Uncle Tom's." Of course, the defenders of this philosophical strategy hold the view that Washington was a realist, a pragmatist, who lived in a terrifying, black lynching, southern white environment, which under no circumstances would tolerate the political empowerment of black people. The reconciliationist ideology, in LeMelle's analysis, exemplified by W. E. B. Du Bois's thinking, differs from the accommodationist in that it does not avoid conflict; it challenges but seeks compromise within "the rules of the game" established by society's white majority. It is assimilationist (it accepts and emulates mainstream culture), and holds that blacks can achieve their goals only if they have a group of highly educated and qualified leaders—*the talented tenth*—who will speak for them and lead them in the crucible of daily confrontation for access to political, social, and economic opportunities.

The black liberal idealists, instead, essentially believe in the goodness of man and the ultimate triumph of good over evil and cherish the democratic and liberal ideals of American society. This type of assimilationist (integrationist) philosophy, identified with Martin Luther King, Jr.'s crusade—the Civil Rights movement of the mid-fifties through the mid-sixties—relies on the good will and the guilty conscience of (white) liberals, who, allied with blacks, in a "rainbow coalition," to use a contemporary phraseology, will peacefully transform America from a racist society to one of brotherhood.

The Marxist-Leninists, clothed in the aura of scientism, adopt and impose a European model on the black community, analyzing its problems on the basis of class (incomes, living standards, and ownership of the means of production) while giving little weight to the race issue which they think will disappear once classes have been eliminated. They focus their hopes on the actions of the workers (the *lumpen proletariat*), both black and white, united, and intent on overthrowing the middle-class or the bourgeoisie.

The problem with this approach, the critics say, is that, as with the liberal idealists, it counts on the good-ness of white workers and their solidarity with their black counterparts, ignoring the fact that, historically, rarely did the two see eye to eye their mutual needs and that, in times of economic crisis, black workers often become the target of white workers, whom they accuse of "stealing their jobs," accepting lower wages, and acting as strike-breakers. Forgetting the perennial reality of race and racial discrimination and the fact that the black middle-class is more of a consuming than a producing and owning society make the Marxist-Leninist position utopian and therefore untenable. LeMelle believes that the Marxist-Leninists constitute one of the most subtle but more dangerous ideologues. Of course, now that communism has lost its grip over important world societies and regimes, the validity of Marxism-Leninism is in serious question as a strategy designed to replace capitalism.

LeMelle defines black nationalism, which emerged out of frustration with American policies and the insignificant gains of the Civil Rights movement, as the "identification with the interests and aspirations of Black people wherever they may be, regardless of state boundaries." As an earlier manifestation of this general category, he includes the slave revolts, the Harlem Renaissance, the Garvey movement, and the philosophy of Carter G. Woodson. Separatist nationalism, often mislabelled as "anti-white," attempts to actually separate black people physically and socially from the majority society and create an independent environment such as a state in which blacks can implement their survival strategies. It appears that the Nation of Islam would fall under this category, if one sees it as "non-anti-white," but "pro-black," to use LeMelle's terminology.

Finally, the psychological black nationalist is "satisfied with his or her own worth and posits self-directed interests and goals," while remaining a part of established society. This approach is exemplified, according to LeMelle, by the attitude of the black students of the 1960s who demanded the establishment of black studies programs across the nation, insisting that they combine relevant and inclusive education with social action to benefit the masses of the black people.

Unfortunately, the tendency of most ideologues is to expect or force everyone to embrace one of these ideologies, and, in specific, theirs, to deserve respect within the black community and the (black) academy. They overlook the fact that most people never consciously formulate or follow a specific philosophy to guide every moment of their lives. In most cases, people may combine one or two or more of these ideologies to face a reality which is not, as they say, all "black or white." The debate on ideological behavior has of late brought about the controversy over "political correctness" mainly on predominantly white campuses and in the political arena across the nation.

Socio-Scientific Trends

While Afrocentricity and ideologies have emerged as debates regarding the proper philosophy and perspective African-American scholars *should* take toward their work and the best action-oriented strategies they should propose to the African-American community, it is helpful to understand what *has been* the nature of the themes and theories guiding their previous efforts, especially in the context of their treatment of the concept of community. The term "African-American (or Black) Community" has been used to mean a) the collectivity of Americans of African ancestry, and b) blacks as a cohesive sociopolitical group. The idea of an African-American or black community has been used most explicitly in the fields of history, sociology and psychology. These disciplines respectively deal with: 1) the historical dimensions of the black experience, 2) the sociological dilemmas of racial stratification and subordination in a democracy, and 3) the impact of the community's historical legacy and its contemporary effects on the mentality of black people.

The philosophies of African-American scholars in these fields appear to have been the result of their own socialization, their individual attitudes toward the canons of their disciplines, the major political and intellectual currents of their eras, and the particular topics, problems, or questions addressed by them. By and large, their ideologies must be inferred from their works. If all of them are unified by any single ideology, it is the ideology of freedom. The individuals and books mentioned below are to be understood as exemplars and examples of the themes and theories of the intellectual cutting edges of their times.

Black scholarly production in the United States originated in the field of history. It began as an effort to have Africa descended people seen as human subjects among humankind and not as inanimate commodities in the economic systems of non-Africans. Consequently, the central theme and objective of black historiography has been the elimination of four centuries of silence, ignorance, and error regarding the human experiences, conditions, and achievements of countless millions once denied voice of standing in Western culture. In the words of historian Earl E. Thorpe, "the central theme of Black History is the quest of Black Americans for freedom, equality and manhood (sic)." The dean of African-American historians, John Hope Franklin, has noted several distinct thematic phases in the evolution of black history.

From the publication of George Washington William's *History of the Negro Race in America* in 1882 to about 1915, writes Franklin, "the common objective of the writers of this period was to define and describe the role of Afro-Americans in the life of the nation." The few black historians of the era tried to counteract this by writing amateur histories and biographies as correctives to the growing belief that Africans anywhere were incapable of making history. To combat this, African-American intellectuals established the American Negro Academy in 1897 with the idea of enhancing, as Alexander Crummell notes, "the civilization of the Negro race in the United States by the scientific processes of literature, art and philosophy through the agency of the cultured men of this same Negro." To this end, its members put out nearly two dozen scholarly publications on the black experience.

The next phase began in 1915 with the founding, by Carter G. Woodson, of the Association for the Study of Negro Life and History. Woodson declared, as noted by Franklin, that the objective of his new national organization was "to save and publish the records of the Negro, that the race may not become a minor factor in the thought of the world"—hence, the establishment of *Journal of Negro History* in 1916 and *the Negro History Bulletin* a decade later. The practical intention of contributionism was the bolstering of community pride and confidence in an era of official racism.

Overlapping the second, the third phase covers the years between 1935 and 1960, a period which saw the rise and fall of Nazism, the urbanization of the black community, and the beginning of the Civil Rights revolution. In 1933, Woodson wrote *The Mis-Education of the Negro* which opened the next stage of black historiography, that of epistemology, or the study of the ideological foundations of knowledge itself. In this work, he urged blacks, the lettered and unlettered alike, not to depend on the majority group for the definition of itself and of social reality. Two years later, the multidisciplinary Du Bois made a declaration of black intellectual independence with a fresh and provocative interpretation of the immediate post-civil war years in *Black Reconstruction*, a magisterial study that placed the African-American community at its center. With this work, black historians quickly evolved from historical narration to historical explanation. The idea of the black community was revised to fit an interactionist interpretation of history. Black history also became overtly critical of the larger social order. This made it possible for historians to use sociology and vice-versa. An excellent example of this is *The Negro in the United*

States (1949), a work of sociological history of the African-American community by the eminent sociologist, E. Franklin Frazier.

The fourth and current phase is one in which no level of historical analysis is omitted. Black historiography now includes work from Thomas Holt's *Black Over White: Negro Political Leadership in South Carolina During Reconstruction* (1977) to the global sweep of St. Clair Drake's *Black Folk Here and There* (1990). Moreover very large numbers of scholars of both races are employing a variety of methods to study and reconstruct the history of the black community from a host of analytical perspectives.

Just as African-American historians moved from narrative to analysis, so did black scholars in the field of sociology. Even before emancipation, free blacks were producing narrative reports on the condition within their communities. In 1897, with his *The Philadelphia Negro*, W. E. B. Du Bois did for African-American sociology what Carter G. Woodson did for history: he used it to explain, in scientific terms, the black community to itself and to others. He and other sociologists such as Charles S. Johnson and E. Franklin Frazier used an evolutionary approach to the study of the black community. Many of these early works measured the development of the black community in terms of rates of growth in income, health, education, and occupational diversity. As a consequence, African-American scholars produced sociological studies with pronounced historical content, Frazier's *The Negro in the United States* being the most notable of them. At the same time, other sociologists stressed the role of contemporary forces in determining the shape and life style of the black community. St. Clair Drake and Horace Clayton produced a classic of this genre in *Black Metropolis* (1945).

By the 1940s, as black historians strove to promote racial and community pride via the contributionist approach, African-American sociologists sought to understand the contemporary status of the race though a number of theories: acculturation, deprivation, segregation, discrimination. Whatever the emphasis, each of the theories presented stressed comparisons between the white and black national communities. By conceptualizing the social conditions within the white community as the norm, inequalities were seen as negatives. The implications of intrinsic human equality espoused by black historians and the sociological observations of group inequalities sparked the search for theories to explain the latter. Thus began the *pathological* theory of the black community. The hypothesis was that the African-American community was "ill," and the white community was not. Sociologists then sought internal and external causes for the "illness" of the community. Some sociologists pointed to the "legacy" of slavery and hypothesized a culture of black dependency it fostered. Others saw the difference in "inappropriate" African cultural "survivals" which had the effect of slowing down the evolution of the race toward a technologically oriented culture. Sociologists who assumed the existence of external sources of the black community's problems called for a return to an interactionist approach as the best way to understand the black community. This meant, again, stressing the conflictive relations and power disparities between the two communities of color. Thus *deprivation* theories were used to guide sociological research on the African-American community. The deprivation argument held that persistent racism and discrimination by white' America had deprived black communities of opportunities to evolve at the same rate as white immigrant communities. In the 1960s, some scholars defined the black community as an internal *colony*, existing to be exploited by a callous "mother country." Some scholars also saw the black community as a "nation" within a nation and several brands of "black nationalism" gained prominence among the more radical black intellectuals.

The internal and external causation theories were blended in the "systems theory" approach which mainstream sociologists applied to the total social order, an approach which at bottom justifies the status quo on a law-and-order basis. In reaction to the inherent conservatism of this conception of the social order, a group of critical sociologists contributed to *The Death of White Sociology*, edited by Joyce Ladner, calling for a new sociology which would supersede black community pathology theories and escape the ideological trap of the systems theory. They sought a black sociology powerful enough to do this. A major volume aimed in this direction is *The Truly Disadvantaged*, written in 1987 by William J. Wilson, the most prominent African-American sociologist in the 1990s. This work places the black community in the vortex of national social forces, but recognizes the role of conscious decision making by government as a major factor influencing the quality of life in black America.

The theories of the African-American community espoused by black psychologists embody the concatenated effects of its historical past and sociological present. Some psychologists (and social psychologists) have argued that polarities of racial status and dualities of black-white interactions have created a cultural schizophrenia resulting in a schizoid mentality for African-Americans, the kind of "two-ness" of identity mentioned by W. E. B. Du Bois at the beginning of the century. The functional stress of this "two-ness" or double consciousness, of being full of but not fully in American society, has created pathological problems for the black community, among them an enervating sense of collective inadequacy and individual impotence. For at least two generations, this was the common theme of both black and white psychologists using "reference group" theory, which asserts that the basic template of personal identity is the group of which the individual is a socialized member, whatever the social status of the group.

The unquestioned low status of the African-American community in the society thus forced self-concept and self-esteem among blacks to be correspondingly low. Beginning in the 1930s, the black psychologists Kenneth and Mamie Clark built national careers featuring this particular theme of the psychological reactions of African-Americans to racial subordination. The white preference responses of children to color-graded dolls and the apparent adoption of Caucasian models by black adults in defining "good features," "good hair," and a "good life," together were seen as creating a psychological dilemma for African-Americans whom neither nature nor society would permit to be what they wished to be. In the 1950–1960 period, themes and theories of deprivation and deficiency undergirded arguments aimed at shaping public and legal policy, particularly in the field of education.

During the 1960s heyday of the Civil Rights movement, however, the thematic emphases of black psychologists began to shift. Black was "beautiful," psychological responses included. Succeeding the prideful contributionism of the historians of the 1930s and rejecting the pathos of the pathogenic sociological themes of the 1940s and early 1950s, black academics began promoting what Maulana Karenga called the "adaptive vitality" model of black sociology and psychology. In his *Introduction to Black Studies* (1982), Karenga declares "the adaptive vitality school contends that adaptation by Blacks to socio-economic pressures and limitations must not be seen as pathologies, but as strength." This was the psychological theme of Andrew Billingsley's highly influential *Black Families in White America* (1968) and Charles W. Thomas in *Boys No More: Black Psychologists Views of Community* (1971). Adelbert Jenkins in *The Psychology of Afro-Americans: A Humanistic Approach* (1992) suggested a revised model of normality based on proven psychological findings and employing a humanistic perspective to promote positive self-concept and esteem among African-Americans. In 1991, William E. Cross in *Shades of Black: Diversity in African American Identity* produced a masterly critique of previous psychological studies and a stimulating African-American-oriented model, an ambitious attempt to create a model of the structures and dynamics determining the nature of black identity in contemporary life.

The overview of the issue addressed by black psychologists suggests that the following tasks are of major interest and importance:

- defining and developing a concept of "normality" which is scientifically sound and socially positive;
- creating "treatment" protocols for the African-American community strong enough to cover the human diversity among its members; and
- generating implementation strategies powerful enough to neutralize the normal human reactions to the impact of community subordination and socialization in a theoretically egalitarian social order.

Whatever the ideological future of Afrocentrism as currently debated, this overview of the themes and theories permeating the work of African-American historians, sociologists, and psychologists indicates that perspectives arise from the nature of the work done as much as they do from the work anticipated. Regardless of their individual ideological "isms," black academics are interested in having their labors make a positive impact in the battle to the African-American community. By ties of affection and circumstance, intellectuals are bound to the primary community through which they, as beings, entered this world. Its struggle is inescapably their own.

JOSEPH E. HARRIS

Return Movements to West and East Africa: A Comparative Approach

The significant crosscurrents of mutual influence between blacks in the United States and the Caribbean, and among those two areas and Africa, as well as between India and Africa, have very deep historical roots that, from the perspective of the African heritage, form a useful Pan-African approach to the study of blacks throughout the world. The key problems of that approach are, first, to trace the changes that occurred among Africans as they adjusted to varied conditions abroad during the period of slavery, abolition, and after; second, to determine the extent to which African customs and memories survived abroad and in what form; third, to analyze the ways in which the idea of Africa arose and manifested itself in the diaspora and related itself to Africa and Africans; fourth, to assess the nature, extent, and significance of contacts between and within Africa and the areas of the diaspora.

The 1770s and 1780s were critical decades in African diaspora history. The key year was 1787. Its significance was twofold: first, because of European decisions about Africans in Europe and America; second, because of the decisions and actions Africans in the Americas were taking. In 1787 Americans wrote into their constitution a provision that permitted the termination of the slave trade in 1807. The consequences of this act resulted in a more limited source of slaves, a federal subsidy for disposal of slaves liberated on the high seas, and cooperation with the American Colonization Society, which founded Liberia in 1821. In Europe in 1787, a group of English abolitionists completed plans for the resettlement in Africa of Africans residing in England. In the wake of the 1772 decision against slavery in England, some abolitionists believed they could found a society of free labor, develop trade in goods, spread Christianity, and contribute to the abolition of slavery and the slave trade in Africa by settling Africa with unwanted, Christianized Africans. Thus, in 1787 some four hundred Africans left to begin that experiment in Sierra Leone; shortly thereafter they were joined by a group from the United States who came by way of Nova Scotia, Canada. A third group from Jamaica, West Indies, followed a few years later.

It was also in 1787 that Africans in the United States were formally organizing their separate institutions: the church, which became the largest black organization in the country; the African lodges; the African Free Schools; and so on. Not only did all these institutions bear the African label, they also expressed interest in the welfare of Africans. Some of them, notably the churches and schools, became seriously involved in the development of a deepening consciousness of and cooperation with Africans in the Caribbean and Africa.

Between 1820 and 1860 there occurred what is sometimes called the first black renaissance in the United States, a period when blacks expressed themselves and their heritage in literature, art, music, and dance. It was also the era when black schools and churches, in particular, sent representatives to Africa and the Caribbean as teachers and preachers. In 1841 Edward Jones, the first black college graduate in the United States, became president of the recently established Fourah Bay College in Sierra Leone. This and other examples confirmed that a situation had developed in the United States that provided a pool of educated and concerned Africans for work in the diaspora and in Africa at a time when such opportunities were rarely available elsewhere.

Because Sierra Leone's repatriates were from England and the Americas, they valued Western culture and education. They enrolled their children in the several mission schools and sent their sons and daughters to English universities. In fact, the liberated African's desire for Western education, and the missionary's commitment to education to "civilize" Africans, had led to the founding of Fourah Bay College by the Church Missionary Society (CMS) in 1826. In 1876 a connection was established between Fourah Bay and Durham University, thereby bringing university education to Sierra Leone, where it became available to students across West Africa, especially British West Africa. In a very real sense, therefore, Western education, in general, and Fourah Bay College, in particular, distinguished Sierra Leone in Africa and the diaspora.[1]

The very nature of these developments, and the fact that the repatriated Africans had not come from that area originally, provided Sierra Leone with the unique opportunity of spearheading a Pan-African tradition. As the repatriates began migrating throughout West Africa in search of their families, a way back home, opportunities to expand their business interests, or, in the case of some, to spread the faith, they took with them aspects of Western education and culture. Those trained at Fourah Bay College were selected by British missionaries, merchants, and colonial officials to entrench British influence. At the same time, however, there were men like Samuel Crowther, who wrote books in the Nupe and Ibo languages and compiled a Yoruba dictionary; Samuel Johnson, who wrote the valuable *History of the Yorubas;* and Thomas Macaulay, father of Herbert and sometimes known as the father of Nigerian nationalism. These were all either repatriates or their descendants and were graduates of Fourah Bay College. Many other examples could be given to show that although they were sometimes exploited for European purposes, the repatriated Africans still forged links in West Africa that broadened the horizons and expanded the channels of communication of several local societies, and thus facilitated Sierra Leone's role in this early Pan-Africanist tradition before a strong, independent base had emerged.

Sierra Leone's experiment had a significant impact on groups in the United States, although repatriation took a somewhat different course. Africans had on their own, early in the eighteenth century, petitioned for freedom and a return to Africa. But the real black repatriationist was Paul Cuffe, that black shipper who organized groups in the United States and Sierra Leone to assist in his efforts to settle Africans from the United States in that colony. He himself financed the settlement of thirty-eight persons in 1815. Cuffe's efforts and the success of Sierra Leone demonstrated the feasibility of black settlement in Africa. Within a few years, colonization schemes to rid America of free Africans became a serious concern of white Americans.

In the United States slave society, Africans were forbidden to speak their language or practice their religion; free blacks were denied many of the rights of freedom. In addition, with the independence of Haiti in 1804, many slave owners in the United States and the Caribbean referred to that black state as the "Black Menace," which could cause blacks elsewhere to revolt for freedom. For these and other reasons, many ordinary and prominent white Americans joined efforts that resulted in the organization of a society to settle "free" blacks in Africa. This endeavor led to the founding of Liberia.

Liberia's development was similar in several aspects to that of Sierra Leone, but there are some differences. First, although the overall number of Liberian settlers was much smaller than Sierra Leone's, the great majority in Liberia had previously resided in the United States. Second, although most of the Liberian settlers were poor, a significant number of them had been born free, were educated, and had owned property in the United States. Their connections with America were, thus, very real and strong. It is not surprising, therefore, that many of Liberia's institutions were patterned after American ones. In addition to the churches, the University of Liberia helped to prepare Liberians as agents of social change, Western-style, as Fourah Bay College was doing in Sierra Leone. But more than in Sierra Leone, Liberian settlers took greater responsibility for their own physical and social survival, which led to their independence in 1847.

With independence, Liberia became unique in Africa and in the diaspora. Not only was Liberia the result of repatriation of Africans from abroad, it also became the only internationally recognized independent black state in Africa until well into the twentieth century. And precisely because of its unique status and history, Liberia became a symbol of hope for many at home and abroad. The pioneer Liberians viewed their venture as an opportunity to exercise their freedom, and within a few years their leaders envisioned the country as destined to become a "province of freedom" for the uplift of all persons of African ancestry. The Liberian constitution noted that the object of forming the state was "to provide a home for the dispersed and oppressed children of Africa." Even more than the case of Sierra Leone, the Liberian situation facilitated continued close relations with Africans overseas, especially in America. The story here is well known: Joseph Roberts from the United States became the first president; John Russwurm, who cofounded with Samuel Cornish the first Afro-American newspa-

per in the United States, also founded the first newspaper in Liberia, the *Liberian Herald*; John Day left the United States to become the country's chief justice; and Edward Blyden, from the West Indies, became Liberia's most distinguished citizen, as publisher, diplomat, minister of state, and intellectual.[2]

Although Blyden is well known, he deserves special attention. His efforts on behalf of unity and freedom for Africa ranged across West Africa, as he held posts in Liberia, Sierra Leone, and Nigeria. His popular appeal to persons of African descent was extended to the diaspora and to the indigenous peoples on the continent. Blyden wanted to make Liberia College (the second Western-style college in Africa) one in which African religion, political systems, and other customs could be studied; and in this sense, he became the major proponent of black studies at the national and international levels. Later, he pioneered a synthesis of African and Western culture, a task that he realized would require the dedication and labor of large numbers of educated and skilled Africans from the diaspora. We will never know whether his objectives and the Liberian goals might have been achieved because the thrust of the nineteenth-century colonial rule diverted and delayed those efforts from establishing tangible and lasting ties between Africa and the American diaspora. Marcus Garvey through his Universal Negro Improvement Association, W. E. B. Du Bois and others through the several Pan-African congresses, the Harlem Renaissance, and Negritude movements, and the Nation of Islam (Black Muslims) continued that trend in the twentieth century and had a significant impact on nationalism in West Africa.[3]

The Brazilian returnees to West Africa are discussed in a later essay by Dr. Boadi-Siaw. However, it is important to note here that those returnees came voluntarily from communities in Brazil that had retained Yoruba language and culture. Indeed, other African cultural influences persisted in Brazil. Thus, the Brazilian returnees not only retained much of their Africanity, they could identify with the area to which they returned, unlike the returnees to Sierra Leone and Liberia. To be sure, they had adopted aspects of Portuguese culture and had not escaped the idea of redemption that motivated so many returnees. They regarded themselves as special agents of cultural change and were regarded by some as "half-baked Europeans," but, as Boadi-Siaw notes, they nonetheless combined their European and African ideas and skills and made notable contributions to Ghana, Togo, Benin, and Nigeria.[4]

Let us now examine developments on the other side of the continent, where the Indian Ocean slave trade was many centuries older than that of the Atlantic, and where Africans had been planted at various points in Asia from the Middle East probably as far as China since the first or second century A.D., if not earlier. These are episodes that require more extensive examination by researchers, for by the time of my own research—which focused on the nineteenth century primarily—African communities were already centuries old in India, Turkey, Arabia, Iraq, Iran, Yemen, Pakistan, China, and possibly elsewhere.[5]

In India, for example, frequent references to Africans may be found in records from the thirteenth century. Groups of Africans (referred to in Asia as *Habshis* and *Siddis*) revolted in Bengal, India, during the latter part of the fifteenth century and established control there for a few years before finally suffering defeat. During the sixteenth and seventeenth centuries, Africans in western India, Gujarat in particular, emerged in positions of prominence in military and administrative affairs. One such person was Malik Ambar, sold as a slave in Ethiopia, in Mocha, in Baghdad and finally in India in 1575. Malik Ambar had been taught clerical skills in Arabia and later was placed in important clerical positions in the Deccan. Because of his loyalty and military skills, he eventually became a commander of the slave guard in Ahmadnagar. Malik Ambar commanded a unit of a thousand African soldiers and built auxiliary units of Asians; with these two groups he seized power and emerged as the undisputed leader of the Ahmadnagar area between 1602 and 1626. In this role he prevented the Great Mughuls of Delhi from conquering the Deccan for more than a quarter of a century.[6]

Other groups of Africans became prominent on Janjira Island, some forty miles south of Bombay. They claim descent from Ethiopians and have several legends to support their claim. In any case, it appears that most of these people arrived by way of the Indian Ocean slave trade. By the seventeenth century the community had become large enough and had built a fleet strong enough to command control over the area between Bombay and Goa; they were therefore sought as allies not only by local Indian groups, Mughuls and Marathas, but also by European merchants—Dutch, Portuguese, and British. At various times during the seventeenth and eighteenth centuries the Janjira Africans played one group against the other and received subsidies to keep open the sea lanes around Bombay. However, when the economic and political stakes became higher during the eighteenth century, Britain invaded the island, destroyed the fleet, and declared it a colony in 1834.[7]

A different kind of African community in Asia sprang from the abolitionist campaign of the nineteenth century. Between 1820 and 1873, after the legal abolition of the West African slave trade in 1807,

Britain negotiated a series of abolitionist treaties with Asian and African sovereigns. In addition to suppressing the slave trade, the British also pressed for the liberation of slaves on the Asian continent itself—and had a measure of success. Thus, Africans liberated from ships on the seas and those freed on the Asian mainland were channeled to three depots for settlement: Aden in Arabia, Bombay in India, and the Seychelles in the Indian Ocean. These places had long been frequented by Africans, and they attracted others seeking the economic and social security these depots provided during the nineteenth century.[8]

Africans resided in Bombay at least as early as the eighteenth century, when British merchants also engaged in the slave trade to India. Several documents refer to British cruiser commanders complaining about the difficulty of controlling the "Madagascar slaves." The British East India Company purchased, trained, and advertised Africans as contract slaves in the eighteenth century. And in the latter part of the century, an official British abstract listing persons who could be called on to defend Bombay included nearly a thousand Africans.

As a depot for liberated Africans, Bombay received its first allotment in 1835. That year a group of 200 African children came from Karachi and was sent to Bombay's police commissioner to place them among families, in employment, or in charitable institutions. From that time until the 1870s at least, European and Indian families in Bombay requested and received liberated Africans as domestics. In addition, the British navy in India enlisted so many liberated Africans that by the 1850s the government observed that the majority of its seamen were Africans.

Mission stations also accepted liberated Africans in India. The principal stations were the Roman Catholic orphanage at Bandora, the American mission at Poona, and the Church Missionary Society (CMS) African Asylum at Nasik. In these cases the government contributed a monthly allowance for the children's upkeep. Thus, by the time of the Treaty of 1873, the East African slave trade was legally ended. When Bartle Frere recommended the establishment of settlements of liberated Africans on the East African coast, liberated Africans in India were prepared to return and make a meaningful contribution to East Africa.

The CMS mission at Nasik, in particular, was called on to provide the initial group. Nasik had been established in 1854 by the Reverend William Price with initial funds from fines imposed on convicted slave dealers in India. In 1857, the government of India began making annual awards from the public revenues. As a center for liberated African children, its responsibilities included the conduct of a school that taught history, geography,

English, arithmetic, and Bible studies; in addition, the girls were trained in sewing and cooking, while the boys were trained as blacksmiths, carpenters, masons, and printers. At that time it was thought that the Africans should be prepared to seek jobs in addition to their missionary work. David Livingstone was one of the staunch supporters of the school. In 1865 he visited the school and returned to Africa with nine of the boys, one of whom was with him when he died.[9]

Now, let us turn to the Kenya connection. In 1874, the CMS sent William Price, who had established the program at Nasik, to organize the station in Mombasa. Prior arrangements had already been undertaken as early as 1864 when William Henry Jones, who had been rescued as a slave and landed at Nasik in 1854, was sent to Mombasa to join Johann Rebmann, the CMS missionary. While on the coast, Jones visited several areas, including Zanzibar, to explore the possibilities of establishing mission stations for the resettlement of liberated Africans. He returned to Bombay in 1871 and appealed to Africans to return to the coast and to Zanzibar under the auspices of the CMS. Clearly, therefore, the movement to return was already in motion when Frere recommended that liberated and captured Africans be repatriated at Mombasa.[10]

The history of Nasik led to the selection of William Price, the former superintendent, to supervise the establishment of the community at Mombasa, which came to be known as Freetown and was patterned after Nasik. The aims of the CMS project were to form an industrial Christian settlement of liberated Africans at Freetown and Rabai, and to expand toward Kilimanjaro. To accomplish these objectives, a church and a school were built, and William Jones, Ismael Semler, David George, and their wives, all Africans formerly at the Nasik school became Price's principal assistants. They were joined later by others from the Bombay area, who, thus, have become known in some quarters as Bombay Africans, Bombay boys, and Nasik boys.[11]

The early settler Africans became pioneers in the Freetown settlement. They helped to set the cultural tone and substance of the community through their leadership roles in the churches, schools, media, trade unions, crafts, and civil service; and neighboring Africans, Europeans, Arabs, and Indians in Kenya viewed the Christian community of Freetown as an influential outpost of Western society.[12]

Freetown poses some contrasts to Sierra Leone and Liberia. First, unlike the two West African examples, Freetown was founded by repatriated Africans who, for the most part, were born in Africa, and who had been away only for up to twenty years before returning. They, therefore, retained much more of their culture, especially language (they spoke Swahili and some of the vernaculars); they also had not been abroad long enough to sever ties with families and friends (indeed, some among them were reunited with members of their families and friends at Freetown and Rabai). In addition, because those who returned came from a mission station apart from Indian society, they had not been exposed to any great extent to the wider Indian community and, therefore, had little reason to identify with it, though several of them had been taught the Hindostani and Gujarati languages.

However, like their West African counterparts in Liberia and Sierra Leone, the Bombay group had had significant exposure to Western cultural values for up to a maximum of twenty years. They were Christians, spoke English, adopted European dress, and acquired skills as blacksmiths, carpenters, masons, and tailors. Some of them gained experience as railroad and dock workers. All of these activities made them attractive potential for European missionaries propagating the faith, for merchants expanding their businesses, for explorers venturing into the interior, and for colonial officials entrenching colonial rule. Thus, some of the repatriated Africans became missionaries who settled widely along the coast, establishing mission stations. The Imperial British East Africa Company (IBEA) and other businesses made use of repatriated Africans as clerks and interpreters, while explorers employed them to accompany caravans into the interior and relied heavily on their accounts of inland societies. William Jones, for example, accompanied Bishop Hannington to Uganda. In addition to returning with news of Hannington's death, Jones also provided valuable information on the state of affairs between the coast and Uganda.

With the establishment of colonial rule, people of Freetown were employed as clerks, interpreters, and advisers in the courts, post office, and other agencies. Indeed, one of the few highly qualified printers, African or otherwise, on the coast in the 1920s was James "Jimmy" Jones, son of William Jones.

No one at Freetown really compares with Blyden of Liberia, but there are some similarities with William Jones. He was an ex-slave who was reared in the Indian mission, where he received a good Western education. Like Blyden, he made several trips from Africa to India to encourage Africans to return to the continent. There seems to be no record of the number who responded to his appeals, but he must be given credit for having been responsible for encouraging some of the several hundred who ultimately joined the community directly from India. In Freetown and Rabai, Jones stimulated pride in Africans and provided a rationale for the responsible involvement of the liberated community on behalf of Africans, especially on the matter of slavery and human dignity. For this stance, Jones was denounced by his fellow European missionaries, but he became a hero to Africans.

Because of their background in a Western setting, the pioneer settlers in Freretown, Sierra Leone, and Liberia identified themselves with European culture and ideas. However, because of the great numbers of other Africans who also accepted Christianity and European ways, intermarriages occurred and—as in Sierra Leone—there emerged the Creole society, which represented a blend of African and European beliefs, languages, cuisine, and so on. This group, thus, became exclusive and achieved the greatest mobility in trade and Western-style professions, where Africans could earn the most money. This also happened in Liberia, where the repatriates believed that theirs was the task of redeeming Africa, which meant a special position for them in the country's affairs. In Liberia the strong impact of American racial denigration of blacks as well as the development of the "providential design" concept caused the "Americo-Liberians" to have a greater commitment to the gradual uplift of the masses than the other areas, especially after independence, which—at least theoretically—provided for greater authority in policy formulation for Liberians. A compulsory educational system to facilitate national integration did emerge in principle in the nineteenth century and slowly proceeded to incorporate other ethnic groups in Western-style activities.

Unlike Liberia, Sierra Leone remained a colony on which Britain placed some priority in Africa. Thus, Creoles received appointments to civil service posts and seats in the executive and legislative councils not only in Sierra Leone but also in other British West African colonies.[13] However, from 1896 when the British declared a colony over the hinterland, Creole fortunes diminished because interior peoples, the Mende and Temne in particular, regarded the Creoles as "black Englishmen."[14] The British then proceeded to limit Creole influence in the colony by restricting the expansion of Christianity in the hinterland and by appointing Englishmen to posts formerly held by the Creoles on the coast. This policy assured greater ethnic particularity.

At the same time, Creole merchants had to compete with European merchants whose presence in Africa increased perceptibly during the last quarter of the nineteenth century. And while the Creole community's influence in Sierra Leone declined during this period, and distrust between them and indigenous Africans increased, one should also note that Creole influence on business, education, journalism, the civil service, and other areas was deeply imprinted in neighboring countries of West Africa. The same imprint was made by

Freretownians in Kenya and to lesser degrees in Uganda, Tanganyika and Zanzibar (Tanzania).

In Freretown there developed a generally steadier trend of identification with neighboring peoples than in either Sierra Leone or Liberia at the early stage of growth. This was probably because Freretownians had not been as completely alienated from the area as their West African counterparts had been and thus could more easily understand the indigenous groups. Certainly this was evident in their language. In addition, better preparations had been made for the return to Africa, which may have resulted in part from prior knowledge of the West African experiences. Jones had surveyed the area, and Frere discussed plans and negotiated an agreement with Arabs on the coast, and they readily accepted the idea and eventually benefited from the community's presence in such things as trade, medicine, and education. The Arab School in Mombasa drew on the Freretown community for some of its teachers in the 1920s, 1930s, and later. Freretownians thus served as a social and economic bridge between Africans and Arabs on the coast.[15]

Further, several of the local missionaries tolerated (and some, especially the Africans, welcomed) the presence of their brothers fleeing slavery. In addition, neighboring Africans were attracted to Freretown for education and economic survival, especially during the several famines of the 1880s and 1890s, and for security (particularly those running away from slavery). The close identification of the area with Swahili culture also facilitated the eventual development of closer cohesion among the repatriates, refugees, and indigenous Africans. Very early, therefore, Freretown became a mixture of several ethnic groups, and although the first settlers were viewed as, and considered themselves, a kind of elite, the fact is that they soon recognized that the Europeans, Arabs, and Asians did not accord them equality but regarded them as inferior, though a step above indigenous Africans. These factors had the effect of facilitating a fusion into the larger African community, a process that continues today.

The Freretown settlers never constituted a large group and were always dependent not only on the European missionaries but also on good relations with their neighbors, among whom they missionized and taught. Indeed, by the turn of the century, the "Bombay group" as a class had greatly diminished, as they moved to coastal towns and into the interior, fusing with other groups. Some of them migrated because of grievances against the white missionaries; others sought economic opportunities in the towns; still others joined different mission stations. Today, therefore, the descendants of the first settlers are widely scattered on the coast, with only a few remaining in Freretown proper.

Many of the migrating Freretownians became teachers in various parts of the country. It is probably no exaggeration to say that most Africans educated in Kenya prior to World War II were taught by Freretownians or Freretown-trained teachers, and most Christian Africans in Kenya probably had close contact with Freretown. The Freretown Divinity School was the main source of primary and secondary education in the country until 1931, when it was relocated near Nairobi at Limuru. This educational and missionary influence was also spread in neighboring Tanganyika and Zanzibar (Tanzania), and Uganda; and Freretownians were also among the first pioneering Kenyan journalists, radio announcers, and trade unionists, especially among the Africans of Mombasa.

The first national political party among Kenya Africans, KASU/KAU (Kenya African Study Union/Kenya African Union), was founded by several repatriates, including Francis Khamisi, the first general secretary; Thomas Mbotela, assistant general secretary and later vice president under Jomo Kenyatta; and "Jimmy" Jeremiah; all from the Freretown tradition. Other leaders then and later received their education and had close contacts with Freretown. Indeed, the influence of ideas such as multiracialism, nonviolence, and a constitutional approach to independence became major objectives of KAU until late 1951, in large measure because of the impact of these men. It is noteworthy that when Jomo Kenyatta returned to Kenya in 1947 after many years abroad, his leadership depended on assistants who knew the country—the Europeans, Africans, and Asians—who could communicate easily in English and local languages and who had a "national image" to underscore the national character of the party. The Freretownians met those criteria better than anyone else and emerged as key party leaders until Mau Mau ushered in a more radical approach to replace the moderate, constitutional approach pursued by the repatriates and others.

In conclusion, Sierra Leone, Liberia, and Freretown are examples of an important physical return of African people from the diaspora to Africa, thereby greatly influencing not only their immediate settlements but surrounding societies as well. Whether the repatriates served as teachers or civil servants, doctors or trade unionists, journalists or politicians, they were conveyors of ideas and skills necessary to modernize Africa. Their contribution to the development of managerial skills and conceptual approaches necessary to understand international problems and interrelationships greatly accelerated modern freedom movements and the emergence of a national consciousness in several African states. This is not an argument that these developments would not have occurred without the returnees; it is an argument that they did occur with critical assistance from the diaspora.

The black returnees could not escape the influence of their physical and social environment abroad. That influence not only accounted for the contributions they made as returnees in Africa but also facilitated their continued links with the diaspora. Although their language and life-styles changed and their values and goals were modified, traces of several African languages persist in the Guianas and the islands of the southeastern United States; Yoruba became widely spoken in parts of Brazil; Swahili was planted in India; and Creole emerged in Africa and several diaspora communities. Indeed, evidence of cultural continuity continues to be uncovered, and it is likely that the continuity in substance rather than form is even greater. Without a doubt, therefore, cultural as well as biological links were forged between Africa and the diaspora communities, and those links facilitated a meaningful return to Africa.

Whether in music or literature, social or economic relations, military or political achievements, Africans in the diaspora have been major contributors to their adopted societies, in spite of inhibiting racial prejudices on the part of Euro-Americans. Perhaps the greatest contribution of Africans abroad was labor, which facilitated the accumulation of capital, the advance of technology, the internationalization of banking and insurance, and the general administrative organization, especially in the West, but also in the Persian Gulf region and southern Asia, where much additional research is needed.

In conclusion, Sierra Leone, Liberia, Freretown, and the scattered areas in Ghana, Togo, Benin, and Nigeria are examples of an important physical return. This comparative approach clearly has potential for the reconstruction of the history of Africa and its influence abroad; it also promises to provide a more realistic perspective on the history of Africa as well as the areas in which the African presence was established—Europe, the Americas, and Asia.

Notes

1. Many sources consider this subject: Christopher Fyfe, *A History of Sierra Leone* (London: Oxford University Press, 1962); John Peterson, *Province of Freedom: A History of Sierra Leone* (Evanston: University of Illinois Press, 1969); Johnson U. J. Asiegbu, *Slavery and the Politics of Liberation, 1787–1861* (New York: Longmans, 1969); Arthur Porter, *Creoledom* (New York, 1963); Leo Spitzer, *The Creoles of Sierra Leone: Responses to Colo-*

nialism, 1870–1945 (Madison: University of Wisconsin Press, 1974); Jean H. Kopytoff, *A Preface to Modern Nigeria: The Sierra Leoneans in Yoruba, 1880–1890* (Madison: University of Wisconsin Press, 1965); Kenneth L. Little, "The Significance of the West African Creole for Africanist and Afro-American Studies," *African Affairs* 49, 197 (1950); John D. Hargreaves, "African Colonization in the 19th Century: Liberia and Sierra Leone," *Sierra Leone Studies* 4. See also chapter 20 by Akintola Wyse in this volume.

2. The following are sources on Liberia: Raymond Buell, *Liberia: A Century of Survival, 1847–1947* (Philadelphia, 1947); Merran Fraenkel, *Tribe and Class in Monrovia* (New York: Oxford, 1964); Hollis Lynch, *Edward Wilmot Blyden: Pan Negro Patriot* (London: Oxford University Press, 1967); C. L. Simpson, *The Symbol of Liberia* (London: Oxford University Press, 1961); and several issues of *The Liberian Historical Review.*

3. These developments have received much scholarly and popular attention and do not need extended discussion here, especially since some of the contributors to this volume consider the topic.

4. See S. Y. Boadi-Siaw, pp. 421–439 of this volume.

5. This is a largely unexplored dimension of the African diaspora. Consequently, most of the published sources are those of the author: Joseph E. Harris, *The African Presence in Asia: Consquences of the East African Slave Trade* (Evanston, Ill.: Northwestern University Press, 1971); *Abolition and Repatriation in Kenya* (Historical Association of Kenya, East African Publishing House, Nairobi, Kenya, 1977); "The Black Peoples of Asia," *World Encyclopedia of Black Peoples* (Scholarly Press, 1975); *Recollections of James Juma Mbotela* (East African Publishing House, Nairobi, Kenya, 1977).

6. Harris, *The African Presence in Asia* 87–98; Sheikh Chand, *Malik Ambar* (Hyderabad, 1931) in Urdu; D. R. Seth, "The Life and Times of Malik Ambar," *Islamic Culture: An English Quarterly* 31 (Hyderabad, January 1957); Bena Rasi Prasad Saksena, "Malik Ambar," *Hindustani Academy* 4 (October 1933), in Hindi; M. S. Commissariat, *A History of Gujarat* (Calcutta, 1957); E. Denison Ross, *An Arabic History of Gujarat* (London, 1921).

7. D. R. Banaji, *Bombay and the Siddis* (Bombay, 1933); R. V. Ramdas, "Relations between the Marathas and the Siddis of Janjira" (Ph.D. diss., University of Bombay, n.d.); Harris, *The African Presence in Asia*, 80–87.

8. India, Political Department, "Report on the Emigration of Siddhies of Hyderabad" (December 1882) 1: 110–13; Harris, *The African Presence in Asia*, 99–114.

9. Harris, *Abolition and Repatriation*, 19.

10. Ibid., 20.

11. Ibid., 21.

12. James Juma Mbotela, *The Freeing of the Slaves in East Africa* (London: Oxford, 1956) and in Swahili, *Uhuru wa Watumwa* (London: Oxford, 1934).

13. Kopytoff, *Preface to Modern Nigeria*; I. K. Sundiata, "Creolization on Fernando Po: The Nature of Society," *The African Diaspora: Interpretive Essays* (Cambridge: Harvard University Press, 1976).

14. Akintola Wyse modifies this characterization. See page 357 of this volume.

15. For a fuller discussion of this and the remainder of this section before the conclusion, see Joseph E. Harris, *Repatriates and Refugees in a Colonial Society: The Case of Kenya* (Washington, D. C.: Howard University Press, 1982).

CHAPTER NINE

Gifts and Reflections

And they said one to another, Behold, this
dreamer cometh. Come now therefore,
and let us slay him, and cast him into some
pit, and we will say, some evil beast hath
devoured him: and We shall see what
will become of his dreams.

Genesis 37:19

BENJAMIN BRAWLEY

The Negro Genius

About the Negro in the United States two things are observable. One is that distinction so far won by members of the race has been most frequently in the arts. The other is that, aside from enforced labor, any influence exerted on civilization has been mainly in the field of aesthetics. As to the first point, we might refer to a long line of beautiful singers, to the sensuous poetry of Dunbar, the picturesque style of Du Bois, the mysticism of the paintings of Tanner, and to the striving of many younger artists. Even Booker T. Washington, most practical of men, is largely remembered for his anecdote and vivid illustration. The influence on the country's life will be referred to more than once as we proceed.

If one has taken note of the homes of Negro peasants in the South, he must have observed that the instinct for beauty insists upon an outlet. If no better picture is available, there will be a flaming advertisement on the walls. Few homes have not at least a rosebush in the garden or a geranium on the windowsill. Conversely, those things that are most picturesque make to the Negro the readiest appeal. *Faust* has been popular with those who would never think of going to another play of its class. The applause leaves one in no doubt as to the reason for Goethe's popularity. It is the suggestiveness of the love scenes, the red costume of Mephistopheles, the electrical effects, and the rain of fire that give the thrill desired. *Faust* is a good show as well as a good play.

In some of our communities Negroes are often known to "get happy" in church. It is never a sermon on the theory of the Atonement that awakens such ecstasy. Instead, this accompanies a vivid description of the beauties of heaven—the walls of jasper, the angels with palms in their hands, and, best of all, the feast of milk and honey. It is the sensuous appeal that is most effective. The untutored Negro is thrilled not so much by the moral as by the artistic and pictorial elements of religion.

Just why this should be so is a question for the anthropologist. At present we are concerned simply with the fact. Behind any achievement of the race is temperament, and that of the Negro has been shown to be pre-eminently imaginative and sensuous. It is subjective too, so that in general Negro authors and composers have been better in poetry and music than in the novel and the drama. The temper seeks an outlet in vivid, striking expression. Naturally this would be seen first of all in the folklore.

In the life and history of the Negro has developed an unusual store of customs, superstitions, and tales. Frederick Douglass and William Wells Brown called attention to this, but Charles W. Chesnutt was the first writer of the race to give it sustained literary treatment. Its chief monument so far has been in the Uncle Remus tales of Joel Chandler Harris. One must be careful of course not to claim too much for the Negro. The study of sources and analogues is far from being as simple as some might suppose. It takes one far afield, not only to Africa but even to India and the Continent of Europe.

Important as is Negro folklore, however, the folk-music is even more so. In recent years this has been claimed for other countries or nations; but, just as in the folklore there is distinctive imagination, so in the music there is a quality peculiarly the Negro's own. One has to consider both the "spirituals" and the secular songs.

Unlike the English and Scottish popular ballads, the spirituals depend for their merit more upon their tunes than their words. They are also more affected by nature. A meteoric shower, a thunder-storm, or the dampness of a furrow was sufficient to give birth to a hymn; and there was the freest possible use of figures of speech. As in the ballads, the sentiment becomes universal, and there is a tendency toward what has been called incremental repetition; thus, after a number of old people had been crooning "I'm a-Rollin'" before a fire, someone would begin a stanza, "O brothers, won't you help me?" Then would follow, "O sisters, won't you help me?" Obviously such a process could be prolonged indefinitely. One soon observes different stages in the development of this music. The first gives that which is simple and elemental, taking one to the African wilderness, as in "See Fo' an' Twenty

Elders on Deir Knees." The second stage exhibits the great class of Afro-American melodies, like "Steal Away" and "I've been a-listenin' all de night long." The third shows a blending of Negro music and that of the adopted country, as in "Bright Sparkles in the Churchyard." Those melodies that are most original are generally sorrowful in tone, growing out of the Negro's trials in slavery, like "Nobody Knows de Trouble I See" and "Sometimes I Feel Like a Motherless Child." In some, however, there is a note of triumph, as in "Oh, Give Way, Jordan" and "I'm Gwine to Jine de Great 'Sociation." No one is able to tell just how many of these melodies are in existence, for, though there have been many collections, there is not yet one that is definitive.

Just as the spirituals reflect the higher life of the Negro—that of prayer and hope and yearning, with some influence from the evangelical hymns—so do the secular songs reflect his lower life—that of the railroad camp, the turpentine camp, and the chaingang. Only within recent years have these received scholarly study. To some extent they were submerged by minstrelsy, and the influence of the churches was naturally against them. In 1911, however, Howard W. Odum began to publish articles on "Folk-Songs and Folk-Poetry as found in the Secular Songs of Southern Negroes," and he and Guy B. Johnson have since produced *The Negro and his Songs* and *Negro Workaday Songs*. Other writers have followed and Professor Johnson has also published *John Henry*, about the "big steel-drivin' man" who died with a hammer in his hand. The ballads that have grown up about this heroic figure are typical of the songs at their best. It appears that John Henry had a contest with a steel-driving machine in which he was victorious at the cost of his life. "There is pretty good evidence that the ballad is based on an incident which occurred about 1871 during the building of the Big Bend Tunnel on the C. & O. Railroad in West Virginia."

John Henry said to his captain,
"Well, a man ain't nothing but a man,
But before I'll be beaten by your old steam drill,
I'll die with my hammer in my han',
Lawd, I'll die with my hammer in my han'."

There are numerous other work songs, songs about women, and "blues," these last being "the sorrowful songs of the workaday Negro." There is also much "bad man stuff," one of the best known songs being about Stacker Lee (more commonly, Stagolee), who could shoot the buttons off a man's coat but whose reputation paled somewhat when he met John Henry.

Stagolee was a bully man an' everybody knowed
When dey seed Stagolee comin' to give Stagolee de road.
Oh, dat man, bad man, Stagolee done come.

This reference to the spirituals and even to songs of a different temper calls up something far deeper than sensuous beauty. No people can rise to the heights of art until it has passed through suffering. The Russians are a case in point; they have endured much and their literature is one of power. The same future beckons to the Negro. There is something elemental about the race—something that finds its origin in the forest and the sighing of the nightwind. There is something grim and stern about it too, something that speaks of the lash, of the child torn from its mother's bosom, of the body riddled with bullets and swinging all night by the roadside.

Naturally one might expect to find this temper best revealed in those members of the race who were strong characters but untouched by the schools. So we do. Harriet Tubman was describing to an audience a great battle in the Civil War. "And then," she said, "we saw the lightning, and that was the guns; and then we heard the thunder, and that was the big guns; and then we heard the rain falling, and that was drops of blood falling; and when we came to git in the craps, it was dead men that we reaped." Sojourner Truth, the old prophetess with inimitable wit, was speaking to one who came to see her in her last illness. "I isn't goin' to die, honey," she said; "I's goin' home like a shootin' star."

John Jasper, of Richmond, Virginia, became famous a few years after the Civil War by reason of his sermon, "De Sun do Move." Even before the war he was well known in the vicinity for his picturesque discourses; and he preached not only on his favorite theme but also on "Dry Bones in the Valley," "The Hebrew Children in the Fiery Furnace," "The Raising of Lazarus," and other subjects that gave scope for his imagination. The Reverend William E. Hatcher, who heard him preach more than once, has described for us the portrayal of the King in his beauty. Said he of Jasper: "His earnestness and reverence passed all speech, and grew as he went. The light from the throne dazzled him from afar. There was the great white throne, there the elders bowing in adoring wonder, there the archangels waiting in silence for the commands of the King, there the King in his resplendent glory, there in hosts innumerable were the ransomed. In point of vivid description it surpassed all I had heard or read. The old Negro seemed glorified. Earth could hardly hold him. He sprang about the platform with a boy's alertness; he was unconsciously waving his handkerchief as if greeting a conqueror; his face was streaming with tears; he was bowing before the Redeemer; he was clapping his hands, laughing, shouting and wiping the blinding tears out of his eyes. It was a moment of transport and unmatched wonder to every one, and I felt as if it could never cease, when suddenly in a new note he broke into his chorus, ending with the soul-melting words, 'Oh, what mus' it be to be thar!' "

It is obvious, then, that if we would have at its best the element of which we have spoken, we must take the race without adulteration or sophistication. It happens that those who belong to the Negro people in the United States form the most variegated group in the world. Ray Stannard Baker said thirty years ago that he had not been studying the South very long before he was forced to ask just what was a Negro. The statement of some persons that they belonged to the race he accepted against the testimony of his own senses. Some had blue eyes and flaxen hair. That is true; and because the persons of fairer hue have generally had better economic and cultural opportunity than others, it was a favorite diversion of some men in the nineteenth century to assert and try to prove that the ability of individuals was in direct proportion to their infusion of white blood.

In some cases this may have been true; but so far was it from being the general truth that we may now affirm that such distinction as the Negro has won in the arts is due primarily to the black rather than the mixed element in the race. People of mixed blood have given us the college presidents, the administrators, the Government employees; but the blacks are the singers and seers. Black slaves gave us the spirituals; modern composers of a lighter hue transcribe them. A modern author may reproduce in verse the sermons of the old exhorters, but it would hardly do to ask him to preach one of them. In other words, the mixed element in the race may represent the Negro's talent, but it is upon the black element that he must rely for his genius.

Let us not be misunderstood. In our emphasis on achievement in the arts, we do not mean to say that the Negro can not rise to distinction in any other sphere. He has recently made notable advance in scholarship, and some of the younger men have been especially brilliant in science. We do suggest, however, that every race has its peculiar genius and that, as far as we can at present judge, the Negro, with all his manual labor, is destined to reach his greatest heights in the field of the artistic. On every hand we have proof of this tendency.

For a long time this inclination was discounted or disregarded. The public associated the Negro simply with minstrelsy, burlesque, and a few stereotyped characters. Then, in 1867, a sympathetic article on the spirituals by Thomas Wentworth Higginson in the *Atlantic* commanded attention, and within the next decade the Fisk Jubilee Singers were received with acclaim. At the close of the century Paul Laurence Dunbar won such success as was never before achieved by a Negro author. Two decades later, in connection with the World

War and after, the change in attitude became general. Where formerly the Negro was ignored, he mounted to the crest of the wave. It became the popular thing to attend night clubs in Harlem. Publishers who formerly had frowned upon Negro novels were now eager to have one or two such books on their lists. By 1925 the new fad was in full career. In literature there was a so-called renaissance.

About the origin of jazz, which was now popular, there was much discussion. Some writers have insisted that the word is primarily a verb rather than a noun. That means, as Sigmund G. Spaeth reminded us (*Forum*, August, 1928), that "jazz is not a form of music. It is a treatment applied to music, and, incidentally, to all the arts, and to modern life in general. The jazz treatment, in brief, is a distortion of the conventional, a revolt against tradition, a deliberate twisting of established formulas. As such, it is thoroughly characteristic of the civilization of today." That may be, but it was generally understood that what was known as jazz in music originated in Negro slums; and it called for serious consideration in view of its far-reaching connections in modern art.

Whether the new impulse was an unmixed good, and whether it tended toward the development of what is best in literature, is an open question. Again we are primarily concerned with a fact. A change had taken place and as never before attention was directed to Negro life and Negro themes. It happened that interest was chiefly in life on the lowest plane, writers seeming to be moved by one or the other of two appeals. One was that of the sensational. Prostitutes and gamblers had to be featured by all means, and a whole stream of novels followed in the wake of Carl Van Vechten's *Nigger Heaven*. The other appeal was that of primitivism. This was more provocative.

It was about 1907 that some modernistic painters in Paris—Picasso, Derain, Matisse, and Vlaminck—in their endeavor to produce certain new effects on canvas, observed that similar effects had been achieved centuries before in primitive African art. About some samples of wood-carving that they found they realized that "these figures were not mere childish attempts to make our kind of statue; they were successful attempts to make an entirely different kind of statue." In some ways they were even "a stage in advance of European evolution." Clive Bell, writing in 1920, said of the efforts of the artists and their literary apostle, Guillaume Apollinaire, to find pieces of African workmanship in old shops: "Thus a demand was created which M. Paul Guillaume was there to meet and stimulate. The part played by that enterprising dealer is highly commendable; it was he who put the most sensitive public in Europe—a little cosmopolitan group of artists, critics, and amateurs—in the way of seeing a number of first-rate things." In 1926, with the co-operation of the Barnes Foundation of Merion, Pennsylvania, Paul Guillaume and Thomas Munro produced *Primitive Negro Sculpture*, a book that became almost the bible of the new movement. It called attention to the fact that Negro sculpture offered a compromise between representation and design, and concluded: "In an age when more than one voice has been heard to say that sculpture is obsolete, and the plastic arts exhausted, Negro art has brought creative forces that may prove to be inexhaustible."

To some extent that statement was a challenge, and there were not lacking those willing to take up the gauntlet. To many it not only seemed that the fad was overdone, and largely promoted by commercialism, but that a fundamental question was raised as to the extent to which primitive African art had anything whatsoever to do with the achievement of Negro artists in America. Some Negroes were opposed to the fad by reason of its social and political implications. They felt that effort in connection with it was a subtle attempt to set them apart and fit them into a groove in American life, and they insisted that for the Negro in the United States the influence of nationalism was stronger than that of race. Even Paul Laurence Dunbar twenty years previously had taken this position. A reporter once asked him about the poetry written by Negroes as compared with that of white people. Dunbar replied, "The predominating power of the African race is lyric. In that I should expect the writers of my race to excel. But, broadly speaking, their poetry will not be exotic or differ much from that of the whites. For two hundred and fifty years the environment of the Negro has been American, in every respect the same as that of all other Americans." George S. Schuyler, writing under the title "The Negro-Art Hokum" in the *Nation* (June 16, 1926), said: "Because a few writers with a paucity of themes have seized upon the imbecilities of the Negro rustics and clowns and palmed them off as authentic and characteristic Aframerican behavior, the common notion that the black American is so 'different' from his white neighbor has gained wide currency. . . . Negro art has been, is, and will be among the numerous black nations of Africa; but to suggest the possibility of any such development among the ten million colored people in this republic is self-evident foolishness."

This attitude of protest is of course largely negative; it does not encourage a distinctive art. On the other hand one might note the position of Langston Hughes, who has also written in the *Nation* (June 23, 1926). Says he: "We younger Negro artists who create now intend to express our individual dark-skinned selves without fear or shame. If the white people are pleased, we are glad. If they are not, it doesn't matter. We know we are beautiful. And ugly too. The tom-tom cries and the tom-tom laughs. If colored people are pleased, we are glad. If they are not, their displeasure doesn't matter either. We build our temples for to-morrow, strong as we know them, and we stand on top of the mountain, free within ourselves."

To some extent the temples have begun to be erected, but there is a shortcoming not always recognized by writers of the school of Mr. Hughes. In their protest against the smugness and the self-consciousness of the bourgeoisie, they laud "the so-called common element," the "lowdown folks," who "live on Seventh Street in Washington or State Street in Chicago," and they present again and again the roustabout, the gambler, and the prostitute. They protest against the older stereotypes; yet, if they do not watch, they will give us new stereotypes hardly better than the old.

It thus appears that in speaking of the Negro Genius we enter a field beset with explosives. At any turn one may run into a contradiction or an inconsistency. We can not reconcile all the differences of opinion, but about one thing at least we must be clear: we emphasize no connection between primitive African art and that of the Negro in America to-day. An individual sculptor may indeed receive some suggestion or inspiration from a piece of African carving, but that would not say that his own culture was basically African. We recall that the English drama, an indigenous growth, at the time of Elizabeth received stimulus from Plautus and Seneca, but that stimulus did not make the English drama Latin. So we shall not attempt to overstate the present case. We do think, however, that the main observation will hold: The temperament of the American Negro is primarily lyrical, imaginative, subjective; and his genius has most frequently sought expression in some one of the arts.

STERLING ALLEN BROWN

Negro Character As Seen by White Authors

Introduction

There are three types of Negroes, says Roark Bradford, in his sprightly manner: "the nigger, the 'colored person,' and the Negro—upper case N." In his foreword to *Ol' Man Adam an' His Chillun*, the source from which Marc Connelly drew *The Green Pastures*, and a book causing the author to be considered, in some circles, a valid interpreter of *the* Negro, Roark Bradford defines *the* Negro's character and potentialities. The Negro, he says, is the race leader, not too militant, concerned more with economic independence than with civil equality. The colored person, "frequently of mixed blood, loathes the blacks and despises the whites. . . . Generally he inherits the weaknesses of both races and seldom inherits the strength of either. He has the black man's emotions and the white man's inhibitions."[1] Together with the "poor white trash" it is the "colored persons" who perpetuate racial hatreds and incite race riots and lynchings. "The nigger" interests Mr. Bradford more than the rest. He is indolent, entirely irresponsible, shiftless, the bugaboo of Anglo-Saxon ideals, a poor fighter and a poor hater, primitively emotional and uproariously funny.

Such are the "original" contributions of Mr. Bradford, who states modestly that, in spite of the Negro's penchant to lying:

> I believe I know them pretty well. I was born on a plantation that was worked by them; I was nursed by one as an infant and I played with one when I was growing up. I have watched them at work in the fields, in the levee camps, and on the river. I have watched them at home, in church, at their picnics and their funerals.[2]

All of this, he believes, gives him license to step forth as their interpreter and repeat stereotypes time-hallowed in the South. It doesn't. Mr. Bradford's stories remain highly amusing; his generalizations about *the* Negro remain a far better analysis of a white man than of *the* Negro. We see that, even in pontifical moments, one white Southerner cannot escape being influenced by current folk-beliefs.

Mr. Bradford's views have been restated at some length to show how obviously dangerous it is to rely upon literary artists when they advance themselves as sociologists and ethnologists. Mr. Bradford's easy pigeonholing of an entire race into three small compartments is a familiar phenomenon in American literature, where the Indian, the Mexican, the Irishman, and the Jew have been similarly treated. Authors are too anxious to have it said, "Here is *the* Negro," rather than here are a few Negroes whom I have seen. If one wishes to learn of Negro individuals observed from very specialized points of view, American literature can help him out. Some books will shed a great deal of light upon Negro experience. But if one wishes to learn of *the* Negro, it would be best to study *the*

Sterling A. Brown and "Duke" Ellington (Courtesy of the Moorland-Spingarn Research Center)

Negro himself; a study that might result in the discovery that *the* Negro is more difficult to find than the countless human beings called Negroes.

The Negro has met with as great injustice in American literature as he has in American life. The majority of books about Negroes merely stereotype Negro character. It is the purpose of this paper to point out the prevalence and history of these stereotypes. Those considered important enough for separate classification, although overlappings *do* occur, are seven in number: (1) The Contented Slave, (2) The Wretched Freeman, (3) The Comic Negro, (4) The Brute Negro, (5) The Tragic Mulatto, (6) The Local Color Negro, and (7) The Exotic Primitive.

A detailed evaluation of each of these is impracticable because of limitations of space. It can be said, however, that all of these stereotypes are marked either by exaggeration or omissions; that they all agree in stressing the Negro's divergence from an Anglo-Saxon norm to the flattery of the latter; they could all be used, as they probably are, as justification of racial proscription; they all illustrate dangerous specious generalizing from a few particulars recorded by a single observer from a restricted point of view—which is itself generally dictated by the desire to perpetuate a stereotype. All of these stereotypes are abundantly to be found in American literature, and are generally accepted as contributions to true racial understanding. Thus one critic, setting out imposingly to discuss "the Negro character"

---

[1] Roark Bradford, *Ol' Man Adam an' His Chillun*. New York: Harper and Bros., 1928, p. xi.

[2] *Ibid.*, p. ix.

in American literature, can still say, unabashedly, that *"The whole range of the Negro character is revealed thoroughly,"*[3] in one twenty-six-line sketch by Joel Chandler Harris of Br'er Fox and Br'er Mud Turtle.

The writer of this essay does not consider everything a stereotype that shows up the weaknesses of Negro character; sometimes the stereotype makes the Negro appear too virtuous. Nor does he believe the stereotypes of contented slaves and buffoons are to be successfully balanced by pictures of Negroes who are unbelievably intellectual, noble, self-sacrificial, and faultless. Any stereotyping is fatal to great, or even to convincing literature. Furthermore, he believes that he has considered to be stereotypes only those patterns whose frequent and tedious recurrence can be demonstrably proved by even a cursory acquaintance with the literature of the subject.

The Contented Slave

"Massa make de darkies lub him
'Case he was so kind. . . ."
　　　　　　　　(Stephen Foster)

The first lukewarm stirrings of abolitionary sentiment in the South were chilled with Eli Whitney's invention of the cotton gin at the close of the 18th Century. Up until this time the *raison d'être* of slavery had not been so powerful. But now there was a way open to quick wealth; Cotton was crowned King, and a huge army of black servitors was necessary to keep him upon the throne; considerations of abstract justice had to give way before economic expediency. A complete rationale of slavery was evolved.

One of the most influential of the authorities defending slavery was President Dew of William and Mary College, who stated, in 1832,

> . . . slavery had been the condition of all ancient culture, that Christianity approved servitude, and that the law of Moses had both assumed and positively established slavery. . . . It is the order of nature and of God that the being of superior faculties and knowledge, and therefore of superior power, should control and dispose of those who are inferior. It is as much in the order of nature that men should enslave each other as that other animals should prey upon each other.[4]

The pamphlet of this young teacher was extensively circulated, and was substantiated by Chancellor Harper of the University of South Carolina in 1838:

> Man is born to subjection. . . . The proclivity of the natural man is to domineer or to be subservient. . . . If there are sordid, servile, and laborious offices to be performed, is it not better that there should be sordid, servile, and laborious beings to perform them?[5]

The economic argument had frequent proponents; an ex-governor of Virginia showed that, although Virginia was denied the tremendous prosperity accruing from cotton raising, it was still granted the opportunity to profit from selling Negroes to the far South. Sociologists and anthropologists hastened forward with proof of the Negro's three-fold inferiority: physically (except for his adaptability to cotton fields and rice swamps), mentally, and morally. Theologians advanced the invulnerable arguments from the Bible; in one of the "Bible Defences of Slavery" we read: "The curse of Noah upon *Ham,* had a *general* and *interminable* application to the whole Hamite race, in placing them under a *peculiar* liability of being enslaved by the races of the two other brothers."[6]

The expressions of these dominant ideas in the fiction and poetry of the period did not lag far behind. In fact, one influential novel was among the leaders of the van, for in 1832, the year in which Professor Dew stated the argument that was to elevate him to the presidency of William and Mary College, John P. Kennedy published a work that was to make him one of the most widely read and praised authors of the Southland. His ideas of the character of the Negro and of slavery are in fundamental agreement with those of Dew and Harper. According to F. P. Gaines, in *The Southern Plantation,* Kennedy's *Swallow Barn* has the historical significance of starting the plantation tradition, a tradition hoary and mildewed in our own day, but by no means moribund.

Swallow Barn is an idyllic picture of slavery on a tidewater plantation. The narrator, imagined to be from the North (Kennedy himself was from Tidewater, Maryland), comes to Virginia, expecting to see a drastic state of affairs. Instead, he finds a kindly patriarchy and grateful, happy slaves. After vignettes of the Negro's laziness, mirth, vanity, improvidence, done with some charm and, for a Southern audience, considerable persuasiveness, the "Northern" narrator concludes:

---

[3]John Herbert Nelson, *The Negro Character in American Literature.* Lawrence, Kansas: The Department of Journalism Press, 1926, p. 118.

[4]William E. Dodd, *The Cotton Kingdom,* Chapter III, Philosophy of the Cotton Planter, p. 53.

---

[5]*Ibid.,* p. 57.

[6]Josiah Priest, *Bible Defence of Slavery.* Glasgow, Ky.: W. S. Brown, 1851, p. 52.

I am quite sure they never could become a happier people than I find them here. . . . No tribe of people has ever passed from barbarism to civilization whose . . . progress has been more secure from harm, more genial to their character, or better supplied with mild and beneficent guardianship, adapted to the actual state of their intellectual feebleness, than the Negroes of *Swallow Barn*. And, from what I can gather, it is pretty much the same on the other estates in this region.[7]

Shortly after the publication of *Swallow Barn*, Edgar Allan Poe wrote:

. . . we must take into consideration the peculiar character (I may say the peculiar nature) of the Negro. . . . [Some believe that Negroes] are, like ourselves, the sons of Adam and must, therefore, have like passions and wants and feelings and tempers in all respects. This we deny and appeal to the knowledge of all who know. . . . We shall take leave to speak as of things *in esse*, in a degree of loyal devotion on the part of the slave to which the white man's heart is a stranger, and of the master's reciprocal feeling of parental attachment to his humble dependent. . . . That these sentiments in the breast of the Negro and his master are stronger than they would be under like circumstances between individuals of the white race, we believe.[8]

In *The Gold-Bug*, Poe shows this reciprocal relationship between Jupiter, a slave, and his master. Southern fiction of the thirties and forties supported the thesis of Kennedy and Poe without being so explicit. The mutual affection of the races, the slave's happiness with his status, and his refusal to accept freedom appear here and there, but the books were dedicated less to the defense of the peculiar institution than to entertainment. William Gilmore Simms, for instance, includes in *The Yemassee*, a novel published in the same year as *Swallow Barn*, the typical pro-slavery situation of a slave's refusing freedom: "I d—n to h—ll, maussa, ef I guine to be free!" roared the *adhesive* black, in a tone of unrestrainable determination.[9] But the burden of this book is not pro-slavery; Hector earns his freedom by the unslavish qualities of physical prowess, foresight, and courage in battle.

In 1853, Simms, in joining forces with Dew and Harper in the *Pro-Slavery Argument*, writes: "Slavery has elevated the Negro from savagery. The black man's

finer traits of fidelity and docility were encouraged in his servile position. . . ."[10] Simms turned from cursory references to slavery to ardent pro-slavery defense, in company with other novelists of the South, for a perfectly definite reason. The abolitionary attacks made by men like Garrison had taken the form of pamphlets, and these had been answered in kind. The publication of *Uncle Tom's Cabin* in 1851, however, showed that the abolitionists had converted the novel into a powerful weapon. Pro-slavery authors were quick to take up this weapon, although their wielding of it was without the power of Harriet Beecher Stowe. *Swallow Barn* was reissued in 1851, and "besides the numerous controversial pamphlets and articles in periodicals there were no fewer than fourteen pro-slavery novels and one long poem published in the three years (1852–54) following the appearance of *Uncle Tom's Cabin*."[11]

These novels are all cut out of the same cloth. Like *Swallow Barn*, they omit the economic basis of slavery, and minimize "the sordid, servile and laborious offices" which Chancellor Harper had considered the due of "sordid, servile, and laborious beings." The pro-slavery authors use the first adjective only in considering free Negroes, or those who, by some quirk of nature, are disobedient; admit the second completely; and deny the third. Slavery to all of them is a beneficent guardianship, the natural and inevitable state for a childish people.

There is very little reference to Negroes working in the fields; even then they are assigned to easy tasks which they lazily perform to the tune of slave melodies. They are generally described as "leaving the fields." They are allowed to have, for additional provisions and huckstering, their own garden-plots, which they attend in their abundant leisure. Their holidays are described at full length: the corn huskings, barbecuing, Yuletide parties, and hunting the possom by the light of a kindly moon.

In *Life at the South, or Uncle Tom's Cabin As It Is* (1852), Uncle Tom, out of hurt vanity, but not for any more grievous cause, runs away. His wife, Aunt Dinah, although loving Tom, realizes that her greater loyalty is due to her master, and not to her errant spouse, and refuses to escape with him. Tom, after experiencing the harshness of the unfeeling North, begs to return to slavery. In *The Planter's Northern Bride*, the bride, having come to the salve South with misgivings, is quickly converted to an enthusiast for slavery, since it presents "an aspect so tender and affectionate." One

---

[7]John P. Kennedy, *Swallow Barn*, p. 453.

[8]Edgar Allan Poe, *Literary Criticism*, Vol. 1, "Slavery in the United States," p. 271.

[9]William Gilmore Simms, *The Yemassee*. Richmond: B. F. Johnson Publishing Co., 1911, p. 423. The italics are mine but not the omissions.

[10]Jeanette Reid Tandy, "Pro-Slavery Propaganda in American Fiction of the Fifties," *South Atlantic Quarterly*, Vol. XXI, No. 1, p. 41.

[11]*Ibid.*

fears that the bride is not unpartisan, however, since her appearance on the plantation elicited wild cries of worship, and her beloved husband is a great ethnologist, proving that the Negro's peculiar skull and skin were decreed by the divine fiat so that he could pick cotton. In *The Yankee Slave Dealer*, the meddling abolitionist cannot persuade any slaves to run off with him except a half-witted rogue. One slave recited to him *verbatim* a miniature *Bible Defence of Slavery*, citing the book of the Bible, the chapter, and the verse. In *The Hireling and the Slave*, William J. Grayson, "poet laureate" of South Carolina, contrasts the lot of the industrial worker of the North with that of the slave. Gems of this widely read poetical disquisition follow:

And yet the life, so unassailed by care,
So blessed with moderate work, with ample fare,
With all the good the starving pauper needs,
The happier slave on each plantation leads. . . . (p. 50)

And Christian slaves may challenge as their own,
The blessings claimed in fabled states alone. . . . (p. 50)

This pattern of the joyous contentment of the slave in a paradisiacal bondage persisted and was strongly reenforced in Reconstruction days. If it was no longer needed for the defense of a tottering institution, it was needed for reasons nearly as exigent. Ancestor worshippers, the sons of a fighting generation, remembering bitterly the deaths or sufferings of their fathers, became elegists of a lost cause and cast a golden glow over the plantation past; unreconstructed "fire-eaters," determined to resurrect slavery as far as they were able, needed as a cardinal principle the belief that Negroes were happy as slaves, and hopelessly unequipped for freedom. Both types were persuasive, the first because the romantic idealizing of the past will always be seductive to a certain large group of readers, and the second because the sincere unremitting harping upon one argument will finally make it seem plausible. We find, therefore, that whereas *Uncle Tom's Cabin* had triumphed in the antebellum controversy, the pro-slavery works of Page, Russell, and Harris swept the field in Reconstruction days. It is from these last skillful authors, undeniably acquainted with Negro folk-life, and affectionate toward certain aspects of it, that the American reading public as a whole has accepted the delusion of the Negro as contented slave, entertaining child, and docile ward.

Mutual affection between the races is a dominant theme. Thus, Irwin Russell, the first American poet to treat Negro life in folk speech, has his ex-slave rhapsodizing about his "Mahsr John." "Washintum an' Franklum . . . wuzn't nar a one . . . come up to Mahsr John":

Well times is changed. De war it come an' sot de
   nigger free
An' now ol' Mahsr John ain't hardly wuf as much
   as me;
He had to pay his debts, an' so his lan' is mos'ly gone—
An' I declar' I's sorry for my pore ol' Mahsr John.[12]

The volume has many other references to the slave's docility toward, and worship of his master.

Irwin Russell implies throughout that the Southern white best understands how to treat the Negro. Perhaps this is one reason for Joel Chandler Harris' praise:

> But the most wonderful thing about the dialect poetry of Irwin Russell is his accurate conception of the negro character. . . . I do not know where could be found today a happier or a more perfect representation of negro character.

On reading Russell's few poems, one is struck by the limited gamut of characteristics allowed to Negroes. Inclined to the peccadilloes of cheating, lying easily; a good teller of comic stories, a child of mirth, his greatest hardship that of being kicked about by refractory mules, and his deepest emotion, compassion for his master's lost estate—surely this is hardly a "perfect" representation of even Negro folk character?

Thomas Nelson Page followed Russell's lead in poetry. In the poems of *Befo' De War*, Page puts into the mouths of his Negroes yearnings for the old days and expressions of the greatest love for old marster. One old slave welcomes death if it will replace him in old "Marster's service." Old Jack entrusts his life-earnings to his son to give to young "Marster," since the latter can't work and needs them more.[13]

In most of Page's widely influential stories, there is the stock situation of the lifelong devotion of master and body-servant. In *Marse Chan*, old "Marse" is blinded in rescuing a slave from a burning barn. Sam accompanies his young Marse Chan to the war, his devotion overcoming "racial cowardice" to such a degree that he rides to the very cannon's mouth with him, and brings back his master's body. Of slavery, Sam speaks thus:

> Dem wuz good old times, marster—de bes' Sam ever see! Dey wuz, in fac'! Niggers didn't hed nothin 't all to do—jes' hed to 'ten to de feedin' an' cleanin' de hosses, an' doin' what de marster tell 'em to do; an' when dey wuz sick, dey had things sont 'em out de

---

[12]Irwin Russell, *Christmas Night in the Quarters*. New York: The Century Co., 1917, pp. 63 ff.

[13]Thomas Nelson Page, *Befo' De War*. New York: Chas. Scribner's Sons, 1906, "Little Jack."

house, an' de same doctor come to see 'em whar ten'
do de white folks when dey wuz po'ly. D'yar warn'
no trouble nor nothin.[14]

Over all his fiction there is the reminiscent melancholy of an exiled Adam, banished by a flaming sword—wielded not by Michael but by a Yankee devil, from what was truly an Eden. In *The Negro: The Southerner's Problem*, we read:

> In fact, the ties of pride were such that it was often remarked that the affection of the slaves was stronger toward the whites than toward their own offspring.[15]

And in the same book there is an apostrophe to the "mammy" that is a worthy forerunner of the bids so many orators make for interracial goodwill, and of the many remunerative songs that emerge from Tin Pan Alley.

Joel Chandler Harris is better known for his valuable contribution to literature and folk-lore in recording the Uncle Remus stories than for his aid in perpetuation of the "plantation Negro" stereotype. Nevertheless, a merely cursory study of Uncle Remus' character would reveal his close relationship to the "Caesars," "Hectors," "Pompeys," *et al.* of the pro-slavery novel, and to Page's "Uncle Jack" and "Uncle Billy." In Uncle Remus' philosophizing about the old days of slavery there is still the wistful nostalgia. Harris comments, "In Middle Georgia the relations between master and slave were as perfect as they could be under the circumstances." This might mean a great deal, or nothing, but it is obvious from other words of Harris that, fundamentally, slavery was to him a kindly institution, and the Negro was contended. Slavery was:

> . . . in some of its aspects far more beautiful and inspiring than *any* of the relations between employers and the employed in this day.[16]

George Washington Cable, although more liberal in his views upon the Negro than his Southern contemporaries, gives an example of the self-abnegating servant in *Posson Jone'*. This slave uses his wits to safeguard his master. A goodly proportion of the Negro servants are used to solve the complications of their "white-folks." They are in a long literacy tradition—that of the faithful, clever servant—and they probably are just as true to Latin prototypes as to real Negroes. In the works of F. Hopkinson Smith, Harry Stilwell Edwards, and in Maurice Thompson's *Balance of Power,* we have this appearance of a black *deus ex machina.*

To deal adequately with the numerous books of elegiac reminiscence of days "befo' de war" would be beyond the scope and purpose of this essay. The tone of them all is to be found in such sad sentences as these:

> Aunt Phebe, Uncle Tom, Black Mammy, Uncle Gus, Aunt Jonas, Uncle Isom, and all the rest—who shall speak all your virtues or enshrine your simple faith and fidelity? It is as impossible as it is to describe the affection showered upon you by those whom you called "Marster" and "Mistis."[17]

Ambrose Gonzales grieves that "the old black folk are going fast" with the passing of the "strict but kindly discipline of slavery," yearning, in Tennysonian accents, "for the tender grace of a day that is dead."[18]

Although the realism of today is successfully discounting the sentimentalizing of the Old South, there are still many contemporary manifestations of the tradition. Hergesheimer, arch-romanticist that he is, writes that he would be happy to pay with everything the wasted presence holds for the return of the pastoral civilization based on slavery.[19]

Donald Davidson, a Tennessee poet, has written this:

Black man, when you and I were young together,
We knew each other's hearts. Though I am no longer
A child, and you perhaps unfortunately
Are no longer a child, we still understand
Better maybe than others. There is the wall
Between us, anciently erected. Once
It might have been crossed, men say. But now I cannot
Forget that I was master, and you can hardly
Forget that you were slave. We did not build
The ancient wall, but there it painfully is.
Let us not bruise our foreheads on the wall.[20]

Ol' Massa's People, by Orlando Kay Armstrong, is one of the most recent of the books in which ex-slaves speak—as in Page apparently with their master's voice—their praise of slavery. The theme seems inexhaustible; in the February issue of the *Atlantic Monthly* it is restated

[14]Thomas Nelson Page, *In Ole Virginia.* New York: Chas. Scribner's Sons, 1889.

[15]Thomas Nelson Page, *The Negro: The Southerner's Problem.* New York: Chas. Scribner's Sons, 1904, p. 174.

[16]Julia Collier Harris, *Joes Chandler Harris, Editor and Essayist.* Chapel Hill: University of North Carolina Press, 1931, "The Old-Time Darky," p. 129.

[17]Essie Collins Matthews, *Aunt Phebe, Uncle Tom and Others.* Columbus, Ohio: The Champlin Press, 1915, p. 13.

[18]Ambrose Gonzales, *With Aesop Along the Black Border.* Columbia, S. C.: The State Co., 1924, p. xiv.

[19]Joseph Hergesheimer, *Quiet Cities.* New York: Alfred A. Knopf, 1928, pp. 14 ff.

[20]Donald Davidson, *The Tall Men.* New York: Houghton Mifflin Co., 1927, p. 39.

in nearly the words that have already been quoted. Designed originally to defend slavery, it is now a convenient argument for those wishing to keep "the Negro in his place"—out of great love for him, naturally—believing that he will be happier so.

The Wretched Freeman

"Go tell Marse Linkum, to tek his freedom back."

As a foil to the contented slave, pro-slavery authors set up another puppet—the wretched free Negro. He was necessary for the argument. Most of the pro-slavery novels paid a good deal of attention to his degradation. Either the novelist interpolated a long disquisition on the disadvantages of his state both to the country and to himself, or had his happy slaves fear contact with him as with a plague.

In *Life at the South, or Uncle Tom's Cabin As It Is,* Uncle Tom experiences harsh treatment from unfeeling Northern employers, sees Negroes frozen to death in snow storms, and all in all learns that the North and freedom is no stopping place for him. In *The Yankee Slave Dealer,* the slaves are insistent upon the poor lot of free Negroes. In *The Planter's Northern Bride,* Crissy runs away from freedom in order to be happy again in servitude. Grayson in *The Hireling and the Slave* prophesies thus:

Such, too, the fate the Negro must deplore
If slavery guards his subject race no more,
If by weak friends or vicious counsels led
To change his blessings for the hireling's bread. . . .
There in the North in surburban dens and human sties,
In foul excesses sung, the Negro lies;
A moral pestilence to taint and stain.
His life a curse, his death a social gain,
Debased, despised, the Northern pariah knows
He shares no good that liberty bestows;
Spurned from her gifts, with each successive year.
In drunken want his numbers disappear.[21]

There was a carry-over of these ideas in the Reconstruction. Harris, in one of his most moving stories, *Free Joe,* showed the tragedy of a free Negro in a slave-holding South, where he was considered a bad model by slaveowners, an economic rival by poor whites, and something to be avoided by the slaves. The story might be considered as a condemnation of a system, but in all probability was taken to be another proof of the Negro's incapacity for freedom. Although Harris wrote generously of Negro advancement since

emancipation, there is little doubt that the implications of many passages furthered the stereotype under consideration.

Page, a bourbon "fire-eater," for all his yearnings for his old mammy, saw nothing of good for Negroes in emancipation:

> Universally, they [Southerners] will tell you that while the old-time Negroes were industrious, saving, and, when not misled, well-behaved, kindly, respectful, and self-respecting, and while the remnant of them who remain still retain generally these characteristics, the "new issue," for the most part, are lazy, thriftless, intemperate, insolent, dishonest, and without the most rudimentary elements of morality. . . . Universally, they report a general depravity and retrogression of the Negroes at large, in sections in which they are left to themselves, closely resembling a reversion to barbarism.[22]

The notion of the Negro's being doomed to extinction was sounded by a chorus of pseudo-scientists, bringing forth a formidable (?) array of proofs. Lafcadio Hearn yielded to the lure of posing as a prophet:

> As for the black man, he must disappear with the years. Dependent like the ivy, he needs some strong oak-like friend to cling to. His support has been cut from him, and his life must wither in its prostrate helplessness. Will he leave no trace of his past? . . . Ah, yes! . . . the weird and beautiful melodies born in the hearts of the poor, child-like people to whom freedom was destruction.[23]

Many were the stories ringing changes on the theme: "Go tell Marse Linkum, to tek his freedom back." Thus, in *The Carolina Low Country,* Mr. Sass writes of Old Aleck, who, on being freed, spoke his little piece: "Miss, I don't want no wagis." "God bless you, old Aleck," signs Mr. Sass.

Modern neo-confederates repeat the stereotype. Allen Tate, co-member with Donald Davidson of the Nashville saviors of the South, implies in *Jefferson Davis, His Rise and Fall,* that to educate a Negro beyond his station brings him unhappiness. One of the chief points of agreement in the Neo-Confederate *I'll Take My Stand* by Davidson, Tate and ten others is that freedom has proved to be a perilous state for the Negro. Joseph Hergesheimer agrees: "A free Negro is more often wretched than not."[24] "Slavery was gone, the old serene days were gone. Negroes were bad because they

---

[21]William J. Grayson, *The Hireling and the Slave.* Charleston, S.C.: McCarter and Co., 1856, pp. 68 ff.

[22]Thomas Nelson Page, *The Negro: The Southerner's Problem, op. cit.,* p. 80.

[23]Lafcadio Hearn, *Letters from the Raven.* New York: A. & C. Boni, 1930, p. 168.

[24]Joseph Hergesheimer, *op. cit.,* p. 137.

were neither slave nor free."[25] And finally, a modern illustration must suffice. Eleanor Mercein Kelly in an elegy for the vanishing South, called *Monkey Motions*, pities "the helplessness of a simple jungle folk, a bandar-log, set down in the life of cities and expected to be men."[26]

It is, all in all, a sad picture that these savants give. What concerns us here, however, is its persistence, a thing inexpressibly more sad.

The Comic Negro

*"That Reminds Me of a Story. There Were Once Two
Ethiopians, Sambo and Rastus. . . ."*
(1,001 After-Dinner Speakers.)

The stereotype of the "comic Negro" is about as ancient as the "contented slave." Indeed, they might be considered complementary, since, if the Negro could be shown as perpetually mirthful, his state could not be so wretched. This is, of course, the familiar procedure when conquerors depict a subject people. English authors at the time of Ireland's greatest persecution built up the stereotype of the comic Irishman, who fascinated English audiences, and unfortunately, in a manner known to literary historians, influenced even Irish authors.[27] Thus, we find, in a melodrama about Irish life, an English officer soliloquizing:

I swear, the Irish nature is beyond my comprehension. A strange people!—merry 'mid their misery— laughing through their tears, like the sun shining through the rain. Yet what simple philosophers they! They tread life's path as if 'twere strewn with roses devoid of thorns, and make the most of life with natures of sunshine and song.[28]

Any American not reading the words "Irish nature" could be forgiven for taking the characterization to refer to American Negroes. Natures of sunshine and song, whose wretchedness becomes nothing since theirs is a simple philosophy of mirth! So runs the pattern.

In her excellent book, *American Humor*, Constance Rourke points out the Negro as one of the chief ingredients of the potpourri of American humor. She traces him as far back as the early '20's when Edwin

Forrest made up as a Southern plantation Negro to excite the risibilities of Cincinnati. In *The Spy*, Cooper belabors the grotesqueness of Caesar's appearance, although Caesar is not purely and simply the buffoon:

. . . But it was in his legs that nature had indulged her most capricious humor. There was an abundance of material injudiciously used. The calves were neither before nor behind, but rather on the outer side of the limb, inclining forward. . . . The leg was placed so near the center (of the foot) as to make it sometimes a matter of dispute whether he was not walking backward.[29]

Kennedy in his *Swallow Barn* not only reveals the Negro as delighted by the master's benevolence, but also as delighting the master by his ludicrous departure from the Anglo-Saxon norm. Kennedy revels in such descriptions as the following:

His face . . . was principally composed of a pair of protuberant lips, whose luxuriance seemed intended as an indemnity for a pair of crushed nostrils. . . . Two bony feet occupied shoes, each of the superfices and figure of a hoe. . . . Wrinkled, decrepit old men, with faces shortened as if with drawing strings, noses that seemed to have run all to nostril, and with feet of the configuration of a mattock. . . .[30]

It was in the early '30's, however, that T. D. Rice first jumped "Jim Crow" in the theatres along the Ohio River and set upon the stage the "minstrel Negro." Apparently immortal, this stereotype was to involve in its perpetuation such famous actors as Joseph Jefferson and David Belasco, to make Amos 'n' Andy as essential to American domesticity as a car in every garage, and to mean affluence for a Jewish comedian of whom only one gesture was asked: that he sink upon one knee, extend his white-gloved hands, and cry out "Mammy."

In pro-slavery fiction the authors seemed to agree on the two aspects of the comic Negro—that he was ludicrous to others, and forever laughing himself. Grayson writes in *The Hireling and the Slave*:

The long, loud laugh, that freemen seldom share,
Heaven's boon to bosoms unapproached by care;
And boisterous jest and humor unrefined. . . .[31]

To introduce comic relief, perhaps, in stories that might defeat their own purposes if confined only to the harrowing details of slavery, anti-slavery authors had their comic characters. Topsy is the classic example; it

[25]*Ibid.*, p. 293.

[26]Blanche Colton Williams, *O. Henry Memorial Award Prize Stories of 1927*. Garden City: Doubleday, Doran & Co., p. 207.

[27]*Vide:* George Bernard Shaw's *John Bull's Other Island*, Daniel Corkery's *Synge and Anglo-Irish Literature*, Yeats's *Plays and Controversies*, Lady Gregory's *Our Irish Theatre*, for attacks upon the "comic" Irishman stereotype.

[28]John Fitzgerald Murphy, *The Shamrock and the Rose*. Boston: Walter H. Baker Co., n.d., p. 25.

[29]James Fenimore Cooper, *The Spy*. New York: Scott, Foresman Co., 1927, p. 45.

[30]Kennedy, *op. cit., passim.*

[31]Grayson, *op. cit.*, p. 51.

is noteworthy that in contemporary acting versions of "Uncle Tom's Cabin," Topsy and the minstrel show note, if not dominant, are at least of equal importance to the melodrama of Eliza and the bloodhounds.

Reconstruction literature developed the stereotype. Russell's Negroes give side-splitting versions of the Biblical story (foreshadowing Bradford's *Ol' Man Adam an' His Chillun*), or have a fatal fondness for propinquity to a mule's rear end. Page's Negroes punctuate their worship of "ole Marse" with "Kyah-kyahs," generally directed at themselves. The humor of Uncle Remus is nearer to genuine folk-humor, which—it might be said in passing—is *not* the same as the "comic Negro" humor. Negroes in general, in the Reconstruction stories, are seen as creatures of mirth—who wouldn't suffer from hardship, even if they had to undergo it. Thus a Negro, sentenced to the chain-gang for stealing a pair of breeches, is made the theme of a comic poem.[32] This is illustrative. There may be random jokes in Southern court rooms, but joking about the Negroes' experiences with Southern "justice" and with the chain-gang is rather ghastly—like laughter at the mouth of hell. Creatures of sunshine and of song!

The "comic Negro" came into his own in the present century, and brought his creators into theirs. Octavius Cohen, who looks upon the idea of Negro doctors and lawyers and society belles as the height of the ridiculous, served such clienteles as that of *The Saturday Evening Post* for a long time with the antics of Florian Slappey. His work is amusing at its best, but is pseudo-Negro. Instead of being a handicap, however, that seems a recommendation to his audience. Trusting to most moth-eaten devices of farce, and interlarding a Negro dialect never heard on land or sea—compounded more of Dogberry and Mrs. Malaprop than of Birmingham Negroes,[33] he has proved to the whites that all along they have known the real Negro—"Isn't he funny, now!"—and has shown to Negroes what whites wanted them to resemble. Mrs. Octavius Roy Cohen follows in the wake of her illustrious husband in *Our Darktown Press,* a gleaning of "boners" from Aframerican newspapers. Editorial carelessness is sadly enough familiar in race journals; every item in the book is vouched for, but the total effect is the reenforcing of a stereotype that America loves to believe in.

Arthur E. Akers, with a following in another widely read magazine, is another farceur. He uses the situation of the domestic difficulty, as old as medieval fabliaux and farces—and places it in a Southern Negro community, and has his characters speak an approximation to Negro dialect—but too slick and 'literary' for conviction. Irate shrews and "Milquetoast" husbands, with razors wielded at departing parts of the anatomy, are Akers' stock-in-trade. Hugh Wiley with his Wildcat, inseparable from his goat, Lady Luck, unsavory but a talisman, is another creator of the farce that Negro life is too generally believed to be. E. K. Means, with obvious knowledge of Southern Negro life, is concerned to show in the main its ludicrous side, and Irvin Cobb, with a reputation of after-dinner wit to uphold, is similarly confined.

The case of Roark Bradford is different. An undoubted humorist, in the great line of Twain and the tall tales of the Southwest, he gleans from a rich store of Negro speech and folk-ways undeniably amusing tales. But as his belief about the Negro (cf. Introduction) might attest, he has a definite attitude to the Negro to uphold. His stories of the easy loves of the levee (frequently found in *Collier's*) concentrate upon the comic aspect of Negro life, although another observer might well see the tragic. In *Ol' Man Adam an' His Chillun* we have farce manufactured out of the Negro's religious beliefs. It seems to the writer that the weakest sections of *Green Pastures* stick closest to Bradford's stories, and that the majesty and reverence that can be found in the play must come from Marc Connelly. In *John Henry,* Bradford has definitely weakened his material by making over a folk-hero into a clown.

Although the situations in which the comic Negro finds himself range from the fantastic as in Cohen, to the possible as in "The Two Black Crows" and in "Amos 'n' Andy," his characteristics are fairly stable. The "comic Negro" is created for the delectation of a white audience, condescending and convinced that any departure from the Anglo-Saxon norm is amusing, and that any attempt to enter the special provinces of whites, such as wearing a dress suit, is doubly so. The "comic Negro" with certain physical attributes exaggerated—with his razor (generally harmless), his love for watermelon and gin, for craps, his haunting of chicken roosts, use of big words he doesn't understand, grandiloquent names and titles, "loud" clothes, bluster, hysterical cowardice, and manufactured word-play—has pranced his way by means of books, vaudeville skits, shows, radio programs, advertisements, and after-dinner speeches, into the folklore of the nation. As Guy B. Johnson urges there is a sort of—

---

[32]Belle Richardson Harrison, *Poetry of the Southern States,* edited by Clement Wood. Girard, Kansas: Haldeman-Julius Co., 1924, p. 36.

[33]"Yeh, an' was he to git one good bite at a cullud man like me, he'd exterminate me so quick I wouldn't even have a chance to notify my heirs," "I ain't hahdly sawn her right recent," are examples of his inimitable (fortunately so, although Amos 'n' Andy try it in "I'se regusted," etc.) dialect; "Drastic" "Unit" "Quinine" "Midnight," and "Sons and Daughters of I Will Arise" are examples of his nomenclature.

... folk attitude of the white man toward the Negro. . . . One cannot help noticing that the white man must have his fun out of the Negro, even when writing serious novels about him. This is partly conscious, indeed a necessity, if one is to portray Negro life as it is, for Negroes are human and behave like other human beings. Sometimes it is unconscious, rising out of our old habit of associating the Negro with the comical.[34]

In pointing out the stereotype, one does not deny the rich comedy to be found in Negro life. One is insisting, however, that any picture concentrating upon this to the exclusion of all else is entirely inadequate, that many of the most popular creators of the "comic Negro," "doctor" their material, and are far from accurate in depicting even the small area of Negro experience they select, and that too often they exceed the prerogative of comedy by making copy out of persecution and injustice.

The Brute Negro

"All Scientific Investigation of the Subject Proves the Negro to Be An Ape."

(Chas. Carroll, *The Negro a Beast.*)

Because the pro-slavery authors were anxious to prove that slavery had been a benefit to the Negro in removing him from savagery to Christianity, the stereotype of the "brute Negro" was relatively insignificant in antebellum days. There were references to vicious criminal Negroes in fiction (vicious and criminal being synonymous to discontented and refractory), but these were considered as exceptional cases of half-wits led astray by abolitionists. *The Bible Defence of Slavery*, however, in which the Rev. Priest in a most unclerical manner waxes wrathful at abolitionists, sets forth with a great array of theological argument and as much ridiculousness, proofs of the Negro's extreme lewdness. Sodom and Gomorrah were destroyed because these were strongholds of *Negro* vice. The book of Leviticus proved that *Negroes*

> outraged all order and decency of human society. Lewdness of the most hideous description was the crime of which they were guilty, blended with idolatry in their adoration of the gods, who were carved out of wood, painted and otherwise made, so as to represent the wild passions of lascivious desires. . . . The baleful fire of unchaste amour rages through the negro's blood more fiercely than in the blood of

any other people . . . on which account they are a people who are suspected of being but little acquainted with the virtue of chastity, and of regarding very little the marriage oath. . . .[35]

H. R. Helper, foe of slavery, was no friend of the Negro, writing, in 1867, *Nojoque*, a lurid condemnation of the Negro, setting up black and beastly as exact synonyms. Van Evrie's *White Supremacy and Negro Subordination, or Negroes A Subordinate Race, and (so-called) Slavery Its Normal Condition* gave "anthropological" support to the figment of the "beastly Negro," and *The Negro a Beast* (1900) gave theological support. The title page of this book runs:

> The Reasoner of the Age, the Revelator of the Century! The Bible As It Is! The Negro and his Relation to the Human Family! The Negro a beast, but created with articulate speech, and hands, that he may be of service to his master—the White Man. . . . by Chas. Carroll, who has spent 15 years of his life and $20,000.00 in its compilation. . . .

Who could ask for anything more?

Authors stressing the mutual affection between the races looked upon the Negro as a docile mastiff. In the Reconstruction this mastiff turned into a mad dog. "Damyanks," carpetbaggers, scalawags, and New England schoolmarms affected him with the rabies. The works of Thomas Nelson Page are good examples of this metamorphosis. When his Negro characters are in their place, loyally serving and worshipping ole Marse, they are admirable creatures, but in freedom they are beasts, as his novel *Red Rock* attests. *The Negro: The Southerner's Problem* says that the state of the Negro since emancipation is one of minimum progress and maximum regress.

> [This] is borne out by the increase of crime among them, by the increase of superstition, with its black trail of unamable immorality and vice; by the homicides and murders, and by the outbreak and growth of that brutal crime which has chiefly brought about the frightful crime of lynching which stains the *good name of the South* and has spread northward with the spread of the ravisher. . . . The crime of rape . . . is the fatal product of new conditions. . . . The Negro's passion, always his controlling force, is now, since the new teaching, for the white woman. [Lynching is justifiable] for it has its root deep in the basic passions of humanity; the determination to put an end to the *ravishing of their women by an inferior race*, or by any race, no matter what the consequence. . . . A crusade has been preached against lynching, even as far as England; but none has been attempted against the

---

[34]Guy B. Johnson, "Folk Values in Recent Literature on the Negro" in *Folk-Say*, edited by B. A. Botkin, Norman, Oklahoma, 1930, p. 371.

[35]Josiah Priest, *op. cit.*, Eighth Section, *passim.*

ravishing and tearing to pieces of white women and children.[36]

The best known author of Ku Klux Klan fiction after Page is Thomas Dixon. Such works as *The Clansman*, and *The Leopard's Spots*, because of their sensationalism and chapter titles (e.g., "The Black Peril," "The Unspoken Terror," "A Thousand Legged Beast," "The Hunt for the Animal"), seemed just made for the mentality of Hollywood, where D. W. Griffith's in *The Birth of a Nation* made for Thomas Dixon a dubious sort of immortality, and finally fixed the stereotype in the mass-mind. The stock Negro in Dixon's books, unless the shuffling hat-in-hand servitor, is a gorilla-like imbecile, who "springs like a tiger" and has the "black claws of a beast." In both books there is a terrible rape, and a glorious ride of the Knights on a Holy Crusade to avenge Southern civilization. Dixon enables his white geniuses to discover the identity of the rapist by using "a microscope of sufficient power [to] reveal on the retina of the dead eyes the image of this devil as if etched there by fire." . . . The doctor sees "The bestial figure of a negro—his huge black hand plainly defined. . . . It was Gus." Will the wonders of science never cease? But, perhaps, after all, Negroes have been convicted on even flimsier evidence. Fortunately for the self-respect of American authors, this kind of writing is in abeyance today. Perhaps it fell because of the weight of its own absurdity. But it would be unwise to underestimate this stereotype. It is probably of great potency in certain benighted sections where Dixon, if he could be read, would be applauded—and it certainly serves as a convenient self-justification for a mob about to uphold white supremacy by a lynching.

The gods bestow on me
A life of hate,
The white man's gift to see
A nigger's fate.

("The Mulatto Addresses His Savior on Christmas Morning," Seymour Gordden Link.)

Stereotyping was by no means the monopoly of pro-slavery authors defending their type of commerce, or justifying their ancestors. Anti-slavery authors, too, fell into the easy habit, but with a striking difference. Where pro-slavery authors had predicated a different set of characteristics for the Negroes, a distinctive sub-human nature, and had stereotyped in accordance with such a comforting hypothesis, anti-slavery authors insisted that the Negro had a common humanity with the whites, that in given circumstances a typically human type of response was to be expected, unless certain other powerful influences were present. The stereotyping in abolitionary literature, therefore, is not stereotyping of *character,* but of *situation.* Since the novels were propagandistic, they concentrated upon abuses: floggings, the slave mart, the domestic slave trade, forced concubinage, runaways, slave hunts, and persecuted freemen—all of these were frequently repeated. Stereotyped or not, heightened if you will, the anti-slavery novel has been supported by the verdict of history—whether recorded by Southern or Northern historians. Facts, after all, are abolitionist. Especially the fact that the Colonel's lady and old Aunt Dinah are sisters under the skin.

Anti-slavery authors did at times help to perpetuate certain pro-slavery stereotypes. Probably the novelists knew that harping upon the gruesome, to the exclusion of all else, would repel readers, who—like their present-day descendants—yearn for happy endings and do not wish their quick consciences to be harrowed. At any rate, comic relief, kindly masters (in contrast to the many brutes), loyal and submissive slaves (to accentuate the wrongs inflicted upon them) were scattered throughout the books. Such tempering of the attacks was turned to pro-slavery uses. Thus, Harris writes:

> It seems to me to be impossible for any unprejudiced person to read Mrs. Stowe's book and fail to see in it a defence of American slavery as she found it in Kentucky. . . . The real moral that Mrs. Stowe's book teaches is that the possibilities of slavery . . . are shocking to the imagination, while the realities, under the best and happiest conditions, possess a romantic beauty and a tenderness all their own. . . .[37]

Anti-slavery did proffer one stereotype, doomed to unfortunate longevity. This is the tragic mulatto. Pro-slavery apologists had almost entirely omitted (with so many other omissions) mention of concubinage. If anti-slavery authors, in accordance with Victorian gentility, were wary of illustrating the practice, they made great use nevertheless of the offspring of illicit unions. Generally the heroes and heroines of their books are near-whites. These are the intransigent, the resentful, the mentally alert, the proofs of the Negro's possibilities. John Herbert Nelson says with some point:

> Abolitionists tried, by making many of their characters almost white, to work on racial feeling as well. This was a curious piece of inconsistency on their part, an indirect admission that a white man in chains was more pitiful to behold than the African similarly placed. Their most impassioned plea was

[36]Page, *The Negro: The Southerner's Problem, passim* (italics mine).

[37]Julia Collier Harris, *op. cit.,* p. 117.

in behalf of a person little resembling their swarthy protegés, the quadroon or octoroon.[38]

Nelson himself, however, shows similar inconsistency, as he infers that the "true African—essentially gay, happy-go-lucky, rarely ambitious or idealistic, the eternal child of the present moment, able to leave trouble behind—is unsuited for such portrayal. . . . Only the mulattoes and others of mixed blood have, so far, furnished us with material for convincing tragedy."[39]

The tragic mulatto appears in both of Mrs. Stowe's abolitionary novels. In *Uncle Tom's Cabin*, the fugitives Liza and George Harris and the rebellious Cassy are mulattoes. Uncle Tom, the pure black, remains the paragon of Christian submissiveness. In *Dred*, Harry Gordon and his wife are nearly white. Harry is an excellent manager, and a proud, unsubmissive type:

> Mr. Jekyl, that humbug don't go down with me! I'm no more of the race of Ham than you are! I'm Colonel Gordon's oldest son—as white as my brother, who you say owns me! Look at my eyes, and my hair, and say if any of the rules about Ham pertain to me.[40]

The implication that there are "rules about Ham" that do pertain to blacks is to be found in other works. Richard Hildreth's *Archy Moore, or The White Slave*, has as its leading character a fearless, educated mulatto, indistinguishable from whites; Boucicault's *The Octoroon* sentimentalizes the hardships of a slave girl; both make the mixed blood the chief victim of slavery.

Cable, in the *Grandissimes*, shows a Creole mulatto educated beyond his means, and suffering ignominy, but he likewise shows in the character of Bras-Coupé that he does not consider intrepidity and vindictiveness the monopoly of mixed-bloods. In *Old Creole Days*, however, he discusses the beautiful octoroons, whose best fortune in life was to become the mistress of some New Orleans dandy. He shows the tragedy of their lives, but undoubtedly contributed to the modern stereotype that the greatest yearning of the girl of mixed life is for a white lover. Harriet Martineau, giving a contemporary portrait of old New Orleans, wrote:

> The quadroon girls . . . are brought up by their mothers to be what they have been; the mistresses of white gentlemen. The boys are some of them sent to France; some placed on land in the back of the

State. . . . The women of their own color object to them, "*ils sont si degoutants!*"[41]

Lyle Saxon says that "the free men of color are always in the background; to use the Southern phrase, 'they know their place.' "

The novelists have kept them in the background. Many recent novels show this: *White Girl, The No-Nation Girl, A Study in Bronze, Gulf Stream, Dark Lustre*—all of these show luridly the melodrama of the lovely octoroon girl. Indeed "octoroon" has come to be a feminine noun in popular usage.

The stereotype that demands attention, however, is the notion of mulatto character, whether shown in male or female. This character works itself out with mathematical symmetry. The older theses ran: First, the mulatto inherits the vices of both races and none of the virtues; second, any achievement of a Negro is to be attributed to the white blood in his veins. The logic runs that even inheriting the worst from whites is sufficient for achieving among Negroes. The present theses are based upon these: The mulatto is a victim of a divided inheritance; from his white blood come his intellectual strivings, his unwillingness to be a slave; from his Negro blood come his baser emotional urges, his indolence, his savagery.

Thus, in *The No-Nation Girl*, Evans Wall writes of his tragic heroine, Précieuse:

> Her dual nature had not developed its points of difference. The warring qualities, her double inheritance of Caucasian and black mingled in her blood, had not yet begun to disturb, and torture, and set her apart from either race. . . .
>
> [As a child,] Précieuse had learned to dance as soon as she could toddle about on her shapely little legs; half-savage little steps with strange movements of her body, exotic gestures and movements that had originated among the remote ancestors of her mother's people in some hot African jungle.
>
> . . . the wailing cry of the guitar was as primitive and disturbing as the beat of a tom-tom to dusky savages gathered for an orgy of dancing and passion in some moon-flooded jungle. . . . Self-control reached its limit. The girl's half-heritage of savagery rose in a flood that washed away all trace of her father's people except the supersensitiveness imparted to her taut nerves. She must dance or scream to relieve the rising torrent of response to the wild, monotonous rhythm.

It is not long before the girl is unable to repress, what Wall calls, the lust inherited from her mother's people; the environment of debauchery, violence, and rapine

---

[38]John Herbert Nelson, *op. cit.*, p. 84.

[39]*Ibid.*, p. 136.

[40]Harriet Beecher Stowe, *Nina Gordon, or Dred*. Boston: Houghton, Mifflin and Co., 1881, p. 142.

[41]Quoted in Lyle Saxon, *Fabulous New Orleans*. New York: The Century Co., 1928, p. 182.

is exchanged for concubinage with a white paragon, which ends, of course, in the inevitable tragedy. The girl "had no right to be born."

Dark Lustre, by Geoffrey Barnes, transfers the main essentials of the foregoing plot to Harlem. Aline, of the darkly lustrous body, thus analyzes herself in accordance with the old clichés: "The black half of me is ashamed of itself for being there, and every now and then crawls back into itself and tries to let the white go ahead and pass. . . ." Says the author: "There was too much of the nigger in her to let her follow a line of reasoning when the black cloud of her emotions settled over it." Half-white equals reason; half-black equals emotion. She too finds her ideal knight in a white man, and death comes again to the tragic octoroon who should never have been born. *White Girl, Gulf Stream, A Study in Bronze* are in substance very similar to these.

Roark Bradford in *This Side of Jordan* gives an unconscious *reductio ad absurdum* of this stereotype.

> The blade of a razor flashed through the air. Scrap has concealed it in the folds of her dress. Her Negro blood sent it unerringly between two ribs. Her Indian blood sent it back for an unnecessary second and third slash.

It might be advanced that Esquimaux blood probably would have kept her from being chilled with horror. The strangest items are attributed to different racial strains: In *No-Nation Girl* a woman cries out in childbirth because of her Negro expressiveness; from the back of Précieuse's "ankles down to her heels, the flesh was slightly thicker"—due to her Negro blood; Lessie in Welbourn Kelley's *Inchin' Along* "strongly felt the urge to see people, to talk to people. . . . That was the white in her maybe. Or maybe it was the mixture of white and black."

This kind of writing should be discredited by its patent absurdity. It is generalizing of the wildest sort, without support from scientific authorities. And yet it has set these *idées fixes* in the mob mind: The Negro of unmixed blood is no theme for tragedy; rebellion and vindictiveness are to be expected only from the mulatto; the mulatto is victim of a divided inheritance and therefore miserable; he is a "man without a race" worshipping the whites and despised by them, despising and despised by Negroes, perplexed by his struggle to unite a white intellect with black sensuousness. The fate of the octoroon girl is intensified—the whole desire of her life is to find a white lover, and then go down, accompanied by slow music, to a tragic end. Her fate is so severe that in some works disclosure of "the single drop of midnight" in her veins makes her commit suicide.

The stereotype is very flattering to a race which, for all its self-assurance, seems to stand in great need of flattery. But merely looking at one of its particulars—that white blood means asceticism and Negro blood means unbridled lust—will reveal how flimsy the whole structure is. It is ingenuous that mathematical computation of the amount of white blood in a mulatto's veins will explain his character. And it is a widely held belief. But it is nonsense, all the same.

The Local Color Negro

"The defects of local color inhere in the constitution of the cult itself, which, as its name suggests, thought . . . first of the piquant surfaces and then— if at all—of the stubborn deeps of human life."
(Carl Van Doren, *Contemporary American Novelists*.)

Local color stresses the quaint, the odd, the picturesque, the different. It is an attempt to convey the peculiar quality of a locality. Good realistic practice would insist upon the localizing of speech, garb, and customs; great art upon the revelation of the universal beneath these local characteristics. Local color is now in disrepute because of its being contented with merely the peculiarity of dialect and manners. As B. A. Botkin, editor of *Folk-Say*, has stated: "In the past [local consciousness] has been narrowly sectional rather than broadly human, superficially picturesque rather than deeply interpretative, provincial without being indigenous."[42]

The "local color Negro" is important in any study of the Negro character in American literature. But, since the local colorists of the Negro were more concerned with fidelity to speech and custom, with revelation of his difference in song and dance and story, than with revelation of Negro character, they accepted at face valuation the current moulds into which Negro character had been forced. Therefore, local colorists have been and will be considered under other heads. Page and Russell were local colorists in that they paid close attention to Negro speech, but the Negro they portrayed was the same old contented slave. Their study of Negro speech, however, was fruitful and needed—for pro-slavery authors had been as false in recording Negro speech as they were in picturing Negro experience. Kennedy, for instance, forces a confessedly wretched dialect into the mouths of poor Negroes, and W. L. G. Smith has his Shenandoah Negroes speak Gullah, because his master, Simms, had written of South Carolina Negroes.

---

[42]B. A. Botkin, *Folk-Say, A Regional Miscellany*. Norman: The Oklahoma Folk-Lore Society, 1929, p. 12.

Cable, one of the best of the local colorists, in *The Grandissimes*, goes a step beyond the mere local color formula; *Old Creole Days* is local color, but has been considered under the "Tragic Mulatto." The Negroes in Lyle Saxon's old and new New Orleans, E. Larocque Tinker's old New Orleans, R. Emmett Kennedy's Gretna Green, are in the main kinsfolk to the contented slave; in Evans Wall's Mississippi cane-brakes are exotic primitives, or tragic mulattoes; on Roark Bradford's levees are primitives; and those on Julia Peterkin's Blue Brook plantation, in Heyward's Catfish Row, and in John Vandercook's Surinam, Liberia, and Haiti, usually surmount, in the writer's opinion, the deficiencies of local color. Stereotyped, or genuinely interpreted, however, they all agree in one respect: they show the peculiar differences of certain Negroes in well-defined localities.

John B. Sale in *The Tree Named John* records with sympathy the dialect, superstitions, folk-ways of Mississippi Negroes. He is meticulous, perhaps to a fault, in his dialectal accuracy; the milieu is correspondingly convincing. His Negroes do carry on the pattern of mutual affection between the races—and yet they are far nearer flesh and blood than those of Page. Samuel Stoney and Gertrude Shelby, in *Black Genesis*, give the peculiarities of the Gullah Negro's cosmogony. Care is paid to fidelity in recording the dialect, but the authors' comments reveal a certain condescension toward quaintness which is the usual bane of local colorists. In *Po' Buckra* the authors reveal the localized tragedy of the "brass-ankle"—the Croatan-Negro-near-white caste. Much of the "tragic mulatto" theme is in this book, as well as the purely local color interest. Ambrose Gonzales in his Gullah renditions of Aesop, and in his tales of the "black border," reveals for the curious the intricacies of a little known Negro dialect, following the lead of Harris, and C. C. Jones, who recorded the Br'er Rabbit tales in the dialect of the Georgia coast.

Although most of these authors who dwell upon quaint and picturesque divergencies are discussed under other headings, it will not do to underestimate this local color Negro. The showing of Negro peculiarities in speech, superstitions, and customs has been popular for many years, and is likely to be for a long while yet. It undoubtedly has its artistic uses; but being an end in itself is surely not the chief of them.

The Exotic Primitive

"Then I saw the Congo, cutting through the black. . . ."
—(Vachel Lindsay)

This stereotype grew up with America's post-war revolt against Puritanism and Babbittry. Literary crit-
ics urged a return to spontaneity, to unrestrained emotions; American literature had been too long conventional, drab, without music and color. Human nature had been viewed with too great a reticence. Sex, which the Victorians had considered unmentionable, was pronounced by the school of Freud to have an overwhelming importance in motivating our conduct. So the pendulum swung from the extreme of Victorian prudishness to that of modern expressiveness.

To authors searching "for life in the raw," Negro life and character seemed to beg for exploitation. There was the Negro's savage inheritance, as they conceived it: hot jungle nights, the tom-tom calling to esoteric orgies. There were the frankness and violence to be found in any underprivileged group, or on any frontier. There were the traditional beliefs of the Negro being a creature of his appetites, and although pro-slavery fiction had usually (because of Victorianism) limited these to his yearnings for hog meat and greens, 'possum and yams, and for whiskey on holidays, Reconstruction fiction had stressed his lustfulness. He seemed to be cut out for the hands of certain authors. They promptly rushed to Harlem for color. In Harlem dives and cabarets they found what they believed to be *the* Negro, *au naturel*.

The figure who emerges from their pages is a Negro synchronized to a savage rhythm, living a life of ecstasy, superinduced by jazz (repetition of the tom-tom, awakening vestigial memories of Africa) and gin, that lifted him over antebellum slavery, and contemporary economic slavery, and placed him in the comforting fastnesses of their "mother-land." A kinship exists between this stereotype and that of the contented slave; one is merely a "jazzed-up" version of the other, with cabarets supplanting cabins, and Harlemized "blues," instead of the spirituals and slave reels. Few were the observers who saw in the Negroes' abandon a release from the troubles of this world similar to that afforded in slavery by their singing. Many there were, however, who urged that the Harlem Negro's state was that of an inexhaustible *joie de vivre*.

Carl Van Vechten was one of the pioneers of the hegira from downtown to Harlem; he was one of the early discoverers of the cabaret; and his novel, *Nigger Heaven*, is to the exotic pattern what *Swallow Barn* was to the contented slave. All of the possibilities of the development of the type are inherent in the book. In the prologue, we have the portrait of the "creeper," Don Juan of Seventh Avenue, whose amatory prowess causes him to be sought by women unknown to him. We feel that this prologue sets the tone of the work: we are going to see the Harlem of gin mills and cabarets, of kept men and loose ladies, of all-day sleepers and all-night roisterers. Van Vechten, who was already famed as a sophisticated romantic novelist, writes graphically of this Harlem. His style invited emulation from young men desiring to be men-about-town first and then novelists, just as Kennedy invited emulation from young Southerners desiring to defend slavery first. Van Vechten's novel does more than present the local color of Harlem; there is as well the character study of a young Negro intellectual who cannot withstand the dissipations of the "greatest Negro city." But the Bohemian life in Harlem is the main thing, even in this youngster's life. According to the publisher's blurb, "Herein is caught the fascination and tortured ecstasies of Harlem. . . . The author tells the story of modern Negro life." The blurb claims too much. There is another, there are many other Harlems. And *the* story of modern Negro life will never be found in one volume, or in a thousand.

Lasca Sartoris, exquisite, gorgeous, golden-brown Messalina of Seventh Avenue, is one of the chief characters of the book. On seeing her one of the characters comments: "Whew! She'll make a dent in Harlem." She does. She causes the young hero, Byron, in a drunken rage, to empty his gun in the body of one of her lovers, although the man was already dead, and a policeman was approaching.

Van Vechten has a noted magazine editor comment pontifically on the possibilities of Negro literature:

> Nobody has yet written a good gambling story; nobody has gone into the curious subject of the divers tribes of the region. . . . There's the servant-girl, for instance. Nobody has ever done the Negro servant-girl, who refuses to 'live in.' Washing dishes in the day-time, she returns at night to her home in Harlem where she smacks her daddy in the jaw or else dances and makes love. On the whole I should say she has the best time of any domestic servant in the world. . . . The Negro fast set does everything the Long Island fast set does, plays bridge, keeps the bootlegger busy, drives around in Rolls-Royces and commits adultery, but it is vastly more amusing than the Long Island set for the simple reason that it is *amused*. . . . Why, Roy McKain visited Harlem just once and then brought me in a cabaret yarn about a Negro pimp. I don't suppose he even saw the fellow. Probably just made him up, imagined him, but his imagination was based on a background of observation. The milieu is correct. . . .[43]

Although these are merely the offhand comments of an editor, and not to be taken too seriously as final critical pronouncements on *the* Negro, still certain implications are obvious. The best Negro characters for literary purposes are suggested: gamblers, fast set, servant-girl-sweet-mamma, etc. All are similar in their great capacity for enjoyment—and it is that side that must be shown. The eternal playboys of the Western hemisphere! Why even one trip to Harlem will reveal the secret of their mystery. The connection of all of this to the contented slave, comic, local color Negro is patent. Another thing to be noticed is the statement issued by the literary market: Stereotypes wanted.

In *Black Sadie*, T. Bowyer Campbell, whose preference is for the stereotype of the contended slave of the South, ironically accounts for the Harlem fad by the desire of jaded sophisticates for a new thrill. But Campbell does agree in some degree with the Harlem stereotype: "Colored people demand nothing but easy happiness, good nature." Black Sadie, child of a man hanged for raping an old white woman, having become the toast of artistic New York, remaining a kleptomaniac—"it was in her blood"—even in affluence, causing a murder, returns—in the best tradition of minstrel songs—to happy Virginia. "Easy come, easy go, niggers," Campbell closes his book, philosophically.

Sherwood Anderson, in *Dark Laughter*, expresses a genuine Rousseauism. Hostile toward the routine of industrialism and Puritanism, Anderson sets up as a foil the happy-go-lucky sensuality of river-front Negroes, who laugh, with genial cynicism, at the self-lacerations of hypersensitive Nordics. His "dark laughter" lacks the sinister undertone of Llwellyn Powys' "black laughter" heard in Africa. Anderson's Negroes are too formalized a chorus, however, for conviction, and are more the dream-children of a romanticist than actual flesh-and-blood creations. Anderson has drawn some excellent Negro characters; in *Dark Laughter*, however, he characterizes the Negroes too straitly. That the chief response of the Negro to his experience is a series of deep rounds of laughter at white sex-tangles is difficult of credence.

William Seabrook in *Magic Island* and *Jungle Ways* writes sensational travel tales—according to some, in the tradition of Munchausen and Marco Polo. He exploits the exotic and primitive, recording voodoo rites, black magic, strange sexual practices, weird superstitions, and cannibalism. His work brings a sort of vicarious satisfaction to Main Street, and advances the stereotype. He traces back to original sources what downtown playboys come up to Harlem to see.

The stereotype of the exotic-primitive would require more than a dogmatic refutation. Not so patently a "wish-fulfillment," as the "contented slave" stereotype was, nor an expression of unreasoning hatred, as the "brute Negro," it is advanced by novelists realistic in technique and rather convincing, although demonstrably

[43]Carl Van Vechten, *Nigger Heaven*. New York: Grosset and Dunlap, 1928, pp. 225 ff.

"romantic" in their choice of the sensational. But it would be pertinent to question the three basic assumptions—either insinuated or expressed—underlying the stereotype: that the "natural" Negro is to be found in Harlem cabarets; that the life and character depicted there are representative of Negro life in general; and that the Negro is "himself," and startlingly different in the sensational aspects of his life.

It is strange that the "natural" Negro should be looked for in the most sophisticated of environment. Even the names "Cotton Club," "Plantation Revue," the lavish, though inaccurate, cotton bolls decorating the walls, the choruses in silken overalls and bandanas do not disguise but rather enforce the fact that Negro entertainers, like entertainers everywhere, give the public what clever managers, generally Caucasian, believe the public wants. Unwise as it is to generalize about America, or New York State, or even Queens from the Great White Way, it is no less unwise to generalize about Negro life and character from Harlem. It is even unwise to generalize about Harlem, from *the* Harlem shown in books. Strange to say, there is a Harlem that can be observed by the cold glare of daylight.

The exotic primitives of Mississippi levees and cane-brakes, of Catfish Row and Blue Brook Plantation are more convincing, as examples of frontier communities, and of underprivileged groups who are known to live violent lives. It is surely not impossible, however, to believe that observers with an eye for environmental factors might see an entirely different picture from the one presented by searchers for exotic-primitive innate tendencies.

Harvey Wickham in *The Impuritans* writes:

> On Pacific Street, San Francisco, there used to be, and probably still is, a Negro dance hall called the So-Different Cafe. The name was deceptive. It was not so different from any other slum-hole. [A slum hole] is tediously the same, whether it be in Harlem, lower Manhattan, London, Paris, Berlin, Rome, Athens, Pekin, or Timbuctoo. There is no possible variety in degradation. . . .[44]

Such a comment surely deserves as careful attention as the stereotype of the exotic-primitive.

Attempts At Realization

"John Henry said to his captain,
A man ain't nothin' but a man. . . ."
(Ballad of John Henry.)

It would be a mistake to believe that the works of all white authors bear out these stereotypes. Some of the best attacks upon stereotyping have come from white authors, and from Southerners, just as some of the strongest upholding of the stereotypes has come from Negroes. Moreover, the writer of this essay hopes that he will not be accused of calling everything a stereotype that does not flatter Negro character, or of insisting that the stereotypes have no basis in reality. Few of the most apologistic of "race" orators could deny the presence of contented slaves, of wretched freemen, in our past; nor of comic Negroes (even in the joke-book tradition), of self-pitying mulattoes, of brutes, of exotic primitives in our present. Negro life does have its local color, and a rich, glowing color it can be at times. What this essay has aimed to point out is the obvious unfairness of hardening racial character into fixed moulds. True in some particulars, each of these popular generalizations is dangerous when applied to the entire group. Furthermore, most of these generalizations spring from a desire to support what is considered social expediency rather than from a sincere attempt at interpretation, and are therefore bad art.

Attempts at sincere "realization" rather than imitation of set patterns can be found in the early works of Eugene O'Neill, whose plays first brought a tragic Negro to Broadway. Ridgeley Torrence saw another side to the familiar guitar playing clown—showing him to be a dreamer of dreams like the other Playboy of the Western World—and saw dignity in his long suffering, hardworking wife. *The Rider of Dreams*, in its quiet way, did much to demolish the old stereotypes.

Julia Peterkin, for all of her tendency to local color (*Bright April* is a storehouse of Negro superstitions and folk customs) and her emphasis on sex and violence,[45] is still of importance in her departure from the stereotypes.

In a simple, effective manner, she reveals the winning humanity of the Gullah people, whom she obviously loves and respects. If critics would refuse to call her the interpreter of *the* Negro, and realize that she writes of a very limited segment of life from a very personal point of view, they would do a service to her and to their own reputations. She has well-nigh surmounted the difficulty of being a plantation owner.

Du Bose Heyward has given us some of the best Negro characterizations in *Porgy* and *Mamba's Daughters*. Though the first is naturalistic with a flair for the exotic-primitive, Heyward does show in it essential humanity. Porgy reveals himself as capable of essential

---

[44]Harvey Wickham, *The Impuritans*. New York: The Dial Press, 1929, p. 284.

[45]*Vide: Black April, Scarlet Sister Mary* for examples of extreme promiscuity, and *Bright Skin* for violent deaths.

fineness, and even Bess is not completely past reclaiming. *Mamba's Daughters* reveals that Negroes, too, can be provident as Mamba was, or heroic as Hagar was, for the sake of the young. The travesty of Southern justice toward the Negro, the difficulties of the aspiring Negro, the artistic potentialities and actualities of Negroes receive ample attention. Except for certain forgivable slips into the "comic," the book is an excellent illustration of the dignity and beauty that can be found in some aspects of lowly Negro life.

E. C. L. Adams, because he seems to let Negro characters speak for themselves, in their own idiom, and as if no white man was overhearing, has been very successful in his interpretation of Negro folk-life. Here the humor expressed by the Negro is miles away from Cohen's buffoonery. There is a sharp, acid flavor to it; in the Negroes' condemnation of the Ben Bess case there is the bitterness that has been stored up for so very long. These folk are not happy-go-lucky, nor contented; they are shrewd, realistic philosophers, viewing white pretense and injustice with cynicism—though not with Sherwood Anderson's "Dark Laughter." Illiterate they may be, but they are not being fooled.

Howard Odum, by letting the Negro speak for himself, presents a similarly convincing folk-Negro, in this case, the rambling man, who has been everywhere, and seen everybody. Many of the stereotypes are overthrown in *Rainbow Round My Shoulder,* although comic, and brutal, and submissive Negroes may be seen there. These are viewed, however, "in the round," not as walking generalizations about *the* Negro, and Odum is intent on making us understand how they got to be what they are.

Evelyn Scott and T. S. Stribling, historical novelists of the Civil War, as different as may be in technique, agree in giving us rounded pictures of antebellum Negroes. Slavery is not a perpetual Mardi Gras in their novels, nor are Negroes cast in the old, rigid moulds. They are characterized as human beings, not as representatives of a peculiar species. Paul Green's *In Abraham's Bosom* shows the Negro's handicapped struggles for education during the Reconstruction; Green has brought great dramatic power to bear upon revealing that the Negro is a figure worthy of tragic dignity. In *The House of Connelly* he has disclosed aspects of the so-called "contented slave" that antebellum authors were either ignorant of, or afraid to show.

Erskine Caldwell, George Milburn, William Faulkner, and Thomas Wolfe, while their metier is the portraiture of poor whites, help in undermining the stereotypes by showing that what have been considered Negro characteristics, such as dialect, illiteracy, superstitions, sexual looseness, violence, etc., are to be found as frequently among poor whites. When they do show Negro characters, they frequently show them to be burdened by economic pressure, the playthings of Southern justice, and the catspaws for sadistic "superiors."

A recent novel, *Amber Satyr,* shows a lynching that follows a white woman's relentless and frenzied pursuit of her hired man, a good-looking Negro. Welbourne Kelley's *Inchin' Along,* although influenced by some stereotypes (his mulatto wife, true to type, is the easy prey of the first white man who rides along), does show the hard-working, provident, stoical Negro. James Knox Millen wrote a powerful attack upon lynching in *Never No More,* showing the precarious hold the Southern Negro has upon peace and happiness. Scott Nearing, with a proletarian emphasis, has presented graphically the new slavery, peonage, in the South, with its horrible concomitant lynchings, and the bitter prejudice of organized labor in the North. And finally, John L. Spivak, in *Georgia Nigger,* has written a second *Uncle Tom's Cabin,* an indictment of peonage, and convict-labor in Georgia, powerful enough to put to shame all the rhapsodists of the folk Negro's happy state.

To trace the frequency with which the Negro author has stepped out of his conventional picture frame, from the spirituals and satiric folk-rhymes down to Langston Hughes, would exceed the bounds of this paper, and for present purposes is not needed. A reading of only a few of the white authors just mentioned (many of whom are from the South) would effectively illustrate the inadequacy of the familiar stereotypes.

It is likely that, in spite of the willingness of some Negro authors to accept at face value some of these stereotypes, the exploration of Negro life and character rather than its exploitation must come from Negro authors themselves. This, of course, runs counter to the American conviction that the Southern white man knows the Negro best, and can best interpret him. Nan Bagby Stephens states what other Southern authors have insinuated:

> Maybe it was because my slave-owning ancestors were fond of their darkies and treated them as individuals that I see them like that. It seems to me that no one, not even the negroes themselves, can get the perspective reached through generations of understanding such as we inherited.[46]

The writer of this essay holds to the contrary opinion, agreeing with another Southerner, F. P. Gaines,[47] that when a white man says that he knows the Negro he generally means that he knows the Negro of the joke-book tradition. Stephen Vincent Benet has written:

---

[46]*Contempo,* Volume II, No. 2, p. 3.

[47]F. P. Gaines, *op. cit.,* p. 17.

Oh, blackskinned epic, epic with the black spear,
I cannot sing you, having too white a heart,
And yet, some day a poet will rise to sing you
And sing you with such truth and mellowness . . .
That you will be a match for any song. . . .[48]

But whether Negro life and character are to be best interpreted from without or within is an interesting by-path that we had better not enter here. One manifest truth, however, is this: the sincere, sensitive artist, willing to go beneath the clichés of popular belief to get at an underlying reality, will be wary of confining a race's entire character to a half-dozen narrow grooves. He will hardly have the temerity to say that his necessarily limited observation of a few Negroes in a restricted environment can be taken as the last word about some mythical *the* Negro. He will hesitate to do this, even though he had a Negro mammy, or spent a night in Harlem, or has been a Negro all his life. The writer submits that such an artist is the only one worth listening to, although the rest are legion.

ALAIN LOCKE

The Negro's Contribution to American Culture

After twenty years or so of continuous discussion, this subject of the cultural contribution of the Negro as a racial group has become trite and well-nigh threadbare. Having undergone much critical wear and tear, and having passed in the process from intriguing novelty to tawdry commonplace and from careful critical delineation to careless propaganda, the whole subject now obviously needs, even to the layman's eye, thoroughgoing renovation. Before we proceed to any further documentation, then, of the Negro's cultural contributions, let us address ourselves to this more difficult and more important task of its critical evaluation.

The crux of the whole issue from the critical point of view is basically the question of the propriety of applying race concepts to cultural products. What makes a work of art Negro, its theme or its idiom? What constitutes a "Negro contribution to culture," its authorship or its cultural base? Is there or should there be any such set of categories in our critical thinking or our creative living? Seldom do we ask such basic questions, and when we do, we too often run off, like Pontius Pilate, without waiting for an answer. Yet by and on

some unequivocal answers to questions like these must our whole philosophy and practise of culture be judged and justified.

As an instance of this dilemma, we find James Weldon Johnson in his anthology,—*The Book of American Negro Poetry*, cautiously accepting Negro authorship as the criterion of Negro cultural contribution in this field, excluding both the folk poetry and the large body of American verse on the Negro theme,[1] but in his celebrated preface to the same, boldly claiming as Negro "contributions" Uncle Remus, with titular white authorship, jazz ragtime and American popular dance forms to the extent they are the derivatives of Negro idioms or source originals. Obviously here is a paradox. Which is the sound position? What is the proper and consistent claim?

Obviously culture politics has a good deal to do with the situation, often forcing both majority and minority partisans into strange and untenable positions. Granted even that the very notion of "Negro art" and of "Negro cultural contributions" is a sequel of minority status, and an unfortunate by-product of racial discrimination and prejudice, it by no means follows that an uncritical acceptance of the situation is necessary or advisable. There is, in fact, a fallacy in both of the extreme positions in this cultural dilemma. Although there is in the very nature of the social situation an unavoidable tendency for the use of literature and art as instruments of minority group expression and counter-assertion, there is a dangerous fallacy of the minority position involved in cultural racialism. Cultural chauvinism is not unique in a racial situation, however; a national literature and art too arbitrarily interpreted has the same unpardonable flaws. However, where as in the case of the Negro there are no group differentials of language or basic culture patterns between the majority and the minority, cultural chauvinism is all the more ridiculous and contrary to fact. Consistently applied it would shut the minority art up in a spiritual ghetto and deny vital and unrestricted creative participation in the general culture.

On the other hand, there is the majority fallacy of regarding the cultural situation of a group like the Negro after the analogy of a "nation within a nation," implying a situation of different culture levels or traditions, a system of cultural bulkheads, so to speak, each racially compartmentalized and water-tight. Like most fallacies, in explicit statement, they reveal their own inner self-contradiction and absurdities. However, hid-

---

[48]Stephen Vincent Benet, *John Brown's Body*. Garden City, N.Y.: Doubleday, Doran and Co., 1928, p. 347.

[1]Calverton's *Anthology of American Negro Literature* includes the folk poetry, and Sterling Brown's *Negro Poetry and Drama* treats the literature of the Negro theme by both white and Negro poets and dramatists.

Alain LeRoy Locke (c. 1925—Pastel on artist board by Winold Reiss [1886–1953]. National Portrait Gallery, Smithsonian Institution. Gift of Lawrence A. Fleischman and Howard Garfinkle with a matching grant from the National Endowment for the Arts.)

tionally current and representative. Incidentally, it is by the same logic and process that the English language, Anglo-Saxon institutions and mores, including English literary and art forms and traditions have become by differential acculturation what we style "American." In culture, it is the slightly but characteristically divergent that counts, and in most cases racial and nationalist distinctions are only shades of degrees apart. The Negro cultural product we find to be in every instance itself a composite, partaking often of the nationally typical and characteristic as well, and thus something which if styled Negro for short, is more accurately to be described as "Afro-American." In spite, then, of the ready tendency of many to draw contrary conclusions, there is little if any evidence and justification for biracialism in the cultural field, if closely scrutinized and carefully interpreted. The subtle interpenetration of the "national" and the "racial" traits is interesting evidence of cultural cross-fertilization and the wide general vogue and often national representativeness of the "racial contribution" is similar evidence of the effective charm and potency of certain cultural hybrids.

And so, we end up by being able to ferret out no other reliable criterion for what we style typically or characteristically "Negro," culturally speaking, than that cultural compounding and variation which has produced what we style "American" out of what was historically and basically English or Anglo-Saxon. This, if sound, destroys completely the "nation within a nation" analogy which has been so overworked a parallel, and makes Negro literature and art a vital, integral part of American cultural expression. Not even the notion of a cultural province will fit the facts, for the Negro variants have wide distribution and partake of the regional characteristics according to geographical distribution. The cultural products of the Negro are distinctive hybrids; culturally "mulatto" generations ahead of the mixed physical condition and ultimate biological destiny, perhaps, of the human stock.

This makes what is Negro in the truest sense, apart from the arbitrary criterion of Negro authorship, hard to define, no doubt; but fortunately in practise, it is easy enough to discriminate on close contact and comparison. Like rum in the punch, that although far from being the bulk ingredient, still dominates the mixture, the Negro elements have in most instances very typical and dominating flavors, so to speak. I know only one racial idiom with equal versatility combined with equally distinctive potency,—and even that with narrower cultural range since it has been almost exclusively musical; the idioms of Gipsy music and dance which blending with as diverse strains as Russian, Hungarian, Roumanian, Spanish, and even Oriental music,

den taint of both these fallacious positions is very common in our popular and critical thinking on this issue of Negro cultural expression and contribution.

Cultural racialism and chauvinism flatter the minority group ego; cultural biracialism not only flatters the majority group ego, but is the extension of discrimination into cultural prejudices and bigotry.[2] Both are contrary to fact, and particularly so in the case of the American Negro. What is "racial" for the American Negro resides merely in the overtones to certain fundamental elements of culture common to white and black and his by adoption and acculturation. What is distinctively Negro in culture usually passes over by rapid osmosis to the general culture, and often as in the case of Negro folklore and folk music and jazz becomes na-

[2]For a particularly trenchant analysis and criticism of this culture prejudice, see Buell Gallagher's *American Caste and the Negro College*, pp. 368–71.

yet succeed in maintaining their own distinctive flavor. The Negro cultural influence, most obvious, too, in music and dance, has a still wider range,—in linguistic influence, in folklore and literary imagery, and in rhythm, the tempo and the emotional overtones of almost any typically Negro version of other cultural art forms. Let us consider a typical, perhaps an extreme instance of this characteristic dominance and its transforming force. Suppose we do laboriously prove the cultural ancestor of the Negro spiritual to be the evangelical hymn forms and themes of white Protestantism; suppose we even find, as the proponents of "White Spirituals" do, interesting parallels and close equivalents, that by no means counters or counteracts the uniqueness in style and appeal of the Negro spiritual, either as folk poetry or folk music. Indeed the formula analysis, showing so many common ingredients, only adds to the wonder and credit of the almost immeasurable difference in total effect. We need scarcely go further to the acid test of comparing the continued spontaneity and fresh creativeness of the one strain with the comparative sterility and stereotyped character of the other. The one hardly moved its own immediate devotees and barely survives culturally; the other has been creatively potent at all musical levels—folk, popular and classical, has been vital out of its original context in instrumental as well as vocal forms, and has moved the whole world.

If this were a single exceptional instance, no weighty issue would be involved. But creative vitality and versatility, this contagious dominance seems in so many cases to be a characteristic trait of the Negro cultural product. This disproportionality of effect in culture contacts and fusions is becoming more and more obvious as we study the ramified influence of Negro cultural strains. Weldon Johnson no doubt had this in mind when he characterized the Negro genius as having great "emotional endowment, originality in artistic conception, and what is more important, the power of creating that which has universal appeal and influence." This truth will become axiomatic, I take it, when we broaden the scope of our studies of the influence of Negro cultural admixture geographically as is now beginning to develop. For the American Negro elements are but one small segment of the whole gamut of Negro cultural influence; there is the very pronounced Afro-Cuban, the Afro-Brazilean, the Caribbean Creole, the Jamaican, the Trinidadian, the Bahamian, the Louisiana Creole together with those better known to us,—the Southern Lowlands Carolinian, the Lower and Upper South and the urbanized or "Harlem" idiom, which it will be noted is in many respects the most hybrid and attenuated of all. In addition to a new perspective on the range and force of Negro cul-

ture contacts, such future study may give us important clues as to the basic African common denominators and some explanation of their unusual vitality and versatility.

It seems reasonable to maintain, therefore, that tracing an arbitrary strand of Negro authorship and narrowly construed race productivity not only does not do the Negro group cultural justice, but that more importantly, it does not disclose the cultural exchanges and interactions which are vital to the process. Following the latter pattern, criticism would teach us to view the cultural scene more in terms of what it actually is, and in addition cut under the superficial bases of the cultural partisanship and chauvinisms of both sides. An increasing number of critical studies and analyses are taking this more modern and more scientific point of view and approach; and a particular series[3] has recently taken as its basic viewpoint the analysis of the Negro idiom and the Negro theme in the various art fields as a gradually widening field of collaboration and interaction between the white and the Negro creative artists. Two schools or recent trends of American letters and criticism have also taken the same composite theory and practise, the one, regionalism—a growing school of critical thought, and Proletarian realism, also a popular and increasing vogue in fiction, drama, and criticism. The former of course is more congenial to the retention of the nation of racial idioms; the latter, over-simplifying the situation in my judgment, discounts and ignores almost completely in its emphasis on class status and class psychology, the idioms of race.

With this background, and with the now almost traditional precedents of claims like that of "Uncle Remus" (with titular white authorship) and jazz music, with its elaborate biracial production, it is to be hoped there will be little or no surprise, as we review rapidly the epochs of Negro cultural activity, in having drama like *The Emperor Jones, The Green Pastures* and *Stevedore*, novels like *Green Thursday* and *Porgy*, poems like Lindsay's *Congo* or Bodenheim's *Jazz Kaleidoscope*, though by white authors, referred to in the context of the cultural influence of the Negro theme and idiom. In art, it is color, not the colorline that counts; and that not so much the hue of the author as the complexion of the idiom.

The cultural history of the Negro himself in America may be broadly traced as falling into two periods,— a long period of creative but unsophisticated expression at the folk level, dating almost from his introduction to

---

[3]*The Bronze Booklets*, Published by Associates in Negro Folk Education, Washington, D.C.

this country up to half a generation after Emancipation, and a shorter period of expression at the cultural, articulate level, stretching back in exceptional, sporadic instances to Phillis Wheatley in 1787, but becoming semiliterary with the anti-slavery controversy from 1835–1860, and literary in the full sense only since 1890.

Between these two levels there is a gap, transitional only in the historical sense, when the main line of Negro expression was motivated by conscious imitation of general American standards and forms, and reacted away from distinctive racial elements in an effort at cultural conformity. This was inevitable and under the circumstances normal; most other literatures and art have passed through such imitative phases; even French and German literature and art; and of course American art itself in the colonial period. But in Negro expression the position of cultural conformity and the suppression of racial emphasis has since been reversed,—first by the dialect school of Negro expression of which Paul Laurence Dunbar was the leading exponent, and more lately still by the younger contemporary school of "racial self-expression," the so-called "New Negro Movement," which since 1917 or thereabouts has produced the most outstanding formal contributions of the Negro to American literature and art.

The importance of this latter movement is not to be underestimated; for, apart from its own creative impulse, it has effected a transformation of race spirit and group attitude, and acted like the creation of a national literature in the vernacular reacted upon the educated classes of other peoples, who, also, at one or another stage of their cultural history, were not integrated with their own particular tradition and folk-background.

There is a division of critical opinion about this so-called "Negro renaissance." In one view, it was a cultural awakening and "coming of age" pivoted on a newly galvanized intelligentsia; according to the other, it was a mass movement of the urban migration of Negroes during the war period, projected on the plane of an increasingly articulate elite. Both interpretations have their share of truth. What is more important than the interpretation is the fact of a new group dynamic acquired at this time and a steadily increasing maturity coming into the Negro's formal self-expression in the arts. The breadth of the cultural stream increased with its depth; for the traditional arts of music, poetry, and oratory were rapidly supplemented by increased productivity in drama, fiction, criticism, painting, and sculpture.

Cultural racialism, with its stirring dynamic and at times its partisan fanaticism, was the keynote of the Negro renaissance. In its first phase, it was naïve, senti-mental, and almost provincial; later, under the influence of the World War principles of self-determination and the rise of other cultural nationalisms (Irish, Czecho-Slovakian, etc.) it was to become sophisticated and grounded in a deliberate revival of folk traditions and a cult of African historical origins. Poems, stories, novels, plays emphasizing such themes and glorifying race pride, race solidarity, folk-origins came in a crescendo of creative effort with the rising talents of Claude McKay, Jean Toomer, Countee Cullen, Langston Hughes, Rudolph Fisher, Jessie Fauset, Eric Walrond, Wallace Thurman, Zora Hurston, and others. This was the first generation of "New Negro" writers. They had their artistic, musical, and dramatic counterparts in Harry Burleigh, Roland Hayes, Paul Robeson, Charles Gilpin, Rose McClendon, the painters Archibald Motley, Aaron Douglas, Laura Wheeler, Edward Harleston, Palmer Hayden, Hale Woodruff, the sculptors—Meta Fuller, May Jackson, Augusta Savage, Sargent Johnson, Richmond Barthe,—to mention just the outstanding names.

But we have little time or space for names; what concerns us more are trends of style and schools of artistic thought. It was this significant decade,—1920–1930, that witnessed the collaboration of white dramatists like Ridgeley Torrence, Eugene O'Neill, Paul Green, and DuBose Heyward, with Negro acting talent like Cooper, Gilpin and Robeson which gave Negro drama its present vital position in serious native American drama; that saw the parallel developments of the new realistic and regional fiction of the liberal "New South" and the development of the Negro novel of both the Harlem and the folk-lore school; that from the world-wide recognition of the serious Negro singers from Roland Hayes to Marion Anderson threaded through first the vocal folk-song arrangements of Negro composers like Burleigh, Diton, Dett, Brown, Boatner, Hall Johnson and then gained audience for the orchestral and chamber music compositions of Coleridge Taylor, William Dawson, Dett and Grant Still. Comparable strides took Negro popular music on an upswing of popularity and influence, carrying the occasionally successful "rag-time composer" to the assured dominance of Negro dance and music in the jazz period. Here, too, was a collaboration and interchange of talent and effort,—perhaps the closest of all the cultural collaborations to date, and one profoundly influential on public opinion as well as upon the professional circles immediately involved. Indeed the competitive use, and sometimes exploitation, of the jazz idioms by the Whitemans, Gershwins and Goodmans on the one side and Fletcher Hendersons, Duke Ellingtons, Count Basies (over the common denominator, often as not, of the Negro jazz "arranger", the true composer for the non-improvising type of jazz orchestra) have made a demonstration of cultural reciprocity and mutual reenforcement that may be prophetic of similar developments in other artistic fields.

But to return to our tracing of literary trends; between 1925 and the present three schools of Negro cultural expression have in succession appeared. But they have overlapped and each has even at the moment its exponents and adherents, though of course with successively diminishing vogue. The first started the Negro renaissance with an enthusiastic cult of idealistic racialism. It made a point of the stressing of special traits of "race temperament," of a group philosophy of life, of the re-expression on the cultural level of the folk-spirit and folk history, including the half-forgotten African background. Many of this school were devoted, if slightly, too romantic Africanists. Toomer's *Cane*, Countee Cullen's *Color*, Langston Hughes' *Weary Blues*, McKay's *Harlem Shadows* were produced in the heyday of this enthusiasm. Social protest and ironic challenge had already had some embodiment, especially with Claude McKay and Fenton Johnson, but romantic and jazz exoticism still were dominant notes. As Harlem became a fashionable fad a certain amount of irresponsible individualism and eccentric exhibitionism inevitably followed, and some of the brightest of these younger talents were warped and diverted from the sounder courses of serious work and development.

Meanwhile, even before the disillusion of the depression became effective, a more serious trend of folk realism was gaining ground. It followed the general trend of American realism in poetry and fiction, and began to develop on the basis of serious local color portraiture the native distinctiveness of Negro life, first in the urban and then in the Southland settings. Hughes' soberer second book of verse *Fine Clothes to the New*, McKay's *Banjo* and *Gingertown*, Sterling Brown's realistic and ironic folk poetry in *Southern Road* are typical of this latter trend. This was a more soberly toned and prosaic racialism, delineating the grimmer side of the Harlem scene, painting the Southern peasant in careful genre studies, exposing the paradoxes and injustices of race prejudice. A few problem novels saw the light,— not too successful because of lack of objectivity and too obvious indignation and indictment, but in drama and poetry some of the best folk portraiture by Negro writers was being produced.

Though not completely diverted, a good deal of this maturing realism has been channeled off, partly by the vogue of proletarian realism and partly by the deepening disillusionment of the Negro's sad economic plight, into a rising school of iconoclast protest fiction, poetry, and drama. *Stevedore* and Erskine Caldwell's novels and stories set the pace for this latest school of Negro expression, which closely parallels the general

vogue in style, theme, and social philosophy. However, in poetry like that of Frank Marshall Davis, the latest work of Sterling Brown and Langston Hughes, and particularly in the brilliant fiction of Richard Wright, the Negro literature of social protest has some distinctive qualities of local color and idiom, quizzical irony, dashing satire, and freedom from unrelieved drabness, all of which make it somewhat distinctive in comparison with the parallel white authors. But the common factors of social reformism and relentless indictment are also there, as characteristic no doubt of the youngest trend in our serious literature.

Enough has been said to show clearly that Negro art follows no peculiar path of its own, but is with slight differences of emphasis or pace, in step with the general aesthetic and social trends of contemporary American art and literature. As aestheticism, realism, regionalism, proletarianism become the general vogue, Negro art is apt to reflect it. But always, as might be expected, these reflections are caught up in the texture of a racially-determined phase of agreement with a difference, sometimes a difference of emphasis, sometimes of motivation, often also a difference of emotional temper and stylistic idiom. It is this that saves a good deal of our art from being a feebly echoed repetition of general situations and attitudes. At times, however, this is not the case, and then in reversion to the subservient imitativeness which it has so largely outgrown, the minority literature and art becomes really minor.

As for the counter-influence, an increasing vogue for Negro themes and materials has certainly been a characteristic feature of the unfinished decade in which we now are, in fiction, drama, and the classical use of Negro musical idioms particularly. A whole generation of younger Southern novelists, Robert Rylee, Hamilton Basso, William March, James Childers, Josephine Johnson, Julian Meade have succeeded the pathbreaking realists, Clement Wood, Stribling, Sherwood Anderson, Faulkner and Caldwell, with telling documentation recanting the Bourbon tradition and the contrary to fact romance of *Gone with the Wind* and *So Red the Rose*. A realistically portrayed and fairly humanized Negro is one of the vital pivots of this new Southern fiction; just as a new economic and social reconstruction is one of its basic creeds. In drama the folk realism of Paul Green and of DuBose Heyward has continued to give moving portraiture of Negro life, though no such level of truth or moving beauty has been reached in drama as has already been attained in fiction on the Negro theme. Jazz music has reached a level of serious cultivation and analysis unprecedented for any previous form of popular music, and in classical jazz, the great talents of Negro composers like

Ellington, Dett, Still, Hall Johnson, Reginald Forsythe have been seriously challenged by Grofé, Gershwin, Gruenberg, Cesana, Lamar, Stringfield, and Morton Gould. Indeed the vogue and use of Negro themes and materials by white creative artists has grown so steadily as quite to challenge the Negro creative artist's natural spokesmanship for his own cultural materials. But this challenge should be stimulating, and the net result in event of any fair competition will doubtless be an enforced maturity of the Negro artist in several fields where he is yet immature, partly from lack of full cultural opportunity, partly through too little objectivity toward his subject-matter. It is to be frankly admitted that in the more objective fields of fiction, playwriting, descriptive portraiture, the white artist working in Negro materials has on the whole an advantage of objective control and technical maturity, while in the more intimately subjective and emotional activities of poetry, acting, music, and dance, the Negro creators and interpreters have their turn of the advantage. Such generalizations have, of course, their exceptions on both sides, but in passing they are typical of the present moment and tentatively true.

Benefiting, even because of the depression, by the Federal Arts Projects and their reasonably democratic inclusion of the Negro artists of various sorts, the growth and geographic spread of Negro art has been materially enhanced. Particularly a whole younger generation of promising painters and sculptors has been incubated by the Federal Art Project, almost too numerous for individual mention. Three Negro dramas, the *Macbeth*, *Haiti*, and the *Swing Mikado*, have been among the ranking successes of the Federal Theatre, a tribute to noncommercial management and in the case of the *Macbeth* and *Mikado* as refreshing and revealing "Negro versions" of familiar classics, almost living texts for the corroboration of the central theme of this discussion;—the compound gain of the distinctive cultural hybrid. Proof also, these experimental ventures of the powerful appeal of Negro idioms in dignified and unstereotyped contexts,—a lesson Broadway and Hollywood have yet to learn. Hollywood particularly, in spite of a new medium, is still snared in a reactionary groove and prostitutes genuine Negro talent to the perpetuation among the masses of reactionary social and racial stereotypes of character and situation. If the persuasiveness of the new art or the pressure of its new social creeds ever leaps the barricades and fences of the "movies" and the popular novel and the popular entertainment stage, as there is faint reason to hope, a revolutionizing force for liberalizing culture will have been set in irresistible motion. Up to this point we have been dealing mainly with the artistic cultural significance of Negro art, but here we cite what is probably the next

objective and the next crusade in the ascending path of Negro art, its use as an instrument for social enlightenment and constructive social reform. This, too, is no racially exclusive job and has no racially partisan objective. It is perhaps, since it is the ultimate goal of cultural democracy, the capstone of the historic process of American acculturation. To be a crucial factor in so vital a general matter will be a cultural contribution of supreme importance.

STEPHEN HENDERSON

Theme

Of the three categories, perhaps the simplest and most apparent is theme. In the following quatrain by George Moses Horton, for example, the "Blackness" is apparent in what he is speaking about, his historical situation as a Black slave in the United States.

Alas! and am I born for this,
To wear this slavish chain
Deprived of all created bliss,
Through hardships, toil and pain!

Or another simple example might be Cullen's "To Make a Poet Black," with its bitter concluding couplet:

Yet do I marvel at this curious thing,
To make a poet black and bid him sing. *

It could be easily argued that both Horton and Cullen are really dealing with the universal theme of rebellion against oppression, and that Black poets have no monopoly on the theme. To that there can be varied response, but the significant point is that poetry because of its very nature—sensuous and rooted in particular experience—is not the same as philosophy or mathematics. Thus, though "slavish chain" might evoke a sympathetic tear from the eye of a white New York professor meditating upon his people's enslavement in ancient Egypt, that makes the poem no less valid as a "Black statement." However, this ambiguity does make it a less precise kind of statement than Cullen's, because in the latter the irony cannot be

---

*All thematic materials are certainly not this obvious and direct, but on a very low level of perception we can be alerted to racial content this way. Ambiguities, of course, exist. For example, if a non-Black writer elected to write on a "Black theme" using a Black persona, and if he were as successful in absorbing Black expressive patterns as some musicians are, then, indeed there would be real problems. As far as I know, there are no poems written by non-Blacks which have that degree of success. But there is a considerable body of "dialect" poetry from whites to indicate what I mean. In addition, there are various poetical works like Blake's "Little Black Boy," as well as prose fiction like *Othello*, *Oroonoko*, *Uncle Remus*.

appreciated without understanding the specific historical debasement of the African psyche in America. Other questions raised under the rubric of "universal theme" can be answered basically in the same way.

It should be understood from the outset that a Black poet may develop a theme which stems directly out of his experience, colored, so to speak, by his Blackness, but not communicate that Blackness, unless one go outside the poem itself. This we may choose not to do. If we do, however, the action, I think, would be perfectly valid. To test the validity of this statement, let us read the following sonnet:

My mistress' eyes are nothing like the sun;
Coral is far more red than her lips' red;
If snow be white, why then her breasts are dun;
If hairs be wires, black wires grow on her head.
I have seen roses damask'd, red and white,
But no such roses see I in her cheeks;
And in some perfumes is there more delight
Than in the breath that from my mistress reeks.
I love to hear her speak, yet well I know
That music hath a far more pleasing sound;
I grant, I never saw a goddess go;
My mistress when she walks treads on the ground:
And yet, by heaven, I think my love as rare
As any she belied with false compare.

This, of course, is Shakespeare's sonnet No. 130. But, if we discovered one day that it had been composed by an African at Elizabeth's court, would not the thematic meaning change? Perhaps formalist critics would not publicly admit the point, but a culturally oriented critic would. So, knowledge of the author's race altered our point of view, i.e., going outside of the poem changed our perspective of it.

There are more difficult questions regarding theme, which cannot be discussed abstractly or by simple example. Such questions are: Is there a special theme or cluster of themes which run throughout Black poetry? Are there Black themes which apparently cannot be handled by non-Black writers? This question was raised by W. S. Braithwaite in "The Negro in American Literature" (*The New Negro*, p. 35) but in the broader context of all of Black literature, not just poetry. He states, ". . . in spite of all good intentions, the true presentation of the real tragedy of Negro life is a task still left for Negro writers to perform. This is especially true for those phases of culturally representative race life that as yet have scarcely at all found treatment by white American authors." Present-day poets and many critics too—as the response to William Styron's *Nat Turner* shows—would deny the ultimate validity of any white presentation of the Black Experience in art.

Historical surveys such as Brawley's *Early Negro American Writers*, Brown, Davis, and Lee's *The Negro Caravan*, and Robinson's *Early Black Poets* suggest that there are indeed thematic clusters in Black poetry around what could be called the idea of Liberation. And when we move to the present, we must consider certainly the essays by Richard Wright and the critical statements by the poets themselves in which they express their intent that, as a rule, follows the historical consciousness of the people. This is to say, that as Black people in the United States refine and clarify their conceptions of themselves the poetry reflects the process.

The early formal Black poetry reflected the concerns of those who were trained to read and to write. Thus, to follow Sterling Brown's account, there were those poets whose chief object was to demonstrate their ability to write as well as the whites, as in the case of Alberry Whitman and the "Mockingbird School of Poets." Other poets, like James Bell and Frances Ellen Harper, used their talents in the abolitionist cause. Another group wrote in dialect and took for their subject matter the lives of the common folk which they sometimes caricatured in the manner of white writers like Thomas Nelson Page. Others, like Paul Laurence Dunbar and James Edwin Campbell, while still influenced by white stereotypes and the expectations of white audiences, presented wholesome, if not altogether realistic, portraits of Black folk life. The period preceding the Harlem Renaissance not only produced the dialect poets but found many Black poets studiously avoiding overt racial considerations in a manner reminiscent of the late forties and the fifties. "Poetry was a romantic escape for many of them," states Brown, "not a perception of reality. . . ."

Although there were attempts at realistic depiction of Black life before they came on the scene, the writers of the Harlem Renaissance were the first to do this in a systematic manner, as even a cursory look at the period will reveal. One recalls Langston Hughes's famous declaration in "The Negro Artist and the Racial Mountain":

These common people are not afraid of spirituals, as for a long time their more intellectual brethren were, and jazz is their child. They furnish a wealth of colorful, distinctive material for any artist because they still hold their own individuality in the face of American standardizations. And perhaps these common people will give to the world its truly great Negro artist, the one who is not afraid to be himself. Whereas the better-class Negro would tell the artist what to do, the people at least let him alone when he does appear. And they are not ashamed of him—if they know he exists at all. And they accept what beauty is their own without question.

[*Black Expression, pp. 259, 260.*]

Notwithstanding the bravery of this kind of effort, Hughes and other realistic writers of his generation were sharply censured by middle-class members of their own race, including W. E. B. Du Bois and Benjamin Brawley (*Negro Genius,* p. 248), for portraying the "seamy side" of Black life. Seen in retrospect, the poetry of this group, the poetry of the twenties, helped to balance the pieties of the abolitionist writers on the one hand and the bucolic idylls of the dialect school on the other. Alain Locke's essay entitled "The New Negro," which appeared in his larger "statement," the epoch-making volume of the same name, brought the issues into focus. Afro-Americans had come of age; they could look at themselves for what they were, without false piety and without shame, rejecting the "social nostrums and the panaceas," and realizing that although religion, freedom, and education were important to their cause, they alone were not sufficient. What was needed was group solidarity and collective effort.

> Each generation . . . will have its creed, and that of the present is the belief in the efficacy of collective effort, in race cooperation. This deep feeling of race is at present the mainspring of Negro life. It seems to be the outcome of the reaction to proscription and prejudice; an attempt, fairly successful on the whole, to convert a defensive into an offensive position, a handicap into an incentive. It is radical in tone, but not in purpose and only the most stupid forms of opposition, misunderstanding or persecution could make it otherwise. Of course, the thinking Negro has shifted a little toward the left with the worldtrend, and there is an increasing group who affiliate with radical and liberal movements. But fundamentally for the present the Negro is radical on race matters, conservative on others, in other words, a "forced radical," a social protestant rather than a genuine radical. Yet under further pressure and injustice, iconoclastic thought and motives will inevitably increase. Harlem's quixotic radicalisms call for their ounce of democracy to-day lest to-morrow they be beyond cure.
>
> [*New Negro, p. 11.*]

Locke's analysis was essentially correct. Unfortunately his warning was not heeded, and although the "stupid forms of opposition," the "misunderstanding," and the "persecution" which he warned against seemed to be abating during the Civil Rights Movement of the fifties and sixties, the failure of Dr. King's Northern Campaign which linked the anti-war and the Civil Rights issues, and his assassination in 1968 indicated that the country still intended to keep its Black citizens in subjection.

Disenchantment with the goals and strategies of the Civil Rights Movement led to the Black Power Movement and the subsequent widespread revival of nationalist and internationalist feeling and thought among Blacks. To the extent that Black artists today have influenced their community to view itself in the larger political and spiritual context of Blackness, they have moved beyond the Harlem Renaissance, though obviously influenced by it. The old theme of liberation took on new meaning. Thus the Black Arts Movement, though emerging before the Black Power Movement, is in some respects the cultural dimension of that phenomenon. Numerous eloquent spokesmen have appeared, among them Imamu Amiri Baraka (LeRoi Jones), Larry Neal, Ron Karenga, and Don L. Lee.

In their statements, one can see the process of self-definition made clearer and sharper as the self-reliance and racial consciousness of an earlier period are revived and raised to the level of revolutionary thought.

The present movement is different from the Harlem Renaissance in the extent of its attempt to speak directly *to* Black people *about themselves* in order to move them toward self-knowledge and collective freedom. It is therefore not "protest" art but essentially an art of liberating vision. Larry Neal is probably its most articulate proponent. He states that when Black artists speak of the need to address the psychic and spiritual needs of their people,

> They are not speaking of an art that screams and masturbates before white audiences. That is the path of Negro literature and civil rights literature. No, they are not speaking about that kind of thing, even though that is what some Negro writers of the past have done. Instead, they are speaking of an art that addresses itself directly to Black People; an art that speaks to us in terms of our feelings and ideas about the world; an art that validates the positive aspects of our life style. Dig: An art that opens us up to the beauty and ugliness within us; that makes us understand our condition and each other in a more profound manner; that unites us, exposing us to our painful weaknesses and strengths; and finally, an art that posits for us the Vision of a Liberated Future.
>
> [*"Any Day Now: Black Art and Black Liberation," Ebony, August, 1969, pp. 55, 56.*]

A difference in emphasis, in depth, in scope, and political maturity is thus evident when one considers the Harlem Renaissance, but many of these developments were possible because of the changing world in which Black Americans of the post-World War II generation found themselves, a world in which articulate men and women rediscovered Africa and Pan-Africanism, rediscovered Du Bois and Garvey, rediscovered the Harlem Renaissance itself and built upon its strengths while seeking to avoid its errors. The process is continuing, as a careful examination of Neal's statement would show, for in its polemical dimension it calls attention, in fact, to the problems which still beset Black art. There is still, for example, a sizeable amount of masturbatory art that screams "whitey" and "honkie." But that too is changing under the advice of artists like Mari Evans, in critical essays and in poems like "Speak the Truth to the People." Askia Touré is another who has contributed to a growing general awareness by Black intellectuals that there are more important things to do than to amuse supercilious whites or to respond to their misunderstanding of Black creative efforts.

In spite of false starts, meandering, backsliding, and illusory goals, the great overarching movement of consciousness for Black people must be called, in contemporary parlance the idea of Liberation—from slavery, from segregation and degradation, from wishful "integration" into the "main stream," to the passionate denial of white middle-class values of the present and an attendant embrace of Africa and the Third World as alternative routes of development. This is not to say, of course, that all contemporary Black poets mean the same thing by Liberation, or even that they speak very precisely for the Black masses when they use that term, but if one substituted the old word "Freedom" for it, there would be no doubt at all that the message is clear. At any rate, it should be clear that not only have the Black professionals organized themselves around varying concepts of Liberation, but so also have innumerable other groups, some representing and having direct contact with the masses. But perhaps the most striking embodiment of this Liberation consciousness has occurred among Black prisoners, as the Attica uprising of September 9, 1971, indicates. Some Blacks see the uprising as a failure of revolutionary resolve because of the divisiveness among the prisoners and their seeming inability to make good on their threats to execute their hostages and fight to the death. Another view appears in a report from The Institute of the Black World, an independent research organization based in Atlanta, Georgia. The report describes the political significance in these terms:

> Attica is a new event in history. Nothing like it has ever happened before. It is a symbol that black men whom white society has consigned to its deepest dungeons have, instead of succumbing, rediscovered themselves and reeducated themselves to rise up and strike back at the system which intended that they should never survive at all—and certainly not as men. But beyond the symbolism are the immense practical achievements of the brothers.

After listing these achievements, it goes on to state:

> The men of Attica were different from their captors. One brother said, "I am Attica." He meant that he was

the new reality, the embodiment of change that Attica and all American institutions must undergo.... In order to sustain the revolt at Attica some new moral and political force had to be created, some new set of values. What was it? What was new about the black prisoners which made their revolt unlike any other that had happened before? ... The prisoners seized Attica and ran it *autonomously* and *humanely*. With compassion for their enemies. This is what is new. This is what the non-official "visitors" who got inside could not believe.

[*IBW Monthly Report, Sept., 1971.*]

Whether the masses of Black people accept this position, the first one, or some other, the cultural dimension of the event lies in the fact that Black writing—not only the works of Malcolm X and Fanon, but the poetry of Etheridge Knight and Don L. Lee and Claude McKay—had helped to shape the prisoners' new values, had increased their self-esteem and sharpened their political awareness, just as it has affected a whole generation of Black college students on all levels. Ironically, for it shows with graphic precision the arrogant ignorance which established institutions have of the Black Arts Movement, and, deeper, of Black history and aspirations—ironically, a *Time* magazine story which purported to be an in-depth study of the rebellion noted that Black prisons were inspired by original writings by the prisoners themselves, among which was "a poem written by an unknown prisoner, crude but touching in its would-be heroic style (*Time*, Sept. 7, 1971, p. 20). And in demonstration of what it meant, the *Time* writer included the opening lines of Claude McKay's famous sonnet, "If We Must Die." This was crude. True, the prisoner who copied the lines had written "unglorious" for McKay's "inglorious." But crude! Winston Churchill, of course, had better taste, and better judgment. In the abysmal early days of World War II when Great Britain was struggling for its very life against Nazi Germany, when all of Western Europe had been overrun, and France itself had been crushed—in those bitter times for the British people—Winston Churchill, the Prime Minister of Great Britain and its greatest leader of modern times, galvanized the British Parliament and the will of the English people with the ringing words of this self-same sonnet, written by a young Jamaican two decades earlier, while he smarted from the same kind of institutionalized racism that Hitler's Germany was inflicting upon its neighbors. The crowning irony, of course, is that few people knew that McKay was Black or bothered to think, if they knew it, that his homeland Jamaica was an exploited British colony with a history of bloody suppression, or, for that matter, that his adopted homeland America though subtle, at times, was hardly less brutal. And now twenty odd years after his death, amidst the intellectual ambivalence which surrounds the Harlem Renaissance, his explosive words, though literally baffled by the sonnet form, still inspire hope and revolutionary courage in the minds of men whom their country had declared to be an economic and spiritual surplus.

But though the great theme of Black poetry, and, indeed, of Black life in the United States is Liberation, there are important complementary patterns, some of which take us outside the dimension of history into the universal realm of the mythical. In the oral tradition, the dogged determination of the work songs, the tough-minded power of the blues, the inventive energy of jazz, and the transcendent vision of God in the spirituals and the sermons, all energize the idea of Liberation, which is itself liberated from the temporal, the societal, and the political—not with the narcotic obsession to remain above the world of struggle and change and death, but with full realization of a return to that world both strengthened and renewed. Thus in the spirituals we have both:

Go down, Moses, way down in Egypt land.
Tell ol Pharaoh to let my people go.

and

Drinkin' of the wine, wine, wine,
Drinkin' of the wine
I ought to bin to Heaven ten thousand years
Drinkin' of the wine.

In the blues we find these haunting lines from Robert Johnson:

I got to keep movinn', I got to keep movinnn',
Blues fallin' down like hail, blues fallin' down like hail,
Mmmmmmmmmmmmm-mmmm-mmm, blues fallin'
   down like hail, blues fallin' down like hail,
And the days keep on worryin' me, for a hell-hound
   on my trail,
Hell-hound on my trail, hell-hound on my trail.

But we also find this famous anonymous line, which seems a distillation of the blues spirit:

I got the blues, but I'm too damn mean to cry.

And in Furry Lewis' "White Lightnin' Blues," the blues not only represent spiritual paralysis, but liberation through sexuality.

Baby, fix my breakfast, so I can go to bed,
Baby, fix my breakfast, so I can go to bed,
I been drinkin' white lightnin' and it's done gone to
   my head.

Got the blues so bad, it hurts my feet to walk,
Got the blues so bad, it hurts my feet to walk;
It wouldn't hurt so bad, but it hurts my tongue to talk.

Not only that, but also this resolution in the affirmative:

The train I ride sixteen coaches long,
The train I ride sixteen coaches long;
She don't haul nothin' but chocolate to the bone.

And even in the contemporary poetry, with all of its preoccupation with the immediate problems of political assertion and the raising of consciousness and the celebration of the Black cities, there is a pronounced concern with the spiritual, sometimes rooted in the idiom of the Black church, sometimes exploring religious concepts of Islam and African religions, sometimes seeking analogues to modern music. Some of the poets who reflect this concern with the spiritual are W. Keorapetse Kgositsile, Don Lee, Imamu Baraka (LeRoi Jones), and Larry Neal. In this volume the pattern is found in poems like Baraka's "I Am Speaking of Future Good-ness and Social Philosophy," Sharon Bourke's "Sopranosound, Memory of John," and Larry Neal's "Morning Raga for Malcolm," with the lines:

I now calm airily float
lift my spirit—Allah you
am me. space undulates
under me, space, to my sides
and under me nothing
I now calm airily float

There are, of course, other thematic patterns that Black poetry handles. But even in the purely personal concerns, say, of some of Paul Laurence Dunbar's "nonracial" poems, or of Countee Cullen's or Walter Dancy's, there are patterns that one can call "Black," if one accepts the critical premises of this essay. So, there are, then, Black poems in which the theme is apparent, such as the personal concern of Horton as a Black person in the previously quoted quatrain. One might also include in this group Dunbar's bitter lament in "The Poet," Cullen's "Heritage" and some of the poetry of Langston Hughes.

A step toward objectification and distancing of personal involvement occurs when the poet depicts either real or imaginary Black figures. Here the technique, of course, merges with that of other literary traditions, at times rather obviously so, as in the case of the realistic writers of the thirties being under the influence of Carl Sandburg, E. A. Robinson, and other American whites. However, it must be remembered that there is a Black storytelling tradition which is also at work, and sometimes it is consciously being followed. At any rate, this depiction of Black character deals with historical figures like Frederick Douglass, in Robert Hayden's poem; Malcolm X, as in Margaret Walker and James Emanuel; Martin L. King, Jr., as in Mari Evans, Margaret Danner, and Donald Graham; Nat

Turner, as in Robert Hayden and Margaret Walker. At times it deals with Black musical figures, whose lives become vehicles for comment by the poet, as in the various poems on Coltrane by Don Lee, Sonia Sanchez, and others; Bessie Smith, by Robert Hayden; Ma Rainey, by Sterling Brown; Duke Ellington, by Sarah Fabio. In addition, there are musical figures who may or may not be historical, such as Dunbar's "Malindy" and "Whistling Sam."

Similarly, Black literary figures also become the subject of various poems. Among the figures thus treated are Countee Cullen, Richard Wright, Paul Dunbar, Langston Hughes, and Gwendolyn Brooks.

A final group of character poems includes larger-than-life figures such as Stack O'Lee, Shine, and John Henry. In all of this, of course, the poet can pursue whatever theme related to the Black Experience he finds meaningful. Of course, few white writers find these subjects meaningful enough to write about.

Some of these concerns, as I have implied earlier, are common to poets outside of the Black tradition as well, so I need not try to enumerate or to discuss them. Others have been dealt with in summary form, but it might be of value to return to the poetry of the Harlem Renaissance and to compare its concerns with those of the present.

Sterling Brown's succinct statement is an indispensable point of departure. Speaking of the Renaissance poetry, he points out its five chief areas of interest:

> (1) a discovery of Africa as a source for race pride, (2) a use of Negro heroes and heroic episodes from American History, (3) propaganda of protest, (4) a treatment of the Negro masses frequently of the folk, less often of the workers with more understanding and less apology, and (5) franker and deeper self-revelation.
>
> [*Negro Poetry & Drama, Atheneum ed., 1969, p. 61.*]

Some of these concerns are also those of contemporary Black poetry, but with an important difference of emphasis. For example, in the rediscovery of Africa as a source for race pride, poets of the sixties were better informed generally about the true nature of African civilizations and, as a rule, were especially concerned about the political relevance of modern Africa to the rest of the Black World. This obviously has been the result of the emergence of free African states during the past two decades as well as the rise of interest among American Blacks in their continental brothers and sisters. The role of the media cannot be overestimated in this phenomenon, especially when Black men in the General Assembly of the United Nations, dressed in their native garb, were shown on television intelligently debating issues of international significance. A further related fac-

tor undoubtedly has been the influx of African students into the colleges and universities of the United States, especially into the Black ones. Then, one must consider the Black Power Movement and its extensions in the Black Arts Movement, the national concern with Black Studies and the subsequent reprinting of quality materials on Africa, and finally the resurgence of interest in Pan-Africanism. In all of this, Alain Locke's essay "The New Negro" presently reads almost like prophecy. In sum, if the concern in the twenties was largely romantic, in the sixties, though at times not unromantic, it has been chiefly political.

With regard to the second point, "a use of Negro heroes and heroic episodes," we have already referred to the contemporary popularity of Black historical figures as subjects of poetry. However, it must be noted that the single most popular hero of contemporary Black poetry is Malcolm X, not Martin Luther King, Jr. And the heroes, whoever they are, do not apologize to America, nor plead, but seek to affirm their right to self-definition and manhood, with all that that implies. And the episodes in American history are viewed as episodes in "Black history," so it is not Peter Salem who interests the present generation but Nat Turner. And Black history also means African history and African heroes, Chaka, Kenyatta, Lumumba, Nyeryere, Nkrumah.

There has been, despite denials, some protest poetry in the sixties, as I have implied, but for the most part the message of that period, unlike that of earlier times, has been directed toward Black audiences, even though the poet knew that the white world was looking over his shoulder.

What Brown stated in his fourth point is still true of Black poetry. Although the "masses" appear frequently in the poetry of the sixties, there is to my knowledge little or no treatment of the Black worker as subject. Perhaps this is due to a comparative lack of sympathy with Marxist thought, perhaps to ideological unclarity, perhaps to a tendency to concentrate on heroic figures, martyrs, hustlers, and other romanticized types who go counter to the "mainstream" of American life.

Point number five, "franker and deeper self-revelation," indicates an important difference between the poetry of the Renaissance and that of the present; the tendency since the sixties has been mainly toward public statement, toward didacticism, and toward collective ritual. Thus it is not surprising that some of the poets are also dramatists and musicians and artists. I think one can safely generalize that much of the poetry of self-revelation written and published during this period is either by poets whose chronological age puts them in the fifties, at least, or by very young poets who are caught up in the introspection of adolescence. Notwithstanding, it is curious that much of contemporary poetry avoids the character drawing which was so prominent a part of the earlier production, from Paul Laurence Dunbar to Gwendolyn Brooks. Again, however, the exceptions are the older poets who have managed to keep attuned to the times. The question of form and personal habit may have something to do with this. At any rate, the younger poet will usually rap or declaim or sing, but if he wants to create a Black character for one purpose or another, he usually turns to drama or to the short story, as in the case of Sonia Sanchez, Carolyn Rodgers, and S. E. Anderson. Perhaps, finally, their method is dictated by their objectives. They want to speak as directly to the community as they can. At times they succeed, even when it entails not only speaking to a college audience but to a cynical gathering of people at a poolroom or bar, as the OBAC writers have done. More recently, the poets have been experimenting with more effective ways of reaching a mass audience, and the result has been the recording of LP albums which are played on the air, the use of the church as a forum, as in the case of Nikki Giovanni, and TV appearances, like those by the Last Poets. As I pointed out earlier, these poets are being heard and they are being understood by the people whom they address.

Sometimes a poet in his effort at self-revelation moves outside of the immediate concerns of the Black Community. Some of the poems of Mari Evans, Gwendolyn Brooks, and Robert Hayden appear to do this. Nevertheless, our mere awareness of them as Black persons helps to shape our response to the poem, and this is so whether or not the poet wants us to consider him as other than a poet pure and simple, or for that matter, pure and complex. The fact of the matter is that the Black Community does not intend to give up any of its beautiful singers, whether Countee Cullen or Melvin Tolson or Robert Hayden. We may quarrel with them sometimes, but ain't never gonna say good-bye.

RALPH ELLISON

Epilogue from *Invisible Man*

So there you have all of it that's important. Or at least you *almost* have it. I'm an invisible man and it placed me in a hole—or showed me the hole I was in, if you will—and I reluctantly accepted the fact. What else could I have done? Once you get used to it, reality is as irresistible as a club, and I was clubbed into the cellar before I caught the hint. Perhaps that's the way it had

to be; I don't know. Nor do I know whether accepting the lesson has placed me in the rear or in the *avant-garde. That*, perhaps, is a lesson for history, and I'll leave such decisions to Jack and his ilk while I try belatedly to study the lesson of my own life.

Let me be honest with you—a feat which, by the way, I find of the utmost difficulty. When one is invisible he finds such problems as good and evil, honesty and dishonesty, of such shifting shapes that he confuses one with the other, depending upon who happens to be looking through him at the time. Well, now I've been trying to look through myself, and there's a risk in it. I was never more hated than when I tried to be honest. Or when, even as just now I've tried to articulate exactly what I felt to be the truth. No one was satisfied—not even I. On the other hand, I've never been more loved and appreciated than when I tried to "justify" and affirm someone's mistaken beliefs; or when I've tried to give my friends the incorrect, absurd answers they wished to hear. In my presence they could talk and agree with themselves, the world was nailed down, and they loved it. They received a feeling of security. But here was the rub: Too often, in order to justify *them*, I had to take myself by the throat and choke myself until my eyes bulged and my tongue hung out and wagged like the door of an empty house in a high wind. Oh, yes, it made them happy and it made me sick. So I became ill of affirmation, of saying "yes" against the nay-saying of my stomach—not to mention my brain.

There is, by the way, an area in which a man's feelings are more rational than his mind, and it is precisely in that area that his will is pulled in several directions at the same time. You might sneer at this, but I know now. I was pulled this way and that for longer than I can remember. And my problem was that I always tried to go in everyone's way but my own. I have also been called one thing and then another while no one really wished to hear what I called myself. So after years of trying to adopt the opinions of others I finally rebelled. I am an *invisible* man. Thus I have come a long way and returned and boomeranged a long way from the point in society toward which I originally aspired.

So I took to the cellar; I hibernated. I got away from it all. But that wasn't enough. I couldn't be still even in hibernation. Because, damn it, there's the mind, the *mind.* It wouldn't let me rest. Gin, jazz and dreams were not enough. Books were not enough. My belated appreciation of the crude joke that had kept me running, was not enough. And my mind revolved again and again back to my grandfather. And, despite the farce that ended my attempt to say "yes" to the Brotherhood, I'm still plagued by his deathbed advice . . .

Perhaps he hid his meaning deeper than I thought, perhaps his anger threw me off—I can't decide. Could he have meant—hell, he *must* have meant the principle, that we were to affirm the principle on which the country was built and not the men, or at least not the men who did the violence. Did he mean say "yes" because he knew that the principle was greater than the men, greater than the numbers and the vicious power and all the methods used to corrupt its name? Did he mean to affirm the principle, which they themselves had dreamed into being out of the chaos and darkness of the feudal past, and which they had violated and compromised to the point of absurdity even in their own corrupt minds? Or did he mean that we had to take the responsibility for all of it, for the men as well as the principle, because we were the heirs who must use the principle because no other fitted our needs? Not for the power or for vindication, but because we, with the given circumstance of our origin, could only thus find transcendence? Was it that we of all, we, most of all, had to affirm the principle, the plan in whose name we had been brutalized and sacrificed—not because we would always be weak nor because we were afraid or opportunistic, but because we were older than they, in the sense of what it took to live in the world with others and because they had exhausted in us, some—not much, but some—of the human greed and smallness, yes, and the fear and superstition that had kept them running. (Oh, yes, they're running too, running all over themselves.) Or was it, did he mean that we should affirm the principle because we, through no fault of our own, were linked to all the others in the loud, clamoring semi-visible world, that world seen only as a fertile field for exploitation by Jack and his kind, and with condescension by Norton and his, who were tired of being the mere pawns in the futile game of "making history"? Had he seen that for these too we had to say "yes" to the principle, lest they turn upon us to destroy both it and us?

"Agree 'em to death and destruction," grandfather had advised. Hell, weren't they their own death and their own destruction except as the principle lived in them and in us? And here's the cream of the joke: Weren't we *part of them* as well as apart from them and subject to die when they died? I can't figure it out; it escapes me. But what do *I* really want, I've asked myself. Certainly not the freedom of a Rinehart or the power of a Jack, nor simply the freedom not to run. No, but the next step I couldn't make, so I've remained in the hole.

I'm not blaming anyone for this state of affairs, mind you; nor merely crying *mea culpa*. The fact is that you carry part of your sickness within you, at least I do as an invisible man. I carried my sickness and though for a long time I tried to place it in the outside world, the attempt to write it down shows me that at least half of it lay within me. It came upon me slowly, like that strange disease that affects those black men whom you see turning slowly from black to albino, their pigment disappearing as under the radiation of some cruel, invisible ray. You go along for years knowing something is wrong, then suddenly you discover that you're as transparent as air. At first you tell yourself that it's all a dirty joke, or that it's due to the "political situation." But deep down you come to suspect that you're yourself to blame, and you stand naked and shivering before the millions of eyes who look through you unseeingly. *That* is the real soul-sickness, the spear in the side, the drag by the neck through the mob-angry town, the Grand Inquisition, the embrace of the Maiden, the rip in the belly with the guts spilling out, the trip to the chamber with the deadly gas that ends in the oven so hygienically clean—only it's worse because you continue stupidly to live. But live you must, and you can either make passive love to your sickness or burn it out and go on to the next conflicting phase.

Yes, but what *is* the next phase? How often have I tried to find it! Over and over again I've gone up above to seek it out. For, like almost everyone else in our country, I started out with my share of optimism. I believed in hard work and progress and action, but now, after first being "for" society and then "against" it, I assign myself no rank or any limit, and such an attitude is very much against the trend of the times. But my world has become one of infinite possibilities. What a phrase—still it's a good phrase and a good view of life, and a man shouldn't accept any other; that much I've learned underground. Until some gang succeeds in putting the world in a strait jacket, its definition is possibility. Step outside the narrow borders of what men call reality and you step into chaos—ask Rinehart, he's a master of it—or imagination. That too I've learned in the cellar, and not by deadening my sense of perception; I'm invisible, not blind.

No indeed, the world is just as concrete, ornery, vile and sublimely wonderful as before, only now I better understand my relation to it and it to me. I've come a long way from those days when, full of illusion, I lived a public life and attempted to function under the assumption that the world was solid and all the relationships therein. Now I know men are different and that all life is divided and that only in division is there true health. Hence again I have stayed in my hole, because up above there's an increasing passion to make men conform to a pattern. Just as in my nightmare, Jack and the boys are waiting with their knives, looking for the slightest excuse to . . . well, to "ball the jack," and I do not refer to the old dance step, although what they're doing is making the old eagle rock dangerously.

Whence all this passion toward conformity anyway?—diversity is the word. Let man keep his many parts and you'll have no tyrant states. Why, if they follow this conformity business they'll end up by forcing me, an invisible man, to become white, which is not a color but the lack of one. Must I strive toward colorlessness? But seriously, and without snobbery, think of what the world would lose if that should happen. America is woven of many strands; I would recognize them and let it so remain. It's "winner take nothing" that is the great truth of our country or of any country. Life is to be lived, not controlled; and humanity is won by continuing to play in face of certain defeat. Our fate is to become one, and yet many—This is not prophecy, but description. Thus one of the greatest jokes in the world is the spectacle of the whites busy escaping blackness and becoming blacker every day, and the blacks striving toward whiteness, becoming quite dull and gray. None of us seems to know who he is or where he's going.

Which reminds me of something that occurred the other day in the subway. At first I saw only an old gentleman who for the moment was lost. I knew he was lost, for as I looked down the platform I saw him approach several people and turn away without speaking. He's lost, I thought, and he'll keep coming until he sees me, then he'll ask his direction. Maybe there's an embarrassment in it if he admits he's lost to a strange white man. Perhaps to lose a sense of *where* you are implies the danger of losing a sense of *who* you are. That must be it, I thought—to lose your direction is to lose your face. So here he comes to ask his direction from the lost, the invisible. Very well, I've learned to live without direction. Let him ask.

But then he was only a few feet away and I recognized him; it was Mr. Norton. The old gentleman was thinner and wrinkled now but as dapper as ever. And seeing him made all the old life live in me for an instant, and I smiled with tear-stinging eyes. Then it was over, dead, and when he asked me how to get to Centre Street, I regarded him with mixed feelings.

"Don't you know me?" I said.

"Should I?" he said.

"You see me?" I said, watching him tensely.

"Why, of course—Sir, do you know the way to Centre Street?"

"So. Last time it was the Golden Day, now it's Centre Street. You've retrenched, sir. But don't you really know who I am?"

"Young man, I'm in a hurry," he said, cupping a hand to his ear. "Why should I know you?"

"Because I'm your destiny."

"My destiny, did you say?" He gave me a puzzled stare, backing away. "Young man, are you well? Which train did you say I should take?"

"I didn't say," I said shaking my head. "Now, aren't you ashamed?"

"Ashamed? ASHAMED!" he said indignantly.

I laughed, suddenly taken by the idea. "Because, Mr. Norton, if you don't know *where* you are, you probably don't know *who* you are. So you came to me out of shame. You are ashamed, now aren't you?"

"Young man, I've lived too long in this world to be ashamed of anything. Are you light-headed from hunger? How do you know my name?"

"But I'm your destiny, I made you. Why shouldn't I know you?" I said, walking closer and seeing him back against a pillar. He looked around like a cornered animal. He thought I was mad.

"Don't be afraid, Mr. Norton," I said. "There's a guard down the platform there. You're safe. Take any train; they all go to the Golden D—"

But now an express had rolled up and the old man was disappearing quite spryly inside one of its doors. I stood there laughing hysterically. I laughed all the way back to my hole.

But after I had laughed I was thrown back on my thoughts—how had it all happened? And I asked myself if it were only a joke and I couldn't answer. Since then I've sometimes been overcome with a passion to return into that "heart of darkness" across the Mason-Dixon line, but then I remind myself that the true darkness lies within my own mind, and the idea loses itself in the gloom. Still the passion persists. Sometimes I feel the need to reaffirm all of it, the whole unhappy territory and all the things loved and unlovable in it, for all of it is part of me. Till now, however, this is as far as I've ever gotten, for all life seen from the hole of invisibility is absurd.

So why do I write, torturing myself to put it down? Because in spite of myself I've learned some things. Without the possibility of action, all knowledge comes to one labeled "file and forget," and I can neither file nor forget. Nor will certain ideas forget me; they keep filing away at my lethargy, my complacency. Why should I be the one to dream this nightmare? Why should I be dedicated and set aside—yes, if not to at least *tell* a few people about it? There seems to be no escape. Here I've set out to throw my anger into the world's face, but now that I've tried to put it all down the old fascination with playing a role returns, and I'm drawn upward again. So that even before I finish I've failed (maybe my anger is too heavy; perhaps, being a talker, I've used too many words). But I've failed. The very act of trying to put it all down has confused me and negated some of the anger and some of the bitterness. So it is that now I denounce and defend, or feel prepared to defend. I condemn and affirm, say no and say yes, say yes and say no. I denounce because though implicated and partially responsible, I have been hurt to the point of abysmal pain, hurt to the point of invisibility. And I defend because in spite of all I find that I love. In order to get some of it down I *have* to love. I sell you no phony forgiveness, I'm a desperate man—but too much of your life will be lost, its meaning lost, unless you approach it as much through love as through hate. So I approach it through division. So I denounce and I defend and I hate and I love.

Perhaps that makes me a little bit as human as my grandfather. Once I thought my grandfather incapable of thoughts about humanity, but I was wrong. Why should an old slave use such a phrase as, "This and this or this has made me more human," as I did in my arena speech? Hell, he never had any doubts about his humanity—that was left to his "free" offspring. He accepted his humanity just as he accepted the principle. It was his, and the principle lives on in all its human and absurd diversity. So now having tried to put it down I have disarmed myself in the process. You won't believe in my invisibility and you'll fail to see how any principle that applies to you could apply to me. You'll fail to see it even though death waits for both of us if you don't. Nevertheless, the very disarmament has brought me to a decision. The hibernation is over. I must shake off the old skin and come up for breath. There's a stench in the air, which, from this distance underground, might be the smell either of death or of spring—I hope of spring. But don't let me trick you, there *is* a death in the smell of spring and in the smell of thee as in the smell of me. And if nothing more, invisibility has taught my nose to classify the stenches of death.

In going underground, I whipped it all except the mind, the *mind*. And the mind that has conceived a plan of living must never lose sight of the chaos against which that pattern was conceived. That goes for societies as well as for individuals. Thus, having tried to give pattern to the chaos which lives within the pattern of your certainties, I must come out, I must emerge. And there's still a conflict within me: With Louis Armstrong one half of me says, "Open the window and let the foul air out," while the other says, "It was good green corn before the harvest." Of course Louie was kidding, *he* wouldn't have thrown old Bad Air out, because it would have broken up the music and the dance, when it was the good music that came from the bell of old Bad Air's horn that counted. Old Bad Air is still around with his music and his dancing and his diversity, and I'll be up and around with mine. And, as I said before, a decision has been made. I'm shaking off

the old skin and I'll leave it here in the hole. I'm coming out, no less invisible without it, but coming out nevertheless. And I suppose it's damn well time. Even hibernations can be overdone, come to think of it. Perhaps that's my greatest social crime, I've overstayed my hibernation, since there's a possibility that even an invisible man has a socially responsible role to play.

"Ah," I can hear you say, "so it was all a build-up to bore us with his buggy jiving. He only wanted us to listen to him rave!" But only partially true: Being invisible and without substance, a disembodied voice, as it were, what else could I do? What else but try to tell you what was really happening when your eyes were looking through? And it is this which frightens me:

Who knows but that, on the lower frequencies, I speak for you?

JOHN T. REILLY

Notes on *Native Son*

The three sections, subtitled "Fear," "Flight," and "Fate," comprise the novel *Native Son*. The first of these places the leading character, Bigger Thomas, in a web of particularized details that establish him as a representative African-American youth living on Chicago's South Side, a "native" figure in the American environment. The plot of the narrative carries him to the home of the wealthy Dalton family for whom he will be employed as a chauffeur. Directed to take the daughter of the family, Mary Dalton, to classes at the university, Bigger discovers that he is expected instead to drive Mary to a meeting with Jan whose left-wing politics have made him an attractive counterpart for her to her conventional parents. During the evening Bigger is made increasingly uncomfortable by Mary's and Jan's drinking and especially by their instruction for him to disregard the code of racially segregated Chicago, treat them as social equals, and accompany them to an African-American club.

When Bigger returns the inebriated Mary from her clandestine meeting, he helps her to her bedroom, falls into an embrace, and is startled by the entrance of Mrs. Dalton into the room. Although Mrs. Dalton is blind and cannot see them Bigger feels he has to quiet Mary, which he accomplishes by placing a pillow over her face. This kills Mary. In a panic, Bigger destroys her body in the basement furnace.

The narrative of "Flight" follows Bigger as he seeks to escape the consequences of the crime. The most compelling feature of this section in the novel, however, is provided by Richard Wright's use of a technique known as "free indirect discourse" to report Bigger's feelings. The technique does not attempt a plausible simulation of the character's thought, nor does it present an internal monologue. Rather it employs the author's skill in language to suggest the consciousness of the fictional character. In that way "free indirect discourse" presents a subjective dimension of the figure, Bigger, who is otherwise known to readers through the objective details of his age, economic class, and race.

The following passage of the novel presents Bigger in "Flight" just after he has departed from his friends and begun the journey back to the Dalton home on the morning after the death of Mary. The text is taken from the Library of America edition of the novel (1991). This edition prepared by Arnold Rampersad recovers the final version Wright prepared of the novel before he undertook changes requested by the publisher Harper & Row for the 1940 first edition.

RICHARD WRIGHT

Flight from *Native Son*

He waved at them and swung through the door. He walked over the snow, feeling giddy and elated. His mouth was open and his eyes shone. It was the first time he had even been in their presence without feeling fearful. He was following a strange path into a strange land and his nerves were hungry to see where it led. He lugged his suitcase to the end of the block, and stood waiting for a street car. He slipped his fingers into his vest pocket and felt the crisp roll of bills. Instead of going to Dalton's, he could take a street car to a railway station and leave town. But what would happen if he left? If he ran away now it would be thought at once that he knew something about Mary, as soon as she was missed. No; it would be far better to stick it out and see what happened. It might be a long time before anyone would think that Mary was killed and a still longer time before anyone would think that he had done it. And when Mary was missed, would they not think of the Reds first?

The street car rumbled up and he got on and rode to Forty-seventh Street, where he transferred to an eastbound car. He looked anxiously at the dim reflection of his black face in the sweaty windowpane. Would any of the white faces all about him think that he had killed a rich white girl? No! They might think he would steal a dime, rape a woman, get drunk, or cut somebody; but to kill a millionaire's daughter and

burn her body? He smiled a little, feeling a tingling sensation enveloping all his body. He saw it all very sharply and simply: act like other people thought you ought to act, yet do what you wanted. In a certain sense he had been doing just that in a loud and rough manner all his life, but it was only last night when he had smothered Mary in her room while her blind mother had stood with outstretched arms that he had seen how clearly it could be done. Although he was trembling a little, he was not really afraid. He was eager, tremendously excited. I can take care of them, he thought, thinking of Mr. and Mrs. Dalton.

There was only one thing that worried him; he had to get that lingering image of Mary's bloody head lying on those newspapers from before his eyes. If that were done, then he would be all right. Gee, what a fool she was, he thought, remembering how Mary had acted. Carrying on that way! Hell, she *made* me do it! I couldn't help it! She should've known better! She should've left me alone, Goddammit! He did not feel sorry for Mary; she was not real to him, not a human being; he had not known her long or well enough for that. He felt that his murder of her was more than amply justified by the fear and shame she had made him feel. It seemed that her actions had evoked fear and shame in him. But when he thought hard about it it seemed impossible that they could have. He really did not know just where that fear and shame had come from; it had just been there, that was all. Each time he had come in contact with her it had risen hot and hard.

It was not Mary he was reacting to when he felt that fear and shame. Mary had served to set off his emotions, emotions conditioned by many Marys. And now that he had killed Mary he felt a lessening of tension in his muscles; he had shed an invisible burden he had long carried.

As the car lurched over the snow he lifted his eyes and saw black people upon the snow-covered sidewalks. Those people had feelings of fear and shame like his. Many a time he had stood on street corners with them and talked of white people as long sleek cars zoomed past. To Bigger and his kind white people were not really people; they were a sort of great natural force, like a stormy sky looming overhead, or like a deep swirling river stretching suddenly at one's feet in the dark. As long as he and his black folks did not go beyond certain limits, there was no need to fear that white force. But whether they feared it or not, each and every day of their lives they lived with it; even when words did not sound its name, they acknowledged its reality. As long as they lived here in this prescribed corner of the city, they paid mute tribute to it.

There were rare moments when a feeling and longing for solidarity with other black people would take hold of him. He would dream of making a stand against that white force, but that dream would fade when he looked at the other black people near him. Even though black like them, he felt there was too much difference between him and them to allow for a common binding and a common life. Only when threatened with death could that happen; only in fear and shame, with their backs against a wall, could that happen. But never could they sink their differences in hope.

As he rode, looking at the black people on the sidewalks, he felt that one way to end fear and shame was to make all those black people act together, rule them, tell them what to do, and make them do it. Dimly, he felt that there should be one direction in which he and all other black people could go wholeheartedly; that there should be a way in which gnawing hunger and restless aspiration could be fused; that there should be a manner of acting that caught the mind and body in certainty and faith. But he felt that such would never happen to him and his black people, and he hated them and wanted to wave his hand and blot them out. Yet, he still hoped, vaguely. Of late he had liked to hear tell of men who could rule others, for in actions such as these he felt that there was a way to escape from this tight morass of fear and shame that sapped at the base of his life. He liked to hear of how Japan was conquering China; of how Hitler was running the Jews to the ground; of how Mussolini was invading Spain. He was not concerned with whether these acts were right or wrong; they simply appealed to him as possible avenues of escape. He felt that some day there would be a black man who would whip the black people into a tight band and together they would act and end fear and shame. He never thought of this in precise mental images; he felt it; he would feel it for a while and then forget. But hope was always waiting somewhere deep down in him.

It was fear that had made him fight Gus in the poolroom. If he had felt certain of himself and of Gus, he would not have fought. But he knew Gus, as he knew himself, and he knew that one of them might fail through fear at the decisive moment. How could he think of going to rob Blum's that way? He distrusted and feared Gus and he knew that Gus distrusted and feared him; and the moment he tried to band himself and Gus together to do something, he would hate Gus and himself. Ultimately, though, his hate and hope turned outward from himself and Gus: his hope toward a vague benevolent something that would help and lead him, and his hate toward the whites; for he felt that they ruled him, even when they were far away and not thinking of him, ruled him by conditioning him in his relations to his own people.

The street car crawled through the snow; Drexel Boulevard was the next stop. He lifted the suitcase and stood at the door. In a few minutes he would know if Mary had burned. The car stopped; he swung off and walked through snow as deep as his ankles, heading for Dalton's.

When he got to the driveway he saw that the car was standing just as he had left it, but all covered with a soft coat of snow. The house loomed white and silent. He unlatched the gate and went past the car, seeing before his eyes an image of Mary, her bloody neck just inside the furnace and her head with its curly black hair lying upon the soggy newspapers. He paused. He could turn round now and go back. He could get into the car and be miles from here before anybody knew it. But why run away unless there was good reason? He had some money to make a run for it when the time came. And he had his gun. His fingers trembled so that he had difficulty in unlocking the door; but they were not trembling from fear. It was a kind of eagerness he felt, a confidence, a fulness, a freedom; his whole life was caught up in a supreme and meaningful act. He pushed the door in, then was stone-still, sucking his breath in softly. In the red glare of the furnace stood a shadowy figure. Is that Mrs. Dalton? But it was taller and stouter than Mrs. Dalton. Oh, it was Peggy! She stood with her back to him, a little bent. She seemed to be peering hard into the furnace. She didn't hear me come in, he thought. *Maybe I ought to go!* But before he could move Peggy turned round.

"Oh, good morning, Bigger."

He did not answer.

"I'm glad you came. I was just about to put more coal into the fire."

"I'll fix it, mam."

He came forward, straining his eyes to see if any traces of Mary were in the furnace. When he reached Peggy's side he saw that she was staring through the cracks of the door at the red bed of livid coals.

"The fire was very hot last night," Peggy said. "But this morning it got low."

"I'll fix it," Bigger said, standing and not daring to open the door of the furnace while she stood there beside him in the red darkness.

He heard the dull roar of the draft going upwards and wondered if she suspected anything. He knew that he should have turned on the light; but what if he did and the light revealed parts of Mary in the furnace?

"I'll fix it, mam," he said again.

Quickly, he wondered if he would have to kill her to keep her from telling if she turned on the light and saw something that made her think that Mary was dead? Without turning his head he saw an iron shovel resting in a near-by corner. His hands clenched. Peggy moved from his side toward a light that swung from the ceiling at the far end of the room near the stairs.

"I'll give you some light," she said.

He moved silently and quickly toward the shovel and waited to see what would happen. The light came on, blindingly bright; he blinked. Peggy stood near the steps holding her right hand tightly over her breast. She had on a kimono and was trying to hold it closely about her. Bigger understood at once. She was not even thinking of the furnace; she was just a little ashamed of having been seen in the basement in her kimono.

"Has Miss Dalton come down yet?" she asked over her shoulder as she went up the steps.

"No'm. I haven't seen her."

"You just come?"

"Yessum."

She stopped and looked back at him.

"But the car, it's in the driveway."

"Yessum," he said simply, not volunteering any information.

"Then it stayed out all night?"

"I don't know, mam."

"Didn't you put it in the garage?"

"No'm. Miss Dalton told me to leave it out."

"Oh! Then it *did* stay out all night. That's why it's covered with snow."

"I reckon so, mam."

Peggy shook her head and sighed.

"Well, I suppose she'll be ready for you to take her to the station in a few minutes."

"Yessum."

"I see you brought the trunk down."

"Yessum. She told me to bring it down last night."

"Don't forget it," she said, going through the kitchen door.

For a long time after she had gone he did not move from his tracks. Then, slowly, he looked round the basement, turning his head like an animal with eyes and ears alert, searching to see if anything was amiss. The room was exactly as he had left it last night. He walked about, looking closer. All at once he stopped, his eyes widening. Directly in front of him he saw a small piece of blood-stained newspaper lying in the livid reflection cast by the cracks in the door of the furnace. Had Peggy seen that? He ran to the light and turned it out and ran back and looked at the piece of paper. He could barely see it. That meant that Peggy had not seen it. How about Mary? Had she burned? He turned the light back on and picked up the piece of paper. He glanced to the left and right to see if anyone was watching, then opened the furnace door and peered in, his eyes filled with the vision of Mary and her bloody throat. The inside of the furnace breathed and quivered in the grip of fiery coals. But there was no sign of the body, even though the body's image hovered before his eyes, between his eyes and the bed of coals burning hotly. Like the oblong mound of fresh clay of a newly made grave, the red coals revealed the bent outline of Mary's body. He had the feeling that if he simply touched that red oblong mound with his finder it would cave in and Mary's body would come into full view, unburnt. The coals had the appearance of having burnt the body beneath, leaving the glowing embers formed into a shell of red hotness with a hollowed space in the center, keeping still in the embrace of the quivering coals the huddled shape of Mary's body. He blinked his eyes and became aware that he still held the piece of paper in his hand. He lifted it to the level of the door and the draft sucked it from his fingers; he watched it fly into the red trembling heat, smoke, turn black, blaze, then vanish.

He shut the door and pulled the lever for more coal. The rattling of the tiny lumps against the tin sides of the chute came loudly to his ears as the oblong mound of red fire turned gradually black and blazed from the fanwise spreading of coal whirling into the furnace. He shut off the lever and stood up; things were all right so far. As long as no one poked round in that fire, things would be all right. He himself did not want to poke in it, for fear that some part of Mary was still there. If things could go on like this until afternoon, Mary would be burned enough to make him safe. He turned and looked at the trunk again. Oh! He must not forget! He had to put those Communist pamphlets in his room right away. He ran back of the furnace, up the steps to his room and placed the pamphlets smoothly and neatly in a corner of his dresser drawer. Yes, they would have to be stacked neatly. No one must think that he had read them.

He went back to the basement, dragged the trunk to the door, lifted it to his back, carried it to the car and fastened it to the running board. He looked at his watch; it was eight-twenty. Now, he would have to wait for Mary to come out. He took his seat at the steering wheel and waited for five minutes. He would ring the bell for her. He looked at the steps leading up to the side door of the house, remembering how Mary had stumbled last night and how he had held her up. Then, involuntarily, he started in fright as a full blast of intense sunshine fell from the sky, making the snow leap and glitter and sparkle about him in a world of magic whiteness without sound. It's getting late! He would have to go in and ask for Miss Dalton. If he stayed here too long it would seem that he was not expecting her to come down. He got out of the car and walked up the steps to the side door. He looked through the glass; no one was in sight. He tried to open the door and found it locked. He pushed the bell, hearing the gong sound softly within. He waited a moment, then saw Peggy hurrying down the hall. She opened the door.

"Hasn't she come out yet?"

"No'm. And it's getting late."

"Wait. I'll call her."

Peggy, still dressed in the kimono, ran up the stairs, the same stairs up which he had half-dragged Mary and the same stairs down which he had stumbled with the trunk last night. Then he saw Peggy coming back down the stairs, much slower than she had gone up. She came to the door.

"She ain't here. Maybe she's gone. What did she tell you?"

"She said to drive her to the station and to take her trunk; mam."

"Well, she ain't in her room and she ain't in Mrs. Dalton's room. And Mr. Dalton's asleep. Did she tell you she was going this morning?"

"That's what she told me last night, mam."

"She told you to bring the trunk down last night?"

"Yessum."

Peggy thought a moment, looking past him at the snow-covered car.

"Well, you better take the trunk on. Maybe she didn't stay here last night."

"Yessum."

He turned and started down the steps.

"Bigger!"

"Yessum."

"You say she told you to leave the car out, all *night?*"

"Yessum."

"Did she say she was going to use it again?"

"No'm. You see," Bigger said, feeling his way, "he was in it. . . ."

"*Who?*"

"The gentleman."

"Oh; yes. Take the trunk on. I suppose Mary was up to some of her pranks."

He got into the car and pulled it down the driveway to the street, then headed northward over the snow. He wanted to look back and see if Peggy was watching him, but dared not. That would make her think that he thought that something was wrong, and he did not want to give that impression now. Well, at least he had one person thinking it as he wanted it thought.

He reached the La Salle Street Station, pulled the car to a platform, backed into a narrow space between other cars; hoisted the trunk up, and waited for a man to give him a ticket for the trunk. He wondered what would happen if no one called for it. Maybe they would notify Mr. Dalton. Well, he would wait and see.

He had done his part. Miss Dalton had asked him to take the trunk to the station and he had done it.

He drove as hurriedly back to the Dalton's as the snow-covered streets would allow him. He wanted to be back on the spot to see what would happen, to be there with his fingers on the pulse of time. He reached the driveway and nosed the car into the garage, locked it, and then stood wondering if he ought to go to his room or to the kitchen. It would be better to go straight to the kitchen as though nothing had happened. He had not as yet eaten his breakfast as far as Peggy was concerned, and his coming into the kitchen would be thought natural. He went through the basement, pausing to look at the roaring furnace, and then went to the kitchen door and stepped in softly. Peggy stood at the gas stove with her back to him. She turned and gave him a brief glance.

"You make it all right?"

"Yessum."

"You see her down there?"

"No'm."

"Hungry?"

"A little, mam."

"A little?" Peggy laughed. "You'll get used to how this house is run on Sundays. Nobody gets up early and when they do they're almost famished."

"I'm all right, mam."

"That was the only kick Green had while he was working here," Peggy said. "He swore we starved him on Sundays."

Bigger forced a smile and looked down at the black and white linoleum on the floor. What would she think if she knew? He felt very kindly toward Peggy just then; he felt he had something of value which she could never take from him even if she despised him. He heard a phone ring in the hallway. Peggy straightened and looked at him as she wiped her hands on her apron.

"Who on earth's calling here this early on a Sunday morning?" she mumbled.

She went out and he sat, waiting. Maybe that was Jan asking about Mary. He remembered that Mary had promised to call him. He wondered how long it took to go to Detroit. Five or six hours? It was not far. Mary's train had already gone. About four o'clock she would be due in Detroit. Maybe someone had planned to meet her? If she was not on the train, would they call or wire about it? Peggy came back, went to the stove and continued cooking.

"Things'll be ready in a minute," she said.

"Yessum."

Then she turned to him.

"Who was the gentleman with Miss Dalton last night?"

"I don't know, mam. I think she called him Jan, or something like that."

"Jan? He just called," Peggy said. She tossed her head and her lips tightened. "He's a no-good one, if there ever was one. One of them anarchists who's agin the government."

Bigger listened and said nothing.

"What on earth a good girl like Mary wants to hang around with that crazy bunch for, God only knows. Nothing good'll come of it, just you mark my word. If it wasn't for that Mary and her wild ways, this household would run like a clock. It's such a pity, too. Her mother's the very soul of goodness. And there never was a finer man than Mr. Dalton. . . . But later on Mary'll settle down. They all do. They think they're missing something unless they kick up their heels when they're young and foolish. . . ."

She brought a bowl of hot oatmeal and milk to him and he began to eat. He had difficulty in swallowing, for he had no appetite. But he forced the food down. Peggy talked on and he wondered what he should say to her; he found that he could say nothing. Maybe she was not expecting him to say anything. Maybe she was talking to him because she had no one else to talk to, like his mother did sometimes. Yes; he would see about the fire again when he got to the basement. He would fill that furnace as full of coal as it would get and make sure that Mary burned in a hurry. The hot cereal was making him sleepy and he suppressed a yawn.

"What all I got to do today, mam?"

"Just wait on call. Sunday's a dull day. Maybe Mr. or Mrs. Dalton'll go out."

"Yessum."

He finished the oatmeal.

"You want me to do anything now?"

"No. But you're not through eating. You want some ham and eggs?"

"No'm. I got a plenty."

"Well, it's right here for you. Don't be afraid to ask for it."

"I reckon I'll see about the fire now."

"All right, Bigger. Just you listen for the bell about two o'clock. Till then I don't think there'll be anything."

He went to the basement. The fire was blazing. The embers glowed red and the draft droned upward. It did not need any coal. Again he looked round the basement, into every nook and corner, to see if he had left any trace of what had happened last night. There was none.

He went to his room and lay on the bed. Well; here he was now. What would happen? The room was quiet. No! He heard something! He cocked his head, listening. He caught faint sounds of pots and pans rattling in the kitchen below. He got up and walked to the far end of the room; the sounds came louder. He heard the soft but firm tread of Peggy as she walked across the kitchen floor. She's right under me, he thought. He stood still, listening. He heard Mrs. Dalton's voice, then Peggy's. He stooped and put his ear to the floor. Were they talking about Mary? He could not make out what they were saying. He stood up and looked round. A foot from him was the door of the clothes closet. He opened it; the voices came clearly. He went into the closet and the planks squeaked; he stopped. Had they heard him? Would they think he was snooping? Oh! He had an idea! He got his suitcase and opened it and took out an armful of clothes. If anyone came into the room it would seem that he was putting his clothes away. He went into the closet and listened.

". . . . you mean the car stayed out all *night* in the driveway?"

"Yes; he said she told him to leave it there."

"What time was that?"

"I don't know, Mrs. Dalton. I didn't ask him."

"I don't understand this at all."

"Oh, she's all right. I don't think you need worry."

"But she didn't even leave a note, Peggy. That's not like Mary. Even when she ran away to New York that time she at least left a note."

"Maybe she hasn't gone. Maybe something came up and she stayed out all night, Mrs. Dalton."

"But why would she leave the car out?"

"I don't know."

"And he said a man was with her?"

"It was that Jan, I think, Mrs. Dalton."

"Jan?"

"Yes; the one who was with her in Florida."

"She just *won't* leave those awful people alone."

"He called here this morning, asking for her."

"Called *here?*"

"Yes."

"And what did he say?"

"He seemed sort of peeved when I told him she was gone."

"What can that poor child be up to? She told me she was not seeing him any more."

"Maybe *she* had him to call, Mrs. Dalton. . . ."

"What do you mean?"

"Well, mam, I was kind of thinking that maybe she's with him again, like that time she was in Florida. And maybe she had him to call to see if we knew she was gone. . . ."

"Oh, Peggy!"

"Oh, I'm sorry, mam. . . . Maybe she stayed with some friends of hers?"

"But she was in her *room* at two o'clock this morning, Peggy. Whose house would she go to at that hour?"

"Mrs. Dalton, I noticed something when I went to her room this morning."

"What?"

"Well, mam, it looks like her bed wasn't slept in at all. The cover wasn't even pulled back. Looks like somebody had just stretched out awhile and then got up. . . ."

"Oh!"

Bigger listened intently, but there was silence. They knew that something was wrong now. He heard Mrs. Dalton's voice again, quavering with doubt and fear.

"Then she *didn't* sleep here last night?"

"Looks like she didn't."

"Did that boy say Jan was in the car?"

"Yes. I thought something was strange about the car being left out in the snow all night, and so I asked him. He said she told him to leave the car there and he said Jan was in it."

"Listen, Peggy. . . ."

"Yes, Mrs. Dalton."

"Mary was drunk last night. I hope nothing's happened to her."

"Oh, what a pity!"

"I went to her room just after she came in. . . . She was too drunk to talk. She was *drunk*, I tell you. I never thought she'd come home in that condition."

"She'll be all right, Mrs. Dalton. I *know* she will."

There was another long silence. Bigger wondered if Mrs. Dalton was on her way to his room. He went back to the bed and lay down, listening. There were no sounds. He lay a long time, hearing nothing; then he heard footsteps in the kitchen again. He hurried into the closet.

"Peggy!"

"Yes, Mrs. Dalton."

"Listen, I just felt around in Mary's room. Something's wrong. She didn't finish packing her trunk. At least half of her things are still there. She said she was planning to go to some dances in Detroit and she didn't take the new things she bought."

"Maybe she didn't go to Detroit."

"But where *is* she?"

Bigger stopped listening, feeling fear for the first time. He had not thought that the trunk was not fully packed. How could he explain that she had told him to take a half-packed trunk to the station? Oh, shucks! The girl was drunk. That was it. Mary was so drunk that she didn't know what she was doing. He would say that she had told him to take it and he had just taken it; that's all. If someone asked him why he had

taken a half-packed trunk to the station, he would tell them that that was no different from all the other foolish things that Mary had told him to do that night. Had not people seen him eating with her and Jan in Ernie's Kitchen Shack? He would say that both of them were drunk and that he had done what they told him because it was his job. He listened again to the voices.

". . . . and after a while send that boy to me. I want to talk to him."

"Yes, Mrs. Dalton."

Again he lay on the bed. He would have to go over his story and make it foolproof. Maybe he had done wrong in taking that trunk? Maybe it would have been better to have carried Mary down in his arms and burnt her? But he had put her in the trunk because of the fear of someone's seeing her in his arms. That was the only way he could have gotten her down out of the room. Oh, hell, what had happened had happened and he would stick to his story. He went over the story again, fastening every detail firmly in his mind. He would say that she had been drunk, sloppy drunk. He lay on the soft bed in the warm room listening to the steam hiss in the radiator and thinking drowsily and lazily of how drunk she had been and of how he had lugged her up the steps and of how he had pushed the pillow over her face and of how he had put her in the trunk and of how he had struggled with the trunk on the dark stairs and of how his fingers had burned while he had stumbled down the stairs with the heavy trunk going *bump-bump-bump* so loud that surely all the world must have heard it. . . .

He jumped awake, hearing a knock at the door. His heart raced. He sat up and stared sleepily around the room. Had someone knocked? He looked at his watch; it was three o'clock. Gee! He must have slept through the bell that was to ring at two. The knock came again.

"O.K.!" he mumbled.

"This is Mrs. Dalton!"

"Yessum. Just a minute."

He reached the door in two long steps, then stood a moment trying to collect himself. He blinked his eyes and wet his lips. He opened the door and saw Mrs. Dalton smiling before him, dressed in white, her pale face held as it had been when she was standing in the darkness while he had smothered Mary on the bed.

"Y-y-yes, mam," he stammered. "I—I was asleep. . . ."

"You didn't get much sleep last night, did you?"

"No'm," he drawled, afraid of what she might mean.

"Peggy rang for you three times, and you didn't answer."

"I'm sorry, mam. . . ."

"That's all right. I wanted to ask you about last night . . . Oh, you took the trunk to the station, didn't you?" she asked.

"Yessum. This morning," he said, detecting hesitancy and confusion in her voice.

"I see," said Mrs. Dalton. She stood with her face tilted upward in the semi-darkness of the hallway. He had his hand on the doorknob, waiting, his muscles taut. He had to be careful with his answers now. And yet he knew he had a certain protection; he knew that a certain element of shame would keep Mrs. Dalton from asking him too much and letting him know that she was worried. He was a boy and she was an old woman. He was the hired and she was the hirer. And there was a certain distance to be kept between them.

"You left the car in the driveway last night, didn't you?"

"Yessum. I was about to put it up," he said, indicating that his only concern was with keeping his job and doing his duties. "But she told me to leave it."

"And was someone with her?"

"Yessum. A gentleman."

"That must have been pretty late, wasn't it?"

"Yessum. A little before two, mam."

"And you took the trunk down a little before two?"

"Yessum. She told me to."

"She took you to her room?"

He did not want her to think that he had been alone in the room with Mary. Quickly, he recast the story in his mind.

"Yessum. They went up. . . ."

"Oh, *he* was with her?"

"Yessum."

"I see. . . ."

"Anything wrong, mam?"

"Oh, no! I—I—I. . . . No; there's nothing wrong."

She stood in the doorway and he looked at her light-grey blind eyes, eyes almost as white as her face and hair and dress. He knew that she was really worried and wanted to ask him more questions. But he knew that she would not want to hear him tell of how drunk her daughter had been. After all, he was black and she was white. He was poor and she was rich. She would be ashamed to let him think that something was so wrong in her family that she had to ask him, a black servant, about it. He felt confident.

"Will there be anything right now, mam?"

"No. In fact, you may take the rest of the day off, if you like. Mr. Dalton is not feeling well and we're not going out."

"Thank you, mam."

She turned away and he shut the door; he stood listening to the soft whisper of her shoes die away down the hall, then on the stairs. He pictured her groping her way, her hands touching the walls. She must know this house like a book, he thought. He trembled with excitement. She was white and he was black; she was rich and he was poor; she was old and he was young; she was the boss and he was the worker. He was safe; yes. When he heard the kitchen door open and shut he went to the closet and listened again. But there were no sounds.

Well, he would go out. To go out now would be the answer to the feeling of strain that had come over him while talking to Mrs. Dalton. He would go and see Bessie. That was it! He got his cap and coat and went to the basement. The suction of air through the furnace moaned and the fire was white-hot; there was enough coal to last until he came back.

He went to Forty-seventh Street and stood on the corner to wait for a car. Yes, Bessie was the one he wanted to see now. Funny, he had not thought of her much during the last day and night. Too many exciting things had been happening. He had had no need to think of her. But now he had to forget and relax and he wanted to see her. She was always home on Sunday afternoons. He wanted to see her very badly; he felt that he would be stronger to go through tomorrow if he saw her.

The street car came and he got on, thinking of how things had gone that day. No; he did not think they would suspect him of anything. He was black. Again he felt the roll of crisp bills in his pocket; if things went wrong he could always run away. He wondered how much money was in the roll; he had not even counted it. He would see when he got to Bessie's. No; he need not be afraid. He felt the gun nestling close to his skin. That gun could always make folks stand away and think twice before bothering him.

But of the whole business there was one angle that bothered him; he should have gotten more money out of it; he should have *planned* it. He had acted too hastily and accidentally. Next time things would be much different; he would plan and arrange so that he would have money enough to keep him a long time. He looked out of the car window and then round at the white faces near him. He wanted suddenly to stand up and shout, telling them that he had killed a rich white girl, a girl whose family was known to all of them. Yes; if he did that a look of startled horror would come over their faces. But, no. He would not do that, even though the satisfaction would be keen. He was so greatly outnumbered that he would be arrested, tried, and executed. He wanted the keen thrill of startling them, but felt that the cost was too great. He wished that he had the power to say what he had done without fear of being arrested; he wished that he could be an idea in their minds; that his black face and the image of his smothering Mary and cutting off her head and burning her could hover before their eyes as a terrible picture of reality which they could see and feel and yet not destroy. He was not satisfied with the way things stood now; he was a man who had come in sight of a goal, then had won it, and in winning it had seen just within his grasp another goal, higher, greater. He had learned to shout and had shouted and no ear had heard him; he had just learned to walk and was walking but could not see the ground beneath his feet; he had long been yearning for weapons to hold in his hands and suddenly found that his hands held weapons that were invisible.

The car stopped a block from Bessie's home and he got off. When he reached the building in which she lived, he looked up to the second floor and saw a light burning in her window. The street lamps came on suddenly, lighting up the snow-covered sidewalks with a yellow sheen. It had gotten dark early. The lamps were round hazy balls of light frozen into motionlessness, anchored in space and kept from blowing away in the icy wind by black steel posts. He went in and rang the bell and, in answer to a buzzer, mounted the stairs and found Bessie smiling at him in her door.

"Hello, stranger!"

"Hi, Bessie."

He stood face to face with her, then reached for her hands. She shied away.

"What's the matter?"

RUDOLPH FISHER

The Caucasian Storms Harlem

It might not have been such a jolt had my five years' absence from Harlem been spent otherwise. But the study of medicine includes no courses in cabareting; and, anyway, the Negro cabarets in Washington, where I studied, are all uncompromisingly black. Accordingly I was entirely unprepared for what I found when I returned to Harlem recently.

I remembered one place especially where my own crowd used to hold forth; and, hoping to find some old-timers there still, I sought it out one midnight. The old, familiar plunkety-plunk welcomed me from below as I entered. I descended the same old narrow stairs, came into the same smoke-misty basement, and found myself a chair at one of the ancient white-porcelain, mirror-smooth tables. I drew a deep breath and looked about, seeking familiar faces. "What a lot of 'fays!" I thought, as I noticed the number of white guests. Presently I grew puzzled and began to stare, then I

gaped—and gasped. I found myself wondering if this was the right place—if, indeed, this was Harlem at all. I suddenly became aware that, except for the waiters and members of the orchestra, I was the only Negro in the place.

After a while I left it and wandered about in a daze from night-club to night-club. I tried the Nest, Small's, Connie's Inn, the Capitol, Happy's, the Cotton Club. There was no mistake; my discovery was real and was repeatedly confirmed. No wonder my old crowd was not to be found in any of them. The best of Harlem's black cabarets have changed their names and turned white.

Such a discovery renders a moment's recollection irresistible. As irresistible as were the cabarets themselves to me seven or eight years ago. Just out of college in a town where cabarets were something only read about. A year of graduate work ahead. A Summer of rest at hand. Cabarets. Cabarets night after night, and one after another. There was no cover-charge then, and a fifteen-cent bottle of Whistle lasted an hour. It was just after the war—the heroes were home—cabarets were the thing.

How the Lybia prospered in those happy days! It was the gathering place of the swellest Harlem set: if you didn't go to the Lybia, why, my dear, you just didn't belong. The people you saw at church in the morning you met at the Lybia at night. What romance in those war-tinged days and nights! Officers from Camp Upton, with pretty maids from Brooklyn! Gay lieutenants, handsome captains—all whirling the lively onestep. Poor non-coms completely ignored; what sensible girl wanted a corporal or even a sergeant? That white, old-fashioned house, standing alone in 138th street, near the corner of Seventh avenue—doomed to be torn down a few months thence—how it shook with the dancing and laughter of the dark merry crowds!

But the first place really popular with my friends was a Chinese restaurant in 136th street, which had been known as Hayne's Café and then became the Oriental. It occupied an entire house of three stories, and had carpeted floors and a quiet, superior air. There was excellent food and incredibly good tea and two unusual entertainers: a Cuban girl, who could so vary popular airs that they sounded like real music, and a slender little "brown" with a voice of silver and a way of singing a song that made you forget your food. One could dance in the Oriental if one liked, but one danced to a piano only, and wound one's way between linen-clad tables over velvety, noiseless floors.

Here we gathered: Fritz Pollard, All-American halfback, selling Negro stock to prosperous Negro physicians; Henry Creamer and Turner Layton, who had written "After You've Gone" and a dozen more songs, and were going to write "Strut, Miss Lizzie"; Paul Robeson,

All-American end, on the point of tackling law, quite un-aware that the stage would intervene; Preacher Harry Bragg, Harvard Jimmie MacLendon and half a dozen others. Here at a little table, just inside the door, Bert Williams had supper every night, and afterward some-times joined us upstairs and sang songs with us and lampooned the Actors' Equity Association, which·had barred him because of his color. Never did white guests come to the Oriental except as guests of Negroes. But the manager soon was stricken with a psychosis of some sort, became a black Jew, grew himself a bushy, square-cut beard, donned a skull-cap and abandoned the Orien-tal. And so we were robbed of our favorite resort, and thereafter became mere rounders.

II

Such places, those real Negro cabarets that we met in the course of our rounds! There was Edmonds' in Fifth avenue at 130th street. It was a sure-enough honky-tonk, occupying the cellar of a saloon. It was the social center of what was then, and still is, Negro Harlem's kitchen. Here a tall brown-skin girl, unmistakably the one guaranteed in the song to make a preacher lay his Bible down, used to sing and dance her own peculiar numbers, vesting them with her own originality. She was known simply as Ethel, and was a genuine draw-ing-card. She knew her importance, too. Other girls wore themselves ragged trying to rise above the inatten-tive din of conversation, and soon, literally, yelled them-selves hoarse; eventually they lost whatever music there was in their voices and acquired that familiar throaty roughness which is so frequent among blues singers, and which, though admired as characteristically Afri-can, is as a matter of fact nothing but a form of chronic laryngitis. Other girls did these things, but not Ethel. She took it easy. She would stride with great leisure and self-assurance to the center of the floor, stand there with a half-contemptuous nonchalance, and wait. All would become silent at once. Then she'd begin her song, gen-uine blues, which, for all their humorous lines, em-anated tragedy and heartbreak:

Woke up this mawnin'
The day was dawnin'
And I was sad and blue, so blue, Lord—
Didn' have nobody
To tell my troubles to—

It was Ethel who first made popular the song, "Tryin' to Teach My Good Man Right from Wrong," in the slow, meditative measures in which she com-plained:

I'm gettin' sick and tired of my railroad man
I'm gettin' sick and tired of my railroad man—
Can't get him when I want him—
I get him when I can.

It wasn't long before this song-bird escaped her dingy cage. Her name is a vaudeville attraction now, and she uses it all—Ethel Waters. Is there anyone who hasn't heard her sing "Shake That Thing!"?

A second place was Connor's in 135th street near Lenox avenue. It was livelier, less languidly sensuous, and easier to breathe in than Edmonds'. Like the latter, it was in a basement, reached by the typical narrow, headlong stairway. One of the girls there specialized in the Jelly-Roll song, and mad habitués used to fling peti-tions of greenbacks at her feet—pretty nimble feet they were, too—when she sang that she loved 'em but she had to turn 'em down. Over in a corner a group of 'fays would huddle and grin and think they were having a wild time. Slumming. But they were still very few in those days.

And there was the Oriental, which borrowed the name that the former Hayne's Café had abandoned. This was beyond Lenox avenue on the south side of 135th street. An upstairs place, it was nevertheless as dingy as any of the cellars, and the music fairly fought its way through the babble and smoke to one's ears, suffering in transit weird and incredible distortion. The prize pet here was a slim, little lad, unbelievably black beneath his high-brown powder, wearing a Mexican bandit costume with a bright-colored head-dress and sash. I see him now, poor kid, in all his glory, shimmy-ing for enraptured women, who marveled at the per-fect control of his voluntary abdominal tremors. He used to let the women reach out and put their hands on his sash to palpate those tremors—for a quarter.

Finally, there was the Garden of Joy, an open-air cabaret between 138th and 139th streets in Seventh avenue, occupying a plateau high above the sidewalk—a large, well-laid, smooth wooden floor with tables and chairs and a tinny orchestra, all covered by a propped-up roof, that resembled an enormous lampshade, di-recting bright light downward and outward. Not far away the Abyssinian Church used to hold its Summer camp-meetings in a great round circus-tent. Night after night there would arise the mingled strains of blues and spirituals, those peculiarly Negro forms of song, the one secular and the other religious, but both born of wretchedness in travail, both with their soarings of exultation and sinkings of despair. I used to wonder if God, hearing them both, found any real distinction.

There were the Lybia, then, and Hayne's, Con-nor's, the Oriental, Edmonds' and the Garden of Joy, each distinctive, standing for a type, some living up to their names, others living down to them, but all predominantly black. Regularly I made the rounds among these places and saw only incidental white people. I have seen them occasionally in numbers, but such parties were out on a lark. They weren't in their natural habitat and they often weren't any too comfortable.

But what of Barron's, you say? Certainly they were at home there. Yes, I know about Barron's. I have been turned away from Barron's because I was too dark to be welcome. I have been a member of a group that was told, "No more room," when we could see plenty of room. Negroes were never actually wanted in Barron's save to work. Dark skins were always discouraged or barred. In short, the fact about Barron's was this: it simply wasn't a Negro cabaret; it was a cabaret run by Negroes for whites. It wasn't even on the lists of those who lived in Harlem—they'd no more think of going there than of going to the Winter Garden Roof. But these other places were Negro through and through. Negroes supported them, not merely in now-and-then parties, but steadily, night after night.

III

Now, however, the situation is reversed. It is I who go occasionally and white people who go night after night. Time and again, since I've returned to live in Harlem, I've been one of a party of four Negroes who went to this or that Harlem cabaret, and on each occasion we've been the only Negro guests in the place. The managers don't hesitate to say that it is upon these predominant white patrons that they depend for success. These places therefore are no longer mine but theirs. Not that I'm barred, any more than they were seven or eight years ago. Once known, I'm even welcome, just as some of them used to be. But the complexion of the place is theirs, not mine. I? Why, I am actually stared at, I frequently feel uncomfortable and out of place, and when I go out on the floor to dance I am lost in a sea of white faces. As another observer has put it to me since, time was when white people went to Negro cabarets to see how Negroes acted; now Negroes go to these same cabarets to see how white people act. Negro clubs have recently taken to hiring a place outright for a presumably Negro party; and even then a goodly percentage of the invited guests are white.

One hurries to account for this change of complexion as a reaction to the Negro invasion of Broadway not long since. One remembers "Shuffle Along" of four years ago, the first Negro piece in the downtown district for many a moon. One says, "Oh yes, Negroes took their stuff to the whites and won attention and praise, and now the whites are seeking this stuff out on its native soil." Maybe. So I myself

thought at first. But one looks for something of oppositeness in a genuine reaction. One would rather expect the reaction to the Negro invasion of Broadway to be apathy. One would expect that the same thing repeated under different names or in imitative fragments would meet with colder and colder reception, and finally with none at all.

A little recollection will show that just what one would expect was what happened. Remember "Shuffle Along's" successors: "Put and Take," "Liza," "Strut Miss Lizzie," "Runnin' Wild," and the others? True, none was so good as "Shuffle Along," but surely they didn't deserve all the roasting they got. "Liza" flared but briefly, during a holiday season. "Put and Take" was a loss, "Strut Miss Lizzie" strutted about two weeks, and the humor of "Runnin' Wild" was derided as Neo-Pleistocene. Here was reaction for—wholesale withdrawal of favor. One can hardly conclude that such withdrawal culminated in the present swamping of Negro cabarets. People so sick of a thing would hardly go out of their way to find it.

And they *are* sick of it—in quantity at least. Only one Negro entertainment has survived this reaction of apathy in any permanent fashion. This is the series of revues built around the personality of Florence Mills. Without that bright live personality the Broadway district would have been swept clean last season of all-Negro bills. Here is a girl who has triumphed over a hundred obstacles. Month after month she played obscure, unnoticed rôles with obscure, unknown dark companies. She was playing such a minor part in "Shuffle Along" when the departure of Gertrude Saunders, the craziest blues-singer on earth, unexpectedly gave her the spotlight. Florence Mills cleaned up. She cleaned up so thoroughly that the same public which grew weary of "Shuffle Along" and sick of its successors still had an eager ear for her. They have yet, and she neither wearies nor disappoints them. An impatient Broadway audience awaits her return from Paris, where she and the inimitable Josephine Baker have been vying with each other as sensations. She is now in London on the way home, but London won't release her; the enthusiasm over her exceeds anything in the memory of the oldest reviewers.

Florence Mills, moreover, is admired by her own people too, because, far from going to her head, her success has not made her forgetful. Not long ago, the rumor goes, she made a fabulous amount of money in the Florida real-estate boom, and what do you suppose she plans to do with it? Build herself an Italian villa somewhere up the Hudson? Not at all. She plans to build a first-rate Negro theatre in Harlem.

But that's Florence Mills. Others have encountered indifference. In vain has Eddie Hunter, for instance, tried for a first-class Broadway showing, despite the fact that he himself has a new kind of Negro-comedian character to portray—the wise darkey, the "bizthniss man," the "fly" rascal who gets away with murder, a character who amuses by making a goat of others instead of by making a goat of himself. They say that some dozen Negro shows have met with similar denials. Yet the same people, presumably, whose spokesmen render these decisions flood Harlem night after night and literally crowd me off the dancing-floor. If this is a reaction, it is a reaction to a reaction, a swinging back of the pendulum from apathy toward interest. Maybe so. The cabarets may present only those special Negro features which have a particular and peculiar appeal, leaving out the high-yaller display that is merely feebly imitative. But a reaction to a reaction—that's differential calculus.

IV

Some think it's just a fad. White people have always more or less sought Negro entertainment as diversion. The old shows of the early nineteen hundreds, Williams and Walker and Cole and Johnson, are brought to mind as examples. The howling success—literally that—of J. Leubrie Hill around 1913 is another; on the road his "Darktown Follies" played in numerous white theatres. In Harlem it played at the black Lafayette and, behold, the Lafayette temporarily became white. And so now, it is held, we are observing merely one aspect of a meteoric phenomenon, which simply presents itself differently in different circumstances: Roland Hayes and Paul Robeson, Jean Toomer and Walter White, Charles Gilpin and Florence Mills—"Green Thursday," "Porgy," "In Abraham's Bosom"—Negro spirituals—the startling new African groups proposed for the Metropolitan Museum of Art. Negro stock is going up, and everybody's buying.

This doesn't sound unreasonable when it refers to certain things. Interest in the shows certainly presents many features of a fad. As in some epidemic fevers, there are sudden onset, swift contagion, brief duration, and a marked tendency to recur. Consider "Shuffle Along," for example, as a fad. Interest waned, as it will with fads. Disruption was hastened by internal dissension in the company: Sissle and Blake had written the songs and insisted on keeping the royalties therefrom, and Miller and Lyles had helped make the songs famous and contended that they too deserved a share of the proceeds. There was a deadlock and a split. "In Bamville" went one way and "Runnin' Wild" another, but neither went the prosperous way of the parent fad, "Shuffle Along."

Meanwhile, Creamer and Layton, among others, had found that the fad no longer infected. But if America was barren ground was not Europe virgin soil?

So, while Creamer remained to run the Cotton Club, Layton packed off to England, where already Hayes had done admirably in recital and Robeson was becoming well known on the stage. Layton and his new partner, Tandy Johnstone, were amazed at their success in England, and there they are at this writing. They earn more in a week there than they used to in many months over here. They have transplanted their fad into other susceptible communities—communities likely to become immune less swiftly. They are London vaudeville headliners, and their jazz has captivated the British. These entertainers will probably not soon lose that peculiar knack of striking a popular response. Turner Layton's father was for many years assistant director of music in the Washington public schools, and it is said that this imposing gentleman could get music out of a hall full of empty chairs. There may be something hereditary therefore in the way in which the most lifeless instrument responds to Turner's touch.

Followed Sissle and Blake to England, whence they have recently returned successful. Noble Sissle was the friend and companion of Jim Europe, who organized the New York Clef Club and was the most popular Negro musician of his day. After Europe's unfortunate death, Sissle and Eubie Blake became an extremely popular vaudeville team. Earlier, Blake used to play the piano for house-parties and dances around Baltimore, and later played in cabarets. Certain of his Baltimore friends point to him proudly now, and well they may: the accuracy and agility with which his fingers scamper over the keyboard is always a breath-taking wonder. Sissle and Blake, too, have learned the lessons taught by struggle and disaster. Time was when the "Shuffle Along" company, coming to Washington from New York for a Sunday afternoon engagement at the world's best Negro theatre, the Lincoln, entered the town with all the triumphal glamor of a circus. Almost every principal in the show had his or her own automobile, and they weren't designed or painted with an eye for modest retirement. The principals drove down from New York in their cars, if you please; which was entirely their own business, of course. The point is that they *could*. Sissle and Blake, it appears, still can. Such is the profitable contagion of a fad.

Pending a contemplated reunion of these unusual teams, Miller and Lyles have been playing with various Broadway revues. These comical fellows are both college graduates, and eminently respectable and conservative in private life. It is, by the way, a noteworthy thing about all of these men, Creamer, Johnstone, Layton, Sissle, Blake, Miller, and Lyles, that one never hears the slightest murmur of social criticism about any one of them. They have managed to conduct themselves off stage entirely above reproach. It is no accident that the private lives of these dark-skinned stars are so circumspect. It is part of the explanation of their success.

V

It is only a part, however; and the fad-like characteristics of their experience may be another part. It may be a season's whim, then, this sudden, contagious interest in everything Negro. If so, when I go into a familiar cabaret, or the place where a familiar cabaret used to be, and find it transformed and relatively colorless, I may be observing just one form that the season's whim has taken.

But suppose it is a fad—to say that explains nothing. How came the fad? What occasions the focusing of attention on this particular thing—rounds up and gathers these seasonal whims, and centers them about the Negro? Cabarets are peculiar, mind you. They're not like theatres and concert halls. You don't just go to a cabaret and sit back and wait to be entertained. You get out on the floor and join the pow-wow and help entertain yourself. Granted that white people have long enjoyed the Negro entertainment as a diversion, is it not something different, something more, when they bodily throw themselves into Negro entertainment in cabarets? "Now Negroes go to their own cabarets to see how white people act."

And what do we see? Why, we see them actually playing Negro games. I watch them in that epidemic Negroism, the Charleston. I look on and envy them. They camel and fish-tail and turkey, they geche and black-bottom and scronch, they skate and buzzard and mess-around—and they do them all better than I! This interest in the Negro is an active and participating interest. It is almost as if a traveler from the North stood watching an African tribe-dance, then suddenly found himself swept wildly into it, caught in its tidal rhythm.

Willingly would I be an outsider in this if I could know that I read it aright—that out of this change in the old familiar ways some finer thing may come. Is this interest akin to that of the Virginians on the veranda of a plantation's big-house—sitting genuinely spellbound as they hear the lugubrious strains floating up from the Negro quarters? Is it akin to that of the African explorer, Stanley, leaving a village far behind, but halting in spite of himself to catch the boom of its distant drum? Is it significant of basic human responses, the effect of which, once admitted, will extend far beyond cabarets? Maybe these Nordics at last have tuned in on our wavelength. Maybe they are at last learning to speak our language.

TONI MORRISON

Excerpt from *Song of Solomon*

The twilight had thickened and all around them it was getting dark. Milkman moved his hand over her chest and stomach, trying to find the place where she might be hit. "Pilate? You okay?" He couldn't make out her eyes. His hand under her head was sweating like a fountain. "Pilate?"

She sighed. "Watch Reba for me." And then, "I wish I'd a knowed more people. I would of loved 'em all. If I'd a knowed more, I would a loved more."

Milkman bent low to see her face and saw darkness staining his hand. Not sweat, but blood oozing from her neck down into his cupped hand. He pressed his fingers against the skin as if to force the life back in her, back into the place it was escaping from. But that only made it flow faster. Frantically he thought of tourniquets and could even hear the rip of cloth he should have been tearing. He shifted his weight and was about to lay her down, the better to wrap her wound, when she spoke again.

"Sing," she said. "Sing a little somethin for me."

Milkman knew no songs, and had no singing voice that anybody would want to hear, but he couldn't ignore the urgency in her voice. Speaking the words without the least bit of a tune, he sang for the lady. "Sugargirl don't leave me here/ Cotton balls to choke me/Sugargirl don't leave me here/ Buckra's arms to yoke me." The blood was not pushing out any longer and there was something black and bubbly in her mouth. Yet when she moved her head a little to gaze at something behind his shoulder, it took a while for him to realize that she was dead. And when he did, he could not stop the worn old words from coming, louder and louder as though sheer volume would wake her. He woke only the birds, who shuddered off into the air. Milkman laid her head down on the rock. Two of the birds circled round them. One dived into the new grave and scooped something shiny in its beak before it flew away.

Now he knew why he loved her so. Without ever leaving the ground, she could fly. "There must be another one like you," he whispered to her. "There's got to be at least one more woman like you."

Even as he knelt over her, he knew there wouldn't be another mistake; that the minute he stood up Guitar would try to blow his head off. He stood up.

"Guitar!" he shouted.

Tar tar tar, said the hills.

"Over here, brother man! Can you see me?" Milkman cupped his mouth with one hand and waved the other over his head. "Here I am!"

Am am am am, said the rocks.

"You want me? Huh? You want my life?"

Life life life life.

Squatting on the edge of the other flat-headed rock with only the night to cover him, Guitar smiled over the barrel of his rifle. "My man," he murmured to himself. "My main man." He put the rifle on the ground and stood up.

Milkman stopped waving and narrowed his eyes. He could just make out Guitar's head and shoulders in the dark. "You want my life?" Milkman was not shouting now. "You need it? Here." Without wiping away the tears, taking a deep breath, or even bending his knees—he leaped. As fleet and bright as a lodestar he wheeled toward Guitar and it did not matter which one of them would give up his ghost in the killing arms of his brother. For now he knew what Shalimar knew: If you surrendered to the air, you could *ride* it.

HENRY DUMAS

Goodbye, Sweetwater

His arms flapping like a bird, Layton Bridges stood on the porch of the shack and listened to the distant whistle of the freight. Its long sustained peal told him that it was carrying a heavy load, maybe enough cars for the sun to set before the last one passed. He rolled up the frayed ends of his jeans above his bare legs so that the air could get to them. Sometimes after a long freight passed, all he could see was the shadow of the last car streaking across the fallen sun, plunging through the dusty evening, leaving behind only an echo and a hush of loneliness.

The little back country district of Sulfur Springs, Arkansas, sits upon a series of bauxite and sulfur layers. The mineral richness below the surface has transformed the once cotton and tobacco lands into little pocket mining communities, sticking like hardened sores beneath the white dust. A cement factory adds to the gray haze that has become the shroud over every village and rural town.

Holly Springs, where Layton lived, got its name because it has spring water untouched by chemical hardness. Most of the well water in the area was known for its hardness and the taste of sulfur, but this one district erupted now and then with fresh spring water. The spring played a hide-and-seek pattern, going underground and reappearing later.

The only source of soft water in Sulfur Springs was a tiny spring in the middle of a stretch of land closed off by the federal government. Located a mile south of the road near Layton's shack, this land was once part of a rich cotton plantation. Now it was broken up and leased to planters and corporations. The rural people, like Layton Bridges and his grandmother, thought of themselves as living on the edge of a great burnt-out plain, thirsty and bitter, cracking daily under the malice of men. Eventually the land would swallow them up. The big companies would move in and buy them out. Already Sulfur Springs was depopulated, as if overnight the earth had reclaimed or frightened away the people. Besides Layton and his grandmother there were five other families. None of them could claim any young people, except for the kids, too young to move out on their own.

Sixteen-year-old Layton went out into the bare yard where the chinaberry tree stood. The hot afternoon dust leaped up between his toes like fire. He put his arms out as if he were going to dive. Then he leaped, caught the limb of the chinaberry tree and swung himself up. The freight train, like a fleeing worm, crawled atop the horizon of distant trees and hills. It was about a mile away, and Layton wanted to get close to it now. He had believed that any day his mother would come for him or the man she had written about, her friend, Mr. Stubbs, would drive by and take him away. But he had been waiting long months now. He would leave soon, he knew, if he had to make a way himself. The only thing Layton could not reconcile with this joy of leaving Holly Springs was the gnawing feeling that his grandmother was not going. She did not want to go. She would shake her head and say, "Son, I reckon the Lord know best what your grandma gwine do. He been keepin me here on this land now since 'fore anything flyin in the sky 'cept the birds. . . . You go on wid your mama. You go to your mama up there in New York. Go on and finish school. Go in the army. Go to college. Get yourself some learnin. Take care of your mama. You do that and your grandma be happy." Layton always felt and trusted the deep faith and nobility in her voice.

Somehow his grandmother was bigger and stronger than the land. No matter how many factories they built nearby, or how many highways they proposed, or how many mines they dug, his grandmother's strength would last when the rest had crumbled to dust.

He climbed to the top of the tree. The freight still passed, its many-colored, many-shaped cars looking like the curious shapes of a puzzle.

Down the road Layton saw his grandmother coming. Beside her walked Mrs. Fields, who lived in the cabin with her ailing husband and his mother,

Granny Lincoln. Nobody knew how old Granny Lincoln was except Granpa Fields. He claimed that his mother was born a slave and when she was a girl had seen Abraham Lincoln campaigning for the presidency. The two old women wore wide straw hats, which cast long boatlike shadows in front of them. Their aprons bulged with vegetables as they approached in the dust, an ancient silence walking beside them, a part of them, and yet, like them, a part of the land.

Leaning out from the tree with his feet firmly set in the notch where the limb sprung from the body of the tree, and holding to the neck of the tree with his left hand, Layton raised his right hand at the train. How many times had he waved at trains? If he could live as long as the number of times he had waved, he knew, without counting them, that he would live to be as old or older than Granny Lincoln. But there was something about waving at a freight train that seemed dry and meaningless. He lowered his hand. He had always waved at the swift passenger trains, and many times when he went across the river and sat by the tracks, people on the train would wave back. He never knew if the white faces waving at him would ever make the engineer stop the train for him. His brother had ridden on a train when he had gone off to Vietnam. But that was two years ago and his brother had been killed over there. They said he had been missing in action. He thought of himself in a few years riding on a train or maybe even an airplane and being a soldier somewhere. He would fight in his brother's place. He would save up all his money and come back to New York, give it all to his mother to help her. Yes, he would do all that and then he would buy a car, come back to Holly Springs and take his grandmother to Illinois where his uncle Joe lived. Uncle Joe had said that he wanted her to stay with him, but she had always refused.

Layton watched the last car on the freight. The hot white dust clung to the smooth hard surfaces of the tree like powder.

Long before the cement factory was built several miles down the road, Layton had fallen from the tree, but it had been because he was careless. Now with the dust from the trucks and cars and the factory, all the trees and shacks in Holly Springs took on the look of the blight. Granny Bridges called it the blight. It had come with the bauxite mines years before and now it had spread over the land like a creeping fever. A dry fever. One that made you sneeze, cough and choke. It killed the trees, the grass and gardens. There were certain vegetables that his grandmother could not grow anymore. Something about the land refused the seed, as if the land was sick, and didn't know any longer what its nature was.

Once he recalled, when Granny Lincoln was brought out to sun, some big trucks loaded with ores stopped in front of the house. The men had heard about some sweet water around somewhere in the area and wanted some. Granny Lincoln had wanted to know what the men were doing carrying away her yard, and when Grandpa Fields tried to console her, she refused to listen. Finally she had taken consolation in the Bible, saying that all of those trucks and men were signs. She said it was written that in the latter days, Satan and his angels would come forth from the earth seeking whom they might devour.

He began to climb down, the deadly powder making his descent as treacherous as his ascent. He had seen no sign of life on the freight. He had only shaken white dust into the air. It was a three-o'clock afternoon sun, hot, direct, lapping at the wounded earth with a dry merciless tongue. Layton did not feel angry at the sun, not really. He had learned somewhere in school that the sun was the source of all power. It was the sun that made the gardens grow, made the fields of hay, and cotton, corn and sorghum. It was the sun that drew up the rain from the ocean and sent rain down to make things green. Yet he knew it was by some terrible agreement, something beyond his comprehension, that allowed the sun and the whitemen to weaken the land. It was the same feeling which took his joy away when he thought of his coming new life in New York. It was like waving at a freight train. Somewhere he felt betrayed. Perhaps he was betraying the land himself. He felt that it all was a part of a great conspiracy . . . with the sun in the center. He did not like to think of leaving her to the mercy of the heat and the dust. And yet . . .

The only thing that gave Layton any real consolation was the fact that his grandmother was indestructible. He watched her slow pace up the road, her blue apron bulging with vegetables she had gotten from Granny Fields. She would sit on the porch in the evenings and the white dust never settled on her. Sometimes, he would think, gwine live forever. . . .

The two old women entered the bald yard in front of the shack. Their heads were bent as if they were watching the direction of their shadows, but Layton felt instinctively that his grandmother knew that he was in the tree. She never had to look at things to recognize them. She knew because it was the same to her as her bones telling when it was going to rain.

Layton was about to swing down to the last limb above the ground when he turned his neck to get a last look at the horizon where the trains passed. The 6:00 P.M. passenger would be the next one on the line, and he imagined that in a few more days he himself would be on it or maybe riding in the car with Mr. Stubbs. They would cross the tracks in Mr. Stubbs's car at the Sulfur Springs Greyhound station and he imagined telling Mr. Stubbs just what time the trains came by. . . . When he recognized the swirling dust as a car in the distance, he was already swinging down to the last limb. He never touched the ground, but swung, toes over head, back up onto the limb, grunting, his mouth open, his stomach flopping down on the limb. Upside down he saw the two figures climb wearily up on the porch. Mrs. Fields sat down in the rocking chair that was especially padded for her, and his grandmother rested in hers. He climbed back to the top. The car he saw had not taken the road which led to the cement plant. It was headed toward their house. He knew that no mistake could be made. There had been signs posted on the road for years. A screen of dust leaped from behind the car as it came like a racing beetle.

He almost blurted out the news of the car, but suddenly felt his throat dry up; in a careless movement of his foot, he slipped. . . .

Even the chinaberry tree, in its struggle with the land, had grown spiteful. It had not produced any berries in two years now, only a few scrawny pits that even the birds would not eat. He fell against the next limb, shaking the tree as if a wind had blown through. Before he caught himself he heard his grandmother's voice, calling him, warning him. He knew she had seen him fall, and in her voice, he could tell that she was saving him. His arms hooked the limb and he held it.

"Grandma," he said, swinging out of the tree and feeling grit in his throat, "yonder come somebody."

The old lady, as if she had known not only that someone was coming, but that her grandson would report it just that way, looked up from her lap where she was shelling green peas. "I reckon, your grandma and Mrs. Fields, 'bout to die of thirst, son."

By her voice he knew that the car was another betrayal. Yet there was no reason why it couldn't be Mr. Stubbs. The letter had said as soon as school was out and school had been out for weeks. He had not told Mr. Purdy at the cement plant that he was leaving, but he had told everybody else. No more night walking and night working. No more sleeping in the daytime and walking the dark roads at night with a flashlight. No more breathing the rock dust and chemicals, breathing them so much that you thought you were going to choke to death. No more looking in that cracked mirror at the plant and seeing a face covered with white dust, a black face underneath covered with a dry white fever. No more of the loneliness of walking to school and finding one less face there each day. . . .

Willy Strom, he gone off to Chicago with his brother. Maybelle Davis, she pregnant and gone to live with her cousin in Little Rock. Jesse Higgins, he left last night with Odell Miller and Claude Sykes. They all

goin to the Job Corps in New Jersey. Louise Watkins, she getting married to a guy some kin to the Lawrences. They goin to Los Angeles.

Layton walked across the yard and stood in front of his grandmother. "I get you some sweet water." He paused. "Grandma, who you reckon comin yonder?" He couldn't really believe that his mother's letters were also betrayals.

Sarah Bridges, her long silver hair tied neatly in a bun, stopped shelling peas and lifted the straw hat to her face to fan. The brim slapped a fly into her lap and Layton watched as the insect regained its wing power and buzzed off.

"Reckon it nothin but somebody lookin for somethin to get, son. Every empty truck and car or wagon come into Holly Springs nowadays, always roll out full. It the change of the seasons, son. You get old as I am and you learn when to see the change of the seasons."

Granny Fields, her black face shining in her perpetual silence, looked up from her lap of peas. Her short arms continued to work as the round peas fell from the shove of her thumb. The empty hulls fell with their brothers on the floor beside her ancient high-top leather shoes. After years of working in the earth, her shoes had taken on the color of the dirt.

"I hear your mama want you up there with her, boy," she said to Layton. She leaned out over the porch and spit a brown stream of snuff.

"Yes mam," Layton said. Something began to ring in his head now, like a kind of church bell. He looked out over the flat land. He could not see the car now, but he picked the point in the distance where he knew it would come into view. "But I reckon if she don't, then I'm gwine go visit her and maybe work for the summer. . . . I might even go to school up there next year."

"You stay outa trouble, you hear. And mind your mama," said Granny Fields. She returned to her accustomed silence now, having gathered up all the forces of her intellect to deliver her familiar warning. Layton liked Granny Fields because she spoke only when she thought it necessary. Almost in his motion to go back into the shack there came the deep and respectful, "Yes mam."

He went through the shack. On his bed he saw the dusty brown suitcase which he had put there every day since he got the word from his mother. Even if she didn't send for him, he was going to use that suitcase.

On the back porch he went to the earthen jug. It was the vessel which he had filled every one or two days since he could remember. He had gone with his mother when he was only a tiny boy, to fill it, and he had gone with Granny and Mr. Fields, and once with a man who Granny had told him was his own father. He couldn't remember his father because it was only that once that he had seen him.

His mother had gone off to get a job, and even though she sent money to his grandmother, Layton felt a kind of dryness, and emptiness, whenever he tried to imagine her living way up in New York. He wanted to go himself, and as he stirred the dipper around in the dark inside of the jug, he could hear the ringing of the train whistle, and the roar of sounds he knew he would have to learn to identify. New sounds. New smells. New sights. No more picking cotton. No more dragging the long sack of cotton over sunbaked fields of dusty stalks, kicking up the red dirt. No more choking on cement dust. No more squinting at the distant death-smoke which began early in the morning as a haze but which by afternoon had become a cloud, a cloud of white gray dust, catching the sun, and choking off the rain and smothering the land. He did not drink. He would have to go out to get some water. There was just about two dippers full left.

He could see the sulfur-water well half hidden by the clothes on the line between the shack and the well. He checked the two sulfur-water buckets at the far edge of the porch; they both were full. A yellowish scale clung to their insides. Layton dipped up some of the water with the dipper, held it in his mouth for a short while, rinsed his mouth as he had seen the old people do after dipping snuff, and then spat. The taste of the water was intensified because the sun had broken through cracks on the porch wall and heated the water. It was not for drinking anyway, only for washing.

He poured the water from each bucket into a large bent tin tub which leaned against the rear of the shack. His grandmother used it to wash and collect rainwater. He would fill both buckets with sweet water at the spring.

When he lifted his head, he could see the pillar of dust swirling like a miniature twister. He went to the earthen jug and poured the contents into one of the buckets. Then he went through the house and stood looking beyond the front porch, beyond the sound of his grandmother humming softly, beyond the almost silent flick of thumbs shelling peas, beyond the chinaberry tree, obstinately clinging to the land, and beyond the edge of the young cotton, that Mr. Fields and he had planted and chopped, to the point where the car now appeared.

His grandmother lifted her head and squinted toward the road. Mrs. Fields in her silence lifted her head also, as if she had waited for the other woman to make the first indication that the car was drawing close enough to look at.

"Granny Fields, you want a dipperful now?" Layton asked, watching the scale from the bucket shine from its slakeness and wondering how it was that sulfur got into the water, and how was it that the sweet water managed to escape the sulfur.

"I can wait for the fresh, son," she said. A pea popped from a shell and rolled off the porch. Layton saw it disappear in the dust, and the neck of a chicken shot from under the porch and struck the pea. He knew his grandmother always waited for fresh water too.

He stepped off the porch around a feathered form of a chicken asleep in the sun, its wing fanned out in the dust as if it were taking a bath. His bare feet slapped the baked clay in a familiar rhythm.

He stepped in a hole, where as a small boy he had played with wooden blocks and tin cans nailed together by his brother for trucks, cars, tractors, airplanes, or anything they wanted them to be. They had played bauxite and coal mining, cement hauling, gold digging and war.

Who would go and get the sweet water from the spring? The trip was too long for any of them to walk. Old Mr. Fields could not walk that far every day for water. They would all have to drink sulfur water, and he knew that was a bad sign. He stood there, paused beside the house watching the rapid approach of the car now, prolonging his own thirst. When he heard his grandmother's call, he felt the same feeling when he slipped on the tree. She did not call him but once, softly, as if she knew he had not gone very far, as if she knew that he was watching the car from the side of the house.

He saw a tailspin of dust rise up and then fall forward over the car. It had stopped in the yard. A whiteman emerged from the dust, wiping his face with a handkerchief. Layton climbed up on the porch and watched the man. He was Yul Stencely who came now and then to collect money, and Granny Bridges always paid it without question, as if it were her duty. He knew that the money he made and the money his mother sometimes sent finally went into the whiteman's hands. He watched the man approach. Yul Stencely looked around the yard expectantly. Layton knew he was looking for a dog to rush out at him.

"How do, Mrs. Bridges," the whiteman spoke, mopping his blond head and then resetting the straw hat he wore back on it. He drew near the steps. Particles of dust floated and settled on the porch. "Mighty hot today."

"How do, Mr. Stencely." She had already put aside the peas in her lap. Now she brought out a paring knife and began to peel a large white potato. "Yes, 'tis hot."

The whiteman drew out a notebook from his bosom pocket. Layton watched him. The man did not once notice the presence of Granny Fields nor did he look at Layton.

Tall, thin and straight, he wore a coat that was too large. Layton looked closely but he could see no signs of sweat, although the man was constantly wiping his face. He would look at the dirty handkerchief, blow his breath into it as the cloth passed over his mouth and then look at his notebook with silent appraisal. He stepped into a tiny shaft of shade near Granny Bridges at the edge of the porch.

"Who told you I had anything for you this time, Mr. Stencely?" There was no real anger in her voice, but Layton could tell that there was a determination, a kind of defiance which always made him feel that his grandmother was indestructible. She kept on peeling potatoes, without looking at the whiteman. He cleared his throat and continued his scrutiny of the notebook. Then he looked around the yard again.

"Well, Mrs. Bridges, aint no harm in comin. Is there? Sides, I reckon you owe since the last time I was here. . . ." He paused. Layton studied the man. Granny was right. He had come like the rest. They come empty and leave full. Layton suddenly wanted to know the reason for this continued payment to the whiteman. Why was it that it was always Negroes who paid money to the whiteman? Yet he knew the answers, but asking the questions over again made him feel a fire rise up from his toes and churn away in his stomach. And the fire gave him direction. "Well, I reckon there aint no harm in comin, Mr. Stencely, and I reckon there aint no harm in me askin you to come again next month. I speck my daughter-in-law gwine send a bit of money . . ."

Layton set the bucket down. It made a noise. The whiteman turned and looked at it. Then he looked away around the house toward the well. Layton felt as if she had said something then to take away all the years of his faith in her strength. If his mother had sent some money, it would go to that man. . . . He knew that. But it just shouldn't. . . . Over and over now he heard the ring of the tin bucket on the ground. . . . The settling of the dust was millions of tiny bells.

The whiteman laughed. He couldn't go any further than the old woman would let him. He knew that they were poor, but that was not his fault. He collected from poor whites as well as poor blacks. He even had some Mexicans he collected from. He was hot and he needed a drink.

"Well, Mrs. Bridges, I tell you what I'm gonna do. You let me have a drink of your good well water and I'll be obliged to come agin when you able . . ."

Granny Bridges flipped a long curled potato peeling out into the yard where a chicken neck grabbed it and fled beneath the house.

"Layton, give Mr. Stencely a drink of water. . . ."

When she called his name, Layton was already in motion. He left the bucket with the two dippers of sweet water from the earthen jug and went to the back and to the sulfur-water well. He let the long aluminum cylinder down into the well shaft. The ringing of the rusty wheel which rode the chain up and down was a kind of music which Layton associated with dryness. The water from the well never really quenched your thirst. Only the spring water could quench your thirst. He felt the cylinder strike bottom, fill, and grow heavy. He coughed and began to pull. His muscles burned and the sun struck him through the hood of the well right in the face. He frowned, and his frowning made him hot. The whiteman would drink what he gave him. He would drink, but he would not lose his thirst. His stomach would swell and almost burst, but he would still be thirsty. Hours after drinking this water you would belch it and want to spit, but your tongue would be dry. Your throat would crack, and you would sweat.

He returned to the front porch with a bucket and a glass from the kitchen. He took the dipper from the sweet-water bucket and watched it sink in the freshly drawn sulfur water. Then he stood in the doorway, motionless. He expected the whiteman to reach and fill the glass and drink. He didn't hear his grandmother's voice calling him. He lifted the sweet water pail and stepped back into the doorway. . . .

"Layton."

The truth still rang in her voice. It halted him. He heard the slosh of the remaining bits of water in the pail against his bare leg. "Yes, mam?"

"Aint you got no manners?"

He returned to the doorway and saw his grandmother lifting the bucket of sulfur water and aiming it out to the yard.

She slung it. "This water aint fit to drink." Layton felt as if the water had been splashed in his face. A shiver went up his legs. He quickly looked at the whiteman, then set down his bucket.

"There be enough for one drink left," announced Granny Fields. She looked up at Layton as if she had suddenly come out of a cave after a long time.

Layton watched as the whiteman carefully drank two full glasses of water. Not one drop fell. He mopped his face again. "Mrs. Bridges, that's the sweetest water in Holly Springs. You sure you aint got a softener hidden out in that well somewhere?"

"The Lord provides." She was not receptive to flattery. She set the bucket down in front of Layton and then sat back down in her chair. Yul Stencely stepped into the sun. He looked at Layton. Their eyes met.

"That's your youngest grandchild," he stated rather than asked, without taking his eyes off Layton.

Layton came out on the porch, picked up the other bucket, walked off the porch in front of Yul and went around the side of the house slinging the two buckets violently. He did not hear what she said anymore. He passed the sulfur well, passed the old grassy area where their hog pen used to be. They could not afford to raise hogs anymore. They had a few chickens. Even dogs would not stay. Dogs would roam and die off, getting run over on the highway or killed by other dogs. Layton could hardly remember when he had a dog. It was his brother's dog that Yul Stencely had seen on his last visit, but that was months ago. His brother had gone off to Vietnam.

Layton felt funny thinking about that whiteman coming to get money when they didn't have any. The few pennies he made at the cement plant would not keep him away. He even began to wonder if his grandmother's sturdiness could keep the dust away any longer. His brother had gone. . . . And yet Layton knew that staying was like dying. He could not die. He would go off and take his chances. At least you had a chance. But staying here trying to finish school, by alternating it with chopping and picking cotton or with pit work at the plant, was sure death.

He pictured one day a whiteman coming after him. But it burned him inside to feel that. He had seen the fire in the eyes of the kids in Holly Springs last year in the marches and demonstrations. He would join in the voter drive, he would get out and work against the dryness.

He moved along a path toward the spring. It was a grassy path. When he reached the sign and the high fence which read GOVERNMENT PROPERTY KEEP OFF, he scanned the fence for a weeded spot, then broke over, throwing the two buckets over ahead of him. The spring lay a half mile within the boundary of the fence. He had to hurry.

When his grandmother threw out that water, it was like seeing her fall down in the dust on the road. No. He rebuked himself for a thought. Even the Bible . . . He didn't know much about the Bible. He could not quote it like she could. The Bible didn't hold that much interest for him. It was those preachers who always came looking for sweet water. He didn't want to distrust the Bible, but then he could not give it all of his trust. She did not really want him to leave and go North like she said; she wanted him to stay. There wasn't nobody around Holly Springs anymore. All gone. And his grandmother wanted him to be like Granny Lincoln and the rest of the old ones. The thought choked him. He reached the spring.

The cool clear water bubbled out of the little opening in the ground near an encirclement of trees. A slight depression in the ground marked the spot. The water flowed for a very short distance and then disappeared again in the earth. His bare feet moved over little stone steps. The spurt of the water from the ground was about seven or eight inches. Layton drank.

Well, maybe she didn't really want him to stay, but then who would take care of her . . . after she couldn't do it herself? But he could not picture her ever reaching the point where she could not take care of herself. When all the rest were down, Granny would still be there.

He noticed that the spurt was thinner than it was yesterday. He wondered if anybody else besides the Negroes who lived near the spring had discovered it. It wouldn't be long before the government found out that it had sweet water on its plantation. By then the spring would disappear and come up again somewhere else.

Or maybe the spring was tired of feeding the sulfurous earth and was going to return to the deep darkness forever. Layton filled the buckets and drank again. . . . When he bent over he felt his head spin as if stars were falling on him. . . .

When he returned to the shack, the sun had gathered itself into a kind of orange brilliance and was aiming toward a line in the distance. Layton filled the earthen jug, letting the water fall to make bubbles like the sound of the spring. He took the women a bucket and a dipper. But before his grandmother drank she called him.

"Son, I reckon you see a lot of things in town and out at that plant that your granny don't see. I reckon you got a right to get mad like the young people these days. I'm all for that, but I aint for you gettin mad like a mad dog. You 'member when your brother's dog got the rabies, don't you, son?"

Layton nodded. He figured he knew what his grandmother was going to say. . . . But he could not run from it. Somehow he wanted to hear it even if it cooled him. The taste of the sweet water seemed to linger in the air. . . .

"A mad dog will bite anybody, son. It don't matter who it used to belong to. It even bite the man what raised it. A mad dog will bite its own mother, son. So I'm sayin, son, be mad but not like a mad dog. Be right first. Be truthful first. And when you get mad at somethin then you got all *that* to back you up. Don't spite that man cause he thirsty and white. That's wrong. Give 'em your best at all times. When you give 'em your best when you don't like him, he be the first to know it. God on your side then."

It never mattered whether he really agreed with Granny or not, because she seemed to be right. Mrs. Fields, in her silence, had only glanced at him, and he knew that she was backing up his grandmother. It was a conspiracy. It was a bond which he could not understand nor defeat, and nothing in his experience seemed full enough to satisfy him. His mother was not sending for him. She too was trapped. In the North she wasn't doing as good as she said. He had heard how that in cities up North they were having race riots and killing Negroes. Then what good was his trying to wait till she sent out Mr. Stubbs? There wasn't no man. His father was dead and that was it. He felt himself now ready to cast off the dreams and things people said. He would believe no one, and if he dreamed something, he would not believe it were true until *he* made it come true. . . . If he were going to leave soon, then it would be because he wanted to. Even if his mother sent a ticket, it would mean nothing unless he wanted to leave. His grandmother would not drink sulfur water unless she had to and he knew that as long as there was sweet water coming out of the ground, she would be strong. . . .

A long whistle broke the late evening heaviness, and Layton stopped packing his suitcase and went out to the bald yard. . . . If he climbed the tree to see the passenger train, he knew that he would not fall.

Jane Gastin and her charges, circa 1900

All the Pretty Little Horses

(An authentic slave lullaby sung by African-American mothers who were forced to take care of the enslavers' children while having to neglect their own.)

Hushaby, don't you cry,
Go to sleepy, little baby.
When you wake, you shall have
        cake,
And all the pretty little horses.
Blacks and bays, dapples and grays,
Coach and six-a little horses.

    Way down yonder in the meadow,
    There's a poor little lambie;
    The bees and the butterflies
        pickin' out his eyes,
    The poor little thing cries:
        "Mammy."

Hushaby, don't you cry,
Go to sleepy, little baby.

FRANCES ELLEN WATKINS HARPER

Bury Me in a Free Land

Make me a grave where'er you will,
In a lowly plain, or a lofty hill;
Make it among earth's humblest graves,
But not in a land where men are slaves.

I could not rest if around my grave
I heard the steps of a trembling slave;
His shadow above my silent tomb
Would make it a place of fearful gloom.

I could not rest if I heard the tread
Of a coffle gang to the shambles led,
And the mother's shriek of wild despair
Rise like a curse on the trembling air.

I could not sleep if I saw the lash
Drinking her blood at each fearful gash,
And I saw her babes torn from her breast,
Like trembling doves from their parent nest.

I'd shudder and start if I heard the bay
Of bloodhounds seizing their human prey,
And I heard the captive plead in vain
As they bound afresh his galling chain.

If I saw young girls from their mothers' arms
Bartered and sold for their youthful charms,
My eye would flash with a mournful flame,
My death-paled cheek grow red with shame.

I would sleep, dear friends, where bloated might
Can rob no man of his dearest right;

My rest shall be calm in any grave
Where none can call his brother a slave.

I ask no monument, proud and high,
To arrest the gaze of the passers-by;
All that my yearning spirit craves,
Is bury me not in a land of slaves.

PAUL LAURENCE DUNBAR

When Malindy Sings

G'way an' quit dat noise, Miss Lucy—
    Put dat music book away;
What's de use to keep on tryin'?
    Ef you practise twell you're gray,
You cain't sta't no notes a-flyin'
    Lak de ones dat rants and rings
F'om de kitchen to de big woods
    When Malindy sings.

You ain't got de nachel o'gans
    Fu' to make de soun' come right,
You ain't got de tu'ns an' twistin's
    Fu' to make it sweet an' light.
Tell you one thing now, Miss Lucy,
    An' I'm tellin' you fu' true,
When hit comes to raal right singin',
    'T ain't no easy thing to do.

Easy 'nough fu' folks to hollah,
    Lookin' at de lines an' dots,
When dey ain't no one kin sence it,
    An' de chune comes in, in spots;
But fu' real melojous music,
    Dat jes' strikes yo' hea't and clings,
Jes' you stan' an' listen wif me
    When Malindy sings.

Paul Laurence Dunbar (Courtesy of the Moorland-Spingarn Research Center)

Ain't you nevah hyeahd Malindy?
    Blessed soul, tek up de cross!
Look hyeah, ain't you jokin', honey?
    Well, you don't know whut you los'.
Y' ought to hyeah dat gal a-wa'blin',
    Robins, la'ks, an' all dem things.
Heish dey moufs an' hides dey faces
    When Malindy sings.

Fiddlin' man jes' stop his fiddlin'.
    Lay his fiddle on de she'f;
Mockin'-bird quit tryin' to whistle,
    'Cause he jes' so shamed hisse'f.
Folks a-playin' on de banjo
    Drap dey fingahs on de strings—
Bless yo' soul—fu'gits to move em,
    When Malindy sings.

She jes' spreads huh mouf and hollahs,
    "Come to Jesus," twell you hyeah

Sinnahs' tremblin' steps and voices
    Timid-lak a-drawin' neah;
Den she tu'ns to "Rock of Ages,"
    Simply to de cross she clings;
An' you fin' yo' teahs a-drappin'
    When Malindy sings.

Who dat says dat humble praises
    Wif de Master nevah counts?
Heish yo' mouf, I hyeah dat music,
    Ez hit rises up an' mounts—
Floatin' by de hills an' valleys,
    Way above dis buryin' sod,
Ez hit makes its way in glory
    To de very gates of God!

Oh, hit's sweetah dan de music
    Of an edicated band;
An hit's dearah dan de battle's
    Song o'triumph in de lan'.
It seems holier dan evenin'
    When de solemn chu'ch bell rings,
Ez I sit an' ca'mly listen
    While Malindy sings.

Towsah, stop dat ba'kin', hyeah me!
    Mandy, mek dat chile keep still;
Don't you hyeah de echoes callin'
    F'om de valley to de hill?
Let me listen, I can hyeah it,
    Th'oo de bresh of angels' wings,
Sof' an' sweet, "Swing Low, Sweet Chariot,"
    Ez Malindy sings.

DUDLEY RANDALL

Booker T. and W. E. B.

Booker T. Washington and W. E. B. Du Bois

"It seems to me," said Booker T.,
"It shows a mighty lot of cheek
To study chemistry and Greek
When Mister Charlie needs a hand
To hoe the cotton on his land,
And when Miss Ann looks for a cook,
Why stick your nose inside a book?"

"I don't agree," said W. E. B.
"If I should have the drive to seek
Knowledge of chemistry or Greek,
I'll do it. Charles and Miss can look

Another place for hand or cook.
Some men rejoice in skill of hand,
And some in cultivating land,
But there are others who maintain
The right to cultivate the brain."

"It seems to me," said Booker T.,
"That all you folks have missed the boat
Who shout about the right to vote,
And spend vain days and sleepless nights
In uproar over civil rights.
Just keep your mouths shut, do not grouse,
But work, and save, and buy a house."

"I don't agree," said W. E. B.
"For what can property avail
If dignity and justice fail?
Unless you help to make the laws,
They'll steal your house with trumped-up clause.
A rope's as tight, a fire as hot,

William Edward Burghardt Du Bois (1925—Pastel on artist board by Winold Reiss [1886–1953]. National Portrait Gallery, Smithsonian Institution. Gift of Lawrence A. Fleischman and Howard Garfinkle with a matching grant from the National Endowment for the Arts.)

No matter how much cash you've got.
Speak soft, and try your little plan,
But as for me, I'll be a man."

"It seems to me," said Booker T.—

"I don't agree,"
Said W. E. B.

LANGSTON HUGHES

The Negro Speaks of Rivers

(To W. E. B. Du Bois)

I've known rivers:
I've known rivers ancient as the world and older
   than the flow of human blood in human veins.

My soul has grown deep like the rivers.

I bathed in the Euphrates when dawns were young.
I built my hut near the Congo and it lulled me to sleep.
I looked upon the Nile and raised the pyramids above it.
I heard the singing of the Mississippi when Abe
   Lincoln went down to New Orleans, and I've seen
   its muddy bosom turn all golden in the sunset.

I've known rivers:
Ancient, dusky rivers.

My soul has grown deep like the rivers.

Langston Hughes (c. 1925—Pastel on artist board by Winold Reiss [1886–1953]. National Portrait Gallery, Smithsonian Institution. Gift of W. Tjark Reiss in memory of his father, Winold Reiss.)

The Dream Keeper

Bring me all of your dreams
You dreamers.
Bring me all of your
Heart melodies.
That I may wrap them
In a blue cloud-cloth
Away from the too rough fingers
Of the world.

STERLING ALLEN BROWN

Strong Men

The strong men keep coming on.

—Sandburg.

They dragged you from homeland,
They chained you in coffles,
They huddled you spoon-fashion in filthy hatches,
They sold you to give a few gentlemen ease.

They broke you in like oxen,
They scourged you,
They branded you,
They made your women breeders,
They swelled your numbers with bastards . . .
They taught you the religion they disgraced.

Langston Hughes signs autographs after delivering the Charles Eaton Burch Memorial Lecture, April 1957. L–R: Dr. Ivan Earle Taylor, Rochelle Reid, Dr. Gertrude Rivers, Mr. Hughes, Professor Sterling A. Brown, and Connie Pindle. (Courtesy of the Moorland-Spingarn Research Center)

You sang:
      Keep a-inchin' along
      Lak a po' inch worm. . . .

You sang:
      Bye and bye
      I'm gonna lay down dis heaby load. . . .

You sang:
      Walk togedder, chillen,
      Dontcha git weary. . . .

            The strong men keep a-comin' on
            The strong men git stronger.

They point with pride to the roads you built for them,
They ride in comfort over the rails you laid for them.
They put hammers in your hands
And said—Drive so much before sundown.

You sang:
      Ain't no hammah
      In dis lan',
      Strikes lak mine, bebby,
      Strikes lak mine.

They cooped you in their kitchens,
They penned you in their factories,
They gave you the jobs that they were too good
      for,
They tried to guarantee happiness to themselves
By shunting dirt and misery to you.

You sang:
      Me an' muh baby gonna shine, shine
      Me an' muh baby gonna shine.
            The strong men keep a-comin' on
            The strong men git stronger. . . .

They bought off some of your leaders
You stumbled, as blind men will . . .
They coaxed you, unwontedly soft-voiced. . . .
You followed a way.
Then laughed as usual.
They heard the laugh and wondered;
Uncomfortable;
Unadmitting a deeper terror. . . .
      The strong men keep a-comin' on
      Gittin' stronger. . . .

What, from the slums
Where they have hemmed you,
What, from the tiny huts
They could not keep from you—
What reaches them
Making them ill at ease, fearful?
Today they shout prohibition at you
"Thou shalt not this"
"Thou shalt not that"
"Reserved for whites only"
You laugh.

One thing they cannot prohibit—
      The strong men . . . coming on
      The strong men gittin' stronger.
      Strong men. . . .
      Stronger. . . .

Old Lem

I talked to old Lem
And old Lem said:
    "They weigh the cotton
    They store the corn
        We only good enough
        To work the rows;
    They run the commissary
    They keep the books
        We gotta be grateful
        For being cheated;
    Whippersnapper clerks
    Call us out of our name
        We got to say mister
        To spindling boys
    They make our figgers

"Old Lem" from THE COLLECTED POEMS OF STERLING A
BROWN, edited by Michael S. Harper. Copyright © 1980 by Sterling
A. Brown. Reprinted by permission of HarperCollins Publishers, Inc.

Turn somersets
We buck in the middle
    Say, 'Thankyuh, sah.'
        They don't come by ones
        They don't come by twos
        But they come by tens.

"They got the judges
They got the lawyers
They got the jury-rolls
They got the law
        They don't come by ones
They got the sheriffs
They got the deputies
        They don't come by twos

They got the shotguns
They got the rope
    We git the justice
    In the end
        And they come by tens.

"Their fists stay closed
Their eyes look straight
    Our hands stay open
    Our eyes must fall
        They don't come by ones
They got the manhood
They got the courage
        They don't come by twos
    We got to slink around,
    Hangtailed hounds.
They burn us when we dogs
They burn us when we men
        They come by tens. . . .

"I had a buddy
Six foot of man
Muscled up perfect
Game to the heart
        They don't come by ones
Outworked and outfought
Any man or two men
        They don't come by twos
He spoke out of turn
At the commissary
They gave him a day
To git out the county.
He didn't take it.
He said "Come and get me."
They came and got him.
        And they came by tens.
He stayed in the county—
He lays there dead.

They don't come by ones
They don't come by twos
But they come by tens."

After Winter

He snuggles his fingers
In the blacker loam
The lean months are done with,
The fat to come.

His eyes are set
On a brushwood-fire
But his heart is soaring
Higher and higher.

Ten acres unplanted
To raise dreams on.

The lean months are done with,
The fat to come.
His hopes, winter wanderers,
Hasten home.

"Butterbeans fo' Clara
Sugar corn fo' Grace
An' fo' de little feller
Runnin' space. . . ."

Robert Hayden

Middle Passage

Jesús, Estrella, Esperanza, Mercy:

Sails flashing to the wind like weapons,
sharks following the moans the fever and the
    dying;
horror the corposant and compass rose.

Middle Passage:
        voyage through death
                to life upon these shores.

---

18 lines from "After Winter" from SOUTHERN ROAD by Sterling A. Brown. Copyright 1932 by Harcourt, Brace & Co. Copyright renewed 1960 by Sterling Brown. Included in THE COLLECTED POEMS OF STERLING A. BROWN, selected by Michael S. Harper. Copyright © 1980 by Sterling A. Brown.

"10 April 1800—
Blacks rebellious. Crew uneasy. Our linguist says
their moaning is a prayer for death,
ours and their own. Some try to starve themselves.
Lost three this morning leaped with crazy laughter
to the waiting sharks, sang as they went under."

Desire, Adventure, Tartar, Ann:

Standing to America, bringing home
black gold, black ivory, black seed.

        Deep in the festering hold thy father lies,
        of his bones New England pews are made,
        those are altar lights that were his eyes.

Jesus   Saviour   Pilot   Me
Over   Life's   Tempestuous   Sea

We pray that Thou wilt grant, O Lord,
safe passage to our vessels bringing
heathen souls unto Thy chastening.

Jesus   Saviour

"8 bells. I cannot sleep, for I am sick
with fear, but writing eases fear a little
since still my eyes can see these words take shape
upon the page & so I write, as one
would turn to exorcism. 4 days scudding,
but now the sea is calm again. Misfortune
follows in our wake like sharks (our grinning
tutelary gods). Which one of us
has killed an albatross? A plague among
our blacks—Ophthalmia: blindness—& we
have jettisoned the blind to no avail.
It spreads, the terrifying sickness spreads.
Its claws have scratched sight from the Capt.'s eyes
& there is blindness in the fo'c'sle
& we must sail 3 weeks before we come
to port."

        What port awaits us, Davy Jones'
        or home? I've heard of slavers drifting,
            drifting,
        playthings of wind and storm and chance,
            their crews
        gone blind, the jungle hatred
        crawling up on deck.

Thou   Who   Walked   On   Galilee

"Deponent further sayeth *The Bella J*
left the Guinea Coast

with cargo of five hundred blacks and odd
for the barracoons of Florida:

"That there was hardly room 'tween-decks for half
the sweltering cattle stowed spoon-fashion there;
that some went mad of thirst and tore their flesh
and sucked the blood:

"That Crew and Captain lusted with the comeliest
of the savage girls kept naked in the cabins;
that there was one they called The Guinea Rose
and they cast lots and fought to lie with her:

"That when the Bo's'n piped all hands, the flames
spreading from starboard already were beyond
control, the negroes howling and their chains
entangled with the flames:

"That the burning blacks could not be reached,
that the Crew abandoned ship,
leaving their shrieking negresses behind,
that the Captain perished drunken with the
     wenches:

"Further Deponent sayeth not."

Pilot   Oh   Pilot   Me

II
Aye, lad, and I have seen those factories,
Gambia, Rio Pongo, Calabar;
have watched the artful mongos baiting traps
of war wherein the victor and the vanquished

Were caught as prizes for our barracoons.
Have seen the nigger kings whose vanity
and greed turned wild black hides of Fellatah,
Mandingo, Ibo, Kru to gold for us.

And there was one—King Anthracite we named
     him—
fetish face beneath French parasols
of brass and orange velvet, impudent mouth
whose cups were carven skulls of enemies:

He'd honor us with drum and feast and conjo
and palm-oil-glistening wenches deft in love,
and for tin crowns that shone with paste,
red calico and German-silver trinkets

Would have the drums talk war and send
his warriors to burn the sleeping villages
and kill the sick and old and lead the young
in coffles to our factories.

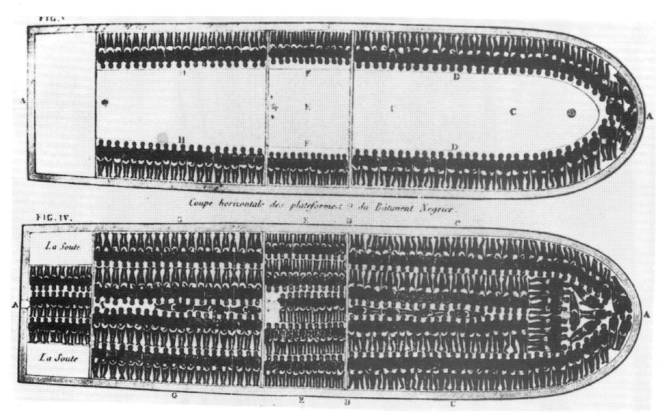

*A deck and a half illustrate how the enslaved Africans were made to lie "spoon fash-
ion." (Brooks/Library of Congress)*

Twenty years a trader, twenty years,
for there was wealth aplenty to be harvested
from those black fields, and I'd be trading still
but for the fevers melting down my bones.

    III
Shuttles in the rocking loom of history,
the dark ships move, the dark ships move,
their bright ironical names
like jests of kindness on a murderer's mouth;
plough through thrashing glister toward
fata morgana's lucent melting shore,
weave toward New World littorals that are
mirage and myth and actual shore.

Voyage through death,
                  voyage whose chartings are
                     unlove.

A charnel stench, effluvium of living death
spreads outward from the hold,
where the living and the dead, the horribly dying,
lie interlocked, lie foul with blood and excrement.

    Deep in the festering hold thy father lies,
    the corpse of mercy rots with him,
    rats eat love's rotten gelid eyes.

    But, oh, the living look at you
    with human eyes whose suffering accuses you,
    whose hatred reaches through the swill of dark
    to strike you like a leper's claw.

    You cannot stare that hatred down
    or chain the fear that stalks the watches
    and breathes on you its fetid scorching breath;
    cannot kill the deep immortal human wish,
    the timeless will.

        "But for the storm that flung up barriers
        of wind and wave, *The Amistad*, señores,
        would have reached the port of Príncipe
            in two,
        three days at most; but for the storm we
            should
        have been prepared for what befell.
        Swift as the puma's leap it came. There was
        that interval of moonless calm filled only
        with the water's and the rigging's usual
            sounds,
        then sudden movement, blows and snarling
            cries
        and they had fallen on us with machete
        and marlinspike. It was as though the very
        air, the night itself were striking us.

        Exhausted by the rigors of the storm,
        we were no match for them. Our men
            went down
        before the murderous Africans. Our loyal
        Celestino ran from below with gun
        and lantern and I saw, before the cane-
        knife's wounding flash, Cinquez,
        that surly brute who calls himself a prince,
        directing, urging on the ghastly work.
        He hacked the poor mulatto down, and
            then
        he turned on me. The decks were slippery

        when daylight finally came. It sickens me
        to think of what I saw, of how these apes
        threw overboard the butchered bodies of
        our men, true Christians all, like so much
            jetsam.
        Enough, enough. The rest is quickly told:
        Cinquez was forced to spare the two of us
        you see to steer the ship to Africa,
        and we like phantoms doomed to rove
            the sea
        voyaged east by day and west by night,
        deceiving them, hoping for rescue,
        prisoners on our own vessel, till
        at length we drifted to the shores of this
        your land, America, where we were freed
        from our unspeakable misery. Now we
        demand, good sirs, the extradition of
        Cinquez and his accomplices to La
        Havana. And it distresses us to know
there are so many here who seem inclined
to justify the mutiny of these blacks.
We find it paradoxical indeed
that you whose wealth, whose tree of liberty
are rooted in the labor of your slaves
should suffer the august John Quincy Adams
to speak with so much passion of the right
of chattel slaves to kill their lawful masters
and with his Roman rhetoric weave a hero's
garland for Cinquez. I tell you that
we are determined to return to Cuba
with our slaves and there see justice done.
    Cinquez—
or let us say 'the Prince'—Cinquez shall die."

The deep immortal human wish,
the timeless will:

    Cinquez its deathless primaveral image,
    life that transfigures many lives.

Voyage through death
               to life upon these shores.

A Ballad of Remembrance

Quadroon mermaids, Afro angels, black saints
balanced upon the switchblades of that air
and sang. Tight streets unfolding to the eye
like fans of corrosion and elegiac lace
crackled with their singing: Shadow of time, Shadow
    of blood.

Shadow, echoed the Zulu king, dangling
from a cluster of balloons. Blood,
whined the gun-metal priestess, floating
over the courtyard where dead men diced.

What will you have? she inquired, the sallow vendeuse
of prepared tarnishes and jokes of nacre and ormolu,
what but those gleamings, oldrose graces,
manners like scented gloves? Contrived ghosts
rapped to metronome clack of lavalieres.

Contrived illuminations riding a threat
of river, masked Negroes wearing chameleon
satins gaudy now as a fortuneteller's
dream of disaster, lighted the crazy flopping
dance of love and hate among joys, rejections.

Accommodate, muttered the Zulu king,
toad on a throne of glaucous poison jewels.
Love, chimed the saints and the angels and the
    mermaids.
Hate, shrieked the gun-metal priestess
from her spiked bellcollar curved like a fleur-de-lis:

As well have a talon as a finger, a muzzle as a mouth,
as well have a hollow as a heart. And she
    pinwheeled
away in coruscations of laughter, scattering
those others before her like foil stars.

But the dance continued—now among metaphorical
doors, coffee cups floating poised
hysterias, decors of illusion; now among
mazurka dolls offering death's-heads
of cocaine roses and real violets.

Then you arrived, meditative, ironic,
richly human; and your presence was shore where I
    rested
released from the hoodoo of that dance, where I
    spoke
with my true voice again.

And therefore this is not only a ballad of
    remembrance

for the down-South arcane city with death
in its jaws like gold teeth and archaic cusswords;
not only a token for the troubled generous friends
held in the fists of that schizoid city like flowers,
but also, Mark Van Doren,
a poem of remembrance, a gift, a souvenir for you.

Runagate Runagate

I.

Runs falls rises stumbles on from darkness into
    darkness
and the darkness thicketed with shapes of terror
and the hunters pursuing and the hounds pursuing
and the night cold and the night long and the river
to cross and the jack-muh-lanterns beckoning
    beckoning
and blackness ahead and when shall I reach that
    somewhere
morning and keep on going and never turn back and
    keep on going

> Runagate
> > Runagate
> > > Runagate

Many thousands rise and go
many thousands crossing over

> > > > O mythic North
> > > > O star-shaped yonder
> > > > Bible city

Some go weeping and some rejoicing
some in coffins and some in carriages
some in silks and some in shackles

> > Rise and go or fare you well

No more auction block for me
no more driver's lash for me

> If you see my Pompey, 30 yrs of age,
> new breeches, plain stockings, negro shoes;
> if you see my Anna, likely young mulatto
> branded E on the right cheek, R on the left,
> catch them if you can and notify subscriber.
> Catch them if you can, but it won't be easy.
> They'll dart underground when you try to catch
>   them,

plunge into quicksand, whirlpools, mazes,
turn into scorpions when you try to catch them.

And before I'll be a slave
I'll be buried in my grave

North star and bonanza gold
I'm bound for the freedom, freedom-bound
and oh Susyanna don't you cry for me

Runagate

Runagate

II.
Rises from their anguish and their power,

Harriet Tubman,

woman of earth,
whipscarred,
a summoning, a shining

Mean to be free

And this was the way of it, brethren brethren,
way we journeyed from Can't to Can.
Moon so bright and no place to hide,
the cry up and the patterollers riding,
hound dogs belling in bladed air.
And fear starts a-murbling, Never make it,
we'll never make it. *Hush that now,*
and she's turned upon us, levelled pistol
glinting in the moonlight:
Dead folks can't jaybird-talk, she says;
you keep on going now or die, she says.

Wanted   Harriet Tubman   alias The General
alias Moses   Stealer of Slaves

In league with Garrison   Alcott   Emerson
Garrett   Douglass   Thoreau   John Brown

Armed and known to be Dangerous

Wanted   Reward   Dead or Alive

Tell me, Ezekiel, oh tell me do you see
mailed Jehovah coming to deliver me?

Hoot-owl calling in the ghosted air,
five times calling to the hants in the air.

Shadow of a face in the scary leaves,
shadow of a voice in the talking leaves:

Come ride-a my train

Oh that train, ghost-story train
through swamp and savanna movering movering,
over trestles of dew, through caves of the wish,
Midnight Special on a sabre track movering
movering,
first stop Mercy and the last Hallelujah.

Come ride-a my train

Mean mean mean to be free.

E. ETHELBERT MILLER

Tomorrow

tomorrow
i will take the
journey back
sail
the
middle passage
it
would be better
to be packed
like spoons again
than
to continue to
live among
knives and forks

W. E. B. Du Bois

in philadelphia
i studied the negro
i knew everything
about him

in atlanta
i lost my first
born

what do i know
about myself?
there is so
much to learn

Malcolm X, August 1952

i suppose i should be
grateful to the white man
letting me out. where can
a black man in america go?
i stand with the prison in
my shadow. elijah muhammad
teaches us that we are not
thieves. we are the lost ones
who have been stolen.

allah bless my tongue as it
prepares to heal. there are
so many who are in need of
the message. i feel this
country changing, the cross
no longer ours to bear.

MARI EVANS

I am a Black Woman

I am a black woman
the music of my song
some sweet arpeggio of tears
is written in a minor key
and I
can be heard humming in the night

Can be heard
                    humming
in the night

I saw my mate leap screaming to the sea
and I/with these hands/cupped the lifebreath
from my issue in the canebrake.
I lost Nat's swinging body in a rain of tears
and heard my son scream all the way from Anzio
for Peace he never knew. . . . I
learned Da Nang and Pork Chop Hill
in anguish
Now my nostrils know the gas
and these trigger tire/d fingers
seek the softness in my warrior's beard

I
am a black woman
tall as a cypress
strong
beyond all definition still
defying place
and time
and circumstance
    assailed
        impervious
            indestructible
Look
    on me and be
renewed

Credits